PRAISE FROM THE EXPERTS
FOR
The PDR Pocket Guide
to Prescription Drugs

"Any patient or family member of a patient should have ready access to this book. It is informative, useful and a pleasure to read."

—Edwin C. Cadman, M.D.,
Ensign Professor and Chairman,
Department of Internal Medicine,
Yale University School of Medicine

"A must for every household where there are concerns about the safe use of medications. It is an ideal way to clarify and supplement the information provided by your health-care provider."

—Jack M. Rosenberg, Pharm.D., Ph.D.,
Professor of Clinical Pharmacy and Pharmacology,
Director, Division of Pharmacy Practice,
Arnold & Marie Schwartz College of
Pharmacy and Health Sciences,
Long Island University

"The premier professional drug reference now gives consumers their best guide to . . . the medications prescribed for them. . . . Clear, readable, comprehensive."

—Barrie R. Cassileth, Ph.D.,
Adjunct Professor,
University of North Carolina and
Duke University Medical Centers

"An excellent supplement to the education that should occur during every health care visit. The Guide allows people to find answers when and where they need them—any time of the day or night in their own home."

—Barbara P. Yawn, M.D., M.S.,
Associate Professor of Clinical Family
Medicine and Community Health,
University of Minnesota

"An easy-to-read guide to medications, side effects, and efficacy . . . Now one can get understandable medical information which can help keep health costs down, yet give patients a fine comfort level with the medicines they take."

—Leon G. Smith, M.D., F.A.C.P.,
Director of Medicine,
Saint Michael's Medical Center

THE PDR

POCKET GUIDE
TO PRESCRIPTION DRUGS

*Based on Physicians' Desk Reference®,
the Nation's Leading Professional
Drug Handbook*

POCKET BOOKS
New York   London   Toronto   Sydney   Tokyo   Singapore

Officers of Medical Economics: President and Chief Executive Officer: **Norman R. Snesil;** President and Chief Operating Officer: **Curtis B. Allen;** Executive Vice President and Chief Financial Officer: **J. Crispin Ashworth;** Senior Vice President—Corporate Operations: **John R. Ware;** Senior Vice President—Corporate Business Development: **Raymond M. Zoeller;** Vice President, Information Services and Chief Information Officer: **Edward J. Zecchini**

POCKET BOOKS, a division of Simon & Schuster Inc.
1230 Avenue of the Americas, New York, NY 10020

Copyright © 1995, 1996 by Medical Economics Company

Published by arrangement with Medical Economics Company, Inc.

ISBN: 0-671-52520-4

First Pocket Books printing February 1996

10 9 8 7 6 5 4 3 2 1

POCKET and colophon are registered trademarks of Simon & Schuster Inc.

Cover art supplied by Medical Economics Company

Printed in the U.S.A.

Publisher's Note

The drug information contained in this book is based on product labeling published in the 1995 edition of Physicians' Desk Reference®, supplemented with facts from other sources the publisher believes reliable. While diligent efforts have been made to assure the accuracy of this information, the book does not list every possible adverse reaction, interaction, precaution, and effect of a drug; and all information is presented without guarantees by the authors, consultants, and publisher, who disclaim all liability in connection with its use.

This book is intended only as a reference for use in an ongoing partnership between doctor and patient in the vigilant management of the patient's health. It is not a substitute for a doctor's professional judgment, and serves only as a reminder of concerns that may need discussion. All readers are urged to consult with a physician before beginning or discontinuing use of any prescription drug or undertaking any form of self-treatment.

Brand names listed in this book are intended to represent only the more commonly used products. Inclusion of a brand name does not signify endorsement of the product; absence of a name does not imply a criticism or rejection of the product. The publisher is not advocating the use of any product described in this book, does not warrant or guarantee any of these products, and has not performed any independent analysis in connection with the product information contained herein.

Contents

Contents

The PDR Guide to Prescription Drugs based on the third edition of The PDR® Family Guide to Prescription Drugs®

Editor-in-Chief: David W. Sifton
Pharmaceutical Director: Mukesh Mehta, RPh
Art Director: Robert Hartman

Assistant Editors: Ann Ben Larbi; Beret R. Erway

Writers: Lynn H. Buechler; Lawrence D. Chilnick; Janet S. Chilnick; Jayne Jacobson; Regina C. Vengrow, Theresa Waldron

Illustrations: Christopher Wikoff, MAMS

Editorial Production: Marjorie Duffy, Director of Production; Carrie Williams, Assistant Director of Production; Vicki Leal, Production Manager; Gregory Thomas, Product Integration Manager; Beret R. Erway, Production Editor; Lisa Best, Production Assistant; Joanne McCloskey, Electronic Publishing Coordinator; Shawn Cahill, Digital Imaging Coordinator; Kimberly Hiller-Vivas, Electronic Publishing Production Manager; Richard Weinstock, Electronic Publishing Design

Business Staff

Product Manager: Karen B. Sperber

Paul Walsh, Product Support Manager; Robin Bartlett, Commercial Sales Manager; Bill Gaffney, Commercial Sales Account Executive; Michele Barth, Marketing Communications Manager; Laurie Roth, Marketing Communications Coordinator; Roni LaVine, Robert Loeser, Fulfillment Managers; Raul Collado, Database and Systems Development Manager; Lynne Handler, Manager, Database Administration; Lynn Whealan, Customer Service Manager; Martina Murtagh, Administrative Assistant

Younghee Limb, MD
Assistant Professor of Internal Medicine
State University of New York, Stony Brook, NY

Gardiner Morse, MS
Executive Editor, AIDS Clinical Care, Waltham, MA

Louis V. Napolitano, MD
Senior Attending Physician
Hackensack Medical Center, Hackensack, NJ

Mark D. Ravenscraft, MD
Medical Director, Renal Transplantation
St. John's Mercy Medical Center, St. Louis, MO

Martin I. Resnick, MD
Professor and Chairman, Department of Urology
Case Western Reserve University, Cleveland, OH

Frank Simo, MD
Assistant Clinical Professor, Department of Otolaryngology
St. Louis University, St. Louis, MO

Karl Singer, MD
Exeter Family Medicine Associates, Exeter, NH

Eugene W. Sweeney, MD
Assistant Clinical Professor of Dermatology
Columbia College of Physicians and Surgeons, New York, NY

Foreword

The PDR Pocket Guide to Prescription Drugs strives to make the many benefits of modern pharmaceuticals—as well as their undeniable risks—as clear and simple as can be. Unlike other books in the field, *The PDR Pocket Guide* discloses all important side effects that the manufacturer has listed in the drug's product labeling. As a safeguard against error, it also provides you with full information on standard dosage recommendations. It tells exactly what to do when you miss a dose of your medication, while alerting you to the warning signs of an overdose. And to help you find all these facts as quickly as possible, it lists each medication under its familiar brand name —with a cross-reference in case the drug is dispensed generically.

Still, despite the depth and detail of the information you'll find here, *The PDR Pocket Guide* is not a replacement for your doctor's advice. Instead, it serves as a reminder of the basic instructions and caveats that all too often are forgotten by the time a patient leaves the doctor's office, as well as providing you with a checklist of the problems and conditions that you must be certain the doctor knows about—facts that might call for a change in your prescription.

In this way, the book is designed to serve as an aid in an ongoing dialogue between you and your doctor—a collaboration that's necessary for any treatment to work. Just as the doctor must tell you how and why to use a particular drug, you must tell the doctor how it affects you, reporting any reactions or drug interactions you suspect you may have. And while it's up to the doctor to devise your treatment strategy, it's up to you to make sure that the right doses are administered at the right times, and that the prescribed course of therapy is completed as planned.

Physicians' Desk Reference has been providing doctors with the information needed for safe, effective drug therapy for 50 years. Designed especially for health-care professionals, it presents the facts in a detailed, technical format approved by the Food and Drug Administration. Now, to make the key facts buried in this wealth of data accessible to everyone, *The PDR Pocket Guide* has stripped away the medical shorthand and technical terminology, and presented the core of this information in a simple, standard format designed for maximum convenience and ease of use by the consumer.

Almost all the information you'll find in *The Pocket Guide*'s consumer drug profiles has been extracted from PDR itself. When necessary, however, selected facts have been added from other sources—in particular, the publisher's Computerized Clinical Information System, used in hospitals throughout the nation. Generally, this extra information describes uses for a drug that are still awaiting formal FDA approval, or supplies instructions meant specifically for the patient, such as how to make up a missed dose.

The PDR Pocket Guide to Prescription Drugs is based on The PDR Family Guide to Prescription Drugs. All the information contained in The PDR Pocket Guide is identical to that contained in The PDR Family Guide, third edition, except that the Pocket Guide edition does not include the Disease Overview Section that appears in The Family Guide. However, all the drug information and profiles, as well as the drug identification guide and appendices, are included in The PDR Pocket Guide without abridgement.

Modern drug therapy is a vast and complicated field—so complicated that, for many questions about medicines, the answer varies with each patient. The PDR Pocket Guide gives you general guidelines for safe drug use; but only your doctor, evaluating the unique details of your case, can give you the exact instructions best suited for you. Our goal in this book is simply to alert you to the most pertinent questions to ask, and to help clarify your doctor's answers—in short, to give you the tools you need to supervise your own medical care as effectively as possible. We wish you good health.

Robert W. Hogan, MD
Chairman, Board of Medical Consultants

How to Use This Book

Modern medicines spare us all an incredible amount of suffering. If you doubt it, imagine a world without antibiotics to cure infections, analgesics to alleviate pain, or any of the many drugs we use to ease stiff joints and help weakened hearts.

But today's potent medicines are not without their risks. For certain people, at certain times, some drugs can cause problems. And for all people, misusing a medication is an invitation to trouble. The purpose of this book is to alert you to those times and those conditions which should make you wary, and to help you use all of your medications safely and effectively.

This book is not a substitute for a visit to the doctor. Only a doctor can weigh all the diverse aspects of your condition and choose the treatment most likely to meet your needs. What we hope this book can do, however, is help you sort out the facts and questions that deserve further discussion. Your doctor, after all, can respond only to the problems and concerns you mention. And a seemingly unimportant question could turn out to be a crucial aspect of your particular case.

The Drug Profiles

The drug profiles are designed to give you detailed information on the nation's most frequently prescribed prescription drugs, plus a few widely used over-the-counter medications. Though the section covers more than 1,000 products, it is not all-inclusive. If you do not find a profile for a particular prescription you've received, you shouldn't be concerned. There are a number of specialized, yet valuable drugs in current use that have been omitted here due to lack of space.

Most prescription products have two names—a generic chemical name and a manufacturer's brand name. Both are listed alphabetically in this book, with a profile of the drug appearing under the more familiar of the two. In most instances, that means the brand name. In a few cases—such as insulin, for example—the generic name heads the profile. In either case, the drug's other name gives you a cross-reference to the profile.

If there is more than one brand of a drug, you'll usually find the profile under the name that's most frequently prescribed. For example, information on amoxicillin can be found in the profile of Amoxil, the nation's leading brand. Other brands of amoxicillin, such as Wymox and Polymox, are cross-referenced to the Amoxil entry.

The drug profiles begin with correct pronunciation of the name, followed by the other brand and generic names for the drug. The information that follows these names is divided into 10 sections. Here's what you'll find in each.

Why is this drug prescribed?

This section provides an overview of the major diseases and disorders for which the drug is generally given. It names each basic problem, but does not go into technical details. For instance, the information here will confirm that a particular antibiotic is used to fight, say, upper respiratory tract infections. The section does not, however, attempt to list all the specific germs that the antibiotic is capable of eliminating.

Most important fact about this drug

Highlighted here is one key point—out of the dozens found in a typical profile—that is especially worthwhile to remember. We've placed it here for the sake of emphasis. Never regard this section as a definitive summary of the drug.

How should you take this medication?

Some drugs should never be taken with meals. Others must be. This section details such special instructions including how and when to take the medication, and any dietary restrictions that may apply. Also found here is advice on what to do when you forget a dose, and any special storage requirements that apply.

What side effects may occur?

Shown here are the potential side effects that the manufacturer has listed in the drug's FDA-approved product labeling. Virtually any drug will occasionally cause an unwanted reaction. However, even the most common of these reactions is generally seen in only a small minority of patients. For that reason, presence of a long list of possible side effects does not mean that the drug is unusually dangerous or trouble-prone. In fact, your odds of experiencing even one of these effects are typically very low. Not listed are the few side effects that can be detected only by a physician or by analysis in a laboratory.

Why should this drug not be prescribed?

A few drugs are known to be harmful under certain specific conditions, which are detailed here—the most common being hypersensitivity to the drug itself. If you think one of these restrictions applies to you, you should alert your doctor immediately. If you're correct, he or she may decide to use an alternative treatment.

Special warnings about this medication

This cautionary information is presented as a double check. If it includes any problems or conditions that your doctor may be unaware of, be sure to bring them to his or her attention. Chances are that no change in treatment will be called for; but it's worth making sure. In any event, do not take this information as a signal to change your dosage or discontinue the drug without consulting your doctor. Such a change might well do more harm than good.

Possible food and drug interactions when taking this medication

In this section you'll find a list of specific drugs—and types of drugs—that have been known to interact with the medicine being profiled. Generally, the list includes a few examples of each type. However, it is far from inclusive. If you're not certain whether a medication you're taking falls into one of these categories, be sure to check with your doctor or pharmacist.

Remember, too, that the chances of an interaction—and its intensity if one occurs—vary from person to person. In many cases, the benefits of the two medicines may outweigh the results of an interaction. Don't stop taking either drug without first consulting your doctor.

Special information
if you are pregnant or breastfeeding

Very few medicines have been definitively proved safe for use during pregnancy. On the other hand, only a handful are known to be inevitably harmful. Most drugs fall in-between, in a gray area where no harm has been reported, but neither has safety been conclusively proved. With many of these drugs, the small theoretical risk they pose may be overshadowed by your need for treatment. This section will tell you whether a drug has been confirmed safe, is known to be dangerous, or is part of that large group about which scientists are not really sure.

Recommended dosage

Shown here are excerpts of the dosage guidelines your doctor uses. They generally present a range of doses recommended for typical cases, and sometimes include a recommended maximum. The information is presented as a convenient double-check in case you suspect a misunderstanding or a typographical error on your prescription label. It is not useful for determining an exact dosage yourself. The dose that's best for you depends on numerous factors—such as your age, weight, physical condition, and response to the drug—that can be properly evaluated only by your doctor.

Overdosage

As another safety measure, this section lists, when available, the signs of an overdose. If the symptoms listed in this section lead you to suspect an overdose, your best response is to seek emergency medical attention immediately.

Other Features

The book includes several other sections that you'll find useful when faced with certain specific problems.

The Disease and Disorder Index

This index enables you to quickly identify drugs available for a particular medical condition. Arranged alphabetically by ailment, it lists all the medications profiled in the book.

Product Identification Guide

It's wise to keep all your prescription medications in their original bottles or vials. However, if they do somehow get mixed up, you may find this section helpful for sorting them out. It includes actual-size photographs of the leading products discussed in the book. Because some of the more common generic alternatives are shown along with the brand-name drugs, the section is arranged by each drug's generic name. Manufacturers occasionally change the color and shape of a product, so if a prescription does not match the photo shown here, check with your pharmacist before assuming there's been a mistake.

The Appendices

In this section you'll find lists of drugs that meet certain special conditions, such as those that are sugar- or alcohol-free, and those that may make you unusually sensitive to light. These lists include prescription and over-the-counter products, and are not limited to brands mentioned in the drug profiles. On the other hand, the lists are not all-inclusive; so even if a medication fails to appear, there's still a chance it may qualify. Check with your pharmacist to be sure.

The Doctor-Patient Partnership

Although doctors today can often work miracles with advanced technology and sophisticated medicines, they still need the help of the patient to make most treatments work. No matter how potent the medication, it can still prove worthless if you fail to take it properly. Likewise, if you react badly to a drug, or have a condition that makes it dangerous, there is nothing any doctor can do about it unless you report the problem.

This book is offered as an aid in this cooperative effort with your doctor. We hope its suggests the right questions to ask, while allaying any unwarranted concerns you might have. Most of all, we hope it helps in some small way to make all of your treatments as effective as they can possibly be.

Drug Profiles

Brand name:

ACCUPRIL

Pronounced: AK-you-prill
Generic name: Quinapril hydrochloride

Why is this drug prescribed?

Accupril is used in the treatment of high blood pressure. It can be taken alone or in combination with a thiazide type of diuretic such as Hydro DIURIL. Accupril is in a family of drugs known as "ACE inhibitors." It works by preventing a chemical in your blood called angiotensin I from converting into a more potent form that increases salt and water retention in your body. Accupril also enhances blood flow throughout your blood vessels. Drugs such as Accupril are sometimes prescribed in the treatment of congestive heart failure.

Most important fact about this drug

You must take Accupril regularly for it to be effective. Since blood pressure declines gradually, it may be several weeks before you get the full benefit of Accupril; and you must continue taking it even if you are feeling well. Accupril does not cure high blood pressure; it merely keeps it under control.

How should you take this medication?

You can take Accupril with or without meals.

Alcohol may increase the effect of Accupril, and could cause dizziness or fainting. Avoid alcohol until you have checked with your doctor.

Take Accupril exactly as prescribed, and see your doctor regularly to make sure the drug is working properly without unwanted side effects. Do not stop taking this drug without first consulting your doctor.

- *If you miss a dose...*
  Take the forgotten dose as soon as you remember. However, if it is almost time for your next dose, skip the one you missed and go back to your regular schedule. Never try to "catch up" by doubling the dose.

- *Storage instructions...*
  Accupril can be stored at room temperature.

What side effects may occur?

Side effects cannot be anticipated. If any develop or change in intensity, inform your doctor as soon as possible. Only your doctor can determine if it is safe for you to continue taking Accupril.

- *More common side effects may include:*
  Dizziness
  Headache

- *Less common side effects may include:*
  Abdominal pain, coughing, fatigue, nausea, vomiting

- *Rare side effects may include:*
  Angina (severe chest pain), back pain, bleeding in the stomach or intestines, bronchitis, changes in heart rhythm, constipation, depression, dimmed vision, dizziness when first standing up, dry mouth or throat, extremely high blood pressure, fainting, heart attack, heart failure, high potassium, increased blood pressure, increased sweating, inflammation of the pancreas, inflammation of the sinuses, itching, kidney failure, nervousness, palpitations, rapid heartbeat, sensitivity to light, skin peeling, sleepiness, sore throat, stroke, swelling of the mouth and throat, vague feeling of illness, vertigo

Why should this drug not be prescribed?
If you are sensitive to or have ever had an allergic reaction to Accupril or similar drugs, such as Capoten and Vasotec, you should not take this medication. Make sure your doctor is aware of any drug reactions you have experienced.

Special warnings about this medication
If you develop swelling of the face, lips, tongue, or throat, or of your arms and legs, or have difficulty swallowing or breathing, you should contact your doctor immediately. You may need emergency treatment.

You may feel light-headed, especially during the first few days of Accupril therapy. If this occurs, notify you doctor. If you actually faint, stop taking the medication until you have consulted with your doctor.

Vomiting, diarrhea, and heavy perspiration can all deplete your body fluid; and dehydration can cause your blood pressure to drop. If this leads to light-headedness or fainting, you should check with your doctor.

Inform your doctor or dentist that you are taking Accupril before undergoing surgery or anesthesia.

Do not use potassium supplements or salt substitutes containing potassium without consulting your doctor.

If you develop a sore throat or fever contact your doctor immediately. It could indicate a more serious illness.

If you are taking Accupril, your doctor will do a complete assessment of your kidney function and will watch it closely as long as you are taking this drug.

Possible food and drug interactions
when taking this medication

If Accupril is taken with certain other drugs, the effects of either could be increased, decreased, or altered. It is especially important to check with your doctor before combining Accupril with the following:

Diuretics such as Lasix
Lithium (Eskalith, Lithobid)
Potassium-sparing diuretics such as Aldactone, Dyazide, and Moduretic
Potassium supplements such as Slow-K and K-Dur
Salt substitutes containing potassium
Tetracycline (Achromycin V, Sumycin)

Special information
if you are pregnant or breastfeeding

ACE inhibitors such as Accupril have been shown to cause injury and even death to the unborn child when used in pregnancy during the second and third trimesters. If you are pregnant, your doctor should discontinue Accupril as soon as possible. If you plan to become pregnant, make sure your doctor knows you are taking this medication. Accupril may appear in breast milk and could affect a nursing infant. If this medication is essential to your health, your doctor may advise you to discontinue breastfeeding until your treatment is finished.

Recommended dosage

ADULTS

The usual starting dose for high blood pressure is 10 milligrams taken once a day. If you have any problems with your kidneys or if you are also taking a diuretic, your starting dose may be lower. Depending on how your blood pressure responds, your doctor may increase your dose up to a total of 80 milligrams a day taken once a day or divided into two doses.

CHILDREN

The safety and effectiveness of Accupril in children have not been established.

Overdosage

Any medication taken in excess can have serious consequences. If you suspect an overdose, seek medical attention immediately.

A severe drop in blood pressure is the primary sign of an Accupril overdose.

Brand name:

ACCUTANE

Pronounced: ACC-u-tane
Generic name: Isotretinoin

Why is this drug prescribed?

Accutane, a chemical cousin of vitamin A, is prescribed for the treatment of severe, disfiguring cystic acne that has not cleared up in response to milder medications such as antibiotics. It works on the oil glands within the skin, shrinking them and diminishing their output. You take Accutane by mouth every day for several months, then stop. The antiacne effect can last even after you have finished your course of medication.

Most important fact about this drug

Because Accutane can cause severe birth defects, including mental retardation and physical malformations, a woman *must not* become pregnant while taking it. If you are a woman of childbearing age, your doctor will ask you to sign a detailed consent form before you start taking Accutane. If you accidentally become pregnant while taking the medication, you should immediately consult your doctor.

How should you take this medication?

Take Accutane with food. Follow your doctor's instructions carefully.

Depending on your reaction to Accutane, your doctor may need to adjust the dosage upward or downward. If you respond quickly and very well, your doctor may take you off Accutane even before the 15 or 20 weeks are up.

After you finish taking Accutane, there should be at least a 2-month "rest period" during which you are off the drug. This is because your acne may continue to get better even though you are no longer taking the medication. Once the 2 months are up, if your acne is still severe, your doctor may want to give you a second course of Accutane.

Avoid consumption of alcoholic beverages.

Read the patient information leaflet available with the product.

Do not crush the capsules.

■ *If you miss a dose...*
Take the forgotten dose as soon as you remember. If it is almost time for your next dose, skip the one you missed and go back to your regular schedule. Do not take 2 doses at the same time.

■ *Storage instructions...*
Store at room temperature, away from light.

What side effects may occur?
Side effects cannot be anticipated. If any develop or change in intensity, inform your doctor as soon as possible. Only your doctor can determine if it is safe for you to continue taking Accutane.

■ *More common side effects may include:*
Conjunctivitis ("pinkeye")
Dry or fragile skin
Dry, cracked, inflamed lips
Dry mouth
Dry nose
Itching
Joint pains
Nosebleed

■ *Less common side effects may include:*
Bowel inflammation and pain, chest pain, decreased night vision, decreased tolerance to contact lenses, depression, fatigue, headache, nausea, peeling palms or soles, rash, skin infections, stomach and intestinal discomfort, sunburn-sensitive skin, thinning hair, urinary discomfort, vision problems, vomiting

Why should this drug not be prescribed?
You should not take Accutane if you are sensitive to or have ever had an allergic reaction to parabens, the preservative used in the capsules.

If you are a woman of childbearing age, you should not take Accutane if you are pregnant, if you think there is a possibility you might get pregnant during the treatment, or if you are unable to keep coming back to the doctor for monthly checkups, including pregnancy testing.

Special warnings about this medication
When you first start taking Accutane, it is possible that your acne will get worse before it starts to get better.

If you are a woman of childbearing age and you are considering taking Accutane, you will be given both spoken and written warnings about the importance of avoiding pregnancy during the treatment. You will be asked to sign a consent form noting that:

- Accutane is a powerful, "last resort" medication for severe acne;
- You must not take Accutane if you are pregnant or may become pregnant during treatment;
- If you get pregnant while taking Accutane, your baby will be at high risk for birth defects;
- If you take Accutane, you must use effective birth control from 1 month before the start of treatment through 1 month after the end of treatment;
- You must test negative for pregnancy within 2 weeks before starting Accutane, and you must start Accutane on the second or third day of your menstrual period;
- You may participate in a program that includes an initial free pregnancy test and birth control counseling session;
- If you become pregnant, you must immediately stop taking Accutane and see your doctor;
- You have read and understood the Accutane patient brochure and asked your doctor any questions you had;
- You are not currently pregnant and do not plan to become pregnant for at least 30 days after you finish taking Accutane;
- You have been invited to participate in a survey of women being treated with Accutane.

Some people taking Accutane, including some who simultaneously took tetracycline, have experienced headache, nausea, and visual disturbances caused by increased pressure within the skull. See a doctor immediately if you have these symptoms; if the doctor finds swelling of the optic nerve at the back of your eye, you must stop taking Accutane at once and see a neurologist for further care.

Be careful driving at night. Some people have experienced a sudden decrease in night vision.

Some people taking Accutane have had problems regulating their blood sugar level.

You may not be able to tolerate your contact lenses during and after your therapy with Accutane.

You should stop taking Accutane immediately if you have abdominal pain, bleeding from the rectum, or severe diarrhea. You may have an inflammatory disease of the bowel.

You should not donate blood during your therapy with Accutane and for at least a month after you stop taking it.

Possible food and drug interactions
when taking this medication

While taking Accutane, do not take vitamin supplements containing vitamin A. Accutane and vitamin A are chemically related; taking them together is like taking an overdose of vitamin A.

Special information
if you are pregnant or breastfeeding

Accutane causes birth defects; do not use it while pregnant. Nursing mothers should not take Accutane because of the possibility of passing the drug on to the baby via breast milk.

Recommended dosage

The recommended dosage range for Accutane is 0.5 to 2 milligrams per 2.2 pounds of body weight, divided into 2 doses daily, for 15 to 20 weeks. The usual starting dose is 0.5 to 1 milligram per 2.2 pounds per day.

People whose disease is very severe or is primarily on the body may have to take up to the maximum recommended dose.

If after a period of 2 months or more off therapy, severe cystic acne persists, your doctor may prescribe a second course of therapy.

Overdosage

Any medication taken in excess can have serious consequences. If you suspect an overdose of Accutane, seek medical attention immediately.

- *Overdosage of Accutane, like overdosage of vitamin A, can cause:*
  Abdominal pain
  Dizziness
  Dry, cracked, inflamed lips
  Facial flushing
  Incoordination and clumsiness
  Headache
  Vomiting

Generic name:

ACEBUTOLOL

See Sectral, page 1002.

Generic name:

ACETAMINOPHEN

See Tylenol, page 1168.

Generic name:

ACETAMINOPHEN WITH CODEINE

See Tylenol with Codeine, page 1171.

Generic name:

ACETAMINOPHEN WITH OXYCODONE

See Percocet, page 831.

Generic name:

ACETAZOLAMIDE

See Diamox, page 324.

Brand name:

ACHROMYCIN V CAPSULES

Pronounced: A-kro-MY-cin Vee
Generic name: Tetracycline hydrochloride
Other brand name: Sumycin

Why is this drug prescribed?
Achromycin V, a "broad-spectrum" antibiotic, is used to treat bacterial infections such as Rocky Mountain spotted fever, typhus fever, and tick fevers; upper respiratory infections; pneumonia; gonorrhea; amoebic infections; and urinary tract infections. It is also used to help treat severe acne and to treat trachoma (a chronic eye infection) and conjunctivitis (pinkeye). Tetracycline is often an alternative drug for people who are allergic to penicillin.

Most important fact about this drug
Tetracycline should not be used during the last half of pregnancy or in children under the age of 8. It may damage developing teeth and cause permanent discoloration.

How should you take this medication?

Achromycin V should be taken exactly as prescribed by your doctor. Be sure to use the entire prescription. If you are taking a liquid form of the drug, shake well before using.

Do not use outdated Achromycin V. Outdated tetracycline is highly toxic to the kidneys.

Do not take antacids containing aluminum, calcium, or magnesium (e.g., Mylanta, Maalox) while taking this medication. They will affect the absorption of the drug.

Take Achromycin V 1 hour before or 2 hours after meals. Foods, milk, and some other dairy products affect absorption of the drug.

Achromycin V should be continued for at least 24 to 48 hours after your symptoms have subsided.

■ *If you miss a dose...*

Take it as soon as you remember. If it is almost time for your next dose and you take Achromycin V once a day (e.g., for acne), take the dose you missed, and then take the next one 10 to 12 hours later; if you take it twice a day, take the dose you missed, and then take the next one 5 to 6 hours later; if you take 3 or more doses a day, take the one you missed, and then take the next one 2 to 4 hours later. Then go back to your regular schedule.

■ *Storage instructions...*

Store capsules at room temperature. Keep the liquid form of tetracycline in the refrigerator, but do not allow it to freeze.

What side effects may occur?

Side effects cannot be anticipated. If any occur or change in intensity, inform your doctor as soon as possible. Only your doctor can determine if it is safe for you to continue taking Achromycin V.

■ *More common side effects may include:*

Anemia, blood disorders, blurred vision and headache (in adults), bulging soft spot on the head (in infants), diarrhea, difficult or painful swallowing, dizziness, extreme allergic reactions, genital or anal sores or rash, hives, inflammation of large bowel, inflammation of the tongue, inflammation of the upper digestive tract, increased sensitivity to light, loss of appetite, nausea, rash, ringing in the ears, swelling due to fluid accumulation, vision disturbance, vomiting

■ *Less common or rare side effects may include:*
Inflamed skin, inflammation of the penis, liver poisoning, muscle weakness, peeling, skin eruptions, throat sores and inflammation

Why should this drug not be prescribed?
Do not take this medication if you are sensitive to or have ever had an allergic reaction to Achromycin V or any other tetracycline medication.

Special warnings about this medication
If you have kidney disease, make sure the doctor knows about it. A lower than usual dose of Achromycin V may be needed.

Tetracycline drugs can make you more prone to sunburn when you are in sunlight or ultraviolet light. Take appropriate precautions.

Some adults may develop a headache and blurred vision while taking tetracycline, and infants may develop a bulging soft spot on the head. Contact your doctor if you experience or notice these symptoms. They usually disappear soon after the medication is stopped.

As with other antibiotics, use of this medication may cause other infections to develop. Contact your doctor if this occurs.

If you are taking Achromycin V over an extended period of time, your doctor will perform blood, kidney, and liver tests periodically.

Possible food and drug interactions
when taking this medication
If Achromycin V is taken with certain other drugs, the effects of either could be increased, decreased, or altered. It is especially important to check with your doctor before combining Achromycin V with the following:

Antacids containing aluminum, calcium, or magnesium, such as Mylanta and Maalox
Blood thinners such as Coumadin
Oral contraceptives
Penicillin (Amoxil, Pen-Vee K, others)

Special information
if you are pregnant or breastfeeding
Achromycin V is not recommended for use during pregnancy. It can affect the development of the unborn child's bones and teeth. If you are pregnant or plan to become pregnant, inform your doctor immediately. Achromycin V appears in breast milk and may affect a nursing infant. If this medication is essential to your health, your doctor may recommend that you stop breastfeeding until your treatment is finished.

Recommended dosage
Your doctor will adjust your dose on the basis of the condition to be treated, your age, and risk factors such as kidney problems.

You should use this drug for at least 24 to 48 hours after symptoms and fever have subsided. For a streptococcal infection, doses should be taken for at least 10 days.

ADULTS

For most infections, the usual daily dose is 1 to 2 grams divided into 2 or 4 equal doses, depending on severity.

For treatment of brucellosis
The usual dose is 500 milligrams 4 times daily for 3 weeks; the drug should be accompanied by streptomycin.

For treatment of syphilis
You should take a total of 30 to 40 grams, divided into equal doses over a period of 10 to 15 days.

Gonorrhea patients sensitive to penicillin can take tetracycline, starting with 1.5 grams, followed by 0.5 gram every 6 hours for 4 days, to a total dosage of 9 grams.

For urethral, endocervical, or rectal infections in adults caused by Chlamydia trachomatis
The usual dose is 500 milligrams, 4 times a day, for at least 7 days.

CHILDREN 8 YEARS OF AGE AND ABOVE

The usual daily dose is 10 to 20 milligrams per pound of body weight divided into 2 or 4 equal doses.

Overdosage
Any medication taken in excess can have serious consequences. Seek medical attention immediately if you suspect an overdose of Achromycin V.

Brand name:

ACLOVATE

Pronounced: AK-low-vait
Generic name: Alclometasone dipropionate

Why is this drug prescribed?
Aclovate, a synthetic steroid medication of the cortisone family, is spread on the skin to relieve certain types of itchy rashes, including psoriasis.

Most important fact about this drug
When you use Aclovate, you inevitably absorb some of the medication through your skin and into the bloodstream. Too much absorption can lead to unwanted side effects elsewhere in the body. To keep this problem to a minimum, avoid using large amounts of Aclovate over large areas, and do not cover it with airtight dressings such as plastic wrap or adhesive bandages unless specifically told to by your doctor.

How should you use this medication?
Use Aclovate exactly as prescribed by your doctor and only to treat the condition for which your doctor prescribed it. The usual procedure is to spread a thin film of Aclovate cream or ointment over the rash and massage gently until the medication disappears. Do this 2 or 3 times a day.

For areas of deep-seated, persistent rash, your doctor may recommend a thick layer of Aclovate cream or ointment topped with waterproof bandaging, to be left in place for 1 to 4 days. If necessary, this procedure may be repeated 3 or 4 times. Do not use bandaging at all, however, unless your doctor so advises.

Aclovate is for use only on the skin. Be careful to keep it out of your eyes.

■ *If you miss a dose...*
Apply it as soon as you remember. If it is almost time for the next dose, skip the one you missed and go back to your regular schedule.

■ *Storage instructions...*
Store at room temperature.

What side effects may occur?
Side effects cannot be anticipated. If any develop or change in intensity, inform your doctor as soon as possible. Only your doctor can determine if it is safe for you to continue taking Aclovate.

■ *Side effects may include:*
Abnormally excessive growth of hair, acne-like pimples, allergic rash, burning, dryness, infection, irritation, itching, maceration (sponginess), pale (depigmented) spots, prickly heat, rash around the mouth, redness, skin inflammation, stretch marks on skin

Why should this drug not be prescribed?
Do not use Aclovate if you are sensitive to or have ever had an allergic reaction to alclometasone dipropionate (the active ingredient) or other corticosteroids, or to any of the oils, waxes, alcohols, or other chemicals in the cream or ointment.

Special warnings about this medication
Aclovate is for external use only. Do not let the cream or ointment get into your eyes.

Avoid covering a treated area with waterproof diapers or plastic pants. They can increase unwanted absorption of Aclovate.

If you use Aclovate over large areas of skin for prolonged periods of time, the amount of hormone absorbed into your bloodstream may eventually lead to Cushing's syndrome: a moon-faced appearance, fattened neck and trunk, and purplish streaks on the skin. Children, because of their relatively larger ratio of skin surface to body weight, are particularly susceptible to overabsorption of hormone from Aclovate.

Possible food and drug interactions
when taking this medication
Check with your doctor before combining Aclovate with other more potent steroids, since this could lead to undesirably large amounts of hormone circulating in your bloodstream.

Special information
if you are pregnant or breastfeeding
Drug absorbed from Aclovate cream or ointment into the bloodstream may find its way into an unborn child's blood, or may seep into breast milk. To avoid any possible harm to your child, use Aclovate very sparingly—and only with your doctor's permission—if you are pregnant or nursing a baby.

Recommended dosage
Apply a thin film of Aclovate cream or ointment to the affected skin areas 2 or 3 times daily; massage gently until the medication disappears.

Bandages that block out air may be used to control psoriasis and other severe skin rashes, if your doctor recommends them. Apply as follows:

1. Cover the affected area with a thick layer of Aclovate cream or ointment and a light gauze dressing, then cover the area with a pliable plastic film.
2. Seal the edges to the normal skin by adhesive tape or other means.

3. Leave the dressing in place 1 to 4 days and repeat the procedure 3 or 4 times as needed.

With this method of treatment, marked improvement is often seen in a few days. If an infection develops, the use of airtight bandages should be discontinued. Your doctor will recommend an alternative treatment.

Overdosage
Any medication taken in excess can have serious consequences. If you suspect an overdose, seek medical attention immediately.

In a child, an overdose of Aclovate may cause increased pressure within the skull leading to bulging soft spots (in an infant's head), headache, and nausea or vomiting. If this happens, see a doctor without delay.

Over the long term, overuse of Aclovate can interfere with a child's normal growth and development.

Generic name:

ACRIVASTINE WITH PSEUDOEPHEDRINE

See Semprex-D, page 1010.

Brand name:

ACTIGALL

Pronounced: AK-ti-gawl
Generic name: Ursodiol

Why is this drug prescribed?
Actigall is used to help dissolve certain kinds of gallstones. If you suffer from gallstones but do not want to undergo surgery to remove them, or if age, infirmity, or a poor reaction to anesthesia makes you a poor candidate for surgery, Actigall treatment may be a good alternative.

Most important fact about this drug
Actigall is not a quick remedy. It takes months of Actigall therapy to dissolve gallstones, and there is a possibility of incomplete dissolution and recurrence of stones. Your doctor will weigh Actigall against alternative treatments and recommend the best one for you.

Actigall is most effective if your gallstones are small or "floatable" (i.e., high cholesterol content). In addition, your gallbladder must still be functioning properly.

How should you take this medication?
Actigall should be taken exactly as prescribed by your doctor; otherwise the gallstones may dissolve slowly or not dissolve at all. During treatment, your doctor will do periodic ultrasound exams to see if your stones are dissolving.

■ *If you miss a dose...*
Take it as soon as you remember, or at the same time as the next dose.

■ *Storage instructions...*
Store at room temperature in a tightly closed container.

What side effects may occur?
Side effects cannot be anticipated. If any develop or change in intensity, inform your doctor as soon as possible. Only your doctor can determine if it is safe for you to continue taking Actigall.

■ *Side effects may include:*
Abdominal pain, anxiety, back pain, constipation, cough, depression, dry skin, fatigue, gas, hair thinning, headache, hives, indigestion, inflammation of the mouth or nose, itching, metallic taste, mild temporary diarrhea, muscle and joint pain, nausea, rash, severe pain in the upper right side of the abdomen, sleep disorders, sweating, vomiting

Why should this drug not be prescribed?
Do not take this medication if you are sensitive to or have ever had an allergic reaction to ursodiol (ursodeoxycholic acid) or to other bile acids.

Actigall will not dissolve certain types of gallstones. If your doctor tells you that your gallstones are calcified cholesterol stones, radio-opaque stones, or radiolucent bile pigment stones, you are not a candidate for treatment with Actigall.

Also, if you have biliary tract (liver, gallbladder, bile duct) problems or certain liver and pancreas diseases, your doctor may not be able to prescribe Actigall for you.

Special warnings about this medication
Although Actigall is not known to cause liver damage, it is theoretically possible in some people. Your doctor may check the levels of liver enzymes in your blood before you start to take Actigall and again while you are taking it.

Possible food and drug interactions
when taking this medication

If Actigall is taken with certain other drugs, the effects of either could be increased, decreased, or altered. It is especially important to check with your doctor before combining Actigall with the following:

Aluminum-based antacid medications (Alu-Cap, Alu-Tab, Rolaids, others)
Certain cholesterol-lowering medications, such as Questran and Colestid
Estrogens, such as Premarin
Lipid-lowering medications, such as Lopid and Mevacor
Oral contraceptives

Special information
if you are pregnant or breastfeeding

If you are pregnant or plan to become pregnant, inform your doctor immediately. So far, there is no evidence that Actigall can harm an unborn baby; but to be safe, the medication is not recommended during pregnancy. Caution is needed during breastfeeding; it is not known whether Actigall taken by a nursing mother passes into her breast milk.

Recommended dosage

The recommended dose for Actigall treatment of radiolucent gallbladder stones is 8 to 10 milligrams per 2.2 pounds of body weight per day divided into 2 or 3 doses.

Overdosage

Although there have been no reports of overdose with Actigall, the most likely symptom of severe overdose would be diarrhea. Since any medication taken in excess can have serious consequences, you should seek medical attention immediately if you suspect an Actigall overdose.

Generic name:

ACYCLOVIR

See Zovirax, page 1245.

Brand name:

ADALAT

See Procardia, page 896.

Brand name:

ADAPIN

See Sinequan, page 1029.

Brand name:

ADVIL

Generic name: Ibuprofen
Other brand names: Motrin, Rufen

Why is this drug prescribed?

Ibuprofen, a nonsteroidal anti-inflammatory drug, is used to relieve the inflammation, swelling, stiffness, and joint pain associated with rheumatoid arthritis and osteoarthritis (the most common form of arthritis). It is also used in the treatment of menstrual and other types of pain.

Ibuprofen suspension (Children's Advil, Children's Motrin) is used for fever reduction in children 6 months of age and older.

Most important fact about this drug

You should have frequent check-ups with your doctor if you take ibuprofen regularly. Ulcers or internal bleeding can occur without warning.

How should you take this medication?

Your doctor may ask you to take ibuprofen with food or an antacid to avoid stomach upset. Ibuprofen suspension can be given with meals or milk if it upsets a child's stomach.

If you are using ibuprofen for arthritis, you should take it regularly, exactly as prescribed.

- *If you miss a dose...*
  Take it as soon as you remember. If it is almost time for your next dose, skip the one you missed and go back to your regular schedule. Never take 2 doses at the same time.

- *Storage information...*
  Store ibuprofen at room temperature.

What side effects may occur?

Side effects cannot be anticipated. If any develop or change in intensity, inform your doctor as soon as possible. Only your doctor can determine if it is safe for you to continue taking ibuprofen.

- *More common side effects may include:*
  Abdominal cramps or pain, abdominal discomfort, bloating and gas, constipation, diarrhea, dizziness, fluid retention and swelling, headache, heartburn, indigestion, itching, loss of appetite, nausea, nervousness, rash, ringing in ears, stomach pain, vomiting

- *Less common or rare side effects may include:*
  Abdominal bleeding, anemia, black stool, blood in urine, blurred vision, changes in heartbeat, chills, confusion, congestive heart failure, depression, dry eyes and mouth, emotional volatility, fever, hair loss, hearing loss, hepatitis, high blood pressure, hives, inability to sleep, inflammation of nose, inflammation of the pancreas or stomach, kidney failure, severe allergic reactions, shortness of breath, skin eruptions, sleepiness, Stevens-Johnson syndrome (peeling skin), stomach or upper intestinal ulcer, ulcer of gums, vision loss, wheezing, yellow eyes and skin

Why should this drug not be prescribed?
If you are sensitive to or have ever had an allergic reaction to ibuprofen, aspirin, or similar drugs, or if you have had asthma attacks caused by aspirin or other drugs of this type, or if you have angioedema, a condition whose symptoms are skin eruptions, you should not take this medication.

Make sure that your doctor is aware of any drug reactions that you have experienced.

Special warnings about this medication
Peptic ulcers and bleeding can occur without warning.

This drug should be used with caution if you have kidney or liver disease, and it can cause liver or kidney inflammation or other problems in some people.

Do not take aspirin or any other anti-inflammatory medications while taking ibuprofen unless your doctor tells you to do so.

Ibuprofen may cause vision problems. If you experience any changes in your vision, inform your doctor.

Ibuprofen may prolong bleeding time. If you are taking blood-thinning medication, this drug should be taken with caution.

This drug can cause water retention. It should be used with caution if you have high blood pressure or poor heart function.

Avoid the use of alcohol while taking this medication.

Ibuprofen may mask the usual signs of infection. Use with care in the presence of an existing infection.

Ibuprofen suspension (Children's Motrin) contains 1.5 grams of sucrose and 8 calories per teaspoonful. If your child needs to watch his or her sugar intake, consult with your doctor.

Possible food and drug interactions when taking this medication

If ibuprofen is taken with certain other drugs, the effects of either could be increased, decreased, or altered. It is especially important to check with your doctor before combining ibuprofen with the following:

Aspirin
Blood pressure medications such as Vasotec and Aldomet
Blood-thinning drugs such as Coumadin
Diuretics such as Lasix and HydroDIURIL
Lithium (Lithonate)
Methotrexate

Special information if you are pregnant or breastfeeding

The effects of ibuprofen during pregnancy have not been adequately studied. If you are pregnant or plan to become pregnant, inform your doctor immediately. Ibuprofen may appear in breast milk and could affect a nursing infant. If this medication is essential to your health, your doctor may advise you to discontinue breastfeeding until your treatment with this medication is finished.

Recommended dosage

ADULTS

Rheumatoid Arthritis and Osteoarthritis
The usual dosage is 1,200 to 3,200 milligrams per day divided into 3 or 4 doses. Your doctor will tailor the dose to your individual needs. Symptoms should be reduced within 2 weeks. Daily dosage should not be greater than 3,200 milligrams.

Mild to Moderate Pain
The usual dose is 400 milligrams every 4 to 6 hours as necessary.

Menstrual Pain
The usual dose is 400 milligrams every 4 hours as necessary. Begin treatment when symptoms first appear.

CHILDREN 6 MONTHS TO 12 YEARS OF AGE

Fever reduction (suspension only)
The recommended dose is 5 milligrams per 2.2 pounds of body weight if temperature is less than 102.5°F or 10 milligrams per 2.2 pounds of body weight if temperature is greater than 102.5°F. The fever should go down for 6 to 8 hours. Do not give the child more than 40 milligrams per 2.2 pounds of body weight in one day.

ELDERLY

The doctor will determine the dosage according to the particular needs of the elderly individual.

Overdosage
Any medication taken in excess can have serious consequences. If you suspect an overdose, seek medical attention immediately.

Brand name:

AEROBID

Pronounced: AIR-oh-bid
Generic name: Flunisolide
Other brand names: AeroBid-M, Nasalide

Why is this drug prescribed?
AeroBid is prescribed for people who need long-term treatment to control the symptoms of bronchial asthma. It contains an anti-inflammatory steroid type of medication.

Most important fact about this drug
AeroBid helps to reduce the likelihood of an asthma attack, but will not relieve one that has already started. To be effective as a preventive measure, it must be taken every day at regularly spaced intervals. It may be several weeks before you receive its full benefit.

How should you take this medication?
Take this medication at regular intervals, exactly as prescribed by your doctor. Taking doses higher than your doctor has prescribed may impair the function of your adrenal glands.

- *Administration technique:*
  1. Remove the cap and hold inhaler upright.
  2. Shake the inhaler thoroughly.
  3. Take a drink of water to moisten the throat.
  4. Tilt your head slightly and breathe out.
  5. While activating the inhaler, take a slow deep breath for 3 to 5 seconds, hold the breath for about 10 seconds, then breathe out slowly.
  6. Allow at least 1 minute between inhalations.

If you are also using a bronchodilator inhalant, it should be used before the AeroBid inhalant to derive the best effects from this drug. Use of the two inhalers should be separated by several minutes.

To help reduce hoarseness, throat irritation, and mouth infection, rinse out with water after each use.

Illustrated instructions for use are available with the product.

- *If you miss a dose...*
  Use it as soon as you remember. If it is almost time for your next dose, skip the one you missed and go back to your regular schedule. Do not take 2 doses at the same time.

- *Storage instructions...*
  Store away from heat or cold and light. Keep away from open flames.

What side effects may occur?
Side effects cannot be anticipated. If any develop or change in intensity, inform your doctor as soon as possible. Only your doctor can determine if it is safe for you to continue taking AeroBid.

- *More common side effects may include:*
  Cold symptoms
  Diarrhea
  Flu
  Headache
  Infection of the upper respiratory tract
  Nasal congestion
  Nausea
  Sore throat
  Unpleasant taste
  Upset stomach
  Vomiting

- *Less common side effects may include:*
Abdominal pain, chest congestion, chest pain, cough, decreased appetite, dizziness, ear infection, eczema (inflamed skin with sores and crusting), fever, heartburn, hoarseness, inflamed lining of the nose, irritability, itching, loss of smell or taste, menstrual disturbances, nervousness, phlegm, rapid, fluttering heartbeat, rash, runny nose, shakiness, sinus congestion, sinus drainage, sinus infection, sinus inflammation, sneezing, swelling due to fluid retention, wheezing, yeastlike fungal infection of the mouth and throat

- *Rare side effects may include:*
Acne, anxiety, blurred vision, bronchitis, chest tightness, chills, constipation, depression, difficult or labored breathing, dry throat, earache, excessive restlessness, eye discomfort, eye infection, faintness, fatigue, gas, general feeling of illness, head stuffiness, high blood pressure, hives, inability to fall or stay asleep, increased appetite, indigestion, inflammation of the tongue, laryngitis, moodiness, mouth irritation, nasal irritation, nosebleed, numbness, pneumonia, rapid heart rate, sinus discomfort, sluggishness, sweating, swelling of the arms and legs, throat irritation, vertigo, weakness, weight gain

Why should this drug not be prescribed?
AeroBid should not be used if your asthma can be controlled with bronchodilators and other nonsteroid medications.

This medication should not be used if you require only occasional corticosteroid treatment for asthma. It is not for treatment of prolonged, severe asthma attacks where more intensive measures are required.

AeroBid should not be used for the treatment of nonasthmatic bronchitis.

If you are allergic or sensitive to AeroBid or other steroid drugs, advise your doctor before using this medication.

Special warnings about this medication
Your asthma should be reasonably stable before treatment with AeroBid Inhaler is started. AeroBid should be started in combination with your usual dose of an oral steroid medication. After approximately 1 week, your doctor will start to withdraw gradually the oral steroid by reducing the daily or alternate daily dose. A slow rate of reduction is very important, as some people have experienced withdrawal symptoms such as joint and/or muscular pain, fatigue, and depression. Tell your doctor if you lose weight or feel light-headed. You may need to take more systemic corticosteroid temporarily.

This medication is not useful when you need rapid relief of asthma symptoms.

Transferring from steroid tablet therapy to AeroBid Inhaler may produce allergic conditions that were previously controlled by the steroid tablet therapy. These include rhinitis (inflammation of the mucous membrane of the nose), conjunctivitis (pinkeye), and eczema.

Contact your doctor immediately if you have an asthma attack that isn't controlled by a bronchodilator while you are being treated with AeroBid. You may need an oral steroid drug.

While you are being treated with AeroBid, particularly at higher doses, your doctor will carefully observe you for any evidence of adverse effects such as the suppression of glandular function and diminished bone growth in children. If you have just had surgery or are under extreme stress, your doctor will also closely monitor you.

The use of AeroBid may cause a yeastlike fungal infection of the mouth, pharynx (throat), or larynx (voice box). If you suspect a fungal infection, notify your doctor. Treatment with antifungal medication may be necessary.

Since the contents of this inhalant are under pressure, do not puncture the container and do not use or store the medication near heat or an open flame. Exposure to temperatures above 120 degrees may cause the container to explode.

People taking drugs such as AeroBid that suppress the immune system are more open to infection. Take extra care to avoid exposure to measles and chickenpox if you've never had them or never had shots. Such diseases can be serious or even fatal when your immune system is below par. If you are exposed, tell your doctor immediately.

Possible food and drug interactions
when taking this medication
No interactions have been reported.

Special information
if you are pregnant or breastfeeding
The effects of AeroBid during pregnancy have not been adequately studied. If you are pregnant or plan to become pregnant, inform your doctor immediately. It is not known whether AeroBid appears in breast milk. If this medication is essential to your health, your doctor may advise you to discontinue breastfeeding your baby until your treatment with this medication is finished.

Recommended dosage

The AeroBid Inhaler system is for oral inhalation only.

ADULTS

The recommended starting dose is 2 inhalations twice daily, in the morning and evening, for a total daily dose of 1 milligram. The daily dose should not exceed 4 inhalations twice a day, for a total daily dose of 2 milligrams.

CHILDREN

For children 6 to 15 years of age, 2 inhalations may be used twice daily, for a total daily dose of 1 milligram.

The safety and effectiveness of this drug have not been established in children under 6 years of age.

Overdosage

Any medication taken in excess can have serious consequences. If you suspect an overdose, seek emergency medical treatment immediately.

Generic name:

ALBUTEROL

See Proventil, page 912.

Generic name:

ALCLOMETASONE

See Aclovate, page 11.

Brand name:

ALDACTAZIDE

Pronounced: al-DAK-tah-zide
Generic ingredients: Spironolactone, Hydrochlorothiazide
Other brand name: Spirozide

Why is this drug prescribed?

Aldactazide is used in the treatment of high blood pressure and other conditions that require the elimination of excess fluid from the body. These conditions include congestive heart failure, cirrhosis of the liver, and kidney disease. Aldactazide combines two diuretic drugs that help your body produce and eliminate more urine. Spironolactone, one of the ingredients, helps to minimize the potassium loss that can be caused by the hydrochlorothiazide component.

Most important fact about this drug
If you have high blood pressure, you must take Aldactazide regularly for it to be effective. Since blood pressure declines gradually, it may be several weeks before you get the full benefit of Aldactazide; and you must continue taking it even if you are feeling well. Aldactazide does not cure high blood pressure; it merely keeps it under control.

How should you take this medication?
Take Aldactazide exactly as prescribed. Stopping Aldactazide suddenly could cause your condition to worsen.

■ *If you miss a dose...*
Take it as soon as you remember. If it is almost time for your next dose, skip the one you missed and go back to your regular schedule. Never take 2 doses at the same time.

■ *Storage instructions...*
Store at room temperature.

What side effects may occur?
Side effects cannot be anticipated. If any develop or change in intensity, inform your doctor as soon as possible. Only your doctor can determine if it is safe for you to continue taking Aldactazide.

■ *Side effects may include:*
Abdominal cramps, breast development in males, change in potassium levels (leading to such symptoms as dry mouth, excessive thirst, weak or irregular heartbeat, and muscle pain or cramps), deepening of the voice, diarrhea, dizziness, dizziness on rising, drowsiness, excessive hairiness, fever, headache, hives, inflammation of blood vessels or lymph vessels, inflammation of the pancreas, irregular menstruation, lack of coordination, loss of appetite, mental confusion, muscle spasms, nausea, postmenopausal bleeding, rash, red or purple spots on skin, restlessness, sensitivity to light, sexual dysfunction, sluggishness, stomach bleeding, stomach inflammation, stomach ulcers, tingling or pins and needles, vertigo, vomiting, weakness, yellow eyes and skin, yellow vision

Why should this drug not be prescribed?

Aldactazide should not be used if you have acute kidney disease or liver failure, have difficulty urinating or are unable to urinate, or have high potassium levels in your blood.

If you are sensitive to or have ever had an allergic reaction to spironolactone, hydrochlorothiazide, or similar drugs, or if you are sensitive to sulfa drugs, you should not take this medication. Make sure your doctor is aware of any drug reactions you may have experienced.

Special warnings about this medication

This medication should be used only if your doctor has determined that the precise amount of each ingredient in Aldactazide meets your specific needs.

Potassium supplements (including salt substitutes) or diuretics that leave high levels of potassium in your body should not be used while taking Aldactazide, unless specifically recommended by your doctor.

If you are taking an ACE-inhibitor type of blood pressure medication such as Vasotec, this drug should be used with extreme caution.

If you have liver disease lupus erythematosus (a disease that causes skin eruptions), Aldactazide should be used with caution.

Excessive sweating, dehydration, severe diarrhea, or vomiting could cause you to lose too much water and cause your blood pressure to become too low. Be careful when exercising and in hot weather.

Notify your doctor or dentist that you are taking Aldactazide if you have a medical emergency, and before you have surgery or dental treatment.

Possible food and drug interactions
when taking this medication

If Aldactazide is taken with certain other drugs, the effects of either could be increased, decreased, or altered. It is especially important to check with your doctor before combining Aldactazide with the following:

ACE-inhibitor blood pressure drugs such as Vasotec
Antigout medications such as Zyloprim
Digoxin (Lanoxin)
Diuretics such as Lasix and Midamor
Indomethacin (Indocin)
Insulin or oral antidiabetic drugs such as Micronase
Lithium (Lithonate)
Norepinephrine (Levophed)
Potassium supplements such as Slow-K
Steroids such as prednisone

Special information
if you are pregnant or breastfeeding
The effects of Aldactazide during pregnancy have not been adequately studied. If you are pregnant or plan to become pregnant, inform your doctor immediately. Aldactazide appears in breast milk and could affect a nursing infant. If this medication is essential to your health, your doctor may advise you to discontinue breastfeeding until your treatment is finished.

Recommended dosage

ADULTS

Congestive Heart Failure, Cirrhosis, Nephrotic Syndrome (Kidney Disorder)
The usual dosage is 100 milligrams each of spironolactone and hydrochlorothiazide daily, taken as a single dose or in divided doses. Dosage may range from 25 milligrams to 200 milligrams of each ingredient daily, depending on your individual needs.

High Blood Pressure
The usual dose is 50 milligrams to 100 milligrams each of spironolactone and hydrochlorothiazide daily, in a single dose divided into smaller doses.

CHILDREN

The usual dose of Aldactazide should provide 0.75 milligram to 1.5 milligrams of spironolactone per pound of body weight.

ELDERLY

Your doctor will determine the dosage according to your needs.

Overdosage
Although there is no information on specific signs of Aldactazide overdose, any medication taken in excess can have serious consequences. If you suspect an overdose, seek medical attention immediately.

Brand name:

ALDACTONE

Pronounced: al-DAK-tone
Generic name: Spironolactone

Why is this drug prescribed?

Aldactone is a diuretic and high blood pressure medication. It is used in the diagnosis and treatment of hyperaldosteronism, a condition in which the adrenal gland secretes too much aldosterone (a hormone that regulates the body's salt and potassium levels). It is also used in treating other conditions that require the elimination of excess fluid from the body. These conditions include congestive heart failure, high blood pressure, cirrhosis of the liver, kidney disease, and unusually low potassium levels in the blood. When used for high blood pressure, Aldactone can be used alone or with other high blood pressure medications. Aldactone causes increased amounts of sodium and water to be eliminated, without potassium loss.

Most important fact about this drug

If you have high blood pressure, you must take Aldactone regularly for it to be effective. Since blood pressure declines gradually, it may be several weeks before you get the full benefit of Aldactone; and you must continue taking it even if you are feeling well. Aldactone does not cure high blood pressure; it merely keeps it under control.

How should you take this medication?

Take Aldactone exactly as prescribed by your doctor. Stopping Aldactone suddenly could cause your condition to worsen.

■ *If you miss a dose...*
Take it as soon as you remember. If it is almost time for your next dose, skip the one you missed and go back to your regular schedule. Never take 2 doses at the same time.

■ *Storage instructions...*
Store at room temperature.

What side effects may occur?

Side effects cannot be anticipated. If any develop or change in intensity, inform your doctor as soon as possible. Only your doctor can determine if it is safe for you to continue taking Aldactone.

■ *Side effects may include:*
Abdominal cramps, breast development in males, change in potassium levels (leading to such symptoms as dry mouth, excessive thirst, weak or irregular heartbeat, and muscle pain or cramps), deepening of voice, diarrhea, drowsiness, excessive hairiness, fever, headache, hives, irregular menstruation, lack of coordination, lethargy, mental confusion, postmeno-

pausal bleeding, sexual dysfunction, skin eruptions, stomach bleeding, stomach inflammation, ulcers, vomiting

Why should this drug not be prescribed?
You should not take Aldactone if you have kidney disease, an inability to urinate, difficulty urinating, or high potassium levels in your blood.

Special warnings about this medication
Potassium supplements or other diuretics that leave your potassium levels high, such as Maxzide, should not be used while taking Aldactone, unless specifically indicated by your doctor.

ACE inhibitors (Vasotec, Capoten), used for blood pressure and heart failure, should not be taken while using Aldactone.

If you are taking Aldactone, your kidney function should be given a complete assessment and should continue to be monitored.

If you have liver disease, your doctor will be cautious about using this medication.

Excessive sweating, dehydration, severe diarrhea, or vomiting could cause you to lose too much water and cause your blood pressure to become too low. Be careful when exercising and in hot weather.

Notify your doctor or dentist that you are taking Aldactone if you have a medical emergency, and before you have surgery or dental treatment.

Possible food and drug interactions
when taking this medication
If Aldactone is taken with certain other drugs, the effects of either could be increased, decreased, or altered. It is especially important to check with your doctor before combining Aldactone with the following:

ACE inhibitors such as Vasotec and Capoten
Digoxin (Lanoxin)
Indomethacin (Indocin)
Norepinephrine (Levophed)
Other diuretics such as Lasix and HydroDIURIL
Other high blood pressure medications such as Aldomet and Procardia
  XL

Special information
if you are pregnant or breastfeeding
The effects of Aldactone during pregnancy have not been adequately studied. If you are pregnant or plan to become pregnant, inform your doctor

immediately. Aldactone appears in breast milk and could affect a nursing infant. If this medication is essential to your health, your doctor may advise you to discontinue breastfeeding until your treatment with this medication is finished.

Recommended dosage

ADULTS

Primary Hyperaldosteronism

Initial dosages of this medication are used to determine the presence of primary hyperaldosteronism (too much secretion of the adrenal hormone aldosterone). People can be tested with this medication over either a long or a short period of time.

In the long test, you take 400 milligrams per day for 3 to 4 weeks. If your potassium levels and blood pressure are corrected with this dosage in this time period, your physician may assume you have this condition.

In the short test, you receive 400 milligrams per day for 4 days. A laboratory test compares potassium levels while on Aldactone and after the medication is stopped. Your doctor may then make a diagnosis.

After the diagnosis of primary hyperaldosteronism is made and confirmed by more tests, the usual dose is 100 to 400 milligrams per day, prior to surgery. In those who are not good candidates for surgery, this drug is given over the long term at the lowest effective dose.

Adult Edema (Congestive Heart Failure, Cirrhosis of the Liver, or Kidney Disorders)

The usual starting dosage is 100 milligrams daily either in a single dose or divided into smaller doses. However, your doctor may have you take daily doses as low as 25 milligrams or as high as 200 milligrams.

Your doctor may choose to adjust your dosage after an initial 5-day trial period or add another diuretic medication to this one.

Essential Hypertension (High Blood Pressure)

The usual starting dosage is 50 to 100 milligrams daily in a single dose or divided into smaller doses. This medication may be given with another diuretic or with other high blood pressure medications.

It may take up to 2 weeks before the full effect of this medication is seen. Your doctor can then adjust the dosage according to your response.

Hypokalemia (Potassium Loss)
Your doctor may have you take daily dosages of 25 milligrams to 100 milligrams when potassium loss caused by the effects of a diuretic cannot be treated by a potassium supplement.

CHILDREN

Edema (Swelling Due to Water Retention)
The usual starting dosage is 1.5 milligrams per pound of body weight daily in a single dose or divided into smaller doses.

Overdosage
Although no specific information on signs of Aldactone overdose is available, any medication taken in excess can have serious consequences. If you suspect an overdose, seek medical attention immediately.

Brand name:

ALDOMET

Pronounced: AL-doe-met
Generic name: Methyldopa

Why is this drug prescribed?
Aldomet is used to treat high blood pressure. It is effective when used alone or with other high blood pressure medications.

Most important fact about this drug
You must take Aldomet regularly for it to be effective. Since blood pressure declines gradually, it may be several weeks before you get the full benefit of Aldomet; and you must continue taking it even if you are feeling well. Aldomet does not cure high blood pressure; it merely keeps it under control.

How should you take this medication?
Take this medication exactly as prescribed. Try not to miss any doses. Do not stop taking the drug without your doctor's knowledge.

Drowsiness may occur when dosage is increased. If your doctor increases the amount of Aldomet you take, start the new dosage in the evening.

■ *If you miss a dose...*
   Take it as soon as you remember. If it is almost time for your next dose, skip the one you missed and go back to your regular schedule. Never take 2 doses at the same time.

■ *Storage instructions...*
Keep Aldomet in the container it came in, tightly closed. Store Aldomet tablets at room temperature. Keep oral suspension in the refrigerator. Protect from light.

What side effects may occur?
Side effects cannot be anticipated. If any develop or change in intensity, inform your doctor as soon as possible. Only your doctor can determine if it is safe for you to continue taking Aldomet.

■ *More common side effects may include:*
Drowsiness during first few weeks of therapy
Fluid retention or weight gain
Headache
Weakness

■ *Less common or rare side effects may include:*
Anemia, Bell's palsy (paralysis of the face, making it look distorted), bloating, blood disorders, breast development in males, breast enlargement, changes in menstruation, chest pain, congestive heart failure, constipation, decreased mental ability, decreased sex drive, depression, diarrhea, dizziness when standing up, dry mouth, fever, gas, hepatitis, impotence, inflammation of the large intestine, inflammation of the pancreas, inflammation of the salivary glands, involuntary movements, joint pain, light-headedness, liver disorders, milk production, muscle pain, nasal stuffiness, nausea, nightmares, parkinsonism (tremors, shuffling walk, stooped posture, muscle weakness), rash, slow heartbeat, sore or "black" tongue, tingling or pins and needles, vomiting, yellow eyes and skin

Why should this drug not be prescribed?
If you have liver disease or cirrhosis, or if you have taken Aldomet before and developed liver disease, do not take this medication.

If you are sensitive to or have ever had an allergic reaction to Aldomet, or if you are taking the oral suspension form of Aldomet and have ever had an allergic reaction to sulfites, you should not take this medication.

Special warnings about this medication
Before you begin taking Aldomet, your doctor should perform a complete study of your liver function, and it should be monitored periodically thereafter.

Aldomet can cause liver disorders. You may develop a fever, jaundice (yellow eyes and skin), or both, usually within the first 2 to 3 months of therapy. If either of these symptoms occurs, stop taking Aldomet and contact your doctor immediately. If the fever and/or jaundice were caused by the medication, your liver function should gradually return to normal.

If you have a history of liver disease, this medication should be used with caution.

Hemolytic anemia, a blood disorder in which red blood cells are destroyed, can develop with long-term use of Aldomet; your doctor will do periodic blood counts to check for this problem.

Aldomet can cause water retention or weight gain in some people. A diuretic will usually relieve these symptoms.

If you have asthma and are taking the liquid form of Aldomet, you could have an allergic reaction to the sulfite component of the liquid.

If you are on dialysis and are taking Aldomet for high blood pressure, your blood pressure may rise after your dialysis treatments.

Aldomet can cause you to become drowsy or less alert, especially during the first few weeks of therapy or when dosage levels are increased. If it affects you this way, driving or operating heavy machinery or participating in any hazardous activity that requires full mental alertness is not recommended.

Notify your doctor or dentist that you are taking Aldomet if you have a medical emergency and before you have surgery or dental treatment.

Possible food and drug interactions
when taking this medication
If Aldomet is taken with certain other drugs, the effects of either could be increased, decreased, or altered. It is especially important to check with your doctor before combining Aldomet with the following:

Dextroamphetamine (Dexedrine)
Imipramine (Tofranil)
Iron-containing products such as Feosol
Lithium (Lithonate)
Other high blood pressure drugs
Phenylpropanolamine (a decongestant used in common cold remedies
    such as Comtrex, Entex LA, and others)
Propranolol (Inderal)
Tolbutamide (Orinase)

Special information
if you are pregnant or breastfeeding
The use of Aldomet during pregnancy appears to be relatively safe. However, if you are pregnant or plan to become pregnant, inform your doctor immediately. Aldomet appears in breast milk and could affect a nursing infant. If this medication is essential to your health, your doctor may advise you to discontinue breastfeeding until your treatment is finished.

Recommended dosage
ADULTS

The usual starting dose is 250 milligrams, 2 or 3 times per day in the first 48 hours of treatment. Your doctor may increase or decrease your dose over the next few days to achieve the correct blood pressure.

To reduce the effect of any sedation the medication may cause, dosage increases will usually be given in the evening.

The usual maintenance dosage is 500 milligrams to 2 grams per day divided into 2 to 4 doses. The maximum dose is usually 3 grams. Some people may be told by their doctor to take the entire daily dose at bedtime.

Your doctor will also adjust your dosage of Aldomet when it is taken in combination with certain other high blood pressure drugs.

If you take Aldomet with a non-thiazide high blood pressure medicine, your doctor will limit the initial dosage to 500 milligrams daily divided into small doses.

Dosages will be adjusted, and other high blood pressure drugs may be added, during the first few months of treatment with Aldomet. Those with reduced kidney function may require smaller doses. Older people who are prone to fainting spells due to arterial disease may also require smaller doses.

CHILDREN

The usual starting dose is 10 milligrams per 2.2 pounds of body weight daily, divided into 2 to 4 doses. Doses will be adjusted until blood pressure is normal. The maximum daily dose is usually 65 milligrams per 2.2 pounds of body weight or 3 grams, whichever is less.

ELDERLY

Dosages of this drug are adjusted to each individual's needs. Lower doses may be prescribed by your doctor.

Overdosage

Any medication taken in excess can have serious consequences. If you suspect an overdose, seek medical attention immediately.

■ *The symptoms of Aldomet overdose may include:*

Bloating, constipation, diarrhea, dizziness, extreme drowsiness, gas, light-headedness, nausea, severely low blood pressure, slow heartbeat, vomiting, weakness

Generic name:

ALLOPURINOL

See Zyloprim, page 1248.

Generic name:

ALPRAZOLAM

See Xanax, page 1211.

Brand name:

ALTACE

Pronounced: AL-tayce
Generic name: Ramipril

Why is this drug prescribed?

Altace is used in the treatment of high blood pressure. It is effective when used alone or in combination with other high blood pressure medications, especially thiazide-type diuretics. Altace works by preventing the conversion of a chemical in your blood called Angiotensin I into a more potent substance that increases salt and water retention in your body. It also enhances blood flow in your circulatory system. It is a member of the group of drugs called ACE inhibitors.

Most important fact about this drug

You must take Altace regularly for it to be effective. Since blood pressure declines gradually, it may be several weeks before you get the full benefit of Altace; and you must continue taking it even if you are feeling well. Altace does not cure high blood pressure; it merely keeps it under control.

How should you take this medication?

Take this medication exactly as prescribed by your doctor. If you have difficulty swallowing the capsule, you can sprinkle the contents on a small amount (about 4 ounces) of apple sauce, or mix the contents with 4 ounces of water or apple juice.

■ *If you miss a dose...*
If you forget to take a dose, take it as soon as you remember. If it is almost time for your next dose, skip the one you missed and go back to your regular schedule. Never take 2 doses at the same time.

■ *Storage instructions...*
Store Altace at room temperature in a tightly closed container.

What side effects may occur?

Side effects cannot be anticipated. If any develop or change in intensity, inform your doctor as soon as possible. Only your doctor can determine if it is safe for you to continue taking Altace.

■ *More common side effects may include:*
Cough
Headache

■ *Less common or rare side effects may include:*
Abdominal pain, angina pectoris (chest pain), anxiety, arthritis, bruises, change in taste, constipation, convulsions, depression, diarrhea, difficulty swallowing, dizziness, dry mouth, fainting, fatigue, feeling of general discomfort, fluid retention, hearing loss, heart attack, impotence, inability to sleep, increased salivation, indigestion, inflammation of the stomach and intestines, irregular heartbeat, itching, joint pain or inflammation, labored breathing, light-headedness, loss of appetite, low blood pressure, memory loss, muscle pain, nausea, nerve pain, nervousness, nosebleed, rash, ringing in ears, skin inflammation, skin sensitivity to light, sleepiness, sudden loss of strength, sweating, tingling or pins and needles, tremors, vertigo, very rapid heartbeat, vision changes, vomiting, weakness, weight gain

Why should this drug not be prescribed?

If you are sensitive to or have ever had an allergic reaction to Altace or similar drugs such as Capoten, Vasotec and Zestril, or if you have a history of swelling of the face, tongue, or throat while taking these drugs, you should not take this medication. Make sure that your doctor is aware of any drug reactions that you have experienced.

Special warnings about this medication

If you develop chest pain, palpitations or other heart effects, swelling of the face around your lips, tongue, or throat or difficulty swallowing, difficulty breathing, swelling of arms and legs or infection, sore throat, and fever, you should contact your doctor immediately. You may have a serious side effect of the drug and need emergency treatment.

If you are taking Altace, your kidney function should be given a complete assessment and should continue to be monitored.

Altace should be used with caution if you have liver disease, diabetes, or a disease of the connective tissue such as lupus erythematosus or scleroderma.

If you are taking high doses of diuretics and Altace, you may develop excessively low blood pressure.

Do not use salt substitutes containing potassium without consulting your doctor.

Altace may cause you to become drowsy or less alert, especially if you are also taking a water pill (diuretic) at the same time. If it has this effect on you, driving or operating dangerous machinery or participating in any hazardous activity that requires full mental alertness is not recommended.

Light-headedness can occur when taking Altace, especially during the first days of therapy, and should be reported to your doctor. If fainting occurs, stop taking the medication and notify your doctor immediately.

Dehydration, excessive sweating, severe diarrhea or vomiting could deplete your body's fluids, causing your blood pressure to drop dangerously.

Possible food and drug interactions
when taking this medication

If Altace is taken with certain other drugs, the effects of either could be increased, decreased, or altered. It is especially important to check with your doctor before combining Altace with the following:

Alcohol
Diuretics such as hydrochlorothiazide (found in many blood pressure
    medicines) and furosemide (Lasix)
Lithium

Potassium-sparing diuretics (found in Dyazide, Maxzide, Moduretic, and others)

Spironolactone (Aldactone)

Potassium supplements such as K-lyte and K-Tab

Potassium-containing salt substitutes

Special information
if you are pregnant or breastfeeding

Altace can cause birth defects, prematurity and death to developing and newborn babies. If you are pregnant or plan to become pregnant and are taking Altace, contact your doctor immediately. Altace may appear in breast milk and could affect a nursing infant. If this medication is essential to your health, your doctor may advise you to discontinue breastfeeding until your treatment is finished.

Recommended dosage

ADULTS

For patients not on diuretics, the usual starting dose is 2.5 milligrams, taken once daily. After blood pressure is under control, the dosage will range from 2.5 to 20 milligrams a day in a single dose or divided into 2 equal doses.

Diuretic use should, if possible, be stopped before using Altace. If not, your physician may give you an initial dose of Altace under his supervision before any further medication is prescribed.

If you have kidney problems, your doctor may prescribe a lower than normal dose.

CHILDREN

The safety and effectiveness of Altace in children have not been established.

ELDERLY

Dosage varies according to the individual's response.

Overdosage

Any medication taken in excess can have serious consequences. If you suspect an overdose, seek medical attention immediately.

A sudden drop in blood pressure is likely to be the primary sign of an Altace overdose.

Brand name:

ALUPENT

Pronounced: AL-yew-pent
Generic name: Metaproterenol sulfate
Other brand name: Metaprel

Why is this drug prescribed?
Alupent is a bronchodilator prescribed for the prevention and relief of bronchial asthma and bronchial spasms (wheezing) associated with bronchitis and emphysema. Alupent Inhalation Solution is also used to treat acute asthmatic attacks in children 6 years of age and older.

Most important fact about this drug
Alupent's effects last up to 6 hours. It should not be used more frequently than your doctor recommends.

Increasing the number of doses can be dangerous and may actually make symptoms of asthma worse. Fatalities have occurred with excessive use of this medication.

If the dose your doctor recommends does not provide relief of your symptoms, if your symptoms become worse, or if side effects occur, seek medical attention immediately.

How should you take this medication?
Take this medication exactly as prescribed by your doctor.

- *If you miss a dose...*
  Take the dose as soon as you remember. Take any remaining doses for the day at equal intervals thereafter. Do not increase the total for the day or take 2 doses at the same time.

- *Storage instructions...*
  Store at room temperature. Protect from light and excessive humidity. Keep out of reach of children.

What side effects may occur?
Side effects cannot be anticipated. If any develop or change in intensity, inform your doctor as soon as possible. Only your doctor can determine if it is safe for you to continue taking Alupent.

■ *Side effects may include:*
Cough, dizziness, headache, high blood pressure, increased heart rate, nausea, nervousness, rapid, strong heartbeat, stomach and intestinal upset, throat irritation, tremors, vomiting, worsening or aggravation of asthma

Side effects can occur when a new aerosol container is used, even though you have had no trouble with the medication in the past. Replacing the container may solve the problem.

Why should this drug not be prescribed?
If you are sensitive to or have ever had an allergic reaction to Alupent or similar drugs, such as Proventil, you should not take this medication. Make sure your doctor is aware of any drug reactions you have experienced.

Unless you are directed to do so by your doctor, do not take this medication if you have an irregular, rapid heart rate.

Special warnings about this medication
When taking Alupent, you should not use other inhaled medications (called sympathomimetics) before checking with your doctor. Only your doctor can determine the sufficient amount of time between inhaled medications.

A single dose of nebulized Alupent used to treat an acute attack of asthma may not completely stop the attack.

Consult your doctor before using this medication if you have a heart condition or convulsive disorder (e.g., epilepsy), high blood pressure, hyperthyroidism, or diabetes mellitus.

Possible food and drug interactions
when taking this medication
If Alupent is taken with certain other drugs, the effects of either could be increased, decreased, or altered. It is especially important to check with your doctor before combining Alupent with the following:

MAO inhibitors (antidepressant drugs such as Nardil and Parnate)
Bronchodilators such as Ventolin and Proventil inhalers
Tricyclic antidepressants such as Elavil and Tofranil

Special information
if you are pregnant or breastfeeding
The effects of Alupent during pregnancy have not been adequately studied. If you are pregnant or plan to become pregnant, inform your doctor immediate-

ly. It is not known whether Alupent appears in breast milk. If this medication is essential to your health, your doctor may advise you to stop nursing your baby until your treatment is finished.

Recommended dosage

ADULTS

Inhalation Aerosol
The usual single dose is 2 to 3 inhalations. Inhalation should usually not be repeated more often than about every 3 to 4 hours. Total dosage per day should not exceed 12 inhalations.

Inhalation Solution 5%
Treatment usually need not be repeated more often than every 4 hours to relieve acute attacks of bronchospasm.

As part of a total treatment program for chronic breathing disorders, the inhalation solution may be taken 3 to 4 times per day, as determined by your doctor.

Inhalation solution is given by oral inhalation with the aid of a hand-bulb nebulizer or an intermittent positive pressure breathing (IPPB) apparatus.

The usual single dose with the nebulizer is 10 inhalations. However, a single dose of 5 to 15 inhalations can be taken, as determined by your doctor. The usual single daily dose with the IPPB is 0.3 milliliter diluted in approximately 2.5 milliliters of saline solution. The dosage range is 0.2 to 0.3 milliliter, as determined by your doctor.

Inhalation Solution 0.4% and 0.6% Unit-Dose Vials
The inhalation solution unit-dose vial is administered by oral inhalation using an intermittent positive pressure breathing (IPPB) apparatus. The usual adult dose is 1 vial per treatment. You should not need to repeat the treatment more often than every 4 hours for severe attacks of wheezing. You can use the unit-dose vials 3 to 4 times a day.

Syrup
The usual dose is 2 teaspoonfuls, 3 or 4 times a day.

Tablets
The usual dose is 20 milligrams, 3 or 4 times per day.

CHILDREN

Inhalation Aerosol
Alupent Inhalation Aerosol is not recommended for use in children under 12 years of age.

Inhalation Solution
For children aged 6 to 12 years, the usual single dose is 0.1 milliliter, given by oral inhalation with a nebulizer. Dosage can be increased to 0.2 milliliter.

The unit-dose vial is not recommended for children under 12 years of age.

Syrup
The usual dose for children 6 to 9 years of age or weighing under 60 pounds is 1 teaspoonful, 3 or 4 times a day.

The usual dose for children over 9 years of age or weighing over 60 pounds is 2 teaspoonfuls, 3 or 4 times a day.

Tablets
The usual dose for children 6 to 9 years of age or weighing under 60 pounds is 10 milligrams, 3 or 4 times a day.

The usual dose for children over 9 years of age or weighing over 60 pounds is 20 milligrams, 3 or 4 times a day.

Tablets are not recommended for use in children under 6 years of age.

Overdosage
Any medication taken in excess can have serious consequences.

If you suspect an overdose, seek medical attention immediately.

■ *Symptoms of Alupent overdose may include:*

Dizziness, dry mouth, fatigue, general feeling of bodily discomfort, headache, high or low blood pressure, inability to fall or stay asleep, irregular heartbeat, nausea, nervousness, rapid, fluttery heartbeat, severe, suffocating chest pain, tremors

Brand name:

AMBIEN

Pronounced: AM-bee-en
Generic name: Zolpidem tartrate

Why is this drug prescribed?
Ambien is used for short-term treatment of insomnia (difficulty falling asleep or staying asleep, or early awakening). A relatively new drug, it is chemically different from other common sleep medications such as Halcion and Dalmane.

Most important fact about this drug
Sleep problems are usually temporary and require medication for a week or two at most. Insomnia that lasts longer could be a sign of another medical problem. If you find that you need this medicine for more than 7 to 10 days, be sure to check with your doctor.

How should you take this medication?
Ambien works very quickly. Take it just before going to bed. Take only the prescribed dose, exactly as instructed by your doctor.

■ *If you miss a dose...*
Take Ambien only as needed. Never double the dose.

■ *Storage instructions...*
Store at room temperature. Protect from extreme heat.

What side effects may occur?
Side effects cannot be anticipated. If any develop or change in intensity, tell your doctor immediately. Only your doctor can determine whether it is safe to continue taking Ambien.

■ *More common side effects may include:*
Abdominal pain, abnormal vision, allergy, back pain, confusion, constipation, daytime drowsiness, depression, dizziness, double vision, drugged feeling, dry mouth, exaggerated feeling of well-being, flu-like symptoms, headache, indigestion, inflammation of the throat, insomnia, joint pain, lack of muscle coordination, lethargy, light-headedness, nausea, rash, sinus inflammation, throbbing heartbeat, upper respiratory infection, urinary tract infection, vertigo

■ *Less common side effects may include:*
Abnormal dreams, agitation, amnesia, anxiety, arthritis, bronchitis, burning sensation, chest pain, constipation, coughing, daytime sleeping, decreased mental alertness, diarrhea, difficulty breathing, difficulty concentrating, difficulty swallowing, diminished sensitivity to touch, dizziness on standing, emotional instability, eye irritation, falling, fatigue, fever, gas, general discomfort, hallucination, hiccup, high blood pressure, high blood

sugar, increased sweating, infection, lack of bladder control, loss of appetite, menstrual disorder, migraine, muscle pain, nasal inflammation, nervousness, numbness, paleness, prickling or tingling sensation, rapid heartbeat, ringing in the ears, sleep disorder, speech difficulties, swelling due to fluid retention, taste abnormalities, tremor, unconsciousness, vomiting, weakness

■ *Rare side effects may include:*
Abnormal tears or tearing, abscess, acne, aggravation of allergies, aggravation of high blood pressure, aggression, allergic reaction, altered production of saliva, anemia, belching, blisters, blood clot in lung, boils, breast pain, breast problems, breast tumors, bruising, chill with high temperature, followed by heat and perspiration, decreased sex drive, delusion, difficulties with blood circulation, difficulty urinating, excess hemoglobin in the blood, excessive urine production, eye pain, facial swelling due to fluid retention, fainting, false perceptions, feeling intoxicated, feeling strange, flushing, frequent urination, glaucoma, gout, heart attack, hemorrhoids, herpes infection, high cholesterol, hives, hot flashes, impotence, inability to urinate, increased appetite, increased tolerance to the drug, intestinal blockage, irregular heartbeat, joint degeneration, kidney failure, kidney pain, laryngitis, leg cramps, loss of reality, low blood pressure, mental deterioration, muscle spasms in arms and legs, muscle weakness, nosebleed, pain, painful urination, panic attacks, paralysis, pneumonia, rectal bleeding, rigidity, sciatica (lower back pain), sensation of seeing flashes of lights or sparks, sensitivity to light, sleepwalking, speech difficulties, swelling of the eye, thinking abnormalities, thirst, tooth decay, uncontrolled leg movements, urge to go to the bathroom, varicose veins, weight loss, yawning

Why should this drug not be prescribed?
There are no known situations in which Ambien cannot be used.

Special warnings about this medication
When Ambien is used every night for more than a few weeks, it loses its effectiveness. Remember, too, that you can become dependent on the drug if you use it for a long time or at high doses.

Some people using Ambien have experienced unusual changes in their thinking and/or behavior. Alert your doctor if you notice a change.

Ambien and other sleep medicines can cause a special type of memory loss. It should not be taken on an overnight airplane flight of less than 7 to 8 hours, since "traveler's amnesia" may occur.

When you first start taking Ambien, until you know whether the medication will have any "carry over" effect the next day, use extreme care while doing anything that requires complete alertness, such as driving a car or operating machinery.

Use Ambien cautiously if you have kidney or liver problems. It will take longer for its effects to wear off.

If you take Ambien for more than 1 or 2 weeks, consult your doctor before stopping. Sudden discontinuation of a sleep medicine can bring on withdrawal symptoms ranging from unpleasant feelings to vomiting and cramps.

When taking Ambien, do *not* drink alcohol. It can increase the drug's side effects.

If you have breathing problems, they may become worse when you use Ambien.

Possible food and drug interactions
when taking this medication

If Ambien is used with certain other drugs, the effects of either drug could be increased, decreased, or altered. It is especially important to check with your doctor before combining Ambien with the following:

The major tranquilizer, chlorpromazine (Thorazine)
The antidepressant drug, imipramine (Tofranil)
Other drugs that depress the central nervous system, including Valium, Percocet, and Benadryl

Special information
if you are pregnant or breastfeeding

If you are pregnant or plan to become pregnant, inform your doctor immediately. Babies whose mothers take sedative/hypnotic drugs such as Ambien may have withdrawal symptoms after birth and may seem limp and flaccid. Ambien is not recommended for use by nursing mothers.

Recommended dosage

ADULTS

The recommended dosage for adults is 10 milligrams right before bedtime. Your doctor will prescribe a smaller dose if you are likely to be sensitive to the drug. Never take more than 10 milligrams of Ambien per day.

CHILDREN

Safety and effectiveness have not been established in children below the age of 18.

ELDERLY

Because older people may be more sensitive to Ambien's effects, the recommended starting dosage is 5 milligrams just before bedtime.

Overdosage

People who take too much Ambien may become excessively sleepy or even go into a light coma. The symptoms of overdose are more severe if the person is also taking other drugs that depress the central nervous system. Some cases of multiple overdose have been fatal.

If you suspect an overdose, seek medical attention immediately.

Generic name:

AMCINONIDE

See Cyclocort, page 255.

Generic name:

AMILORIDE WITH HYDROCHLOROTHIAZIDE

See Moduretic, page 678.

Generic name:

AMITRIPTYLINE

See Elavil, page 386.

Generic name:

AMITRIPTYLINE WITH PERPHENAZINE

See Triavil, page 1147.

Generic name:

AMLODIPINE

See Norvasc, page 764.

Generic name:

AMOXICILLIN

See Amoxil, page 47.

Generic name:

AMOXICILLIN WITH CLAVULANATE

See Augmentin, page 88.

Brand name:

AMOXIL

Pronounced: a-MOX-il
Generic name: Amoxicillin
Other brand names: Trimox, Wymox

Why is this drug prescribed?
Amoxil, an antibiotic, is used to treat a wide variety of infections, including gonorrhea, middle ear infections, skin infections, upper and lower respiratory tract infections, and infections of genital and urinary tract.

Most important fact about this drug
If you are allergic to either penicillin or cephalosporin antibiotics in any form, consult your doctor before taking Amoxil. There is a possibility that you are allergic to both types of medication; and if a reaction occurs, it could be extremely severe. If you take the drug and feel signs of a reaction, seek medical attention immediately.

How should you take this medication?
Amoxil can be taken with or without food. If you are using Amoxil suspension, shake it well before using.

- *If you miss a dose...*
  Take it as soon as you remember. If it is almost time for the next dose, and you take 2 doses a day, take the one you missed and the next dose 5 to 6 hours later. If you take 3 or more doses a day, take the one you missed and the next dose 2 to 4 hours later. Then go back to your regular schedule.

- *Storage instructions...*
  Amoxil suspension and pediatric drops should be stored in a tightly closed bottle. Discard any unused medication after 14 days. Refrigeration is preferable.

What side effects may occur?
Side effects cannot be anticipated. If any develop or change in intensity, inform your doctor as soon as possible. Only your doctor can determine if it is safe for you to continue taking Amoxil.

- *Side effects may include:*
   Agitation, anemia, anxiety, changes in behavior, confusion, diarrhea, dizziness, hives, hyperactivity, insomnia, nausea, rash, vomiting

Why should this drug not be prescribed?
You should not use Amoxil if you are allergic to penicillin or cephalosporin antibiotics (for example, Ceclor).

Special warnings about this medication
If you have ever had asthma, hives, hay fever, or other allergies, consult with your doctor before taking Amoxil.

You should stop using Amoxil if you experience reactions such as bruising, fever, skin rash, itching, joint pain, swollen lymph nodes, and/or sores on the genitals. If these reactions occur, stop taking Amoxil unless your doctor advises you to continue.

For infections such as strep throat, it is important to take Amoxil for the entire amount of time your doctor has prescribed. Even if you feel better, you need to continue taking Amoxil. If you stop taking Amoxil before your treatment time is complete, you may get other infections, such as glomerulonephritis (a kidney infection) or rheumatic fever.

If you are diabetic, be aware that Amoxil may cause a *false positive* Clinitest (urine glucose test) result to occur. You should consult with your doctor about using different tests while taking Amoxil.

Before taking Amoxil, tell your doctor if you have ever had asthma, colitis (inflammatory bowel disease), diabetes, or kidney or liver disease.

Possible food and drug interactions
when taking this medication
If Amoxil is taken with certain other drugs, the effects of either could be increased, decreased, or altered. It is especially important to check with your doctor before combining Amoxil with the following:

   Chloramphenicol (Chloromycetin)
   Erythromycin (E.E.S., PCE, others)
   Oral contraceptives
   Probenecid (Benemid)
   Tetracycline (Achromycin V, others)

Special information
if you are pregnant or breastfeeding
Amoxil should be used during pregnancy only when clearly needed. If you are pregnant or plan to become pregnant, inform your doctor immediately. Since

Amoxil may appear in breast milk, you should consult your doctor if you plan to breastfeed your baby.

Recommended dosage
Dosages will be determined by the type of infection being treated.

ADULTS

Ear, Nose, Throat, Skin, Genital, and Urinary Tract Infections
The usual dosage is 250 milligrams, taken every 8 hours.

Infections of the Lower Respiratory Tract
The usual dosage is 500 milligrams, taken every 8 hours.

Gonorrhea
The usual dosage is 3 grams in a single oral dose.

Gonococcal Infections Such as Acute, Uncomplicated Anogenital, and Urethral Infections
3 grams as a single oral dose.

CHILDREN

Children weighing 44 pounds and over should follow the recommended adult dose schedule.

Children weighing under 44 pounds will have their dosage determined by their weight.

Dosage of Pediatric Drops:
Use the dropper provided with the medication to measure all doses.

All Infections Except Those of the Lower Respiratory Tract
Under 13 pounds:
0.75 milliliter every 8 hours.
13 to 15 pounds:
1 milliliter every 8 hours.
16 to 18 pounds:
1.25 milliliters every 8 hours.

Infections of the Lower Respiratory Tract
Under 13 pounds:
1.25 milliliters every 8 hours.
13 to 15 pounds:
1.75 milliliters every 8 hours.
16 to 18 pounds:
2.25 milliliters every 8 hours.

Children weighing more than 18 pounds should take the oral liquid. The required amount of suspension should be placed directly on the child's tongue for swallowing. It can also be added to formula, milk, fruit juice, water, ginger ale, or cold drinks. The preparation should be taken immediately. To be certain the child is getting the full dose of medication, make sure he or she drinks the entire preparation.

ELDERLY
The elderly should use Amoxil cautiously.

Overdosage
Any medication taken in excess can have serious consequences. If you suspect an overdose, seek medical attention immediately.

■ *Symptoms of Amoxil overdose may include:*
Diarrhea
Nausea
Stomach cramps
Vomiting

Generic name:

AMPICILLIN

See Omnipen, page 772.

Brand name:

ANAFRANIL

Pronounced: an-AF-ran-il
Generic name: Clomipramine hydrochloride

Why is this drug prescribed?
Anafranil, a chemical cousin of tricyclic antidepressant medications such as Tofranil and Elavil, is used to treat people who suffer from obsessions and compulsions.

An obsession is a persistent, disturbing idea, image, or urge that keeps coming to mind despite the person's efforts to ignore or forget it—for example, a preoccupation with avoiding contamination.

A compulsion is an irrational action that the person knows is senseless but feels driven to repeat again and again—for example, hand-washing perhaps dozens or even scores of times throughout the day.

Most important fact about this drug
Serious, even fatal, reactions have been known to occur when drugs such as Anafranil are taken along with the antidepressant drugs known as MAO inhibitors. Drugs in this category include Nardil, Marplan, and Parnate. Never take Anafranil with one of these drugs.

How should you take this medication?
Take Anafranil with meals, at first, to avoid stomach upset. After your regular dosage has been established, you can take 1 dose at bedtime to avoid sleepiness during the day. Always take it exactly as prescribed.

This medicine may cause dry mouth. Hard candy, chewing gum, or bits of ice may relieve this problem

- *If you miss a dose...*
  If you take 1 dose at bedtime, consult your doctor. Do not take the missed dose in the morning. If you take 2 or more doses a day, take the missed dose as soon as you remember. If it is almost time for your next dose, skip the one you missed and go back to your regular schedule. Do not take 2 doses at the same time.

- *Storage instructions...*
  Store at room temperature in a tightly closed container, away from moisture.

What side effects may occur?
Side effects cannot be anticipated. If any develop or change in intensity, inform your doctor as soon as possible. Only your doctor can determine if it is safe for you to continue taking Anafranil.

The most significant risk is that of seizures (convulsions). Headache, fatigue, and nausea can be a problem. Men are likely to experience problems with sexual function. Unwanted weight gain is a potential problem for many people who take Anafranil, although a small number actually lose weight.

■ *More common side effects may include:*
Abdominal pain, abnormal dreaming, abnormal tearing, abnormal milk secretion, agitation, allergy, anxiety, appetite loss, back pain, chest pain, confusion, constipation, coughing, depression, diarrhea, dizziness, dry mouth, extreme sleepiness, failure to ejaculate, fast heartbeat, fatigue, fever, flushing, fluttery heartbeat, frequent urination, gas, headache, hot flushes, impotence, inability to concentrate, increased appetite, increased sweating, indigestion, inflamed lining of nose or sinuses, itching, joint pain, light-headedness on standing up, memory problems, menstrual pain and disorders, middle ear infection (children), migraine, muscle pain or tension, nausea, nervousness, pain, rash, red or purple areas on the skin, ringing in the ears, sex-drive changes, sleeplessness, sleep disturbances, sore throat, speech disturbances, taste changes, tingling or pins and needles, tooth disorder, tremor, twitching, urinary problems, urinary tract infection, vision problems, vomiting, weight gain, weight loss (children), yawning

■ *Less common side effects may include:*
Abnormal skin odor (children), acne, aggression (children), eye allergy (children), anemia (children), bad breath (children), belching (children), breast enlargement, breast pain, chills, conjunctivitis (pinkeye), difficult or labored breathing (children), difficulty swallowing, difficulty or pain in urinating, dilated pupils, dry skin, emotional instability, eye twitching (children), fainting (children), hearing disorder (children), hives, irritability, lack of menstruation, loss of sense of identity, mouth inflammation (children), muscle weakness, nosebleed, panic, paralysis (children), skin inflammation, sore throat (children), stomach and intestinal problems, swelling due to fluid retention, thirst, unequal size of pupils of the eye (children), vaginal inflammation, weakness (children), wheezing, white or yellow vaginal discharge

Why should this drug not be prescribed?
Do not take this medication if you are sensitive to or have ever had an allergic reaction to a tricyclic antidepressant such as Tofranil and Elavil.

Be sure to avoid Anafranil if you are taking, or have taken within the past 14 days, an MAO inhibitor antidepressant such as Parnate, Nardil, or Marplan. Combining Anafranil with one of these medications could lead to fever, seizures, coma, and even death.

Do not take Anafranil if you have recently had a heart attack.

Special warnings about this medication
If you have narrow-angle glaucoma (increased pressure in the eye) or are
having difficulty urinating, Anafranil could make these conditions worse. Use
Anafranil with caution if your kidney function is not normal.

If you have a tumor of the adrenal gland, this medication could cause your
blood pressure to rise suddenly and dangerously.

Because Anafranil poses a possible risk of seizures, and because it may
impair mental or physical ability to perform complicated tasks, your doctor
will probably warn you to take special precautions if you need to drive a car,
operate complicated machinery, or take part in activities such as swimming
or climbing, in which suddenly losing consciousness could be dangerous.
Note that your risk of seizures is increased:

- If you have ever had a seizure
- If you have a history of brain damage or alcoholism
- If you are taking another medication that might predispose you to seizures

As with Tofranil, Elavil, and other tricyclic antidepressants, an overdose of
Anafranil can be fatal. Do not be surprised if your doctor prescribes only a
small quantity of Anafranil at a time. This is standard procedure to minimize
the risk of overdose.

Anafranil may cause your skin to become more sensitive to sunlight. Avoid
prolonged exposure to sunlight.

Before having any kind of surgery involving the use of general anesthesia, tell
your doctor or dentist that you are taking Anafranil. You may be advised to
discontinue the drug temporarily.

When it is time to stop taking Anafranil, do not stop abruptly. Your doctor
will have you taper off gradually to avoid withdrawal symptoms such as
dizziness, fever, general feeling of illness, headache, high fever, irritability or
worsening emotional or mental problems, nausea, sleep problems, vomiting.

**Possible food and drug interactions
when taking this medication**
Avoid alcoholic beverages while taking Anafranil.

If Anafranil is taken with certain other drugs, the effects of either could be
increased, decreased, or altered. It is especially important to check with your
doctor before combining Anafranil with the following:

Antispasmodic drugs such as Donnatal, Cogentin, and Bentyl
Barbiturates such as phenobarbital
Certain blood pressure drugs such as Ismelin and Catapres-TTS

Cimetidine (Tagamet)
Digoxin (Lanoxin)
Fluoxetine (Prozac)
Haloperidol (Haldol)
Methylphenidate (Ritalin)
Major tranquilizers such as Thorazine
MAO inhibitors such as Nardil and Parnate
Phenytoin (Dilantin)
Thyroid medications such as Synthroid
Tranquilizers such as Xanax and Valium
Warfarin (Coumadin)

Special information
if you are pregnant or breastfeeding

If you are pregnant or plan to become pregnant, inform your doctor immediately. Anafranil should not be used during pregnancy unless absolutely necessary; some babies born to women who took Anafranil have had withdrawal symptoms such as jitteriness, tremors, and seizures. Anafranil appears in breast milk. Your doctor may advise you to stop breastfeeding while you are taking Anafranil.

Recommended dosage

ADULTS

The usual recommended initial dose is 25 milligrams daily. Your doctor may gradually increase this dosage to 100 milligrams during the first 2 weeks. During this period you will be asked to take this drug, divided into smaller doses, with meals. The maximum daily dosage is 250 milligrams. After the dose has been determined, your doctor may direct you to take a single dose at bedtime, to avoid sleepiness during the day.

CHILDREN

The usual recommended initial dose is 25 milligrams daily, divided into smaller doses and taken with meals. Your doctor may gradually increase the dose to a maximum of 100 milligrams or 3 milligrams per 2.2 pounds of body weight per day, whichever is smaller. The maximum dose is 200 milligrams or 3 milligrams per 2.2 pounds of body weight, whichever is smaller. Once the dose has been determined, the child can take it in a single dose at bedtime.

Overdosage

An overdose of Anafranil can be fatal. If you suspect an overdose, seek medical attention immediately.

- *Early signs and symptoms of Anafranil overdose may include:*
  Agitation, coma, convulsions, delirium, drowsiness, grimacing, exaggerated reflexes, loss of coordination, restlessness, rigid muscles, staggering gait, stupor, sweating, twitching, writhing

- *Other signs and symptoms of overdosage may include:*
  Bluish skin color, dilated pupils, excessive perspiration, fever, irregular heartbeat, little or no urine, low blood pressure, rapid heartbeat, shallow breathing, shock, vomiting

There is a danger of heart malfunction and even, in rare cases, cardiac arrest.

Brand name:

ANAPROX

Pronounced: AN-uh-procks
Generic name: Naproxen sodium

Why is this drug prescribed?
Anaprox, a nonsteroidal anti-inflammatory drug, is used to relieve mild to moderate pain and menstrual cramps. It is also prescribed for relief of the inflammation, swelling, stiffness, and joint pain associated with rheumatoid arthritis, osteoarthritis (the most common form of arthritis), and for juvenile arthritis, ankylosing spondylitis (spinal arthritis), tendinitis, bursitis, acute gout, and other conditions.

Most important fact about this drug
You should have frequent checkups with your doctor if you take Anaprox regularly. Ulcers or internal bleeding can occur without warning.

How should you take this medication?
Your doctor may ask you to take Anaprox with food or an antacid to avoid stomach upset.

Take this medication exactly as prescribed by your doctor.

If you are using Anaprox for arthritis, it should be taken regularly.

- *If you miss a dose...*
  Take the forgotten dose as soon as you remember. If it is almost time for your next dose, skip the one you missed and go back to your regular schedule. Never take 2 doses at the same time.

■ *Storage instructions...*
Store at room temperature in a tightly closed container.

What side effects may occur?
Side effects cannot be anticipated. If any develop or change in intensity, inform your doctor as soon as possible. Only your doctor can determine if it is safe for you to continue taking Anaprox.

■ *More common side effects may include:*
Abdominal pain, bruising, constipation, diarrhea, difficult or labored breathing, dizziness, drowsiness, headache, hearing changes, heartburn, indigestion, inflammation of the mouth, itching, light-headedness, nausea, rapid, fluttery heartbeat, red or purple spots on the skin, ringing in the ears, skin eruptions, sweating, swelling due to fluid retention, thirst, vertigo, vision changes

■ *Less common or rare side effects may include:*
Abdominal bleeding, black stools, blood in the urine, change in dream patterns, changes in hearing, chills and fever, colitis (inflammation of the large intestine), congestive heart failure, depression, general feeling of illness, hair loss, inability to concentrate, inability to sleep, inflammation of the lungs, kidney disease or failure, menstrual problems, muscle weakness and/or pain, peptic ulcer, severe allergic reactions, skin inflammation due to sensitivity to light, skin rashes, vomiting, vomiting blood, yellow skin and eyes

Why should this drug not be prescribed?
If you are sensitive to or have ever had an allergic reaction to Anaprox, aspirin, or similar drugs such as Motrin, or if you have had asthma attacks caused by aspirin or other drugs of this type, you should not take this medication. Make sure your doctor is aware of any drug reactions you have experienced.

Special warnings about this medication
Remember that peptic ulcers and bleeding can occur without warning.

This drug should be used with caution if you have kidney or liver disease. It can cause liver inflammation in some people.

Do not take aspirin or any other anti-inflammatory medications while taking Anaprox, unless your doctor tells you to do so.

Anaprox contains sodium. If you are on a low-sodium diet, discuss this with your doctor.

Use with caution if you have heart disease or high blood pressure. This drug can increase water retention.

Anaprox may cause vision problems. If you experience any changes in your vision, inform your doctor.

Anaprox may cause you to become drowsy or less alert; therefore, driving or operating dangerous machinery or participating in any hazardous activity that requires full mental alertness is not recommended.

Possible food and drug interactions when taking this medication

If Anaprox is taken with certain other drugs, the effects of either could be increased, decreased, or altered. It is especially important to check with your doctor before combining Anaprox with the following:

Antiseizure drugs such as Dilantin
Aspirin
Beta blockers, including blood pressure drugs such as Inderal
Blood thinners such as Coumadin
Lithium (Lithonate)
Loop diuretics such as Lasix
Methotrexate
Naproxen in other forms such as Naprosyn
Oral diabetes drugs such as Micronase
Probenecid (Benemid)

Special information if you are pregnant or breastfeeding

The effects of Anaprox during pregnancy have not been adequately studied. If you are pregnant or plan to become pregnant, inform your doctor immediately. Anaprox appears in breast milk and could affect a nursing infant. If this medication is essential to your health, your doctor may advise you to discontinue breastfeeding until your treatment with this medication is finished.

Recommended dosage

ADULTS

Mild to Moderate Pain, Menstrual Cramps, Acute Tendinitis and Bursitis
The starting dose is 550 milligrams, followed by 275 milligrams every 6 to 8 hours. You should not take more than 1,375 milligrams a day.

Rheumatoid Arthritis, Osteoarthritis, and Ankylosing Spondylitis

The starting dose is 275 milligrams or 550 milligrams 2 times a day (morning and evening). Your physician can adjust the doses for maximum benefit. Symptoms should improve within 2 to 4 weeks.

Acute Gout

The starting dose is 825 milligrams, followed by 275 milligrams every 8 hours, until symptoms subside.

CHILDREN

Juvenile Arthritis

The usual daily dosage is a total of 10 milligrams per 2.2 pounds of body weight, divided into 2 doses. Dosage should not exceed 15 milligrams per 2.2 pounds per day.

The safety and effectiveness of Anaprox have not been established in children under 2 years of age.

ELDERLY

Your doctor will determine the dosage based on your particular needs. Adjustments in the normal adult dosage may be needed.

Overdosage

Any medication taken in excess can cause symptoms of overdose. If you suspect an overdose of Anaprox, seek medical attention immediately.

- *The symptoms of Anaprox overdose may include:*
  Drowsiness
  Heartburn
  Indigestion
  Nausea
  Vomiting

Brand name:

ANASPAZ

See Levsin, page 567.

Brand name:

ANEXSIA

See Vicodin, page 1193.

Generic name:

ANOLOR 300

See Fioricet, page 433.

Brand name:

ANSAID

Pronounced: AN-sed
Generic name: Flurbiprofen

Why is this drug prescribed?

Ansaid, a nonsteroidal anti-inflammatory drug, is used to relieve the inflammation, swelling, stiffness, and joint pain associated with rheumatoid arthritis and osteoarthritis (the most common form of arthritis).

Most important fact about this drug

You should have frequent checkups with your doctor if you take Ansaid regularly. Ulcers or internal bleeding can occur without warning.

How should you take this medication?

Your doctor may ask you to take Ansaid with food or an antacid.

Take this medication exactly as prescribed by your doctor.

If you are using Ansaid for arthritis, it should be taken regularly.

- *If you miss a dose...*
  Take the forgotten dose as soon as you remember. If it is almost time for your next dose, skip the one you missed and go back to your regular schedule. Never take 2 doses at the same time.

- *Storage instructions...*
  Store at room temperature.

What side effects may occur?
Side effects cannot be anticipated. If any develop or change in intensity, inform your doctor as soon as possible. Only your doctor can determine if it is safe for you to continue taking Ansaid.

■ *More common side effects may include:*
Abdominal bleeding, abdominal pain, anxiety, constipation, depression, diarrhea, dizziness, gas, general feeling of illness, headache, inflammation of the nose, indigestion, loss of memory, nausea, nervousness, rash, ringing in ears, sleepiness, swelling due to fluid retention, tremors, trouble sleeping, urinary tract infection, vision changes, vomiting, weakness, weight changes

■ *Less common or rare side effects may include:*
Altered sense of smell, anemia, asthma, blood in the urine, bloody diarrhea, bruising, chills and fever, confusion, conjunctivitis (pinkeye), heart failure, hepatitis, high blood pressure, hives, inflammation of the mouth and tongue, inflammation of the stomach, itching, kidney failure, lack of coordination, nosebleed, peptic ulcer, pins and needles, sensitivity of skin to light, severe allergic reaction, skin inflammation with or without sores and crusting, swelling of throat, twitching, vomiting blood, welts, yellow eyes and skin

Why should this drug not be prescribed?
If you are sensitive to or have ever had an allergic reaction to Ansaid, aspirin, or similar drugs such as Motrin, or if you have had asthma attacks caused by aspirin or other drugs of this type, you should not take this medication. Make sure your doctor is aware of any drug reactions you have experienced.

Special warnings about this medication
This drug should be used with caution if you have kidney or liver disease. Kidney problems are most likely to develop in such people, as well as in those with heart failure, those taking diuretics (water pills), and the elderly.

Do not take aspirin or similar drugs while taking Ansaid, unless your doctor tells you to do so.

Ansaid can cause vision problems. If you experience a change in your vision, inform your doctor. Blurred and/or decreased vision has occurred while taking this medication.

Ansaid prolongs bleeding time. If you are taking blood-thinning medication, this drug should be taken with caution.

This drug can increase water retention. If you have heart disease or high blood pressure, use with caution.

If you want to take Ansaid for pain less serious than that of arthritis, be sure to discuss the risks of using this drug with your doctor.

Possible food and drug interactions
when taking this medication

If Ansaid is taken with certain other drugs, the effects of either could be increased, decreased, or altered. It is especially important to check with your doctor before combining Ansaid with the following:

Aspirin
Beta blockers such as Inderal and Tenormin
Blood thinners such as Coumadin
Cimetidine (Tagamet)
Diuretics such as Lasix and Bumex
Methotrexate
Oral diabetes drugs such as Micronase

Special information
if you are pregnant or breastfeeding

The effects of Ansaid during pregnancy have not been adequately studied. If you are pregnant or plan to become pregnant, inform your doctor immediately. Ansaid appears in breast milk and could affect a nursing infant. If this medication is essential to your health, your doctor may advise you to discontinue breastfeeding until your treatment is finished.

Recommended dosage

ADULTS

Rheumatoid Arthritis or Osteoarthritis:
The usual starting dosage is a total of 200 to 300 milligrams a day, divided into 2, 3, or 4 smaller doses (usually 3 or 4 for rheumatoid arthritis). Your doctor will tailor the dose to suit your needs, but you should not take more than 100 milligrams at any one time or more than 300 milligrams in a day.

CHILDREN

The safety and effectiveness of Ansaid have not been established in children.

ELDERLY

The elderly are among those most apt to develop kidney problems while taking this drug.

Your doctor will determine the dosage according to your needs.

Overdosage

Any medication taken in excess can cause symptoms of overdose. If you suspect an overdose of Ansaid, seek medical attention immediately.

- *The symptoms of Ansaid overdose may include:*

  Agitation, change in pupil size, coma, disorientation, dizziness, double vision, drowsiness, headache, nausea, semiconsciousness, shallow breathing, stomach pain

Category:

ANTACIDS

Brand names: Gaviscon, Gelusil, Maalox, Mylanta, Rolaids, Tums

Why is this drug prescribed?

Available under a number of brand names, antacids are used to relieve the uncomfortable symptoms of acid indigestion, heartburn, gas, and sour stomach.

Most important fact about this drug

Do not take antacids for longer than 2 weeks or in larger than recommended doses unless directed by your doctor. If your symptoms persist, contact your doctor. Antacids should be used only for occasional relief of stomach upset.

How should you take this medication?

If you take a chewable antacid tablet, chew thoroughly before swallowing so that the medicine can work faster and be more effective. Allow Mylanta Soothing Lozenges to completely dissolve in your mouth. Shake liquids well before using.

- *If you miss a dose...*
  Take this medication only as needed or as instructed by your doctor.

- *Storage instructions...*
  Store at room temperature. Keep liquids tightly closed and protect from freezing.

What side effects may occur?

When taken as recommended, antacids are relatively free of side effects. Occasionally, one of the following symptoms may develop.

■ *Side effects may include:*
  Chalky taste
  Constipation
  Diarrhea
  Increased thirst
  Stomach cramps

Why should this drug not be prescribed?

Do not take antacids if you have signs of appendicitis or an inflamed bowel; symptoms include stomach or lower abdominal pain, cramping, bloating, soreness, nausea, or vomiting.

If you are sensitive to or have ever had an allergic reaction to aluminum, calcium, magnesium, or simethicone, do not take an antacid containing these ingredients. If you are elderly and have bone problems or if you are taking care of an elderly person with Alzheimer's disease, do not use an antacid containing aluminum.

Special warnings about this medication

If you are taking any prescription drug, check with your doctor before you take an antacid. Also, tell your doctor or pharmacist about any drug allergies or medical conditions you have.

If you have kidney disease, do not take an antacid containing aluminum or magnesium. If you are on a sodium-restricted diet, do not take Gaviscon without checking first with your doctor or pharmacist.

Possible food and drug interactions
when taking this medication

If antacids are taken with certain other medications, the effects of either could be increased, decreased, or altered. It is especially important to check with your doctor before combining antacids with the following:

  Cellulose sodium phosphate (Calcibind)
  Isoniazid (Rifamate)
  Ketoconazole (Nizoral)
  Mecamylamine (Inversine)
  Methenamine (Mandelamine)
  Sodium polystyrene sulfonate resin (Kayexalate)
  Tetracycline antibiotics (Achromycin, Minocin)

**Special information
if you are pregnant or breastfeeding**
As with all medications, ask your doctor or health care professional whether
it is safe for you to use antacids while you are pregnant or breastfeeding.

Recommended dosage

ADULTS

Take antacids according to the following schedules, or as directed by your
doctor.

*Gaviscon and Gaviscon Extra Strength Relief Formula
Chewable Tablets*
Chew 2 to 4 tablets 4 times a day after meals and at bedtime or as needed.
Follow with half a glass of water or other liquid. Do not swallow the tablets
whole.

Gaviscon Extra Strength Relief Formula Liquid
Take 2 to 4 teaspoonfuls 4 times a day after meals and at bedtime. Follow
with half a glass of water or other liquid.

Gaviscon Liquid
Take 1 or 2 tablespoonfuls 4 times a day after meals and at bedtime. Follow
with half a glass of water.

Gelusil Liquid and Chewable Tablets
Take 2 or more teaspoonfuls or tablets 1 hour after meals and at bedtime.
The tablets should be chewed.

Maalox Antacid Caplets
Take 1 caplet as needed. Swallow the tablets whole; do not chew them.

Maalox Heartburn Relief Chewable Tablets
Chew 2 to 4 tablets after meals and at bedtime. Follow with half a glass of
water or other liquid.

*Maalox Heartburn Relief Suspension, Maalox Magnesia
and Alumina Oral Suspension, and Extra Strength Maalox
Antacid Plus Anti-Gas Suspension*
Take 2 to 4 teaspoonfuls 4 times a day, 20 minutes to 1 hour after meals
and at bedtime.

Maalox Plus Chewable Tablets
Chew 1 to 4 tablets 4 times a day, 20 minutes to 1 hour after meals and at bedtime.

Extra Strength Maalox Antacid Plus Anti-Gas Chewable Tablets
Chew 1 to 3 tablets 20 minutes to 1 hour after meals and at bedtime.

Mylanta and Mylanta Double Strength Liquid and Chewable Tablets Antacid/Anti-Gas
Take 2 to 4 teaspoonfuls of liquid or chew 2 to 4 tablets between meals and at bedtime.

Mylanta Gelcaps
Take 2 to 4 gelcaps as needed.

Mylanta Soothing Lozenges
Dissolve 1 lozenge in your mouth. If needed, follow with a second. Repeat as needed.

Rolaids, Calcium-Rich/Sodium Free Rolaids, and Extra Strength Rolaids
Chew 1 or 2 tablets as symptoms occur. Repeat hourly if symptoms return.

Tums, Tums E-X, and Tums Anti-Gas Formula
Chew 1 or 2 tablets as symptoms occur. Repeat hourly if symptoms return. You may also hold the tablet between your gum and cheek and let it dissolve gradually.

CHILDREN

Do not give to children under 6 years of age, unless directed by your doctor.

Overdosage
Any medication taken in excess can have serious consequences. If you suspect an overdose, seek medical attention immediately.

■ *Symptoms of antacid overdose may include:*

For aluminum-containing antacids (Gaviscon, Gelusil, Maalox, Mylanta)
Bone pain, constipation (severe and continuing), feeling of discomfort

(continuing), loss of appetite (continuing), mood or mental changes, muscle weakness, swelling of wrists or ankles, weight loss (unusual)

For calcium-containing antacids (Mylanta, Rolaids, Tums)
Constipation (severe and continuing), difficult or painful urination, frequent urge to urinate, headache (continuing), loss of appetite (continuing), mood or mental changes, muscle pain or twitching, nausea or vomiting, nervousness or restlessness, slow breathing, unpleasant taste, unusual tiredness or weakness

For magnesium-containing antacids (Gaviscon, Gelusil, Maalox, Mylanta)
Difficult or painful urination, dizziness or light-headedness, irregular heartbeat, mood or mental changes, unusual tiredness or weakness

Generic name:

ANTIPYRINE, BENZOCAINE, AND GLYCERIN

See Auralgan, page 91.

Brand name:

ANTIVERT

Pronounced: AN-tee-vert
Generic name: Meclizine hydrochloride
Other brand names: Bonine

Why is this drug prescribed?

Antivert, an antihistamine, is prescribed for the management of nausea, vomiting, and dizziness associated with motion sickness.

Antivert may also be prescribed for the management of vertigo (a spinning sensation or a feeling that the ground is tilted) due to diseases affecting the vestibular system (the bony labyrinth of the ear, which contains the sensors that control your balance).

Most important fact about this drug

Antivert may cause you to become drowsy or less alert; therefore, driving a car or operating dangerous machinery is not recommended.

How should you take this medication?
Take this medication exactly as prescribed by your doctor.

■ *If you miss a dose...*
Take it as soon as you remember. If it is almost time for your next dose, skip the one you missed and go back to your regular schedule. Do not take 2 doses at the same time.

■ *Storage instructions...*
Store away from heat, light, and moisture.

What side effects may occur?
Side effects cannot be anticipated. If any develop or change in intensity, inform your doctor as soon as possible. Only your doctor can determine if it is safe for you to continue taking Antivert.

■ *More common side effects may include:*
Drowsiness
Dry mouth

■ *Rare side effects may include:*
Blurred vision

Why should this drug not be prescribed?
If you are sensitive to or have ever had an allergic reaction to Antivert or similar drugs, do not take this drug. Make sure that your doctor is aware of any drug reactions you have experienced.

Special warnings about this medication
If you have asthma, glaucoma, or an enlarged prostate gland, check with your doctor before using Antivert.

**Possible food and drug interactions
when taking this medication**
Antivert may intensify the effects of alcohol. Do not drink alcohol while taking this medication.

**Special information
if you are pregnant or breastfeeding**
Studies regarding the use of Antivert in pregnant women do not indicate that this drug increases the risk of abnormalities. However, if you are pregnant or

plan to become pregnant, inform your doctor before using Antivert. Check with him, too, if you are breastfeeding your baby.

Recommended dosage

ADULTS AND CHILDREN 12 AND OVER

Motion Sickness:
For protection against motion sickness, take 25 to 50 milligrams 1 hour before traveling. You may repeat the dose every 24 hours for the duration of the journey.

Vertigo:
The recommended dosage is 25 to 100 milligrams per day, divided into equal, smaller doses as determined by your doctor.

CHILDREN

The safety and effectiveness of Antivert have not been established in children under 12 years of age.

Overdosage
Any medication taken in excess can have serious consequences. If you suspect an overdose of Antivert, seek emergency medical treatment immediately.

Brand name:

ANUSOL-HC

Pronounced: AN-yoo-sol AICH-SEE
Generic name: Hydrocortisone
Other brand names: Hytone, proctoCream-HC

Why is this drug prescribed?
Anusol is a steroid cream for use on the skin. It is prescribed to treat certain itchy rashes and other inflammatory skin conditions.

Most important fact about this drug
When you use Anusol-HC, you inevitably absorb some of the medication through your skin and into the bloodstream. Too much absorption can lead to unwanted side effects elsewhere in the body. To keep this problem to a minimum, avoid using large amounts of Anusol-HC over extensive areas, and

do not cover it with airtight dressings such as plastic wrap or adhesive bandages unless specifically told to by your doctor.

How should you use this medication?
Use Anusol-HC exactly as directed, and only to treat the condition for which your doctor prescribed it.

Anusol-HC is for use only on the skin. Be careful to keep it out of your eyes.

Apply the medication directly to the affected area.

If you are using Anusol-HC for psoriasis or a condition that has been difficult to cure, your doctor may advise you to use a bandage or covering over the affected area. If an infection develops, remove the bandage and contact your doctor.

■ *If you miss a dose...*
Apply it as soon as you remember. If it is almost time for the next dose, skip the one you missed and go back to your regular schedule.

■ *Storage instructions...*
Keep the container tightly closed, and store it at room temperature, away from heat. Protect from freezing.

What side effects may occur?
Side effects cannot be anticipated. If any develop or change in intensity, inform your doctor as soon as possible. Only your doctor can determine if it is safe for you to continue using Anusol-HC.

■ *Side effects may include:*
Acne-like skin eruptions, burning, dryness, growth of excessive hair, inflammation of the hair follicles, inflammation around the mouth, irritation, itching, peeling skin, prickly heat, secondary infection, skin inflammation, skin softening, stretch marks, unusual lack of skin color

Why should this drug not be prescribed?
Do not use Anusol-HC if you are sensitive to or have ever had an allergic reaction to any of its ingredients.

Special warnings about this medication
Avoid covering a treated area with waterproof diapers or plastic pants. They can increase unwanted absorption of Anusol-HC.

If you use this medication over large areas of skin for prolonged periods of time—or cover the treated area—the amount of the hormone absorbed into your bloodstream may eventually lead to Cushing's syndrome: a moon-faced appearance, fattened neck and trunk, and purplish streaks on the skin. You can also develop glandular problems or high blood sugar, or show sugar in your urine. Children, because of their relatively larger ratio of skin surface area to body weight, are particularly susceptible to overabsorption of hormone from Anusol-HC.

Long-term treatment of children with steroids such as Anusol-HC may interfere with growth and development.

If an irritation develops, stop using the medication and contact your doctor.

**Possible food and drug interactions
when using this medication**
No interactions have been reported.

**Special information
if you are pregnant or breastfeeding**
The effects of Anusol-HC during pregnancy have not been adequately studied. If you are pregnant or plan to become pregnant, inform your doctor immediately. It is not known whether this medication appears in breast milk in sufficient amounts to affect a nursing baby. To avoid any possible harm to your baby, use Anusol-HC sparingly, and only with your doctor's permission, when breastfeeding.

Recommended dosage

ADULTS

Apply Anusol-HC to the affected area 2 to 4 times a day, depending on the severity of the condition.

CHILDREN

Limit use to the least amount necessary, as directed by your doctor.

Overdosage
Extensive or long-term use can cause Cushing's syndrome (see "Special warnings about this medication"), glandular problems, higher than normal amounts of sugar in the blood, and high amounts of sugar in the urine. If you suspect an overdose of Anusol-HC, seek medical treatment immediately.

Brand name:

ARMOUR THYROID

Pronounced: ARE-more THIGH-roid
Generic name: Natural thyroid hormones TC and TD

Why is this drug prescribed?

Armour Thyroid is prescribed when your thyroid gland is unable to produce enough hormone. It is also used to treat or prevent goiter (enlargement of the thyroid gland), and is given in a "suppression test" to diagnose an overactive thyroid.

Most important fact about this drug

Although Armour Thyroid will speed up your metabolism, it is not effective as a weight-loss drug and should not be used for that purpose. Too much Armour Thyroid may cause severe side effects, especially if you are also taking appetite suppressants.

How should you take this medication?

Take Armour Thyroid exactly as prescribed by your doctor. There is no "typical" dosage; the amount you need to take will depend on how much thyroid hormone your body is able to produce. Take no more or less than the amount your doctor prescribes. Take your dose at the same time every day for consistent effect.

Do not change brands of medication without consulting your doctor.

If you are taking Armour Thyroid to compensate for an underactive thyroid gland, you will probably need to take the medication indefinitely.

■ *If you miss a dose...*
Take it as soon as you remember. If it is almost time for your next dose, skip the one you missed and go back to your regular schedule. Do not take 2 doses at the same time. If you miss 2 or more doses in a row, consult your doctor.

■ *Storage instructions...*
Store at room temperature in a tightly closed container.

What side effects may occur?

Side effects are rare when Armour Thyroid is taken at the correct dosage. However, taking too much medication or increasing the dosage too quickly may lead to overstimulation of the thyroid gland.

■ *Symptoms of overstimulation may include:*
  Changes in appetite, diarrhea, fever, headache, increased heart rate, irritability, nausea, nervousness, sleeplessness, sweating, weight loss

Although children treated with Armour Thyroid may initially lose some hair, the hair loss is temporary.

Why should this drug not be prescribed?

You should not take Armour Thyroid if you have ever had an allergic reaction to this drug, your thyroid gland is overactive, or your adrenal glands are not making enough corticosteroid hormone.

Special warnings about this medication

If you are elderly, particularly if you suffer from angina (chest pain due to a heart condition), you should take Armour Thyroid at a lower dosage, and your doctor should schedule frequent checkups.

Armour Thyroid tends to aggravate symptoms of diabetes and underactive adrenal glands. If you take medication to treat one of these disorders, your dosage of that medication will probably need to be adjusted once you start taking Armour Thyroid.

Possible food and drug interactions
when taking this medication

If you take Armour Thyroid with certain other drugs, the effect of either drug could be increased, decreased, or altered. It is especially important to check with your doctor before combining Armour Thyroid with the following:

  Asthma medications such as Theo-Dur
  Blood thinners such as Coumadin
  Cholestyramine (Questran)
  Colestipol (Colestid)
  Estrogen preparations (including some birth control pills such as Ortho-
    Novum and Premarin)
  Insulin
  Oral diabetes drugs (such as Diabinese and Glucotrol)

Special information
if you are pregnant or breastfeeding

If you need to take Armour Thyroid because of a thyroid hormone deficiency, you may continue using the medication during pregnancy, but your doctor will test you regularly and may change your dosage. Once your baby is born, you may breastfeed while continuing treatment with Armour Thyroid.

Recommended dosage

ADULTS

Your doctor will tailor the dosage of Armour Thyroid to meet your individual requirements, taking into consideration the status of your thyroid gland and any other medical conditions you may have.

Overdosage

An overdose of Armour Thyroid will speed up all of the body's vital processes, causing physical and mental hyperactivity, increased appetite, excessive sweating, chest pain, increased pulse rate, palpitations, nervousness, intolerance to heat, and possibly tremors or a rapid heartbeat.

Brand name:

ARTANE

Pronounced: AR-tane
Generic name: Trihexyphenidyl hydrochloride

Why is this drug prescribed?

Artane is used, in conjunction with other drugs, for the relief of certain symptoms of Parkinson's disease, a brain disorder that causes muscle tremor, stiffness, and weakness. It is also used to control certain side effects induced by antipsychotic drugs such as Thorazine and Haldol. Artane works by correcting the chemical imbalance that causes Parkinson's disease.

Most important fact about this drug

Artane is not a cure for Parkinson's disease; it merely minimizes and reduces the frequency of symptoms such as tremors.

How should you take this medication?

You may take Artane either before meals or after meals, whichever you find more convenient. Your doctor will probably start you on a small amount and increase the dosage gradually. Take Artane exactly as prescribed.

If the medication makes your mouth feel dry, try chewing gum, sucking mints, or simply sipping water.

Artane comes in tablet and liquid form. With either, you will probably need to take 3 or 4 doses a day.

Once you have reached the dosage that is best for you, your doctor may switch you to sustained-release capsules ("sequels"), which are to be taken only once or twice a day. Do not open or crush the sequels. Always swallow them whole.

■ *If you miss a dose...*
Take it as soon as you remember. If it is within 2 hours of your next dose, skip the one you missed and go back to your regular schedule. Do not take 2 doses at the same time.

■ *Storage instructions...*
Store at room temperature. Do not allow the liquid to freeze.

What side effects may occur?
Side effects cannot be anticipated. If any develop or change in intensity, inform your doctor as soon as possible. Only your doctor can determine if it is safe for you to continue taking Artane.

■ *Common side effects may include:*
Blurred vision
Dry mouth
Nausea
Nervousness

These side effects, which appear in 30% to 50% of all people who take Artane, tend to be mild. They may disappear as your body gets used to the drug; if they persist, your doctor may want to lower your dosage slightly.

■ *Other potential side effects include:*
Agitation, bowel obstruction, confusion, constipation, delusions, difficulty urinating, dilated pupils, disturbed behavior, drowsiness, hallucinations, headache, pressure in the eye, rapid heartbeat, rash, vomiting, weakness

Why should this drug not be prescribed?
Do not take Artane if you are known to be sensitive to it or if you have ever had an allergic reaction to it or to other antiparkinson medications of this type.

Special warnings about this medication
The elderly are highly sensitive to drugs such as Artane and should use it with caution.

Artane can reduce the body's ability to perspire, one of the key ways your body prevents overheating. Avoid excess sun or exercise that also cause you to become overheated.

If you have any of the following conditions, make sure your doctor knows about them, since Artane could make them worse:

Enlarged prostate
Glaucoma
Stomach/intestinal obstructive disease
Urinary tract obstructive disease

It is important to stick to the prescribed dosage; taking larger amounts "for kicks" could lead to an overdose.

Your doctor should watch you carefully if you have heart, liver, or kidney disease or high blood pressure, and should check your eyes frequently. You should also be watched for the development of any allergic reactions.

Possible food and drug interactions when taking this medication

If you take Artane along with any of the drugs listed below, your doctor may need to adjust the dosage of Artane, the other medication, or possibly both.

Amantadine (Symmetrel)
Amitriptyline (Elavil)
Chlorpromazine (Thorazine)
Doxepin (Sinequan)
Haloperidol (Haldol)

Special information if you are pregnant or breastfeeding

No specific information is available concerning the use of Artane during pregnancy or breastfeeding. If you are pregnant or plan to become pregnant while taking Artane, inform your doctor immediately.

Recommended dosage

Your doctor will individualize the dose to your needs, starting with a low dose and then increasing it gradually, especially if you are over 60 years of age.

ADULTS

Parkinson's Disease:
The usual starting dose, in tablet or liquid form, is 1 milligram on the first day.

After the first day, your doctor may increase the dose by 2 milligrams at intervals of 3 to 5 days, until you are taking a total of 6 to 10 milligrams a day.

Your total daily dose will depend upon what is found to be the most effective level. For many people, 6 to 10 milligrams is most effective. Some, however, may require a total daily dose of 12 to 15 milligrams.

Drug-Induced Parkinsonism:

Your doctor will have to determine by trial and error the size and frequency of the dose of Artane needed to control the tremors and muscle rigidity that sometimes result from commonly used tranquilizers.

The total daily dosage usually ranges between 5 and 15 milligrams, although, in some cases, symptoms have been satisfactorily controlled on as little as 1 milligram daily.

Your doctor may start you on 1 milligram of Artane a day. If your symptoms are not controlled in a few hours, he or she may slowly increase the dose until satisfactory control is achieved.

Use of Artane with Levodopa:

When Artane is used at the same time as levodopa, the usual dose of each may need to be reduced. Your doctor will adjust the dosages carefully, depending on the side effects and the degree of symptom control. Artane dosage of 3 to 6 milligrams daily, divided into equal doses, is usually adequate.

Artane Tablets and Liquid:

You will be able to handle the total daily intake of Artane tablets or liquid best if the medication is divided into 3 doses and taken at mealtimes. If you are taking high doses (more than 10 milligrams daily), your doctor may divide them into 4 parts, so that you take 3 doses at mealtimes and the fourth at bedtime.

Overdosage

Overdosage with Artane may cause agitation, delirium, disorientation, hallucinations, or psychotic episodes.

■ *Other symptoms may include:*
Clumsiness or unsteadiness, fast heartbeat, flushing of skin, seizures, severe drowsiness, shortness of breath or troubled breathing, trouble sleeping, unusual warmth

If you suspect an overdose of Artane, seek medical attention immediately.

Brand name:

ASACOL

See Rowasa, page 984.

Generic name:

ASPIRIN

Pronounced: ASS-per-in
Brand names: Empirin, Ecotrin, Genuine Bayer, Halfprin

Why is this drug prescribed?
Aspirin is an anti-inflammatory pain medication (analgesic) that is used to relieve headaches, toothaches, and minor aches and pains, and to reduce fever. It also temporarily relieves the minor aches and pains of arthritis, muscle aches, colds, flu, and menstrual discomfort. In some patients, a small daily dose of aspirin may be used to ensure sufficient blood flow to the brain and prevent stroke. Aspirin may also be taken to decrease recurrence of a heart attack or other heart problems.

Most important fact about this drug
Aspirin should not be used during the last 3 months of pregnancy unless specifically prescribed by a doctor. It may cause problems in the unborn child or complications during delivery.

How should you take this medication?
Do not take more than the recommended dose.

Do not use aspirin if it has a strong, vinegar-like odor.

If aspirin upsets your stomach, use of a coated or buffered brand may reduce the problem.

Do not chew or crush sustained-release brands, such as Bayer time-release aspirin, or pills coated to delay breakdown of the drug, such as Ecotrin. To make them easier to swallow, take them with a full glass of water.

■ *If you miss a dose...*
Take it as soon as you remember. If it is almost time for your next dose, skip the one you missed and go back to your regular schedule. Never take 2 doses at the same time.

■ *Storage instructions...*
Store at room temperature.

What side effects may occur?
Side effects cannot be anticipated. If any develop or change in intensity, inform your doctor as soon as possible. Only your doctor can determine if it is safe for you to continue using aspirin.

■ *Side effects may include:*
Heartburn
Nausea and/or vomiting
Possible involvement in formation of stomach ulcers and bleeding
Small amounts of blood in stool
Stomach pain
Stomach upset

Why should this drug not be prescribed?
Do not take aspirin if you are allergic to it, if you have asthma, ulcers or ulcer symptoms, or if you are taking a medication that affects the clotting of your blood, unless specifically told to do so by your doctor.

Special warnings about this medication
Aspirin should not be given to children or teenagers for flu symptoms or chickenpox. Aspirin has been associated with the development of Reye's syndrome, a dangerous disorder characterized by disorientation, and lethargy leading to coma.

If you have a continuous or high fever, or a severe or persistent sore throat, especially with a high fever, vomiting and nausea, consult your doctor. It could indicate a more serious illness.

If pain persists for more than 10 days or if redness or swelling appears at the site of inflammation, consult your doctor immediately.

If you experience ringing in the ears, hearing loss, upset stomach, or dizziness, consult your doctor before taking more aspirin.

Check with your doctor before giving aspirin for arthritis or rheumatism to a child under 12.

Possible food and drug interactions when taking this medication
If aspirin is taken with certain other drugs, the effects of either could be increased, decreased, or altered. It is especially important to check with your doctor before combining aspirin with the following:

Acetazolamide (Diamox)
ACE-inhibitor-type blood pressure medications such as Capoten
Anti-gout medications such as Zyloprim
Arthritis medications such as Motrin and Indocin
Blood thinners such as Coumadin
Certain diuretics such as Lasix
Diabetes medications such as DiaBeta and Micronase
Diltiazem (Cardizem)
Dipyridamole (Persantine)
Insulin
Seizure medications such as Depakene
Steroids such as prednisone

Special information
if you are pregnant or breastfeeding

The use of aspirin during pregnancy should be discussed with your doctor.
Aspirin should not be used during the last 3 months of pregnancy unless
specifically indicated by your doctor. It may cause problems in the fetus and
complications during delivery. Aspirin may appear in breast milk and could
affect a nursing infant. Ask your doctor whether it is safe to take aspirin
while you are breastfeeding.

Recommended dosage

ADULTS

Treatment of Minor Pain and Fever
The usual dose is 1 or 2 tablets every 3 to 4 hours up to 6 times a day.

Prevention of Stroke
The usual dose is 1 tablet 4 times daily or 2 tablets 2 times a day.

Prevention of Heart Attack
The usual dose is 1 tablet daily. Your physician may suggest that you take a
larger dose, however. If you use Halfprin low-strength tablets (162
milligrams), adjust dosage accordingly.

CHILDREN

Consult your doctor.

Overdosage

Any medication used in excess can have serious consequences. If you
suspect symptoms of an aspirin overdose, seek medical treatment immediately.

Brand name:

ASPIRIN FREE ANACIN

See Tylenol, page 1168.

Generic name:

ASPIRIN WITH CODEINE

See Empirin with Codeine, page 397.

Generic name:

ASTEMIZOLE

See Hismanal, page 487.

Brand name:

ATARAX

Pronounced: AT-a-raks
Generic name: Hydroxyzine hydrochloride
Other brand name: Vistaril

Why is this drug prescribed?

Atarax is an antihistamine used to relieve the symptoms of common anxiety and tension and, in combination with other medications, to treat anxiety that results from physical illness. It also relieves itching from allergic reactions and can be used as a sedative before and after general anesthesia. Antihistamines work by decreasing the effects of histamine, a chemical the body releases that narrows air passages in the lungs and contributes to inflammation. Antihistamines reduce itching and swelling and dry up secretions from the nose, eyes, and throat.

Most important fact about this drug

Atarax is not intended for long-term use (more than 4 months). Your doctor should re-evaluate the prescription periodically.

How should you take this medication?

Take this medication exactly as prescribed by your doctor.

■ *If you miss a dose...*
Take it as soon as you remember. If it is almost time for your next dose, skip the one you missed and go back to your regular schedule. Do not take 2 doses at once.

■ *Storage instructions...*
Store tablets and syrup away from heat, light, and moisture. Keep the syrup from freezing.

What side effects may occur?
Side effects cannot be anticipated. If any develop or change in intensity, inform your doctor as soon as possible. Only your doctor can determine if it is safe for you to continue taking Atarax.

Drowsiness, the most common side effect of Atarax, is usually temporary and may disappear in a few days or when dosage is reduced. Other side effects include dry mouth, twitches, tremors, and convulsions. The last two usually occur with higher than recommended doses of Atarax.

Why should this drug not be prescribed?
Atarax should not be taken in early pregnancy or if you are sensitive to or have ever had an allergic reaction to it. Make sure your doctor is aware of any drug reactions you have experienced.

Special warnings about this medication
Atarax increases the effects of drugs that depress the activity of the central nervous system. If you are taking narcotics, non-narcotic analgesics, or barbiturates in combination with Atarax, their dosage should be reduced.

This medication can cause drowsiness. Driving or operating dangerous machinery or participating in any hazardous activity that requires full mental alertness is not recommended until you know how you react to Atarax.

Possible food and drug interactions
when taking this medication
Atarax may increase the effects of alcohol. Avoid alcohol while taking this medication.

If Atarax is taken with certain other drugs, the effects of either could be increased, decreased, or altered. It is especially important to check with your doctor before combining Atarax with the following:

Barbiturates such as Seconal and Phenobarbital
Narcotics such as Demerol and Percocet
Non-narcotic analgesics such as Motrin and Tylenol

Special information
if you are pregnant or breastfeeding
Although the effects of Atarax during pregnancy have not been adequately
studied in humans, birth defects have appeared in animal studies with this
medication. You should not take Atarax in early pregnancy. If you are
pregnant or plan to become pregnant, inform your doctor immediately. Atarax
may appear in breast milk and could affect a nursing infant. If this medication
is essential to your health, your doctor may advise you to discontinue
breastfeeding until your treatment is finished.

Recommended dosage
When treatment begins with injections, it can be continued in tablet form.

Your doctor will adjust your dosage based on your response to the drug.

FOR ANXIETY AND TENSION

Adults
The usual dose is 50 to 100 milligrams 4 times per day.

Children under Age 6
The total dose is 50 milligrams daily, divided into several smaller doses.

Children over Age 6
The total dose is 50 to 100 milligrams daily, divided into several smaller
doses.

FOR ITCHING DUE TO ALLERGIC CONDITIONS

Adults
The usual dose is 25 milligrams 3 or 4 times a day.

Children under Age 6
The total dose is 50 milligrams daily, divided into several smaller doses.

Children over Age 6
The total dose is 50 to 100 milligrams daily, divided into several smaller
doses.

BEFORE AND AFTER GENERAL ANESTHESIA

Adults
The usual dose is 50 to 100 milligrams.

Children
The usual dose is 0.6 milligram per 2.2 pounds of body weight.

Overdosage
Any medication taken in excess can have serious consequences. If you suspect an overdose of Atarax, seek medical attention immediately.

The most common symptom of Atarax overdose is excessive calm; your blood pressure may drop, although it is not likely.

Generic name:

ATENOLOL

See Tenormin, page 1090.

Generic name:

ATENOLOL WITH CHLORTHALIDONE

See Tenoretic, page 1087.

Brand name:

ATIVAN

Pronounced: AT-i-van
Generic name: Lorazepam

Why is this drug prescribed?
Ativan is used in the treatment of anxiety disorders and for short-term (up to 4 months) relief of the symptoms of anxiety. It belongs to a class of drugs known as benzodiazepines.

Most important fact about this drug
Tolerance and dependence can develop with the use of Ativan. You may experience withdrawal symptoms if you stop using it abruptly. Only your doctor should advise you to discontinue or change your dose.

How should you take this drug?
Take this medication exactly as prescribed by your doctor.

■ *If you miss a dose...*
If it is within an hour or so of the scheduled time, take the forgotten dose as soon as you remember. Otherwise, skip the dose and go back to your regular schedule. Do not take 2 doses at once.

■ *Storage instructions...*
Store at room temperature in a tightly closed container, away from light.

What side effects may occur?
Side effects cannot be anticipated. If any develop or change in intensity, inform your doctor as soon as possible. Only your doctor can determine if it is safe for you to continue taking Ativan.

If you experience any side effects, it will usually be at the beginning of your treatment; they will probably disappear as you continue to take the drug, or if your dosage is reduced.

■ *More common side effects may include:*
Dizziness
Sedation (excessive calm)
Unsteadiness
Weakness

■ *Less common or rare side effects may include:*
Agitation, change in appetite, depression, eye function disorders, headache, memory impairment, mental disorientation, nausea, skin problems, sleep disturbance, stomach and intestinal disorders

■ *Side effects due to rapid decrease or abrupt withdrawal of Ativan:*
Abdominal and muscle cramps, convulsions, depressed mood, inability to fall or stay asleep, sweating, tremors, vomiting

Why should this drug not be prescribed?
If you are sensitive to or have ever had an allergic reaction to Ativan or similar drugs such as Valium, you should not take this medication.

Also avoid Ativan if you have the eye disease acute narrow-angle glaucoma.

Anxiety or tension related to everyday stress usually does not require treatment with Ativan. Discuss your symptoms thoroughly with your doctor.

Special warnings about this medication

Ativan may cause you to become drowsy or less alert; therefore, driving or operating dangerous machinery or participating in any hazardous activity that requires full mental alertness is not recommended.

If you are severely depressed or have suffered from severe depression, consult with your doctor before taking this medication.

If you have decreased kidney or liver function, use of this drug should be discussed with your doctor.

If you are elderly or if you have been using Ativan for a prolonged period of time, your doctor will watch you closely for stomach and upper intestinal problems.

Possible food and drug interactions
when taking this medication

Ativan may intensify the effects of alcohol. Avoid alcohol while taking this medication.

If Ativan is taken with certain other drugs, the effects of either could be increased, decreased, or altered. It is especially important to check with your doctor before combining Ativan with barbiturates (phenobarbital, Seconal, Amytal) or sedative-type medications such as Valium and Halcion.

Special information
if you are pregnant or breastfeeding

Do not take Ativan if you are pregnant or planning to become pregnant. There is an increased risk of birth defects. It is not known whether Ativan appears in breast milk. If this medication is essential to your health, your doctor may advise you to discontinue breastfeeding until your treatment is finished.

Recommended dosage

ADULTS

The usual recommended dosage is a total of 2 to 6 milligrams per day divided into smaller doses. The largest dose should be taken at bedtime. The daily dose may vary from 1 to 10 milligrams.

Anxiety

The usual starting dose is a total of 2 to 3 milligrams per day taken in 2 or 3 smaller doses.

Insomnia Due to Anxiety

A single daily dose of 2 to 4 milligrams may be taken, usually at bedtime.

CHILDREN

The safety and effectiveness of Ativan have not been established in children under 12 years of age.

ELDERLY

The usual starting dosage for the elderly and those in a weakened condition should not exceed a total of 1 to 2 milligrams per day, divided into smaller doses, to avoid oversedation. This dose can be adjusted by your doctor as needed.

Overdosage

Any medication taken in excess can have serious consequences. If you suspect an overdose, seek medical attention immediately.

■ *The symptoms of Ativan overdose may include:*
Coma
Confusion
Low blood pressure
Sleepiness

Brand name:

ATRETOL

See Tegretol, page 1076.

Brand name:

ATROVENT

Pronounced: AT-row-vent
Generic name: Ipratropium bromide

Why is this drug prescribed?

Atrovent is a bronchodilator prescribed for long-term treatment of bronchial spasms (wheezing) associated with chronic obstructive pulmonary disease, including chronic bronchitis and emphysema. A bronchodilator improves the passage of air into the lungs.

Most important fact about this drug

This medication is not for initial use in acute attacks of bronchial spasm when fast action is needed.

How should you take this medication?
Atrovent is not intended for occasional use. To get the most benefit from this drug, you must use it consistently throughout your course of treatment, as prescribed by your doctor.

■ *If you miss a dose...*
Take it as soon as you remember. If it is almost time for your next dose, skip the one you missed and go back to your regular schedule. Do not take 2 doses at once.

■ *Storage instructions...*
Store at room temperature. Protect from excess humidity.

What side effects may occur?
Side effects cannot be anticipated. If any develop or change in intensity, inform your doctor as soon as possible. Only your doctor can determine if it is safe for you to continue taking Atrovent.

■ *More common side effects may include:*
Blurred vision, cough, dizziness, dry mouth, fluttering heartbeat, headache, irritation from aerosol, nausea, nervousness, rash, stomach and intestinal upset, worsening of symptoms

■ *Less common or rare side effects may include:*
Allergic reactions, constipation, coordination difficulty, difficulty in urinating, drowsiness, fatigue, flushing, hives, hoarseness, inability to fall or stay asleep, increased heart rate, itching, low blood pressure, loss of hair, mouth sores, sharp eye pain, swelling of the tongue, lips, and face, tightening of the throat, tingling sensation, tremors

Why should this drug not be prescribed?
If you are sensitive to or have ever had an allergic reaction to Atrovent or any of its ingredients, or to soybeans, soy lecithin, or peanuts, you should not take this medication.

You should also avoid Atrovent if you are allergic to drugs based on atropine. Make sure your doctor is aware of any drug reactions you have experienced.

Special warnings about this medication
Unless you are directed to do so by your doctor, do not take this medication if you have the eye condition called narrow-angle glaucoma, an enlarged prostate, or obstruction in the neck of the bladder.

Your vision may be temporarily blurred if you accidentally spray the aerosol in your eyes.

Possible food and drug interactions
when taking this medication

No interactions have been reported.

Special information
if you are pregnant or breastfeeding

The effects of Atrovent during pregnancy have not been adequately studied. If you are pregnant or plan to become pregnant, inform your doctor immediately. It is not known whether Atrovent may appear in breast milk. If this drug is essential to your health, your doctor may advise you to stop nursing your baby until your treatment is finished.

Recommended dosage

ADULTS

The usual starting dose is 2 inhalations, 4 times per day. Additional inhalations may be taken, but the total should not exceed 12 in 24 hours.

CHILDREN

Safety and effectiveness have not been established in children below 12 years of age.

Overdosage

There is no information on specific symptoms of Atrovent overdose. However, any drug taken in excess can have serious consequences. If you suspect an overdose of Atrovent, seek medical attention immediately.

Brand name:

A/T/S

See Erythromycin, Topical, page 409.

Brand name:

AUGMENTIN

Pronounced: awg-MENT-in
Generic ingredients: Amoxicillin, Clavulanate potassium

Why is this drug prescribed?

Augmentin is used in the treatment of lower respiratory, middle ear, sinus, skin, and urinary tract infections that are caused by certain specific bacteria. These bacteria produce a chemical enzyme called beta lactamase that makes some infections particularly difficult to treat.

Most important fact about this drug

If you are allergic to either penicillin or cephalosporin antibiotics in any form, consult your doctor *before taking Augmentin*. There is a possibility that you are allergic to both types of medication and if a reaction occurs, it could be extremely severe. If you take the drug and feel signs of a reaction, seek medical attention immediately.

How should you take this medication?

Augmentin may be taken with or without food.

Shake the suspension well before using.

- *If you miss a dose...*
  Take it as soon as you remember. If it is almost time for the next dose, and you take 2 doses a day, take the one you missed and the next dose 5 to 6 hours later. If you take 3 or more doses a day, take the one you missed and the next dose 2 to 4 hours later. Then go back to your regular schedule.

- *Storage instructions...*
  Store the suspension under refrigeration and discard after 10 days. Store tablets away from heat, light, and moisture.

What side effects may occur?

Side effects cannot be anticipated. If any develop or change in intensity, inform your doctor as soon as possible. Only your doctor can determine if it is safe for you to continue taking Augmentin.

- *More common side effects may include:*
  Diarrhea/loose stools
  Nausea
  Skin rashes and hives

- *Less common side effects may include:*
  Abdominal discomfort, anemia, arthritis, black "hairy" tongue, blood disorders, fever, gas, headache, indigestion, intestinal inflammation, itching, itching or burning of the vagina, joint pain, muscle pain, skin

inflammation, skin peeling, sores and inflammation in the mouth and on the tongue and gums, stomach inflammation, vomiting, yeast infection

- *Rare side effects may include:*
  Agitation, anxiety, behavioral changes, blood in the urine, change in liver function, confusion, dizziness, hyperactivity, insomnia, kidney problems

Why should this drug not be prescribed?

If you are sensitive to or have ever had an allergic reaction to any penicillin medication, do not take this drug.

Also avoid taking Augmentin if it has ever given you liver problems or yellowing of the skin and eyes.

Special warnings about this medication

Augmentin and other penicillin-like medicines are generally safe; however, anyone with liver, kidney, or blood disorders is at increased risk when using this drug. Alternative choices may be available to your doctor.

If you have diabetes and test your urine for the presence of sugar, you should ask your doctor or pharmacist if this medication will interfere with the type of test you use.

Allergic reactions to this medication can be serious and possibly fatal. Let your doctor know about previous allergic reactions to medicines, food, or other substances before using Augmentin. If you experience a reaction, report it to your doctor immediately and seek medical treatment.

If you develop diarrhea while taking Augmentin, inform your doctor. It could be a sign of a potentially dangerous form of bowel inflammation.

Possible food and drug interactions
when taking this medication

Augmentin may react with the antigout medication Benemid, resulting in changes in blood levels. A reaction with another antigout drug, Zyloprim, may cause rashes. Notify your doctor if you are taking either of these drugs.

Do not take Augmentin when using Antabuse (disulfiram).

Special information
if you are pregnant or breastfeeding

The effects of Augmentin during pregnancy have not been adequately studied. Because there may be risk to the developing baby, doctors usually recommend Augmentin to pregnant women only when the benefits of therapy outweigh any potential danger. Augmentin appears in breast milk and could affect a nursing infant. If Augmentin is essential to your health, your doctor may advise you to stop nursing your baby until your treatment with this drug is finished.

Recommended dosage

ADULTS

The usual adult dose is one 250-milligram tablet every 8 hours. For more severe infections and infections of the respiratory tract, the dose should be one 500-milligram tablet every 8 hours. It is essential that you take this medicine according to your doctor's directions.

CHILDREN

The usual total daily dosage is 20 milligrams per 2.2 pounds of body weight per day, divided into 4 doses and taken every 8 hours. For middle ear infections, sinus infections, and lower respiratory infections, the dose should be 40 milligrams per 2.2 pounds per day, divided into smaller doses and taken every 8 hours. Severe infections should be treated with the higher recommended dose. Children weighing 88 pounds or more will take the adult dosage.

Overdosage

Augmentin is generally safe; however, large amounts may cause overdose symptoms, including exaggerated side effects listed above. Suspected overdoses of Augmentin must be treated immediately; contact your physician or an emergency room.

Brand name:

AURALGAN

Pronounced: Aw-RAL-gan
Generic ingredients: Antipyrine, Benzocaine, Glycerin
Other brand name: Auroto Otic

Why is this drug prescribed?

Auralgan is prescribed to reduce the inflammation and congestion and relieve the pain and discomfort of severe middle ear infections. This drug may be used in combination with an antibiotic for curing the infection.

Auralgan is also used to remove excessive or impacted earwax.

Most important fact about this drug

Discard this product 6 months after the dropper is first placed in the drug solution.

How should you use this medication?
Use this medication exactly as prescribed. Administer as follows:

1. Warm the drops to body temperature by holding the bottle in your hand for a few minutes.
2. Shake the bottle.
3. Lie on your side or tilt the affected ear up.
4. Gently pull the ear lobe up.
5. Administer the prescribed number of drops.
6. Avoid touching the dropper to the ear.
7. Keep the ear tilted up for about 5 to 7 minutes.

Do not rinse the dropper; replace it in the bottle after each use. Hold the dropper assembly by the screw cap and, without squeezing the rubber bulb, insert the dropper into the bottle and screw down tightly.

■ *If you miss a dose...*
Use it as soon as you remember. If it is almost time for your next dose, skip the one you missed and go back to your regular schedule.

■ *Storage instructions...*
Store at room temperature.

What side effects may occur?
Side effects cannot be anticipated. If any develop or change in intensity, inform your doctor as soon as possible. For Auralgan, no specific side effects have been reported.

Why should this drug not be prescribed?
If you are sensitive to or allergic to any of the ingredients contained in Auralgan or similar drugs, you should not take this medication. Make sure your doctor is aware of any drug reactions you have experienced.

Unless directed to do so by your doctor, do not use this medication if you have a punctured eardrum.

Special warnings about this medication
Notify your doctor if irritation occurs or if you develop an allergic reaction to this medication.

Possible food and drug interactions when taking this medication
No food or drug interactions have been reported.

Special information
if you are pregnant or breastfeeding

The effects of Auralgan during pregnancy have not been adequately studied. If you are pregnant or plan to become pregnant, notify your doctor immediately. It is not known whether Auralgan appears in breast milk. If this medication is essential to your health, your doctor may advise you to discontinue breastfeeding until your treatment is finished.

Recommended dosage

ADULTS AND CHILDREN

Acute Otitis Media (Severe Middle Ear Infection):
Apply the medication drop by drop into the ear, permitting the solution to run along the wall of the ear canal until it is filled. Avoid touching the ear with the dropper. Then moisten a piece of cotton dressing material, such as gauze, with Auralgan and insert it into the opening of the ear. Repeat every 1 to 2 hours until pain and congestion are relieved.

Removal of Earwax:
Apply Auralgan drop by drop into the ear 3 times daily for 2 or 3 days to help detach and remove earwax from the wall of the ear canal.

After the wax has been removed, Auralgan is useful for drying out the canal or relieving discomfort.

Before and after the removal of earwax, cotton dressing material such as gauze should be moistened with Auralgan and inserted into the opening of the ear following use of the medication.

Overdosage
No information on overdosage with Auralgan is available.

Generic name:

AURANOFIN

See Ridaura, page 959.

Brand name:

AUROTO OTIC

See Auralgan, page 91.

Brand name:

AVENTYL

See Pamelor, page 792.

Brand name:

AXID

Pronounced: AK-sid
Generic name: Nizatidine

Why is this drug prescribed?

Axid is prescribed for the treatment of duodenal ulcers and noncancerous stomach ulcers. Full-dose therapy for these problems lasts no longer than 8 weeks. However, your doctor may prescribe Axid at a reduced dosage after a duodenal ulcer has healed. The drug is also prescribed for the heartburn and the inflammation that result when acid stomach contents flow backward into the esophagus. Axid belongs to a class of drugs known as histamine H_2 blockers.

Most important fact about this drug

Although Axid can be used for up to 8-12 weeks, most ulcers are healed within 4 weeks of therapy.

How should you take this medication?

Take this medication exactly as prescribed by your doctor.

- *If you miss a dose...*
  Take it as soon as you remember. If it is almost time for your next dose, skip the one you missed and go back to your regular schedule. Do not take 2 doses at once.

- *Storage instructions...*
  Store at room temperature.

What side effects may occur?

Side effects cannot be anticipated. If any develop or change in intensity, inform your doctor as soon as possible. Only your doctor can determine if it is safe for you to continue taking Axid.

- *More common side effects may include:*
  Abdominal pain

Diarrhea
Dizziness
Gas
Headache
Indigestion
Inflammation of the nose
Nausea
Pain
Sore throat
Vomiting
Weakness

■ *Less common or rare side effects may include:*
Abnormal dreams, anxiety, back pain, chest pain, constipation, dimmed vision, dry mouth, fever, inability to sleep, increased cough, infection, itching, loss of appetite, muscle pain, nervousness, rash, sleepiness, stomach/intestinal problems, tooth problems

Why should this drug not be prescribed?
If you are sensitive to or have ever had an allergic reaction to Axid or similar drugs such as Zantac, you should not take this medication. Make sure your doctor is aware of any drug reactions you have experienced.

Special warnings about this medication
Axid could mask a stomach malignancy. If you continue to have any problems, notify your doctor.

If you have moderate to severe kidney disease, your doctor will reduce your dosage.

Possible food and drug interactions
when taking this medication
If Axid is taken with certain other drugs, the effects of either could be increased, decreased, or altered. It is especially important to check with your doctor before combining Axid with aspirin, especially in high doses.

Special information
if you are pregnant or breastfeeding
The effects of Axid during pregnancy have not been adequately studied. If you are pregnant or plan to become pregnant, inform your doctor immediately. Axid appears in breast milk and could affect a nursing infant. If this medication is essential to your health, your doctor may advise you to

discontinue breastfeeding until your treatment with this medication is finished.

Recommended dosage

ADULTS

Active Duodenal Ulcer:
The usual dose is 300 milligrams once a day at bedtime, but your doctor may have you take 150 milligrams twice a day.

Active Noncancerous Stomach Ulcer:
The usual dose is 150 milligrams twice a day or 300 milligrams once a day at bedtime.

Maintenance of a Healed Duodenal Ulcer:
The usual dose is 150 milligrams once a day at bedtime.

If you have moderate to severe kidney disease, your doctor will prescribe a lower dose.

CHILDREN

The safety and effectiveness of Axid have not been established in children.

ELDERLY

Your doctor will determine the dosage based on your needs.

Overdosage

No specific information on Axid overdose is available. However, any medication taken in excess can have serious consequences. If you suspect an overdose of Axid, seek medical attention immediately.

Generic name:

AZATADINE WITH PSEUDOEPHEDRINE

See Trinalin Repetabs, page 1158.

Generic name:

AZITHROMYCIN

See Zithromax, page 1234.

Brand name:

AZMACORT

Pronounced: AZ-ma-court
Generic name: Triamcinolone acetonide
Other brand name: Nasacort

Why is this drug prescribed?

Azmacort and Nasacort are metered-dose inhalers containing the anti-inflammatory steroid medication triamcinolone acetonide. Azmacort is used as long-term therapy to control bronchial asthma attacks. Nasacort is prescribed to relieve the symptoms of hay fever and other nasal allergies. Nasacort is also used in the treatment of nasal polyps (projecting masses if tissue in the nose.)

Most important fact about this drug

Azmacort does not provide rapid relief in an asthma attack. Instead, it reduces the frequency and severity of attacks when taken on a regular basis. For quick relief, you must still use airway-opening medications.

How should you take this medication?

Take these drugs on a regular daily basis, exactly as prescribed.

Shake the canister before each use. Do not use an Azmacort inhaler more than 240 times. Discard the Nasacort canister after 100 inhalations.

If the drug irritates your throat, gargling and rinsing your mouth with water after each dose can help to relieve the problem.

If you are using a bronchodilator inhalant, it should be used before the Azmacort inhalant to derive the best effects from this drug. Use of the two inhalers should be separated by several minutes.

Illustrated instructions for use are available with the product.

- *If you miss a dose...*
  Use it as soon as you remember. If it is almost time for your next dose, skip the one you missed and go back to your regular schedule. Do not take 2 doses at once.

- *Storage instructions...*
  Store at room temperature.

Since the contents of this inhalant are under pressure, do not puncture the container and do not use or store the medication near heat or open flame. Exposure to temperatures above 120°F may cause the container to explode.

What side effects may occur?
Side effects cannot be anticipated. If any develop or change in intensity, inform your doctor as soon as possible. Only your doctor can determine if it is safe for you to continue taking these medications.

■ *More common side effects of Azmacort may include:*
Dry mouth
Dry throat
Hoarseness
Irritated throat

■ *Less common side effects of Azmacort may include:*
Facial swelling, increased wheezing and cough, mouth and throat infections

■ *More common side effects of Nasacort may include:*
Headache

■ *Less common side effects of Nasacort may include:*
Dryness of the membranes lining the nose, mouth, and throat, nasal irritation, nasal and sinus congestion, nosebleeds, sneezing, throat discomfort

Why should this drug not be prescribed?
Do not use either of these medications if you are allergic to or sensitive to any of the ingredients.

Do not use Azmacort if:

your asthma can be controlled with airway openers and other non-steroid medications.
you require only occasional steroid treatment for asthma. (Azmacort is not for treatment of prolonged, severe asthma attacks where fast-acting measures are required.)
you have bronchitis not associated with asthma.

Special warnings about this medication
Your doctor will see that your asthma is reasonably under control before starting you on Azmacort Inhaler. For about a week, he or she will have you take Azmacort along with your usual dose of oral steroid. After that, you will

gradually take less and less of the oral drug. If you develop joint or muscular pain, weariness, and depression, contact your doctor immediately. If you feel light-headed or find that you are losing weight, also tell your doctor.

If you are using Azmacort and your airway-opening medication is not effective during an asthma attack, contact your doctor immediately.

The use of triamcinolone acetonide may cause a yeast-like fungal infection in the mouth and throat (Azmacort) or nose and throat (Nasacort). If you suspect a fungal infection, notify your doctor. Treatment with antifungal medication may be necessary.

Children using steroid medications such as these are more susceptible to infection. Chickenpox and measles, for example, can be far more serious for these children and for adults who have not had them. Try to avoid exposure, but if you are exposed, inform your doctor. Medication may be needed.

Switching from steroid tablet therapy to Azmacort Inhaler may allow allergic conditions to surface that were previously controlled by the tablets. These include rhinitis (inflammation of the inside of the nose), conjunctivitis (pinkeye), and eczema.

If your child is using Azmacort, your doctor will watch to be sure he or she is growing properly. If you have just had an operation, or if you are experiencing extreme stress, your doctor will watch you closely.

Use these medications with extreme caution if you have tuberculosis, untreated fungal, bacterial, or systemic viral infections, or herpes infections of the eye.

Use Nasacort with caution if you have not fully healed from nasal ulcers, or an injury to your nose. Steroids can slow wound healing, and there have been rare cases of perforation inside the nose caused by inhaled steroids.

If you are using Nasacort, contact your doctor if your symptoms don't improve after 3 weeks or if they get worse. Also notify your doctor if you have nasal irritation, burning, or stinging after you use the spray.

Possible food and drug interactions
while taking this medication
Inhaled steroids such as Azmacort and Nasacort are not recommended for long-term use with alternate-day prednisone treatment.

Special information
if you are pregnant or breastfeeding
The effects of triamcinolone acetonide during pregnancy have not been adequately studied. If you are pregnant or plan to become pregnant, inform

your doctor immediately. It is not known whether triamcinolone acetonide appears in breast milk. If this medication is essential to your health, your doctor may advise you to discontinue breastfeeding until your treatment with this medication is finished.

Recommended dosage

AZMACORT

The Azmacort Inhaler unit is for oral inhalation only.

Adults

The usual dose is 2 inhalations (about 200 micrograms), taken 3 or 4 times a day. The daily dose should not exceed 16 inhalations.

Children 6 to 12 Years of Age

The usual dose is 1 or 2 inhalations (100 to 200 micrograms), taken 3 or 4 times a day. The daily dose should not exceed 12 inhalations.

Children Under 6 Years of Age

The safety and effectiveness of this drug have not been established in children under 6 years of age.

NASACORT

Adults and Children Aged 12 and Older

The usual starting dose is 220 micrograms a day, taken as 2 sprays in each nostril once a day. (One spray is 55 micrograms.) If necessary, your doctor may increase the dose up to 440 micrograms a day, taken all at once, twice a day, or 4 times a day. Once Nasacort has started to work, your doctor may decrease the dose to 110 micrograms a day.

Children Under 12 Years of Age

The safety and effectiveness of Nasacort in children under 12 years of age have not been established.

Overdosage

Any medication taken in excess can have serious consequences. If you suspect an overdose, seek emergency medical treatment immediately. An overdose is likely to be signaled by an increase in side effects. Accidentally getting the contents of the canister on your skin would most likely irritate your nose and give you a headache.

Brand name:

AZULFIDINE

Pronounced: A-ZUL-fi-deen
Generic name: Sulfasalazine

Why is this drug prescribed?
Azulfidine, an anti-inflammatory medicine, is prescribed for the treatment of mild to moderate ulcerative colitis (a long-term, progressive bowel disease) and as an added treatment in severe ulcerative colitis (chronic inflammation and ulceration of the lining of large bowel and rectum, the main symptom of which is bloody diarrhea). This medication is also prescribed to decrease severe attacks of ulcerative colitis.

Azulfidine EN-tabs are prescribed for people who cannot take the regular Azulfidine tablet because of symptoms of stomach and intestinal irritation such as nausea and vomiting when taking the first few doses of the drug, or for those in whom a reduction in dosage does not lessen the stomach or intestinal side effects.

Most important fact about this drug
Although ulcerative colitis rarely disappears completely, the risk of recurrence can be substantially reduced by the continued use of this drug.

How should you take this medication?
Take this medication in evenly spaced, equal doses, as determined by your doctor, preferably after meals or with food to avoid stomach upset.

It is important that you drink plenty of fluids while taking this medication to avoid kidney stones.

- *If you miss a dose...*
  Take it as soon as you remember. If it is almost time for your next dose, skip the one you missed and go back to your regular schedule. Do not take 2 doses at once.

- *Storage instructions...*
  Store at room temperature.

What side effects may occur?
Side effects cannot be anticipated. If any develop or change in intensity, inform your doctor as soon as possible. Only your doctor can determine if it is safe for you to continue taking Azulfidine.

■ *More common side effects may include:*
Headache
Lack or loss of appetite
Nausea
Stomach distress
Vomiting

■ *Less common side effects may include:*
Anemia, bluish discoloration of the skin, fever, hives, itching, skin rash

■ *Rare side effects may include:*
Abdominal pain, blood disorders, blood in the urine, bloody diarrhea, convulsions, diarrhea, drowsiness, hallucinations, hearing loss, hepatitis, inability to fall or stay asleep, inflammation of the mouth, intestinal inflammation, itchy skin eruptions, joint pain, kidney disorders, lack of muscle coordination, loss of hair, mental depression, red, raised rash, ringing in the ears, sensitivity to light, severe allergic reaction, skin discoloration, skin disorders, spinal cord defects, swelling around the eye, urine discoloration, vertigo

Why should this drug not be prescribed?
If you are sensitive to or have ever had an allergic reaction to Azulfidine, salicylates (aspirin), or other sulfa drugs, you should not take this medication. Make sure your doctor is aware of any drug reactions you have experienced.

Unless you are directed to do so by your doctor, do not take Azulfidine if you have an intestinal or urinary obstruction or if you have porphyria (an inherited disorder involving the substance that gives color to the skin and iris of the eyes).

Special warnings about this medication
If you have kidney or liver damage or any blood disease, your doctor will check you very carefully before prescribing Azulfidine. Deaths have been reported from allergic reactions, blood diseases, kidney or liver damage, changes in nerve and muscle impulses, and fibrosing alveolitis (inflammation of the lungs due to a thickening or scarring of tissue). Signs such as sore throat, fever, abnormal paleness of the skin, purple or red spots on the skin, or jaundice (yellowing of the skin) may be an indication of a serious blood disorder. Your doctor will do frequent blood counts and urine tests. Use caution taking Azulfidine if you have a severe allergy or bronchial asthma.

If Azulfidine EN-tabs are eliminated undisintegrated, stop taking the drug and notify your doctor immediately. (You may lack the intestinal enzymes necessary to dissolve this medication.)

Men taking Azulfidine may experience temporary infertility and a low sperm count.

Skin and urine may become yellow-orange in color while taking Azulfidine.

In addition, prolonged exposure to the sun should be avoided.

Possible food and drug interactions
when taking this medication
If Azulfidine is taken with certain other drugs, the effects of either could be increased, decreased, or altered. It is especially important to check with your doctor before combining Azulfidine with the following:

Digoxin (Lanoxin)
Folic acid (a B-complex vitamin)

Special information
if you are pregnant or breastfeeding
The effects of Azulfidine during pregnancy have not been adequately studied. If you are pregnant or plan to become pregnant, inform your doctor immediately. Azulfidine is secreted in breast milk and could affect a nursing infant. If this medication is essential to your health, your doctor may advise you to discontinue breastfeeding until your treatment is finished.

Recommended dosage
Your doctor will carefully individualize your dosage and monitor your response periodically.

ADULTS

The usual recommended initial dose is 3 to 4 grams daily divided into smaller doses (intervals between nighttime doses should not exceed 8 hours). In some cases the initial dosage is 1 to 2 grams daily to lessen side effects.

Maintenance Therapy
The usual maintenance dose is 2 grams daily.

CHILDREN AGED 2 AND OLDER

The usual recommended initial dose is 40 to 60 milligrams per 2.2 pounds of body weight in each 24-hour period, divided into 3 to 6 doses.

Maintenance Therapy

The usual maintenance is 30 milligrams per 2.2 pounds of body weight in each 24-hour period, divided into 4 doses.

Overdosage

Any medication taken in excess can have serious consequences. If you suspect an Azulfidine overdose, seek emergency medical attention immediately.

- ■ *Symptoms of Azulfidine overdose may include:*
  Abdominal pain
  Convulsions
  Drowsiness
  Nausea
  Stomach upset
  Vomiting

Brand name:

BACTICORT

See Cortisporin Ophthalmic Suspension, page 241.

Brand name:

BACTRIM

Pronounced: BAC-trim
Generic ingredients: Trimethoprim, Sulfamethoxazole
Other brand names: Cotrim, Co-Trimoxazole, Septra

Why is this drug prescribed?

Bactrim, an antibacterial combination drug, is prescribed for the treatment of certain urinary tract infections, severe middle ear infections in children, long-lasting or frequently recurring bronchitis in adults that has increased in seriousness, inflammation of the intestine due to a severe bacterial infection, pneumonia in patients who have a suppressed immune system (*Pneumocystis carinii* pneumonia) and for travelers' diarrhea in adults.

Most important fact about this drug

Sulfamethoxazole, an ingredient in Bactrim, is one of a group of drugs called sulfonamides, which prevent the growth of bacteria in the body. Rare but sometimes fatal reactions have occurred with use of sulfonamides. These reactions include Stevens-Johnson syndrome (severe eruptions around the mouth, anus, or eyes), progressive disintegration of the outer layer of the skin, sudden and severe liver damage, a severe blood disorder (agranulocytosis), and a lack of red and white blood cells because of a bone marrow disorder.

Notify your doctor at the first sign of an adverse reaction such as skin rash, sore throat, fever, joint pain, cough, shortness of breath, abnormal skin paleness, reddish or purplish skin spots, or yellowing of the skin or whites of the eyes.

Frequent blood counts by a doctor are recommended for patients taking sulfonamide drugs.

How should you take this medication?
It is important that you drink plenty of fluids while taking this medication in order to prevent sediment in the urine and the formation of stones.

Bactrim works best when there is a constant amount in the blood. Take Bactrim exactly as prescribed; try not to miss any doses. It is best to take doses at evenly spaced times day and night.

If you are taking Bactrim suspension, ask your pharmacist for a specially marked measuring spoon that delivers accurate doses.

■ *If you miss a dose...*
Take the forgotten dose as soon as you remember. If it is almost time for your next dose, skip the one you missed and go back to your regular schedule. Do not take 2 doses at once.

■ *Storage instructions...*
Store tablets and suspension at room temperature and protect from light. Keep tablets in a dry place. Protect the suspension from freezing.

What side effects may occur?
Side effects cannot be anticipated. If any develop or change in intensity, inform your doctor as soon as possible. Only your doctor can determine if it is safe for you to continue taking Bactrim.

■ *More common side effects may include:*
Hives
Lack or loss of appetite
Nausea
Skin rash
Vomiting

■ *Less common or rare side effects may include:*
Abdominal pain, allergic reactions, anemia, chills, convulsions, depression, diarrhea, eye irritation, fatigue, fever, hallucinations, headache, hepatitis, inability to fall or stay asleep, inability to urinate, increased urination, inflammation of heart muscle, inflammation of the mouth and/or tongue, itching, joint pain, kidney failure, lack of feeling or concern, lack of muscle coordination, loss of appetite, low blood sugar, meningitis (inflammation of the brain or spinal cord), muscle pain, nausea, nervousness, red, raised rash, redness and swelling of the tongue, ringing in the ears, scaling of dead skin due to inflammation, sensitivity to light, severe skin welts or swelling, skin eruptions, skin peeling, vertigo, weakness, yellowing of eyes and skin

Why should this drug not be prescribed?

If you are sensitive to or have ever had an allergic reaction to trimethoprim, sulfamethoxazole, or other sulfa drugs such as Septra, you should not take this medication. Make sure that your doctor is aware of any drug reactions that you have experienced.

Unless you are directed to do so by your doctor, do not take this medication if you have been diagnosed as having megaloblastic anemia, which is a blood disorder due to a deficiency of folic acid.

This drug should not be prescribed for infants less than 2 months of age.

Bactrim is not recommended for preventative or prolonged use in middle ear infections and should not be used in the treatment of streptococcal pharyngitis (inflammation or infection of the pharynx due to streptococcus bacteria).

You should not take Bactrim if you are pregnant or nursing a baby.

Special warnings about this medication

Make sure your doctor knows if you have impaired kidney or liver function, have a folic acid deficiency, are a chronic alcoholic, are taking anticonvulsants, have been diagnosed as having malabsorption syndrome (abnormal intestinal absorption), are in a state of poor nutrition, or have severe allergies or bronchial asthma. Bactrim should be used cautiously under these conditions.

If you have AIDS (acquired immunodeficiency syndrome) and are being treated for *Pneumocystis carinii* pneumonia, you will experience more side effects than will someone without AIDS.

Possible food and drug interactions
when taking this medication

If Bactrim is taken with certain other drugs, the effects of either could be increased, decreased, or altered. It is especially important to check with your doctor before combining Bactrim with the following:

Amantadine (Symmetrel)
Anticonvulsants such as Dilantin
Blood thinners such as Coumadin
Diuretics (in the elderly) such as HydroDIURIL
Methotrexate (Rheumatrex)
Oral diabetes medications such as Micronase

Special information
if you are pregnant or breastfeeding

Bactrim should not be taken during pregnancy. If you are pregnant or plan to become pregnant, notify your doctor immediately. Bactrim does appear in breast milk and could affect a nursing infant. It should not be taken while breastfeeding.

Recommended dosage

ADULTS

Urinary Tract Infections and Intestinal Inflammation

The usual adult dosage in the treatment of urinary tract infection is 1 Bactrim DS (double strength tablet) or 2 Bactrim tablets, or 4 teaspoonfuls (20 milliliters) of Bactrim Pediatric Suspension every 12 hours for 10 to 14 days. The dosage for inflammation of the intestine is the same but is taken for 5 days.

Worsening of Chronic Bronchitis

The usual recommended dosage is 1 Bactrim DS (double strength tablet), 2 Bactrim tablets, or 4 teaspoonfuls (20 milliliters) of Bactrim Pediatric Suspension every 12 hours for 14 days.

Pneumocystis Carinii Pneumonia

The recommended dosage is 20 milligrams of trimethoprim and 100 milligrams of sulfamethoxazole per 2.2 pounds of body weight per 24 hours divided into equal doses every 6 hours for 14 days.

Travelers' Diarrhea

The usual recommended dosage is 1 Bactrim DS (double strength tablet), 2 Bactrim tablets, or 4 teaspoonfuls (20 milliliters) of Bactrim Pediatric Suspension every 12 hours for 5 days.

CHILDREN

Urinary Tract Infections or Middle Ear Infections

The recommended dose for children 2 months of age or older, given every 12 hours for 10 days, is determined by weight. The following table is a guideline for this dosage:

22 pounds, 1 teaspoonful (5 milliliters)

44 pounds, 2 teaspoonfuls (10 milliliters) or 1 tablet

66 pounds, 3 teaspoonfuls (15 milliliters) or 1½ tablets

88 pounds, 4 teaspoonfuls (20 milliliters) or 2 tablets or 1 DS tablet

Intestinal Inflammation

The recommended dose is identical to the dosage recommended for urinary tract and middle ear infections; however, it should be taken for 5 days.

Pneumocystis Carinii Pneumonia

The recommended dose, taken every 6 hours for 14 days, is determined by weight. The following table is a guideline for this dosage:

18 pounds, 1 teaspoonful (5 milliliters)

35 pounds, 2 teaspoonfuls (10 milliliters) or 1 tablet

53 pounds, 3 teaspoonfuls (15 milliliters) or 1½ tablets

70 pounds, 4 teaspoonfuls (20 milliliters) or 2 tablets or 1 DS tablet

The safety of repeated use of Bactrim in children under 2 years of age has not been established.

ELDERLY

There may be an increased risk of severe side effects when Bactrim is taken by the elderly, especially in those who have impaired kidney and/or liver function or who are taking other medication. Consult with your doctor before taking Bactrim.

Overdosage

If you suspect an overdose of Bactrim, seek emergency medical attention immediately.

■ *Symptoms of an overdose of Bactrim include:*
  Blood or sediment in the urine, colic, confusion, dizziness, drowsiness,

fever, headache, lack or loss of appetite, mental depression, nausea, unconsciousness, vomiting, yellowed eyes and skin

Brand name:

BACTROBAN

Pronounced: BAC-tro-ban
Generic name: Mupirocin

Why is this drug prescribed?
Bactroban is prescribed for the treatment of impetigo, a bacterial infection of the skin.

Most important fact about this drug
If the use of Bactroban does not clear your skin infection within 3 to 5 days, or if the infection becomes worse, notify your doctor.

How should you use this medication?
This drug is for external use only.

- *If you miss a dose...*
  Apply it as soon as you remember. If it is almost time for the next dose, skip the one you missed and go back to your regular schedule.

- *Storage instructions...*
  Store at room temperature.

What side effects may occur?
Side effects cannot be anticipated. If any develop or change in intensity, inform your doctor as soon as possible. Only your doctor can determine if it is safe for you to continue using Bactroban.

- *More common side effects may include:*
  Burning
  Pain
  Stinging

- *Less common side effects may include:*
  Itching

- *Rare side effects may include:*
  Abnormal redness, dry skin, inflammation of the skin, nausea, oozing, skin rash, swelling, tenderness

Why should this drug not be prescribed?

If you are sensitive to or have ever had an allergic reaction to Bactroban or similar drugs, you should not use this medication. Make sure your doctor is aware of any drug reactions you have experienced.

Special warnings about this medication

Continued or prolonged use of Bactroban may result in the growth of bacteria that do not respond to this medication and can cause a secondary infection.

This drug is not intended for use in the eyes.

If your skin shows signs of an allergic reaction or irritation, stop using Bactroban and consult your doctor.

Possible food and drug interactions when taking this medication

There are no known interactions.

Special information if you are pregnant or breastfeeding

The effects of Bactroban during pregnancy have not been adequately studied. If you are pregnant or plan to become pregnant, inform your doctor immediately. Bactroban may appear in breast milk and could affect a nursing infant. Your doctor may advise you to discontinue breastfeeding until your treatment with this medication is finished.

Recommended dosage

Apply a small amount of this medication to the affected area 3 times a day. Cover the treated area with gauze if you want.

Overdosage

There is no information available on overdosage.

Generic name:

BECLOMETHASONE DIPROPRIONATE

Pronounced: BECK-low-METH-ah-sone dye-PRO-pee-uh-nate

Brand names: Beclovent Inhalation Aerosol, Beconase AQ Nasal Spray, Beconase Inhalation Aerosol, Vancenase AQ Nasal Spray, Vancenase Nasal Inhaler, Vanceril Inhaler

Why is this drug prescribed?

Beclomethasone is a type of steroid used for respiratory problems. Beclovent and Vanceril are prescribed for the treatment of recurring symptoms of bronchial asthma.

Beconase and Vancenase are used for the symptomatic relief of hay fever and for the prevention of the recurrence of nasal polyps following surgical removal.

Most important fact about this drug

Beclomethasone is not a bronchodilator medication (it does not quickly open the airways); and it should not be used for relief of asthma when bronchodilators and other nonsteroid drugs prove effective. Do not expect immediate relief from beclomethasone, and do not take higher doses in an attempt to make it work. It is not intended for rapid relief, but it will help control symptoms when taken routinely.

How should you take this medication?

Beclomethasone is prescribed in an oral inhalant or a nasal spray form. Use this medication only as preventive therapy exactly as prescribed by your doctor. Many people will require additional drugs to control asthma symptoms fully, but this drug may allow other drugs to be used in smaller doses.

If you are also using a bronchodilator inhalant, take it before inhaling beclomethasone. This will improve the effect of the second drug. Take the two inhalations several minutes apart.

To use the inhaler:
1. Remove the cap and hold inhaler upright.
2. Shake the inhaler thoroughly.
3. Take a drink of water to moisten the throat.
4. Tilt your head slightly and breathe out.
5. While activating the inhaler, take a slow deep breath for 3 to 5 seconds, hold the breath for about 10 seconds, then breathe out slowly.
6. Allow at least 1 minute between inhalations.

Gargling and rinsing your mouth with water after each dose may help prevent hoarseness and throat irritation. Do not swallow the water after you rinse.

This medication comes with directions. Read them carefully before using this medicine.

■ *If you miss a dose...*
Take it as soon as you remember and take the remaining doses for that day at evenly spaced intervals. If it is time for your next dose, skip the one you missed. Never take 2 doses at the same time.

■ *Storage instructions...*
Store at room temperature, away from heat and cold. Do not puncture the container, store it near open flame, or dispose of it in a fire or incinerator.

What side effects may occur?
Side effects cannot be anticipated. If any develop or change in intensity, inform your doctor as soon as possible. Only your doctor can determine if it is safe for you to continue taking this medication.

■ *Side effects may include:*
Dry mouth
Fluid retention
Hives
Hoarseness
Skin rash
Wheezing

■ *When using a nasal spray, other possible side effects are:*
Headache, light-headedness, nasal burning, nasal irritation, nausea, nose and throat infections, nosebleed, runny nose, sneezing, stuffy nose, tearing eyes

Why should this drug not be prescribed?
Your doctor will prescribe beclomethasone only if your asthma cannot be controlled with bronchodilators and other non-steroid medications.

Beclomethasone is not used for the treatment of non-asthmatic bronchitis, or for intermittent asthma therapy.

If you are sensitive to or have ever had an allergic reaction to beclomethasone or other steroid drugs, you should not take this medication. Make sure that your doctor is aware of any drug reactions that you have experienced.

Special warnings about this medication
When steroid drugs are taken by mouth they substitute for and decrease the body's normal ability to make its own steroids as well as its ability to respond to stress.

There is a risk of causing a serious condition called "adrenal insufficiency" when people change from steroid tablets taken by mouth to aerosol beclomethasone dipropionate. Although the aerosol may provide adequate control of asthma during the changeover period, it does not provide the normal amount of steroid the body needs during acute stress situations. If you are being transferred from steroid tablets to beclomethasone and you experience a period of stress or a severe asthma attack, your doctor may prescribe additional treatment with steroid tablets.

Transfer from steroid tablet therapy to beclomethasone dipropionate aerosol may reactivate allergic conditions that were previously suppressed by the steroid tablet therapy, such as runny nose, inflamed eyelids, and eczema. Inform your doctor if you experience any of these symptoms.

High doses of steroids can suppress your immune system. Take extra care to avoid exposure to measles or chickenpox if you have never had them or never had shots. These infections can be serious or even fatal if your immune system is below par. If you are exposed, seek medical advice immediately.

Symptoms such as mental disturbances, increased bruising, weight gain, facial swelling (moon-faced), and reduced growth in children may occur with orally inhaled corticosteroids such as Beclovent. If you experience any of these symptoms, notify your doctor immediately.

Recommended dosage

ADULTS

Beclomethasone Oral Inhalant
The usual recommended dose for adults and children 12 years of age and over is 2 inhalations given 2 to 4 times a day. Four inhalations given twice daily have been shown to be effective in some people. If you have severe asthma, your doctor may advise you to start with 12 to 16 inhalations a day. Daily intake should not exceed 20 inhalations.

Beclomethasone Nasal Spray
The usual dosage is 1 or 2 inhalations in each nostril 2 to 4 times a day for adults and children 12 years of age and over.

CHILDREN

Beclomethasone Oral Inhalant
Children 6 to 12 years of age: The usual recommended dose is 1 or 2 inhalations given 3 or 4 times a day. Four inhalations given twice daily have been effective for some children. Daily intake should not exceed 10 inhalations.

Beclomethasone Nasal Spray
Children 6 to 12 years of age: The usual dosage is 1 inhalation in each nostril 3 times daily.

Beclomethasone should not be given to children under the age of 6 unless advised by your doctor.

Overdosage
Any medication taken in excess can have serious consequences. If you suspect an overdose, seek medical attention immediately.

Brand name:

BECLOVENT

See Beclomethasone Diproprionate, page 110.

Brand name:

BECONASE

See Beclomethasone Diproprionate, page 110.

Brand name:

BEEPEN VK

See Penicillin V Potassium, page 824.

Generic name:

BELLATAL

See Donnatal, page 360.

Brand name:

BENADRYL

Pronounced: BEN-ah-dril
Generic name: Diphenhydramine hydrochloride

Why is this drug prescribed?
Benadryl is an antihistamine with drying and sedative effects. It relieves red, inflamed eyes caused by food allergies and the itching, swelling, and redness from hives and other rashes that are caused by mild allergic reactions. It also relieves the sneezing, coughing, runny or stuffy nose, and red, teary, itching

eyes caused by seasonal allergies (hay fever) and the common cold. Antihistamines work by decreasing the effects of histamine, a chemical released in the body that narrows air passages in the lungs and contributes to inflammation. Antihistamines reduce itching and swelling and dry up secretions from the nose, eyes, and throat.

Benadryl is also used to treat allergic reactions to blood transfusions, to prevent and treat motion sickness, and, with other drugs, to treat anaphylactic shock (severe allergic reaction) and Parkinson's disease, a nerve disorder characterized by tremors, stooped posture, shuffling walk, muscle weakness, drooling, and emotional instability.

Most important fact about this drug
Antihistamines may produce excitability in children. In the elderly they may cause dizziness, excessive calm, or low blood pressure.

How should you take this medication?
Benadryl should be taken exactly as prescribed, or follow instructions on the label.

■ *If you miss a dose...*
Take it as soon as you remember. If it is almost time for your next dose, skip the one you missed and go back to your regular schedule. Do not take 2 doses at once.

■ *Storage instructions...*
Store at room temperature. Protect from moisture.

What side effects may occur?
Side effects cannot be anticipated. If any develop or change in intensity, inform your doctor as soon as possible. Only your doctor can determine if it is safe for you to continue taking Benadryl.

■ *More common side effects may include:*
Disturbed coordination
Dizziness
Excessive calm
Increased chest congestion
Sleepiness
Stomach upset

■ *Less common or rare side effects may include:*
Anaphylactic shock (extreme allergic reaction), anemia, blurred vision, chills, confusion, constipation, convulsions, diarrhea, difficulty sleeping,

double vision, dry mouth, nose, throat, early menstruation, excessive perspiration, excitation, fast, fluttery heartbeat, fatigue, frequent or difficult urination, headache, hives, inability to urinate, increased sensitivity to light, irregular heartbeat, irritability, loss of appetite, low blood pressure, nausea, nervousness, rapid heartbeat, rash, restlessness, ringing in the ears, stuffy nose, tightness of chest and wheezing, tingling or pins and needles, tremor, unreal or exaggerated sense of well-being, vertigo, vomiting

Why should this drug not be prescribed?

Benadryl should not be used in newborn or premature infants, or if you are breastfeeding your infant.

Do not take this medication if you are sensitive to or have ever had an allergic reaction to diphenhydramine hydrochloride or other antihistamines.

Special warnings about this medication

In general, you should use antihistamines very cautiously if you have the eye condition called narrow-angle glaucoma, narrowing of the stomach or intestine because of peptic ulcer or other stomach problems, intestinal blockage, symptoms of an enlarged prostate, or difficulty urinating due to obstruction in the bladder.

Antihistamines can make adults and children less alert and, in young children, may cause excitability.

Elderly people (60 years or older) are more likely to experience dizziness, extreme calm, and low blood pressure.

Use Benadryl cautiously if you have a history of asthma or other chronic lung disease, an overactive thyroid, high blood pressure, or heart disease.

This medication can cause drowsiness. Driving or operating dangerous machinery or participating in any hazardous activity that requires full mental alertness is not recommended until you know how you react to Benadryl.

Possible food and drug interactions
when taking this medication

Benadryl may increase the effects of alcohol, and alcohol may increase the sedative effects of Benadryl. Do not drink alcohol while taking this medication.

If Benadryl is taken with certain other drugs, the effects of either could be increased, decreased, or altered. It is especially important to check with your doctor before combining Benadryl with the following:

Antidepressant drugs known as MAO inhibitors, such as Marplan and Nardil

Sedative/hypnotics such as Halcion, Nembutal, and Seconal

Tranquilizers such as Xanax and Valium

Special information
if you are pregnant or breastfeeding

The effects of Benadryl during pregnancy have not been adequately studied. If you are pregnant or plan to become pregnant, inform your doctor immediately. Benadryl should be used during pregnancy only if clearly needed. Antihistamine therapy is not advised for nursing mothers. If this medication is essential to your health, your doctor may advise you to discontinue breastfeeding until your treatment with Benadryl is finished.

Recommended dosage

Your doctor will tailor the dosage to suit your needs. Benadryl reaches its peak effect in 1 hour, and 1 dose will continue to work for 4 to 6 hours.

ADULTS

The usual recommended dose is 25 to 50 milligrams 3 or 4 times daily. The sleep-aid dosage is 50 milligrams at bedtime.

Motion Sickness

For prevention of motion sickness, take the first dose 30 minutes before exposure to motion; take the other doses before meals and at bedtime for as long as the motion continues.

CHILDREN (OVER 20 POUNDS)

The usual dose is 12.5 to 25 milligrams, 3 to 4 times daily. A child should not take more than 300 milligrams a day.

This medication should not be used as a sleep aid for children under age 12.

Your physician will determine the best use of the drug in response to its effects on the child.

Overdosage

Any medication taken in excess can have serious consequences. If you suspect an overdose, seek medical attention immediately. Antihistamine overdose has caused hallucinations, convulsions, and death in children.

■ *Symptoms of Benadryl overdose may include:*
Central nervous system depression or stimulation, especially in children.

Dry mouth
Fixed, dilated pupils
Flushing
Stomach and intestinal symptoms

Generic name:

BENAZEPRIL

See Lotensin, page 609.

Brand name:

BENTYL

Pronounced: BEN-til
Generic name: Dicyclomine hydrochloride

Why is this drug prescribed?
Bentyl is prescribed for the treatment of functional bowel/irritable bowel syndrome (abdominal pain, accompanied by diarrhea and constipation associated with stress).

Most important fact about this drug
Heat prostration (fever and heat stroke due to decreased sweating) can occur with use of this drug in hot weather. If symptoms occur, stop taking the drug and notify your doctor immediately.

How should you take this medication?
Take this medication exactly as prescribed.

■ *If you miss a dose...*
Take it as soon as you remember. If it is almost time for your next dose, skip the one you missed and go back to your regular schedule. Do not take 2 doses at once.

■ *Storage instructions...*
Store at room temperature. Keep tablets out of direct sunlight. Keep syrup away from excessive heat.

What side effects may occur?
Side effects cannot be anticipated. If any develop or change in intensity, inform your doctor as soon as possible. Only your doctor can determine if it is safe for you to continue taking Bentyl.

■ *Side effects may include:*
Blurred vision
Dizziness
Drowsiness
Dry mouth
Light-headedness
Nausea
Nervousness
Weakness

Not all of the following side effects have been reported with dicyclomine hydrochloride, but they have been reported for similar drugs with antispasmodic action; contact your doctor if they occur.

Abdominal pain, bloated feeling, constipation, decreased sweating, difficulty in urinating, double vision, enlargement of the pupil of the eye, eye paralysis, fainting, headache, hives, impotence, inability to urinate, increased pressure in the eyes, itching, labored, difficult breathing, lack of coordination, lack or loss of appetite, nasal stuffiness or congestion, numbness, rapid heartbeat, rash, severe allergic reaction, sluggishness, sneezing, suffocation, suppression of breast milk, taste loss, temporary cessation of breathing, throat congestion, tingling, vomiting

Why should this drug not be prescribed?
If you are sensitive to or have ever had an allergic reaction to Bentyl, you should not take this medication. Make sure your doctor is aware of any drug reactions you have experienced.

Unless you are directed to do so by your doctor, do not take this drug if you have a blockage of the urinary tract, stomach, or intestines; severe ulcerative colitis (inflammatory disease of the large intestine); reflux esophagitis (inflammation of the esophagus usually caused by the backflow of acid stomach contents); glaucoma; or myasthenia gravis (a disease characterized by long-lasting fatigue and muscle weakness).

This drug should not be given to infants less than 6 months of age or used by women who are nursing an infant.

Special warnings about this medication
Bentyl may produce drowsiness or blurred vision. Therefore, driving a car, operating machinery, or participating in any activity that requires full mental alertness is not recommended.

Diarrhea may be an early symptom of a partial intestinal blockage, especially in people who have had bowel removals and an ileostomy or colostomy. If this occurs, notify your doctor immediately.

You should use this medication with caution if you have autonomic neuropathy (a nerve disorder); liver or kidney disease; hyperthyroidism; high blood pressure; coronary heart disease; congestive heart failure; rapid, irregular heartbeat; hiatal hernia (protrusion of part of the stomach through the diaphragm); or enlargement of the prostate gland.

Possible food and drug interactions
when taking this medication

If Bentyl is taken with certain other drugs, the effects of either could be increased, decreased, or altered. It is especially important to check with your doctor before combining Bentyl with the following:

Airway-opening drugs such as Proventil and Ventolin
Amantadine (Symmetrel)
Antacids such as Maalox
Antiarrhythmics such as quinidine (Quinidex)
Antiglaucoma drugs such as Pilopine
Antihistamines such as Tavist
Benzodiazepines (tranquilizers) such as Valium and Xanax
Corticosteroids such as prednisone (Deltasone)
Digoxin (the heart failure medication Lanoxin)
Major tranquilizers such as Mellaril and Thorazine
MAO inhibitors (antidepressants such as Nardil and Parnate)
Metoclopramide (the gastrointestinal stimulant Reglan)
Narcotic analgesics (pain relievers such as Demerol)
Nitrates and nitrites (heart medications such as nitroglycerin)
Tricyclic antidepressant drugs such as Elavil and Tofranil

Special information
if you are pregnant or breastfeeding

The effects of Bentyl during pregnancy have not been adequately studied. If you are pregnant or plan to become pregnant, notify your doctor. Bentyl does appear in breast milk and could affect a nursing infant. Do not use it when breastfeeding.

Recommended dosage

ADULTS

The usual dosage is 160 milligrams per day divided into 4 equal doses. Since this dose is associated with a significant incidence of side effects, your doctor may recommend a starting dose of 80 milligrams per day divided into 4 equal doses. If no side effects appear, the doctor will then increase the dose.

If this drug is not effective within 2 weeks or side effects require doses below 80 milligrams per day, your doctor may discontinue it.

Overdosage

Any medication taken in excess can have serious consequences. If you suspect an overdose, seek medical attention immediately.

■ *Symptoms of a Bentyl overdose include:*
Blurred vision, difficulty in swallowing, dilated pupils, dizziness, dryness of the mouth, headache, hot, dry skin, nausea, nerve blockage causing weakness and possible paralysis, vomiting

Brand name:

BENZAC W

See Desquam-E, page 308.

Brand name:

BENZAGEL

See Desquam-E, page 308.

Brand name:

BENZAMYCIN

Pronounced: BEN-za-MI-sin
Generic ingredients: Erythromycin, Benzoyl peroxide

Why is this drug prescribed?

A combination of the antibiotic erythromycin and the antibacterial agent benzoyl peroxide, Benzamycin is effective in stopping the bacteria that cause acne and in reducing acne infection.

Most important fact about this drug

If you experience excessive irritation or dryness, stop using Benzamycin and notify your doctor.

How should you use this medication?

Use Benzamycin 2 times per day, once in the morning and once in the evening, or as directed by your doctor. Apply to the affected areas after thoroughly washing, rinsing with warm water, and then gently patting dry.

■ *If you miss a dose...*
  Apply it as soon as you remember. If it is almost time for your next dose, skip the one you missed and go back to your regular schedule.

■ *Storage instructions...*
  This medication should be stored in your refrigerator in a tightly closed container and discarded after 3 months. Do not freeze.

What side effects may occur?
Very few side effects have been reported with the use of Benzamycin. However, those reported include:

  Abnormal redness of the skin
  Dryness
  Itching

If any develop or change in intensity, inform your doctor as soon as possible. Only your doctor can determine if it is safe for you to continue taking Benzamycin.

Why should this drug not be prescribed?
If you are sensitive to or have ever had an allergic reaction to erythromycin or benzoyl peroxide, or any other ingredients in Benzamycin, you should not take this medication. Make sure your doctor is aware of any drug reactions you have experienced.

Special warnings about this medication
Benzamycin Topical Gel is for external use only. Avoid contact with your eyes and mucous membranes.

Benzamycin may bleach hair or colored fabric. Avoid contact with scalp and clothes.

As you use this antibiotic, organisms that are resistant to it may start to grow. Your doctor will have you stop taking Benzamycin and will give you a medication to fight the new bacteria.

Possible food and drug interactions
when using this medication
If Benzamycin is used with other acne medications, the effects of either could be increased, decreased, or altered. Always check with your doctor before combining any other prescription or over-the-counter acne remedy with Benzamycin.

Special information
if you are pregnant or breastfeeding

The effects of Benzamycin during pregnancy have not been adequately studied. If you are pregnant or plan to become pregnant, inform your doctor immediately. It is not known whether Benzamycin appears in breast milk. If this medication is essential to your health, your doctor may advise you to discontinue breastfeeding your baby until your treatment with this medication is finished.

Recommended dosage

ADULTS

Apply to affected areas twice daily, once in the morning and once in the evening.

CHILDREN

The safety and effectiveness of Benzamycin have not been established in children under 12 years of age.

Overdosage

There is no information available on overdosage.

Brand name:

BENZASHAVE

See Desquam-E, page 308.

Generic name:

BENZONATATE

See Tessalon, page 1100.

Generic name:

BENZOYL PEROXIDE

See Desquam-E, page 308.

Generic name:

BENZTROPINE

See Cogentin, page 219.

Brand name:

BETAGAN

Pronounced: BAIT-ah-gan
Generic name: Levobunolol hydrochloride

Why is this drug prescribed?
Betagan eyedrops are given to treat chronic open-angle glaucoma (increased pressure inside the eye). This medication is a beta blocker. It works by lowering pressure within the eyeball.

Most important fact about this drug
Although Betagan eyedrops are applied to the eye, the medication is absorbed and may have effects in other parts of the body. If you have diabetes, asthma or other respiratory diseases, or decreased heart function, make sure your doctor is aware of the problem.

How should you use this medication?
Use Betagan eyedrops exactly as prescribed. Some people also need to use eyedrops that constrict their pupils.

Administer Betagan eyedrops as follows:

1. Wash your hands thoroughly.
2. Gently pull your lower eyelid down to form a pocket between your eye and eyelid.
3. Hold the bottle on the bridge of your nose or on your forehead.
4. Do not touch the applicator tip to any surface, including your eye.
5. Tilt your head back and squeeze the medication into your eye.
6. Close your eyes gently.
7. Keep your eyes closed for 1 to 2 minutes.
8. Wait 5 to 10 minutes before using any other eyedrops.
9. Do not rinse the dropper.

■ *If you miss a dose...*
   If you take Betagan once a day, use it as soon as you remember. If you do not remember until the next day, skip the dose you missed and go back to your regular schedule. Do not take 2 doses at once. If you take Betagan 2 or more times a day, use it as soon as you remember. If it is almost time for your next dose, skip the one you missed and go back to your regular schedule. Do not take 2 doses at once.

■ *Storage instructions...*
Store at room temperature, away from light.

What side effects may occur?

Side effects from Betagan cannot be anticipated. If any develop or change in intensity, inform your doctor. Only your doctor can determine whether it is safe for you to continue using this medication. You may feel a momentary burning and stinging when you place the drops in your eyes. More rarely, you may develop an eye inflammation.

Beta blockers may cause muscle weakness; weakened muscles around the eyes may cause double vision or drooping eyelids.

■ *Other potential side effects include:*
Burning and tingling (pins and needles), chest pain, congestive heart failure, depression, diarrhea, difficult or labored breathing, dizziness, fainting, headache, heart palpitations, hives, low blood pressure, nasal congestion, nausea, rash, slow or irregular heartbeat, stroke, temporary heart stoppage, vision problems, weakness, wheezing

Why should this drug not be prescribed?

Do not use Betagan if you have ever had an allergic reaction to it or are sensitive to it.

You should not use Betagan if you have any of the following conditions:

Asthma
Cardiogenic shock (shock due to insufficient heart action)
Certain heart irregularities
Heart failure
Severe chronic obstructive lung disease
Slow heartbeat (sinus bradycardia)

Special warnings about this medication

Betagan contains a sulfite preservative. In a few people, sulfites can cause an allergic reaction, which may be life-threatening. If you suffer from asthma, you are at increased risk for sulfite allergy.

Betagan may be absorbed into your bloodstream. If too much of the drug is absorbed, this may worsen asthma or other lung diseases or lead to heart failure, which sometimes happens with oral beta-blocker medications.

Beta blockers may increase the risks of anesthesia. If you are facing elective surgery, your doctor may want you to taper off Betagan prior to your operation.

Use Betagan cautiously if you have diminished lung function.

Since beta blockers may mask some signs and symptoms of low blood sugar (hypoglycemia), you should use Betagan very carefully if you have low blood sugar, or if you have diabetes and are taking insulin or an oral antidiabetic medication.

If your body tends to produce too much thyroid hormone, you should taper off Betagan very gradually rather than stopping the drug all at once. Abrupt withdrawal of any beta blocker may provoke a rush of thyroid hormone ("thyroid storm").

Do not use 2 or more beta-blocker eye medications at the same time.

Possible food and drug interactions
when taking this medication
If Betagan is used with certain other drugs, the effects of either could be increased, decreased, or altered. It is especially important to check with your doctor before combining Betagan with the following:

Calcium-blocking blood pressure medications such as Calan and
    Cardizem
Digitalis (the heart medication Lanoxin)
Epinephrine (Epifrin)
Oral beta blockers such as Inderal and Tenormin
Reserpine (Serpasil)

Special information
if you are pregnant or breastfeeding
The use of Betagan in pregnancy has not been adequately studied. If you are pregnant or plan to become pregnant, notify your doctor immediately. Betagan eyedrops should be used during pregnancy only if the benefit justifies the potential risk to the unborn child. Since other beta blocker medications are known to appear in breast milk, use Betagan eyedrops with caution if you are breastfeeding.

Recommended dosage

ADULTS

The recommended starting dose is 1 or 2 drops of Betagan 0.5% in the affected eye(s) once a day.

The typical dose of Betagan 0.25% is 1 or 2 drops twice daily.

For more severe glaucoma, your doctor may have you use Betagan 0.5% twice a day.

Overdosage

Overuse of Betagan eyedrops may produce symptoms of beta blocker overdosage—slowed heartbeat, low blood pressure, breathing difficulty, and/or heart failure. Any medication taken in excess can have serious consequences. If you suspect an overdose of Betagan, seek medical attention immediately.

Generic name:

BETAMETHASONE

See Diprolene, page 345.

Generic name:

BETAXOLOL

See Betoptic, page 127.

Brand name:

BETOPTIC

Pronounced: bet-OP-tick
Generic name: Betaxolol hydrochloride

Why is this drug prescribed?

Betoptic Ophthalmic Solution and Betoptic S Ophthalmic Suspension contain a medication that lowers internal eye pressure and is used to treat open-angle glaucoma (high pressure of the fluid in the eye).

Most important fact about this drug

Although Betoptic, a type of drug called a beta blocker, is applied directly to the eye, it may be absorbed into the bloodstream. Because it may have effects in other parts of the body, you should use Betoptic cautiously if you have diabetes, asthma or other respiratory diseases, or decreased heart function.

How should you use this medication?

Use this medication exactly as prescribed. You may need to use other medications at the same time.

Betoptic S Suspension should be shaken well before each dose.

Administer Betoptic as follows:

1. Wash your hands thoroughly.
2. Gently pull your lower eyelid down to form a pocket between your eye and eyelid.
3. Hold the bottle on the bridge of your nose or on your forehead.
4. Do not touch the applicator tip to any surface, including your eye.
5. Tilt your head back and squeeze the medication into your eye.
6. Close your eyes gently.
7. Keep your eyes closed for 1 to 2 minutes.
8. Wait for 5 to 10 minutes before using any other eyedrops.
9. Do not rinse the dropper.

■ *If you miss a dose...*
Use it as soon as you remember. If it is almost time for your next dose, skip the one you missed and go back to your regular schedule. Do not use 2 doses at once.

■ *Storage instructions...*
Store at room temperature.

What side effects may occur?
Side effects cannot be anticipated. If any develop or change in intensity, inform your doctor as soon as possible. Only your doctor can determine if it is safe for you to continue using Betoptic.

■ *More common side effects may include:*
Temporary eye discomfort

■ *Less common or rare side effects may include:*
Allergic reactions, asthma, congestive heart failure, decreased corneal sensitivity, dead skin, depression, difficulty breathing, difficulty sleeping or drowsiness, dizziness, hair loss, headache, hives, inflammation of the cornea, inflammation of the tongue, intolerance to light, itching, peeling skin, pupils of different sizes, red eyes and skin, slow heartbeat, sluggishness, tearing, thickening chest secretions, vertigo, wheezing

Why should this drug not be prescribed?
Do not use Betoptic if you are sensitive to or have ever had an allergic reaction to it.

People with certain heart conditions should not use Betoptic.

Special warnings about this medication

Before you use Betoptic, tell your doctor if you have any of the following:

Asthma
Diabetes
Heart disease
Thyroid disease

If you are having surgery, your doctor may advise you to gradually stop using Betoptic before general anesthesia.

This drug may lose some of its effectiveness for glaucoma after you have been taking it a long time.

Possible food and drug interactions
when using this medication

If Betoptic is used with certain other drugs, the effects of either could be increased, decreased, or altered. It is especially important to check with your doctor before combining Betoptic with the following:

Drugs that alter mood, such as Nardil and Elavil
Oral beta blockers such as Inderal and Tenormin
Reserpine (Serpasil)

Special information
if you are pregnant or breastfeeding

The effects of Betoptic during pregnancy have not been adequately studied. If you are pregnant or plan to become pregnant, inform your doctor immediately. Betoptic may appear in breast milk and could affect a nursing infant. If this medication is essential to your health, your doctor may advise you to stop breastfeeding until your treatment with Betoptic is finished.

Recommended dosage

Your doctor may have you take another medication with Betoptic or Betoptic-S.

ADULTS

Betoptic
The usual recommended dose is 1 to 2 drops of Betoptic in the affected eye(s) twice daily.

Betoptic S
The usual recommended dose is 1 to 2 drops of Betoptic S in the affected eye(s) twice daily.

Overdosage

Any medication used in excess can have serious consequences. If you suspect an overdose of Betoptic, seek medical attention immediately.

With an oral beta blocker, symptoms of overdose might include:

Heart failure
Low blood pressure
Slow heartbeat

Brand name:

BIAXIN

Pronounced: buy-AX-in
Generic name: Clarithromycin

Why is this drug prescribed?

Biaxin, an antibiotic chemically related to erythromycin, is used to treat certain bacterial infections of the respiratory tract, including:

Strep throat
Pneumonia
Sinusitis (inflammation of sinuses due to infection)
Tonsillitis (inflammation of tonsils due to infection)
Acute middle ear infections

It is also used to treat infections of the skin.

Most important fact about this drug

Biaxin, like any other antibiotic, works best when there is a constant amount of drug in the blood. To keep the amount constant, try not to miss any doses.

How should you take this medication?

You may take Biaxin with or without food. Take it exactly as prescribed; continue taking it for the full course of treatment.

■ *If you miss a dose...*
Take it as soon as you remember. If it is almost time for your next dose, take the one you missed and take the next one 5 to 6 hours later. Then go back to your regular schedule.

■ *Storage instructions...*
Store at room temperature in a tightly closed container, away from light. Do not refrigerate the suspension.

What side effects may occur?

Side effects cannot be anticipated. If any side effects develop or change in intensity, tell your doctor immediately. Only your doctor can determine whether it is safe for you to continue taking Biaxin.

■ *Side effects may include:*
Abdominal pain/discomfort
Altered sense of taste
Diarrhea
Headache
Indigestion
Nausea

Why should this drug not be prescribed?

Do not take Biaxin if you have ever had an allergic reaction to it, or if you are sensitive to it or erythromycin, or similar antibiotics such as Tao and Zithromax.

Special warnings about this medication

If you have severe kidney disease, the doctor may need to prescribe a smaller dose of Biaxin. Make sure the doctor is aware of any kidney problems you may have.

Like other antibiotics, Biaxin may cause a potentially life-threatening form of diarrhea that signals a condition called pseudomembranous colitis (inflammation of the large intestine). Mild diarrhea, a fairly common Biaxin side effect, may disappear as your body gets used to the drug. However, if Biaxin gives you prolonged or severe diarrhea, stop taking the drug and call your doctor immediately.

Possible food and drug interactions
when taking this medication

If Biaxin is taken with certain other drugs, the effects of either can be increased, decreased, or altered. It is especially important to check with your doctor before combining Biaxin with the following:

Carbamazepine (Tegretol)
Terfenadine (Seldane)
Theophylline (Slo-Phyllin, Theo-Dur, others)
Zidovudine (Retrovir)

Biaxin is chemically related to erythromycin. It is possible that other drugs reported to interact with erythromycin could also interact with Biaxin. They include:

Astemizole (Hismanal)
Blood thinners such as Coumadin
Cyclosporine (Sandimmune)
Digoxin (Lanoxin)
Ergotamine (Cafergot)
Hexobarbital
Phenytoin (Dilantin)
Triazolam (Halcion)

Special information
if you are pregnant or breastfeeding

If you are pregnant or plan to become pregnant, notify your doctor immediately. Since Biaxin may have the potential to produce birth defects, it is prescribed during pregnancy only when there is no alternative. Caution is advised when using Biaxin while breastfeeding. Biaxin may appear in breast milk, as does its chemical cousin, erythromycin.

Recommended dosage

ADULTS

Your doctor will carefully tailor your individual dosage of Biaxin depending upon the type of infection and organism causing it.

The usual dose varies from 250 to 500 milligrams every 12 hours for 7 to 14 days.

CHILDREN

Biaxin is not recommended for children under 6 months of age.

The dose for children older than 6 months depends on how much the child weighs. Biaxin is usually given twice a day for 10 days.

Overdosage

Although no specific information is available, any medication taken in excess can have serious consequences. If you suspect an overdose of Biaxin, seek medical attention immediately.

Brand name:

BLEPH-10

See Sodium Sulamyd, page 1033.

Brand name:

BONINE

See Antivert, page 66.

Brand name:

BRETHAIRE

See Brethine, page 133.

Brand name:

BRETHINE

Pronounced: Breath-EEN
Generic name: Terbutaline sulfate
Other brand names: Bricanyl, Brethaire

Why is this drug prescribed?
Brethine is a bronchodilator (a medication that opens the bronchial tubes), prescribed for the prevention and relief of bronchial spasms in asthma. This medication is also used for the relief of bronchial spasm associated with bronchitis and emphysema.

Most important fact about this drug
If you experience an immediate allergic reaction and a worsening of a bronchial spasm, notify your doctor immediately.

How should you take this medication?
Take this drug exactly as prescribed by your doctor.

The action of Brethine may last up to 8 hours. Do not use it more frequently than recommended.

- *If you miss a dose...*
  Take it as soon as you remember. Then take the rest of your medication for that day in evenly spaced doses. Do not take 2 doses at once.

- *Storage instructions...*
  Store at room temperature in a tightly closed container, away from light.

What side effects may occur?

Side effects cannot be anticipated. If any develop or change in intensity, inform your doctor as soon as possible. Only your doctor can determine if it is safe for you to continue taking Brethine.

■ *More common side effects may include:*
Chest discomfort, difficulty in breathing, dizziness, drowsiness, fast, fluttery heartbeat, flushed feeling, headache, increased heart rate, nausea, nervousness, pain at injection site, rapid heartbeat, sweating, tremors, vomiting, weakness

■ *Less common side effects may include:*
Anxiety, dry mouth, muscle cramps

■ *Rare side effects may include:*
Inflamed blood vessels

Why should this drug not be prescribed?

If you are sensitive to or have ever had an allergic reaction to Brethine or similar drugs such as Ventolin, you should not take this medication. Make sure your doctor is aware of any drug reactions you have experienced.

Special warnings about this medication

When taking Brethine, you should not use other asthma medications before checking with your doctor. Only your doctor can determine what is a sufficient amount of time between doses.

Consult with your doctor before using this medication if you have diabetes, high blood pressure, or an overactive thyroid gland, or if you have had seizures at any time.

Unless you are directed to do so by your doctor, do not take this medication if you have heart disease, especially if you also have an irregular heart rate.

Possible food and drug interactions
when taking this medication

If Brethine is taken with certain other drugs, the effects of either could be increased, decreased, or altered. It is especially important to check with your doctor before combining Brethine with the following:

Antidepressant drugs known as MAO inhibitors (Nardil, Parnate, others)
Beta blockers (blood pressure medications such as Inderal and
Tenormin)

Other bronchodilators such as Proventil and Ventolin
Tricyclic antidepressant drugs such as Elavil and Tofranil

**Special information
if you are pregnant or breastfeeding**
The effects of Brethine during pregnancy have not been adequately studied.
If you are pregnant or plan to become pregnant, inform your doctor
immediately. It is not known whether Brethine appears in breast milk. If this
drug is essential to your health, your doctor may advise you to stop nursing
your baby until your treatment is finished.

Recommended dosage

FOR BRETHINE

Adults

The usual tablet dose is 5 milligrams taken at approximately 6-hour intervals,
3 times per day during waking hours. If side effects are excessive, your
doctor may reduce your dose to 2.5 milligrams, 3 times per day.

Do not take more than 15 milligrams in a 24-hour period.

Children

This medication is not recommended for use in children below 12 years of
age.

For children 12 to 15 years of age, the usual dose is 2.5 milligrams, 3 times
per day, not to exceed a total of 7.5 milligrams in a 24-hour period.

FOR BRETHAIRE

The usual dosage for adults and children 12 years and older is 2 inhalations
separated by a 60-second interval, repeated every 4 to 6 hours.

Overdosage
Any drug taken or used in excess can have serious consequences. Signs of a
Brethine overdose are the same as the side effects. If you suspect an
overdose, seek medical attention immediately.

Brand name:

BREVICON

See Oral Contraceptives, page 775.

Brand name:

BRICANYL

See Brethine, page 133.

Generic name:

BROMOCRIPTINE

See Parlodel, page 800.

Generic name:

BROMPHENIRAMINE, PHENYLPROPANOLAMINE, AND CODEINE

See Dimetane-DC, page 340.

Generic name:

BRONTEX

See Tussi-Organidin NR, page 1165.

Generic name:

BUDESONIDE

See Rhinocort, page 956.

Generic name:

BUMETANIDE

See Bumex, page 136.

Brand name:

BUMEX

Pronounced: BYOO-meks
Generic name: Bumetanide

Why is this drug prescribed?
Bumex is used to lower the amount of excess salt and water in your body by increasing the output of urine. It is prescribed in the treatment of edema, or

fluid retention, associated with congestive heart failure and liver or kidney disease. It is also occasionally prescribed, along with other drugs, to treat high blood pressure.

Most important fact about this drug

Bumex is a powerful drug. If taken in excessive amounts, it can severely decrease the levels of water and minerals, especially potassium, your body needs to function. Therefore, your doctor should monitor your dose carefully.

How should you take this medication?

Bumex can increase the frequency of urination and may cause loss of sleep if taken at night. Therefore, if you are taking a single dose of Bumex daily, it should be taken in the morning after breakfast. If you take more than one dose a day, take the last dose no later than 6:00 P.M.

- *If you miss a dose...*
  Take the forgotten dose as soon as you remember. If it is almost time for your next dose, skip the one you missed and go back to your regular schedule. Never take 2 doses at the same time.

- *Storage instructions...*
  Store at room temperature.

What side effects may occur?

Side effects cannot be anticipated. If any develop or change in intensity, inform your doctor as soon as possible. Only your doctor can determine if it is safe for you to continue taking Bumex.

- *More common side effects may include:*
  Dizziness
  Headache
  Low blood pressure
  Muscle cramps
  Nausea

- *Signs of too much potassium loss are:*
  Dry mouth
  Irregular heartbeat
  Muscle cramps or pains
  Unusual tiredness or weakness

■ *Less common or rare side effects may include:*
Abdominal pain, black stools, chest pain, dehydration, diarrhea, dry mouth, ear discomfort, fatigue, hearing loss, itching, joint pain, kidney failure, muscle and bone pain, nipple tenderness, premature ejaculation and difficulty maintaining erection, rapid breathing, skin rash or hives, sweating, upset stomach, vertigo, vomiting, weakness

Why should this drug not be prescribed?

Bumex should not be used if you are unable to urinate or if you are dehydrated.

If you are sensitive to or have ever had an allergic reaction to Bumex or similar drugs such as Lasix, you should not take this medication. Make sure your doctor is aware of any drug reactions you have experienced.

Special warnings about this medication

If you are allergic to sulfur-containing drugs such as sulfonamides (antibacterial drugs), check with your doctor before taking Bumex.

Bumex can decrease the number of platelets in your blood. Your doctor should monitor your blood status regularly.

Bumex can cause a loss of potassium from the body. Your doctor may recommend foods or fluids high in potassium or may want you to take a potassium supplement to help prevent this. Follow your doctor's recommendation carefully.

While taking this medication you may feel dizzy or light-headed or actually faint when getting up from a lying or sitting position. If getting up slowly does not help or if this problem continues, notify your doctor.

Possible food and drug interactions
when taking this medication

If Bumex is taken with certain other drugs, the effects of either could be increased, decreased, or altered. It is especially important to check with your doctor before combining Bumex with the following:

Blood pressure medications such as Vasotec and Tenormin
Indomethacin (Indocin) and other nonsteroidal anti-inflammatory drugs
Probenecid (Benemid)

The combination of Bumex and certain antibiotics or cisplatin (Platinol) may increase the risk of hearing loss.

Because Bumex can lower potassium levels, the combination of Bumex and digitalis or digoxin (Lanoxin) may increase the risk of changes in heartbeat.

The combination of Bumex and lithium (Lithonate) may increase the levels of lithium in the body, causing it to become poisonous.

Special information
if you are pregnant or breastfeeding

The effects of Bumex during pregnancy have not been adequately studied. If you are pregnant or plan to become pregnant, inform your doctor immediately. It is not known if this medication appears in breast milk. Your doctor may advise you to discontinue breastfeeding your baby until your treatment with Bumex is finished.

Recommended dosage

ADULTS

The usual total daily dose is 0.5 to 2.0 milligrams a day. For most people, this is taken as a single dose. However, if the initial dose is not adequate, your doctor may have you take a second and, possibly, a third dose at 4- to 5-hour intervals, up to a maximum daily dose of 10 milligrams.

For the continuing control of edema, your doctor may tell you to take Bumex on alternate days or for 3 to 4 days at a time with rest periods of 1 to 2 days in between.

If you have liver failure, your dose will be kept to a minimum and increased very carefully.

CHILDREN

The safety and effectiveness of Bumex have not been established in children below the age of 18.

Overdosage

An overdose of Bumex can lead to severe dehydration, reduction of blood volume, and severe problems with the circulatory system.

- *The signs of an overdose include:*
  Cramps
  Dizziness
  Lethargy (sluggishness)
  Loss or lack of appetite
  Mental confusion
  Vomiting
  Weakness

If you suspect an overdose, get medical attention immediately.

Generic name:

BUPROPION

See Wellbutrin, page 1204.

Brand name:

BUSPAR

Pronounced: BYOO-spar
Generic name: Buspirone hydrochloride

Why is this drug prescribed?
BuSpar is used in the treatment of anxiety disorders and for short-term relief of the symptoms of anxiety.

Most important fact about this drug
BuSpar should not be used with antidepressant drugs known as monoamine oxidase (MAO) inhibitors. Brands include Nardil and Parnate.

How should you take this medication?
Take BuSpar exactly as prescribed. Do not be discouraged if you feel no immediate effect. The full benefit of this drug may not be seen for 1 to 2 weeks after you start to take it.

■ *If you miss a dose...*
   Take the forgotten dose as soon as you remember. If it is almost time for your next dose, skip the one you missed and go back to your regular schedule. Never take 2 doses at the same time.

■ *Storage instructions...*
   Store at room temperature in a tightly closed container, away from light.

What side effects may occur?
Side effects cannot be anticipated. If any develop or change in intensity, inform your doctor as soon as possible. Only your doctor can determine if it is safe for you to continue taking BuSpar.

■ *More common side effects may include:*
   Dizziness, dry mouth, fatigue, headache, light-headedness, nausea, nervousness, unusual excitement

■ *Less common or rare side effects may include:*
Anger/hostility, blurred vision, bone aches/pain, confusion, constipation, decreased concentration, depression, diarrhea, fast, fluttery heartbeat, incoordination, muscle pain/aches, numbness, pain or weakness in hands or feet, rapid heartbeat, rash, restlessness, stomach and abdominal upset, sweating/clamminess, tingling or pins and needles, tremor, urinary incontinence, vomiting, weakness

Why should this drug not be prescribed?
If you are sensitive to or have ever had an allergic reaction to BuSpar or similar mood-altering drugs, you should not take this medication. Make sure your doctor is aware of any drug reactions you have experienced.

Anxiety or tension related to everyday stress usually does not require treatment with BuSpar. Discuss your symptoms thoroughly with your doctor.

The use of BuSpar is not recommended if you have severe kidney or liver damage.

Special warnings about this medication
The effects of BuSpar on the central nervous system (brain and spinal cord) are unpredictable. Therefore, you should not drive or operate dangerous machinery or participate in any hazardous activity that requires full mental alertness while you are taking BuSpar.

Possible food and drug interactions when taking this medication
Although BuSpar does not intensify the effects of alcohol, it is best to avoid alcohol while taking this medication.

If BuSpar is taken with certain other drugs, the effects of either can be increased, decreased, or altered. It is especially important to check with your doctor before combining BuSpar with the following:

The blood-thinning drug Coumadin
Haloperidol (Haldol)
MAO inhibitors (antidepressant drugs such as Nardil and Parnate)
Trazodone (Desyrel)

Special information if you are pregnant or breastfeeding
The effects of BuSpar during pregnancy have not been adequately studied. If you are pregnant or plan to become pregnant, inform your doctor immediate-

ly. It is not known whether BuSpar appears in breast milk. If this medication is essential to your health, your doctor may advise you to discontinue breastfeeding until your treatment is finished.

Recommended dosage

ADULTS

The recommended starting dose is a total of 15 milligrams per day divided into smaller doses, usually 5 milligrams 3 times a day. Every 2 to 3 days, your doctor may increase the dosage 5 milligrams per day as needed. The daily dose should not exceed 60 milligrams.

CHILDREN

The safety and effectiveness of BuSpar have not been established in children under 18 years of age.

ELDERLY

The use of BuSpar in the elderly has not been thoroughly researched. However, no unusual age-related effects have been identified. The usual dose is 15 milligrams per day divided into smaller doses.

Overdosage

Any medication taken in excess can have serious consequences. If you suspect an overdose of BuSpar, seek medical attention immediately.

■ *The symptoms of BuSpar overdose may include:*
Dizziness
Drowsiness
Nausea or vomiting
Severe stomach upset
Unusually small pupils

Generic name:

BUSPIRONE

See BuSpar, page 140.

Generic name:

BUTALBITAL, ACETAMINOPHEN, AND CAFFEINE

See Fioricet, page 433.

Generic name:

BUTALBITAL, ASPIRIN, AND CAFFEINE

See Fiorinal, page 437.

Generic name:

BUTALBITAL, CODEINE, ASPIRIN, AND CAFFEINE

See Fiorinal with Codeine, page 440.

Generic name:

BUTOCONAZOLE

See Femstat, page 431.

Brand name:

CAFERGOT

Pronounced: KAF-er-got
Generic ingredients: Ergotamine tartrate, Caffeine

Why is this drug prescribed?

Cafergot is prescribed for the relief or prevention of vascular headaches—for example, migraine, migraine variants, or cluster headaches.

Most important fact about this drug

The excessive use of Cafergot can lead to ergot poisoning, resulting in symptoms such as headache, pain in the legs when walking, muscle pain, numbness, coldness, and abnormal paleness of the fingers and toes. If this condition is not treated, it can lead to gangrene (tissue death due to decreased blood supply).

How should you take this medication?

Cafergot is available in both tablet and suppository form. Be sure to take it exactly as prescribed, remaining within the limits of your recommended dosage.

Cafergot works best if you use it at the first sign of a migraine attack. If you get warning signals of a coming migraine, take the drug before the headache actually starts.

Lie down and relax in a quiet, dark room for at least a couple of hours or until you feel better.

Avoid exposure to cold.

To use the suppositories, follow these steps:

1. If the suppository feels too soft, leave it in the refrigerator for about 30 minutes or put it, still wrapped, in ice water until it hardens.
2. Remove the foil wrapper and dip the tip of the suppository in water.
3. Lie down on your side and with a finger insert the suppository into the rectum. Hold it in place for a few moments.

■ *If you miss a dose...*
Take this medication only when threatened with an attack.

■ *Storage instructions*
Store at room temperature in a tightly closed container away from light. Keep suppositories away from heat.

What side effects may occur?
Side effects cannot be anticipated. If any develop or change in intensity, inform your doctor as soon as possible. Only your doctor can determine if it is safe for you to continue taking Cafergot.

■ *Side effects may include:*
Fluid retention
High blood pressure
Itching
Nausea
Numbness
Rapid heart rate
Slow heartbeat
Tingling or pins and needles
Vertigo
Vomiting
Weakness

■ *Complications caused by constriction of the blood vessels can be serious. They include:*
Bluish tinge to the skin
Chest pain
Cold arms and legs

Gangrene
Muscle pains

Although these symptoms occur most commonly with long-term therapy at relatively high doses, they have been reported with short-term or normal doses. A few people on long-term therapy have developed heart valve problems.

Why should this drug not be prescribed?
If you are sensitive to or have ever had an allergic reaction to ergotamine tartrate, caffeine, or similar drugs, you should not take this medication. Make sure your doctor is aware of any drug reactions you have experienced.

Unless directed to do so by your doctor, do not take this medication if you have coronary heart disease, circulatory problems, high blood pressure, impaired liver or kidney function, or an infection, or if you are pregnant.

Special warnings about this medication
It is extremely important that you do not exceed your recommended dosage, especially when Cafergot is used over long periods. There have been reports of psychological dependence in people who have abused this drug over long periods of time. Discontinuance of the drug may produce withdrawal symptoms such as sudden, severe headaches.

If you experience excessive nausea and vomiting during attacks, making it impossible for you to retain oral medication, your doctor will probably tell you to use rectal suppositories.

This drug is effective only for migraine and migraine-type headaches. Do not use it for any other kind of headache.

Possible food and drug interactions
when taking this medication
If Cafergot is taken with certain other drugs, the effects of either could be increased, decreased, or altered. It is especially important to check with your doctor before combining Cafergot with the following:

Beta-blocker drugs (blood pressure medications such as Inderal and Tenormin)
Drugs that constrict the blood vessels, such as EpiPen and the oral decongestant Sudafed
Macrolide antibiotics such as PCE, E.E.S., and Biaxin
Nicotine (Nicoderm, Habitrol, others)

Special information
if you are pregnant or breastfeeding
Do not take Cafergot if you are pregnant. Cafergot appears in breast milk and may have serious effects in your baby. If this medication is essential for your health, your doctor may advise you to discontinue breastfeeding.

Recommended dosage
Dosage should start at the first sign of an attack.

ADULTS

Orally
The total dose for any single attack should not exceed 6 tablets.

Rectally
The maximum dose for an individual attack is 2 suppositories.

The total weekly dosage should not exceed 10 tablets or 5 suppositories.

A preventive, short-term dose may be given at bedtime to certain people, but only as prescribed by a doctor.

Overdosage
If you suspect an overdose of Cafergot, seek emergency medical treatment immediately.

■ *Symptoms of Cafergot overdose include:*
  Coma, convulsions, diminished or absent pulses, drowsiness, high or low blood pressure, numbness, shock, stupor, tingling, pain and bluish discoloration of the limbs, unresponsiveness, vomiting

Brand name:

CALAN

Pronounced: CAL-an
Generic name: Verapamil hydrochloride
Other brand names: Calan SR, Isoptin, Isoptin SR, Verelan

Why is this drug prescribed?
Verapamil, the active ingredient in Calan, Isoptin, and Verelan, is prescribed for the treatment of various types of angina (chest pain, often accompanied by a feeling of choking, usually caused by lack of oxygen to the heart due to clogged arteries). It is also used for irregular heartbeat and for high blood

pressure. The sustained release formula (SR) is used only for the treatment of high blood pressure. Verapamil is a type of medication called a calcium channel blocker. It eases the heart's workload by slowing down the passage of nerve impulses through it, and hence the contractions of the heart muscle. This improves blood flow through the heart and throughout the body, reduces blood pressure, corrects irregular heartbeat, and helps prevent angina pain.

Some doctors also prescribe verapamil to prevent migraine headache and asthma and to treat manic depression and panic attacks.

Most important fact about this drug
If you have high blood pressure, you must take verapamil regularly for it to be effective. Since blood pressure declines gradually, it may be several weeks before you get the full benefit of verapamil; and you must continue taking it even if you are feeling well. Verapamil does not cure high blood pressure; it merely keeps it under control.

How should you take this medication?
Calan, Isoptin, and Verelan tablets can be taken with or without food. Calan SR and Isoptin SR should be taken with food.

Calan SR, Isoptin SR, and Verelan must be swallowed whole and should not be crushed or chewed.

Take this medication exactly as prescribed, even if you are feeling well. Try not to miss any doses. If the drug is not taken regularly, your condition can get worse.

Check with your doctor before you stop taking this drug; a slow reduction in the dose may be required.

- *If you miss a dose...*
  Take it as soon as you remember. If it is almost time for your next dose, skip the one you missed and go back to your regular schedule. Never take 2 doses at the same time.

- *Storage instructions...*
  Store at room temperature away from light and moisture.

What side effects may occur?
Side effects cannot be anticipated. If any develop or change in intensity, inform your doctor as soon as possible. Only your doctor can determine if it is safe for you to continue taking verapamil.

■ *More common side effects may include:*
Congestive heart failure, constipation, dizziness, fatigue, fluid retention, headache, low blood pressure, nausea, rash, shortness of breath, slow heartbeat

■ *Less common or rare side effects may include:*
Angina, blurred vision, breast development in males, bruising, chest pain, confusion, diarrhea, difficulty sleeping, drowsiness, dry mouth, excessive milk secretion, fainting, fever and rash, flushing, hair loss, heart attack, hives, impotence, increased urination, joint pain, limping, loss of balance, muscle cramps, pounding heartbeat, rash, shakiness, skin peeling, sleepiness, spotty menstruation, sweating, tingling or pins and needles, upset stomach

Why should this drug not be prescribed?
If you have low blood pressure or certain types of heart disease or heartbeat irregularities, you should not take verapamil. Make sure the doctor is aware of any cardiac problems you may have.

If you are sensitive to or have ever had an allergic reaction to Calan or any other brands of verapamil, or other calcium channel blockers, do not take this medication.

Special warnings about this medication
Verapamil can reduce or eliminate angina pain caused by exertion or exercise. Be sure to discuss with your doctor how much exertion is safe for you.

Verapamil may cause your blood pressure to become too low. If you experience dizziness or light-headedness, notify your doctor.

Congestive heart failure and fluid in the lungs have occurred in people taking verapamil together with other heart drugs known as beta blockers. Make sure your doctor is aware of all medications you are taking.

If you have a heart condition, liver disease, kidney disease, or Duchenne's dystrophy (the most common type of muscular dystrophy), make certain your doctor knows about it. Verapamil should be used with caution.

Possible food and drug interactions
when taking this medication
If verapamil is taken with certain other drugs, the effects of either could be increased, decreased, or altered. It is especially important to check with your doctor before combining verapamil with the following:

Amiodarone (Cordarone)
ACE inhibitor-type blood pressure drugs such as Capoten and Vasotec
Beta-blocker-type blood pressure drugs such as Lopressor, Tenormin,
 and Inderal
Carbamazepine (Tegretol)
Chloroquine (Aralen)
Cimetidine (Tagamet)
Cyclosporine (Sandimmune)
Dantrolene (Dantrium)
Digitalis (Lanoxin)
Disopyramide (Norpace)
Diuretics such as Lasix, HydroDIURIL
Flecainide (Tambocor)
Glipizide (Glucotrol)
Imipramine (Tofranil)
Inhalation anesthetics
Lithium (Lithonate)
Nitrates such as Transderm Nitro and Isordil
Phenobarbital
Phenytoin (Dilantin)
Quinidine (Quinidex)
Rifampin (Rifadin)
Theophylline (Theo-Dur)
Vasodilator-type blood pressure drugs such as Loniten
Other high blood pressure drugs such as Minipress

Special information
if you are pregnant or breastfeeding

The effects of verapamil during pregnancy have not been adequately studied.
If you are pregnant or plan to become pregnant, inform your doctor
immediately. The drug appears in breast milk and could affect a nursing
infant. If this medication is essential to your health, your doctor may advise
you to discontinue breastfeeding until your treatment is finished.

Recommended dosage

FOR CALAN AND ISOPTIN

Dosages of this medication must be adjusted to meet individual needs. In
general, dosages of this medication should not exceed 480 milligrams per
day. Your doctor will closely monitor your response to this drug, usually
within 8 hours of the first dose.

Safety and effectiveness of this drug in children have not been established.

Angina

The usual initial dose is 80 to 120 milligrams, 3 times a day. Lower doses of 40 milligrams 3 times a day may be used by people who have a stronger response to this medication, such as the elderly or those with decreased liver function. The dosage may be increased by your doctor either daily or weekly until the desired response is seen.

Irregular Heartbeat

The usual dose in people who are also on digitalis ranges from 240 to 320 milligrams per day divided into 3 or 4 doses.

In those not on digitalis, doses range from a total of 240 to 480 milligrams per day divided into 3 or 4 doses.

Maximum effects of this drug should be seen in the first 48 hours of use.

High Blood Pressure

Effects of this drug on blood pressure should be seen within the first week of use. Any adjustment of this medication to a higher dose will be based on its effectiveness as determined by your doctor.

The usual dose of this drug, when used alone for high blood pressure, is 80 milligrams, 3 times per day. Total daily doses of 360 milligrams and 480 milligrams may be used. Smaller doses of 40 milligrams 3 times per day may be taken by smaller individuals and the elderly.

FOR CALAN SR, ISOPTIN SR, AND VERELAN

Dosages for high blood pressure should be adjusted to meet each individual's needs.

Adults

The usual starting dose of Calan SR and Isoptin SR is 180 milligrams taken in the morning. For Verelan, it is 240 milligrams. A lower starting dose of 120 milligrams may be taken if the person is smaller. Your doctor will monitor your response to this drug and may adjust it each week. In addition, your doctor may increase the dose and add evening doses to the morning dose, based on the effectiveness of the drug.

You should see results from the drug within a week.

Children

The safety and effectiveness of this drug in children under age 18 have not been established.

Elderly
Your doctor may start you at a lower dose of 120 milligrams and then adjust it according to your response.

Overdosage
Any medication taken in excess can have serious consequences. If you suspect an overdose, seek medical attention immediately.

An overdose of Calan can cause dangerously low blood pressure and life-threatening heart problems. After treatment for an overdose, you should remain under observation in the hospital for at least 48 hours, especially if you have taken the sustained-release form of the drug.

Brand name:

CALCIMAR

Pronounced: KAL-si-mar
Generic name: Calcitonin-salmon

Why is this drug prescribed?
Calcimar is a synthetic form of calcitonin, a naturally occurring hormone produced by the thyroid gland. Calcimar reduces the rate of calcium loss from bones. Since less calcium passes from the bones to the blood, Calcimar also helps control blood calcium levels. Calcimar is used to treat:

Paget's disease (abnormal bone growth leading to deformities)
Hypercalcemia (abnormally high calcium blood levels)
Postmenopausal osteoporosis (bone loss occurring after menopause)

Most important fact about this drug
Calcimar has been reported to cause serious allergic reactions (such as shock, difficulty breathing, wheezing, and swelling of the throat or tongue) in a few people.

How should you take this medication?
Calcimar is taken by injection, given by either you or your doctor. If you are injecting Calcimar yourself, it is important to follow your doctor's instructions carefully so that you inject Calcimar correctly. Calcimar is for injection under the skin or into a muscle; do not inject it into a vein.

You can minimize side effects such as nausea, vomiting, and skin flushing by taking the injection at bedtime.

Do not use Calcimar solution if it has changed color or has particles floating in it.

If you are taking Calcimar for postmenopausal bone loss, you should be sure your diet provides enough calcium and vitamin D. Foods that are good sources of calcium include dairy products (such as milk and cheese) and fish. Good sources of vitamin D include fish (such as salmon, sardines, and tuna), liver, and dairy products. Sunlight is an indirect source of vitamin D.

■ *If you miss a dose...*
If you take Calcimar twice a day, take it as soon as you remember if it is within 2 hours of your scheduled time. Then go back to your regular schedule. If you do not remember until later, skip the dose you missed and go back to your regular schedule.

If you take Calcimar once a day, take it as soon as you remember, then go back to your regular schedule. If you do not remember until the next day, skip the dose you missed and go back to your regular schedule.

If you take Calcimar every other day, take it as soon as you remember if it is the day you are scheduled to take it. Then go back to your regular schedule. If you do not remember until the next day, take the dose you missed when you remember it, then skip a day and start your schedule again.

If you take a dose of Calcimar 3 times a week, take the dose you missed the next day, then set each injection back a day for the rest of the week. The following week, go back to your regular 3 days.

Whatever your schedule, never take 2 doses at once.

■ *Storage instructions...*
Store in the refrigerator.

What side effects may occur?
Side effects cannot be anticipated. If any develop or change in intensity, inform your doctor as soon as possible. Only your doctor can determine if it is safe for you to continue taking Calcimar.

■ *More common side effects may include:*
Inflamed skin where Calcimar has been injected
Nausea
Vomiting

■ *Less common side effects may include:*
Flushed face, flushed hands, severe allergic reaction, skin rashes

Why should this drug not be prescribed?
You should not be using Calcimar if you are allergic to it.

Special warnings about this medication
Calcimar may cause an abnormally low blood level of calcium, resulting in muscle cramps, spasms, and twitches in the face, feet, and hands.

Before taking Calcimar for the first time, you should consider having a skin test to determine whether you are allergic to the drug.

People who take Calcimar on a long-term basis should have periodic urine and blood tests to determine the ongoing effects of Calcimar.

It is important to let your doctor know how you respond to this drug; some people may develop an antibody to Calcimar, and it may become less effective.

**Possible food and drug interactions
when taking this medication**
There are no interactions listed for this drug.

**Special information
if you are pregnant or breastfeeding**
The effects of Calcimar in pregnancy have not been adequately studied.

Pregnant women should use Calcimar only if the potential benefits clearly outweigh any potential risks to the unborn child. It is not known whether Calcimar appears in breast milk. Women are usually advised not to take Calcimar while breastfeeding an infant.

Recommended dosage
Your doctor will tailor the dosage according to your individual requirements and the condition being treated. Do not change the dose without consulting your doctor.

If you are taking Calcimar for postmenopausal osteoporosis, ask your doctor about taking supplemental Vitamin D and calcium.

Overdosage
Any medication taken in excess can have serious consequences. If you suspect an overdose, seek medical help immediately.

■ *Symptoms of Calcitonin overdose may include:*
Nausea
Vomiting

Generic name:

CALCITONIN-SALMON

See Calcimar, page 151.

Generic name:

CALCITRIOL

See Rocaltrol, page 975.

Brand name:

CAPOTEN

Pronounced: KAP-o-ten
Generic name: Captopril

Why is this drug prescribed?

Capoten is used in the treatment of high blood pressure and congestive heart failure. When prescribed for high blood pressure, it is effective used alone or combined with diuretics. If it is prescribed for congestive heart failure, it is used in combination with digitalis and diuretics. Capoten is in a family of drugs known as "ACE (angiotensin converting enzyme) inhibitors." It works by preventing a chemical in your blood called angiotensin I from converting into a more potent form that increases salt and water retention in your body. Capoten also enhances blood flow throughout your blood vessels.

In addition, Capoten is used to improve survival in certain people who have suffered heart attacks and to treat kidney disease in diabetics.

Some doctors also prescribe Capoten for angina pectoris (crushing chest pain), Raynaud's phenomenon (a disorder of the blood vessels that causes the fingers to turn white when exposed to cold), and rheumatoid arthritis.

Most important fact about this drug

If you have high blood pressure, you must take Capoten regularly for it to be effective. Since blood pressure declines gradually, it may be several weeks before you get the full benefit of Capoten; you must continue taking it even if you are feeling well. Capoten does not cure high blood pressure; it merely keeps it under control.

How should you take this medication?

Capoten should be taken 1 hour before meals. If you are taking an antacid such as Mylanta, take it 2 hours prior to Capoten.

Take this medication exactly as prescribed. Stopping Capoten suddenly could cause your blood pressure to increase.

- *If you miss a dose...*
  Take it as soon as you remember. If it is almost time for your next dose, skip the one you missed and go back to your regular schedule. Never take 2 doses at the same time.

- *Storage instructions...*
  Store Capoten at room temperature, away from moisture, in a tightly closed container.

What side effects may occur?

Side effects cannot be anticipated. If any develop or change in intensity, inform your doctor as soon as possible. Only your doctor can determine if it is safe for you to continue taking Capoten.

- *More common side effects may include:*
  Itching
  Loss of taste
  Low blood pressure
  Rash

- *Less common or rare side effects may include:*
  Abdominal pain, anemia, angina pectoris (severe chest pain), blisters, blurred vision, breast development in males, cardiac arrest, changes in heart rhythm, chest pain, confusion, constipation, cough, depression, diarrhea, difficulty swallowing, dizziness, dry mouth, fatigue, fever and chills, flushing, general feeling of ill health, hair loss, headache, heart attack, heart failure, impotence, inability to sleep, indigestion, inflammation of the nose, inflammation of the tongue, labored breathing, lack of coordination, loss of appetite, lung inflammation, muscle pain and/or weakness, nausea, nervousness, pallor, palpitations, peptic ulcer, rapid heartbeat, sensitivity to light, skin inflammation, skin peeling, sleepiness, sore throat, stomach irritation, stroke, sudden fainting or loss of strength, swelling of face, lips, tongue, throat, or arms and legs, tingling or pins and needles, vomiting, weakness, wheezing, yellow eyes and skin

Why should this drug not be prescribed?

If you are sensitive to or have ever had an allergic reaction to Capoten or similar drugs such as Vasotec, you should not take this medication. Make sure that your doctor is aware of any drug reactions that you have experienced.

Special warnings about this medication

If you develop swelling of the face around your lips, tongue or throat (or of your arms and legs) or have difficulty swallowing, you should stop taking Capoten and contact your doctor immediately. You may need emergency treatment.

If you are receiving bee or wasp venom to prevent an allergic reaction to stings, use of Capoten at the same time may cause a severe allergic reaction.

If you are taking Capoten, a complete assessment of your kidney function should be done; and your kidney function should continue to be monitored. If you have kidney disease, Capoten should be used only if you have taken other blood pressure medications and your doctor has determined that the results were unsatisfactory.

Some people taking Capoten have had a severe allergic reaction during kidney dialysis.

If you are taking Capoten for your heart, be careful not to increase physical activity too quickly. Check with your doctor as to how much exercise is safe for you.

If you are taking Capoten for congestive heart failure, your blood pressure may drop temporarily after the first few doses and you may feel light-headed for a time. Your doctor should monitor you closely when you start taking the medication or when your dosage is increased.

If you are taking high doses of diuretics and Capoten, you may develop excessively low blood pressure. Your doctor may reduce your diuretic dose so that your blood pressure doesn't drop too far.

If you notice a yellow coloring to your skin or the whites of your eyes, stop taking the drug and notify your doctor immediately. You could be developing a liver problem.

Capoten may cause you to become drowsy or less alert, especially if you are also taking a diuretic at the same time. If it has this effect on you, driving or participating in any potentially hazardous activity is not recommended.

Dehydration may cause a drop in blood pressure. If you experience symptoms such as excessive perspiration, vomiting, and/or diarrhea, notify your doctor immediately.

If you develop a sore throat or fever, you should contact your doctor immediately. It could indicate a more serious illness.

If you develop a persistent, dry cough, tell your doctor. It may be due to the medication and, if so, will disappear if you stop taking Capoten.

Possible food and drug interactions
when taking this medication

If Capoten is taken with certain other drugs, the effects of either could be increased, decreased, or altered. It is especially important to check with your doctor before combining Capoten with the following:

Allopurinol (Zyloprim)
Aspirin
Blood pressure drugs known as beta blockers, such as Inderal and Tenormin
Cyclosporine (Sandimmune)
Digoxin (Lanoxin)
Diuretics such as HydroDIURIL
Lithium (Lithonate)
Nitroglycerin and similar heart medicines (Nitro-Dur, Transderm-Nitro, others)
Nonsteroidal anti-inflammatory drugs such as Indocin and Feldene
Potassium preparations such as Micro-K and Slow-K
Potassium-sparing diuretics such as Aldactone and Midamor

Do not use potassium-containing salt substitutes while taking Capoten.

Special information
if you are pregnant or breastfeeding

ACE inhibitors such as Capoten have been shown to cause injury and even death to the developing baby when used in pregnancy during the second and third trimesters. If you are pregnant or plan to become pregnant, contact your doctor immediately. Capoten appears in breast milk and could affect a nursing infant. If this medication is essential to your health, your doctor may advise you to discontinue breastfeeding until your treatment is finished.

Recommended dosage

ADULTS

High Blood Pressure

The usual starting dose is 25 milligrams taken 2 or 3 times a day. If you have any problems with your kidneys or suffer from other major health problems, your starting dose may be lower. Depending on how your blood pressure responds, your doctor may increase your dose later, up to a total of 150 milligrams 2 or 3 times a day. The maximum recommended daily dose is 450 milligrams.

Heart Failure
For most people, the usual dose is 25 milligrams taken 3 times a day. A daily dosage of 450 milligrams should not be exceeded.

After a Heart Attack
The usual starting dose is 6.25 milligrams, taken once, followed by 12.5 milligrams 3 times a day. Your doctor will increase the dose over the next several days to 25 milligrams taken 3 times a day and then, over the next several weeks, to 50 milligrams 3 times a day.

Kidney Disease in Diabetes
The usual dose is 25 milligrams taken 3 times a day.

CHILDREN
The safety and effectiveness of Capoten in children have not been established.

ELDERLY
Your doctor will determine the dosage according to your particular needs.

Overdosage
Any medication taken in excess can cause symptoms of overdose. If you suspect an overdose of Capoten, seek medical attention immediately.

Light-headedness or dizziness due to a sudden drop in blood pressure is the primary effect of a Capoten overdose.

Brand name:

CAPOZIDE

Pronounced: KAP-oh-zide
Generic ingredients: Captopril, Hydrochlorothiazide

Why is this drug prescribed?
Capozide is used in the treatment of high blood pressure. It combines an ACE inhibitor with a thiazide diuretic. Captopril, the ACE inhibitor, works by preventing a chemical in your blood called angiotensin I from converting into a more potent form that increases salt and water retention in your body.

Captopril also enhances blood flow throughout your blood vessels. Hydro-chlorothiazide, the diuretic, helps your body produce and eliminate more urine, which helps in lowering blood pressure.

Most important fact about this drug
You must take Capozide regularly for it to be effective. Since blood pressure declines gradually, it may be several weeks before you get the full benefit of Capozide; and you must continue taking it even if you are feeling well. Capozide does not cure high blood pressure; it merely keeps it under control.

How should you take this medication?
Capozide should be taken 1 hour before meals. Take it exactly as prescribed. Stopping Capozide suddenly could cause your blood pressure to increase.

- *If you miss a dose...*
  Take it as soon as you remember. If it is almost time for your next dose, skip the one you missed and go back to your regular schedule. Never take 2 doses at the same time.

- *Storage instructions...*
  Capozide should be stored at room temperature in a tightly closed container away from moisture.

What side effects may occur?
Side effects can't be anticipated. If any develop or change in intensity, inform your doctor as soon as possible. Only your doctor can determine if it is safe for you to continue taking Capozide.

- *More common side effects may include:*
  Itching
  Loss of taste
  Low blood pressure
  Rash

- *Less common or rare side effects may include:*
  Abdominal pain, anemia, angina pectoris (severe chest pain), angioedema (swelling of the arms and legs, face, lips, tongue, or throat), blurred vision, breast development in males, bronchitis, bronchospasm, changes in heart rhythm, chest pain, confusion, constipation, cough, cramping, depression, diarrhea, dizziness, dizziness upon standing up, dry mouth, fainting, fatigue, fever, flushing, general feeling of ill health, hair loss, headache, heart attack, heart failure, hepatitis, hives, inability to sleep,

indigestion, impotence, inflammation of nose, inflammation of tongue, labored breathing, lack of coordination, loss of appetite, low potassium levels leading to symptoms such as dry mouth, excessive thirst, weak or irregular heartbeat, muscle pain or cramps, muscle pain and/or weakness, muscle spasm, nausea, nervousness, pallor, peptic ulcer, rapid heartbeat, Raynaud's Syndrome (circulatory disorder), restlessness, sensitivity to light, severe allergic reactions, skin inflammation and/or peeling, sleepiness, stomach irritation, stroke, tingling or pins and needles, vomiting, vertigo, weakness, wheezing, yellow eyes and skin

Why should this drug not be prescribed?

If you are sensitive to or have ever had an allergic reaction to captopril or hydrochlorothiazide or similar drugs, or if you are sensitive to other sulfonamide-derived drugs, you should not take this medication. If you have a history of angioedema (swelling of face, extremities, and throat) or inability to urinate, you should not take this medication.

Special warnings about this medication

If you develop swelling of your face around your lips, tongue, or throat, or in your arms and legs, or if you begin to have difficulty swallowing, you should contact your doctor immediately. You may need emergency treatment.

If you develop a sore throat or fever you should contact your doctor immediately. It could indicate a more serious illness.

If you are taking Capozide, a complete assessment of your kidney function should be done; kidney function should continue to be monitored.

If you have impaired kidney function, Capozide should be used only if you have taken other blood pressure medications and your doctor has determined that the results were unsatisfactory.

If you have liver disease or a disease of the connective tissue called lupus erythematosus, Capozide should be used with caution.

If you have congestive heart failure, you should be carefully watched for low blood pressure. You should not increase your physical activity too quickly.

Excessive sweating, dehydration, severe diarrhea, or vomiting could deplete your fluids and cause your blood pressure to become too low. Be careful when exercising and in hot weather.

This drug should be used with caution if you are on dialysis. There have been reports of extreme allergic reactions during dialysis in people taking ACE-inhibitor medications such as Capozide.

While taking Capozide, do not use potassium-sparing diuretics (such as

Moduretic), potassium supplements, or salt substitutes containing potassium without talking to your doctor first.

Possible food and drug interactions
when taking this medication

Capozide may intensify the effects of alcohol. Do not drink alcohol while taking this medication.

If Capozide is taken with certain other drugs, the effects of either could be increased, decreased, or altered. It is especially important to check with your doctor before combining Capozide with the following:

Alcohol
Antigout drugs such as Zyloprim
Barbiturates such as phenobarbital or Seconal
Calcium
Cardiac glycosides such as Lanoxin
Cholestyramine (Questran)
Colestipol (Colestid)
Corticosteroids such as prednisone
Diabetes medications
Diazoxide (Proglycem)
Heart medications such as Lanoxin
Lithium (Lithonate)
MAO inhibitors (antidepressants such as Nardil)
Methenamine (Mandelamine)
Narcotics such as Percocet
Nitroglycerin or other nitrates such as Transderm-Nitro
Nonsteroidal anti-inflammatory drugs such as Naprosyn
Norepinephrine (Levophed)
Oral blood thinners such as Coumadin
Other blood pressure drugs such as Vasotec and Procardia XL
Potassium-sparing diuretics such as Moduretic
Potassium supplements such as Slow K
Probenecid (Benemid)
Salt substitutes containing potassium
Sulfinpyrazone (Anturane)

Special information
if you are pregnant or breastfeeding

ACE inhibitors such as Capozide have been shown to cause injury and even death to the developing baby when used in pregnancy during the second or third trimesters. If you are pregnant, your doctor should discontinue your use of this medication as soon as possible. If you plan to become pregnant and are taking Capozide, contact your doctor immediately to discuss the potential hazard to your unborn child. Capozide appears in breast milk and could affect a nursing infant. If this medication is essential to your health, your doctor may advise you to discontinue breastfeeding until your treatment is finished.

Recommended dosage

ADULTS

Dosages of this drug are always individualized, and your doctor will determine what combination works best for you. This medication can be used in conjunction with other blood pressure medications such as beta blockers. Dosages are also adjusted for people with decreased kidney function.

The initial dose is one 25 milligram/15 milligram tablet, once a day. If this is not effective, your doctor may adjust the dosage upward every 6 weeks. The daily dose should not exceed 150 milligrams captopril and 50 milligrams hydrochlorothiazide.

CHILDREN

The safety and effectiveness of Capozide in children have not been established. Capozide should be used in children only if other measures for controlling blood pressure have not been effective.

ELDERLY

Your doctor will determine the dosage according to your particular needs.

Overdosage

Any medication taken in excess can have serious consequences. If you suspect an overdose, seek medical attention immediately.

■ *The symptoms of Capozide overdose may include:*
Coma
Hypermotility
Lethargy
Low blood pressure
Sluggishness
Stomach and intestinal irritation

Generic name:

CAPTOPRIL

See Capoten, page 154.

Generic name:

CAPTOPRIL WITH HYDROCHLOROTHIAZIDE

See Capozide, page 158.

Brand name:

CARAFATE

Pronounced: CARE-uh-fate
Generic name: Sucralfate

Why is this drug prescribed?
Carafate Tablets and Suspension are used for the short-term treatment (up to 8 weeks) of an active duodenal ulcer; Carafate Tablets are also used for longer-term therapy at a reduced dosage after a duodenal ulcer has healed.

Carafate helps ulcers heal by forming a protective coating over them.

Some doctors also prescribe Carafate for ulcers in the mouth and esophagus that develop during cancer therapy, for digestive tract irritation caused by drugs, for long-term treatment of stomach ulcers, and to relieve pain following tonsil removal.

Most important fact about this drug
A duodenal ulcer is a recurring illness. While Carafate can cure an acute ulcer, it cannot prevent other ulcers from developing or lessen their severity.

How should you take this medication?
Carafate works best when taken on an empty stomach. If you take an antacid to relieve pain, avoid doing it within one half-hour before or after you take Carafate. Always take Carafate exactly as prescribed.

- *If you miss a dose...*
  Take it as soon as you remember. If it is almost time for your next dose, skip the one you missed and go back to your regular schedule. Never take 2 doses at the same time.

- *Storage instructions...*
  Store at room temperature. Protect the suspension from freezing.

What side effects may occur?
Side effects cannot be anticipated. If any develop or change in intensity, inform your doctor as soon as possible. Only your doctor can determine if it is safe for you to continue taking Carafate.

■ *More common side effects may include:*
Constipation

■ *Less common or rare side effects may include:*
Back pain, diarrhea, dizziness, dry mouth, gas, headache, indigestion, insomnia, itching, nausea, possible allergic reactions, including hives and breathing difficulty, rash, sleepiness, stomach upset, vertigo, vomiting

Why should this drug not be prescribed?
There are no restrictions on the use of this drug.

Special warnings about this medication
If you have kidney failure or are on dialysis, the doctor will be cautious about prescribing this drug. Use of Carafate while taking aluminum-containing antacids may increase the possibility of aluminum poisoning in those with kidney failure.

**Possible food and drug interactions
when taking this medication**
If Carafate is taken with certain other drugs, the effects of either could be increased, decreased, or altered. It is especially important to check with your doctor before combining Carafate with the following:

Antacids such as Mylanta and Maalox
Blood-thinning drugs such as Coumadin
Cimetidine (Tagamet)
Digoxin (Lanoxin)
Drugs for controlling spasms, such as Bentyl
Ketoconazole (Nizoral)
Phenytoin (Dilantin)
Quinidine (Quinidex)
Quinolone antibiotics such as Cipro and Floxin
Ranitidine (Zantac)
Tetracycline (Achromycin V)
Theophylline (Theo-Dur)

**Special information
if you are pregnant or breastfeeding**
The effects of Carafate during pregnancy have not been adequately studied. If you are pregnant or plan to become pregnant, inform your doctor immediately. Carafate may appear in breast milk and could affect a nursing infant. If this medication is essential to your health, your doctor may advise

you to discontinue breastfeeding until your treatment with this medication is finished.

Recommended dosage

ADULTS

Active Duodenal Ulcer:
The usual dose is 1 gram (1 tablet or 2 teaspoonfuls of suspension) 4 times a day on an empty stomach. Although your ulcer may heal during the first 2 weeks of therapy, Carafate should be continued for 4 to 8 weeks.

Maintenance Therapy:
The usual dose is 1 gram (1 tablet) 2 times a day.

CHILDREN

The safety and effectiveness of Carafate in children have not been established.

Overdosage

Although the risk of overdose with Carafate is low and no specific symptoms of overdose have been reported, any medication taken in excess can have serious consequences. If you suspect an overdose, seek medical attention immediately.

Generic name:

CARBAMAZEPINE

See Tegretol, page 1076.

Generic name:

CARBIDOPA WITH LEVODOPA

See Sinemet CR, page 1025.

Generic name:

CARBINOXAMINE WITH PSEUDOEPHEDRINE

See Rondec, page 981.

Brand name:

CARDENE

Pronounced: CAR-deen
Generic name: Nicardipine hydrochloride

Why is this drug prescribed?

Cardene, a type of medication called a calcium channel blocker, is prescribed for the treatment of chronic stable angina (chest pain usually caused by lack of oxygen to the heart resulting from clogged arteries, brought on by exertion) and for high blood pressure. When used to treat angina, Cardene is effective alone or in combination with beta-blocking medications such as Tenormin or Inderal. If it is used to treat high blood pressure, Cardene is effective alone or in combination with other high blood pressure medications. Calcium channel blockers ease the workload of the heart by slowing down its muscle contractions and the passage of nerve impulses through it. This improves blood flow through the heart and throughout the body, reducing blood pressure.

Cardene SR, a long-acting form of the drug, is prescribed only for high blood pressure.

Some doctors also prescribe Cardene to prevent migraine headache and to treat congestive heart failure. In combination with other drugs, such as Amicar, Cardene is also prescribed to manage neurological problems following certain kinds of stroke.

Most important fact about this drug

If you have high blood pressure, you must take Cardene regularly for it to be effective. Since blood pressure declines gradually, it may be several weeks before you get the full benefit of Cardene, and you must continue taking it even if you are feeling well. Cardene does not cure high blood pressure; it merely keeps it under control.

How should you take this medication?

Take this medication exactly as prescribed, even if your symptoms have disappeared.

If you are taking Cardene SR, swallow the capsule whole; do not chew, crush, or divide it.

Try not to miss any doses. If Cardene is not taken regularly, your condition may worsen.

■ *If you miss a dose...*
Take it as soon as you remember. If it is almost time for the next dose, skip the one you missed and go back to your regular schedule. Do not take 2 doses at the same time.

■ *Storage instructions...*
Store at room temperature, away from light and moisture.

What side effects may occur?
Side effects cannot be anticipated. If any develop or change in intensity, inform your doctor as soon as possible. Only your doctor can determine if it is safe for you to continue taking Cardene.

■ *More common side effects may include:*
Dizziness
Flushing
Headache
Increased chest (angina) pain
Indigestion
Nausea
Pounding or rapid heartbeat
Sleepiness
Swelling of feet
Weakness

■ *Less common side effects may include:*
Abnormal dreaming, constipation, difficulty sleeping, drowsiness, dry mouth, excessive nighttime urination, fainting, fluid retention, muscle pain, nervousness, rash, shortness of breath, tingling or pins and needles, tremors, vomiting, vague feeling of bodily discomfort

■ *Rare side effects may include:*
Allergic reactions, anxiety, blurred vision, confusion, dizziness when standing, depression, hot flashes, increased movements, infection, inflammation of the nose, inflammation of the sinuses, impotence, joint pain, low blood pressure, more frequent urination, ringing in ears, sore throat, unusual chest pain, vertigo, vision changes

Why should this drug not be prescribed?
If you have advanced aortic stenosis (a narrowing of the aortic valve that causes obstruction of blood flow from the heart to the body), you should not take this medication.

If you are sensitive to or have ever had an allergic reaction to Cardene, you should not take this medication. Make sure your doctor is aware of any drug reactions you may have experienced.

Special warnings about this medication

Cardene can reduce or eliminate chest (angina) pain caused by exertion or exercise. Be sure to discuss with your doctor how much exercise or exertion is safe for you.

If you experience increased chest pain when you start taking Cardene or when your dosage is increased, contact your doctor immediately.

Your doctor will monitor your progress especially carefully if you have congestive heart failure, particularly if you are also taking a beta-blocking medication such as Tenormin or Inderal.

Cardene can cause your blood pressure to become too low, making you feel light-headed or faint. Your doctor should check your blood pressure when you start taking Cardene and continue to monitor it while your dosage is being adjusted.

If you have liver disease or decreased liver function, use this drug with caution.

Possible food and drug interactions
when taking this medication

If Cardene is taken with certain other drugs, the effects of either could be increased, decreased, or altered. It is especially important to check with your doctor before combining Cardene with the following:

Amiodarone (Cordarone)
Cimetidine (Tagamet)
Cyclosporine (Sandimmune)
Digoxin (Lanoxin)
Phenytoin (Dilantin)
Propranolol (Inderal)

Special information
if you are pregnant or breastfeeding

The effects of Cardene during pregnancy have not been adequately studied. If you are pregnant or plan to become pregnant, inform your doctor immediately. Cardene may appear in breast milk and could affect a nursing infant. If this medication is essential to your health, your doctor may advise you to discontinue breastfeeding until your treatment with Cardene is finished.

Recommended dosage

ADULTS

Angina

Your doctor will adjust the dosage according to your needs, usually beginning with 20 milligrams 3 times a day. The usual regular dose is 20 to 40 milligrams 3 times a day. Your physician may monitor your condition for at least 3 days before adjusting your dose.

High Blood Pressure

Your doctor will adjust the dosage to suit your needs. The starting dose of Cardene is usually 20 milligrams 3 times a day. The regular dose ranges from 20 to 40 milligrams 3 times a day.

The starting dose of Cardene SR is usually 30 milligrams 2 times a day. The regular dose ranges from 30 to 60 milligrams 2 times a day.

Your doctor may monitor your response to this medication for a few hours after the first dose, and will check your condition for at least 3 days before adjusting your dose.

CHILDREN

The safety and effectiveness of this drug in children under age 18 have not been established.

ELDERLY

The elderly should use this drug with caution.

Overdosage

■ *The symptoms of overdose may include:*
Confusion
Drowsiness
Severe low blood pressure
Slow heartbeat
Slurred speech

If you suspect a Cardene overdose, seek medical attention immediately.

Brand name:

CARDIZEM

Pronounced: CAR-di-zem
Generic name: Diltiazem hydrochloride

Why is this drug prescribed?

Cardizem and Cardizem CD (a controlled release form of diltiazem) are used in the treatment of angina pectoris (chest pain usually caused by lack of oxygen to the heart due to clogged arteries) and chronic stable angina (caused by exertion). Cardizem CD is also used to treat high blood pressure. Another controlled release form, Cardizem SR, is used only in the treatment of high blood pressure. Cardizem, a calcium channel blocker, dilates blood vessels and slows the heart to reduce blood pressure and the pain of angina.

Doctors sometimes prescribe Cardizem for loss of circulation in the fingers and toes (Raynaud's Syndrome), for involuntary movements (tardive dyskinesia), and to prevent heart attack.

Most important fact about this drug

If you are taking Cardizem for high blood pressure, remember that it does not cure the problem; it merely controls it. You may need to take a blood pressure medication for the rest of your life.

If you are taking Cardizem for angina, do not stop suddenly. This can lead to an increase in your attacks.

How should you take this medication?

Cardizem should be taken before meals and at bedtime. Cardizem CD and Cardizem SR should be swallowed whole; do not chew, crush, or divide.

Take this medication exactly as prescribed by your doctor, even if your symptoms have disappeared.

- *If you miss a dose...*
  If you forget to take a dose, take it as soon as you remember. If it's almost time for your next dose, skip the missed dose and go back to your regular schedule. Never take 2 doses at the same time.

- *Storage instructions...*
  Cardizem should be stored at room temperature.

What side effects may occur?

Side effects cannot be anticipated. If any develop or change in intensity, inform your doctor as soon as possible. Only your doctor can determine if it is safe for you to continue taking Cardizem.

- *More common side effects may include:*
  Abnormally slow heartbeat (more common with Cardizem SR and Cardizem CD)

Dizziness
Fluid retention
Flushing (more common with Cardizem SR and Cardizem CD)
Headache
Nausea
Rash
Weakness

- *Less common or rare side effects may include:*
  Abnormal dreams, amnesia, anemia, angina (severe chest pain), blood disorders, congestive heart failure, constipation, depression, diarrhea, difficulty sleeping, drowsiness, dry mouth, excessive urination at night, eye irritation, fainting, hair loss, hallucinations, heart attack, high blood sugar, hives, impotence, increased output of pale urine, indigestion, insomnia, irregular heartbeat, itching, joint pain, labored breathing, loss of appetite, low blood pressure, low blood sugar, muscle cramps, nasal congestion, nervousness, nosebleed, palpitations, personality change, rapid heartbeat, reddish or purplish spots on skin, ringing in ears, sexual difficulties, skin peeling, sensitivity to light, sleepiness, taste alteration, thirst, tingling or pins and needles, tremor, unusual gait, vision changes, vomiting, welts, weight increase

Why should this drug not be prescribed?
If you suffer from "sick sinus" syndrome or second- or third-degree heart block (various types of irregular heartbeat), you should not take this drug unless you have a ventricular pacemaker.

Do not take Cardizem if you have low blood pressure or an allergy to the drug.

Special warnings about this medication
If you have congestive heart failure or suffer from kidney or liver disease, use Cardizem with caution.

This medication may cause your heart rate to become too slow. You should check your pulse regularly.

Possible food and drug interactions
when taking this medication
If Cardizem is taken with certain other drugs, the effects of either could be increased, decreased, or altered. It is especially important to check with your doctor before combining Cardizem with the following:

Beta-blockers (heart and blood pressure drugs such as Tenormin and Inderal)

Carbamazepine (Tegretol)

Cimetidine (Tagamet)

Cyclosporine (Sandimmune)

Digoxin (Lanoxin)

Special information
if you are pregnant or breastfeeding

The effects of Cardizem during pregnancy have not been adequately studied. If you are pregnant or plan to become pregnant, inform your doctor immediately. Cardizem appears in breast milk and could affect a nursing infant. If this medication is essential to your health, your doctor may advise you to discontinue breastfeeding until your treatment with this medication is finished.

Recommended dosage

ADULTS

Dosage levels must be determined by each patient's needs. However, the average daily dosage is between 180 milligrams and 360 milligrams, divided into 3 or 4 smaller doses.

The recommended starting dosage for Cardizem SR is 60 to 120 milligrams 2 times a day, to be increased to 240 to 360 milligrams a day. Cardizem CD is a once-a-day form of this drug. For hypertension, starting doses of Cardizem CD range from 180 to 240 milligrams; for angina, 120 to 180 milligrams.

CHILDREN

Safety and effectiveness in children have not been established.

Overdosage

Any medication taken in excess can cause overdose. If you suspect an overdose of Cardizem, seek medical attention immediately.

■ *The symptoms of Cardizem overdose may include:*
Fainting, dizziness, and irregular pulse
Heart failure
Low blood pressure
Very slow heartbeat

Brand name:

CARDURA

Pronounced: car-DUHR-uh
Generic name: Doxazosin mesylate

Why is this drug prescribed?
Cardura is used in the treatment of high blood pressure. It is effective when used alone or in combination with diuretics or beta-blocking medications.

Doctors also prescribe Cardura to treat symptoms of benign prostatic hyperplasia (BPH), an abnormal enlargement of the prostate gland, and, along with other drugs such as digitalis and diuretics, for treatment of congestive heart failure.

Most important fact about this drug
If you have high blood pressure, you must take Cardura regularly for it to be effective. Since blood pressure declines gradually, it may be several weeks before you get the full benefit of Cardura; and you must continue taking it even if you are feeling well. Cardura does not cure high blood pressure; it merely keeps it under control.

How should you take this medication?
This medication can be taken with or without food.

Cardura should be taken exactly as prescribed, even if your symptoms have disappeared. Try not to miss any doses. If this medication is not taken regularly, your condition may worsen.

- *If you miss a dose...*
  Take it as soon as you remember. If it is almost time for your next dose, skip the one you missed and go back to your regular schedule. Never take 2 doses at the same time.

- *Storage instructions...*
  Store at room temperature.

What side effects may occur?
Side effects cannot be anticipated. If any develop or change in intensity, inform your doctor as soon as possible. Only your doctor can determine if it is safe for you to continue taking Cardura.

■ *More common side effects may include:*
Dizziness
Drowsiness
Fatigue
Headache

■ *Less common side effects may include:*
Arthritis, constipation, depression, difficulty sleeping, eye pain, flushing, gas, inability to hold urine, indigestion, inflammation of conjunctiva (pinkeye), itching, joint pain, lack of muscle coordination, low blood pressure, motion disorders, muscle cramps, muscle pain, muscle weakness, nausea, nervousness, nosebleeds, rash, ringing in ears, shortness of breath, tingling or pins and needles, weakness

■ *Rare side effects may include:*
Abnormal thinking, abnormal vision, agitation, altered sense of smell, amnesia, back pain, breast pain, changeable emotions, changes in taste, chest pain, confusion, coughing, decreased sense of touch, diarrhea, dizziness when standing up, dry mouth, dry skin, earache, excessive urination, fainting, fecal incontinence, fever, fluid retention, flu-like symptoms, gout, hair loss, heart attack, hot flushes, inability to concentrate, inability to tolerate light, increased appetite, increased sweating, increased thirst, infection, inflammation of the nose, loss of appetite, loss of sense of personal identity, migraine headache, morbid dreams, nausea, nervousness, pain, pallor, rapid pounding heartbeat, sexual problems, sinus inflammation, slight or partial paralysis, sore throat, tremors, twitching, vertigo, weight gain, weight loss, wheezing

Why should this drug not be prescribed?
Cardura should not be taken if you are sensitive to or have ever had an allergic reaction to Cardura or such drugs as Minipress or Hytrin. Make sure your doctor is aware of any drug reactions you may have experienced.

Special warnings about this medication
Cardura can cause low blood pressure, especially when you first start taking the medication and when dosage is increased. This can cause you to become faint, dizzy, or light-headed, particularly when first standing up. You should avoid driving or any hazardous tasks where injury could occur for 24 hours after taking the first dose, after your dose has been increased, or if Cardura has been stopped and then restarted.

If you have liver disease or are taking other medications that alter liver function, your doctor will monitor you closely when you take Cardura.

Cardura may lower blood counts. Your doctor will most likely monitor your blood counts while you are taking this medication.

This medication may cause you to become drowsy or sleepy. For this reason, too, driving or operating dangerous machinery or participating in any hazardous activity that requires full mental alertness is not recommended.

Possible food and drug interactions
when taking this medication
No significant interactions have been reported.

Special information
if you are pregnant or breastfeeding
The effects of Cardura during pregnancy have not been adequately studied. If you are pregnant or plan to become pregnant, inform your doctor immediately. Cardura may appear in breast milk and could affect a nursing infant. If this medication is essential to your health, your doctor may advise you to discontinue breastfeeding until your treatment with this medication is finished.

Recommended dosage

ADULTS

Your doctor will adjust the dosage to fit your needs.

The usual starting dose is 1 milligram taken once a day. To minimize the potential for dizziness or fainting associated with Cardura, which may occur between 2 and 6 hours after a dose, your doctor will monitor your blood pressure during this period and afterwards.

After the effects of the starting dose are measured, your doctor may increase the dose to 2 milligrams per day and then, if necessary, to 4 milligrams, 8 milligrams, or 16 milligrams. As the dose increases, the potential for side effects such as dizziness, vertigo, light-headedness, and fainting also increases.

CHILDREN

The safety and effectiveness of this drug in children have not been established.

ELDERLY

This drug is prescribed cautiously for the elderly.

Overdosage

Any medication taken in excess can have serious consequences. Although no specific information is available, low blood pressure is the most likely symptom of an overdose of Cardura.

If you suspect an overdose, seek medical attention immediately.

Generic name:

CARISOPRODOL

See Soma, page 1035.

Brand name:

CATAFLAM

See Voltaren, page 1200.

Brand name:

CATAPRES

Pronounced: KAT-uh-press
Generic name: Clonidine hydrochloride

Why is this drug prescribed?

Catapres is prescribed for high blood pressure. It is effective when used alone or with other high blood pressure medications.

Doctors also prescribe Catapres for alcohol, nicotine, or benzodiazepine (tranquilizer) withdrawal; migraine headaches; smoking cessation programs; Tourette's syndrome (tics and uncontrollable utterances); narcotic/methadone detoxification; premenstrual tension; and diabetic diarrhea.

Most important fact about this drug

If you have high blood pressure, you must take Catapres regularly for it to be effective. Since blood pressure declines gradually, it may be several weeks before you get the full benefit of Catapres; and you must continue taking it even if you are feeling well. Catapres does not cure high blood pressure; it merely keeps it under control.

How should you take this medication?

Take this medication exactly as prescribed, even if you are feeling well.

Try not to miss any doses. If Catapres is not taken regularly, your condition may worsen.

■ *If you miss a dose...*
Take is as soon as you remember, then go back to your regular schedule. If you forget to take the medication 2 or more times in a row, or if you forget to change the transdermal patch for 3 or more days, contact your doctor.

■ *Storage instructions...*
Store at room temperature in a tightly closed container away from light.

What side effects may occur?
Side effects cannot be anticipated. If any develop or change in intensity, inform your doctor as soon as possible. Only your doctor can determine if it is safe for you to continue taking Catapres.

■ *More common side effects may include:*
Constipation
Dizziness
Drowsiness
Dry mouth
Sedation (calm)
Skin reactions (Catapres-TTS)

■ *Less common side effects may include:*
Agitation, breast development in males, changes in heartbeat, changes in taste, decreased sexual activity, difficulty sleeping, difficulty urinating, dizziness on standing up, excessive nighttime urination, fatigue, fluid retention, hair loss, headache, hives, impotence, itching, joint pain, leg cramps, loss of appetite, loss of sexual drive, mental depression, muscle pain, nausea, nervousness, rash, retention of urine, sluggishness, vague bodily discomfort, vomiting, weakness, weight gain

■ *Rare side effects may include:*
Anxiety, behavior changes, blurred vision, burning eyes, congestive heart failure, delirium, dry eyes, dry nasal passages, fever, greater sensitivity to alcohol, hallucinations, hepatitis, pallor, restlessness, vivid dreams or nightmares

Why should this drug not be prescribed?
Do not take this medication if you have ever had an allergic reaction to Catapres or to any of the components of the adhesive layer of the transdermal patch.

Special warnings about this medication

Catapres should not be stopped suddenly. Headache, nervousness, agitation, and rapid rise in blood pressure can occur. Severe reactions such as disruption of brain functions and death have also been reported. Your doctor should therefore gradually reduce your dosage over several days to avoid withdrawal symptoms.

If your doctor has switched you to oral Catapres (tablet) because you had an allergic reaction, such as a rash or hives, to the transdermal skin patch, be aware that you may have a similar reaction to the Catapres tablet.

If you have severe heart or kidney disease, are recovering from a heart attack, or have a disease of the blood vessels of the brain, your doctor will prescribe Catapres with caution.

If you are taking Catapres and a beta blocker such as Inderal or Tenormin, and your doctor wants to stop your medication, the beta blocker should be stopped several days before the gradual withdrawal of Catapres.

Catapres may cause you to become drowsy or less alert; therefore, you should avoid driving, operating dangerous machinery, or participating in any hazardous activity that requires full mental alertness.

Possible food and drug interactions
when taking this medication

Catapres may increase the effects of alcohol. Do not drink alcohol while taking this medication.

If Catapres is taken with certain other drugs, the effects of either could be increased, decreased, or altered. It is especially important to check with your doctor before combining Catapres with the following:

Barbiturates such as Nembutal and Seconal
Sedatives such as Valium, Xanax, and Halcion
Tricyclic antidepressants such as Elavil and Tofranil

Special information
if you are pregnant or breastfeeding

The effects of Catapres during pregnancy have not been adequately studied. If you are pregnant or plan to become pregnant, inform your doctor immediately. Catapres appears in breast milk and could affect a nursing infant. If this medication is essential to your health, your doctor may advise you to discontinue breastfeeding until your treatment with this medication is finished.

Recommended dosage

ADULTS

The dosage will be adjusted to your individual needs.

The usual starting dose is 0.1 milligram, twice a day (usually in the morning and at bedtime).

The regular dose of Catapres is determined by increasing the starting dose by 0.1 milligram per day until the desired response is achieved. A larger portion of the increased dose can be taken at bedtime to reduce potential side effects of drowsiness and dry mouth that may appear when you begin taking this drug.

The most common effective dosages range from 0.2 milligram to 0.6 milligram per day divided into smaller doses. The maximum effective dose is 2.4 milligrams per day; however, this dose is not usually prescribed.

Transdermal Patch

The patch comes in different strengths, and your doctor will determine which is best for you based on your blood pressure response.

People who are using another high blood pressure medication should not stop taking it abruptly when they begin using the patch, because the medication in the patch may take a few days to work. The other medication should be discontinued slowly as the patch begins to work.

The Catapres-TTS patch should be put on a hairless, clean area of the upper arm or body. Normally, a new one is applied every 7 days to a new area of the skin. If the patch becomes loose, use some adhesive tape or an adhesive bandage to keep it in place.

CHILDREN

Safety and effectiveness of Catapres in children have not been established. Safety of Catapres-TTS has not been established in children under 12.

ELDERLY

Dosages are generally as above; however, the initial dosage for an older person may be lower than the regular starting dose.

Overdosage

- *Symptoms of Catapres overdose may include:*
  Changes in heart function, constriction of pupils of the eye, high blood pressure, irritability, low blood pressure, reduced rate of breathing,

seizures, sleepiness, slow heartbeat, slowed reflexes, sluggishness, temporary failure to breathe, vomiting, weakness

If you suspect symptoms of a Catapres overdose, seek medical attention immediately.

Brand name:

CECLOR

Pronounced: SEE-klor
Generic name: Cefaclor

Why is this drug prescribed?

Ceclor, a cephalosporin antibiotic, is used in the treatment of ear, nose, throat, respiratory tract, urinary tract, and skin infections caused by specific bacteria, including staph, strep, and *E. coli*. Uses include treatment of sore or strep throat, pneumonia, and tonsillitis.

Most important fact about this drug

If you are allergic to either penicillin or cephalosporin antibiotics in any form, consult your doctor *before taking* Ceclor. There is a possibility that you are allergic to both types of medication; and if a reaction occurs, it could be extremely severe. If you take the drug and feel signs of a reaction, seek medical attention immediately.

How should you take this medication?

Take this medication exactly as prescribed. It is important that you finish taking all of this medication to obtain the maximum benefit.

This medication works fastest when taken on an empty stomach. However, your doctor may ask you to take this drug with food to avoid stomach upset.

Ceclor suspension should be shaken well before using.

- *If you miss a dose...*
  Take it as soon as you remember. If it is almost time for your next dose, skip the one you missed and go back to your regular schedule. Never take 2 doses at the same time.

- *Storage instructions...*
  Keep Ceclor capsules in the container they came in, tightly closed. Store at room temperature.

  Refrigerate Ceclor suspension. Discard any unused portion after 14 days.

What side effects may occur?
Side effects cannot be anticipated. If any develop or change in intensity, inform your doctor as soon as possible. Only your doctor can determine if it is safe for you to continue taking Ceclor.

- *More common side effects may include:*
  Diarrhea
  Hives
  Itching

- *Less common or rare side effects may include:*
  Blood disorders (an increase in certain types of white blood cells), liver disorders, nausea, skin rashes accompanied by joint pain, vaginal inflammation, vomiting

Other problems have been reported in patients taking Ceclor, although it is not known whether the drug was the cause. Check with your doctor if you suspect a side effect.

Why should this drug not be prescribed?
If you are sensitive to or have ever had an allergic reaction to Ceclor or any other cephalosporin antibiotic, you should not take this medication. Make sure your doctor is aware of any drug reactions you have experienced.

Unless you are directed to do so by your doctor, do not take this medication if you have a history of gastrointestinal problems, particularly bowel inflammation (colitis). You may be at increased risk for side effects.

Special warnings about this medication
Ceclor may cause a false positive result with some urine sugar tests for diabetics. Your doctor can advise you of any adjustments you may need to make in your medication or diet.

Ceclor occasionally causes diarrhea. Some diarrhea medications can make this diarrhea worse. Check with your doctor before taking any diarrhea remedy.

Oral contraceptives may not work properly while you are taking Ceclor. For greater certainty, use other measures while taking Ceclor.

Possible food and drug interactions
when taking this medication
If Ceclor is taken with certain other drugs, the effects of either could be increased, decreased, or altered. It is especially important to check with your doctor before combining Ceclor with the following:

Certain antibiotics such as Amikin
Certain potent diuretics such as Edecrin and Lasix
Oral contraceptives
Probenecid (Benemid)

Special information
if you are pregnant or breastfeeding

The effects of Ceclor during pregnancy have not been adequately studied. If you are pregnant or plan to become pregnant, this drug should be used only when prescribed by your doctor. Ceclor appears in breast milk and could affect a nursing infant. If this medication is essential to your health, your doctor may advise you to stop nursing your baby until your treatment with Ceclor is finished.

Recommended dosage

ADULTS

The usual adult dose is 250 milligrams every 8 hours. For more severe infections (such as pneumonia), your doctor may increase the dosage.

CHILDREN

The usual daily dosage is 20 milligrams per 2.2 pounds of body weight per day divided into smaller doses and taken every 8 hours. In more serious infections, such as middle ear infection, the usual dose is 40 milligrams per 2.2 pounds of body weight per day divided into smaller doses. The total daily dose should not exceed 1 gram.

Overdosage

■ *Symptoms of Ceclor overdose may include:*
Diarrhea
Nausea
Stomach upset
Vomiting

If other symptoms are present, they may be related to an allergic reaction or other underlying disease. In any case, you should contact your doctor or an emergency room immediately.

Generic name:

CEFACLOR

See Ceclor, page 180.

Generic name:

CEFADROXIL

See Duricef, page 371.

Generic name:

CEFIXIME

See Suprax, page 1050.

Generic name:

CEFPROZIL

See Cefzil, page 186.

Brand name:

CEFTIN

Pronounced: SEF-tin
Generic name: Cefuroxime axetil

Why is this drug prescribed?
Ceftin, a cephalosporin antibiotic, is prescribed for mild to moderately severe bacterial infections of the throat, lungs, ears, skin, and urinary tract, and for gonorrhea.

Most important fact about this drug
If you are allergic to either penicillin or cephalosporin antibiotics such as Ceclor, Cefzil, or Keflex, consult your doctor *before taking* Ceftin. There is a possibility that you are allergic to both types of medication; if a reaction occurs, it could be extremely severe. If you take the drug and develop shortness of breath, a pounding heartbeat, a skin rash, or hives, seek medical attention immediately.

How should you take this medication?
Ceftin tablets can be taken on a full or empty stomach. However, this drug enters the bloodstream and works faster when taken after meals. Ceftin oral suspension must be taken with food.

Take this medication exactly as prescribed: It is important that you finish taking all of this medication to obtain the maximum benefit.

The crushed tablet has a strong, persistent, bitter taste. Children who cannot swallow the tablet whole should take the oral suspension. Shake the oral suspension well before each use.

■ *If you miss a dose...*
Take it as soon as you remember. If it is almost time for your next dose, skip the one you missed and go back to the regular schedule. Do not take 2 doses at once.

■ *Storage instructions...*
Store tablets at room temperature in a tightly closed container. Protect from moisture. The oral suspension may be stored either in the refrigerator or at room temperature. Discard any unused suspension after 10 days.

What side effects may occur?
Side effects cannot be anticipated. If any develop or change in intensity, inform your doctor as soon as possible. Only your doctor can determine if it is safe for you to continue taking Ceftin.

■ *More common side effects may include:*
Diaper rash in infants
Diarrhea
Nausea
Vomiting

■ *Rare side effects of the tablets include:*
Abdominal pain or cramps, chest pain, chills, gas, headache, hives, indigestion, itch, loss of appetite, mouth ulcers, rash, shortness of breath, sleepiness, swollen tongue, thirst, urinary problems, vaginitis

■ *Rare side effects of the oral suspension include:*
Abdominal pain, cough, drooling, fever, gas, gastrointestinal infection, hyperactivity, inflamed sinuses, irritability, joint pain and swelling, rash, upper respiratory infection, urinary infection, vaginal irritation, virus infection, yeast infection

Why should this drug not be prescribed?
Ceftin should not be prescribed if you have a known allergy to penicillin or cephalosporin antibiotics.

Special warnings about this medication

Inflammation of the bowel (colitis) has been reported with the use of Ceftin; therefore, if you develop diarrhea while taking this medication, notify your doctor.

Continued or prolonged use of Ceftin may result in an overgrowth of bacteria that do not respond to this medication and can cause a second infection. You should take this drug only when it is prescribed by your doctor, even if you have symptoms like those of a previous infection. Tell your doctor if you have any kidney problems. Your dosage may need to be lowered.

Possible food and drug interactions
when taking this medication

It is important to consult your doctor before taking this drug with probenecid, a gout medication.

If diarrhea occurs while taking Ceftin, consult your doctor before taking an antidiarrhea medication. Certain drugs, such as Lomotil, may cause your diarrhea to become worse.

Be cautious if you are taking potent water pills (diuretics) while on Ceftin. The combination could affect your kidneys.

Special information
if you are pregnant or breastfeeding

The effects of Ceftin during pregnancy have not been adequately studied. If you are pregnant or plan to become pregnant, inform your doctor immediately. Ceftin appears in breast milk and could affect a nursing infant. If this medication is essential to your health, your doctor may advise you to discontinue breastfeeding until your treatment with this medication is finished.

Recommended dosage

ADULTS

The usual dose for adults and children over 12 years of age is 250 milligrams, 2 times a day for 10 days. For more severe infections the dose may be increased to 500 milligrams, 2 times a day.

The usual dose for urinary tract infection is 125 milligrams, 2 times a day for 7 to 10 days. This dose may be increased to 250 milligrams 2 times a day for severe infection.

The usual dosage for gonorrhea is a single dose of 1 gram.

CHILDREN

Ceftin oral suspension may be given to children ranging in age from 3 months to 12 years.

Your doctor will determine the dosage based on your child's weight and the type of infection being treated. Ceftin oral suspension is given twice a day for 10 days. The usual total daily amount is 500 to 1000 milligrams.

Overdosage

Any medication taken in excess can have serious consequences. Overdosage with cephalosporin antibiotics can cause brain irritation, leading to convulsions. If you suspect an overdose, seek medical attention immediately.

Generic name:

CEFUROXIME

See Ceftin, page 183.

Brand name:

CEFZIL

Pronounced: SEFF-zil
Generic name: Cefprozil

Why is this drug prescribed?

Cefzil, a cephalosporin antibiotic, is prescribed for mild to moderately severe bacterial infections of the throat, ear, respiratory tract, and skin. Among these infections are strep throat, tonsillitis, bronchitis, and pneumonia.

Most important fact about this drug

If you are allergic to either penicillin or cephalosporin antibiotics in any form, consult your doctor *before taking* Cefzil. There is a possibility that you are allergic to both types of medication; and if a reaction occurs, it could be extremely severe. If you take the drug and feel signs of a reaction, seek medical attention immediately.

How should you use this medication?

Take this medication exactly as prescribed. It is important that you finish all of the medication to obtain the maximum benefit.

Cefzil works fastest when taken on an empty stomach, but can be taken with food to avoid stomach upset.

Cefzil oral suspension should be shaken well before using.

- *If you miss a dose...*
  Take it as soon as you remember. If it is almost time for your next dose, skip the one you missed and go back to your regular schedule. Never take 2 doses at the same time.

- *Storage instructions...*
  Store Cefzil tablets at room temperature. Keep the oral suspension in the refrigerator. Discard any unused portion after 14 days.

What side effects may occur?
Side effects cannot be anticipated. If any develop or change in intensity, notify your doctor as soon as possible. Only your doctor can determine whether it is safe for you to continue taking Cefzil.

The most common side effect is nausea.

- *Less common or rare side effects may include:*
  Abdominal pain, confusion, diaper rash, diarrhea, difficulty sleeping, dizziness, genital itching, headache, hives, hyperactivity, nervousness, rash, sleepiness, superinfection (additional infection), vaginal inflammation, vomiting, yellow eyes and skin

Although not reported for Cefzil, similar antibiotics have been known occasionally to have severe side effects such as anaphylaxis (a severe allergic reaction), skin rash with blisters, Stevens-Johnson syndrome (a rare skin condition characterized by severe blisters and bleeding in the lips, eyes, mouth, nose and genitals), and "serum-sickness" (itchy rash, fever, and pain in the joints).

Why should this drug not be prescribed?
If you are sensitive to or have ever had an allergic reaction to Cefzil or other cephalosporin antibiotics, do not take this medication. Make sure your doctor is aware of any drug reactions you have experienced.

Special warnings about this medication
Cefzil occasionally causes colitis (inflammation of the bowel), leading to diarrhea. Some diarrhea medications can make this diarrhea worse. Check with your doctor before taking any diarrhea remedy.

Oral contraceptives may not work properly while you are taking Cefzil. For greater certainty, use other measures while taking Cefzil.

Your doctor will check your kidney function before and during your treatment with this medication.

Use Cefzil with caution if you are taking a strong diuretic, or if you have ever had stomach and intestinal disease, particularly colitis.

If new infections (called superinfections) occur, talk to your doctor. You may need to be treated with a different antibiotic.

Cefzil may alter the results of some urine sugar tests for diabetics. Your doctor can advise you of any adjustments you may need to make in your medication or diet.

Possible food and drug interactions
when taking this medication
When Cefzil is taken with certain other drugs, the effects of either could be increased, decreased, or altered. It is especially important to check with your doctor before combining Cefzil with the following:

    Certain other antibiotics such as Amikin
    Certain potent diuretics such as Edecrin and Lasix
    Oral contraceptives
    Probenecid (Benemid)
    Propantheline (Pro-Banthine)

Special information
if you are pregnant or breastfeeding
The effects of Cefzil during pregnancy have not been adequately studied. If you are pregnant or plan to become pregnant, inform your doctor immediately. Cefzil may appear in breast milk and could affect a nursing infant. If this medication is essential to your health, your doctor may advise you to stop breastfeeding until your treatment with this medication is finished.

Recommended dosage

ADULTS

Throat and Respiratory Tract Infections
The usual dose is 500 milligrams, taken once or twice a day for 10 days.

Skin Infections
The dosage is usually either 250 milligrams taken 2 times a day, or 500 milligrams taken once or twice a day for 10 days.

CHILDREN 2 TO 12 YEARS OF AGE

Throat Infections and Tonsillitis
The usual dose is 7.5 milligrams for each 2.2 pounds of body weight, taken 2 times a day for 10 days.

INFANTS AND CHILDREN 6 MONTHS TO 12 YEARS OF AGE

Ear Infections
The usual dose is 15 milligrams for each 2.2 pounds of body weight, taken 2 times a day for 10 days.

INFANTS UNDER 6 MONTH OF AGE

The safety and effectiveness of Cefzil in children below the age of 6 months have not been established.

Overdosage
Although no specific information is available, any medication taken in excess can have serious consequences. If you suspect an overdose of Cefzil, seek medical attention immediately.

Brand name:

CENTRAX

Pronounced: SEN-tracks
Generic name: Prazepam

Why is this drug prescribed?
Centrax is used in the treatment of anxiety disorders and for short-term relief of the symptoms of anxiety. In addition, doctors sometimes prescribe it to treat alcohol and narcotic withdrawal. It belongs to a class of drugs known as benzodiazepines.

Most important fact about this drug
Tolerance and dependence can occur with the use of Centrax. You may experience withdrawal symptoms if you stop using this drug abruptly. Discontinue or change your dose only in consultation with your doctor.

How should you take this medication?
Take this medication exactly as prescribed by your doctor.

■ *If you miss a dose...*
Take it as soon as you remember. If it is almost time for your next dose, skip the one you missed and go back to your regular schedule. Never take 2 doses at the same time.

■ *Storage instructions...*
Store Centrax at room temperature, protected from moisture.

What side effects may occur?
Side effects cannot be anticipated. If any develop or change in intensity, inform your doctor as soon as possible. Only your doctor can determine if it is safe for you to continue taking Centrax.

■ *More common side effects may include:*
Dizziness
Drowsiness
Fatigue
Lack of muscular coordination
Light-headedness
Weakness

■ *Less common or rare side effects may include:*
Blurred vision, confusion, dry mouth, excessive sweating, fainting, genital and urinary tract disorders, headache, itching, joint pain, palpitations, skin rashes, slurred speech, stomach and intestinal disorders, swelling of feet, tremors, vivid dreams

Why should this drug not be prescribed?
If you are sensitive to or have ever had an allergic reaction to Centrax or similar drugs, you should not take this medication.

Unless you are directed to do so by your doctor, do not take this medication if you have the eye condition known as acute narrow-angle glaucoma.

Centrax should not be prescribed if you are being treated for other emotional disorders more serious than anxiety.

Anxiety or tension related to everyday stress usually does not require treatment with Centrax. Discuss your symptoms thoroughly with your doctor.

Special warnings about this medication
Centrax may cause you to become drowsy or less alert; therefore, driving or

operating dangerous machinery or participating in any hazardous activity that requires full mental alertness is not recommended.

If you are severely depressed or have suffered from severe depression, consult with your doctor before taking this medication.

If you take Centrax for a prolonged period of time, your doctor should perform periodic blood and liver tests.

If you have kidney or liver disease, this drug should be used with caution.

Possible food and drug interactions when taking this medication

Like alcohol, Centrax is a central nervous system depressant. Do not drink alcohol while taking this medication.

If Centrax is taken with certain other drugs, the effects of either could be increased, decreased, or altered. It is especially important to check with your doctor before combining Centrax with antidepressants and central nervous system depressants, including the following:

Barbiturates (Phenobarbital)
Cimetidine (Tagamet)
Guanabenz (Wytensin)
MAO inhibitors (antidepressant drugs such as Nardil, Marplan, and Parnate)
Major tranquilizers such as Mellaril and Thorazine
Narcotic pain medications such as Demerol and Percocet

Special information if you are pregnant or breastfeeding

Do not take Centrax if you are pregnant or planning to become pregnant. There may be an increased risk of birth defects. This drug may appear in breast milk and could affect a nursing infant. If this medication is essential to your health, your doctor may advise you to discontinue breastfeeding until your treatment with this medication is finished.

Recommended dosage

ADULTS

The usual dosage is a total of 30 milligrams per day divided into small doses. Your doctor will adjust the dose gradually to between 20 and 60 milligrams per day, depending on what you need.

Centrax can also be taken as a single dose at bedtime. The recommended starting dose is 20 milligrams. To maximize the anti-anxiety effect with a minimum of daytime drowsiness, your doctor may increase the dose up to a total of 40 milligrams.

CHILDREN

Safety and effectiveness have not been established in children under 18 years of age.

ELDERLY

In the elderly, the usual daily dose is 10 to 15 milligrams, divided into smaller doses.

Overdosage
Any medication taken in excess can have serious consequences. If you suspect an overdose, seek medical attention immediately.

Generic name:

CENTRUM

See Multivitamins, page 693.

Generic name:

CEPHALEXIN

See Keflex, page 542.

Generic name:

CHLORDIAZEPOXIDE

See Librium, page 574.

Generic name:

CHLORDIAZEPOXIDE WITH CLIDINIUM

See Librax, page 571.

Generic name:

CHLORHEXIDINE

See Peridex, page 837.

Generic name:

CHLOROTHIAZIDE

See Diuril, page 353.

Generic name:

CHLORPHENIRAMINE WITH PHENYLEPHRINE

See Rynatan, page 992.

Generic name:

CHLORPHENIRAMINE WITH PSEUDOEPHEDRINE

See Deconamine, page 289.

Generic name:

CHLORPROMAZINE

See Thorazine, page 1107.

Generic name:

CHLORPROPAMIDE

See Diabinese, page 320.

Generic name:

CHLORTHALIDONE

See Hygroton, page 496.

Generic name:

CHLORZOXAZONE

See Parafon Forte DSC, page 798.

Generic name:

CHOLESTYRAMINE

See Questran, page 928.

Generic name:

CHOLINE MAGNESIUM TRISALICYLATE

See Trilisate, page 1155.

Brand name:

CHRONULAC SYRUP

Pronounced: KRON-yoo-lak
Generic name: Lactulose
Other brand name: Duphalac

Why is this drug prescribed?
Chronulac treats constipation. In people who are chronically constipated, Chronulac increases the number and frequency of bowel movements.

Most important fact about this drug
It may take 24 to 48 hours to produce a normal bowel movement.

How should you take this medication?
Take this medication exactly as prescribed. If you find the taste of Chronulac unpleasant, it can be taken with water, fruit juice, or milk.

■ *If you miss a dose...*
   Take the forgotten dose as soon as you remember; but do not try to "catch up" by taking a double dose.

■ *Storage instructions...*
   Store at room temperature. Avoid excessive heat or direct light. The liquid may darken in color, which is normal.

What side effects may occur?
Side effects cannot be anticipated. If any develop or change in intensity, inform your doctor as soon as possible. Only your doctor can determine if it is safe for you to continue taking Chronulac.

■ *Side effects may include:*
   Diarrhea
   Gas (temporary, at the beginning of use)
   Intestinal cramps (temporary, at the beginning of use)
   Nausea
   Potassium and fluid loss
   Vomiting

Why should this drug not be prescribed?
Chronulac contains galactose, a simple sugar. If you are on a low-galactose diet, do not take this medication.

Special warnings about this medication
Because of its sugar content, this medication should be used with caution if you have diabetes.

If unusual diarrhea occurs, contact your doctor.

Possible food and drug interactions when taking this medication
If Chronulac is taken with certain other drugs, the effects of either could be increased, decreased, or altered. It is especially important to check with your doctor before combining Chronulac with non-absorbable antacids such as Maalox and Mylanta.

Special information if you are pregnant or breastfeeding
The effects of Chronulac during pregnancy have not been adequately studied. If you are pregnant or plan to become pregnant, inform your doctor immediately. Chronulac may appear in breast milk and could affect a nursing infant. If this medication is essential to your health, your doctor may advise you to stop breastfeeding until your treatment is finished.

Recommended dosage
The usual dose is 1 to 2 tablespoonfuls (15 to 30 milliliters) daily. Your doctor may increase the dose to 60 milliliters a day, if necessary.

Overdosage
Any medication taken in excess can have serious consequences. If you suspect an overdose, seek medical treatment immediately.

- *Symptoms of Chronulac overdose may include:*
  Abdominal cramps
  Diarrhea

Brand name:

CIBALITH-S

See Lithonate, page 581.

Generic name:

CICLOPIROX

See Loprox, page 599.

Generic name:

CIMETIDINE

See Tagamet, page 1062.

Brand name:

CIPRO

Pronounced: SIP-roh
Generic name: Ciprofloxacin hydrochloride

Why is this drug prescribed?
Cipro is used to treat infections of the lower respiratory tract, the skin, the bones and joints, and the urinary tract. It is also prescribed for infectious diarrhea; and some doctors also prescribe Cipro for certain serious ear infections, tuberculosis, and some of the infections common in AIDS patients.

Because Cipro is effective only for certain types of bacterial infections, before beginning treatment your doctor may perform tests to identify the specific organisms causing your infection.

Most important fact about this drug
Cipro kills a variety of bacteria, and is frequently used to treat infections in many parts of the body. However, be sure to notify your doctor immediately at the first sign of a skin rash or any other allergic reaction. Although quite rare, serious and occasionally fatal allergic reactions—some following the first dose—have been reported in patients receiving this type of antibacterial drug. Some reactions have been accompanied by collapse of the circulatory system, loss of consciousness, swelling of the face and throat, shortness of breath, tingling, itching, and hives.

How should you take this medication?
Cipro may be taken with or without meals but is best tolerated when taken 2 hours after a meal.

Drink plenty of fluids while taking this medication.

Cipro, like other antibiotics, works best when there is a constant amount in the blood and urine. To help keep the level constant, try not to miss any doses, and take them at evenly spaced intervals around the clock.

■ *If you miss a dose...*
Take it as soon as you remember. If it is almost time for your next dose, skip the one you missed and go back to your regular schedule. Never take 2 doses at the same time.

■ *Storage instructions...*
Cipro should be stored at room temperature.

What side effects may occur?
Side effects cannot be anticipated. If any develop or change in intensity, inform your doctor as soon as possible. Only your doctor can determine if it is safe for you to continue taking Cipro.

■ *More common side effects may include:*
Abdominal pain/discomfort
Diarrhea
Headache
Nausea
Rash
Restlessness
Vomiting

■ *Less common side effects may include:*
Abnormal dread or fear, achiness, bleeding in the stomach and/or intestines, blood clots in the lungs, blurred vision, change in color perception, chills, confusion, constipation, convulsions, coughing up blood, decreased vision, depression, difficulty in swallowing, dizziness, double vision, drowsiness, eye pain, fainting, fever, flushing, gas, gout flare-up, hallucinations, hearing loss, heart attack, hiccups, high blood pressure, hives, inability to fall or stay asleep, inability to urinate, indigestion, intestinal inflammation, involuntary eye movement, irregular heartbeat, irritability, itching, joint or back pain, joint stiffness, kidney failure, labored breathing, lack of muscle coordination, lack or loss of appetite, large volumes of urine, light-headedness, loss of sense of identity, loss of sense of smell, mouth sores, neck pain, nightmares, nosebleed, pounding heartbeat, ringing in the ears, seizures, sensitivity to light, severe allergic reaction, skin peeling, redness, sluggishness, speech difficulties, swelling

of the face, neck, lips, eyes, or hands, swelling of the throat, tender, red bumps on skin, tingling sensation, tremors, unpleasant taste, unusual darkening of the skin, vaginal inflammation, vague feeling of illness, weakness, yellowed eyes and skin

Why should this drug not be prescribed?
If you are sensitive to or have ever had an allergic reaction to Cipro or certain other antibiotics of this type, you should not take this medication. Make sure that your doctor is aware of any drug reactions that you have experienced.

Special warnings about this medication
Cipro may cause you to become dizzy or light-headed; therefore, you should not drive a car, operate dangerous machinery, or participate in any hazardous activity that requires full mental alertness until you know how the drug affects you.

Continued or prolonged use of this drug may result in a growth of bacteria that do not respond to this medication and can cause a secondary infection. Therefore, it is important that your doctor monitor your condition on a regular basis.

Convulsions have been reported in people receiving Cipro. If you experience a seizure or convulsion, notify your doctor immediately.

This medication may stimulate the central nervous system, which may lead to tremors, restlessness, light-headedness, confusion, and hallucinations. If these reactions occur, consult your doctor at once.

If you have a known or suspected central nervous system disorder such as epilepsy or hardening of the arteries in the brain, make sure your doctor knows about it when prescribing Cipro.

You may become more sensitive to light while taking this drug. Try to stay out of the sun as much as possible.

If you must take Cipro for an extended period of time, your doctor will probably order blood tests and tests for urine, kidney, and liver function.

Possible food and drug interactions
when taking this medication
Serious and fatal reactions have occurred when Cipro was taken in combination with theophylline (Theo-Dur). These reactions have included cardiac arrest, seizures, status epilepticus (continuous attacks of epilepsy with no periods of consciousness), and respiratory failure.

Products containing iron, multivitamins containing zinc, or antacids containing magnesium, aluminum, or calcium, when taken in combination with Cipro, may interfere with absorption of this medication.

Cipro may increase the effects of caffeine.

If Cipro is taken with certain other drugs, the effects of either also could be increased, decreased, or altered. These drugs include:

Cyclophosphamide (Cytoxan)
Cyclosporine (Sandimmune)
Metoprolol (Lopressor)
Phenytoin (Dilantin)
Probenecid (Benemid)
Sucralfate (Carafate)
Theophylline (Theo-Dur)
Warfarin (Coumadin)

Special information
if you are pregnant or breastfeeding
The effects of Cipro during pregnancy have not been adequately studied. If you are pregnant or plan to become pregnant, notify your doctor immediately. Cipro does appear in breast milk and could affect a nursing infant. If this medication is essential to your health, your doctor may advise you to discontinue breastfeeding your baby until your treatment is finished.

Recommended dosage

ADULTS

The length of treatment with Cipro depends upon the severity of infection. Generally, Cipro should be continued for at least 2 days after the signs and symptoms of infection have disappeared. The usual length of time is 7 to 14 days; however, for severe and complicated infections, treatment may be prolonged.

Bone and joint infections may require treatment for 4 to 6 weeks or longer.

Infectious diarrhea may be treated for 5 to 7 days.

Urinary Tract Infections
The usual adult dosage is 250 milligrams taken every 12 hours. Complicated infections, as determined by your doctor, may require 500 milligrams taken every 12 hours.

Lower Respiratory Tract, Skin, Bone, and Joint Infections
The usual recommended dosage is 500 milligrams taken every 12 hours.
Complicated infections, as determined by your doctor, may require a dosage
of 750 milligrams taken every 12 hours.

Infectious Diarrhea
The recommended dosage is 500 milligrams taken every 12 hours.

CHILDREN

Safety and effectiveness have not been established in children and
adolescents under 18 years of age.

Overdosage
Any medication taken in excess can have serious consequences. If you
suspect an overdose, seek medical attention immediately.

Generic name:

CIPROFLOXACIN

See Cipro, page 196.

Generic name:

CISAPRIDE

See Propulsid, page 903.

Generic name:

CLARITHROMYCIN

See Biaxin, page 130.

Brand name:

CLARITIN

Pronounced: CLAR-i-tin
Generic name: Loratadine

Why is this drug prescribed?
Claritin is an antihistamine that relieves the sneezing, runny nose, stuffiness,
itching, and tearing eyes caused by hay fever.

Most important fact about this drug

If you have liver disease, your doctor should prescribe a lower starting dose of Claritin.

How should you take this medication?

Claritin should be taken on an empty stomach. Take it exactly as prescribed by your doctor.

■ *If you miss a dose...*

Take the forgotten dose as soon as you remember. If it is almost time for your next dose, skip the one you missed. Never take 2 doses at the same time.

■ *Storage instructions...*

Claritin can be stored at room temperature.

What side effects may occur?

Side effects cannot be anticipated. If any develop or change in intensity, inform your doctor as soon as possible. Only your doctor can determine if it is safe for you to continue taking Claritin.

■ *More common side effects may include:*

Dry mouth
Fatigue
Headache
Sleepiness

■ *Less common or rare side effects may include:*

Abdominal discomfort or pain, abnormal dreams, agitation, anxiety, back pain, blurred vision, breast enlargement, breast pain, bronchitis, change in salivation, change in taste, chest pain, chills and fever, confusion, conjunctivitis (pinkeye), constipation, coughing up blood, coughing, decreased sensitivity to touch, decreased sex drive, depression, diarrhea, difficult or labored breathing, difficulty concentrating, difficulty speaking, discoloration of urine, dizziness, dry hair, dry skin, earache, eye pain, fainting, fever, flushing, gas, general feeling of illness, hair loss, hepatitis, high blood pressure, hives, hyperactivity, impotence, increased appetite, increased or decreased eye tearing, increased sweating, indigestion, inflammation of the mouth, insomnia, itching, joint pain, laryngitis, leg cramps, loss of appetite, low blood pressure, memory loss, menstrual changes, migraine, muscle pain, nasal congestion, dryness, or inflammation, nausea, nervousness, nosebleeds, palpitations, rapid heartbeat, rash, ringing in ears, seizures, sensitivity to light, sinus inflammation, skin inflammation, sneezing, sore throat, stomach inflammation, swelling, thirst, tingling, toothache, tremor, twitching of the eye, upper respiratory infection, urinary changes, vaginal inflammation, vertigo, vomiting, weakness, weight gain, wheezing, yellow eyes and skin

Why should this drug not be prescribed?

Do not take Claritin if you are sensitive to or have ever had an allergic reaction to it. Make sure your doctor is aware of any drug reactions that you have experienced.

Special warnings about this medication

This medication may cause excessive sleepiness in people with liver or kidney disease, or the elderly, and should be used with caution.

Possible food and drug interactions
when taking this medication

Although no interactions with Claritin have been reported, there is a theoretical possibility of an interaction with the following drugs:

Antibiotics such as erythromycin and Biaxin
Cimetidine (Tagamet)
Ketoconazole (Nizoral)
Ranitidine (Zantac)
Theophylline (Theo-Dur)

Special information
if you are pregnant or breastfeeding

The effects of Claritin during pregnancy have not been adequately studied. If you are pregnant or plan to become pregnant, inform your doctor immediately. Claritin appears in breast milk and could affect a nursing infant. If this medication is essential to your health, your doctor may advise you to discontinue breastfeeding until your treatment with Claritin is finished.

Recommended dosage

ADULTS AND CHILDREN 12 YEARS OF AGE AND OVER

The usual dose is one 10-milligram tablet taken once a day. In people with liver disease, the usual dose is one 10-milligram tablet taken every other day.

Overdosage

Any medication taken in excess can have serious consequences. If you suspect an overdose, seek medical attention immediately.

- *Symptoms of Claritin overdose may include:*
  Headache
  Rapid heartbeat
  Sleepiness

Brand name:

CLARITIN-D

Pronounced: CLAR-i-tin dee
Generic ingredients: Loratadine, Pseudoephedrine sulfate

Why is this drug prescribed?
Claritin-D is an antihistamine and decongestant that relieves the sneezing, runny nose, stuffiness, and itchy, tearing eyes caused by hay fever.

Most important fact about this drug
If you have liver disease, make sure the doctor is aware of it. Claritin-D is not recommended in this situation.

How should you take this medication?
Take Claritin-D on an empty stomach. Take it exactly as prescribed by your doctor. Do not break or chew the tablet.

- *If you miss a dose...*
  Take it as soon as you remember. If it almost time for your next dose, skip the one you missed. Never take 2 doses at the same time.

- *Storage instructions...*
  Store at room temperature.

What side effects may occur?
Side effects cannot be anticipated. If any develop or change in intensity, inform your doctor as soon as possible. Only your doctor can determine if it is safe for you to continue taking Claritin-D.

- *More common side effects may include:*
  Dry mouth
  Insomnia

- *Less common or rare side effects may include:*
  Dizziness, fatigue, headache, indigestion, insomnia, nausea, nervousness, sleepiness, sore throat

Why should this drug not be prescribed?

Do not take Claritin-D if you have ever had an allergic reaction to any of its ingredients.

Avoid Claritin-D if you have the eye condition called narrow-angle glaucoma, very high blood pressure, or coronary artery disease; and do not take the drug if you have difficulty urinating. Also avoid taking Claritin-D within 14 days of taking any antidepressant drug classified as an MAO inhibitor, including Nardil, Marplan, and Parnate.

Special warnings about this medication

If you are taking Claritin-D and experience insomnia, dizziness, weakness, tremor, or unusual heartbeats, tell your doctor; you may be having an allergic reaction.

You must be careful using Claritin-D if you have diabetes, heart disease, an overactive thyroid gland, kidney or liver problems, or an enlarged prostate gland.

Do not use Claritin-D with over-the-counter antihistamines and decongestants.

Possible food and drug interactions
when taking this medication

Check with your doctor before combining Claritin-D with any of the following:

　　Antidepressant drugs classified as MAO inhibitors, including Nardil and
　　　　Parnate
　　Blood pressure medications classified as beta blockers, such as Inderal
　　　　and Tenormin
　　Digoxin (Lanoxin)
　　Mecamylamine (Inversine)
　　Methyldopa (Aldomet)
　　Reserpine (Serpasil)

Special information
if you are pregnant or breastfeeding

The effects of Claritin-D during pregnancy have not been adequately studied. If you are pregnant or plan to become pregnant, inform your doctor immediately. Claritin-D may appear in breast milk. If this medication is essential to your health, your doctor may advise you not to breastfeed until your treatment is finished.

Recommended dosage

ADULTS AND CHILDREN 12 YEARS OF AGE AND OVER

The usual dose is 1 tablet every 12 hours. If you have kidney trouble, your doctor will start you on 1 tablet a day.

Overdosage

Any medication taken in excess can have serious consequences. If you suspect an overdose, seek medical attention immediately.

■ *Symptoms of Claritin-D overdose may include:*
Anxiety, breathing difficulty, chest pain, coma, convulsions, delusions, difficulty urinating, fast, fluttery heartbeat, giddiness, hallucinations, headache, insomnia, irregular heartbeat, nausea, rapid heartbeat, restlessness, sleepiness, sweating, tension, thirst, vomiting, weakness

Generic name:

CLEMASTINE

See Tavist, page 1073.

Brand name:

CLEOCIN T

Pronounced: KLEE-oh-sin tee
Generic name: Clindamycin phosphate

Why is this drug prescribed?

Cleocin T is an antibiotic used to treat acne.

Most important fact about this drug

Although applied only to the skin, some of this medication could be absorbed into the bloodstream; and it has been known to cause severe—sometimes even fatal—colitis (an inflammation of the lower bowel) when taken internally. Symptoms, which can occur a few days, weeks, or months after beginning treatment with this drug, include severe diarrhea, severe abdominal cramps, and the possibility of the passage of blood.

How should you take this medication?

Use this medication exactly as prescribed. Excessive use of Cleocin T can cause your skin to become too dry or irritated.

■ *If you miss a dose...*
Apply it as soon as you remember. If it is almost time for your next dose, skip the one you missed and go back to your regular schedule.

■ *Storage instructions...*
Store at room temperature. Keep from freezing.

What side effects may occur?
Side effects cannot be anticipated. If any develop or change in intensity, inform your doctor as soon as possible. Only your doctor can determine if it is safe for you to continue taking Cleocin T.

The most common side effect is skin dryness.

■ *Less common or rare side effects may include:*
Abdominal pain, bloody diarrhea, burning or abnormal redness of skin, colitis, diarrhea, oily skin, peeling skin, skin inflammation and irritation, stomach and intestinal disturbances

Why should this drug not be prescribed?
If you are sensitive to or have ever had an allergic reaction to Cleocin T or similar drugs, you should not use this medication. Make sure your doctor is aware of any drug reactions you have experienced.

Unless you are directed to do so by your doctor, do not take this medication if you have ever had an intestinal inflammation, ulcerative colitis, or antibiotic-associated colitis.

Special warnings about this medication
Cleocin T contains an alcohol base, which can cause burning and irritation of the eyes. It also has an unpleasant taste. Use caution when applying this medication so as not to get it in the eyes, nose, mouth, or skin abrasions. In the event of accidental contact, rinse the affected area with cool water.

Use with caution if you have hay fever, asthma, or eczema.

Possible food and drug interactions
when taking this medication
If you have diarrhea while taking Cleocin T, check with your doctor before taking an antidiarrhea medication, as certain drugs may cause your diarrhea to become worse.

The diarrhea should not be treated with the commonly used drugs that slow movement through the intestinal tract, such as Lomotil or products containing paregoric.

Special information
if you are pregnant or breastfeeding
The effects of Cleocin T during pregnancy have not been adequately studied. If you are pregnant or plan to become pregnant, inform your doctor immediately. Cleocin T may appear in breast milk and could affect a nursing infant. If this medication is essential to your health, your doctor may advise you to discontinue breastfeeding your baby until your treatment with this medication is finished.

Recommended dosage

ADULTS

Apply a thin film of gel, solution, or lotion to the affected area 2 times a day.

If you are using the lotion, shake it well immediately before using.

CHILDREN

The safety and effectiveness of Cleocin T have not been established in children under 12 years of age.

Overdosage
Although there is no information on Cleocin T overdose, any medication taken in excess can have serious consequences. If you suspect an overdose, seek medical attention immediately.

Generic name:

CLINDAMYCIN

See Cleocin T, page 205.

Brand name:

CLINDEX

See Librax, page 571.

Brand name:

CLINORIL

Pronounced: CLIN-or-il
Generic name: Sulindac

Why is this drug prescribed?

Clinoril, a nonsteroidal anti-inflammatory drug, is used to relieve the inflammation, swelling, stiffness and joint pain associated with rheumatoid arthritis, osteoarthritis (the most common form of arthritis), and ankylosing spondylitis (stiffness and progressive arthritis of the spine.) It is also used to treat bursitis, tendinitis, acute gouty arthritis, and other types of pain.

The safety and effectiveness of this medication in the treatment of people with rheumatoid arthritis who are incapacitated, almost or completely bedridden, in wheelchairs, or unable to care for themselves, have not been established.

Most important fact about this drug

You should have frequent checkups with your doctor if you take Clinoril regularly. Ulcers or internal bleeding can occur without warning.

How should you take this medication?

Take this medication exactly as prescribed by your doctor.

If you are using Clinoril for arthritis, it should be taken regularly.

- *If you miss a dose...*
  Take it as soon as you remember. If it is almost time for your next dose, skip the one you missed and go back to your regular schedule. Never take 2 doses at the same time.

- *Storage instructions...*
  Do not store in damp places like the bathroom.

What side effects may occur?

Side effects cannot be anticipated. If any develop or change in intensity, inform your doctor as soon as possible. Only your doctor can determine if it is safe for you to continue taking Clinoril.

- *More common side effects may include:*
  Abdominal pain, constipation, diarrhea, dizziness, gas, headache, indigestion, itching, loss of appetite, nausea, nervousness, rash, ringing in ears, stomach cramps, swelling due to fluid retention, vomiting

- *Less common or rare side effects may include:*
  Abdominal bleeding, abdominal inflammation, anemia, appetite change, bloody diarrhea, blurred vision, change in color of urine, chest pain, colitis, congestive heart failure, depression, fever, hair loss, hearing loss, hepatitis, high blood pressure, inability to sleep, inflammation of lips and

tongue, kidney failure, liver failure, loss of sense of taste, low blood pressure, muscle and joint pain, nosebleed, painful urination, pancreatitis, peptic ulcer, sensitivity to light, shortness of breath, skin eruptions, sleepiness, Stevens-Johnson syndrome (blisters in the mouth and eyes), vaginal bleeding, weakness, yellow eyes and skin

Why should this drug not be prescribed?

If you are sensitive to or have ever had an allergic reaction to Clinoril, aspirin, or similar drugs, or if you have had asthma attacks caused by aspirin or other drugs of this type, you should not take this medication. Make sure that your doctor is aware of any drug reactions that you have experienced.

Special warnings about this medication

Peptic ulcers and bleeding can occur without warning.

This drug should be used with caution if you have kidney or liver disease; it can cause liver inflammation in some people.

Do not take aspirin or any other anti-inflammatory medications while taking Clinoril, unless your doctor tells you to do so.

Nonsteroidal anti-inflammatory drugs such as Clinoril can hide the signs and symptoms of an infection. Be sure your doctor knows about any infection you may have.

Clinoril can cause vision problems. If you experience a change in your vision, inform your doctor.

If you have heart disease or high blood pressure, this drug can increase water retention. Use with caution.

If you develop pancreatitis (inflammation of the pancreas), Clinoril should be stopped immediately and not restarted.

Clinoril may cause you to become drowsy or less alert. If this happens, driving or operating dangerous machinery or participating in any hazardous activity that requires full mental alertness is not recommended.

Possible food and drug interactions
when taking this medication

If Clinoril is taken with certain other drugs, the effects of either could be increased, decreased, or altered. It is especially important to check with your doctor before combining Clinoril with the following:

Aspirin
Blood thinners such as Coumadin and Panwarfin
Cyclosporine (Sandimmune)

Diflunisal (Dolobid)
Dimethyl sulfoxide (dmso)
Lithium
Loop diuretics such as Lasix
Methotrexate
Oral diabetes medications
The anti-gout medication Benemid

Special information
if you are pregnant or breastfeeding

The effects of Clinoril during pregnancy have not been adequately studied; drugs of this class are known to cause birth defects. If you are pregnant or plan to become pregnant, inform your doctor immediately. Clinoril may appear in breast milk and could affect a nursing infant. If this medication is essential to your health, your doctor may advise you to discontinue breastfeeding until your treatment with Clinoril is finished.

Recommended dosage

ADULTS

Osteoarthritis, Rheumatoid Arthritis, Ankylosing Spondylitis

Starting dosage is 150 milligrams 2 times a day. Take with food. Doses should not exceed 400 milligrams per day.

Acute Gouty Arthritis or Arthritic Shoulder and Joint Condition

400 milligrams daily taken in doses of 200 milligrams 2 times a day.

For acute painful shoulder, therapy lasting 7 to 14 days is usually adequate.

For acute gouty arthritis, therapy lasting 7 days is usually adequate.

The lowest dose that proves beneficial should be used.

CHILDREN

The safety and effectiveness of Clinoril have not been established in children.

Overdosage

Any medication taken in excess can cause symptoms of overdose. If you suspect an overdose, seek medical attention immediately.

■ *Symptoms of Clinoril overdose may include:*
Coma

Low blood pressure
Reduced output of urine
Stupor

Generic name:

CLOBETASOL

See Temovate, page 1081.

Brand name:

CLOMID

See Clomiphene Citrate, page 211.

Generic name:

CLOMIPHENE CITRATE

Pronounced: KLAHM-if-een SIT-rate
Brand names: Clomid, Serophene

Why is this drug prescribed?
Clomiphene is prescribed for the treatment of ovulatory failure in women who wish to become pregnant and whose partners are fertile and potent.

Most important fact about this drug
Properly timed sexual intercourse is very important to increase the chances of conception. The likelihood of conception diminishes with each succeeding course of treatment. Your doctor will determine the need for continuing therapy after the first course. If you do not become pregnant after 3 courses, your doctor will stop the therapy.

How should you take this medication?
Take this medication exactly as prescribed by your doctor.

■ *If you miss a dose...*
Take it as soon as you remember. If it is time for your next dose, take the 2 doses together and go back to your regular schedule. If you miss more than 1 dose, contact your doctor.

■ *Storage instructions...*
Store at room temperature in a tightly closed container, away from light, moisture, and excessive heat.

What side effects may occur?
Side effects occur infrequently and generally do not interfere with treatment at the recommended dosage of clomiphene. They tend to occur more frequently at higher doses and during long-term treatment.

- *More common side effects include:*
  Abdominal discomfort
  Enlargement of the ovaries
  Hot flushes

- *Less common side effects include:*
  Abnormal uterine bleeding, breast tenderness, depression, dizziness, fatigue, hair loss, headache, hives, inability to fall or stay asleep, increased urination, inflammation of the skin, light-headedness, nausea, nervousness, ovarian cysts, visual disturbances, vomiting, weight gain

Why should this drug not be prescribed?
If you are pregnant or think you may be, do not take this drug.

Unless directed to do so by your doctor, do not use this medication if you have an uncontrolled thyroid or adrenal gland disorder, an abnormality of the brain such as a pituitary gland tumor, a liver disease or a history of liver problems, abnormal uterine bleeding of undetermined origin, ovarian cysts, or enlargement of the ovaries not caused by polycystic ovarian syndrome (a hormonal disorder causing lack of ovulation).

Special warnings about this medication
Your doctor will evaluate you for normal liver function and normal estrogen levels before considering you for treatment with clomiphene.

Your doctor will also examine you for pregnancy, ovarian enlargement, or cyst formation prior to treatment with this drug and between each treatment cycle. He or she will do a complete pelvic examination before each course of this medication.

Clomiphene treatment increases the possibility of multiple births; also, birth defects have been reported following treatment to induce ovulation with clomiphene, although no direct effects of the drug on the unborn child have been established.

Because blurring and other visual symptoms may occur occasionally with clomiphene treatment, you should be cautious about driving a car or operating dangerous machinery, especially under conditions of variable lighting.

If you experience visual disturbances, notify your doctor immediately. Symptoms of visual disturbance may include blurring, spots or flashes, double vision, intolerance to light, decreased visual sharpness, loss of peripheral vision, and distortion of space. Your doctor may recommend a complete evaluation by an eye specialist.

Ovarian hyperstimulation syndrome (or OHSS, enlargement of the ovary) has occurred in women receiving treatment with clomiphene. OHSS may progress rapidly and become serious. The early warning signs are severe pelvic pain, nausea, vomiting, and weight gain. Symptoms include abdominal pain, abdominal enlargement, nausea, vomiting, diarrhea, weight gain, difficult or labored breathing, and less urine production. If you experience any of these warning signs or symptoms, notify your doctor immediately.

To lessen the risks associated with abnormal ovarian enlargement during treatment with clomiphene, the lowest effective dose should be prescribed. Women with the hormonal disorder polycystic ovarian syndrome may be unusually sensitive to certain hormones and may respond abnormally to usual doses of this drug. If you experience pelvic pain, notify your doctor, who may discontinue your use of clomiphene until the ovaries return to pretreatment size.

Because the safety of long-term treatment with clomiphene has not been established, your doctor will not prescribe more than 3 courses of therapy.

**Possible food and drug interactions
when taking this medication**
No food or drug interactions have been reported with clomiphene therapy.

**Special information
if you are pregnant or breastfeeding**
If you become pregnant, notify your doctor immediately. You should not be taking this drug while you are pregnant.

Recommended dosage
The recommended dosage for the first course of treatment is 50 milligrams (1 tablet) daily for 5 days. If ovulation does not appear to have occurred, your doctor may prescribe up to 2 more courses of treatment.

Overdosage
Taking any medication in excess can have serious consequences. If you suspect an overdose of clomiphene, contact your doctor immediately.

Generic name:

CLOMIPRAMINE

See Anafranil, page 50.

Generic name:

CLONAZEPAM

See Klonopin, page 546.

Generic name:

CLONIDINE

See Catapres, page 176.

Generic name:

CLORAZEPATE

See Tranxene, page 1140.

Generic name:

CLOTRIMAZOLE

See Gyne-Lotrimin, page 476.

Generic name:

CLOTRIMAZOLE WITH BETAMETHASONE

See Lotrisone, page 612.

Generic name:

CLOZAPINE

See Clozaril, page 214.

Brand name:

CLOZARIL

Pronounced: KLOH-zah-ril
Generic name: Clozapine

Why is this drug prescribed?

Clozaril is given to help people with severe schizophrenia who have failed to respond to standard treatments. Clozaril is not a cure, but it can help some people return to more normal lives.

Most important fact about this drug

Even though it does not produce some of the disturbing side effects of other antipsychotic medications, Clozaril may cause agranulocytosis, a potentially lethal disorder of the white blood cells. Because of the risk of agranulocytosis, anyone who takes Clozaril is required to have a blood test once a week. The drug is carefully controlled so that those taking it must get their weekly blood test before receiving the following week's supply of medication. Anyone whose blood test results are abnormal will be taken off Clozaril either temporarily or permanently, depending on the results of an additional 4 weeks of testing.

How should you take this medication?

Take Clozaril exactly as directed by your doctor. Because of the significant risk of serious side effects associated with this drug, your doctor will periodically reassess the need for continued Clozaril therapy. Clozaril is distributed *only* through the Clozaril Patient Management System, which ensures weekly white blood cell testing, monitoring, and pharmacy services prior to delivery of the next week's supply.

Clozaril may be taken with or without food.

■ *If you miss a dose...*
Take it as soon as you remember. If it is almost time for your next dose, skip the one you missed and go back to your regular schedule. Do not take 2 doses at once.

If you stop taking Clozaril for more than 2 days, do not start taking it again without consulting your physician.

■ *Storage instructions...*
Store at room temperature.

What side effects may occur?

Side effects cannot be anticipated. If any develop or change in intensity, inform your doctor as soon as possible. Only your doctor can determine if it is safe for you to continue taking Clozaril.

The most feared side effect is agranulocytosis, a dangerous drop in the number of a certain kind of white blood cell. Symptoms include fever, lethargy, sore throat, and weakness. If not caught in time, agranulocytosis can be fatal. That is why all people who take Clozaril must have a blood test every week. About 1 percent develop agranulocytosis and must stop taking the drug.

Seizures are another potential side effect, occurring in some 5 percent of people who take Clozaril. The higher the dosage, the greater the risk of seizures.

■ *More common side effects may include:*
Abdominal discomfort, agitation, confusion, constipation, disturbed sleep, dizziness, drowsiness, dry mouth, fainting, fever, headache, heartburn, high blood pressure, inability to sit down, loss or slowness of muscle movement, low blood pressure, nausea, nightmares, rapid heartbeat and other heart conditions, restlessness, rigidity, salivation, sedation, sweating, tremors, vertigo, vision problems, vomiting, weight gain

■ *Less common side effects may include:*
Abdominal distention, abnormal stools, anemia, angina (severe, crushing chest pain), anxiety, appetite increase, belching, bitter taste, blood clots, bloodshot eyes, bluish tinge in the skin, breast pain or discomfort, bronchitis, bruising, chest pain, chills or chills and fever, constant involuntary eye movement, coughing, delusions, depression, diarrhea, difficult or labored breathing, dilated pupils, disorientation, dry throat, ear disorders, ejaculation problems, excessive movement, eyelid disorder, fast, fluttery heartbeat, fatigue, fluid retention, frequent urination, hallucinations, heart problems, hives, hot flashes, impotence, inability to fall asleep or stay asleep, inability to hold urine, inability to urinate, increase or decrease in sex drive, inflamed stomach and intestines, involuntary movement, irritability, itching, jerky movements, joint pain, lack of coordination, laryngitis, lethargy, light-headedness (especially when rising quickly from a seated or lying position), loss of appetite, loss of speech, low body temperature, memory loss, muscle pain or ache, muscle spasm, muscle weakness, nervous stomach, nosebleed, numbness, pain in back, neck, or legs, painful menstruation, pallor, paranoia, pneumonia or pneumonia-like symptoms, poor coordination, rapid breathing, rash, rectal bleeding, runny nose, shakiness, shortness of breath, skin inflammation, redness, scaling, slow heartbeat, slurred speech, sneezing, sore or numb tongue, speech difficulty, stomach pain, stomach ulcer, stuffy nose, stupor, stuttering, thirst, throat discomfort, tics, twitching, urination problems, vaginal infection, vaginal itch, a vague feeling of being sick, vomiting blood, weakness, wheezing

Why should this drug not be prescribed?
Clozaril is considered a somewhat risky medication because of its potential to cause agranulocytosis and seizures. It should be taken only by people whose condition is serious, and who have not been helped by more traditional antipsychotic medications such as Haldol or Mellaril.

You should not take Clozaril if:

- You have a bone marrow disease or disorder;
- You have epilepsy that is not controlled;
- You ever developed an abnormal white blood cell count while taking Clozaril;
- You are currently taking some other drug, such as Tegretol, that could cause a decrease in white blood cell count or a drug that could affect the bone marrow.

Special warnings about this medication
Clozaril can cause drowsiness, especially at the start of treatment. For this reason, and also because of the potential for seizures, you should not drive, swim, climb, or operate dangerous machinery while you are taking this medication, at least in the early stages of treatment.

Even though you will have weekly blood tests while taking Clozaril, you should stay alert for early symptoms of agranulocytosis: weakness, lethargy, fever, sore throat, a general feeling of illness, a flu-like feeling, or ulcers of the lips, mouth, or other mucous membranes. If any such symptoms develop, tell your doctor immediately.

Especially during the first 3 weeks of treatment, you may develop a fever. If you do, notify your doctor.

While taking Clozaril, do not drink alcohol or use drugs of any kind, including over-the-counter medicines, without first checking with your doctor.

If you take Clozaril, you must be monitored especially closely if you have either the eye condition called narrow-angle glaucoma or an enlarged prostate; Clozaril could make these conditions worse.

Especially when you begin taking Clozaril, you may feel light-headed upon standing up, to the point where you pass out.

If you have kidney, liver, lung or heart disease; or a history of seizures or prostate problems, you should discuss these with your doctor before taking Clozaril.

Drugs such as Clozaril can sometimes cause a set of symptoms called neuroleptic malignant syndrome. Symptoms include high fever, muscle rigidity, irregular pulse or blood pressure, rapid heartbeat, excessive perspiration, and changes in heart rhythm. Your doctor will have you stop taking Clozaril while this condition is being treated.

There is also a risk of developing tardive dyskinesia, a condition of involuntary, slow, rhythmical movements. It happens more often in the elderly, especially elderly women.

Possible food and drug interactions
when taking this medication

If Clozaril is taken with certain other drugs, the effects of either could be increased, decreased, or altered. It is especially important to check with your doctor before combining Clozaril with the following:

Antidepressants such as Prozac and Zoloft
Antipsychotic drugs such as Thorazine and Mellaril
Blood pressure medication such as Aldomet and Hytrin
Cimetidine (Tagamet)
Digitoxin (Crystodigin)
Digoxin (Lanoxin)
Drugs that depress the central nervous system, such as phenobarbital
    and Seconal
Drugs that contain atropine, such as Donnatal and Levsin
Epilepsy drugs, such as Tegretol and Dilantin
Epinephrine (EpiPen)
Heart rhythm stabilizers such as Quinidex and Tambocor
Tranquilizers such as Valium and Xanax
Warfarin (Coumadin and Panwarfin)

Special information
if you are pregnant or breastfeeding

The effects of Clozaril during pregnancy have not been adequately studied. If you are pregnant or plan to become pregnant, inform your doctor immediately. Clozaril treatment should be continued during pregnancy only if absolutely necessary. You should not breastfeed if you are taking Clozaril, since the drug may appear in breast milk.

Recommended dosage

ADULTS

Your doctor will carefully individualize your dosage and monitor your response weekly.

The usual recommended initial dose is half of a 25-milligram tablet (12.5

milligrams) 1 or 2 times daily. Your doctor may increase the dosage in increments of 25 to 50 milligrams a day to achieve a daily dose of 300 to 450 milligrams a day by the end of 2 weeks. Dosage increases after that will be only once or twice a week and will be no more than 100 milligrams each time. The most you can take is 900 milligrams a day divided into 2 or 3 doses.

Your doctor will determine long-term dosage depending upon your response and results of the weekly blood test.

CHILDREN

Safety and efficacy have not been established for children up to 16 years of age.

Overdosage

Any medication taken in excess can have serious consequences. If you suspect an overdose, seek emergency medical attention immediately.

■ *Symptoms of overdose with Clozaril may include:*
   Coma
   Delirium
   Drowsiness
   Excess salivation
   Low blood pressure, faintness
   Pneumonia
   Rapid heartbeat
   Seizures
   Shallow breathing or absence of breathing

Brand name:

COGENTIN

Pronounced: co-JEN-tin
Generic name: Benztropine mesylate

Why is this drug prescribed?
Cogentin is given to help relieve the symptoms of "parkinsonism": the muscle rigidity, tremors, and difficulties with posture and balance that occur in Parkinson's disease and that sometimes develop as unwanted side effects of antipsychotic drugs such as Haldol and Thorazine.

Cogentin is an "anticholinergic" medication, a drug that controls spasms. It reduces the symptoms of parkinsonism, but it is not a cure.

Most important fact about this drug

When starting Cogentin, you may not feel its effect for 2 or 3 days. Symptoms caused by drugs such as Haldol and Thorazine are often temporary, so if drug-induced parkinsonism is your problem, you may need to take Cogentin for only a couple of weeks.

How should you take this medication?

Take Cogentin exactly as prescribed. Unlike some of the other antiparkinsonian medications, Cogentin acts over a long period of time. It is thus particularly suitable as a bedtime medication because it lasts through the night. Taken at bedtime, it may help a person regain enough muscle control to move and roll over during sleep and to arise unaided in the morning.

Cogentin causes dry mouth. Sucking on sugarless hard candy or sipping water can relieve this problem.

Cogentin can reduce the ability to sweat, one of the key ways your body prevents overheating. Avoid excess sun or exercise that may cause overheating.

■ *If you miss a dose...*
Take it as soon as you remember. If it is within 2 hours of your next dose, skip the one you missed and go back to your regular schedule. Do not take 2 doses at once.

■ *Storage instructions...*
Store away from heat, light, and moisture.

What side effects may occur?

Side effects cannot be anticipated. If any develop or change in intensity, inform your doctor as soon as possible. Only your doctor can determine if it is safe for you to continue taking Cogentin.

■ *Side effects may include:*
Blurred vision, bowel blockage, confusion, constipation, depression, dilated pupils, disorientation, dry mouth, fever, hallucinations, heat stroke, impaired memory, inability to urinate, listlessness, nausea, nervousness, numbness in fingers, painful urination, rapid heartbeat, rash, vomiting

Why should this drug not be prescribed?

Do not take Cogentin if you are sensitive to it or if you have ever had an allergic reaction to it or to any similar antispasmodic medication.

Do not take Cogentin if you have an eye condition called angle-closure glaucoma.

Some people who take certain antipsychotic medications develop tardive dyskinesia, a syndrome of involuntary movements of the mouth, jaw, arms, and legs. Cogentin should not be given to treat tardive dyskinesia; it will not help, and it may make the condition worse.

Cogentin should not be given to children under the age of 3; it should be used with caution in older children.

Special warnings about this medication

Do not drive or operate dangerous machinery while taking Cogentin, since the drug may impair your mental or physical abilities.

Be sure to tell your doctor if you have ever had tachycardia (excessively rapid heartbeats) or if you have an enlarged prostate; you will require especially close monitoring while taking Cogentin in these cases.

Tell your doctor if Cogentin produces weakness in particular muscle groups. For example, if you have been suffering from neck rigidity and Cogentin suddenly causes your neck to relax so much that it feels weak, you may be taking more Cogentin than you need.

If you have been taking another antiparkinsonism drug, do not stop taking it abruptly when you start taking Cogentin. If you are to stop taking the other drug, your doctor will have you taper off gradually.

Cogentin has a drying effect on the mouth and other moist tissues. If you take it along with another drug that also has a drying effect, you are at risk for anhidrosis (inability to sweat), heat stroke, and even death from hyperthermia (high fever). Chronic illness, alcoholism, central nervous system (brain and spinal cord) disease, or heavy manual labor in a hot environment can increase this risk. In hot weather, your doctor may lower your dosage of Cogentin.

Possible food and drug interactions when taking this medication

When taken simultaneously with an antipsychotic medication (Thorazine, Stelazine, Haldol, others) or a tricyclic antidepressant medication (Elavil, Norpramin, Tofranil, others), Cogentin has occasionally caused bowel blockage or heat stroke that proved dangerous or even fatal. If you are taking Cogentin along with an antipsychotic or with a tricyclic antidepressant, tell your doctor immediately if you begin to have any stomach or bowel complaint, fever, or heat intolerance.

Antacids, such at Tums, Maalox, Mylanta, may decrease the effects of Cogentin. Do not take them within 1 hour of taking Cogentin.

Certain other drugs may also interact with Cogentin. Consult your doctor before combining Cogentin with any of the following:

Amantadine (Symmetrel)
Doxepin (Sinequan)
Antihistamines such as Benadryl and Tavist
Other anticholinergic agents such as Bentyl

Special information
if you are pregnant or breastfeeding
If you are pregnant or plan to become pregnant, inform your doctor immediately. No information is available about the safety of taking Cogentin during pregnancy or while you are breastfeeding.

Recommended dosage
Your doctor will individualize the dose of Cogentin, taking into consideration your age and weight, the condition being treated, the presence of other diseases, and any physical disorder.

In general, the usual oral dose is 1 to 2 milligrams a day, but it can range from 0.5 to 6 milligrams a day.

Overdosage
Any medication taken in excess can have serious consequences. If you suspect symptoms of an overdose of Cogentin, seek medical attention immediately. Symptoms of overdose may include any of those listed in the "side effects section" (see above) or any of the following:

Blurred vision, confusion, coma, constipation, convulsions, delirium, difficulty swallowing or breathing, dilated pupils, dizziness, dry mouth, flushed, dry skin, glaucoma, hallucinations, headache, high blood pressure, high body temperature, inability to sweat, listlessness, muscle weakness, nausea, nervousness, numb fingers, painful urination, palpitations, rapid heartbeat, rash, shock, uncoordinated movements, vomiting

Brand name:

COGNEX

Pronounced: COG-necks
Generic name: Tacrine hydrochloride

Why is this drug prescribed?
Cognex is used for the treatment of mild to moderate Alzheimer's disease. This progressive, degenerative disorder causes physical changes in the brain

that disrupt the flow of information and affect memory, thinking, and behavior. As someone caring for an Alzheimer's patient, you should be aware that Cognex is not a cure, but has helped some patients.

Most important fact about this drug
Do not abruptly stop Cognex treatment, or reduce the dosage, without consulting the doctor. A sudden reduction can cause the person you are caring for to become more disturbed and forgetful. Taking more Cognex than the doctor advises can also cause serious problems. Do not change the dosage of Cognex unless instructed by the doctor.

How should this medication be taken?
This medication will work better if taken at regular intervals, usually 4 times a day. Cognex is best taken between meals; however, if it is irritating to the stomach, the doctor may advise taking it with meals. If Cognex is not taken regularly, as the doctor directs, the condition may get worse.

■ *If you miss a dose...*
  Give the forgotten dose as soon as possible. If it is within 2 hours of the next dose, skip the missed dose and go back to the regular schedule. Do not double the doses.

■ *Storage instructions...*
  Store at room temperature away from moisture.

What side effects may occur?
Side effects cannot be anticipated. If any develop or change in intensity, tell the doctor as soon as possible. Only the doctor can determine if it is safe to continue giving Cognex.

■ *More common side effects may include:*
  Abdominal pain, abnormal thinking, agitation, anxiety, chest pain, clumsiness or unsteadiness, confusion, constipation, coughing, depression, diarrhea, dizziness, fatigue, flushing, frequent urination, gas, headache, inflamed nasal passages, insomnia, indigestion, liver function disorders, loss of appetite, muscle pain, nausea, rash, sleepiness, upper respiratory infection, urinary tract infection, vomiting, weight loss

■ *Less common side effects may include:*
  Back pain, hallucinations, hostile attitude, purple or red spots on the skin, skin discoloration, tremor, weakness

Be sure to report any symptoms that develop while on Cognex therapy. You should alert the doctor if the person you are caring for develops nausea, vomiting, loose stools, or diarrhea at the start of therapy or when the dosage is increased. Later in therapy, be on the lookout for rash, yellowing of the eyes and skin, or changes in the color of the stool.

Why should this drug not be prescribed?

People who are sensitive to or have ever had an allergic reaction to Cognex should not take this medication. Before starting treatment with Cognex, it is important to discuss any medical problems with the doctor. If during previous Cognex therapy the person you are caring for developed jaundice (yellow skin and eyes), which signals that something is wrong with the liver, Cognex should not be used again.

Special warnings about this medication

Use Cognex with caution if the person you are caring for has a history of liver disease, certain heart disorders, stomach ulcers, or asthma.

Because of the risk of liver problems when taking Cognex, the doctor will schedule weekly blood tests to monitor liver function for the first 18 weeks on treatment. After 18 weeks, blood tests will be given every 3 months. When the doctor increases the dose of Cognex, he or she will resume weekly monitoring of the liver for at least 6 weeks. If the person you are caring for develops any liver problems, the doctor may temporarily discontinue Cognex treatment until further testing shows that the liver has returned to normal. If the doctor resumes Cognex treatment, he or she will reinstate weekly monitoring of the liver.

Before having any surgery, including dental surgery, tell the doctor that the person is being treated with Cognex.

Cognex can cause seizures, and may cause difficulty urinating.

Possible food and drug interactions
when taking this medication

If Cognex is taken with certain other drugs, the effects of either could be increased, decreased, or altered. It is especially important that you check with your doctor before combining Cognex with the following:

Antispasmodic drugs such as Bentyl and Cogentin
Bethanechol chloride (Urecholine)
Cimetidine (Tagamet)
Theophylline (Theo-Dur)

Special information
regarding pregnancy or breastfeeding
The effects of Cognex during pregnancy have not been studied, and it is not known whether Cognex appears in breast milk.

Recommended dosage

ADULTS

The usual starting dose is 10 milligrams 4 times a day, for at least 6 weeks. Do not increase the dose during this 6-week period unless directed by the doctor. The doctor may then increase the dosage to 20 milligrams 4 times a day.

Restarting Cognex Therapy
The recommended restarting dose is 10 milligrams 4 times a day for 6 weeks.

The doctor may adjust the dose at regular intervals.

CHILDREN

The safety and effectiveness of Cognex have not been established in children.

Overdosage
Any medication taken in excess can have serious consequences. If you suspect an overdose, seek medical attention immediately.

- *Symptoms of Cognex overdose include:*
  Collapse
  Convulsions
  Extreme muscle weakness, possibly ending in death (if breathing
    muscles are affected)
  Low blood pressure
  Nausea
  Salivation
  Slowed heart rate
  Sweating
  Vomiting

Brand name:

COLACE

Pronounced: KOH-lace
Generic name: Docusate sodium

Why is this drug prescribed?

Colace, a stool softener, promotes easy bowel movements without straining. It softens the stool by mixing in fat and water. Colace is helpful for people who have had recent rectal surgery, people with heart problems or high blood pressure, patients with hernias, and women who have just had babies.

Most important fact about this drug

Colace is for short-term relief only, unless your doctor directs otherwise. It usually takes a day or two for the drug to achieve its laxative effect; some people may need to wait 4 or 5 days.

How should you take this medication?

To conceal the drug's bitter taste, take Colace liquid in half a glass of milk or fruit juice; it can be given in infant formula. The proper dosage of this medication may also be added to a retention or flushing enema.

■ *If you miss a dose...*
Take this medication only as needed.

■ *Storage instructions...*
Store at room temperature. Keep from freezing.

What side effects may occur?

Side effects are unlikely. The main ones reported are bitter taste, throat irritation, and nausea (mainly associated with use of the syrup and liquid). Rash has occurred.

Why should this drug not be prescribed?

There are no known reasons this drug should not be prescribed.

Possible food and drug interactions
when taking this medication

No interactions have been reported with Colace.

Special information
if you are pregnant or breastfeeding

If you are pregnant, plan to become pregnant, or are breastfeeding your baby, notify your doctor before using this medication.

Recommended dosage

Your doctor will adjust the dosage according to your needs.

You will be using higher doses at the start of treatment with Colace. You should see an effect on stools 1 to 3 days after the first dose.

ADULTS AND CHILDREN 12 AND OLDER

The suggested daily dosage is 50 to 200 milligrams.

In enemas, add 50 to 100 milligrams of Colace or 5 to 10 milliliters of Colace liquid to a retention or flushing enema, as prescribed by your doctor.

CHILDREN UNDER 12

The suggested daily dosage for children 6 to 12 years of age is 40 to 120 milligrams; for children 3 to 6 years of age, it is 20 to 60 milligrams; for children under 3 years of age, it is 10 to 40 milligrams.

Overdosage
Overdose is unlikely with the normal use of Colace.

Brand name:

COLESTID

Pronounced: Koh-LESS-tid
Generic name: Colestipol hydrochloride

Why is this drug prescribed?
Colestid, in conjunction with diet, is used to help lower high levels of cholesterol in the blood. It is available in plain and orange-flavored varieties.

Most important fact about this drug
Accidentally inhaling Colestid may cause serious effects. To avoid this, NEVER take it in its dry form. Colestid should always be mixed with water or other liquids BEFORE you take it.

How should you take this medication?
Colestid should be mixed with liquids such as:
   Carbonated beverages (may cause stomach or intestinal discomfort)
   Flavored drinks
   Milk
   Orange juice
   Pineapple juice
   Tomato juice
   Water

Colestid may also be mixed with:
   Milk used on breakfast cereals
   Pulpy fruit (such as crushed peaches, pears, or pineapple) or fruit
      cocktail
   Soups with a high liquid content (such as chicken noodle or tomato)

To take Colestid with beverages:
1. Measure at least 3 ounces of liquid into a glass.
2. Add the prescribed dose of Colestid to the liquid.
3. Stir until Colestid is completely mixed (it will not dissolve) and then drink the mixture.
4. Pour a small amount of the beverage into the glass, swish it around, and drink it. This will help make sure you have taken all the medication.

■ *If you miss a dose...*
Take the forgotten dose as soon as you remember. If it is almost time for the next dose, skip the one you missed and go back to your regular schedule. Never try to "catch up" by doubling the dose.

■ *Storage instructions...*
Store Colestid at room temperature.

What side effects may occur?
Side effects cannot be anticipated. If any develop or change in intensity, inform your doctor as soon as possible. Only your doctor can determine if it is safe for you to continue taking Colestid.

■ *Most common side effects:*
Constipation
Worsening of hemorrhoids

■ *Less common or rare side effects may include:*
Abdominal bloating or distention/cramping/pain, arthritis, diarrhea, dizziness, fatigue, gas, headache, hives, joint pain, loss of appetite, muscle pain, nausea, shortness of breath, skin inflammation, vomiting, weakness

■ *Additional side effects from regular Colestid may include:*
Anxiety, belching, drowsiness, vertigo

■ *Additional side effects from Flavored Colestid may include:*
Aches and pains in arms and legs, angina (crushing chest pain), backache, bleeding hemorrhoids, blood in the stool, bone pain, chest pain, indigestion, insomnia, light-headedness, loose stools, migraine, rapid heartbeat, rash, sinus headache, swelling of hands or feet

Why should this drug not be prescribed?
You should not be using Colestid if you are allergic to it or any of its components.

Special warnings about this medication

Before starting treatment with Colestid, you should:

- Be tested (and treated) for diseases that may contribute to increased blood cholesterol, such as an underactive thyroid gland, diabetes, nephrotic syndrome (a kidney disease), dysproteinemia (a blood disease), obstructive liver disease, and alcoholism.
- Be on a diet plan (approved by your doctor) that stresses low-cholesterol foods and weight loss (if necessary).

Because certain medications may increase cholesterol, you should tell your doctor all of the medications you use.

Colestid may prevent the absorption of vitamins such as A, D, K, and folic acid. Long-term use of Colestid may be connected to increased bleeding from a lack of vitamin K. Taking vitamin K_1 will help relieve this condition and prevent it in the future.

Your cholesterol and triglyceride levels should be checked regularly while you are taking Colestid.

Colestid may cause or worsen constipation. Dosages should be adjusted by your doctor. You may need to increase your intake of fiber and fluid. A stool softener also may be needed occasionally. People with coronary artery disease should be especially careful to avoid constipation. Hemorrhoids may be worsened by constipation related to Colestid.

If you have phenylketonuria (a hereditary disease caused by your body's inability to handle the amino acid phenylalanine), be aware that Flavored Colestid contains phenylalanine.

Possible food and drug interactions
when taking this medication

Colestid may delay or reduce the absorption of other drugs. The time period between taking Colestid and taking other medications should be as long as possible. Other drugs should be taken at least 1 hour before or 4 hours after taking Colestid.

If Colestid is taken with certain other drugs, the effects of either could be increased, decreased, or altered. It is especially important to check with your doctor before combining Colestid with the following:

Chlorothiazide (Diuril)
Digitalis (Lanoxin)
Furosemide (Lasix)
Gemfibrozil (Lopid)

Hydrochlorothiazide (HydroDIURIL)
Penicillin G, including brands such as Pentids
Phosphate supplements
Propranolol (Inderal)
Tetracycline drugs such as Sumycin
Vitamins such as A, D, and K

Special information
if you are pregnant or breastfeeding

The effects of Colestid during pregnancy have not been adequately studied. If you are pregnant or planning to become pregnant, or plan to breastfeed, check with your doctor.

Recommended dosage

ADULTS

One packet or 1 level scoopful of Flavored Colestid contains 5 grams of Colestipol.

The usual starting dose is 1 packet or 1 level scoopful once or twice a day. Your doctor may increase this by 1 dose a day every month or every other month, up to 6 packets or 6 level scoopfuls taken once a day or divided into smaller doses.

CHILDREN

The safety and effectiveness of Colestid have not been established for children.

Overdosage

Overdoses of Colestid have not been reported. If an overdose occurred, the most likely harmful effect would be obstruction of the stomach and/or intestines. If you suspect an overdose, seek medical help immediately.

Generic name:

COLESTIPOL HYDROCHLORIDE

See Colestid, page 227.

Generic name:

COLISTIN, NEOMYCIN, HYDROCORTISONE, AND THONZONIUM

See Coly-Mycin S Otic, page 231.

Brand name:

COLY-MYCIN S OTIC

Pronounced: KOH-lee-MY-sin ESS OH-tic
Generic ingredients: Colistin sulfate, Neomycin sulfate,
Hydrocortisone acetate, Thonzonium bromide

Why is this drug prescribed?

Coly-Mycin S Otic is a liquid solution used to treat ear infections. Colistin sulfate and neomycin sulfate are antibiotics used to treat the bacterial infection itself, while hydrocortisone acetate is a steroid that helps reduce the inflammation, swelling, itching, and other skin reactions associated with an ear infection; thonzonium bromide facilitates the drug's effects.

Most important fact about this drug

As with other antibiotics, long-term treatment may encourage other infections. Therefore, if your ear infection does not improve within a week, your physician may want to change your medication.

How should you use this medication?

Use Coly-Mycin S for the full course of treatment (but no more than 10 days) even if you start to feel better in a few days.

Shake well before using.

The external ear canal should be thoroughly cleaned and dried with a sterile cotton swab (applicator). The person should lie with the infected ear facing up. Pull the earlobe down and back (for children) or up and back (for adults) to straighten the ear canal. Drop the solution into the ear. The person should lie in this position for 5 minutes to help the drops penetrate into the ear. If necessary, this procedure should be repeated for the other ear. To keep the medicine from leaking out, you can gently insert a sterile cotton plug.

If you prefer, a sterile cotton wick or plug may be inserted into the ear canal and then soaked with the Coly-Mycin S Otic solution. This cotton wick should be moistened every 4 hours with more solution and replaced at least once every 24 hours.

Avoid touching the dropper to the ear or other surfaces.

- *If you miss a dose...*
  Apply it as soon as you remember. If it is almost time for your next dose, skip the one you missed and go back to your regular schedule.

■ *Storage instructions...*
Store at room temperature; avoid prolonged exposure to high temperatures.

What side effects may occur?
No specific side effects have been reported; however, neomycin (an ingredient in Coly-Mycin S Otic) may be associated with an increased risk of allergic skin reaction.

Why should this drug not be prescribed?
You should not take this drug if you have had an allergic reaction to any of the ingredients, or if you suffer from herpes simplex, vaccinia (cowpox), or varicella (chickenpox).

Special warnings about this medication
Treatment should not continue for more than 10 days.

If you warm Coly-Mycin S Otic before applying, do not heat the solution to above body temperature, since this will lessen its potency. Warm the drops by holding the bottle in your hand for a few minutes.

If an allergic reaction occurs, you should stop using Coly-Mycin S Otic immediately. Your doctor may also recommend that future treatment with kanamycin, paromomycin, streptomycin, and possibly gentamicin be avoided, since you may also be allergic to these medications.

Use Coly-Mycin S Otic with care if you have a perforated eardrum or chronic otitis media (inflammation of the middle ear).

Possible food and drug interactions
when using this medication
No interactions have been reported.

Special information
if you are pregnant or breastfeeding
The effects of Coly-Mycin S Otic during pregnancy have not been adequately studied. If you are pregnant or plan to become pregnant, inform your doctor immediately. Coly-Mycin S Otic may appear in breast milk and could affect a nursing infant. If this medication is essential to your health, your doctor may advise you to stop breastfeeding until your treatment is finished.

Recommended dosage
ADULTS

The usual dose is 5 drops (when using the supplied measured dropper) or 4 drops (when using the dropper-bottle container) in the affected ear, 3 or 4 times daily.

INFANTS AND CHILDREN

The usual dose is 4 drops (when using the supplied measured dropper) or 3 drops (when using the dropper-bottle container) in the affected ear 3 or 4 times daily.

Please see the "How should you use this medication?" section above for more information on applying Coly-Mycin S Otic.

Overdosage
Although no specific information is available, any medication taken in excess can have serious consequences. If you suspect an overdose of Coly-Mycin S Otic, seek medical treatment immediately.

Brand name:

COMPAZINE

Pronounced: KOMP-ah-zeen
Generic name: Prochlorperazine

Why is this drug prescribed?
Compazine is used to control severe nausea and vomiting. It is also used to treat symptoms of mental disorders such as schizophrenia, and is occasionally prescribed for anxiety.

Most important fact about this drug
Compazine may cause tardive dyskinesia—involuntary muscle spasms and twitches in the face and body. This condition may be permanent. It appears to be most common among the elderly, especially women. Ask your doctor for information about this possible risk.

How should you take this medication?
Never take more Compazine than prescribed. It can increase the risk of serious side effects.

If you are using the suppository form of Compazine and find it is too soft to insert, you can chill it in the refrigerator for about 30 minutes or run cold water over it before removing the wrapper.

To insert a suppository, first remove the wrapper and moisten the suppository with cold water. Then lie down on your side and use a finger to push the suppository well up into the rectum.

- *If you miss a dose...*
Take the forgotten dose as soon as you remember. If it is almost time for the next dose, skip the one you missed and go back to your regular schedule. Never try to "catch up" by doubling the dose.

- *Storage instructions...*
Store at room temperature. Protect from heat and light.

What side effects may occur?
Side effects cannot be anticipated. If any develop or change in intensity, inform your doctor as soon as possible. Only your doctor can determine if it is safe for you to continue taking Compazine.

- *Side effects may include:*
Abnormal muscle rigidity, abnormal secretion of milk, abnormal sugar in urine, abnormalities of posture and movement, agitation, anemia, appetite changes, asthma, blurred vision, breast development in males, chewing movements, constipation, convulsions, difficulty swallowing, discolored skin tone, dizziness, drooling, drowsiness, dry mouth, ejaculation problems, exaggerated reflexes, fever, fluid retention, head arched backward, headache, heart attack, heels bent back on legs, high or low blood sugar, hives, impotence, inability to urinate, increased psychotic symptoms, increased weight, infection, insomnia, intestinal obstruction, involuntary movements of arms, hands, legs, and feet, involuntary movements of face, tongue, and jaw, irregular movements, jerky movements, jitteriness, light sensitivity, low blood pressure, mask-like face, menstrual irregularities, narrowed or dilated pupils, nasal congestion, nausea, pain in the shoulder and neck area, painful muscle spasm, parkinsonism-like symptoms, persistent, painful erections, pill-rolling motion, protruding tongue, puckering of the mouth, puffing of the cheeks, rigid arms, feet, head, and muscles, rotation of eyeballs or state of fixed gaze, shock, shuffling gait, skin peeling, rash and inflammation, sore throat, mouth, and gums, spasms in back, feet and ankles, jaw, and neck, swelling and itching skin, swelling in throat, tremors, yellowed eyes and skin

Why should this drug not be prescribed?
Do not take Compazine if you are sensitive to or have ever had an allergic reaction to prochlorperazine or other phenothiazine drugs such as Thorazine, Prolixin, Triavil, Mellaril, or Stelazine.

Special warnings about this medication
Never take large amounts of alcohol, barbiturates, or narcotics when taking Compazine. Serious problems can result.

If you suddenly stop taking Compazine, you may experience a change in appetite, dizziness, nausea, vomiting, and tremors. Follow your doctor's instructions closely when discontinuing this drug.

Make sure the doctor knows if you are being treated for a brain tumor, intestinal blockage, heart disease, glaucoma, or an abnormal blood condition such as leukemia, or if you are exposed to extreme heat or pesticides.

This drug may impair your ability to drive a car or operate potentially dangerous machinery. Do not participate in any activities that require full alertness if you are unsure about your ability.

While taking Compazine, try to stay out of the sun. Use sun block and wear protective clothing. Your eyes may become more sensitive to sunlight, too, so keep sunglasses handy.

Compazine interferes with your ability to shed extra heat. Be cautious in hot weather.

Compazine may cause false-positive pregnancy tests.

Possible food and drug interactions
when taking this medication
If Compazine is taken with certain other drugs, the effects of either could be increased, decreased, or altered. It is especially important to check with your doctor before combining Compazine with the following:

Anticonvulsants such as Dilantin and Tegretol
Anticoagulants such as Coumadin
Guanethidine (Ismelin)
Lithium (Lithobid, Eskalith)
Narcotic pain killers such as Demerol and Tylenol with Codeine
Other central nervous system depressants such as Xanax, Valium, Seconal, Halcion
Propranolol (Inderal)
Thiazide diuretics such as Dyazide

Special information
if you are pregnant or breastfeeding
Compazine is not usually recommended for pregnant women. However, your doctor may prescribe it for severe nausea and vomiting if the potential benefits of the drug outweigh the potential risks. Compazine appears in breast milk and may affect a nursing infant. If this drug is essential to your health, your doctor may recommend that you stop breastfeeding until your treatment is finished.

Recommended dosage

ADULTS

To Control Severe Nausea and Vomiting
Tablets: The usual dosage is one 5-milligram or 10-milligram tablet 3 or 4 times a day.

"Spansule" Capsules: The usual starting dose is one 15-milligram capsule on getting out of bed or one 10-milligram capsule every 12 hours.

The usual rectal dosage (suppository) is 25 milligrams taken 2 times a day.

For Non-psychotic Anxiety
Tablets: The usual dose is 5 milligrams taken 3 or 4 times a day.

"Spansule" capsule: The usual starting dose is one 15-milligram capsule on getting up or one 10-milligram capsule every 12 hours.

Treatment should not continue for longer than 12 weeks, and daily doses should not exceed 20 milligrams.

Relatively Mild Psychotic Disorders
The usual dose is 5 or 10 milligrams taken 3 or 4 times daily.

Moderate to Severe Psychotic Disorders
Dosages usually start at 10 milligrams taken 3 or 4 times a day. If needed, dosage may be gradually increased; 50 to 75 milligrams daily has been helpful for some people.

More Severe Psychotic Disorders
Dosages may range from 100 to 150 milligrams per day.

CHILDREN

Children under 2 years of age or weighing less than 20 pounds should not be given Compazine. If a child becomes restless or excited after taking Compazine, do not give the child another dose.

For Severe Nausea and Vomiting
An oral or rectal dose of Compazine is usually not needed for more than 1 day.

Children 20 to 29 Pounds
The usual dose is 2½ milligrams 1 or 2 times daily. Total daily amount should not exceed 7.5 milligrams.

Children 30 to 39 Pounds
The usual dose is 2½ milligrams 2 or 3 times daily. Total daily amount should not exceed 10 milligrams.

Children 40 to 85 Pounds
The usual dose is 2½ milligrams 3 times daily, or 5 milligrams 2 times daily.

Total daily amount should not exceed 15 milligrams.

For Psychotic Disorders

Children 2 to 5 Years Old
The starting oral or rectal dose is 2½ milligrams 2 or 3 times daily. Do not exceed 10 milligrams the first day or 20 milligrams thereafter.

Children 6 to 12 Years Old
The starting oral or rectal dose is 2½ milligrams 2 or 3 times daily. Do not exceed 10 milligrams the first day or 25 milligrams thereafter.

ELDERLY

In general, elderly people take lower dosages of Compazine. Because they may develop low blood pressure while taking the drug, the doctor should monitor them closely. Elderly people (especially elderly women) may be more susceptible to tardive dyskinesia—a possibly permanent condition. Tardive dyskinesia causes involuntary muscle spasms and twitches in the face and body. Consult your doctor for more information about these potential risks.

Overdosage
An overdose of Compazine can be fatal. If you suspect an overdose, seek medical help immediately.

- *Symptoms of Compazine overdose may include:*
  Agitation
  Coma
  Convulsions
  Dry mouth
  Extreme sleepiness
  Fever
  Intestinal blockage
  Irregular heart rate
  Restlessness

Generic name:

CONJUGATED ESTROGENS

See Premarin, page 883.

Brand name:

CORGARD

Pronounced: CORE-guard
Generic name: Nadolol

Why is this drug prescribed?

Corgard is used in the treatment of angina pectoris (chest pain, usually caused by lack of oxygen to the heart due to clogged arteries) and to reduce high blood pressure.

When prescribed for high blood pressure, it is effective when used alone or in combination with other high blood pressure medications. Corgard is a type of drug known as a beta blocker. It decreases the force and rate of heart contractions, reducing the heart's demand for oxygen and lowering blood pressure.

Most important fact about this drug

If you have high blood pressure, you must take Corgard regularly for it to be effective. Since blood pressure declines gradually, it may be several weeks before you get the full benefit of Corgard; and you must continue taking it even if you are feeling well. Corgard does not cure high blood pressure; it merely keeps it under control.

How should you take this medication?

Corgard can be taken with or without food. Take it exactly as prescribed even if your symptoms have disappeared.

Try not to miss any doses. Corgard is taken once a day. If it is not taken regularly, your condition may worsen.

■ *If you miss a dose...*
   Take it as soon as you remember. If it is within 8 hours of your next scheduled dose, skip the one you missed and go back to your regular schedule. Never take 2 doses at the same time.

■ *Storage instructions...*
Store at room temperature, away from light and heat, in a tightly closed container.

What side effects may occur?
Side effects cannot be anticipated. If any develop or change in intensity, inform your doctor as soon as possible. Only your doctor can determine if it is safe for you to continue taking Corgard.

■ *More common side effects may include:*
Change in behavior
Changes in heartbeat
Dizziness or light-headedness
Mild drowsiness
Slow heartbeat
Weakness or tiredness

■ *Less common or rare side effects may include:*
Abdominal discomfort, asthma-like symptoms, bloating, confusion, constipation, cough, decreased sex drive, diarrhea, dry eyes, dry mouth, dry skin, facial swelling, gas, headache, heart failure, impotence, indigestion, itching, loss of appetite, low blood pressure, nasal stuffiness, nausea, rash, ringing in ears, slurred speech, vision changes, vomiting, weight gain

Why should this drug not be prescribed?
If you have a slow heartbeat, bronchial asthma, certain types of heartbeat irregularity, cardiogenic shock (shock due to inadequate blood supply from the heart), or active heart failure, you should not take this medication.

Special warnings about this medication
If you have a history of congestive heart failure, your doctor will prescribe Corgard with caution.

Corgard should not be stopped suddenly. This can cause increased chest pain and even a heart attack. Dosage should be gradually reduced.

If you suffer from asthma, chronic bronchitis, emphysema, seasonal allergies or other bronchial conditions, or kidney or liver disease, this medication should be used with caution.

Ask your doctor if you should check your pulse while taking Corgard. It can cause your heartbeat to become too slow.

This medication may mask the symptoms of low blood sugar or alter blood sugar levels. If you are diabetic, discuss this with your doctor.

This medication may cause you to become drowsy or less alert; therefore, driving or operating dangerous machinery or participating in any hazardous activity that requires full mental alertness is not recommended until you know how you respond to this medication.

Notify your doctor or dentist that you are taking Corgard if you have a medical emergency or before you have surgery or dental treatment.

Possible food and drug interactions
when taking this medication

If Corgard is taken with certain other drugs, the effects of either could be increased, decreased, or altered. It is especially important to check with your doctor before combining Corgard with the following:

Antidiabetic drugs, including insulin and oral drugs such as Micronase
Certain blood pressure drugs such as Diupres and Ser-Ap-Es
Epinephrine (EpiPen)

Special information
if you are pregnant or breastfeeding

The effects of Corgard during pregnancy have not been adequately studied. If you are pregnant or plan to become pregnant, inform your doctor immediately. Corgard appears in breast milk and could affect a nursing infant. If this medication is essential to your health, your doctor may advise you to discontinue breastfeeding until your treatment with this medication is finished.

Recommended dosage

ADULTS

Dosage is tailored to each individual's needs.

Angina Pectoris

The usual starting dose is 40 milligrams once daily. The usual long-term dose is 40 or 80 milligrams, once a day. Doses up to 160 or 240 milligrams, once a day, may be needed.

High Blood Pressure

The usual starting dose is 40 milligrams once daily.

The usual long-term dose is 40 or 80 milligrams, once a day. Doses up to 240 or 320 milligrams, once a day, may be needed.

CHILDREN

The safety and effectiveness of Corgard have not been established in children.

ELDERLY

The doctor will determine the dosage according to the particular needs of the elderly person.

Overdosage

Any medication taken in excess can have serious consequences. If you suspect an overdose, seek medical attention immediately.

■ *The symptoms of Corgard overdose may include:*
Difficulty in breathing
Heart failure
Low blood pressure
Slow heartbeat

Brand name:

CORTISPORIN OPHTHALMIC SUSPENSION

Pronounced: KORE-ti-SPORE-in off-THAL-mick suss-PEN-shun
Generic ingredients: Polymyxin B sulfate, Neomycin sulfate, Hydrocortisone
Other brand name: Bacticort

Why is this drug prescribed?

Cortisporin Ophthalmic Suspension is a combination of the steroid drug hydrocortisone and two antibiotics. It is prescribed to relieve inflammatory conditions such as irritation, swelling, redness, and general eye discomfort, and to treat superficial bacterial infections of the eye.

Most important fact about this drug

Prolonged use of this medication may increase pressure within the eye, leading to potential damage to the optic nerve and visual problems. Prolonged use also may suppress your immune response and thus increase the hazard of secondary eye infections. Your doctor should measure your eye pressure periodically if you are using this product for 10 days or longer.

How should you use this medication?
To help clear up your infection completely, use this medication exactly as prescribed for the full time of treatment, even if your symptoms have disappeared.

Administer the eyedrops as follows:

1. Shake the dropper bottle well.
2. Wash your hands thoroughly.
3. Gently pull your lower eyelid down to form a pocket between your eye and eyelid.
4. Hold the bottle on the bridge of your nose or on your forehead.
5. Tilt your head back and squeeze the medication into your eye.
6. Do not touch the applicator tip to any surface, including your eye.
7. Close your eyes gently, and keep them closed for 1 to 2 minutes.
8. Do not rinse the dropper.
9. Wait 5 to 10 minutes before using any other eyedrops.

If you do not improve after 2 days, your doctor should re-evaluate your case.

Do not share this medication with anyone else; you may spread the infection.

■ *If you miss a dose...*
Apply it as soon as you remember. If it is almost time for your next dose, skip the one you missed and go back to your regular schedule.

■ *Storage instructions...*
Store at room temperature. Keep tightly closed and protect from freezing.

What side effects may occur?
Side effects cannot be anticipated. If any develop or change in intensity, inform your doctor as soon as possible. Only your doctor can determine if it is safe for you to continue using Cortisporin.

■ *Side effects may include:*
Cataract formation (results in blurred vision)
Delayed wound healing
Increased eye pressure with possible development of glaucoma and, infrequently, optic nerve damage
Irritation when drops are instilled
Local allergic reactions (itching, swelling, redness)
Other infections—particularly fungal infections of the cornea and bacterial eye infection
Severe allergic reactions

Why should this drug not be prescribed?

Cortisporin should not be used if you have certain viral or fungal diseases of the eye, including inflammation of the cornea caused by herpes simplex, chickenpox, or cowpox, or if you are sensitive to or have ever had an allergic reaction to any of its ingredients.

Special warnings about this medication

Remember that steroids such as hydrocortisone may hide the existence of an infection or worsen an existing one.

If you are using this medication for more than 10 days, your doctor should routinely check your eye pressure. If you already have high pressure within the eye (glaucoma), use this medication cautiously.

Neomycin, one of the ingredients in Cortisporin, may cause an allergic reaction—usually itching, redness, and swelling—or failure to heal. If you develop any of these signs, stop using Cortisporin; the symptoms should quickly subside. If the condition persists or gets worse, or if a rash or allergic reaction develops, call your doctor immediately. You are more likely to be sensitive to neomycin if you are sensitive to the following antibiotics: kanamycin, paromomycin, streptomycin, and possibly gentamicin.

The use of steroids in the eye can prolong and worsen many viral infections of the eye, including herpes simplex. Use this medication with extreme caution if you have this infection.

If you develop a sensitivity to Cortisporin, avoid other topical medications that contain neomycin.

Eye products that are not handled properly can become contaminated with bacteria that cause eye infections. If you use a contaminated product, you can seriously damage your eyes, even to the point of blindness.

Possible food and drug interactions
when taking this medication

No interactions have been reported.

Special information
if you are pregnant or breastfeeding

Although the effects of Cortisporin during pregnancy have not been adequately studied, steroids should be used during pregnancy only if the benefits outweigh the dangers to the fetus. If you are pregnant or plan to become pregnant, inform your doctor immediately. Hydrocortisone, when taken orally, appears in breast milk. Since medication may be absorbed into the bloodstream when it is applied to the eye, your doctor may advise you to stop breastfeeding until your treatment with Cortisporin is finished.

Recommended dosage

ADULTS

The usual recommended dose is 1 or 2 drops in the affected eye every 3 or 4 hours, depending on the severity of the condition. Cortisporin may be used more often if necessary.

Overdosage

Any medication used in excess can have serious consequences. If you suspect an overdose of Cortisporin Ophthalmic Suspension, seek medical treatment immediately.

Brand name:

CORZIDE

Pronounced: CORE-zide
Generic ingredients: Nadolol, Bendroflumethiazide

Why is this drug prescribed?

Corzide is a combination drug used in the treatment of high blood pressure. It combines a beta blocker and a thiazide diuretic. Nadolol, the beta blocker, decreases the force and rate of heart contractions thereby reducing blood pressure. Bendroflumethiazide, the diuretic, helps your body produce and eliminate more urine, which also helps in lowering blood pressure.

Most important fact about this drug

You must take Corzide regularly for it to be effective. Since blood pressure declines gradually, it may be several weeks before you get the full benefit of Corzide; and you must continue taking it even if you are feeling well. Corzide does not cure high blood pressure; it merely keeps it under control.

How should you take this medication?

Corzide may be taken with or without food. Take it exactly as prescribed, even if your symptoms have disappeared.

Try not to miss any doses. Corzide is taken once a day. If this medication is not taken regularly, your condition may worsen.

- ■ *If you miss a dose...*
  Take it as soon as you remember. If it's within 8 hours of your next scheduled dose, skip the one you missed and go back to your regular schedule. Never take 2 doses at the same time.

■ *Storage instructions...*
Store at room temperature, away from heat, in a tightly closed container.

What side effects may occur?
Side effects cannot be anticipated. If any develop or change in intensity, inform your doctor as soon as possible. Only your doctor can determine if it is safe for you to continue taking Corzide.

■ *More common side effects may include:*
Asthma-like symptoms
Changes in heart rhythm
Cold hands and feet
Dizziness
Fatigue
Low blood pressure
Low potassium levels (symptoms include dry mouth, excessive thirst, weak or irregular heartbeat, muscle pain or cramps)
Slow heartbeat

■ *Less common or rare side effects may include:*
Abdominal discomfort, anemia, bloating, blurred vision, certain types of irregular heartbeat, change in behavior, constipation, cough, diarrhea, dry mouth, eyes, or skin, facial swelling, gas, headache, heart failure, hepatitis, impotence, indigestion, inflammation of the pancreas, itching, loss of appetite, lowered sex drive, muscle spasm, nasal stuffiness, nausea, rash, ringing in ears, sedation, sensitivity to light, slurred speech, sweating, tingling or pins and needles, vertigo, vomiting, weakness, weight gain, wheezing, yellowed eyes and skin

Why should this drug not be prescribed?
If you have bronchial asthma, slow heartbeat, certain heartbeat irregularities (heart block), inadequate blood supply to the circulatory system (cardiogenic shock), active congestive heart failure, inability to urinate, or if you are sensitive to or have ever had an allergic reaction to Corzide, its ingredients, or similar drugs, you should not take this medication.

Special warnings about this medication
If you have a history of congestive heart failure, your doctor will prescribe Corzide with caution.

Corzide should not be stopped suddenly. This can cause increased chest pain and even a heart attack. Dosage should be gradually reduced.

If you suffer from asthma, seasonal allergies, emphysema or other bronchial conditions, or kidney or liver disease, this medication should be used with caution.

Ask your doctor if you should check your pulse while taking Corzide. It can cause your heartbeat to become too slow.

Corzide may mask the symptoms of low blood sugar or alter blood sugar levels. If you are diabetic, discuss this with your doctor.

This medication can cause you to become drowsy or less alert; therefore, activity that requires full mental alertness is not recommended until you know how you respond to this medication.

Notify your doctor or dentist that you are taking Corzide if you have a medical emergency, or before you have surgery or dental treatment.

Possible food and drug interactions
when taking this medication

Corzide may intensify the effects of alcohol. Do not drink alcohol while taking this medication.

If Corzide is taken with any other drug, the effects of either could be increased, decreased, or altered. It is especially important to check with your doctor before combining Corzide with the following:

Amphotericin B
Antidepressant drugs known as MAO inhibitors, such as Nardil and
   Parnate
Antidiabetic drugs, including insulin and oral drugs such as Micronase
Antigout drugs such as Benemid
Barbiturates such as phenobarbital
Blood thinners such as Coumadin
Calcium salt
Certain blood pressure drugs such as Diupres and Ser-Ap-Es
Cholestyramine (Questran)
Colestipol (Colestid)
Diazoxide (Proglycem)
Digitalis medications such as Lanoxin
Lithium (Lithonate)
Methenamine (Mandelamine)
Narcotics such as Percocet
Nonsteroidal anti-inflammatory drugs, such as Motrin, Naprosyn, and
   Nuprin
Other antihypertensives such as Vasotec
Steroid medications such as prednisone
Sulfinpyrazone (Anturane)

Special information
if you are pregnant or breastfeeding

The effects of Corzide during pregnancy have not been adequately studied. If you are pregnant or plan to become pregnant, inform your doctor immediately. Corzide appears in breast milk and could affect a nursing infant. If this medication is essential to your health, your doctor may advise you to discontinue breastfeeding until your treatment with Corzide is finished.

Recommended dosage

ADULTS

Dosages of this drug are always tailored to the individual's needs.

The usual dose is 1 Corzide 40/5 milligram tablet per day or, if necessary, 1 Corzide 80/5 milligram tablet per day. Your doctor may gradually add another high blood pressure medication to this drug.

CHILDREN

The safety and effectiveness of Corzide have not been established in children.

ELDERLY

Your doctor will determine the dosage according to your particular needs.

Overdosage

Any medication taken in excess can have serious consequences. If you suspect an overdose, seek medical attention immediately.

- *The symptoms of Corzide overdose may include:*
  Abdominal irritation
  Central nervous system depression
  Coma
  Extremely slow heartbeat
  Heart failure
  Lethargy
  Low blood pressure
  Wheezing

Brand name:

COTRIM

See Bactrim, page 104.

Brand name:

CO-TRIMOXAZOLE

See Bactrim, page 104.

Brand name:

COUMADIN

Pronounced: COO-muh-din
Generic name: Warfarin sodium

Why is this drug prescribed?
Coumadin is an anticoagulant (blood thinner). It is prescribed to:

Prevent and/or treat a blood clot that has formed within a blood vessel or in the lungs;

Prevent and/or treat blood clots associated with certain heart conditions or replacement of a heart valve;

Aid in the prevention of blood clots that may form in blood vessels anywhere in the body after a heart attack.

Some doctors prescribe Coumadin to prevent heart attack or the symptoms that precede a stroke.

Most important fact about this drug
The most serious risks associated with Coumadin treatment are hemorrhage (severe bleeding resulting in the loss of a large amount of blood) in any tissue or organ and, less frequently, the destruction of skin tissue cells (necrosis) or gangrene. The risk of hemorrhage usually depends on the dosage and length of treatment with this drug.

Hemorrhage and necrosis have been reported to result in death or permanent disability. Severe necrosis can lead to the removal of damaged tissue or amputation of a limb. Necrosis appears to be associated with blood clots located in the area of tissue damage and usually occurs within a few days of starting Coumadin treatment.

How should you take this medication?
The objective of treatment with a blood-thinner is to control the blood-clotting process without causing severe bleeding, so that a clot does not form and cut off the blood supply necessary for normal body function. Therefore, it is very important that you take this medication exactly as prescribed by your doctor and that your doctor monitor your condition on a

regular basis. Be especially careful to stick to the exact dosage schedule your doctor prescribes.

Effective treatment with minimal complications depends on your cooperation and communication with the doctor.

Do not take or discontinue any other medication unless directed to do so by your doctor. Avoid alcohol, salicylates such as aspirin, larger than usual amounts of foods rich in vitamin K (including asparagus, bacon, beef liver, cabbage, cauliflower, fish, and green leafy vegetables), or any other drastic change in diet.

Note that Coumadin often turns urine reddish-orange.

You should carry an identification card that indicates you are taking Coumadin.

Do not change from one brand of this drug to another without consulting your doctor or pharmacist.

■ *If you miss a dose...*
Take the forgotten dose as soon as you remember, then go back to your regular schedule. If you do not remember until the next day, skip the dose. Never try to "catch up" by doubling the dose. Keep a record for your doctor of any doses you miss.

■ *Storage instructions...*
Coumadin can be stored at room temperature. Close the container tightly and protect from light.

What side effects may occur?
Side effects cannot be anticipated. If any develop or change in intensity, inform your doctor as soon as possible. Only your doctor can determine if it is safe for you to continue taking Coumadin.

■ *More common side effects may include:*
Hemorrhage: Signs of severe bleeding resulting in the loss of large amounts of blood depend upon the location and extent of bleeding. Symptoms include: Chest, abdomen, joint, or other pain, difficult breathing or swallowing, headache, paralysis, shortness of breath, unexplained shock, unexplained swelling

■ *Less common side effects may include:*
Abdominal cramping, allergic reactions, diarrhea, fever, hives, liver damage, loss of hair, nausea, necrosis (gangrene), purple toes, severe or long-lasting inflammation of the skin

Why should this drug not be prescribed?

This drug should not be prescribed for any condition where the danger of hemorrhage may be greater than the potential benefits of treatment. Unless directed to do so by your doctor, do not take this medication if one of the following conditions or situations applies to you:

A tendency to hemorrhage

Alcoholism

An abnormal blood condition

Aneurysm (balloon-like swelling of a blood vessel) in the brain or heart

Bleeding tendencies associated with ulceration or bleeding of the stomach, intestines, respiratory tract, or the genital or urinary system

Eclampsia (a rare and serious pregnancy disorder producing life-threatening convulsions)

Excessive bleeding of brain blood vessels

Inflammation, due to bacterial infection, of the membrane that lines the inside of the heart

Inflammation of the sac that surrounds the heart or an escape of fluid from the heart sac

Malignant hypertension (extremely elevated blood pressure that damages the inner linings of blood vessels, the heart, spleen, kidneys, and brain)

Pregnancy

Recent or contemplated surgery

Special warnings about this medication

Treatment with blood thinners may increase the risk that fatty plaque will break away from the wall of an artery and lodge at another point, causing the blockage of a blood vessel. If you notice any of the following symptoms, contact your doctor immediately:

Abdominal pain; abrupt and intense pain in the leg, foot, or toes; bluish mottling of the skin of the legs and hands; foot ulcers; gangrene; high blood pressure; muscle pain; rash; or thigh or back pain.

There is an increased risk of developing blood clots if you have one of the following conditions:

An infectious disease or intestinal disorder

A history of recurrent blood clot disorders in you or your family

Dental procedures

Inflammation of a blood vessel

Moderate to severe high blood pressure

Moderate to severe kidney or liver dysfunction

Polycythemia vera (blood disorder)

Severe allergic disorders
Severe diabetes
Any trauma or injury that may result in internal bleeding

Purple toes syndrome can occur when taking Coumadin, usually 3 to 10 weeks after the start of anticoagulation therapy. Symptoms include dark purplish or mottled color of the toes that turns white when pressure is applied and fades when you elevate your legs, pain and tenderness of the toes, and change in intensity of the color over a period of time. If any of these symptoms develop, notify your doctor immediately.

If you are taking Coumadin, your doctor should periodically check the time it takes for your blood to start the clotting process (prothrombin time). Numerous factors such as travel and changes in diet, environment, physical state, and medication may alter your response to treatment with an anticoagulant. Clotting time should also be monitored after your release from the hospital and whenever other medications are started, discontinued, or taken haphazardly.

Notify your doctor if any illness, such as diarrhea, infection, or fever develops; if any unusual symptoms, such as pain, swelling, or discomfort, appear; or if you see prolonged bleeding from cuts, increased menstrual flow, vaginal bleeding, nosebleeds, bleeding of gums from brushing, unusual bleeding or bruising, red or dark brown urine, or red or tarry black stool.

Possible food and drug interactions when taking this medication

Avoid taking aspirin and other nonsteroidal anti-inflammatory drugs such as Advil and Motrin. They can increase the effect of Coumadin. Do not eat large amounts of leafy green vegetables. They contain vitamin K and can counteract the effect of Coumadin.

Make sure the doctor knows you are taking Coumadin before administering clot-dissolving drugs such as streptokinase (Streptase), urokinase (Abbokinase), and anistreplase (Eminase).

A great many medications can change the effects of Coumadin, so be sure to tell your doctor every drug you're taking. The following drugs may increase the time it takes for your blood to begin the clotting process when taken alone or in combination with Coumadin:

Acetaminophen (Tylenol)
Alcohol
Allopurinol (Zyloprim)
Aminosalicylic acid
Amiodarone hydrochloride (Cordarone)

Anabolic steroids such as Anadrol-50
Antibiotics such as Keflex
Aspirin
Bromelains
Chenodiol (Chenix)
Chloral hydrate (Noctec)
Chlorpropamide (Diabinese)
Chymotrypsin (Catarase)
Cimetidine (Tagamet)
Clofibrate (Atromid-S)
Dextrothyroxine (Choloxin)
Diazoxide (Proglycem)
Diflunisal (Dolobid)
Disulfiram (Antabuse)
Diuretics such as Hydromox
Ethacrynic acid (Edecrin)
Fenoprofen (Nalfon)
Glucagon (used to treat low blood sugar)
Ibuprofen (Motrin)
Indomethacin (Indocin)
Influenza virus vaccine (Flu-Imune)
Lovastatin (Mevacor)
Mefenamic acid (Ponstel)
Methyldopa (Aldomet)
Methylphenidate (Ritalin)
Metronidazole (Flagyl)
Miconazole (Monistat)
MAO inhibitors (such as Nardil, Marplan, and Parnate)
Moricizine hydrochloride (Ethmozine)
Nalidixic acid (NegGram)
Naproxen (Naprosyn)
Narcotics such as Percocet and Demerol
Pentoxifylline (Trental)
Phenobarbital
Phenytoin (Dilantin)
Propafenone (Rythmol)
Quinidine (Quinidex)
Quinine (Quinamm)
Ranitidine (Zantac)
Sulfa drugs such as Bactrim, Gantrisin, and Septra
Sulfinpyrazone (Anturane)
Sulindac (Clinoril)

Tamoxifen (Nolvadex)
Thyroid drugs (Synthroid)
Tolbutamide (Orinase)

The following drugs may decrease the time it takes for your blood to begin the clotting process if taken alone or in combination with Coumadin:

Adrenocortical steroids such as prednisone
Alcohol
Aminoglutethimide (Cytadren)
Antacids such as Maalox
Antihistamines such as Benadryl
Barbiturates such as phenobarbital
Carbamazepine (Tegretol)
Chloral hydrate (Noctec)
Chlordiazepoxide (Librium)
Cholestyramine (Questran)
Diuretics such as Hydromox
Ethchlorvynol (Placidyl)
Glutethimide (Doriden)
Griseofulvin (Gris-PEG)
Haloperidol (Haldol)
Meprobamate (Miltown)
Moricizine hydrochloride (Ethmozine)
Nafcillin (Unipen)
Oral contraceptives
Paraldehyde
Primidone (Mysoline)
Ranitidine (Zantac)
Rifampin (Rifadin)
Sucralfate (Carafate)
Trazodone (Desyrel)
Vitamin C

Special information
if you are pregnant or breastfeeding

Coumadin should not be taken by women who are or may become pregnant since the drug may cause fatal hemorrhage in the developing baby. There have also been reports of birth malformations in children born to mothers who have been treated with Coumadin during pregnancy. Spontaneous abortions and stillbirths are also known to occur. If you become pregnant while taking this drug, inform your doctor immediately. Coumadin may appear in breast milk and could affect a nursing infant. If this medication is essential to your health, your doctor may advise you to stop nursing your baby until your treatment with this drug is finished.

Recommended dosage

ADULTS

The administration and dosage of Coumadin must be individualized by your doctor according to your sensitivity to the drug.

A common starting dosage for adults is 2 to 5 milligrams per day. Individualized daily dosage adjustments are based on the results of tests that determine the amount of time it takes for the blood clotting process to begin.

A maintenance dose of 2 to 10 milligrams per day is satisfactory for most people. The duration of treatment will be determined by your physician.

CHILDREN

Safety and effectiveness have not been established in children below the age of 18.

Overdosage

Signs and symptoms of Coumadin overdose reflect abnormal bleeding. They include:

Blood in stools or urine
Excessive menstrual bleeding
Black stools
Reddish or purplish spots on skin
Excessive bruising
Persistent bleeding from superficial injuries

If you suspect an overdose, seek emergency medical treatment immediately.

Generic name:

CROMOLYN

See Intal, page 533.

Generic name:

CYCLOBENZAPRINE

See Flexeril, page 448.

Brand name:

CYCLOCORT

Pronounced: SIKE-low-court
Generic name: Amcinonide

Why is this drug prescribed?
Cyclocort is prescribed for the relief of the inflammatory and itchy symptoms of skin disorders that are responsive to corticosteroid treatment.

Most important fact about this drug
When you use Cyclocort, you inevitably absorb some of the medication through your skin and into the bloodstream. Too much absorption can lead to unwanted side effects elsewhere in the body. To keep this problem to a minimum, avoid using large amounts of Cyclocort over large areas, and do not cover it with airtight dressings such as plastic wrap or adhesive bandages unless specifically told to by your doctor.

How should you use this medication?
Use this medication exactly as prescribed by your doctor. It is for use only on the skin. Be careful to keep it out of your eyes.

Apply Cyclocort sparingly. Rub it in gently.

- *If you miss a dose...*
  Apply the forgotten dose as soon as you remember. Use the remaining doses for that day at evenly spaced intervals. Never try to "catch up" by doubling the amount applied.

- *Storage instructions...*
  Cyclocort can be stored at room temperature. Protect from freezing.

What side effects may occur?
Side effects cannot be anticipated. If any develop or change in intensity, inform your doctor as soon as possible. Only your doctor can determine if it is safe for you to continue taking Cyclocort.

- *More common side effects may include:*
  Burning
  Itching
  Soreness
  Stinging

■ *Less common or rare side effects may include:*
Dryness, excessive growth of hair, infection, inflammation of hair follicles, inflammation of the skin around the mouth, irritation, prickly heat, skin eruptions resembling acne, softening of the skin, stretch marks

Why should this drug not be prescribed?
If you are sensitive to or have ever had an allergic reaction to amcinonide or other steroid medications, you should not use Cyclocort. Make sure your doctor is aware of any drug reactions you have experienced.

Special warnings about this medication
Do not use this drug for any disorder other than the one for which it was prescribed.

The use of tight-fitting diapers or plastic pants is not recommended for a child being treated in the diaper area. These garments may act as airtight dressings or bandages.

The treated skin area should not be bandaged, covered, or wrapped unless you have been directed to do so by your doctor.

If an irritation or allergic reaction develops while you are using Cyclocort, notify your doctor.

Possible food and drug interactions
when taking this medication
No interactions with food or other drugs have been reported.

Special information
if you are pregnant or breastfeeding
The effects of Cyclocort during pregnancy have not been adequately studied. If you are pregnant or plan to become pregnant, inform your doctor immediately. It is not known whether this medication appears in breast milk. If this drug is essential to your health, your doctor may advise you to discontinue breastfeeding until your treatment is finished.

Recommended dosage

ADULTS

Apply a thin film of Cyclocort to the affected area 2 or 3 times a day, depending on the severity of the condition.

Cyclocort lotion may be applied to the affected areas, particularly hairy areas, 2 times per day. The lotion should be rubbed in completely, and the area should not be washed and should be protected from clothing until the lotion has dried.

Your doctor may recommend airtight bandages or dressings if you are being treated for psoriasis (a skin disorder characterized by patches of red, dry, scale-covered skin) or other stubborn skin conditions. If an infection develops, stop bandaging the area.

CHILDREN

Topical use of Cyclocort on children should be limited to the smallest amount that is effective. Long-term treatment may interfere with children's growth and development.

Overdosage

A severe overdosage is unlikely with the use of Cyclocort; however, long-term or prolonged use can produce side effects throughout the body (see "Most important fact about this drug").

Generic name:

CYCLOPHOSPHAMIDE

See Cytoxan, page 263.

Generic name:

CYCLOSPORINE

See Sandimmune, page 998.

Brand name:

CYCRIN

See Provera, page 916.

Brand name:

CYLERT

Pronounced: SIGH-lert
Generic name: Pemoline

Why is this drug prescribed?

Cylert is used to help treat children who have attention deficit disorder with hyperactivity. However, this condition does not always require drug treatment. Drugs such as Cylert should be taken as part of a comprehensive treatment plan offering psychological and educational support to help the child become more stable.

Children who have attention deficit disorder with hyperactivity may show signs of:

Emotional mood swings
Hyperactivity
Impulsive actions
Moderate to severe distractibility
Short attention span

Most important fact about this drug
Because long-term use of drugs such as Cylert may affect a child's growth, your doctor will monitor your child carefully if he or she is taking this drug for an extended period.

How should you take this medication?
Cylert should be taken once a day, in the morning.

■ *If you miss a dose...*
Have your child take it as soon as you remember, then go back to the regular schedule. If you do not remember it until the next day, skip the missed dose and go back to the regular schedule. Do not give 2 doses at once.

■ *Storage instructions...*
Store at room temperature.

What side effects may occur?
Side effects cannot be anticipated. If any develop or change in intensity, inform your doctor as soon as possible. Only your doctor can determine if it is safe for your child to continue taking Cylert.

■ *More common side effects may include:*
Insomnia

■ *Less common side effects may include:*
Dizziness, drowsiness, hallucinations, headache, hepatitis and other liver problems, increased irritability, involuntary fragmented movements of the face, eyes, lips, tongue, arms, and legs, loss of appetite, mild depression, nausea, seizures, skin rash, stomachache, suppressed growth (in children), uncontrolled vocal outbursts (such as grunts, shouts, and obscene language), weight loss, yellowing of skin or eyes

■ *Rare side effects may include:*
   A rare form of anemia with symptoms such as bleeding gums, bruising, chest pain, fatigue, headache, nosebleeds, and abnormal paleness

Why should this drug not be prescribed?
Your child should not be using Cylert if he or she is allergic to it or if he or she has liver problems.

Special warnings about this medication
Cylert may cause dizziness. Warn your child to be careful climbing stairs or participating in activities that require mental alertness.

Although there have been no reports that Cylert is physically addictive, it is chemically similar to a class of drugs that are potentially addictive. Therefore, anyone who has a history of drug or alcohol abuse should use Cylert cautiously.

Remember that children who take this drug on a long-term basis should be carefully monitored for signs of stunted growth.

Use Cylert cautiously if your child has kidney problems.

Psychotic children who take Cylert may experience increasingly disordered thoughts and behavioral disturbances.

Possible food and drug interactions
when taking this medication
If Cylert is taken with certain other drugs, the effects of either could be increased, decreased, or altered. It is especially important to check with your doctor before combining Cylert with the following:

   Antiepileptic medications such as Tegretol
   Other drugs that affect the central nervous system (brain and spinal cord) such as Ritalin

Special information
if you are pregnant or breastfeeding
The effects of Cylert in pregnancy have not been adequately studied. Pregnant women should use Cylert only if it is clearly necessary. Women who breastfeed should use this drug cautiously because it might appear in breast milk and affect the baby.

Recommended dosage
The recommended beginning dose is 37.5 milligrams daily. Dosages may be gradually increased if needed. Most children take doses ranging from 56.25 to 75 milligrams a day. The maximum recommended daily dose of Cylert is

112.5 milligrams. Significant improvement is gradual and may not be apparent until the third or fourth week of treatment with Cylert.

Your doctor may occasionally stop treatment with Cylert to see whether behavioral problems return and whether further treatment with Cylert is necessary.

Overdosage

Any medication taken in excess can have serious consequences. If you suspect an overdose, seek medical help immediately.

- *Symptoms of Cylert overdose may include:*
  Agitation, coma, confusion, convulsions, delirium, dilated pupils, exaggerated feeling of well-being, extremely high temperature, flushing, hallucinations, headache, high blood pressure, increased heart rate, increased reflex reactions, muscle twitches, sweating, tremors, vomiting

Generic name:

CYPROHEPTADINE

See Periactin, page 834.

Brand name:

CYTOTEC

Pronounced: SITE-oh-tek
Generic name: Misoprostol

Why is this drug prescribed?

Cytotec, a synthetic prostaglandin (hormone-like substance), reduces the production of stomach acid and protects the stomach lining. People who take nonsteroidal anti-inflammatory drugs (NSAIDs) may be given Cytotec tablets to help prevent stomach ulcers.

Aspirin and other NSAIDs such as Motrin, Naprosyn, Feldene, and others, which are widely used to control the pain and inflammation of arthritis, are generally hard on the stomach. If you must take an NSAID for a prolonged period of time, and if you are elderly or have ever had a stomach ulcer, your doctor may want you to take Cytotec for as long as you take the NSAID.

Most important fact about this drug

You must not become pregnant while using Cytotec. This drug causes uterine contractions that could lead to a miscarriage. If you do have a miscarriage, there is a risk that it might be incomplete. This could lead to bleeding, hospitalization, surgery, infertility, or even death. It is vitally important to use reliable contraception while taking Cytotec.

How should you take this medication?
Take Cytotec with meals, exactly as prescribed.

Take Cytotec for the full course of NSAID treatment, even if you notice no stomach problems.

Take the final dosage at bedtime.

■ *If you miss a dose...*
Take it as soon as you remember. If it is almost time for your next dose, skip the one you missed and go back to your regular schedule. Do not take 2 doses at once.

■ *Storage instructions...*
Store at room temperature in a dry place.

What side effects may occur?
Cytotec may cause abdominal cramps, diarrhea, and/or nausea, especially during the first few weeks of treatment. These symptoms may disappear as your body gets used to the drug. Taking Cytotec with food can help minimize diarrhea. If you have prolonged difficulty (more than 8 days), or if you have severe diarrhea, cramping and/or nausea, call your doctor.

■ *Other side effects may include:*
Constipation, gas, indigestion, headache, heavy menstrual bleeding, menstrual disorder, menstrual pain or cramps, paleness, spotting (light bleeding between menstrual periods), stomach or intestinal bleeding, vomiting

Cytotec may cause uterine bleeding even if you have gone through menopause. However, postmenopausal bleeding could be a sign of some other gynecological problem. If you experience any such bleeding while taking Cytotec, notify your doctor at once.

Why should this drug not be prescribed?
Do not take Cytotec if you are sensitive to or have ever had an allergic reaction to it or to another prostaglandin medication.

Do not take Cytotec if you are pregnant or might become pregnant while taking it.

Special warnings about this medication

Since Cytotec may cause diarrhea, you should use this drug very cautiously if you have inflammatory bowel disease or any other condition in which the loss of fluid caused by diarrhea would be particularly dangerous.

To reduce the risk of diarrhea, take Cytotec with food and avoid taking it with a magnesium-containing antacid, such as Di-Gel, Gelusil, Maalox, Mylanta, and others. Have frequent medical checkups.

Never give Cytotec to anyone else; the dosage might be wrong, and if the other person is pregnant, the drug might harm the unborn baby or cause a miscarriage.

Possible food and drug interactions
when taking this medication

Cytotec does not interfere with arthritis medications such as aspirin and ibuprofen.

Special information
if you are pregnant or breastfeeding

If you are pregnant or plan to become pregnant, inform your doctor immediately. Because Cytotec can cause miscarriage, it should not be taken during pregnancy. If you are a woman of childbearing age, you should not take Cytotec unless you have thoroughly discussed the risks with your doctor and believe you are able to take effective contraceptive measures.

You will need to take a pregnancy test about 2 weeks before starting to take Cytotec. To be sure you are not pregnant at the start of Cytotec treatment, your doctor will have you take your first dose on the second or third day of your menstrual period.

Even the most scrupulous contraceptive measures sometimes fail. If you believe you may have become pregnant while taking Cytotec, stop taking the drug and contact your doctor immediately.

It is not known if Cytotec appears in breast milk. Because of the potential for severe diarrhea in a nursing infant, your doctor may have you stop breastfeeding until your treatment is finished.

Recommended dosage

ADULTS

The recommended oral dose of Cytotec for the prevention of NSAID-induced stomach ulcers is 200 micrograms 4 times daily with food. Take the last dose of the day at bedtime.

If you cannot tolerate this dosage, your doctor can prescribe a dose of 100 micrograms.

Your should take Cytotec for the duration of NSAID therapy, as prescribed by your doctor.

For People with Kidney Impairment
You will not normally need an adjustment in the dosing schedule, but your doctor can reduce the dosage if you have trouble handling the usual dose.

Overdosage
Any medication taken in excess can have serious consequences. If you suspect symptoms of an overdose of Cytotec, seek medical attention immediately.

■ *Symptoms of Cytotec overdose may include:*
Abdominal pain
Breathing difficulty
Convulsions
Diarrhea
Fever
Heart palpitations
Low blood pressure
Sedation (extreme drowsiness)
Slowed heartbeat
Stomach or intestinal discomfort
Tremors

Brand name:

CYTOXAN

Pronounced: sigh-TOKS-an
Generic name: Cyclophosphamide

Why is this drug prescribed?
Cytoxan, an anticancer drug, works by interfering with the growth of malignant cells. It may be used alone but is often given with other anticancer medications.

Cytoxan is used in the treatment of the following types of cancer:

Breast cancer
Leukemias (cancers affecting the white blood cells)

Malignant lymphomas (Hodgkin's disease or cancer of the lymph nodes)
Multiple myeloma (a malignant condition or cancer of the plasma cells)
Advanced mycosis fungoides (cancer of the skin and lymph nodes)
Neuroblastoma (a malignant tumor of the adrenal gland or sympathetic nervous system)
Ovarian cancer (adenocarcinoma)
Retinoblastoma (a malignant tumor of the retina)

In addition, Cytoxan may sometimes be given to children who have "minimal change" nephrotic syndrome (kidney damage resulting in loss of protein in the urine) and who have not responded well to treatment with steroid medications.

Most important fact about this drug
Cytoxan may cause bladder damage, probably from toxic byproducts of the drug that are excreted in the urine. Potential problems include bladder infection with bleeding and fibrosis of the bladder.

While you are being treated with Cytoxan, drink 3 or 4 liters of fluid a day to help prevent bladder problems. The extra fluid will dilute your urine and make you urinate frequently, thus minimizing the Cytoxan byproducts' contact with your bladder.

How should you take this medication?
Take Cytoxan exactly as prescribed. You will undergo frequent blood tests, and the doctor will adjust your dosage depending on the evolution of your white blood cell count; a dosage reduction is necessary if the count drops below a certain level. You will also have frequent urine tests to check for blood in the urine, a sign of bladder damage.

Take Cytoxan on an empty stomach. If you have severe stomach upset, then you may take it with food.

If you are unable to swallow the tablet form, you may be given an oral solution made from the injectable form of Cytoxan and Aromatic Elixir. This solution should be used within 14 days.

■ *If you miss a dose...*
Do not take the dose you missed. Go back to your regular schedule and contact your doctor. Do not take 2 doses at once.

■ *Storage instructions...*
Store tablets at room temperature. Store the oral solution in the refrigerator.

What side effects may occur?

Side effects cannot be anticipated. If any develop or change in intensity, inform your doctor immediately. Only your doctor can determine if it is safe for you to continue using Cytoxan.

One possible Cytoxan side effect is the development of a secondary cancer, typically of the bladder, lymph nodes, or bone marrow. A secondary cancer may occur up to several years after the drug is given.

Cytoxan can lower the activity of your immune system, making you more vulnerable to infection.

Noncancerous bladder problems may occur during Cytoxan therapy (see "Most important fact about this drug" section, above).

■ *More common side effects may include:*
Loss of appetite
Nausea and vomiting
Temporary hair loss

■ *Less common or rare side effects may include:*
Abdominal pain, anemia, bleeding, inflamed colon, darkening of skin and changes in fingernails, decreased sperm count, diarrhea, impaired wound healing, mouth sores, new tumor growth, prolonged impairment of fertility or temporary sterility in men, rash, severe allergic reaction, temporary failure to menstruate, yellowing of eyes and skin

Why should this drug not be prescribed?

Do not take this medication if you have ever had an allergic reaction to it.

Also, tell your doctor if you have ever had an allergic reaction to another alkylating anticancer drug such as Alkeran, CeeNU, Emcyt, Leukeran, Myleran, or Zanosar.

In adults, Cytoxan should not be given for "minimal change" nephrotic syndrome or any other kidney disease.

Also, Cytoxan should not be given to anyone who is unable to produce normal blood cells because the bone marrow—where blood cells are made—is not functioning well.

Special warnings about this medication

You are at increased risk for toxic side effects from Cytoxan if you have any of the following conditions:

Blood disorder (low white blood cell or platelet count)
Bone marrow tumors
Kidney disorder
Liver disorder
Past anticancer therapy
Past X-ray therapy

Possible food and drug interactions
when taking this medication

If Cytoxan is taken with certain other drugs, the effects of either could be increased, decreased, or altered. It is especially important to check with your doctor before combining Cytoxan with the following:

Adriamycin (another anticancer drug)
Allopurinol (the gout medicine Zyloprim)
Anectine (used in anesthesia)
Digoxin (the heart medication Lanoxin)
Phenobarbital

If you take adrenal steroid hormones because you have had your adrenal glands removed, you are at increased risk for toxic effects from Cytoxan; your dosage of both steroids and Cytoxan may need to be modified.

Special information
if you are pregnant or breastfeeding

If you are pregnant or plan to become pregnant, inform your doctor immediately. When taken during pregnancy, Cytoxan can cause defects in the unborn baby. Women taking Cytoxan should use effective contraception. Cytoxan does appear in breast milk. A new mother will need to choose between taking this drug and nursing her baby.

Recommended dosage

ADULTS AND CHILDREN

Malignant Diseases

Your doctor will tailor your dosage according to your condition and other drugs taken with Cytoxan.

The recommended oral dosage range is 1 to 5 milligrams per 2.2 pounds of body weight per day.

CHILDREN

"Minimal Change" Nephrotic Syndrome
The recommended oral dosage is 2.5 to 3 milligrams per 2.2 pounds of body weight per day for a period of 60 to 90 days.

Overdosage
Although there is no specific information on Cytoxan overdose, any medication taken in excess can have serious consequences. If you suspect an overdose of Cytoxan, seek medical attention immediately.

Brand name:

DALMANE

Pronounced: DAL-main
Generic name: Flurazepam hydrochloride

Why is this drug prescribed?
Dalmane is used for the relief of insomnia, defined as difficulty falling asleep, waking up frequently at night, or waking up early in the morning. It can be used by people whose insomnia keeps coming back and in those who have poor sleeping habits. It belongs to a class of drugs known as benzodiazepines.

Most important fact about this drug
Tolerance and dependence can occur with the use of Dalmane. You may experience withdrawal symptoms if you stop using this drug abruptly. Discontinue or change your dose only in consultation with your doctor.

How should you take this medication?
Take this medication exactly as prescribed.

- *If you miss a dose...*
  Take the dose you missed as soon as you remember, if it is within an hour or so of the scheduled time. If you do not remember it until later, skip the dose you missed and go back to your regular schedule. Do not take 2 doses at once.

- *Storage instructions...*
  Store away from heat, light, and moisture.

What side effects may occur?

Side effects cannot be anticipated. If any develop or change in intensity, inform your doctor as soon as possible. Only your doctor can determine if it is safe for you to continue taking Dalmane.

■ *More common side effects may include:*
Dizziness
Drowsiness
Falling
Lack of muscular coordination
Light-headedness
Staggering

■ *Less common or rare side effects may include:*
Apprehension, bitter taste, blurred vision, body and joint pain, burning eyes, chest pains, confusion, constipation, depression, diarrhea, difficulty in focusing, dry mouth, exaggerated feeling of well-being, excessive salivation, excitement, faintness, flushes, genital and urinary tract disorders, hallucinations, headache, heartburn, hyperactivity, irritability, itching, loss of appetite, low blood pressure, nausea, nervousness, rapid, fluttery heartbeat, restlessness, shortness of breath, skin rash, slurred speech, stimulation, stomach and intestinal pain, stomach upset, sweating, talkativeness, vomiting, weakness

■ *Side effects due to rapid decrease or abrupt withdrawal from Dalmane:*
Abdominal and muscle cramps
Convulsions
Depressed mood
Inability to fall asleep or stay asleep
Sweating
Tremors
Vomiting

Why should this drug not be prescribed?

If you are sensitive to or have had an allergic reaction to Dalmane or similar drugs such as Valium, you should not take this medication. Make sure your doctor is aware of any drug reactions you have experienced.

Special warnings about this medication

Dalmane will cause you to become drowsy or less alert; therefore, you should not drive or operate dangerous machinery or participate in any hazardous activity that requires full mental alertness after taking Dalmane.

If you are severely depressed or have suffered from severe depression, consult with your doctor before taking this medication.

If you have decreased kidney or liver function or chronic respiratory or lung disease, discuss use of this drug with your doctor.

Possible food and drug interactions
when taking this medication

Alcohol intensifies the effects of Dalmane. Do not drink alcohol while taking this medication.

If Dalmane is taken with certain other drugs, the effects of either could be increased, decreased, or altered. It is especially important to check with your doctor before combining Dalmane with the following:

Antidepressants such as Elavil and Tofranil
Antihistamines such as Benadryl and Tavist
Barbiturates such as Seconal and phenobarbital
Major tranquilizers such as Mellaril and Thorazine
Narcotic pain-killers such as Demerol and Tylenol with Codeine
Sedatives such as Xanax and Halcion
Tranquilizers such as Librium and Valium

Special information
if you are pregnant or breastfeeding

Do not take Dalmane if you are pregnant or planning to become pregnant. There is an increased risk of birth defects. This drug may appear in breast milk and could affect a nursing infant. If this medication is essential to your health, your doctor may advise you to discontinue breastfeeding until your treatment with Dalmane is finished.

Recommended dosage

ADULTS

The usual recommended dose is 30 milligrams at bedtime; however, 15 milligrams may be all that is necessary. Your doctor will adjust the dose to your needs.

CHILDREN

Safety and effectiveness of Dalmane have not been established in children under 15 years of age.

ELDERLY

Your doctor will limit the dosage to the smallest effective amount to avoid oversedation, dizziness, confusion, or lack of muscle coordination. The usual starting dose is 15 milligrams.

Overdosage

Any medication taken in excess can cause symptoms of overdose. If you suspect an overdose of Dalmane, seek medical attention immediately.

- *The symptoms of Dalmane overdose may include:*
  Coma
  Confusion
  Low blood pressure
  Sleepiness

Brand name:

DARVOCET-N

Pronounced: DAR-voe-set en
Generic ingredients: Propoxyphene napsylate,
  Acetaminophen
Other brand names: Darvon-N (propoxyphene napsylate),
  Darvon (propoxyphene hydrochloride), Darvon
  Compound-65 (propoxyphene hydrochloride, aspirin, and
  caffeine)

Why is this drug prescribed?

Darvocet-N and Darvon Compound-65 are mild narcotic analgesics prescribed for the relief of mild to moderate pain, with or without fever.

Darvon-N and Darvon are prescribed for the relief of mild to moderate pain.

Most important fact about this drug

You can build up tolerance to, and become dependent on, these drugs if you take them in higher than recommended doses over long periods of time.

How should you take this medication?

Take these drugs exactly as prescribed. Do not increase the amount you take without your doctor's approval. Do not take them for any reason other than those for which they are prescribed. Do not give them to others who may have similar symptoms.

- *If you miss a dose...*
  Take it as soon as you remember. If it is almost time for your next dose, skip the one you missed and go back to your regular schedule. Do not take 2 doses at once.

- *Storage instructions...*
  Store at room temperature.

What side effects may occur?
Side effects cannot be anticipated. If any develop or change in intensity, inform your doctor as soon as possible. Only your doctor can determine if it is safe for you to continue taking one of these medications.

- *More common side effects may include:*
  Drowsiness
  Dizziness
  Nausea
  Sedation
  Vomiting

If these side effects occur, it may help if you lie down after taking the medication.

- *Less common side effects may include:*
  Abdominal pain, constipation, feelings of elation or depression, hallucinations, headache, kidney problems, light-headedness, liver problems, minor visual disturbances, skin rashes, weakness, yellowed eyes and skin

Why should this drug not be prescribed?
If you are sensitive to or have ever had an allergic reaction to propoxyphene, any of the other ingredients in these drugs, or other pain relievers of this type, you should not take this medication. Make sure your doctor is aware of any drug reactions you have experienced.

Special warnings about this medication
These medicines may cause you to become drowsy or less alert; therefore, you should not drive or operate dangerous machinery or participate in any hazardous activity that requires full mental alertness until you know how the drug affects you.

If you have a kidney or liver disorder, consult your doctor before taking Darvocet-N.

Darvon Compound-65 contains aspirin and caffeine. If you have an ulcer or a blood clotting problem, consult your doctor before taking this medication. Aspirin may irritate the stomach lining and could cause bleeding.

Because there is a possible association between aspirin and the severe neurological disorder known as Reye's syndrome, children and teenagers with chickenpox or flu should not take Darvon Compound-65 unless prescribed by a doctor.

Aspirin may cause asthma attacks. If you have had an asthma attack while taking aspirin, consult your doctor before you take Darvon Compound-65.

Possible food and drug interactions when taking this medication

The propoxyphene in these drugs slows down the central nervous system and intensifies the effects of alcohol. Heavy use of alcohol with this drug may cause overdose symptoms. Therefore, limit or avoid use of alcohol while you are taking this medication.

If these medications are taken with certain other drugs, the effects of either could be increased, decreased, or altered. It is especially important to check with your doctor before combining them with the following:

Anticonvulsant medications such as Tegretol
Antidepressant drugs such as Elavil
Antihistamines such as Benadryl
Muscle relaxants such as Flexeril
Narcotic pain relievers such as Demerol
Sleep aids such as Halcion
Tranquilizers such as Xanax and Valium
Warfarin-like drugs such as Coumadin

The use of these drugs with propoxyphene can lead to potentially fatal overdose symptoms.

Severe neurologic disorders, including coma, have occurred with the use of propoxyphene in combination with Tegretol.

The use of anticoagulants (blood thinners such as Coumadin) in combination with Darvon Compound-65 may cause bleeding. If you are taking an anticoagulant, consult your doctor before taking this drug.

The use of aspirin with drugs for gout may alter the effects of the antigout medication. Consult your doctor before taking Darvon Compound-65.

Special information
if you are pregnant or breastfeeding

Do not take these medications if you are pregnant or planning to become pregnant unless you are directed to do so by your doctor. Temporary drug dependence may occur in newborns when the mother has taken this drug consistently in the weeks before delivery. The use of Darvon Compound-65 (which contains aspirin) during pregnancy may cause problems in the developing baby or complications during delivery. Do not take it during the last 3 months of pregnancy. Darvocet-N does appear in breast milk. However, no adverse effects have been found in nursing infants.

Recommended dosage

ADULTS

These medicines may be taken every 4 hours as needed for pain. The usual doses are:

Darvocet-N 50: 2 tablets

Darvocet-N 100: 1 tablet

Darvon: 1 capsule

Darvon Compound-65: 1 capsule

Your doctor may lower the total daily dosage if you have kidney or liver problems.

The most you should take of Darvon or Darvon Compound-65 is 6 capsules a day.

CHILDREN

The safety and effectiveness of Darvocet-N has not been established in children.

ELDERLY

Your doctor may lengthen the time between doses.

Overdosage

Any medication taken in excess can have serious consequences. If you suspect an overdose, seek medical attention immediately.

- *Symptoms of a propoxyphene overdose may include:*
  Bluish tinge to the skin, coma, convulsions, decreased or difficult breathing

to the point of temporary stoppage, decreased heart function, extreme sleepiness, irregular heartbeat, low blood pressure, pinpoint pupils becoming dilated later, stupor

■ *Additional symptoms of overdose with Darvocet-N:*
Abdominal pain, excessive sweating, general feeling of illness, kidney failure, liver problems, loss of appetite, nausea, vomiting

■ *Additional symptoms of overdose with Darvon Compound-65:*
Confusion, deafness, excessive perspiration, headache, mental dullness, nausea, rapid breathing, rapid pulse, ringing in the ears, vertigo, vomiting

Extreme overdosage may lead to unconsciousness and death.

Brand name:

DARVON

See Darvocet-N, page 270.

Brand name:

DARVON COMPOUND-65

See Darvocet-N, page 270.

Brand name:

DARVON-N

See Darvocet-N, page 270.

Brand name:

DAYPRO

Pronounced: DAY-pro
Generic name: Oxaprozin

Why is this drug prescribed?
Daypro is a nonsteroidal anti-inflammatory drug used to relieve the inflammation, swelling, stiffness, and joint pain associated with rheumatoid arthritis and osteoarthritis (the most common kind of arthritis).

Most important fact about this drug

You should have frequent check-ups with your doctor if you take Daypro regularly. Ulcers and internal bleeding can occur without warning.

How should you take this medication?

Take Daypro with a full glass of water. If the drug upsets your stomach, your doctor may recommend taking Daypro with food, milk, or an antacid, even though food may delay onset of relief.

It will also help to prevent irritation in your upper digestive tract if you avoid lying down for about 20 minutes after taking Daypro.

Take this medication exactly as prescribed.

■ *If you miss a dose...*
Try to take Daypro at the same time each day, for example, after breakfast. If you forget to take a dose and remember later in the day, you can still take it. If you completely forget to take your medication, do *not* double the dose the next day to make up for the missed dose. You should get back on your normal schedule as soon as possible.

■ *Storage instructions...*
Store at room temperature in a tightly closed container, away from light.

What side effects may occur?

Side effects cannot be anticipated. If any develop or change in intensity, tell your doctor as soon as possible. Only your doctor can decide if it is safe for you to continue taking Daypro.

■ *More common side effects may include:*
Constipation
Diarrhea
Indigestion
Nausea
Rash

■ *Less common side effects may include:*
Abdominal pain, confusion, depression, frequent or painful urination, gas, loss of appetite, ringing in the ears, sleep disturbances, sleepiness, vomiting

■ *Rare side effects may include:*
Anaphylaxis (a severe allergic reaction), anemia, blood in the urine, blood pressure changes, blurred vision, bruising, changes in kidney and liver function, decreased menstrual flow, fluid retention, general feeling of

illness, hemorrhoidal or rectal bleeding, hepatitis, hives, inflammation of the mouth, irritated eyes, itching, peptic ulcerations, respiratory infection, sensitivity to light, stomach and intestinal bleeding, weight gain or loss, weakness

Why should this drug not be prescribed?

If you are sensitive to or have ever had an allergic reaction to Daypro, or if you have ever developed asthma, nasal tumors, or other allergic reactions due to aspirin or other nonsteroidal anti-inflammatory drugs, you should not take this medication. Make sure your doctor is aware of any drug reactions you have experienced.

Special warnings about this medication

Use Daypro with caution if you have kidney or liver disease.

Do not take aspirin or any other anti-inflammatory medications while taking Daypro, unless your doctor tells you to do so.

Daypro can increase water retention. Use with caution if you have heart disease or high blood pressure.

If you are taking Daypro for an extended period, your doctor should check your blood for anemia.

Daypro can prolong bleeding time. If you are taking a blood-thinning medication, use Daypro with caution.

Daypro may cause sensitivity to sunlight. Avoid prolonged exposure to the sun. Use sunscreens and wear protective clothing.

Do not use Daypro if you are planning to have surgery in the immediate future.

Possible food and drug interactions
when taking this medication

If you take Daypro with certain other drugs, the effects of either medication could be increased, decreased, or altered. It is especially important to check with your doctor before combining Daypro with following medications:

Aspirin
Beta-blocking blood pressure medications such as Inderal and Tenormin
Blood thinners such as Coumadin
Diuretics such as Lasix and Midamor
Lithium (Lithonate)

Avoid alcoholic beverages while taking Daypro.

Special information
if you are pregnant or breastfeeding

The effects of Daypro during pregnancy have not been adequately studied. If you are pregnant or plan to become pregnant, tell your doctor immediately. Since the effects of Daypro on nursing infants are not known, tell you doctor if you are nursing or plan to nurse. If Daypro treatment is necessary for your health, your doctor may tell you to discontinue nursing until your treatment is finished.

Recommended dosage

ADULTS

Your doctor will adjust the dose based on your needs.

Rheumatoid Arthritis

The usual daily dose is 1200 milligrams (two 600-milligram caplets) once a day.

Osteoarthritis

The usual starting dose for moderate to severe osteoarthritis is 1200 milligrams (two 600-milligram caplets) once a day.

The most you should take in a day is 1800 milligrams divided into smaller doses, or 26 milligrams per 2.2 pounds of body weight, whichever is lower.

CHILDREN

The safety and efficacy of Daypro in children have not been determined.

Overdosage

If you take too much of any medication, it can have serious consequences. If you suspect an overdose, seek medical attention immediately.

- *Symptoms of Daypro overdose may include:*
  Coma
  Drowsiness
  Fatigue
  Nausea
  Pain in the stomach
  Stomach and intestinal bleeding
  Vomiting

Acute kidney failure, high blood pressure, and a slowdown in breathing have occurred rarely.

Brand name:

DDAVP

Pronounced: dee-dee-ai-vee-pee
Generic name: Desmopressin acetate
Other brand name: Stimate

Why is this drug prescribed?
DDAVP is given to prevent or control the frequent urination and loss of water associated with diabetes insipidus (a rare condition characterized by very large quantities of diluted urine and excessive thirst). It is also used to treat frequent passage of urine and increased thirst in people with certain brain injuries, and those who have undergone surgery in the pituitary region of the brain. It is prescribed to help stop some types of bedwetting.

Stimate nasal spray is used to stop bleeding in certain types of hemophilia (failure of the blood to clot).

DDAVP is available as a nasal spray in a pump bottle, or as nose drops to be taken using a soft plastic tube. An injectable form of DDAVP is also available.

Most important fact about this drug
When taking DDAVP, elderly and young people in particular should limit their fluid intake to no more than satisfies thirst. Although extremely rare, there is a possibility of water intoxication, in which reduced sodium levels in the blood can lead to seizures.

How should you use this medication?
Use DDAVP exactly as prescribed. The spray and drops are for nasal use only; never swallow the medication or allow the liquid to run into your mouth.

Your doctor may increase or decrease your dosage, depending on how you respond to DDAVP. Your response will be judged by how long you are able to sleep without having to get up to urinate and how much urine your kidneys produce.

The DDAVP nasal spray pump bottle accurately delivers 50 doses of the medication. After the 50th dose, the amount of medication that comes out with each spray will no longer be a full dose. When this happens, throw the bottle away even if it is not completely empty. Stimate nasal spray delivers

25 doses; the same instructions apply. The Stimate nasal spray pump must be primed before you use it for the first time: Press down 4 times.

Since the DDAVP spray bottle delivers only a standard-sized dose, those who need more or less medication should use the nose drops instead of the spray.

If nasal congestion, scars, or swelling inside the nose make it difficult to absorb DDAVP, your doctor may temporarily stop the drug or give you an injectable form.

■ *If you miss a dose...*
Take the forgotten dose as soon as you remember. If you take 1 dose a day and don't remember until the next day, skip the dose. If you take DDAVP more than once a day and it is almost time for the next dose, skip the one you missed and go back to your regular schedule. Never try to "catch up" by doubling the dose.

■ *Storage instructions...*
Both spray and drops should be stored in the refrigerator. If you are traveling, they will stay fresh at room temperature for up to 3 weeks.

What side effects may occur?
Too high a dosage of DDAVP may produce headache, nausea, mild abdominal cramps, stuffy nose, irritation of the nose, or flushing. These symptoms will probably disappear when the dosage is reduced. Some people have complained of nosebleed, sore throat, cough, or a cold or other upper respiratory infections after taking DDAVP.

■ *Other potential side effects include:*
Abdominal pain, chills, conjunctivitis (pinkeye), depression, dizziness, inability to produce tears, leg rash, nostril pain, rash, stomach or intestinal upset, swelling around the eyes, weakness

■ *Side effects of Stimate nasal spray may include:*
Agitation, chest pain, chills, dizziness, fast, fluttery heartbeat, fluid retention and swelling, indigestion, inflammation of the penis, insomnia, itchy or light-sensitive eyes, pain, rapid heartbeat, sleepiness, vomiting, warm feeling

Why should this drug not be prescribed?
Do not use DDAVP if you are sensitive to it or have ever had an allergic reaction to it.

Special warnings about this medication

If you have cystic fibrosis or any other condition in which there is fluid and electrolyte imbalance, you should use DDAVP with extreme caution.

Because DDAVP may cause a rise in blood pressure, use this medication cautiously if you have high blood pressure and/or coronary artery disease. Your blood pressure could also fall temporarily. If you continue to experience bleeding after using Stimate nasal spray, contact your doctor.

Possible food and drug interactions
when taking this medication

If DDAVP is taken with certain other drugs, the effects of either could be increased, decreased, or altered. It is especially important to check with your doctor before combining DDAVP with the following:

Any drug used to increase blood pressure
Clofibrate (Atromid-S)
Glyburide (Micronase)
Epinephrine (EpiPen)

Special information
if you are pregnant or breastfeeding

If you are pregnant or plan to become pregnant, inform your doctor immediately. Although DDAVP is not known to cause birth defects, it should be used with caution. DDAVP should be taken during pregnancy only if clearly needed. DDAVP is not believed to appear in breast milk. However, check with your doctor before using the drug while breastfeeding.

Recommended dosage

Your doctor will carefully tailor your dosage to meet your individual needs.

CENTRAL CRANIAL DIABETES INSIPIDUS

Adults

The usual recommended dosage range is 0.1 to 0.4 milliliter daily, either as a single dose or divided into 2 or 3 doses. Most adults require 0.2 milliliter per day divided into 2 doses.

Children

The usual dosage range for children aged 3 months to 12 years is 0.05 to 0.3 milliliter daily, either as a single dose or divided into 2 doses.

PRIMARY NOCTURNAL ENURESIS (BED-WETTING)

Children 6 Years of Age and Older

The usual recommended dose is 20 micrograms or 0.2 milliliter at bedtime. Dosage requirements range from 10 to 40 micrograms. One-half the dose should be taken in each nostril.

To stop bleeding in some types of hemophilia

The usual dose is one 150-microgram spray in each nostril. If you use the spray more frequently than every 48 hours, you may find you are not responding as well as you should to the drug.

Overdosage

An overdose of DDAVP may cause abdominal cramps, flushing, headache or nausea. If you suspect an overdose of DDAVP, seek medical attention immediately.

Brand name:

DECADRON TABLETS

Pronounced: DECK-uh-drohn
Generic name: Dexamethasone

Why is this drug prescribed?

Decadron, a corticosteroid drug, is used to reduce inflammation and relieve symptoms in a variety of disorders, including rheumatoid arthritis and severe cases of asthma. It may be given to people to treat primary or secondary adrenal cortex insufficiency (lack of sufficient adrenal hormone). It is also given to help treat the following disorders:

Severe allergic conditions such as drug-induced allergies
Blood disorders such as various anemias
Certain cancers (along with other drugs)
Skin diseases such as severe psoriasis
Collagen (connective tissue) diseases such as systemic lupus
    erythematosus
Digestive tract disease such as ulcerative colitis
High serum levels of calcium associated with cancer
Fluid retention due to nephrotic syndrome (a condition in which damage
    to the kidneys causes the body to lose protein in the urine)

Eye diseases such as allergic conjunctivitis
Lung diseases such as tuberculosis (along with other drugs)

Most important fact about this drug

Decadron lowers your resistance to infections and can make them harder to treat. Decadron may also mask some of the signs of an infection, making it difficult for your doctor to diagnose the actual problem.

How should you take this medication?

Decadron should be taken exactly as prescribed by your doctor.

If you are taking large doses, your doctor may advise you to take Decadron with meals and to take antacids between meals, to prevent a peptic ulcer from developing.

Check with your doctor before stopping Decadron abruptly. If you have been taking the drug for a long time, you may need to reduce your dose gradually over a period of days or weeks.

The lowest possible dose should always be used, and as symptoms subside, dosage should be reduced gradually.

■ *If you miss a dose...*
Take the forgotten dose as soon as you remember. If it is almost time for the next dose, skip the one you missed and go back to your regular schedule. Never try to "catch up" by doubling the dose.

■ *Storage instructions...*
There are no special storage requirements.

What side effects may occur?

Side effects cannot be anticipated. If any develop or change in intensity, inform your doctor as soon as possible. Only your doctor can determine if it is safe for you to continue taking Decadron.

■ *Side effects may include:*
Abdominal distention, allergic reactions, blood clots, bone fractures and degeneration, bruises, cataracts, congestive heart failure, convulsions, "cushingoid" symptoms (moon face, weight gain, high blood pressure, emotional disturbances, growth of facial hair in women), emotional disturbances, excessive hairiness, fluid and salt retention, general feeling of illness, glaucoma, headache, hiccups, high blood pressure, hives, increased appetite, increased eye pressure, increased pressure in head, increased sweating, increases in amounts of insulin or hypoglycemic

medications needed in diabetes, inflammation of the esophagus, inflammation of the pancreas, irregular menstruation, loss of muscle mass, low potassium levels in blood (leading to symptoms such as dry mouth, excessive thirst, weak or irregular heartbeat, and muscle pain or cramps), muscle weakness, nausea, osteoporosis, peptic ulcer, perforated small and large bowel, poor healing of wounds, protruding eyeballs, ruptured tendons, suppression of growth in children, thin skin, tiny red or purplish spots on the skin, vertigo, weight gain

Why should this drug not be prescribed?

Decadron should not be used if you have a fungal infection, or if you are sensitive or allergic to any of its ingredients.

Special warnings about this medication

Decadron can alter the way your body responds to unusual stress. If you are injured, need surgery, or develop an acute illness, inform your doctor. Your dosage may need to be increased.

Corticosteroids such as Decadron can lower your resistance to infection. Diseases such as measles and chickenpox can be serious and even fatal in adults. If you are taking Decadron and are exposed to chickenpox or measles, notify your doctor immediately.

Do not get a smallpox vaccination or any other immunizations while taking Decadron, especially in high doses. The vaccination might not take, and could do harm to the nervous system.

Decadron may reactivate a dormant case of tuberculosis. If you have inactive tuberculosis and must take Decadron for an extended period, your doctor will prescribe anti-TB medication as well.

When you stop taking Decadron after long-term therapy, you may develop withdrawal symptoms such as fever, muscle or joint pain, and a feeling of illness.

Long-term use of Decadron may cause cataracts, glaucoma, and eye infections.

If you have any of the following conditions, make sure your doctor knows about it:

Allergy to any cortisone-like drug
Cirrhosis
Diabetes
Diverticulitis
Eye infection (herpes simplex)

Glaucoma
High blood pressure
Impaired thyroid function
Kidney disease (impaired kidney function)
Myasthenia gravis (a muscle disorder)
Osteoporosis (brittle bones)
Peptic ulcer
Recent heart attack
Tuberculosis
Ulcerative colitis

Steroids may alter male fertility.

This medication can aggravate existing emotional problems or cause emotional disturbances. Symptoms range from an exaggerated sense of well-being and difficulty sleeping to mood swings and psychotic episodes. If you experience any changes in mood, contact your doctor.

If you have recently been to the tropics or are suffering from diarrhea with no apparent cause, inform your doctor before taking Decadron.

Possible food and drug interactions
when taking this medication

If Decadron is taken with certain other drugs, the effects of either could be increased, decreased, or altered. It is especially important to check with your doctor before combining Decadron with the following:

Aspirin
Blood-thinning medications such as Coumadin and Panwarfin
Ephedrine (a decongestant in drugs such as Marax and Rynatuss)
Indomethacin (Indocin)
Phenobarbital
Phenytoin (Dilantin)
Potassium-depleting diuretics such as HydroDIURIL
Rifampin (Rifadin, Rimactane)

Special information
if you are pregnant or breastfeeding

The effects of Decadron during pregnancy have not been adequately studied. If you are pregnant or plan to become pregnant, inform your doctor immediately. Infants born to mothers who have taken substantial doses of corticosteroids during pregnancy should be carefully watched for adrenal problems. Corticosteroids appear in breast milk and can suppress growth in infants. If Decadron is essential to your health, your doctor may advise you to stop breastfeeding until your treatment with Decadron is finished.

Recommended dosage

ADULTS

Your doctor will tailor your individual dose to the condition being treated. Initial doses range from 0.75 milligram to 9 milligrams a day.

After the drug produces a satisfactory response, your doctor will gradually lower the dose to the minimum effective level.

Overdosage

Reports of overdose with this medication are rare. However, if you suspect an overdose, seek medical treatment immediately.

Brand name:

DECADRON TURBINAIRE AND RESPIHALER

Pronounced: DECK-ah-drahn tur-bin-AIR and RESS-pi-hail-er
Generic name: Dexamethasone sodium phosphate
Other brand name: Dexacort

Why is this drug prescribed?

Decadron is a synthetic adrenocortical steroid (a hormone created in the laboratory). Decadron Turbinaire is used to treat hay fever and other nasal allergies, and to assist in the treatment of nasal polyps. Decadron Respihaler is prescribed for bronchial asthma in people who need sustained treatment.

Most important fact about this drug

Decadron lowers your resistance to infections and can make them harder to treat. Decadron may also mask some of the signs of an infection, making it difficult for your doctor to diagnose the actual problem.

How should you take this medication?

These medications come with directions. Read them carefully before using the medicine. To work, the medications must be used exactly as directed.

If you are using the Decadron Respihaler, gargling and rinsing your mouth with water after each dose may help prevent hoarseness and throat irritation. Do not swallow the water after you rinse.

■ *If you miss a dose...*
Take the forgotten dose as soon as possible and take the remaining doses for that day at evenly spaced intervals. If it is time for your next dose, skip the one you missed. Never take a double dose.

■ *Storage instructions...*
Store Decadron at room temperature. Since the contents are under pressure, keep the container away from fire or extreme heat.

What side effects may occur?
Side effects cannot be anticipated. If any develop or change in intensity, inform your doctor as soon as possible. Only your doctor can determine whether it is safe to continue using Decadron.

■ *More common side effects of Decadron Turbinaire may include:*
Nasal dryness
Nasal irritation

■ *Less common side effects of Decadron Turbinaire may include:*
Bronchial asthma, headache, hives, light-headedness, loss of smell, nausea, nosebleeds, perforated nasal septum (dividing wall of the nose), rebound nasal congestion

■ *Side effects of Decadron Respihaler may include:*
Coughing
Fungal infections in the throat
Hoarseness
Throat irritation

■ *Side effects that may occur when Decadron is absorbed into the bloodstream:*
Abdominal distention, abnormal skin redness, allergic reactions, blood clots, bruising, cataracts, congestive heart failure, convulsions, development of Cushing's syndrome (moon face, emotional disturbances, high blood pressure, weight gain, and growth of facial and body hair in women), diabetes, emotional disturbances, excessive hairiness, fractures of the long bones, fractures of the vertebrae, fragile skin, glaucoma, headache, hiccups, high blood pressure, hives, increased appetite, increased eye pressure, increased pressure in head, increased sweating, loss of muscle mass, menstrual irregularities, muscle weakness, nausea, osteoporosis, perforated small or large bowel, poor wound healing, potassium loss, protruding eyeballs, reddish or purplish spots on the skin, ruptured tendons, salt and fluid retention, stomach ulcer, ulcer of the esophagus, vague feeling of weakness, vertigo, weight gain

Why should this drug not be prescribed?

Do not use Decadron if you have a fungal infection or if you have ever had an allergic reaction or are sensitive to any cortisone-like medication such as Beclovent. Decadron Turbinaire should not be used if you have tuberculosis or a nasal condition caused by a virus or a fungus, or if you have herpes simplex infection of the eye. Decadron Respihaler should not be used if tests show that you have a yeast infection (*Candida albicans*).

Special warnings about this medication

Decadron does not expand the bronchial passages, and should be used for asthma only if bronchodilators and other asthma medications are not effective. Decadron does not provide rapid relief of symptoms, but does help to control asthma when taken routinely.

Decadron can alter the way your body responds to unusual stress. If you are injured, need surgery, or develop an acute illness, tell your doctor. Your dosage may need to be increased.

If you develop an infection of the throat or voice box while using the Decadron Respihaler, stop using the Respihaler and notify your doctor. You will need medication.

Corticosteroids such as Decadron may mask the symptoms of infection and make you more susceptible to infections. Diseases such as chickenpox and measles can be serious and even fatal in adults who have never had these illnesses. If you are using Decadron Turbinaire or Respihaler and are exposed to chickenpox or measles, notify your doctor immediately. Do not get a smallpox vaccination or any other immunizations while taking Decadron, especially in high doses. The vaccination might not take, and could do harm to the nervous system.

Using Decadron for a long time may cause cataracts, glaucoma, and eye infections.

Large doses of Decadron may raise blood pressure and increase salt and water retention. If this happens, your doctor may tell you to restrict salt in your diet.

Decadron should be used with extreme caution if you have dormant tuberculosis or test positive for tuberculosis. Decadron may reactivate the disease.

When you stop taking Decadron after long-term therapy, you may develop withdrawal symptoms such as fever, muscle or joint pain, and weakness.

Decadron should be used with care if you have an underactive thyroid or cirrhosis.

Your doctor will prescribe the lowest possible dose to control your condition, and reduce your dosage of Decadron gradually. Do not suddenly stop taking it.

Decadron may aggravate existing emotional problems or cause emotional disturbances. Symptoms range from euphoria (an exaggerated sense of well-being) and difficulty sleeping to mood swings, personality changes, severe depression, and psychotic episodes. If you experience any changes in mood, call your doctor.

Decadron should be used with care if you have ulcerative colitis, diverticulitis (an inflammation of the digestive tract), peptic ulcer, kidney disease, high blood pressure, osteoporosis, or myasthenia gravis (muscle weakness, especially in the face and neck), or if you have recently had a heart attack.

Long-term therapy with Decadron may affect the growth and development of children and should be carefully checked by your doctor. Decadron Turbinaire is not recommended for children under 6 years of age.

If you have recently been to the tropics or are suffering from diarrhea with no apparent cause, inform your doctor before using Decadron.

Possible food and drug interactions
when taking this medication

If Decadron is taken with certain other drugs, the effects of either could be increased, decreased, or altered. It is especially important to check with your doctor before combining Decadron with the following:

Aspirin
Blood thinners such as Coumadin
Ephedrine
Phenytoin (Dilantin)
Phenobarbital (Bellergal-S, Donnatal, others)
Potassium-depleting diuretics such as Dyazide and Esidrix
Rifampin (Rifadin, Rimactane)

Special information
if you are pregnant or breastfeeding

The effects of Decadron during pregnancy have not been adequately studied. If you are pregnant or plan to become pregnant, inform your doctor immediately. Infants born to mothers who have taken substantial doses of steroids during pregnancy may have problems with their adrenal glands. Corticosteroids appear in breast milk and could affect infant growth or cause other damaging effects. Decadron is not recommended for nursing mothers. If Decadron is essential to your health, your doctor may advise you to stop breastfeeding until your treatment with Decadron is finished.

Recommended dosage

TURBINAIRE

Adults

The usual initial dosage is 2 sprays in each nostril, 2 or 3 times a day.

Children (6 to 12 Years of Age)

The usual initial dosage is 1 or 2 sprays in each nostril 2 times a day, depending on age.

Dosage should be gradually reduced when improvement occurs. The maximum daily dosage for adults is 12 sprays and for children, 8 sprays. Therapy should be stopped as soon as possible. If symptoms return, your doctor may start the medication again.

RESPIHALER

Adults

The recommended initial dose is 3 inhalations, 3 or 4 times a day.

Children

The recommended initial dose is 2 inhalations, 3 or 4 times a day.

Dosage should be gradually reduced when improvement occurs. The maximum daily dosage for adults is 3 inhalations per dose, 12 inhalations per day; and for children, 2 inhalations per dose, 8 inhalations per day.

Overdosage

There have been rare reports of toxicity (poisoning) and death following steroid overdose. If you suspect Decadron overdose, seek medical treatment immediately.

Brand name:

DECONAMINE

Pronounced: dee-CON-uh-meen
Generic ingredients: Chlorpheniramine maleate,
   d-Pseudoephedrine hydrochloride

Why is this drug prescribed?

Deconamine is an antihistamine and decongestant used for the temporary relief of persistent runny nose, sneezing, and nasal congestion caused by upper respiratory infections (the common cold), sinus inflammation, or hay fever. It is also used to help clear nasal passages and shrink swollen membranes and to drain the sinuses and relieve sinus pressure.

Most important fact about this drug
Deconamine may cause you to become drowsy or less alert. You should not drive or operate machinery or participate in any activity that requires full mental alertness until you know how you react to Deconamine.

How should you take this medication?
If Deconamine makes you nervous or restless, or you have trouble sleeping, take the last dose of the day a few hours before you go to bed. Take Deconamine exactly as prescribed.

Antihistamines can make your mouth and throat dry. It may help to suck on hard candy, chew gum, or melt bits of ice in your mouth.

■ *If you miss a dose...*
Take it as soon as you remember. If it is almost time for your next dose, skip the one you missed and go back to your regular schedule. Never take 2 doses at once.

■ *Storage instructions...*
Store at room temperature.

What side effects may occur?
Side effects cannot be anticipated. If any develop or change in intensity, inform your doctor as soon as possible. Only your doctor can determine if it is safe for you to continue taking Deconamine.

The most common side effect is mild to moderate drowsiness.

■ *Less common or rare side effects may include:*
Anaphylactic shock (extreme allergic reaction), anemia, anxiety, blurred vision, breathing difficulty, chills, confusion, constipation, convulsion, diarrhea, difficulty sleeping, difficulty in carrying out movements, disturbed coordination, dizziness, double vision, dry mouth, nose, and throat, early menstruation, exaggerated sense of well being, excessive perspiration, excitation, fatigue, extreme calm (sedation), fear, frequent or difficult urination, hallucinations, headache, hives, hysteria, increased chest congestion, irregular heartbeat, irritability, light-headedness, loss of appetite, low blood pressure, nausea, nervousness, painful urination, pallor, pounding heartbeat, rapid heartbeat, restlessness, ringing in ears, sensitivity to light, skin rash, stomach upset or pain, stuffy nose,

tenseness, tightness of chest, tingling or numbness, tremor, unusual bleeding or bruising, vertigo, vomiting, weakness, wheezing

Why should this drug not be prescribed?

Do not use Deconamine if you have severe high blood pressure or severe heart disease, are taking an antidepressant drug known as an MAO inhibitor (Nardil, Parnate, others), or are sensitive to or have ever had an allergic reaction to antihistamines or decongestants.

Special warnings about this medication

Use Deconamine with extreme caution if you have the eye condition called glaucoma, peptic ulcer or stomach obstructions, an enlarged prostate, or difficulty urinating.

Also use caution if you have bronchial asthma, emphysema, chronic lung disease, high blood pressure, heart disease, diabetes, or an overactive thyroid.

Deconamine may cause excitability, especially in children.

Possible food and drug interactions
when taking this medication

Alcohol increases the sedative effect of Deconamine. Avoid it while taking this medication.

If Deconamine is taken with certain other drugs, the effects of either may be increased, decreased, or altered. It is especially important to check with your doctor before combining Deconamine with the following:

Antidepressant drugs such as the MAO inhibitors Nardil and Parnate
Asthma medications such as Ventolin and Proventil
Bromocriptine (Parlodel)
Mecamylamine (Inversine)
Methyldopa (Aldomet)
Narcotic pain killers such as Demerol and Percocet
Phenytoin (Dilantin)
Reserpine (Ser-Ap-Es, others)
Sleep aids such as Halcion and Seconal
Tranquilizers such as Valium and Xanax

Special information
if you are pregnant or breastfeeding

The effects of Deconamine during pregnancy have not been adequately studied. If you are pregnant or plan to become pregnant, notify your doctor immediately. Deconamine appears in breast milk and could affect a nursing infant. If this medication is essential to your health, your doctor may advise you to discontinue breastfeeding until your treatment with Deconamine is finished.

Recommended dosage

DECONAMINE TABLETS

Adults and Children over 12 Years
The usual dosage is 1 tablet 3 or 4 times daily.

Children under 12 Years
Use Deconamine Syrup instead of the tablets.

DECONAMINE SYRUP

Adults and Children over 12 Years
The usual dose is 1 to 2 teaspoonfuls (5 to 10 milliliters) 3 or 4 times daily.

Children 6 to 12 Years
The usual dose is ½ to 1 teaspoonful (2.5 to 5 milliliters) 3 or 4 times daily, not to exceed 4 teaspoonfuls in 24 hours.

Children 2 to 6 Years
The usual dose is ½ teaspoonful (2.5 milliliters) 3 or 4 times daily, not to exceed 2 teaspoonfuls in 24 hours.

Children under 2 Years
Use as directed by your doctor.

DECONAMINE SR CAPSULES

Adults and Children over 12 Years
The usual dose is 1 capsule every 12 hours.

Children under 12 Years
Use Deconamine Syrup instead of the capsules.

Overdosage
Any medication taken in excess can have serious consequences. If you suspect an overdose, seek medical attention immediately.

■ *Symptoms of Deconamine overdose include:*
Convulsions
Diminished alertness
Hallucinations
Severe drowsiness
Severe dryness of mouth, nose, and throat
Shortness of breath/difficulty breathing
Sleep problems
Slow or rapid heartbeat
Tremors

Brand name:

DELTASONE

Pronounced: DELL-tuh-zone
Generic name: Prednisone
Other brand name: Orasone

Why is this drug prescribed?
Deltasone, a steroid drug, is used to reduce inflammation and alleviate symptoms in a variety of disorders, including rheumatoid arthritis and severe cases of asthma. It may be given to treat primary or secondary adrenal cortex insufficiency (lack of sufficient adrenal hormone in the body). It is used in treating all of the following:

Allergic conditions (severe)
Blood disorders
Certain cancers (along with other drugs)
Diseases of the connective tissue including systemic lupus
    erythematosus
Eye diseases of various kinds
Flare-ups of multiple sclerosis
Fluid retention due to "nephrotic syndrome" (a condition in which
    damage to the kidneys causes protein to be lost in the urine)
Lung diseases, including tuberculosis
Prevention of organ rejection
Rheumatoid arthritis and related disorders
Severe flare-ups of ulcerative colitis or enteritis (inflammation of the
    intestines)
Skin diseases
Trichinosis (with complications)

Most important fact about this drug

Deltasone lowers your resistance to infections and can make them harder to treat. Deltasone may also mask some of the signs of an infection, making it difficult for your doctor to diagnose the actual problem.

How should you take this medication?

Take Deltasone exactly as prescribed. Dosages are kept to an absolute minimum.

If you need long-term Deltasone treatment, your doctor may prescribe alternate-day therapy, in which you take the medication only every other morning. The "resting day" gives your adrenal glands a chance to produce some hormone naturally so they will not lose the ability.

If you have been taking Deltasone for a period of time, you will probably need an increased dosage of the medication before, during, and after any stressful situation. Always consult your doctor if you are anticipating stress and think you may need a temporary dosage increase.

When stopping Deltasone treatment, tapering off is better than quitting abruptly. Your doctor will probably have you decrease the dosage very gradually over a period of days or weeks.

You should take Deltasone with food to avoid stomach upset.

If you are on alternate-day therapy or have been prescribed a single daily dose, take Deltasone in the morning with breakfast (about 8 A.M.). If you have been prescribed several doses per day, take them at evenly spaced intervals around the clock.

Patients on long-term Deltasone therapy should wear or carry identification.

■ *If you miss a dose...*

If you take your dose once a day, take it as soon as you remember. If you don't remember until the next day, skip the one you missed.

If you take several doses a day, take the forgotten dose as soon as you remember and then go back to your regular schedule. If you don't remember until your next dose, double the dose you take.

If you take your dose every other day, and you remember it the same morning, take it as soon as you remember, then go back to your regular schedule. If you don't remember until the afternoon, do not take a dose until the following morning, then skip a day.

- *Storage instructions...*
  Store in tightly closed container away from heat, light, and moisture.

What side effects may occur?
Side effects cannot be anticipated. If any develop or change in intensity, inform your doctor as soon as possible. Only your doctor can determine if it is safe for you to continue taking Deltasone.

Deltasone may cause euphoria, insomnia, mood changes, personality changes, psychotic behavior, or severe depression. It may worsen any existing emotional instability.

At a high dosage, Deltasone may cause fluid retention and high blood pressure. If this happens, you may need a low-salt diet and a potassium supplement.

With prolonged Deltasone treatment, eye problems may develop (e.g., a viral or fungal eye infection, cataracts, or glaucoma).

If you take Deltasone over the long term, the buildup of adrenal hormones in your body may cause a condition called Cushing's syndrome, marked by weight gain, a "moon-faced" appearance, thin, fragile skin, muscle weakness, brittle bones, and purplish stripe marks on the skin. Women are more vulnerable to this problem than men. Alternate-day therapy may help prevent its development.

- *Other potential side effects from Deltasone include:*
  Bone fractures, bulging eyes, convulsions, distended abdomen, face redness, glaucoma, headache, hives and other allergic-type reactions, increased pressure inside eyes or skull, inflamed esophagus or pancreas, irregular menstrual periods, muscle weakness or disease, osteoporosis, peptic ulcer, poor healing of wounds, stunted growth (in children), sweating, thin, fragile skin, vertigo

Why should this drug not be prescribed?
Do not take Deltasone if you have ever had an allergic reaction to it.

You should not be treated with Deltasone if you have a body-wide fungus infection, such as candidiasis or cryptococcosis.

Special warnings about this medication
Do not get a smallpox vaccination or any other immunization while you are taking Deltasone. The vaccination might not "take," and could do harm to the nervous system.

Deltasone may reactivate a dormant case of tuberculosis. If you have inactive TB and must take Deltasone for an extended time, you should be given anti-TB medication as well.

If you have an underactive thyroid gland or cirrhosis of the liver, your doctor will probably need to prescribe Deltasone for you at a lower-than-average dosage.

If you have an eye infection caused by the herpes simplex virus, Deltasone should be used with great caution; there is a potential danger that the cornea will become perforated.

Deltasone should also be taken with caution if you have any of the following conditions:

Diverticulitis or other disorder of the intestine
High blood pressure
Kidney disorder
Myasthenia gravis (a muscle-weakness disorder)
Osteoporosis (brittle bones)
Peptic ulcer
Ulcerative colitis (inflammation of the bowel)

Long-term treatment with Deltasone may stunt growth. If this medication is given to a child, the youngster's growth should be monitored carefully.

Diseases such as chickenpox or measles can be very serious or even fatal in both children and adults who are taking this drug. Try to avoid exposure to these diseases.

Possible food and drug interactions
when taking this medication
Deltasone may decrease your carbohydrate tolerance or activate a latent case of diabetes. If you are already taking insulin or oral medication for diabetes, make sure your doctor knows this; you may need an increased dosage while you are being treated with Deltasone.

If you have a blood-clotting disorder caused by a vitamin K deficiency and are taking Deltasone, check with your doctor before you use aspirin.

You may be at risk of convulsions if you take the immunosuppressant drug cyclosporine (Sandimmune) while being treated with Deltasone.

If Deltasone is taken with certain other drugs, the effects of either could be increased, decreased, or altered. Check with your doctor before combining Deltasone with any of the following:

Amphotericin B (Fungizone)
Carbamazepine (Tegretol)
Estrogen drugs such as Premarin
Ketoconazole (Nizoral)
Oral contraceptives
Phenytoin (Dilantin)
Potent diuretics such as Lasix
Rifampin (Rifadin)

Special information
if you are pregnant or breastfeeding
If you are pregnant or plan to become pregnant, inform your doctor immediately. Deltasone should be taken during pregnancy or while breast-feeding only if clearly needed and only if the benefit outweighs the potential risks to the child.

Recommended dosage
Dosage is determined by the condition being treated and your response to the drug. Typical starting doses can range from 5 milligrams to 60 milligrams a day. Once you respond to the drug, your doctor will lower the dose gradually to the minimum effective amount. For treatment of acute attacks of multiple sclerosis, doses of as much as 200 milligrams per day may be given for a week.

Overdosage
Long-term high doses of Deltasone may produce Cushing's syndrome (see "What side effects may occur?"). Although no specific information is available regarding short-term overdosage, any medication taken in excess can have serious consequences. If you suspect an overdose of Deltasone, seek medical attention immediately.

Brand name:

DEMEROL

Pronounced: DEM-er-awl
Generic name: Meperidine hydrochloride

Why is this drug prescribed?
Demerol, a narcotic analgesic, is prescribed for the relief of moderate to severe pain.

Most important fact about this drug
Do not take Demerol if you are currently taking antidepressant drugs known

as MAO inhibitors or have used them in the previous 2 weeks. Drugs in this category include Nardil, Parnate, and Marplan. When taken with Demerol, they can cause unpredictable, severe, and occasionally fatal reactions.

How should you take this medication?

Take Demerol exactly as prescribed. Do not increase the amount or length of time you take this drug without your doctor's approval.

If you are using Demerol in syrup form, take each dose in a half glass of water.

■ *If you miss a dose...*
Take it as soon as you remember. If it is almost time for your next dose, skip the one you missed and go back to your regular schedule. Never take 2 doses at once.

■ *Storage instructions...*
Store away from heat, light, and moisture.

What side effects may occur?

Side effects cannot be anticipated. If any develop or change in intensity, inform your doctor as soon as possible. Only your doctor can determine if it is safe for you to continue taking Demerol.

■ *More common side effects may include:*
Dizziness
Light-headedness
Nausea
Sedation
Sweating
Vomiting

If any of these side effects occur, it may help if you lie down after taking the medication.

■ *Less common or rare side effects may include:*
Agitation, constipation, difficulty urinating, disorientation, dry mouth, fainting, fast heartbeat, feeling of elation or depression, flushing of the face, hallucinations, headache, hives, impairment of physical performance, itching, low blood pressure, mental sluggishness or clouding, palpitations, rashes, restlessness, severe convulsions, slow heartbeat, tremors, troubled and slowed breathing, uncoordinated muscle movements, visual disturbances, weakness

Why should this drug not be prescribed?

If you are sensitive to or have ever had an allergic reaction to Demerol or other narcotic painkillers, you should not use this medication. Make sure your doctor is aware of any drug reactions you have experienced.

Do not take Demerol with MAO inhibitors such as Nardil and Parnate.

Special warnings about this medication

Demerol may affect you both mentally and physically. You should not drive a car, operate machinery, or perform any other potentially hazardous activities until you know how the drug affects you.

You can build up tolerance to, and both mental and physical dependence on, Demerol if you take it repeatedly. If you have ever had a problem with drug abuse, consult with your doctor before taking this drug.

Use Demerol with caution if you have a severe liver or kidney disorder, hypothyroidism (underactive thyroid gland), Addison's disease (adrenal gland failure), an enlarged prostate, a urethral stricture (narrowing of the tube leading from the bladder), a head injury, a severe abdominal condition, or an irregular heartbeat, or if you have ever had convulsions.

Be very careful taking this drug if you are having a severe asthma attack, if you have frequently recurring lung disease, if you are unable to inhale or exhale extra air when needed, or if you have any pre-existing breathing difficulties.

Because Demerol may cause unusually slow or troubled breathing and may increase the pressure from fluid surrounding the brain and spinal cord, this drug should be used by people with head injury only if the doctor considers it absolutely necessary.

Demerol may make you feel light-headed or dizzy when you get up from lying down.

Before having surgery, make sure the doctor knows you are taking Demerol.

Possible food and drug interactions
when taking this medication

Demerol slows brain activity and intensifies the effects of alcohol. Do not drink alcohol while taking this medication.

If Demerol is taken with certain other drugs, the effects of either could be increased, decreased, or altered. It is especially important to check with your doctor before combining Demerol with the following:

Antidepressant drugs such as Elavil, Tofranil
Antihistamines such as Benadryl
Cimetidine (Tagamet)
Major tranquilizers such as Mellaril and Thorazine
MAO inhibitors such as Nardil and Parnate
Other narcotic pain killers such as Percocet and Tylenol with Codeine
Phenytoin (Dilantin)
Sedatives such as Halcion and Restoril
Tranquilizers such as Xanax and Valium

Special information
if you are pregnant or breastfeeding

Do not take Demerol if you are pregnant or planning to become pregnant unless you are directed to do so by your doctor. Demerol appears in breast milk and could affect a nursing infant. If this medication is essential to your health, your doctor may advise you to discontinue breastfeeding your baby until your treatment is finished.

Recommended dosage

ADULTS

The usual dosage of Demerol is 50 milligrams to 150 milligrams every 3 or 4 hours, determined according to your response and the severity of the pain.

CHILDREN

The usual dosage is 0.5 milligram to 0.8 milligram per pound of body weight, taken every 3 or 4 hours, as determined by your doctor.

ELDERLY

Your doctor may reduce the dosage.

Overdosage

■ *Symptoms of Demerol overdose include:*
Bluish discoloration of the skin
Cold and clammy skin
Coma or extreme sleepiness
Limp, weak muscles
Low blood pressure
Slow heartbeat
Troubled or slowed breathing

With severe overdose, a person may stop breathing, have a heart attack, and even die.

If you suspect an overdose, seek emergency medical treatment immediately.

Brand name:

DEMULEN

See Oral Contraceptives, page 775.

Brand name:

DEPAKENE

Pronounced: DEP-uh-keen
Generic name: Valproic acid

Why is this drug prescribed?
Depakene, an epilepsy medicine, is used to treat certain types of seizures and convulsions. It may be prescribed alone or with other anticonvulsant medications.

Most important fact about this drug
Depakene can cause serious liver damage, especially during the first 6 months of treatment. Children under 2 years of age are the most vulnerable, especially if they are also taking other anticonvulsant medicines and have certain other disorders such as mental retardation. The risk of liver damage decreases with age; but you should always be alert for the following symptoms: loss of seizure control, weakness, dizziness, drowsiness, a general feeling of ill health, facial swelling, loss of appetite, vomiting, and yellowing of the skin and eyes. If you suspect a liver problem, call your doctor immediately.

How should you take this medication?
If Depakene irritates your digestive system, take it with food. To avoid irritating your mouth and throat, swallow Depakene capsules whole; do not chew them.

■ *If you miss a dose...*
If you take 1 dose a day, take the dose you missed as soon as you remember. If you do not remember until the next day, skip the dose you missed and go back to your regular schedule.

If you take more than 1 dose a day and you remember the missed dose within 6 hours of the scheduled time, take it immediately. Take the rest of the doses for that day at equally spaced intervals. Never take 2 doses at once.

■ *Storage instructions...*
Store at room temperature.

What side effects may occur?
Side effects cannot be anticipated. If any develop or change in intensity, inform your doctor as soon as possible. Only your doctor can determine if it is safe for you to continue taking Depakene.

■ *More common side effects may include:*
Indigestion
Nausea
Vomiting

■ *Less common or rare side effects may include:*
Abdominal cramps, aggression, anemia, bleeding, blood disorders, breast enlargement, breast milk not associated with pregnancy or nursing, bruising, changes in behavior, coma, constipation, depression, diarrhea, difficulty in speaking, dizziness, double vision, drowsiness, emotional upset, excessive urination (mainly children), fever, growth failure in children, hair loss (temporary), hallucinations, headache, involuntary eye movements, involuntary jerking or tremors, irregular menstrual periods, itching, lack of coordination, liver disease, loss of bladder control, loss of or increased appetite, overactivity, rash, rickets (mainly children), sedation, sensitivity to light, skin eruptions or peeling, spots before the eyes, swelling of the arms and legs due to fluid retention, swollen glands, weakness, weight loss or gain

Why should this drug not be prescribed?
You should not take this drug if you have liver disease or your liver is not functioning properly, or if you have had an allergic reaction to it.

Special warnings about this medication
Remember that liver failure is possible when taking Depakene (see "Most important fact about this drug"). Your doctor should test your liver function at regular intervals.

Because of the potential for side effects involving blood disorders, your doctor will probably test your blood before prescribing Depakene and at regular intervals while you are taking it. Bruising, hemorrhaging, or clotting disorders usually mean the dosage should be reduced or the drug should be stopped altogether.

Since Depakene may cause drowsiness, you should not drive a car, operate heavy machinery, or engage in hazardous activity until you know how you react to the drug.

Do not abruptly stop taking this medicine without first consulting your doctor. A gradual reduction in dosage is usually required.

This drug can also increase the effect of pain killers and anesthetics. Before any surgery or dental procedure, make sure the doctor knows you are taking Depakene.

Possible food and drug interactions
when taking this medication
If Depakene is taken with certain other drugs, the effects of either could be increased, decreased, or altered. It is especially important to check with your doctor before combining Depakene with the following:

Aspirin
Barbiturates such as phenobarbital and Seconal
Blood-thinning drugs such as Coumadin and Dicumarol
Carbamazepine (Tegretol)
Clonazepam (Klonopin)
Felbamate (Felbatol)
Oral contraceptives
Phenytoin (Dilantin)
Primidone (Mysoline)

Extreme drowsiness and other serious effects may occur if Depakene is taken with alcohol or other central nervous system depressants such as Halcion, Restoril, or Xanax.

Special information
if you are pregnant or breastfeeding
If taken during pregnancy, Depakene may harm the baby. The drug is not recommended for pregnant women unless the benefits of therapy clearly outweigh the risks. In fact, women in their childbearing years should take Depakene only if it has been shown to be essential in the control of seizures. Since Depakene appears in breast milk, nursing mothers should use it only with caution.

Recommended dosage
The usual starting dose is 15 milligrams per 2.2 pounds of body weight per day. Your doctor may increase the dose at weekly intervals by 5 to 10

milligrams per 2.2 pounds per day until seizures are controlled or side effects become too severe. The daily dose should not exceed 60 milligrams per 2.2 pounds per day.

Overdosage
Any medication taken in excess can have serious consequences. An overdose of Depakene can be fatal. If you suspect an overdose, seek medical help immediately.

■ *Symptoms of Depakene overdose may include:*
Coma
Extreme drowsiness
Heart problems

Brand name:

DEPAKOTE

Pronounced: DEP-uh-coat
Generic name: Divalproex sodium (Valproic acid)

Why is this drug prescribed?
Depakote, an epilepsy medicine, is used to treat certain types of seizures and convulsions. It may be prescribed alone or with other anticonvulsant medications.

Most important fact about this drug
Depakote can cause serious liver damage, especially during the first 6 months of treatment. Children under 2 years of age are the most vulnerable, especially if they are also taking other anticonvulsant medicines and have certain other disorders such as mental retardation. The risk of liver damage decreases with age; but you should always be alert for the following symptoms: loss of seizure control, weakness, dizziness, drowsiness, a general feeling of ill health, facial swelling, loss of appetite, vomiting, and yellowing of the skin and eyes. If you suspect a liver problem, call your doctor immediately.

How should you take this medication?
Take the tablet with water and swallow it whole (don't chew it or crush it). It has a special coating to avoid upsetting your stomach.

If you are taking the sprinkle capsule, you can swallow it whole or open it and sprinkle the contents on a teaspoon of soft food such as applesauce or pudding. Swallow it immediately, without chewing. The sprinkle capsules are large enough to be opened easily.

Depakote can be taken with meals or snacks to avoid stomach upset. Take it exactly as prescribed.

■ *If you miss a dose...*
If you take Depakote once a day, take your dose as soon as you remember. If you don't remember until the next day, skip the missed dose and return to your regular schedule. Never take 2 doses at the same time.

If you take more than one dose a day, take your dose right away if it's within 6 hours of the scheduled time, and take the rest of the day's doses at equal intervals during the day. Never take 2 doses at the same time.

■ *Storage instructions...*
Store at room temperature.

What side effects may occur?
Side effects cannot be anticipated. If any develop or change in intensity, inform your doctor as soon as possible. Because Depakote is often used with other antiseizure drugs, it may not be possible to determine whether a side effect is due to Depakote alone. Only your doctor can determine if it is safe for you to continue taking Depakote.

■ *More common side effects may include:*
Indigestion
Nausea
Vomiting

■ *Less common or rare side effects may include:*
Abdominal cramps, abnormal milk secretion, aggression, anemia, behavior problems, bleeding, blood disorders, breast enlargement, bruising, coma, constipation, depression, diarrhea, dizziness, double vision, drowsiness, emotional upset, excessive urination (mainly children), fever, growth failure in children, hallucinations, headache, increased appetite, involuntary rapid movement of eyeball, irregular menstruation, itching, jerky movements, lack of muscular coordination, liver problems, loss of appetite, loss of bladder control, overactivity, rickets (mainly children), sedation, seeing "spots before your eyes," sensitivity to light, skin eruptions or peeling, skin rash, speech difficulties, swelling of arms and legs due to fluid retention, swollen glands, temporary hair loss, tremor, weakness, weight loss or gain

Why should this drug not be prescribed?

You should not take this medication if you have liver disease or your liver is not functioning well.

If you are sensitive to or have ever had an allergic reaction to Depakote, you should not take this medication.

Special warnings about this medication

This medication can severely damage the liver (see "Most important fact about this drug").

Depakote causes some people to become drowsy or less alert. You should not drive or operate dangerous machinery or participate in any hazardous activity that requires full mental alertness until you are certain the drug does not have this effect on you.

Do not abruptly stop taking this medicine without first consulting your doctor. A gradual reduction in dosage is usually required.

Depakote prolongs the time it takes blood to clot, which increases your chances of serious bleeding.

This drug can also increase the effect of painkillers and anesthetics. Before any surgery or dental procedure, make sure the doctor knows you are taking Depakote.

Possible food and drug interactions
when taking this medication

Depakote depresses activity of the central nervous system, and may increase the effects of alcohol. Do not drink alcohol while taking this medication.

If Depakote is taken with certain other drugs, the effects of either could be increased, decreased, or altered. It is especially important to check with your doctor before combining Depakote with the following:

Aspirin
Barbiturates such as phenobarbital and Seconal
Blood thinners such as Coumadin
Cyclosporine (Sandimmune)
Oral contraceptives
Other seizure medications, including carbamazepine (Tegretol),
    clonazepam (Klonopin), ethosuximide (Zarontin), felbamate (Felbatol),
    and phenytoin (Dilantin)
Primidone (Mysoline)
Sleep aids such as Halcion
Tranquilizers such as Valium and Xanax

Special information
if you are pregnant or breastfeeding

Depakote may produce birth defects if it is taken during pregnancy. If you are pregnant or plan to become pregnant, inform your doctor immediately. Depakote appears in breast milk and could affect a nursing infant. If Depakote is essential to your health, your doctor may advise you to discontinue breastfeeding until your treatment with this medication is finished.

Recommended dosage

ADULTS AND CHILDREN

Dosage is determined by your body weight. The usual recommended starting dose is 15 milligrams per 2.2 pounds per day; your doctor may increase the dose at 1-week intervals by 5 to 10 milligrams per 2.2 pounds per day until your seizures are controlled or the side effects become too severe. The most you should take is 60 milligrams per 2.2 pounds per day. If your total dosage is more than 250 milligrams a day, your doctor will divide it into smaller individual doses.

Overdosage

Any medication taken in excess can have serious consequences. An overdose of Depakote can be fatal. If you suspect an overdose, seek medical attention immediately.

- *Symptoms of Depakote overdose may include:*
  Coma
  Extreme sleepiness
  Heart problems

Generic name:

DERMACIN

See Lidex, page 578.

Generic name:

DESIPRAMINE

See Norpramin, page 760.

Generic name:

DESMOPRESSIN

See DDAVP, page 278.

Brand name:

DESOGEN

See Oral Contraceptives, page 775.

Generic name:

DESONIDE

See Tridesilon, page 1152.

Brand name:

DESOWEN

See Tridesilon, page 1152.

Generic name:

DESOXIMETASONE

See Topicort, page 1134.

Brand name:

DESQUAM-E

Pronounced: DES-kwam ee
Generic name: Benzoyl peroxide
Other brand names: Benzac W, Benzagel, BenzaShave,
   Theroxide

Why is this drug prescribed?
Desquam-E gel is used to treat various types of acne. It can be used alone or with other treatments, including antibiotics and products that contain retinoic acid, sulfur, or salicylic acid.

Most important fact about this drug
Significant clearing of the skin should occur after 2 to 3 weeks of treatment with Desquam-E. If used with sunscreens such as PreSun 15, which contain PABA (para-amino benzoic acid), it may cause temporary skin discoloration.

How should you use this medication?
Cleanse the affected area thoroughly before applying the medication. Desquam-E should then be gently rubbed in.

- *If you miss a dose...*
  Apply it as soon as you remember. Then go back to your regular schedule.

- *Storage instructions...*
  Store at room temperature.

What side effects may occur?
Side effects cannot be anticipated. If any develop or change in intensity, notify your doctor as soon as possible. Only your doctor can determine whether it is safe for you to continue using Desquam-E.

- *Side effects may include:*
  Allergic reaction (itching, rash in area where the medication was applied)
  Excessive drying (red and peeling skin and possible swelling)

Why should this drug not be prescribed?
Do not use Desquam-E if you are sensitive to or allergic to benzoyl peroxide.

Special warnings about this medication
Desquam-E is for external use only. Avoid contact with your eyes, nose, or throat.

If you are sensitive to medications derived from benzoic acid (including certain topical anesthetics) or to cinnamon, you may also be sensitive to Desquam-E.

Desquam-E can bleach hair or colored fabric.

Possible food and drug interactions
when taking this medication
When used with sunscreens containing PABA (para-amino benzoic acid), Desquam-E may cause temporary skin discoloration.

Special information
if you are pregnant or breastfeeding

The effects of Desquam-E during pregnancy have not been adequately studied. It should be used only if clearly needed. If you are pregnant or plan to become pregnant, inform your doctor immediately. This medication may appear in breast milk and could affect a nursing infant. If this medication is essential to your health, your doctor may advise you to stop breastfeeding until your treatment with Desquam-E is finished.

Recommended dosage

ADULTS AND CHILDREN 12 YEARS AND OVER

Gently rub Desquam-E gel into all affected areas once or twice a day. If you are fair-skinned or live in an excessively dry climate, you should probably start with one application a day. You can continue to use Desquam-E for as long as your doctor thinks it is necessary.

Overdosage

Overdosage of Desquam-E can result in excessive scaling of the skin, reddening skin, or swelling due to fluid retention. Any medication taken in excess can have serious consequences. If you suspect an overdose, seek medical attention.

Brand name:

DESYREL

Pronounced: DES-ee-rel
Generic name: Trazodone hydrochloride

Why is this drug prescribed?

Desyrel is prescribed for the treatment of depression.

Most important fact about this drug

Desyrel does not provide immediate relief. It may take up to 4 weeks before you begin to feel better, although most patients notice improvement within 2 weeks.

How should you take this medication?

Take Desyrel shortly after a meal or light snack. You may be more apt to feel dizzy or light-headed if you take the drug before you have eaten.

Desyrel may cause dry mouth. Sucking on a hard candy, chewing gum, or melting bits of ice in your mouth can relieve the problem.

- *If you miss a dose...*
  Take it as soon as you remember. If it is within 4 hours of your next dose, skip the one you missed and go back to your regular schedule. Never take 2 doses at once.

- *Storage instructions...*
  Store at room temperature in a tightly closed container away from light and excessive heat.

What side effects may occur?
Side effects cannot be anticipated. If any develop or change in intensity, inform your doctor as soon as possible. Only your doctor can determine if it is safe for you to continue taking Desyrel.

- *More common side effects may include:*
  Abdominal or stomach disorder, aches or pains in muscles and bones, anger or hostility, blurred vision, brief loss of consciousness, confusion, constipation, decreased appetite, diarrhea, dizziness or light-headedness, drowsiness, dry mouth, excitement, fainting, fast or fluttery heartbeat, fatigue, fluid retention and swelling, headache, inability to fall or stay asleep, low blood pressure, nasal or sinus congestion, nausea, nervousness, nightmares or vivid dreams, tremors, uncoordinated movements, vomiting, weight gain or loss

- *Less common or rare side effects may include:*
  Allergic reactions, anemia, bad taste in mouth, blood in the urine, chest pain, delayed urine flow, decreased concentration, decreased sex drive, disorientation, ejaculation problems, excess salivation, gas, general feeling of illness, hallucinations or delusions, high blood pressure, impaired memory, impaired speech, impotence, increased appetite, increased sex drive, menstrual problems, more frequent urination, muscle twitches, numbness, prolonged erections, red, tired, itchy eyes, restlessness, ringing in the ears, shortness of breath, sweating or clammy skin, tingling or pins and needles

Why should this drug not be prescribed?
If you are sensitive to or have ever had an allergic reaction to Desyrel or similar drugs, you should not take this medication. Make sure your doctor is aware of any drug reactions you have experienced.

Special warnings about this medication
Desyrel may cause you to become drowsy or less alert and may affect your judgment. Therefore, you should not drive or operate dangerous machinery or

participate in any hazardous activity that requires full mental alertness until you know how this drug affects you.

Desyrel has been associated with priapism, a persistent, painful erection of the penis. Men who experience prolonged or inappropriate erections should stop taking this drug and consult their doctor.

Notify your doctor or dentist that you are taking this drug if you have a medical emergency, and before you have surgery or dental treatment. Your doctor will ask you to stop using the drug if you are going to have elective surgery.

Be careful taking this drug if you have heart disease. Desyrel can cause irregular heartbeats.

Possible food and drug interactions
when taking this medication
Desyrel may intensify the effects of alcohol. Do not drink alcohol while taking this medication.

If Desyrel is taken with certain other drugs, the effects of either could be increased, decreased, or altered. It is especially important to check with your doctor before combining Desyrel with the following:

Antidepressant drugs known as MAO inhibitors, including Nardil and
    Parnate
Barbiturates such as Seconal
Central nervous system depressants such as Demerol and Halcion
Chlorpromazine (Thorazine)
Digoxin (Lanoxin)
Drugs for high blood pressure such as Catapres and Wytensin
Other antidepressants such as Prozac and Norpramin
Phenytoin (Dilantin)
Warfarin (Coumadin)

Special information
if you are pregnant or breastfeeding
The effects of Desyrel during pregnancy have not been adequately studied. If you are pregnant or planning to become pregnant, inform your doctor immediately. This medication may appear in breast milk. If treatment with this drug is essential to your health, your doctor may advise you to discontinue breastfeeding your baby until your treatment is finished.

Recommended dosage

ADULTS

The usual starting dosage is a total of 150 milligrams per day, divided into 2 or more smaller doses. Your doctor may increase your dose by 50 milligrams per day every 3 or 4 days. Total dosage should not exceed 400 milligrams per day, divided into smaller doses. Once you have responded well to the drug, your doctor may gradually reduce your dose. Because this medication makes you drowsy, your doctor may tell you to take the largest dose at bedtime.

CHILDREN

The safety and effectiveness of Desyrel have not been established in children below 18 years of age.

Overdosage

Any medication taken in excess can have serious consequences. An overdose of Desyrel in combination with other drugs can be fatal.

■ *Symptoms of a Desyrel overdose may include:*
Breathing failure
Drowsiness
Irregular heartbeat
Prolonged, painful erection
Seizures
Vomiting

If you suspect an overdose, seek medical attention immediately.

Generic name:

DEXACORT

See Decadron Turbinaire and Respihaler, page 285.

Generic name:

DEXAMETHASONE

See Decadron Tablets, page 281.

Generic name:

DEXAMETHASONE SODIUM PHOSPHATE

See Decadron Turbinaire and Respihaler, page 285.

Generic name:

DEXAMETHASONE WITH NEOMYCIN

See Neodecadron Ophthalmic Ointment and Solution, page 716.

Generic name:

DEXCHLORPHENIRAMINE MALEATE

See Polaramine, page 868.

Brand name:

DEXEDRINE

Pronounced: DEX-eh-dreen
Generic name: Dextroamphetamine sulfate

Why is this drug prescribed?
Dexedrine, a stimulant drug available in tablet or sustained-release capsule form, is prescribed to help treat the following conditions:

1. Narcolepsy (recurrent "sleep attacks")
2. Attention deficit disorder with hyperactivity. (The total treatment program should include social, psychological, and educational guidance along with Dexedrine.)
3. Short-term treatment of obesity (along with a behavioral modification program).

Most important fact about this drug
Because it is a stimulant, this drug has high abuse potential. The stimulant effect may give way to a letdown period of depression and fatigue. Although the letdown can be relieved by taking another dose, this soon becomes a vicious circle.

If you habitually take Dexedrine in doses higher than recommended, or if you take it over a long period of time, you may eventually become dependent on the drug and suffer from withdrawal symptoms when it is unavailable.

How should you take this medication?
Take Dexedrine exactly as prescribed. If it is prescribed in tablet form, you may need up to 3 doses a day. Take the first dose when you wake up; take

the next 1 or 2 doses at intervals of 4 to 6 hours. You can take the sustained-release capsules only once a day.

Do not take Dexedrine late in the day, since this could cause insomnia. If you experience insomnia or an unwanted loss of appetite while taking this drug, notify your doctor; you may need a lower dosage.

It is likely that your doctor will periodically take you off Dexedrine to determine whether you still need it.

Do not chew or crush the sustained release form, Dexedrine Spansules.

Do not increase the dosage, except on your doctor's advice.

Do not use Dexedrine to improve mental alertness or stay awake. Do not share it with others.

■ *If you miss a dose...*
If you take 1 dose a day, take it as soon as you remember, but not within 6 hours of going to bed. If you do not remember until the next day, skip the dose you missed and go back to your regular schedule.

If you take 2 or 3 doses a day, take the dose you missed if it is within and hour or so of the scheduled time. Otherwise, skip the dose and go back to your regular schedule. Never take 2 doses at once.

■ *Storage instructions...*
Store at room temperature in a tightly closed container, away from light.

What side effects may occur?
Side effects cannot be anticipated. If any develop or change in intensity, inform your doctor as soon as possible. Only your doctor can determine if it is safe for you to continue taking Dexedrine.

■ *More common side effects may include:*
Excessive restlessness
Overstimulation

■ *Other side effects may include:*
Changes in sex drive, constipation, diarrhea, dizziness, dry mouth, exaggerated feeling of well-being or depression, headache, heart palpitations, high blood pressure, hives, impotence, rapid heartbeat, sleeplessness, stomach and intestinal disturbances, tremors, uncontrollable twitching or jerking, unpleasant taste in the mouth

Unless you are being treated for obesity, you may find appetite suppression and weight loss to be unwanted side effects.

■ *Effects of chronic heavy abuse of Dexedrine may include:*
Hyperactivity, irritability, personality changes, schizophrenia-like thoughts and behavior, severe insomnia, severe skin disease

Why should this drug not be prescribed?
Do not take Dexedrine if you are sensitive to or have ever had an allergic reaction to it.

Do not take Dexedrine for at least 14 days after taking a monoamine oxidase inhibitor (MAO inhibitor) type of antidepressant such as Marplan, Nardil, or Parnate. Dexedrine and MAO inhibitor antidepressants may interact to cause a sharp, potentially life-threatening rise in blood pressure.

Your doctor will not prescribe Dexedrine for you if you suffer from any of the following conditions:

Agitation
Cardiovascular disease
Glaucoma
Hardening of the arteries
High blood pressure
Overactive thyroid gland
Substance abuse

Special warnings about this medication
In the treatment of obesity, only a short course of Dexedrine should be prescribed. When the drug's appetite-suppressing effect no longer seems to work, it is time to stop taking Dexedrine—not take more of it. Increasing the dosage will lead to drug dependence.

Be aware that one of the inactive ingredients in Dexedrine is a yellow food coloring called tartrazine (Yellow No. 5). In a few people, particularly those who are allergic to aspirin, tartrazine can cause a severe allergic reaction.

Dexedrine may impair judgment or coordination. Do not drive or operate dangerous machinery until you know how you react to the medication.

There is some concern that Dexedrine may stunt a child's growth. For the sake of safety, any child who takes Dexedrine should have his or her growth monitored.

Possible food and drug interactions when taking this medication

If Dexedrine is taken with certain foods or drugs, the effects of either could be increased, decreased, or altered. It is especially important to check with your doctor before combining Dexedrine with the following:

■ *Substances that dampen the effects of Dexedrine:*
Ammonium chloride
Chlorpromazine (Thorazine)
Fruit juices
Glutamic acid hydrochloride
Guanethidine (Ismelin)
Haloperidol (Haldol)
Lithium carbonate (Lithonate)
Methenamine (Urised)
Reserpine (Diupres)
Sodium acid phosphate
Vitamin C (as ascorbic acid)

■ *Substances that boost the effects of Dexedrine:*
Acetazolamide (Diamox)
MAO-inhibitor antidepressants such as Marplan, Nardil, and Parnate
Propoxyphene (Darvon)
Sodium bicarbonate (baking soda)
Thiazide diuretics such as Diuril

■ *Substances that have decreased effect when taken with Dexedrine:*
Antihistamines such as Benadryl
Blood pressure medications such as Catapres, Hytrin, and Minipress
Ethosuximide (Zarontin)
Veratrum alkaloids (found in certain blood pressure drugs)

■ *Substances that have increased effect when taken with Dexedrine:*
Antidepressants such as Norpramin and Vivactil
Meperidine (Demerol)
Norepinephrine (Levophed)
Phenobarbital
Phenytoin (Dilantin)

Special information
if you are pregnant or breastfeeding

The effects of Dexedrine during pregnancy have not been adequately studied. If you are pregnant or plan to become pregnant, inform your doctor immediately. Babies born to women taking Dexedrine may be premature or have low birth weight. They may also be depressed, agitated, or apathetic due to withdrawal symptoms. Since Dexedrine appears in breast milk, it should not be taken by a nursing mother.

Recommended dosage

Regardless of what the drug is to be used for, take no more Dexedrine than your doctor prescribes. Intake should be kept to the lowest level that proves effective.

NARCOLEPSY

Adults

The usual dose is 5 to 60 milligrams per day, divided into smaller, equal doses.

Children

Narcolepsy seldom occurs in children under 12 years of age; however, when it does, Dexedrine may be used.

The suggested initial dose for children between 6 and 12 years of age is 5 milligrams per day. Your doctor may increase the daily dose in increments of 5 milligrams at weekly intervals until it becomes effective.

Children 12 years of age and older will be started with 10 milligrams daily. The daily dosage may be raised in increments of 10 milligrams at weekly intervals until effective. If side effects such as insomnia or anorexia appear, the dosage will probably be reduced.

ATTENTION DEFICIT DISORDER WITH HYPERACTIVITY

This drug is not recommended for children under 3 years of age.

Children from 3 to 5 Years of Age

The usual starting dose is 2.5 milligrams daily, in tablet form. Your doctor may raise the daily dosage by 2.5 milligrams at weekly intervals until the drug becomes effective.

Children 6 Years of Age and Older

The usual starting dose is 5 milligrams once or twice a day. Your doctor may raise the dose by 5 milligrams at weekly intervals until he or she is satisfied with the response. Only in rare cases will the child take more than 40 milligrams per day.

The doctor may prescribe "Spansule" capsules for your child. They are taken once a day.

Your child should take the first dose when he or she wakes up; the remaining 1 or 2 doses are taken at intervals of 4 to 6 hours. Your doctor may interrupt the schedule occasionally to see if behavioral symptoms come back enough to require continued therapy.

OBESITY

The usual dosage is one 10- or 15-milligram "Spansule" capsule daily, taken in the morning, or up to 30 milligrams daily as tablets divided into doses of 5 to 10 milligrams taken 30 to 60 minutes before meals.

Dexedrine is not recommended for this use in children under 12 years of age.

Overdosage

An overdose of Dexedrine can be fatal. If you suspect an overdose, seek medical attention immediately.

- *Symptoms of an acute Dexedrine overdose may include:*
  Abdominal cramps, assaultiveness, coma, confusion, convulsions, depression, diarrhea, fatigue, hallucinations, high fever, heightened reflexes, high or low blood pressure, irregular heartbeat, nausea, panic, rapid breathing, restlessness, tremor, vomiting

Generic name:

DEXTROAMPHETAMINE

See Dexedrine, page 314.

Brand name:

DIABETA

See Micronase, page 661.

Brand name:

DIABINESE

Pronounced: dye-AB-in-eez
Generic name: Chlorpropamide

Why is this drug prescribed?
Diabinese is an oral antidiabetic medication used to treat Type II (non-insulin-dependent) diabetes. Diabetes occurs when the body fails to produce enough insulin or is unable to use it properly. Insulin is believed to work by helping sugar penetrate the cell wall so it can be used by the cell.

There are two forms of diabetes: Type I insulin-dependent and Type II non-insulin-dependent. Type I usually requires insulin injection for life, while Type II diabetes can usually be treated by dietary changes and oral antidiabetic medications such as Diabinese. Apparently, Diabinese controls diabetes by stimulating the pancreas to secrete more insulin. Occasionally, Type II diabetics must take insulin injections on a temporary basis, especially during stressful periods or times of illness.

Most important fact about this drug
Always remember that Diabinese is an aid to, not a substitute for, good diet and exercise. Failure to follow a sound diet and exercise plan can lead to serious complications, such as dangerously high or low blood sugar levels. Remember, too, that Diabinese is *not* an oral form of insulin, and cannot be used in place of insulin.

How should you take this medication?
Ordinarily, your doctor will ask you to take a single daily dose of Diabinese each morning with breakfast. However, if this upsets your stomach, he or she may ask you to take Diabinese in smaller doses throughout the day.

To prevent low blood sugar levels (hypoglycemia):

- You should understand the symptoms of hypoglycemia
- Know how exercise affects your blood sugar levels
- Maintain an adequate diet
- Keep a source of quick-acting sugar with you all the time

- *If you miss a dose...*
  Take it as soon as you remember. If it is almost time for the next dose, skip the one you missed and go back to your regular schedule. Do not take 2 doses at the same time.

- *Storage instructions...*
  Store at room temperature.

What side effects may occur?

Side effects cannot be anticipated. If any develop or change in intensity, inform your doctor as soon as possible. Only your doctor can determine if it is safe for you to continue taking Diabinese.

Side effects from Diabinese are rare and seldom require discontinuation of the medication.

- *More common side effects include:*
  Diarrhea
  Hunger
  Itching
  Loss of appetite
  Nausea
  Stomach upset
  Vomiting

- *Less common or rare side effects may include:*
  Anemia and other blood disorders, hives, inflammation of the rectum and colon, sensitivity to light, yellowing of the skin and eyes

Diabinese, like all oral antidiabetics, can cause hypoglycemia (low blood sugar). The risk of hypoglycemia is increased by missed meals, alcohol, other medications, and excessive exercise. To avoid hypoglycemia, closely follow the dietary and exercise regimen suggested by your physician.

- *Symptoms of mild hypoglycemia may include:*
  Cold sweat
  Drowsiness
  Fast heartbeat
  Headache
  Nausea
  Nervousness

- *Symptoms of more severe hypoglycemia may include:*
  Coma
  Pale skin
  Seizures
  Shallow breathing

Contact your doctor immediately if these symptoms of severe low blood sugar occur.

Why should this drug not be prescribed?
You should not take Diabinese if you have ever had an allergic reaction to it.

Do not take Diabinese if you are suffering from diabetic ketoacidosis (a life-threatening medical emergency caused by insufficient insulin and marked by excessive thirst, nausea, fatigue, pain below the breastbone, and a fruity breath).

Special warnings about this medication
It's possible that drugs such as Diabinese may lead to more heart problems than diet treatment alone, or diet plus insulin. If you have a heart condition, you may want to discuss this with your doctor.

If you are taking Diabinese, you should check your blood and urine periodically for the presence of abnormal sugar levels.

Remember that it is important that you closely follow the diet and exercise regimen established by your doctor.

Even people with well-controlled diabetes may find that stress, illness, surgery, or fever results in a loss of control. If this happens, your doctor may recommend that Diabinese be discontinued temporarily and insulin used instead.

In addition, the effectiveness of any oral antidiabetic, including Diabinese, may decrease with time. This may occur because of either a diminished responsiveness to the medication or a worsening of the diabetes.

**Possible food and drug interactions
when taking this medication**
When you take Diabinese with certain other drugs, the effects of either could be increased, decreased, or altered. It is important that you consult with your doctor before taking Diabinese with the following:

Anabolic steroids
Aspirin in large doses
Barbiturates such as Seconal
Beta-blocking blood pressure medications such as Inderal and Tenormin
Calcium-blocking blood pressure medications such as Cardizem and
    Procardia
Chloramphenicol (Chloromycetin)
Coumarin (Coumadin)
Diuretics such as Diuril and HydroDIURIL
Epinephrine (EpiPen)
Estrogen medications such as Premarin
Isoniazid (Nydrazid)

Major tranquilizers such as Mellaril and Thorazine
MAO inhibitor-type antidepressants such as Nardil and Parnate
Nicotinic acid (Nicobid, Nicolar)
Nonsteroidal anti-inflammatory agents such as Advil, Motrin, Naprosyn, and Nuprin
Oral contraceptives
Phenothiazines
Phenylbutazone (Butazolidin)
Phenytoin (Dilantin)
Probenecid (Benemid, ColBENEMID)
Steroids such as prednisone
Sulfa drugs such as Bactrim and Septra
Thyroid medications such as Synthroid

Avoid alcohol since excessive alcohol consumption can cause low blood sugar, breathlessness, and facial flushing.

Special information
if you are pregnant or breastfeeding

The effects of Diabinese during pregnancy have not been adequately established. If you are pregnant or plan to become pregnant you should inform your doctor immediately. Since studies suggest the importance of maintaining normal blood sugar (glucose) levels during pregnancy, your physician may prescribe injected insulin.

To minimize the risk of low blood sugar (hypoglycemia) in newborn babies, Diabinese, if prescribed during pregnancy, should be discontinued at least 1 month before the expected delivery date.

Since Diabinese appears in breast milk, it is not recommended for nursing mothers. If diet alone does not control glucose levels, then insulin should be considered.

Recommended dosage

Dosage levels are determined by each individual's needs.

ADULTS

Usually, an initial daily dose of 250 milligrams is recommended for stable, middle-aged, non-insulin-dependent diabetics. After 5 to 7 days, your doctor may adjust this dosage in increments of 50 to 125 milligrams every 3 to 5 days to achieve the best benefit. People with mild diabetes may respond well to daily doses of 100 milligrams or less of Diabinese, while those with severe diabetes may require 500 milligrams daily. Maintenance doses above 750 milligrams are not recommended.

ELDERLY

People who are elderly, malnourished, or debilitated and those with impaired kidney and liver function usually take an initial dose of 100 to 125 milligrams.

CHILDREN

Safety and effectiveness have not been established.

Overdosage

An overdose of Diabinese can cause low blood sugar (see "What side effects may occur?" for symptoms).

Eating sugar or a sugar-based product will often correct the condition. If you suspect an overdose, seek medical attention immediately.

Brand name:

DIAMOX

Pronounced: DYE-uh-mocks
Generic name: Acetazolamide

Why is this drug prescribed?

Diamox controls fluid secretion. It is used in the treatment of glaucoma (excessive pressure in the eyes), epilepsy (for both brief and unlocalized seizures), and fluid retention due to congestive heart failure or drugs. It is also used to prevent or relieve the symptoms of acute mountain sickness in climbers attempting a rapid climb and those who feel sick even though they are making a gradual climb.

Most important fact about this drug

This drug is considered to be a sulfa drug because of its chemical properties. Although rare, severe reactions have been reported with sulfa drugs. If you develop a rash, bruises, sore throat, or fever, contact your doctor immediately.

How should you take this medication?

Take this medication exactly as prescribed by your doctor.

- *If you miss a dose...*
  Take it as soon as you remember. If it is almost time for your next dose, skip the one you missed and go back to your regular schedule. Never take 2 doses at the same time.

■ *Storage instructions...*
  Store at room temperature.

What side effects may occur?
Side effects cannot be anticipated. If any develop or change in intensity, inform your doctor as soon as possible. Only your doctor can determine if it is safe for you to continue taking Diamox.

■ *More common side effects may include:*
  Change in taste
  Diarrhea
  Increase in amount or frequency of urination
  Loss of appetite
  Nausea
  Ringing in the ears
  Tingling or pins and needles in hands or feet
  Vomiting

■ *Less common or rare side effects may include:*
  Anemia, black or bloody stools, blood in urine, confusion, convulsions, drowsiness, fever, hives, liver dysfunction, nearsightedness, paralysis, rash, sensitivity to light, severe allergic reaction, skin peeling

Why should this drug not be prescribed?
Your doctor will not prescribe this medication for you if your sodium or potassium levels are low, or if you have kidney or liver disease, including cirrhosis.

Diamox should not be used as a long-term treatment for the type of glaucoma called chronic noncongestive angle-closure glaucoma.

Special warnings about this medication
Be very careful about taking high doses of aspirin if you are also taking Diamox. Effects of this combination can range from loss of appetite, sluggishness, and rapid breathing to unresponsiveness; the combination can be fatal.

If you have emphysema or other breathing disorders, use this drug with caution.

If you are taking Diamox to help in rapid ascent of a mountain, you must still come down promptly if you show signs of severe mountain sickness.

Possible food and drug interactions
when taking this medication

If Diamox is taken with certain other drugs, the effects of either could be increased, decreased, or altered. It is especially important to check with your doctor before combining Diamox with the following:

Amitriptyline (Elavil)
Amphetamines such as Dexedrine
Aspirin
Cyclosporine (Sandimmune)
Lithium (Lithonate)
Methenamine (Urex)
Oral diabetes drugs such as Micronase
Quinidine (Quinidex)

Special information
if you are pregnant or breastfeeding

The effects of Diamox during pregnancy have not been adequately studied. If you are pregnant or plan to become pregnant, inform your doctor immediately. Diamox may appear in breast milk and could affect a nursing infant. If this medication is essential to your health, your doctor may advise you to discontinue breastfeeding until your treatment with Diamox is finished.

Recommended dosage

ADULTS

This medication is available in both oral and injectable form. Dosages are for the oral form only.

Glaucoma

This medication is used as an addition to regular glaucoma treatment. Dosages for open-angle glaucoma range from 250 milligrams to 1 gram per 24 hours in 2 or more smaller doses. Your doctor will supervise your dosage and watch the effect of this medication carefully if you are using it for glaucoma. In secondary glaucoma and before surgery in acute congestive (closed-angle) glaucoma, the usual dosage is 250 milligrams every 4 hours or, in some cases, 250 milligrams twice a day. Some people may take 500 milligrams to start, and then 125 or 250 milligrams every 4 hours. The injectable form of this drug is occasionally used in acute cases.

The usual dosage of Diamox Sequels (sustained-release capsules) is 1 capsule (500 milligrams) twice a day, usually in the morning and evening.

Your doctor may adjust the dosage, as needed.

Epilepsy

The daily dosage is 8 to 30 milligrams per 2.2 pounds of body weight in 2 or more doses. Typical dosage may range from 375 to 1,000 milligrams per day. Your doctor will adjust the dosage to suit your needs; Diamox can be used with other anticonvulsant medication.

Congestive Heart Failure

The usual starting dosage to reduce fluid retention in people with congestive heart failure is 250 milligrams to 375 milligrams per day or 5 milligrams per 2.2 pounds of body weight, taken in the morning. Diamox works best when it is taken every other day—or 2 days on, 1 day off—for this condition.

Edema Due to Medication

The usual dose is 250 milligrams to 375 milligrams daily for 1 or 2 days, alternating with a day of rest.

Acute Mountain Sickness

The usual dose is 500 milligrams to 1,000 milligrams a day in 2 or more doses, using either tablets or sustained-release capsules. Doses of this medication are often begun 1 or 2 days before attempting to reach high altitudes.

CHILDREN

The safety and effectiveness of Diamox in children have not been established. However, doses of 8 milligrams to 30 milligrams per 2.2 pounds of body weight have been used in children with various forms of epilepsy.

Overdosage

There is no specific information available on Diamox overdose, but any medication taken in excess can have serious consequences. If you suspect an overdose, seek medical attention immediately.

Generic name:

DIAZEPAM

See Valium, page 1180.

Generic name:

DICLOFENAC

See Voltaren, page 1200.

Generic name:

DICLOXACILLIN

See Pathocil, page 805.

Generic name:

DICYCLOMINE

See Bentyl, page 118.

Generic name:

DIETHYLPROPION

See Tenuate, page 1094.

Generic name:

DIFLORASONE

See Psorcon, page 924.

Brand name:

DIFLUCAN

Pronounced: Dye-FLEW-can
Generic name: Fluconazole

Why is this drug prescribed?
Diflucan is used to treat fungal infections called candidiasis (also known as thrush or yeast infections). These include throat infections and fungal infections elsewhere in the body, such as infections of the urinary tract, peritonitis (inflammation of the lining of the abdomen), and pneumonia. This drug is also used to treat meningitis (brain or spinal cord inflammation) caused by another type of fungus.

In addition, Diflucan is now being prescribed for vaginal yeast infections, fungal infections in kidney and liver transplant patients, and fungal infections in patients with AIDS.

Most important fact about this drug
Strong allergic reactions to Diflucan, although rare, have been reported. Symptoms may include hives, itching, swelling, sudden drop in blood

pressure, difficulty breathing or swallowing, diarrhea, or abdominal pain. If you experience any of these symptoms, notify your doctor immediately.

How should you take this medication?
You can take Diflucan with or without meals.

Take this medication exactly as prescribed, and continue taking it for as long as your doctor instructs. You may begin to feel better after the first few days, but it takes weeks or even months of treatment to completely cure certain fungal infections.

■ *If you miss a dose...*
Take the forgotten dose as soon as you remember. However, if it is almost time for your next dose, skip the one you missed and return to your regular schedule. Do not take double doses.

■ *Storage instructions...*
Diflucan tablets should be stored at normal room temperature. Avoid exposing them to temperatures above 86°F.

What side effects may occur?
Side effects cannot be anticipated. If any develop or change in intensity, inform your doctor as soon as possible. Only your doctor can determine if it is safe for you to continue taking Diflucan.

The most common side effect is nausea.

■ *Less common side effects may include:*
Abdominal pain, diarrhea, headache, skin rash, vomiting

Why should this drug not be prescribed?
Do not take Diflucan if you are sensitive to any of its ingredients or have ever had an allergic reaction to similar drugs, such as Nizoral. Make sure your doctor is aware of any drug reactions you have experienced.

Special warnings about this medication
Your doctor will watch your liver function carefully while you are taking Diflucan.

If your immunity is low and you develop a rash, your doctor should monitor your condition closely. You may have to stop taking Diflucan if the rash gets worse.

Possible food and drug interactions
when taking this medication

If Diflucan is taken with certain other drugs, the effects of either could be increased, decreased, or altered. It is especially important to check with your doctor before combining Diflucan with the following:

Anticoagulants (Coumadin)
Antidiabetic drugs such as Orinase, DiaBeta and Glucotrol
Certain antihistamines, such as Hismanal
Cyclosporine (Sandimmune)
Hydrochlorothiazide (HydroDIURIL)
Phenytoin (Dilantin)
Rifampin (Rifadin)
Ulcer medications such as Tagamet

Special information
if you are pregnant or breastfeeding

The effects of Diflucan during pregnancy have not been adequately studied. If you are pregnant or plan to become pregnant, inform your doctor immediately. Diflucan appears in breast milk and could affect a nursing infant. If this medication is essential to your health, your doctor may advise you to stop breastfeeding until your treatment with Diflucan is finished.

Recommended dosage

ADULTS

For throat infections

The usual dose for candidiasis of the mouth and throat is 200 milligrams on the first day, followed by 100 milligrams once a day. Treatment should continue for at least 2 weeks to avoid a relapse. For candidiasis of the esophagus (gullet) the usual dose is 200 milligrams on the first day, followed by 100 milligrams once a day. Treatment should continue for a minimum of 3 weeks and for at least 2 weeks after symptoms have stopped.

For systemic (bodywide) infections

The usual dose is 400 milligrams on the first day, followed by 200 milligrams once a day. Treatment should continue for a minimum of 4 weeks and for at least 2 weeks after symptoms have stopped.

For cryptococcal meningitis

The usual dose is 400 milligrams on the first day, followed by 200 milligrams once a day. Treatment should continue for 10 to 12 weeks once tests of spinal fluid come back negative. For AIDS patients, a 200-milligram dose taken once a day is recommended to prevent relapse.

If you have kidney disease, your doctor may have to reduce your dosage.

CHILDREN

Efficacy has not been established in children, although a small number of children have been treated safely with Diflucan.

Overdosage
Any medication taken in excess can have serious consequences. If you suspect an overdose, seek medical treatment immediately.

■ *Symptoms of Diflucan overdose may include:*
Hallucinations
Paranoia

Generic name:

DIFLUNISAL

See Dolobid, page 357.

Generic name:

DIGOXIN

See Lanoxin, page 556.

Generic name:

DIHYDROCODEINE, ASPIRIN, AND CAFFEINE

See Synalgos-DC, page 1056.

Brand name:

DILANTIN

Pronounced: dye-LAN-tin
Generic name: Phenytoin sodium

Why is this drug prescribed?
Dilantin is an antiepileptic drug, prescribed to control grand mal seizures (a type of seizure in which the patient experiences a sudden loss of

consciousness immediately followed by generalized convulsions) and temporal lobe seizures (a type of seizure caused by disease in the cortex of the temporal [side] lobe of the brain affecting smell, taste, sight, hearing, memory, and movement).

Dilantin may also be used to prevent and treat seizures occurring during and after neurosurgery (surgery of the brain and spinal cord).

Most important fact about this drug
If you have been taking Dilantin regularly, do not stop abruptly. This may precipitate prolonged or repeated epileptic seizures without any recovery of consciousness between attacks—a condition called status epilepticus that can be fatal if not treated promptly.

How should you take this medication?
It is important that you strictly follow the prescribed dosage regimen and tell your doctor about any condition that makes it impossible for you to take Dilantin as prescribed.

If you are given Dilantin Oral Suspension, shake it well before using. Use the specially marked measuring spoon, a plastic syringe, or a small measuring cup to measure each dose accurately.

Swallow Dilantin Kapseals whole. Dilantin Infatabs can be either chewed thoroughly and then swallowed, or swallowed whole. The Infatabs are not to be used for once-a-day dosing.

Do not change from one form of Dilantin to another without consulting your doctor. Different products may not work the same way.

Depending on the type of seizure disorder, your doctor may give you another drug with Dilantin.

■ *If you miss a dose...*
If you take one dose a day, take the dose you missed as soon as you remember. If you do not remember until the next day, skip the missed dose and go back to your regular schedule. Do not take 2 doses at once.

If you take more than 1 dose a day, take the missed dose as soon as possible. If it is within 4 hours of your next dose, skip the one you missed and go back to your regular schedule. Do not take 2 doses at once.

If you forget to take your medication 2 or more days in a row, check with your doctor.

■ *Storage instructions...*
Store at room temperature away from light and moisture.

What side effects may occur?
Side effects cannot be anticipated. If any develop or change in intensity, inform your doctor as soon as possible. Only your doctor can determine whether it is safe for you to continue taking Dilantin.

■ *More common side effects may include:*
Decreased coordination
Involuntary eye movement
Mental confusion
Slurred speech

■ *Other side effects may include:*
Abnormal hair growth, abnormal muscle tone, blood disorders, coarsening of facial features, constipation, dizziness, enlargement of lips, fever, headache, inability to fall asleep or stay asleep, joint pain, nausea, nervousness, overgrowth of gum tissue, Peyronie's disease (a disorder of the penis that causes the penis to bend on an angle during erection, often making intercourse painful or difficult), rapid and spastic involuntary movement, skin peeling or scaling, skin rash, tremors, twitching, vomiting, yellowing of skin and eyes

Why should this drug not be prescribed?
If you have ever had an allergic reaction to or are sensitive to phenytoin or similar epilepsy medications such as Peganone or Mesantoin, do not take Dilantin. Make sure your doctor is aware of any drug reactions you have experienced.

Special warnings about this medication
Tell your doctor if you develop a skin rash. If the rash is scale-like, characterized by reddish or purplish spots, or consists of (fluid-filled) blisters, your doctor may stop Dilantin and prescribe an alternative treatment. If the rash is more like measles, your doctor may have you stop taking Dilantin until the rash is completely gone.

Because Dilantin is processed by the liver, people with impaired liver function, the elderly, and those who are seriously ill may show early signs of drug poisoning.

Practicing good dental hygiene minimizes the development of gingival hyperplasia (excessive formation of the gums over the teeth) and its complications.

Avoid drinking alcoholic beverages while taking Dilantin.

Possible food and drug interactions when taking this medication

If Dilantin is taken with certain other drugs, the effects of either could be increased, decreased, or altered. It is especially important to check with your doctor before combining Dilantin with the following:

Alcohol
Amiodarone (Cordarone)
Antacids containing calcium
Blood-thinning drugs such as Coumadin
Chloramphenicol (Chloromycetin)
Chlordiazepoxide (Librium)
Diazepam (Valium)
Dicumarol
Digitoxin (Crystodigin)
Disulfiram (Antabuse)
Doxycycline (Vibramycin)
Estrogens such as Premarin
Felbamate (Felbatol)
Fluoxetine (Prozac)
Furosemide (Lasix)
Isoniazid (Nydrazid)
Major tranquilizers such as Mellaril and Thorazine
Methylphenidate (Ritalin)
Molindone hydrochloride (Moban)
Oral contraceptives
Phenobarbital
Quinidine (Quinidex)
Reserpine (Diupres)
Rifampin (Rifadin)
Salicylates such as aspirin
Seizure medications such as Depakene, Depakote, Tegretol, and Zarontin
Steroid drugs such as prednisone
Sucralfate (Carafate)
Sulfa drugs such as Gantrisin
Theophylline (Theo-Dur, others)
Tolbutamide (Orinase)
Trazodone (Desyrel)
Ulcer medications such as Tagamet and Zantac

Tricyclic antidepressants (such as Elavil, Norpramin, and others) may cause seizures in susceptible people, making a dosage adjustment of Dilantin necessary.

Hyperglycemia (high blood sugar) may occur in people taking Dilantin, which blocks the release of insulin. People with diabetes may experience increased blood sugar levels due to Dilantin.

Abnormal softening of the bones may occur in people taking Dilantin because of Dilantin's interference with vitamin D metabolism.

Special information
if you are pregnant or breastfeeding
If you are pregnant or plan to become pregnant, inform your doctor immediately. Because of the possibility of birth defects with antiepileptic drugs such as Dilantin, you may need to discontinue the drug. Do not, however, stop taking it without first consulting your doctor. Dilantin appears in breast milk; breastfeeding is not recommended during treatment with this drug.

Recommended dosage
Dosage is tailored to each individual's needs. Your doctor will monitor blood levels of the drug closely, particularly when switching you from one drug to another.

ADULTS

Standard Daily Dosage
If you have not had any previous treatment, your doctor will have you take one 100-milligram Dilantin Capsule 3 times daily to start.

On a continuing basis, most adults need 1 capsule 3 to 4 times a day. Your doctor may increase that dosage to 2 capsules 3 times a day, if necessary.

Once-A-Day Dosage
If your seizures are controlled on 100-milligram Dilantin capsules 3 times daily, your doctor may allow you to take the entire 300 milligrams as a single dose once daily.

CHILDREN

The starting dose is 5 milligrams per 2.2 pounds of body weight per day, divided into 2 or 3 equal doses; the most a child should take is 300 milligrams a day. The regular daily dosage is usually 4 to 8 milligrams per 2.2 pounds. Children over 6 years of age may need the minimum adult dose (300 milligrams per day).

Overdosage

An overdose of Dilantin can be fatal. If you suspect an overdose, seek medical attention immediately.

■ *Symptoms of Dilantin overdose may include:*
Coma
Difficulty in pronouncing words correctly
Involuntary eye movement
Lack of muscle coordination
Low blood pressure
Nausea
Sluggishness
Slurred speech
Tremors
Vomiting

Brand name:

DILAUDID

Pronounced: Dye-LAW-did
Generic name: Hydromorphone hydrochloride

Why is this drug prescribed?

Dilaudid, a narcotic analgesic, is prescribed for the relief of moderate to severe pain such as that due to:

Biliary colic (pain caused by an obstruction in the gallbladder or bile
    duct)
Burns
Cancer
Heart attack
Injury (soft tissue and bone)
Renal colic (sharp lower back and groin pain usually caused by the
    passage of a stone through the ureter)
Surgery

Most important fact about this drug

High dose tolerance leading to mental and physical dependence can occur with the use of Dilaudid when it is taken repeatedly. Physical dependence (need for continual doses to prevent withdrawal symptoms) can occur after only a few days of narcotic use, although it usually takes several weeks.

How should you take this medication?
Take Dilaudid exactly as prescribed by your doctor. Never increase the amount you take without your doctor's approval.

■ *If you miss a dose...*
Take the forgotten dose as soon as you remember. If it is almost time for the next dose, skip the one you missed and go back to your regular schedule. Never try to "catch up" by doubling the dose.

■ *Storage instructions...*
Tablets and liquid should be stored at room temperature. Protect from light and extreme cold or heat. Suppositories should be stored in the re-frigerator.

What side effects may occur?
Side effects cannot be anticipated. If any develop or change in intensity, inform your doctor as soon as possible. Only your doctor can determine if it is safe for you to continue taking Dilaudid.

■ *More common side effects may include:*
Anxiety, constipation, dizziness, drowsiness, fear, impairment of mental and physical performance, inability to urinate, mental clouding, mood changes, nausea, restlessness, sedation, sluggishness, troubled and slowed breathing, vomiting

■ *Less common side effects may include:*
Agitation, blurred vision, chills, cramps, diarrhea, difficulty urinating, disorientation, double vision, dry mouth, exaggerated feelings of depres-sion or well-being, failure of breathing or heartbeat, faintness/fainting, flushing, hallucinations, headache, increased pressure in the head, insomnia, involuntary eye movements, itching, light-headedness, loss of appetite, low or high blood pressure, muscle rigidity or tremor, muscle spasms of the throat or air passages, palpitations, rashes, shock, slow or rapid heartbeat, small pupils, sudden dizziness on standing, sweating, taste changes, tingling and/or numbness, tremor, uncoordinated muscle movements, visual disturbances, weakness

Why should this drug not be prescribed?
If you are sensitive to or have ever had an allergic reaction to Dilaudid or narcotic painkillers, you should not take this medication. Make sure that your doctor is aware of any drug reactions that you have experienced.

Special warnings about this medication

Dilaudid may impair the mental and/or physical abilities required for the performance of potentially hazardous tasks such as driving a car or operating machinery.

Dilaudid should be used with caution if you are in a weakened condition or if you have a severe liver or kidney disorder, hypothyroidism (underactive thyroid gland), Addison's disease (adrenal gland failure), an enlarged prostate, a urethral stricture (narrowing of the urethra), low blood pressure or a head injury.

Dilaudid suppresses the cough reflex; therefore, the doctor will be cautious about prescribing Dilaudid after an operation or for patients with a lung disease.

High doses of Dilaudid may produce labored or slowed breathing. This drug also affects centers that control breathing rhythm and may produce irregular breathing. People who already have breathing difficulties should be very careful about taking Dilaudid.

Narcotics such as Dilaudid may mask or hide the symptoms of sudden or severe abdominal conditions, making diagnosis and treatment difficult.

If you are prone to convulsions, your doctor may not prescribe Dilaudid. It can make seizures worse.

Possible food and drug interactions
when taking this medication

Dilaudid is a central nervous system depressant and intensifies the effects of alcohol. Do not drink alcohol while taking this medication.

If Dilaudid is taken with certain other drugs, the effects of either could be increased, decreased, or altered. It is especially important to check with your doctor before combining Dilaudid with the following:

Antiemetics (drugs that prevent or lessen nausea and vomiting such as
    Compazine and Phenergan)
Antihistamines such as Benadryl
General anesthetics
Other central nervous system depressants such as Nembutal and
    Restoril
Other narcotic analgesics such as Demerol and Percocet
Phenothiazines such as Thorazine
Sedative/hypnotics such as Valium and Halcion
Tranquilizers such as Xanax
Tricyclic antidepressants such as Elavil and Tofranil

Special information
if you are pregnant or breastfeeding

Do not take Dilaudid if you are pregnant or plan to become pregnant unless you are directed to do so by your doctor. Drug dependence occurs in newborns when the mother has taken narcotic drugs regularly during pregnancy. Withdrawal signs include irritability and excessive crying, tremors, overactive reflexes, increased breathing rate, increased stools, sneezing, yawning, vomiting, and fever. Dilaudid may appear in breast milk and could affect a nursing infant. If this medication is essential to your health, your doctor may advise you to discontinue breastfeeding your baby until your treatment is finished.

Recommended dosage

ADULTS

Tablets
The usual starting dose of Dilaudid tablets is 2 to 4 milligrams every 4 to 6 hours as determined by your doctor. Severity of pain, your individual response, and your size are used to determine your exact dosage.

Liquid
The usual dose of Dilaudid liquid is ½ to 2 teaspoonfuls every 3 to 6 hours. In some cases, the dosage may be higher.

Suppositories
Dilaudid suppositories (3 milligrams) may provide relief for a longer period of time. The usual adult dose is 1 suppository inserted rectally every 6 to 8 hours or as directed by your doctor.

CHILDREN

The safety and effectiveness of Dilaudid have not been established in children.

ELDERLY

Elderly patients should be very careful when using Dilaudid. Your doctor will prescribe a dose individualized to suit your needs.

Overdosage

■ *Symptoms of Dilaudid overdose include:*
Bluish tinge to skin, cold and clammy skin, constricted pupils, coma,

extreme sleepiness progressing to a state of unresponsiveness, labored or slowed breathing, limp, weak muscles, low blood pressure, slow heart rate

In severe overdosage, the patient may stop breathing. Shock, heart attack, and death can occur.

If you suspect an overdose, seek emergency medical treatment immediately.

Generic name:

DILTIAZEM

See Cardizem, page 169.

Brand name:

DIMETANE-DC

Pronounced: DYE-meh-tayne DEE SEE
Generic ingredients: Brompheniramine maleate,
    Phenylpropanolamine hydrochloride, Codeine phosphate

Why is this drug prescribed?

Dimetane-DC cough syrup is an antihistamine/decongestant/cough suppressant combination that relieves coughs and nasal congestion caused by allergies and the common cold. Brompheniramine, the antihistamine, reduces itching and dries up secretions from the nose, eyes, and throat. Phenylpropanolamine, the decongestant, clears nasal stuffiness and makes breathing easier. Codeine calms a cough.

Most important fact about this drug

Dimetane-DC may cause you to become drowsy or less alert. You should not drive or operate dangerous machinery or participate in any hazardous activity that requires full mental alertness until you know how you react to Dimetane-DC.

How should you take this medication?

Take this medication exactly as prescribed.

Do not exceed the directed dosage.

■ *If you miss a dose...*
   Take it as soon as you remember. If it is almost time for your next dose, skip the one you missed and go back to your regular schedule. Do not take 2 doses at once.

- *Storage instructions...*
  Store at room temperature in a tightly closed container, away from light.

What side effects may occur?
Side effects cannot be anticipated. If any side effects develop or change in intensity, tell your doctor as soon as possible. Only your doctor can determine whether it is safe for you to continue taking Dimetane-DC.

- *More common side effects may include:*
  Dizziness/light-headedness
  Drowsiness
  Dry mouth, nose, and throat
  Sedation
  Thickening of phlegm

- *Less common or rare side effects may include:*
  Anemia, constipation, convulsions, diarrhea, difficulty sleeping, difficulty urinating, disturbed coordination, exaggerated sense of well-being or depression, frequent urination, headache, high blood pressure, hives, increased sensitivity to light, irregular heartbeat, irritability, itching, loss of appetite, low blood pressure, nausea, nervousness, rash, shortness of breath, stomach upset, tightness in chest, tremor, vision changes, vomiting, weakness, wheezing

Why should this drug not be prescribed?
This medication should not be given to children under 2 years of age or used by nursing mothers.

Do not take Dimetane-DC if you have severe high blood pressure or heart disease, or if you are taking antidepressant drugs known as MAO inhibitors (Nardil, Parnate and others). Dimetane-DC is not for treatment of asthma or other breathing disorders. Avoid Dimetane-DC if you have ever had an allergic reaction or are sensitive to any of its ingredients.

Special warnings about this medication
Use Dimetane-DC cautiously if you have, or have ever had, bronchial asthma, the eye condition called narrow-angle glaucoma, stomach, intestinal, or bladder obstruction, diabetes, high blood pressure, heart disease, or thyroid disease.

Codeine can cause drug dependence and tolerance with continued use; your doctor will monitor your use of this drug carefully.

Antihistamines can make young children excited.

**Possible food and drug interactions
when taking this medication**
Dimetane-DC may increase the effects of alcohol. Do not drink alcohol while taking this medication.

If Dimetane-DC is taken with certain other drugs, the effects of either drug could be increased, decreased, or altered. It is especially important to check with your doctor before combining Dimetane-DC with the following:

MAO inhibitor-type antidepressant drugs such as Nardil and Marplan
Medications for high blood pressure such as Aldomet
Sedatives/hypnotics such as phenobarbital, Halcion, and Seconal
Tranquilizers such as Xanax, BuSpar, Librium and Valium

**Special information
if you are pregnant or breastfeeding**
No information is available about the safety of Dimetane-DC during pregnancy. If you are pregnant or plan to become pregnant, inform your doctor immediately.

Dimetane-DC should not be taken if you are breastfeeding. If Dimetane-DC is essential to your health, your doctor may advise you to stop breastfeeding until your treatment is finished.

Recommended dosage
Do not take more than 6 doses in 24 hours.

ADULTS AND CHILDREN 12 YEARS OLD AND OVER

The recommended dosage is 2 teaspoonfuls every 4 hours.

CHILDREN 6 TO UNDER 12 YEARS OLD

The usual dosage is 1 teaspoonful every 4 hours.

CHILDREN 2 TO UNDER 6 YEARS OLD

The dosage is one-half teaspoonful every 4 hours.

Overdosage
An overdose of antihistamines may cause hallucinations, convulsions, and death, especially in infants and small children. If you suspect an overdose, seek medical treatment immediately.

■ *Symptoms of Dimetane-DC overdose may include:*
Anxiety, breathing difficulty, convulsions, delirium, depression, dilated pupils, excessive excitement or stimulation, extreme sleepiness leading to loss of consciousness, hallucinations, heart attack, high blood pressure, irregular heartbeat, rapid heartbeat, restlessness, tremors

Brand name:

DIPENTUM

Pronounced: dye-PENT-um
Generic name: Olsalazine sodium

Why is this drug prescribed?
Dipentum is an anti-inflammatory drug used to maintain long-term freedom from symptoms of ulcerative colitis (chronic inflammation and ulceration of the large intestine and rectum). It is prescribed for people who cannot take sulfasalazine (Azulfidine).

Most important fact about this drug
If you have kidney disease, Dipentum could cause further damage. You'll need regular checks on your kidney function, so be sure to keep all regular appointments with your doctor.

How should you take this medication?
Take Dipentum for as long as your doctor has directed, even if you feel better.

Take Dipentum with food.

■ *If you miss a dose...*
Take it as soon as you remember. If it is almost time for your next dose, skip the one you missed and go back to your regular schedule. Do not take 2 doses at once.

■ *Storage instructions...*
Store at room temperature.

What side effects may occur?
Side effects cannot be anticipated. If any develop or change in intensity, inform your doctor as soon as possible. Only your doctor can determine if it is safe for you to continue taking Dipentum.

Diarrhea or loose stools are the most common side effects.

■ *Other side effects may include:*
Abdominal pain/cramping, bloating, depression, dizziness, drowsiness, headache, heartburn, indigestion, inflammation of the mouth, insomnia, joint pain, light-headedness, loss of appetite, nausea, rectal bleeding, skin itching, skin rash, sluggishness, upper respiratory infection, vertigo, vomiting

Rare cases of hepatitis have been reported in people taking Dipentum. Symptoms may include aching muscles, chills, fever, headache, joint pain, loss of appetite, vomiting, and yellowish skin.

Why should this drug not be prescribed?
You should not be using Dipentum if you are allergic to salicylates such as aspirin.

Special warnings about this medication
If diarrhea occurs, contact your doctor.

**Possible food and drug interactions
when taking this medication**
If Dipentum is taken with certain other drugs, the effects of either could be increased, decreased, or altered. It is especially important to check with your doctor before combining Dipentum with warfarin (Coumadin).

**Special information
if you are pregnant or breastfeeding**
The effects of Dipentum in pregnancy have not been adequately studied. Pregnant women should use Dipentum only if the possible gains warrant the possible risks to the unborn child. Women who breastfeed an infant should use Dipentum cautiously, because it is not known whether this drug appears in breast milk and what effect it might have on a nursing infant.

Recommended dosage

ADULTS

The usual dose is a total of 1 gram per day, divided into 2 equal doses.

CHILDREN

Safety and effectiveness have not been established in children.

Overdosage
There have been no reports of Dipentum overdose. However, should you suspect one, seek medical help immediately.

Generic name:

DIPHENHYDRAMINE

See Benadryl, page 114.

Generic name:

DIPHENOXYLATE WITH ATROPINE

See Lomotil, page 588.

Generic name:

DIPIVEFRIN

See Propine, page 900.

Brand name:

DIPROLENE

Pronounced: dye-PROH-leen
Generic name: Betamethasone dipropionate

Why is this drug prescribed?
Diprolene, a synthetic cortisone-like steroid available in cream, gel, lotion, or ointment form, is used to treat certain itchy rashes and other inflammatory skin conditions.

Most important fact about this drug
When you use Diprolene, you inevitably absorb some of the medication through your skin and into the bloodstream. Too much absorption can lead to unwanted side effects elsewhere in the body. To keep this problem to a minimum, avoid using large amounts of Diprolene over large areas, and do not cover it with airtight dressings such as plastic wrap or adhesive bandages.

How should you use this medication?
Apply Diprolene in a thin film, exactly as prescribed by your doctor. A typical regimen is 1 or 2 applications per day. Do not use the medication for longer than prescribed.

Diprolene is for use only on the skin. Be careful to keep it out of your eyes.

Once you have applied Diprolene, never cover the skin with an airtight bandage or other tight dressing.

For a fungal or bacterial skin infection, you will need antifungal or antibacterial medication in addition to Diprolene. If improvement is not prompt, you should stop using Diprolene until the infection is visibly clearing.

■ *If you miss a dose...*
Apply it as soon as you remember. If it is almost time for the next dose, skip the one you missed and go back to your regular schedule.

■ *Storage instructions...*
Store at room temperature.

What side effects may occur?
Side effects cannot be anticipated. A possible side effect of Diprolene is stinging or burning of the skin where the medication is applied.

■ *Other side effects on the skin may include:*
Acne-like eruptions, atrophy, "broken" capillaries (fine reddish lines), cracking or tightening, dryness, infected hair follicles, irritation, itching, prickly heat, rash, redness, sensitivity

Using too much Diprolene, or using Diprolene for too long, may produce side effects elsewhere in the body; see the "Overdosage" section below.

Why should this drug not be prescribed?
Do not use Diprolene if you are sensitive to it or have ever had an allergic reaction to it.

Special warnings about this medication
Do not use Diprolene to treat any condition other than the one for which it was prescribed.

Possible food and drug interactions
when using this medication
No interactions have been reported.

Special information
if you are pregnant or breastfeeding
It is not known whether Diprolene, when applied to skin, causes any problem during pregnancy or while breastfeeding. Nevertheless, let your doctor know if you are pregnant or are planning to become pregnant.

Recommended dosage

ADULTS

Diprolene products are not to be used with airtight dressings.

Cream or ointment
Apply a thin film to the affected skin areas once or twice daily. Treatment should be limited to 45 grams per week.

Lotion
Apply a few drops of Diprolene Lotion to the affected area once or twice daily and massage lightly until the lotion disappears.

Treatment must be limited to 14 days; do not use any more than 50 milliliters per week.

Gel
Apply a thin layer of Diprolene Gel to the affected area once or twice daily and rub in gently and completely.

Treatment must be limited to 14 days; do not use any more than 50 grams per week.

CHILDREN

Use of Diprolene Gel, Lotion, Ointment, and AF Cream is not recommended for children under 12 years of age.

Overdosage
With copious or prolonged use of Diprolene, hormone absorbed into the bloodstream may cause high blood sugar, sugar in the urine, and a group of symptoms called Cushing's syndrome.

- *Symptoms of Cushing's syndrome may include:*
  Acne, depression, high blood pressure, humped upper back, insomnia, moonfaced appearance, muscle weakness, obese trunk, paranoia, stretch marks, susceptibility to bruising, fractures, infections, retardation of growth, delayed weight gain, wasted limbs

Cushing's syndrome may also trigger the development of diabetes mellitus. Left uncorrected, the syndrome may become serious. If you suspect your use of Diprolene has led to this problem, seek medical attention immediately.

Generic name:

DIPYRIDAMOLE

See Persantine, page 840.

Brand name:

DISALCID

Pronounced: dye-SAL-sid
Generic name: Salsalate

Why is this drug prescribed?

Disalcid, a nonsteroidal anti-inflammatory drug, is used to relieve the symptoms of rheumatoid arthritis, osteoarthritis (the most common form of arthritis), and other rheumatic disorders (conditions that involve pain and inflammation in joints and the tissues around them).

Most important fact about this drug

Disalcid contains salicylate, an ingredient that may be associated with the development of Reye's syndrome (a disorder that causes abnormal brain and liver function). It occurs mostly in children who have taken aspirin or other medications containing salicylate to relieve symptoms of the flu or chickenpox. Do not take Disalcid if you have flu symptoms or chickenpox.

How should you take this medication?

Take Disalcid exactly as prescribed. Food may slow its absorption. However, your doctor may ask you to take Disalcid with food in order to avoid stomach upset.

■ *If you miss a dose...*
Take it as soon as you remember. If it is almost time for your next dose, skip the one you missed and go back to your regular schedule. Never take two doses at once.

■ *Storage instructions...*
Store at room temperature. Keep out of the reach of children.

What side effects may occur?

Side effects cannot be anticipated. If any develop or change in intensity, inform your doctor as soon as possible. Only your doctor can determine if it is safe for you to continue taking Disalcid.

- *Side effects may include:*
Hearing impairment
Nausea
Rash
Ringing in the ears
Vertigo

Why should this drug not be prescribed?
Disalcid should not be taken if you are sensitive to or have ever had an allergic reaction to salsalate.

Special warnings about this medication
Use Disalcid with extreme caution if you have chronic kidney disease or a peptic ulcer.

Salicylates occasionally cause asthma in people who are sensitive to aspirin. Although Disalcid contains a salicylate, it is less likely than aspirin to cause this reaction.

Possible food and drug interactions
when taking this medication
If Disalcid is taken with certain other drugs, the effects of either could be increased, decreased, or altered. It is especially important to check with your doctor before combining Disalcid with the following:

ACE inhibitor-type blood pressure drugs such as Capoten and Vasotec
Acetazolamide (Diamox)
Aspirin and other drugs containing salicylates such as Bufferin and
    Empirin
Blood-thinning medications such as Coumadin
Medications for gout such as Zyloprim and Benemid
Methotrexate (Rheumatrex)
Naproxen (Anaprox, Naprosyn)
Oral diabetes drugs such as Glucotrol and Tolinase
Penicillin (Pen-Vee K)
Phenytoin (Dilantin)
Steroids such as Deltasone and Decadron
Sulfinpyrazone (Anturane)
Thyroid medications such as Synthroid

Special information
if you are pregnant or breastfeeding
The effects of Disalcid during pregnancy have not been adequately studied. If you are pregnant or plan to become pregnant, inform your doctor immediate-

ly. Disalcid may appear in breast milk and could affect a nursing infant. If this medication is essential to your health, your doctor may advise you to stop breastfeeding until your treatment with Disalcid is finished.

Recommended dosage

You may not feel the full benefit of this medication for 3 to 4 days.

ADULTS

The usual dosage is 3,000 milligrams daily, divided into smaller doses as follows:

1. 2 doses of two 750-milligram tablets

2. 2 doses of three 500-milligram tablets or capsules

3. 3 doses of two 500-milligram tablets or capsules

CHILDREN

Safety and effectiveness of Disalcid use in children have not been established.

ELDERLY

A lower dosage may be sufficient to achieve desired blood levels without the more common side effects.

Overdosage

Any medication taken in excess can have serious consequences. Deaths have occurred from salicylate overdose. If you suspect an overdose, seek medical treatment immediately.

- *Symptoms of Disalcid overdose may include:*
  Confusion, dehydration, diarrhea, drowsiness, headache, high body temperature, hyperventilation, ringing in the ears, sweating, vertigo, vomiting

Generic name:

DISOPYRAMIDE

See Norpace, page 757.

Brand name:

DITROPAN

Pronounced: DYE-tro-pan
Generic name: Oxybutynin chloride

Why is this drug prescribed?

Ditropan relaxes the bladder muscle and reduces spasms. It is used to treat the urgency, frequency, leakage, incontinence, and painful or difficult urination caused by a neurogenic bladder (altered bladder function due to a nervous system abnormality).

Most important fact about this drug

Ditropan can cause heat prostration (fever and heat stroke due to decreased sweating) in high temperatures. If you live in a hot climate or will be exposed to high temperatures, take appropriate precautions.

How should you take this medication?

Take this medication exactly as prescribed.

Ditropan can make your mouth dry. Sucking hard candies or melting bits of ice in your mouth can remedy the problem.

- *If you miss a dose...*
  Take the forgotten dose as soon as you remember. If it is almost time for your next dose, skip the one you missed and go back to your regular schedule. Never take 2 doses at once.

- *Storage...*
  Keep this medication in a tightly closed container and store it at room temperature. Protect the syrup from direct light.

What side effects may occur?

Side effects cannot be anticipated. If any develop or change in intensity, inform your doctor as soon as possible. Only your doctor can determine if it is safe for you to continue taking Ditropan.

- *Side effects may include:*
  Constipation, decreased production of tears, decreased sweating, difficulty falling or staying asleep, dilation of the pupil of the eye, dim vision, dizziness, drowsiness, dry mouth, eye paralysis, hallucinations, impotence,

inability to urinate, nausea, palpitations, rapid heartbeat, rash, restlessness, suppression of milk production, weakness

Why should this drug not be prescribed?

You should not take Ditropan if you have certain types of untreated glaucoma (excessive pressure in the eye), partial or complete blockage of the gastrointestinal tract, or paralytic ileus (obstructed bowel). Ditropan should also be avoided if you have severe colitis (inflamed colon), myasthenia gravis (abnormal muscle weakness), or urinary tract obstruction. This drug is usually not prescribed for the elderly or debilitated.

Do not take this medication if you are sensitive or have ever had an allergic reaction to it. Make sure your doctor is aware of any allergic reactions you have experienced.

Special warnings about this medication

If you have an ileostomy or colostomy (an artificial opening to the bowel) and develop diarrhea while taking Ditropan, inform your doctor immediately.

Ditropan may cause drowsiness or blurred vision. Driving or operating dangerous machinery or participating in any hazardous activity that requires full mental alertness is not recommended until you know how this medication affects you.

Your doctor will prescribe Ditropan with caution if you have liver disease, kidney disease, or a nervous system disorder.

Ditropan may aggravate the symptoms of overactive thyroid, heart disease or congestive heart failure, irregular or rapid heartbeat, high blood pressure, or enlarged prostrate.

Possible food and drug interactions
when taking this medication

If Ditropan is taken with certain other drugs, the effects of either may be increased, decreased or altered. It is especially important to check with your doctor before combining Ditropan with alcohol or sedatives such as Halcion or Restoril because increased drowsiness may occur.

Special information
if you are pregnant or breastfeeding

The effects of Ditropan during pregnancy have not been adequately studied. If you are pregnant or plan to become pregnant, inform your doctor immediately. Ditropan may appear in breast milk and could affect a nursing infant. If this medication is essential to your health, your doctor may advise you to stop breastfeeding until your treatment is finished.

Recommended dosage

ADULTS

Tablets
The usual dose is one 5-milligram tablet taken 2 to 3 times a day. You should not take more than 4 tablets a day.

Syrup
The usual dose is 1 teaspoonful 2 to 3 times a day, but not more than 4 times a day.

CHILDREN OVER 5 YEARS OF AGE

Tablets
The usual dose is one 5 milligram tablet taken twice a day. The most a child should take is 3 tablets a day.

Syrup
The usual dose is 1 teaspoonful 2 times a day, but not more than 3 times a day.

Ditropan is not recommended for children under 5 years of age.

Overdosage

Any medication taken in excess can have serious consequences. If you suspect an overdose, seek medical attention immediately.

- *Symptoms of Ditropan overdose may include:*
  Coma, convulsions, delirium, difficulty breathing, fever, flushing, hallucinations, irritability, low or high blood pressure, nausea, paralysis, rapid heartbeat, restlessness, tremor, vomiting

Brand name:

DIURIL

Pronounced: DYE-your-il
Generic name: Chlorothiazide

Why is this drug prescribed?

Diuril is used in the treatment of high blood pressure and other conditions that require the elimination of excess fluid (water) from the body. These conditions include congestive heart failure, cirrhosis of the liver, corticosteroid and estrogen therapy, and kidney disease. When used for high blood pressure, Diuril can be used alone or with other high blood pressure medications. Diuril contains a form of thiazide, a diuretic that prompts your body to eliminate more fluid, which helps lower blood pressure.

Most important fact about this drug

If you have high blood pressure, you must take Diuril regularly for it to be effective. Since blood pressure declines gradually, it may be several weeks before you get the full benefit of Diuril; and you must continue taking it even if you are feeling well. Diuril does not cure high blood pressure; it merely keeps it under control.

How should you take this medication?

Take Diuril exactly as prescribed. Stopping Diuril suddenly could cause your condition to worsen.

■ *If you miss a dose...*
   Take it as soon as you remember. If it is almost time for your next dose, skip the one you missed and go back to your regular schedule. Never take 2 doses at the same time.

■ *Storage instructions...*
   Store at room temperature in a tightly closed container. Protect from moisture and freezing.

What side effects may occur?

Side effects cannot be anticipated. If any develop or change in intensity, inform your doctor as soon as possible. Only your doctor can determine if it is safe for you to continue taking Diuril.

■ *Side effects may include:*
   Abdominal cramps, anemia, changes in blood sugar, constipation, diarrhea, difficulty breathing, dizziness, dizziness on standing up, fever, fluid in lungs, hair loss, headache, high levels of sugar in urine, hives, hypersensitivity reactions, impotence, inflammation of the pancreas, inflammation of the salivary glands, loss of appetite, low blood pressure, low potassium (leading to symptoms such as dry mouth, excessive thirst, weak or irregular heartbeat, muscle pain or cramps), lung inflammation, muscle spasms, nausea, rash, reddish or purplish spots on skin,

restlessness, sensitivity to light, Stevens-Johnson syndrome, stomach irritation, stomach upset, tingling or pins and needles, vertigo, vision changes, vomiting, weakness, yellow eyes and skin

Why should this drug not be prescribed?

If you are unable to urinate, you should not take this medication. If you are sensitive to or have ever had an allergic reaction to Diuril or other thiazide-type diuretics, or if you are sensitive to sulfa drugs, you should not take this medication.

Special warnings about this medication

Diuretics can cause your body to lose too much potassium. Signs of an excessively low potassium level include muscle weakness and rapid or irregular heartbeat. To boost your potassium level, your doctor may recommend eating potassium-rich foods or taking a potassium supplement.

If you are taking Diuril, your doctor will do a complete assessment of your kidney function and continue to monitor it. Use with caution if you have severe kidney disease.

If you have liver disease, diabetes, gout, or the connective tissue disease lupus erythematosus, your doctor will prescribe Diuril cautiously.

If you have bronchial asthma or a history of allergies, you may be at greater risk for an allergic reaction to this medication.

Dehydration, excessive sweating, severe diarrhea, or vomiting could deplete your body's fluids and lower your blood pressure too much. Be careful when exercising and in hot weather.

Notify your doctor or dentist that you are taking Diuril if you have a medical emergency, and before you have surgery or dental treatment.

Possible food and drug interactions
when taking this medication

Diuril may increase the effects of alcohol. Do not drink alcohol while taking this medication.

If Diuril is taken with certain other drugs, the effects of either may be increased, decreased, or altered. It is especially important to check with your doctor before combining Diuril with the following:

Barbiturates such as phenobarbital and Seconal
Cholesterol-lowering drugs such as Questran and Colestid
Drugs to treat diabetes such as Insulin and Micronase
Lithium (Lithonate)
Narcotic painkillers such as Percocet

Nonsteroidal anti-inflammatory drugs such as Naprosyn and Motrin
Norepinephrine (Levophed)
Other drugs for high blood pressure such as Capoten and Procardia XL
Steroids such as prednisone

Special information
if you are pregnant or breastfeeding

The effects of Diuril during pregnancy have not been adequately studied. If
you are pregnant or plan to become pregnant, inform your doctor immediately. Diuril appears in breast milk and could affect a nursing infant. If this
medication is essential to your health, your doctor may advise you to
discontinue breastfeeding until your treatment is finished.

Recommended dosage

ADULTS

Diuril comes in tablets, an oral suspension, and an intravenous preparation,
reserved for emergencies. Dosages below are for the oral preparations.

Swelling due to excess water

The usual dose is 0.5 gram to 1 gram 1 or 2 times per day. Your doctor may
have you take this medication on alternate days or on some other on-off
schedule.

High Blood Pressure

The starting dose is 0.5 gram to 1 gram per day, taken as one dose or two or
more smaller doses. Your doctor will adjust the dosage to suit your needs.

CHILDREN

Dosages for children are adjusted according to weight, generally 10
milligrams per pound of body weight daily in 2 doses.

Under 6 months

Dosage may be up to 15 milligrams per pound of body weight per day in 2
doses.

Under 2 years

The usual dosage is 125 milligrams to 375 milligrams per day in 2 doses.
The liquid form of this drug may be used in children under 2 years of age at
½ to 1½ teaspoons (2.5 to 7.5 milliliters) per day.

2 to 12 years

The usual dosage is 375 milligrams to 1 gram daily in 2 doses. The liquid form of this medication may be used in children 2 to 12 years at 1½ to 4 teaspoons (7.5 milliliters to 20 milliliters) per day.

ELDERLY

The doctor will determine the dosage based on the particular needs of the individual.

Overdosage

Any medication taken in excess can have serious consequences. If you suspect an overdose, seek medical attention immediately.

- *Signs of Diuril overdose may include:*
  Dehydration
  Symptoms of low potassium (dry mouth, excessive thirst, weak or irregular heartbeat, muscle pain or cramps)

Generic name:

DIVALPROEX SODIUM

See Depakote, page 304.

Generic name:

DOCUSATE

See Colace, page 225.

Brand name:

DOLOBID

Pronounced: DOLL-oh-bid
Generic name: Diflunisal

Why is this drug prescribed?

Dolobid, a nonsteroidal anti-inflammatory drug, is used to treat mild to moderate pain and relieve the inflammation, swelling, stiffness, and joint pain associated with rheumatoid arthritis and osteoarthritis (the most common form of arthritis).

Most important fact about this drug
You should have frequent check-ups with your doctor if you take Dolobid regularly. Ulcers or internal bleeding can occur without warning.

How should you take this medication?
Dolobid should be taken with food or food together with an antacid, and with a full glass of water or milk. Never take it on an empty stomach.

Tablets should be swallowed whole, not chewed or crushed.

Take this medication exactly as prescribed by your doctor. If you are using Dolobid for arthritis, it should be taken regularly.

- *If you miss a dose...*
  Take it as soon as you remember. If it is almost time for your next dose, skip the one you missed and go back to your regular schedule. Never take 2 doses at the same time.

- *Storage instructions...*
  Do not store in damp places, like the bathroom.

What side effects may occur?
Side effects cannot be anticipated. If any develop or change in intensity, inform your doctor as soon as possible. Only your doctor can determine if it is safe for you to continue taking Dolobid.

- *More common side effects may include:*
  Abdominal pain, constipation, diarrhea, dizziness, fatigue, gas, headache, inability to sleep, indigestion, nausea, rash, ringing in ears, sleepiness, vomiting

- *Less common or rare side effects may include:*
  Abdominal bleeding, anemia, blurred vision, confusion, depression, disorientation, dry mouth and nose, fluid retention, flushing, hepatitis, hives, inflammation of lips and tongue, itching, kidney failure, light-headedness, loss of appetite, nervousness, painful urination, peptic ulcer, pins and needles, protein or blood in urine, rash, sensitivity to light, skin eruptions, Stevens-Johnson syndrome, vertigo, weakness, yellow eyes and skin

Why should this drug not be prescribed?
If you are sensitive to or have had an allergic reaction to Dolobid, aspirin, or similar drugs, or if you have had asthma attacks caused by aspirin or other drugs of this type, you should not take this medication. Make sure that your doctor is aware of any drug reactions that you have experienced.

Special warnings about this medication

Peptic ulcers and bleeding can occur without warning.

This drug should be used with caution if you have kidney or liver disease; it can cause liver inflammation in some people.

Do not take aspirin or any other anti-inflammatory medications while taking Dolobid, unless your doctor tells you to do so.

Nonsteroidal anti-inflammatory drugs such as Dolobid can hide the signs and symptoms of infection. Be sure your doctor knows about any infection you may have.

Dolobid can cause vision problems. If you experience any changes in your vision, inform your doctor.

Dolobid may prolong bleeding time. If you are taking blood-thinning medication, take Dolobid with caution.

If you have heart disease or high blood pressure, use Dolobid with caution. It can increase water retention.

Dolobid may cause you to become drowsy or less alert; therefore, driving or operating dangerous machinery or participating in any hazardous activity that requires full mental alertness is not recommended.

Possible food and drug interactions
when taking this medication

If Dolobid is taken with certain other drugs, the effects of either could be increased, decreased, or altered. It is especially important to check with your doctor before combining Dolobid with the following:

Acetaminophen (Tylenol)
Antacids taken regularly
Aspirin
Cyclosporine (Sandimmune)
Methotrexate (Rheumatrex)
Naproxen (Naprosyn)
Oral anticoagulants (blood thinners)
The arthritis medication sulindac (Clinoril)
The diuretic hydrochlorothiazide

Special information
if you are pregnant or breastfeeding

The effects of Dolobid during pregnancy have not been adequately studied. If you are pregnant or plan to become pregnant, inform your doctor immediately. Dolobid appears in breast milk and could affect a nursing infant. If this medication is essential to your health, your doctor may advise you to discontinue breastfeeding until your treatment with Dolobid is finished.

Recommended dosage

ADULTS

Mild to Moderate Pain
Starting dose is 1,000 milligrams, followed by 500 milligrams every 8 to 12 hours, depending on the individual. Your physician may adjust your dosage according to your age and weight, and the severity of your symptoms.

Osteoarthritis and Rheumatoid Arthritis
The usual dose is 500 to 1,000 milligrams per day in 2 doses of 250 milligrams or 500 milligrams.

The lowest dose that proves beneficial should be used.

The maximum recommended dosage is 1,500 milligrams per day.

CHILDREN

The safety and effectiveness of Dolobid have not been established in children under 12 years of age. However, your doctor may decide that the benefits of this medication may outweigh the potential risks.

Overdosage

Any medication taken in excess can cause symptoms of overdose. If you suspect an overdose, seek medical attention immediately.

■ *Symptoms of Dolobid overdose may include:*
Abnormally rapid heartbeat, coma, diarrhea, disorientation, drowsiness, hyperventilation, nausea, ringing in the ears, stupor, sweating, vomiting

Brand name:

DONNATAL

Pronounced: DON-nuh-tal
Generic ingredients: Phenobarbital, Hyoscyamine sulfate, Atropine sulfate, Scopolamine hydrobromide
Other brand name: Bellatal

Why is this drug prescribed?

Donnatal is a mild antispasmodic medication; it has been used with other drugs for relief of cramps and pain associated with various stomach, intestinal, and bowel disorders, including irritable bowel syndrome, acute colitis, and duodenal ulcer.

One of its ingredients, phenobarbital, is a mild sedative.

Most important fact about this drug
Phenobarbital, one of the ingredients of Donnatal, can be habit-forming. If you have ever been dependent on drugs, do not take Donnatal.

How should you take this medication?
Take Donnatal one-half hour to 1 hour before meals. Use it exactly as prescribed.

■ *If you miss a dose...*
Take it as soon as you remember. If it is almost time for your next dose, skip the one you missed and go back to your regular schedule. Never take 2 doses at the same time.

■ *Storage instructions...*
Store at room temperature in a tightly closed container. Protect from light.

What side effects may occur?
Side effects cannot be anticipated. If any develop or change in intensity, inform your doctor as soon as possible. Only your doctor can determine if it is safe for you to continue taking Donnatal.

■ *Side effects may include:*
Agitation, allergic reaction, bloated feeling, blurred vision, constipation, decreased sweating, difficulty sleeping, difficulty urinating, dilation of the pupil of the eye, dizziness, drowsiness, dry mouth, excitement, fast or fluttery heartbeat, headache, hives, impotence, muscular and bone pain, nausea, nervousness, rash, reduced sense of taste, suppression of lactation, vomiting, weakness

Why should this drug not be prescribed?
Do not take Donnatal if you suffer from the eye condition called glaucoma, diseases that block the urinary or gastrointestinal tracts, or myasthenia gravis, a condition in which the muscles become progressively paralyzed. Also, you should not use Donnatal if you have intestinal atony (loss of strength in the intestinal muscles), unstable cardiovascular status, severe ulcerative colitis (chronic inflammation and ulceration of the bowel), or hiatal hernia (a rupture in the diaphragm above the stomach). You should also avoid Donnatal if you have acute intermittent porphyria—a disorder of the metabolism in which there is severe abdominal pain and sensitivity to light.

If you are sensitive to or have ever had an allergic reaction to Donnatal, its ingredients, or similar drugs, you should not take this medication. Also avoid Donnatal if phenobarbital makes you excited or restless, instead of calming you down. Make sure your doctor is aware of any drug reactions you have experienced.

Special warnings about this medication

Be cautious in using Donnatal if you suffer from high blood pressure, overactive thyroid (hyperthyroidism), irregular or rapid heartbeat, or heart, kidney, or liver disease.

Donnatal can decrease sweating. If you are exercising or are subjected to high temperatures, be alert for heat prostration.

If you develop diarrhea, especially if you have an ileostomy or colostomy (artificial openings to the bowel), check with your doctor.

If you have a gastric ulcer, use this medication with caution.

Donnatal may cause you to become drowsy or less alert. You should not drive or operate dangerous machinery or participate in any hazardous activity that requires full mental alertness until you know how this drug affects you.

Possible food and drug interactions
when taking this medication

Donnatal may intensify the effects of alcohol. Check with your doctor before using alcohol with this medication.

Avoid taking antacids within 1 hour of a dose of Donnatal; they may reduce its effectiveness.

If Donnatal is taken with certain other drugs, the effects of either could be increased, decreased, or altered. It is especially important to check with your doctor before combining Donnatal with the following:

Antidepressants such as Elavil and Tofranil
Antidepressants known as MAO inhibitors, including Nardil and Parnate
Antihistamines such as Benadryl
Antispasmodic drugs such as Bentyl and Cogentin
Barbiturates such as Seconal
Blood-thinning drugs such as Coumadin
Diarrhea medications containing Kaolin or attapulgite
Digitalis (Lanoxin)
Narcotics such as Percocet
Potassium (Slow-K, K-Dur, others)
Steroids such as Medrol and Deltasone
Tranquilizers such as Valium

Special information
if you are pregnant or breastfeeding

The effects of Donnatal during pregnancy have not been adequately studied. If you are pregnant or plan to become pregnant, this drug should be used only when prescribed by your doctor. It is not known whether Donnatal appears in breast milk. If this medication is essential to your health, your doctor may advise you to discontinue breastfeeding until your treatment is finished.

Recommended dosage

ADULTS

Your doctor will adjust the dosage to your needs.

Tablets or Capsules
The usual dosage is 1 or 2 tablets or capsules, 3 or 4 times a day.

Liquid
The usual dosage is 1 or 2 teaspoonfuls, 3 or 4 times a day.

Donnatal Extentabs
The usual dosage is 1 tablet every 12 hours. Your doctor may tell you to take 1 tablet every 8 hours, if necessary.

CHILDREN

Dosage of the elixir is determined by body weight; it can be given every 4 to 6 hours. Follow your doctor's instructions carefully when giving this medication to a child.

Overdosage

Any medication taken in excess can cause symptoms of overdose. If you suspect an overdose, seek medical attention immediately.

■ *The symptoms of Donnatal overdose may include:*
   Blurred vision
   Central nervous system stimulation
   Difficulty swallowing
   Dilated pupils
   Dizziness
   Dry mouth
   Headache
   Hot and dry skin
   Nausea
   Vomiting

Brand name:

DORAL

Pronounced: DOHR-al
Generic name: Quazepam

Why is this drug prescribed?

Doral, a sleeping medication available in tablet form, is taken as short-term treatment for insomnia. Symptoms of insomnia may include difficulty falling asleep, frequent awakenings throughout the night, or very early morning awakening.

Most important fact about this drug

Doral is a chemical cousin of Valium and is potentially addictive. Over time, your body will get used to the prescribed dosage of Doral, and you will no longer derive any benefit from it. If you were to increase the dosage against medical advice, the drug would again work as a sleeping pill—but only until your body adjusted to the higher dosage. This is a vicious circle that can lead to addiction. To avoid this danger, use Doral only as prescribed.

How should you take this medication?

Take Doral exactly as prescribed by your doctor—one dose per day, at bedtime. Keep in touch with your doctor; if you respond very well, it may be possible to cut your dosage in half after the first few nights. The older or more run-down you are, the more desirable it is to try for this early dosage reduction.

If you have been taking Doral regularly for 6 weeks or so, you may experience withdrawal symptoms if you stop suddenly, or even if you reduce the dosage without specific instructions on how to do it. Always follow your doctor's advice for tapering off gradually from Doral.

■ *If you miss a dose...*
Take this medication only if needed.

■ *Storage instructions...*
Store at room temperature, away from moisture.

What side effects may occur?

Side effects cannot be anticipated. If any develop or change in intensity, inform your doctor as soon as possible. Only your doctor can determine if it is safe for you to continue taking Doral.

- *More common side effects may include:*
  Drowsiness during the day
  Headache

- *Less common side effects may include:*
  Changes in sex drive, dizziness, dry mouth, fatigue, inability to urinate, incontinence, indigestion, irregular menstrual periods, irritability, muscle spasms, slurred or otherwise abnormal speech, yellowed eyes and skin

In rare instances, Doral produces agitation, sleep disturbances, hallucinations, or stimulation—exactly the opposite of the desired effect. If this should happen to you, tell your doctor; he or she will take you off the medication.

Why should this drug not be prescribed?
Do not take Doral if you are sensitive to it, or if you have ever had an allergic reaction to it or to another Valium-type medication.

You should not take Doral if you know or suspect that you have sleep apnea (short periods of interrupted breathing that occur during sleep).

You should not take Doral if you are pregnant.

Special warnings about this medication
Because Doral may decrease your daytime alertness, do not drive, climb, or operate dangerous machinery until you find out how the drug affects you. In some cases, Doral's sedative effect may last for several days after the last dose.

If you are suffering from depression, Doral may make your depression worse.

If you have ever abused alcohol or drugs, you are at special risk for addiction to Doral.

Never increase the dosage of Doral on your own. Tell your doctor right away if the medication no longer seems to be working.

Possible food and drug interactions
when taking this medication
If Doral is taken with certain other drugs, the effects of either could be increased, decreased, or altered. It is especially important to check with your doctor before combining Doral with the following:

Antihistamines such as Benadryl
Antiseizure medications such as Dilantin and Tegretol

Mood-altering medications such as Thorazine and Clozaril
Other central nervous system depressants such as Xanax and Valium

Do not drink alcohol while taking Doral; it can increase the drug's effects.

Special information
if you are pregnant or breastfeeding

Because Doral may cause harm to the unborn child, it should not be taken during pregnancy. If you want to have a baby, tell your doctor, and plan to discontinue taking Doral before getting pregnant.

Babies whose mothers are taking Doral at the time of birth may experience withdrawal symptoms from the drug. Such babies may be "floppy" (flaccid) instead of having normal muscle tone.

Since Doral does appear in breast milk, you should not take this medication if you are nursing a baby.

Recommended dosage

ADULTS

The recommended initial dose is 15 milligrams daily. Your doctor may later reduce this dosage to 7.5 milligrams.

CHILDREN

Safety and efficacy of Doral in children under 18 years old have not been established.

ELDERLY

The elderly may be more sensitive to this drug, and the doctor may reduce the dosage after only 1 or 2 nights.

Overdosage

Any medication taken in excess can have serious consequences. If you suspect an overdose of Doral, seek medical attention immediately.

■ *Symptoms of an overdose of Doral may include:*
Coma
Confusion
Extreme sleepiness

Brand name:

DORYX

Pronounced: DORE-icks
Generic name: Doxycycline hyclate
Other brand names: Vibramycin, Vibra-Tabs

Why is this drug prescribed?

Doxycycline is a broad-spectrum tetracycline antibiotic used against a wide variety of bacterial infections, including Rocky Mountain spotted fever and other fevers caused by ticks, fleas, and lice; urinary tract infections; trachoma (chronic infections of the eye); and some gonococcal infections in adults. It is also used with other medications to treat severe acne and amoebic dysentery (diarrhea caused by severe parasitic infection of the intestines).

Doxycycline may also be taken for the prevention of malaria on foreign trips of less than 4 months duration.

Occasionally doctors prescribe doxycycline to treat early Lyme disease and to prevent "traveler's diarrhea." These are not yet officially approved uses for this drug.

Most important fact about this drug

Children under 8 years old and women in the last half of pregnancy should not take this medication. It may cause developing teeth to become permanently discolored (yellow-gray-brown).

How should you take this medication?

Take doxycycline with a full glass of water or other liquid to avoid irritating your throat or stomach. Doxycycline can be taken with or without food. However, if the medicine does upset your stomach, you may wish to take it with a glass of milk or after you have eaten. Doxycycline tablets should be swallowed whole.

Take this medication exactly as prescribed by your doctor, even if your symptoms have disappeared.

If you are taking an oral suspension form of doxycycline, shake the bottle well before using. Do not use outdated doxycycline.

■ *If you miss a dose...*
Take the forgotten dose as soon as you remember. If it is almost time for the next dose, put it off for several hours after taking the missed dose.

Specifically, if you are taking one dose a day, take the next one 10 to 12 hours after the missed dose. If you are taking two doses a day, take the next one 5 to 6 hours after the missed dose. If you are taking three doses a day, take the next one 2 to 4 hours after the missed dose. Then return to your regular schedule.

■ *Storage instructions...*
Doxycycline can be stored at room temperature. Protect from light and excessive heat.

What side effects may occur?
Side effects cannot be anticipated. If any develop or change in intensity, inform your doctor as soon as possible. Only your doctor can determine if it is safe for you to continue taking doxycycline.

■ *More common side effects may include:*
Angioedema (chest pain; swelling of face, around lips, tongue and throat, arms and legs; difficulty swallowing), bulging foreheads in infants, diarrhea, difficulty swallowing, discolored teeth in infants and children (more common during long-term use of tetracycline), inflammation of the tongue, loss of appetite, nausea, rash, rectal or genital itching, severe allergic reaction (hives, itching, and swelling), skin sensitivity to light, vomiting

■ *Less common or rare side effects may include:*
Aggravation of lupus erythematosus (disease of the connective tissue), skin inflammation and peeling, throat inflammation and ulcerations

Why should this drug not be prescribed?
If you are sensitive to or have ever had an allergic reaction to doxycycline or drugs of this type, you should not take this medication. Make sure your doctor is aware of any drug reactions that you have experienced.

Special warnings about this medication
As with other antibiotics, treatment with doxycycline may result in a growth of bacteria that do not respond to this medication and can cause a secondary infection.

Bulging foreheads in infants and headaches in adults have occurred. These symptoms disappeared when doxycycline was discontinued.

You may become more sensitive to sunlight while taking doxycycline. Be careful if you are going out in the sun or using a sunlamp. If you develop a skin rash, notify your doctor immediately.

Birth control pills that contain estrogen may not be as effective while you are taking tetracycline drugs. Ask your doctor or pharmacist if you should use another form of birth control while taking doxycycline.

Doxycycline syrup (Vibramycin) contains a sulfite that may cause allergic reactions in certain people. This reaction happens more frequently to people with asthma.

Possible food and drug interactions
when taking this medication

If doxycycline is taken with certain other drugs, the effects of either could be increased, decreased, or altered. It is especially important to check with your doctor before combining doxycycline with the following:

Antacids containing aluminum, calcium, or magnesium, and iron-
    containing preparations such as Maalox, Mylanta, and others
Barbiturates such a Phenobarbital
Bismuth subsalicylate (Pepto-Bismol)
Blood-thinning medications such as Coumadin and Panwarfin
Carbamazepine (Tegretol)
Oral contraceptives
Penicillin (V-Cillin K, Pen VK, others)
Phenytoin (Dilantin)
Sodium bicarbonate

Special information
if you are pregnant or breastfeeding

Doxycycline should not be used during pregnancy. Tetracycline can damage developing teeth during the last half of pregnancy. If you are pregnant or plan to become pregnant, inform your doctor immediately. Tetracyclines such as doxycycline appear in breast milk and can affect a nursing infant. If this medication is essential to your health, your doctor may advise you to discontinue breastfeeding until your treatment is finished.

Recommended dosage

ADULTS

The usual dose of oral doxycycline is 200 milligrams on the first day of treatment (100 milligrams every 12 hours) followed by a maintenance dose of 100 milligrams per day. The maintenance dose may be taken as a single dose or as 50 milligrams every 12 hours.

Your doctor may prescribe 100 milligrams every 12 hours for severe infections such as chronic urinary tract infection.

For Uncomplicated Gonorrhea (Except Anorectal Infections in Men)
The usual dose is 100 milligrams by mouth, twice a day for 7 days. An alternate, single-day treatment is 300 milligrams, followed in 1 hour by a second 300-milligram dose.

For Primary and Secondary Syphilis
The usual dose is 200 milligrams a day, divided into smaller, equal doses for 14 days.

For Prevention of Malaria
The usual dose is 100 milligrams a day. Treatment should begin 1 to 2 days before travel to the area where malaria is found, then continued daily during travel in the area and 4 weeks after leaving.

CHILDREN

For children above 8 years of age, the recommended dosage schedule for those weighing 100 pounds or less is 2 milligrams per pound of body weight, divided into 2 doses, on the first day of treatment, followed by 1 milligram per pound of body weight given as a single daily dose or divided into 2 doses on subsequent days.

For more severe infections, up to 2 milligrams per pound of body weight may be used.

For prevention of malaria, the recommended dose is 2 milligrams per 2.2 pounds of body weight up to 100 milligrams.

For children over 100 pounds, the usual adult dose should be used.

Overdosage
Any medication taken in excess can have serious consequences. If you suspect an overdose, seek medical treatment immediately.

Generic name:

DOXAZOSIN

See Cardura, page 173.

Generic name:

DOXEPIN

See Sinequan, page 1029.

Generic name:

DOXYCYCLINE

See Doryx, page 367.

Brand name:

DUPHALAC

See Chronulac Syrup, page 194.

Brand name:

DURICEF

Pronounced: DUHR-i-sef
Generic name: Cefadroxil monohydrate
Other brand name: Ultracef

Why is this drug prescribed?
Duricef, a cephalosporin antibiotic, is used in the treatment of nose, throat, urinary tract, and skin infections that are caused by specific bacteria, including staph, strep, and *E. coli.*

Most important fact about this drug
If you are allergic to either penicillin or cephalosporin antibiotics in any form, consult your doctor *before taking* Duricef. There is a possibility that you are allergic to both types of medication, and if a reaction occurs, it could be extremely severe. If you take the drug and feel signs of a reaction, seek medical attention immediately.

How should you take this medication?
Take this medication exactly as prescribed. It is important that you finish all of it to obtain the maximum benefit.

- *If you miss a dose...*
  Take it as soon as you remember. If it is almost time for the next dose, and you take it once a day, take the one you missed and the next dose 10 to 12

hours later. If you take 2 doses a day, take the one you missed and the next dose 5 to 6 hours later. If you take it 3 or more times a day, take the one you missed and the next dose 2 to 4 hours later. Then go back to your regular schedule.

■ *Storage information...*
Store at room temperature.

What side effects may occur?
Side effects cannot be anticipated. If any develop or change in intensity, inform your doctor as soon as possible. Only your doctor can determine if it is safe for you to continue taking Duricef.

■ *More common side effects may include:*
Diarrhea

■ *Less common or rare side effects may include:*
Inflammation of the bowel (colitis), nausea, redness and swelling of skin, skin rash and itching, vaginal inflammation, vomiting

Why should this drug not be prescribed?
If you are sensitive to or have ever had an allergic reaction to a cephalosporin antibiotic, you should not take Duricef.

Special warnings about this medication
If you have allergies, particularly to drugs, or often develop diarrhea when taking other antibiotics, you should tell your doctor before taking Duricef.

Use with caution if you have a history of gastrointestinal disease, particularly inflammation of the bowel (colitis).

Continued or prolonged use of Duricef may result in a growth of bacteria that do not respond to this medication and can cause a second infection.

Possible food and drug interactions
when taking this medication
No significant interactions have been reported.

Special information
if you are pregnant or breastfeeding
The effects of Duricef during pregnancy have not been adequately studied. If you are pregnant or plan to become pregnant, inform your doctor immediate-

ly. Duricef may appear in breast milk and could affect a nursing infant. If this medication is essential to your health, your doctor may advise you to stop nursing your baby until your treatment time with Duricef is finished.

Recommended dosage

ADULTS

Urinary Tract Infections
The usual dosage for uncomplicated infections is a total of 1 to 2 grams per day in a single dose or 2 smaller doses. For all other urinary tract infections, the usual dosage is a total of 2 grams per day taken in 2 doses.

Skin and Skin Structure Infections
The usual dose is a total of 1 gram per day in a single dose or 2 smaller doses.

Throat Infections—Strep Throat and Tonsillitis:
The usual dosage is a total of 1 gram per day in a single dose or 2 smaller doses for 10 days.

CHILDREN

For urinary tract and skin infections, the usual dose is 30 milligrams per 2.2 pounds of body weight per day, divided into 2 doses and taken every 12 hours. For throat infections, the recommended dose per day is 30 milligrams per 2.2 pounds of body weight in a single dose or 2 smaller doses. In the treatment of strep throat, the dose should be taken for at least 10 days.

ELDERLY

If you are elderly, your dose may be reduced by your doctor.

Overdosage
Duricef is generally safe. However, large amounts may cause seizures or the side effects listed above. If you suspect an overdose of Duricef, seek medical attention immediately.

Brand name:

DYAZIDE

Pronounced: DYE-uh-zide
Generic ingredients: Hydrochlorothiazide, Triamterene

Why is this drug prescribed?

Dyazide is a combination of diuretic drugs used in the treatment of high blood pressure and other conditions that require the elimination of excess fluid from the body. When used for high blood pressure, Dyazide can be taken alone or with other high blood pressure medications. Diuretics help your body produce and eliminate more urine, which helps lower blood pressure. Triamterene, one of the ingredients of Dyazide, helps to minimize the potassium loss that can be caused by the other component, hydrochlorothiazide.

Most important fact about this drug

If you have high blood pressure, you must take Dyazide regularly for it to be effective. Since blood pressure declines gradually, it may be several weeks before you get the full benefit of Dyazide; and you must continue taking it even if you are feeling well. Dyazide does not cure high blood pressure; it merely keeps it under control.

How should you take this medication?

Dyazide should be taken early in the day. To avoid stomach upset, take it with food.

- *If you miss a dose...*
  Take it as soon as you remember. If it is almost time for the next dose, skip the one you missed and go back to your regular schedule. Do not take 2 doses at the same time.

- *Storage instructions...*
  Store at room temperature, away from light.

What side effects may occur?

Side effects cannot be anticipated. If any occur or change in intensity, inform your doctor as soon as possible. Only your doctor can determine if it is safe for you to continue taking Dyazide.

- *Side effects may include:*
  Abdominal pain, anemia, breathing difficulty, change in potassium level (causing symptoms such as numbness, tingling, muscle weakness, slow heart rate, shock), constipation, diabetes, diarrhea, dizziness, dizziness when standing up, dry mouth, fatigue, headache, hives, impotence, irregular heartbeat, kidney stones, muscle cramps, nausea, rash, sensitivity to light, strong allergic reaction (localized hives, itching, and swelling or, in severe cases, shock), vomiting, weakness, yellow eyes and skin

Why should this drug not be prescribed?

If you are unable to urinate or have any serious kidney disease, if you have high potassium levels in your blood, or if you are taking other drugs that prevent loss of potassium, you should not take Dyazide.

If you are sensitive to or have ever had an allergic reaction to triamterene (Dyrenium), hydrochlorothiazide (Oretic), or sulfa drugs such as Gantrisin, you should not take this medication.

Special warnings about this medication

When taking Dyazide, do not use potassium-containing salt substitutes. Take potassium supplements only if specifically directed to by your doctor. Your potassium level should be checked frequently.

If you are taking Dyazide and have kidney disease, you doctor should monitor your kidney function closely.

If you have liver disease, diabetes, cirrhosis of the liver, heart failure, or kidney stones, this medication should be used with care.

Possible food and drug interactions
when taking this medication

Dyazide should be used with caution if you are taking a type of blood pressure medication called an ACE inhibitor, such as Vasotec or Capoten.

If Dyazide is taken with certain other drugs, the effects of either could be increased, decreased, or altered. It is especially important to check with your doctor before combining Dyazide with the following:

Blood-thinning medications such as Coumadin and Panwarfin
Corticosteroids such as Deltasone
Drugs for diabetes such as Micronase
Gout medications such as Zyloprim
Laxatives
Lithium (Lithonate)
Methenamine (Urised)
Nonsteroidal anti-inflammatory drugs such as Indocin and Dolobid
Other drugs that minimize potassium loss or contain potassium
Other high blood pressure medications such as Minipress
Salt substitutes containing potassium
Sodium polystyrene sulfonate (Kayexalate)

Special information
if you are pregnant or breastfeeding

The effects of Dyazide during pregnancy have not been adequately studied. If you are pregnant or plan to become pregnant, inform your doctor immediately. Dyazide appears in breast milk and could affect a nursing infant. If this medication is essential to your health, your doctor may advise you to discontinue breastfeeding until your treatment is finished.

Recommended dosage

ADULTS

The usual dose of Dyazide is 1 or 2 capsules once daily, with appropriate monitoring of blood potassium levels by your doctor.

CHILDREN

Safety and effectiveness in children have not been established.

Overdosage

Any medication taken in excess can have serious consequences. If you suspect an overdose, seek medical treatment immediately.

■ *Symptoms of Dyazide overdose may include:*
  Fever
  Flushed face
  Nausea
  Production of large amounts of pale urine
  Vomiting
  Weakness
  Weariness

Brand name:

DYNACIN

See Minocin, page 674.

Brand name:

DYNACIRC

Pronounced: DYE-na-serk
Generic name: Isradipine

Why is this drug prescribed?

DynaCirc, a type of medication called a calcium channel blocker, is prescribed for the treatment of high blood pressure. It is effective when used alone or with a thiazide-type diuretic. Calcium channel blockers ease the workload of the heart by slowing down the passage of nerve impulses through the heart muscle, thereby slowing the beat. This improves blood flow through the heart and throughout the body and reduces blood pressure.

Most important fact about this drug
You must take DynaCirc regularly for it to be effective. Since blood pressure declines gradually, it may be several weeks before you get the full benefit of DynaCirc; and you must continue taking it even if you are feeling well. DynaCirc does not cure high blood pressure; it merely keeps it under control.

How should you take this medication?
Take this medication exactly as prescribed, even if your symptoms have disappeared. Try not to miss any doses. If DynaCirc is not taken regularly, your condition may worsen.

Swallow the capsule whole, without crushing or chewing it.

■ *If you miss a dose...*
Take it as soon as you remember. If it is almost time for your next dose, skip the one you missed and go back to your regular schedule. Never take 2 doses at the same time.

■ *Storage instructions...*
Store at room temperature, away from light, in a tightly closed container.

What side effects may occur?
Side effects cannot be anticipated. If any develop or change in intensity, inform your doctor as soon as possible. Only your doctor can determine if it is safe for you to continue taking DynaCirc.

■ *More common side effects may include:*
Dizziness
Fluid retention
Flushing
Headache
Pounding heartbeat

■ *Less common side effects may include:*
Chest pain, diarrhea, fatigue, nausea, rapid heartbeat, rash, shortness of breath, stomach upset, unusually frequent urination, vomiting, weakness

■ *Rare side effects may include:*
Constipation, cough, decreased sex drive, depression, difficulty sleeping, drowsiness, dry mouth, excessive sweating, fainting, changes in heartbeat, heart attack, heart failure, hives, impotence, itching, leg and foot

cramps, low blood pressure, nervousness, numbness, severe dizziness, sluggishness, stroke, throat discomfort, tingling or pins and needles, vision changes

Why should this drug not be prescribed?
If you are sensitive to or have ever had an allergic reaction to DynaCirc or other calcium channel blockers such as Vascor and Procardia, you should not take this medication. Tell your doctor about any drug reactions you have experienced.

Special warnings about this medication
DynaCirc can cause your blood pressure to become too low. If you feel light-headed or faint, contact your doctor.

This medication should be carefully monitored if you have congestive heart failure, especially if you are also taking a beta-blocking medication such as Tenormin or Inderal.

Before having surgery, including dental surgery, tell the doctor that you are taking DynaCirc.

Possible food and drug interactions
when taking this medication
If DynaCirc is taken with certain other drugs, the effects of either could be increased, decreased, or altered. It is especially important to check with your doctor before combining DynaCirc with the following:

  Beta-blocking blood pressure drugs such as Tenormin, Inderal, and
    Lopressor
  Cimetidine (Tagamet)
  Rifampicin (Rifadin)

Special information
if you are pregnant or breastfeeding
The effects of DynaCirc during pregnancy have not been adequately studied. If you are pregnant or plan to become pregnant, consult your doctor immediately. DynaCirc may appear in breast milk and could affect a nursing infant. If this medication is essential to your health, your doctor may advise you to discontinue breastfeeding until your treatment with DynaCirc is finished.

Recommended dosage

ADULTS

Your dosage will be adjusted to meet your individual needs.

The usual starting dose is 2.5 milligrams, 2 times a day, either alone or in combination with a thiazide diuretic drug. DynaCirc may lower blood pressure 2 to 3 hours after taking the first dose, but the full effect of the drug may not take place for 2 to 4 weeks.

After a 2- to 4-week trial, your doctor may increase the dosage by 5 milligrams per day every 2 to 4 weeks until a maximum dose of 20 milligrams per day is reached. Side effects may increase or become more common after a 10-milligram dose.

If you have kidney or liver disease, you should still begin treatment with a 2.5-milligram dose 2 times per day; however, your doctor will monitor you closely, since your condition may alter the effects of this drug.

ELDERLY

This drug's effects may be stronger in the elderly. The usual starting dose should still be 2.5 milligrams 2 times per day.

Overdosage

Although there is little information on DynaCirc, overdose has resulted in sluggishness, low blood pressure, and rapid heartbeat. The symptoms of overdose with other calcium channel blockers include drowsiness, severe low blood pressure, and rapid heartbeat.

If you suspect a DynaCirc overdose, seek medical attention immediately.

Generic name:

ECHOTHIOPHATE IODIDE

See Phospholine Iodide, page 854.

Generic name:

ECONAZOLE

See Spectazole Cream, page 1038.

Brand name:

ECOTRIN

See Aspirin, page 77.

Brand name:

E.E.S.

See Erythromycin, Oral, page 405.

Brand name:

EFFEXOR

Pronounced: ef-ecks-OR
Generic name: Venlafaxine hydrochloride

Why is this drug prescribed?

Effexor is prescribed for the treatment of depression—that is, a continuing depression that interferes with daily functioning. The symptoms usually include changes in appetite, sleep habits, and mind/body coordination, decreased sex drive, increased fatigue, feelings of guilt or worthlessness, difficulty concentrating, slowed thinking, and suicidal thoughts.

Most important fact about this drug

Serious, sometimes fatal reactions have occurred when Effexor is used in combination with other antidepressant drugs known as MAO inhibitors, including Nardil, Parnate, and Marplan. Never take Effexor with one of these drugs; and do not begin therapy with Effexor within 14 days of discontinuing treatment with one of them. Also, allow at least 7 days between the last dose of Effexor and the first dose of an MAO inhibitor.

How should you take this medication?

Take Effexor with food, exactly as prescribed. It may take several weeks before you begin to feel better. Your doctor should check your progress periodically.

- If you miss a dose...
  It is not necessary to make it up. Skip the missed dose and continue with your next scheduled dose. Do not take 2 doses at once.

■ *Storage instructions...*
Store in a tightly closed container at room temperature. Protect from excessive heat and moisture.

What side effects may occur?

Side effects cannot be anticipated. If any develop or change in intensity, tell your doctor as soon as possible. Only your doctor can determine if it is safe for you to continue taking Effexor.

■ *More common side effects may include:*
Abnormal dreams, abnormal ejaculation/orgasm, anxiety, blurred vision, chills, constipation, diarrhea, dizziness, dry mouth, extreme muscle tension, flushing, frequent urination, gas, headache, impotence, inability to sleep, indigestion, loss of appetite, nausea, nervousness, prickling or burning sensation, rash, sleepiness, sweating, tremor, vomiting, weakness, yawning

■ *Less common side effects may include:*
Abnormal thinking, abnormal vision, accidental injury, agitation, belching, blood in the urine, bronchitis, bruising, changeable emotions, chest pain, confusion, decreased sex drive, depression, difficult or painful urination, difficulty in breathing, difficulty swallowing, dilated pupils, ear pain, high or low blood pressure, inflammation of the vagina, injury, itching, lack of orgasm, light-headedness on standing up, lockjaw, loss of touch with reality, menstrual problems, migraine headache, neck pain, orgasm disturbance, rapid heartbeat, ringing in the ears, taste changes, twitching, uterine bleeding between menstrual periods, vague feeling of illness, vertigo, weight loss or gain

■ *Rare side effects may include:*
Abnormally slow movements, abnormal movements, abnormal sensitivity to sound, abnormal speech, abortion, abuse of alcohol, acne, alcohol intolerance, allergic reaction, anemia, angina pectoris (crushing chest pain), apathy, appendicitis, arthritis, asthma, bad breath, black stools, bleeding gums, blocked intestine, blood clots, blood clots in the lungs, blood disorders, bluish color to the skin, body odor, bone disease and/or pain, including osteoporosis, breast enlargement or swelling, breast pain, brittle nails, bulging eyes, cancerous growth, cataracts, changed sense of smell, chest congestion, cold hands and feet, colitis (inflamed bowel), confusion, conjunctivitis ("pinkeye"), coughing up blood, deafness, delusions, depression, diabetes, double vision, drug withdrawal symp-

toms, dry eyes, dry skin, ear infection, eczema, enlarged abdomen, enlarged thyroid gland, exaggerated feeling of well-being, excessive hair growth, excessive menstrual flow, eye disorders, eye pain, fainting, fungus infection, gallstones, glaucoma, gout, hair discoloration, hair loss, hallucinations, hangover effect, heart disorders, hemorrhoids, hepatitis, herpes infections, high cholesterol, hives, hostility, hyperventilation (fast, deep breathing), inability to communicate, increased mucus, increased physical activity, increased salivation, increased sensitivity to touch, increased sex drive, inflammation of the stomach, intestines, anus and rectum, gums, tongue, eyelid, or inner ear, intolerance to light, involuntary eye movements, irregular or slow heartbeat, kidney disorders, lack of menstruation, large amounts of urine, laryngitis, loss of consciousness, loss of muscle movement, low or high blood sugar, menstrual problems, middle ear infection, mouth fungus, mouth sores, muscle spasms, muscle weakness, nosebleeds, over- and underactive thyroid gland, overdose, paranoia, pelvic pain, pinpoint pupils, "pins and needles" around the mouth, pneumonia, prolonged erection, psoriasis, rectal hemorrhage, reduced menstrual flow, restlessness, secretion of milk, sensitivity to light, skin disorders, skin eruptions or hemorrhage, skin inflammation, sleep disturbance, soft stools, stiff neck, stomach or peptic ulcer, stroke, stupor, sugar in the urine, swelling due to fluid retention, swollen or discolored tongue, taste loss, temporary failure to breathe, thirst, twisted neck, ulcer, unconsciousness, uncoordinated movements, urgent need to urinate, urination at night, uterine and vaginal hemorrhage, varicose veins, voice changes, vomiting blood, yellowed eyes and skin

Why should this drug not be prescribed?
Never take Effexor while taking other antidepressants known as MAO inhibitors. (See "Most important fact about this drug.")

Special warnings about this medication
Your doctor will prescribe Effexor with caution if you have high blood pressure, heart, liver, or kidney disease, or a history of seizures or mania (extreme agitation or excitability). You should discuss all of your medical problems with your doctor before taking Effexor.

Effexor may cause you to feel drowsy or less alert and may affect your judgment. Therefore, avoid driving or operating dangerous machinery or participating in any hazardous activity that requires full mental alertness until you know how this drug affects you.

If you have ever been addicted to drugs, tell your doctor before you start taking Effexor.

If you develop a skin rash or hives while taking Effexor, notify your doctor.

Do not stop taking the drug without consulting your doctor. If you stop suddenly, you may have withdrawal symptoms, even though this drug does not seem to be habit-forming. Your doctor will have you taper off gradually.

Possible food and drug interactions
when taking this medication
Combining Effexor with MAO inhibitors could cause a fatal reaction. (See "Most important fact about this drug.")

Although Effexor does not interact with alcohol, the manufacturer recommends avoiding alcohol while taking this medication.

If you have high blood pressure or liver disease, or are elderly, check with your doctor before combining Effexor with cimetidine (Tagamet).

Effexor does not interact with Lithium or Valium. However, you should consult your doctor before combining Effexor with other drugs that affect the central nervous system, including narcotic painkillers, sleep aids, tranquilizers, and other antidepressants.

Special information
if you are pregnant or breastfeeding
The effects of Effexor during pregnancy have not been adequately studied. If you are pregnant or are planning to become pregnant, tell your doctor immediately. Effexor should be used during pregnancy only if clearly needed. Effexor may appear in breast milk. If this medication is essential to your health, your doctor may tell you to discontinue breastfeeding your baby until your treatment with Effexor is finished.

Recommended dosage

ADULTS

The usual starting dose is 75 milligrams a day, divided into 2 or 3 smaller doses, and taken with food. If needed, your doctor may increase your dose to 150 to 225 milligrams a day up to a maximum of 375 milligrams per day.

If you have kidney or liver disease or are taking other medications, your doctor will adjust your dosage accordingly.

CHILDREN

The safety and effectiveness of Effexor have not been established in children under 18 years of age.

Overdosage

Any medication taken in excess can have serious consequences. If you suspect an overdose, seek medical attention immediately.

■ *Symptoms of Effexor overdose include:*
Convulsions
Rapid heartbeat
Sleepiness

Brand name:

EFUDEX

Pronounced: EFF-you-decks
Generic name: Fluorouracil

Why is this drug prescribed?

Efudex is an prescribed for the treatment of actinic or solar keratoses (small red horny growths or flesh-colored wartlike growths caused by overexposure to ultraviolet radiation or the sun). Such growths may develop into skin cancer. When conventional methods are impractical—as when the affected sites are hard to get at—Efudex is useful in the treatment of superficial basal cell carcinomas, or slow-growing malignant tumors of the face usually found at the edge of the nostrils, eyelids, or lips. Efudex is available in cream and solution forms.

Most important fact about this drug

If you use an airtight dressing to cover the skin being treated, there may be inflammatory reactions in the normal skin around the treated area. If it is necessary to cover the treated area, use a porous gauze dressing to avoid skin reactions.

How should you take this medication?

Use care when applying Efudex around the eyes, nose, and mouth. Wash your hands immediately after applying this medication.

■ *If you miss a dose...*
Apply it as soon as you remember. If more than a few hours have passed, skip the dose you missed and go back to your regular schedule. If you miss more than 1 dose, contact your doctor.

- *Storage instructions...*
  Store away from heat, light, and moisture.

What side effects may occur?
Side effects cannot be anticipated. If any develop or change in intensity, inform your doctor as soon as possible. Only your doctor can determine if it is safe for you to continue using Efudex.

- *More common side effects may include:*
  Burning
  Discoloration of the skin
  Itching
  Pain

- *Less common side effects may include:*
  Allergic skin inflammation, pus, scaling, scarring, soreness, swelling, tenderness

Why should this drug not be prescribed?
If you are sensitive to or have ever had an allergic reaction to Efudex or similar drugs, you should not take this medication. Make sure your doctor is aware of any drug reactions you have experienced.

Special warnings about this medication
Avoid prolonged exposure to ultraviolet rays while you are under treatment with Efudex.

Skin may be unsightly during treatment with this drug and, in some cases, for several weeks after treatment has ended.

If your solar keratoses do not clear up with use of this drug, your doctor will probably order a biopsy (removal of small amount of tissue to be examined under a microscope) to confirm the skin disease.

Your doctor will perform follow-up biopsies if you are being treated for superficial basal cell carcinoma.

Possible food and drug interactions
when taking this medication
There are no reported food or drug interactions.

Special information
if you are pregnant or breastfeeding
The effects of Efudex during pregnancy have not been adequately studied. If you are pregnant, plan to become pregnant, or are breastfeeding your baby, consult your doctor immediately.

Recommended dosage
When Efudex is applied to affected skin, the skin becomes abnormally red, blisters form, and the surface skin wears away. A lesion or sore forms at the affected site, and the diseased or cancerous skin cells die before a new layer of skin forms.

ADULTS

Actinic or Solar Keratosis
Apply cream or solution 2 times a day in an amount sufficient to cover the affected area. Continue using the medication until the inflammatory response reaches the stage where the skin wears away, a sore or lesion forms, and the skin cells die; your doctor will then have you stop using the medication. The usual length of treatment is from 2 to 4 weeks. You may not see complete healing of the affected area for 1 to 2 months after ending the treatment.

Superficial Basal Cell Carcinomas
You should use only the 5% strength of this medication. Twice a day, apply enough cream or solution to cover the affected area. Continue the treatment for at least 3 to 6 weeks; it may take 10 to 12 weeks of application before the lesions are gone.

Your doctor will want to monitor your condition to make sure it has been cured.

Overdosage
Although no specific information is available on Efudex overdosage, any medication used in excess can have serious consequences. If you suspect an overdosage, seek medical attention immediately.

Brand name:

ELAVIL

Pronounced: ELL-uh-vil
Generic name: Amitriptyline hydrochloride
Other brand name: Endep

Why is this drug prescribed?
Elavil is prescribed for the relief of symptoms of mental depression. It is a member of the group of drugs called tricyclic antidepressants. Some doctors also prescribe Elavil to treat bulimia (an eating disorder), to control chronic pain, to prevent migraine headaches, and to treat a pathological weeping and laughing syndrome associated with multiple sclerosis.

Most important fact about this drug
You may need to take Elavil regularly for several weeks before it becomes fully effective. Do not skip doses, even if they seem to make no difference or you feel you don't need them.

How should you take this medication?
Take Elavil exactly as prescribed. You may experience side effects, such as mild drowsiness, early in therapy. However, they usually disappear after a few days.

Elavil may cause dry mouth. Sucking a hard candy, chewing gum or melting bits of ice in your mouth can provide relief.

■ *If you miss a dose...*
Take it as soon as you remember. If it is almost time for your next dose, skip the one you missed and go back to your regular schedule. Never take 2 doses at the same time.

If you take a single daily dose at bedtime, do not make up for it in the morning. It may cause side effects during the day.

■ *Storage instructions...*
Keep Elavil in a tightly closed container. Store at room temperature. Protect from light and excessive heat.

What side effects may occur?
Side effects cannot be anticipated. If any develop or change in intensity, inform your doctor as soon as possible. Only your doctor can determine if it is safe for you to continue taking Elavil.

■ *Side effects may include:*
Abnormal movements, anxiety, black tongue, blurred vision, breast development in males, breast enlargement, coma, confusion, constipation, delusions, diarrhea, difficult or frequent urination, difficulty in speech, dilation of pupils, disorientation, disturbed concentration, dizziness on getting up, dizziness or light-headedness, drowsiness, dry mouth, excessive or spontaneous flow of milk, excitement, fatigue, fluid retention, hair

loss, hallucinations, headache, heart attack, hepatitis, high blood pressure, high fever, high or low blood sugar, hives, impotence, inability to sleep, increased or decreased sex drive, increased perspiration, increased pressure within the eye, inflammation of the mouth, intestinal obstruction, irregular heartbeat, lack or loss of coordination, loss of appetite, low blood pressure, nausea, nightmares, numbness, rapid and/or fast, fluttery heartbeat, rash, red or purple spots on skin, restlessness, ringing in the ears, seizures, sensitivity to light, stomach upset, strange taste, stroke, swelling due to fluid retention in the face and tongue, swelling of testicles, swollen glands, tingling and pins and needles in the arms and legs, tremors, vomiting, weakness, weight gain or loss, yellowed eyes and skin

■ *Side effects due to rapid decrease or abrupt withdrawal from Elavil include:*
Headache
Nausea
Vague feeling of bodily discomfort

■ *Side effects due to gradual dosage reduction may include:*
Dream and sleep disturbances
Irritability
Restlessness

These side effects do not signify an addiction to the drug.

Why should this drug not be prescribed?
If you are sensitive to or have ever had an allergic reaction to Elavil or similar drugs such as Norpramin and Tofranil, you should not take this medication. Make sure your doctor is aware of any drug reactions you have experienced.

Do not take Elavil while taking other antidepressants known as MAO inhibitors. Drugs in this category include Nardil, Parnate, and Marplan.

Unless you are directed to do so by your doctor, do not take this medication if you are recovering from a heart attack.

Special warnings about this medication
Do not stop taking Elavil abruptly, especially if you have been taking large doses for a long time. Your doctor probably will want to decrease your dosage gradually. This will help prevent a possible relapse and will reduce the possibility of withdrawal symptoms.

Elavil may make your skin more sensitive to sunlight. Try to stay out of the sun, wear protective clothing, and apply a sun block.

Elavil may cause you to become drowsy or less alert; therefore, you should not drive or operate dangerous machinery or participate in any hazardous activity that requires full mental alertness until you know how this drug affects you.

While taking this medication, you may feel dizzy or light-headed or actually faint when getting up from a lying or sitting position. If getting up slowly doesn't help or if this problem continues, notify your doctor.

Use Elavil with caution if you have ever had seizures, urinary retention, glaucoma or other chronic eye conditions, a heart or circulatory system disorder, or liver problems. Be cautious, too, if you are receiving thyroid medication. You should discuss all of your medical problems with your doctor before starting Elavil therapy.

Before having surgery, dental treatment or any diagnostic procedure, tell the doctor that you are taking Elavil. Certain drugs used during surgery, such as anesthetics and muscle relaxants, and drugs used in certain diagnostic procedures may react badly with Elavil.

Possible food and drug interactions
when taking this medication

Elavil may intensify the effects of alcohol. Do not drink alcohol while taking this medication.

If Elavil is taken with certain other drugs, the effects of either could be increased, decreased, or altered. It is especially important that you consult with your doctor before taking Elavil in combination with the following:

Acetazolamide (Diamox)
Airway-opening drugs such as Proventil and Ventolin
Allergy and cold medicines such as Comtrex and Dristan
Antispasmodic drugs such as Bentyl
Antihistamines such as Benadryl and Tavist
Barbiturates such as phenobarbital
Certain blood pressure medicines such as Catapres
Cimetidine (Tagamet)
Disulfiram (Antabuse)
Estrogen drugs such as Premarin
Ethchlorvynol (Placidyl)
Fluoxetine (Prozac)
Guanethidine (Ismelin)
Levodopa (Larodopa)
Major tranquilizers such as Mellaril and Thorazine
Muscle relaxants such as Lioresal

Oral contraceptives
Painkillers such as Demerol and Percocet
Parkinsonism drugs such as Cogentin
Quinidine (Quinidex)
Seizure medications such as Tegretol and Dilantin
Sleep medicines such as Halcion and Dalmane
Thyroid hormones (Synthroid)
Tranquilizers such as Librium and Xanax
Vitamin C in large doses
Warfarin (Coumadin)

Special information
if you are pregnant or breastfeeding

The effects of Elavil during pregnancy have not been adequately studied. If you are pregnant or planning to become pregnant, inform your doctor immediately. This medication appears in breast milk. If Elavil is essential to your health, your doctor may advise you to discontinue breastfeeding until your treatment is finished.

Recommended dosage

ADULTS

The usual starting dosage is 75 milligrams per day divided into 2 or more smaller doses. Your doctor may gradually increase this dose to 150 milligrams per day. The total daily dose is generally never higher than 200 milligrams.

Alternatively, your doctor may want you to start with 50 milligrams to 100 milligrams at bedtime. He or she may increase this bedtime dose by 25 or 50 milligrams up to a total of 150 milligrams a day.

For long-term use, the usual dose ranges from 40 to 100 milligrams taken once daily, usually at bedtime.

CHILDREN

Use of Elavil is not recommended for children under 12 years of age.

The usual dose for adolescents 12 years of age and over is 10 milligrams 3 times a day, with 20 milligrams taken at bedtime.

ELDERLY

The usual dose is 10 milligrams taken 3 times a day, with 20 milligrams taken at bedtime.

Overdosage
An overdose of Elavil can prove fatal.

- *Symptoms of Elavil overdose may include:*
  Abnormally low blood pressure
  Congestive heart failure
  Convulsions
  Dilated pupils
  Drowsiness
  Rapid or irregular heartbeat
  Reduced body temperature
  Stupor
  Unresponsiveness or coma

- *Symptoms contrary to the effect of this medication are:*
  Agitation
  Extremely high body temperature
  Rigid muscles
  Vomiting

If you suspect an overdose, seek medical attention immediately.

Brand name:

ELDEPRYL

Pronounced: ELL-dep-rill
Generic name: Selegiline hydrochloride

Why is this drug prescribed?
Eldepryl is prescribed along with Sinemet (levodopa/carbidopa) for people
with Parkinson's disease. It is used when Sinemet no longer seems to be
working well. Eldepryl has no effect when taken by itself; it works only in
combination with Larodopa (levodopa) or Sinemet.

Parkinson's disease, which causes muscle rigidity and difficulty with walking
and talking, involves the progressive degeneration of a particular type of
nerve cell. Early on, Larodopa or Sinemet alone may alleviate the symptoms
of the disease. In time, however, these medications work less well; their
effectiveness seems to switch on and off at random, and the individual may
begin to experience side effects such as involuntary movements and
"freezing" in mid-motion.

Eldepryl may be prescribed at this stage of the disease to help restore the effectiveness of Larodopa or Sinemet. When you begin to take Eldepryl, you may need a reduced dosage of the other medication.

Most important fact about this drug

Eldepryl belongs to a class of drugs known as MAO inhibitors. These drugs can interact with certain foods—including aged cheeses and meats, pickled herring, beer, and wine—to cause a life-threatening surge in blood pressure. At the dose recommended for Eldepryl, this interaction is not a problem. But for safety's sake, you may want to watch your diet; and you should never take more Eldepryl than the doctor prescribed.

How should you take this medication?

Take Eldepryl and your other Parkinson's medication exactly as prescribed.

■ *If you miss a dose...*
Take it as soon as you remember. If you do not remember until late afternoon or evening, skip the dose you missed and go back to your regular schedule. Never take 2 doses at once.

■ *Storage instructions...*
Store at room temperature.

What side effects may occur?

Side effects cannot be anticipated. If any develop or change in intensity, inform your doctor as soon as possible. Only your doctor can determine if it is safe for you to continue taking Eldepryl.

■ *Side effects may include:*
Abdominal pain, abnormal movements, abnormally fast walking, aches, agitation, angina (crushing chest pain), anxiety, apathy, asthma, back pain, behavior or mood changes, bleeding from the rectum, blurred vision, body ache, burning lips and mouth or throat, chills, confusion, constipation, delusions, depression, diarrhea, difficulty swallowing, disorientation, dizziness, double vision, drowsiness, dry mouth, excessive urination at night, eyelid spasm, facial grimace, facial hair, fainting, falling down, freezing, frequent urination, general feeling of illness, hair loss, hallucinations, headache, heartburn, heart palpitations, heart rhythm abnormalities, "heavy leg," high blood pressure, hollow feeling, inability to carry out purposeful movements, inability to urinate, increased sweating, increased tremor, insomnia, involuntary movements, irritability, lack of appetite, leg pain, lethargy, light-headedness upon standing up, loss of balance, low blood pressure, lower back pain, migraine, muscle cramps, nausea,

nervousness, numbness in toes/fingers, overstimulation, pain over the eyes, personality change, poor appetite, rapid heartbeat, rash, restlessness (desire to keep moving), ringing in the ear, sensitivity to light, sexual problems, shortness of breath, sleep disturbance, slow heartbeat, slow urination, slowed body movements, speech problems, stiff neck, stomach and intestinal bleeding, swelling of the ankles or arms and legs, taste disturbance, tension, tiredness, twitching, urinary problems, vertigo, vivid dreams or nightmares, vomiting, weakness, weight loss

Why should this drug not be prescribed?
Do not take Eldepryl if you are sensitive to or have ever had an allergic reaction to it.

Special warnings about this medication
Never take Eldepryl at a higher dosage than prescribed; doing so could put you at risk for a dangerous rise in blood pressure. If you develop a severe headache or any other unusual symptoms, contact your doctor immediately.

Possible food and drug interactions
when taking this medication
If Eldepryl is taken with certain other drugs, the effects of either could be increased, decreased, or altered. It is especially important to check with your doctor before combining Eldepryl with the following:

Amphetamines such as Dexedrine
Antidepressant medications such as Elavil and Tofranil
Diabetes medications, including insulin and drugs such Micronase
Fluoxetine (Prozac)
Narcotic painkillers such as Demerol, Percocet, and Tylenol with
    Codeine

If you have taken Prozac, you should wait at least 5 weeks after the last dose before starting to take Eldepryl.

If you anticipate taking Prozac, do not take the first dose until at least 14 days after your last dose of Eldepryl.

Eldepryl may worsen side effects caused by your usual dosage of levodopa.

Special information
if you are pregnant or breastfeeding
The effects of Eldepryl during pregnancy have not been adequately studied. If you are pregnant or plan to become pregnant, inform your doctor immediate-

ly. Although Eldepryl is not known to cause specific birth defects, it should not be taken during pregnancy unless it is clearly needed. It is not known whether Eldepryl appears in breast milk. As a general rule, a nursing mother should not take any drug unless it is clearly necessary.

Recommended dosage

ADULTS

The recommended dose of Eldepryl is 10 milligrams per day divided into 2 smaller doses of 5 milligrams each, taken at breakfast and lunch. There is no evidence of additional benefit from higher doses, and they increase the risk of side effects.

CHILDREN

The use of Eldepryl in children has not been evaluated.

Overdosage

Although no specific information is available about Eldepryl overdosage, it is assumed, because of chemical similarities, that the symptoms would resemble those of overdose with an MAO inhibitor antidepressant.

■ *Symptoms of MAO inhibitor overdose may include:*
Agitation, chest pain, clammy skin, coma, convulsions, dizziness, drowsiness, extremely high fever, faintness, fast and irregular pulse, hallucinations, headache (severe), high blood pressure, hyperactivity, inability to breathe, irritability, lockjaw, low blood pressure (severe), shallow breathing, spasm of the entire body, sweating

It is important to note that after a large overdose, symptoms may not appear for up to 12 hours and may not reach their full force for 24 hours or more. An overdose can be fatal. If you suspect an Eldepryl overdose, seek medical attention immediately. Hospitalization is recommended, with continuous observation and monitoring for at least 2 days.

Brand name:

ELOCON

Pronounced: ELL-oh-con
Generic name: Mometasone furoate

Why is this drug prescribed?
Elocon is a cortisone-like steroid available in cream, ointment, and lotion form. It is used to treat certain itchy rashes and other inflammatory skin conditions.

Most important fact about this drug
When you use Elocon, you inevitably absorb some of the medication through your skin and into the bloodstream. Too much absorption can lead to unwanted side effects elsewhere in the body. To keep this problem to a minimum, avoid using large amounts of Elocon over large areas, and do not cover it with airtight dressings such as plastic wrap or adhesive bandages unless specifically told to by your doctor.

How should you use this medication?
Apply a thin film of the cream or ointment or a few drops of the lotion to the affected skin once a day. Massage it in until it disappears.

Elocon is for use only on the skin. Be careful to keep it out of your eyes.

For the most effective and economical use of Elocon lotion, hold the tip of the bottle very close to (but not touching) the affected skin and squeeze the bottle gently.

Once you have applied Elocon, never cover the skin with an airtight bandage, a tight diaper, plastic pants, or any other airtight dressing. This could encourage excessive absorption of the medication into your bloodstream.

Be careful not to use Elocon for a longer time than prescribed. If you do, you may disrupt your ability to make your own natural adrenal corticoid hormones (hormones secreted by the outer layer of the adrenal gland).

- *If you miss a dose...*
  Apply it as soon as you remember. If it is almost time for your next dose, skip the one you missed and go back to your regular schedule.

- *Storage instructions...*
  Store at room temperature.

What side effects may occur?
Side effects cannot be anticipated. If any develop or change in intensity, notify your doctor as soon as possible. Only your doctor can determine if it is safe for you to continue using Elocon.

■ *Side effects may include:*
  Acne-like pimples, allergic skin rash, boils, burning, damaged skin, dryness, excessive hairiness, infected hair follicles, infection of the skin, irritation, itching, light colored patches on skin, prickly heat, rash around the mouth, skin atrophy and wasting, softening of the skin, stretch marks, tingling or stinging

Why should this drug not be prescribed?

Do not use Elocon if you are sensitive to it or have ever had an allergic reaction to it or any other steroid medication.

Special warnings about this medication

Remember, Elocon is for external use only. Avoid getting it into your eyes. Do not use it to treat anything other than the condition for which it was prescribed.

Possible food and drug interactions
when using this medication

No interactions have been noted.

Special information
if you are pregnant or breastfeeding

If you are pregnant or plan to become pregnant, inform your doctor immediately. Elocon should not be used during pregnancy unless the benefit outweighs the potential risk to the unborn child.

You should not use Elocon while breastfeeding, since absorbed hormone could make its way into the breast milk and perhaps harm the nursing baby. If you are a new mother, you should contact your doctor, who will help you decide between breastfeeding and using Elocon.

Recommended dosage

ADULTS

Apply once daily.

CHILDREN

Use should be limited to the least amount necessary. Use of steroids over a long period of time may interfere with growth and development.

Overdosage

With extensive or long-term use of Elocon, hormone absorbed into the bloodstream may cause a group of symptoms called Cushing's syndrome.

- *Symptoms of Cushing's syndrome may include:*
  Acne, depression, excessive hair growth, high blood pressure, humped upper back, insomnia, moon-faced appearance, obese trunk, paranoia, stretch marks, wasted limbs, stunted growth (in children), susceptibility to bruising, fractures, and infections

Cushing's syndrome may also trigger diabetes mellitus.

If it is left uncorrected, Cushing's syndrome may become serious. If you suspect your long-term use of Elocon has led to this problem, seek medical attention immediately.

Brand name:

EMPIRIN

See Aspirin, page 77.

Brand name:

EMPIRIN WITH CODEINE

Pronounced: EM-pir-in with KOE-deen
Generic ingredients: Aspirin, Codeine phosphate

Why is this drug prescribed?
Empirin with Codeine is a narcotic pain reliever and anti-inflammatory medication. It is prescribed for mild, moderate, and moderate to severe pain.

Most important fact about this drug
Codeine can be habit-forming when taken over a long period of time or in high doses. Do not take more of the drug, or use it for a longer period of time than your doctor has indicated.

How should you take this medication?
Take Empirin with Codeine with food or a full glass of milk or water to reduce stomach irritation. Take it exactly as prescribed.

- *If you miss a dose...*
  Take it as soon as you remember. If it is almost time for your next dose, skip the one you missed and go back to your regular schedule. Never take 2 doses at once.

- *Storage instructions...*
  Storage at room temperature in a dry place; protect from light.

What side effects may occur?
Side effects cannot be anticipated. If any develop or change in intensity, inform your doctor as soon as possible. Only your doctor can determine if it is safe for you to continue using Empirin with Codeine.

- *More common side effects may include:*
  Constipation
  Dizziness
  Drowsiness
  Light-headedness
  Nausea
  Shallow breathing
  Vomiting

- *Less common side effects may include:*
  Abdominal pain, aggravation of peptic ulcer, anaphylactic shock (severe allergic reaction), asthma, bruising or bleeding, confusion, dizziness, drowsiness, exaggerated sense of well-being or depression, excessive bleeding following injury or surgery, fatigue, headache, hearing problems, heartburn, hives, indigestion, itching, nausea, rapid heartbeat, ringing in ears, runny nose, skin rashes, sweating, thirst, vision problems, vomiting, weakness

Why should this drug not be prescribed?
Empirin with Codeine should not be used if you: are sensitive or allergic to aspirin or codeine, experience severe bleeding, have a blood clotting disorder or severe vitamin K deficiency, are taking blood-thinning medications, have a peptic ulcer, or have liver damage. Children or teenagers with symptoms of chickenpox or the flu should not take Empirin with Codeine because of the danger of contracting Reye's syndrome, a condition characterized by nausea, vomiting, and lethargy and disorientation deepening to coma.

Special warnings about this medication
Aspirin can cause severe allergic reactions including anaphylactic shock (difficulty breathing, bluish skin color caused by lack of oxygen, fever, rash or hives, irregular pulse, convulsions, or collapse).

Aspirin can cause bleeding if you have a peptic ulcer, open sores in the stomach or intestines, or a bleeding disorder. It may also prolong bleeding time after an injury or surgery.

Codeine can hide symptoms of serious abdominal conditions.

Use Codeine with care if you have a head or brain injury. It can slow your breathing, make you drowsy, and increase pressure in your head.

Be careful taking Empirin with Codeine if you are elderly or in a weakened condition or have severe kidney or liver disease, gallstones or gallbladder disease, a breathing disorder, an irregular heartbeat, an inflamed stomach or intestines, an underactive thyroid gland, Addison's disease (a disorder of the adrenal glands), or an enlarged prostate or narrowing of the urethra.

Use aspirin with care if you have ever had any allergies. Sensitivity reactions are relatively common in people with asthma and nasal polyps (swollen growths in the nose).

Empirin with Codeine may make you drowsy or less alert. Be careful driving, operating machinery, or using appliances that require full mental alertness until you know how you react to this medication.

Remember, this medication can be habit-forming and should be taken exactly as prescribed. Do not take more of the medication, or use it more often, than your doctor has indicated.

Possible food and drug interactions when taking this medication

The effects of alcohol may be increased if taken with Empirin with Codeine. Avoid using alcohol while taking this medication.

If Empirin with Codeine is taken with certain other drugs, the effects of either could be increased, decreased, or altered. It is especially important to check with your doctor before combining Empirin with Codeine with the following:

Blood thinners such as Coumadin and Panwarfin
Furosemide (Lasix)
Insulin
MAO inhibitors such as the antidepressants Marplan and Nardil
Methotrexate (Rheumatrex)
Mercaptopurine
Nonsteroidal anti-inflammatory drugs such as Advil, Motrin, and Indocin
Oral diabetes medications such as Diabinese and Tolinase
Other narcotic analgesics such as Percodan and Tylox
Para-amino salicylic acid
Penicillin
Probenecid (Benemid)
Sedatives such as phenobarbital and Nembutal

Steroids such as Medrol and prednisone
Sulfa drugs such as Azo Gantrisin and Septra
Sulfinpyrazone (Anturane)
Tranquilizers such as Xanax and Valium
Vitamin C

Special information
if you are pregnant or breastfeeding

The effects of Empirin with Codeine during pregnancy have not been adequately studied. If you are pregnant or plan to become pregnant, inform your doctor immediately. Aspirin and codeine appear in small amounts in breast milk and may affect a nursing infant. If this medication is essential to your health, your doctor may advise you to stop breastfeeding until your treatment with this medication is finished.

Recommended dosage

Dosage is determined by the severity of your pain and your response to this medication. Your doctor may prescribe more than the usual recommended dose if your pain is severe or if you are no longer getting enough pain relief from the dose you have been taking.

The usual adult dose for Empirin with Codeine No. 3 is 1 or 2 tablets every 4 hours as needed. The usual adult dose for Empirin with Codeine No. 4 is 1 tablet every 4 hours as required.

Overdosage

■ *In adults, symptoms of Empirin with Codeine overdose may include:*
Bluish skin color due to lack of oxygen, circulatory collapse, clammy skin, coma, constricted pupils, delirium, delusions, difficult or labored breathing, double vision, excitability, flabby muscles, garbled speech, hallucinations, restlessness, skin eruptions, slow and shallow breathing, stupor, vertigo

■ *In children, symptoms of Empirin with Codeine overdose may include:*
Confusion, convulsions, dehydration, difficulty hearing, dim vision, dizziness, drowsiness, extremely high body temperature, headache, nausea, rapid breathing, ringing in ears, sweating, thirst, vomiting

If you suspect an overdose, seek medical treatment immediately.

Brand name:

E-MYCIN

See Erythromycin, Oral, page 405.

Generic name:

ENALAPRIL

See Vasotec, page 1188.

Generic name:

ENALAPRIL WITH HYDROCHLOROTHIAZIDE

See Vaseretic, page 1184.

Brand name:

ENDEP

See Elavil, page 386.

Generic name:

ENOXACIN

See Penetrex, page 821.

Brand name:

ENTEX LA

Pronounced: ENN-teks ell ai
Generic ingredients: Guaifenesin, Phenylpropanolamine
* hydrochloride*
Other brand name: Exgest LA

Why is this drug prescribed?
Entex LA is used to treat bronchitis, the common cold, sinus inflammation, nasal congestion, and sore throat.

Entex LA is a combination of two medications, phenylpropanolamine (a decongestant) and guaifenesin (an expectorant), specially formulated to deliver prolonged action. Phenylpropanolamine helps reduce congestion in the nasal passages, while guaifenesin breaks up mucus in the lower respiratory tract, making it easier to clear the passages.

Most important fact about this drug

Certain medical conditions can affect your use of Entex LA. If you have heart disease, high blood pressure, or diabetes, make sure the doctor knows about it. The phenylpropanolamine in Entex LA can raise blood pressure and speed up the heart, and can put you at a greater risk of heart or blood-vessel disease if you are diabetic.

How should you take this medication?

You may break Entex LA tablets in half to make them easier to swallow, but you must not chew or crush them.

■ *If you miss a dose...*
Take it as soon as you remember. If it is almost time for your next dose, skip the one you missed and go back to your regular schedule. Never take 2 doses at once.

■ *Storage instructions...*
Store at room temperature.

What side effects may occur?

Side effects cannot be anticipated. If any develop or change in intensity, inform your doctor as soon as possible. Only your doctor can determine if it is safe for you to continue taking Entex LA.

■ *Side effects may include:*
Difficulty urinating (in men with an enlarged prostate)
Headache
Inability to sleep or difficulty sleeping
Irritated stomach
Nausea
Nervousness
Restlessness

Why should this drug not be prescribed?

You should not use Entex LA if you have severe high blood pressure, are sensitive to other stimulating drugs such as Dristan Decongestant, or take antidepressant medications known as MAO inhibitors, including Nardil, Parnate, and Marplan.

Special warnings about this medication

Use Entex LA cautiously if you have any of the following conditions:

Diabetes
Glaucoma (excessive pressure in the eyes)
Heart disease
High blood pressure
Hyperthyroidism (excessive thyroid gland activity)
Prostate enlargement

Possible food and drug interactions
when taking this medication

Do not take Entex LA if you are taking an antidepressant medication classified as an MAO inhibitor, including Nardil, Parnate, and Marplan. Avoid other stimulating drugs such as Proventil, Ventolin, and many decongestants. Interactions can also occur with the following:

Bromocriptine (Parlodel)
Methyldopa (Aldomet)

Special information
if you are pregnant or breastfeeding

The effects of Entex LA during pregnancy have not been adequately studied. If you are pregnant or plan to become pregnant, notify your doctor immediately. It is not known whether Entex LA appears in breast milk. If this medication is essential to your health, your doctor may advise you to discontinue breastfeeding until treatment with this drug is finished.

Recommended dosage

ADULTS AND CHILDREN 12 YEARS AND OLDER

The usual dosage is 1 tablet every 12 hours.

CHILDREN 6 TO 12 YEARS OLD

The usual dosage is one-half tablet every 12 hours.

The safety and effectiveness of Entex LA have not been established in children under the age of 6.

Overdosage

Any medication taken in excess can have serious consequences. If you suspect an overdose, seek medical help immediately.

■ *Symptoms of Entex LA overdose may include:*
Coma
Convulsions
High blood pressure

Brand name:

EPITOL

See Tegretol, page 1076.

Brand name:

EQUANIL

See Miltown, page 667.

Generic name:

ERGOLOID MESYLATES

See Hydergine, page 490.

Generic name:

ERGOTAMINE WITH CAFFEINE

See Cafergot, page 143.

Brand name:

ERYC

See Erythromycin, Oral, page 405.

Brand name:

ERYCETTE

See Erythromycin, Topical, page 409.

Brand name:

ERY-TAB

See Erythromycin, Oral, page 405.

Brand name:

ERYTHROCIN

See Erythromycin, Oral, page 405.

Generic name:

ERYTHROMYCIN ETHYLSUCCINATE WITH SULFISOXAZOLE

See Pediazole, page 818.

Generic name:

ERYTHROMYCIN, ORAL

Pronounced: er-ITH-row MY-sin
Brand names: E.E.S., E-Mycin, ERYC, Ery-Tab,
* Erythrocin, Ilosone, PCE*

Why is this drug prescribed?

Erythromycin is an antibiotic used to treat many kinds of infections, including:

Acute pelvic inflammatory disease
Gonorrhea
Intestinal parasitic infections
Legionnaires' disease
Pinkeye
Skin infections
Syphilis
Upper and lower respiratory tract infections
Urinary tract infections
Whooping cough

Erythromycin is also prescribed to prevent infections of the heart (rheumatic fever and bacterial endocarditis) in people who are allergic to penicillin and who have congenital or rheumatic heart disease.

Most important fact about this drug

Erythromycin, like any other antibiotic, works best when there is a constant amount of drug in the blood. To help keep the drug amount constant, it is important not to miss any doses. Also, it is advisable to take the doses at evenly spaced times around the clock.

How should you take this medication?

Your doctor may advise you to take erythromycin at least 1 hour before or 2 hours after meals. If the drug upsets your stomach, taking it with meals may help. Ask your doctor whether this is advisable for you.

Chewable forms of erythromycin should be crushed or chewed before being swallowed.

Delayed-release brands and tablets and capsules that are coated to slow their breakdown should be swallowed whole. Do not crush or break. If you are not sure about the form of erythromycin you are taking, ask your pharmacist.

The liquid should be shaken well before each use.

■ *If you miss a dose...*
Take it as soon as you remember. If it is almost time for your next dose, and you take 2 doses a day, space the missed dose and the next dose 5 to 6 hours apart; if you take 3 or more doses a day, space the missed dose and the next one 2 to 4 hours apart. Never take 2 doses at the same time.

■ *Storage instructions...*
The liquid form of erythromycin should be kept in the refrigerator. Do not freeze. Store tablets and capsules at room temperature.

What side effects may occur?

Side effects cannot be anticipated. If any develop or change in intensity, inform your doctor as soon as possible. Only your doctor can determine whether it is safe to continue taking this medication.

■ *More common side effects may include:*
Abdominal pain
Diarrhea
Loss of appetite
Nausea
Vomiting

■ *Less common side effects may include:*
Hives, rash, skin eruptions, yellow eyes and skin

■ *Rare side effects may include:*
Hearing loss (temporary), inflammation of the large intestine, irregular heartbeat, skin reddening and/or peeling, severe allergic reaction

Why should this drug not be prescribed?

You should not use erythromycin if you have ever had an allergic reaction to it or are sensitive to it. Erythromycin should not be used with Seldane or Hismanal.

Special warnings about this medication

If you have ever had liver disease, consult your doctor before taking erythromycin.

If a new infection (called superinfection) develops, talk to your doctor. You may need to be treated with a different antibiotic.

Possible food and drug interactions
when taking this medication

If erythromycin is taken with certain other drugs, the effects of either could be increased, decreased, or altered. It is especially important to check with your doctor before combining erythromycin with the following:

Astemizole (Hismanal)
Blood-thinning drugs such as Coumadin
Bromocriptine (Parlodel)
Carbamazepine (Tegretol)
Cyclosporine (Sandimmune)
Digoxin (Lanoxin)
Dihydroergotamine (D.H.E. 45)
Disopyramide (Norpace)
Ergotamine (Cafergot)
Hexobarbital
Lovastatin (Mevacor)
Phenytoin (Dilantin)
Terfenadine (Seldane)
Theophylline (Theo-Dur)
Triazolam (Halcion)

Special information
if you are pregnant or breastfeeding

If you are pregnant or plan to become pregnant, inform your doctor immediately. Erythromycin appears in breast milk and could affect a nursing infant. If this medication is essential to your health, your doctor may advise you to discontinue breastfeeding until your treatment is finished.

Recommended dosage

Dosage instructions are determined by the type (and severity) of infection being treated and may vary slightly for different brands of erythromycin. The following are recommended dosages for PCE, one of the most commonly prescribed brands.

ADULTS

Streptococcal Infections

The usual dose is 333 milligrams every 8 hours, or 500 milligrams every 12 hours. Depending on the severity of the infection, the dose may be increased to a total of 4 grams a day. However, when the daily dosage is larger than 1 gram, twice-a-day doses are not recommended, and the drug should be taken more often in smaller doses.

To treat streptococcal infections of the upper respiratory tract (tonsillitis or strep throat), erythromycin should be taken for 10 days.

To Prevent Bacterial Endocarditis (Inflammation and Infection of the Heart Lining and Valves) in Those Allergic to Penicillin

The oral regimen is 1 gram of erythromycin taken 1 hour before dental surgery or surgical procedures of the upper respiratory tract, followed by 500 milligrams 6 hours later.

Urinary Tract Infections Due to Chlamydia Trachomatis During Pregnancy

The usual dosage is 500 milligrams of erythromycin orally 4 times a day or 666 milligrams every 8 hours on an empty stomach for at least 7 days. For women who cannot tolerate this regimen, a decreased dose of 500 milligrams every 12 hours or 333 milligrams every 8 hours a day should be used for at least 14 days.

For Those with Uncomplicated Urinary, Reproductive Tract, or Rectal Infections Caused by Chlamydia Trachomatis When Tetracycline Cannot Be Taken

The usual oral dosage is 500 milligrams of erythromycin 4 times a day or 666 milligrams every 8 hours for at least 7 days.

For Those with Nongonococcal Urethral Infections When Tetracycline Cannot Be Taken

The usual dosage is 500 milligrams of erythromycin by mouth 4 times a day or 666 milligrams orally every 8 hours for at least 7 days.

Acute Pelvic Inflammatory Disease Caused by Neisseria gonorrhoeae

The usual treatment is three days of intravenous erythromycin followed by 500 milligrams orally every 12 hours or 333 milligrams orally every 8 hours for 7 days.

Syphilis

The usual dosage is 30 to 40 grams divided into smaller doses over a period of 10 to 15 days.

Intestinal Infections

The usual dosage is 500 milligrams every 12 hours, or 333 milligrams every 8 hours, for 10 to 14 days.

Legionnaires' Disease

The usual dosage ranges from 1 to 4 grams daily, divided into smaller doses.

CHILDREN

Age, weight, and severity of the infection determine the correct dosage.

The usual dosage is from 30 to 50 milligrams daily for each 2.2 pounds of body weight, divided into equal doses.

For more severe infections, this dosage may be doubled, but it should not exceed 4 grams per day.

Children weighing over 44 pounds should follow the recommended adult dose schedule.

Overdosage

Any medication taken in excess can have serious consequences. If you suspect an overdose, seek medical help immediately.

■ *Symptoms of erythromycin overdose may include:*
Diarrhea
Nausea
Stomach cramps
Vomiting

Generic name:

ERYTHROMYCIN, TOPICAL

Pronounced: err-rith-ro-MY-sin
Brand names: A/T/S, Erycette, T-Stat

Why is this drug prescribed?

Topical Erythromycin (applied directly to the skin) is used for the treatment of acne.

Most important fact about this drug

For best results, you should continue the treatment for as long as prescribed, even if your acne begins to clear up. This medicine is not an instant cure.

How should you use this medication?

Use exactly as prescribed by your doctor.

Thoroughly wash the affected area with soap and water and pat dry before applying medication.

Moisten the applicator or pad with the medication and lightly spread it over the affected area. A/T/S Topical Gel should not be rubbed in.

- *If you miss a dose...*
  Apply the forgotten dose as soon as you remember. If it is almost time for the next application, skip the one you missed and go back to your regular schedule.

- *Storage instructions...*
  This medicine can be stored at room temperature.

What side effects may occur?

Side effects cannot be anticipated. If any develop or change in intensity, inform your doctor as soon as possible. Only your doctor can determine if it is safe for you to continue using topical erythromycin.

- *Side effects may include:*
  Burning sensation
  Dryness
  Hives
  Irritation of the eyes
  Itching
  Oiliness
  Peeling
  Scaling
  Tenderness
  Unusual redness of the skin

Why should this drug not be prescribed?

Erythromycin should not be used if you are sensitive to or have ever had an allergic reaction to any of the ingredients.

Special warnings about this medication

This type of erythromycin is for external use only. Do not use it in the eyes, nose, or mouth.

If the acne does not improve after 6 to 8 weeks of treatment, or if it gets worse, stop using the topical erythromycin preparation and call your doctor.

The use of antibiotics can stimulate the growth of other bacteria that are resistant to the antibiotic you are taking. If new infections (called superinfections) occur, talk to your doctor. You may need to be treated with a different antibiotic drug.

The use of other topical acne medications in combination with topical erythromycin may cause irritation, especially with the use of peeling, scaling, or abrasive medications.

The safety and effectiveness of A/T/S have not been established in children.

Possible food and drug interactions
when using this medication

If topical erythromycin is used with certain other drugs, the effects of either could be increased, decreased, or altered. It is especially important to check with your doctor before combining topical erythromycin with other topical acne medications.

Special information
if you are pregnant or breastfeeding

The effects of topical erythromycin during pregnancy have not been adequately studied. If you are pregnant or plan to become pregnant, inform your doctor immediately. Erythromycin may appear in breast milk and could affect a nursing infant. If this medication is essential to your health, your doctor may advise you to stop breastfeeding until your treatment with erythromycin is finished.

Recommended dosage

Apply medication to the affected area 2 times a day, in the morning and at night. Moisten the applicator or a pad, then rub over the affected area. Use additional pads as needed. Apply gel products as a thin film over the affected area. Make sure the area is thoroughly washed with soap and water and patted dry before applying medication. Thoroughly wash your hands after application of the medication.

Reducing the frequency of applications may reduce peeling and drying.

Overdosage

Although overdosage is unlikely, any medication used in excess can have serious consequences. If you suspect an overdose, seek medical treatment immediately.

Generic name:

ERYTHROMYCIN WITH BENZOYL PEROXIDE

See Benzamycin, page 121.

Brand name:

ESGIC

See Fioricet, page 433.

Brand name:

ESIDRIX

See HydroDIURIL, page 492.

Brand name:

ESKALITH

See Lithonate, page 581.

Generic name:

ESTAZOLAM

See ProSom, page 908.

Brand name:

ESTRACE

See Estraderm, page 413.

Brand name:

ESTRADERM

Pronounced: ESS-tra-derm
Generic name: Estradiol
Other brand name: Estrace

Why is this drug prescribed?

Estraderm is an estrogen replacement drug. It is used to reduce symptoms of menopause, including feelings of warmth in face, neck, and chest, and the sudden intense episodes of heat and sweating known as "hot flashes." It is also used for other conditions caused by lack of estrogen, such as dry, itchy external genitals and vaginal irritation, and may be prescribed for teenagers who fail to mature at the usual rate.

Along with diet, calcium supplements, and exercise, Estraderm is also prescribed to prevent osteoporosis, a condition in which the bones become brittle and easily broken.

Estrace is also used to treat low levels of estrogen in certain people and to provide relief in breast or prostate cancer.

Most important fact about this drug

Because estrogens have been linked with increased risk of endometrial cancer (cancer in the lining of the uterus), it is essential to have regular checkups and to report any unusual vaginal bleeding to your doctor immediately.

How should you take this medication?

Each Estraderm patch is individually sealed in a protective pouch and is applied directly to the skin.

A stiff protective liner covers the adhesive side of the patch. Remove the liner by sliding it sideways between your thumb and index finger. Holding the patch at one edge, remove the protective liner and discard it. Try to avoid touching the adhesive. Use immediately after removing the liner.

Apply the adhesive side to a clean, dry area of your skin on the trunk of your body (including the buttocks and abdomen). Do not apply to your breasts or waist. Firmly press the patch in place with the palm of your hand for about 10 seconds, to make sure the edges are flat against your skin.

Contact with water during bathing, swimming, or showering will not affect the patch.

The application site must be rotated. Allow an interval of at least 1 week between applications to a particular site.

Estrace Tablets are taken orally.

If you are using Estrace vaginal cream, follow these steps to apply:

1. Load the supplied applicator to the fill line.
2. Lie on your back with your knees drawn up.
3. Gently insert the applicator high into the vagina. Release the medicine by pushing the plunger.
4. Withdraw the applicator.
5. Wash the applicator with soap and water.

■ *If you miss a dose...*
If you forget to apply a new patch when you are supposed to, do it as soon as you remember. If it is almost time to change patches anyway, skip the one you missed and go back to your regular schedule. Do not apply more than one patch at a time.

If you miss a dose of the tablets, take it as soon as you remember. If it is almost time for your next dose, skip the one you missed and go back to your regular schedule. Do not take 2 doses at once.

■ *Storage instructions...*
Store Estraderm at room temperature, in its sealed pouch. Store Estrace at room temperature.

What side effects may occur?
Side effects cannot be anticipated. If any develop or change in intensity, notify your doctor as soon as possible. Only your doctor can determine if it is safe for you to continue taking Estraderm.

■ *The most common side effect is:*
Skin redness and irritation at the site of the patch.

■ *Less common or rare side effects may include:*
Abdominal cramps, bloating, breakthrough bleeding, breast enlargement, breast tenderness, change in cervical secretions, change in menstrual flow, change in sex drive, change in weight, darkening of skin, dizziness, fluid retention, growth of benign fibroid tumors in the uterus, headache, intolerance to contact lenses, migraine, nausea, rash, severe allergic reaction, spotting, vomiting, yellowing of eyes and skin

- *Other side effects reported with estradiol include:*
  Abnormal withdrawal bleeding, certain cancers, cardiovascular disease, depression, excessive growth of hair, gallbladder disease, hair loss, high blood pressure, reddened skin, skin discoloration, skin eruptions, twitching, vaginal yeast infection

Why should this drug not be prescribed?

Estraderm should not be used if you are sensitive to or have ever had an allergic reaction to any of its components.

Estrogens should not be used if you have ever had breast or uterine cancer or a tumor promoted by estrogen. Also avoid estrogens if you are pregnant or think you are pregnant, if you have abnormal, undiagnosed genital bleeding, if you have blood clots or a blood clotting disorder, or if you have a history of blood clotting disorders associated with previous estrogen use.

Special warnings about this medication

The risk of cancer of the uterus increases when estrogen is used for a long time or taken in large doses. There also may be increased risk of breast cancer in women who take estrogen for an extended period of time.

Women who take estrogen after menopause are more likely to develop gallbladder disease.

Estrogen also increases the risk of blood clots. These blood clots can cause stroke, heart attack, or other serious disorders.

While taking Estraderm, get in touch with your doctor right away if you notice any of the following:

  Abdominal pain, tenderness, or swelling
  Abnormal bleeding of the vagina
  Breast lumps
  Coughing up blood
  Pain in your chest or calves
  Severe headache, dizziness, or faintness
  Sudden shortness of breath
  Vision changes
  Yellowing of the skin

A complete medical and family history should be taken by your doctor before starting any estrogen therapy.

In general, you should not take estrogen for more than 1 year without another physical examination by your doctor.

Estraderm may cause fluid retention in some people. If you have asthma, epilepsy, migraine, or heart or kidney disease, use this medication cautiously.

Estrogen therapy may cause uterine bleeding or breast pain.

**Possible food and drug interactions
when taking this medication**
If you take certain other drugs while using Estraderm, the effects of either could be increased, decreased, or altered. It is especially important to check with your doctor before taking the following:

  Barbiturates such as phenobarbitol and Seconal
  Blood thinners such as Coumadin
  Dantrolene (Dantrium)
  Epilepsy drugs such as Tegretol and Dilantin
  Rifampin (Rifadin)
  Steroids such as Deltasone
  Tricyclic antidepressants such as Elavil and Tofranil

**Special information
if you are pregnant or breastfeeding**
Estrogens should not be used during pregnancy or immediately after childbirth. If you are pregnant or plan to become pregnant, notify your doctor immediately. Estraderm may appear in breast milk and could affect a nursing infant. If this medication is essential to your health, your doctor may advise you to discontinue breastfeeding until your treatment is finished.

Recommended dosage

SYMPTOMS OF MENOPAUSE

Estraderm
The usual starting dose is one 0.05-milligram patch applied to the skin 2 times a week. Dosage should be decreased at 3- to 6-month intervals.

Estrace
The usual starting dose is 1 or 2 milligrams a day; you will take the tablets for 3 weeks and then have 1 week off for each cycle.

PREVENTION OF OSTEOPOROSIS

Estraderm
The usual starting dose is 0.05 milligram per day.

Estrace
The usual dose is 0.5 milligram taken every day for 23 days, followed by 5 days off.

LOW ESTROGEN LEVELS

Estrace
The usual starting dose is 1 or 2 milligrams a day.

RELIEF IN BREAST CANCER

Estrace
The usual dose is 10 milligrams 3 times a day for at least 3 months.

RELIEF IN PROSTATE CANCER

Estrace
The usual dose is 1 to 2 milligrams 3 times a day.

VAGINAL ITCHING AND DRYNESS

Estrace Vaginal Cream
The usual dosage is 2 to 4 grams (marked on the applicator) inserted into the vagina once a day for 1 to 2 weeks. The dosage and frequency may be reduced after your condition improves.

To prevent recurrence, a dosage of 1 gram 1 to 3 times a week is recommended.

Overdosage
Any medication taken in excess can have serious consequences. If you suspect an overdose, seek medical attention immediately.

■ *Symptoms of Estraderm overdose may include:*
Nausea
Vomiting
Withdrawal bleeding

Generic name:

ESTRADIOL

See Estraderm, page 413.

Generic name:

ESTROPIPATE

See Ogen, page 768.

Generic name:

ETODOLAC

See Lodine, page 585.

Brand name:

EULEXIN

Pronounced: you-LEKS-in
Generic name: Flutamide

Why is this drug prescribed?
Eulexin is used along with drugs such as Lupron to treat prostate cancer. Eulexin belongs to a class of drugs known as antiandrogens. It blocks the effect of the male hormone testosterone. Giving Eulexin with Lupron, which reduces the body's testosterone levels, is one way of treating prostate cancer.

Most important fact about this drug
Taking Eulexin and Lupron together is essential in this form of treatment. You should not interrupt their doses or stop taking either of these medications without consulting your doctor.

How should you take this medication?
Take Eulexin exactly as prescribed. Do not use more or less, and do not take it more often than instructed.

■ *If you miss a dose...*
   Take it as soon as you remember. If it is almost time for your next dose, skip the one you missed and go back to your regular schedule. Never take 2 doses at once.

■ *Storage instructions...*
Store at room temperature.

What side effects may occur?
Side effects cannot be anticipated. If any develop or change in intensity, inform your doctor immediately. Since Eulexin is always given with another antiandrogen drug, when a side effect develops, it is difficult to know which drug is responsible. Only your doctor can determine if it is safe for you to continue taking Eulexin.

■ *More common side effects may include:*
Breast tissue swelling and tenderness
Diarrhea
Hot flashes
Impotence
Loss of sex drive
Nausea
Vomiting

■ *Less common side effects may include:*
Confusion, decreased sexual ability, jaundice and liver damage, rash, sun sensitivity (rashes, blisters upon exposure to sun), urine discoloration (amber or yellow-green)

Why should this drug not be prescribed?
Do not take Eulexin if you have ever had an allergic reaction to it or are sensitive to it or to any of the colorings or other inactive ingredients in the capsules.

Special warnings about this medication
Eulexin may cause liver damage in some people. Your doctor will do blood tests to check your liver function before you start treatment with Eulexin, and at regular intervals thereafter. If a liver problem does develop, you may need to take less Eulexin or stop taking the drug altogether. Report any signs or symptoms that might suggest liver damage to your doctor right away. Warning signs include dark urine, itching, flu-like symptoms, jaundice (a yellowing of the skin and eyes), persistent appetite loss, and persistent tenderness on the right side of the upper abdomen.

Possible food and drug interactions
when taking this medication
If you are already taking the anticoagulant drug warfarin (Coumadin,

Panwarfin), you will need to be monitored especially closely after treatment with Eulexin begins. Your doctor may need to lower your dosage of warfarin.

Recommended dosage
The recommended adult Eulexin dosage is 2 capsules 3 times a day at 8-hour intervals for a total daily dosage of 750 milligrams.

Overdosage
You may notice breast development or tenderness with an overdose of Eulexin. Any medication taken in excess can have serious consequences. If you suspect an overdose, seek medical attention immediately.

Generic name:

EXGEST LA

See Entex LA, page 401.

Generic name:

FAMCICLOVIR

See Famvir, page 420.

Generic name:

FAMOTIDINE

See Pepcid, page 828.

Brand name:

FAMVIR

Pronounced: FAM-veer
Generic name: Famciclovir

Why is this drug prescribed?
Famvir tablets are used to treat herpes zoster, commonly referred to as "shingles," in adults. Shingles is a painful rash with raised, red pimples on the trunk of the body, usually the back. Because it is caused by the same virus that causes chickenpox, only people who have had chickenpox can get shingles.

Most important fact about this drug
Famvir is most effective if started within the first 48 hours after shingles first appears. The effectiveness of Famvir if treatment is begun more than 72 hours after the rash first appears is not known. Thus, it is important to see your doctor as soon as possible after symptoms appear.

How should you take this medication?
Take this medication exactly as prescribed by your doctor. You may take Famvir with meals or in between.

- *If you miss a dose...*
  Take the forgotten dose as soon as you remember. If it is almost time for your next dose, skip the one you missed and go back to your regular schedule. Never take two doses at the same time.

- *Storage instructions...*
  Store at room temperature.

What side effects may occur?
Side effects cannot be anticipated. If any develop or change in intensity, inform your doctor as soon as possible. Only your doctor can determine if it is safe for you to continue taking Famvir.

- *More common side effects may include:*
  Constipation
  Diarrhea
  Dizziness
  Fatigue
  Fever
  Headache
  Nausea
  Vomiting

- *Less common side effects may include:*
  Abdominal pain, back pain, chills and fever, injury, irritated sinuses, itching, joint pain, loss of appetite, pain, prickling or burning sensation of the skin, sleepiness, sore throat

Why should this drug not be prescribed?
Do not take Famvir if you are sensitive to it or have ever had an allergic reaction to it.

Special warnings about this medication

Famvir helps relieve the rash associated with shingles, but it is not a cure. Studies of the drug have found that the rash and pimples healed faster with Famvir than they did in people not taking Famvir. If you have any kidney problems, be sure your doctor knows about them before prescribing Famvir for you.

Possible food and drug interactions when taking this medication

If Famvir is taken with certain other drugs, the effects of either could be increased, decreased, or altered. It is especially important to check with your doctor before combining Famvir with probenecid (Benemid), a drug used to treat gout (a type of arthritis).

Special information if you are pregnant or breastfeeding

The effects of Famvir during pregnancy have not been adequately studied. If you are pregnant or plan to become pregnant, inform your doctor immediately. Famvir should be used during pregnancy only when the benefit to the mother clearly outweighs the potential risk to the baby. Famvir may appear in breast milk, and could affect a nursing infant. If this drug is essential to your health, your doctor may advise you to discontinue breastfeeding until your treatment with Famvir is finished.

Recommended dosage

ADULTS

The usual adult dose is 500 milligrams every 8 hours for 7 days.

Overdosage

There have been no reported cases of Famvir overdose, but any medication taken in excess can have serious consequences. If you suspect an overdose, seek medical attention immediately.

Brand name:

FASTIN

Pronounced: FAS-tin
Generic name: Phentermine hydrochloride
Other brand names: Ionamin, Oby-Cap

Why is this drug prescribed?
Fastin, an appetite suppressant, is prescribed for short-term use (a few weeks) as part of an overall diet plan for weight reduction. Fastin should be used along with a behavior modification program.

Most important fact about this drug
Always remember that Fastin is an aid to, not a substitute for, good diet and exercise. Take Fastin only as directed by your doctor. Do not take it more often or for a longer time than your doctor has ordered. Fastin can lose its effectiveness after a few weeks.

How should you take this medication?
Take Fastin about 2 hours after breakfast. Do not take it late in the evening because it may keep you from sleeping.

Take Ionamin before breakfast or 10 to 14 hours before you go to bed. Ionamin capsules should be swallowed whole.

- *If you miss a dose...*
  Skip the missed dose completely; then take the next dose at the regularly scheduled time.

- *Storage instructions...*
  Store away from heat, light, and moisture.

What side effects may occur?
Side effects cannot be anticipated. If any develop or change in intensity, inform your doctor as soon as possible. Only your doctor can determine if it is safe for you to continue taking this medication.

- *Side effects may include:*
  Changes in sex drive, constipation, diarrhea, dizziness, dry mouth, exaggerated feelings of depression or elation, headache, high blood pressure, hives, impotence, inability to fall or stay asleep, increased heart rate, overstimulation, restlessness, stomach or intestinal problems, throbbing heartbeat, tremors, unpleasant taste

Why should this drug not be prescribed?
If you are sensitive to or have ever had an allergic reaction to phentermine hydrochloride or other drugs that stimulate the nervous system, you should not take this medication. Make sure your doctor is aware of any drug reactions you have experienced.

Do not take this drug if you have hardening of the arteries, symptoms of heart or blood vessel disease, an overactive thyroid gland, the eye condition known as glaucoma, or moderate to severe high blood pressure. Also avoid this drug if you are agitated, have ever abused drugs, or have taken an MAO inhibitor, including antidepressant drugs such as Nardil and Parnate, within the last 14 days.

Special warnings about this medication

Fastin may affect your ability to perform potentially hazardous activities. Therefore, you should be extremely careful if you have to drive a car or operate machinery.

You can become psychologically dependent on this drug. Consult your doctor if you rely on this drug to maintain a state of well-being.

If you stop taking Fastin suddenly after you have taken high doses for a long time, you may find you are extremely fatigued or depressed, or that you have trouble sleeping.

If you continually take too much of any appetite suppressant it can cause severe skin disorders, a pronounced inability to fall or stay asleep, irritability, hyperactivity, and personality changes.

Even if your blood pressure is only mildly high, be careful taking this drug.

Possible food and drug interactions
when taking this medication

This drug may intensify the effects of alcohol. Avoid alcoholic beverages while you are taking it.

If Fastin is taken with certain other drugs, the effects of either can be increased, decreased, or altered. It is especially important that you check with your doctor before combining Fastin with the following:

Antidepressants classified as MAO inhibitors, including Nardil and
   Parnate
Diabetes medications such as insulin and Micronase
High blood pressure medications such as guanethidine (Ismelin)

Special information
if you are pregnant or breastfeeding

The effects of Fastin during pregnancy have not been adequately studied. If you are pregnant, plan to become pregnant, or are breastfeeding, notify your doctor immediately.

Recommended dosage

ADULTS

Fastin or Oby-Cap
The usual dosage is 1 capsule approximately 2 hours after breakfast. One capsule should suppress your appetite for 12 to 14 hours.

Ionamin
The usual dose is 1 capsule a day, taken before breakfast or 10 to 14 hours before bedtime.

CHILDREN

This drug is not recommended for use in children under 12 years of age.

Overdosage

Any medication taken in excess can have serious consequences. An overdose of Fastin can be fatal. If you suspect an overdose, seek emergency medical treatment immediately.

- *Symptoms of Fastin overdose may include:*
  Abdominal cramps, aggressiveness, confusion, diarrhea, exaggerated reflexes, hallucinations, high or low blood pressure, irregular heartbeat, nausea, panic states, rapid breathing, restlessness, tremors, vomiting

Fatigue and depression may follow the stimulant effects of Fastin.

In cases of fatal poisoning, convulsions and coma usually precede death.

Generic name:

FELBAMATE

See Felbatol, page 425.

Brand name:

FELBATOL

Pronounced: FELL-ba-tohl
Generic name: Felbamate

Why is this drug prescribed?

Felbatol, a relatively new epilepsy medication, is used alone or with other drugs to treat partial seizures with or without generalization (seizures in which consciousness may be retained or lost). It is also used with other medications to treat seizures associated with Lennox-Gastaut syndrome (a childhood condition characterized by brief loss of awareness and muscle tone).

Felbatol is prescribed only when other medications have failed to control severe cases of epilepsy.

Most important fact about this drug
When taking Felbatol, be alert for signs of a very rare but dangerous side effect called aplastic anemia, in which the red blood cell count declines drastically. Warning signs include weakness, fatigue, and a tendency to easily bruise or bleed.

How should you take this medication?
Take this medication exactly as prescribed by your doctor. Felbatol should not be stopped suddenly. This could increase the frequency of your seizures.

If you are taking Felbatol liquid, shake well before using.

- *If you miss a dose...*
  Take the forgotten dose as soon as you remember. If it is almost time for your next dose, skip the one you missed and go back to your regular schedule. Never take a double dose.

- *Storage instructions...*
  Felbatol should be stored in a tightly closed container, at room temperature, away from excessive heat and moisture.

What side effects may occur?
Side effects cannot be anticipated. If any develop or change in intensity, notify your doctor as soon as possible. Only your doctor can determine if it is safe for you to continue taking Felbatol.

- *Side effects in adults taking Felbatol alone may include:*
  Acne, anxiety, constipation, diarrhea, double vision, ear infection, facial swelling, fatigue, headache, inability to fall or stay asleep, indigestion, loss of appetite, menstrual irregularities, nausea, nasal inflammation, rash, upper respiratory infection, urinary tract infection, vomiting, weight decrease

- *Side effects in adults taking Felbatol with other medication may include:*
Abdominal pain, abnormal stride, abnormal taste, abnormal vision, anxiety, chest pain, constipation, depression, diarrhea, dizziness, double vision, dry mouth, fatigue, fever, headache, inability to fall or stay asleep, indigestion, lack of muscle coordination, loss of appetite, muscle pain, nausea, nervousness, pins and needles, rash, sinus inflammation, sleepiness, sore throat, stupor, tremor, upper respiratory infection, vomiting

- *Side effects in children taking Felbatol with other medication may include:*
Abnormal stride, abnormal thinking, abnormally small pupils (pinpoint pupils), constipation, coughing, diarrhea, ear infection, fatigue, fever, headache, hiccups, inability to control urination, inability to fall or stay asleep, indigestion, lack of muscle coordination, loss of appetite, mood changes, nausea, nervousness, pain, rash, red or purple spots on skin, sleepiness, sore throat, taste changes, unstable emotions, upper respiratory infection, vomiting, weight decrease

Why should this drug not be prescribed?
If you are sensitive to or have ever had an allergic reaction to Felbatol or similar drugs, or if you have ever been diagnosed with bone marrow depression, do not take this medication. Make sure your doctor is aware of any drug reactions you have experienced.

Special warnings about this medication
Remember to watch for signs of aplastic anemia. (See "Most important fact about this drug.")

Expect your doctor to monitor your response carefully when you start taking Felbatol.

Possible food and drug interactions
when taking this medication
If you are taking Felbatol with certain other drugs, the effects of either could be increased, decreased, or altered. It is especially important to check with your doctor before combining Felbatol with other epilepsy drugs, such as Dilantin, Depakene, and Tegretol.

Special information
if you are pregnant or breastfeeding
The effects of Felbatol during pregnancy have not been adequately studied. If you are pregnant or plan to become pregnant, inform your doctor immediate-

ly. Felbatol appears in breast milk and could affect a nursing infant. If this medication is essential to your health, your doctor may advise you to discontinue breastfeeding until your treatment is finished.

Recommended dosage

ADULTS 14 YEARS OF AGE AND OVER

Whether Felbatol is taken alone or with other antiepileptic drugs, the usual starting dose is 1,200 milligrams per day divided into smaller doses and taken 3 or 4 times daily. Your doctor may gradually increase your daily dose to as much as 3,600 milligrams.

If you are already taking a drug to control your epilepsy, your doctor will reduce its dosage when you add Felbatol.

CHILDREN WITH LENNOX-GASTAUT SYNDROME (2 TO 14 YEARS)

The usual dose is 15 milligrams per 2.2 pounds of body weight per day divided into smaller doses taken 3 or 4 times daily. Your doctor may gradually increase your child's dose to 45 milligrams per 2.2 pounds of body weight per day. The doctor will reduce the amount of any other epilepsy drug your child is taking when starting Felbatol.

Overdosage

Any medication taken in excess can have serious consequences. If you suspect an overdose, seek medical treatment immediately.

■ *Symptoms of Felbatol overdose may include:*
Mild stomach upset
Unusually fast heartbeat

Brand name:

FELDENE

Pronounced: FELL-deen
Generic name: Piroxicam

Why is this drug prescribed?

Feldene, a nonsteroidal anti-inflammatory drug, is used to relieve the inflammation, swelling, stiffness, and joint pain associated with rheumatoid arthritis and osteoarthritis (the most common form of arthritis). It is prescribed both for sudden flare-ups and for long-term treatment.

Most important fact about this drug

In a few patients on long-term therapy, Feldene can cause stomach ulcers and bleeding. Warning signs include severe abdominal or stomach cramps, pain or burning in the stomach, and black, tarry stools. Inform your doctor immediately if you develop any of these symptoms.

How should you take this medication?

To avoid digestive side effects, take Feldene with food or an antacid, and with a full glass of water. Never take it on an empty stomach.

Take this medication exactly as prescribed by your doctor. Avoid alcohol and aspirin while taking this drug.

■ *If you miss a dose...*
If you forget to take a dose, take it as soon as you remember. If it is almost time for your next dose, skip the one you missed and go back to your regular schedule. Never take two doses at the same time.

■ *Storage instructions...*
Store at room temperature. Protect from light and heat.

What side effects may occur?

Side effects cannot be anticipated. If any develop or change in intensity, inform your doctor as soon as possible. Only your doctor can determine if it is safe for you to continue taking Feldene.

■ *More common side effects may include:*
Abdominal pain or discomfort, anemia, constipation, diarrhea, dizziness, fluid retention, gas, general feeling of ill health, headache, heartburn, indigestion, inflammation inside the mouth, itching, loss of appetite, nausea, rash, ringing in ears, sleepiness, stomach upset, vertigo

■ *Less common or rare side effects may include:*
Abdominal bleeding, severe allergic reactions, angioedema (swelling of lips, face, tongue and throat), black stools, blood in the urine, blurred vision, bruising, colicky pain, congestive heart failure (worsening of), depression, dry mouth, eye irritations, fatigue, fever, flu-like symptoms, hepatitis, high blood pressure, hives, inability to sleep, joint pain, labored breathing, low or high blood sugar, nervousness, nosebleed, serum sickness (fever, painful joints, enlarged lymph nodes, skin rash), skin allergy to sunlight, skin eruptions, Stevens-Johnson syndrome (blisters in the mouth and eyes), sweating, swollen eyes, vomiting, vomiting blood, weight loss or gain, wheezing, worsening of angina, yellow eyes and skin

Why should this drug not be prescribed?

If you are sensitive to or have ever had an allergic reaction to Feldene, aspirin, or similar drugs, or if you have had asthma attacks caused by aspirin or other drugs of this type, you should not take this medication. Make sure that your doctor is aware of any drug reactions that you have experienced.

Special warnings about this medication

If you have heart disease, or high blood pressure, or other conditions that cause fluid retention, use this drug with caution. Feldene can increase water retention.

This drug should be used with caution if you have kidney or liver disease; it can cause liver inflammation in some people.

Drugs such as Feldene may cause eye disturbances in some people. If you develop visual problems, notify your eye doctor.

Possible food and drug interactions
when taking this medication

If Feldene is taken with certain other drugs, the effects of either could be increased, decreased, or altered. It is especially important to check with your doctor before combining Feldene with the following:

Anticoagulants (blood thinners such as Coumadin)
Aspirin
Lithium

Special information
if you are pregnant or breastfeeding

Feldene is not recommended for use in nursing mothers or pregnant women. If you are pregnant or plan to become pregnant, inform your doctor immediately.

Recommended dosage

ADULTS

Rheumatoid Arthritis and Osteoarthritis:
The usual dose is 20 milligrams a day in one dose. Your doctor may want you to divide this dose into smaller ones. You will not feel Feldene's full effects for 7 to 12 days, although some relief of symptoms will start to occur soon after you take the medication.

CHILDREN

The safety and effectiveness of Feldene have not been established in children.

ELDERLY

Your doctor will determine your dosage according to your particular needs.

Overdosage

Although there are no specific symptoms of a Feldene overdose, any medication taken in excess can have serious consequences. If you suspect an overdose, seek medical attention immediately.

Generic name:

FELODIPINE

See Plendil, page 865.

Brand name:

FEMSTAT

Pronounced: FEM-stat
Generic name: Butoconazole nitrate

Why is this drug prescribed?

Femstat Vaginal Cream is prescribed for the treatment of yeast-like fungal infections of the vulva and vagina.

Most important fact about this drug

To obtain maximum benefit, it is important that you continue to use Femstat Vaginal Cream during menstruation and that you finish using all of the medication, even if your symptoms have disappeared.

How should you use this medication?

Use this medication exactly as prescribed. To keep it from getting on your clothing, wear a sanitary napkin. Do not use a tampon; it will absorb the drug. Do not douche unless your doctor tells you to do so.

While using Femstat, wear cotton underwear or pantyhose with a cotton crotch. Avoid synthetic fabrics such as rayon and nylon.

- *To apply Femstat:*
  1. Fill the applicator that comes with the vaginal cream to the level indicated.
  2. Lie on your back with your knees drawn up.
  3. Gently insert the applicator high into vagina and push the plunger.
  4. Withdraw the applicator and discard if disposable or wash with soap and water.

To avoid reinfection, refrain from intercourse during treatment or ask your partner to use a condom.

- *If you miss a dose...*
  Insert it as soon as you remember. If it is almost time for your next dose, skip the one you missed and go back to your regular schedule.

- *Storage instructions...*
  Store at room temperature, away from heat. Do not freeze.

What side effects may occur?
Side effects cannot be anticipated. If any develop or change in intensity, inform your doctor as soon as possible. Only your doctor can determine if it is safe for you to continue using Femstat.

- *Side effects may include:*
  Itching of the fingers
  Soreness
  Swelling
  Vaginal discharge
  Vulvar itching
  Vulvar or vaginal burning

Why should this drug not be prescribed?
If you are sensitive to or have ever had an allergic reaction to butoconazole nitrate or any other ingredients in Femstat Cream, you should not use this medication. Make sure your doctor is aware of any drug reactions you have experienced.

Special warnings about this medication
If your symptoms persist, or if you become irritated or have an allergic reaction while using this medication, notify your doctor.

Possible food and drug interactions
when taking this medication
No interactions with other drugs have been reported.

**Special information
if you are pregnant or breastfeeding**
The effects of Femstat Cream during the first trimester (first 3 months) of pregnancy have not been adequately studied. However, women using this cream for 3 to 6 days during the second or third trimester of pregnancy have experienced no adverse effects or complications, nor have their infants. It is not known whether this drug appears in breast milk. If Femstat is essential to your health, your doctor may advise you to discontinue breastfeeding until your treatment is finished.

Recommended dosage

ADULTS

Non-pregnant Women
The recommended dose is 1 applicatorful of cream inserted in the vagina at bedtime for 3 days. Your doctor may extend your treatment for an additional 3 days if necessary.

Pregnant Women (Second and Third Trimesters Only)
The recommended dose is 1 applicatorful of cream inserted in the vagina at bedtime for 6 days.

CHILDREN

Safety and effectiveness have not been established in children.

Overdosage
No overdosage has been reported.

Generic name:

FINASTERIDE

See Proscar, page 906.

Brand name:

FIORICET

Pronounced: fee-OAR-i-set
Generic ingredients: Butalbital, Acetaminophen, Caffeine
Other brand names: Anolor 300, Esgic, Esgic Plus

Why is this drug prescribed?

Fioricet, a strong, nonnarcotic pain reliever and relaxant, is prescribed for the relief of tension headache symptoms caused by muscle contractions in the head, neck, and shoulder area. It combines a sedative barbiturate (butalbital), a non-aspirin pain reliever (acetaminophen), and caffeine.

Most important fact about this drug

Mental and physical dependence can occur with the use of barbiturates such as butalbital when these drugs are taken in higher than recommended doses over long periods of time.

How should you take this medication?

Take Fioricet exactly as prescribed. Do not increase the amount you take without your doctor's approval.

■ *If you miss a dose...*
Take it as soon as you remember. If it is almost time for your next dose, skip the one you missed and go back to your regular schedule. Never take 2 doses at the same time.

■ *Storage instructions...*
Store at room temperature in a tight, light-resistant container.

What side effects may occur?

Side effects cannot be anticipated. If any develop or change in intensity, inform your doctor as soon as possible. Only your doctor can determine if it is safe for you to continue taking Fioricet.

■ *More common side effects may include:*
Abdominal pain
Dizziness
Drowsiness
Intoxicated feeling
Light-headedness
Nausea
Sedation
Shortness of breath
Vomiting

■ *Less common or rare side effects may include:*
Agitation, allergic reactions, constipation, depression, difficulty swallowing, dry mouth, earache, exaggerated feeling of well-being, excessive sweating, excessive urination, excitement, fainting, fatigue, fever, flatu-

lence, headache, heartburn, heavy eyelids, high energy, hot spells, itching, leg pain, mental confusion, muscle fatigue, numbness, rapid heartbeat, ringing in the ears, seizure, shaky feeling, skin redness and/or peeling, sluggishness, stuffy nose, tingling

Why should this drug not be prescribed?

If you are sensitive to or have ever had an allergic reaction to barbiturates, acetaminophen, or caffeine, you should not take this medication. Make sure that your doctor is aware of any drug reactions that you have experienced.

Unless you are directed to do so by your doctor, do not take this medication if you have porphyria (an inherited metabolic disorder affecting the liver or bone marrow).

Special warnings about this medication

Fioricet may cause you to become drowsy or less alert; therefore, driving or operating dangerous machinery or participating in any hazardous activity that requires full mental alertness is not recommended until you know your response to this drug.

If you are being treated for severe depression or have a history of severe depression or drug abuse, consult with your doctor before taking Fioricet.

Use this drug with caution if you are elderly or in a weakened condition, if you have liver or kidney problems, or if you have severe abdominal trouble.

Possible food and drug interactions
when taking this medication

Butalbital is a central nervous system (brain and spinal cord) depressant and intensifies the effects of alcohol and other CNS depressants. Use of alcohol with this drug may also cause overdose symptoms. Therefore, use of alcohol should be avoided.

If Fioricet is taken with certain other drugs, the effects of either could be increased, decreased, or altered. It is especially important to check with your doctor before combining Fioricet with the following:

Antidepressant drugs known as monoamine oxidase inhibitors, including Nardil, Marplan, and Parnate
Antihistamines such as Benadryl
Antipsychotics such as Haldol and Thorazine
Drugs to treat depression such as Elavil
Muscle relaxants such as Flexeril
Narcotic pain relievers such as Darvon
Sleep aids such as Halcion
Tranquilizers such as Xanax and Valium

Special information
if you are pregnant or breastfeeding

If you are pregnant or plan to become pregnant, inform your doctor immediately. Fioricet can affect a developing baby. It also appears in breast milk. If this medication is essential to your health, your doctor may advise you to discontinue breastfeeding your baby until your treatment is finished.

Recommended dosage

ADULTS

The usual dose of Fioricet is 1 or 2 tablets taken every 4 hours as needed. Do not exceed a total dose of 6 tablets per day.

The usual dose of Esgic-Plus is 1 tablet every 4 hours as needed. Do not take more than 6 tablets a day.

CHILDREN

The safety and effectiveness of Fioricet have not been established in children under 12 years of age.

ELDERLY

Fioricet may cause excitement, depression, and confusion in the elderly. Therefore, your doctor will prescribe a dose individualized to suit your needs.

Overdosage

Symptoms of Fioricet overdose can be due to its barbiturate or its acetaminophen component.

■ *Symptoms of barbiturate poisoning may include:*
  Coma
  Confusion
  Drowsiness
  Low blood pressure
  Shock
  Slow or troubled breathing

Overdose due to the acetaminophen component of Fioricet may cause kidney and liver damage, blood disorders, or coma due to low blood sugar. Massive doses may cause liver failure.

■ *Symptoms of liver damage include:*
  Excess perspiration
  Feeling of bodily discomfort

Nausea
Vomiting

If you suspect an overdose, seek emergency medical treatment immediately.

Brand name:

FIORINAL

Pronounced: fee-OR-i-nahl
Generic ingredients: Butalbital, Aspirin, Caffeine
Other brand name: Isollyl Improved

Why is this drug prescribed?
Fiorinal, a strong, non-narcotic pain reliever and muscle relaxant, is prescribed for the relief of tension headache symptoms caused by stress or muscle contraction in the head, neck, and shoulder area. It combines a non-narcotic, sedative barbiturate (butalbital) with a pain reliever (aspirin) and a stimulant (caffeine).

Most important fact about this drug
Barbiturates such as butalbital can be habit-forming if you take them over long periods of time.

How should you take this medication?
For best relief, take Fiorinal as soon as a headache begins.

Take the medication with a full glass of water or food to reduce stomach irritation. Do not take this medication if it has a strong odor of vinegar.

Take Fiorinal exactly as prescribed. Do not increase the amount you take without your doctor's approval.

- *If you miss a dose...*
  If you take Fiorinal on a regular schedule, take the forgotten dose as soon as you remember. If it is almost time for your next dose, skip the one you missed and go back to your regular schedule. Do not take 2 doses at once.

- *Storage instructions...*
  Store at room temperature. Keep the container tightly closed.

What side effects may occur?
Side effects cannot be anticipated. If any develop or change in intensity, inform your doctor as soon as possible. Only your doctor can determine if it is safe for you to continue taking Fiorinal.

- *More common side effects may include:*
  Dizziness
  Drowsiness

- *Less common or rare side effects may include:*
  Gas, light-headedness, nausea, skin problems, vomiting

Why should this drug not be prescribed?

If you are sensitive to or have ever had an allergic reaction to barbiturates, aspirin, caffeine, or other sedatives and pain relievers, you should not take this medication. Make sure your doctor is aware of any drug reactions you have experienced.

Unless you are directed to do so by your doctor, do not take this medication if you have porphyria (an inherited metabolic disorder affecting the liver or bone marrow).

Because aspirin, when given to children and teenagers suffering from flu or chickenpox, can cause a dangerous neurological disease called Reye's syndrome, do not use Fiorinal under these circumstances.

Special warnings about this medication

Fiorinal may make you drowsy or less alert; therefore, you should not drive or operate dangerous machinery or participate in any hazardous activity that requires full mental alertness until you know your response to this drug.

Fiorinal contains aspirin. If you have a stomach (peptic) ulcer or a disorder affecting the blood clotting process, consult your doctor before taking Fiorinal. Aspirin may irritate the stomach lining and may cause bleeding.

If you have chronic (long-lasting or frequently recurring) tension headaches and your prescribed dose of Fiorinal does not relieve the pain, consult with your doctor. Taking more of this drug than your doctor has prescribed may cause dependence and symptoms of overdose.

Possible food and drug interactions
when taking this medication

Butalbital decreases the activity of the central nervous system and intensifies the effects of alcohol. Avoid drinking alcohol while you are taking Fiorinal.

If Fiorinal is taken with certain other drugs, the effects of either could be increased, decreased, or altered. It is especially important to check with your doctor before combining Fiorinal with the following:

Acetazolamide (Diamox)
Antidepressant drugs such as Elavil, Norpramin, Nardil, and Parnate

Beta-blocking blood pressure drugs such as Inderal and Tenormin
Blood-thinning drugs such as Coumadin
Insulin
Narcotic pain relievers such as Darvon and Percocet
Oral contraceptives
Oral diabetes drugs such as Micronase
Sleep aids such as Halcion, Nembutal, and phenobarbital
Steroid medications such as prednisone
Theophylline (Theo-Dur, others)
Tranquilizers such as Librium, Valium, and Xanax
Valproic acid (Depakene, Depakote)

Special information
if you are pregnant or breastfeeding

The effects of Fiorinal during pregnancy have not been adequately studied. If you are pregnant or plan to become pregnant, inform your doctor immediately. Butalbital and aspirin appear in breast milk. If this medication is essential to your health, your doctor may advise you to discontinue breastfeeding until your treatment with this medication is finished.

Recommended dosage

ADULTS

The usual dose of Fiorinal is 1 or 2 tablets or capsules taken every 4 hours. You should not take more than 6 tablets or capsules in a day.

CHILDREN

The safety and effectiveness of Fiorinal have not been established in children under 12 years of age.

Overdosage

Any medication taken in excess can have serious consequences. If you suspect an overdose, seek medical attention immediately.

- *Symptoms of an overdose of Fiorinal are mainly attributed to its barbiturate component. These symptoms may include:*
  Coma
  Confusion
  Drowsiness
  Low blood pressure
  Shock
  Slow or troubled breathing

- *Symptoms attributed to the aspirin and caffeine components of Fiorinal may include:*
  Abdominal pain
  Deep, rapid breathing
  Delirium
  High fever
  Inability to fall or stay asleep
  Rapid or irregular heartbeat
  Restlessness
  Ringing in the ears
  Seizures
  Tremor
  Vomiting

Brand name:

FIORINAL WITH CODEINE

Pronounced: fee-OR-i-nahl with KO-deen
Generic ingredients: Butalbital, Codeine phosphate, Aspirin, Caffeine

Why is this drug prescribed?

Fiorinal with Codeine, a strong narcotic pain reliever and muscle relaxant, is prescribed for the relief of tension headache caused by stress and muscle contraction in the head, neck, and shoulder area. It combines a sedative-barbiturate (butalbital), a narcotic pain reliever and cough suppressant (codeine), a non-narcotic pain and fever reliever (aspirin), and a stimulant (caffeine).

Most important fact about this drug

Barbiturates such as butalbital and narcotics such as codeine can be habit-forming when taken in higher than recommended doses over long periods of time.

How should you take this medication?

Take Fiornal with Codeine with a full glass of water or food to reduce stomach irritation. Do not take this medication if it has a strong odor of vinegar.

Take Fiorinal with Codeine exactly as prescribed. Do not increase the amount you take without your doctor's approval.

Do not take it more frequently than your doctor has prescribed.

■ *If you miss a dose...*
If you take the drug on a regular schedule, take the forgotten dose as soon as you remember. If it is almost time for your next dose, skip the one you missed and go back to your regular schedule. Do not take 2 doses at once.

■ *Storage instructions...*
Store at room temperature. Keep the container tightly closed.

What side effects may occur?
Side effects cannot be anticipated. If any develop or change in intensity, inform your doctor as soon as possible. Only your doctor can determine if it is safe for you to continue taking Fiorinal with Codeine.

■ *More common side effects may include:*
Abdominal pain
Dizziness
Drowsiness
Nausea

■ *Additional side effects, which can be caused by this drug's components, may include:*
Anemia, blocked air passages, hepatitis, high blood sugar, internal bleeding, intoxicated feeling, irritability, kidney damage, lack of clotting, light-headedness, peptic ulcer, stomach upset, tremors

Why should this drug not be prescribed?
If you are sensitive to or have ever had an allergic reaction to butalbital, codeine, aspirin, caffeine, or other pain relievers, you should not take this medication. Make sure your doctor is aware of any drug reactions you have experienced.

Unless you are directed to do so by your doctor, do not take this medication if you have: a tendency to bleed too much, severe vitamin K deficiency, severe liver damage, nasal polyps (growths or nodules), asthma due to aspirin or other nonsteroidal anti-inflammatory drugs such as Motrin, swelling due to fluid retention, peptic ulcer, or porphyria (an inherited metabolic disorder affecting the liver and bone marrow).

Because aspirin, when given to children and teenagers with chickenpox or flu, can cause a dangerous neurological disease called Reye's syndrome, do not use Fiorinal with Codeine under these circumstances.

Special warnings about this medication

Fiorinal with Codeine may make you drowsy or less alert; therefore, you should not drive or operate dangerous machinery or participate in any hazardous activity that requires full mental alertness until you know how this drug affects you.

Codeine may cause unusually slow or troubled breathing and may increase the pressure caused by fluid surrounding the brain and spinal cord in people with head injury. Codeine also affects brain and spinal cord function and makes it hard for the doctor to see how people with head injuries are doing.

If you have chronic (long-lasting or frequently recurring) tension headaches and your prescribed dose of Fiorinal with Codeine does not relieve the pain, consult with your doctor. Taking more of this drug than your doctor has prescribed may cause dependence and symptoms of overdose.

Aspirin can cause internal bleeding in people with ulcers or bleeding disorders.

Codeine can hide signs of severe abdominal problems.

If you have ever developed dependence on a drug, consult with your doctor before taking Fiorinal with Codeine.

If you are being treated for a kidney, liver, or blood clotting disorder, consult with your doctor before taking Fiorinal with Codeine.

If you are older or in a weakened condition, be very careful taking Fiornal with Codeine.

Possible food and drug interactions
when taking this medication

Fiorinal with Codeine reduces the activity of the central nervous system and intensifies the effects of alcohol. Use of alcohol with this drug may also cause overdose symptoms. Therefore, use of alcohol should be avoided.

If Fiornal with Codeine is taken with certain other drugs, the effects of either could be increased, decreased, or altered. It is especially important to check with your doctor before combining Fiorinal with Codeine with the following:

Acetazolamide (Diamox)
Antidepressant drugs such as Elavil, Sinequan, Nardil, and Parnate
Antigout medications such as Zyloprim
Antihistamines such as Benadryl
Beta-blocking blood pressure drugs such as Inderal and Tenormin
Blood-thinning drugs such as Coumadin

Insulin
6-Mercaptopurine
Methotrexate (Rheumatrex)
Narcotic pain relievers such as Darvon and Vicodin
Nonsteroidal anti-inflammatory drugs such as Motrin and Indocin
Oral contraceptives
Oral diabetes drugs such as Micronase
Sleep aids such as Nembutal and phenobarbital
Steroid drugs such as prednisone
Theophylline (Theo-Dur, others)
Tranquilizers such as Librium, Xanax, and Valium
Valproic acid (Depakone, Depakote)

**Special information
if you are pregnant or breastfeeding**
The effects of Fiorinal with Codeine during pregnancy have not been adequately studied. If you are pregnant or plan to become pregnant, inform your doctor immediately. Butalbital, aspirin, caffeine, and codeine appear in breast milk. If this medication is essential to your health, your doctor may advise you to discontinue breastfeeding until your treatment with this medication is finished.

Recommended dosage

ADULTS

The usual dose of Fiorinal with Codeine is 1 or 2 capsules taken every 4 hours. Do not take more than 6 capsules per day.

CHILDREN

The safety and effectiveness of butalbital have not been established in children under 12 years of age.

Overdosage
Symptoms of an overdose of Fiorinal with Codeine are mainly attributed to its barbiturate and codeine ingredients.

- *Symptoms attributed to the barbiturate ingredient of Fiorinal with Codeine may include:*
  Coma
  Confusion
  Dizziness

Drowsiness
Low blood pressure
Shock
Slow or troubled breathing

■ *Symptoms attributed to the codeine ingredient of*
Fiorinal with Codeine may include:
Convulsions
Loss of consciousness
Pinpoint pupils
Troubled and slowed breathing

■ *Symptoms attributed to the aspirin ingredient of Fiorinal*
with Codeine may include:
Abdominal pain
Deep, rapid breathing
Delirium
High fever
Restlessness
Ringing in the ears
Seizures
Vomiting

Though caffeine poisoning occurs only at very high doses, it can cause
delirium, insomnia, irregular heartbeat, rapid heartbeat, restlessness, and
tremor.

If you suspect an overdose of Fiorinal with Codeine, seek emergency medical
treatment immediately.

Brand name:

FLAGYL

Pronounced: FLAJ-ill
Generic name: Metronidazole
Other brand name: Protostat

Why is this drug prescribed?
Flagyl is an antibacterial drug prescribed for certain vaginal and urinary tract
infections in men and women; amebic dysentery and liver abscess; and
infections of the abdomen, skin, bones and joints, brain, lungs, and heart
caused by certain bacteria.

Most important fact about this drug
Do not drink alcoholic beverages while taking Flagyl. The combination can cause abdominal cramps, nausea, vomiting, headaches, and flushing. It can also change the taste of the alcoholic beverage. When you have stopped taking Flagyl, wait another 24 hours (one day) before consuming any alcohol. Also avoid over-the-counter medications containing alcohol, such as certain cough and cold products.

How should you take this medication?
Flagyl works best when there is a constant amount in the blood. Take your doses at evenly spaced intervals, day and night, and try to avoid missing any.

If you are being treated for the sexually transmitted genital infection called trichomoniasis, your doctor may want to treat your partner at the same time, even if there are no symptoms. Try to avoid sexual intercourse until infection is cured. If you do have sex, use a condom.

Flagyl can be taken with or without food. It may cause dry mouth. Hard candy, chewing gum, or bits of ice can help to relieve the problem.

■ *If you miss a dose...*
Take it as soon as you remember. If it is almost time for your next dose, skip the one you missed and go back to your regular schedule. Do not take 2 doses at once.

■ *Storage Instructions...*
Store at room temperature. Protect from light.

What side effects may occur?
Side effects cannot be anticipated. If any develop or change in intensity, tell your doctor immediately. Only your doctor can determine whether it is safe for you to continue taking Flagyl.

Two serious side effects that have occurred with Flagyl are seizures and numbness or tingling in the arms, legs, hands, and feet. If you experience either of these symptoms, stop taking the medication and call your doctor immediately.

■ *More common side effects may include:*
Abdominal cramps
Constipation
Diarrhea
Headache

Loss of appetite
Nausea
Upset stomach
Vomiting

■ *Less common side effects may include:*
Blood disorders, confusion, dark urine, decreased sex drive, depression, difficulty sleeping, dizziness, dry mouth (or vagina or vulva), fever, flushing, furry tongue, hives, inability to hold urine, increased production of pale urine, inflamed mouth or tongue, inflammation of the rectum, irritability, lack of muscle coordination, metallic taste, occasional joint pain, pain during sexual intercourse, painful or difficult urination, pelvic pressure, rash, stuffy nose, vertigo, weakness, yeast infection (candida) in vagina

Why should this drug not be prescribed?
Flagyl should not be used during the first 3 months of pregnancy to treat vaginal infections. Do not take Flagyl if you have ever had an allergic reaction to or are sensitive to metronidazole or similar drugs. Tell your doctor about any drug reactions you have experienced.

Special warnings about this medication
If you experience seizures or numbness or tingling in your arms, legs, hands, or feet, remember that you should stop taking Flagyl and call your doctor immediately.

If you have liver disease, make sure the doctor is aware of it. Flagyl should be used with caution.

Active or undiagnosed yeast infections may appear or worsen when you take Flagyl.

Possible food and drug interactions
when taking this medication
Do not drink alcohol while taking Flagyl and for another 24 hours after your last dose.

If Flagyl is taken with certain other drugs, the effects of either could be increased, decreased, or altered. It is especially important to check with your doctor before combining Flagyl with any of the following:

Blood thinners such as Coumadin
Cholestyramine (Questran)
Cimetidine (Tagamet)
Disulfiram (Antabuse)

Lithium (Lithonate)
Phenobarbital
Phenytoin (Dilantin)

**Special information
if you are pregnant or breastfeeding**
The effects of Flagyl in pregnancy have not been adequately studied. If you are pregnant or plan to become pregnant, notify your doctor. This medication should be used during pregnancy only if it is clearly needed. Flagyl appears in breast milk and could affect a nursing infant. If Flagyl is essential to your health, your doctor may advise you to stop breastfeeding until your treatment is finished.

Recommended dosage

ADULT

Trichomoniasis
One-day treatment: 2 grams of Flagyl, taken as a single dose or divided into 2 doses (1 gram each) taken in the same day.

Seven-day course of treatment: 250 milligrams 3 times daily for 7 consecutive days.

Acute Intestinal Amebiasis (Acute Amebic Dysentery)
The usual dose is 750 milligrams taken by mouth 3 times daily for 5 to 10 days.

Amebic Liver Abscess
The usual dose is 500 milligrams or 750 milligrams taken by mouth 3 times daily for 5 to 10 days.

Anaerobic Bacterial Infections
The usual adult oral dosage is 7.5 milligrams per 2.2 pounds of body weight every 6 hours.

CHILDREN

Amebiasis
The usual dose is 35 to 50 milligrams for each 2.2 pounds of body weight per day, divided into 3 doses taken for 10 days.

The safety and efficacy of Flagyl for any other condition in children have not been established.

ELDERLY

Your doctor will test to see how much medication is in your blood and will adjust your dosage if necessary.

Overdosage

Any medication taken in excess can have serious consequences. If you suspect an overdose, seek medical treatment immediately.

■ *Symptoms of Flagyl overdose may include:*
Lack of muscle coordination
Nausea
Vomiting

Generic name:

FLAVOXATE

See Urispas, page 1178.

Generic name:

FLECAINIDE

See Tambocor, page 1069.

Brand name:

FLEXERIL

Pronounced: FLEX-eh-rill
Generic name: Cyclobenzaprine hydrochloride

Why is this drug prescribed?

Flexeril is a muscle relaxant prescribed to relieve muscle spasms resulting from injuries such as sprains, strains, or pulls. Combined with rest and physical therapy, Flexeril provides relief of muscular stiffness and pain.

Most important fact about this drug

Flexeril is not a substitute for the physical therapy, rest, or exercise that your doctor orders for proper healing. Although Flexeril relieves the pain of strains and sprains, it is not useful for other types of pain.

How should you take this medication?
Flexeril may be taken with or without food.

Flexeril should be used only for short periods (no more than 3 weeks). Since the type of injury that Flexeril treats should improve in a few weeks, there is no reason to use it for a longer period.

Flexeril may cause dry mouth. Sucking a hard candy, chewing gum, or melting ice chips in your mouth can provide temporary relief.

■ *If you miss a dose...*
Take it as soon as you remember, if it is within an hour or so of your scheduled time. If you do not remember until later, skip the missed dose and go back to your regular schedule. Do not take 2 doses at once.

■ *Storage instructions...*
Store away from heat, light, and moisture.

What side effects may occur?
Side effects cannot be anticipated. If any develop or change in intensity, inform your doctor as soon as possible. Only your doctor can determine if it is safe for you to continue taking Flexeril.

■ *More common side effects may include:*
Dizziness
Drowsiness
Dry mouth

■ *Less common or rare side effects may include:*
Abnormal heartbeats, abnormal sensations, abnormal thoughts or dreams, agitation, anxiety, bloated feeling, blurred vision, confusion, constipation, convulsions, decreased appetite, depressed mood, diarrhea, difficulty falling or staying asleep, difficulty speaking, disorientation, double vision, excitement, fainting, fatigue, fluid retention, gas, hallucinations, headache, heartburn, hepatitis, hives, increased heart rate, indigestion, inflammation of the stomach, itching, lack of coordination, liver diseases, loss of sense of taste, low blood pressure, muscle twitching, nausea, nervousness, palpitations, rash, ringing in the ears, severe allergic reaction, stomach and intestinal pain, sweating, swelling of the tongue or face, thirst, tingling in hands or feet, tremors, unpleasant taste in the mouth, urinating more or less than usual, vague feeling of bodily discomfort, vertigo, vomiting, weakness, yellow eyes and skin

Why should this drug not be prescribed?
You should not take this drug if you are taking an antidepressant drug known as an MAO inhibitor (such as Nardil or Parnate) or have taken an MAO inhibitor within the last 2 weeks. Also avoid Flexeril if you have ever had an allergic reaction to it, or if your thyroid gland is overactive.

In addition, you should not take Flexeril if you have recently had a heart attack or if you have congestive heart failure, or suffer from irregular heartbeat.

Special warnings about this medication
Flexeril may cause you to become drowsy or less alert; therefore, you should not drive or operate dangerous machinery or participate in any hazardous activity that requires full mental alertness until you know how this drug affects you.

You should use Flexeril with caution if you have ever been unable to urinate or if you have ever had the eye condition called glaucoma.

**Possible food and drug interactions
when taking this medication**
Serious, potentially fatal reactions may occur if you take Flexeril with an antidepressant drug known as an MAO inhibitor (such as Nardil, Parnate) or if it has been less than 2 weeks since you last took an MAO inhibitor. You should closely follow your doctor's advice regarding discontinuation of MAO inhibitors before taking Flexeril.

Avoid alcoholic beverages while taking Flexeril.

If Flexeril is taken with certain other drugs, the effects of either could be increased, decreased, or altered. It is especially important to check with your doctor before combining Flexeril with the following:

  Antispasmodic drugs such as Donnatal or Bentyl
  Barbiturates such as phenobarbital
  Guanethidine (Esimil, Ismelin) and other high blood pressure drugs
  Other drugs that slow the central nervous system, such as Halcion and
     Xanax

**Special information
if you are pregnant or breastfeeding**
The effects of Flexeril during pregnancy have not been adequately studied. If you are pregnant or plan to become pregnant, inform your doctor immediately. It is not known if Flexeril appears in breast milk. However, cyclobenzaprine is related to tricyclic antidepressants, and some of those drugs do

appear in breast milk. If this medication is essential to your health, your doctor may advise you to discontinue breastfeeding your baby until your treatment is finished.

Recommended dosage

ADULTS

The usual dose is 10 milligrams 3 times a day. You should not take more than 60 milligrams a day.

CHILDREN

The safety and effectiveness of Flexeril have not been established for children under the age of 15.

Overdosage

Any medication taken in excess can have serious consequences. If you suspect a Flexeril overdose, seek medical attention immediately.

■ *Symptoms of Flexeril overdose may include:*
Agitation, coma, confusion, congestive heart failure, convulsions, dilated pupils, disturbed concentration, drowsiness, hallucinations, high or low temperature, increased heartbeats, irregular heart rhythms, muscle stiffness, overactive reflexes, severe low blood pressure, stupor, vomiting

High doses also may cause any of the conditions listed in "What side effects may occur?"

Brand name:

FLOXIN

Pronounced: FLOCKS-in
Generic name: Ofloxacin

Why is this drug prescribed?

Floxin is an antibiotic. It has been used effectively to treat lower respiratory tract infections, including chronic bronchitis and pneumonia, sexually transmitted diseases (except syphilis), and infections of the urinary tract, prostate gland, and skin.

Most important fact about this drug

Floxin kills a variety of bacteria, and is frequently used to treat infections in many parts of the body. However, you should stop taking the drug and notify your doctor immediately at the first sign of a skin rash or any other allergic reaction. Although quite rare, serious and occasionally fatal allergic reactions have been reported, some after only one dose. Signs of an impending reaction include swelling of the face and throat, shortness of breath, difficulty swallowing, rapid heartbeat, tingling, itching, and hives.

How should you take this medication?

Do not take Floxin with food. Be sure to drink plenty of fluids while taking this medication.

Do not take mineral supplements, vitamins with iron or minerals, or antacids containing calcium, aluminum, or magnesium within 2 hours of taking Floxin.

Take Floxin exactly as prescribed. You need to complete the full course of therapy to obtain best results and decrease the risk of a recurrence of the infection.

■ *If you miss a dose...*
Take it as soon as you remember. If it is almost time for your next dose, skip the one you missed and go back to your regular schedule. Never take 2 doses at the same time.

■ *Storage instructions...*
Store at room temperature in a tightly closed container.

What side effects may occur?

Side effects cannot be anticipated. If any develop or change in intensity, inform your doctor as soon as possible. Only your doctor can determine if it is safe for you to continue taking Floxin.

■ *More common side effects may include:*
Diarrhea
Difficulty sleeping
Dizziness
Headache
Itching of genital area in women
Nausea
Vaginal inflammation
Vomiting

■ *Less common or rare side effects may include:*
Abdominal pain and cramps, aggressiveness or hostility, agitation, anemia, anxiety, asthma, blood in the urine, blurred vision, body pain, bruising, burning or rash of the female genitals, burning sensation in the upper chest, changeable emotions, changes in thinking and perception, chest

pain, confusion, conjunctivitis (pinkeye), continual runny nose, constipation, cough, decreased appetite, depression, difficult or labored breathing, disorientation, disturbed dreams, disturbed sense of smell, double vision, dry mouth, exaggerated sense of well-being, excessive perspiration, fainting, fatigue, fear, fever, fluid retention, frequent urination, gas, hallucinations, hearing disturbance or loss, hepatitis, hiccups, high or low blood pressure, high or low blood sugar, hives, inability to urinate, increased urination, indigestion, inflammation of the colon, inflammation or rupture of tendons, intolerance to light, involuntary eye movement, itching, joint pain, kidney problems, lack of coordination, light-headedness, liver problems, menstrual changes, muscle pain, nervousness, nightmares, nosebleed, pain, pain in arms and legs, painful or difficult urination, purple or red areas/spots on the skin, rapid heartbeat, rash, reddened skin, restlessness, ringing in the ears, seizures, sensitivity to light, severe allergic reaction, skin inflammation and flaking or eruptions, sleepiness, sleep problems, sore mouth or throat, speech difficulty, Stevens-Johnson syndrome (severe skin eruptions), stomach and intestinal upset or bleeding, taste distortion, thirst, throbbing or fluttering heartbeat, tingling or pins and needles, tremor, unexplained bleeding from the uterus, vaginal discharge, vaginal yeast infection, vague feeling of illness, vertigo, visual disturbances, weakness, weight loss, yellowing of eyes and skin

Why should this drug not be prescribed?

Do not take Floxin if you are sensitive to or have ever had an allergic reaction to it or other quinolone antibiotics such as Cipro and Noroxin.

Special warnings about this medication

Floxin, used in high doses for short periods of time, may hide or delay the symptoms of syphilis, but is not effective in treating syphilis. If you are taking Floxin for gonorrhea, your doctor will test you for syphilis and then perform a follow-up test after 3 months of treatment.

Convulsions, increased pressure in the head, psychosis, tremors, restlessness, light-headedness, nervousness, confusion, depression, nightmares, insomnia, and hallucinations have occasionally been reported with this type of antibiotic. If you experience any of these symptoms, stop taking the drug and contact your doctor immediately.

If you are prone to seizures due to kidney disease, a brain disorder, or epilepsy, make sure your doctor knows about it. Floxin should be used with caution under these conditions.

If you have liver or kidney disease, your doctor will watch you closely while you are taking Floxin.

Avoid being in the sun too much; you can develop sun poisoning while you are taking Floxin.

Floxin may make you feel dizzy or light-headed. Be careful driving, operating machinery, or doing any activity that requires full mental alertness until you know how you react to this medication.

Safety has not been established for children under 18 years of age.

Possible food and drug interactions
when taking this medication
If Floxin is taken with certain other drugs, the effects of either could be increased, decreased, or altered. It is especially important to check with your doctor before combining Floxin with the following:

Antacids containing calcium, magnesium, or aluminum
Blood thinners such as Coumadin
Calcium supplements such as Caltrate
Cyclosporine (Sandimmune)
Insulin
Iron supplements such as Feosol
Multivitamins containing zinc
Nonsteroidal anti-inflammatory drugs such as Motrin and Naprosyn
Oral diabetes drugs such as Diabinese and Micronase
Sucralfate (Carafate)
Theophylline-containing drugs, such as Theo-Dur

Special information
if you are pregnant or breastfeeding
The effects of Floxin during pregnancy have not been adequately studied. If you are pregnant or plan to become pregnant, inform your doctor immediately. This medication should not be used during pregnancy unless your doctor has determined that the benefit to you outweighs the risk to the unborn baby. Floxin appears in breast milk and could affect a nursing infant. If this medication is essential to your health, your doctor may advise you to stop breastfeeding until your treatment with Floxin is finished.

Recommended dosage

LOWER RESPIRATORY TRACT INFECTIONS

Worsening of Chronic Bronchitis
The usual dose is 400 milligrams every 12 hours for 10 days, for a total daily dose of 800 milligrams.

Pneumonia
The usual dose is 400 milligrams every 12 hours for 10 days, for a total daily dose of 800 milligrams.

SEXUALLY TRANSMITTED DISEASES

Gonorrhea
The usual dose is 400 milligrams taken once.

Infections of the Cervix or Urethra
The usual dose is 300 milligrams every 12 hours for 7 days, for a total daily dose of 600 milligrams.

MILD TO MODERATE SKIN INFECTIONS

The usual dose is 400 milligrams every 12 hours for 10 days, for a total daily dose of 800 milligrams.

URINARY TRACT INFECTIONS

Bladder Infections
The usual dose is 200 milligrams every 12 hours for a total daily dose of 400 milligrams. This dose is taken for 3 days for infections due to *E. Coli* or *K. Pneumoniae*. For infections due to other microbes, it is taken for 7 days.

Complicated Urinary Tract Infections
The usual dose is 200 milligrams every 12 hours for 10 days, for a total daily dose of 400 milligrams.

Prostatitis
The usual dose is 300 milligrams every 12 hours for 6 weeks, for a total daily dose of 600 milligrams.

Overdosage
Although no specific information is available, any medication taken in excess can have serious consequences. If you suspect an overdose, seek medical treatment immediately.

Generic name:

FLUCONAZOLE

See Diflucan, page 328.

Generic name:

FLUNISOLIDE

See AeroBid, page 20.

Generic name:

FLUOCINONIDE

See Lidex, page 578.

Generic name:

FLUOROMETHOLONE

See FML, page 457.

Generic name:

FLUOROURACIL

See Efudex, page 384.

Generic name:

FLUOXETINE

See Prozac, page 920.

Generic name:

FLURAZEPAM

See Dalmane, page 267.

Generic name:

FLURBIPROFEN

See Ansaid, page 59.

Generic name:

FLUTAMIDE

See Eulexin, page 418.

Generic name:

FLUVASTATIN

See Lescol, page 563.

Generic name:

FLUVOXAMINE

See Luvox, page 621.

Brand name:

FML

Generic name: Fluorometholone

Why is this drug prescribed?

FML is a steroid (cortisone-like) eye ointment that is used to treat inflammation of the eyelid and the eye itself.

Most important fact about this drug

Do not use FML more often or for a longer period of time than you doctor orders. Overuse can increase the risk of side effects and lead to eye damage. Also, if your eye problems return, do not use any leftover FML without first consulting your doctor.

How should you use this medication?

FML may increase the chance of infection from contact lenses. Your doctor may advise you to stop wearing your contacts while using this medication.

Use FML exactly as prescribed. Do not stop until your doctor advises you to do so. To avoid spreading infection, do not let anyone else use your prescription.

To administer FML eye drops:

1. Wash your hands thoroughly.
2. Shake well before using.
3. Gently pull your lower eyelid down to form a pocket between your eye and eyelid.
4. Hold the eye drop bottle on the bridge of your nose or on your forehead.
5. Do not touch the applicator tip to any surface, including your eye.

6. Tilt your head back and squeeze the medication into your eye.
7. Close your eyes gently. Keep them closed for 1 to 2 minutes.
8. Do not rinse the dropper.
9. Wait for 5 to 10 minutes before using a second eye medication.

■ *If you miss a dose...*
Apply it as soon as you remember. If it is almost time for your next dose, skip the one you missed and return to your regular schedule. Do not apply a double dose.

■ *Storage instructions...*
Store at room temperature. Protect from extreme heat.

What side effects may occur?
Side effects cannot be anticipated. If any develop or change in intensity, inform your doctor as soon as possible. Only your doctor can determine if it is safe for you to continue using FML.

■ *Side effects may include:*
Cataract formation
Corneal ulcers
Dilation of the pupil
Drooping eyelids
Eye inflammation and infection including pinkeye
Glaucoma
Increased eye pressure
Slow wound healing

Why should this drug not be prescribed?
Do not use FML if you have ever had an allergic reaction to or are sensitive to fluorometholone or similar drugs (anti-inflammatories and steroids) such as Decadron. Tell your doctor about any drug reactions you have experienced.

FML is not prescribed for patients with certain viral, fungal, and bacterial infections of the eye.

Special warnings about this medication
Prolonged use of FML may result in glaucoma (elevated pressure in the eye causing optic nerve damage and loss of vision), cataract formation (an eye disorder causing the lens of the eye to cloud up), or the development or worsening of eye infections.

Steroids such as FML have been known to cause punctures when used in the presence of diseases that cause thinning of the cornea or the sclera (tough, opaque covering at the back of the eyeball).

The use of a corticosteroid medication could hide the presence of a severe eye infection or cause the infection to become worse.

Internal pressure of the eye should be checked frequently by your doctor.

This medication should be used with caution after cataract surgery.

If pain or inflammation lasts longer than 48 hours, or becomes worse, discontinue use of FML and notify your doctor.

**Possible food and drug interactions
when taking this medication**
No interactions with food or other drugs have been reported.

**Special information
if you are pregnant or breastfeeding**
The effects of FML in pregnancy have not been adequately studied. If you are pregnant or plan to become pregnant, tell your doctor immediately. FML may appear in breast milk and could affect a nursing infant. If using FML is essential to your health, your doctor may advise you to stop breastfeeding until your treatment is finished.

Recommended dosage

ADULTS

FML Ointment
Apply a small amount of ointment (a ½-inch ribbon) between the lower eyelid and eyeball 1 to 3 times a day. During the first 24 to 48 hours, your doctor may increase the dosage to 1 application every 4 hours.

FML Liquifilm
Place 1 drop of suspension between the lower eyelid and eyeball 2 to 4 times a day. During the first 24 to 48 hours, the dosage may be increased to 1 application every 4 hours.

CHILDREN

The safety and effectiveness of FML have not been established in children under 2 years of age.

Overdosage

Overdosage with FML will not ordinarily cause severe problems. If FML is accidentally swallowed, drink fluids to dilute the medication.

Generic name:

FOSINOPRIL

See Monopril, page 685.

Brand name:

FULVICIN P/G

See Gris-PEG, page 472.

Generic name:

FUROSEMIDE

See Lasix, page 559.

Generic name:

GABAPENTIN

See Neurontin, page 721.

Brand name:

GANTRISIN

Pronounced: GAN-tris-in
Generic name: Sulfisoxazole

Why is this drug prescribed?

Gantrisin is prescribed for the treatment of severe, repeated, or long-lasting urinary tract infections. These include pyelonephritis (bacterial kidney inflammation), pyelitis (inflammation of the part of the kidney that drains urine into the ureter), and cystitis (inflammation of the bladder).

This drug is also used to treat bacterial meningitis, and is prescribed as a preventive measure for people who have been exposed to meningitis.

Some middle ear infections are treated with Gantrisin in combination with penicillin or erythromycin.

Toxoplasmosis (parasitic disease transmitted by infected cats, their feces or litter boxes, and by undercooked meat) can be treated with Gantrisin in combination with pyrimethamine (Daraprim).

Malaria that does not respond to the drug chloroquine (Aralen) can be treated with Gantrisin in combination with other drug treatment.

Gantrisin is also used in the treatment of bacterial infections such as trachoma and inclusion inflammation conjunctivitis (eye infections), nocardiosis (bacterial disease affecting the lungs, skin, and brain), and chancroid (venereal disease causing enlargement and ulceration of lymph nodes in the groin).

Most important fact about this drug

Notify your doctor at the first sign of a reaction such as skin rash, sore throat, fever, joint pain, cough, shortness of breath, or other breathing difficulties, abnormal skin paleness, reddish or purplish skin spots, or yellowing of the skin or whites of the eyes.

Rare but severe reactions, sometimes fatal, have occurred with the use of sulfa drugs such as Gantrisin. These reactions include sudden and severe liver damage, agranulocytosis (a severe blood disorder), aplastic anemia (a lack of red and white blood cells because of a bone marrow disorder), and Stevens-Johnson syndrome (severe blistering).

Patients taking sulfa drugs such as Gantrisin should have frequent blood counts.

How should you take this medication?

Take Gantrisin exactly as prescribed. It is important that you drink plenty of fluids while taking this medication in order to prevent crystals in the urine and the formation of stones.

Gantrisin Pediatric Suspension should be shaken well before each dose. To assure an accurate dose, ask you pharmacist for a specially marked measuring spoon.

Gantrisin, like other antibacterials, works best when there is a constant amount in the blood and urine. To help keep a constant level, try not to miss any doses and take them at evenly spaced intervals, around the clock.

■ *If you miss a dose...*
Take it as soon as you remember. If it is almost time for your next dose, skip the one you missed and go back to your regular schedule. Never take 2 doses at the same time.

■ *Storage instructions...*
Keep this medication in the container it came in, tightly closed. Store it at room temperature, away from moist places and direct light.

What side effects may occur?
Side effects cannot be anticipated. If any develop or change in intensity, inform your doctor as soon as possible. Only your doctor can determine if it is safe for you to continue taking Gantrisin.

■ *Side effects may include:*
Abdominal bleeding, abdominal pain, allergic reactions, anemia and other blood disorders, angioedema (swelling of face, lips, tongue and throat), anxiety, bluish discoloration of the skin, chills, colitis, convulsions, cough, dark, tarry stools, depression, diarrhea, disorientation, dizziness, drowsiness, enlarged salivary glands, enlarged thyroid, exhaustion, fainting, fatigue, fever, flushing, gas, hallucinations, headache, hearing loss, hepatitis, hives, inability to fall or stay asleep, inability to urinate, increased urination, inflammation of the mouth or tongue, itching, joint pain, kidney failure, lack of feeling or concern, lack of muscle coordination, lack or loss of appetite, low blood sugar, muscle pain, nausea, palpitations, presence of blood or crystals in urine, rapid heartbeat, reddish or purplish skin spots, retention of urine, ringing in the ears, sensitivity to light, serum sickness (fever, painful joints, enlarged lymph nodes, skin rash), severe skin welts or swelling, shortness of breath, skin eruptions, skin rash, swelling due to fluid retention, tingling or pins and needles, vertigo, vomiting, weakness, yellow eyes and skin

Why should this drug not be prescribed?
If you are sensitive to or have ever had an allergic reaction to Gantrisin or other sulfa drugs, you should not take this medication. Make sure that your doctor is aware of any drug reactions that you have experienced.

Except in rare cases, doctors do not prescribe Gantrisin for infants less than 2 months of age. Also, you should not take Gantrisin if you are at the end of your pregnancy or if you are nursing a baby under 2 months.

Special warnings about this medication
If you have impaired kidney or liver function, or if you have severe allergies or bronchial asthma make sure your doctor knows about it. Caution should be exercised when taking Gantrisin.

An analysis of your urine and kidney function should be performed by your doctor during treatment with Gantrisin, especially if you have a kidney problem.

If you develop diarrhea while taking Gantrisin, notify your doctor.

Possible food and drug interactions
when taking this medication

If Gantrisin is taken with certain other drugs, the effects of either could be increased, decreased, or altered. It is especially important to check with your doctor before combining this drug with the following:

Blood-thinning drugs such as Coumadin
Methotrexate, an anticancer drug
Oral contraceptives
Oral diabetes drugs such as Micronase

Special information
if you are pregnant or breastfeeding

There are no adequate and well-controlled studies in pregnant women. This medication should not be used during pregnancy unless your doctor has determined that the benefits outweigh the potential risks. Gantrisin appears in breast milk. If this medication is essential to your health, your doctor may advise you to discontinue breastfeeding until your treatment with this drug is finished.

Recommended dosage

ADULTS

The recommended starting dose is 2 to 4 grams. Later, regular dose of 4 to 8 grams per day, divided into 4 to 6 doses, is recommended.

CHILDREN

This medication should not be prescribed for infants under 2 months of age except in the treatment of congenital toxoplasmosis (a parasitic infection contracted by pregnant women and passed along to the fetus).

The usual dose for children 2 months of age or older is 150 milligrams per 2.2 pounds of body weight divided into 4 to 6 doses taken over 24 hours.

The usual starting dose is one-half of the regular dose, or 75 milligrams per 2.2 pounds of body weight divided into 4 to 6 doses taken over 24 hours. Doses should not exceed 6 grams over 24 hours.

Gantrisin tablets come in a half-gram (500 milligram) strength. Gantrisin pediatric suspension and syrup supply a half-gram (500 milligram) in each teaspoonful.

Overdosage
Any medication taken in excess can have serious consequences. If you suspect an overdose, seek emergency medical treatment immediately.

■ *Symptoms of an overdose of Gantrisin include:*
   Blood or sediment in the urine, blue tinge to the skin, colic, dizziness, drowsiness, fever, headache, lack or loss of appetite, nausea, unconsciousness, vomiting, yellowing of skin and whites of eyes

Brand name:

GARAMYCIN OPHTHALMIC

Pronounced: gar-uh-MY-sin off-THAL-mick
Generic name: Gentamicin sulfate

Why is this drug prescribed?
Garamycin Ophthalmic, an antibiotic, is applied to the eye for treatment of infections such as conjunctivitis (pinkeye) and other eye infections.

Most important fact about this drug
To help clear up your infection completely, keep using Garamycin eyedrops or ointment for the full time of treatment, even if your symptoms have disappeared. Do not allow anyone else to use this medication, and do not save it for use on another infection.

How should you use this medication?
Use this medication exactly as prescribed. To administer Garamycin, follow these steps:

Eyedrops

1. Wash your hands thoroughly.
2. Gently pull your lower eyelid down to form a pocket between your eye and the lid.
3. Brace the eyedrop bottle on your forehead or on the bridge of your nose.
4. Do not touch the applicator tip to your eye or any other surface.
5. Close your eyes gently and keep them closed for a minute or two.

6. Do not rinse the dropper.
7. If you are using a second type of eyedrop, wait 5 to 10 minutes before applying it.

Eye Ointment

1. Wash your hands thoroughly.
2. Pull your lower eyelid down and away from the eye to form a pocket.
3. Squeeze a thin strip of ointment into the pouch.
4. Avoid touching the tip of the tube to your eye or any other surface.
5. Close your eyes for a couple of minutes.
6. Wipe the tip of the tube with tissue and immediately replace the cap tightly.

Your vision may be blurred for a few minutes following application of the ointment.

- *If you miss a dose...*
  Apply it as soon as you remember. If it is almost time for your next dose, skip the one you missed and go back to your regular schedule.

- *Storage instructions...*
  Store away from heat and light. Do not freeze.

What side effects may occur?
Occasional eye irritation—with itching, redness and swelling—may occur with use of the eyedrops.

Occasional burning or stinging in the eye may occur with use of the ointment.

Why should this drug not be prescribed?
If you are sensitive to or have ever had an allergic reaction to Garamycin or certain other antibiotics, such as Tobrex, you should not take this medication. Make sure your doctor is aware of any drug reactions you have experienced.

Special warnings about this medication
Continued or prolonged use of this drug may result in a growth of bacteria or fungi that do not respond to this medication and can cause a second infection. Should this occur, notify your doctor.

Ophthalmic ointments may slow corneal healing.

**Possible food and drug interactions
with this medication**
No interactions have been reported.

**Special information
if you are pregnant or breastfeeding**
There are no special recommendations for this medication. If you are pregnant or plan to become pregnant, ask your doctor for the best advice in your personal situation.

Recommended dosage

ADULTS AND CHILDREN

Garamycin Ophthalmic Solution
Put 1 or 2 drops into the affected eye every 4 hours. For severe infections, your doctor may increase your dosage up to a maximum of 2 drops once every hour.

Garamycin Ophthalmic Ointment
Apply a thin strip—about one-third inch—of ointment to the affected eye 2 or 3 times a day.

Overdosage
Although there is no information on overdose with Garamycin ophthalmic products, any medication taken in excess can have serious consequences. If you suspect an overdose, seek medical attention immediately.

Generic name:

GAVISCON

See Antacids, page 62.

Generic name:

GELUSIL

See Antacids, page 62.

Generic name:

GEMCOR

See Lopid, page 592.

Generic name:

GEMFIBROZIL

See Lopid, page 592.

Brand name:

GENORA

See Oral Contraceptives, page 775.

Generic name:

GENTAMICIN

See Garamycin Ophthalmic, page 464.

Brand name:

GENUINE BAYER

See Aspirin, page 77.

Generic name:

GLIPIZIDE

See Glucotrol, page 467.

Brand name:

GLUCOTROL

Pronounced: GLUE-kuh-troll
Generic name: Glipizide

Why is this drug prescribed?

Glucotrol is an oral antidiabetic medication used to treat Type II (non-insulin-dependent) diabetes. In diabetics the body either does not make enough insulin or the insulin that is produced no longer works properly.

There are actually two forms of diabetes: Type I, insulin-dependent, and Type II, non-insulin-dependent. Type I usually requires insulin injections for life, while Type II diabetes can usually be treated by dietary changes and/or oral antidiabetic medications such as Glucotrol. Apparently, Glucotrol controls diabetes by stimulating the pancreas to secrete more insulin. Occasionally,

Type II diabetics must take insulin injections on a temporary basis, especially during stressful periods or times of illness.

Most important fact about this drug
Always remember that Glucotrol is an aid to, not a substitute for, good diet and exercise. Failure to follow a sound diet and exercise plan can lead to serious complications, such as dangerously high or low blood sugar levels. Remember, too, that Glucotrol is *not* an oral form of insulin, and cannot be used in place of insulin.

How should you take this medication?
In general, to achieve the best control over blood sugar levels, Glucotrol should be taken 30 minutes before a meal. However, the exact dosing schedule as well as the dosage amount must be determined by your physician.

▪ *If you miss a dose...*
Take it as soon as you remember. If it is almost time for your next dose, skip the one you missed and go back to your regular schedule. Never take 2 doses at the same time.

▪ *Storage instructions...*
Glucotrol should be stored at room temperature.

What side effects may occur?
Side effects from Glucotrol are rare and seldom require discontinuation of the medication.

▪ *More common side effects may include:*
Constipation, diarrhea, dizziness, drowsiness, headache, hives, itching, low blood sugar, nausea, sensitivity to light, skin rash and eruptions, stomach pain

▪ *Less common or rare side effects may include:*
Anemia and other blood disorders, yellow eyes and skin

Glucotrol, like all oral antidiabetic drugs, can cause low blood sugar. This risk is increased by missed meals, alcohol, other medications, and/or excessive exercise. To avoid low blood sugar, you should closely follow the dietary and exercise regimen suggested by your physician.

▪ *Symptoms of mild low blood sugar may include:*
Blurred vision
Cold sweats

Dizziness
Fast heartbeat
Fatigue
Headache
Hunger
Light-headedness
Nausea
Nervousness

■ *Symptoms of more severe low blood sugar may include:*
Coma
Disorientation
Pale skin
Seizures
Shallow breathing

Ask your doctor what steps you should take if you experience mild hypoglycemia. If symptoms of severe low blood sugar occur, contact your doctor immediately. Severe hypoglycemia should be considered a medical emergency, and prompt medical attention is essential.

Why should this drug not be prescribed?
You should not take Glucotrol if you have had an allergic reaction to it previously.

Glucotrol will be stopped if you are suffering from diabetic ketoacidosis (a life-threatening medical emergency caused by insufficient insulin and marked by excessive thirst, nausea, fatigue, pain below the breastbone, and a fruity breath).

Special warnings about this medication
It's possible that drugs such as Glucotrol may lead to more heart problems than diet treatment alone, or diet plus insulin. If you have a heart condition, you may want to discuss this with your doctor.

If you are taking Glucotrol, you should check your blood and urine periodically for the presence of abnormal sugar (glucose) levels.

Even people with well-controlled diabetes may find that injury, infection, surgery, or fever results in a lack of control over their diabetes. In these cases, the physician may recommend that you stop taking Glucotrol temporarily and use insulin instead.

In addition, the effectiveness of any oral antidiabetic, including Glucotrol, may decrease with time. This may occur because of either a diminished responsiveness to the medication or a worsening of the diabetes.

Possible food and drug interactions
when taking this medication

It is essential that you closely follow your physician's dietary guidelines and that you inform your physician of any medication, either prescription or nonprescription, that you are taking. Specific medications that affect Glucotrol include:

Airway-opening drugs such as Sudafed
Antacids such as Mylanta
Aspirin
Chloramphenicol (Chloromycetin)
Cimetidine (Tagamet)
Clofibrate (Atromid-S)
Corticosteroids such as prednisone (Deltasone)
Coumarin (Coumadin)
Diuretics such as HydroDIURIL
Estrogens such as Premarin
Fluconazole (Diflucan)
Gemfibrozil (Lopid)
Heart and blood pressure medications called beta blockers such as
    Tenormin and Lopressor
Heart medications called calcium channel blockers such as Cardizem
    and Procardia XL
Isoniazid (Nydrazid)
Itraconazole (Sporanox)
MAO inhibitors (antidepressant drugs such as Nardil)
Major tranquilizers such as Thorazine and Mellaril
Miconazole (Monistat)
Nicotinic acid (Nicobid)
Nonsteroidal anti-inflammatory drugs such as Motrin
Oral contraceptives
Phenytoin (Dilantin)
Probenecid (Benemid)
Rifampin (Rifadin)
Sulfa drugs such as Bactrim
Thyroid medications such as Synthroid

Alcohol must be used carefully, since excessive alcohol consumption can cause low blood sugar.

Special information
if you are pregnant or breastfeeding

The effects of Glucotrol during pregnancy have not been adequately studied. Therefore, if you are pregnant, or planning to become pregnant, you should take Glucotrol only on the advice of your physician. Since studies suggest the importance of maintaining normal blood sugar (glucose) levels during pregnancy, your physician may prescribe insulin during pregnancy. To minimize the risk of low blood sugar in newborn babies, Glucotrol, if taken during pregnancy, should be discontinued at least one month before the expected delivery date. Although it is not known if Glucotrol appears in breast milk, other oral antidiabetics do. Because of the potential for hypoglycemia in nursing infants, your doctor may advise you either to discontinue Glucotrol or to stop nursing. If Glucotrol is discontinued and if diet alone does not control glucose levels, your doctor may prescribe insulin.

Recommended dosage
Dosage levels must be determined by each patient's needs.

ADULTS

The usual recommended starting dose is 5 milligrams taken before breakfast. Depending upon blood glucose response, this initial dose may be increased in increments of 2.5 to 5 milligrams. The maximum recommended daily dose is 40 milligrams; total daily dosages above 15 milligrams are usually divided into 2 equal doses that are taken before meals.

CHILDREN

The safety and effectiveness of this drug in children have not been established.

ELDERLY

The elderly or those with liver disease usually start with 2.5 milligrams.

Overdosage
An overdose of Glucotrol can cause low blood sugar.

■ *Symptoms of mild low blood sugar include:*
 Blurred vision
 Cold sweats
 Dizziness
 Fatigue
 Headache
 Hunger
 Light-headedness
 Nausea

Nervousness
Rapid heartbeat

Eating sugar or a sugar-based product will often correct the condition. Otherwise, seek medical attention immediately.

■ *Symptoms of more severe low blood sugar include:*
Coma
Disorientation
Pale skin
Seizures
Shallow breathing

Contact your doctor immediately if these symptoms occur.

Generic name:

GLYBURIDE

See Micronase, page 661.

Brand name:

GLYNASE

See Micronase, page 661.

Brand name:

GRISACTIN

See Gris-PEG, page 472.

Generic name:

GRISEOFULVIN

See Gris-PEG, page 472.

Brand name:

GRIS-PEG

Pronounced: GRISS-peg
Generic name: Griseofulvin
Other brand names: Grisactin, Fulvicin P/G

Why is this drug prescribed?
Gris-PEG is prescribed for the treatment of the following ringworm infections:

Athlete's foot
Barber's itch (inflammation of the facial hair follicles)
Ringworm of the body
Ringworm of the groin and thigh
Ringworm of the nails
Ringworm of the scalp

Because Gris-PEG is effective for only certain types of fungal infections, before treatment your doctor may perform tests to identify the source of infection.

Most important fact about this drug
To clear up your infection completely, continue taking Gris-PEG as prescribed until your doctor tells you to stop. Although some improvement may appear within a few days, you need to take Gris-PEG for an extended period.

How should you take this medication?
To minimize stomach irritation and help your body absorb the drug, take Gris-PEG at mealtimes or with food or whole milk. If you are on a low-fat diet, check with your doctor.

Observe good hygiene during treatment to help control infection and prevent reinfection.

- *If you miss a dose...*
  Take it as soon as you remember. If it is almost time for your next dose, skip the one you missed and go back to your regular schedule. Do not take 2 doses at once.

- *Storage instructions...*
  Store at room temperature in a tightly closed container. Protect from light. Keep the liquid from freezing.

What side effects may occur?
Side effects cannot be anticipated. If any develop or change in intensity, inform your doctor as soon as possible. Only your doctor can determine if it is safe for you to continue taking Gris-PEG.

- *More common side effects may include:*
  Hives
  Skin rashes

- *Less common side effects may include:*
  Confusion, diarrhea, dizziness, fatigue, headache, impairment of performance of routine activities, inability to fall or stay asleep, nausea, oral thrush (mouth inflammation), upper abdominal pain, vomiting

- *Rare side effects may include:*
  Swelling and itching of areas of skin, tingling sensation in hands and feet

Why should this drug not be prescribed?

If you are sensitive to or have ever had an allergic reaction to Gris-PEG or other drugs of this type, you should not take this medication. Make sure your doctor is aware of any drug reactions you have experienced.

Unless you are directed to do so by your doctor, do not take this medication if you have liver damage or porphyria (an inherited disorder of the liver or bone marrow).

Do not take Gris-PEG while pregnant.

Special warnings about this medication

Gris-PEG is similar to penicillin. Although penicillin-sensitive people have used Gris-PEG without difficulty, notify your doctor if you are sensitive to or allergic to penicillin.

Because Gris-PEG can make you sensitive to light, avoid exposure to intense natural or artificial sunlight.

Notify your doctor if you develop lupus erythematosus (a form of rheumatism) or a lupus-like condition. Signs and symptoms of lupus include arthritis, red butterfly rash over the nose and cheeks, tiredness, weakness, sensitivity to sunlight, and skin eruptions.

If you are being treated with Gris-PEG for an extended period of time, your doctor should perform regular tests, including periodic monitoring of kidney function, liver function, and blood cell production.

Gris-PEG has not been proved safe and effective for the prevention of fungal infections.

Gris-PEG may decrease the effectiveness of birth-control pills. Use additional protection while you are taking Gris-PEG.

Possible food and drug interactions
when taking this medication

Gris-PEG may intensify the effects of alcohol. If you drink alcohol while taking this medication, your heart may start beating faster and your skin may be flushed.

If Gris-PEG is taken with certain other drugs, the effects of either could be increased, decreased, or altered. It is especially important to check with your doctor before combining Gris-PEG with the following:

Blood-thinning drugs such as Coumadin
Barbiturates such as phenobarbital
Oral contraceptives

Special information
if you are pregnant or breastfeeding
Do not take Gris-PEG if you are pregnant. If you become pregnant while taking this drug, notify your doctor immediately. There is a potential hazard to the developing baby.

If you are breastfeeding, consult with your doctor before taking Gris-PEG.

Recommended dosage
The usual treatment periods for various ringworm infections are:

Ringworm of the scalp—4 to 6 weeks
Ringworm of the body—2 to 4 weeks
Athlete's foot—4 to 8 weeks

The usual treatment period, depending on the rate of growth, for ringworm of the fingernails is at least 4 months and for ringworm of the toenails at least 6 months.

ADULTS

Ringworm of the Body, Groin and Thigh, Scalp
The usual dosage is 375 milligrams a day taken as a single dose or divided into smaller doses, as determined by your doctor.

Athlete's Foot, Ringworm of the Nails
The usual dosage is 750 milligrams a day divided into smaller doses, as determined by your doctor.

CHILDREN

A single daily dose is effective in children with ringworm of the scalp.

The usual dosage is 3.3 milligrams per pound of body weight per day. This means that children weighing 35 to 60 pounds will take 125 to 187.5 milligrams a day, and children weighing more than 60 pounds will take 187.5 to 375 milligrams a day.

No dosage has been established for children 2 years of age and under.

Overdosage

Any medication taken in excess can have dangerous consequences. If you suspect an overdose of Gris-PEG, seek emergency medical treatment immediately.

Generic name:

GUAIFENESIN WITH CODEINE

See Tussi-Organidin NR, page 1165.

Generic name:

GUAIFENESIN WITH PHENYLPROPANOLAMINE

See Entex LA, page 401.

Generic name:

GUANABENZ

See Wytensin, page 1208.

Generic name:

GUANFACINE

See Tenex, page 1084.

Brand name:

GYNE-LOTRIMIN

Pronounced: GUY-nuh-LOW-trim-in
Generic name: Clotrimazole
Other brand names: Lotrimin, Mycelex, Mycelex-7

Why is this drug prescribed?

Clotrimazole, the active ingredient in these medications, is used to treat fungal infections. In preparations for the skin, it is effective against ringworm, athlete's foot, and jock itch. In vaginal creams and tablets, it is used against vaginal yeast infections. In lozenge form, it is taken for oral yeast infections (thrush).

Most important fact about this drug
Keep using this medicine for the full time of treatment, even if the infection seems to have disappeared. If you stop too soon, the infection could return. You should continue using the vaginal forms of this medicine even during your menstrual period.

How should you take this medication?
Keep all forms of this medicine away from your eyes.

Before applying the skin preparations, be sure to wash your hands. Massage the medication gently into the affected area and the surrounding skin.

If you are taking Mycelex troches, place the lozenge in your mouth and let it dissolve slowly for 15 to 30 minutes. Do not chew the lozenge or swallow it whole.

If you are using a vaginal cream or tablet, use the following administration technique:

1. Load the applicator to the fill line with cream, or unwrap a tablet, wet it with warm water, and place it in the applicator as shown in the instructions you receive with the product.
2. Lie on your back with your knees drawn up.
3. Gently insert the applicator high into the vagina and push the plunger.
4. Withdraw the applicator and discard it if disposable, or wash with soap and water.

To keep the vaginal medication from getting on your clothing, wear a sanitary napkin. Do not use a tampon, because it will absorb the medicine. Wear underwear or pantyhose with a cotton crotch—avoid synthetic fabrics such as nylon or rayon. Do not douche unless your doctor tells you to do so.

■ *If you miss a dose...*
Make up for it as soon as you remember. If it is almost time for the next dose, skip the one you missed and go back to your regular schedule.

■ *Storage instructions...*
Store at room temperature, away from heat, light, and moisture.

What side effects may occur?
Side effects cannot be anticipated. If any develop or change in intensity, inform your doctor as soon as possible. Only your doctor can determine if it is safe for you to continue using this medication.

- *Side effects may include:*
  Blistering
  Burning
  Hives
  Irritated skin
  Itching
  Peeling
  Reddened skin
  Stinging
  Swelling due to fluid retention

- *Side effects of clotrimazole vaginal preparations may include:*
  Abdominal/stomach cramps/pain
  Burning/irritation of penis of sexual partner
  Headache
  Pain during sexual intercourse
  Skin rash, hives
  Vaginal burning
  Vaginal irritation
  Vaginal itching
  Vaginal soreness during sexual intercourse

An unpleasant mouth sensation has been reported by some people taking Mycelex.

Why should this drug not be prescribed?
You should not be using this medication if you have had an allergic reaction to any of its ingredients.

Special warnings about this medication
Contact your doctor if you experience increased skin irritations (such as redness, itching, burning, blistering, swelling, or oozing).

Check with your doctor before using this medication on a child.

In general, if your symptoms have not improved within 2 to 4 weeks of treatment, notify your doctor.

Clotrimazole vaginal preparations should not be used if you have abdominal pain, fever, or a foul-smelling vaginal discharge. Contact your doctor immediately.

While using the vaginal preparations, either avoid sexual intercourse or make sure your partner uses a condom. This will prevent reinfection. Oils used in some vaginal preparations can weaken latex condoms or diaphragms. To find out whether you can use your medication with latex products, check with your pharmacist.

**Possible food and drug interactions
when taking this medication**
None have been reported.

**Special information
if you are pregnant or breastfeeding**
The use of clotrimazole during the first trimester of pregnancy has not been adequately studied. It should be used during the first trimester only if clearly needed. Do not use clotrimazole at any time during pregnancy without the advice and supervision of your doctor.

It is not known whether clotrimazole appears in breast milk. Nursing mothers should use this medication cautiously and only when clearly needed.

Recommended dosage

LOTRIMIN

Adults and Children

Wash your hands before and after you use Lotrimin. Apply in the morning and evening. Use enough Lotrimin to massage into the affected area.

Symptoms usually improve during the first week of treatment with Lotrimin.

GYNE-LOTRIMIN CREAM

Adults

Fill the applicator with the cream and insert 1 applicatorful into the vagina every day, preferably at bedtime. Repeat this procedure for 7 consecutive days.

MYCELEX TROCHE

Adults

The recommended dosage is 1 troche slowly dissolved in the mouth 5 times daily for 14 consecutive days. To prevent recurrence, the recommended dose is 1 troche 3 times daily.

Overdosage
Although any medication used in excess can have serious consequences, an overdose of clotrimazole is unlikely. If you suspect an overdose, however, seek medical help immediately.

Brand name:

HABITROL

See Nicotine Patches, page 729.

Brand name:

HALCION

Pronounced: HAL-see-on
Generic name: Triazolam

Why is this drug prescribed?
Halcion is used for short-term treatment of insomnia. It is a member of the benzodiazepine class of drugs, many of which are used as tranquilizers.

Most important fact about this drug
Sleep problems are usually temporary, requiring treatment for only a short time, usually 1 or 2 days and no more than 1 to 2 weeks. Insomnia that lasts longer than this may be a sign of another medical problem. If you find you need this medicine for more than 7 to 10 days, be sure to check with your doctor.

How should you take this medication?
Take this medication exactly as directed; never take more than your doctor has prescribed.

As with all prescription medications, never share Halcion with anyone else.

To help avoid upset stomach, Halcion can be taken with food.

- *If you miss a dose...*
  Take Halcion only as needed.

- *Storage instructions...*
  Keep this medication in the container it came in, tightly closed, and out of reach of children. Store it at room temperature.

What side effects may occur?
Side effects cannot be anticipated. If any develop or change in intensity, inform your doctor as soon as possible. Only your doctor can determine if it is safe for you to continue taking Halcion.

■ *More common side effects may include:*
Coordination problems
Dizziness
Drowsiness
Headache
Light-headedness
Nausea/vomiting
Nervousness

■ *Less common or rare side effects may include:*
Aggressiveness, agitation, behavior problems, burning tongue, changes in sexual drive, chest pain, confusion, congestion, constipation, cramps/pain, delusions, depression, diarrhea, disorientation, dreaming abnormalities, drowsiness, dry mouth, exaggerated sense of well-being, excitement, fainting, falling, fatigue, hallucinations, impaired urination, inappropriate behavior, incontinence, inflammation of the tongue and mouth, irritability, itching, loss of appetite, loss of sense of reality, memory impairment, memory loss (e.g., traveler's amnesia), menstrual irregularities, morning "hangover" effects, muscle spasms in the shoulders or neck, nightmares, rapid heart rate, restlessness, ringing in the ears, skin inflammation, sleep disturbances including insomnia, sleepwalking, slurred or difficult speech, stiff or awkward movements, taste changes, tingling or pins and needles, tiredness, visual disturbances, weakness, yellowing of the skin and whites of the eyes

Why should this drug not be prescribed?
You should not take this drug if you are pregnant or if you have had an allergic reaction to it or to other benzodiazepine drugs such as Valium.

Special warnings about this medication
When Halcion is used every night for more than a few weeks, it loses its effectiveness to help you sleep. This is known as tolerance. Also, it can cause dependence, especially when it is used regularly for longer than a few weeks or at high doses.

Abrupt discontinuation of Halcion should be avoided, since it has been associated with withdrawal symptoms (convulsions, cramps, tremor, vomiting, sweating, feeling ill, perceptual problems, and insomnia). A gradual dosage tapering schedule is usually recommended for patients taking more than the lowest dose of Halcion for longer than a few weeks. The usual treatment period is 7 to 10 days.

If you develop unusual and disturbing thoughts or behavior during treatment with Halcion, you should discuss them with your doctor immediately.

"Traveler's amnesia" has been reported by patients who took Halcion to induce sleep while traveling. To avoid this condition, do not take Halcion on an overnight airplane flight of less than 7 to 8 hours.

You may suffer increased anxiety during the daytime while taking Halcion.

When you first start taking Halcion, until you know whether the medication will have any "carry over" effect the next day, use extreme care while doing anything that requires complete alertness such as driving a car or operating machinery.

After discontinuing the drug, you may experience a "rebound insomnia" for the first 2 nights—that is, insomnia may be worse than before you took the sleeping pill.

You should be aware that anterograde amnesia (forgetting events after an injury) has been associated with benzodiazepine drugs such as Halcion.

You should be cautious about using this drug if you have liver or kidney problems, lung problems, or a tendency to temporarily stop breathing while you are asleep.

Possible food and drug interactions
when taking this medication
Avoid alcoholic beverages.

If Halcion is taken with certain other drugs, the effects of either could be increased, decreased, or altered. It is especially important to check with your doctor before combining Halcion with the following:

Antidepressant medications, including "tricyclic" drugs such as Elavil
    and MAO inhibitors such as Nardil and Parnate
Antihistamines such as Benadryl and Tavist
Barbiturates such as phenobarbital and Seconal
Cimetidine (Tagamet)
Erythromycin (E.E.S., PCE, E-Mycin, others)
Isoniazid (Nydrazid)
Narcotic pain killers such as Demerol
Major tranquilizers such as Mellaril and Thorazine
Other tranquilizers such as BuSpar, Valium, and Xanax
Oral contraceptives
Seizure medications such as Dilantin and Tegretol

Special information
if you are pregnant or breastfeeding
Since benzodiazepines have been associated with damage to the developing baby, you should not take Halcion if you are pregnant, think you may be pregnant, or are planning to become pregnant; or if you are breastfeeding.

Recommended dosage

ADULTS

The usual dose is 0.25 milligram before bedtime. The dose should never be more than 0.5 milligram.

CHILDREN

Safety and effectiveness for children under the age of 18 have not been established.

ELDERLY

To decrease the possibility of oversedation, dizziness, or impaired coordination, the usual starting dose is 0.125 milligram. This may be increased to 0.25 milligram if necessary.

Overdosage

Any medication taken in excess can have serious consequences. Severe overdosage of Halcion can be fatal. If you suspect an overdose, seek medical help immediately.

- *Symptoms of Halcion overdose may include:*
  Apnea (temporary cessation of breathing)
  Coma
  Confusion
  Excessive sleepiness
  Problems in coordination
  Seizures
  Shallow or difficult breathing
  Slurred speech

Brand name:

HALDOL

Pronounced: HAL-dawl
Generic name: Haloperidol

Why is this drug prescribed?

Haldol is used to reduce the symptoms of mental disorders such as schizophrenia. It is also prescribed to control tics (uncontrolled muscle contractions of face, arms, or shoulders) and the unintended utterances that mark Gilles de la Tourette's syndrome. In addition, it is used in short-term treatment of children with severe behavior problems, including hyperactivity and combativeness.

Some doctors also prescribe Haldol to relieve severe nausea and vomiting caused by cancer drugs, to treat drug problems such as LSD flashback and PCP intoxication, and to control symptoms of hemiballismus, a condition that causes involuntary writhing of one side of the body.

Most important fact about this drug
Haldol may cause tardive dyskinesia—a condition characterized by involuntary muscle spasms and twitches in the face and body. This condition can be permanent, and appears to be most common among the elderly, especially women. Ask your doctor for information about this possible risk.

How should you take this medication?
Haldol may be taken with food or after eating. If taking Haldol in a liquid concentrate form, you will need to dilute it with milk or water.

You should not take Haldol with coffee, tea, or other caffeinated beverages, or with alcohol.

Haldol causes dry mouth. Sucking on a hard candy or ice chips may help alleviate the problem.

■ *If you miss a dose...*
Take it as soon as you remember. Take the rest of the doses for that day at equally spaced intervals. Do not take 2 doses at once.

■ *Storage instructions...*
Store away from heat, light, and moisture in a tightly closed container. Do not freeze the liquid.

What side effects may occur?
Side effects cannot be anticipated. If any side effects develop or change in intensity, inform your doctor as soon as possible. Only your doctor can determine if it is safe for you to continue taking Haldol.

■ *Side effects may include:*
Abnormal secretion of milk, acne-like skin reactions, agitation, anemia, anxiety, blurred vision, breast pain, breast development in males, cataracts, catatonic (unresponsive) state, chewing movements, confusion, constipation, coughing, deeper breathing, dehydration, depression, diarrhea, dizziness, drowsiness, dry mouth, epileptic seizures, exaggerated feeling of well-being, exaggerated reflexes, excessive perspiration, exces-

sive salivation, hair loss, hallucinations, headache, heat stroke, high fever, high or low blood pressure, high or low blood sugar, impotence, inability to urinate, increased sex drive, indigestion, involuntary movements, irregular menstrual periods, irregular pulse, lack of muscular coordination, liver problems, loss of appetite, muscle spasms, nausea, Parkinson-like symptoms, persistent abnormal erections, physical rigidity and stupor, protruding tongue, puckering of mouth, puffing of checks, rapid heartbeat, restlessness, rigid arms, feet, head, and muscles, rotation of eyeballs, sensitivity to light, skin rash, skin eruptions, sleeplessness, sluggishness, swelling of breasts, twitching in the body, neck, shoulders, and face, vertigo, visual problems, vomiting, wheezing or asthma-like symptoms, yellowing of skin and whites of eyes

Why should this drug not be prescribed?
You should not take Haldol if you have Parkinson's disease or are sensitive to or allergic to the drug.

Special warnings about this medication
You should use Haldol cautiously if you have ever had breast cancer, a severe heart or circulatory disorder, chest pain, the eye condition known as glaucoma, seizures, or any drug allergies.

Temporary muscle spasms and twitches may occur if you suddenly stop taking Haldol. Follow your doctor's instructions closely when discontinuing the drug.

This drug may impair your ability to drive a car or operate potentially dangerous machinery. Do not participate in any activities that require full alertness if you are unsure of your reaction to Haldol.

Haldol may make your skin more sensitive to sunlight. When spending time in the sun, use a sunscreen or wear protective clothing.

Avoid exposure to extreme heat or cold. Haldol interferes with the body's temperature-regulating mechanism, so you could become overheated or suffer severe chills.

Possible food and drug interactions
when taking this medication
Extreme drowsiness and other potentially serious effects can result if Haldol is combined with alcohol, narcotics, painkillers, sleeping medications, or other drugs that slow down the central nervous system.

If Haldol is taken with certain other drugs, the effects of either could be increased, decreased, or altered. It is especially important to check with your doctor before combining Haldol with the following:

Anticonvulsants such as Dilantin or Tegretol
Antispasmodic drugs such as Bentyl and Cogentin
Blood-thinning medications such as Coumadin
Certain antidepressants, including Elavil, Tofranil, and Prozac
Epinephrine (EpiPen)
Lithium (Lithonate)
Methyldopa (Aldomet)
Propranolol (Inderal)
Rifampin (Rifadin)

Special information
if you are pregnant or breastfeeding

The effects of Haldol during pregnancy have not been adequately studied.
Pregnant women should use Haldol only if clearly needed. If you are pregnant
or plan to become pregnant, inform your doctor immediately. Haldol should
not be used by women who are breastfeeding an infant.

Recommended dosage

ADULTS

Moderate Symptoms

The usual dosage is 1 to 6 milligrams daily. This amount should be divided
into 2 or 3 smaller doses.

Severe Symptoms

The usual dosage is 6 to 15 milligrams daily, divided into 2 or 3 smaller
doses.

CHILDREN

Children younger than 3 years old should not take Haldol.

For children between the ages of 3 and 12, weighing approximately 33 to 88
pounds, doses should start at 0.5 milligram per day. Your doctor will
increase the dose if needed.

For Psychotic Disorders

The daily dose may range from 0.05 milligram to 0.15 milligram for every
2.2 pounds of body weight.

*For Non-psychotic Behavior Disorders and Tourette's
Syndrome*

The daily dose may range from 0.05 milligram to 0.075 milligram for every
2.2 pounds of body weight.

ELDERLY

In general, elderly people take dosages of Haldol in the lower ranges. Elderly people (especially elderly women) may be more susceptible to tardive dyskinesia—a possibly irreversible condition marked by involuntary muscle spasms and twitches in the face and body. Elderly people should consult their doctor for information about these potential risks.

Doses may range from 1 to 6 milligrams daily.

Overdosage

Any medication taken in excess can have serious consequences. If you suspect an overdose, seek medical help immediately.

- *Symptoms of Haldol overdose may include:*
  Catatonic (unresponsive) state
  Coma
  Decreased breathing
  Low blood pressure
  Rigid muscles
  Sedation
  Tremor
  Weakness

Generic name:

HALFPRIN

See Aspirin, page 77.

Generic name:

HALOPERIDOL

See Haldol, page 483.

Brand name:

HISMANAL

Pronounced: HISS-man-al
Generic name: Astemizole

Why is this drug prescribed?

Hismanal is an antihistamine prescribed to relieve hay fever and to treat chronic hives. Hismanal is for long-term use; it will not provide immediate relief.

Most important fact about this drug
Never take more than the prescribed dose of Hismanal in an attempt to speed its action. Higher doses have been known to cause dangerously irregular heartbeats.

How should you take this medication?
Hismanal should be taken on an empty stomach—for example, 1 hour before you eat or 2 hours after eating. Taking the drug with food may make it less effective.

■ *If you miss a dose...*
Take it as soon as you remember. If it is almost time for your next dose, skip the one you missed and go back to your regular schedule. Never take 2 doses at the same time.

■ *Storage instructions...*
Store at room temperature. Protect from moisture.

What side effects may occur?
Side effects cannot be anticipated. If any develop or change in intensity, inform your doctor as soon as possible. Only your doctor can determine if it is safe for you to continue taking Hismanal.

■ *More common side effects may include:*
Drowsiness
Dry mouth
Fatigue
Headache
Increase in appetite
Weight gain

■ *Less common side effects may include:*
Asthma-like symptoms, burning, prickling, or tingling, depression, diarrhea, dizziness, fluid retention, hepatitis, inflammation of the eyelids, itching, joint pain, muscle pain, nausea, nervousness, nosebleed, palpitations, sensitivity to light, skin rash, sore throat, stomach and intestinal pain

■ *Rare side effects may include:*
Low blood pressure

Why should this drug not be prescribed?
Avoid Hismanal if you have a known allergy to it.

Special warnings about this medication

Rare, serious, heart-related side effects have been reported when Hismanal is used with erythromycin (PCE, E-Mycin) or ketoconazole (Nizoral), a medicine for fungal infections. If you are taking these medicines, do not take Hismanal.

If you are being treated for a lower respiratory tract disease such as asthma or for liver or kidney disease, consult with your doctor before taking Hismanal.

Possible food and drug interactions
when taking this medication

Taking this drug with food can decrease its effectiveness.

If Hismanal is taken with certain other drugs, the effects of either may be increased, decreased, or altered. It is especially important to check with your doctor before combining Hismanal with the following:

Antibiotics such as Flagyl
Antifungal drugs such as Diflucan, Nizoral, Monistat, and Sporanox
Drugs that affect heart rhythms such as Vascor, Elavil, and Thorazine
"Macrolide" antibiotics such as Zithromax, Biaxin, E-Mycin, PCE, and Tao

See "Special warnings about this medication" for more information.

Special information
if you are pregnant or breastfeeding

The effects of Hismanal during pregnancy have not been adequately studied. Therefore, this medication should be prescribed only when the benefits of therapy outweigh any potential risk to the fetus. It is not known whether Hismanal appears in breast milk. If this medication is essential to your health, your doctor may advise you to stop nursing your baby until your treatment with this drug is finished.

Recommended dosage

ADULTS

The usual dose for adults and children 12 years and over is 10 milligrams (1 tablet) once daily.

CHILDREN

Safety and effectiveness in children under 12 have not been established.

Overdosage

Hismanal is generally safe; however, large amounts may cause serious symptoms. If you suspect an overdose, get medical help immediately.

- *Symptoms of Hismanal overdose may include:*
  Cardiac arrest
  Fainting
  Irregular heartbeat
  Seizures

Brand name:

HUMULIN

See Insulin, page 527.

Brand name:

HYDERGINE

Pronounced: HY-der-jeen
Generic name: Ergoloid mesylates

Why is this drug prescribed?

Hydergine helps relieve symptoms of declining mental capacity, thought to be related to aging or dementia, seen in some people over age 60. The symptoms include reduced understanding and motivation, and a decline in self-care and interpersonal skills.

Most important fact about this drug

It may take several weeks or more for Hydergine to produce noticeable results. In fact, your doctor may need up to 6 months to determine whether the drug is right for you. Keep taking your regular doses even if you feel no effect.

How should you take this medication?

Take Hydergine exactly as prescribed.

If you are taking sublingual tablets, allow them to dissolve completely under the tongue. Do not crush or chew them.

- *If you miss a dose...*
  Skip the dose you missed and go back to your regular schedule. Do not take 2 doses at once. If you miss 2 or more doses in a row, consult your doctor.

■ *Storage instructions...*
Store away from heat, light, and moisture. Do not freeze the oral solution.

What side effects may occur?
Side effects cannot be anticipated. If any develop or change in intensity, notify your doctor as soon as possible. Only your doctor can determine whether it is safe to continue taking Hydergine.

■ *Side effects may include:*
Irritation below the tongue (with sublingual tablets)
Stomach upset
Temporary nausea

Why should this drug not be prescribed?
Do not use Hydergine if you have ever had an allergic reaction to or are sensitive to the drug, or if you have a mental disorder.

Special warnings about this medication
Since the symptoms treated with Hydergine are of unknown origin and may change or evolve into a specific disease, your doctor will make a careful diagnosis before prescribing Hydergine and then watch closely for any changes in your condition.

**Possible food and drug interactions
when taking this medication**
No interactions have been reported.

**Special information
if you are pregnant or breastfeeding**
Hydergine is not intended for use by women of childbearing age.

Recommended dosage

ADULTS

The usual dose of Hydergine is 1 milligram, 3 times a day.

Overdosage
Any medication taken in excess can have serious consequences. If you suspect an overdose of Hydergine, seek medical attention immediately.

Generic name:

HYDROCHLOROTHIAZIDE

See HydroDIURIL, page 492.

Generic name:

HYDROCHLOROTHIAZIDE WITH TRIAMTERENE

See Dyazide, page 373.

Generic name:

HYDROCODONE WITH ACETAMINOPHEN

See Vicodin, page 1193.

Generic name:

HYDROCODONE WITH CHLORPHENIRAMINE

See Tussionex, page 1162.

Generic name:

HYDROCORTISONE

See Anusol-HC, page 68.

Brand name:

HYDRODIURIL

Pronounced: High-dro-DYE-your-il
Generic name: Hydrochlorothiazide
Other brand name: Esidrix

Why is this drug prescribed?

HydroDIURIL is used in the treatment of high blood pressure and other conditions that require the elimination of excess fluid (water) from the body. These conditions include congestive heart failure, cirrhosis of the liver, corticosteroid and estrogen therapy, and kidney disorders. When used for high blood pressure, HydroDIURIL can be used alone or with other high blood pressure medications. HydroDIURIL contains a form of thiazide, a diuretic that prompts your body to produce and eliminate more urine, which helps lower blood pressure.

Most important fact about this drug:

If you have high blood pressure, you must take HydroDIURIL regularly for it to be effective. Since blood pressure declines gradually, it may be several weeks before you get the full benefit of HydroDIURIL; and you must continue taking it even if you are feeling well. HydroDIURIL does not cure high blood pressure; it merely keeps it under control.

How should you take this medication?

Take HydroDIURIL exactly as prescribed by your doctor.

■ *If you miss a dose...*
If you forget a dose, take it as soon as you remember. If it is almost time for your next dose, skip the one you missed and go back to your regular schedule. Never take 2 doses at the same time.

■ *Storage instructions...*
Keep container tightly closed. Protect from light, moisture, and freezing cold. Store at room temperature.

What side effects may occur?

Side effects cannot be anticipated. If any develop or change in intensity, inform your doctor as soon as possible. Only your doctor can determine if it is safe for you to continue taking HydroDIURIL.

■ *Side effects may include:*
Abdominal cramping
Diarrhea
Dizziness upon standing up
Headache
Loss of appetite
Low blood pressure
Low potassium leading to symptoms such as dry mouth, excessive
    thirst, weak or irregular heartbeat, muscle pain or cramps
Stomach irritation
Stomach upset
Weakness

■ *Less common or rare side effects may include:*
Anemia, blood disorders, changes in blood sugar, constipation, difficulty breathing, dizziness, fever, fluid in the lung, hair loss, high levels of sugar

in the urine, hives, hypersensitivity reactions, impotence, inflammation of the lung, inflammation of the pancreas, inflammation of the salivary glands, kidney failure, muscle spasms, nausea, rash, reddish or purplish spots on the skin, restlessness, sensitivity to light, skin disorders including Stevens-Johnson syndrome (blisters in the mouth and eyes), skin peeling, tingling or pins and needles, vertigo, vision changes, vomiting, yellow eyes and skin

Why should this drug not be prescribed?

If you are unable to urinate, you should not take this medication.

If you are sensitive to or have ever had an allergic reaction to HydroDIURIL or similar drugs, or if you are sensitive to sulfa or other sulfonamide-derived drugs, you should not take this medication.

Special warnings about this medication

Diuretics can cause your body to lose too much potassium. Signs of an excessively low potassium level include muscle weakness and rapid or irregular heartbeat. To boost your potassium level, your doctor may recommend eating potassium-rich foods or taking a potassium supplement.

If you are taking HydroDIURIL, your kidney function should be given a complete assessment, and should continue to be monitored.

If you have liver disease, diabetes, gout, or lupus erythematosus (a form of rheumatism), HydroDIURIL should be used with caution.

If you have bronchial asthma or a history of allergies, you may be at greater risk for an allergic reaction to this medication.

Dehydration, excessive sweating, severe diarrhea or vomiting could deplete your body's fluids and cause your blood pressure to become too low. Be careful when exercising and in hot weather.

Possible food and drug interactions
when taking this medication

HydroDIURIL may increase the effects of alcohol. Do not drink alcohol while taking this medication.

If HydroDIURIL is taken with certain other drugs, the effects of either could be increased, decreased, or altered. It is especially important to check with your doctor before combining HydroDIURIL with the following:

Barbiturates such as phenobarbital
Cholestyramine (Questran)
Colestipol (Colestid)
Corticosteroids such as prednisone and ACTH

Drugs to treat diabetes such as insulin or Micronase
Lithium
Narcotics such as Percocet
Nonsteroidal anti-inflammatory drugs such as Naprosyn
Norepinephrine (Levophed)
Other high blood pressure medications
Skeletal muscle relaxants, such as tubocurarine

Special information
if you are pregnant or breastfeeding

The effects of HydroDIURIL during pregnancy have not been adequately studied. If you are pregnant or plan to become pregnant, inform your doctor immediately. HydroDIURIL appears in breast milk and could affect a nursing infant. If this medication is essential to your health, your doctor may advise you to discontinue breastfeeding until your treatment is finished.

Recommended dosage

Dosage should be adjusted to each individual's needs. The smallest dose that is effective should be used.

ADULTS

Water Retention

The usual dose is 25 milligrams to 100 milligrams per day. Your doctor may tell you to take the drug in a single dose or to divide the total amount into more than one dose. Your doctor may put you on a day-on, day-off schedule or some other alternate-day schedule to suit your needs.

High Blood Pressure

The usual dose is 25 milligrams as a single dose. Your doctor may increase the dose to 50 milligrams, as a single dose or divided into 2 doses. Dosages should be adjusted when used with other high blood pressure medications.

CHILDREN

Dosages for children should be adjusted according to weight, generally 1 milligram per pound of body weight in 2 doses per day. Children with high blood pressure only rarely will benefit from doses larger than 50 milligrams per day. Infants under 6 months may need 1.5 milligrams per pound per day in 2 doses.

Under 2 years

Based on age and body weight, the dosage is 12.5 milligrams to 37.5 milligrams per day in 2 doses.

2 to 12 years
The dosage, based on body weight, is 37.5 milligrams to 100 milligrams in 2 doses.

HydroDIURIL tablets come in strengths of 25, 50, and 100 milligrams.

Overdosage
Any medication taken in excess can cause symptoms of overdose. If you suspect an overdose, seek medical attention immediately.

■ *The Symptoms of HydroDIURIL overdose may include:*
Dry mouth
Electrolyte imbalance
Excessive thirst
Muscle pain or cramps
Symptoms of low potassium such as dehydration
Weak or irregular heartbeat

Generic name:

HYDROMORPHONE

See Dilaudid, page 336.

Generic name:

HYDROXYCHLOROQUINE

See Plaquenil, page 860.

Generic name:

HYDROXYZINE

See Atarax, page 80.

Brand name:

HYGROTON

Pronounced: HIGH-grow-ton
Generic name: Chlorthalidone
Other brand name: Thalitone

Why is this drug prescribed?

Hygroton is a diuretic (water pill) used to treat high blood pressure and fluid retention associated with congestive heart failure, cirrhosis of the liver (a disease of the liver caused by damage to its cells), corticosteroid and estrogen therapy, and kidney disease. When used for high blood pressure, Hygroton may be used alone or in combination with other high blood pressure medications. Diuretics help your body produce and eliminate more urine, which helps lower blood pressure.

Most important fact about this drug

If you have high blood pressure, you must take Hygroton regularly for it to be effective. Since blood pressure declines gradually, it may be several weeks before you get the full benefit of Hygroton; and you must continue taking it even if you are feeling well. Hygroton does not cure high blood pressure; it merely keeps it under control.

How should you take this medication?

Diuretics such as Hygroton increase urination; therefore Hygroton should be taken in the morning.

Do not interchange Hygroton or generic chlorthalidone with Thalitone without consulting your doctor or pharmacist.

Hygroton may be taken with food. Take it exactly as prescribed.

- *If you miss a dose...*
  Take it as soon as you remember. If it is almost time for the next dose, skip the one you missed and go back to your regular schedule. Do not take 2 doses at the same time.

- *Storage instructions...*
  Store at room temperature.

What side effects may occur?

Side effects cannot be anticipated. If any side effects develop or change in intensity, tell your doctor immediately. Only your doctor can determine whether it is safe to continue taking Hygroton.

- *Side effects may include:*
  Allergic reaction, anemia, changes in blood sugar, change in potassium levels (causing such symptoms as dry mouth, excessive thirst, weak or irregular heartbeat, and muscle pain or cramps), constipation, cramping,

diarrhea, dizziness, dizziness upon standing up, flaky skin, headache, hives, impotence, inflammation of the pancreas, itching, loss of appetite, low blood pressure, muscle spasms, nausea, rash, restlessness, sensitivity to light, stomach irritation, tingling or pins and needles, vision changes, vomiting, weakness, yellow eyes and skin

Why should this drug not be prescribed?
If you are unable to urinate or if you have ever had an allergic reaction to or are sensitive to chlorthalidone or other sulfa drugs, do not take Hygroton.

Special warnings about this medication
Diuretics can cause your body to lose too much potassium. Signs of an excessively low potassium level include muscle weakness and rapid or irregular heartbeat. To boost your potassium level, your doctor may recommend eating potassium-rich foods or taking a potassium supplement.

Tell your doctor if you have ever had an allergic reaction to other diuretics or if you have asthma, kidney or liver disease, gout, or lupus.

If you have a history of bronchial asthma, you are more likely to have an allergic reaction to Hygroton.

Be careful in hot weather not to become dehydrated. Contact your doctor if you experience excessive thirst, tiredness, restlessness, muscle pains or cramps, nausea, vomiting, or increased heart rate or pulse.

This medication may aggravate lupus erythematosus, a disease of the connective tissue.

Avoid prolonged exposure to sunlight.

Possible food and drug interactions
when taking this medication
Drinking alcohol may increase the chance of dizziness. Do not drink alcohol while taking this medication.

If Hygroton is taken with certain other drugs, the effects of either could be increased, decreased, or altered. It is especially important to check with your doctor before combining Hygroton with the following:

Appetite-control medicines such as Tenuate
Cholestyramine (Questran)
Colestipol (Colestid)
Decongestants (medicines for colds, cough, hay fever, or sinus)
Digitalis (Lanoxin)
Insulin
Lithium (Lithonate)

Oral diabetes drugs such as Micronase
Other high blood pressure medications such as Catapres and Aldomet
Steroids such as prednisone

Special information
if you are pregnant or breastfeeding

Information is not available about the safety of Hygroton during pregnancy. If you are pregnant or plan to become pregnant, inform your doctor immediately. Hygroton may appear in breast milk and could affect a nursing infant. If Hygroton is essential to your health, your doctor may advise you to stop breastfeeding until your treatment is finished.

Recommended dosage

Your doctor will tailor your individual dose to the lowest possible amount that delivers a satisfactory response.

Once desired control of blood pressure or fluid retention has been achieved, your doctor may adjust your dose downward.

HIGH BLOOD PRESSURE

Hygroton

The usual initial dosage is a single dose of 25 milligrams. Your doctor may increase the dose to 100 milligrams once daily.

Thalitone

The usual initial dose is a single dose of 15 milligrams. Your doctor may increase the dose to 45 to 50 milligrams once daily.

FLUID RETENTION

Hygroton

The usual recommended initial dose is 50 to 100 milligrams daily or 100 milligrams every other day. Some people may require up to 150 to 200 milligrams at these intervals.

Thalitone

The usual initial dose is 30 to 60 milligrams daily or 60 milligrams on alternate days. Some people may require up to 90 to 120 milligrams at these intervals.

Overdosage

Any medication taken in excess can have serious consequences. If you suspect an overdose, seek medical treatment immediately.

■ *Symptoms of Hygroton overdose may include:*
Confusion
Dizziness
Nausea
Weakness

Generic name:

HYOSCYAMINE

See Levsin, page 567.

Brand name:

HYTONE

See Anusol-HC, page 68.

Brand name:

HYTRIN

Pronounced: HIGH-trin
Generic name: Terazosin hydrochloride

Why is this drug prescribed?

Hytrin is prescribed to reduce high blood pressure. It may be used alone or in combination with other blood pressure lowering drugs, such as HydroDIURIL (a diuretic) or Inderal, a beta blocker.

Hytrin is also prescribed to relieve the symptoms of benign prostatic hyperplasia, or BPH. BPH is an enlargement of the prostate gland that surrounds the urinary canal. It leads to the following symptoms:

■ a weak or interrupted stream when urinating
■ a feeling that you cannot empty your bladder completely
■ a feeling of delay when you start to urinate
■ a need to urinate often, especially at night
■ a feeling that you must urinate right away

Hytrin relaxes the tightness of a certain type of muscle in the prostate and at the opening of the bladder. This can reduce the severity of the symptoms.

Most important fact about this drug

If you have high blood pressure, you must take Hytrin regularly for it to be effective. Since blood pressure declines gradually, it may be several weeks before you get the full benefit of Hytrin; and you must continue taking it even if you are feeling well. Hytrin does not cure high blood pressure; it merely keeps it under control.

How should you take this medication?
You may take Hytrin with or without food. Take your first dose at bedtime. Do not take more than the 1 milligram your doctor has prescribed.

■ *If you miss a dose...*
Take it as soon as you remember. If it is almost time for the next dose, skip the one you missed and go back to your regular schedule. Do not take 2 doses at the same time.

■ *Storage instructions...*
Store at room temperature in a cool, dry place.

What side effects may occur?
Side effects cannot be anticipated. If any develop or change in intensity, inform your doctor as soon as possible. Only your doctor can determine if it is safe for you to continue taking Hytrin.

■ *More common side effects may include:*
Difficult or labored breathing
Dizziness
Headache
Heart palpitations
Light-headedness upon standing
Nausea
Pain in the arms and legs
Sleepiness
Stuffy nose
Swollen wrists and ankles
Weakness

If these symptoms persist, tell your doctor. Your dosage of Hytrin may be higher than needed.

■ *Less common or rare side effects may include:*
Anxiety, back pain, blurred vision, bronchitis, conjunctivitis (inflamed eyes), constipation, decreased sex drive, depression, diarrhea, dimmed vision, dry mouth, facial swelling, fainting, fever, flu or cold symptoms (cough, sore throat, runny nose), fluid retention, frequent urination, gas, gout, impotence, inability to hold urine, increased heart rate, indigestion, inflamed sinuses, insomnia, irregular heartbeat, itching, joint pain and inflammation, low blood pressure, muscle aches, nasal inflammation,

nervousness, nosebleed, numbness or tingling, pain in the abdomen, chest, neck, or shoulder, rash, ringing in the ears, severe allergic reaction, sweating, urinary tract infection, vertigo, vision changes, vomiting, weight gain

Why should this drug not be prescribed?

Do not take Hytrin if you are sensitive to it or have ever had an allergic reaction to it.

Special warnings about this medication

When your blood pressure falls in response to Hytrin, you may faint. Other less severe reactions include dizziness, heart palpitations, light-headedness, and drowsiness. You are also likely to feel dizzy or faint whenever you rise from a sitting or lying position; this should disappear as your body becomes accustomed to Hytrin. If your occupation is such that these symptoms might cause serious problems, make sure your doctor knows this from the start; he or she will increase your Hytrin dosage very cautiously.

Regardless of your occupation, avoid driving, climbing, and other hazardous tasks at the following times:

- For 12 hours after your first dose of Hytrin
- With each new dosage increase
- When you re-start Hytrin after any treatment interruption

If you are taking Hytrin for benign prostatic hyperplasia, remember that although Hytrin helps relieve the symptoms of BPH, it does *not* change the size of the prostate, which may continue to grow. You may still need surgery in the future. In addition, it *is* possible to have BPH and prostate cancer at the same time.

Possible food and drug interactions
when taking this medication

If Hytrin is taken with certain other drugs, the effects of either could be increased, decreased, or altered. It is especially important to check with your doctor before combining Hytrin with the following:

Nonsteroidal anti-inflammatory painkillers such as Motrin and Naprosyn
Other blood pressure medications, such as Dyazide, Vasotec, Calan, and Verelan

Special information
if you are pregnant or breastfeeding

The effects of Hytrin during pregnancy have not been adequately studied. If you are pregnant or plan to become pregnant, notify your doctor immediately.

Hytrin is not recommended during pregnancy unless the benefit outweighs the potential risk to the unborn baby. It is not known whether Hytrin appears in breast milk. Because many drugs do appear in breast milk, your doctor may advise you to stop breastfeeding until your treatment with this drug is finished.

Recommended dosage

ADULTS

High blood pressure
The usual initial dose is 1 milligram at bedtime. Your doctor may slowly increase the dose until your blood pressure has been lowered sufficiently. The usual recommended dosage range is 1 milligram to 5 milligrams taken once a day; however, some people may benefit from doses as high as 20 milligrams per day.

Benign prostatic hyperplasia
The starting dose is 1 milligram at bedtime. Your doctor will gradually increase the dose to 10 milligrams, taken once a day for 4 to 6 weeks. A few men have needed a dose of 20 milligrams a day.

If you stop taking Hytrin for several days or longer, your doctor will re-start your treatment with 1 milligram at bedtime.

CHILDREN

The safety and effectiveness of Hytrin in children have not been established.

Overdosage
If you take too much Hytrin, dizziness, light-headedness, and fainting may occur within 90 minutes. A large overdose may lead to shock. If you suspect an overdose of Hytrin, seek medical attention immediately.

Generic name:

IBUPROFEN

See Advil, page 17.

Brand name:

ILETIN

See Insulin, page 527.

Brand name:

ILOSONE

See Erythromycin, Oral, page 405.

Brand name:

IMDUR

Pronounced: IM-duhr
Generic name: Isosorbide mononitrate
Other brand names: Ismo, Monoket

Why is this drug prescribed?
Imdur is prescribed to prevent angina pectoris (crushing chest pain that results when partially clogged arteries restrict the flow of needed oxygen-rich blood to the heart). This medication does not relieve angina attacks already underway.

Most important fact about this drug
Imdur may cause severe low blood pressure (possibly marked by dizziness or fainting), especially when you are standing or if you sit up quickly. People taking blood pressure medication or those who have low blood pressure should use Imdur with caution.

How should you take this medication?
To maintain this drug's protective effect, it is important that you take it exactly as prescribed.

Take Imdur once a day, when you get up in the morning. It may be taken with or without food. Imdur tablets should not be crushed or chewed. Swallow them with half a glass of liquid.

Do not switch to another brand of isosorbide mononitrate without consulting your doctor or pharmacist.

■ *If you miss a dose...*
    Take it as soon as you remember. If it is almost time for your next dose, skip the one you missed and go back to your regular schedule. Do not take 2 doses at the same time.

■ *Storage instructions...*
    Store at room temperature.

What side effects may occur?
Side effects cannot be anticipated. If any develop or change in intensity, tell your doctor as soon as possible. Only your doctor can determine if it is safe for you to continue taking Imdur.

Headache is the most common side effect; usually, aspirin or acetaminophen will relieve the pain. The headaches associated with Imdur usually subside within a short time after treatment with the drug begins. Check with your doctor if your headaches persist or become more intense. Another common side effect is dizziness.

■ *Less common or rare side effects may include:*
Abdominal pain, abnormal hair texture, abnormal heart sounds, abnormal or terrifying dreams, abnormal vision, acne, anemia, anxiety, back pain, bacterial infection, black stools, breast pain, bronchitis, chest pain, confusion, constipation, coughing, decreased sex drive, depression, diarrhea, difficult or labored breathing, difficulty concentrating, diminished sense of touch, drooping eyelid, dry mouth, earache, excessive amount of urine, fatigue, fever, fluid retention and swelling, flu-like symptoms, flushing, frozen shoulder, gas, general feeling of illness, heart attack, heart failure, heart murmur, hemorrhoids, high blood pressure, hot flashes, impotence, inability to sleep, increased mucus from the lungs, increased sweating, indigestion, inflamed eyes, inflammation of the stomach, inflammation of the tongue, inflammation of the vagina, intolerance of light, irregular heartbeat, itching, joint pain, kidney stones, leg ulcer, loose stools, low blood pressure, migraine, muscle and/or bone pain, muscle weakness, nasal or sinus inflammation, nausea, nervousness, palpitations (throbbing or fluttering heartbeat), paralysis, perforated eardrum, pneumonia, purple or red spots on the skin, rapid heartbeat, rash, ringing in the ears, severe pain in calf muscles during walking, sleepiness, slow heartbeat, sore throat, stomach ulcer with or without bleeding, stuffy nose, tingling or pins and needles, tremor, twisted neck, urinary tract infection, varicose veins, vertigo, viral infection, vomiting, weakness, wheezing, worsening of angina pectoris, yeast infection

Why should this drug not be prescribed?
You should not take Imdur if you have had a previous allergic reaction to it or ot other heart medications containing nitrates or nitrites. Your doctor will probably not prescribe Imdur if you have had a recent heart attack or congestive heart failure. If the doctor decides that this medication is essential, your heart function and blood pressure will need to be closely monitored to avoid potential side effects.

Special warnings about this medication

Do not abruptly stop taking this medication. Follow your doctor's plan for a gradual withdrawal.

Since Imdur can cause dizziness, you should be careful while driving, operating machinery, or performing other tasks that demand concentration.

Nitrate-type medications such as Imdur may aggravate angina caused by certain heart conditions.

Do not try to avoid a headache by changing your dose. If your headache stops, it may mean the drug has lost its effectiveness.

Be sure to tell your doctor about any medical conditions you have before starting Imdur therapy.

Possible food and drug interactions
when taking this medication

If Imdur is taken with certain other drugs, the effects of either could be increased, decreased, or altered. Extreme low blood pressure with dizziness and fainting upon standing up may occur if Imdur is taken with calcium-blocking blood pressure medications such as Calan, Cardizem, and Procardia.

Alcohol may interact with Imdur and cause a swift decrease in blood pressure, possibly resulting in light-headedness.

Special information
if you are pregnant or breastfeeding

The effects of Imdur during pregnancy have not been adequately studied. If you are pregnant or plan to become pregnant, tell your doctor immediately. Imdur should be used during pregnancy only if it is clearly needed.

It is not known whether Imdur appears in breast milk. If the drug is essential to your health, your doctor may advise you to stop nursing until your treatment is finished.

Recommended dosage

ADULTS

The usual starting dose is 30 milligrams (taken as one-half of a 60-milligram tablet) or 60 milligrams once a day.

After several days, your doctor may increase the dose to 120 milligrams (two 60-milligrams tablets) once daily.

Your doctor may further adjust the dosage according to your response to the medication.

CHILDREN

The safety and effectiveness of Imdur in children have not been established.

Overdosage

Any medication taken in excess can have serious consequences. Severe overdosage of Imdur can be fatal. If you suspect an overdose, seek medical help immediately.

- *Symptoms of Imdur overdose may include:*
  Air hunger, bloody diarrhea, coma, confusion, difficulty breathing, fainting, fever, nausea, palpitations, paralysis, pressure in the head, profuse sweating, seizures, skin either cold and clammy or flushed, slow heartbeat, throbbing headache, vertigo, visual disturbances, vomiting

Generic name:

IMIPRAMINE

See Tofranil, page 1124.

Brand name:

IMITREX INJECTION

Pronounced: IM-i-trex in-JECK-shun
Generic name: Sumatriptan succinate

Why is this drug prescribed?

Imitrex Injection is prescribed for the treatment of a migraine attack with or without the presence of an aura (visual disturbances, usually sensations of halos or flickering lights, which precede an attack). This medication will not prevent or reduce the number of attacks you may experience.

Most important fact about this drug

Imitrex Injection should be used only to treat an acute, classic migraine attack. It should not be used for headaches or certain unusual types of migraine.

How should you take this medication?

Imitrex is injected just below the skin with an autoinjector (self-injection device). Your doctor should carefully instruct you on how to use the autoinjector and how to dispose of the empty syringes. You should carefully read the instruction pamphlet that comes with the medication.

Imitrex should be injected as soon as your migraine symptoms appear, but may be used at any time during an attack.

A second injection may be given if your migraine symptoms return; however, never take more than 2 injections within 24 hours, and be sure to wait 1 hour between doses.

■ *If you miss a dose...*
Imitrex is *not* for regular use. Take it only during an attack.

■ *Storage instructions...*
Store Imitrex Injection away from heat and light, at room temperature, in the case provided. If your medication has expired (the expiration date is printed on the treatment pack), throw it away as instructed, but keep the autoinjector. If your doctor decides to stop your treatment, do not keep any leftover medicine unless your doctor tells you to. Throw away your medicine as instructed.

What side effects may occur?

Side effects cannot be anticipated. If any develop or change in intensity, inform your doctor as soon as possible. Only your doctor can determine if it is safe for you to continue taking Imitrex Injection.

■ *More common side effects may include:*
Burning sensation, dizziness or vertigo, feeling of heaviness, feeling of tightness, flushing, mouth and tongue discomfort, muscle weakness, neck pain and stiffness, numbness, pressure sensation, redness at the site of injection, sore throat, tingling, warm/hot sensation

■ *Less common or rare side effects may include:*
Abdominal discomfort, allergic reactions (severe), anxiety, changes in heart rhythm, cold sensation, difficulty swallowing, drowsiness/calmness, fatigue, feeling strange, general feeling of illness, headache, hives, itching, jaw discomfort, muscle cramps, muscle pain or tenderness, pressure in chest, rash, rise in blood pressure (temporary), shortness of breath, sinus or nasal discomfort, sweating, tight feeling in head, tightness in chest, vision changes

Why should this drug not be prescribed?

If you are sensitive to or have an allergic reaction to sumatriptan you should not use this drug again. Make sure your doctor is aware of any drug reactions you have experienced.

Imitrex Injection should not be used if you have certain types of heart disease, including angina (crushing chest pain) or a history of heart attack, if you suffer from irregular heartbeat, shortness of breath, or uncontrolled blood pressure, or if you are taking a medication containing ergotamine (often used in other migraine medications).

You should not use Imitrex with antidepressant drugs known as MAO inhibitors, such as Nardil and Parnate, or within 2 weeks of discontinuing treatment with an MAO inhibitor.

Special warnings about this medication

Your doctor may administer the first dose of Imitrex Injection in his office. Although extremely rare, serious heart problems have occurred in people with heart disease when receiving an injection of this medication, and you should be carefully observed after the initial dose to make sure this medication is safe for you to use.

Do not use Imitrex Injection intravenously. This can cause a serious heart irregularity.

This medication should not be used for other types of migraine headache. If the first dose does not relieve your symptoms, your doctor will re-evaluate you; you may not have a migraine.

Use Imitrex Injection cautiously if you have liver or kidney disease.

Although very rare, severe and even fatal allergic reactions have occurred in people taking Imitrex. Such reactions are more likely in people who have several allergies. If you are sensitive to sulfa drugs such as Gantrisin or Bactrim, there is a greater chance of an allergic reaction to Imitrex.

If you have epilepsy, make sure the doctor is aware of it. In rare cases, people have suffered seizures after taking Imitrex.

Possible food and drug interactions
while taking this medication

If Imitrex Injection is taken with certain other drugs, the effects of either may be increased, decreased, or altered. It is especially important to check with your doctor before combining Imitrex Injection with the following:

Antidepressants classified as MAO inhibitors, including Nardil and
  Parnate
Ergot-containing drugs such as Cafergot and Ergostat

Special information
if you are pregnant or breastfeeding

The effects of Imitrex Injection during pregnancy have not been adequately studied. If you are pregnant or plan to become pregnant, inform your doctor immediately. Imitrex Injection may appear in breast milk and could affect a nursing infant. If this medication is essential to your health, your doctor may advise you to discontinue breastfeeding until your treatment with Imitrex Injection is finished.

Recommended dosage

ADULTS

The maximum single recommended dose of Imitrex Injection is 6 milligrams injected under the skin.

The maximum recommended dose that may be given within 24 hours is two 6-milligram injections taken at least 1 hour apart.

CHILDREN

The safety and effectiveness of Imitrex Injection in children have not been established.

ELDERLY

The safety and effectiveness of Imitrex Injection in people 65 and older have not been established.

Overdosage

Any medication taken in excess can have serious consequences. If you suspect an overdose, seek medical attention immediately.

- *Symptoms of Imitrex overdose may include:*
  Bluish tinge to the skin
  Convulsions
  Dilated pupils
  Inactivity
  Lack of coordination
  Paralysis
  Redness in the arms and legs
  Skin changes at the site of injection
  Slow breathing
  Tremor

Brand name:

IMODIUM

Pronounced: i-MOH-dee-um
Generic name: Loperamide hydrochloride

Why is this drug prescribed?

Imodium is prescribed for the control and relief of symptoms of diarrhea not known to be caused by a specific germ, and for diarrhea associated with long-term inflammatory bowel disease. This drug is also prescribed for reducing the volume of discharge from an ileostomy (a surgical opening of the small intestine onto the abdominal wall for purposes of elimination).

Some doctors also prescribe Imodium, along with antibiotics such as Septra or Bactrim, to treat traveler's diarrhea.

Most important fact about this drug

If your diarrhea does not stop after a couple of days, if you have blood in your stools, or a fever develops, notify your doctor immediately.

How should you take this medication?

Do not take more than the prescribed dose of this medication.

Imodium may cause dryness of the mouth. Sucking on a hard candy or chewing gum can help relieve the problem.

- *If you miss a dose...*
  If you are taking Imodium on a regular schedule for chronic diarrhea and miss a dose, take it as soon as you remember, then take the remaining doses for that day at evenly spaced intervals. However, if you are not having diarrhea, skip the missed dose completely.

- *Storage instructions...*
  Imodium should be stored at room temperature.

What side effects may occur?

Side effects reported from the use of Imodium are difficult to distinguish from symptoms associated with diarrhea. Those reported, however, were more commonly observed during the treatment of long-lasting diarrhea.

- *Side effects may include:*
  Abdominal distention
  Abdominal pain or discomfort

Allergic reactions, including skin rash
Constipation
Dizziness
Drowsiness
Dry mouth
Nausea and vomiting
Tiredness

Why should this drug not be prescribed?

If you are sensitive to or have ever had an allergic reaction to Imodium, you should not take this medication. Make sure that your doctor is aware of any drug reactions that you have experienced.

Unless you are directed to do so by your doctor, do not take Imodium if constipation must be avoided.

Special warnings about this medication

Imodium may cause drowsiness and/or dizziness. You should exercise extra caution while driving or performing tasks requiring mental alertness.

Imodium is not good for all types of diarrhea. It is not prescribed for acute dysentery (an inflammation of the intestines characterized by abdominal pain, watery—sometimes bloody—stools, and fever, caused by bacteria, viruses, or parasites).

Dehydration can be a problem when you have diarrhea. It is important that you drink plenty of fluids while taking Imodium.

Use special caution when giving Imodium to a young child. Response to the drug can be unpredictable.

If you have a liver problem, your doctor should closely watch for signs of central nervous system reactions, such as drowsiness or convulsions.

If you have colitis and develop abdominal distention, constipation or an intestinal blockage, notify your doctor immediately. The use of Imodium should be discontinued.

Possible food and drug interactions
when taking this medication

There are no reported food or drug interactions.

Special information
if you are pregnant or breastfeeding

The effects of Imodium during pregnancy have not been adequately studied. If you are pregnant or plan to become pregnant, notify your doctor. It is not known whether Imodium appears in breast milk. If this medication is essential to your health, your doctor may advise you to discontinue breastfeeding until your treatment is finished.

Recommended dosage

ADULTS

Severe Diarrhea
The recommended starting dosage is 2 capsules (4 milligrams) followed by 1 capsule (2 milligrams) after each unformed stool. Daily dosage should not exceed 8 capsules (16 milligrams). Improvement should be observed within 48 hours.

Long-Lasting or Frequently Recurring Diarrhea
The recommended starting dosage is 2 capsules (4 milligrams) followed by 1 capsule (2 milligrams) after each unformed stool until diarrhea is controlled, after which the dosage of Imodium should be reduced by your doctor to meet your individual needs. When the ideal daily dosage has been established, this amount may then be given as a single dose or in divided doses. The average maintenance dosage is 2 to 4 capsules per day, not to exceed 8 capsules. If improvement is not observed after treatment with 8 capsules (16 milligrams) per day for at least 10 days, notify your doctor.

CHILDREN

Imodium is not recommended in children under 2 years of age.

Severe Diarrhea
In children 2 to 5 years of age or 44 pounds or less, the nonprescription liquid medication (Imodium A-D) should be used. For children between the ages of 6 and 12, either Imodium capsules (2 milligrams per capsule) or Imodium A-D Liquid (1 milligram per teaspoonful) may be used.

For children 2 to 12 years of age, the following schedule for capsules or liquid will usually fulfill starting dosage requirements:

  2 to 5 years (28-44 pounds):
    1 milligram (1 teaspoonful of Imodium
    A-D liquid) taken 3 times a day (3
    milligrams daily)
  6 to 8 years (45-66 pounds):
    2 milligrams taken 2 times a day (4
    milligrams daily)

8 to 12 years (67 pounds and over):
2 milligrams taken 3 times a day (6
milligrams daily)

After the first day of treatment, additional Imodium doses (1 milligram per 22 pounds of body weight) should be given only after a loose stool. The total daily dosage should not exceed the recommended dosages for the first day.

Long-Lasting or Frequently Recurring Diarrhea
A dosage has not been established for children with long-lasting or frequently recurring diarrhea.

Overdosage
Any medication taken in excess can have serious consequences. If you suspect an Imodium overdose, seek medical attention immediately.

■ *Symptoms of an Imodium overdosage may include:*
Constipation
Drowsiness, lethargy, and depression
Nausea

Generic name:

INDAPAMIDE

See Lozol, page 615.

Brand name:

INDERAL

Pronounced: IN-der-al
Generic name: Propranolol hydrochloride

Why is this drug prescribed?
Inderal, a type of medication known as a beta blocker, is used in the treatment of high blood pressure, angina pectoris (chest pain, usually caused by lack of oxygen to the heart due to clogged arteries), changes in heart rhythm, prevention of migraine headache, hereditary tremors, hypertrophic subaortic stenosis (a condition related to exertional angina), and tumors of the adrenal gland. It is also used to reduce the risk of death from recurring heart attack. When used for the treatment of high blood pressure, it is

effective alone or combined with other high blood pressure medications, particularly thiazide-type diuretics. Beta blockers decrease the force and rate of heart contractions, reducing the heart's demand for oxygen and lowering blood pressure.

Most important fact about this drug

If you have high blood pressure, you must take Inderal regularly for it to be effective. Since blood pressure declines gradually, it may be several weeks before you get the full benefit of Inderal; and you must continue taking it even it you are feeling well. Inderal does not cure high blood pressure; it merely keeps it under control.

How should you take this medication?

Inderal works best when taken before meals. Take it exactly as prescribed, even if your symptoms have disappeared.

Try not to miss any doses. If this medication is not taken regularly, your condition may worsen.

- *If you miss a dose...*
  Take it as soon as you remember. If it is within 8 hours of your next scheduled dose, skip the one you missed and go back to your regular schedule. Never take 2 doses at the same time.

- *Storage instructions...*
  Store at room temperature in a tightly closed, light-resistant container.

What side effects may occur?

Side effects cannot be anticipated. If any develop or change in intensity, inform your doctor as soon as possible. Only your doctor can determine if it is safe for you to continue taking Inderal.

- *Side effects may include:*
  Abdominal cramps, colitis, congestive heart failure, constipation, decreased sexual ability, depression, diarrhea, difficulty breathing, disorientation, dry eyes, fever with sore throat, hair loss, hallucinations, headache, light-headedness, low blood pressure, lupus erythematosus (a disease of the connective tissue), nausea, rash, reddish or purplish spots on the skin, short-term memory loss, slow heartbeat, tingling, prickling in hands, tiredness, trouble sleeping, upset stomach, visual changes, vivid dreams, vomiting, weakness, worsening of certain heartbeat irregularities

Why should this drug not be prescribed?

If you have inadequate blood supply to the circulatory system (cardiogenic shock), certain types of irregular heartbeat, a slow heartbeat, bronchial asthma, or severe congestive heart failure, you should not take this medication.

Special warnings about this medication

If you have a history of congestive heart failure, your doctor will prescribe Inderal cautiously.

Inderal should not be stopped suddenly. This can cause increased chest pain and heart attack. Dosage should be gradually reduced.

If you suffer from asthma or other bronchial conditions, coronary artery disease, or kidney or liver disease, this medication should be used with caution.

Ask your doctor if you should check your pulse while taking Inderal. This medication can cause your heartbeat to become too slow.

This medication may mask the symptoms of low blood sugar or alter blood sugar levels. If you are diabetic, discuss this with your doctor.

Notify your doctor or dentist that you are taking Inderal if you have a medical emergency, and before you have surgery or dental treatment.

Possible food and drug interactions
when taking this medication

If Inderal is taken with certain other drugs, the effects of either could be increased, decreased, or altered. It is especially important to check with your doctor before combining Inderal with the following:

Aluminum hydroxide gel (Amphojel)
Calcium-blocking blood pressure drugs such as Cardizem, Procardia, and Calan
Certain high blood pressure medications such as Diupres and Ser-Ap-Es
Chlorpromazine (Thorazine)
Cimetidine (Tagamet)
Epinephrine (EpiPen)
Haloperidol (Haldol)
Insulin
Lidocaine (Xylocaine)
Nonsteroidal anti-inflammatory drugs such as Motrin and Naprosyn
Oral diabetes drugs such as Micronase
Phenobarbitone

Phenytoin (Dilantin)
Rifampin (Rifadin)
Theophylline (Theo-Dur, others)
Thyroid medications such as Synthroid

Special information
if you are pregnant or breastfeeding

The effects of Inderal during pregnancy have not been adequately studied. If you are pregnant or plan to become pregnant, inform your doctor immediately. Inderal appears in breast milk and could affect a nursing infant. If this medication is essential to your health, your doctor may advise you to discontinue breastfeeding until your treatment with this medication is finished.

Recommended dosage

ADULTS

All dosages of Inderal, for any problem, must be tailored to the individual. Your doctor will determine when and how often you should take this drug. Remember to take it exactly as directed.

Hypertension

The usual starting dose is 40 milligrams 2 times a day. This dose may be in combination with a diuretic. Dosages are gradually increased to between 120 milligrams and 240 milligrams per day for maintenance. In some cases, a dose of 640 milligrams per day may be needed. Depending on the individual, maximum effect of this drug may not be reached for a few days or even several weeks. Some people may do better taking this medication 3 times a day.

Angina Pectoris

The usual daily dosage is 80 milligrams to 320 milligrams, divided into 2, 3 or 4 smaller doses. When your treatment is being discontinued, your doctor will reduce the dosage gradually over a period of several weeks.

Irregular Heartbeat

The usual dose is 10 milligrams to 30 milligrams 3 or 4 times a day, before meals and at bedtime.

Heart Attack

The usual daily dosage is 180 milligrams to 240 milligrams divided into smaller doses. The usual maximum dose is 240 milligrams, although your doctor may increase the dose when treating heart attack with angina or high blood pressure.

Migraine
The usual starting dosage is 80 milligrams per day divided into smaller doses. Dosages can be increased gradually to between 160 milligrams and 240 milligrams per day. If this dose does not relieve your symptoms in 4 to 6 weeks, your doctor will slowly take you off the drug.

Tremors
The usual starting dose is 40 milligrams, 2 times per day. Symptoms will usually be relieved with a dose of 120 milligrams per day; however, on occasion, dosages of 240 milligrams to 320 milligrams per day may be necessary.

Hypertrophic Subaortic Stenosis
The usual dose is 20 milligrams to 40 milligrams, 3 to 4 times a day, before meals and at bedtime.

Before Adrenal Gland Surgery
The usual dose is 60 milligrams a day divided into smaller doses for 3 days before surgery in combination with an alpha-blocker drug.

Inderal may also be taken by people with inoperable tumors in doses of 30 milligrams a day, divided into smaller doses.

CHILDREN

Inderal will be carefully individualized for use in children and is used only for high blood pressure. Doses in children are calculated by body weight, and range from 2 milligrams to 4 milligrams per 2.2 pounds daily, divided into 2 equal doses. The maximum dose is 16 milligrams per 2.2 pounds per day.

If treatment is stopped, this drug must be gradually reduced over a 7- to 14-day period.

ELDERLY

Your doctor will determine the dosage according to your needs.

Inderal is also available in a sustained-release formulation, called Inderal LA, for once-a-day dosing.

Overdosage
No specific information on Inderal overdosage is available; however, overdose symptoms with other beta blockers include:

Extremely slow heartbeat
Irregular heartbeat
Low blood pressure
Severe congestive heart failure
Seizures
Wheezing

Any medication taken in excess can have serious consequences. If you
suspect an overdose, seek medical attention immediately.

Brand name:

INDERIDE

Pronounced: IN-deh-ride
Generic ingredients: Inderal (Propranolol hydrochloride),
*   Hydrochlorothiazide*

Why is this drug prescribed?
Inderide is used in the treatment of high blood pressure. It combines a beta
blocker (Inderal) with a thiazide diuretic (hydrochlorothiazide). Beta blockers
decrease the force and rate of heart contractions, thus lowering blood
pressure. Diuretics help your body produce and eliminate more urine, which
also helps lower blood pressure.

Most important fact about this drug
You must take Inderide regularly for it to be effective. Since blood pressure
declines gradually, it may be several weeks before you get the full benefit of
Inderide; and you must continue taking it even if you are feeling well.
Inderide does not cure high blood pressure; it merely keeps it under control.

How should you take this medication?
Take Inderide exactly as prescribed, even if your symptoms have disappeared.

Try not to miss any doses. If this medication is not taken regularly, your
condition may worsen.

■ *If you miss a dose...*
Take it as soon as you remember. If the next dose is within 8 hours, skip
the one you missed and go back to your regular schedule. Do not take 2
doses at the same time.

■ *Storage instructions...*
Store at room temperature in a tightly closed container, protected from
moisture, freezing, and excessive heat.

What side effects may occur?

Side effects cannot be anticipated. If any develop or change in intensity, inform your doctor as soon as possible. Only your doctor can determine if it is safe for you to continue taking Inderide.

■ *Side effects may include:*

Allergic reactions (including fever, rash, aching and sore throat), anemia, blood disorders, blurred vision, constipation, congestive heart failure, cramps, decreased mental clarity, depression, diarrhea, difficulty breathing, difficulty sleeping, disorientation, dizziness, dizziness when standing, dry eyes, emotional changeability, exhaustion, fatigue, hair loss, hallucinations, headache, high blood sugar, hives, increased skin sensitivity to sunlight, inflammation of the large intestine or the pancreas, inflammation of the salivary glands, light-headedness, loss of appetite, low blood pressure, lupus erythematosus (a connective tissue disease), male impotence, muscle spasms, nausea, restlessness, short-term memory loss, slow heartbeat, stomach irritation, sugar in the urine, tingling or pins and needles, upset stomach, vertigo, visual disturbances, vivid dreams, vomiting, weakness, wheezing, yellow eyes and skin

Why should this drug not be prescribed?

If you have inadequate blood supply to the circulatory system (cardiogenic shock), certain types of irregular heartbeat, slow heartbeat, bronchial asthma, or congestive heart failure, you should not take this medication.

Do not take Inderide if you are unable to urinate or if you are sensitive to or have ever had an allergic reaction to any of its ingredients or to sulfa drugs.

Special warnings about this medication

Inderide should not be stopped suddenly. This can cause chest pain and even heart attack. Dosage should be gradually reduced.

Diuretics can cause your body to lose too much potassium. Signs of an excessively low potassium level include muscle weakness and rapid or irregular heartbeat. To boost your potassium level, your doctor may recommend eating potassium-rich foods or taking a potassium supplement.

If you suffer from asthma, seasonal allergies or other bronchial conditions, or kidney or liver disease, your doctor will prescribe this medication with caution.

This medication may mask the symptoms of low blood sugar or alter blood sugar levels. If you are diabetic, discuss this with your doctor.

If you have a history of allergies or bronchial asthma, you are more likely to have an allergic reaction to Inderide.

Inderide may interfere with the screening test for glaucoma (excessive pressure in the eyes) and pressure within the eyes may increase when the medication is stopped.

Notify your doctor or dentist that you are taking Inderide if you have a medical emergency, and before you have surgery or dental treatment.

Possible food and drug interactions
when taking this medication
If Inderide is taken with certain other drugs, the effects of either could be increased, decreased, or altered. It is especially important to check with your doctor before combining Inderide with the following:

ACTH (adrenocorticotropic hormone)
Alcohol
Aluminum hydroxide gel (Mylanta)
Calcium-blocking blood pressure drugs such as Calan, Cardizem, and
    Procardia XL
Certain blood pressure medications such as Diupres and Ser-Ap-Es
Chlorpromazine (Thorazine)
Cimetidine (Tagamet)
Corticosteroids such as prednisone
Digitalis (Lanoxin)
Epinephrine (EpiPen)
Haloperidol (Haldol)
Insulin
Lidocaine (Xylocaine)
Nonsteroidal anti-inflammatory drugs such as Motrin
Norepinephrine (Levophed)
Oral diabetes drugs such as Micronase
Phenobarbitone
Phenytoin (Dilantin)
Rifampin (Rifadin)
Theophylline (Theo-Dur)
Thyroid medications such as Synthroid

Special information
if you are pregnant or breastfeeding
The effects of Inderide during pregnancy have not been adequately studied. If you are pregnant or plan to become pregnant, inform your doctor immediately. Inderide appears in breast milk and could affect a nursing infant. If Inderide is essential to your health, your doctor may advise you to discontinue breastfeeding until your treatment is finished.

Recommended dosage

ADULTS

Your doctor will tailor your dosage according to your response to Inderide's main ingredients.

The usual dose is one Inderide tablet, 2 times per day.

Your doctor may use this medication in combination with other high blood pressure drugs to achieve the desired effect.

CHILDREN

The safety and effectiveness of this drug in children have not been established.

ELDERLY

Your doctor will adjust your dosage with extra caution.

Overdosage

Any medication taken in excess can have severe consequences. If you suspect an overdose, seek medical attention immediately.

■ *The symptoms of Inderide overdose may include:*
Coma
Extremely slow heartbeat
Heart failure
Increased urination
Irritation and overactivity of the stomach and intestines
Low blood pressure
Sluggishness
Stupor
Wheezing

Brand name:

INDOCIN

Pronounced: IN-doh-sin
Generic name: Indomethacin

Why is this drug prescribed?

Indocin, a nonsteroidal anti-inflammatory drug, is used to relieve the inflammation, swelling, stiffness and joint pain associated with moderate or severe rheumatoid arthritis and osteoarthritis (the most common form of arthritis), and ankylosing spondylitis (arthritis of the spine). It is also used to treat bursitis, tendinitis (acute painful shoulder), acute gouty arthritis, and other kinds of pain.

Most important fact about this drug
You should have frequent checkups with your doctor if you take Indocin regularly. Ulcers or internal bleeding can occur without warning.

How should you take this medication?
Indocin should be taken with food or an antacid, and with a full glass of water. Never take on an empty stomach.

Take this medication exactly as prescribed by your doctor.

If you are using Indocin for arthritis, it should be taken regularly.

If you are taking the liquid form of this medicine, shake the bottle well before each use.

Indocin SR capsules should be swallowed whole, not crushed or broken.

Do not lie down for about 20 to 30 minutes after taking Indocin. This helps prevent irritation that could lead to trouble in swallowing.

If you are using suppository form of this medicine:

1. If the suppository is too soft to insert, hold it under cool water or chill it before removing the wrapper
2. Remove the foil wrapper and moisten your rectal area with cool tap water.
3. Lie down your side and use your finger to push the suppository well up into the rectum. Hold your buttocks together for a few seconds.
4. Indocin suppositories should be kept inside the rectum for at least one hour so that all of the medicine can be absorbed by your body.

■ *If you miss a dose...*
Take the forgotten dose as soon as you remember. If it is time for your next dose, skip the one you missed and return to your regular schedule. Never take a double dose.

■ *Storage instructions...*
The liquid and suppository forms of Indocin may be stored at room temperature. Keep both forms from extreme heat, and protect the liquid from freezing.

What side effects may occur?
Side effects cannot be anticipated. If any develop or change in intensity, inform your doctor as soon as possible. Only your doctor can determine if it is safe for you to continue taking Indocin.

■ *More common side effects may include:*
Abdominal pain, constipation, depression, diarrhea, dizziness, fatigue, headache, heartburn, indigestion, nausea, ringing in the ears, sleepiness or excessive drowsiness, stomach pain, stomach upset, vertigo, vomiting

■ *Less common or rare side effects may include:*
Anemia, anxiety, asthma, behavior disturbances, bloating, blurred vision, breast changes, changes in heart rate, chest pain, coma, congestive heart failure, convulsions, decrease in white blood cells, fever, fluid in lungs, fluid retention, flushing, gas, hair loss, hepatitis, high or low blood pressure, hives, itching, increase in blood sugar, insomnia, kidney failure, labored breathing, light-headedness, loss of appetite, mental confusion, muscle weakness, nosebleed, peptic ulcer, problems in hearing, rash, rectal bleeding, Stevens-Johnson syndrome (skin peeling), stomach or intestinal bleeding, sweating, twitching, unusual redness of skin, vaginal bleeding, weight gain, worsening of epilepsy, yellow eyes and skin

Why should this drug not be prescribed?
If you are sensitive to or have ever had an allergic reaction to Indocin, aspirin, or similar drugs, or if you have had asthma attacks caused by aspirin or other drugs of this type, you should not take this medication. Make sure that your doctor is aware of any drug reactions that you have experienced.

Do not use Indocin suppositories if you have a history of rectal inflammation or recent rectal bleeding.

Special warnings about this medication
Indocin prolongs bleeding time. If you are taking blood-thinning medication, this drug should be taken with caution.

Your doctor should prescribe the lowest possible effective dose. The incidence of side effects increases as dosage increases.

Peptic ulcers and bleeding can occur without warning.

This drug should be used with caution if you have kidney or liver disease, and it can cause liver inflammation in some people.

Do not take aspirin or any other anti-inflammatory medications while taking Indocin, unless your doctor tells you to do so.

If you have heart disease or high blood pressure, this drug can increase water retention.

This drug can mask the symptoms of an existing infection.

Indocin may cause you to become drowsy or less alert; therefore, driving or operating dangerous machinery or participating in any hazardous activity that requires full mental alertness is not recommended.

Possible food and drug interactions
when taking this medication
If Indocin is taken with certain other drugs, the effects of either could be increased, decreased or altered. It is especially important to check with your doctor before combining Indocin with the following:

Aspirin
Beta-adrenergic blockers such as Tenormin, Inderal
Blood-thinning medicines such as Coumadin
Captopril (Capoten)
Cyclosporine (Sandimmune)
Diflunisal (Dolobid)
Digoxin (Lanoxin)
Lithium (Eskalith)
Loop diuretics (Lasix)
Potassium-sparing diuretics such as Aldactone
Probenecid (Benemid, ColBENEMID)
The anticancer drug methotrexate
Thiazide-type diuretics such as Diuril
Triamterene (Dyazide)

Special information
if you are pregnant or breastfeeding
The effects of Indocin during pregnancy have not been adequately studied. If you are pregnant or plan to become pregnant, inform your doctor immediately. Indocin appears in breast milk and could affect a nursing infant. If this medication is essential to your health, your doctor may advise you to discontinue breastfeeding until your treatment is finished.

Recommended dosage

ADULTS

This medication is available in liquid, capsule, and suppository form. The following dosages are for the capsule form. If you prefer the liquid form, ask your doctor to make the proper substitution. Do not try to convert the medication or dosage yourself.

Moderate to Severe Rheumatoid Arthritis, Osteoarthritis, Ankylosing Spondylitis

The usual dose is 25 milligrams 2 or 3 times a day, increasing to a total daily dose of 150 to 200 milligrams. Your doctor should monitor you carefully for side effects when you are taking this drug.

Your doctor may prescribe a single daily 75-milligram capsule of Indocin SR in place of regular Indocin.

Bursitis or Tendinitis

The usual dose is 75 to 150 milligrams daily divided into 3 to 4 small doses for 1 to 2 weeks, until symptoms disappear.

Acute Gouty Arthritis

The usual dose is 50 milligrams 3 times a day until pain is reduced to a tolerable level (usually 3 to 5 days). Your doctor will advise you when to stop taking this drug for this condition. Keep him informed of its effects on your symptoms.

CHILDREN

The safety and effectiveness of Indocin have not been established in children under 14 years of age. However, your doctor may decide that the benefits of this medication may outweigh the potential risks.

ELDERLY

Your doctor will adjust the dosage as needed.

Overdosage

Any medication taken in excess can cause symptoms of overdose. If you suspect an overdose, seek medical attention immediately.

- *The symptoms of Indocin overdose may include:*
  Convulsions
  Disorientation
  Dizziness
  Intense headache
  Lethargy
  Mental confusion
  Nausea, vomiting
  Numbness
  Tingling or pins and needles

Generic name:

INDOMETHACIN

See Indocin, page 522.

Generic name:

INSULIN

Pronounced: IN-suh-lin
Available formulations:
Insulin, Human:
  Humulin
Insulin, Human Isophane Suspension:
  Humulin N
Insulin, Human NPH:
  Insulatard NPH Human
  Novolin N
Insulin, Human Regular:
  Novolin R
  Humulin BR & R
  Velosulin Human
Insulin, Human Regular and Human NPH mixture:
  Humulin 70/30
  Mixtard Human 70/30
  Novolin 70/30
Insulin, Human, Zinc Suspension:
  Humulin L & U
  Novolin L
Insulin, NPH:
  NPH Iletin I (also II, Beef; II, Pork)
  Insulatard NPH
  NPH Insulin
Insulin, Regular and NPH mixture:
  Mixtard 70/30
Insulin, Zinc Crystals:
  NPH Iletin I
Insulin, Regular:
  Iletin I Regular (also II, Beef; II, Pork)
  Regular Insulin
  Velosulin

Insulin, Zinc Suspension:
  Iletin I, Lente
  Protamine, Zinc and Iletin
  Iletin I, Semilente
  Iletin I
  Lente Insulin
  Ultralente Insulin

Why is this drug prescribed?

Insulin is prescribed for diabetes mellitus when this condition does not improve with oral medications or by modifying your diet. Insulin is a hormone produced by the pancreas, a large gland that lies near the stomach. This hormone is necessary for the body's correct use of food, especially sugar. Insulin apparently works by helping sugar penetrate the cell wall, where it is then utilized by the cell. In people with diabetes, the body either does not make enough insulin, or the insulin that is produced cannot be used properly.

There are actually two forms of diabetes: Type I, insulin-dependent, and Type II, non-insulin-dependent. Type I usually requires insulin injection for life, while Type II diabetes can usually be treated by dietary changes and/or oral antidiabetic medications such as Diabinese and Glucotrol. Occasionally, Type II diabetics must take insulin injections on a temporary basis, especially during stressful periods or times of illness.

The various insulin brands above differ in several ways: in the source (animal, human, or genetically engineered), in the time requirements for the insulin to take effect, and in the length of time the insulin remains working.

Regular insulin is manufactured from beef and pork pancreas, begins working within 30 to 60 minutes, and lasts for 6 to 8 hours. Variations of insulin have been developed to satisfy the needs of individual patients. For example, zinc suspension insulin is an intermediate-acting insulin that starts working within 1 to 1½ hours and lasts approximately 24 hours. Insulin combined with zinc and protamine is a longer-acting insulin that takes effect within 4 to 6 hours and lasts up to 36 hours. The time and course of action may vary considerably in different individuals or at different times in the same individual.

Animal-based insulin is a very safe product. However, some components may cause an allergic reaction (see "What side effects may occur?"). Therefore, genetically engineered human insulin has been developed to lessen the chance of an allergic reaction. It is structurally identical to the insulin produced by your body's pancreas. However, some human insulin may be produced in a semi-synthetic process that begins with animal-based ingredients, which may cause an allergic reaction.

Most important fact about this drug

Regardless of the type of insulin your doctor has prescribed, you should follow carefully the dietary and exercise guidelines he or she has recommended. Failure to follow these guidelines or to take your insulin as prescribed may result in serious and potentially life-threatening complications such as hypoglycemia (lowered blood sugar levels).

How should you take this medication?

Take your insulin exactly as prescribed, being careful to follow your doctor's dietary and exercise recommendations.

■ *If you miss a dose...*
Your doctor should tell you what to do if you miss an insulin injection or meal.

■ *Storage instructions...*
Store insulin in a refrigerator (but not in the freezer) or in another cool, dark place. Do not expose insulin to heat or direct sunlight.

Some brands of prefilled syringes can be kept at room temperature for a week or a month. Check your product's label. Never use insulin after the expiration date that is printed on the label and carton.

What side effects may occur?

While side effects from insulin use are rare, allergic reactions or low blood sugar (sometimes called "an insulin reaction") may pose significant health risks. Your doctor should be notified if any of the following occur:

■ *Mild allergic reactions:*
Swelling, itching or redness at the injection site (usually disappears within a few days or weeks)

■ *More serious allergic reactions:*
Fast pulse
Low blood pressure
Perspiration
Rash over the entire body
Shortness of breath, shallow breathing, or wheezing

Other side effects are virtually eliminated when the correct dose of insulin is matched with the proper diet and level of physical activity. Low blood sugar may develop in poorly controlled or unstable diabetes. Consuming sugar or a sugar-containing product will usually correct the condition, which can be brought about by taking too much insulin, missing or delaying meals, exercising or working more than usual, an infection or illness, a change in the body's need for insulin, drug interactions, or consuming alcohol.

■ *Symptoms of low blood sugar include:*
Abnormal behavior, anxiety, blurred vision, cold sweat, confusion, depressed mood, dizziness, drowsiness, fatigue, headache, hunger, inability to concentrate, light-headedness, nausea, nervousness, personality changes, rapid heartbeat, restlessness, sleep disturbances, slurred speech, sweating, tingling in the hands, feet, lips, or tongue, tremor, unsteady movement

Contact your physician if these symptoms persist.

■ *Symptoms of more severe low blood sugar include:*
Coma
Disorientation

Remember, too, the symptoms associated with an under-supply of insulin, which can be brought on by taking too little of it, overeating, or fever and infection.

■ *Symptoms of insufficient insulin include:*
Drowsiness
Flushing
Fruity breath
Heavy breathing
Loss of appetite
Rapid pulse
Thirst

If you are ill, you should check your urine for ketones (acetone), and notify your doctor if the test is positive. This condition can be life-threatening.

Why should this drug not be prescribed?
Insulin should be used only to correct diabetic conditions.

Special warnings about this medication
Wear personal identification that states clearly that you are diabetic. Carry a sugar-containing product such as hard candy to offset any symptoms of low blood sugar.

Do not change the type of insulin or even the model and brand of syringe or needle you use without your physician's instruction. Failure to use the proper syringe may lead to improper dosage levels of insulin.

If you become ill from any cause, especially with nausea and vomiting or fever, your insulin requirements may change. It is important to eat as normally as possible. If you have trouble eating, drink fruit juices, soda, or clear soups, or eat small amounts of bland foods. Test your urine and/or blood sugar and tell your doctor at once. If you have severe and prolonged vomiting, seek emergency medical care.

If you are taking insulin, you should check your glucose levels with home blood and urine testing devices. If your blood tests consistently show above-normal sugar levels or your urine tests consistently show the presence of sugar, your diabetes is not properly controlled, and you should tell your doctor.

To avoid infection or contamination, use disposable needles and syringes or sterilize your reusable syringe and needle carefully.

Always keep handy an extra supply of insulin as well as a spare syringe and needle.

Possible food and drug interactions
when taking this medication
Follow your physician's dietary guidelines as closely as you can and inform your physician of any medication, either prescription or nonprescription, that you are taking. Specific medications, depending on the amount present, that affect insulin levels or its effectiveness include:

Anabolic steroids such as Androl-50
Appetite suppressants such as Tenuate
Aspirin
Beta-blocking blood pressure medicines such as Tenormin and Lopressor
Diuretics such as Lasix and Dyazide
Epinephrine (EpiPen)
Estrogens such as Premarin
MAO inhibitors (antidepressant drugs such as Nardil and Parnate)
Phenytoin (Dilantin)
Steroid medications such as prednisone
Thyroid medications such as Synthroid and Proloid

Use alcohol carefully, since excessive alcohol consumption can cause low blood sugar. Don't drink unless your doctor has approved it.

Special information
if you are pregnant or breastfeeding
Insulin is considered safe for pregnant women, but pregnancy may make managing your diabetes more difficult.

Properly controlled diabetes is essential for the health of the mother and the developing baby; therefore, it is extremely important that pregnant women follow closely their physician's dietary and exercise guidelines and prescribing instructions.

Since insulin does not pass into breast milk, it is safe for nursing mothers.

Recommended dosage
Your doctor will specify which insulin to use, how much, when, and how often to inject it. Your dosage may be affected by changes in food, activity, illness, medication, pregnancy, exercise, travel, or your work schedule. Proper control of your diabetes requires close and constant cooperation with your doctor. Failure to use your insulin as prescribed may result in serious and potentially fatal complications.

Some insulins should be clear, and some have a cloudy precipitate. Find out what your insulin should look like and check it carefully before using.

Overdosage
An overdose of insulin can cause low blood sugar (hypoglycemia). Symptoms include:

Depressed mood, dizziness, drowsiness, fatigue, headache, hunger, inability to concentrate, irritability, nausea, nervousness, personality changes, rapid heartbeat, restlessness, sleep disturbances, slurred speech, sweating, tingling, tremor, unsteady movements

■ *Symptoms of more severe low blood sugar include:*
  Coma
  Disorientation
  Pale skin
  Seizures

Your doctor should be contacted immediately if these symptoms of severe low blood sugar occur.

Eating sugar or a sugar-based product will often correct the condition. If you suspect an overdose, seek medical attention immediately.

Brand name:

INTAL

Pronounced: IN-tahl
Generic name: Cromolyn sodium
Other brand name: Nasalcrom

Why is this drug prescribed?

Intal contains the antiasthmatic/antiallergic medication cromolyn sodium.

Different forms of the drug are used to manage bronchial asthma, to prevent asthma attacks, and to prevent and treat seasonal and chronic allergies.

The drug works by preventing certain cells in the body from releasing substances that can cause allergic reactions or prompt too much bronchial activity. It also helps prevent bronchial constriction caused by exercise, aspirin, cold air, and certain environmental pollutants such as sulfur dioxide.

Most important fact about this drug

Intal does not help an acute asthma attack. When taken to prevent severe bronchial asthma, it can be 4 weeks before you feel its maximum benefit, though some people get relief sooner. Do not discontinue the inhalation capsules or nasal solution abruptly without the advice of your doctor.

How should you take this medication?

Intal capsules should not be swallowed. They are for inhalation using the Spinhaler turbo-inhaler. The contents of 1 capsule is usually inhaled 4 times daily at regular intervals. Wash the Spinhaler in warm water at least once a week; dry thoroughly. Replace the Spinhaler every 6 months.

Intal nebulizer solution should be inhaled using a power-operated nebulizer equipped with an appropriate face mask or mouthpiece. Hand-operated nebulizers are not suitable. It is important that the solution be inhaled at regular intervals, usually 4 times per day.

Intal aerosol spray can be used either for chronic asthma or to prevent an asthma attack. For chronic asthma, it must be inhaled at regular intervals, as directed by your doctor, usually 2 sprays inhaled 4 times daily. To prevent an asthma attack caused by exercise, cold air, or other irritants, the usual dose of 2 inhalation sprays should be taken between 10 and 60 minutes before exercising or exposure to cold or pollutants.

Nasalcrom nasal solution should be used with a metered nasal spray device, which should be replaced every 6 months. Blow your nose to clear your nasal passages before administering the spray. The nasal solution is used for nasal congestion due to seasonal or chronic allergies. For seasonal allergies, treatment is more effective if begun before the start of the allergy season. Treatment should then continue throughout the season. For year-round allergies, treatment may be required for up to 4 weeks before results are seen. Your doctor may find it necessary to add other allergy medications, such as antihistamines or decongestants, during initial treatment.

■ *If you miss a dose...*
Take it as soon as you remember. Then take the rest of that day's doses at equally spaced intervals. Do not take 2 doses at once.

■ *Storage instructions...*
Store at room temperature, away from light and heat. Keep the ampules in their foil pouch until you are ready to use them.

What side effects may occur?
Side effects cannot be anticipated. If any develop or change in intensity, inform your doctor as soon as possible. Only your doctor can determine if it is safe for you to continue taking Intal.

■ *More common side effects may include:*
Cough
Nasal congestion or irritation
Nausea
Sneezing
Throat irritation
Wheezing

■ *Less common or rare side effects may include:*
Angioedema (swelling of face around lips, tongue, and throat, swollen arms and legs), bad taste in mouth, burning in chest, difficulty swallowing, dizziness, ear problems, headache, hives, joint swelling and pain, nosebleed, painful urination or frequent urination, postnasal drip, rash, severe allergic reaction, swollen glands, swollen throat, teary eyes, tightness in throat

Why should this drug not be prescribed?
If you are sensitive to or have ever had an allergic reaction to cromolyn sodium or lactose, you should not take this medication. Make sure your doctor is aware of any drug reactions you have experienced.

Special warnings about this medication

Asthma symptoms may recur if the recommended dosage of Intal is reduced or discontinued. Intal has no role in the treatment of an acute asthmatic attack once it has begun. Obtain medical help immediately if you experience a severe attack.

If you have liver or kidney problems, your doctor may have to reduce the dosage or even take you off the drug altogether.

When using the capsules, you may accidentally inhale some powder, which can irritate your throat or make you cough. Try rinsing your mouth or taking a drink of water immediately before and/or after using the Spinhaler.

If your heartbeat is ever irregular or if you have any other kind of heart trouble, be sure your doctor knows about it before you use Intal aerosol spray.

Intal aerosol spray may not help you if your attack has been brought on by exercise.

Possible food and drug interactions
when taking this medication

If you are taking other prescription or nonprescription drugs, discuss this with your doctor to determine if these drugs would interact with Intal.

Special information
if you are pregnant or breastfeeding

The effects of Intal during pregnancy have not been adequately studied. If you are pregnant or plan to become pregnant, inform your doctor immediately. It is not known whether Intal appears in breast milk. As with all medication, a nursing woman should use this drug only after careful consultation with her doctor.

Recommended dosage

INTAL CAPSULES FOR INHALATION
INTAL NEBULIZER SOLUTION

Adults and Children 2 Years Old and Over

For management of bronchial asthma, the usual dosage is 20 milligrams (1 capsule or ampule) inhaled 4 times daily at regular intervals, using the Spinhaler turbo-inhaler or power-operated nebulizer. If you have chronic asthma, this drug's effectiveness depends on your taking it regularly, as directed, and only after an attack has been controlled and you can inhale adequately.

For the prevention of an acute attack following exercise or exposure to cold, dry air or environmental irritants, the usual dose is 1 capsule or ampule inhaled shortly before exposure to the irritant. You may repeat the inhalation as needed for continued protection during prolonged exposure.

INTAL INHALER AEROSOL SPRAY

Adults and Children 5 Years Old and Over

For the management of bronchial asthma, the usual starting dose is 2 metered sprays taken at regular intervals, 4 times daily. This is the maximum dose that should be taken, and lower dosages may be effective in children. This drug should be used only after an asthma attack has been controlled and you can inhale adequately.

For the prevention of an acute asthma attack following exercise, exposure to cold air or environmental agents, the usual dose is inhalation of 2 metered sprays shortly (10 to 15 minutes but not more than 60 minutes) before exposure to the irritant.

NASALCROM NASAL SOLUTION

Adults ana Children 6 Years Old and Over

For the prevention and treatment of allergies caused by exposure to certain irritants, the usual dosage is 1 spray in each nostril 3 to 4 times per day at regular intervals, using the metered spray device. Your doctor may have you use the spray 6 times a day if you need it.

Overdosage

Any medication taken in excess can have serious consequences. If you suspect an overdose, seek medical attention immediately.

■ *Symptoms of Intal overdose may include:*
Difficulty breathing
Heart failure
Low blood pressure
Slow heartbeat

Generic name:

IODINATED GLYCEROL WITH DEXTROMETHORPHAN HYDROBROMIDE

See Tussi-Organidin NR, page 1165.

Brand name:

IONAMIN

See Fastin, page 422.

Generic name:

IPRATROPIUM BROMIDE

See Atrovent, page 86.

Brand name:

ISMO

See Imdur, page 504.

Brand name:

ISOLLYL IMPROVED

See Fiorinal, page 437.

Generic name:

ISOMETHEPTENE, DICHLORALPHENAZONE, AND ACETAMINOPHEN

See Midrin, page 665.

Brand name:

ISOPTIN

See Calan, page 146.

Brand name:

ISOPTO CARPINE

See Pilocar, page 857.

Brand name:

ISORDIL

Pronounced: ICE-or-dill
Generic name: Isosorbide dinitrate
Other brand name: Sorbitrate

Why is this drug prescribed?
Isordil is prescribed to relieve or prevent angina pectoris (suffocating chest pain). Angina pectoris occurs when the arteries and veins become constricted and sufficient oxygen does not reach the heart. Isordil dilates the blood vessels by relaxing the muscles in their walls. Oxygen flow improves as the vessels relax, and chest pain subsides.

In swallowed capsules or tablets, Isordil helps to increase the amount of exercise you can do before chest pain begins.

In chewable or sublingual (held under the tongue) tablets, Isordil can help relieve chest pain that has already started or prevent pain expected from a strenuous activity such as walking up a hill or climbing stairs.

Most important fact about this drug
Isordil may cause severe low blood pressure (possibly marked by dizziness or fainting), especially when you stand or sit up quickly. People taking diuretic medication or those who have low blood pressure should use Isordil with caution.

How should you take this medication?
Swallowed capsules or tablets should be taken on an empty stomach. While regular tablets may be crushed for easier use, sustained- or prolonged-release products should not be chewed, crushed or altered.

Chewable tablets should be chewed thoroughly and held in the mouth for a couple of minutes. Do not eat, drink, smoke, or use chewing tobacco while a sublingual tablet is dissolving.

- *If you miss a dose...*
  If you are taking this drug regularly, take the forgotten dose as soon as you remember. If your next dose is within 2 hours—or 6 hours for controlled-release tablets and capsules—skip the one you missed and go back to your regular schedule. Do not take 2 doses at once.

■ *Storage information...*
Store at room temperature in a tightly closed container, away from light.

What side effects may occur?
Side effects cannot be anticipated. If any develop or change in intensity, inform your doctor as soon as possible. Only your doctor can determine if it is safe for you to continue taking Isordil.

Headache is the most common side effect; usually, standard headache treatments with over-the-counter pain products will relieve the pain. The headaches associated with Isordil usually subside within 2 weeks after treatment with the drug begins.

■ *Other common side effects may include:*
Dizziness
Low blood pressure
Weakness

■ *Less common or rare side effects may include:*
Collapse, fainting, flushed skin, nausea, pallor, perspiration, rash, restlessness, skin inflammation and flaking, vomiting

Why should this drug not be prescribed?
You should not take Isordil if you have had a previous allergic reaction to it or to other nitrates or nitrites.

Special warnings about this medication
You should use Isordil with caution if you have anemia, the eye condition called glaucoma, a previous head injury or heart attack, heart disease, low blood pressure, or thyroid disease.

If you stop using Isordil, you should follow your doctor's plan for a gradual withdrawal schedule. Abruptly stopping this medication could result in additional chest pain.

Some people may develop a tolerance to Isordil, which causes its effects to be reduced over time. Tell your doctor if you think Isordil is starting to lose its effectiveness.

Possible food and drug interactions
when taking this medication
If Isordil is taken with certain other drugs, the effects of either could be increased, decreased, or altered.

Extreme low blood pressure (marked by dizziness, fainting, and numbness) may occur if you take Isordil with certain other high blood pressure drugs such as Cardizem and Procardia.

Alcohol may interact with Isordil and produce a swift decrease in blood pressure, possibly causing dizziness and fainting.

Special information
if you are pregnant or breastfeeding

The effects of Isordil in pregnancy have not been adequately studied. Isordil should be used only when the benefits of therapy clearly outweigh the potential risks to the developing baby. If you are pregnant or plan to become pregnant, inform your doctor immediately. It is not known if Isordil appears in breast milk; therefore, nursing mothers should use Isordil with caution.

Recommended dosage

ADULTS

The usual sublingual starting dose for the treatment of angina pectoris is 2.5 milligrams to 5 milligrams. Your doctor will increase this initial dose gradually until the pain subsides or side effects prove bothersome.

The usual sublingual starting dose for the prevention of an impending attack of angina pectoris is usually 5 or 10 milligrams every 2 to 3 hours.

To prevent chronic stable angina pectoris, the usual starting dose for swallowed, immediately released Isordil is 5 to 20 milligrams. Your doctor may increase this initial dose to 10 to 40 milligrams every 6 hours.

To prevent chronic stable angina pectoris with controlled-release Isordil, the usual initial dose is 40 milligrams. Your doctor may increase this dose from 40 to 80 milligrams given every 8 to 12 hours.

CHILDREN

The safety and effectiveness of Isordil have not been established for children.

Overdosage

Any medication taken in excess can have serious consequences. Severe overdosage of Isordil can be fatal. If you suspect an overdose, seek medical help immediately.

■ *Symptoms of Isordil overdose may include:*
  Bloody diarrhea, coma, confusion, convulsions, fainting, fever, flushed and

perspiring skin (later cold and blue), nausea, palpitations, paralysis, rapid decrease in blood pressure, rapid, then difficult and slow breathing, slow pulse, throbbing headache, vertigo, visual disturbances, vomiting

Generic name:

ISOSORBIDE DINITRATE

See Isordil, page 538.

Generic name:

ISOSORBIDE MONONITRATE

See Imdur, page 504.

Generic name:

ISOTRETINOIN

See Accutane, page 4.

Generic name:

ISRADIPINE

See DynaCirc, page 376.

Generic name:

ITRACONAZOLE

See Sporanox, page 1040.

Brand name:

KAON-CL

See Micro-K, page 658.

Brand name:

K-DUR

See Micro-K, page 658.

Brand name:

KEFLEX

Pronounced: KEF-lecks
Generic name: Cephalexin hydrochloride
Other brand name: Keftab

Why is this drug prescribed?

Keflex and Keftab are cephalosporin antibiotics. They are prescribed for bacterial infections of the respiratory tract, including middle ear infection, bone, skin, and the reproductive and urinary systems. Because they are effective for only certain types of bacterial infections, before beginning treatment your doctor may perform tests to identify the organisms causing the infection.

Keflex is available in capsules and an oral suspension form for use in children. Keftab, available only in tablet form, is prescribed exclusively for adults.

Most important fact about this drug

If you are allergic to either penicillin or cephalosporin antibiotics in any form, consult your doctor *before taking Keflex*. There is a possibility that you are allergic to both types of medication and if a reaction occurs, it could be extremely severe. If you take the drug and feel signs of a reaction, seek medical attention immediately.

How should you take this medication?

Keflex may be taken with or without meals. However, if the drug upsets your stomach, you may want to take it after you have eaten.

Take Keflex at even intervals around the clock as prescribed by your doctor.

If you are taking the liquid form of Keflex, use the specially marked spoon to measure each dose accurately.

To obtain maximum benefit, it is important that you finish taking all of this medication, even if you are feeling better.

■ *If you miss a dose...*
Take it as soon as you remember. If it is almost time for the next dose, and you take 2 doses a day, take the one you missed and the next dose 5 to 6 hours later. If you take 3 or more doses a day, take the one you missed and the next dose 2 to 4 hours later, or double the next dose. Then go back to your regular schedule.

■ *Storage instructions...*
Store capsules and tablets at room temperature. Store the liquid suspension in a refrigerator; discard any unused medication after 14 days.

What side effects may occur?
Side effects cannot be anticipated. If any develop or change in intensity, inform your doctor as soon as possible. Only your doctor can determine if it is safe for you to continue taking Keflex.

■ *More common side effects may include:*
Diarrhea

■ *Less common or rare side effects may include:*
Abdominal pain, agitation, colitis (inflammation of the large intestine), confusion, dizziness, fatigue, fever, genital and rectal itching, hallucinations, headache, hepatitis, hives, indigestion, inflammation of joints, inflammation of the stomach, joint pain, nausea, rash, seizures, severe allergic reaction, skin peeling, skin redness, swelling due to fluid retention, vaginal discharge, vaginal inflammation, vomiting, yellowing of skin and whites of eyes

Why should this drug not be prescribed?
If you are sensitive to or have ever had an allergic reaction to the cephalosporin group of antibiotics, you should not use this medication. Make sure your doctor is aware of any drug reactions you have experienced.

Special warnings about this medication
If you have a history of stomach or intestinal disease, especially colitis, check with your doctor before taking Keflex.

If you have ever had an allergic reaction, particularly to drugs, be sure to tell your doctor.

If diarrhea occurs while taking cephalexin, check with your doctor before taking a remedy. Certain diarrhea medications (for instance, Lomotil) may increase your diarrhea or make it last longer.

Prolonged use of Keflex may result in an overgrowth of bacteria that do not respond to the medication, causing a secondary infection. Your doctor will monitor your use of this drug on a regular basis.

If you have a kidney disorder, check with your doctor before taking Keflex. You may need a reduced dose.

If you are diabetic, it is important to note that Keflex may cause false results in tests for urine sugar. Notify your doctor that you are taking this medication before being tested. Do not change your diet or dosage of diabetes medication without first consulting with your doctor.

If your symptoms do not improve within a few days, or if they get worse, notify your doctor immediately.

Do not give this medication to other people or use it for other infections before checking with your doctor.

Possible food and drug interactions
when taking this medication
If Keflex is taken with certain other drugs, the effects of either could be increased, decreased, or altered. It is especially important to check with your doctor before combining Keflex with the following:

Certain diarrhea medications such as Lomotil
Oral contraceptives

Special information
if you are pregnant or breastfeeding
The effects of Keflex during pregnancy have not been adequately studied. If you are pregnant or plan to become pregnant, notify your doctor immediately. Keflex appears in breast milk and could affect a nursing infant. If this medication is essential to your health, your doctor may advise you to discontinue breastfeeding until your treatment is finished.

Recommended dosage

ADULTS

Throat, Skin, and Urinary Tract Infections
The usual adult dosage is 500 milligrams taken every 12 hours. Cystitis (bladder infection) therapy should be continued for 7 to 14 days.

Other Infections
The usual recommended dosage is 250 milligrams taken every 6 hours. For more severe infections, larger doses may be needed, as determined by your doctor.

CHILDREN

Keflex
The usual dose is 25 to 50 milligrams for each 2.2 pounds of body weight per day, divided into smaller doses.

For strep throat in children over 1 year of age and for skin infections, the dose may be divided into 2 doses taken every 12 hours. For strep infections, the medication should be taken for at least 10 days. Your doctor may double the dose if your child has a severe infection.

For middle ear infection, the dose is 75 to 100 milligrams per 2.2 pounds per day, divided into 4 doses.

Keftab
Safety and effectiveness have not been established in children.

Overdosage
Any medication taken in excess can have serious consequences.

If you suspect an overdose, seek emergency medical treatment immediately.

■ *Symptoms of Keflex overdose may include:*
Blood in the urine
Diarrhea
Nausea
Upper abdominal pain
Vomiting

Brand name:

KEFTAB

See Keflex, page 542.

Generic name:

KETOCONAZOLE

See Nizoral, page 739.

Generic name:

KETOPROFEN

See Orudis, page 786.

Generic name:

KETOROLAC

See Toradol, page 1137.

Brand name:

KLONOPIN

Pronounced: KLON-uh-pin
Generic name: Clonazepam

Why is this drug prescribed?

Klonopin is used alone or along with other medications to treat convulsive disorders such as epilepsy. It belongs to a class of drugs known as benzodiazepines.

Most important fact about this drug

Klonopin works best when there is a constant amount in the bloodstream. To keep blood levels as constant as possible, take your doses at regularly spaced intervals and try not to miss any.

How should you take this medication?

Klonopin should be taken exactly as prescribed by your doctor.

- *If you miss a dose...*
  If it is within an hour after the missed time, take the dose as soon as you remember. If you do not remember until later, skip the dose and go back to your regular schedule. Never take 2 doses at the same time.

- *Storage instructions...*
  Store away from heat, light, and moisture.

What side effects may occur?

Side effects cannot be anticipated. If any develop or change in intensity, inform your doctor as soon as possible. Only your doctor can determine if it is safe for you to continue taking Klonopin.

- *More common side effects may include:*
  Behavior problems
  Drowsiness
  Lack of muscular coordination

- *Less common or rare side effects may include:*
  Abnormal eye movements, anemia, bed wetting, chest congestion, coated tongue, coma, confusion, constipation, dehydration, depression, diarrhea, double vision, dry mouth, excess hair, fever, fluttery or throbbing heartbeat, "glassy-eyed" appearance, hair loss, headache, hallucinations, inability to fall or stay asleep, inability to urinate, increased sex drive,

involuntary rapid movement of the eyeballs, loss of or increased appetite, loss of voice, memory loss, muscle and bone pain, muscle weakness, nausea, nighttime urination, painful or difficult urination, partial paralysis, runny nose, shortness of breath, skin rash, slowed breathing, slurred speech, sore gums, speech difficulties, stomach inflammation, swelling of ankles and face, tremor, uncontrolled body movement or twitching, vertigo, weight loss or gain

■ *Side effects due to rapid decrease or abrupt withdrawal from Klonopin may include:*
Abdominal and muscle cramps
Behavior disorders
Convulsions
Depressed feeling
Hallucinations
Restlessness
Sleeping difficulties
Tremors

Why should this drug not be prescribed?
If you are sensitive to or have ever had an allergic reaction to Klonopin or similar drugs, such as Librium and Valium, you should not take this medication. Make sure your doctor is aware of any reactions you have experienced.

You should not take this medication if you have severe liver disease or the eye condition known as acute narrow-angle glaucoma.

Special warnings about this medication
Klonopin may cause you to become drowsy or less alert; therefore, you should not drive or operate dangerous machinery or participate in any hazardous activity that requires full mental alertness until you know how this drug affects you.

If you have several types of seizures, this drug may increase the possibility of grand mal seizures (epilepsy). Inform your doctor if this occurs. Your doctor may wish to prescribe an additional anticonvulsant drug or increase your dose.

Klonopin can be habit-forming and can lose its effectiveness as you build up a tolerance to it. You may experience withdrawal symptoms—such as convulsions, hallucinations, tremor, and abdominal and muscle cramps—if you stop using this drug abruptly. Discontinue or change your dose only in consultation with your doctor.

**Possible food and drug interactions
when taking this medication**
Klonopin slows the nervous system and its effects may be intensified by
alcohol. Do not drink while taking this medication.

If Klonopin is taken with certain other drugs, the effects of either could be
increased, decreased, or altered. It is especially important to check with your
doctor before combining Klonopin with the following:

Antianxiety drugs such as Valium
Antidepressant drugs such as Elavil, Nardil, Parnate, and Tofranil
Barbiturates such as phenobarbital
Major tranquilizers such as Haldol, Navane, and Thorazine
Narcotic pain relievers such as Demerol and Percocet
Other anticonvulsants such as Dilantin, Depakene, and Depakote
Sedatives such as Halcion

**Special information
if you are pregnant or breastfeeding**
The effects of Klonopin during pregnancy have not been adequately studied.
If you are pregnant or plan to become pregnant, inform your doctor
immediately. Klonopin appears in breast milk and could affect a nursing
infant. If this medication is essential to your health, you should not
breastfeed until your treatment with this medication is finished.

Recommended dosage

ADULTS

The starting dose should be no more than 1.5 milligrams per day, divided into
3 doses. Your doctor may increase your daily dosage by 0.5 to 1 milligram
every 3 days until your seizures are controlled or the side effects become too
bothersome. The most you should take in 1 day is 20 milligrams.

CHILDREN

The starting dose for infants and children up to 10 years old or up to 66
pounds should be 0.01 to 0.03 milligram—no more than 0.05 milligram—per 2.2 pounds of body weight daily. The daily dosage should be
given in 2 or 3 smaller doses. Your doctor may increase the dose by 0.25 to
0.5 milligram every 3 days until seizures are controlled or side effects
become too bad. If the dose cannot be divided into 3 equal doses, the largest
dose should be given at bedtime. The maximum maintenance dose is 0.1 to
0.2 milligram per 2.2 pounds daily.

Overdosage
Any medication taken in excess can have serious consequences. If you suspect an overdose, seek medical attention immediately.

■ *The symptoms of Klonopin overdose may include:*
Coma
Confusion
Sleepiness
Slowed reaction time

Brand name:

KLOR-CON

See Micro-K, page 658.

Brand name:

KWELL

Pronounced: QUELL
Generic name: Lindane

Why is this drug prescribed?
Kwell cream and lotion are used to treat scabies, a contagious skin disease caused by an almost invisible organism known as the "itch mite." Kwell shampoo is used to treat people with head lice and pubic (crab) lice and their eggs.

Most important fact about this drug
Use Kwell only as directed by your doctor. Using too much or applying it more often than directed can result in seizures or even death, particularly in the young. Read the "Instructions to Patients" information sheet accompanying the Kwell package before using. If you have any questions, call your doctor.

How should you use this medication?

CREAM AND LOTION

Shake the lotion well before using. Apply cream or lotion in a thin layer to dry skin, starting from the neck and working down, including the soles of your feet (unless otherwise directed by your doctor), and rub in thoroughly. Trim your nails and apply the medication under the nails with a toothbrush, then throw the toothbrush away. If you take a warm bath or shower before using Kwell, dry your skin thoroughly and let it cool completely before applying the medication. Leave the cream or lotion on for no less than 8 and no more than 12 hours (usually overnight), then take a shower or bath to wash it off thoroughly. Apply only once, and use only enough to cover the body in a thin layer.

SHAMPOO

Before applying Kwell shampoo, wash your hair with regular shampoo, without conditioners, then rinse it and dry it completely. Shake the shampoo well, then apply directly to dry hair, without adding water. Work thoroughly into your hair and leave it on for 4 minutes. After 4 minutes, add a little water until you have a good lather. Immediately rinse all the lather away. Do not let the lather touch any other part of the body any more than necessary. Towel-dry your hair. Remove nits (eggs) with a nit comb or tweezers. If you are using Kwell on another person, try to keep it off your skin as much as possible. If you are using Kwell on more than one person, wear rubber gloves (this applies especially to pregnant women and nursing mothers).

■ *If you miss a dose...*
Use Kwell only once per infection. Multiple applications are dangerous.

■ *Storage instructions...*
Store away from heat and direct light. Keep out of the reach of children.

What side effects may occur?
Side effects are extremely rare, but can be serious. If any develop, contact your doctor as soon as possible.

■ *Side effects may include:*
Convulsions
Dizziness
Seizures
Skin eruptions
Skin rash

Why should this drug not be prescribed?
If you are sensitive to or have ever had an allergic reaction to Kwell or any of its ingredients, do not use it again. Do not use Kwell on premature infants; their skin is more sensitive and more drug could be absorbed into the body. Do not use Kwell if you have any kind of seizure disorder; and do not use the cream or lotion for Norwegian scabies (an extremely contagious skin disease with a thin, flaky, rash).

Special warnings about this medication

Be careful to avoid contact with your eyes. If any Kwell does get in your eyes, immediately flush them with cold water; if they become irritated or you have an allergic reaction, call your doctor.

Do not swallow Kwell. If you accidentally swallow any, call your doctor or your local poison control center immediately. Do not allow your child to apply Kwell without close adult supervision.

Be sure to cover an infant's hands and feet during treatment with Kwell cream or lotion to prevent the child from sucking or licking the medication.

Do not use Kwell on open wounds such as cuts or sores unless directed by your doctor. After one application of Kwell cream or lotion, your itching may continue for several weeks. The itching is quite normal and does not require a reapplication of Kwell. You will not usually need a second treatment with Kwell shampoo, but if you find living lice in your hair 7 days after treatment, call your doctor. You may need retreatment.

Wash all recently worn clothing, underwear and pajamas, used sheets, pillow cases, and towels in very hot water or have them dry cleaned.

Use Kwell cream or lotion cautiously on young children and the elderly because their skin may absorb more of the medication. To avoid reinfection, make sure that any sexual partners are treated at the same time that you are. Kwell cannot be used to prevent scabies or lice, since no effects remain after it has been washed off.

Possible food and drug interactions
when taking this medication

Oils may cause more Kwell to be absorbed through the skin into the body, possibly causing serious side effects. Therefore, do not use oils, creams, or ointments at the same time you are using Kwell cream or lotion and do not use oil treatments or oil-based hair dressings or conditioners immediately before and after you apply Kwell shampoo.

Special information
if you are pregnant or breastfeeding

If you are pregnant, follow your doctor's directions carefully. Do not use more Kwell than your doctor recommends, and do not use it more than twice during your pregnancy.

If you are breastfeeding, be sure to check with your doctor before using Kwell. Small amounts pass into breast milk, so even though Kwell has not been found to cause problems in nursing infants, your doctor may have you give up breast feeding for 4 days after using Kwell.

Recommended dosage

CREAM AND LOTION

Adults and Children Aged 6 and Over
Use 1 to 2 ounces. Apply only once; and do not leave on for more than 12 hours.

Children Under Age 6
Use 1 ounce (half of a 2-ounce container). Apply only once.

SHAMPOO

Use 1 ounce (½ bottle) for short hair, 1½ ounces (¾ bottle) for medium-length hair, and 2 ounces (1 bottle) for long hair. Do not use more than 2 ounces.

Overdosage

Any medication used in excess can have serious consequences. If you suspect an overdose, seek medical attention immediately.

■ *Symptoms of Kwell overdose may include:*
Convulsions
Dizziness

Generic name:

LABETALOL

See Normodyne, page 750.

Generic name:

LACTULOSE

See Chronulac Syrup, page 194.

Brand name:

LAMICTAL

Pronounced: LAM-ic-tal
Generic name: Lamotrigine

Why is this drug prescribed?
Lamictal is prescribed to control partial seizures in people with epilepsy. It is used in combination with other antiepileptic medications such as Tegretol and Depakene.

Most important fact about this drug
You may develop a rash during the first 4 to 6 weeks of Lamictal therapy, particularly if you are also taking Depakene. If this happens, notify your doctor immediately. The rash could become severe and even dangerous.

How should you take this medication?
Take Lamictal exactly as prescribed by your doctor. Do not stop taking this medication without first discussing it with your doctor. An abrupt halt could increase your seizures. Your doctor can schedule a gradual reduction in dosage.

■ *If you miss a dose...*
Take it as soon as you remember. If it is almost time for your next dose, skip the one you missed and go back to your regular schedule. Do not take 2 doses at once.

■ *Storage instructions...*
Store in a tightly closed container at room temperature. Keep dry and protect from light.

What side effects may occur?
Side effects cannot be anticipated. If any develop or change in intensity, tell your doctor as soon as possible. Only your doctor can determine if it is safe for you to continue taking Lamictal.

■ *More common side effects may include:*
Blurred vision, dizziness, double vision, headache, nausea, rash, sleepiness, uncoordinated movements, vomiting

■ *Less common side effects may include:*
Abdominal pain, accidental injury, anxiety, constipation, depression, diarrhea, fever, "flu-like" symptoms, increased cough, inflammation of vagina, irritability, painful menstruation, sore throat, tremor

■ *Rare side effects may include:*
Absence of menstrual periods, chills, confusion, dry mouth, ear pain, emotional changes, heart palpitations, hot flashes, joint disorders, memory

decrease, mind racing, muscle weakness, muscle spasm, poor concentration, ringing in ears, sleep disorder, speech disorder

Why should this drug not be prescribed?
If you are sensitive to or have ever had an allergic reaction to Lamictal, you should not take this medication. Make sure your doctor is aware of any drug reactions you have experienced.

Special warnings about this medication
Lamictal may cause some people to become drowsy, dizzy, or less alert. Do not drive or operate dangerous machinery or participate in any activity that requires full mental alertness until you are certain the drug does not have this kind of effect on you. Remember to be alert for development of any type of rash, especially during the first 4 to 6 weeks of treatment.

Be sure to tell your doctor about any medical problems you have before starting therapy with Lamictal. If you have kidney or liver disease, or heart problems, Lamictal should be used with caution.

Lamictal may cause vision problems. If any develop, notify your doctor immediately. Also be sure to call your doctor if you find you have less control over your seizures.

Possible food and drug interactions when taking this medication
Lamictal is not used alone; it is combined with other medications used to treat epilepsy, including the following:

Carbamazepine (Tegretol)
Phenobarbital (Donnatal, Quadrinal, others)
Phenytoin (Dilantin)
Primidone (Mysoline)
Valproic acid (Depakene)

Be sure to check with your doctor before combining any other drugs with your seizure medications. Lamictal, in particular, may inhibit the action of sulfa drugs such as Bactrim, Prolorim, and Septra.

Special information if you are pregnant or breastfeeding
The effects of Lamictal during pregnancy have not been adequately studied. If you are pregnant or plan to become pregnant, tell your doctor immediately. Lamictal should be used during pregnancy only if clearly needed. Lamictal

appears in breast milk. Because the effects of Lamictal on an infant exposed to this medication are unknown, breastfeeding is not recommended.

Recommended dosage

ADULTS

Lamictal combined with Tegretol, Dilantin, Phenobarbital, and Mysoline:

One 50-milligram dose per day for 2 weeks, then two 50-milligram doses per day for 2 weeks. After that, your doctor will have you take a total of 300 milligrams to 500 milligrams a day, divided into 2 doses.

Lamictal combined with Depakene and any of the above medications:

One 25-milligram dose every other day for 2 weeks, then 25 milligrams once a day for 2 weeks. After that, the doctor will prescribe a total of 100 milligrams to 150 milligrams a day, divided into 2 doses. You should not take more than 25 milligrams every other day because of the increased risk of rash with this combination of drugs.

CHILDREN

Safety and effectiveness of Lamictal in children below the age of 16 have not been studied.

Overdosage

Any medication taken in excess can have serious consequences. If you suspect an overdose, seek medical treatment immediately. There has been little experience with Lamictal overdose. However, the following symptoms might be seen.

- *Symptoms of Lamictal overdose may include:*
  Coma
  Dizziness
  Headache
  Sleepiness

Generic name:

LAMOTRIGINE

See Lamictal, page 552.

Brand name:

LANOXIN

Pronounced: la-NOCKS-in
Generic name: Digoxin

Why is this drug prescribed?
Lanoxin is used in the treatment of congestive heart failure, irregular heartbeat, and other heart problems. It improves the strength and efficiency of your heart, which leads to better circulation of blood and reduction of the uncomfortable swelling that is common in people with congestive heart failure. Lanoxin is in a class of drugs known as cardiac glycosides.

Most important fact about this drug
You should not stop taking Lanoxin without first consulting your doctor. A sudden absence of the drug could cause a serious change in your heart function. You will probably have to take Lanoxin for a long time—possibly for the rest of your life.

How should you take this medication?
Lanoxin usually is taken once daily. To help you remember your dose, try to take it at the same time every day—for instance, when brushing your teeth in the morning or going to bed at night.

If you are taking the liquid form of Lanoxin, use the specially marked dropper that comes with it.

It's best to take this medicine on an empty stomach. However, if this upsets your stomach, you can take Lanoxin with food.

Avoid taking this medicine with high-bran/high-fiber foods, such as certain breakfast cereals.

Do not change from one brand of this drug to another without first consulting your doctor or pharmacist.

Your doctor may ask you to check your pulse rate while taking Lanoxin. Slowing or quickening of your pulse could mean you are developing side effects to your prescribed dose. The amount of Lanoxin needed to help most people is very close to the amount that could cause serious problems from overdose, so monitoring your pulse can be very important.

■ *If you miss a dose...*
  If you remember within 12 hours, take it immediately. If you remember later, skip the dose you missed and go back to your regular schedule.

Never take 2 doses at the same time. If you miss doses 2 or more days in a row, consult your doctor.

■ *Storage instructions...*
Store this medication at room temperature in the container it came in, tightly closed, and away from moist places and direct light. Keep out of reach of children. Digitalis is a major cause of accidental poisoning in the young.

What side effects may occur?
Side effects cannot be anticipated. If any develop or change in intensity, inform your doctor as soon as possible. Only your doctor can determine if it is safe for you to continue taking Lanoxin.

■ *Side effects may include:*
Apathy, blurred vision, breast development in males, change in heartbeat, diarrhea, dizziness, headache, loss of appetite, lower stomach pain, nausea, psychosis, rash, vomiting, weakness, yellow vision

Why should this drug not be prescribed?
If you are sensitive to or have ever had an allergic reaction to Lanoxin or other digitalis preparations, you should not take this medication. Make sure your doctor is aware of any drug reactions you have experienced.

Lanoxin should not be taken by people with the heart irregularity known as ventricular fibrillation.

Lanoxin should not be used, alone or with other drugs, for weight reduction. It can cause irregular heartbeat and other dangerous, even fatal, reactions.

Special warnings about this medication
Tell the doctor that you are taking Lanoxin if you have a medical emergency and before you have surgery or dental treatment.

Even if you have no symptoms, do not change your dose or discontinue the use of Lanoxin before consulting with your doctor.

Possible food and drug interactions when taking this medication
In general, you should avoid nonprescription medicines, such as antacids; laxatives; cough, cold, and allergy remedies; and diet aids, except on professional advice.

If Lanoxin is taken with certain other drugs, the effects of either can be increased, decreased, or altered. It is especially important to check with your doctor before combining Lanoxin with the following:

Airway-opening drugs such as Proventil and Ventolin
Alprazolam (Xanax)
Amiloride (Midamor)
Amiodarone (Cordarone)
Antacids such as Maalox and Mylanta
Antiarrhythmic drugs such as Quinidex
Antibiotics such as neomycin and tetracycline
Beta-blocking blood pressure drugs such as Tenormin and Inderal
Calcium (injectable form)
Calcium-blocking blood pressure drugs such as Calan SR, Cardizem, and Procardia
Certain anticancer drugs such as Neosar
Cholestyramine (Questran)
Colestipol (Colestid)
Cyclosporine (Sandimmune)
Diphenoxylate (Lomotil)
Disopyramide (Norpace)
Diuretics such as Lasix
Indomethacin (Indocin)
Itraconazole (Sporanox)
Kaolin-pectin
Metoclopramide (Reglan)
Propafenone (Rythmol)
Propantheline (Pro-Banthine)
Rifampin (Rifadin)
Steroids such as Decadron and Deltasone
Succinylcholine (Anectine)
Sucralfate (Carafate)
Sulfasalazine (Azulfidine)
Thyroid hormones such as Synthroid

Special information
if you are pregnant or breastfeeding
The effects of Lanoxin during pregnancy have not been adequately studied. If you are pregnant or plan to become pregnant, inform your doctor immediately. Lanoxin appears in breast milk and could affect a nursing infant. If this medication is essential to your health, your doctor may advise you to discontinue breastfeeding.

Recommended dosage

Your doctor will determine your dosage based on several factors: (1) the disease being treated; (2) your body weight; (3) your kidney function; (4) your age; and (5) other diseases you have or drugs you are taking.

ADULTS

If you are receiving Lanoxin for the first time, you may be rapidly "digitalized" (a larger first dose may be taken, followed by smaller maintenance doses), or gradually "digitalized" (maintenance doses only), depending on your doctor's recommendation. A typical maintenance dose might be a 0.125-milligram or 0.25-milligram tablet once daily, but individual requirements vary widely. The exact dose will be determined by your doctor, based on your needs.

CHILDREN

Infants and young children usually have their daily dose divided into smaller doses; children over age 10 need adult dosages in proportion to body weight as determined by your doctor.

Overdosage

Suspected overdoses of Lanoxin must be treated immediately; you should contact your doctor or emergency room without delay.

■ *Symptoms of Lanoxin overdose include:*
Abdominal pain
Diarrhea
Irregular heartbeat
Loss of appetite
Nausea
Very slow pulse
Vomiting

In infants and children, irregular heartbeat is the most common sign of overdose.

Brand name:

LASIX

Pronounced: LAY-six
Generic name: Furosemide

Why is this drug prescribed?

Lasix is used in the treatment of high blood pressure and other conditions that require the elimination of excess fluid (water) from the body. These conditions include congestive heart failure, cirrhosis of the liver, and kidney disease. When used to treat high blood pressure, Lasix is effective alone or in combination with other high blood pressure medications. Diuretics help your body produce and eliminate more urine, which helps lower blood pressure. Lasix is classified as a "loop diuretic" because of its point of action in the kidneys.

Most important fact about this drug

Lasix acts quickly, usually within 1 hour. However, since blood pressure declines gradually, it may be several weeks before you get the full benefit of Lasix; and you must continue taking it even if you are feeling well. Lasix does not cure high blood pressure; it merely keeps it under control.

How should you take this medication?

Take this medication exactly as prescribed by your doctor.

■ *If you miss a dose...*
Take the forgotten dose as soon as you remember. If it is almost time for your next dose, skip the one you missed and go back to your regular schedule. Never take two doses at the same time.

■ *Storage instructions...*
Keep this medication in the container it came in, tightly closed, and away from moist places and direct light. Store Lasix tablets at room temperature. Store the oral solution in the refrigerator; discard an open bottle after 60 days.

What side effects may occur?

Side effects cannot be anticipated. If any develop or change in intensity, inform your doctor as soon as possible. Only your doctor can determine if it is safe for you to continue taking Lasix.

■ *Side effects may include:*
Anemia, blood disorders, blurred vision, constipation, cramping, diarrhea, dizziness, dizziness upon standing, fever, headache, hearing loss, high blood sugar, hives, itching, loss of appetite, low potassium (leading to symptoms like dry mouth, excessive thirst, weak or irregular heartbeat, muscle pain or cramps), muscle spasms, nausea, rash, reddish or purplish spots on the skin, restlessness, ringing in the ears, sensitivity to light,

skin eruptions, skin inflammation and flaking, stomach or mouth irritation, tingling or pins and needles, vertigo, vision changes, vomiting, weakness, yellow eyes and skin

Why should this drug not be prescribed?

If you are sensitive to or have ever had an allergic reaction to Lasix or diuretics, or if you are unable to urinate, you should not take this medication.

Special warnings about this medication

Lasix can cause your body to lose too much potassium. Signs of an excessively low potassium level include muscle weakness and rapid or irregular heartbeat. To improve your potassium level, your doctor may prescribe a potassium supplement or recommend potassium-rich foods, such as bananas, prunes, raisins, orange juice, and whole and skim milk.

Make sure the doctor knows if you have kidney disease, liver disease, diabetes, gout, or the connective tissue disease lupus erythematosus. Lasix should be used with caution.

If you are allergic to sulfa drugs, you may also be allergic to Lasix.

If you have high blood pressure, avoid over-the-counter medications that may increase blood pressure, including cold remedies and appetite suppressants.

Your skin may be more sensitive to the effects of sunlight.

Possible food and drug interactions
when taking this medication

If Lasix is taken with certain other drugs, the effects of either could be increased, decreased, or altered. It is especially important to consult with your doctor before taking Lasix with any of the following:

Aminoglycoside antibiotics such as Garamycin
Aspirin
Barbiturates such as phenobarbital
Ethacrynic acid (Edecrin)
Indomethacin (Indocin)
Lithium (Lithonate)
The muscle-relaxing drug Tubocurarine
Narcotics such as Darvon and Percocet
Nonsteroidal anti-inflammatory drugs such as Advil and Naprosyn
Norepinephrine (Levophed)
Other high blood pressure medications such as Vasotec and Aldomet
Succinylcholine (Anectine)
Sucralfate (Carafate)

**Special information
if you are pregnant or breastfeeding**
The effects of Lasix during pregnancy have not been adequately studied. If you are pregnant or plan to become pregnant, inform your doctor immediately. Lasix appears in breast milk and could affect a nursing infant. If this medication is essential to your health, your doctor may advise you to discontinue breastfeeding until your treatment is finished.

Recommended dosage
Your doctor will adjust the dosages of this medication, which is a strong diuretic, to meet your specific needs. It is available in both oral and injectable form. The injectable form is used only in emergency situations or in cases where patients cannot take oral medication. Dosages shown here are for oral tablets or solution only.

ADULTS

Edema Fluid Retention
You will be started at a single dose of 20 to 80 milligrams. If needed, the same dose can be repeated 6 to 8 hours later. Your doctor may raise the dosage by 20 milligrams or 40 milligrams with each successive administration— each 6 to 8 hours after the previous dose—until the desired effect is achieved. This dosage is then taken once or twice daily thereafter. Your doctor will monitor you carefully using laboratory tests. The maximum daily dose is 600 milligrams.

High Blood Pressure
The usual starting dose is 80 milligrams per day divided into 2 doses. Your doctor will adjust the dosages and may add other high blood pressure medications if Lasix is not enough.

CHILDREN

The usual initial dose is 2 milligrams per 2.2 pounds of body weight. The doctor may increase subsequent doses by 1 to 2 milligrams per 2.2 pounds. Doses are spaced 6 to 8 hours apart. A child's dosage will be adjusted to the lowest needed to achieve maximum effect, and should not exceed 6 milligrams per 2.2 pounds.

ELDERLY

The doctor will determine the dosage based on the particular needs of the individual.

Overdosage

Any medication taken in excess can cause symptoms of overdose. If you suspect an overdose, seek medical attention immediately.

- *The symptoms of Lasix overdose may include:*
 Dehydration
 Dry mouth
 Excessive thirst
 Low blood pressure
 Muscle pain or cramps
 Weak or irregular heartbeat

Brand name:

LESCOL

Pronounced: LESS-cahl
Generic name: Fluvastatin sodium

Why is this drug prescribed?

Lescol is a cholesterol-lowering drug. Your doctor may prescribe Lescol if you have been unable to reduce your blood cholesterol level sufficiently with a low-fat, low-cholesterol diet alone.

Most important fact about this drug

Lescol is usually prescribed only if diet, exercise, and weight loss fail to bring your cholesterol levels under control. It's important to remember that Lescol is a supplement—not a substitute—for those other measures. To get the full benefit of the medication, you need to stick to the diet and exercise program prescribed by your doctor. All these efforts to keep your cholesterol levels normal are important because together they may lower your risk of heart disease.

How should you take this medication?

Take Lescol at bedtime; you may take it with or without food.

- *If you miss a dose...*
 If you miss a dose of this medication, take it as soon as you remember. However, if it is almost time for your next dose, skip the one you missed and go back to your regular schedule. Do not take 2 doses at the same time.

- *Storage instructions...*
 Store at room temperature. Protect from direct light and excessive heat. Keep out of reach of children.

What side effects may occur?
Side effects cannot be anticipated. If any develop or change in intensity, tell your doctor as soon as possible. Only your doctor can determine if it is safe for you to continue taking Lescol.

- *More common side effects may include:*
  Abdominal pain, accidental injury, back pain, diarrhea, fatigue, flu-like symptoms, headache, indigestion, joint disease, muscle pain, nasal inflammation, nausea, sour throat, upper respiratory infection

- *Less common side effects may include:*
  Allergy, bronchitis, constipation, coughing, dizziness, dental problems, gas, inflamed sinuses, insomnia, rash

Why should this drug not be prescribed?
Do not take Lescol while pregnant or nursing. Also avoid Lescol if you are experiencing liver problems, or if you have ever been found to be sensitive to it.

Special warnings about this medication
Because Lescol may damage the liver, your doctor may order a blood test to check your liver enzyme levels before you start taking this medication. Blood tests will probably be done at 6 and 12 weeks after you start Lescol therapy and periodically after that. If your liver enzymes rise too high, your doctor may tell you to stop taking Lescol. Your doctor will monitor you especially closely if you have ever had liver disease or if you are, or have ever been, a heavy drinker.

Since Lescol may cause damage to muscle tissue, be sure to tell your doctor of any unexplained muscle pain, tenderness, or weakness right away, especially if you also have a fever or feel sick. Your doctor may want to do a blood test to check for signs of muscle damage. If your blood test shows signs of muscle damage, your doctor may suggest discontinuing this medication.

If your risk of muscle and/or kidney damage suddenly increases because of major surgery or injury, or conditions such as low blood pressure, severe infection, or seizures, your doctor may tell you to stop taking Lescol for a while.

Be sure to tell your doctor about any medical conditions you may have before starting therapy with Lescol.

Possible food and drug interactions when taking this medication

If you take Lescol with certain drugs, the effects of either could be increased, decreased, or altered. It is especially important to check with your doctor before combining Lescol with the following:

Cholestyramine (Questran)
Cimetidine (Tagamet)
Clofibrate (Atromid-S)
Cyclosporine (Sandimmune)
Digoxin (Lanoxin, Lanoxicaps)
Erythromycin (E-Mycin, E.E.S.)
Gemfibrozil (Lopid)
Ketoconazole (Nizoral)
Omeprazole (Prilosec)
Ranitidine (Zantac)
Rifampin (Rifadin)
Spironolactone (Aldactone, Aldactazide)

Special information if you are pregnant or breastfeeding

You must not become pregnant while taking Lescol. This medication lowers cholesterol, and cholesterol is needed for a baby to develop properly. Because of the possible risk of birth defects, your doctor will prescribe Lescol only if you are highly unlikely to get pregnant while taking this medication. If you do become pregnant while taking Lescol, stop taking the drug and notify your doctor right away.

Lescol does appear in breast milk. Therefore, Lescol could cause severe side effects in a nursing baby. Do not take Lescol while breastfeeding your baby.

Recommended dosage

Your doctor will put you on a cholesterol-lowering diet before starting treatment with Lescol. You should continue on this diet while you are taking Lescol.

ADULTS

The usual starting dose is 20 milligrams per day, taken as a single dose at bedtime. The usual range after that is 20 to 40 milligrams per day as a single dose at bedtime. After 4 weeks of therapy with Lescol, your doctor will check your cholesterol level and adjust your dosage if necessary.

Combined Drug Therapy
If you are taking Lescol with another cholesterol medication such as Questran, make sure you take the other drug at least 2 hours before your dose of Lescol.

CHILDREN

The safety and effectiveness of Lescol in children under 18 years old have not been established. Do not give Lescol to children under 18 years of age.

Overdosage
Although no specific information about Lescol overdose is available, any medication taken in excess can have serious consequences. If you suspect an overdose of Lescol, seek medical attention immediately.

Brand name:

LEVLEN

See Oral Contraceptives, page 775.

Generic name:

LEVOBUNOLOL

See Betagan, page 124.

Brand name:

LEVOTHROID

See Synthroid, page 1059.

Generic name:

LEVOTHYROXINE

See Synthroid, page 1059.

Brand name:

LEVOXYL

See Synthroid, page 1059.

Brand name:

LEVSIN

Pronounced: LEV-sin
Generic name: Hyoscyamine sulfate
Other brand name: Anaspaz

Why is this drug prescribed?

Levsin is an antispasmodic medication given to help treat various stomach, intestinal, and urinary tract disorders that involve cramps, colic, or other painful muscle contractions. Because Levsin has a drying effect, it may also be used to dry a runny nose or to dry excess secretions before anesthesia is administered.

For inflammation of the pancreas, Levsin may be used to help control excess secretions and reduce pain. Levsin may also be taken in Parkinson's disease to help reduce muscle rigidity and tremors and to help control drooling and excess sweating.

Doctors also give Levsin as part of the preparation for certain diagnostic x-rays (for example, of the stomach, intestines, or kidneys).

Levsin comes in several forms, including regular tablets, tablets to be dissolved under the tongue, sustained-release capsules, liquid, drops, and an injectable solution.

Most important fact about this drug

Levsin may make you sweat less, causing your body temperature to increase and putting you at the risk of heatstroke. Try to stay inside as much as possible on hot days, and avoid warm places such as very hot baths and saunas.

How should you take this medication?

If you take Levsin for a stomach disorder, you may also need to take antacid medication. However, antacids make Levsin more difficult for the body to absorb. To minimize this problem, take Levsin before meals and the antacids after meals.

Take Levsin exactly as prescribed. Although the sublingual tablets (Levsin/SL) are designed to be dissolved under the tongue, they may also be chewed or swallowed. The regular tablets may also be dissolved under the tongue or swallowed.

Levsin can cause dry mouth. For temporary relief, suck on a hard candy or chew gum.

- *If you miss a dose...*
  Take it as soon as you remember. If it is almost time for your next dose, skip the one you missed and go back to your regular schedule. Do not take 2 doses at once.

- *Storage instructions...*
  Store at room temperature.

What side effects may occur?
Side effects cannot be anticipated. If any side effects develop or change in intensity, tell your doctor immediately. Only your doctor can determine whether it is safe for you to continue taking Levsin.

- *Side effects may include:*
  Allergic reactions, bloating, blurred vision, confusion, constipation, decreased sweating, dilated pupils, dizziness, drowsiness, dry mouth, excitement, headache, hives, impotence, inability to urinate, insomnia, itching, heart palpitations, lack of coordination, loss of sense of taste, nausea, nervousness, rapid heartbeat, skin reactions, speech problems, vomiting, weakness

Why should this drug not be prescribed?
Do not take Levsin if you have ever had an allergic reaction to it or similar drugs such as scopolamine. Also, you should not be given Levsin if you have any of the following:

Bowel or digestive tract obstruction or paralysis
Glaucoma (excessive pressure in the eyes)
Myasthenia gravis (a disorder in which muscles become weak and tire easily)
Ulcerative colitis (severe bowel inflammation)
Urinary obstruction

Levsin is not appropriate if you have diarrhea, especially if you have a surgical opening to the bowels (an ileostomy or colostomy).

Special warnings about this medication
Be careful using Levsin if you have an overactive thyroid gland, heart disease, congestive heart failure, irregular heartbeats, high blood pressure, or kidney disease.

Because Levsin may make you dizzy or drowsy, or blur your vision, do not drive, operate other machinery, or do any other hazardous work while taking this medication.

While you are taking Levsin, you may experience confusion, disorientation, short-term memory loss, hallucinations, difficulty speaking, lack of coordination, coma, an exaggerated sense of well-being, decreased anxiety, fatigue, sleeplessness and agitation. These symptoms should disappear 12 to 48 hours after you stop taking the drug.

Possible food and drug interactions
when taking this medication

If Levsin is taken with certain other drugs, the effects of either drug could be increased, decreased, or altered. It is especially important to check with your doctor before combining Levsin with the following:

Amantadine (Symmetrel)
Antacids
Antidepressant drugs such as Elavil, Nardil, Parnate, and Tofranil
Antihistamines such as Benadryl
Major tranquilizers such as Thorazine and Haldol
Other antispasmodic drugs such as Bentyl
Potassium supplements such as Slow-K

Special information
if you are pregnant or breastfeeding

If you are pregnant or plan to become pregnant, inform your doctor immediately. Although it is not known whether Levsin can cause birth defects, pregnant women should avoid all drugs except those necessary to health.

Levsin appears in breast milk. Your doctor may ask you to forgo breastfeeding when taking this drug.

Recommended dosage

LEVSIN/SL AND LEVSIN TABLETS

The tablets may be swallowed or placed under the tongue. Levsin/SL tablets may also be chewed.

Adults and Children 12 Years of Age and Older

The usual dose is 1 to 2 tablets every 4 hours or as needed. Do not take more than 12 tablets in 24 hours.

Children 2 to Under 12 Years of Age

The usual dose is one-half to 1 tablet every 4 hours or as needed. Do not give a child more than 6 tablets in 24 hours.

LEVSIN ELIXIR

Adults and Children 12 Years of Age and Older

The recommended dosage is 1 to 2 teaspoonfuls every 4 hours or as needed, but no more than 12 teaspoonfuls in 24 hours.

Children 2 to 12 Years of Age

The usual dosage is one-quarter to 1 teaspoonful every 4 hours or as needed. Do not give a child more than 6 teaspoonfuls in 24 hours.

LEVSIN DROPS

Adults and Children 12 Years of Age and Older

The recommended dosage is 1 to 2 milliliters every 4 hours or as needed, but no more than 12 milliliters in 24 hours.

Children 2 to 12 Years of Age

The usual dosage is one-quarter to 1 milliliter every 4 hours or as needed. Do not give a child more than 6 milliliters in 24 hours.

Children Under 2 Years of Age

Your doctor will determine the dosage based on body weight. The doses may be repeated every 4 hours or as needed.

WEIGHT	USUAL DOSAGE	DO NOT EXCEED IN 24 HOURS
2.3 kilograms (5 lbs)	3 drops	18 drops
3.4 kilograms (7.5 lbs)	4 drops	24 drops
5 kilograms (11 lbs)	5 drops	30 drops
7 kilograms (15 lbs)	6 drops	36 drops
10 kilograms (22 lbs)	8 drops	48 drops
15 kilograms (33 lbs)	11 drops	66 drops

LEVSINEX TIMECAPS

Adults and Children 12 Years of Age and Older

The recommended dosage is 1 to 2 Timecaps every 12 hours. Your doctor may adjust the dosage to 1 Timecap every 8 hours if needed. Do not take more than 4 Timecaps in 24 hours.

Children 2 to 12 Years of Age

The usual dosage is 1 Timecap every 12 hours. Do not give a child more than 2 Timecaps in 24 hours.

Overdosage

Any medication taken in excess can have serious consequences. If you suspect an overdose, seek medical attention immediately.

- *Symptoms of Levsin overdose may include:*
  Blurred vision
  Dilated pupils
  Dizziness
  Dry mouth
  Excitement
  Headache
  Hot, dry skin
  Nausea
  Swallowing difficulty
  Vomiting

Brand name:

LIBRAX

Pronounced: LIB-racks
Generic ingredients: Chlordiazepoxide hydrochloride,
   Clidinium bromide
Other brand name: Clindex

Why is this drug prescribed?

Librax is used, in combination with other therapy, for the treatment of peptic ulcer, irritable bowel syndrome (spastic colon), and acute enterocolitis (inflammation of the colon and small intestine). Librax is a combination of a benzodiazepine (chlordiazepoxide) and an antispasmodic medication (clidinium).

Most important fact about this drug
Because of its sedative effects, you should not operate heavy machinery, drive, or engage in other hazardous tasks that require you to be mentally alert while you are taking Librax.

How should you take this medication?
Take Librax as directed by your doctor. Other therapy may be prescribed to be used at the same time.

Librax can make your mouth dry. For temporary relief, suck a hard candy or chew gum.

Take Librax before meals and at bedtime.

■ *If you miss a dose...*
Take it as soon as you remember. If it is almost time for your next dose, skip the one you missed and go back to your regular schedule. Do not take 2 doses at once.

■ *Storage instructions...*
Store away from heat, light, and moisture.

What side effects may occur?
Side effects cannot be anticipated. If any develop or change in intensity, inform your doctor as soon as possible. Only your doctor can determine if it is safe for you to continue taking Librax.

■ *Side effects may include:*
Blurred vision, changes in sex drive, confusion, constipation, drowsiness, dry mouth, fainting, lack of coordination, liver problems, minor menstrual irregularities, nausea, skin eruptions, swelling due to fluid retention, urinary difficulties, yellowing of skin and eyes

Why should this drug not be prescribed?
You should not take this drug if you have glaucoma (elevated pressure in the eye), prostatic hypertrophy (enlarged prostate), or a bladder obstruction. If you are sensitive to or have ever had an allergic reaction to Librax or any of its ingredients, you should not take this medication. Make sure your doctor is aware of any drug reactions you have experienced.

Special warnings about this medication
Librax can be habit-forming and has been associated with drug dependence and addiction. Be very careful taking this medication if you have ever had problems with alcohol or drug abuse. Never take more than the prescribed amount.

In addition, you should not stop taking Librax suddenly, because of the risk of withdrawal symptoms (convulsions, cramps, tremors, vomiting, sweating, feeling depressed, and insomnia). If you have been taking Librax over a long period of time, your doctor will have you taper off gradually.

The elderly are more likely to develop side effects such as confusion, excessive drowsiness, and uncoordinated movements when taking Librax. The doctor will probably prescribe a low dose.

Long-term treatment with Librax may call for periodic blood and liver function tests.

Possible food and drug interactions
when taking this medication
If Librax is taken with certain other drugs, the effects of either can be increased, decreased, or altered. It is especially important to check with your doctor before combining Librax with the following:

Antidepressant drugs known as MAO inhibitors, such as Nardil and Parnate
Blood-thinning drugs such as Coumadin
Certain diarrhea medications such as Donnagel and Kaopectate
Ketoconazole (Nizoral)
Major tranquilizers such as Stelazine and Thorazine
Potassium supplements such as Micro-K

In addition, you may experience excessive drowsiness and other potentially dangerous side effects if you combine Librax with alcohol or other drugs, such as Benadryl and Valium, that make you drowsy.

Special information
if you are pregnant or breastfeeding
Several studies have found an increased risk of birth defects if Librax is taken during the first 3 months of pregnancy. Therefore, Librax is rarely recommended for use by pregnant women. If you are pregnant, plan to become pregnant, or are breastfeeding, inform your doctor immediately.

Recommended dosage

ADULTS

The usual dose is 1 or 2 capsules, 3 or 4 times a day before meals and at bedtime.

ELDERLY

Your doctor will have you take the lowest dose that is effective.

Overdosage

Any medication taken in excess can have serious consequences. A severe overdose of Librax can be fatal. If you suspect an overdose, seek medical help immediately.

- *Symptoms of Librax overdose may include:*
  Blurred vision
  Coma
  Confusion
  Constipation
  Excessive sleepiness
  Excessively dry mouth
  Slow reflexes
  Urinary difficulties

Brand name:

LIBRITABS

See Librium, page 574.

Brand name:

LIBRIUM

Pronounced: LIB-ree-um
Generic name: Chlordiazepoxide
Other brand name: Libritabs

Why is this drug prescribed?

Librium is used in the treatment of anxiety disorders. It is also prescribed for short-term relief of the symptoms of anxiety, symptoms of withdrawal in acute alcoholism, and anxiety and apprehension before surgery. It belongs to a class of drugs known as benzodiazepines.

Most important fact about this drug

Librium is habit-forming and you can become dependent on it. You could experience withdrawal symptoms if you stopped taking it abruptly (see "What side effects may occur?"). Discontinue or change your dose only on advice of your doctor.

How should you take this medication?

Take this medication exactly as prescribed.

■ *If you miss a dose...*
Take it as soon as you remember if it is within an hour or so of your scheduled time. If you do not remember until later, skip the dose you missed and go back to your regular schedule. Do not take 2 doses at once.

■ *Storage instructions...*
Store away from heat, light, and moisture.

What side effects may occur?
Side effects cannot be anticipated. If any develop or change in intensity, inform your doctor as soon as possible. Only your doctor can determine if it is safe for you to continue taking Librium.

■ *Side effects may include:*
Confusion, constipation, drowsiness, fainting, increased or decreased sex drive, liver problems, lack of muscle coordination, minor menstrual irregularities, nausea, skin rash or eruptions, swelling due to fluid retention, yellow eyes and skin

■ *Side effects due to rapid decrease or abrupt withdrawal from Librium include:*
Abdominal and muscle cramps
Convulsions
Exaggerated feeling of depression
Sleeplessness
Sweating
Tremors
Vomiting

Why should this drug not be prescribed?
If you are sensitive to or have ever had an allergic reaction to Librium or similar tranquilizers, you should not take this medication.

Anxiety or tension related to everyday stress usually does not require treatment with Librium. Discuss your symptoms thoroughly with your doctor.

Special warnings about this medication
Librium may cause you to become drowsy or less alert; therefore, you should not drive or operate dangerous machinery or participate in any hazardous activity that requires full mental alertness until you know how you react to this drug.

If you are severely depressed or have suffered from severe depression, consult with your doctor before taking this medication.

This drug may cause children to become less alert.

If you have a hyperactive, aggressive child taking Librium, inform your doctor if you notice contrary reactions such as excitement, stimulation, or acute rage.

Consult with your doctor before taking Librium if you are being treated for porphyria (a rare metabolic disorder) or kidney or liver disease.

Possible food and drug interactions
when taking this medication

Librium is a central nervous system depressant and may intensify the effects of alcohol or have an additive effect. Do not drink alcohol while taking this medication.

If Librium is taken with certain other drugs, the effects of either can be increased, decreased, or altered. It is especially important to check with your doctor before combining Librium with the following:

Antacids such as Maalox and Mylanta
Antidepressant drugs known as MAO inhibitors, including Nardil and
    Parnate
Barbiturates such as phenobarbital
Blood-thinning drugs such as Coumadin
Cimetidine (Tagamet)
Disulfiram (Antabuse)
Levodopa (Laradopa)
Major tranquilizers such as Stelazine and Thorazine
Narcotic pain relievers such as Demerol and Percocet
Oral contraceptives

Special information
if you are pregnant or breastfeeding

Do not take Librium if you are pregnant or planning to become pregnant. There may be an increased risk of birth defects. This drug may appear in breast milk and could affect a nursing infant. If the medication is essential to your health, your doctor may advise you to discontinue breastfeeding until your treatment with the drug is finished.

Recommended dosage

ADULTS

Mild or Moderate Anxiety
The usual dose is 5 or 10 milligrams, 3 or 4 times a day.

Severe Anxiety
The usual dose is 20 to 25 milligrams, 3 or 4 times a day.

Apprehension and Anxiety before Surgery
On days preceding surgery, the usual dose is 5 to 10 milligrams, 3 or 4 times a day.

Withdrawal Symptoms of Acute Alcoholism
The usual starting oral dose is 50 to 100 milligrams; the doctor will repeat this dose, up to a maximum of 300 milligrams per day, until agitation is controlled. The dose will then be reduced as much as possible.

CHILDREN

The usual dose for children 6 years of age and older is 5 milligrams, 2 to 4 times per day. Some children may need to take 10 milligrams, 2 or 3 times per day. The drug is not recommended for children under 6.

ELDERLY

Your doctor will limit the dose to the smallest effective amount in order to avoid oversedation or lack of coordination. The usual dose is 5 milligrams, 2 to 4 times per day.

Overdosage

Any medication taken in excess can cause symptoms of overdose. If you suspect an overdose, seek medical attention immediately.

■ *The symptoms of Librium overdose may include:*
Coma
Confusion
Slow reflexes
Sleepiness

Brand name:

LIDEX

Pronounced: LYE-decks
Generic name: Fluocinonide
Other brand name: Dermacin

Why is this drug prescribed?
Lidex is a steroid medication that relieves the itching and inflammation of a wide variety of skin problems, including redness and swelling.

Most important fact about this drug
When you use Lidex, you inevitably absorb some of the medication through your skin and into the bloodstream. Too much absorption can lead to unwanted side effects elsewhere in the body. To keep this problem to a minimum, avoid using large amounts of Lidex over large areas, and do not cover it with airtight dressings such as plastic wrap or adhesive bandages unless specifically told to by your doctor.

How should you use this medication?
Lidex is for use only on the skin. Be careful to keep it out of your eyes. If the medication gets in your eyes and causes irritation, immediately flush your eyes with a large amount of water.

Apply Lidex as directed by your doctor. Do not use more of the medication than suggested by your doctor.

- *If you miss a dose...*
  Apply it as soon as you remember. If it is almost time for the next dose, skip the one you missed and go back to your regular schedule.

- *Storage instructions...*
  Store at room temperature. Avoid excessive heat.

What side effects may occur?
Side effects cannot be anticipated. If any develop or change in intensity, inform your doctor immediately. Only your doctor can determine if it is safe for you to continue using Lidex.

- *Side effects may include:*
  Acne-like eruptions, burning, dryness, excessive hair growth, infection of the skin, irritation, itching, lack of skin color, prickly heat, skin inflammation, skin loss or softening, stretch marks

Why should this drug not be prescribed?
You should not be using Lidex if you are allergic to any of its components.

Special warnings about this medication
Do not use Lidex more often or for a longer time than your doctor ordered. If enough of the drug is absorbed through the skin, it may produce unusual side effects, including increased sugar in your blood and urine and a group of symptoms called Cushing's syndrome, characterized by a moon-shaped face, emotional disturbances, high blood pressure, weight gain, and growth of body hair in women.

Some factors that may increase absorption include:

Using bandages over the area where the medication is applied;
Using the medication over a large area of skin or on broken skin; or
Using the medication for an extended period of time.

Children may absorb a proportionally greater amount of steroid drugs and may be more sensitive to the effects of these drugs. Avoid covering a treated area with waterproof diapers or plastic pants. They can increase absorption of Lidex.

- *Effects experienced by children may include:*
  Bulges on the head
  Delayed weight gain
  Headache
  Slow growth

Lidex should be discontinued if irritation develops, and another treatment should be used.

Extended treatment time with any steroid product may cause skin to waste away. This may also occur with short-term use on the face, armpits, and skin creases.

**Possible food and drug interactions
when taking this medication**
No interactions have been reported with Lidex.

**Special information
if you are pregnant or breastfeeding**
Pregnant women should not use steroids on the skin in large amounts or for long periods of time. During pregnancy, these medications should be used only if the possible gains outweigh the possible risks to the baby.

Steroids do appear in breast milk. Women who breastfeed an infant should use them cautiously.

Recommended dosage

ADULTS

Lidex is applied to the affected areas in a thin film 2 to 4 times a day. If hair covers the infected area, part the hair so that the medication can be applied directly.

CHILDREN

Children should be given the smallest effective dose.

Overdosage

Lidex can be absorbed in amounts large enough to have temporary effects on the adrenal, hypothalamic, and pituitary glands.

- *Some effects of steroid drugs may include:*
  Abnormal sugar levels in urine
  Excessive blood sugar levels
  Symptoms of Cushing's syndrome

- *Symptoms of Cushing's syndrome may include:*
  Easily bruised skin
  Increased blood pressure
  Mood swings
  Water retention
  Weak muscles
  Weight gain

If you suspect a Lidex overdose, seek medical help immediately.

Generic name:

LINDANE

See Kwell, page 549.

Generic name:

LISINOPRIL

See Zestril, page 1230.

Generic name:

LISINOPRIL WITH HYDROCHLOROTHIAZIDE

See Zestoretic, page 1226.

Generic name:

LITHIUM

See Lithonate, page 581.

Brand name:

LITHONATE

Pronounced: LITH-oh-nate
Generic name: Lithium carbonate
Other brand names: Cibalith-S (lithium citrate), Eskalith,
  Lithotabs

Why is this drug prescribed?

Lithonate is used to treat the manic episodes of manic-depressive illness, a condition in which a person's mood swings from depression to excessive excitement. A manic episode may involve some or all of the following symptoms:

  Aggressiveness
  Elation
  Fast, urgent talking
  Frenetic physical activity
  Grandiose, unrealistic ideas
  Hostility
  Little need for sleep
  Poor judgment

Once the mania subsides, Lithonate treatment may be continued over the long term, at a somewhat lower dosage, to prevent or reduce the intensity of future manic episodes.

Some doctors also prescribe lithium for premenstrual tension, eating disorders such as bulimia, certain movement disorders, and sexual addictions.

Most important fact about this drug

If the Lithonate dosage is too low, you will derive no benefit; if it is too high, you could suffer lithium poisoning. You and your doctor will need to work together to find the correct dosage. Initially, this means frequent blood tests to find out how much of the drug is actually circulating in your bloodstream. As long as you take Lithonate, you will need to watch for side effects. Signs of lithium poisoning include vomiting, unsteady walking, diarrhea, drowsiness, tremor and weakness. Stop taking the drug and call your doctor if you have any of these symptoms.

How should you take this medication?
To avoid stomach upset, take Lithonate immediately after meals or with food or milk.

Do not change from one brand of lithium to another without consulting your doctor or pharmacist. Take the drug exactly as prescribed.

While taking Lithonate, you should drink 10 to 12 glasses of water or fluid a day. To minimize the risk of harmful side effects, eat a balanced diet that includes some salt and lots of liquids. If you have been sweating a great deal or have had diarrhea, make sure you get extra liquids and salt.

If you develop an infection with a fever, you may need to cut back on your Lithonate dosage or even quit taking it temporarily. While you are ill, keep in close touch with your doctor.

Long-acting forms of lithium, such as Eskalith CR, should be swallowed whole. Do not chew, crush, or break.

If you are taking a syrup form of lithium, such as Cibalith-S, dilute it with fruit juice or another flavored beverage. You may obtain a specially marked measuring spoon from your pharmacist to ensure an accurate dose.

■ *If you miss a dose...*
Ask your doctor what to do; requirements vary for each individual. Do not take 2 doses at once.

■ *Storage instructions...*
Store at room temperature.

What side effects may occur?
The possibility of side effects varies with the level of lithium in your bloodstream. If you experience unfamiliar symptoms of any kind, inform your doctor as soon as possible.

■ *Side effects that may occur when you start taking lithium include:*
Discomfort
Frequent urination

Hand tremor
Mild thirst
Nausea

■ *Side effects that may occur at a high dosage include:*
Diarrhea, drowsiness, lack of coordination, muscular weakness, vomiting

Why should this drug not be prescribed?
Although your doctor will be cautious under certain conditions, lithium may be prescribed for anyone.

Special warnings about this medication
Lithonate may affect your judgment or coordination. Do not drive, climb, or perform hazardous tasks until you find out how this drug affects you.

Your doctor will prescribe Lithonate with extra caution if you have a heart or kidney problem, or have been weak, run-down, or dehydrated.

Also make sure your doctor is aware of any medical problems you may have, including diabetes, epilepsy, thyroid problems, Parkinson's disease, and difficulty urinating.

You should be careful in hot weather to avoid activities that cause you to sweat heavily. Also avoid drinking large amounts of coffee, tea, or cola, which can cause dehydration through increased urination. Do not make a major change in your eating habits or go on a weight loss diet without consulting your doctor. The loss of water and salt from your body could lead to lithium poisoning.

Possible food and drug interactions when taking this medication
Lithonate may intensify or prolong the effects of certain drugs used in anesthesia. If you are facing surgery, make sure the surgeon and anesthesiologist know you are taking Lithonate.

If Lithonate is taken with certain other drugs, the effects of either could be increased, decreased, or altered. It is especially important to check with your doctor before combining Lithonate with the following:

ACE-inhibitor blood pressure drugs such as Capoten or Vasotec
Acetazolamide (Diamox)
Amphetamines such as Dexedrine
Anti-inflammatory drugs such as Indocin and Feldene
Bicarbonate of soda
Caffeine (No-Doz)
Calcium-blocking blood pressure drugs such as Calan and Cardizem

Carbamazepine (Tegretol)
Diuretics such as Lasix or HydroDIURIL
Fluoxetine (Prozac)
Iodine-containing preparations such as potassium iodide (Quadrinal)
Major tranquilizers such as Haldol and Thorazine
Methyldopa (Aldomet)
Metronidazole (Flagyl)
Tetracyclines such as Achromycin V and Sumycin
Theophylline (Theo-Dur, Quibron, others)

Special information
if you are pregnant or breastfeeding

The use of Lithonate during pregnancy is usually not recommended because of the possibility that it might cause birth defects. If you are pregnant or plan to become pregnant, inform your doctor immediately.

Lithonate is excreted in breast milk and is considered potentially harmful to a nursing infant. If this medication is essential to your health, your doctor may advise you to discontinue breastfeeding while you are taking it.

Recommended dosage

ADULTS

Acute Episodes

The usual dosage is a total of 1,800 milligrams per day. Immediate-release forms are taken in 3 doses per day; long-acting forms are taken twice a day. The usual dose of syrup is 2 teaspoons, taken 3 times a day.

Your doctor will individualize your dosage according to the levels of the drug in your blood. Your blood levels will be checked at least twice a week when the drug is first prescribed and on a regular basis thereafter.

Long-term Control

Dosage will vary from one individual to another, but a total of 900 milligrams to 1,200 milligrams per day is typical. Immediate-release forms are taken in 3 or 4 doses per day; long-acting forms are taken twice a day. The usual dose of syrup is 1 teaspoon 3 or 4 times a day.

Blood levels in most cases should be checked every 2 months.

CHILDREN

The safety and effectiveness of Lithonate in children under 12 years of age have not been established.

ELDERLY

The elderly often need less Lithonate and may show signs of overdose at a dosage younger people can handle well.

Overdosage

Any medication taken in excess can have serious consequences. If you suspect symptoms of an overdose of Lithonate, seek medical attention immediately.

The harmful levels are close to those that will treat your condition. Watch for early signs of overdose, such as diarrhea, drowsiness, lack of coordination, vomiting, and weakness. If you develop any of these signs, stop taking the drug and call your doctor.

Brand name:

LITHOTABS

See Lithonate, page 581.

Brand name:

LODINE

Pronounced: LOW-deen
Generic name: Etodolac

Why is this drug prescribed?

Lodine, a nonsteroidal anti-inflammatory drug, is used to relieve the inflammation, swelling, stiffness, and joint pain associated with acute and long-term treatment of osteoarthritis (the most common form of arthritis).

Most important fact about this drug

You should have frequent checkups with your doctor if you take Lodine regularly. Ulcers or internal bleeding can occur without warning.

How should you take this medication?

Your doctor may ask you to take Lodine with food or an antacid, and with a full glass of water. Never take it on an empty stomach.

Take this medication exactly as prescribed by your doctor.

If you are using Lodine for arthritis, it should be taken regularly.

■ *If you miss a dose...*
Take the forgotten dose as soon as you remember. If it is almost time for the next dose, skip the one you missed and go back to your regular schedule. Never try to "catch up" by doubling the dose.

■ *Storage instructions...*
Store at room temperature. Protect from moisture.

What side effects may occur?
Side effects cannot be anticipated. If any develop or change in intensity, inform your doctor as soon as possible. Only your doctor can determine if it is safe for you to continue taking Lodine.

■ *More common side effects may include:*
Abdominal pain, black stools, blurred vision, chills, constipation, depression, diarrhea, dizziness, fever, gas, increased frequency of urination, indigestion, itching, nausea, nervousness, rash, ringing in ears, painful or difficult urination, vomiting, weakness

■ *Less common or rare side effects may include:*
Abdominal bleeding, abnormal intolerance of light, anemia, asthma, blood disorders, congestive heart failure, dry mouth, fainting, flushing, hepatitis, high blood pressure, high blood sugar in some diabetics, hives, inability to sleep, inflammation of mouth, kidney problems, including kidney failure, loss of appetite, peptic ulcer, rapid heartbeat, rash, skin disorders, including increased pigmentation, sleepiness, Stevens-Johnson syndrome (peeling skin), sweating, swelling (fluid retention), thirst, visual disturbances, yellowed skin and eyes

Why should this drug not be prescribed?
If you are sensitive to or have ever had an allergic reaction to Lodine, aspirin, or similar drugs, or if you have had asthma attacks caused by aspirin or other drugs of this type, you should not take this medication. Make sure that your doctor is aware of any drug reactions that you have experienced.

Special warnings about this medication
Peptic ulcers and bleeding can occur without warning.

This drug should be used with caution if you have kidney or liver disease; and it can cause liver inflammation in some people.

Do not take aspirin or any other anti-inflammatory medications while taking Lodine, unless your doctor tells you to do so.

If you are taking Lodine over an extended period of time, your doctor should check your blood for anemia.

This drug can increase water retention. Use with caution if you have heart disease or high blood pressure.

Possible food and drug interactions when taking this medication

If Lodine is taken with certain other drugs, the effects of either could be increased, decreased, or altered. It is especially important to check with your doctor before combining Lodine with the following:

Aspirin
Cyclosporine (Sandimmune)
Diuretics such as HydroDIURIL
Digoxin (Lanoxin)
Lithium (Lithobid, others)
Methotrexate
Phenylbutazone (Butazolidin)
The blood-thinning drug warfarin (Coumadin)

Special information if you are pregnant or breastfeeding

The effects of Lodine during pregnancy have not been adequately studied. If you are pregnant or plan to become pregnant, inform your doctor immediately. Lodine may appear in breast milk and could affect a nursing infant. If this medication is essential to your health, your doctor may advise you to discontinue breastfeeding until your treatment with this medication is finished.

Recommended dosage

ADULTS

General Pain Relief

Take 200 to 400 milligrams every 6 to 8 hours as needed. Do not take more than 1,200 milligrams a day. For individuals weighing less than 132 pounds, the maximum dose is 20 milligrams per 2.2 pounds.

Osteoarthritis

Starting dose is a total of 800 to 1,200 milligrams per day divided into smaller doses, followed by 600 to 1,200 milligrams per day in divided doses (i.e., 400 milligrams 2 or 3 times a day; 300 milligrams 2, 3 or 4 times a day). For those weighing less than 132 pounds the maximum dose is 20 milligrams per 2.2 pounds.

The lowest dose that proves beneficial should be used.

CHILDREN

The safety and effectiveness of Lodine have not been established in children.

Overdosage

Any medication taken in excess can cause symptoms of overdose. If you suspect an overdose, seek medical attention immediately.

■ *The symptoms of Lodine overdose may include:*
Drowsiness
Lethargy
Nausea
Stomach pain
Vomiting

Brand name:

LOESTRIN

See Oral Contraceptives, page 775.

Generic name:

LOMEFLOXACIN

See Maxaquin, page 628.

Brand name:

LOMOTIL

Pronounced: loe-MOE-till
Generic ingredients: Diphenoxylate hydrochloride, Atropine sulfate

Why is this drug prescribed?

Lomotil is used, along with other drugs, in the treatment of diarrhea.

Most important fact about this drug

Lomotil is not a harmless drug, so never exceed your recommended dosage. An overdose could be fatal.

How should you take this medication?

Lomotil can be habit-forming. Take it exactly as prescribed.

Be sure to drink plenty of liquids to replace lost body fluids. Eat bland foods, such as cooked cereals, breads and crackers.

Lomotil may cause dry mouth. Suck on a hard candy or chew gum to relieve this problem.

■ *If you miss a dose...*
Take it as soon as you remember. If it is almost time for your next dose, skip the one you missed and go back to your regular schedule. Do not take 2 doses at once.

■ *Storage instructions...*
Store away from heat, light, and moisture. Keep the liquid from freezing.

What side effects may occur?
Side effects cannot be anticipated. If any develop or change in intensity, inform your doctor as soon as possible. Only your doctor can determine if it is safe for you to continue taking Lomotil.

■ *Side effects may include:*
Abdominal discomfort, confusion, depression, difficulty urinating, dizziness, dry mouth and skin, exaggerated feeling of elation, fever, flushing, general feeling of not being well, headache, hives, intestinal blockage, itching, lack or loss of appetite, nausea, numbness of arms and legs, rapid heartbeat, restlessness, sedation/drowsiness, severe allergic reaction, sluggishness, swelling due to fluid retention, swollen gums, vomiting

Why should this drug not be prescribed?
If you are sensitive to or have ever had an allergic reaction to the ingredients of Lomotil, diphenoxylate or atropine, you should not take this medication. Make sure your doctor is aware of any drug reactions you have experienced.

Unless you are directed to do so by your doctor, do not take Lomotil if you have obstructive jaundice (a disease in which bile made in the liver does not reach the intestines because of a bile duct obstruction such as gallstones). Do not take Lomotil if you have diarrhea associated with pseudomembranous enterocolitis (inflammation of the intestines) or an infection with enterotoxin-producing bacteria (an enterotoxin is a poisonous substance that affects the stomach and intestines).

Special warnings about this medication
Certain antibiotics such as Ceclor, Cleocin, PCE and Achromycin V may cause

diarrhea. Lomotil can make this type of diarrhea worse and longer-lasting. Check with your doctor before using Lomotil while taking an antibiotic.

Lomotil may cause drowsiness or dizziness. Therefore, you should not drive a car, operate dangerous machinery, or participate in any hazardous activity that requires full mental alertness until you know how this drug affects you.

Lomotil slows activity of the digestive system; this can result in a buildup of fluid in the intestine, which may worsen the dehydration and imbalance in normal body salts that usually occur with diarrhea.

If you have severe ulcerative colitis (an inflammation of the intestines), your doctor will want to monitor your condition while you are taking this drug. If your abdomen becomes distended, or enlarged, notify your doctor.

Use Lomotil with extreme caution if you have kidney and liver disease or if your liver is not functioning normally.

Lomotil should be used with caution in children, since side effects may occur even with recommended doses, especially in children with Down's syndrome (congenital mental retardation).

Since addiction to diphenoxylate hydrochloride is possible at high doses, you should never exceed the recommended dosage.

Possible food and drug interactions
when taking this medication
Lomotil may intensify the effects of alcohol. It's better not to drink alcohol while taking this medication.

If Lomotil is taken with certain other drugs, the effects of either could be increased, decreased, or altered. It is especially important to check with your doctor before combining Lomotil with the following:

Barbiturates (anticonvulsants and sedatives such as phenobarbital)
MAO inhibitors (antidepressants such as Nardil and Parnate)
Tranquilizers (such as Valium and Xanax)

Special information
if you are pregnant or breastfeeding
The effects of Lomotil during pregnancy have not been adequately studied. If you are pregnant or plan to become pregnant, notify your doctor immediately. Lomotil appears in breast milk and could affect a nursing infant. If this medication is essential to your health, your doctor may advise you to discontinue breastfeeding until your treatment is finished.

Recommended dosage

ADULTS

The recommended starting dosage is 2 tablets 4 times a day or 2 regular teaspoonfuls (10 milliliters) of liquid 4 times per day.

Once your diarrhea is under control, your doctor may reduce the dosage; you may need as little as 5 milligrams (2 tablets or 10 milliliters of liquid) per day.

You should see improvement within 48 hours. If your diarrhea persists after you have taken 20 milligrams a day for 10 days, the drug is not likely to work for you.

CHILDREN

Lomotil is not recommended in children under 2 years of age.

Your doctor will take into account your child's nutritional status and degree of dehydration before prescribing this drug.

In children under 13 years of age, use only Lomotil liquid and administer with the plastic dropper. The recommended starting dosage is 0.3 to 0.4 milligram per 2.2 pounds of body weight per day, divided into 4 equal doses. The following table provides approximate starting dosage recommendations for children:

2 years (24-31 pounds):
   1.5-3.0 milligrams, 4 times daily
3 years (26-35 pounds):
   2.0-3.0 milligrams, 4 times daily
4 years (31-44 pounds):
   2.0-4.0 milligrams, 4 times daily
5 years (35-51 pounds):
   2.5-4.5 milligrams, 4 times daily
6-8 years (38-71 pounds):
   2.5-5.0 milligrams, 4 times daily
9-12 years (51-121 pounds):
   3.5-5.0 milligrams, 4 times daily

Your doctor may reduce the dosage as soon as symptoms are controlled. A maintenance dosage may be as low as one-quarter of the starting dose. If your child does not show improvement within 48 hours, Lomotil is unlikely to work.

Overdosage

An overdose of Lomotil can be dangerous and even fatal. If you suspect an overdose, seek medical attention immediately.

■ *Symptoms of Lomotil overdose may include:*
Coma, dry skin and mucous membranes, enlarged pupils of the eyes, extremely high body temperature, flushing, involuntary eyeball movement, lower than normal muscle tone, pinpoint pupils, rapid heartbeat, restlessness, sluggishness, suppressed breathing

Suppressed breathing may be seen as late as 30 hours after an overdose.

Brand name:

LO/OVRAL

See Oral Contraceptives, page 775.

Generic name:

LOPERAMIDE

See Imodium, page 511.

Brand name:

LOPID

Pronounced: LOH-pid
Generic name: Gemfibrozil
Other brand name: Gemcor

Why is this drug prescribed?

Lopid is prescribed, along with a special diet, for treatment of people with very high levels of serum triglycerides (a fatty substance in the blood) who are at risk of developing pancreatitis (inflammation of the pancreas) and who do not respond adequately to a strict diet.

This drug can also be used to reduce the risk of coronary heart disease in people who have failed to respond to weight loss, diet, exercise, and other triglyceride- or cholesterol-lowering drugs.

Most important fact about this drug

Lopid is usually prescribed only if diet, exercise, and weight-loss fail to bring your cholesterol levels under control. It's important to remember that Lopid is a supplement—not a substitute—for these other measures. To get the full benefit of the medication, you need to stick to the diet and exercise program prescribed by your doctor. All these efforts to keep your cholesterol levels normal are important because together they may lower your risk of heart disease.

How should you take this medication?
Take this medication 30 minutes before the morning and evening meal, exactly as prescribed.

■ *If you miss a dose...*
Take it as soon as you remember. If it is almost time for the next dose, skip the one you missed and go back to your regular schedule. Do not take 2 doses at the same time.

■ *Storage instructions...*
Store at room temperature.

What side effects may occur?
Side effects cannot be anticipated. If any develop or change in intensity, inform your doctor as soon as possible. Only your doctor can determine if it is safe for you to continue taking Lopid.

■ *More common side effects may include:*
Abdominal pain, acute appendicitis, constipation, diarrhea, eczema, fatigue, headache, indigestion, nausea/vomiting, rash, vertigo

■ *Less common or rare side effects may include:*
Anemia, blood disorders, blurred vision, confusion, convulsions, decreased male fertility, decreased sex drive, depression, dizziness, fainting, hives, impotence, inflammation of the colon, irregular heartbeat, itching, joint pain, laryngeal swelling, muscle disease, muscle pain, muscle weakness, painful extremities, sleepiness, tingling sensation, weight loss, yellow eyes and skin

Why should this drug not be prescribed?
There is a slight possibility that Lopid may cause malignancy, gallbladder disease, abdominal pain leading to appendectomy, or other serious, possibly fatal, abdominal disorders. This drug should not be used by those who have only mildly elevated cholesterol levels, since the benefits do not outweigh the risk of these severe side effects.

If you are sensitive to or have ever had an allergic reaction to Lopid or similar drugs such as Atromid-S, you should not take this medication. Make sure your doctor is aware of any drug reactions you have experienced.

Unless you are directed to do so by your doctor, do not take this medication if you are being treated for severe kidney or liver disorders or gallbladder disease.

Special warnings about this medication

Excess body weight and excess alcohol intake may be important risk factors leading to unusually high levels of fats in the body. Your doctor will probably want you to lose weight and stop drinking before he or she tries to treat you with Lopid.

Your doctor will probably do periodic blood level tests during the first 12 months of therapy with Lopid because of blood diseases associated with the use of this medication.

Liver disorders have occurred with the use of this drug. Therefore, your doctor will probably test your liver function periodically.

If you are being treated for any disease that contributes to increased blood cholesterol, such as an overactive thyroid, diabetes, nephrotic syndrome (kidney and blood vessel disorder), dysproteinemia (excess of protein in the blood), or obstructive liver disease, consult with your doctor before taking Lopid.

Lopid should begin to reduce cholesterol levels during the first 3 months of therapy. If your cholesterol is not lowered sufficiently, this medication should be discontinued. Therefore, it is important that your doctor check your progress regularly.

The use of this medication may cause gallstones, leading to possible gallbladder surgery. If you develop gallstones, your doctor will have you stop taking the drug.

The use of this drug may be associated with myositis, a muscle disease. If you have muscle pain, tenderness, or weakness, consult with your doctor. If myositis is suspected, your doctor will stop treating you with this drug.

Possible food and drug interactions
when taking this medication

If Lopid is taken with certain other drugs, the effects of either could be increased, decreased, or altered. It is especially important to check with your doctor before combining Lopid with the following:

Blood-thinning drugs such as Coumadin
Fluvastatin (Lescol)
Lovastatin (Mevacor)
Pravastatin (Pravachol)
Simvastatin (Zocor)

Special information
if you are pregnant or breastfeeding

The effects of Lopid during pregnancy have not been adequately studied. If you are pregnant or plan to become pregnant, inform your doctor immediately. Because this medication causes tumors in animals, it may have an effect on nursing infants. If Lopid is essential to your health, your doctor may advise you to discontinue breastfeeding until your treatment with Lopid is finished.

Recommended dosage

ADULTS

The recommended dose is 1,200 milligrams divided into 2 doses, given 30 minutes before the morning and evening meals.

CHILDREN

Safety and effectiveness of Lopid have not been established for use in children.

ELDERLY

This drug should be used with caution by the elderly.

Overdosage

There have been no reported cases of overdose with Lopid. However, should you suspect a Lopid overdose, seek medical attention immediately.

Brand name:

LOPRESSOR

Pronounced: low-PRESS-or
Generic name: Metoprolol tartrate

Why is this drug prescribed?

Lopressor, a type of medication known as a beta blocker, is used in the treatment of high blood pressure, angina pectoris (chest pain, usually caused by lack of oxygen to the heart due to clogged arteries), and heart attack. When prescribed for high blood pressure, it is effective when used alone or in combination with other high blood pressure medications. Beta blockers decrease the force and rate of heart contractions, thereby reducing the demand for oxygen and lowering blood pressure.

Occasionally doctors prescribe Lopressor for the treatment of aggressive behavior, prevention of migraine headache, and relief of temporary anxiety.

Most important fact about this drug
If you have high blood pressure, you must take Lopressor regularly for it to be effective. Since blood pressure declines gradually, it may be several weeks before you get the full benefit of Lopressor; and you must continue taking it even if you are feeling well. Lopressor does not cure high blood pressure; it merely keeps it under control.

How should you take this medication?
Lopressor should be taken with food or immediately after you have eaten.

Take Lopressor exactly as prescribed, even if your symptoms have disappeared.

Try not to miss any doses. If this medication is not taken regularly, your condition may worsen.

■ *If you miss a dose...*
If it is within 4 hours of your next dose, skip the one you missed and go back to your regular schedule. Never take 2 doses at the same time.

■ *Storage instructions...*
Store at room temperature in a tightly closed container, away from light. Protect from moisture.

What side effects may occur?
Side effects cannot be anticipated. If any develop or change in intensity, inform your doctor as soon as possible. Only your doctor can determine if it is safe for you to continue taking Lopressor.

■ *More common side effects may include:*
Depression
Diarrhea
Dizziness
Itching
Rash
Shortness of breath
Slow heartbeat
Tiredness

■ *Less common or rare side effects may include:*
Blurred vision, cold hands and feet, confusion, congestive heart failure, constipation, difficult or labored breathing, dry eyes, dry mouth, gas, hair loss, headache, heart attack, heartburn, low blood pressure, muscle pain, nausea, nightmares, rapid heartbeat, ringing in the ears, short-term memory loss, stomach pain, swelling due to fluid retention, trouble sleeping, wheezing, worsening of heart irregularities

Why should this drug not be prescribed?
If you have a slow heartbeat, certain heart irregularities, low blood pressure, inadequate output from the heart, or heart failure, you should not take this medication.

Special warnings about this medication
If you have a history of congestive heart failure, Lopressor should be used with caution.

Do not stop Lopressor abruptly. This can cause increased chest pain and heart attack. Dosage should be gradually reduced.

If you suffer from asthma, seasonal allergies or other bronchial conditions, or liver disease, this medication should be used with caution.

Ask your doctor if you should check your pulse while taking Lopressor. This medication can cause your heartbeat to become too slow.

This medication may mask some symptoms of low blood sugar in diabetics or alter blood sugar levels. If you are diabetic, discuss this with your doctor.

Lopressor may cause you to become drowsy or less alert; therefore, driving or operating dangerous machinery or participating in any hazardous activity that requires full mental alertness is not recommended until you know how you respond to this medication.

Notify your doctor or dentist that you are taking Lopressor if you have a medical emergency, or before you have surgery or dental treatment.

Notify your doctor if you have any difficulty in breathing.

Possible food and drug interactions
when taking this medication
If Lopressor is taken with certain other drugs, the effects of either could be increased, decreased, or altered. It is especially important to check with your doctor before combining Lopressor with certain high blood pressure drugs such as reserpine (Ser-Ap-ES).

- *Other medications that might interact with Lopressor
  include:*
  Albuterol (Proventil, Ventolin)
  Amiodarone (Cordarone)
  Barbiturates such as phenobarbital
  Calcium channel blockers such as Calan and Cardizem
  Cimetidine (Tagamet)
  Ciprofloxacin (Cipro)
  Clonidine (Catapres)
  Epinephrine (EpiPen)
  Hydralazine (Apresoline)
  Insulin
  Nonsteroidal anti-inflammatory drugs such as Motrin and Indocin
  Oral diabetes drugs such as Glucotrol and Micronase
  Prazosin (Minipress)
  Quinidine (Quinaglute)
  Ranitidine (Zantac)
  Rifampin (Rifadin)

Special information
if you are pregnant or breastfeeding

The effects of Lopressor during pregnancy have not been adequately studied. If you are pregnant or plan to become pregnant, inform your doctor immediately. Lopressor appears in breast milk and could affect a nursing infant. If this medication is essential to your health, your doctor may advise you to discontinue breastfeeding until your treatment with this medication is finished.

Recommended dosage

ADULTS

Dosages of Lopressor should be individualized by your doctor. It should be taken with or immediately following meals.

Hypertension

The usual starting dosage is a total of 100 milligrams a day taken in 1 or 2 doses, whether taken alone or with a diuretic. Your doctor may gradually increase the dosage up to 400 milligrams a day. Generally, the effectiveness of each dosage increase will be seen within a week.

Angina Pectoris

The usual starting dosage is a total of 100 milligrams a day taken in 2 doses. Your doctor may gradually increase the dosage up to 400 milligrams a day.

Generally, the effectiveness of each dosage increase will be seen within a week. If treatment is to be discontinued, your doctor will withdraw the drug gradually over a period of 1 to 2 weeks.

Heart Attack

Lopressor can be used for treatment of heart attack both in the hospital during the early phases and after the individual's condition has stabilized. Your doctor will determine the dosage according to your needs.

CHILDREN

The safety and effectiveness of Lopressor have not been established in children.

Overdosage

Any medication taken in excess can cause symptoms of overdose. If you suspect an overdose, seek medical attention immediately.

■ *The symptoms of Lopressor overdose may include:*
Asthma-like symptoms
Heart failure
Low blood pressure
Slow heartbeat

Brand name:

LOPROX

Pronounced: LOW-prox
Generic name: Ciclopirox olamine

Why is this drug prescribed?

Loprox is prescribed for the treatment of the following fungal skin infections:

Athlete's foot
Fungal infection of the groin (jock itch)
Fungal infection of non-hairy parts of the skin
Candidiasis (yeastlike fungal infection of the skin, nails, mouth, vagina, and lungs)
Tinea versicolor—infection of the skin that is characterized by brown or tan patches on the trunk.

Loprox is available in cream and lotion forms.

Most important fact about this drug
Loprox is for external treatment of skin infections. Do not use Loprox in the eyes.

How should you use this medication?
Use this medication for the full treatment time even if your symptoms have improved. Notify your doctor if there is no improvement after 4 weeks.

Shake Loprox lotion vigorously before each use.

■ *If you miss a dose...*
Apply the forgotten dose as soon as you remember. If it is almost time for your next dose, skip the one you missed and go back to your regular schedule.

■ *Storage instructions...*
Store at room temperature.

What side effects may occur?
Loprox rarely causes side effects. If any develop or change in intensity, inform your doctor as soon as possible. Only your doctor can determine if it is safe for you to continue using Loprox.

■ *Rare side effects may include:*
Burning
Itching
Redness
Worsening of infection symptoms

Why should this drug not be prescribed?
If you are sensitive to or have ever had an allergic reaction to ciclopirox olamine or any other ingredient in Loprox, you should not take this medication. Make sure your doctor is aware of any drug reactions you have experienced.

Special warnings about this medication
If the affected area of skin shows signs of increased irritation (redness, itching, burning, blistering, swelling, oozing), notify your doctor.

Avoid the use of airtight dressings or bandages.

Special information
if you are pregnant or breastfeeding

The effects of Loprox during pregnancy have not been adequately studied. If you are pregnant or plan to become pregnant, inform your doctor immediately. It is not known whether this drug appears in breast milk. If this medication is essential to your health, your doctor may advise you to discontinue breastfeeding your baby until your treatment is finished.

Recommended dosage

ADULTS

Gently massage Loprox into the affected and surrounding skin areas 2 times a day, in the morning and evening. For most infections, improvement usually occurs within the first week of treatment. People with tinea versicolor usually show signs of improvement after 2 weeks of treatment.

CHILDREN

Safety and effectiveness have not been established in children under 10 years of age.

Overdosage

Any medication taken in excess can have serious consequences. If you suspect an overdose, seek medical treatment immediately.

Brand name:

LOPURIN

See Zyloprim, page 1248.

Brand name:

LORABID

Pronounced: LOR-a-bid
Generic name: Loracarbef

Why is this drug prescribed?

Lorabid is used to treat mild-to-moderate bacterial infections of the lungs, ears, throat, sinuses, skin, urinary tract, and kidneys.

Most important fact about this drug

If you have ever had an allergic reaction to Lorabid, penicillin, cephalosporins, or any other drug, be sure your doctor is aware of it before you take Lorabid. You may experience a severe reaction if you are sensitive to penicillin-type medications.

How should you take this medication?
Take Lorabid at least 1 hour before or 2 hours after eating. It is best to take your medication at evenly spaced intervals, day and night.

Do not stop taking your medication even if you begin to feel better after a few days. If you stop taking your medicine too soon, your symptoms may return. If you have a "strep" infection, you should take your medication for at least 10 days.

- *If you miss a dose...*
  Take it as soon as possible. This will help keep a constant amount of medicine in your system. If it is almost time for your next dose, skip the one you missed and go back to your regular schedule. Do not take 2 doses at once.

- *Storage instructions...*
  Lorabid can be stored at room temperature. The liquid form can be kept in the refrigerator, but not in the freezer. Discard any unused portion.

What side effects may occur?
Side effects cannot be anticipated. If any develop or change in intensity, tell your doctor as soon as possible. Only your doctor can determine if it is safe for you to continue taking Lorabid.

- *More common side effects in children may include:*
  Diarrhea
  Inflamed, runny nose
  Vomiting

- *Less common or rare side effects in children may include:*
  Headache
  Loss of appetite
  Rash
  Sleepiness

- *More common side effects in adults may include:*
  Diarrhea
  Headache

■ *Less common side effects in adults may include:*
Abdominal pain
Nausea
Rhinitis
Skin rashes
Vaginitis (inflammation of the vaginal tissues)
Vomiting
Yeast infection

■ *Rare side effects may include:*
Blood disorders
Dizziness
Hives
Insomnia
Itching
Loss of appetite
Nervousness
Red bumps on skin
Sleepiness
Vasodilation (widening of the blood vessels)

■ *Side effects for other drugs of this class may include:*
Allergic reactions (sometimes severe), anemia, blood disorders, hemorrhage, kidney problems, serum sickness (fever, skin rash, joint pain, swollen lymph nodes), skin peeling

Why should this drug not be prescribed?
If you are allergic to penicillin, cephalosporins, or other medications, you should not take Lorabid. Make sure you tell your doctor about any drug reactions you have experienced.

Special warnings about this medication
As with many antibiotics, Lorabid can cause colitis—an inflammation of the bowel. This condition can range from mild to life-threatening. If you develop diarrhea while taking Lorabid, notify your doctor, and do not take any diarrhea medication without your doctor's approval.

Prolonged use of Lorabid may result in development of bacteria that do not respond to the medication, leading to a second infection. Because of this danger, you should not use any left-over Lorabid for later infections, even if they have similar symptoms. Take Lorabid only when your doctor prescribes it for you.

If you have known or suspected kidney problems, your doctor will perform blood tests to check your urine and kidney function before and during Lorabid therapy.

**Possible food and drug interactions
when taking this medication**
If Lorabid is taken with certain other drugs, the effects of either could be increased, decreased, or altered. It is especially important to check with your doctor before combining Lorabid with the following:

Diuretics such as Lasix and Bumex
Probenecid (the gout medication Benemid)

**Special information
if you are pregnant or breastfeeding**
The effects of Lorabid during pregnancy have not been adequately studied. If you are pregnant or plan to become pregnant, tell your doctor immediately. Lorabid should be used during pregnancy only if clearly needed. It is not known whether Lorabid appears in human breast milk. Your doctor will determine whether it is safe for you to take Lorabid while breastfeeding.

Recommended dosage

ADULTS (13 YEARS AND OLDER)

Bronchitis
The usual dose is 200 to 400 milligrams every 12 hours for 7 days.

Pneumonia
The usual dose is 400 milligrams every 12 hours for 14 days.

Sinusitis
The usual dose is 400 milligrams every 12 hours for 10 days.

Skin and Soft Tissue Infections
The usual dose is 200 milligrams every 12 hours for 7 days.

Streptococcal Pharyngitis ("Strep Throat") and Tonsillitis
The usual dose is 200 milligrams every 12 hours for 10 days. For strep throat, take Lorabid for at least 10 days.

Bladder Infections
The usual dose is 200 milligrams every 24 hours for 7 days.

Kidney Infections
The usual dose is 400 milligrams every 12 hours for 14 days.

If you have impaired kidney function, your doctor will adjust the dosage according to your needs.

CHILDREN (6 MONTHS TO 12 YEARS OF AGE)

Otitis Media
This infection of the middle ear should be treated with the suspension. Do not use the pulvules.

The dose is based on body weight. The usual dose is 30 milligrams of liquid per 2.2 pounds of body weight per day in divided doses (half the dose every 12 hours), for 10 days.

Streptococcal Pharyngitis ("Strep Throat") and Tonsillitis
The dose is based on body weight. The usual dose is 15 milligrams per 2.2 pounds of body weight per day in divided doses (half the dose every 12 hours), for at least 10 days.

Impetigo (Skin Infection)
The dose is based on body weight. The usual dose is 15 milligrams of liquid per 2.2 pounds of body weight per day in divided doses (half the dose every 12 hours), for 7 days.

Overdosage
Any medication taken in excess can have serious consequences. If you suspect an overdose, seek medical attention immediately.

■ *Symptoms of Lorabid overdose may include:*
Diarrhea
Nausea
Stomach upset
Vomiting

Generic name:

LORACARBEF

See Lorabid, page 601.

Generic name:

LORATADINE

See Claritin, page 200.

Generic name:

LORATADINE WITH PSEUDOEPHEDRINE

See Claritin-D, page 203.

Generic name:

LORAZEPAM

See Ativan, page 83.

Brand name:

LORELCO

Pronounced: Lore-ELL-Koh
Generic name: Probucol

Why is this drug prescribed?

Lorelco is used, along with diet, to lower cholesterol levels in the blood of people with primary hypercholesterolemia (a genetic defect that causes a lack of low-density lipoprotein [LDL] receptors, which remove cholesterol from the bloodstream). Lorelco lowers *total serum cholesterol*, which means that it not only reduces LDL, or "bad," cholesterol but may reduce HDL (high-density lipoprotein), or "good," cholesterol. The risk of lowering HDL cholesterol while lowering LDL cholesterol is unknown.

Most important fact about this drug

Lorelco is usually prescribed only if diet, exercise, and weight loss fail to bring your cholesterol levels under control. It's important to remember that Lorelco is a supplement—not a substitute—for these other measures. To get the full benefit of the medication, you need to stick to the diet and exercise program prescribed by your doctor. All these efforts to keep your cholesterol levels normal are important because together they may lower your risk of heart disease.

How should you take this medication?
Take Lorelco with meals, exactly as prescribed.

■ *If you miss a dose...*
Take it as soon as you remember. If it is almost time for the next dose, skip the one you missed and go back to your regular schedule. Do not take 2 doses at the same time.

■ *Storage instructions...*
Store in a tightly closed container away from excessive heat and moisture.

What side effects may occur?
Side effects cannot be anticipated. If any develop or change in intensity, inform your doctor as soon as possible. Only your doctor can determine if it is safe for you to continue taking Lorelco.

■ *Side effects when treatment with Lorelco begins may include:*
Brief loss of consciousness or fainting
Chest pain
Dizziness
Nausea
Rapid, strong heartbeat
Vomiting

■ *Side effects during treatment may include:*
Abdominal pain, blurred vision, bruising, diarrhea, diminished sense of taste and smell, dizziness, excessive nighttime urination, excessive perspiration, fainting, gas, headache, impotence, inability to fall or stay asleep, indigestion, inflammation of the eyelid, irregular heartbeat, itching, loss of appetite, nausea, rash, ringing in the ears, stomach or intestinal bleeding, swelling due to fluid retention, tearing, tingling sensation, vomiting

Why should this drug not be prescribed?
If you are sensitive to or have ever had an allergic reaction to Lorelco or similar drugs, you should not use this medication. Make sure that your doctor is aware of any drug reactions you have experienced.

Unless you are directed to do so by your doctor, do not take this medication if you have had recent heart damage, have progressive heart disease, have serious abnormal heart rhythm, or experience unexplained fainting spells or other conditions that your doctor considers dangerous.

Special warnings about this medication

If you are being treated for any disease that contributes to increased blood cholesterol, such as hyperthyroidism, diabetes, nephrotic syndrome (kidney and blood vessel disorder), or obstructive liver disease, consult with your doctor before taking this medication.

Lorelco should begin to reduce cholesterol levels during the first 3 to 4 months of therapy. If your cholesterol is not lowered sufficiently, your doctor will have you stop taking this medication. Therefore, it is important that your doctor check your progress regularly.

Possible food and drug interactions
when taking this medication

If Lorelco is taken with certain other drugs, the effects of either could be increased, decreased, or altered. It is especially important to check with your doctor before combining Lorelco with the following:

Certain antidepressants such as Elavil and Norpramin
Clofibrate (Atromid-S)
Drugs for irregular heartbeat such as Norpace and Quinidex
Major tranquilizers such as Mellaril and Thorazine

Special information
if you are pregnant or breastfeeding

The effects of Lorelco during pregnancy have not been adequately studied. If you are pregnant or plan to become pregnant, inform your doctor immediately. It is recommended that women who plan to become pregnant stop taking this drug and delay the pregnancy with some form of birth control for at least six months. Lorelco may appear in breast milk and could affect a nursing infant. If this medication is essential to your health, your doctor may advise you to discontinue breastfeeding until your treatment is finished.

Recommended dosage

ADULTS

The recommended and maximum dose is 1,000 milligrams per day, divided into 2 doses of 500 milligrams each (two 250-milligram tablets or one 500-milligram tablet), taken with the morning and evening meals.

CHILDREN

The safety and effectiveness of this drug have not been established in children.

ELDERLY

This drug should be used with caution by the elderly.

Overdosage

Any medication taken in excess can cause symptoms of overdose. If you suspect a Lorelco overdose, seek medical attention immediately.

Brand name:

LORTAB

See Vicodin, page 1193.

Brand name:

LOTENSIN

Pronounced: Lo-TEN-sin
Generic name: Benazepril hydrochloride

Why is this drug prescribed?

Lotensin, an angiotensin-converting enzyme (ACE), is used in the treatment of high blood pressure. It is effective when used alone or in combination with thiazide diuretics. Lotensin is in a family of drugs called ACE inhibitors. It works by preventing a chemical in your blood called angiotensin I from converting into a more potent enzyme that increases salt and water retention in your body. Lotensin also enhances blood flow throughout your blood vessels.

Most important fact about this drug

You must take Lotensin regularly for it to be effective. Since blood pressure declines gradually, it may be several weeks before you get the full benefit of Lotensin; and you must continue taking it even if you are feeling well. Lotensin does not cure high blood pressure; it merely keeps it under control.

How should you take this medication?

Lotensin can be taken with or without food. Do not use salt substitutes containing potassium.

Take Lotensin exactly as prescribed. Suddenly stopping Lotensin could cause your blood pressure to increase.

■ *If you miss a dose...*
Take the forgotten dose as soon as you remember. If it is almost time for the next dose, skip the one you missed and go back to your regular schedule. Never try to "catch up" by doubling the dose.

■ *Storage instructions...*
Store at room temperature in a tightly closed container. Protect from light.

What side effects may occur?
Side effects cannot be anticipated. If any develop or change in intensity, inform your doctor as soon as possible. Only your doctor can determine if it is safe for you to continue taking Lotensin.

■ *More common side effects may include:*
Cough
Dizziness
Fatigue
Headache
High potassium levels (dry mouth, excessive thirst, weak or irregular heartbeat, muscle pain or cramps)
Nausea

If you develop swelling of your face, around the lips, tongue, or throat; swelling of arms and legs; sore throat, fever, and chills; or difficulty swallowing, you should contact your doctor immediately. You may need emergency treatment.

■ *Less common or rare side effects may include:*
Allergic reactions, anxiety, arthritis, asthma, bronchitis, chest pain, constipation, dark tarry stool containing blood, decreased sex drive, difficulty sleeping, dizziness when standing, fainting, fluid retention, flushing, impotence, infection, inflammation of the skin, inflammation of the stomach, itching, joint pain, low blood pressure, muscle pain, nervousness, pounding heartbeat, rash, sensitivity to light, shortness of breath, sinus inflammation, sweating, swelling of arms, legs, face, tingling or pins and needles, urinary infections, vomiting, weakness

Why should this drug not be prescribed?
If you are sensitive to or have ever had an allergic reaction to Lotensin or other angiotensin-converting enzyme (ACE) inhibitors, do not take this medication.

Special warnings about this medication

Your kidney function should be assessed when you start taking Lotensin and then monitored for the first few weeks. If you are on kidney dialysis, your doctor may need to use a different medication.

Lotensin can cause low blood pressure, especially if you are also taking a diuretic. You may feel light-headed or faint, especially during the first few days of therapy. If these symptoms occur, contact your doctor. Your dosage may need to be adjusted or discontinued.

If you have congestive heart failure, this drug should be used with caution.

Do not use potassium supplements or salt substitutes containing potassium without talking to your doctor first.

If you develop a sore throat or fever, you should contact your doctor immediately. It could indicate a more serious illness.

Excessive sweating, dehydration, severe diarrhea, or vomiting could make you lose too much water, causing your blood pressure to become too low.

Possible food and drug interactions
when taking this medication

If Lotensin is taken with certain other drugs, the effects of either could be increased, decreased, or altered. It is especially important to check with your doctor before combining Lotensin with the following:

Diuretics such as Dyazide, Lasix
Lithium (Lithonate)
Potassium supplements such as Slow-K
Potassium-sparing diuretics such as Moduretic

Special information
if you are pregnant or breastfeeding

Lotensin can cause injury or death to developing and newborn babies, especially if taken during the second and third trimesters of pregnancy. If you are pregnant or plan to become pregnant and are taking Lotensin, contact your doctor immediately to discuss the potential hazard to your unborn child. Minimal amounts of Lotensin appear in breast milk. If this medication is essential to your health, your doctor may advise you to discontinue breastfeeding until your treatment with this medication is finished.

Recommended dosage

ADULTS

For people not taking a diuretic drug, the usual starting dose is 10 milligrams, 1 time per day. Regular total dosages range from 20 to 40 milligrams per day taken in either a single dose or divided into 2 equal doses. The maximum dose is 80 milligrams per day. Your doctor will closely monitor the effect of this drug and adjust it according to your individual needs.

For people already taking a diuretic, the diuretic should be stopped, if possible, 2 to 3 days before taking Lotensin. This reduces the possibility of fainting or light-headedness. If blood pressure cannot be controlled by Lotensin alone, then diuretic use should begin again. If the diuretic cannot be discontinued, the starting dosage of Lotensin should be 5 milligrams.

For patients with reduced kidney function, the dosages should be individualized according to the amount of reduced function. The usual starting dose in these instances is 5 milligrams per day, adjusted upwards to a maximum of 40 milligrams per day. If you are on kidney dialysis, your doctor may need to use a different medication.

CHILDREN

The safety and effectiveness of Lotensin have not been established in children.

ELDERLY

Lotensin should be used with caution in the elderly.

Overdosage

Although there is no specific information available, a sudden drop in blood pressure would most likely be the primary symptom of Lotensin overdose.

If you suspect a Lotensin overdose, seek medical attention immediately.

Brand name:

LOTRIMIN

See Gyne-Lotrimin, page 476.

Brand name:

LOTRISONE

Pronounced: LOE-trih-sone
Generic ingredients: Clotrimazole, Betamethasone
  dipropionate

Why is this drug prescribed?

Lotrisone, a combination of a steroid (betamethasone) and an antifungal drug (clotrimazole), is used to treat skin infections caused by fungus, such as athlete's foot, jock itch, and ringworm of the·body.

Betamethasone treats symptoms (such as itching, redness, swelling, and inflammation) that result from fungus infections, while clotrimazole treats the cause of the infection by inhibiting the growth of certain yeast and fungus organisms.

Most important fact about this drug

When you use Lotrisone, you inevitably absorb some of the medication through your skin and into the bloodstream. Too much absorption can lead to unwanted side effects elsewhere in the body. To keep this problem to a minimum, avoid using large amounts of Lotrisone over wide areas, and do not cover it with airtight dressings such as plastic wrap or adhesive bandage unless specifically told to by your doctor.

How should you use this medication?

Wash your hands before and after applying Lotrisone. Gently massage it into the affected area and surrounding skin twice a day, in the morning and evening. Do not get it in your eyes.

Use Lotrisone for the full time prescribed, even if your condition has improved.

Lotrisone should be applied sparingly to the groin area, and it should not be used for longer than 2 weeks. Wear loose-fitting clothing.

■ *If you miss a dose...*
  Apply it as soon as you remember. If it is almost time for your next dose, skip the one you missed and go back to your regular schedule.

■ *Storage instructions...*
  Store at room temperature.

What side effects may occur?

Side effects cannot be anticipated. If any develop or change in intensity, inform your doctor as soon as possible. Only your doctor can determine if it is safe for you to continue using Lotrisone.

■ *More common side effects may include:*
  Blistering, hives, infection, irritated skin, itching, peeling, reddened skin, skin eruptions and rash, stinging, swelling due to fluid retention, tingling sensation

■ *Less common side effects may include:*
Acne, burning, dryness, excessive hair growth, inflamed hair follicles, inflamed skin, irritated skin around mouth, loss of skin color, softening of the skin, streaks in the skin

Why should this drug not be prescribed?
You should not use Lotrisone if you are sensitive to clotrimazole or betamethasone or any of its other ingredients, or to similar steroid and antifungal medications.

Special warnings about this medication
Steroid drugs (such as betamethasone) can affect the functioning of the adrenal, hypothalamic, and pituitary glands and temporarily produce sugar in the urine, excessive blood sugar levels, and a disorder called Cushing's syndrome. Symptoms of Cushing's syndrome include easily bruised skin, increased blood pressure, low potassium levels, low sex hormone levels, mood swings, water retention, weak muscles, and weight gain.

Do not take Lotrisone internally and be sure to keep it away from your eyes.

If you are using Lotrisone to treat jock itch (tinea cruris) or a fungal infection of the skin called tinea corporis, and there has been no improvement after 1 week, notify your doctor.

If you are using Lotrisone to treat athlete's foot (tinea pedis), notify your doctor if there is no improvement after 2 weeks of treatment.

Do not use Lotrisone for any condition other than the one for which it was prescribed, and do not use it for longer than 4 weeks.

Lotrisone is not for use on diaper rash.

Possible food and drug interactions
when taking this medication
No interactions have been reported.

Special information
if you are pregnant or breastfeeding
Pregnant women should not use steroid drugs in large amounts or for prolonged periods of time. The effects of Lotrisone during pregnancy have not been adequately studied. The medication should be used during pregnancy only if the potential benefits justify the potential risk to the developing baby. It is not known whether Lotrisone appears in breast milk. Nursing mothers should use Lotrisone with caution and only when clearly needed.

Recommended dosage

ADULTS AND CHILDREN OVER 12 YEARS OLD

"Jock Itch" (Tinea Cruris) or Fungal Skin Infections (Tinea Corporis)
Gently massage Lotrisone into the affected and surrounding skin areas twice a day, in the morning and the evening, for 2 weeks. Lotrisone should be applied sparingly to the groin area. Notify your doctor if there has been no improvement after 1 week of treatment.

Athlete's Foot (Tinea Pedis)
Gently massage Lotrisone into the affected and surrounding skin areas twice a day, in the morning and the evening, for 4 weeks. Notify your doctor if there has been no improvement after 2 weeks of treatment.

CHILDREN

The safety and effectiveness of Lotrisone have not been established for children under 12 years of age. Children may absorb proportionally larger amounts of topical Lotrisone and be more sensitive to its effects than are adults.

Overdosage
Any medication used in excess can have serious consequences. A serious overdose of Lotrisone, which is applied to the skin, is unlikely. However, seek medical help immediately if you suspect an overdose.

Generic name:

LOVASTATIN

See Mevacor, page 651.

Brand name:

LOZOL

Pronounced: LOW-zoll
Generic name: Indapamide

Why is this drug prescribed?
Lozol is used in the treatment of high blood pressure, either alone or in combination with other high blood pressure medications. Lozol is also used

to relieve salt and fluid retention. During pregnancy, your doctor may prescribe Lozol to relieve fluid retention caused by a specific condition or when fluid retention causes extreme discomfort that is not relieved by rest.

Most important fact about this drug
If you have high blood pressure, you must take Lozol regularly for it to be effective. Since blood pressure declines gradually, it may be several weeks before you get the full benefit of Lozol; and you must continue taking it even if you are feeling well. Lozol does not cure high blood pressure; it merely keeps it under control.

How should you take this medication?
Take Lozol exactly as prescribed by your doctor. Suddenly stopping Lozol could cause your condition to worsen.

Lozol is best taken in the morning.

■ *If you miss a dose...*
Take the forgotten dose as soon as you remember. If it is almost time for your next dose, skip the one you missed and go back to your regular schedule. Never take two doses at the same time.

■ *Storage instructions...*
Store Lozol at room temperature. Protect from excessive heat. Keep the container tightly closed.

What side effects may occur?
Side effects cannot be anticipated. If any side effects develop or change in intensity, tell your doctor immediately. Only your doctor can determine whether it is safe to continue taking Lozol. Most side effects are mild and temporary.

■ *More common side effects may include:*
Agitation
Anxiety
Back pain
Dizziness
Headache
Infection
Irritability
Muscle cramps or spasms
Nasal inflammation
Nervousness

Numbness in hands and feet
Pain
Tension
Weakness, fatigue, loss of energy or tiredness

■ *Less common or rare side effects may include:*
Abdominal pain or cramps, blurred vision, chest pain, conjunctivitis, constipation, cough, depression, diarrhea, dizziness when standing up too quickly, drowsiness, dry mouth, excessive urination at night, fluid retention, flu-like symptoms, flushing, fluttering heartbeat, frequent urination, hives, impotence or reduced sex drive, indigestion, insomnia, irregular heartbeat, itching, light-headedness, loss of appetite, nausea, nervousness, premature heart contractions, production of large amounts of pale urine, rash, runny nose, sore throat, stomach irritation, tingling in hands and feet, vertigo, vomiting, weakness, weak or irregular heartbeat, weight loss

Why should this drug not be prescribed?
Avoid using Lozol if you are unable to urinate or if you have ever had an allergic reaction or are sensitive to indapamide or other sulfa-containing drugs.

Special warnings about this medication
Diuretics such as Lozol can cause the body to lose too much salt and potassium, especially among elderly women. Signs of an excessively low potassium level include muscle weakness and rapid or irregular heartbeat. To boost your potassium level, your doctor may recommend eating potassium-rich foods or taking a potassium supplement.

The risk of potassium loss increases when larger doses are used, if you have cirrhosis, or if you are also using corticosteroids or ACTH. Your doctor should check your blood regularly, especially if you have an irregular heartbeat or are taking heart medications.

Lozol should be used with care if you have gout or high uric acid levels, liver disease, diabetes, or lupus erythematosus, a disease of the connective tissue.

This medication should be used with caution if you have severe kidney disease. Your kidney function should be given a complete assessment and should continue to be monitored.

In general, diuretics should not be taken if you are taking lithium, as they increase the risk of lithium poisoning.

**Possible food and drug interactions
when taking this medication**

If Lozol is taken with certain other drugs, the effects of either could be increased, decreased, or altered. It is especially important to check with your doctor before combining Lozol with the following:

Lithium (Eskalith)
Norepinephrine (a drug used to treat cardiac arrest and to maintain blood pressure)
Other high blood pressure medications such as Aldomet and Tenormin

**Special information
if you are pregnant or breastfeeding**

If you are pregnant or plan to become pregnant, tell your doctor immediately. No information is available about the safety of Lozol during pregnancy.

Lozol may appear in breast milk and could affect a nursing infant. If Lozol is essential to your health, your doctor may advise you to stop breastfeeding until your treatment is finished.

Recommended dosage

ADULTS

High Blood Pressure

The usual starting dose is 1.25 milligrams as a single daily dose taken in the morning. If Lozol does not seem to be working for you, your doctor may gradually increase your dosage up to 5 milligrams taken once a day.

Fluid Buildup in Congestive Heart Failure

The usual starting dose is 2.5 milligrams as a single daily dose taken in the morning. Your doctor may increase your dosage to 5 milligrams taken once daily.

Overdosage

Any medication taken in excess can have serious consequences. If you suspect an overdose, seek medical treatment immediately.

■ *Symptoms of Lozol overdose may include:*
Electrolyte imbalance (potassium or salt depletion due to too much fluid loss)
Nausea
Stomach disorders
Vomiting
Weakness

Brand name:

LURIDE

Pronounced: LUHR-ide
Generic name: Sodium fluoride

Why is this drug prescribed?

Luride is prescribed to strengthen children's teeth against decay during the period when the teeth are still developing.

Studies have shown that children who live where the drinking water contains a certain level of fluoride have fewer cavities than others. Fluoride helps prevent cavities in three ways: by increasing the teeth's resistance to dissolving on contact with acid, by strengthening teeth, and by slowing down the growth of mouth bacteria.

Luride may be given to children who live where the water fluoride level is 0.6 parts per million or less.

Most important fact about this drug

Before Luride is prescribed, it is important for the doctor to know the fluoride content of the water your child drinks every day. Your water company, or a private laboratory, can tell you the level of fluoride in your water.

How should you take this medication?

Give your child Luride exactly as prescribed by your doctor. It is preferable to give the tablet at bedtime after the child's teeth have been brushed. The youngster may chew and swallow the tablet or simply suck on it until it dissolves. The liquid form of this medicine is to be taken by mouth. It may be dropped directly into the mouth or mixed with water or fruit juice. Always store Luride drops in the original plastic dropper bottle.

■ *If you miss a dose...*
Administer it as soon as you remember. If it is almost time for the next dose, skip the one your child missed and go back to the regular schedule. Do not give 2 doses at once.

■ *Storage instructions...*
Store away from heat, light, and moisture. Keep the liquid from freezing.

What side effects may occur?

Side effects cannot be anticipated. If any develop, tell your doctor immediately. Only your doctor can determine whether it is safe for your child to continue taking Luride.

In rare cases, Luride may cause an allergic rash or some other unexpected effect.

Why should this drug not be prescribed?

Your child should not take Luride if he or she is sensitive to it or has had an allergic reaction to it in the past.

Your child should not take the 1-milligram strength of Luride if the drinking water in your area contains 0.3 parts per million of fluoride or more. He or she should not take the other forms of Luride if the water contains 0.6 parts per million of fluoride or more.

Special warnings about this medication

Do not give full-strength tablets (1 milligram) to children under the age of 6.

Possible food and drug interactions
when taking this medication

Avoid giving your child Luride with dairy products. The calcium in dairy products may interact with the fluoride to create calcium fluoride, which the body cannot absorb well.

Recommended dosage

Since this drug is used to supplement water with low fluoride content, consult your physician to determine the proper amount based on the local water content. Also check with your doctor if you move to a new area, change to bottled water, or begin using a water-filtering device. Dosages are determined by both age and the fluoride content of the water.

INFANTS AND CHILDREN

The following daily dosages are recommended for areas where the drinking water contains fluoride at less than 0.3 parts per million:

Children 6 Months to 3 Years of Age
1 quarter-strength (0.25 milligram) tablet or ½ dropperful of liquid

3 to 6 Years of Age
1 half-strength (0.5 milligram) tablet or 1 dropperful of liquid

6 to 16 Years of Age
1 full-strength (1 milligram) tablet or 2 droppersful of liquid

For areas where the fluoride content of drinking water is between 0.3 and 0.6 parts per million, the recommended daily dosage of the tablets is one-half the above dosages. Dosage of the liquid should be reduced to ½ dropperful for children ages 3 to 6 and 1 dropperful for children over 6.

Overdosage

Any medication taken in excess can have serious consequences. Taking too much fluoride for a long period of time may cause discoloration of the teeth. Notify your doctor or dentist if you notice white, brown, or black spots on the teeth.

Brand name:

LUVOX

Pronounced: LOO-voks
Generic name: Fluvoxamine maleate

Why is this drug prescribed?

Luvox is prescribed for obsessive-compulsive behavior. Obsessive behavior may include continual, unwanted thoughts that prevent functioning properly in everyday living. Compulsive behavior is typified by ritualistic actions such as repetitive washing, repeating certain phrases, completing steps in a process over and over, counting and recounting, checking and rechecking to make sure that something has not been forgotten, excessive neatness, and hoarding of useless items.

Most important fact about this drug

Before starting therapy with Luvox, it is very important to tell your doctor what medications you are taking, either prescription or over-the-counter, since combining Luvox with certain drugs may cause serious or even life-threatening effects. You should never take Luvox with the antihistamines Seldane and Hismanal. You should also avoid taking Luvox within 14 days of taking an antidepressant drug known as an MAO inhibitor, including Nardil and Parnate.

How should you take this medication?

Take this medication only as directed by your doctor.

Luvox may be taken with or without food.

■ *If you miss a dose...*
   If you are taking 1 dose a day, skip the missed dose and go back to your regular schedule. If you are taking 2 doses a day, take the missed dose as soon as possible, then go back to your regular schedule. Never take 2 doses at the same time.

■ *Storage instructions...*
Store at room temperature and protect from humidity.

What side effects may occur?
Side effects cannot be anticipated. If any develop or change in intensity, tell your doctor immediately. Only your doctor can determine if it is safe for you to continue taking Luvox.

■ *More common side effects may include:*
Abnormal ejaculation, abnormal tooth decay and toothache, anxiety, blurred vision, constipation, decreased appetite, diarrhea, dizziness, dry mouth, feeling "hot or flushed," "flu-like" symptoms, frequent urination, gas and bloating, headache, heart palpitations, inability to fall asleep, indigestion, nausea, nervousness, sleepiness, sweating, taste alteration, tremor, unusual tiredness or weakness, upper respiratory infection, vomiting

■ *Less common side effects may include:*
Abnormal muscle tone, agitation, chills, decreased sex drive, depression, difficult or labored breathing, difficulty swallowing, extreme excitability, impotence, inability to urinate, lack of orgasm, yawning

Why should this drug not be prescribed?
If you are sensitive to or have ever had an allergic reaction to Luvox or similar drugs, such as Prozac and Zoloft, do not take this medication. Make sure your doctor is aware of any drug reactions you have experienced.

Never combine Luvox with Seldane or Hismanal, or take it within 14 days of taking an MAO inhibitor such as Nardil or Parnate. (See "Most important fact about this drug.")

Special warnings about this medication
You should discuss all your medical problems with your doctor before starting therapy with Luvox, as certain physical conditions or diseases may affect your reaction to Luvox.

If you suffer from seizures, use this medication catiously. If you experience a seizure while taking Luvox, stop taking the drug and call your doctor immediately.

If you have or have ever had suicidal thoughts, be sure to tell your doctor, as your dosage may need to be adjusted.

If you have a history of mania (excessively energetic, out-of-control behavior), use this medication cautiously.

If you have liver disease, your doctor will adjust the dosage.

Luvox may cause you to become drowsy or less alert and may affect your judgment. Therefore, avoid driving, operating dangerous machinery, or participating in any hazardous activity that requires full mental alertness until you know your reaction to this medication.

If you develop a rash or hives, or any other allergic-type reaction, notify your physician immediately.

Possible food and drug interactions
when taking this medication

Do not drink alcohol while taking this medication. If you smoke, be sure to tell your doctor before starting Luvox therapy, as your dosage may need adjustment.

If Luvox is taken with certain other drugs, the effects of either could be increased, decreased, or altered. It is especially important to check with your doctor before combining Luvox with the following:

Anticoagulant drugs such as Coumadin
Antidepressant medications such as Anafranil, Elavil, and Tofranil, as well as the MAO inhibitors Nardil and Parnate
Blood pressure medications known as beta blockers, including Inderal and Lopressor
Carbamazepine (Tegretol)
Clozapine (Clozaril)
Diazepam (Valium)
Diltiazem (Cardizem)
Lithium (Lithonate)
Methadone (Dolophine)
Phenytoin (Dilantin)
Theophylline (Theo-Dur)
Tranquilizers and sedatives such as Halcion, Valium, Versed, and Xanax
Tryptophan

Special information
if you are pregnant or breastfeeding

The effects of Luvox in pregnancy have not been adequately studied. If you are pregnant or plan to become pregnant, consult your doctor immediately. Luvox passes into breast milk and may cause serious reactions in a nursing baby. If this medication is essential your health, your doctor may advise you to discontinue breastfeeding until your treatment with Luvox is finished.

Recommended dosage

ADULTS

The usual starting dose is one 50-milligram tablet taken at bedtime.

Your doctor may increase your dose, depending upon your response. The maximum daily dose is 300 milligrams. If you take more than 100 milligrams a day, your doctor will divide the total amount into 2 doses; if the doses are not equal, you should take the larger dose at bedtime.

CHILDREN

The safety and effectiveness of Luvox have not been established in children under age 18.

Overdosage

Any medication taken in excess can have serious consequences. If you suspect an overdose, seek medical attention immediately.

- *Symptoms of Luvox overdose may include:*
  Breathing difficulties
  Changes in pulse rate
  Coma
  Convulsions
  Diarrhea
  Dizziness
  Drowsiness
  Low blood pressure
  Liver problems
  Vomiting

Generic name:

MAALOX

See Antacids, page 62.

Brand name:

MACROBID

See Macrodantin, page 625.

Brand name:

MACRODANTIN

Pronounced: Mack-row-DAN-tin
Generic name: Nitrofurantoin
Other brand name: Macrobid

Why is this drug prescribed?
Nitrofurantoin, an antibacterial drug, is prescribed for the treatment of urinary tract infections caused by certain strains of bacteria.

Most important fact about this drug
Breathing disorders have occurred in patients taking nitrofurantoin. The drug can cause inflammation of the lungs characterized by coughing, difficulty breathing, and wheezing. Pulmonary fibrosis (an abnormal increase in fibrous tissue of the lungs) can develop gradually without symptoms and can cause death. An allergic reaction to this drug is also possible and may occur without warning. Symptoms include a feeling of ill health and a persistent cough. However, these reactions occur rarely and generally in those receiving nitrofurantoin therapy for 6 months or longer.

Sudden and severe lung reactions are characterized by fever, chills, cough, chest pain, and difficulty breathing. These acute reactions usually occur within the first week of treatment and subside when therapy with nitrofurantoin is stopped.

Your doctor should monitor your condition closely, especially if you are receiving long-term treatment with this medication.

How should you take this medication?
To improve absorption of the drug, nitrofurantoin should be taken with food.

Follow your doctor's instructions carefully. Take the full amount prescribed, even if you are feeling better.

This medication works better if your urine is acidic. Ask your doctor whether you should be taking special measures to assure its acidity.

Nitrofurantoin may turn the urine brown.

- *If you miss a dose...*
  Take the forgotten dose as soon as you remember, then space out the rest of the day's doses at equal intervals.

■ *Storage instructions...*
Store at room temperature. Protect from light and keep the container tightly closed.

What side effects may occur?
Side effects cannot be anticipated. If any develop or change in intensity, inform your doctor as soon as possible. Only your doctor can determine if it is safe for you to continue taking nitrofurantoin.

■ *More common side effects may include:*
Lack or loss of appetite
Nausea
Vomiting

■ *Less common or rare side effects may include:*
Abdominal pain/discomfort, chills, confusion, cough, chest pain, depression, diarrhea, difficulty breathing, dizziness, drowsiness, exaggerated sense of well-being, fever, hair loss, headache, hepatitis, hives, inflammation of the nerves causing symptoms of numbness, tingling, pain, or muscle weakness, involuntary eye movement, itching, itchy, red skin patches, joint pain, muscle pain, peeling skin, psychotic reactions, rash, severe allergic reactions, skin inflammation with flaking, skin swelling or welts, vertigo, yellowing of the skin and whites of the eyes, weakness

Why should this drug not be prescribed?
If you are sensitive to or have ever had an allergic reaction to nitrofurantoin or other drugs of this type, such as Furoxone, you should not take this medication. Make sure that your doctor is aware of any drug reactions that you have experienced.

Unless you are directed to do so by your doctor, do not take this medication if your kidneys are not functioning properly, if they are unable to produce urine, or if they produce only a small amount.

Nitrofurantoin should not be taken at term of pregnancy or during labor and delivery; it should not be given to infants under 1 month of age.

Special warnings about this medication
Tell your doctor if you have any unusual symptoms while you are taking this drug.

Fatalities have been reported from hepatitis (liver disease) during treatment with nitrofurantoin. Long-lasting, active hepatitis can occur without symptoms; therefore, if you are receiving long-term treatment with this drug, your doctor should check you periodically for changes in liver function.

Fatalities from peripheral neuropathy—disease of the nerves—have been reported in people taking nitrofurantoin.

If you have a kidney disorder, anemia, diabetes mellitus, a debilitating disease, or a vitamin B deficiency, caution should be exercised when taking this medication. These conditions make peripheral neuropathy more likely. Consult with your doctor.

Hemolytic anemia (below-normal hemoglobin content in the blood caused by the destruction of red blood cells) has occurred in people taking nitrofurantoin.

Continued or prolonged use of this drug may result in growth of bacteria that do not respond to it. This can cause a secondary infection, so it is important that your doctor monitor your condition on a regular basis.

Possible food and drug interactions
when taking this medication

If nitrofurantoin is taken with certain other drugs, the effects of either could be increased, decreased, or altered. It is especially important to check with your doctor before combining nitrofurantoin with the following:

Drugs for spasms of the digestive tract, such as Bentyl and Donnatal
Magnesium trisilicate (Gaviscon Antacid Tablets)
Uricosuric drugs (medications that increase the amount of the uric acid eliminated in the urine, such as the antigout drugs Benemid and Anturane)

Special information
if you are pregnant or breastfeeding

The safety of nitrofurantoin during pregnancy and breastfeeding has not been established. If you are pregnant or breastfeeding or you plan to become pregnant or breastfeed, inform your doctor immediately.

Recommended dosage

Treatment with nitrofurantoin should be continued for 1 week or for at least 3 days after obtaining a urine specimen free of infection. If your infection has not cleared up, your doctor should re-evaluate your case.

ADULTS

The recommended dosage of Macrodantin is 50 to 100 milligrams taken 4 times a day. For long-term treatment, your doctor may reduce your dosage to 50 to 100 milligrams taken at bedtime.

The recommended dosage of Macrobid is one 100-milligram capsule every 12 hours for 7 days.

CHILDREN

This medication should not be prescribed for children under 1 month of age.

The recommended daily dosage of Macrodantin for infants and children over 1 month of age is 5 to 7 milligrams per 2.2 pounds of body weight, divided into 4 doses over 24 hours.

For the long-term treatment of children, the doctor may prescribe daily doses as low as 1 milligram per 2.2 pounds of body weight, taken in 1 or 2 doses per day.

The dosage of Macrobid for children over 12 years of age is one 100-milligram capsule every 12 hours for 7 days. Safety and effectiveness have not been established for children under 12.

Overdosage

An overdose of nitrofurantoin has not resulted in any specific symptoms other than vomiting. If vomiting does not occur soon after an excessive dose, it should be induced.

If you suspect an overdose, seek emergency medical treatment immediately.

Brand name:

MATERNA

See Stuartnatal Plus, page 1048.

Brand name:

MAXAQUIN

Pronounced: MAX-ah-kwin
Generic name: Lomefloxacin hydrochloride

Why is this drug prescribed?

Maxaquin is a quinolone antibiotic used to treat lower respiratory infections, including chronic bronchitis, and urinary tract infections, including cystitis (inflammation of the inner lining of the bladder). Maxaquin is also given before bladder surgery to prevent the infections that sometimes follow this operation.

Most important fact about this drug

During and following treatment, Maxaquin causes sensitivity reactions in patients exposed to sunlight or sunlamps. The reactions can occur despite use of sunscreens and sunblocks, and can be prompted by shaded or diffused light or exposure through glass. Avoid even indirect sunlight while taking Maxaquin and for several days following therapy.

How should you take this medication?
It is important to finish your prescription of Maxaquin completely. If you stop taking your medication too soon, your symptoms may return.

Maxaquin may be taken with or without food. Take it with a full 8-ounce glass of water; and be sure to drink plenty of fluids while on this medication.

■ *If you miss a dose...*
Take it as soon as you remember. If it is almost time for your next dose, skip the one you missed and go back to your regular schedule. Do not take 2 doses at the same time.

■ *Storage instructions...*
Store at room temperature.

What side effects may occur?
Side effects cannot be anticipated. If any develop or change in intensity, tell your doctor as soon as possible. Only your doctor can determine if it is safe for you to continue taking Maxaquin.

■ *More common side effects may include:*
Headache
Nausea

■ *Less common side effects may include:*
Diarrhea
Dizziness
Sensitivity to light

■ *Rare side effects may include:*
Abdominal pain, abnormal or terrifying dreams, abnormal vision, agitation, allergic reaction, altered taste, angina pectoris (crushing chest pain), anxiety, back pain, bleeding between menstrual periods, bleeding in the stomach and intestines, blood clots in the lungs, blood in the urine, blue skin color, chest pain, chills, coma, confusion, conjunctivitis (pinkeye), constipation, convulsions, cough, decreased heat tolerance, depression, difficult or labored breathing, difficulty swallowing, dry mouth, earache, eye pain, facial swelling, fainting, fatigue, fluid retention and swelling, flu-

like symptoms, flushing, gas, general feeling of illness, gout, harsh, high-pitched sound during breathing, heart attack, heart failure, high blood pressure, hives, inability to sleep, increased appetite, increased mucus from the lungs, increased sweating, indigestion, inflammation in the male genital area, inflammation of the stomach and intestines, inflammation of the vagina, irregular heartbeat, itching, joint pain, lack of urine, leg cramps, loss of appetite, loss of sense of identity, low blood pressure, low blood sugar, lung infection or other problems, muscle pain, nervousness, nosebleed, overactivity, pain in the genital-rectal area, problems with urination, purple or red spots on the skin, rapid heartbeat, rash, ringing in the ears, skin disorders, skin eruptions or peeling, sleepiness, slow heartbeat, thirst, tingling or "pins and needles," tongue discoloration, tremor, vaginal yeast infection, vertigo, vomiting, weakness, wheezing, white or yellow vaginal discharge

Why should this drug not be prescribed?

If you are sensitive to or have ever had an allergic reaction to Maxaquin or other quinolone antibiotics such as Cipro and Floxin, you should not take this medication. Make sure your doctor is aware of any drug reactions you have experienced.

Special warnings about this medication

Use Maxaquin cautiously if you have disorders such as epilepsy, severe hardening of the arteries in the brain, and other conditions that can lead to seizures. Maxaquin may cause convulsions.

In rare cases, people taking antibiotics similar to Maxaquin have experienced severe, even fatal reactions, sometimes after only one dose. These reactions may include confusion, convulsions, difficulty breathing, hallucinations, hives, itching, light-headedness, loss of consciousness, rash, restlessness, swelling in the face or throat, tingling, and tremors. If you develop any of these symptoms, stop taking Maxaquin immediately and seek medical help.

If other antibiotics have given you diarrhea, or it develops while you are taking Maxaquin, be sure to tell your doctor. Maxaquin may cause inflammation of the bowel, ranging from mild to life-threatening.

Maxaquin may cause dizziness or light-headedness and may impair your ability to drive a car or operate potentially dangerous machinery. Do not participate in any activities that require full alertness until you know how Maxaquin affects you.

Possible food and drug interactions
when taking this medication

If Maxaquin is taken with certain other drugs, the effects of either could be increased, decreased, or altered. It is especially important to check with your doctor before combining Maxaquin with the following:

Antacids containing magnesium or aluminum, such as Maalox or Tums
Caffeine (including coffee, tea, and some soft drinks)
Cimetidine (Tagamet)
Cyclosporine (Sandimmune)
Probenecid (Benemid)
Sucralfate (Carafate)
Theophylline (Theo-Dur)
Warfarin (Coumadin)
Vitamins or products containing iron or zinc

Special information
if you are pregnant or breastfeeding

The effects of Maxaquin in pregnancy have not been adequately studied. If you are pregnant or plan to become pregnant, notify your doctor immediately. It is not known if Maxaquin appears in breast milk. Because many drugs do make their way into breast milk, your doctor may have you stop nursing while you are taking Maxaquin.

Recommended dosage

ADULTS

Chronic Bronchitis
The usual dosage is 400 milligrams once a day for 10 days.

Cystitis
The usual dosage is 400 milligrams once a day for 10 days.

Urinary Tract Infections
The dosage is 400 milligrams once a day for 14 days.

Patients with Impaired Renal Function or Cirrhosis
Your doctor will adjust the dosage according to your needs.

Dialysis Patients
The recommended dosage for people on dialysis is 400 milligrams, followed by daily maintenance doses of 200 milligrams (one-half tablet) once a day for the duration of treatment.

CHILDREN

Safety and efficacy have not been established for children under the age of 18.

Overdosage

There is no information on overdosage with Maxaquin. However, any medication taken in excess can have serious consequences. If you suspect an overdose, seek medical help immediately.

Brand name:

MAXZIDE

Pronounced: MAX-ide
Generic ingredients: Triamterene, Hydrochlorothiazide

Why is this drug prescribed?

Maxzide is a diuretic combination used in the treatment of high blood pressure or other conditions that require the elimination of excess fluid (water) from the body. When used for high blood pressure, Maxzide can be used alone or with other high blood pressure medications. Diuretics help your body produce and eliminate more urine, which helps lower blood pressure. Triamterene, one of the ingredients, helps to minimize potassium loss, which can be caused by the other component, hydrochlorothiazide.

Most important fact about this drug

If you have high blood pressure, you must take Maxzide regularly for it to be effective. Since blood pressure declines gradually, it may be several weeks before you get the full benefit of Maxzide; and you must continue taking it even if you are feeling well. Maxzide does not cure high blood pressure; it merely keeps it under control.

How should you take this medication?

Take Maxzide exactly as prescribed. Stopping Maxzide suddenly could cause your condition to worsen.

■ *If you miss a dose...*
Take it as soon as you remember. If it is almost time for the next dose, skip the one you missed and go back to your regular schedule. Do not take 2 doses at the same time.

■ *Storage instructions...*
Store at room temperature in a tightly closed container away from light.

What side effects may occur?
Side effects cannot be anticipated. If any develop or change in intensity, inform your doctor as soon as possible. Only your doctor can determine if it is safe for you to continue taking Maxzide.

■ *Side effects may include:*
Abdominal cramps, anemia, anxiety, change in potassium levels (causing such symptoms as dry mouth, excessive thirst, weak or irregular heartbeat, muscle pain or cramps), change in taste, chest pain, constipation, decreased sexual performance, depression, diarrhea, difficulty breathing, difficulty sleeping, discolored urine, dizziness, dizziness on standing up, drowsiness, dry mouth, fatigue, fever, headache, hives, hypersensitivity reaction, inflammation of the pancreas, inflammation of the salivary glands, kidney stones, loss of appetite, muscle cramps, muscle weakness, nausea, rapid heartbeat, rash, reddish or purplish spots on the skin, restlessness, sensitivity to light, shortness of breath, stomach irritation, tingling or pins and needles, vertigo, vision changes, vomiting, yellow eyes and skin

Why should this drug not be prescribed?
If you are unable to urinate or have any serious kidney disease, if you have high potassium levels in your blood, or if you are taking other drugs that prevent loss of potassium, you should not take this medication.

If you are sensitive to or have ever had an allergic reaction to triamterene, hydrochlorothiazide, or similar drugs, or if you are sensitive to other sulfa drugs, you should not take this medication. Make sure your doctor is aware of any drug reactions you may have experienced.

Special warnings about this medication
This medication should be used only if your doctor has determined that the precise amount of each ingredient in Maxzide meets your specific needs. It cannot be exchanged with Dyazide, a combination of the same ingredients in different amounts.

If you are taking Maxzide and have kidney disease, your doctor will do a complete assessment of your kidney function and will continue to monitor it.

If you are taking an ACE-inhibitor type of blood pressure medication such as Vasotec, Maxzide should be used with extreme caution.

If you have liver disease, diabetes, gout, or the connective tissue disease lupus erythematosus, make sure your doctor knows about it. Maxzide should be prescribed with caution.

If you have bronchial asthma or a history of allergies, you may be at greater risk for an allergic reaction to this medication.

Dehydration, excessive sweating, severe diarrhea, or vomiting could deplete your fluids and cause your blood pressure to become too low. Be careful when exercising and in hot weather.

Avoid potassium-containing salt substitutes, potassium supplements, and potassium-enriched diets.

Notify your doctor or dentist that you are taking Maxzide if you have a medical emergency, and before you have surgery.

Possible food and drug interactions
when taking this medication
Maxzide may increase the effects of alcohol. Avoid alcohol while taking this medication.

If Maxzide is taken with certain other drugs, the effects of either could be increased, decreased, or altered. It is especially important to check with your doctor before taking Maxzide with the following:

ACE inhibitors such as Vasotec
Amantadine (Symmetrel)
Barbiturates such as phenobarbital
Beta-blocking blood pressure medications such as Inderal
Cholestyramine (Questran)
Fluconazole (Diflucan)
Indomethacin (Indocin)
Lithium (Lithonate)
Narcotics such as Percocet
Norepinephrine (Levophed)
Oral diabetes drugs such as Micronase
Other diuretics that minimize loss of potassium, such as Midamor
Other high blood pressure medications (Aldomet)
Potassium-containing salt substitutes
Tubocurarine

Special information
if you are pregnant or breastfeeding
The effects of Maxzide during pregnancy have not been adequately studied. If you are pregnant or plan to become pregnant, inform your doctor immediate-

ly. Maxzide appears in breast milk and could affect a nursing infant. If this medication is essential to your health, your doctor may advise you to discontinue breastfeeding until your treatment with this medication is finished.

Recommended dosage

ADULTS

It is important that potassium levels be carefully monitored when you are taking either strength of this medication. Your doctor will adjust your dosage based on your individual condition.

The usual dose of Maxzide-25 MG is 1 or 2 tablets a day in a single dose.

The usual dose of Maxzide is 1 tablet daily.

CHILDREN

The safety and effectiveness of Maxzide have not been established in children.

Overdosage

Any medication taken in excess can have serious consequences. If you suspect an overdose, seek medical attention immediately.

No specific information is available on Maxzide. However, an overdose of triamterene can cause dehydration, nausea, vomiting, and weakness. An overdose of hydrochlorothiazide can cause dehydration, sluggishness—possibly leading to coma—and stomach and intestinal irritation.

Generic name:

MECLIZINE

See Antivert, page 66.

Brand name:

MEDROL

Pronounced: MED-rohl
Generic name: Methylprednisolone

Why is this drug prescribed?

Medrol, a corticosteroid drug, is used to reduce inflammation and improve symptoms in a variety of disorders, including rheumatic arthritis, acute gouty arthritis, and severe cases of asthma. Medrol may be given to people to treat primary or secondary adrenal cortex insufficiency (lack of or insufficient adrenal cortical hormone in the body). It is also given to help treat the following disorders:

Severe allergic conditions (drug-induced allergic state)
Blood disorders (leukemia and various anemias)
Certain cancers (along with other drugs)
Skin diseases (severe psoriasis)
Connective tissue diseases such as systemic lupus erythematosus
Digestive tract diseases such as ulcerative colitis
High serum levels of calcium associated with cancer
Fluid retention due to nephrotic syndrome (a condition in which damage to the kidney causes loss of protein in urine)
Various eye diseases
Lung diseases such as tuberculosis

Most important fact about this drug
Medrol lowers your resistance to infections and can make them harder to treat. Medrol may also mask some of the signs of an infection, making it difficult for your doctor to diagnose the actual problem.

How should you take this medication?
Take Medrol exactly as prescribed. It can be taken every day or every other day, depending on the condition being treated.

Do not abruptly stop taking Medrol without checking with your doctor. If you have been using Medrol for a long time, the dose should be reduced gradually.

Medrol may cause stomach upset. Take Medrol with meals or snacks.

If your doctor has prescribed a single daily dose or alternate-day doses, take this medicine in the morning with breakfast, about 8 A.M. If you are taking multiple doses, take Medrol at evenly spaced intervals throughout the day.

■ *If you miss a dose...*
If you take your dose once a day, take it as soon as you remember. Then go back to your regular schedule. If you don't remember until the next day, skip the one you missed. Do not take 2 doses at once.

If you take it several times a day, take it as soon as you remember. Then go back to your regular schedule. If you don't remember until your next dose, double the dose you take.

If you take your dose every other day, and you remember it the same morning, take it as soon as you remember and go back to your regular schedule. If you don't remember until the afternoon, do not take it until the following morning, then skip a day and go back to your regular schedule.

■ *Storage instructions...*
Store at room temperature.

What side effects may occur?
Side effects cannot be anticipated. If any develop or change in intensity, tell your doctor immediately. Only your doctor can determine whether it is safe for you to continue taking Medrol.

■ *Side effects may include:*
Abdominal swelling, allergic reactions, bone fractures, bruising, congestive heart failure, cataracts, convulsions, Cushingoid symptoms (moon face, weight gain, high blood pressure, emotional disturbances, growth of facial hair in women), face redness, fluid and salt retention, high blood pressure, increased eye pressure, increased sweating, increase in amounts of insulin or hypoglycemic medications needed, inflammation of the upper digestive tract, inflammation of the pancreas, irregular menstruation, muscle wasting and weakness, poor healing of wounds, protruding eyes, stomach ulcer, suppression of growth in children, symptoms of diabetes, thin, fragile skin, tiny red or purplish spots on the skin, vertigo

Why should this drug not be prescribed?
Medrol should not be used if you have a fungal infection or if you are sensitive to or allergic to steroids (corticosteroids).

Special warnings about this medication
The 24-milligram Medrol tablet contains FD&C Yellow No. 5 (tartrazine), which has caused allergic reactions (including asthma) in some people. Although this is rare, it is more common in people who are sensitive to aspirin.

Medrol can alter the way your body responds to unusual stress. If you are injured, need surgery, or develop an acute illness, inform your doctor. Your dosage may need to be increased.

You should not be vaccinated or immunized while taking Medrol, especially in high doses. Medrol may prevent your body from producing the proper antibodies to build up immunity and may cause nervous system problems.

Long-term use of Medrol may cause cataracts, glaucoma (increased eye pressure), and eye infections.

Large doses of Medrol may cause high blood pressure, salt and water retention, and potassium and calcium loss. It may be necessary to restrict your salt intake and take a potassium supplement.

Medrol may reactivate dormant cases of tuberculosis. If you have inactive tuberculosis and must take Medrol for an extended period of time, your doctor will prescribe anti-TB medication as well.

Medrol should be used cautiously if you have an underactive thyroid, liver cirrhosis, or herpes simplex (virus) infection of the eye.

This medication may aggravate existing emotional problems or cause new ones. You may experience euphoria (an exaggerated sense of well-being) and difficulty sleeping, mood swings, or mental problems. If you have any changes in mood, contact your doctor.

Medrol should also be taken with caution if you have any of the following conditions:

Diverticulitis or other inflammatory conditions of the intestine
High blood pressure
Certain kidney diseases
Active or dormant peptic ulcer
Myasthenia gravis (a muscle weakness disorder)
Osteoporosis (brittle bones)
Ulcerative colitis with impending danger of infection

Long-term use of Medrol can slow the growth and development of infants and children.

Use aspirin cautiously with Medrol if you have a blood-clotting disorder.

Avoid exposure to chickenpox and measles.

Possible food and drug interactions
when taking this medication
If Medrol is taken with certain other drugs, the effects of either drug could be increased, decreased, or altered. It is especially important to check with your doctor before combining Medrol with the following:

Aspirin
Barbiturates such as phenobarbital
Carbamazepine (Tegretol)
Cholestyramine (Questran)

Cyclosporine (Sandimmune)
Diuretics such as Lasix and HydroDIURIL
Estrogen medications such as Premarin
Indomethacin (Indocin)
Insulin
Ketoconazole (Nizoral)
Oral diabetes drugs such as Glucotrol
Phenytoin (Dilantin)
Rifampin (Rifadin)

Special information
if you are pregnant or breastfeeding

If you are pregnant or plan to become pregnant, tell your doctor immediately. There is no information about the safety of Medrol during pregnancy. Babies born to mothers who have taken doses of Medrol (corticosteroids) during pregnancy should be carefully watched for adrenal problems. Medrol may appear in breast milk and could affect a nursing infant. If Medrol is essential to your health, your doctor may advise you to stop breastfeeding until your treatment with Medrol is finished.

Recommended dosage

The starting dose of Medrol tablets may vary from 4 milligrams to 48 milligrams per day, depending on the specific problem being treated.

Once the doctor is satisfied with your response, he or she will gradually lower the dosage to the smallest effective amount.

Overdosage

Any medication taken in excess can have serious consequences. If you suspect an overdose, seek medical treatment immediately.

- *Symptoms of Medrol overdose may include:*
  Acid indigestion
  Excessive sweating
  Fatigue
  Muscle weakness
  Swelling of arms and legs
  Upset stomach

Generic name:

MEDROXYPROGESTERONE

See Provera, page 916.

Generic name:

MEFENAMIC ACID

See Ponstel, page 874.

Brand name:

MELLARIL

Pronounced: *MEL-ah-rill*
Generic name: *Thioridazine hydrochloride*

Why is this drug prescribed?

Mellaril is used to reduce the symptoms of psychotic disorders such as schizophrenia, and to treat depression and anxiety in adults. Mellaril is also used in the treatment of agitation, fears, sleep disturbances, tension, depression, and anxiety in elderly people, and for certain behavior problems in children.

Most important fact about this drug

Mellaril may cause tardive dyskinesia—a condition marked by involuntary muscle spasms and twitches in the face and body. This condition may be permanent, and appears to be most common among the elderly, especially women. Ask your doctor for information about this possible risk.

How should you take this medication?

If you are taking Mellaril in a liquid concentrate form, you can dilute it with a liquid such as distilled water, soft tap water, or juice just before taking it.

Do not change from one brand to another without consulting your doctor.

- *If you miss a dose...*
  If you take 1 dose a day and remember later in the day, take the dose immediately. If you don't remember until the next day, skip the dose and go back to your regular schedule.

  If you take more than 1 dose a day and remember the forgotten dose within an hour or so after its scheduled time, take it immediately. If you don't remember until later, skip the dose and go back to your regular schedule.

  Never try to "catch up" by doubling a dose.

- *Storage instructions...*
  Store at room temperature, tightly closed, in the container the medication came in.

What side effects may occur?
Side effects cannot be anticipated. If any develop or change in intensity, inform your doctor as soon as possible. Only your doctor can determine if it is safe for you to continue taking Mellaril.

■ *Side effects may include:*
Abnormal and excessive secretion of milk, agitation, anemia, asthma, blurred vision, body spasm, breast development in males, changed mental state, changes in sex drive, chewing movements, confusion (especially at night), constipation, diarrhea, discolored eyes, drowsiness, dry mouth, excitement, eyeball rotation, fever, fluid accumulation and swelling, headache, inability to hold urine, inability to urinate, inhibition of ejaculation, intestinal blockage, involuntary movements, irregular blood pressure, pulse, and heartbeat, irregular or missed menstrual periods, jaw spasm, loss of appetite, loss of muscle movement, mouth puckering, muscle rigidity, nasal congestion, nausea, overactivity, painful muscle spasm, paleness, pinpoint pupils, protruding tongue, psychotic reactions, puffing of cheeks, rapid heartbeat, redness of the skin, restlessness, rigid and masklike face, sensitivity to light, skin pigmentation and rash, sluggishness, stiff, twisted neck, strange dreams, sweating, swelling in the throat, swelling or filling of breasts, swollen glands, tremors, vomiting, weight gain, yellowing of the skin and whites of eyes

Why should this drug not be prescribed?
Never combine this drug with excessive amounts of central nervous system depressants such as alcohol, barbiturates, or narcotics. Do not take Mellaril if you have heart disease accompanied by severe high or low blood pressure.

Special warnings about this medication
This drug may impair your ability to drive a car or operate potentially dangerous machinery. Do not participate in any activities that require full alertness until you are certain the drug will not interfere.

If you have ever had breast cancer, make sure your doctor is aware of it.

Mellaril may cause false positive results in tests for pregnancy.

**Possible food and drug interactions
when taking this medication**
If Mellaril is taken with certain other drugs, the effects of either could be increased, decreased, or altered. It is especially important to check with your doctor before combining Mellaril with the following:

Epinephrine (EpiPen)
Phosphorus insecticides

Pindolol (Visken)
Propranolol (Inderal)

Extreme drowsiness and other potentially serious effects can result if Mellaril is combined with alcohol or other central nervous system depressants such as narcotics, painkillers, and sleeping medications.

Special information
if you are pregnant or breastfeeding
Pregnant women should use Mellaril only if clearly needed. If you are pregnant or plan to become pregnant, inform your doctor immediately.

Recommended dosage
Your doctor will tailor your dose to your needs, using the smallest effective amount.

ADULTS

Psychotic Disorders
The starting dose ranges from 150 to 300 milligrams a day, divided into 3 equal doses. Your doctor may increase your dosage to as much as 800 milligrams a day, taken in 2 to 4 small doses. Once your symptoms improve, your doctor will decrease the dosage to the lowest effective amount.

Depression and Anxiety
The initial dose is 75 milligrams a day, divided into 3 doses per day. Dosage may range from 20 to 200 milligrams a day, divided into 2 to 4 doses.

CHILDREN

Behavior Problems
Mellaril should not be given to children younger than 2 years old. For children 2 to 12 years old, doses are determined by body weight. Total daily doses range from 0.5 milligram to 3 milligrams for every 2.2 pounds of body weight.

The usual beginning dose for children with moderate disorders is from 20 to 30 milligrams a day, divided into 2 or 3 doses.

ELDERLY

In general, elderly people take dosages of Mellaril in the lower range. Elderly people (especially elderly women) may be more susceptible to tardive

DRUG IDENTIFICATION GUIDE

ACCUPRIL

QUINAPRIL HCL
PARKE-DAVIS

5 MG   10 MG

20 MG   40 MG

ACCUTANE

ISOTRETINOIN
ROCHE

10 MG   20 MG

40 MG

ACHROMYCIN V

TETRACYCLINE HCL
LEDERLE

250 MG

500 MG

ACTIGALL

URSODIOL
SUMMIT

300 MG

ADIPEX-P

PHENTERMINE HCL
TEVA

37.5 MG

ALDACTAZIDE

SPIRONOLACTONE/
HYDROCHLOROTHIAZIDE
G. D. SEARLE

25 MG / 25 MG

50 MG / 50 MG

ALDACTONE

SPIRONOLACTONE
G. D. SEARLE

25 MG   50 MG

100 MG

ALDOMET

METHYLDOPA
MERCK

125 MG   250 MG

500 MG

ALTACE

RAMIPRIL
HOECHST-ROUSSEL

1.25 MG

2.5 MG

5 MG

10 MG

AMBIEN

ZOLPIDEM TARTRATE
G. D. SEARLE

5 MG

10 MG

AMOXIL

AMOXICILLIN
SMITHKLINE BEECHAM

250 MG

500 MG

125 MG
CHEWABLE

250 MG
CHEWABLE

ANAFRANIL

CLOMIPRAMINE HCL
BASEL

25 MG

50 MG

75 MG

ANAPROX

NAPROXEN SODIUM
SYNTEX

275 MG

ANAPROX DS

NAPROXEN SODIUM
SYNTEX

550 MG

ANSAID

FLURBIPROFEN
UPJOHN

50 MG

100 MG

ANTIVERT

MECLIZINE HCL
ROERIG

12.5 MG

ANTIVERT/25

MECLIZINE HCL
ROERIG

25 MG

ANTIVERT/50

MECLIZINE HCL
ROERIG

50 MG

APRESAZIDE

**HYDRALAZINE HCL/
HYDROCHLOROTHIAZIDE**
CIBA

25 MG / 25 MG

50 MG / 50 MG

100 MG / 50 MG

ARMOUR THYROID

THYROID
FOREST

15 MG   30 MG

60 MG   90 MG

120 MG   180 MG

240 MG   300 MG

ARTANE

TRIHEXYPHENIDYL HCL
LEDERLE LABORATORIES

2 MG

5 MG

5 MG
SEQUELS

ATARAX

HYDROXYZINE HCL
ROERIG

10 MG

25 MG

50 MG

100 MG

ATIVAN

LORAZEPAM
WYETH-AYERST

0.5 MG

1 MG

2 MG

ATROMID-S

CLOFIBRATE
WYETH-AYERST

500 MG

AUGMENTIN

**AMOXICILLIN/
CLAVULANATE POTASSIUM**
SMITHKLINE BEECHAM

250 MG / 125 MG

500 MG / 125 MG

125 MG/31.25 MG
CHEWABLE

250 MG/62.5 MG
CHEWABLE

AXID

NIZATIDINE
ELI LILLY

150 MG

300 MG

AZULFIDINE EN-TABS

SULFASALAZINE
KABI

500 MG

BACTRIM

**SULFAMETHOXAZOLE/
TRIMETHOPRIM**
ROCHE

400 MG / 80 MG

BACTRIM DS

**SULFAMETHOXAZOLE/
TRIMETHOPRIM**
ROCHE

800 MG / 160 MG

BEEPEN-VK

PENICILLIN V POTASSIUM
SMITHKLINE BEECHAM

250 MG

500 MG

BENADRYL

DIPHENHYDRAMINE HCL
WARNER WELLCOME

25 MG

BENADRYL KAPSEALS

DIPHENHYDRAMINE HCL
WARNER WELLCOME

25 MG

50 MG

BENTYL

DICYCLOMINE HCL
MARION MERRELL DOW

10 MG

20 MG

BIAXIN

CLARITHROMYCIN
ABBOTT

250 MG

500 MG

BLOCADREN

TIMOLOL MALEATE
MERCK

5 MG   10 MG

20 MG

BUMEX

BUMETANIDE
ROCHE

0.5 MG   1 MG

2 MG

BUSPAR

BUSPIRONE HCL
BRISTOL-MYERS SQUIBB

5 MG   10 MG

CALAN

VERAPAMIL HCL
G. D. SEARLE

40 MG   80 MG

120 MG

CALAN SR

VERAPAMIL HCL
G. D. SEARLE

120 MG

180 MG

240 MG

CAPOTEN

CAPTOPRIL
BRISTOL-MYERS SQUIBB

12.5 MG

25 MG

50 MG

100 MG

CAPOZIDE

**CAPTOPRIL/
HYDROCHLOROTHIAZIDE**
BRISTOL-MYERS SQUIBB

25 MG/15 MG

25 MG/25 MG

50 MG/15 MG

50 MG/25 MG

CARAFATE

SUCRALFATE
MARION MERRELL DOW

1 GM

CARDENE

NICARDIPINE HCL
SYNTEX

20 MG

30 MG

CARDENE SR

NICARDIPINE HCL
SYNTEX

30 MG

45 MG

60 MG

CARDIZEM

DILTIAZEM HCL
MARION MERRELL DOW

30 MG   60 MG

90 MG

120 MG

CARDIZEM CD

DILTIAZEM HCL
MARION MERRELL DOW

120 MG

180 MG

240 MG

300 MG

CARDIZEM SR

DILTIAZEM HCL
MARION MERRELL DOW

60 MG

90 MG

120 MG

CARDURA

DOXAZOSIN MESYLATE
ROERIG

1 MG   2 MG

4 MG   8 MG

CATAPRES

CLONIDINE HCL
BOEHRINGER INGELHEIM

0.1 MG

0.2 MG

0.3 MG

CECLOR

CEFACLOR
ELI LILLY

250 MG

500 MG

CEFTIN

CEFUROXIME AXETIL
GLAXO

125 MG

250 MG

500 MG

CEFZIL

CEFPROZIL
BRISTOL-MYERS SQUIBB

250 MG

500 MG

CIPRO

CIPROFLOXACIN HCL
MILES

250 MG

500 MG

750 MG

CLARITIN

LORATADINE
SCHERING

10 MG

CLARITIN D

LORATADINE/
PSEUDOEPHEDRINE SULFATE
SCHERING

5 MG/120 MG

CLINORIL

SULINDAC
MERCK

150 MG

200 MG

CLOMID

CLOMIPHENE CITRATE
MARION MERRELL DOW

50 MG

CLOXAPEN

CLOXACILLIN SODIUM
SMITHKLINE BEECHAM

250 MG

500 MG

CO-GESIC

HYDROCODONE
BITARTRATE/
ACETAMINOPHEN
CENTRAL

5 MG / 500 MG

COGENTIN

BENZTROPINE MESYLATE
MERCK

0.5 MG

1 MG

2 MG

COGNEX

TACRINE HCL
PARKE-DAVIS

10 MG

20 MG

30 MG

40 MG

COLACE

DOCUSATE SODIUM
ROBERTS

50 MG

100 MG

COMPAZINE

PROCHLORPERAZINE
SMITHKLINE BEECHAM

5 MG   10 MG

25 MG

COMPAZINE SPANSULE

PROCHLORPERAZINE
SMITHKLINE BEECHAM

10 MG

15 MG

CORGARD

NADOLOL
BRISTOL-MYERS SQUIBB

20 MG   40 MG

80 MG

120 MG

160 MG

CORZIDE

NADOLOL/
BENDROFLUMETHIAZIDE
PRINCETON

40 MG / 5 MG

COUMADIN

WARFARIN SODIUM
DUPONT PHARMA

1 MG   2 MG

2.5 MG   4 MG

5 MG   7.5 MG

10 MG

CYLERT

PEMOLINE
ABBOTT

18.75 MG

37.5 MG

75 MG

CYTOTEC

MISOPROSTOL
G. D. SEARLE

100 MCG   200 MCG

DALMANE

FLURAZEPAM HCL
ROCHE

15 MG

30 MG

DARVOCET-N 100

ACETAMINOPHEN/
PROPOXYPHENE NAPSYLATE
ELI LILLY

650 MG/100 MG

DARVON

PROPOXYPHENE HCL
ELI LILLY

65 MG

DARVON COMPOUND-65

PROPOXYPHENE HCL/
ASPIRIN/CAFFEINE
ELI LILLY

65 MG/389 MG/32.4 MG

DARVON-N

PROPOXYPHENE NAPSYLATE
ELI LILLY

100 MG

DECADRON

DEXAMETHASONE
MERCK

0.25 MG   0.5 MG

0.75 MG   1.5 MG

4 MG   6 MG

DELTASONE

PREDNISONE
UPJOHN

2.5 MG   5 MG

10 MG   20 MG

50 MG

DEMEROL

MEPERIDINE HCL
SANOFI WINTHROP

50 MG   100 MG

DEPAKOTE

DIVALPROEX SODIUM
ABBOTT

125 MG

250 MG

500 MG

DEPAKOTE SPRINKLE

DIVALPROEX SODIUM
ABBOTT

125 MG

DEXEDRINE

DEXTROAMPHETAMINE SULFATE
SMITHKLINE BEECHAM

5 MG

5 MG
EXTENDED RELEASE

15 MG
EXTENDED RELEASE

DIABETA

GLYBURIDE
HOECHST-ROUSSEL

1.25 MG

2.5 MG

5 MG

DIABINESE

CHLORPROPAMIDE
PFIZER

100 MG   250 MG

DIAMOX

ACETAZOLAMIDE
LEDERLE

125 MG   250 MG

DIAMOX SEQUELS

ACETAZOLAMIDE
LEDERLE

500 MG

DIFLUCAN	DISALCID	DONNATAL

DIFLUCAN

FLUCONAZOLE
ROERIG

50 MG   100 MG

150 MG   200 MG

DILANTIN INFATABS

PHENYTOIN
PARKE-DAVIS

50 MG
CHEWABLE

DILANTIN KAPSEALS

PHENYTOIN SODIUM
PARKE-DAVIS

30 MG

100 MG

DILAUDID

HYDROMORPHONE HCL
KNOLL

2 MG   4 MG

DISALCID

SALSALATE
RIKER

500 MG

500 MG

750 MG

DITROPAN

OXYBUTYNIN CHLORIDE
MARION MERRELL DOW

5 MG

DIURIL

CHLOROTHIAZIDE
MERCK

250 MG   500 MG

DOLOBID

DIFLUNISAL
MERCK

250 MG

500 MG

DONNATAL

**BELLADONNA ALKALOIDS/
PHENOBARBITAL**
A. H. ROBINS

DONNATAL EXTENTABS

**BELLADONNA ALKALOIDS/
PHENOBARBITAL**
A. H. ROBINS

DORAL

QUAZEPAM
WALLACE

7.5 MG   15 MG

DORYX

DOXYCYCLINE HYCLATE
PARKE-DAVIS

100 MG

DURICEF

**CEFADROXIL
MONOHYDRATE**
BRISTOL-MYERS SQUIBB

500 MG

1GM

DYCILL

DICLOXACILLIN SODIUM
SMITHKLINE BEECHAM

250 MG

500 MG

DYNACIRC

ISRADIPINE
SANDOZ

2.5 MG

5 MG

E.E.S. 400 FILMTAB

ERYTHROMYCIN ETHYLSUCCINATE
ABBOTT

400 MG

E-MYCIN

ERYTHROMYCIN
BOOTS

250 MG   333 MG

EFFEXOR

VENLAFAXINE HCL
WYETH-AYERST

25 MG   37.5 MG

50 MG   75 MG

100 MG

ELAVIL

AMITRIPTYLINE HCL
STUART

10 MG   25 MG

50 MG   75 MG

100 MG

150 MG

ELDEPRYL

SELEGILINE HCL
SOMERSET

5 MG

ENTEX LA

PHENYLPROPANOLAMINE HCL/GUAIFENESIN
PROCTER & GAMBLE

75 MG / 400 MG

EQUANIL

MEPROBAMATE
WYETH-AYERST

200 MG

400 MG

ERGOSTAT

ERGOTAMINE TARTRATE
PARKE-DAVIS

2 MG
SUBLINGUAL

ERYPED CHEWABLE

ERYTHROMYCIN ETHYLSUCCINATE
ABBOTT

200 MG

ERY-TAB

ERYTHROMYCIN
ABBOTT

250 MG

333 MG

500 MG

ERYTHROMYCIN

ERYTHROMYCIN
ABBOTT

250 MG

ERYTHROMYCIN FILMTAB

ERYTHROMYCIN
ABBOTT

250 MG

500 MG

ESIDRIX

HYDROCHLOROTHIAZIDE
CIBA

25 MG   50 MG

100 MG

ESKALITH

LITHIUM CARBONATE
SMITHKLINE BEECHAM

300 MG

ESKALITH CR

LITHIUM CARBONATE
SMITHKLINE BEECHAM

450 MG

EULEXIN

FLUTAMIDE
SCHERING

125 MG

FAMVIR

FAMCICLOVIR
SMITHKLINE BEECHAM

500 MG

FASTIN

PHENTERMINE HCL
SMITHKLINE BEECHAM

30 MG

FELBATOL

FELBAMATE
WALLACE

400 MG

600 MG

FELDENE

PIROXICAM
PRATT

10 MG

20 MG

FIORINAL

**BUTALBITAL/ASPIRIN/
CAFFEINE**
SANDOZ

50 MG / 325 MG / 40 MG

50 MG / 325 MG / 40 MG

FIORINAL W/CODEINE

**BUTALBITAL/ASPIRIN/
CAFFEINE/CODEINE**
SANDOZ

50 MG / 325 MG/
40 MG / 30 MG

FIORICET

**ACETAMINOPHEN/
BUTALBITAL/CAFFEINE**
SANDOZ

325 MG / 50 MG / 40 MG

FIORICET W/CODEINE

**ACETAMINOPHEN/
BUTALBITAL/CAFFEINE/
CODEINE**
SANDOZ

325 MG / 50 MG /
40 MG / 30 MG

FLAGYL

METRONIDAZOLE
G.D. SEARLE & CO.

250 MG

500 MG

FLEXERIL

CYCLOBENZAPRINE HCL
MERCK

10 MG

FLOXIN

OFLOXACIN
MCNEIL

200 MG

300 MG

400 MG

GANTRISIN

SULFISOXAZOLE
ROCHE

500 MG

GLUCOTROL

GLIPIZIDE
PRATT

5 MG

10 MG

HALCION

TRIAZOLAM
UPJOHN

0.125 MG   0.25 MG

HALDOL

HALOPERIDOL
MCNEIL

0.5 MG   1 MG

2 MG   5 MG

10 MG   20 MG

HISMANAL

ASTEMIZOLE
JANSSEN

10 MG

HYDERGINE

ERGOLOID MESYLATES
SANDOZ

0.5 MG   1 MG

1 MG
SUBLINGUAL

HYDERGINE LC

ERGOLOID MESYLATES
SANDOZ

1 MG

HYDROCET

HYDROCODONE BITARTRATE/ ACETAMINOPHEN
CARNRICK

5 MG / 500 MG

HYDRODIURIL

HYDROCHLOROTHIAZIDE
MERCK

25 MG   50 MG

100 MG

HYGROTON

CHLORTHALIDONE
RHONE-POULENC RORER

25 MG   50 MG

100 MG

HYTRIN

TERAZOSIN HCL
ABBOTT

1 MG   2 MG

5 MG   10 MG

IMODIUM A-D

LOPERAMIDE HCL
MCNEIL

2 MG

INDERAL

PROPRANOLOL HCL
WYETH-AYERST

10 MG   20 MG

40 MG   60 MG

80 MG

INDERAL LA

PROPRANOLOL HCL
WYETH-AYERST

60 MG

80 MG

120 MG

160 MG

INDERIDE

PROPRANOL HCL/ HYDROCHLOROTHIAZIDE
WYETH-AYERST

40 MG /   80 MG /
25 MG   25 MG

INDERIDE LA

PROPRANOL HCL/ HYDROCHLOROTHIAZIDE
WYETH-AYERST

80 MG / 50 MG

120 MG / 50 MG

160 MG / 50 MG

INDOCIN

INDOMETHACIN
MERCK

25 MG

50 MG

INDOCIN-SR

INDOMETHACIN
MERCK

75 MG

IMDUR

ISOSORBIDE MONONITRATE
KEY

60 MG

IONAMIN

PHENTERMINE RESIN
FISONS

15 MG

30 MG

ISOPTIN

VERAPAMIL HCL
KNOLL

40 MG   80 MG

120 MG

ISOPTIN SR

VERAPAMIL HCL
KNOLL

120 MG

180 MG

240 MG

ISORDIL

ISOSORBIDE DINITRATE
WYETH-AYERST

2.5 MG
SUBLINGUAL

5 MG
SUBLINGUAL

10 MG
SUBLINGUAL

ISORDIL TEMBIDS

ISOSORBIDE DINITRATE
WYETH-AYERST

40 MG

40 MG

ISORDIL TITRADOSE

ISOSORBIDE DINITRATE
WYETH-AYERST

5 MG   10 MG

20 MG   30 MG

40 MG

K-DUR

POTASSIUM CHLORIDE
KEY

10 MEQ

20 MEQ

KEFLEX

CEPHALEXIN
DISTA

250 MG

500 MG

KEFTAB

CEPHALEXIN HCL
DISTA

250 MG

500 MG

KLONOPIN

CLONAZEPAM
ROCHE

0.5 MG   1 MG

2 MG

KLOR-CON 8

POTASSIUM CHLORIDE
UPSHER-SMITH

8 MEQ

KLOR-CON 10

POTASSIUM CHLORIDE
UPSHER-SMITH

10 MEQ

LAMICTAL

LAMOTRIGINE
BURROUGHS WELLCOME

25 MG   100 MG

150 MG   200 MG

LANOXIN

DIGOXIN
BURROUGHS WELLCOME

0.125 MG   0.25 MG

0.5 MG

LASIX

FUROSEMIDE
HOECHST-ROUSSEL

20 MG   40 MG

80 MG

LEDERCILLIN VK

PENICILLIN V POTASSIUM
LEDERLE

250 MG   500 MG

LESCOL

FLUVASTATIN SODIUM
SANDOZ

20 MG

40 MG

LEVSIN

HYOSCYAMINE SULFATE
SCHWARZ

0.125 MG

LEVSIN / SL

HYOSCYAMINE SULFATE
SCHWARZ

0.125 MG

LEVSIN TIMECAPS

HYOSCYAMINE SULFATE
SCHWARZ

0.375 MG

LIBRIUM

CHLORDIAZEPOXIDE HCL
ROCHE

5 MG

10 MG

25 MG

LIBRAX

**CHLORDIAZEPOXIDE HCL/
CLIDINIUM BR**
ROCHE LABORATORIES

5 MG/2.5 MG

LODINE

ETODOLAC
WYETH-AYERST

200 MG

300 MG

400 MG

LONITEN

MINOXIDIL
UPJOHN

2.5 MG   10 MG

LOMOTIL

**DIPHENOXYLATE HCL/
ATROPINE SULFATE**
G. D. SEARLE

2.5 MG / 0.025 MG

LOPID

GEMFIBROZIL
PARKE-DAVIS

600 MG

LOPRESSOR

METOPROLOL TARTRATE
GEIGY

50 MG

100 MG

LOPURIN

ALLOPURINOL
BOOTS

100 MG   300 MG

LORABID

LORACARBEF
ELI LILLY

200 MG

400 MG

LORCET PLUS

**HYDROCODONE
BITARTRATE/
ACETAMINOPHEN**
UAD

7.5 MG / 650 MG

LORELCO

PROBUCOL
MARION MERRELL DOW

250 MG

500 MG

LOTENSIN

BENAZEPRIL HCL
CIBA

5 MG   10 MG

20 MG   40 MG

LOZOL

INDAPAMIDE
RHONE-POULENC RORER

1.25 MG   2.5 MG

LURIDE SF LOZI-TABS

SODIUM FLUORIDE
COLGATE-HOYT

1 MG

LUVOX

FLUVOXAMINE MALEATE
SOLVAY

50 MG

100 MG

MACRODANTIN

NITROFURANTOIN
PROCTER & GAMBLE

25 MG

50 MG

100 MG

MACROBID

NITROFURANTOIN MONOHYDRATE/ MACROCRYSTALS
PROCTER & GAMBLE

75 MG / 25 MG

MAXAQUIN

LOMEFLOXACIN HCL
G. D. SEARLE

400 MG

MAXZIDE

TRIAMTERENE/ HYDROCHLOROTHIAZIDE
LEDERLE

37.5 MG/ 25 MG	75 MG/ 50 MG

MEDROL

METHYLPREDNISOLONE
UPJOHN

2 MG	4 MG

8 MG	16 MG

24 MG	32 MG

MELLARIL

THIORIDAZINE HCL
SANDOZ

10 MG	15 MG

25 MG	50 MG

100 MG	150 MG

200 MG

METHOTREXATE SODIUM

METHOTREXATE SODIUM
LEDERLE

2.5 MG

MEVACOR

LOVASTATIN
MERCK

10 MG

20 MG

40 MG

MEXITIL

MEXILETINE HCL
BOEHRINGER INGELHEIM

150 MG

200 MG

250 MG

MICRO-K EXTENCAPS

POTASSIUM CHLORIDE
A. H. ROBINS

8 MEQ

MICRO-K 10 EXTENCAPS

POTASSIUM CHLORIDE
A. H. ROBINS

10 MEQ

MICRONASE

GLYBURIDE
UPJOHN

1.25 MG

2.5 MG

5 MG

MIDRIN

ISOMETHEPTENE MUCATE/
DICHLORALPHENAZONE/
ACETAMINOPHEN
CARNRICK

65 MG / 100 MG / 325 MG

MILTOWN

MEPROBAMATE
WALLACE

200 MG

400 MG

600 MG

MINIPRESS

PRAZOSIN HCL
PFIZER

1 MG

2 MG

5 MG

MINOCIN

MINOCYCLINE HCL
LEDERLE

50 MG

100 MG

MODURETIC

AMILORIDE HCL/
HYDROCHLOROTHIAZIDE
MERCK

5 MG / 50 MG

MONOPRIL

FOSINOPRIL SODIUM
BRISTOL-MYERS SQUIBB

10 MG   20 MG

MOTRIN

IBUPROFEN
UPJOHN

300 MG   400 MG

600 MG

800 MG

MS CONTIN

MORPHINE SULFATE
PURDUE FREDERICK

15 MG   30 MG

60 MG   100 MG

200 MG

MYCOSTATIN

NYSTATIN
APOTHECON

500,000 UNITS

MYCOSTATIN PASTILLES

NYSTATIN
BRISTOL-MYERS ONCOLOGY

200,000 UNITS

MYSOLINE

PRIMIDONE
WYETH-AYERST

50 MG   250 MG

NAPROSYN

NAPROXEN
SYNTEX

250 MG

375 MG

500 MG

NARDIL

PHENELZINE SULFATE
PARKE-DAVIS

15 MG

NAVANE

THIOTHIXENE
ROERIG

1 MG

2 MG

5 MG

10 MG

20 MG

NEPTAZANE

METHAZOLAMIDE
LEDERLE

25 MG   50 MG

NEURONTIN

GABAPENTIN
PARKE-DAVIS

100 MG   300 MG

400 MG

NIZORAL

KETOCONAZOLE
JANSSEN

200 MG

NOLAMINE

**CHLORPHENIRAMINE
MALEATE/PHENINDAMINE
TARTRATE/PHENYL-
PROPANOLAMINE HCL**
CARNRICK

4 MG / 24 MG / 50 MG

NOLVADEX

TAMOXIFEN CITRATE
ZENECA

10 MG

NORFLEX

ORPHENADRINE CITRATE
3M

100 MG

NOROXIN

NORFLOXACIN
MERCK

400 MG

NORMODYNE

LABETALOL HCL
SCHERING

100 MG   200 MG

300 MG

NORPACE

**DISOPYRAMIDE
PHOSPHATE**
G. D. SEARLE

100 MG

150 MG

NORPACE CR

DISOPYRAMIDE PHOSPHATE
G. D. SEARLE

100 MG

150 MG

NORPRAMIN

DESIPRAMINE HCL
MARION MERRELL DOW

10 MG   25 MG

50 MG   75 MG

100 MG   150 MG

NORVASC

AMLODIPINE BESYLATE
PFIZER

2.5 MG

5 MG

10 MG

OGEN

ESTROPIPATE
UPJOHN

0.625 MG

1.25 MG

2.5 MG

OMNIPEN

AMPICILLIN
WYETH-AYERST

250 MG

500 MG

ORASONE

PREDNISONE
SOLVAY

1 MG

ORETIC

HYDROCHLOROTHIAZIDE
ABBOTT

50 MG

ORGANIDIN-NR

GUAIFENESIN
WALLACE

200 MG

ORINASE

TOLBUTAMIDE
UPJOHN

250 MG   500 MG

ORUDIS

KETOPROFEN
WYETH-AYERST

25 MG

50 MG

75 MG

PAMELOR

NORTRIPTYLINE HCL
SANDOZ

10 MG

25 MG

50 MG

75 MG

PANCREASE	**PARLODEL**	**PENETREX**

PANCREASE

PANCRELIPASE
MCNEIL

PARLODEL

BROMOCRIPTINE MESYLATE
SANDOZ

2.5 MG

5 MG

PENETREX

ENOXACIN
RHONE-POULENC RORER

200 MG

400 MG

PANCREASE MT 4

PANCRELIPASE
MCNEIL

PAXIL

PAROXETINE HCL
SMITHKLINE BEECHAM

20 MG

30 MG

PEN-VEE K

PENICILLIN V POTASSIUM
WYETH-AYERST

250 MG   500 MG

PANCREASE MT 10

PANCRELIPASE
MCNEIL

PBZ-SR

TRIPELENNAMINE HCL
GEIGY

100 MG

PEPCID

FAMOTIDINE
MERCK

20 MG   40 MG

PANCREASE MT 16

PANCRELIPASE
MCNEIL

PCE

ERYTHROMYCIN
ABBOTT

333 MG

500 MG

PERCOCET

**OXYCODONE HCL/
ACETAMINOPHEN**
DUPONT

5 MG / 325 MG

PANCREASE MT 20

PANCRELIPASE
MCNEIL

PARAFON FORTE DSC

CHLORZOXAZONE
MCNEIL

500 MG

PERIACTIN

CYPROHEPTADINE HCL
MERCK

4 MG

PERSANTINE

DIPYRIDAMOLE
BOEHRINGER INGELHEIM

25MG   50 MG

75 MG

PHENAPHEN W/CODEINE NO.3

ACETAMINOPHEN/ CODEINE PHOSPHATE
A. H. ROBINS

325 MG / 30 MG

PHENAPHEN W/CODEINE NO.4

ACETAMINOPHEN/ CODEINE PHOSPHATE
A. H. ROBINS

325 MG / 60 MG

PHENERGAN

PROMETHAZINE HCL
WYETH-AYERST

12.5 MG   25 MG

50 MG

PLAQUENIL

HYDROXCHLOROQUINE SULFATE
SANOFI WINTHROP

200 MG

PLENDIL

FELODIPINE
MERCK

5 MG   10 MG

POLARAMINE

DEXCHLORPHENIRAMINE MALEATE
SCHERING

2 MG

POLARAMINE REPETABS

DEXCHLORPHENIRAMINE MALEATE
SCHERING

4 MG   6 MG

POLYMOX

AMOXICILLIN
APOTHECON

250 MG

500 MG

POLY-VI-FLOR

SODIUM FLUORIDE/ MULTIVITAMINS
MEAD JOHNSON

0.5 MG
CHEWABLE

1 MG
CHEWABLE

PONSTEL KAPSEALS

MEFENAMIC ACID
PARKE-DAVIS

250 MG

PRAVACHOL

PRAVASTATIN SODIUM
BRISTOL-MYERS SQUIBB

10 MG

20 MG

PRILOSEC

OMEPRAZOLE
ASTRA MERCK

20 MG

PRINIVIL

LISINOPRIL
MERCK

2.5 MG

5 MG

10 MG

20 MG

40 MG

PROCAN SR

PROCAINAMIDE HCL
PARKE-DAVIS

500 MG

750 MG

1000 MG

PROCARDIA

NIFEDIPINE
PRATT

10 MG

20 MG

PROCARDIA XL

NIFEDIPINE
PRATT

30 MG

60 MG

90 MG

PROPULSID

CISAPRIDE
JANSSEN

10 MG

PROSCAR

FINASTERIDE
MERCK

5 MG

PROSOM

ESTAZOLAM
ABBOTT

1 MG

2 MG

PROVENTIL

ALBUTEROL SULFATE
SCHERING

2 MG

4 MG

PROVENTIL REPETABS

ALBUTEROL SULFATE
SCHERING

4 MG

PROZAC

FLUOXETINE HCL
DISTA

10 MG

20 MG

PYRIDIUM

PHENAZOPYRIDINE HCL
PARKE-DAVIS

100 MG   200 MG

QUINIDEX EXTENTABS

QUINIDINE SULFATE
A. H. ROBINS

300 MG

REGLAN

METOCLOPRAMIDE HCL
A. H. ROBINS

5 MG   10 MG

RELAFEN	**RIDAURA**	**ROBAXIN-750**
NABUMETONE	AURANOFIN	METHOCARBAMOL
SMITHKLINE BEECHAM	SMITHKLINE BEECHAM	A. H. ROBINS

500 MG

750 MG

RESTORIL

TEMAZEPAM
SANDOZ

7.5 MG

15 MG

30 MG

RETROVIR

ZIDOVUDINE
BURROUGHS WELLCOME

100 MG

REVIA

NALTREXONE HCL
DUPONT

50 MG

3 MG

RIFATER

ISONIAZID/ RIFAMPIN/
PYRAZINAMIDE
MARION MERRELL DOW

50 MG / 120 MG / 300 MG

RITALIN

METHYLPHENIDATE HCL
CIBA

5 MG   10 MG

20 MG

RITALIN-SR

METHYLPHENIDATE HCL
CIBA

20 MG

ROBAXIN

METHOCARBAMOL
A. H. ROBINS

500 MG

750 MG

ROCALTROL

CALCITRIOL
ROCHE

0.25 MCG   0.5 MCG

RONDEC

CARBINOXAMINE MALEATE/
PSEUDOEPHEDRINE HCL
ROSS

4 MG / 60 MG

RUFEN

IBUPROFEN
BOOTS

IBU 400

400 MG

IBU 600

600 MG

IBU 800

800 MG

RU-TUSS

**PHENYLEPHRINE/
PHENYLPROPANOLAMINE/
CHLORPHENIRAMINE/
BELLADONNA ALKALOIDS**
BOOTS

RYNATAN

**PHENYLEPHRINE/
CHLORPHENIRAMINE/
PYRILAMINE TANNATES**
WALLACE

25 MG / 8 MG / 25 MG

RYTHMOL

PROPAFENONE HCL
KNOLL

150 MG   225 MG

300 MG

SANDIMMUNE

CYCLOSPORINE
SANDOZ

25 MG

50 MG

100 MG

SECTRAL

ACEBUTOLOL HCL
WYETH-AYERST

200 MG

400 MG

SELDANE

TERFENADINE
MARION MERRELL DOW

60 MG

SEMPREX D

**ACRIVASTINE/
PSEUDOEPHEDRINE HCL**
BURROUGHS WELLCOME

8 MG / 60 MG

SEPTRA

**SULFAMETHOXAZOLE/
TRIMETHOPRIM**
BURROUGHS WELLCOME

400 MG / 80 MG

SEPTRA DS

**SULFAMETHOXAZOLE/
TRIMETHOPRIM**
BURROUGHS WELLCOME

800 MG / 160 MG

SERAX

OXAZEPAM
WYETH-AYERST

10 MG   15 MG

15 MG

30 MG

SERZONE

NEFAZODONE HCL
BRISTOL-MYERS SQUIBB

100 MG   150 MG

200 MG

250 MG

SINEQUAN

DOXEPIN HCL
ROERIG

10 MG

25 MG

50 MG

75 MG

100 MG

150 MG

SLO-BID GYROCAPS

THEOPHYLLINE
RHONE-POULENC RORER

50 MG

75 MG

100 MG

125 MG

200 MG

300 MG

SLO-PHYLLIN

THEOPHYLLINE
RHONE-POULENC RORER

100 MG   200 MG

SLO-PHYLLIN GYROCAPS

THEOPHYLLINE
RHONE-POULENC RORER

125 MG

250 MG

SLOW-K

POTASSIUM CHLORIDE
SUMMIT

8 MEQ

SORBITRATE

ISOSORBIDE DINITRATE
ZENECA

5 MG   10 MG

20 MG   30 MG

40 MG

5 MG   10 MG
CHEWABLE   CHEWABLE

2.5 MG   5 MG
SUBLINGUAL   SUBLINGUAL

10 MG
SUBLINGUAL

SPORANOX

ITRACONAZOLE
JANSSEN

100 MG

STELAZINE

TRIFLUOPERAZINE HCL
SMITHKLINE BEECHAM

1 MG   2 MG

STUARTNATAL PLUS

VITAMINS, PRENATAL
WYETH-AYERST

SUPRAX

CEFIXIME
LEDERLE

200 MG

400 MG

SURMONTIL

TRIMIPRAMINE MALEATE
WYETH-AYERST

25 MG

50 MG

100 MG

SYNTHROID

LEVOTHYROXINE SODIUM
BOOTS

0.025 MG

0.05 MG

0.075 MG

0.088 MG

0.1 MG

0.112 MG

0.125 MG

0.15 MG

0.175 MG

0.2 MG

0.3 MG

TAGAMET

CIMETIDINE
SMITHKLINE BEECHAM

200 MG

300 MG

400 MG

800 MG

TALWIN NX

PENTAZOCINE HCL/
NALOXONE HCL
SANOFI WINTHROP

50 MG / 0.5 MG

TAVIST

CLEMASTINE FUMARATE
SANDOZ

2.68 MG

TEGRETOL

CARBAMAZEPINE
BASEL

200 MG

100 MG
CHEWABLE

TENORETIC 50

ATENOLOL/
CHLORTHALIDONE
ZENECA

50 MG/25 MG

TENORETIC 100

ATENOLOL/
CHLORTHALIDONE
ZENECA

100 MG/25 MG

TENORMIN

ATENOLOL
ZENECA

25 MG

50 MG

100 MG

TENUATE

DIETHYLPROPION HCL
MARION MERRELL DOW

25 MG

TENUATE DOSPAN

DIETHYLPROPION HCL
MARION MERRELL DOW

75 MG

TESSALON PERLES

BENZONATATE
FOREST

100 MG

THEOCHRON	THEOLAIR	THYROLAR-1/4

THEOCHRON
THEOPHYLLINE
FOREST

100 MG

200 MG

300 MG

THEO-DUR
THEOPHYLLINE
KEY

100 MG   200 MG

300 MG

450 MG

THEO-DUR SPRINKLE
THEOPHYLLINE
KEY

50 MG

75 MG

125 MG

200 MG

THEOLAIR
THEOPHYLLINE
3M

125 MG

250 MG

THEOLAIR-SR
THEOPHYLLINE
3M

200 MG   250 MG

300 MG

500 MG

THORAZINE
CHLORPROMAZINE HCL
SMITHKLINE BEECHAM

25 MG   50 MG

THORAZINE SPANSULES
CHLORPROMAZINE HCL
SMITHKLINE BEECHAM

75 MG

THYROLAR-1/4
LIOTRIX
FOREST

15 MG

THYROLAR-1/2
LIOTRIX
FOREST

30 MG

THYROLAR-1
LIOTRIX
FOREST

60 MG

THYROLAR-2
LIOTRIX
FOREST

120 MG

THYROLAR-3
LIOTRIX
FOREST

180 MG

TIGAN
TRIMETHOBENZAMIDE HCL
SMITHKLINE BEECHAM

100 MG

250 MG

TOFRANIL

IMIPRAMINE HCL
GEIGY

10 MG

25 MG

50 MG

TOLECTIN

TOLMETIN SODIUM
MCNEIL

200 MG

TOLECTIN DS

TOLMETIN SODIUM
MCNEIL

400 MG

TOLECTIN 600

TOLMETIN SODIUM
MCNEIL

600 MG

TONOCARD

TOCAINIDE HCL
MERCK

400 MG

600 MG

TORADOL

KETOROLAC TROMETHAMINE
SYNTEX

10 MG

TRANDATE

LABETALOL HCL
ALLEN & HANBURYS

100 MG   200 MG

300 MG

TRANXENE - SD

**CLORAZEPATE
DIPOTASSIUM**
ABBOTT

11.25 MG   22.5 MG

TRANXENE T-TAB

**CLORAZEPATE
DIPOTASSIUM**
ABBOTT

3.75 MG   7.5 MG

15 MG

TRENTAL

PENTOXIFYLLINE
HOECHST-ROUSSEL

400 MG

TRILAFON

PERPHENAZINE
SCHERING

2 MG   4 MG

8 MG   16 MG

TRILISATE

**CHOLINE MAGNESIUM
TRISALICYLATE**
PURDUE FREDERICK

500 MG

750 MG

1000 MG

TRINALIN REPETABS

AZATADINE MALEATE/
PSEUDOEPHEDRINE
SULFATE
KEY

1 MG / 120 MG

TYLENOL W/CODEINE NO.2

ACETAMINOPHEN/ CODEINE
PHOSPHATE
MCNEIL

300 MG / 15 MG

TYLENOL W/CODEINE NO.3

ACETAMINOPHEN/ CODEINE
PHOSPHATE
MCNEIL

300 MG / 30 MG

TYLENOL W/CODEINE NO.4

ACETAMINOPHEN/ CODEINE
PHOSPHATE
MCNEIL

300 MG / 60 MG

TYLOX

OXYCODONE HCL/
ACETAMINOPHEN
MCNEIL

5 MG / 500 MG

UNIPHYL

THEOPHYLLINE
PURDUE FREDERICK

400 MG

URISED

ATROPINE SULFATE/
BENZOIC ACID/
HYOSCYAMINE/
METHENAMINE/
METHYLENE BLUE/
PHENYL SALICYLATE
POLYMEDICA

0.03 MG / 4.5 MG / 0.03 MG /
40.8 MG / 5.4 MG / 18.1 MG

URISPAS

FLAVOXATE HCL
SMITHKLINE BEECHAM

100 MG

VALIUM

DIAZEPAM
ROCHE

2 MG   5 MG

10 MG

VASERETIC

ENALAPRIL MALEATE/
HYDROCHLOROTHIAZIDE
MERCK

10 MG / 25 MG

VASOTEC

ENALAPRIL MALEATE
MERCK

2.5 MG   5 MG

10 MG   20 MG

V-CILLIN K

PENICILLIN V POTASSIUM
ELI LILLY

125 MG

250 MG

500 MG

VIBRAMYCIN

DOXYCYCLINE HYCLATE
PFIZER

VIBRA | PFIZER 094

50 MG

VIBRA | PFIZER 095

100 MG

VIBRA-TABS

DOXYCYCLINE HYCLATE
PFIZER

100 MG

VICODIN

**HYDROCODONE
BITARTRATE/
ACETAMINOPHEN**
KNOLL

5 MG / 500 MG

VISKEN

PINDOLOL
SANDOZ

5 MG

10 MG

VOLTAREN

DICLOFENAC SODIUM
GEIGY

25 MG   50 MG

75 MG

WELLBUTRIN

BUPROPION HCL
BURROUGHS WELLCOME

75 MG   100 MG

WYMOX

AMOXICILLIN
WYETH-AYERST

WYETH 559

250 MG

WYETH 560

500 MG

XANAX

ALPRAZOLAM
UPJOHN

0.25 MG   0.5 MG

1 MG

2 MG

YOCON

YOHIMBINE HCL
PALISADES

5.4 MG

YOHIMEX

YOHIMBINE HCL
KRAMER

'5.4 MG

ZANTAC

RANITIDINE HCL
GLAXO

150 MG

300 MG

ZANTAC GELDOSE

RANITIDINE HCL
GLAXO

150 MG

300 MG

ZANTAC EFFERDOSE

RANITIDINE HCL
GLAXO

150 MG

ZAROXOLYN

METOLAZONE
FISONS

2.5 MG

5 MG

10 MG

ZERIT

STAVUDINE
BRISTOL-MYERS ONCOLOGY

15 MG

20 MG

30 MG

40 MG

ZESTORETIC

**LISINOPRIL/
HYDROCHLOROTHIAZIDE**
STUART

10 MG/12.5 MG

20 MG/12.5 MG

20 MG/25 MG

ZESTRIL

LISINOPRIL
STUART

5 MG   10 MG

20 MG   40 MG

ZITHROMAX

AZITHROMYCIN DIHYDRATE
PFIZER

250 MG

ZOCOR

SIMVASTATIN
MERCK

5 MG   10 MG

20 MG   40 MG

ZOFRAN

ONDANSETRON HCL
CERENEX

4 MG

8 MG

ZOVIRAX

ACYCLOVIR
BURROUGHS WELLCOME

200 MG

400 MG

800 MG

ZYLOPRIM

ALLOPURINOL
BURROUGHS WELLCOME

100 MG

300 MG

dyskinesia—a possibly irreversible condition marked by involuntary muscle spasms and twitches in the face and body. Elderly people should consult their doctor for information about these potential risks.

Depression, Anxiety and Sleep Disturbances
The starting dose is 75 milligrams a day, divided into 3 doses per day. The dosage may range from 20 to 200 milligrams a day, divided into 2 to 4 doses.

Overdosage
Any medication taken in excess can have serious consequences. An overdose of Mellaril can be fatal. If you suspect an overdose, seek medical help immediately.

■ *Symptoms of Mellaril overdose may include:*
Agitation
Coma
Convulsions
Dry mouth
Extreme drowsiness
Extreme low blood pressure
Fever
Intestinal blockage
Irregular heart rate
Restlessness

Generic name:

MEPERIDINE

See Demerol, page 297.

Generic name:

MEPROBAMATE

See Miltown, page 667.

Generic name:

MESALAMINE

See Rowasa, page 984.

Brand name:

METAPREL

See Alupent, page 39.

Generic name:

METAPROTERENOL

See Alupent, page 39.

Generic name:

METHAZOLAMIDE

See Neptazane, page 719.

Generic name:

METHENAMINE

See Urised, page 1176.

Brand name:

METHERGINE

Pronounced: METH-er-jin
Generic name: Methylergonovine maleate

Why is this drug prescribed?
Methergine, a blood-vessel constrictor, is given to prevent or control excessive bleeding following childbirth. It works by causing the uterine muscles to contract, therefore reducing the mother's blood loss.

Methergine comes in tablet and injectable forms.

Most important fact about this drug
Some blood-vessel disorders and certain infections make the use of Methergine dangerous. Make sure your doctor is aware of any medical conditions you may have.

How should you take this medication?
Take Methergine tablets exactly as prescribed.

■ *If you miss a dose...*
Do not take the missed dose at all and do not double the next one. Instead, go back to your regular schedule.

■ *Storage instructions...*
Store at room temperature in a tightly closed container, away from light.

What side effects may occur?
Side effects cannot be anticipated. If any develop or change in intensity, inform your doctor as soon as possible. Only your doctor can determine if it is safe for you to continue taking Methergine.

The most common side effect is high blood pressure, which may cause a headache or even a seizure. In some people, however, Methergine may cause low blood pressure.

■ *Less common or rare side effects may include:*
Bad taste, blood clots, blood in urine, chest pains (temporary), diarrhea, difficult or labored breathing, dizziness, edema, hallucinations, leg cramps, nasal congestion, nausea, palpitations (throbbing heartbeat), ringing in the ears, sweating, vomiting

Why should this drug not be prescribed?
You should not take Methergine if you are allergic to it, if you are pregnant, or if you have high blood pressure or toxemia (poisons circulating in the blood).

Special warnings about this medication
It may be dangerous to take Methergine if you have an infection, certain blood vessel disorders, or a liver or kidney problem. Inform your doctor if you think you have any such condition.

Possible food and drug interactions
when taking this medication
If Methergine is taken with certain other drugs, the effects of either may be increased, decreased, or altered. It is especially important to check with your doctor before combining Methergine with the following:

Other blood-vessel constrictors such as EpiPen
Other ergot-derived medications such as Ergotrate

Special information
if you are pregnant or breastfeeding
Methergine should not be taken during pregnancy. Methergine appears in breast milk. Although no specific information is available about possible effects of Methergine on a nursing baby, the general rule is that a mother who is breastfeeding should not take any drug unless it is clearly needed.

Recommended dosage
The usual dose is 1 tablet, 0.2 milligram, 3 or 4 times daily after childbirth for a maximum of 1 week.

Overdosage
Any medication taken in excess can have serious consequences. If you suspect symptoms of a Methergine overdose, seek medical attention immediately.

- *Symptoms of Methergine overdose may include:*
  Abdominal pain, coma, convulsions, elevated blood pressure, hypothermia (drop in body temperature), lowered blood pressure, nausea, numbness, slowed breathing, tingling of the arms and legs, vomiting

Generic name:

METHOCARBAMOL

See Robaxin, page 973.

Generic name:

METHOTREXATE

Pronounced: meth-oh-TREX-ate
Brand name: Rheumatrex

Why is this drug prescribed?
Methotrexate is an anticancer drug used in the treatment of lymphoma (cancer of the lymph nodes) and certain forms of leukemia. It is also given to treat some forms of cancers of the uterus, breast, lung, head, neck, and ovary. Methotrexate is also given to treat rheumatoid arthritis when other treatments have proved ineffective, and is sometimes used to treat very severe and disabling psoriasis (a skin disease characterized by thickened patches of red, inflamed skin often covered by silver scales).

Most important fact about this drug

Be certain to remember that in the treatment of psoriasis and rheumatoid arthritis, methotrexate is taken once a *week*, not once a day. Accidentally taking the recommended weekly dosage on a daily basis can lead to fatal overdosage. Be sure to read the patient instructions that come with the package.

How should you take this medication?

Take methotrexate exactly as prescribed, and promptly report to your doctor any new symptoms that may develop.

Methotrexate is given at a higher dosage for cancer than for psoriasis or rheumatoid arthritis. After high-dose methotrexate treatment, a drug called leucovorin may be given to limit the toxic effects.

■ *If you miss a dose...*
Skip it and go back to your regular schedule. Do not take 2 doses at once.

■ *Storage instructions...*
Store at room temperature, away from light.

What side effects may occur?

Side effects cannot be anticipated. If any develop or change in intensity, inform your doctor as soon as possible. Only your doctor can determine whether it is safe for you to continue taking methotrexate.

■ *More common side effects may include:*
Abdominal pain and upset
Chills and fever
Decreased resistance to infection
Dizziness
Fatigue
General feeling of illness
Mouth ulcers
Nausea

■ *Less common side effects may include:*
Abortion, acne, anemia, birth defects, black or tarry stool, blurred vision, boils, bruises, changes in skin coloration, convulsions, diarrhea, drowsiness, fatigue, hair loss, headaches, hives, inability to speak, infection of hair follicles, infertility, inflammation of the gums or mouth, intestinal inflammation, kidney failure, loss of appetite, lung disease, menstrual

problems, partial or complete paralysis, rash or itching, red patches on skin, sensitivity to light, sore throat, stomach and intestinal ulcers and bleeding, stomach pain, vaginal discharge, vomiting, vomiting blood

■ *Rare side effects may include:*
Diabetes, impotence, infection, joint pain, loss of sexual desire, muscular pain, osteoporosis, ringing in the ears, severe allergic reaction, shortness of breath, sleepiness, sudden death, sweating

If you are taking methotrexate for psoriasis, you may also experience hair loss and/or sun sensitivity, and your patches of psoriasis may give a burning sensation.

Methotrexate can sometimes cause serious lung damage that makes it necessary to limit the treatment. If you experience a dry cough, fever, or breathing difficulties while taking methotrexate, be sure to tell your doctor right away.

During and immediately after treatment with methotrexate, fertility may be impaired. Men may have an abnormally low sperm count; women may have menstrual irregularities.

Why should this drug not be prescribed?
Do not take this medication if you are sensitive to it or it has given you an allergic reaction.

Do not take this medication if you are pregnant.

Methotrexate treatment is not suitable for you if you suffer from psoriasis or rheumatoid arthritis and also have one of the following conditions:

Abnormal blood cell count
Alcoholic liver disease or other chronic liver disease
Alcoholism
Anemia
Immune-system deficiency

Special warnings about this medication
Before you start taking methotrexate, your doctor will do a chest X-ray plus blood tests to determine your blood cell counts, liver enzyme levels, and the efficiency of your kidney function. While you are taking methotrexate, the blood tests will be repeated at regular intervals; if you develop a cough or chest pain, the chest X-ray will be repeated.

Older or physically debilitated people are particularly vulnerable to toxic effects from methotrexate.

Your doctor will prescribe methotrexate with great caution if you have any of the following:

    Active infection
    Liver disease
    Peptic ulcer
    Ulcerative colitis

Possible food and drug interactions
when taking this medication

If you are being given methotrexate for the treatment of cancer or psoriasis, you should not take aspirin or other nonsteroidal painkillers such as Advil or Naprosyn; this combination could increase the toxic effects of methotrexate. If you are taking methotrexate for rheumatoid arthritis, you may be able to continue taking aspirin or a nonsteroidal painkiller, but your doctor should monitor you carefully.

Other drugs that may increase the toxic effects of methotrexate include:

    Cisplatin (Platinol)
    Phenylbutazone (Butazolidin)
    Phenytoin (Dilantin)
    Probenecid (Benemid)
    Sulfa drugs such as Bactrim and Gantrisin

Sulfa drugs may increase methotrexate's toxic effect on the bone marrow, where new blood cells are made.

Certain antibiotics, including tetracycline (Achromycin) and chloramphenicol (Chloromycetin) may reduce the effectiveness of methotrexate. This is also true of vitamin preparations that contain folic acid.

Special information
if you are pregnant or breastfeeding

A woman should not start methotrexate therapy until the doctor is sure she is not pregnant. Because methotrexate causes birth defects and miscarriages, it must not be taken during pregnancy by women with psoriasis or rheumatoid arthritis. It should be taken by women being treated for cancer only if the potential benefit outweighs the risk to the developing baby. In fact, a couple should avoid pregnancy if either the man or the woman is taking methotrexate. After the end of methotrexate treatment, a man should wait at least 3 months, and a woman should wait for the completion of at least one menstrual cycle, before attempting to conceive a child.

Methotrexate should not be taken by a woman who is breastfeeding; it does pass into breast milk and may harm a nursing baby.

Recommended dosage
Treatment with methotrexate is highly individualized. Your doctor will carefully tailor your dosage of methotrexate in order to avoid serious side effects and possible under- or overdosing.

Overdosage
Taken in excess, methotrexate can cause serious and even fatal damage to the liver, kidneys, bone marrow, lungs, or other parts of the body. Symptoms of overdosage may include lung or breathing problems, mouth ulcers, or diarrhea. Initially, however, serious damage caused by methotrexate may be apparent only in the results of blood tests. For this reason, careful, regular monitoring by your doctor is necessary. If for any reason you suspect symptoms of an overdose of methotrexate, seek medical attention immediately.

Generic name:

METHYLDOPA

See Aldomet, page 31.

Generic name:

METHYLERGONOVINE

See Methergine, page 644.

Generic name:

METHYLPHENIDATE

See Ritalin, page 969.

Generic name:

METHYLPREDNISOLONE

See Medrol, page 635.

Generic name:

METOCLOPRAMIDE

See Reglan, page 937.

Generic name:

METOLAZONE

See Zaroxolyn, page 1220.

Generic name:

METOPROLOL

See Lopressor, page 595.

Generic name:

METRONIDAZOLE

See Flagyl, page 444.

Brand name:

MEVACOR

Pronounced: MEV-uh-core
Generic name: Lovastatin

Why is this drug prescribed?

Mevacor is used, along with diet, to lower cholesterol levels in the blood of patients with primary hypercholesterolemia (too much cholesterol), a condition caused by a lack of the low-density lipoprotein (LDL) receptors that remove cholesterol from the bloodstream. However, Mevacor is usually prescribed only when a low-fat, low-cholesterol diet does not lower cholesterol levels enough.

Most important fact about this drug

Mevacor is usually prescribed only if diet, exercise, and weight loss fail to bring your cholesterol levels under control. It's important to remember that Mevacor is a supplement—not a substitute—for these other measures. To get the full benefit of the medication, you need to stick to the diet and exercise program prescribed by your doctor. All these efforts to keep your cholesterol levels normal are important because together they may lower your risk of heart disease.

How should you take this medication?

Take Mevacor exactly as prescribed by your doctor.

Mevacor should be taken with meals.

■ *If you miss a dose...*
Take it as soon as you remember. If it is almost time for your next dose, skip the one you missed and go back to your regular schedule. Never take 2 doses at the same time.

■ *Storage instructions...*
Protect Mevacor from light. Store at room temperature. Keep container tightly closed.

What side effects may occur?
Mevacor is generally well tolerated. Any side effects that have occurred have usually been mild and short-lived. If any side effects develop or change in intensity, inform your doctor as soon as possible. Only your doctor can determine if it is safe for you to continue taking Mevacor.

■ *Side effects may include:*
Abdominal pain/cramps, altered sense of taste, blurred vision, constipation, diarrhea, dizziness, gas, headache, heartburn, indigestion, itching, muscle cramps, muscle pain, nausea, rash, weakness

Why should this drug not be prescribed?
If you are sensitive to or have ever had an allergic reaction to Mevacor or similar anticholesterol drugs, you should not take this medication. Make sure that your doctor is aware of any drug reactions that you have experienced.

Unless you are directed to do so by your doctor, do not take this medication if you are being treated for liver disease.

Do not take this drug if you are pregnant or nursing.

Special warnings about this medication
If you are being treated for any disease that contributes to increased blood cholesterol, such as hypothyroidism, diabetes, nephrotic syndrome (kidney and blood vessel disorder), dysproteinemia (an excess of protein in the blood), or liver disease, your doctor will closely monitor your reaction to Mevacor.

It is recommended that liver function tests be performed by your doctor before treatment with Mevacor begins, every 6 weeks during the first 3 months of therapy, every 8 weeks during the rest of the first year, and periodically (about 6-month intervals) thereafter.

This drug should be used with caution if you consume substantial quantities of alcohol or have a past history of liver disease.

Possible food and drug interactions
when taking this medication

If Mevacor is taken with certain other drugs, the effects of either could be increased, decreased, or altered. It is especially important to check with your doctor before combining Mevacor with the following:

Blood-thinning drugs such as Coumadin
Cyclosporine (Sandimmune) and other immunosuppressive drugs
   (medication that lowers the body's defense reaction to a foreign or
   invading substance)
Erythromycin (E.E.S., PCE, others)
Gemfibrozil (Lopid)
Itraconazole (Sporanox)
Nicotinic acid or niacin (Nicobid)

If you are taking Mevacor in combination with nicotinic acid, Lopid, or immunosuppressive drugs such as cyclosporine, alert your doctor immediately if you experience muscle pain, tenderness, or weakness, especially with fever or general bodily discomfort. This could be the first sign of impending kidney damage.

If you are taking cyclosporine and need to take Sporanox as well, the doctor will temporarily take you off Mevacor.

Special information
if you are pregnant or breastfeeding

You should take Mevacor only if pregnancy is highly unlikely. If you become pregnant while taking this drug, discontinue using it and notify your physician immediately. There may be a potential hazard to the developing baby. This medication may appear in breast milk and may have an effect on nursing infants. If this medication is essential to your health, you should discontinue breastfeeding until your treatment with this medication is finished.

Recommended dosage

ADULTS

The recommended starting dose is 20 milligrams once a day, taken with the evening meal. The maximum recommended dose is 80 milligrams per day, taken as a single dose or divided into smaller doses, as determined by your doctor. Adjustments to any dose, as determined by your doctor, should be made at intervals of 4 weeks or more.

If you are taking immunosuppressive drugs in combination with Mevacor, your dose of Mevacor should begin with 10 milligrams and should not exceed 20 milligrams per day.

Cholesterol levels should be monitored periodically by your doctor, who may decide to reduce the dose if your cholesterol level falls below the targeted range.

If you have reduced kidney function, your doctor will be cautious about increasing your dosage.

CHILDREN

The safety and effectiveness of this drug have not been established in children.

Overdosage
There have been no reported cases of overdose with Mevacor. However, if you suspect an overdose, seek medical attention immediately.

Generic name:

MEXILETINE HYDROCHLORIDE

See Mexitil, page 654.

Brand name:

MEXITIL

Pronounced: MEX-ih-till
Generic name: Mexiletine hydrochloride

Why is this drug prescribed?
Mexitil is used to treat severe irregular heartbeat (arrhythmia). Irregular heart rhythms are generally divided into two main types: heartbeats that are faster than normal (tachycardia) and heartbeats that are slower than normal (bradycardia). Arrhythmias are often caused by drugs or disease but can occur in otherwise healthy people with no history of heart disease or other illness.

Most important fact about this drug
While you are taking Mexitil, your doctor should carefully monitor your heartbeat to make sure the drug is working properly.

How should you take this medication?
Take Mexitil with food or an antacid. Take it exactly as prescribed.

■ *If you miss a dose...*
If you remember within 4 hours, take it immediately. If more than 4 hours have passed, skip the missed dose and return to your regular schedule. Never take 2 doses at the same time.

■ *Storage instructions...*
Store at room temperature.

What side effects may occur?
Side effects cannot be anticipated. If any develop or change in intensity, inform your doctor as soon as possible. Only your doctor can determine if it is safe for you to continue taking Mexitil.

■ *More common side effects may include:*
Blurred vision, changes in sleep habits, chest pain, constipation, depression, diarrhea, difficult or labored breathing, dizziness, headache, heartburn, light-headedness, nausea, nervousness, numbness, poor coordination, rash, swelling due to fluid retention, throbbing heartbeat, tingling or pins and needles, tremors, upset stomach, vision changes, vomiting

■ *Less common or rare side effects may include:*
Abdominal pain/cramps, angina (crushing chest pain), appetite changes, behavior changes, bleeding from the stomach, confusion, congestive heart failure, decreased sex drive, depression, difficulty swallowing, difficulty urinating, dry mouth, dry skin, excessive perspiration, fainting, fatigue, fever, hallucinations, hair loss, hepatitis, hiccups, high blood pressure, hot flashes, impotence, joint pain, loss of consciousness, low blood pressure, peptic ulcer, ringing in the ears, seizures, short-term memory loss, skin inflammation and flaking, skin peeling, slow heartbeat, sore throat, speech difficulties, taste changes, vague feeling of bodily discomfort, weakness, worsening of irregular heartbeat

Why should this drug not be prescribed?
This drug should not be used if you have heart failure, a heartbeat irregularity called heart block that has not been corrected by a pacemaker, structural heart disease, or if you have recently had a heart attack.

Special warnings about this medication
If you have heart block and a pacemaker, Mexitil may be prescribed, but you should be continuously monitored while taking it.

Mexitil can aggravate low blood pressure and severe congestive heart failure, so it will be prescribed cautiously for people with these conditions.

You should be monitored carefully if you have liver disease or abnormal liver function as a result of congestive heart failure.

Diets that change the pH (acid/alkaline content) of your urine can alter the excretion of Mexitil from your body. Talk to your doctor or pharmacist about proper diet.

Blood disorders have occurred with Mexitil use. Make sure your doctor performs periodic blood tests while you are using this medication.

If you have a seizure disorder, use Mexitil with caution.

Possible food and drug interactions
when taking this medication
If Mexitil is taken with certain other drugs, the effects of either may be increased, decreased, or altered. It is especially important that you consult with your doctor before taking any of the following:

Antacids such as Maalox
Caffeine products such as No-Doz
Cimetidine (Tagamet)
Other antiarrhythmic drugs such as Norpace and Quinidex
Phenobarbital
Phenytoin (Dilantin)
Rifampin (Rifadin)
Theophylline products such as Theo-Dur

Special information
if you are pregnant or breastfeeding
The effects of Mexitil during pregnancy have not been adequately studied. If you are pregnant or plan to become pregnant, inform your doctor immediately. Mexitil appears in breast milk and could affect a nursing infant. If this medication is essential to your health, your doctor may advise you to discontinue breastfeeding until your treatment is finished.

Recommended dosage
Treatment is usually begun in the hospital.

ADULTS

The dosage of Mexitil will be adjusted to your individual needs on the basis of your response to the drug.

The usual starting dose is 200 milligrams every 8 hours when quick control of an irregular heartbeat is not necessary. Your doctor may adjust the dose by 50 or 100 milligrams up or down every 2 to 3 days.

Most people will do well on 200 to 300 milligrams taken every 8 hours with food or antacids. If you do not, your doctor may raise your dose to 400 milligrams every 8 hours. You should not take more than 1,200 milligrams in a day.

When fast relief is needed, your doctor may start you on 400 milligrams of Mexitil, followed by 200 milligrams in 8 hours. You should see the effects of this drug within 30 minutes to 2 hours.

In general, people with reduced kidney function are prescribed the usual doses of Mexitil, but those with severe liver disease may require lower doses and will be monitored closely.

Some people who handle this drug well may be transferred to a 12-hour dosage schedule that will make it easier and more convenient to take Mexitil. If you do well on a Mexitil dose of 300 milligrams or less every 8 hours, your doctor may decide to divide the daily total into 2 doses taken every 12 hours.

CHILDREN

The safety and efficacy of this drug have not been established in children.

ELDERLY

Dosages will be adjusted according to the individual's needs. Elderly patients should be carefully monitored.

Overdosage

Any medication taken in excess can have serious consequences. There have been deaths from Mexitil overdose. If you suspect an overdose, seek medical attention immediately.

■ *The symptoms of Mexitil overdose may include:*
Low blood pressure
Nausea
Seizures
Slow heartbeat
Tingling or pins and needles

Generic name:

MICONAZOLE

See Monistat, page 681.

Brand name:

MICRO-K

Pronounced: MY-kroe kay
Generic name: Potassium chloride
Other brand names: Klor-Con, K-DUR, KAON-CL,
Slow-K, Ten-K

Why is this drug prescribed?

Micro-K is used to treat or prevent low potassium levels in people who may face potassium loss caused by digitalis (Lanoxin) and non-potassium-sparing diuretics (such as Diuril and Dyazide) and certain diseases.

Potassium plays an essential role in the proper functioning of a wide range of systems in the body, including the kidneys, muscles, and nerves. As a result, a potassium deficiency may have a wide range of effects, including dry mouth, thirst, reduced urination, weakness, fatigue, drowsiness, low blood pressure, restlessness, muscle cramps, abnormal heart rate, nausea, and vomiting.

Micro-K, Klor-Con, K-DUR, KAON-CL, Slow-K and Ten-K are slow-release potassium formulations.

Most important fact about this drug

There have been reports of intestinal and gastric ulcers and bleeding associated with use of slow-release potassium chloride medications. Micro-K should be used only by people who cannot take potassium chloride in liquid or effervescent forms.

Do not change from one brand of potassium chloride to another without consulting your doctor or pharmacist.

How should you take this medication?

Take Micro-K with meals and with water or some other liquid.

Tell your doctor if you have difficulty swallowing Micro-K. You may sprinkle the contents of the capsule onto a spoonful of soft food. Capsules should not be crushed, chewed, or sucked.

- *If you miss a dose...*
  If it is within 2 hours of the scheduled time, take it as soon as you remember. If you do not remember until later, skip the dose you missed and go back to your regular schedule. Do not take 2 doses at once.

■ *Storage instructions...*
Store at room temperature in a tightly closed container.

What side effects may occur?
Side effects cannot be anticipated. If any develop or change in intensity, inform your doctor as soon as possible. Only your doctor can determine if it is safe for you to continue taking Micro-K.

■ *Side effects may include:*
Abdominal pain or discomfort
Diarrhea
Nausea
Stomach and intestinal ulcers and bleeding, blockage, or perforation
Vomiting

Why should this drug not be prescribed?
You should not be using Micro-K in a solid form if you are taking any drug or have any condition that could stop or slow Micro-K as it goes through the gastrointestinal tract.

If you have high potassium levels, you should not use Micro-K.

Special warnings about this medication
Before taking Micro-K, tell your doctor if you have ever had acute dehydration, heat cramps, adrenal insufficiency, diabetes, heart disease, kidney disease, liver disease, ulcers, or severe burns.

Tell your doctor immediately if you notice that your stools are black or tarry.

Possible food and drug interactions
when taking this medication
If Micro-K is taken with certain other drugs, the effects of either could be increased, decreased, or altered. It is important to check with your doctor before combining Micro-K with the following:

Antispasmodic drugs such as Bentyl
Blood pressure medications classified as ACE inhibitors, such as Vasotec and Capoten
Digitalis (Lanoxin)
Potassium-sparing diuretics such as Midamor and Aldactone

Also tell your doctor if you use salt substitutes.

Special information
if you are pregnant or breastfeeding
Micro-K is generally considered safe for pregnant women or women who breastfeed their babies.

Recommended dosage
Dosages must be adjusted for each individual. Safety and effectiveness in children have not been established. The following are typical dosages for Micro-K and other leading slow-release potassium supplements.

TO TREAT LOW POTASSIUM LEVELS

Micro-K, Klor-Con 8, Slow-K
The usual dosage is 5 to 12 tablets or capsules per day.

Micro-K 10, Klor-Con 10, K-DUR 10, KAON-CL 10, Ten-K
The usual dose is 4 to 10 tablets or capsules per day.

K-DUR 20
The usual dose is 2 to 5 tablets per day.

TO PREVENT LOW POTASSIUM LEVELS

Micro-K, Klor-Con 8, Slow-K, K-DUR 10, KAON-CL 10, Ten-K
The usual dosage is 2 or 3 tablets or capsules per day.

Micro-K 10, Klor-Con 10
The usual dose is 2 tablets or capsules per day.

If you are taking more than 2 tablets or capsules per day, your total daily dose will be divided into smaller doses.

Overdosage
Any medication taken in excess can have serious consequences. Overdoses of these supplements can result in potentially fatal levels of potassium. Overdose symptoms may not be noticeable in their early stages. Therefore, if you have any reason to suspect an overdose, seek medical help immediately.

■ *Symptoms of potassium overdose may include:*
Blood in stools
Cardiac arrest
Irregular heartbeat
Muscle paralysis
Muscle weakness

Brand name:

MICRONASE

Pronounced: MIKE-roh-naze
Generic name: Glyburide
Other brand names: DiaBeta, Glynase

Why is this drug prescribed?
Micronase is an oral antidiabetic medication used to treat Type II (non-insulin-dependent) diabetes. Diabetes occurs either when the body does not make enough insulin or when the insulin that is produced no longer works properly. Insulin works by helping sugar get inside the cell, where it is then used for energy.

There are two forms of diabetes: Type I (insulin-dependent) and Type II (non-insulin-dependent). Type I diabetes usually requires insulin injections for life, while Type II diabetes can usually be treated by dietary changes, exercise, and/or oral antidiabetic medications such as Micronase. This medication controls diabetes by stimulating the pancreas to secrete more insulin and by helping insulin to work better. Type II diabetics may need insulin injections, sometimes only temporarily during stressful periods such as illness, or if an oral antidiabetic medication fails to control blood sugars, on a long-term basis.

Most important fact about this drug
Always remember that Micronase is an aid to, not a substitute for, good diet and exercise. Failure to follow a sound diet and exercise plan can lead to serious complications, such as dangerously high or low blood sugar levels. Remember, too, that Micronase is *not* an oral form of insulin, and cannot be used in place of insulin.

How should you take this medication?
In general, Micronase should be taken with breakfast or the first main meal of the day.

■ *If you miss a dose...*
Take it as soon as you remember. If it is almost time for your next dose, skip the one you missed and go back to your regular schedule. Never take 2 doses at the same time.

■ *Storage instructions...*
Keep this medication in the container it came in, tightly closed. Store it at room temperature.

What side effects may occur?
Side effects cannot be anticipated. If any develop or change in intensity, inform your doctor as soon as possible. Only your doctor can determine if it is safe for you to continue taking Micronase.

Many side effects from Micronase are rare and seldom require discontinuation of the medication.

■ *More common side effects may include:*
Bloating
Heartburn
Nausea

■ *Less common or rare side effects may include:*
Anemia and other blood disorders, blurred vision, changes in taste, headache, hives, itching, joint pain, liver problems, muscle pain, reddening of the skin, skin eruptions, skin rash, yellowing of the skin

Micronase, like all oral antidiabetics, may cause hypoglycemia (low blood sugar) especially in elderly, weak, and undernourished people, and those with kidney, liver, adrenal, or pituitary gland problems. The risk of hypoglycemia can be increased by missed meals, alcohol, other medications, fever, trauma, infection, surgery, or excessive exercise. To avoid hypoglycemia, you should closely follow the dietary and exercise plan suggested by your physician.

■ *Symptoms of mild hypoglycemia may include:*
Cold sweat
Drowsiness
Fast heartbeat
Headache
Nausea
Nervousness

■ *Symptoms of more severe hypoglycemia may include:*
Coma
Pale skin
Seizures
Shallow breathing

Eating sugar or a sugar-based product will often correct mild hypoglycemia.

Severe hypoglycemia should be considered a medical emergency, and prompt medical attention is essential.

Why should this drug not be prescribed?

You should not take Micronase if you have had an allergic reaction to it or to similar drugs such as Glucotrol or Diabinese.

Micronase should not be taken if you are suffering from diabetic ketoacidosis (a life-threatening medical emergency caused by insufficient insulin and marked by excessive thirst, nausea, fatigue, pain below the breastbone, and fruity breath).

Special warnings about this medication

It's possible that drugs such as Micronase may lead to more heart problems than diet treatment alone, or diet plus insulin. If you have a heart condition, you may want to discuss this with your doctor.

If you are taking Micronase, you should check your blood or urine periodically for abnormal sugar (glucose) levels.

It is important that you closely follow the diet and exercise plan recommended by your doctor.

The effectiveness of any oral antidiabetic, including Micronase, may decrease with time. This may occur either because of a diminished responsiveness to the medication or a worsening of the diabetes.

Possible food and drug interactions
when taking this medication

If Micronase is taken with certain other drugs, the effects of either could be increased, decreased, or altered. It is especially important to check with your doctor before combining Micronase with the following:

Airway-opening drugs such as Proventil and Ventolin
Anabolic steroids such as testosterone and Danazol
Antacids such as Mylanta
Aspirin
Beta blockers such as Inderal and Tenormin
Blood thinners such as Coumadin
Calcium channel blockers such as Cardizem and Procardia
Certain antibiotics such as Cipro
Chloramphenicol (Chloromycetin)
Cimetidine (Tagamet)
Clofibrate (Atromid-S)
Estrogens such as Premarin
Fluconazole (Diflucan)

Furosemide (Lasix)
Gemfibrozil (Lopid)
Isoniazid (a drug used for tuberculosis)
Itraconazole (Sporanox)
Major tranquilizers such as Stelazine and Mellaril
MAO inhibitors (antidepressants such as Nardil and Parnate)
Niacin (Nicolar, Nicobid)
Nonsteroidal anti-inflammatory drugs such as Advil, Motrin, Naprosyn, and Voltaren
Oral contraceptives
Phenytoin (Dilantin)
Probenecid (Benemid, ColBENEMID)
Steroids such as prednisone
Sulfa drugs such as Gantrisin
Thiazide diuretics such as Diuril and HydroDIURIL
Thyroid medications such as Synthroid

Be careful about drinking alcohol, since excessive alcohol consumption can cause low blood sugar.

Special information
if you are pregnant or breastfeeding
The effects of Micronase during pregnancy have not been adequately studied in humans. This drug should be used during pregnancy only if the benefit outweighs the potential risk to the unborn baby. Since studies suggest the importance of maintaining normal blood sugar (glucose) levels during pregnancy, your physician may prescribe insulin injections during pregnancy.

While it is not known if Micronase appears in breast milk, other oral diabetes medications do. Therefore, women should discuss with their doctors whether to discontinue the medication or to stop breastfeeding. If the medication is discontinued, and if diet alone does not control glucose levels, then your doctor may consider insulin injections.

Recommended dosage
Your doctor will tailor your dosage to your individual needs.

ADULTS

Usually the doctor will prescribe an initial daily dose of 2.5 to 5 milligrams. Maintenance therapy usually ranges from 1.25 to 20 milligrams daily. Daily doses greater than 20 milligrams are not recommended. In most cases, Micronase is taken once a day; however, people taking more than 10 milligrams a day may respond better to twice-a-day dosing.

CHILDREN

The safety and effectiveness of Micronase have not been established in children.

ELDERLY

Elderly, malnourished or debilitated individuals, or those with impaired kidney and liver function, usually receive lower initial and maintenance doses to minimize the risk of low blood sugar (hypoglycemia).

Overdosage

An overdose of Micronase can cause low blood sugar (hypoglycemia).

- *Symptoms of severe hypoglycemia include:*
  Coma
  Pale skin
  Seizure
  Shallow breathing

If you suspect a Micronase overdose, seek medical attention immediately.

Brand name:

MICRONOR

See Oral Contraceptives, page 775.

Brand name:

MIDRIN

Pronounced: MID-rin
Generic ingredients: Isometheptene mucate,
  Dichloralphenazone, Acetaminophen

Why is this drug prescribed?

Midrin is prescribed for the treatment of tension headaches. It is also used to treat vascular headaches such as migraine.

Most important fact about this drug

Midrin can be used only after the headache starts. It does not prevent headaches.

How should you take this medication?
You should start taking Midrin at the first sign of a migraine attack.

Do not take more than the maximum dose of Midrin.

Take this medication exactly as prescribed by your doctor.

■ *If you miss a dose...*
Take this medication only as needed.

■ *Storage instructions...*
Store at room temperature in a dry place.

What side effects may occur?
Side effects cannot be anticipated. If any develop or change in intensity, tell your doctor immediately. Only your doctor can determine whether it is safe for you to continue taking Midrin.

■ *Side effects may include:*
Short periods of dizziness
Skin rash

Why should this drug not be prescribed?
Unless directed to do so by your doctor, do not take Midrin if you have the eye condition called glaucoma or severe kidney disease, high blood pressure, a physical defect of the heart, or liver disease, or if you are currently taking antidepressant drugs known as MAO inhibitors, including Nardil and Parnate.

Special warnings about this medication
Take Midrin cautiously if you have high blood pressure or any abnormal condition of the blood vessels outside of the heart, or have recently had a cardiovascular attack such as a heart attack or stroke.

Possible food and drug interactions
when taking this medication
Avoid alcoholic beverages.

If Midrin is taken with certain other drugs, the effects of either drug could be increased, decreased, or altered. It is especially important to check with your doctor before combining Midrin with the following:

Acetaminophen-containing pain relievers such as Tylenol
Antidepressants classified as MAO inhibitors, including Nardil and
Parnate

Antihistamines such as Benadryl
Central nervous system depressants such as Halcion, Valium and Xanax

Special information
if you are pregnant or breastfeeding
If you are pregnant, plan to become pregnant, or are breastfeeding your baby, check with your doctor before taking Midrin.

Recommended dosage

ADULTS

Relief of Migraine Headache
The usual dosage is 2 capsules at once, followed by 1 capsule every hour until the headache is relieved; do not take more than 5 capsules within a 12-hour period.

Relief of Tension Headache
The usual dosage is 1 or 2 capsules every 4 hours up to a maximum of 8 capsules a day.

Overdosage
Any medication taken in excess can have serious consequences. If you suspect a Midrin overdose, seek emergency medical treatment immediately.

Brand name:

MILTOWN

Pronounced: MILL-town
Generic name: Meprobamate
Other brand name: Equanil

Why is this drug prescribed?
Miltown is a tranquilizer used in the treatment of anxiety disorders and for short-term relief of the symptoms of anxiety.

Most important fact about this drug
Miltown can be habit forming. You can develop tolerance and dependence, and you may experience withdrawal symptoms if you stop using this drug abruptly. Discontinue this drug or change your dose only on your doctor's advice.

How should you take this medication?
Take Miltown exactly as prescribed.

■ *If you miss a dose...*
Take it as soon as you remember if it is within an hour of your scheduled time. If you do not remember until later, skip the dose you missed and go back to your regular schedule. Never take 2 doses at the same time.

■ *Storage instructions...*
Store at room temperature in a tightly closed container.

What side effects may occur?
Side effects cannot be anticipated. If any develop or change in intensity, inform your doctor as soon as possible. Only your doctor can determine if it is safe for you to continue taking Miltown.

■ *More common side effects may include:*
Allergic reactions, blood disorders, bruises, diarrhea, dizziness, drowsiness, exaggerated feeling of well-being, fainting, fast throbbing heartbeat, fever, headache, inappropriate excitement, itchy rash, loss of muscle coordination, nausea, rapid or irregular heartbeat, skin eruptions, slurred speech, small, purplish spots on the skin, sudden severe drop in blood pressure, swelling due to fluid retention, tingling sensation or numbness, vertigo, vision problems, vomiting, weakness

■ *Less common or rare side effects may include:*
Breathing difficulty, chills, high fever, inflammation of mouth, inflammation of the rectum, little or no urine, redness and swelling of skin, severe allergic reaction, skin inflammation and flaking, Stevens-Johnson syndrome (peeling skin)

■ *Side effects due to rapid decrease in dose or abrupt withdrawal from Miltown:*
Anxiety, confusion, convulsions, hallucinations, inability to fall or stay asleep, loss of appetite, loss of coordination, muscle twitching, tremors, vomiting

Withdrawal symptoms usually become apparent within 12 to 48 hours after discontinuation of this medication and should disappear in another 12 to 48 hours.

Why should this drug not be prescribed?
If you are sensitive to or have ever had an allergic reaction to Miltown or related drugs such as carisoprodol (Soma), you should not take this medication.

You should not take Miltown if you have acute intermittent porphyria, an inherited disease of the body's metabolism. It can make your symptoms worse.

Anxiety or tension related to everyday stress usually does not require treatment with Miltown. Discuss your symptoms thoroughly with your doctor.

Special warnings about this medication
If you develop a skin rash, sore throat, fever, or shortness of breath, contact your doctor immediately. You may be having an allergic reaction to the drug.

Miltown may cause you to become drowsy or less alert; therefore, you should not drive or operate dangerous machinery, or participate in any hazardous activity that requires full mental alertness until you know how this drug affects you.

Long-term use of this drug should be evaluated by your doctor periodically for its usefulness.

If you have liver or kidney disorders, make sure your doctor is aware of these conditions before you begin using this medication.

If you have epilepsy, use of this drug may bring on seizures. Consult your doctor before taking it.

Possible food and drug interactions
when taking this medication
Miltown may intensify the effects of alcohol. Do not drink alcohol while taking this medication.

If Miltown is taken with certain other drugs, the effects of either could be increased, decreased, or altered. It is especially important to check with your doctor before combining Miltown with mood-altering drugs and central nervous system depressants such as the following:

Antidepressant drugs such as Elavil, Nardil, and Tofranil
Barbiturates such as Seconal and phenobarbital
Major tranquilizers such as Thorazine and Mellaril
Narcotics such as Percocet or Demerol
Tranquilizers such as Halcion, Restoril, and Valium

**Special information
if you are pregnant or breastfeeding**
Do not take Miltown if you are pregnant or planning to become pregnant. There is an increased risk of birth defects. Miltown appears in breast milk and could affect a nursing infant. If this medication is essential to your health, your doctor may advise you to discontinue breastfeeding until your treatment is finished.

Recommended dosage

ADULTS

Miltown 200 and 400
The usual dosage is 1,200 milligrams to 1,600 milligrams per day divided into 3 or 4 doses. You should not take more than 2,400 milligrams a day.

Miltown 600
The usual dose is one 600-milligram tablet, 2 times a day. Do not take more than 2,400 milligrams a day.

CHILDREN

Miltown 200 and 400
The usual dose for children 6 to 12 years of age is 200 to 600 milligrams per day divided into 2 or 3 doses.

Miltown 200 and 400 are not recommended for use in children under age 6. Miltown 600 is not recommended for use in children.

ELDERLY

Your doctor will limit your dose to the smallest effective amount to avoid oversedation.

Overdosage
Any medication taken in excess can cause symptoms of overdose. If you suspect an overdose, seek emergency medical attention immediately.

■ *The symptoms of Miltown overdose may include:*
Coma
Drowsiness
Loss of muscle control
Severely impaired breathing
Shock
Sluggishness and unresponsiveness

Brand name:

MINIPRESS

Pronounced: MIN-ee-press
Generic name: Prazosin hydrochloride

Why is this drug prescribed?

Minipress is used to treat high blood pressure. It is effective used alone or with other high blood pressure medications such as diuretics or beta-blocking medications (drugs that ease heart contractions) such as Tenormin.

Minipress is also prescribed for the treatment of benign prostatic hyperplasia (BPH), an abnormal enlargement of the prostate gland.

Most important fact about this drug

If you have high blood pressure, you must take Minipress regularly for it to be effective. Since blood pressure declines gradually, it may be several weeks before you get the full benefit of Minipress; and you must continue taking it even if you are feeling well. Minipress does not cure high blood pressure; it merely keeps it under control.

How should you take this medication?

Minipress can be taken with or without food.

This medication should be taken exactly as prescribed by your doctor even if your symptoms have disappeared. Try not to miss any doses. If this medication is not taken regularly, your blood pressure will increase.

- *If you miss a dose...*
  Take it as soon as you remember. If it is almost time for your next dose, skip the one you missed and go back to your regular schedule. Never take 2 doses at the same time.

- *Storage instructions...*
  Protect from heat, light, and moisture.

What side effects may occur?

Side effects cannot be anticipated. If any develop or change in intensity, inform your doctor as soon as possible. Only your doctor can determine if it is safe for you to continue taking Minipress.

- *More common side effects may include:*
  Dizziness
  Drowsiness
  Headache
  Lack of energy
  Nausea
  Palpitations (pounding heartbeat)
  Weakness

- *Less common side effects may include:*
  Blurred vision, constipation, depression, diarrhea, dizziness on standing up, dry mouth, fainting, fluid retention, frequent urination, nasal congestion, nervousness, nosebleeds, rash, red eyes, shortness of breath, vertigo, vomiting

- *Rare side effects may include:*
  Abdominal discomfort/pain, excessive perspiration, fever, hair loss, hallucinations, impotence, inability to hold urine, inflammation of the pancreas, itching, itchy, purple spots on wrists, forearms, and thighs, joint pain, persistent, painful erection, rapid heartbeat, ringing in ears, tingling or pins and needles

Why should this drug not be prescribed?
There are no known reasons to avoid this drug.

Special warnings about this medication
Minipress can cause low blood pressure, especially when you first start taking the medication. This can cause you to become faint, dizzy, or light-headed, particularly on standing up. You should avoid driving or any hazardous tasks where injury could occur for 24 hours after taking the first dose or after your dose has been increased. Dizziness, fainting, or light-headedness may also occur in hot weather, when exercising, or when standing for long periods of time. Ask your doctor what precautions you should take.

Possible food and drug interactions
when taking this medication
Minipress can intensify the effects of alcohol. Be careful of the amount you drink.

If Minipress is taken with certain other drugs, the effects of either could be increased, decreased, or altered. It is especially important that you check with your doctor before combining Minipress with the following:

Beta blockers such as Inderal
Dextroamphetamine (Dexedrine)
Diuretics such as Dyazide
Ibuprofen (Motrin, Advil, others)
Other high blood pressure medications
Verapamil (Calan, Verelan)

Special information
if you are pregnant or breastfeeding

The effects of Minipress during pregnancy have not been adequately studied. If you are pregnant or plan to become pregnant, notify your doctor immediately. Minipress appears in breast milk and can affect a nursing infant. If this medication is essential to your health, your doctor may advise you to discontinue breastfeeding until your treatment is finished.

Recommended dosage

ADULTS

Dosages of this drug should be adjusted by your doctor according to your response.

The usual starting dose is 1 milligram, 2 or 3 times per day.

To determine your regular dose, your doctor may slowly increase this medication to as much as 20 milligrams per day, divided into smaller doses. The commonly prescribed daily dose is 6 milligrams to 15 milligrams per day, divided into smaller doses. Although doses higher than 20 milligrams per day have not been found to be effective, there are some people who may benefit from a daily dose of 40 milligrams, divided into smaller doses.

If Minipress is used with a diuretic or other high blood pressure drug, the dose can be reduced to 1 to 2 milligrams, 3 times a day.

CHILDREN

Safety and effectiveness of this drug have not been established in children.

Overdosage

Any medication taken in excess can have serious consequences. If you suspect a Minipress overdose, seek medical treatment immediately.

- *The symptoms of Minipress overdose may include:*
  Extreme drowsiness
  Low blood pressure

Brand name:

MINOCIN

Pronounced: MIN-o-sin
Generic name: Minocycline hydrochloride
Other brand name: Dynacin

Why is this drug prescribed?
Minocin is a form of the antibiotic tetracycline.

It is given to help treat many different kinds of infection, including:

Acne
Amebic dysentery
Anthrax (a rare skin infection)
Cholera
Gonorrhea (when penicillin cannot be given)
Plague
Respiratory infections such as pneumonia
Rocky Mountain spotted fever
Syphilis (when penicillin cannot be given)
Urinary tract infections caused by certain microbes

Most important fact about this drug
To help clear up your infection completely, keep taking Minocin for the full time of treatment, even if you begin to feel better after a few days. Minocin, like other antibiotics, works best when there is a constant amount in the body. To help keep the level constant, take the doses at evenly spaced times around the clock.

How should you take this medication?
You may take the capsules with or without food. Take Minocin exactly as directed. Your doctor will prescribe it for a specific number of days according to the condition you are being treated for; keep taking the medication until you have used it all up.

To reduce the risk of throat irritation, take the capsule form of Minocin with plenty of fluids.

You should avoid use of antacids that contain aluminum, calcium, or magnesium, such as Maalox and Mylanta, and iron preparations such as Feosol. If you must take these medicines, take them 2 to 3 hours before or after taking Minocin.

- *If you miss a dose...*
  Take it as soon as you remember, then space out evenly any remaining doses for that day. Never take 2 doses at the same time.

- *Storage instructions...*
  Store capsules at room temperature, away from moist places and direct light. The liquid form of Minocin may be kept in the refrigerator. Do not freeze. Shake well before using.

What side effects may occur?
Side effects cannot be anticipated. If any develop or change in intensity, inform your doctor as soon as possible. Only your doctor can determine if it is safe for you to continue taking Minocin.

- *Side effects may include:*
  Aching, inflamed joints, anal or genital sores with fungus infection, anaphylaxis (life-threatening allergic reaction), anemia, appetite loss, blurry vision, bulging of soft spots in infants' heads, decreased hearing, diarrhea, difficulty swallowing, discoloration of children's teeth, fever, fluid retention, headache, hepatitis, hives, inflammation of the penis, inflammation of the intestines, inflammation of the tongue, joint pain, liver failure, nausea, rash, sensitivity to light, skin coloration, skin eruptions, skin inflammation and peeling, throat irritation, thyroid gland problems, vomiting

Why should this drug not be prescribed?
Do not take Minocin if you have ever had an allergic reaction to it or to any other tetracycline antibiotic.

Although Minocin may be given to kill meningococcal (spinal) bacteria in people who are carriers, it should not be given to treat actual meningococcal meningitis (inflammation in the spinal canal).

Minocin is not a first-choice drug for treating any staphylococcal ("staph") infection.

Special warnings about this medication
If you have a kidney problem, a normal dose of Minocin may amount to an overdose for you. It is likely that you will need a lower-than-average dosage; if you need to take Minocin for an extended period of time, your doctor may order frequent blood tests to make sure you are not getting too much of the drug.

Because Minocin may make you dizzy or light-headed or cause a whirling feeling, do not drive, climb, or perform hazardous tasks until you know how the medication affects you.

Minocin should not be given to children 8 years old or younger, since it may cause discoloration of the teeth. Occasionally, Minocin has also caused tooth discoloration in adults.

Like other tetracycline antibiotics, Minocin may cause a sensitivity to light, and you may sunburn very easily. Be careful in sun and under sunlamps. If your skin turns red and hot, stop taking Minocin immediately.

While taking Minocin you may be especially susceptible to fungus infections such as vaginal yeast infection. If you do get a fungus infection, check with your doctor immediately.

If you get a headache and blurry vision while taking Minocin, or if an infant receiving Minocin develops bulging of the "soft spots" (fontanels) on the head, this could mean that the drug is causing a buildup of fluid within the skull. It is important to stop taking Minocin and see a doctor immediately.

Possible food and drug interactions
when taking this medication

If Minocin is taken with certain other drugs, the effects of either could be increased, decreased, or altered. It is especially important to check with your doctor before combining Minocin with the following:

Antacids containing aluminum, calcium, or magnesium, such as Mylanta
Blood thinners such as Coumadin
Iron-containing preparations such as Feosol
Oral contraceptives
Penicillin (Pen-Vee K)

Special information
if you are pregnant or breastfeeding

If you are pregnant or plan to become pregnant, inform your doctor immediately. If you take Minocin during the second half of pregnancy, it may cause permanent yellow, gray, or brown discoloration of your baby's teeth.

There is reason to believe that taking Minocin during pregnancy could also harm the baby in other ways. Therefore, Minocin should be taken during pregnancy only if an antibiotic is clearly needed and only if a non-tetracycline antibiotic cannot be used instead. Because Minocin appears in breast milk and could harm the baby, it should not be taken by a woman who is breastfeeding. If this drug is essential to your health, your doctor may advise you to discontinue breastfeeding until treatment is finished.

Recommended dosage

Minocin differs from the other tetracyclines in the usual dosage and number of times it is taken per day.

You may experience more side effects if you take more than the recommended dosage.

ADULTS

The usual dosage of Minocin is 200 milligrams to start with, followed by 100 milligrams every 12 hours. If your doctor wants you to take more frequent doses, he or she may prescribe two or four 50-milligram capsules initially, and then one 50-milligram capsule 4 times daily.

CHILDREN ABOVE 8 YEARS OF AGE

The usual dosage of Minocin is 4 milligrams per 2.2 pounds of body weight to start, followed by 2 milligrams per 2.2 pounds every 12 hours.

Overdosage

Although no specific information is available, any medication taken in excess can have serious consequences. If you suspect symptoms of an overdose of Minocin, seek medical attention immediately.

Generic name:

MINOCYCLINE

See Minocin, page 674.

Generic name:

MINOXIDIL

See Rogaine, page 978.

Generic name:

MISOPROSTOL

See Cytotec, page 260.

Brand name:

MIXTARD

See Insulin, page 527.

Brand name:

MODICON

See Oral Contraceptives, page 775.

Brand name:

MODURETIC

Pronounced: mod-your-ET-ik
Generic ingredients: Amiloride, Hydrochlorothiazide

Why is this drug prescribed?

Moduretic is a diuretic combination used in the treatment of high blood pressure and congestive heart failure, conditions which require the elimination of excess fluid (water) from the body. When used for high blood pressure, Moduretic can be used alone or with other high blood pressure medications. Diuretics help your body produce and eliminate more urine, which helps lower blood pressure. Amiloride, one of the ingredients, helps minimize the potassium loss that can be caused by the other component, hydrochlorothiazide.

Most important fact about this drug

If you have high blood pressure, you must take Moduretic regularly for it to be effective. Since blood pressure declines gradually, it may be several weeks before you get the full benefit of Moduretic; and you must continue taking it even if you are feeling well. Moduretic does not cure high blood pressure; it merely keeps it under control.

How should you take this medication?

Take this medication with food.

Take Moduretic exactly as prescribed by your doctor. Stopping Moduretic suddenly could cause your condition to worsen.

■ *If you miss a dose...*
Take the forgotten dose as soon as you remember. If it is almost time for your next dose, skip the one you missed and go back to your regular schedule. Never take a double dose.

■ *Storage instructions...*
Store at room temperature. Keep this medication in the container it came in, tightly closed, and protected from moisture, light, and freezing.

What side effects may occur?

Side effects cannot be anticipated. If any develop or change in intensity, inform your doctor as soon as possible. Only your doctor can determine if it is safe for you to continue taking Moduretic.

■ *More common side effects may include:*
Diarrhea, dizziness, elevated potassium levels, fatigue, headache, irregular heartbeat, itching, leg pain, loss of appetite, nausea, rash, shortness of breath, stomach and intestinal pain, weakness

■ *Less common or rare side effects may include:*
Anemia, appetite changes, back pain, bad taste, breast development in males, changes in liver function, changes in potassium levels leading to symptoms such as dry mouth, excessive thirst, weak or irregular heartbeat, muscle pain or cramps, chest pain, constipation, cough, decreased sex drive, dehydration, depression, dermatitis, dizziness on standing up, dry mouth, excessive perspiration, excessive urination at night, fainting, fever, fluid in lungs, flushing, frequent urination, fullness in abdomen, gas, gout, hair loss, heartburn, hiccups, hives, impotence, incontinence, indigestion, insomnia, itching, joint pain, mental confusion, muscle cramps, nasal congestion, neck and shoulder ache, nervousness, numbness, painful or difficult urination, rapid heartbeat, ringing in ears, sensitivity to light, sleepiness, Stevens-Johnson Syndrome (severe blisters), stomach and intestinal bleeding, stupor, sugar in blood or urine, thirst, tingling or pins and needles, tremors, vague feeling of bodily discomfort, vertigo, vision changes, vomiting, yellow eyes and skin

Why should this drug not be prescribed?

If you are unable to urinate or have serious kidney disease, or if you have high potassium levels in your blood, you should not take this medication.

If you are sensitive to or have ever had an allergic reaction to amiloride, hydrochlorothiazide or similar drugs, or if you are sensitive to other sulfonamide-derived drugs, you should not take this medication. Make sure your doctor is aware of any drug reactions you may have experienced.

Special warnings about this medication

Potassium supplements, potassium-containing salt substitutes, and other diuretics (such as Dyazide) that minimize loss of potassium should not be used while you are taking Moduretic unless your doctor specifically says otherwise. You should also limit your consumption of potassium-rich foods such as bananas, prunes, raisins, orange juice, and whole and skim milk. Ask your doctor for advice on how much of these foods to consume.

If you are taking Moduretic, a complete assessment of your kidney function should be done; kidney function should continue to be monitored.

If you are taking an ACE-inhibitor type of blood pressure medication such as Vasotec, this drug should be used with extreme caution.

If you have liver disease, diabetes, gout, or collagen vascular disease (lupus erythematosus), Moduretic should be used with caution.

If you have bronchial asthma or a history of allergies, you may be at risk for an allergic reaction to this medication.

Dehydration, excessive sweating, severe diarrhea or vomiting could deplete your fluids and cause your blood pressure to become too low. Be careful when exercising and in hot weather.

Notify your doctor or dentist that you are taking Moduretic if you have a medical emergency or before you have surgery.

Possible food and drug interactions
when taking this medication

Moduretic may increase the effects of alcohol. Avoid alcohol while taking this medication.

If Moduretic is taken with certain other drugs, the effects of either could be increased, decreased, or altered. It is especially important to check with your doctor before combining Moduretic with the following:

ACE inhibitors such as Vasotec
Barbiturates such as phenobarbital
Cholestyramine (Questran)
Colestipol (Colestid)
Corticosteroids such as prednisone
Insulin
Lithium (Lithonate)
Muscle relaxants such as tubocurarine
Narcotics such as Percocet
Nonsteroidal anti-inflammatory drugs such as Naprosyn
Norepinephrine (Levophed)
Oral drugs for treating diabetes such as Micronase, DiaBeta
Other high blood pressure medications

Special information
if you are pregnant or breastfeeding

The effects of Moduretic during pregnancy have not been adequately studied. If you are pregnant or plan to become pregnant, inform your doctor immediately. Moduretic appears in breast milk and could affect a nursing infant. If this medication is essential to your health, your doctor may advise you to discontinue breastfeeding until your treatment is finished.

Recommended dosage
Your doctor will tailor the dosage to meet your individual requirements, taking into consideration other medical conditions you may have and other medications you may be taking.

ADULTS

The usual starting dose is 1 tablet per day, which may be increased to 2 tablets per day taken at the same time or separately.

CHILDREN

The safety and effectiveness of Moduretic have not been established in children.

Overdosage
Any medication taken in excess can cause symptoms of overdose. If you suspect an overdose, seek medical attention immediately.

No specific information or symptoms or Moduretic overdose is available, but dehydration might be expected.

Generic name:

MOMETASONE FUROATE

See Elocon, page 394.

Brand name:

MONISTAT

Pronounced: MON-ih-stat
Generic name: Miconazole nitrate

Why is this drug prescribed?
Monistat is available in several formulations, including Monistat 3 vaginal suppositories, Monistat 7 vaginal cream and suppositories, and Monistat-Derm skin cream. Monistat's active ingredient, Miconazole, fights fungal infections.

Monistat 3 and Monistat 7 are used for vaginal yeast infections. Monistat-Derm is used for skin infections such as athlete's foot, ringworm, jock itch, yeast infection on the skin (cutaneous candidiasis), and tinea versicolor (a common skin condition that produces patches of white, tan, or brown finely flaking skin over the neck and trunk).

Most important fact about this drug

Keep using this medicine regularly for the full time of the treatment, even if the infection seems to have disappeared. If you stop too soon, the infections could return. You should continue using the vaginal forms of the medicine even during your menstrual period.

How should you use this medication?

Use this medication exactly as prescribed.

Keep all forms of this medicine away from your eyes.

Before applying Monistat-Derm to your skin, be sure to wash your hands. Massage the medication gently into the affected area and the surrounding skin.

If you are using the vaginal cream or suppository, follow these steps:

1. Load the applicator to the fill line with cream, or unwrap a tablet, wet it with warm water, and place it in the applicator as shown in the instructions you received with the product.
2. Lie on your back with your knees drawn up.
3. Gently insert the application high into the vagina and push the plunger.
4. Withdraw the applicator and discard it if disposable, or wash with soap and water.

To keep the vaginal medication from getting on your clothing, wear a sanitary napkin. Do not use tampons, because they will absorb the medicine. Wear cotton underwear—avoid synthetic fabrics such as rayon or nylon. Do not douche unless your doctor tells you to do so.

Dry the genital area thoroughly after a shower, bath, or swim. Change out of a wet bathing suit or damp workout clothes as soon as possible. Yeast is less likely to flourish in a dry environment.

Do not scratch if you can help it. Scratching can cause more irritation and can spread the infection.

■ *If you miss a dose...*
  Make up for it as soon as you remember. However, if it is almost time for your next dose, skip the one you missed and go back to your regular schedule.

■ *Storage instructions...*
Store at room temperature.

What side effects may occur?
Side effects cannot be anticipated. If any develop or change in intensity, inform your doctor. Only your doctor can determine whether it is safe for you to continue taking Monistat.

■ *Side effects may include:*
Burning sensation
Cramping
Headaches
Hives
Irritation
Rash
Vulval or vaginal itching

Why should this drug not be prescribed?
If you have ever had an allergic reaction to or are sensitive to miconazole nitrate, you should not use this medication. Make sure your doctor is aware of any drug reactions you have experienced.

Special warnings about this medication
If symptoms persist, or if an irritation or allergic reaction develops while you are using Monistat, notify your doctor.

The hydrogenated vegetable oil base of Monistat 3 may interact with the latex in vaginal diaphragms, so concurrent use of these two products is not recommended.

Your doctor may recommend Monistat 7 Vaginal Cream if you are using a diaphragm. However, you should be aware that the mineral oil in the vaginal cream can weaken the latex in condoms and diaphragms, making them less reliable for prevention of pregnancy or sexually transmitted disease.

If you are using Monistat 3 or Monistat 7 suppositories, you should either avoid sexual intercourse or make sure your partner uses a condom.

Do not give Monistat 7 to girls less than 12 years of age. Also avoid using Monistat 7 if you have any of the following symptoms:

Fever above 100°F orally
Foul-smelling vaginal discharge
Pain in the lower abdomen, back, or either shoulder

If these symptoms develop while you are using Monistat 7, stop treatment and contact your doctor right away. You may have a more serious infection.

If the infection fails to improve or worsens within 3 days, or you do not obtain complete relief within 7 days, or symptoms return within two months, you may have something other than a yeast infection.

Possible food and drug interactions when taking this medication
No interactions have been reported.

Special information if you are pregnant or breastfeeding
Unless you are directed to do so by your doctor, do not use Monistat during the first trimester (three months) of pregnancy because it is absorbed in small amounts from the vagina. It is not known whether miconazole appears in breast milk. If Monistat is essential to your health, your doctor may advise you to discontinue breastfeeding until your treatment with this medication is finished.

Recommended dosage

MONISTAT-7 VAGINAL CREAM

The usual daily dose is 1 applicatorful inserted into the vagina at bedtime for 7 consecutive days.

MONISTAT-7 VAGINAL SUPPOSITORIES

The usual daily dose is 1 suppository inserted into the vagina at bedtime for 7 consecutive days.

MONISTAT-DERM

For jock itch, ringworm, athlete's foot, or yeast infection of the skin, apply a thin layer of Monistat-Derm over the affected area morning and night. For tinea versicolor, apply a thin layer over the affected area once daily.

Overdosage
Overdose of Monistat has not been reported. However, any medication used in excess can have serious consequences. If you suspect an overdose, seek medical attention immediately.

Brand name:

MONOKET

See Imdur, page 504.

Brand name:

MONOPRIL

Pronounced: MON-oh-prill
Generic name: Fosinopril sodium

Why is this drug prescribed?
Monopril is a high blood pressure medication known as an ACE inhibitor. It is effective when used alone or in combination with other medications for the treatment of high blood pressure.

Monopril works by preventing the conversion of a chemical in your blood called angiotensin I into a more potent substance that increases salt and water retention in your body. Monopril also enhances blood flow in your circulatory system.

Most important fact about this drug
You must take Monopril regularly for it to be effective. Since blood pressure declines gradually, it may be several weeks before you get the full benefit of Monopril; and you must continue taking it even if you are feeling well. Monopril does not cure high blood pressure; it merely keeps it under control.

How should you take this medication?
Monopril is best taken one hour before meals; but it can be taken with food if it upsets your stomach.

Take this medication exactly as prescribed by your doctor.

- *If you miss a dose...*
  Suddenly stopping Monopril could cause your blood pressure to increase. If you forget to take a dose, take it as soon as you remember. If it is almost time for your next dose, skip the one you missed and go back to your regular schedule. Never take 2 doses at the same time.

- *Storage instructions...*
  Store Monopril at room temperature in a tightly closed container to protect the medication from moisture.

What side effects may occur?
Side effects cannot be anticipated. If any develop or change in intensity, inform your doctor as soon as possible. Only your doctor can determine if it is safe for you to continue taking Monopril.

■ *More common side effects may include:*
Cough
Diarrhea
Dizziness
Fatigue
Headache
Nausea
Vomiting

■ *Less common or rare side effects may include:*
Abdominal pain, anaphylaxis (severe allergic reaction), changes in appetite and weight, changes in sexual performance, confusion, constipation, decreased sex drive, drowsiness, dry mouth, excessive sweating, eye irritation, gas, heartburn, itching, kidney failure, liver failure, muscle cramps, rash, ringing in ears, skin sensitivity to sunlight, sleep disturbances, tremors, vertigo, vision disturbances, weakness, yellow eyes and skin

Why should this drug not be prescribed?
If you are sensitive to or have ever had an allergic reaction to Monopril or similar drugs, you should not take this medication. Make sure that your doctor is aware of any drug reactions that you have experienced.

Special warnings about this medication
If you develop a sore throat or fever, you should contact your doctor immediately for medical attention. It could indicate a more serious illness.

If you develop swelling of your face, lips, tongue or throat, or arms and legs, or have difficulty swallowing, you should contact your doctor immediately. You may need emergency treatment.

Make sure your doctor knows about any kidney or liver problems you may have. If you notice your skin or the whites of your eyes turning yellow, stop taking Monopril and contact your doctor immediately.

Your kidney function should be monitored while you are taking Monopril. Also, certain blood tests may be needed if you have a disease of the connective tissue.

If you are taking high doses of diuretic and Monopril, you may develop excessively low blood pressure.

You may experience light-headedness while taking Monopril, especially during the first few days of therapy. If this occurs, notify your doctor. If you actually faint, discontinue the use of this medication and notify your doctor immediately.

Do not use potassium-containing salt substitutes without consulting your doctor.

If you have congestive heart failure, this drug should be started under close medical supervision. Your doctor should continue to monitor your progress for the first 2 weeks of treatment and whenever your dosage is increased.

Excessive sweating, dehydration, severe diarrhea, or vomiting could lead to excessive loss of water and cause your blood pressure to drop dangerously. Take precautions to avoid excessive water loss while exercising.

This drug should be used with caution if you are on dialysis. There have been reports of extreme allergic reactions during dialysis in people taking ACE inhibitors such as Monopril. There have also been reports of severe allergic reactions in people given bee or wasp venom to protect against stings.

Possible food and drug interactions when taking this medication

If Monopril is taken with certain other drugs, the effects of either could be increased, decreased, or altered. It is especially important to check with your doctor before combining Monopril with the following:

Antacids such as Mylanta and Maalox
Lithium (Eskalith, Lithonate)
Potassium preparations such as K+10 and K-Lyte
Potassium-sparing diuretics such as Moduretic and Aldactone
Thiazide diuretics such as Esidrix and Diuril

Special information if you are pregnant or breastfeeding

ACE inhibitors such as Monopril have been shown to cause injury and even death in the developing baby when used in pregnancy during the second or third trimesters. If you are pregnant your doctor should discontinue the use of this medication as soon as possible. If you plan to become pregnant and are taking Monopril, contact your doctor immediately to discuss the potential hazard to your unborn child. Monopril appears in breast milk and could affect a nursing infant. If this medication is essential to your health, your doctor may advise you to discontinue breastfeeding until your treatment with this medication is finished.

Recommended dosage

ADULTS

The usual initial dose is 10 milligrams, taken once a day, either alone or when added to a diuretic. Dosage, after blood pressure is adjusted, should be 20 to 40 milligrams a day in a single dose.

Diuretic use should, if possible, be stopped before using Monopril. If not, your physician may give an initial dose of 10 milligrams under his supervision before any further medication is prescribed.

CHILDREN

The safety and effectiveness of Monopril have not been established in children.

ELDERLY

Your physician will determine the dosage that meets your particular needs.

Overdosage

Any medication taken in excess can have serious consequences. If you suspect an overdose, seek medical attention immediately.

The primary effect of a Monopril overdose is likely to be a sudden drop in blood pressure.

Generic name:

MORPHINE

See MS Contin, page 688.

Brand name:

MOTRIN

See Advil, page 17.

Brand name:

MS CONTIN

Pronounced: em-ess KON-tin
Generic name: Morphine sulfate

Why is this drug prescribed?

MS Contin, a controlled-release tablet containing morphine, is used to relieve moderate to severe pain. While regular morphine is usually given every 4 hours, MS Contin is typically given every 12 hours—only twice a day. MS Contin is intended for people who need a morphine painkiller for more than just a few days.

Most important fact about this drug

Like other narcotics, MS Contin is potentially addictive. If you take MS Contin for some time and then stop abruptly, you could experience withdrawal symptoms. For this reason, do not make dosage changes on your own; always consult your doctor.

How should you take this medication?

Take MS Contin exactly as prescribed by your doctor—typically one tablet every 12 hours. Swallow the tablets whole. If you crush or chew the tablets, a dangerously large amount of morphine could enter your bloodstream all at once.

Do not increase the dose or take the drug more frequently than prescribed. It will take a little time for the drug to begin working.

Do not drink alcoholic beverages while using MS Contin.

- *If you miss a dose...*
  Take the forgotten dose as soon as you remember. If it is almost time for your next dose, skip the one you missed and go back to your regular schedule. Do not take 2 doses at once.

- *Storage instructions...*
  Store at room temperature in a tightly closed container, away from light.

What side effects may occur?

Side effects cannot be anticipated. If any develop or change in intensity, tell your doctor immediately. Only your doctor can determine whether it is safe for you to continue taking MS Contin.

As with other narcotics, the most hazardous potential side effect of MS Contin is respiratory depression (dangerously slow breathing). If you are older or in a weakened condition, you are particularly vulnerable to respiratory depression; you may be at special risk at any age if you have a lung or breathing problem.

■ *More common side effects may include:*
Constipation
Depressed or irritable mood
Dizziness
Exaggerated sense of well-being
Light-headedness
Nausea
Sedation
Sweating
Vomiting

You may be able to lessen some of these side effects by lying down.

■ *Less common side effects may include:*
Agitation, appetite loss, apprehension, blurred vision, chills, constipation, cramps, depression, diarrhea, difficult urination, disorientation, double vision, dreams, dry mouth, facial flushing, fainting, faintness, floating feeling, hallucinations, headache, high blood pressure, hives, inability to urinate, insomnia, involuntary movement of the eyeball, itching, low blood pressure, mood changes, nervousness, "pinpoint" pupils, rapid heartbeat, rash, rigid muscles, seizure, sexual drive or performance problems, slow heartbeat, sweating, swelling due to fluid retention, taste alterations, throbbing heartbeat, tingling or pins and needles, tremor, uncoordinated muscle movements, vision disturbances, weakness

If you stop taking MS Contin after a long period of use, you will probably experience some degree of narcotic withdrawal syndrome. During the first 24 hours, you may have: dilated pupils, goose bumps, restlessness, restless sleep, runny nose, sweating, tearing, or yawning.

Over the next 72 hours, the following may be added:

Abdominal and leg pains, abdominal and muscle cramps, anxiety, diarrhea, hot and cold flashes, inability to fall or stay asleep, increase in body temperature, blood pressure and breathing and heart rate, kicking movements, loss of appetite, nasal discharge, nausea, severe backache, sneezing, twitching and spasm of muscles, vomiting, weakness

Even without treatment, your withdrawal symptoms will probably disappear within a week or two. However, you could experience a second phase of withdrawal, involving aching muscles, irritability, and insomnia, which might last for 2 to 6 months.

Why should this drug not be prescribed?

Do not take MS Contin if you have ever had an allergic reaction to morphine or are sensitive to it, or if you have bronchial asthma.

If your breathing is abnormally slow, you should not be given MS Contin unless there is resuscitation equipment nearby.

MS Contin should not be prescribed if you are suffering an intestinal blockage.

Special warnings about this medication

MS Contin should not be given to anyone who might have a brain injury, or the beginnings of an abdominal problem requiring surgery; the drug could mask the symptoms, making correct diagnosis difficult or impossible.

Caution is advised in giving MS Contin to people facing biliary tract surgery, since the drug could make their condition worse. Your doctor will also prescribe MS Contin with extreme caution if you have any of the following conditions:

Alcoholism
Coma
Curvature of the spine
Delirium tremens (severe alcohol withdrawal)
Drug-related psychosis
Enlarged prostate or constricted urinary canal
Kidney disorder
Liver disorder
Low adrenalin levels
Low thyroid levels
Lung disorder
Swallowing difficulty

If taken by an epileptic person, MS Contin could increase the likelihood of a seizure.

Since MS Contin can impair judgment and coordination, do not drive, climb, or operate hazardous equipment while taking this drug.

MS Contin can lower blood pressure; you may feel dizzy or light-headed, especially when you just stand up.

Possible food and drug interactions
when taking this medication

If MS Contin is taken with certain other drugs, the effects of either could be increased, decreased, or altered. It is especially important to check with your doctor before combining MS Contin with the following:

Alcohol
Certain analgesics such as Talwin, Nubain, Stadol, and Buprenex
Major tranquilizers such as Thorazine and Phenergan
Muscle relaxants such as Flexeril and Valium
Sedatives such as Dalmane and Halcion
Tranquilizers such as Librium and Xanax

Special information
if you are pregnant or breastfeeding

If you are pregnant or plan to become pregnant, inform your doctor immediately. Although there is no evidence so far that a pregnant woman's short-term use of MS Contin can harm her unborn baby, this drug should be taken during pregnancy only if the benefit to the mother outweighs a possible risk to the child.

MS Contin is not recommended for use as a painkiller during childbirth. If a woman takes this drug shortly before giving birth, her baby may have trouble breathing. Babies born to mothers who use morphine chronically may suffer from drug withdrawal symptoms.

Since some of the morphine from MS Contin appears in breast milk, do not take this medication while breastfeeding. If you do nurse while using MS Contin, your baby could experience withdrawal symptoms once you stop taking this medication.

Recommended dosage

ADULTS

MS Contin tablets are swallowed whole, and are not to be broken, chewed, or crushed.

Because MS Contin is so potent, your doctor will determine which dosage form will work best and how often you should take the drug, based on your individual needs.

Overdosage

Any medication taken in excess can have serious consequences. An overdose of MS Contin can be fatal. If you suspect an overdose, seek medical attention immediately.

■ *Symptoms of MS Contin overdose may include:*
 Cold, clammy skin
 Flaccid muscles
 Lowered blood pressure
 "Pinpoint" pupils

Sleepiness leading to stupor and coma
Slowed breathing
Slow pulse rate

Category:

MULTIVITAMINS

Brand names: Centrum, Theragran, Vi-Daylin

Why is this supplement prescribed?

Multivitamins are nutritional supplements for people whose diet may be deficient in certain vitamins and minerals. You may need a supplement if you are on a special diet, or don't eat the right foods. A supplement may also be necessary if you are a strict vegetarian, take medications that prevent the body from using certain nutrients, or have an illness that affects your appetite. In addition, special formulas are available for use during pregnancy.

Vitamin/mineral supplements come in a wide range of formulations. Three of the most widely used are Centrum, Theragran, and Vi-Daylin. Each of these brands offers a variety of formulas tailored to the needs of different groups.

Centrum is a multivitamin/multimineral supplement that includes all antioxidants, the vitamins that strengthen the body's natural defenses against cell damage. *Centrum Silver* contains higher strengths of the vitamins that people 50 years of age or older need the most. *Centrum, Jr.* formulations are geared to children's needs.

Theragran is a multivitamin supplement. *Theragran-M* adds minerals to the formulation. *Theragran Stress Formula* contains higher strengths of the B vitamins that may be needed for people under stress, plus extra vitamin C.

Vi-Daylin is a multivitamin supplement; *Vi-Daylin + Iron* is a multivitamin plus iron, which may be needed by women who have heavy menstrual periods. Some Vi-Daylin formulations also contain fluoride. *Vi-Daylin drops* are be given to infants and young children.

Most important fact about this supplement

Do not use supplements as a replacement for a diet rich in essential vitamins and minerals. Food contains many important ingredients not available in supplements.

How should you take this supplement?

Follow the dosing instructions on the bottle, or use as directed by your doctor.

Do not take more than suggested.

■ *If you miss a dose...*
If you forget to take your multivitamin for a day, don't be concerned. Resume your regular schedule the following day.

■ *Storage instructions...*
Keep out of the reach of children. Store at room temperature, and keep tightly closed.

Why should this supplement not be used?
If you have any serious chronic medical conditions check with your doctor before starting on a multivitamin supplement. You may have special requirements.

If your multivitamin supplement contains fluoride, check with your doctor. You should not use it if your drinking water contains more than 0.7 parts per million of fluoride.

Special warnings about this supplement
Do not take more of a multivitamin supplement than suggested on the packaging, or directed by your doctor. Very high doses of some vitamins and minerals can be harmful or even dangerous.

Possible food and drug interactions
when taking this supplement
When taken as suggested on the packaging, there are no known supplement interactions.

Special information
if you are pregnant or breastfeeding
Ask your doctor whether you should take a multivitamin supplement while you are pregnant or breastfeeding. Taking too much of any supplement may be harmful to you or your unborn child.

Recommended dosage
ADULTS

The usual dose is 1 tablet, teaspoonful, or tablespoonful daily according to package instructions, or as directed by your doctor.

CHILDREN

The usual dose of children's formulations is 1 tablet, teaspoonful, or dropperful daily or as directed by your doctor. Younger children may require only half this dose. Check the instructions on the package.

Overdosage

Megadoses of some vitamins and minerals can be harmful when taken for extended periods. If you have unexplained symptoms and suspect an overdose, check with your doctor.

Generic name:

MUPIROCIN

See Bactroban, page 109.

Brand name:

MYCELEX

See Gyne-Lotrimin, page 476.

Brand name:

MYCELEX-7

See Gyne-Lotrimin, page 476.

Brand name:

MYCOLOG-II

Pronounced: MY-koe-log too
Generic ingredients: Nystatin, Triamcinolone acetonide
Other brand names: Myco-Triacet II, Mytrex

Why is this drug prescribed?

Mycolog-II Cream and Ointment are prescribed for the treatment of candidiasis (a yeast-like fungal infection) of the skin. The combination of an antifungal (nystatin) and a steroid (triamcinolone acetonide) provides greater benefit than nystatin alone during the first few days of treatment. Nystatin kills the fungus or prevents its growth; triamcinolone helps relieve the redness, swelling, itching, and other discomfort that can accompany a skin infection.

Most important fact about this drug

Absorption of this drug through the skin can affect the whole body instead of just the surface of the skin being treated. Although unusual, it is possible that you could experience symptoms of steroid excess such as weight gain, reddening and rounding of the face and neck, growth of excess body and facial hair, high blood pressure, emotional disturbances, increased blood sugar, and urinary excretion of glucose (marked by an increase in frequency of urination).

Use of this medication over large surface areas, for prolonged periods, or with airtight dressings or bandages, could cause these problems. Your doctor will watch your condition and periodically check for symptoms.

How should you use this medication?

Use this medicine for the full course of treatment, even if your symptoms are gone. Apply a thin layer to the affected area and gently rub it in. Do not bandage or wrap the area being treated, unless your doctor tells you to. Keep the area cool and dry.

Use this medication exactly as prescribed by your doctor. Do not use it more often or for a longer time. It is for external use only. Avoid contact with the eyes.

■ *If you miss a dose...*
  Apply it as soon as you remember. If it is almost time for your next dose, skip the one you missed and go back to your regular schedule.

■ *Storage instructions...*
  Store away from heat and light. Do not freeze.

What side effects may occur?

Side effects cannot be anticipated. If any develop or change in intensity, inform your doctor as soon as possible. Only your doctor can determine if it is safe for you to continue taking Mycolog-II.

■ *Side effects may include:*
  Blistering, burning, dryness, eruptions resembling acne, excessive discoloring of the skin, excessive growth of hair (especially on the face), hair loss (especially on the scalp), inflammation around the mouth, inflammation of hair follicles, irritation, itching, peeling, prickly heat, reddish purple lines on skin, secondary infection, severe inflammation of the skin, softening of the skin, stretch marks, stretching or thinning of the skin

Why should this drug not be prescribed?

If you are sensitive to or have ever had an allergic reaction to nystatin, triamcinolone acetonide, or other antifungals or steroids, you should not take this medication. Make sure your doctor is aware of any drug reactions you have experienced.

Special warnings about this medication

Do not use this drug for any disorder other than the one for which it was prescribed.

Remember to avoid wrapping or bandaging the affected area. The use of tight-fitting diapers or plastic pants is not recommended for a child being treated in the diaper area with Mycolog-II. These garments may act in the same way as airtight dressings or bandages.

If an irritation or allergic reaction develops while using Mycolog-II, notify your doctor.

If used in the groin area, apply Mycolog-II sparingly and wear loose-fitting clothing.

If your condition does not show improvement after 2 to 3 weeks, or if it gets worse, consult your doctor.

Possible food and drug interactions
when taking this medication

No interactions have been reported.

Special information
if you are pregnant or breastfeeding

The effects of Mycolog-II in pregnancy have not been adequately studied. If you are pregnant or plan to become pregnant, inform your doctor before using Mycolog-II.

It is not known whether this medication appears in breast milk. If this drug is essential to your health, your doctor may advise you to discontinue breastfeeding until your treatment with this medication is finished.

Recommended dosage

ADULTS

Mycolog-II Cream

Mycolog-II Cream is usually applied to the affected areas 2 times a day, in the morning and evening, by gently and thoroughly massaging the preparation into the skin. Your doctor will have you stop using the cream if your symptoms persist after 25 days of treatment.

Mycolog-II Ointment

A thin film of Mycolog-II Ointment is usually applied to the affected areas 2 times a day, in the morning and the evening. Your doctor will have you stop using the ointment if your symptoms persist after 25 days of treatment.

CHILDREN

Your doctor will limit use of Mycolog-II for children to the least amount that is effective. Long-term treatment may interfere with the growth and development of children.

Overdosage

An acute overdosage is unlikely with the use of Mycolog-II; however, long-term or prolonged use can produce reactions throughout the body. See "Most important fact about this drug."

Brand name:

MYCO-TRIACET II

See Mycolog-II, page 695.

Brand name:

MYKROX

See Zaroxolyn, page 1220.

Generic name:

MYLANTA

See Antacids, page 62.

Brand name:

MYSOLINE

Pronounced: MY-soh-leen
Generic name: Primidone

Why is this drug prescribed?

Mysoline is used to treat epileptic and other seizures. It can be used alone or with other anticonvulsant drugs. It is chemically similar to barbiturates.

Most important fact about this drug

Mysoline should not be stopped suddenly; this could cause you to have seizures. If you no longer need the medication, your doctor will reduce the dosage gradually.

How should you take this medication?

Take Mysoline exactly as prescribed. Do not change from one manufacturer's product to another without consulting your doctor.

If using Mysoline Suspension, shake well before using.

■ *If you miss a dose...*
Take it as soon as you remember. If it is within an hour of your next dose, skip the one you missed and go back to your regular schedule. Never take 2 doses at the same time.

■ *Storage instructions...*
Store at room temperature in a tightly closed container, away from light.

What side effects may occur?

Side effects cannot be anticipated. If any develop or change in intensity, inform your doctor as soon as possible. Only your doctor can determine if it is safe for you to continue taking Mysoline.

■ *More common side effects may include:*
Lack of muscle coordination
Vertigo or severe dizziness

■ *Less common side effects may include:*
Double vision, drowsiness, emotional disturbances, excessive irritability, fatigue, impotence, loss of appetite, nausea, skin eruptions that resemble measles, uncontrolled movement of the eyeballs, vomiting

Why should this drug not be prescribed?

You should not take Mysoline if you have porphyria (an inherited metabolic disorder) or if you are allergic to phenobarbital.

Special warnings about this medication

Remember that you must not stop taking Mysoline suddenly.

It can take several weeks for the full effectiveness of Mysoline to be seen.

Since Mysoline is generally given for long periods of time, your doctor will check your blood count every 6 months.

Possible food and drug interactions
when taking this medication

If Mysoline is taken with certain other drugs, the effects of either could be increased, decreased, or altered. It is especially important to check with your doctor before combining Mysoline with the following:

Antidepressants called MAO inhibitors, such as Parnate and Nardil
Blood-thinning drugs such as Coumadin and Panwarfin
Doxycycline (Doryx, Vibramycin)
Estrogen-containing oral contraceptives such as Ortho-Novum and
    Triphasil
Griseofulvin (Fulvicin-U/F, Grifulvin V)
Steroid drugs such as Decadron

Avoid alcoholic beverages while you are taking Mysoline.

Special information
if you are pregnant or breastfeeding

Although the effects of Mysoline in pregnancy and nursing infants are not known, recent studies show an increase in birth defects in infants born to epileptic women taking anticonvulsant medications (particularly Dilantin and phenobarbital). Although most pregnant women taking anticonvulsant medication give birth to normal, healthy babies, this possibility may also exist with Mysoline. If you are pregnant or plan to become pregnant, inform your doctor immediately. Mysoline appears in breast milk and can affect a nursing infant, causing excessive sleepiness and drowsiness. If this medication is essential to your health, your doctor may advise you to stop breastfeeding.

Recommended dosage

ADULTS AND CHILDREN 8 YEARS AND OLDER

For people 8 years of age and older who have not been treated before, the doctor will start Mysoline as follows, using either 50-milligram or scored 250-milligram Mysoline tablets:

Days 1 to 3: 100 to 125 milligrams at bedtime

Days 4 to 6: 100 to 125 milligrams 2 times a day

Days 7 to 9: 100 to 125 milligrams 3 times a day

Day 10 to maintenance: 250 milligrams 3 times a day

For most adults and children 8 years of age and over, the usual maintenance dosage is 250 milligrams 3 or 4 times a day. If you need more, your doctor may increase the dose to five or six 250-milligram tablets. You should not take more than 500 milligrams 4 times a day (2,000 milligrams or 2 grams).

In patients already receiving other anticonvulsants, the usual starting dose of Mysoline is 100 to 125 milligrams at bedtime; your doctor will gradually increase this dose to a maintenance level as the other drug is gradually decreased. Your doctor will either find a working level for the combination or withdraw the other medication completely. When Mysoline is to be used as a single drug, it will take at least 2 weeks to make the transition from two drugs to one.

CHILDREN UNDER AGE 8

Days 1 to 3: 50 milligrams at bedtime

Days 4 to 6: 50 milligrams 2 times a day

Days 7 to 9: 100 milligrams 2 times a day

Day 10 to maintenance: 125 milligrams 3 times a day to 250 milligrams 3 times day

The usual maintenance dosage is 125 to 250 milligrams 3 times daily or 10 to 25 milligrams per 2.2 pounds of body weight per day, divided into smaller doses.

Overdosage
Any medication taken in excess can have serious consequences. If you suspect a Mysoline overdose, seek medical attention immediately.

Brand name:

MYTREX

See Mycolog-II, page 695.

Generic name:

NABUMETONE

See Relafen, page 941.

Generic name:

NADOLOL

See Corgard, page 238.

Generic name:

NADOLOL WITH BENDROFLUMETHIAZIDE

See Corzide, page 244.

Generic name:

NALTREXONE

See ReVia, page 953.

Generic name:

NAPHAZOLINE WITH PHENIRAMINE

See Naphcon-A, page 702.

Brand name:

NAPHCON-A

Pronounced: NAFF-kon ay
Generic ingredients: Naphazoline hydrochloride,
Pheniramine maleate

Why is this drug prescribed?
Naphcon-A, an eyedrop containing both a decongestant and an antihistamine, is used to relieve eye irritation and allergic or inflammatory eye conditions.

Most important fact about this drug
This medication may cause temporarily blurred vision. Be careful when driving or performing other tasks that could be hazardous.

How should you use this medication?
Remove contact lenses before administering this medication. Do not use the solution if it becomes cloudy or changes color.

To administer the eyedrops, follow these steps:

1. Wash your hands thoroughly.
2. Gently pull your lower eyelid down to form a pocket between your eye and the lid.
3. Hold the eyedrop bottle on your forehead or the bridge of your nose.
4. Do not touch the applicator tip to your eye or any other surface.
5. Tilt your head back and squeeze the medication into your eye.
6. Close your eyes gently and keep them closed for a minute or two.
7. Do not rinse the dropper.

■ *If you miss a dose...*
Use this medication only as needed.

■ *Storage instructions...*
Store at room temperature in a tightly closed bottle. Protect from light and excessive heat.

What side effects may occur?
Side effects cannot be anticipated. If any side effects develop or change in intensity, tell your doctor immediately. Only your doctor can determine whether it is safe for you to continue using this medicine.

Although you apply these drops to the surface of your eye, some of the ingredients may be absorbed from the eyeball into the bloodstream.

■ *Side effects may include:*
Dilated pupils
Drowsiness
High blood pressure
High blood sugar
Increased pressure inside the eyeball
Irregular heartbeat

Why should this drug not be prescribed?
Do not take Naphcon-A if you have ever had an allergic reaction to it or are sensitive to any of its ingredients.

Do not use this medication if you have glaucoma.

Special warnings about this medication
You should use this medication with caution in the following circumstances:

■ If you have severe heart disease (including any heartbeat irregularity),
■ If you have high blood pressure that is not well controlled,
■ If you have diabetes (especially if you are prone to diabetic ketoacidosis, a dangerous surge in blood pressure that can lead to coma).

Do not give Naphcon-A to infants or children. This medication can cause stupor or coma and a serious drop in body temperature in a child.

Possible food and drug interactions
when taking this medication

Do not use Naphcon-A simultaneously with an antidepressant classified as an MAO inhibitor, such as Marplan, Nardil, or Parnate. This drug combination could cause your blood pressure to rise suddenly and dangerously.

Special information
if you are pregnant or breastfeeding

If you are pregnant or plan to become pregnant, inform your doctor immediately. Naphcon-A should be used during pregnancy only if the potential benefit to the mother outweighs the potential risk to the unborn child. It is not known whether Naphcon-A appears in breast milk. To be safe, consult your doctor before using this medication while breastfeeding.

Recommended dosage

ADULTS

Place 1 or 2 drops in each eye every 3 to 4 hours or less to relieve symptoms.

Overdosage

Overdose from accidental oral use or excessive use in the eye can have serious consequences, especially in young children. If you suspect you may have used too much of this medication, seek medical attention immediately.

Brand name:

NAPROSYN

Pronounced: NA-proh-sinn
Generic name: Naproxen

Why is this drug prescribed?

Naprosyn, a nonsteroidal anti-inflammatory drug, is used to relieve the inflammation, swelling, stiffness, and joint pain associated with rheumatoid arthritis, osteoarthritis (the most common form of arthritis), juvenile arthritis, ankylosing spondylitis (spinal arthritis), tendinitis, bursitis, and acute gout; it is also used to relieve menstrual cramps and other types of mild to moderate pain.

Most important fact about this drug
You should have frequent checkups with your doctor if you take Naprosyn regularly. Ulcers or internal bleeding can occur without warning.

How should you take this medication?
Naprosyn may be taken with food or an antacid, and with a full glass of water to avoid stomach upset. Avoid taking it on an empty stomach.

If you are using Naprosyn for arthritis, it should be taken regularly; take it exactly as prescribed.

■ *If you miss a dose...*
  And you take the drug on a regular schedule, take the dose as soon as you remember. If it is almost time for your next dose, skip the one you missed and go back to your regular schedule. Do not take 2 doses at once.

■ *Storage instructions...*
  Store Naprosyn tablets at room temperature in a well-closed container, away from light. Store Naprosyn suspension at room temperature; protect from light and extreme heat.

What side effects may occur?
Side effects cannot be anticipated. If any develop or change in intensity, inform your doctor as soon as possible. Only your doctor can determine if it is safe for you to continue taking Naprosyn.

■ *More common side effects may include:*
  Abdominal pain, bruising, constipation, difficult or labored breathing, dizziness, drowsiness, headache, heartburn, itching, nausea, ringing in ears, skin eruptions, swelling due to fluid retention

■ *Less common or rare side effects may include:*
  Abdominal bleeding, black stools, blood in the urine, changes in liver function, chills and fever, colitis, congestive heart failure, depression, diarrhea, dream abnormalities, general feeling of illness, hair loss, hearing disturbances or loss, inability to concentrate, inability to sleep, indigestion, inflammation of the lungs, inflammation of the mouth, kidney disease or failure, light-headedness, menstrual disorders, muscle pain and weakness, peptic ulcer, red or purple spots on the skin, severe allergic reaction, skin inflammation due to sensitivity to light, skin rashes, sweating, thirst, throbbing heartbeat, vertigo, visual disturbances, vomiting, vomiting of blood, yellow skin and eyes

Why should this drug not be prescribed?

If you are sensitive to or have ever had an allergic reaction to Naprosyn, Anaprox or Anaprox DS, you should not take this drug. Also, if aspirin or other nonsteroidal anti-inflammatory drugs have ever given you asthma or nasal inflammation or tumors, you should not take this medication. Make sure your doctor is aware of any drug reactions you have experienced.

Special warnings about this medication

Remember that peptic ulcers and bleeding can occur without warning. Call your doctor immediately if you suspect a problem.

Use this drug with caution if you have kidney or liver disease; it can cause liver inflammation in some people.

Naprosyn may prolong bleeding time. If you are taking blood-thinning medication, your doctor will prescribe Naprosyn with caution.

This medication may cause vision problems. If you experience any changes in your vision, inform your doctor.

This drug can increase water retention. It will be prescribed with caution if you have heart disease or high blood pressure. Naprosyn suspension contains a significant amount of sodium. If you are on a low-sodium diet, discuss this with your doctor.

Naprosyn may cause you to become drowsy or less alert; therefore, avoid driving, operating dangerous machinery, or participating in any hazardous activity that requires full mental alertness until you are sure of the drug's effect on you.

Possible food and drug interactions
when taking this medication

If Naprosyn is taken with certain other drugs, the effects of either could be increased, decreased, or altered. It is especially important to check with your doctor before combining Naprosyn with the following:

Aspirin
Beta blockers such as Tenormin
Blood-thinning drugs such as Coumadin
Furosemide (Lasix)
Lithium (Lithonate)
Methotrexate
Naproxen sodium (Anaprox)
Phenytoin (Dilantin)
Probenecid (Benemid)
Sulfa drugs such as Bactrim and Septra
Oral diabetes drugs such as Diabinese and Micronase

Special information
if you are pregnant or breastfeeding
The effects of Naprosyn during pregnancy have not been adequately studied. If you are pregnant or plan to become pregnant, inform your doctor immediately. Naprosyn appears in breast milk and could affect a nursing infant. If this medication is essential to your health, your doctor may advise you to discontinue breastfeeding until your treatment with this medication is finished.

Recommended dosage
Naprosyn is available in tablet and liquid form. When taking the liquid, use a teaspoon or the measuring cup, marked in half-teaspoon and 2.5-milliliter increments, that comes with Naprosyn.

ADULTS

Rheumatoid Arthritis, Osteoarthritis, and Ankylosing Spondylitis
The usual dose is 250 milligrams (10 milliliters or 2 teaspoons of suspension), 375 milligrams (15 milliliters or 3 teaspoons), or 500 milligrams (20 milliliters or 4 teaspoons) 2 times a day (morning and evening). Your dose may be adjusted by your doctor over your period of treatment. Improvement of symptoms should be seen in 2 to 4 weeks.

Acute Gout
Starting dose is 750 milligrams (30 milliliters or 6 teaspoons), followed by 250 milligrams (10 milliliters or 2 teaspoons) every 8 hours until the symptoms are relieved.

Mild to Moderate Pain, Menstrual Cramps, Acute Tendinitis and Bursitis
Starting dose is 500 milligrams (20 milliliters or 4 teaspoons of suspension), followed by 250 milligrams (10 milliliters or 2 teaspoons) every 6 to 8 hours as needed. The most you should take in a day is 1,250 milligrams (50 milliliters or 10 teaspoons).

CHILDREN

Juvenile Arthritis
The usual dose is 10 milligrams per 2.2 pounds of body weight, 2 times a day. Follow your doctor's directions carefully when giving a child this medicine.

The safety and effectiveness of Naprosyn have not been established in children under 2 years of age.

Overdosage

Any medication taken in excess can have serious consequences. If you suspect an overdose, seek medical attention immediately.

■ *Symptoms of Naprosyn overdose may include:*
Drowsiness
Heartburn
Indigestion
Nausea
Vomiting

Generic name:

NAPROXEN

See Naprosyn, page 704.

Generic name:

NAPROXEN SODIUM

See Anaprox, page 55.

Brand name:

NARDIL

Pronounced: NAHR-dill
Generic name: Phenelzine sulfate

Why is this drug prescribed?

Nardil is a monoamine oxidase (MAO) inhibitor used to treat depression as well as anxiety or phobias mixed with depression. MAO is an enzyme responsible for breaking down certain neurotransmitters (chemical messengers) in the brain. By inhibiting MAO, Nardil helps restore more normal mood states. Unfortunately, MAO inhibitors such as Nardil also block MAO activity throughout the body, an action that can have serious, even fatal, side effects—especially if MAO inhibitors are combined with other foods or drugs containing a substance called tyramine.

Most important fact about this drug

Avoid the following foods, beverages, and medications while taking Nardil and for 2 weeks thereafter:

Beer (including alcohol-free or reduced-alcohol beer)
Caffeine (in excessive amounts)
Cheese (except for cottage cheese and cream cheese)
Chocolate (in excessive amounts)
Dry sausage (including Genoa salami, hard salami, pepperoni, and Lebanon bologna)
Fava bean pods
Liver
Meat extract
Pickled herring
Pickled, fermented, aged, or smoked meat, fish, or dairy products
Sauerkraut
Spoiled or improperly stored meat, fish, or dairy products
Wine (including alcohol-free or reduced-alcohol wine)
Yeast extract (including large amounts of brewer's yeast)
Yogurt

■ *Medications to avoid:*
Amphetamines
Appetite suppressants such as Tenuate
Antidepressants and related medications such as Prozac, Elavil, Triavil, Tegretol, and Flexeril
Asthma inhalants such as Proventil and Ventolin
Cold and cough preparations including those with dextromethorphan, such as Robitussin DM
Hay fever medications such as Contac, Dristan, and Sudafed
L-tryptophan-containing products
Nasal decongestants in tablet, drop, or spray form
Sinus medications
Weight-loss medications

Taking Nardil with any of the above foods, beverages, or medications can cause serious, potentially fatal, high blood pressure. Therefore, when taking Nardil you should immediately report the occurrence of a headache, heart palpitations, or any other unusual symptom. In addition, make certain that you inform any other physician or dentist you see that you are currently taking Nardil or have taken Nardil within the last 2 weeks.

How should you take this medication?

Nardil may be taken with or without food. Take it exactly as prescribed. It can take up to 4 weeks for the drug to begin working.

Use of Nardil may complicate other medical treatment. Always carry a card that says you take Nardil, or wear a Medic Alert bracelet.

■ *If you miss a dose...*
Take it as soon as you remember. If it is within 2 hours of your next dose, skip the one you missed and go back to your regular schedule. Do not take 2 doses at once.

■ *Storage instructions...*
Store at room temperature.

What side effects may occur?

Side effects cannot be anticipated. If any develop or change in intensity, inform your doctor as soon as possible. Only your doctor can determine if it is safe for you to continue taking Nardil.

■ *More common side effects may include:*
Constipation, disorders of the stomach and intestines, dizziness, drowsiness, dry mouth, excessive sleeping, fatigue, headache, insomnia, low blood pressure (especially when rising quickly from lying down or sitting up), muscle spasms, sexual difficulties, strong reflexes, swelling due to fluid retention, tremors, twitching, weakness, weight gain

■ *Less common or rare side effects may include:*
Anxiety, blurred vision, coma, convulsions, delirium, exaggerated feeling of well-being, fever, glaucoma, inability to urinate, involuntary eyeball movements, jitteriness, lack of coordination, liver damage, mania, muscular rigidity, onset of the mental disorder schizophrenia, rapid breathing, rapid heart rate, repetitious use of words and phrases, skin rash, sweating, swelling in the throat, tingling sensation, yellowed skin and whites of eyes

Why should this drug not be prescribed?

You should not take this drug if you have pheochromocytoma (a tumor of the adrenal gland), congestive heart failure, or a history of liver disease, or if you have had an allergic reaction to it.

You should not take Nardil if you are taking medications that may increase blood pressure (such as amphetamines, cocaine, allergy and cold medications, or Ritalin), other MAO inhibitors, L-dopa, methyldopa (Aldomet), phenylalanine, L-tryptophan, L-tyrosine, fluoxetine (Prozac), buspirone (BuSpar), bupropion (Wellbutrin), guanethidine (Ismelin), meperidine (Demerol), dextromethorphan, or central nervous system depressants such as alcohol and narcotics; or if you must consume the foods, beverages, or medications listed above in the "Most important fact about this drug" section.

Special warnings about this medication

You must follow the food and drug limitations established by your physician; failure to do so may lead to potentially fatal side effects. While taking Nardil, you should promptly report the occurrence of a headache or any other unusual symptoms.

If you are diabetic, your doctor will prescribe Nardil with caution, since it is not clear how MAO inhibitors affect blood sugar levels.

If you are taking Nardil, talk to your doctor before you decide to have elective surgery.

If you stop taking Nardil abruptly, you may have withdrawal symptoms. They may include nightmares, agitation, strange behavior, and convulsions.

Possible food and drug interactions
when taking this medication

If Nardil is taken with certain other drugs, the effects of either could be increased, decreased, or altered. It is important that you closely follow your doctor's dietary and medication limitations when taking Nardil. Consult the "Most important fact about this drug" and "Why should this drug not be prescribed?" sections for lists of the foods, beverages, and medications that should be avoided while taking Nardil.

In addition, you should use blood pressure medications (including diuretics and beta blockers) with caution when taking Nardil, since excessively low blood pressure may result. Symptoms of low blood pressure include dizziness when rising from a lying or sitting position, fainting, and tingling in the hands or feet.

Special information
if you are pregnant or breastfeeding

The effects of Nardil during pregnancy have not been adequately studied. Nardil should be used during pregnancy only if the benefits of therapy clearly outweigh the potential risks to the fetus. If you are pregnant or plan to become pregnant, inform your doctor immediately. Nursing mothers should use Nardil only after consulting their physician, since it is not known whether Nardil appears in human milk.

Recommended dosage

ADULTS

The usual starting dose is 15 milligrams (1 tablet) 3 times a day. Your doctor may increase the dosage to 90 milligrams per day.

It may be 4 weeks before the drug starts to work.

Once you have had good results, your doctor may gradually reduce the dose, possibly to as low as 15 milligrams daily or every 2 days.

CHILDREN

Nardil is not recommended, since safety and efficacy for children under the age of 16 have not been determined.

Overdosage

Any medication taken in excess can have serious consequences. An overdose of Nardil can be fatal. If you suspect an overdose, seek medical help immediately.

- *Symptoms of overdose may include:*
  Agitation, backward arching of the head, neck, and back, cool, clammy skin, coma, convulsions, difficult breathing, dizziness, drowsiness, faintness, hallucinations, high blood pressure, high fever, hyperactivity, irritability, jaw muscle spasms, low blood pressure, pain in the heart area, rapid and irregular pulse, severe headache, sweating

Brand name:

NASACORT

See Azmacort, page 97.

Brand name:

NASALCROM

See Intal, page 533.

Brand name:

NASALIDE

See AeroBid, page 20.

Brand name:

NATALINS

See Stuartnatal Plus, page 1048.

See Stuartnatal Plus, page 1048.

Brand name:

NAVANE

Pronounced: NA-vain
Generic name: Thiothixene

Why is this drug prescribed?
Navane is used to treat psychotic disorders (a severe sense of distorted reality). Researchers theorize that antipsychotic medications such as Navane work by lowering levels of dopamine, a neurotransmitter (or chemical messenger) in the brain. Excessive levels of dopamine are believed to be related to psychotic behavior.

Most important fact about this drug
Navane may cause tardive dyskinesia—a condition marked by involuntary muscle spasms and twitches in the face and body. This condition can be permanent and appears to be most common among the elderly, especially women. Ask your doctor for information about this possible risk.

How should you take this medication?
Navane may be taken in liquid or capsule form. In liquid form, a dropper is supplied.

- *If you miss a dose...*
  Take it as soon as you remember. If it is within 2 hours of your next dose, skip the one you missed and go back to your regular schedule. Do not take 2 doses at once.

- *Storage instructions...*
  Store at room temperature away from heat, light, and moisture. Keep the liquid form from freezing.

What side effects may occur?
Side effects cannot be anticipated. If any develop or change in intensity, inform your doctor as soon as possible. Only your doctor can determine if it is safe for you to continue taking Navane.

- *Side effects may include:*
Abnormal muscle rigidity, abnormal secretion of milk, abnormalities in movements and posture, agitation, anemia, blurred vision, breast development in males, chewing movements, constipation, diarrhea, dizziness, drowsiness, dry mouth, excessive thirst, eyeball rotation or state of fixed gaze, fainting, fatigue, fluid accumulation and swelling, headache, high fever, high or low blood sugar, hives, impotence, insomnia, intestinal blockage, involuntary movements of the arms and legs, irregular menstrual periods, itching, light-headedness, loss or increase of appetite, low blood pressure, narrow or dilated pupils of the eye, nasal congestion, nausea, painful muscle spasm, protruding tongue, puckering of mouth, puffing of cheeks, rapid heartbeat, rash, restlessness, salivation, sedation, seizures, sensitivity to light, severe allergic reaction, skin inflammation and peeling, strong reflexes, sweating, swelling of breasts, tremors, twitching in the body, neck, shoulders, and face, visual problems, vomiting, weakness, weight increase, worsening of psychotic symptoms

Why should this drug not be prescribed?
Do not give Navane to comatose individuals. Do not take Navane if you are known to be hypersensitive to it. Also, you should not be using Navane if the activity of your central nervous system is slowed down for any reason—for example, by a sleeping medication, if you have had circulatory system collapse, or if you have an abnormal bone marrow or blood condition.

Special warnings about this medication
Navane may hide symptoms of brain tumor and intestinal obstruction. Your doctor will prescribe Navane cautiously if you have or have ever had a brain tumor, breast cancer, convulsive disorders, the eye condition called glaucoma, intestinal blockage, or heart disease; or if you are exposed to extreme heat or are recovering from alcohol addiction.

This drug may impair your ability to drive a car or operate potentially dangerous machinery. Do not participate in any activities that require full alertness if you are unsure of your ability.

Possible food and drug interactions
when taking this medication
If Navane is taken with certain other drugs, the effects of either could be increased, decreased, or altered. It is especially important to check with your doctor before combining Navane with the following:

Antihistamines such as Benadryl
Barbiturates such as phenobarbital
Drugs that contain atropine, such as Donnatal

Extreme drowsiness and other potentially serious effects can result if Navane is combined with alcohol or other central nervous system depressants such as painkillers, narcotics, or sleeping medications.

Special information
if you are pregnant or breastfeeding

If you are pregnant or plan to become pregnant, inform your doctor immediately; pregnant women should use Navane only if clearly needed. Consult your doctor if you are breastfeeding; he or she may have you stop while you are taking Navane.

Recommended dosage

Dosages of Navane are tailored to the individual. Usually treatment begins with a small dose, which is increased if needed.

ADULTS

For Milder Conditions

The usual starting dosage is a daily total of 6 milligrams, divided into doses of 2 milligrams and taken 3 times a day. Your doctor may increase the dose to a total of 15 milligrams a day.

For More Severe Conditions

The usual starting dosage is a daily total of 10 milligrams, taken in 2 doses of 5 milligrams each. Your doctor may increase this dose to a total of 60 milligrams a day.

Taking more than 60 milligrams a day rarely increases the benefits of Navane.

Some people are able to take Navane once a day. Check with your doctor to see whether you can follow this schedule.

CHILDREN

Navane is not recommended for children younger than 12 years old.

ELDERLY

In general, elderly people are prescribed dosages of Navane in the lower ranges. Because elderly people may develop low blood pressure while taking Navane, their doctors will monitor them closely. Elderly people (especially women) may be more susceptible to such side effects as involuntary muscle spasms and twitches in the face and body. Check with your doctor for more information about these potential risks.

Overdosage

Any medication taken in excess can have serious consequences. If you suspect an overdose, seek medical help immediately.

■ *Symptoms of Navane overdose may include:*
   Central nervous system depression
   Coma
   Difficulty swallowing
   Dizziness
   Drowsiness
   Head tilted to the side
   Low blood pressure
   Muscle twitching
   Rigid muscles
   Salivation
   Tremors
   Walking disturbances
   Weakness

Generic name:

NEDOCROMIL

See Tilade, page 1115.

Generic name:

NEFAZODONE

See Serzone, page 1019.

Brand name:

NEODECADRON OPHTHALMIC OINTMENT AND SOLUTION

Pronounced: Nee-oh-DECK-uh-drohn
Generic ingredients: Dexamethasone sodium phosphate,
   Neomycin sulfate

Why is this drug prescribed?

Neodecadron is a steroid and antibiotic combination that is used to treat inflammatory eye conditions in which there is also a bacterial infection or the possibility of a bacterial infection. Dexamethasone (the steroid) decreases inflammation. Neomycin, the antibiotic, kills some of the more common bacteria.

Most important fact about this drug
The prolonged use of Neodecadron may increase the possibility of developing additional eye infections. It could also cause vision problems or even result in glaucoma and cataracts. If you take this medication for 10 days or longer, your doctor will routinely check your eye pressure.

How should you use this medication?

Neodecadron Ophthalmic Solution
1. Wash your hands thoroughly before use.
2. Tilt your head backward or lie down and gaze upward.
3. Gently pull the lower eyelid away from the eye to form a pouch.
4. Drop the medicine in the pouch and gently close your eyes. Try not to blink.
5. Keep your eye closed for a couple of minutes. Do not rub the eye.
6. Do not touch the applicator tip or dropper to any surface (including the eye).

Neodecadron Ophthalmic Ointment
1. Wash your hands thoroughly before use.
2. Hold the ointment tube in your hand for a few minutes to warm the ointment and make it flow more smoothly.
3. Tilt your head backward or lie down and gaze upward.
4. Gently pull the lower eyelid away from the eye to form a pouch.
5. Squeeze the tube gently, and with a sweeping motion along the inside of the lower lid, apply 0.25 to 0.5 inch of ointment.
6. Close your eyes for a couple of minutes and roll them in all directions.

■ *If you miss a dose...*
Take the forgotten dose as soon as you remember. If it is almost time for the next dose, skip the one you missed and go back to your regular schedule. Never try to "catch up" by doubling the dose.

■ *Storage instructions...*
There are no special storage requirements.

What side effects may occur?
Side effects cannot be anticipated. If any develop or change in intensity, notify your doctor as soon as possible. Only your doctor can determine whether it is safe to continue using Neodecadron.

■ *Side effects may include:*
Allergic skin reactions
Cataracts
Delay in healing of wounds
Development of additional eye infections
Increased eye pressure with possible glaucoma and optic nerve damage

Why should this drug not be prescribed?

Neodecadron should be avoided if you have an inflammation of the cornea (lens); chickenpox; other bacterial, fungal, or viral eye infections; or if you have recently had a foreign body removed from your cornea. Do not use Neodecadron if you have ever had an allergic reaction or are sensitive to any of its ingredients.

Neodecadron solution contains a sulfite that can cause an allergic reaction in susceptible people.

Special warnings about this medication

Neodecadron is absorbed into your bloodstream when applied to your eye. Its steroid component can lower your resistance to infection. Diseases such as measles and chickenpox can be serious and even fatal in adults. If you are using Neodecadron and are exposed to chickenpox or measles, notify your doctor immediately.

Using Neodecadron for a long time may result in glaucoma, vision changes, and cataracts. Long-term use also increases the chances of developing an additional eye infection. If you use Neodecadron for 10 days or longer, your doctor should check your eye pressure regularly.

If you develop a skin rash or any other allergic reaction, stop using the ointment and contact your doctor.

Neodecadron may cause temporary blurring of vision or stinging.

This prescription should not be renewed unless your doctor has re-examined your eyes.

Possible food and drug interactions
when taking this medication

No interactions have been reported.

**Special information
if you are pregnant or breastfeeding**
No information is available about the safety of Neodecadron during pregnancy and when breastfeeding.

If you are pregnant or plan to become pregnant, inform your doctor immediately.

Recommended dosage
The length of treatment varies with the type of condition being treated. Treatment can take a few days or several weeks.

NEODECADRON OPHTHALMIC OINTMENT

Apply a thin coating of Neodecadron Ophthalmic Ointment 3 or 4 times a day. When the condition gets better, daily applications should be reduced to 2 and later to 1 if a maintenance dose is required to control the symptoms.

NEODECADRON OPHTHALMIC SOLUTION

The recommended initial dose is to place 1 or 2 drops into the conjunctival sac every hour during the day and every 2 hours during the night.

Overdosage
Any medication taken in excess can have serious consequences. If you suspect a Neodecadron overdose, seek medical treatment immediately.

Brand name:

NEPTAZANE

Pronounced: NEP-tuh-zayne
Generic name: Methazolamide

Why is this drug prescribed?
Neptazane anhydrase is used to treat the eye condition called chronic open-angle glaucoma. This type of glaucoma is caused by a gradual blockage of the outflow of fluid in the front compartment of the eye over a period of years, causing a slow rise in pressure. It rarely occurs before the age of 40. Neptazane is also used in the type called acute angle-closure glaucoma when pressure within the eye must be lowered before surgery.

Most important fact about this drug

This medication is related to sulfa drugs and can cause allergic reactions, including fever, rash, redness and peeling of the skin, hives, difficulty breathing, serious skin and blood disorders, and even death. Make sure your doctor is aware of any drug reactions you have experienced. He or she should monitor your blood while you are taking this drug. Call your doctor immediately if you experience any allergic symptoms.

How should you take this medication?

Take Neptazane exactly as prescribed. Your doctor may have you use it with other eye medications.

■ *If you miss a dose...*
Take it as soon as you remember. If it is almost time for your next dose, skip the one you missed and go back to your regular schedule. Do not take 2 doses at once.

■ *Storage instructions...*
Store at room temperature.

What side effects may occur?

Side effects cannot be anticipated. If any occur or change in intensity, inform your doctor as soon as possible. Only your doctor can determine if it is safe for you to continue taking Neptazane. Most reactions to Neptazane have been mild and disappear when the medication is stopped or the dosage is adjusted.

■ *More common side effects may include:*
Confusion, depression, diarrhea, dizziness, drowsiness, excessive urination, fatigue, fever, general feeling of not being well, headache, hearing problems, loss of appetite, nausea and vomiting, rash, ringing in the ears, severe allergic reaction, taste changes, temporary nearsightedness, tingling in fingers, toes, hands, or feet

■ *Rare side effects may include:*
Black, tarry stools, blood in the urine, convulsions, hives, increased sensitivity to light, kidney stones, paralysis

Why should this drug not be prescribed?

Neptazane is not for use against all types of glaucoma—only the ones mentioned in "Why is this drug prescribed?" Also, you should not use Neptazane if you have kidney or liver disease, adrenal gland disorders, or low sodium or potassium levels.

Special warnings about this medication

Neptazane can aggravate acidosis, a condition in which the blood is too acidic.

If you have emphysema or a lung blockage, this drug will be prescribed cautiously.

Possible food and drug interactions
when taking this medication

If Neptazane is taken with certain other drugs, the effects of either could be increased, decreased, or altered.

Neptazane and high-dose aspirin taken at the same time can cause loss of appetite, rapid breathing, lethargy, coma, and even death.

Use of Neptazane with steroids may lower your potassium level.

Special information
if you are pregnant or breastfeeding

The effects of Neptazane in pregnancy have not been adequately studied. Neptazane should be used by a pregnant woman only if the potential benefit outweighs the potential risk to the developing baby. If you are pregnant or plan to become pregnant, inform your doctor immediately. Neptazane may appear in breast milk and could affect a nursing infant. If this medication is essential to your health, your doctor may advise you to stop breastfeeding until your treatment with Neptazane is finished.

Recommended dosage

ADULTS

The usual dosage is 50 milligrams to 100 milligrams taken 2 to 3 times a day.

Overdosage

Any drug taken in excess can have serious consequences. If you suspect an overdose of Neptazane, seek medical attention immediately.

Brand Name:

NEURONTIN

Pronounced: NUHR-on-tin
Generic name: Gabapentin

Why is this drug prescribed?

Neurontin, an epilepsy medication, is used with other medications to treat certain types of difficult-to-manage seizures, including elementary partial seizures (brief and no loss of consciousness) and complex partial seizures (consciousness impaired), with and without secondary generalization (grand mal epilepsy with loss of consciousness).

Most important fact about this drug

Take Neurontin exactly as directed by your doctor. To effectively control your seizures, it is important that you take Neurontin 3 times a day, approximately every 8 hours. You should not go longer than 12 hours without a dose of medication.

How should you take this medication?

Do not increase or decrease dosage of this medication without your doctor's approval; and do not suddenly stop taking it, as this may cause an increase in the frequency of your seizures. If you are taking an antacid such as Maalox, take Neurontin at least 2 hours after the antacid.

You may take Neurontin with or without food.

■ *If you miss a dose...*
Try not to allow more than 12 hours to pass between doses. Do not double doses.

■ *Storage instructions...*
Store at room temperature.

What side effects may occur?

Side effects cannot be anticipated. If any develop or change in intensity, inform your doctor as soon as possible. Because Neurontin is used with other antiseizure drugs, it may not be possible to determine whether a side effect is due to Neurontin alone. Only your doctor can determine if it is safe for you to continue taking Neurontin.

■ *More common side effects may include:*
Blurred, dimmed, or double vision, dizziness, drowsiness, fatigue, involuntary eye movement, itchy, runny nose, lack of muscular coordination, nausea, tremor, vomiting

■ *Less common or rare side effects may include:*
Abnormal coordination, abnormal dreams, abnormal thinking, agitation, allergy, altered reflexes, anemia, angina pectoris (crushing chest pain),

anxiety, apathy, arthritis, back pain, behavioral or psychological problems, bladder problems, bleeding gums, bloody stools, bruising, cataracts, chill, conjunctivitis (pinkeye), constipation, cough, cysts, decreased sensitivity to touch, depression, difficult or labored breathing, dry eyes, dry mouth or throat, dry or scaly skin, ear problems, exaggerated feeling of well-being, excessive body hair, eye pain or disorder, fainting, feeling "high", "fever" blisters on lips and mouth, fluid retention, fracture, gas, general feeling of illness, hair loss, hallucination, heart murmur, heartburn, hemorrhoids, high blood pressure, hostility, hyperactivity, increased appetite, increased salivation, increased sweating, indigestion, inflammation of the mouth, gums, or tongue, inflammation of the stomach and intestinal lining, irregular heartbeat, itching, joint pain, stiffness, or swelling, liver enlargement, loss of appetite, loss of bowel control, loss of memory, low blood pressure, menstrual problems, migraines, mouth sores, muscle pain or weakness, nervousness, nosebleeds, paralysis, pneumonia, sexual problems, shortness of breath, skin disorders, sore throat, speech difficulties, stupor, swelling of the face, taste loss, tendinitis, thirst, tingling or pins and needles, twitching, vaginal hemorrhage, vertigo, weight increase or decrease

Why should this drug not be prescribed?

You should not take Neurontin if you have ever had an allergic reaction to it.

Special warnings about this medication

Neurontin causes some people to become drowsy and less alert. Do not drive or operate dangerous machinery or participate in any hazardous activity that requires full mental alertness until you are certain Neurontin does not have this effect on you.

Be sure to tell your doctor if you have any kidney problems or are on hemodialysis, as your doctor will need to adjust your dosage of Neurontin.

Tell your doctor about any medications you are taking, including over-the-counter drugs.

Possible food and drug interactions
when taking this medication

If Neurontin is taken with certain other drugs, the effects of either can be increased, decreased, or altered. It is especially important to check with your doctor before combining Neurontin with the following:

Antacids such as Maalox

Special information
if you are pregnant or breastfeeding

The effects of Neurontin on pregnant women have not been adequately studied, although birth defects have occurred in babies whose mothers took an antiepileptic drug while they were pregnant. It should be used during pregnancy only if clearly needed. If you are pregnant or plan to become pregnant, tell your doctor immediately. This medication may appear in breast milk and could affect a nursing infant. Check with your doctor if you plan to breastfeed your baby.

Recommended dosage

ADULTS AND CHILDREN 12 YEARS AND OVER

Your doctor will probably start your therapy with one 300-milligram dose at bedtime on the first day, two 300-milligram doses the second day, and three 300-milligram doses the third day. After that, the usual daily dosage ranges from 900 to 1,800 milligrams divided into 3 doses, using 300-milligram or 400-milligram capsules.

If Neurontin is discontinued or another drug added to therapy, your doctor will do this gradually, over a 1-week period.

Overdosage

Any medication taken in excess can have serious consequences. If you suspect an overdose, seek medical treatment immediately.

■ *Symptoms of Neurontin overdose may include:*
  Diarrhea
  Double vision
  Drowsiness
  Lethargy
  Slurred speech

Generic name:

NICARDIPINE

See Cardene, page 166.

Brand name:

NICODERM

See Nicotine Patches, page 729.

Brand name:

NICORETTE

Pronounced: Nik-ho-RET
Generic name: Nicotine polacrilex

Why is this drug prescribed?
Nicorette and Nicorette DS (double strength) are used as a temporary aid by cigarette smokers who want to stop smoking.

Nicorette is most effective when used in a medically supervised behavior modification program offering education, counseling, and psychological support.

Most important fact about this drug
Nicorette contains nicotine—an addicting and toxic substance. Nicorette is a powerful, potentially addicting medication that must be used according to your doctor's instructions.

How should you take this medication?
The following are general, medically approved guidelines for taking Nicorette, but you should carefully follow your doctor's instructions to avoid side effects and addiction to Nicorette.

1. You must give up smoking completely and immediately when you start using Nicorette.
2. When you want to smoke, put 1 piece of Nicorette in your mouth.
3. Chew Nicorette very slowly; chewing Nicorette too fast may release the nicotine in the product too quickly, causing the same effects as inhaling for the first time or smoking too fast (e.g., light-headedness, nausea, vomiting, throat and mouth soreness, hiccups, and upset stomach).
4. Stop chewing when you get a peppery taste or feel a slight tingling in your mouth. This usually happens after about 15 chews.
5. "Park" the gum by placing it between your cheek and gums.
6 Start slowly chewing again when the peppery taste or tingling feeling is almost gone (about 1 minute). Stop chewing when the peppery taste or tingling returns.
7. "Park" the gum again in a different part of the mouth.
8. Repeat this procedure until most of the nicotine is gone from the gum (about 30 minutes).

9. Do not use more than 30 pieces of Nicorette or 20 pieces of Nicorette DS a day.

10. As your urge to smoke fades, gradually use fewer pieces of Nicorette. This may be possible in 2 to 3 months.

11. Stop using Nicorette when you are satisfied with 1 or 2 pieces a day, unless your doctor tells you otherwise. If you have trouble reducing your use of Nicorette, contact your doctor. Do not use Nicorette for more than 6 months.

12. Carry Nicorette with you at all times in case you feel the urge to smoke again.

The effects of Nicorette may be reduced by many foods or drinks such as coffee, juices, wine or soft drinks. Do not eat or drink 15 minutes before or while chewing Nicorette.

■ *If you miss a dose...*
With Nicorette, the goal is to take as few doses as possible. Don't make up a missed dose, and never double the dose.

■ *Storage instructions...*
Keep Nicorette below 86 degrees. (Remember, the inside of a parked car can get much hotter than this.) Protect the chewing pieces from light.

What side effects may occur?
Side effects cannot be anticipated. If any develop or change in intensity, inform your doctor as soon as possible. Only your doctor can determine if it is safe for you to continue taking this medication.

■ *More common side effects may include:*
Bleeding gums, excessive saliva in mouth, hiccups, indigestion, inflammation of the mouth, injury to teeth or cheeks, nausea, stomach and intestinal discomfort, throat soreness, tingling or pins and needles

■ *Less common or rare side effects may include:*
Diarrhea, dry mouth, inflammation of the gums, tongue, or throat, mouth sores, muscle pain, rash, sweating, tongue sores

Why should this drug not be prescribed?
Do not use Nicorette if you are sensitive to or have ever had an allergic reaction to nicotine or any of the other ingredients of Nicorette.

Special warnings about this medication

Using Nicorette on a long-term basis is not recommended because nicotine, if consumed for a long enough time, can be harmful and addicting.

You must chew Nicorette slowly and follow your doctor's instructions carefully to avoid side effects and addiction.

If you develop an allergic reaction such as hives or rash, stop using Nicorette and contact your doctor.

Before using Nicorette, tell your doctor if you have ever had angina (severe chest pain), Buerger's disease (disease of the arteries), diabetes or other endocrine (hormone) diseases, dental problems, difficulty swallowing, drug allergies, heartburn, heart disease, high blood pressure, kidney or liver disease, peptic ulcer, throat or mouth inflammation, or overactive thyroid or TMJ (disease at the joint of the jaw).

Nicorette should be used with caution if you have recently had a heart attack or have a seriously irregular heartbeat.

Nicorette may stick to dentures; if this becomes a problem, stop chewing Nicorette and tell your doctor.

Possible food and drug interactions
when taking this medication

If Nicorette is taken with other drugs, the effects of either could be increased, decreased, or altered. It is especially important to check with your doctor before combining Nicorette with the following:

Acetaminophen (Tylenol)
Caffeine
Furosemide (Lasix)
Glutethimide
Imipramine (Tofranil)
Insulin
Isoproterenol (Isuprel)
Labetalol (Normodyne)
Oxazepam (Serax)
Pentazocine (Talwin)
Phenacetin, the pain and fever reducer
Phenylephrine (Entex)
Prazosin (Minipress)
Propoxyphene (Darvon)
Propranolol (Inderal)
Theophylline (Theo-Dur)

Special information
if you are pregnant or breastfeeding

If you are pregnant or nursing your baby, you should not use Nicorette. If you become pregnant while using Nicorette, contact your doctor immediately.

Nicotine, either from smoking or from chewing Nicorette, does appear in breast milk and can affect the baby.

Recommended dosage

ADULTS

Nicorette—2 milligram

Chew 1 piece of Nicorette every 1 to 2 hours. Most adults require 9 to 12 pieces of Nicorette a day during the first month of treatment. Follow your doctor's advice to be sure you are using Nicorette correctly. Do not use more than 30 pieces a day. After 2 to 3 months, follow your doctor's plan for gradual withdrawal of Nicorette.

Nicorette DS—4 milligram

Chew 1 piece of Nicorette every 1 to 2 hours. Most adults require 9 to 12 pieces of Nicorette a day during the first months of treatment. Follow your doctor's advice to be sure you are using Nicorette correctly. Do not use more than 20 pieces a day. After 2 to 3 months, follow your doctor's plan for gradual withdrawal of Nicorette.

Gradual withdrawal of Nicorette is recommended to avoid the return of symptoms that may lead you to start smoking again. Suggested procedures are as follows:

1. Decrease the total number of pieces of Nicorette used per day by 1 or more pieces every 4 to 7 days.
2. Decrease the chewing time with each piece of Nicorette from the normal 30 minutes to 10 to 15 minutes. Then gradually decrease the total number of pieces used per day. You can also chew each piece longer than 30 minutes and cut down the number of pieces you chew a day.
3. Substitute 1 or more pieces of sugarless gum for an equal number of pieces of Nicorette. Increase the number of pieces of sugarless gum substituted for Nicorette every 4 to 7 days.

CHILDREN

Safety and effectiveness for children and adolescents who smoke have not been established. If a child swallows a piece of Nicorette accidentally, contact your doctor or local poison control center immediately.

ELDERLY

Elderly individuals should use Nicorette cautiously.

Overdosage

Any medication taken in excess can have serious consequences. Overdose may occur if you chew many pieces of Nicorette at one time or in rapid succession, or if you smoke while you are using Nicorette. Accidentally swallowing a piece of Nicorette will probably not cause side effects, but if you have any reason to suspect an overdose, seek medical help immediately.

■ *Symptoms of Nicorette overdose are similar to symptoms of acute nicotine poisoning and may include:*
Abdominal pain, blurred vision, cold sweat, diarrhea, difficulty breathing, disturbed hearing, dizziness, exhaustion, fainting, headache, low blood pressure, mental confusion, nausea, paleness, rapid and irregular pulse, salivation, tremor, upset stomach, vomiting, weakness

A large overdose can result in prostration and respiratory failure.

Category:

NICOTINE PATCHES

Brand names: Habitrol, Nicoderm, Nicotrol, ProStep

Why is this drug prescribed?

Nicotine patches, which are available under several brand names, are designed to help you quit smoking by reducing your craving for tobacco. Each adhesive patch contains a specific amount of nicotine embedded in a pad or gel.

Nicotine, the habit-forming ingredient in tobacco, is a stimulant and a mood lifter. When you give up smoking, lack of nicotine makes you crave cigarettes and may also cause anger, anxiety, concentration problems, irritability, frustration, or restlessness.

When you wear a nicotine patch, a specific amount of nicotine steadily travels out of the patch, through your skin, and into your bloodstream, keeping a constant low level of nicotine in your body. Although the resulting level of nicotine is less than you would get from smoking, it may be enough to keep you from craving cigarettes or experiencing other withdrawal symptoms.

Habitrol patches are round and come in three strengths: 21, 14, or 7 milligrams of nicotine per patch. You wear a Habitrol patch 24 hours a day.

Nicoderm patches are rectangular and come in three strengths: 21, 14, or 7 milligrams of nicotine per patch. You wear a Nicoderm patch 24 hours a day.

Nicotrol patches are rectangular and come in three strengths: 15, 10, or 5 milligrams of nicotine per patch. You put on a Nicotrol patch in the morning, wear it all day, and remove it at bedtime. You do not use it when you sleep.

ProStep patches are round and come in two strengths: 22 or 11 milligrams of nicotine per patch. You wear a Prostep patch 24 hours a day.

Most important fact about this drug
Nicotine patch therapy should be part of an overall stop-smoking program that also includes behavior modification, counseling, and support. The goal of the therapy should be complete cessation of smoking, not just "cutting down."

How should you use this medication?
Use nicotine patches exactly as prescribed. The general procedure is as follows:

- Take a fresh patch out of its packaging and remove the protective liner from the adhesive. Save the wrapper for later disposal of the used patch.
- Stick the patch onto your outer upper arm or any clean, non-hairy part of your trunk.
- Press the patch firmly onto your skin for about 10 seconds, making sure that the edges are sticking well.
- Wash your hands. Any nicotine sticking to your hands could get into your eyes or nose, causing irritation.
- After 16 or 24 hours (depending on the brand), remove that patch and apply a fresh patch to a different spot on your body. To reduce the chances of irritation, do not return to a previously used spot for at least a week.
- Fold the used patch in half, place it back in its own wrapper, and throw it in a trash container that cannot be reached by children or pets.

Water will not harm the nicotine patch. You may keep wearing your patch while bathing, showering, swimming, or using a hot tub.

If your patch does fall off, dispose of it carefully and apply a new patch.

As a memory aid, pick a specific time of day and always apply a fresh patch at that time. You may change the schedule if you need to. Just remember not to wear any single patch for more than the recommended time (16 or 24 hours), since after that time the patch will begin to lose strength and may begin to irritate your skin.

Do not change brands without consulting your doctor.

If you are unable to stop smoking by your fourth week of wearing nicotine patches, it is likely that patch treatment will not work for you. At this point, your doctor may stop prescribing the patches for you.

■ *If you miss a dose...*
Apply the patch as soon as you remember. Never use 2 patches at once.

■ *Storage instructions.*
Do not remove a patch from its wrapping until you are ready to use it. Store your supply of patches at temperatures no higher than 86 degrees Fahrenheit; remember that in warm weather the inside of a car can get much hotter than this.

What side effects may occur?
Side effects cannot be anticipated. If any develop or change in intensity, inform your doctor as soon as possible. Only your doctor can determine if it is safe for you to continue using nicotine patches.

■ *Most common side effects may include:*
Itching and burning at the application site
Rash
Redness of the skin

■ *Less common side effects may include:*
Abnormal dreaming, allergic reactions, back pain, chest pain, constipation, cough, diarrhea, dizziness, drowsiness, dry mouth, headache, high blood pressure, impaired concentration, indigestion, inflammation of sinuses, menstrual irregularities, nausea, nervousness, numbness, pain, pins and needles sensation, sleeplessness, sore throat, stomach pain, sweating, taste changes, tingling, vomiting, weakness

Why should this drug not be prescribed?
Do not take this medication if you are sensitive to or have ever had an allergic reaction to nicotine. Be cautious if you have ever had a bad reaction to a different brand of nicotine patch or to adhesive tape or other adhesive material.

Special warnings about this medication
Do not smoke any form of tobacco while wearing a patch; doing so could give you an overdose of nicotine. Be aware that for several hours after you remove a patch, nicotine from the patch is still in your skin and passing into your bloodstream.

The use of nicotine patches may aggravate certain medical conditions. Before you use any brand of nicotine patch, make sure your doctor knows if you have, or have ever had, any of the following conditions:

Allergies to drugs, adhesive tape, or bandages
Chest pain from a heart condition (angina)
Diabetes requiring insulin injections
Heart attack
High blood pressure (severe)
Irregular heartbeat (heart arrhythmia)
Kidney disease
Liver disease
Overactive thyroid
Skin disease
Stomach ulcer

Nicotine, from any source, can be toxic and addictive. Thoroughly discuss with your doctor the benefits and risks of nicotine replacement therapy.

Because a used nicotine patch still contains enough nicotine to poison a child or a pet, you must dispose of used patches with special care. Wrap each patch in the opened pouch or aluminum foil in which it came and throw it in a trash receptacle that is out of the reach of youngsters and animals.

Possible food and drug interactions when taking this medication

If nicotine patches are used with certain other drugs, the effects of either could be increased, decreased, or altered. It is especially important to check with your doctor before combining nicotine patches with the following:

Acetaminophen-containing drugs such as Tylenol
Caffeine-containing drugs such as No Doz
Certain airway-opening drugs such as Isuprel, Dristan, and Neo-Synephrine
Certain blood pressure medicines such as Minipress, Trandate, and Normodyne
Cimetidine (Tagamet)
Haloperidol (Haldol)
Imipramine (Tofranil)
Insulin
Lithium (Lithonate)
Oxazepam (Serax)
Pentazocine (Talwin)
Propranolol (Inderal)
Theophylline (Theo-Dur)

Special information
if you are pregnant or breastfeeding
If you are pregnant or plan to become pregnant, inform your doctor immediately. Ideally, a pregnant woman should not take nicotine in any form. Do your best to quit smoking with the aid of counseling and support and without drug therapy. If you are unable to quit, you and your doctor should discuss which is more likely to harm your unborn baby: continued smoking or use of nicotine patches to help you quit smoking. Because nicotine passes very readily into breast milk, ideally it should not be taken in any form during breastfeeding. If you are breastfeeding and are unable to quit smoking, discuss with your doctor the pros and cons of using nicotine patches.

Remember that if you smoke while wearing a patch, you are giving your body a "double dose" of nicotine; if you are pregnant or breastfeeding, your baby will get the "double dose" too.

Recommended dosage
Nicotine patches come in two or three strengths, depending on the brand; larger patches contain higher doses of nicotine. The usual starting dose is 1 high-strength patch per day. If you weigh less than 100 pounds, however, or if you smoke less than half a pack of cigarettes a day or have heart disease, your doctor may start you on a lower-dose patch.

Your doctor will work closely with you to determine the best product and the most effective cessation program.

Overdosage
Any medication used in excess, including nicotine patches, can have serious consequences. If you suspect symptoms of an overdose of nicotine, either from a patch or from smoking while wearing a patch, seek medical attention immediately.

- *Symptoms of nicotine overdose may include:*
  Abdominal pain, blurred vision, breathing abnormalities, cold sweat, confusion, diarrhea, dizziness, drooling, fainting, hearing difficulties, heart palpitations, low blood pressure, nausea, pallor, salivation, severe headaches, sweating, tremor, upset stomach, vision problems, vomiting, weakness

Generic name:

NICOTINE POLACRILEX

See Nicorette, page 725.

Brand name:

NICOTROL

See Nicotine Patches, page 729.

Generic name:

NIFEDIPINE

See Procardia, page 896.

Brand name:

NITRO-BID

See Nitroglycerin, page 734.

Brand name:

NITRO-DUR

See Nitroglycerin, page 734.

Generic name:

NITROFURANTOIN

See Macrodantin, page 625.

Generic name:

NITROGLYCERIN

Pronounced: NIGHT-row-GLISS-err-in
Brand names: Nitro-Bid, Nitro-Dur, Nitrolingual Spray,
Nitrostat Tablets, Transderm-Nitro

Why is this drug prescribed?

Nitroglycerin is prescribed to prevent and treat angina pectoris (suffocating chest pain). This condition occurs when the arteries and veins become constricted and are not able to carry sufficient oxygen to the heart. Nitroglycerin is thought to improve oxygen flow by relaxing the muscles of arteries and veins, thus allowing them to dilate.

Nitroglycerin is used in different forms. As a patch or ointment, nitroglycerin may be applied to the skin. The patch and the ointment are for *prevention* of chest pain.

Swallowing nitroglycerin in capsule or tablet form also helps to *prevent* chest pain from occurring.

In the form of sublingual (held under the tongue) or buccal (held in the cheek) tablets, or in oral spray (sprayed on or under the tongue), nitroglycerin helps relieve chest pain that has *already occurred*. The spray can also prevent anginal pain. The type of nitroglycerin you use will depend on your condition.

Most important fact about this drug
Nitroglycerin may cause severe low blood pressure (possibly marked by dizziness or light-headedness), especially if you are in an upright position or have just gotten up from sitting or lying down. You may also find your heart rate slowing and your chest pain increasing. People taking diuretic medication, or who have low systolic blood pressure (less than 90 mmHg) should use nitroglycerin with caution.

How should you take this medication?
Since nitroglycerin is available in many forms, it is crucial for you to follow your doctor's directions for taking the type of nitroglycerin prescribed for you. Never interchange brands.

Ideally, you should take nitroglycerin while sitting down—especially if you feel dizzy or light-headed—so as to avoid a fall.

■ *If you miss a dose...*
If you are using a skin patch or ointment:

Apply it as soon as you remember. If it is almost time for your regular dose, skip the one you missed and go back to your regular schedule. Never apply 2 skin patches at the same time.

If you are taking oral tablets or capsules:

Take the forgotten dose as soon as you remember. However, if it is within 2 hours of your next dose, skip the one you missed and go back to your regular schedule. Never take 2 doses at the same time.

■ *Storage instructions...*
Keep this medication in the container it came in, tightly closed. Store it at room temperature.

Avoid puncturing the spray container and keep it away from excess heat.

Do not open the container of sublingual tablets until you need a dose. Close the container tightly immediately after each use. Do not put other medications, a cotton plug, or anything else in the container. Keep the sublingual tablets handy at all times. Keep the patches in the protective pouches they come in until use.

What side effects may occur?

Side effects cannot be anticipated. If any develop or change in intensity, inform your doctor as soon as possible. Only your doctor can determine if it is safe for you to continue taking nitroglycerin.

- More common side effects may include:
  Dizziness
  Flushed skin (neck and face)
  Headache
  Light-headedness
  Worsened angina pain

- Less common or rare side effects may include:
  Diarrhea, fainting, heart pounding, low blood pressure, nausea, numbness, pallor, restlessness, skin rashes, sweating, vertigo, vomiting, weakness

Why should this drug not be prescribed?

You should not be using nitroglycerin if you are allergic to it or to the adhesive in the patch, if you have a head injury, or if you have any condition caused by increased fluid pressure in your head. Nitroglycerin should not be taken if you have severe anemia or if you recently had a heart attack. The capsule form should not be used if you have closed-angle glaucoma (pressure in the eye) or suffer from postural hypotension (dizziness upon standing up).

Special warnings about this medication

If your vision becomes blurry or your mouth becomes dry while taking nitroglycerin, it should be discontinued. Contact your doctor immediately if these symptoms develop.

You may develop acute headaches if you take nitroglycerin excessively. Also, some people may develop a tolerance to nitroglycerin, and it may become less beneficial over time, especially if used in excess.

Take no more than the smallest possible amount needed to relieve pain.

Daily headaches may be an indicator of the drug's activity. Do not change your dose to avoid the headache, because you may reduce the drug's effectiveness at the same time.

Before taking nitroglycerin, tell your doctor if you have had a recent heart attack, head injury, or stroke; or if you have anemia, glaucoma (pressure in the eye), or heart, kidney, liver, or thyroid disease.

If you use a patch, dispose of it carefully. There is enough drug left in a used patch to be harmful to children and pets.

Since nitroglycerin can cause dizziness, you should observe caution while driving, operating machinery, or performing other tasks that demand concentration.

The benefits of applying nitroglycerin to the skin of people experiencing heart attacks or congestive heart failure have not been established. If you are using the medication for these conditions, your doctor will monitor you to prevent low blood pressure and pounding heartbeat.

Possible food and drug interactions
when taking this medication
If nitroglycerin is taken with certain other drugs, the effects of either could be increased, decreased, or altered.

Taken with many high blood pressure drugs, nitroglycerin may cause extreme low blood pressure (dizziness, fainting, numbness). Take particular care with calcium channel blockers such as Calan and Procardia XL, with isosorbide dinitrate (Sorbitrate, Isordil, others), isosorbide mononitrate (Ismo, others), blood vessel dilators such as Loniten, and beta-blocker medications such as Tenormin.

Alcohol may interact with nitroglycerin and cause a swift decrease in blood pressure, possibly causing dizziness and fainting.

Also be alert for an interaction with dihydroergotamine (D.H.E.). Check with your doctor if you are uncertain about any combination.

Special information
if you are pregnant or breastfeeding
It has not been determined whether nitroglycerin might harm a fetus or a pregnant woman. As a result, nitroglycerin should be used only when the benefits of therapy clearly outweigh the potential risks to the fetus and woman. It is not known if nitroglycerin appears in breast milk; therefore, a nursing mother should use nitroglycerin only on advice of her doctor.

Recommended dosage
The following section is intended to provide guidelines for taking nitroglycerin. Follow your doctor's instructions carefully for using nitroglycerin in the form prescribed for you.

ADULTS

Sublingual or Buccal Tablets

At the first sign of chest pain, 1 tablet should be dissolved under the tongue or inside the cheek. You may repeat the dose every 5 minutes until the pain is relieved. If your pain continues after you have taken 3 tablets in a 15-minute period, notify your doctor or seek medical attention immediately.

You may take sublingual or buccal nitroglycerin from 5 to 10 minutes before starting activities that may cause chest pain.

Patch Form

A patch is applied to the skin for 12 to 14 hours. After this time, the patch is removed; it is not applied again for 10 to 12 hours (a "patch-off" period). Apply the patch as soon as you remove it from its protective pouch.

Spray Form

At the first sign of chest pain, spray 1 or 2 pre-measured doses onto or under the tongue. You should not use more than 3 doses within a 15-minute period. If your chest pain continues, you should contact your doctor or seek medical attention immediately.

The spray can be used 5 to 10 minutes before activity that might precipitate an attack.

Ointment Form

Your initial dose may be a daily total of 1 inch of ointment. Apply one-half inch on rising in the morning, and the remaining one-half inch 6 hours later. If needed, follow your doctor's instructions for increasing your dosage. Apply in a thin, uniform layer, regardless of the amount of your dosage. There should be a daily period where no ointment is applied. Usually, the "ointment-off" period will last from 10 to 12 hours.

Absorption varies with site of application—more is absorbed through the chest.

Sustained-Release Capsules or Tablets

The smallest effective amount should be taken 2 or 3 times a day at 8- to 12-hour intervals.

CHILDREN

The safety and effectiveness of nitroglycerin have not been established for children.

ELDERLY

In general, dosages less than the above adult dosages are recommended, since the elderly may be more susceptible to low blood pressure and headaches.

Overdosage

Any medication taken in excess can have serious consequences. Severe overdosage of nitroglycerin may result in death. If you suspect an overdose, seek medical attention immediately.

- *Symptoms of overdose may include:*
  Bluish skin, clammy skin, colic, coma, confusion, diarrhea (may be bloody), difficult and/or slow breathing, dizziness, fainting, fever, flushed skin, headache (persistent, throbbing), increased pressure within the skull, irregular pulse, loss of appetite, nausea, palpitations (an abnormally rapid throbbing or fluttering of the heart), paralysis, rapid decrease in blood pressure, seizures, slow pulse/heartbeat, sweating, vertigo, visual disturbances, vomiting

Brand name:

NITROLINGUAL SPRAY

See Nitroglycerin, page 734.

Brand name:

NITROSTAT TABLETS

See Nitroglycerin, page 734.

Generic name:

NIZATIDINE

See Axid, page 94.

Brand name:

NIZORAL

Pronounced: NYE-zore-al
Generic name: Ketoconazole

Why is this drug prescribed?

Nizoral, a broad-spectrum antifungal drug available in tablet form, may be given to treat several fungal infections within the body, including oral thrush and candidiasis.

It may also be given to treat severe, hard-to-treat fungal skin infections that have not cleared up after treatment with creams or ointments, or the oral drug griseofulvin (Fulvicin, Grisactin).

Most important fact about this drug

In some people, Nizoral may cause serious or even fatal damage to the liver. Before starting to take Nizoral, and at frequent intervals while you are taking it, you should have blood tests to evaluate your liver function. Tell your doctor immediately if you experience any signs or symptoms that could mean liver damage: these include unusual fatigue, loss of appetite, nausea or vomiting, jaundice, dark urine, or pale stools.

How should you take this medication?

Take Nizoral exactly as prescribed.

You should keep taking the drug until tests show that your fungal infection has subsided. If you stop too soon, the infection might return.

You may want to take Nizoral Tablets with meals to avoid stomach upset.

Avoid alcohol and do not take with antacids. If antacids are necessary, you should wait 2 to 3 hours before taking them.

- *If you miss a dose...*
  Take the forgotten dose as soon as you remember. This will help to keep the proper amount of medicine in the body. However, if it is almost time for your next dose, skip the one you missed and go back to your regular schedule. Do not take double doses.

- *Storage instructions...*
  Nizoral should be stored at room temperature.

What side effects may occur?

Side effects from Nizoral cannot be anticipated. If any develop or change in intensity, inform your doctor as soon as possible. Only your doctor can determine if it is safe for you to continue taking Nizoral.

- *More common side effects may include:*
  Nausea
  Vomiting

- *Less common side effects may include:*
  Abdominal pain
  Itching

- *Rare side effects may include:*
  Breast swelling (in men), depression, diarrhea, dizziness, drowsiness, fever and chills, headache, hives, impotence, light-sensitivity, rash

Why should this drug not be prescribed?
Do not take Nizoral if you are sensitive to it or have ever had an allergic reaction to it. Never take Nizoral together with Seldane, Hismanal, or Propulsid. Rare, but sometimes fatal, reactions have been reported when these drugs are combined.

Special warnings about this medication
In rare cases, people have had anaphylaxis (a life-threatening allergic reaction) after taking their first dose of Nizoral.

Observe caution when driving or performing other tasks requiring alertness, due to potential side effects of headache, dizziness, and drowsiness.

Possible food and drug interactions
when taking this medication
If Nizoral is taken with certain other drugs, the effects of either could be increased, decreased, or altered. It is especially important to check with your doctor before combining Nizoral with the following:

Alcoholic beverages
Antacids such as Di-Gel, Maalox, Mylanta, and others
Anticoagulants such as Coumadin, Dicumarol, and others
Anti-ulcer medications such as Axid, Pepcid, Tagamet, and Zantac
Astemizole (Hismanal)
Cisapride (Propulsid)
Corticosteroids such as Prednisone and Medrol
Cyclosporine (Sandimmune)
Isoniazid (Nydrazid)
Phenytoin (Dilantin)
Rifampin (Rifadin, Rifamate, and Rimactane)
Terfenadine (Seldane)
Theophyllines such as Theo 24, Slo-Phyllin, Theo-Dur, and others

Special information
if you are pregnant or breastfeeding
If you are pregnant or plan to become pregnant, inform your doctor

immediately. Nizoral should be taken during pregnancy only if the benefit outweighs the possible harm to your unborn child.

Since Nizoral can probably make its way into breast milk, it should not be taken during breastfeeding. If you are a new mother, check with your doctor. You may need to stop breastfeeding while you are taking Nizoral.

Recommended dosage

ADULTS

The recommended starting dose of Nizoral is a single daily dose of 200 milligrams (1 tablet).

In very serious infections, or if the problem does not clear up within the expected time, the dose of Nizoral may be increased to 400 milligrams (2 tablets) once daily. Treatment lasts at least 1 to 2 weeks, and for some infections much longer.

CHILDREN

In small numbers of children over 2 years of age, a single daily dose of 3.3 to 6.6 milligrams per 2.2 pounds of body weight has been used.

Nizoral has not been studied in children under 2 years of age.

Overdosage

Although no specific information is available, any medication taken in excess can have serious consequences. If you suspect an overdose of Nizoral, seek medical attention immediately.

Brand name:

NOLAMINE

Pronounced: NOE-luh-meen
Generic ingredients: Phenindamine tartrate,
    Chlorpheniramine maleate, Phenylpropanolamine
    hydrochloride

Why is this drug prescribed?

Nolamine is a nasal decongestant that relieves stuffiness caused by the common cold, inflamed sinuses, or hay fever and other allergies. Nolamine's ingredients include antihistamines (chlorpheniramine maleate and phenindamine tartrate) that reduce itching and swelling and dry up secretions from the nose, eyes, and throat, and a decongestant (phenylpropanolamine hydrochloride) that improves breathing.

Most important fact about this drug

Nolamine can cause drowsiness. You should not drive, operate dangerous machinery, or participate in any hazardous activity that requires full mental alertness until you know how you react to Nolamine.

How should you take this medication?

Nolamine should be taken exactly as prescribed by your doctor.

- *If you miss a dose...*
  Take it as soon as you remember. If it is almost time for your next dose, skip the one you missed and go back to your regular schedule. Do not take 2 doses at once.

- *Storage instructions...*
  Store at room temperature, away from light.

What side effects may occur?

Side effects cannot be anticipated. If any develop or change in intensity, inform your doctor as soon as possible. Only your doctor can determine if it is safe for you to continue taking Nolamine.

- *Side effects may include:*
  Difficulty sleeping
  Dizziness
  Drowsiness
  Nervousness
  Tremors

Why should this drug not be prescribed?

Nolamine should not be taken if you are sensitive to or have ever had an allergic reaction to any of its ingredients, or if you are taking MAO inhibitor medications such as the antidepressant drugs Nardil and Parnate.

Special warnings about this medication

Use Nolamine cautiously if you have high blood pressure, heart disease, diabetes, an overactive thyroid gland, the eye condition called glaucoma, or an enlarged prostate gland.

Before getting behind the wheel, remember that Nolamine can make you drowsy.

Possible food and drug interactions
when taking this medication
Avoid alcoholic beverages while taking this medicine.

If Nolamine is taken with certain other drugs, the effects of either could be increased, decreased, or altered. It is especially important to check with your doctor before combining Nolamine with the following:

MAO inhibitor drugs such as the antidepressants Nardil and Parnate.
Bromocriptine (Parlodel)
Central nervous system depressants such as Valium, Demerol, and Dalmane.
Methyldopa (Aldomet)

Recommended dosage
The usual adult dose is 1 tablet every 8 hours. The dosage in mild cases is 1 tablet every 10 to 12 hours.

Overdosage
Although there are no reports of Nolamine overdose, any medication taken in excess can have serious consequences. If you suspect an overdose, seek medical attention immediately.

Brand name:

NOLVADEX

Pronounced: NOLL-vah-decks
Generic name: Tamoxifen citrate

Why is this drug prescribed?
Nolvadex, an anticancer drug, may be given to treat breast cancer. It also has proved effective when cancer has spread to other parts of the body. Nolvadex is most effective in stopping the kind of breast cancer that thrives on estrogen.

Most important fact about this drug
Women taking Nolvadex should have routine gynecological examinations and report any abnormal vaginal bleeding to the doctor immediately.

How should you take this medication?
Take Nolvadex exactly as prescribed. Do not stop taking this medication without first consulting your doctor. It may be necessary to continue taking the drug for several years.

■ *If you miss a dose...*
Do not try to make it up. Go back to your regular schedule with the next dose.

■ *Storage instructions...*
Nolvadex should be stored away from heat and light.

What side effects may occur?
Side effects from Nolvadex are usually mild and rarely require the drug to be stopped. If any develop or change in intensity, inform your doctor as soon as possible. Only your doctor can determine if it is safe for you to continue taking Nolvadex.

■ *More common side effects may include:*
Hot flashes
Nausea
Vomiting

■ *Less common side effects may include:*
Bone pain, diarrhea, menstrual irregularities, skin rash, tumor pain, vaginal bleeding, vaginal discharge

■ *Rare side effects may include:*
Blood clots, depression, distaste for food, dizziness, hair thinning or partial loss, headache, light-headedness, liver disorders, swelling of arms or legs, vaginal itching, visual problems

Why should this drug not be prescribed?
Do not take Nolvadex if you are sensitive to it or have ever had an allergic reaction to it.

Special warnings about this medication
If you experience visual problems while taking Nolvadex, notify your doctor immediately.

In a few patients Nolvadex may raise the level of cholesterol and other fats in the blood. Your doctor may periodically do blood tests to check your cholesterol and triglyceride levels.

Nolvadex may produce an abnormally high level of calcium in the blood. Symptoms include muscle pain and weakness, loss of appetite, and, if severe, kidney failure. If you experience any of these symptoms, notify your doctor as soon as possible.

If tests show that your blood contains too few white blood cells or platelets while you are taking Nolvadex, your doctor should monitor you with special care. These problems have sometimes been found in patients taking Nolvadex; whether the drug caused the blood-cell abnormalities is uncertain.

Possible food and drug interactions
when taking this medication
If Nolvadex is taken with certain other drugs, the effects of either could be increased, decreased, or altered. It is especially important to check with your doctor before combining Nolvadex with the following:

Blood-thinning drugs such as Coumadin
Bromocriptine (Parlodel)
Phenobarbital

Special information
if you are pregnant or breastfeeding
It is important to avoid pregnancy while taking Nolvadex, because the drug could harm the unborn child. Since Nolvadex is an anti-estrogen drug, you will need to use a non-hormonal form of contraception, such as a condom and/or diaphragm, and not birth control pills. If you accidentally become pregnant while taking Nolvadex, or within 2 months after you have stopped taking it, discuss this with your doctor immediately.

Because Nolvadex might cause serious harm to a nursing infant, you should not breastfeed your baby while taking this drug. If this medication is essential to your health, your doctor may advise you to discontinue breastfeeding until your treatment is finished.

Recommended dosage

ADULTS

The recommended dosage is one or two 10-milligram tablets in the morning and evening.

Overdosage
Any medication taken in excess can have serious consequences. If you suspect an overdose of Nolvadex, seek medical attention immediately.

■ *Symptoms of Nolvadex overdose may include:*
Dizziness
Overactive reflexes
Tremor
Unsteady gait

Brand name:

NORDETTE

See Oral Contraceptives, page 775.

Brand name:

NORETHIN

See Oral Contraceptives, page 775.

Generic name:

NORFLOXACIN

See Noroxin, page 753.

Brand name:

NORGESIC

Pronounced: nor-JEE-zic
Generic ingredients: Orphenadrine citrate, Aspirin,
  Caffeine
Other brand name: Norgesic Forte

Why is this drug prescribed?
Norgesic is prescribed, along with rest, physical therapy, and other measures, for the relief of mild to moderate pain of severe muscle disorders.

Most important fact about this drug
Norgesic may impair your ability to drive a car or operate dangerous machinery. Do not participate in potentially hazardous activities until you know how you react to this medication.

How should you take this medication?
If aspirin upsets your stomach, you may take Norgesic with food. Take it exactly as prescribed.

■ *If you miss a dose...*
If it is within an hour of your scheduled time, take it as soon as you remember. If you do not remember until later, skip the dose you missed and go back to your regular schedule. Do not take 2 doses at once.

■ *Storage instructions...*
Store at room temperature.

What side effects may occur?
Side effects cannot be anticipated. If any develop or change in intensity, inform your doctor as soon as possible. Only your doctor can determine if it is safe for you to continue taking Norgesic.

■ *Side effects may include:*
Blurred vision, confusion (in the elderly), constipation, difficulty in urinating, dilation of the pupils, dizziness, drowsiness, dry mouth, fainting, hallucinations, headache, hives, light-headedness, nausea, palpitations, rapid heart rate, skin diseases, stomach and intestinal bleeding, vomiting, weakness

Why should this drug not be prescribed?
If you are sensitive to or have ever had an allergic reaction to the ingredients of Norgesic—orphenadrine, aspirin, and caffeine—you should not take this medication. Make sure your doctor is aware of any drug reactions you have experienced.

You should not be taking Norgesic if you have the eye condition called glaucoma, a stomach or intestinal blockage, an enlarged prostate gland, a bladder obstruction, achalasia (failure of stomach or intestinal muscles to relax), or myasthenia gravis (muscle weakness and fatigue).

Because taking aspirin while you have chickenpox or flu may cause a rare but serious condition called Reye's syndrome, do not give Norgesic to anyone with these diseases. Call your doctor if fever or swelling develops.

Special warnings about this medication
Because the safety of continuous, long-term therapy with Norgesic has not been established, your doctor should monitor your blood, urine, and liver function if you use this drug for a prolonged period of time.

Because Norgesic contains aspirin, you should be careful taking it if you have a peptic ulcer or problems with blood clotting.

Possible food and drug interactions
when taking this medication

If Norgesic is taken with certain other drugs, the effects of either could be increased, decreased, or altered. It is especially important to check with your doctor before combining Norgesic with propoxyphene (Darvon). The combination can cause confusion, anxiety, and tremors.

Special information
if you are pregnant or breastfeeding

The effects of Norgesic during pregnancy have not been adequately studied. If you are pregnant or plan to become pregnant, inform your doctor immediately. This drug may appear in breast milk and could affect a nursing infant. If this medication is essential to your health, your doctor may advise you to discontinue breastfeeding until your treatment is finished.

Recommended dosage

ADULTS

The usual dose of Norgesic is 1 to 2 tablets taken 3 or 4 times a day.

The usual dosage of Norgesic Forte, which is exactly twice the strength of Norgesic, is one-half to 1 tablet taken 3 or 4 times per day.

CHILDREN

The safety and effectiveness of Norgesic have not been established in children. It is not recommended for children under 12 years of age.

ELDERLY

Some elderly people have experienced confusion when taking this drug. Your doctor may adjust the dosage accordingly.

Overdosage

Any medication taken in excess can have serious consequences. If you suspect an overdose of Norgesic, seek emergency medical treatment immediately.

Brand name:

NORINYL

See Oral Contraceptives, page 775.

Brand name:

NORMODYNE

Pronounced: NORM-oh-dine
Generic name: Labetalol hydrochloride
Other brand name: Trandate

Why is this drug prescribed?
Normodyne is used in the treatment of high blood pressure. It is effective when used alone or in combination with other high blood pressure medications, especially thiazide diuretics such as HydroDIURIL and "loop" diuretics such as Lasix.

Most important fact about this drug
You must take Normodyne regularly for it to be effective. Since blood pressure declines gradually, it may be several weeks before you get the full benefit of Normodyne; and you must continue taking it even if you are feeling well. Normodyne does not cure high blood pressure; it merely keeps it under control.

How should you take this medication?
Normodyne can be taken with or without food. The amount of Normodyne absorbed into your bloodstream is actually increased by food.

This medication should be taken exactly as prescribed by your doctor, even if your symptoms have disappeared.

Try not to miss any doses. If Normodyne is not taken regularly, your condition may worsen.

- *If you miss a dose...*
  Take it as soon as you remember. If it is almost time for your next dose, skip the one you missed and go back to your regular schedule. Never take 2 doses at the same time.

- *Storage instructions...*
  Store at room temperature.

What side effects may occur?
Side effects cannot be anticipated. If any develop or change in intensity, inform your doctor as soon as possible. Only your doctor can determine if it is safe for you to continue taking Normodyne.

■ *More common side effects may include:*
Dizziness
Fatigue
Indigestion
Nausea
Stuffy nose

■ *Less common or rare side effects may include:*
Anaphylaxis (severe allergic reaction), angioedema (swelling of the face, lips, tongue and throat, difficulty swallowing), changes in taste, depression, diarrhea, difficulty urinating, dizziness upon standing up (especially among the elderly), drowsiness, dry eyes, ejaculation failure, fainting, fluid retention, hair loss, headache, heart block (conduction disorder), hives, impotence, increased sweating, itching, low blood pressure, lupus erythematosus (fever, arthritis, skin eruptions), muscle cramps, rash, shortness of breath, slow heartbeat, tingling or pins and needles, tingling scalp, vertigo, vision changes, weakness, wheezing or asthma-like symptoms, vomiting, yellow eyes and skin

Why should this drug not be prescribed?
You should not take Normodyne if you are currently suffering from bronchial asthma, congestive heart failure, heart block (a heart irregularity), inadequate blood supply to the circulatory system (cardiogenic shock), a severely slow heartbeat, or any other condition that causes severe and continued low blood pressure.

If you are sensitive to or have ever had an allergic reaction to Normodyne or any of its ingredients you should not take this medication.

Special warnings about this medication
Normodyne has caused severe liver damage in some people. Although this is a rare occurrence, if you develop any symptoms of abnormal liver function—itching, dark urine, continuing loss of appetite, yellow eyes and skin, or unexplained "flu-like" symptoms—contact your doctor immediately.

If you have a history of congestive heart failure, or kidney or liver disease, Normodyne should be used with caution.

Normodyne should not be stopped suddenly. This can cause chest pain and heart attack. Dosage should be gradually reduced.

If you suffer from asthma, chronic bronchitis, emphysema, or other bronchial diseases, Normodyne should be used cautiously.

If you are prone to severe allergic reactions, you are more likely to have a severe allergic reaction to Normodyne.

This medication may mask the symptoms of low blood sugar or alter blood sugar levels. If you are diabetic, discuss this with your doctor.

Notify your doctor or dentist that you are taking Normodyne if you have a medical emergency, and before you have surgery or dental treatment.

Possible food and drug interactions
when taking this medication

If Normodyne is taken with certain other drugs, the effects of either could be increased, decreased, or altered. It is especially important to check with your doctor before taking Normodyne with the following:

Airway opening drugs such as Proventil and Ventolin
Antidepressant medications such as Elavil
Cimetidine (Tagamet)
Diabetes drugs such as Micronase
Epinephrine (EpiPen)
Insulin
Nitroglycerin products such as Transderm-Nitro
Nonsteroidal anti-inflammatory drugs such as Advil and Motrin
Ritodrine (Yutopar)
Verapamil (Calan)

Special information
if you are pregnant or breastfeeding

The effects of Normodyne during pregnancy have not been adequately studied. If you are pregnant or plan to become pregnant, inform your doctor immediately. Normodyne appears in breast milk and could affect a nursing infant. If this medication is essential to your health, your doctor may advise you to discontinue breastfeeding until your treatment is finished.

Recommended dosage

ADULTS

Your doctor will adjust the dosages to fit your needs. Your doctor may observe the drug's effect in his or her office over a 1- to 3-hour period after you begin taking it, and then check your pressure again at regular office visits (12 hours after a dose) to make sure that the medicine is effective.

The usual starting dose is 100 milligrams, 2 times per day, alone or with a diuretic drug. After 2 to 3 days of checking your blood pressure, your doctor may begin increasing your dose by 100 milligrams, 2 times per day, at intervals of 2 to 3 days.

The regular dose ranges from 200 to 400 milligrams, 2 times per day. Some people may require total daily dosage of as much as 1,200 to 2,400 milligrams, either alone or with a thiazide diuretic. In these cases, your doctor will observe the drug's effect and adjust your dose accordingly.

CHILDREN

The safety and effectiveness of this drug in children have not been established.

ELDERLY

The usual starting dose is the same as younger people's—100 milligrams twice a day. Your doctor may increase the dose, but usually to no more than 200 milligrams twice a day.

Overdosage

Any medication taken in excess can have serious consequences. If you suspect an overdose, seek medical treatment immediately.

- *The symptoms of Normodyne overdose may include:*
  Dizziness when standing up
  Severely low blood pressure
  Severely slow heartbeat

Brand name:

NOROXIN

Pronounced: Nor-OX-in
Generic name: Norfloxacin

Why is this drug prescribed?

Noroxin is an antibacterial used to treat infections of the urinary tract, including cystitis (inflammation of the inner lining of the bladder caused by a bacterial infection), and certain sexually transmitted diseases, such as gonorrhea.

Most important fact about this drug

Noroxin is not given for the treatment of syphilis. When used in high doses for a short period of time to treat gonorrhea, it may actually mask or delay the symptoms of syphilis. Your doctor may perform certain tests for syphilis at the time of diagnosing gonorrhea, and after treatment with Noroxin.

How should you take this medication?
Noroxin should be taken, with a glass of water, either 1 hour *before* or 2 hours *after* eating a meal. Do not take more than the dosage prescribed by your doctor.

It is important to drink plenty of fluids while taking Noroxin.

Take all the Noroxin your doctor prescribes. If you stop taking the medicine too soon, you may have a relapse.

■ *If you miss a dose...*
Be sure to take it as soon as possible. This will help to keep a constant amount of Noroxin in your body. However, if it is almost time for your next dose, skip the one you missed and go back to your regular schedule. Do not take 2 doses at the same time.

■ *Storage instructions...*
Store at room temperature. Keep container tightly closed. Store out of reach of children.

What side effects may occur?
Side effects cannot be anticipated. If any develop or change in intensity, inform your doctor as soon as possible. Only your doctor can determine whether it is safe for you to continue taking Noroxin.

■ *More common side effects may include:*
Dizziness
Fatigue
Headache
Nausea

■ *Other side effects may include:*
Abdominal cramping, arthritis, back pain, bitter taste, blood abnormalities, confusion, constipation, convulsions, dead skin, depression, diarrhea, dizziness, dry mouth, double vision, extreme sleepiness, fever, flushing, reddish skin, gas, hallucinations, headache, heartburn, hives, indigestion, insomnia, itching, joint pain, kidney failure (symptoms may include reduced amount of urine, drowsiness, nausea, vomiting and coma), lack of coordination, light-headedness, loss of appetite, low blood sugar, muscle pain, nausea, peeling skin, psychotic reactions, rash (such as pimples, blisters, and nodules) on skin and mucous membranes, reduced blood

platelets causing bleeding disorders (such as bleeding into the skin), restlessness, severe blisters and bleeding in genitals and in mucous membranes of eyes, lips, mouth, and nasal passages, severe skin reaction to sun, shock, shortness of breath, stomach pain, sweating, temporary hearing loss, tingling (pins and needles sensation), vomiting, weakness, yellow eyes and skin

Why should this drug not be prescribed?
You should not be using Noroxin if you are sensitive to it or to other drugs of the same type, such as Cipro.

Special warnings about this medication
Noroxin is not recommended for:

Children (under the age of 18)
Nursing mothers
Pregnant women

People with disorders such as epilepsy, severe cerebral arteriosclerosis, and other conditions that might lead to seizures should use Noroxin cautiously. There have been reports of convulsions in some people taking Noroxin.

Some people taking drugs chemically similar to Noroxin have experienced severe, sometimes fatal reactions, occasionally after only one dose.

These reactions may include:
Confusion, convulsions, difficulty breathing, hallucinations, heart collapse, hives, increased pressure in the head, itching, light-headedness, loss of consciousness, psychosis, rash, restlessness, shock, swelling in the face or throat, tingling, tremors.

If you experience any of these reactions you should immediately stop taking Noroxin and seek medical help.

Some people find needle-shaped crystals in their urine after taking Noroxin. Drink plenty of fluids while taking Noroxin. This will increase urine output and reduce crystallization.

Noroxin may cause dizziness or light-headedness and might impair your ability to drive a car or operate potentially dangerous machinery. Use caution when undertaking any activities that require full alertness if you are unsure of your ability.

You should avoid excessive exposure to direct sunlight while taking Noroxin. Stop taking Noroxin immediately if you have a severe reaction to sunlight, such as a skin rash.

Possible food and drug interactions
when taking this medication

If Noroxin is taken with certain other drugs, the effects of either could be increased, decreased, or altered. It is especially important to check with your doctor before combining Noroxin with the following:

Antacids such as Maalox and Tums
Caffeine (including coffee, tea, and some soft drinks)
Calcium supplements
Cyclosporine (Sandimmune)
Multivitamins and other products containing iron or zinc
Nitrofurantoin (Macrodantin, Macrobid)
Oral anticoagulants, such as warfarin (Coumadin)
Probenecid (Benemid)
Sucralfate (Carafate)
Theophylline (Theo-Dur)

Special information
if you are pregnant or breastfeeding

The effects of Noroxin during pregnancy have not been adequately studied. Inform your doctor if you are pregnant or planning a pregnancy.

Do not take Noroxin while breastfeeding. There is a possibility of harm to the infant.

Recommended dosage

Take Noroxin with a full glass of water 1 hour before, or 2 hours after, eating a meal. Drink plenty of liquids while taking Noroxin.

Uncomplicated Urinary Tract Infections

The suggested dose is 800 milligrams per day. 400 milligrams should be taken twice a day for 3 to 10 days, depending upon the kind of bacteria causing the infection. People with impaired kidney function may take 400 milligrams once a day for 3 to 10 days.

Complicated Urinary Tract Infections

The suggested dose is 800 milligrams per day. 400 milligrams should be taken twice a day for 10 to 21 days.

Sexually Transmitted Diseases (Gonorrhea)

The usual recommended dose is one single dose of 800 milligrams for 1 day.

The maximum total daily dosage of Noroxin should not be more than 800 milligrams.

Overdosage
The symptoms of overdose with Noroxin are not known. However, any medication taken in excess can have serious consequences. If you suspect a Noroxin overdose, seek medical help immediately.

Brand name:

NORPACE

Pronounced: NOR-pace
Generic name: Disopyramide phosphate
Other brand name: Norpace CR

Why is this drug prescribed?
Norpace is used to treat severe irregular heartbeat. It relaxes an overactive heart and improves the efficiency of the heart's pumping action.

Most important fact about this drug
Do not stop taking Norpace without first consulting your doctor. Stopping suddenly can serious changes in heart function.

How should you take this medication?
Be sure to take this medication exactly as prescribed.

Norpace may cause dry mouth. For temporary relief suck on a hard candy, chew gum, or melt ice chips in your mouth.

■ *If you miss a dose...*
   Take it as soon as you remember, if the next dose is 4 or more hours away. If you do not remember until later, skip the dose you missed and go back to your regular schedule. Do not take 2 doses at once.

■ *Storage instructions...*
   Store at room temperature.

What side effects may occur?
Side effects cannot be anticipated. If any develop or change in intensity, inform your doctor as soon as possible. Only your doctor can determine if it is safe for you to continue taking Norpace.

■ *More common side effects may include:*
   Abdominal pain, bloating, and gas, aches and pains, blurred vision, constipation, dizziness, dry eyes, nose, and throat, dry mouth, fatigue,

headache, inability to urinate, increased urinary frequency and urgency, muscle weakness, nausea, vague feeling of bodily discomfort

■ *Less common or rare side effects may include:*
Breast development in males, chest pain, congestive heart failure, depression, diarrhea, difficulty breathing, difficulty sleeping, fainting, fever, itching, impotence, low blood pressure, low blood sugar (hypoglycemia), nervousness, numbness or tingling, painful urination, rash, psychosis, shortness of breath, skin diseases, swelling due to fluid retention, vomiting, weight gain, yellow eyes and skin

Why should this drug not be prescribed?
This drug should not be used if the output of your heart is inadequate (cardiogenic shock) or if you are sensitive to or have ever had an allergic reaction to Norpace.

Norpace can be used for only certain types of irregular heartbeat, and must not be used for others.

Special warnings about this medication
If you have structural heart disease, inflammation of the heart muscle, or other heart disorders, use this medication with extreme caution.

Norpace may cause or worsen congestive heart failure and can cause severe low blood pressure. If you have a history of heart failure, your doctor will carefully monitor your heart function while you are taking this medication.

Norpace can cause low blood sugar (hypoglycemia), especially if you have congestive heart failure; poor nutrition; or kidney, liver, or other diseases; or if you are taking beta-blocking blood pressure drugs such as Tenormin or drinking alcohol.

Your doctor will prescribe Norpace along with other heart-regulating drugs, such as quinidine, procainamide, encainide, flecainide, propafenone, and propranolol, only if the irregular rhythm is considered life-threatening and other antiarrhythmic medication has not worked.

If you have the eye condition called glaucoma, myasthenia gravis, or difficulty urinating (particularly if you have a prostate condition), use this drug cautiously.

You will take lower dosages if you have liver or kidney disease.

Your doctor should check your potassium levels before starting you on Norpace. Low potassium levels may make this drug ineffective; high levels may increase its toxic effects.

**Possible food and drug interactions
when taking this medication**
Avoid alcoholic beverages while taking Norpace.

If Norpace is taken with certain other drugs, the effects of either could be increased, decreased, or altered. It is especially important to check with your doctor before combining Norpace with the following:

Other heart-regulating drugs such as quinidine (Quinidex), procainamide (Procan SR), lidocaine (Xylocaine), propranolol (Inderal), Verapamil (Calan)
Phenytoin (Dilantin)

**Special information
if you are pregnant or breastfeeding**
The effects of Norpace during pregnancy have not been adequately studied. If you are pregnant or plan to become pregnant, inform your doctor immediately. Norpace appears in breast milk and may affect a nursing infant. If this medication is essential to your health, your doctor may advise you to discontinue breastfeeding until your treatment with this medication is finished.

Recommended dosage
Treatment with Norpace should be started in the hospital.

ADULTS

Your doctor will adjust your dosage according to your own response to, and tolerance of, Norpace or Norpace CR.

The usual dosage range of Norpace and Norpace CR is 400 milligrams to 800 milligrams per day, divided into smaller doses.

The recommended dosage for most adults is 600 milligrams per day, divided into smaller doses (either 150 milligrams every 6 hours for immediate-release Norpace or 300 milligrams every 12 hours for Norpace CR).

For those who weigh less than 110 pounds, the recommended dosage is 400 milligrams per day, divided into smaller doses (either 100 milligrams every 6 hours for immediate-release Norpace or 200 milligrams every 12 hours for Norpace CR).

For people with severe heart disease, the starting dose will be 100 milligrams of immediate-release Norpace every 6 to 8 hours. Your doctor will adjust the dosage gradually and watch you closely for any signs of low blood pressure or heart failure.

For people with moderately reduced kidney or liver function, the dosage is 400 milligrams per day, divided into smaller doses (either 100 milligrams every 6 hours for immediate-release Norpace or 200 milligrams every 12 hours for Norpace CR).

For those who have severe kidney impairment, the dosage of immediate-release Norpace is 100 milligrams; the times will vary with the individual as determined by your doctor.

Norpace CR is not recommended for people with severe kidney disease.

CHILDREN

Dosage in children to age 18 is based on body weight. The total daily dosage should be divided into equal doses taken orally every 6 hours or at intervals that are best for the individual.

Overdosage

Any medication taken in excess can have serious consequences. An overdose of Norpace can be fatal. If you suspect an overdose, seek medical treatment immediately.

- *The symptoms of Norpace overdose may include:*
  Cessation of breathing
  Irregular heartbeat
  Loss of consciousness
  Low blood pressure
  Slow heartbeat
  Worsening of congestive heart failure

Brand name:

NORPRAMIN

Pronounced: NOR-pram-in
Generic name: Desipramine hydrochloride

Why is this drug prescribed?

Norpramin is used in the treatment of depression. It is one of a family of drugs called tricyclic antidepressants. Drugs in this class are thought to work by affecting the levels of the brain's natural chemical messengers (called neurotransmitters), and adjusting the brain's response to them.

Norpramin has also been used to treat bulimia and attention deficit disorders, and to help with cocaine withdrawal.

Most important fact about this drug

Serious, sometimes fatal, reactions have been known to occur when drugs such as Norpramin are taken with another type of antidepressant called an MAO inhibitor. Drugs in this category include Nardil, Marplan, and Parnate. Do not take Norpramin within 2 weeks of taking one of these drugs. Make sure your doctor and pharmacist know of all the medications you are taking.

How should you take this medication?

Norpramin should be taken exactly as prescribed.

Do not stop taking Norpramin if you feel no immediate effect. It can take up to 2 or 3 weeks for improvement to begin.

Norpramin can cause dry mouth. Sucking hard candy or chewing gum can help this problem.

■ *If you miss a dose...*
If you take several doses per day, take the forgotten dose as soon as you remember, then take any remaining doses for the day at evenly spaced intervals. If you take Norpramin once a day at bedtime and don't remember until morning, skip the missed dose. Never try to "catch up" by doubling the dose.

■ *Storage instructions...*
Norpramin can be stored at room temperature. Protect it from excessive heat.

What side effects may occur?

Side effects cannot be anticipated. If any develop or change in intensity, inform your doctor as soon as possible. Only your doctor can determine if it is safe for you to continue taking Norpramin.

■ *Side effects may include:*
Abdominal cramps, agitation, anxiety, black tongue, black, red, or blue spots on skin, blurred vision, breast development in males, breast enlargement in females, confusion, constipation, delusions, diarrhea, dilated pupils, disorientation, dizziness, drowsiness, dry mouth, excessive or spontaneous flow of milk, fatigue, fever, flushing, frequent urination or difficulty or delay in urinating, hallucinations, headache, heart attack, heartbeat irregularities, hepatitis, high or low blood pressure, high or low blood sugar, hives, impotence, increased or decreased sex drive, inflammation of the mouth, insomnia, intestinal blockage, lack of coordination, light-headedness (especially when rising from lying down), loss of

appetite, loss of hair, mild elation, nausea, nightmares, odd taste in mouth, painful ejaculation, palpitations, purplish spots on the skin, rapid heartbeat, restlessness, ringing in the ears, seizures, sensitivity to light, skin itching and rash, sore throat, stomach pain, stroke, sweating, swelling due to fluid retention (especially in face or tongue), swelling of testicles, swollen glands, tingling, numbness and pins and needles in hands and feet, tremors, urinating at night, visual problems, vomiting, weakness, weight gain or loss, worsening of psychosis, yellowed skin and whites of eyes

Why should this drug not be prescribed?

Norpramin should not be used if you are known to be hypersensitive to it, or if you have had a recent heart attack.

People who take antidepressant drugs known as MAO inhibitors (including Nardil, Parnate, and Marplan) should not take Norpramin.

Special warnings about this medication

Before using Norpramin, tell your doctor if you have heart or thyroid disease, a seizure disorder, a history of being unable to urinate, or glaucoma.

Nausea, headache, and uneasiness can result if you suddenly stop taking Norpramin. Consult your doctor and follow instructions closely when discontinuing Norpramin.

This drug may impair your ability to drive a car or operate potentially dangerous machinery. Do not participate in any activities that require full alertness if you are unsure about your ability.

Norpramin may increase your skin's sensitivity to sunlight. Overexposure could cause rash, itching, redness, or sunburn. Avoid direct sunlight or wear protective clothing.

If you are planning to have elective surgery, make sure that your doctor is aware that you are taking Norpramin. It should be discontinued as soon as possible prior to surgery.

Tell your doctor if you develop a fever and sore throat while you are taking Norpramin. He may want to do some blood tests.

Possible food and drug interactions
when taking this medication

People who take antidepressant drugs known as MAO inhibitors (including Nardil, Parnate, and Marplan) should not take Norpramin.

If Norpramin is taken with certain other drugs, the effects of either could be increased, decreased, or altered. It is especially important to check with your doctor before combining Norpramin with the following:

Cimetidine (Tagamet)
Drugs that improve breathing, such as Proventil
Drugs that relax certain muscles, such as Bentyl
Fluoxetine (Prozac)
Guanethidine (Ismelin)
Sedatives/hypnotics (Halcion, Valium)
Thyroid medications (Synthroid)

Extreme drowsiness and other potentially serious effects can result if Norpramin is combined with alcohol or other depressants, including narcotic painkillers such as Percocet and Demerol, sleeping medications such as Halcion and Nembutal, and tranquilizers such as Valium and Xanax.

Special information
if you are pregnant or breastfeeding
Pregnant women or mothers who are nursing an infant should use Norpramin only when the potential benefits clearly outweigh the potential risks. If you are pregnant or planning to become pregnant, inform your doctor immediately.

Recommended dosage
Your doctor will tailor the dose to your individual needs.

ADULTS

The usual dose ranges from 100 to 200 milligrams per day, taken in 1 dose or divided into smaller doses. If needed, dosages may gradually be increased to 300 milligrams a day. Dosages above 300 milligrams per day are not recommended.

CHILDREN

Norpramin is not recommended for children.

ELDERLY AND ADOLESCENTS

The usual dose ranges from 25 to 100 milligrams per day. If needed, dosages may gradually be increased to 150 milligrams a day. Doses above 150 milligrams per day are not recommended.

Overdosage

Any medication taken in excess can have serious consequences. An overdosage of Norpramin can be fatal. If you suspect an overdose, seek medical help immediately.

- *Symptoms of overdose may include:*
  Agitation, coma, confusion, delirium, difficult breathing, dilated pupils, extremely low blood pressure, fever, inability to urinate, irregular heart rate, kidney failure, restlessness, rigid muscles, seizures, shock, stupor, vomiting

Generic name:

NORTRIPTYLINE

See Pamelor, page 792.

Brand name:

NORVASC

Pronounced: NOR-vask
Generic name: Amlodipine besylate

Why is this drug prescribed?

Norvasc is prescribed for angina, a condition characterized by episodes of crushing chest pain usually resulting from a lack of oxygen in the heart due to clogged arteries. Norvasc is also prescribed for high blood pressure. It is a type of medication called a calcium channel blocker. These drugs dilate blood vessels and slow the heart to reduce blood pressure and the pain of angina.

Most important fact about this drug

If you have high blood pressure, you must take Norvasc regularly for it to be effective. Since blood pressure declines gradually, it may be several weeks before you get the full benefit of Norvasc; and you must continue taking it even if you are feeling well. Norvasc does not cure high blood pressure; it merely keeps it under control.

How should you take this medication?

Norvasc may be taken with or without food. A once-a-day medication, Norvasc may be used alone or in combination with other drugs for high blood pressure or angina.

You should take this medication exactly as prescribed, even if your symptoms have disappeared.

- *If you miss a dose...*
  If you forget to take a dose, take it as soon as you remember. If it is almost time for your next dose, skip the one you missed and go back to your regular schedule. Never take 2 doses at the same time.

- *Storage instructions...*
  Store at room temperature in a tightly closed container, away from light.

What side effects may occur?
Side effects cannot be anticipated. If any develop or change in intensity, tell your doctor as soon as possible. Only your doctor can determine if it is safe for you to continue taking Norvasc.

- *More common side effects may include:*
  Dizziness
  Fatigue
  Flushing
  Fluid retention and swelling
  Headache
  Palpitations (fluttery or throbbing heartbeat)

- *Less common side effect may include:*
  Abdominal pain
  Nausea
  Sleepiness

- *Rare side effects may include:*
  Abnormal dreams, agitation, altered sense of smell or taste, anxiety, apathy, back pain, chest pain, cold and clammy skin, conjunctivitis (pinkeye), constipation, coughing, depression, diarrhea, difficult or labored breathing, difficult or painful urination, difficulty swallowing, dizziness or light-headedness when standing, double vision, dry mouth, dry skin, excessive urination, eye pain, fainting, frequent urination, gas, general feeling of illness, hair loss, heart failure, hives, hot flashes, inability to sleep, increased appetite, increased sweating, indigestion, irregular heartbeat, irregular pulse, itching, joint pain or problems, lack of coordination, lack of sensation, loose stools, loss of appetite, loss of memory, loss of sense of identity, low blood pressure, migraine, muscle cramps or pain, muscle weakness, nasal inflammation, nervousness, nosebleed, pain, purple or red spots on the skin, rapid heartbeat, rash, ringing in the ears, sexual problems, skin discoloration, skin inflammation, slow heartbeat, stomach inflammation, thirst, tingling or "pins and needles,"   tremor,

twitching, urinating at night, urinating problems, vertigo, vision problems, vomiting, weakness, weight gain

Why should this drug not be prescribed?
If you are sensitive to or have ever had an allergic reaction or Norvasc, do not take this medication.

Special warnings about this medication
Check with your doctor before you stop taking Norvasc, as a slow reduction in the dose may be needed.

Your doctor will prescribe Norvasc with caution if you have certain heart conditions or liver disease. Make sure the doctor is aware of all your medical problems before you start therapy with Norvasc.

Although very rare, if you have severe heart disease, you may experience an increase in frequency and duration of angina attacks, or even have a heart attack, when you are starting on Norvasc or your dosage is increased.

Safety and effectiveness in children have not been established.

Possible food and drug interactions
There are no known food or drug interactions with this medication.

Special information
if you are pregnant or breastfeeding
The effects of Norvasc during pregnancy have not been adequately studied. If you are pregnant or planning to become pregnant, tell your doctor immediately. Norvasc should be used during pregnancy only if clearly needed. Norvasc may appear in breast milk. If this medication is essential to your health, your doctor may tell you to discontinue breastfeeding your baby until your treatment with Norvasc is finished.

Recommended dosage

HIGH BLOOD PRESSURE

Adults

The usual starting dose is 5 milligrams taken once a day. The most you should take in a day is 10 milligrams. If your doctor is adding Norvasc to other high blood pressure medications, the dose is 2.5 milligrams once daily. The lower 2.5-milligram starting dose also applies if you have liver disease.

Elderly

You will be prescribed a lower starting dose of 2.5 milligrams.

ANGINA

Adults

The usual starting dose is 5 to 10 milligrams once daily. If you have liver disease, the lower 5-milligram dose will be used at the start.

Elderly

The usual starting dose is 5 milligrams. Your doctor may adjust the dose based on your response to the drug.

Overdosage

Experience with Norvasc is limited; but if you suspect an overdose of Norvasc, seek medical attention immediately. The most likely symptoms are a drop in blood pressure and a faster heartbeat.

Brand name:

NOVOLIN

See Insulin, page 527.

Generic name:

NYSTATIN WITH TRIAMCINOLONE

See Mycolog-II, page 695.

Generic name:

OBY-CAP

See Fastin, page 422.

Generic name:

OFLOXACIN

See Floxin, page 451.

Brand name:

OGEN

Pronounced: OH-jen
Generic name: Estropipate
Other brand name: Ortho-Est

Why is this drug prescribed?

Ogen and Ortho-Est are estrogen replacement drugs. The tablets are used to reduce symptoms of menopause, including feelings of warmth in face, neck, and chest, and the sudden intense episodes of heat and sweating known as "hot flashes." They also may be prescribed for teenagers who fail to mature at the usual rate.

In addition, either the tablets or Ogen vaginal cream can be used for other conditions caused by lack of estrogen, such as dry, itchy external genitals and vaginal irritation.

Along with diet, calcium supplements, and exercise, Ogen tablets are also prescribed to prevent osteoporosis, a condition in which the bones become brittle and easily broken.

Some doctors also prescribe these drugs to treat breast cancer and cancer of the prostate.

Most important fact about this drug

Because estrogens have been linked with increased risk of endometrial cancer (cancer in the lining of the uterus) in women who have had their menopause, it is essential to have regular check-ups and to report any unusual vaginal bleeding to your doctor immediately.

How should you take this medication?

Be careful to follow the cycle of administration your doctor establishes for you. Take the medication exactly as prescribed.

When using Ogen Vaginal Cream, follow the instructions printed on the carton. It is for short-term use only. Remove the cap from the tube and make sure the plunger of the applicator is all the way into the barrel. Screw the nozzle of the applicator onto the tube and squeeze the cream into the applicator. The number on the plunger, which indicates the dose you should take, should be level with the top of the barrel. Unscrew the applicator and replace the cap on the tube. Insert the applicator into the vagina and push the plunger all the way down. Between uses, take the plunger out of the barrel and wash the applicator with warm, soapy water. Never use hot or boiling water.

■ *If you miss a dose...*
Take the forgotten dose as soon as you remember. If it is almost time for the next dose, skip the one you missed and go back to your regular schedule. Never try to "catch up" by doubling the dose.

■ *Storage instructions...*
Store at room temperature.

What side effects may occur?
Side effects cannot be anticipated. If any develop or change in intensity, notify your doctor as soon as possible. Only your doctor can determine if it is safe for you to continue taking estrogen.

■ *Side effects may include:*
Abdominal cramps, bloating, breakthrough bleeding, breast enlargement, breast tenderness and secretions, change in amount of cervical secretion, changes in sex drive, changes in vaginal bleeding patterns, chorea (irregular, rapid, jerky movements, usually affecting the face and limbs), depression, dizziness, enlargement of benign tumors (fibroids), excessive hairiness, fluid retention, hair loss, headache, inability to use contact lenses, menstrual changes, migraine, nausea, reduced ability to tolerate carbohydrates, spotting, spotty darkening of the skin, especially around the face, skin eruptions (especially on the legs and arms) with bleeding, skin irritation, skin redness and scaling, vaginal yeast infection, vision problems, vomiting, weight gain or loss, yellow eyes and skin

Why should this drug not be prescribed?
Estrogens should not be used if you know or suspect you have breast cancer or other cancers promoted by estrogen. Do not use estrogen if you are pregnant or think you may be pregnant. Also avoid estrogen if you have abnormal, undiagnosed genital bleeding, or if you have blood clots or a blood clotting disorder or a history of blood clotting disorders associated with previous estrogen use.

Ogen Vaginal Cream should not be used if you are sensitive to or have ever had an allergic reaction to any of its components.

Special warnings about this medication
The risk of cancer of the uterus increases when estrogen is used for a long time or taken in large doses. There also may be increased risk of breast cancer in women who take estrogen for an extended period of time.

Women who take estrogen after menopause are more likely to develop gallbladder disease.

Ogen also increases the risk of blood clots. These blood clots can cause stroke, heart attack, or other serious disorders.

Your doctor will check your blood pressure regularly. It could go up or down.

While taking estrogen, get in touch with your doctor right away if you notice any of the following:

Abdominal pain, tenderness, or swelling
Abnormal bleeding from the vagina
Breast lumps
Coughing up blood
Pain in your chest or calves
Severe headache, dizziness, or faintness
Speech changes
Sudden shortness of breath
Vision changes
Vomiting
Weakness or numbness in an arm or leg
Yellowing of the skin

Ogen may cause fluid retention in some people. If you have asthma, epilepsy, migraine, or heart or kidney disease, use this medication with care.

Estrogen therapy may cause uterine bleeding or breast pain.

Possible food and drug interactions
when taking this medication

If Ogen is taken with certain other drugs, the effects of either could be increased, decreased, or altered. It is especially important to check with your doctor before combining Ogen with the following:

Barbiturates such as phenobarbital
Blood thinners such as Coumadin
Epilepsy drugs (Tegretol, Dilantin, others)
Insulin
Tricyclic antidepressants (Elavil, Tofranil, others)
Rifampin (Rifadin)

Special information
if you are pregnant or breastfeeding

Estrogens should not be used during pregnancy. If you are pregnant or plan to become pregnant, notify your doctor immediately. These drugs may appear in breast milk and could affect a nursing infant. If this medication is essential to your health, your doctor may advise you to discontinue breastfeeding until your treatment is finished.

Recommended dosage

HOT FLASHES AND NIGHT SWEATS

Ogen Tablets: The usual dose ranges from one 0.625 tablet to two 2.5 tablets per day. Tablets should be taken in cycles, according to your doctor's instructions.

Ortho-Est Tablets: The usual dose ranges from ½ tablet to 4 tablets per day of Ortho-Est 1.25 or 1 to 8 tablets of Ortho-Est 6.25. Tablets should be taken in cycles, according to your doctor's instructions.

VAGINAL INFLAMMATION AND DRYNESS

Ogen Tablets: The usual dose ranges from one 0.625 tablet to two 2.5 tablets per day. Tablets should be taken in cycles, according to your doctor's instructions.

Ortho-Est Tablets: The usual dose ranges from ½ tablet to 4 tablets per day of Ortho-Est 1.25 or 1 to 8 tablets of Ortho-Est .625. Tablets should be taken in cycles, according to your doctor's instructions.

Ogen Vaginal Cream: The usual dose is 2 to 4 grams daily. Cream should be used in cycles, and only for limited periods of time.

ESTROGEN HORMONE DEFICIENCY

Ogen Tablets: The usual dose ranges from one 1.25 tablet to three 2.5 tablets per day, taken for 3 weeks, followed by a rest period of 8 to 10 days.

Ortho-Est Tablets: The usual dose ranges from 1 to 6 tablets per day of Ortho-Est 1.25 or 2 to 12 tablets of Ortho-Est .625, given for 3 weeks, followed by a rest period of 8 to 10 days.

OVARIAN FAILURE

Ogen Tablets: The usual dose ranges from one 1.25 tablet to three 2.5 tablets per day for 3 weeks, followed by a rest period of 8 to 10 days. Your doctor may increase or decrease your dosage according to your response.

Ortho-Est Tablets: The usual dose ranges from 1 to 6 tablets per day of Ortho-Est 1.25 or 2 to 12 tablets of Ortho-Est. .625 for 3 weeks, followed by a rest period of 8 to 10 days. Your doctor may increase or decrease your dosage according to your response.

PREVENTION OF OSTEOPOROSIS

Ogen Tablets: The usual dose is one 0.625 tablet per day for 25 days of a 31-day monthly cycle.

Overdosage

Any medication taken in excess can have serious consequences. If you suspect an overdose, seek emergency medical treatment immediately.

■ *Symptoms of Ogen overdose may include:*
Nausea
Vomiting
Withdrawal bleeding

Generic name:

OLSALAZINE

See Dipentum, page 343.

Generic name:

OMEPRAZOLE

See Prilosec, page 888.

Brand name:

OMNIPEN

Pronounced: AHM-nee-pen
Generic name: Ampicillin
Other Brands: Polycillin, Principen, Totacillin

Why is this drug prescribed?

Omnipen is a penicillin-like antibiotic prescribed for a wide variety of infections, including gonorrhea and other genital and urinary infections, respiratory infections, and gastrointestinal infections, as well as meningitis (inflamed membranes of the spinal cord or brain).

Most important fact about this drug

If you are allergic to either penicillin or cephalosporin antibiotics in any form, consult your doctor *before taking Omnipen.* There is a possibility that you are allergic to both types of medication; and if a reaction occurs, it could be extremely severe. If you take the drug and develop a skin reaction, diarrhea, shortness of breath, wheezing, sore throat, or fever, seek medical attention immediately.

How should you use this medication?

Take Omnipen capsules with a full glass of water, a half hour before or 2 hours after a meal.

Omnipen Oral Suspension should be shaken well before using.

Take Omnipen exactly as prescribed. It works best when there is a constant amount in the body. Take your doses at evenly spaced times around the clock, and try not to miss a dose.

■ *If you miss a dose...*
Take it as soon as you remember. If it is almost time for the next dose, and you take 2 doses a day, take the one you missed and the next dose 5 to 6 hours later. If you take 3 or more doses a day, take the one you missed and the next dose 2 to 4 hours later. Then go back to your regular schedule. Do not take 2 doses at once.

■ *Storage information...*
Store Omnipen Capsules at room temperature in a tightly closed container.

Keep Omnipen Oral Suspension in the refrigerator, in a tightly closed container. Discard the unused portion after 14 days.

What side effects may occur?
Side effects cannot be anticipated. If any develop or change in intensity, inform your doctor as soon as possible. Only your doctor can determine whether it is safe for you to continue taking Omnipen.

■ *Side effects may include:*
Colitis (inflammation of the bowel), diarrhea, fever, itching, nausea, rash or other skin problems, sore tongue or mouth, vomiting

Why should this drug not be prescribed?
You should not take Omnipen if you are allergic to penicillin or cephalosporin antibiotics.

Special warnings about this medication
If you have an allergic reaction, stop taking Omnipen and contact your doctor immediately.

After you have taken Omnipen for a long time, you may get a new infection (called a superinfection) due to an organism this medication cannot treat. Consult your doctor if your symptoms do not improve or seem to get worse.

Omnipen sometimes causes diarrhea. Some diarrhea medications can make the diarrhea worse. Check with your doctor before taking any diarrhea remedy.

Oral contraceptives may not work properly while you are taking Omnipen. For greater certainty, use other measures while taking Omnipen.

If you are diabetic, be aware that Omnipen may cause a *false positive* in certain urine glucose tests. You should talk to your doctor about the right tests to use while you are taking Omnipen.

For infections such as strep throat, it is important to take Omnipen for the entire amount of time your doctor has prescribed. Even if you feel better, you need to continue taking the medication.

Possible food and drug interactions
when taking this medication

If Omnipen is taken with certain other drugs the effects of either could be increased, decreased, or altered. It is especially important to check with your doctor before combining Omnipen with any of the following:

Allopurinol (Zyloprim)
Atenolol (Tenormin)
Chloroquine (Aralen)
Mefloquine (Lariam)
Oral contraceptives

Special information
if you are pregnant or breastfeeding

The effects of Omnipen during pregnancy have not been adequately studied. If you are pregnant or plan to become pregnant, inform your doctor immediately. Omnipen should be used during pregnancy only if the potential benefit justifies the potential risk to the developing baby.

Omnipen appears in breast milk and could affect a nursing infant. If this medication is essential to your health, your doctor may advise you to stop breastfeeding until your treatment with Omnipen is finished.

Recommended dosage

Unless you are being treated for gonorrhea, your doctor will have you continue taking Omnipen for 2 to 3 days after your symptoms have disappeared. Dosages are for capsules and oral suspension.

ADULTS

Infections of the Genital, Urinary, or Gastrointestinal Tracts
The usual dose is 500 milligrams, taken every 6 hours.

Gonorrhea
The usual dose is 3.5 grams in a single oral dose along with 1 gram of probenecid

Respiratory Tract Infections
The usual dose is 250 milligrams, taken every 6 hours.

CHILDREN

Children weighing over 44 pounds should follow the adult dose schedule.

Children weighing 44 pounds or less should have their dosage determined by their weight.

Infections of the Genital, Urinary, or Gastrointestinal Tracts
The usual dose is 100 milligrams for each 2.2 pounds of body weight daily, divided into 4 doses for the capsules, and 3 to 4 doses for the suspension.

Respiratory Tract Infections
The usual dose is 50 milligrams for each 2.2 pounds of body weight daily, divided into 3 or 4 doses.

Overdosage
Although no specific symptoms have been reported, any medication taken in excess can have serious consequences. If you suspect an overdose of Omnipen, seek medical attention immediately.

Generic name:

ONDANSETRON

See Zofran, page 1239.

Category:

ORAL CONTRACEPTIVES

Brand names: Brevicon, Demulen, Desogen, Genora, Levlen, Loestrin, Lo/Ovral, Micronor, Modicon, Nordette, Norethin, Norinyl, Ortho-Cept, Ortho-Cyclen, Ortho-Novum, Ortho Tri-Cyclen, Ovcon, Ovral, Triphasil

Why is this drug prescribed?

Oral contraceptives (also known as "The Pill") are highly effective means of preventing pregnancy. Oral contraceptives consist of synthetic forms of two hormones produced naturally in the body: either progestin alone or estrogen and progestin. Estrogen and progestin regulate a woman's menstrual cycle, and the fluctuating levels of these hormones play an essential role in fertility.

To reduce side effects, oral contraceptives are available in a wide range of estrogen and progestin concentrations. Progestin-only products (such as Micronor) are usually prescribed for women who should avoid estrogens; however, they may not be as effective as estrogen/progestin contraceptives.

Most important fact about this drug

Cigarette smoking increases the risk of serious heart-related side effects (stroke, heart attack, blood clots, etc.) in women who use oral contraceptives. This risk increases with heavy smoking (15 or more cigarettes per day) and with age. There is an especially significant increase in heart disease risk in women over 35 years old who smoke and use oral contraceptives.

How should you take this medication?

Oral contraceptives should be taken daily, no more than 24 hours apart, for the duration of the prescribed cycle of 21 or 28 days. Ideally, you should take your pill at the same time every day to reduce the chance of forgetting a dose.

■ *If you miss a dose...*

If you neglect to take only one estrogen/ progestin pill, take it as soon as you remember, take the next pill at your regular time, and continue taking the rest of the medication cycle. The risk of pregnancy is small if you miss only one combination pill per cycle. If you miss more than one tablet, do not take the missed tablets; instead resume the normal medication cycle while *employing another form of contraceptive.* Check your product's patient information for further instructions.

Missing a single progestin-only tablet increases the chance of pregnancy. Consult your doctor immediately if you miss a single dose and use another method of birth control until your next period begins or pregnancy is ruled out.

■ *Storage instructions...*

To help keep track of your doses, use the original container. Store at room temperature.

What side effects may occur?
Side effects cannot be anticipated. If any develop or change in intensity, inform your doctor as soon as possible. Only your doctor can determine if it is safe for you to continue taking an oral contraceptive.

■ *Side effects may include:*
Abdominal cramps, acne, appetite changes, bladder infection, bleeding in spots during a menstrual period, bloating, blood clots, breast tenderness or enlargement, cataracts, chest pain, contact lens discomfort, decreased flow of milk when given immediately after birth, depression, difficulty breathing, dizziness, fluid retention, gallbladder disease, growth of face, back, chest, or stomach hair, hair loss, headache, heart attack, high blood pressure, inflammation of the large intestine, kidney trouble, lack of menstrual periods, liver tumors, lumps in the breast, menstrual pattern changes, migraine, muscle, joint, or leg pain, nausea, nervousness, premenstrual syndrome (PMS), secretion of milk, sex drive changes, skin infection, skin rash or discoloration, stomach cramps, stroke, swelling, temporary infertility, unexplained bleeding in the vagina, vaginal discharge, vaginal infections (and/or burning and itching), visual disturbances, vomiting, weight gain or loss, yellow skin or whites of eyes

Why should this drug not be prescribed?
You should not take oral contraceptives if you have had an allergic reaction to them or if you are pregnant (or think you might be).

If you have ever had breast cancer or cancer in the reproductive organs or liver tumors, you should not take oral contraceptives.

If you have or have ever had a stroke, heart disease, angina (severe chest pain), or blood clots, you should not take oral contraceptives. Women who have had pregnancy-related jaundice or jaundice stemming from previous use of oral contraceptives should not take them.

If you have undiagnosed and/or unexplained abnormal vaginal bleeding, do not take oral contraceptives.

Special warnings about this medication
Oral contraceptives should be used with caution if you are over 40 years old; smoke tobacco; have liver, heart, gallbladder, kidney, or thyroid disease; have high blood pressure, high cholesterol, diabetes, epilepsy, asthma, or porphyria (a blood disorder); or are obese.

In addition, you should use oral contraceptives with caution if you have a family history of breast cancer or other cancers, or you have a personal history of depression, migraine or other headaches, irregular menstrual periods, or visual disturbances.

Since the blood's clotting ability may be affected by oral contraceptives, your doctor may take you off them prior to surgery. If bleeding lasts more than 8 days while you are on a progestin-only oral contraceptive, be sure to let your doctor know.

Oral contraceptives do not protect against HIV infection (AIDS) or any other sexually transmitted disease.

If you miss a menstrual period but have taken your pills regularly, contact your doctor but do not stop taking your pills. If you miss a period and have not taken your pills regularly, or if you miss two consecutive periods, you may be pregnant; stop taking your pills and check with your doctor immediately to see if you are pregnant. Use another form of birth control while you are not taking your pills.

Possible food and drug interactions when taking this medication

If oral contraceptives are taken with certain other drugs, the effects of either could be increased, decreased, or altered. It is especially important to check with your doctor before combining oral contraceptives with the following:

Amitriptyline (Elavil, Endep)
Ampicillin (Principen, Totacillin)
Barbiturates (phenobarbital, Seconal)
Carbamazepine (Tegretol)
Chloramphenicol (Chloromycetin)
Clomipramine (Anafranil)
Diazepam (Valium)
Doxepin (Sinequan)
Glipizide (Glucotrol)
Griseofulvin (Fulvicin, Grisactin)
Imipramine (Tofranil)
Lorazepam (Ativan)
Metoprolol (Lopressor)
Oxazepam (Serax)
Penicillin (Veetids, Pen-Vee K)
Phenylbutazone (Butazolidin)
Phenytoin (Dilantin)
Prednisolone (Prelone, Pediapred)
Prednisone (Deltasone)
Primidone (Mysoline)
Propranolol (Inderal)

Rifampin (Rifadin, Rimactane)
Sulfonamides (Bactrim, Septra)
Tetracycline (Achromycin V, Sumycin)
Theophylline (Theo-Dur, Slo-bid)
Warfarin (Coumadin, Panwarfin)

In addition, oral contraceptives may affect tests for blood sugar levels and thyroid function and may cause an increase in blood cholesterol levels.

Special information
if you are pregnant or breastfeeding
If you are pregnant (or think you might be), you should not use oral contraceptives, since they are not safe during pregnancy. In addition, wait at least 4 weeks after delivery before starting an oral contraceptive.

In general, nursing mothers should not use oral contraceptives, since these drugs can appear in breast milk and may cause jaundice and enlarged breasts in nursing infants. Your doctor may advise you to use a different form of contraception while you are nursing your baby.

Recommended dosage
If you have any questions about how you should take oral contraceptives, consult your doctor or the patient instructions that come in the drug package. The following is a partial list of instructions for taking oral contraceptives; it should not be used as a substitute for consultation with your doctor.

Some brands can be started on the first day of your menstrual cycle or on the first Sunday afterwards. Others must be started on the fifth day of the cycle or the first Sunday afterwards. The instructions below are for the first-Sunday schedule.

Oral contraceptives are supplied in 21-day and 28-day packages.

For a 21-day schedule
Oral contraceptives are taken every day for a 3-week period, followed by 1 week of no oral contraceptives; this cycle is repeated each month.

1. Starting on the first Sunday after the beginning of your menstrual period, take one tablet daily (at the same time each day) for the next 21 days. Note: If your period begins on Sunday, take the first tablet that day.

2. Wait 1 week before taking any tablets. Your menstrual period should occur during this time.

3. Following this 1-week waiting time, begin taking a daily tablet again for the next 21 days.

For a 28-day schedule
Starting on the first Sunday after the beginning of your menstrual period, take one tablet daily (at the same time each day) for the next 28 days. Continue taking the oral contraceptives according to your physician's instructions. Note: If your period begins on Sunday, take the first tablet that day.

For both 21- and 28-day regimens
When following a regimen with a Sunday or Day 5 start, use an additional method of birth control for the first 7 days of the cycle.

Progestin-only tablets should be taken every day of the year.

Overdosage
While any medication taken in excess can cause overdose, the risk associated with oral contraceptives is minimal. Even young children who have taken large amounts of oral contraceptives have not experienced serious adverse effects. However, if you suspect an overdose, seek medical help immediately.

■ *Symptoms of overdose may include:*
  Nausea
  Withdrawal bleeding in females

Brand name:

ORASONE

See Deltasone, page 293.

Brand name:

ORINASE

Pronounced: OR-in-aze
Generic name: Tolbutamide

Why is this drug prescribed?
Orinase is an oral antidiabetic medication used to treat Type II (non-insulin-dependent) diabetes. Diabetes occurs when the body does not make enough insulin, or when the insulin that is produced no longer works properly. Insulin works by helping sugar get inside the body's cells, where it is then used for energy.

There are two forms of diabetes: Type I (insulin-dependent) and Type II (non-insulin-dependent). Type I diabetes usually requires taking insulin injections for life, while Type II diabetes can usually be treated by dietary changes, exercise, and/or oral antidiabetic medications such as Orinase. Orinase controls diabetes by stimulating the pancreas to secrete more insulin and by helping insulin work better.

Occasionally, Type II diabetics must take insulin injections temporarily during stressful periods or times of illness. When diet, exercise, and an oral antidiabetic medication fail to reduce symptoms and/or blood sugar levels, a person with Type II diabetes may require long-term insulin injections.

Most important fact about this drug

Always remember that Orinase is an aid to, not a substitute for, good diet and exercise. Failure to follow a sound diet and exercise plan can lead to serious complications, such as dangerously high or low blood sugar levels. Remember, too, that Orinase is *not* an oral form of insulin, and cannot be used in place of insulin.

How should you take this medication?

In general, Orinase should be taken 30 minutes before a meal to achieve the best control over blood sugar levels. However, the exact dosing schedule, as well as the dosage amount, must be determined by your physician. Ask your doctor when it is best for you to take this medication.

To help prevent low blood sugar levels (hypoglycemia) you should:

Understand the symptoms of hypoglycemia.
Know how exercise affects your blood sugar levels.
Maintain an adequate diet.
Keep a product containing quick-acting sugar with you at all times.
Limit alcohol intake. If you drink alcohol, it may cause breathlessness
     and facial flushing.

■ *If you miss a dose...*
Take it as soon as you remember. If it is almost time for the next dose, skip the one you missed and go back to your regular schedule. Do not take 2 doses at the same time.

■ *Storage instructions...*
Store at room temperature.

What side effects may occur?

Side effects cannot be anticipated. If any develop or change in intensity, inform your doctor as soon as possible. Only your doctor can determine if it is safe for you to continue taking Orinase.

Side effects from Orinase are rare and seldom require discontinuation of the medication.

■ *More common side effects may include:*
Bloating
Heartburn
Nausea

■ *Less common or rare side effects may include:*
Anemia and other blood disorders, blistering, changes in taste, headache, hepatic porphyria (a condition frequently characterized by sensitivity to light, stomach pain, and nerve damage, caused by excessive levels of a substance called porphyrin in the liver), hives, itching, redness of the skin, skin eruptions, skin rash

Orinase, like all oral antidiabetics, may cause hypoglycemia (low blood sugar). The risk of hypoglycemia can be increased by missed meals, alcohol, other medications, fever, trauma, infection, surgery, or excessive exercise. To avoid hypoglycemia, you should closely follow the dietary and exercise plan suggested by your physician.

■ *Symptoms of mild hypoglycemia may include:*
Cold sweat, drowsiness, fast heartbeat, headache, nausea, nervousness.

■ *Symptoms of more severe hypoglycemia may include:*
Coma, pale skin, seizures, shallow breathing.

Contact your doctor immediately if these symptoms of severe low blood sugar occur.

Ask your doctor what you should do if you experience mild hypoglycemia. Severe hypoglycemia should be considered a medical emergency, and prompt medical attention is essential.

Why should this drug not be prescribed?
You should not take Orinase if you have had an allergic reaction to it.

Orinase should not be taken if you are suffering from diabetic ketoacidosis (a life-threatening medical emergency caused by insufficient insulin and marked by excessive thirst, nausea, fatigue, pain below the breastbone, and fruity breath).

In addition, Orinase should not be used as the sole therapy in treating Type I (insulin-dependent) diabetes.

Special warnings about this medication

It's possible that drugs such as Orinase may lead to more heart problems than diet treatment alone, or diet plus insulin. If you have a heart condition, you may want to discuss this with your doctor.

If you are taking Orinase, you should check your blood or urine periodically for abnormal sugar (glucose) levels.

It is important that you closely follow the diet and exercise plan recommended by your doctor.

Even people with well-controlled diabetes may find that stress, illness, surgery, or fever results in a loss of control over their diabetes. In these cases, your physician may recommend that you temporarily stop taking Orinase and use injected insulin instead.

In addition, the effectiveness of any oral antidiabetic, including Orinase, may decrease with time. This may occur because of either a diminished responsiveness to the medication or a worsening of the diabetes.

Like other antidiabetic drugs, Orinase may produce severe low blood sugar if the dosage is wrong. While taking Orinase, you are particularly susceptible to episodes of low blood sugar if:

You suffer from a kidney or liver problem;

You have a lack of adrenal or pituitary hormone;

You are elderly, run-down, malnourished, hungry, exercising heavily, drinking alcohol, or using more than one glucose-lowering drug.

Possible food and drug interactions when taking this medication

If Orinase is taken with certain other drugs, the effects of either could be increased, decreased, or altered. It is especially important to check with your doctor before combining Orinase with the following:

Adrenal corticosteroids such as prednisone (Deltasone) and cortisone (Cortone)
Airway-opening drugs such as Proventil and Ventolin
Anabolic steroids such as testosterone
Barbiturates such as Amytal, Seconal, and phenobarbital
Beta blockers such as Inderal and Tenormin
Blood-thinning drugs such as Coumadin
Calcium channel blockers such as Cardizem and Procardia
Chloramphenicol (Chloromycetin)
Cimetidine (Tagamet)

Clofibrate (Atromid-S)
Colestipol (Colestid)
Epinephrine (EpiPen)
Estrogens (Premarin)
Fluconazole (Diflucan)
Furosemide (Lasix)
Isoniazid (Laniazid, Rifamate)
Itraconazole (Sporanox)
Major tranquilizers such as Stelazine and Mellaril
MAO inhibitors such as Nardil and Parnate
Methyldopa (Aldomet)
Miconazole (Monistat)
Niacin (Nicobid, Nicolar)
Nonsteroidal anti-inflammatory agents such as Advil, aspirin, Motrin, Naprosyn, and Voltaren
Oral contraceptives
Phenytoin (Dilantin)
Probenecid (Benemid)
Rifampin (Rifadin)
Sulfa drugs such as Bactrim and Septra
Thiazide and other diuretics such as Diuril and HydroDIURIL
Thyroid medications such as Synthroid

Be cautious about drinking alcohol, since excessive alcohol can cause low blood sugar.

Special information
if you are pregnant or breastfeeding

The effects of Orinase during pregnancy have not been adequately established in humans. Since Orinase has caused birth defects in rats, it is not recommended for use by pregnant women. Therefore, if you are pregnant or planning to become pregnant, you should take Orinase only on the advice of your physician. Since studies suggest the importance of maintaining normal blood sugar (glucose) levels during pregnancy, your physician may prescribe injected insulin during your pregnancy. While it is not known if Orinase enters breast milk, other similar medications do. Therefore, you should discuss with your doctor whether to discontinue the medication or to stop breastfeeding. If the medication is discontinued, and if diet alone does not control glucose levels, your doctor will consider giving you insulin injections.

Recommended dosage

Dosage levels are based on individual needs.

ADULTS

Usually an initial daily dose of 1 to 2 grams is recommended. Maintenance therapy usually ranges from 0.25 to 3 grams daily. Daily doses greater than 3 grams are not recommended.

CHILDREN

Safety and effectiveness have not been established in children.

ELDERLY

Elderly, malnourished, or debilitated people, or those with impaired kidney or liver function, are usually prescribed lower initial and maintenance doses to minimize the risk of low blood sugar (hypoglycemia).

Overdosage

Any medication taken in excess can have serious consequences. An overdose of Orinase can cause low blood sugar (see "Special warnings about this medication"). Eating sugar or a sugar-based product will often correct mild hypoglycemia. If you suspect an overdose, seek medical attention immediately.

Generic name:

ORPHENADRINE, ASPIRIN, AND CAFFEINE

See Norgesic, page 747.

Brand name:

ORTHO-CEPT

See Oral Contraceptives, page 775.

Brand name:

ORTHO-CYCLEN

See Oral Contraceptives, page 775.

Brand name:

ORTHO-EST

See Ogen, page 768.

Brand name:

ORTHO-NOVUM

See Oral Contraceptives, page 775.

Brand name:

ORTHO TRI-CYCLEN

See Oral Contraceptives, page 775.

Brand name:

ORUDIS

Pronounced: Oh-ROO-dis
Generic name: Ketoprofen
Other brand name: Oruvail

Why is this drug prescribed?

Orudis, a nonsteroidal anti-inflammatory drug, is used to relieve the inflammation, swelling, stiffness, and joint pain associated with rheumatoid arthritis and osteoarthritis (the most common form of arthritis). It is also used to relieve mild to moderate pain, as well as menstrual pain. Oruvail, an extended-release form of the drug, is used to treat the signs and symptoms of rheumatoid arthritis and osteoarthritis over the long term, not severe attacks that come on suddenly.

Most important fact about this drug

You should have frequent check-ups with your doctor if you take Orudis regularly. Ulcers or internal bleeding can occur without warning.

How should you take this medication?

To minimize side effects, your doctor may recommend that you take Orudis with food, an antacid, or milk.

Take this medication exactly as prescribed by your doctor.

If you are using Orudis for arthritis, it should be taken regularly.

■ *If you miss a dose...*
  If you take Orudis on a regular schedule, take the forgotten dose as soon as you remember. If it is almost time for your next dose, skip the one you missed and go back to your regular schedule. Do not take 2 doses at once.

■ *Storage instructions...*
Store at room temperature in a tightly closed container.

What side effects may occur?
Side effects cannot be anticipated. If any develop or change in intensity, inform your doctor as soon as possible. Only your doctor can determine if it is safe for you to continue taking Orudis.

■ *More common side effects may include:*
Abdominal pain, changes in kidney function, constipation, diarrhea, dreams, fluid retention, gas, headache, inability to sleep, indigestion, nausea

■ *Less common or rare side effects may include:*
Allergic reaction, amnesia, anemia, asthma, belching, blood in the urine, bloody or black stools, change in taste, chills, confusion, congestive heart failure, coughing up blood, conjunctivitis (pinkeye), depression, difficult or labored breathing, dizziness, dry mouth, eye pain, facial swelling due to fluid retention, general feeling of illness, hair loss, high blood pressure, hives, impaired hearing, impotence, increase in appetite, increased salivation, infection, inflammation of the mouth, irregular or excessive menstrual bleeding, itching, kidney failure, loosening of fingernails, loss of appetite, migraine, muscle pain, nasal inflammation, nosebleed, pain, peptic or intestinal ulcer, rapid heartbeat, rash, rectal bleeding, red or purple spots on the skin, ringing in the ears, sensitivity to light, skin discoloration, skin eruptions, skin inflammation and flaking, sleepiness, sore throat, stomach inflammation, sweating, swelling of the throat, thirst, throbbing heartbeat, tingling or pins and needles, vertigo, visual disturbances, vomiting, vomiting blood, weight gain or loss

Why should this drug not be prescribed?
If you are sensitive to or have ever had an allergic reaction to Orudis, or if you have had asthma attacks, hives, or other allergic reactions caused by aspirin or other nonsteroidal anti-inflammatory drugs, you should not take this medication. Make sure your doctor is aware of any drug reactions you have experienced.

Special warnings about this medication
Remember that stomach ulcers and bleeding can occur without warning.

This drug should be used with caution if you have kidney or liver disease.

If you are taking Orudis for an extended period of time, your doctor will check your blood for anemia.

This drug can increase water retention. Use with caution if you have heart disease or high blood pressure.

Possible food and drug interactions when taking this medication

If Orudis is taken with certain other drugs, the effects of either could be increased, decreased, or altered. It is especially important to check with your doctor before combining Orudis with the following:

Aspirin
Blood thinners such as Coumadin
Diuretics such as hydrochlorothiazide (HydroDIURIL)
Lithium (Lithonate)
Methotrexate
Probenecid (the gout medication Benemid)

Orudis can prolong bleeding time. If you are taking blood-thinning medication, use this drug cautiously.

Special information if you are pregnant or breastfeeding

The effects of Orudis during pregnancy have not been adequately studied. If you are pregnant or plan to become pregnant, inform your doctor immediately. Orudis may appear in breast milk and could affect a nursing infant. If this medication is essential to your health, your doctor may advise you to discontinue breastfeeding until your treatment with this medication is finished.

Recommended dosage

ADULTS

Rheumatoid Arthritis and Osteoarthritis

The starting dose of Orudis is 75 milligrams 3 times a day or 50 milligrams 4 times a day; for Oruvail, 200 milligrams taken once a day. The most you should take in a day is 300 milligrams. Some side effects, such as headache or upset stomach, increase in severity as the dose gets higher. Smaller people may need smaller doses.

Mild to Moderate Pain and Menstrual Pain

The usual dose of Orudis is 25 to 50 milligrams every 6 to 8 hours as needed. Your doctor may adjust the dosage if you are small or if you have kidney or liver disease.

CHILDREN

The safety and effectiveness of Orudis have not been established in children.

ELDERLY

You may need a lower dosage.

Overdosage

Any medication taken in excess can have serious consequences. If you suspect an overdose of Orudis, seek medical attention immediately.

- *Signs and symptoms of Orudis overdose may include:*
  Breathing difficulty
  Coma
  Convulsions
  Drowsiness
  High blood pressure
  Kidney failure
  Low blood pressure
  Nausea
  Sluggishness
  Stomach and intestinal bleeding
  Stomach pain
  Vomiting

Brand name:

ORUVAIL

See Orudis, page 786.

Brand name:

OVCON

See Oral Contraceptives, page 775.

Brand name:

OVRAL

See Oral Contraceptives, page 775

Generic name:

OXAPROZIN

See Daypro, page 274.

Generic name:

OXAZEPAM

See Serax, page 1016.

Generic name:

OXICONAZOLE

See Oxistat, page 790.

Brand name:

OXISTAT

Pronounced: OX-ee-stat
Generic name: Oxiconazole nitrate

Why is this drug prescribed?
Oxistat is used to treat fungal skin diseases commonly called ringworm (tinea). Oxistat is prescribed for athlete's foot (tinea pedis), jock itch (tinea cruris), and ringworm of the entire body (tinea corporis). It is available as a cream or lotion.

Most important fact about this drug
Oxistat should not be used in, on, or near the eyes, or applied to the vagina.

How should you use this medication?
Use Oxistat exactly as prescribed.

Wash and dry the area to be treated before applying Oxistat and then apply the cream or lotion so that it covers the entire affected area and the area right around it.

Be careful when applying to raw, blistered, or oozing skin.

■ *If you miss a dose...*
  Apply the cream or lotion when you remember, then return to your regular schedule.

■ *Storage instructions...*
Store Oxistat at room temperature.

What side effects may occur?
Side effects cannot be anticipated. If any develop or change in intensity, notify your doctor as soon as possible. Only your doctor can determine whether it is safe for you to continue using Oxistat.

■ *Side effects may include:*
Allergic skin inflammation, burning, cracks in the skin, eczema, irritation, itching, pain, rash, scaling, skin redness, skin softening, small, firm, raised skin eruptions similar to those of chickenpox, stinging, tingling

Why should this drug not be prescribed?
Do not use Oxistat if you have ever had an allergic reaction or are sensitive to oxiconazole or any other ingredients in the cream.

Special warnings about this medication
If you develop an irritation or sensitivity to the medication, notify your doctor.

Possible food and drug interactions
when taking this medication
No interactions have been reported.

Special information
if you are pregnant or breastfeeding
Oxistat has not been proved safe during pregnancy. If you are pregnant or plan to become pregnant, inform your doctor immediately.

Oxistat appears in breast milk and could affect a nursing infant. If Oxistat is essential to your health, your doctor may advise you to stop breastfeeding until your treatment is finished.

Recommended dosage

ADULTS AND CHILDREN

Apply Oxistat Cream or Lotion to cover the affected area once or twice a day. Athlete's foot (tinea pedis) is treated for 1 month. Jock itch (tinea cruris) and ringworm of the body (tinea corporis) are treated for 2 weeks. If your condition does not improve, your doctor will re-evaluate the diagnosis.

Overdosage
Overdose of Oxistat has not been reported. However, if you suspect an overdose, seek medical attention immediately.

Generic name:

OXYBUTYNIN

See Ditropan, page 351.

Brand name:

PAMELOR

Pronounced: PAM-eh-lore
Generic name: Nortriptyline hydrochloride
Other brand name: Aventyl

Why is this drug prescribed?
Pamelor is prescribed for the relief of symptoms of depression. Pamelor is in the class of drugs known as tricyclic antidepressants.

Some doctors also prescribe Pamelor to treat chronic hives, premenstrual depression, attention deficit hyperactivity disorder in children, and bed-wetting.

Most important fact about this drug
Pamelor must be taken regularly to be effective and it may be several weeks before you begin to feel better. Do not skip doses, even if they seem to make no difference.

How should you take this medication?
Take Pamelor exactly as prescribed. Pamelor may make your mouth dry. Sucking on hard candy, chewing gum, or melting ice chips in your mouth can provide relief.

- *If you miss a dose...*
  Take it as soon as you remember. If it is almost time for the next dose, skip the one you missed and go back to your regular schedule. If you take Pamelor once a day at bedtime and you miss a dose, do not take it in the morning, since disturbing side effects could occur. Never take 2 doses at once.

- *Storage instructions...*
  Keep Pamelor in the container it came in, tightly closed and away from light. Be sure to keep this drug out of reach of children; an overdose is particularly dangerous in the young. Store at room temperature.

What side effects may occur?

Side effects cannot be anticipated. If any develop or change in intensity, inform your doctor as soon as possible. Only your doctor can determine if it is safe for you to continue taking Pamelor.

■ *Side effects may include:*

Abdominal cramps, agitation, anxiety, black tongue, blurred vision, breast development in males, breast enlargement, confusion, constipation, delusions, diarrhea, dilation of pupils, disorientation, dizziness, drowsiness, dry mouth, excessive or spontaneous flow of milk, excessive urination at night, fatigue, fever, fluid retention, flushing, frequent urination, hair loss, hallucinations, headache, heart attack, high or low blood pressure, high or low blood sugar, hives, impotence, inability to sleep, inability to urinate, increased or decreased sex drive, inflammation of the mouth, intestinal blockage, itching, loss of appetite, loss of coordination, nausea, nightmares, numbness, panic, perspiration, pins and needles in the arms and legs, rapid, fluttery, or irregular heartbeat, rash, reddish or purplish spots on skin, restlessness, ringing in the ears, seizures, sensitivity to light, stomach upset, strange taste, stroke, swelling of the testicles, swollen glands, tingling, tremors, vision problems, vomiting, weakness, weight gain or loss, yellow eyes and skin

■ *Side effects due to rapid decrease or abrupt withdrawal from Pamelor after a long term of treatment include:*

Headache
Nausea
Vague feeling of bodily discomfort

These side effects do not indicate addiction to this drug.

Why should this drug not be prescribed?

If you are sensitive to or have ever had an allergic reaction to Pamelor or similar drugs, you should not take this medication. Make sure your doctor is aware of any drug reactions you have experienced.

Do not take Pamelor if you are taking—or have taken within the past 14 days—an antidepressant drug classified as an MAO inhibitor. Drugs in this category include Nardil, Parnate, and Marplan. Combining these drugs with Pamelor can cause fever and convulsions, and could even be fatal.

Unless you are directed to do so by your doctor, do not take this medication if you are recovering from a heart attack or are taking any other antidepressant drugs.

Special warnings about this medication

Pamelor may cause you to become drowsy or less alert; therefore, you should not drive or operate dangerous machinery or participate in any hazardous activity that requires full mental alertness until you know how this drug affects you.

Use Pamelor with caution if you have a history of seizures, difficulty urinating, diabetes, or chronic eye conditions such as glaucoma. Be careful, also, if you have heart disease, high blood pressure, an overactive thyroid, or are receiving thyroid medication. You should discuss all of your medical problems with your doctor before taking this medication.

If you are being treated for a severe mental disorder (schizophrenia or manic depression), tell your doctor before taking Pamelor.

Pamelor may make your skin more sensitive to sunlight. Try to stay out of the sun, wear protective clothing, and apply a sun block.

Before having surgery, dental treatment or any diagnostic procedure, tell your doctor that you are taking Pamelor. Certain drugs used during these procedures, such as anesthetics and muscle relaxants, may interact with Pamelor.

Possible food and drug interactions
when taking this medication

Combining Pamelor and MAO inhibitors can be fatal.

Pamelor may intensify the effects of alcohol. Do not drink alcohol while taking this medication.

If Pamelor is taken with certain other drugs, the effects of either can be increased, decreased, or altered. It is especially important to check with your doctor before combining Pamelor with the following:

Acetazolamide (Diamox)
Airway-opening drugs such as Ventolin and Proventil
Amphetamines such as Dexedrine
Antispasmodic drugs such as Donnatal and Bentyl
Blood pressure medications such Catapres and Ismelin
Cimetidine (Tagamet)
Levodopa (Larodopa)
Other antidepressants such as Prozac
Quinidine (Quinaglute)
Reserpine (Diupres)
Thyroid medication such as Synthroid
Vitamin C (in large doses)
Warfarin (Coumadin)

Special information
if you are pregnant or breastfeeding
The effects of Pamelor during pregnancy have not been adequately studied. If you are pregnant or planning to become pregnant, inform your doctor immediately. Also consult your doctor before breastfeeding.

Recommended dosage
This medication is available in tablet and liquid form. Only tablet dosages are listed. Consult your doctor if you cannot take the tablet form of this medication.

ADULTS
Your doctor will monitor your response to this medication carefully and will gradually increase or decrease the dose to suit your needs.

The usual starting dosage is 25 milligrams, 3 or 4 times per day.

Alternatively, your doctor may prescribe that the total daily dose be taken once a day.

Doses above 150 milligrams per day are not recommended.

Your doctor may want to perform a blood test to help in deciding the best dose you should receive.

CHILDREN
The safety and effectiveness of Pamelor have not been established for children and its use is not recommended. However, adolescents may be given 30 to 50 milligrams per day, either in a single dose or divided into smaller doses, as determined by your doctor.

ELDERLY
The usual dose is 30 to 50 milligrams taken in a single dose or divided into smaller doses, as determined by your doctor.

Overdosage
An overdose of this type of antidepressant can be fatal. If you suspect an overdose, seek medical help immediately.

■ *Symptoms of Pamelor overdose may include:*
Agitation, coma, confusion, congestive heart failure, convulsions, decreased breathing, excessive reflexes, extremely high fever, rapid heartbeat, restlessness, rigid muscles, shock, stupor, vomiting

If you suspect a Pamelor overdose, seek medical attention immediately.

Brand name:

PANADOL

See Tylenol, page 1168.

Brand name:

PANCREASE

Pronounced: PAN-kree-ace
Generic name: Pancrelipase
Other brand names: Pancrease MT, Viokase, Ultrase

Why is this drug prescribed?

Pancrease is used to treat pancreatic enzyme deficiency. It is often prescribed for people with cystic fibrosis, chronic inflammation of the pancreas, or blockages of the pancreas or common bile duct caused by cancer. It is also taken by people who have had their pancreas removed or who have had gastrointestinal bypass surgery. Pancrease is taken to help with digestion of proteins, starches, and fats.

Most important fact about this drug

Pancrease capsules should not be chewed or crushed.

How should you take this medication?

Take this medication exactly as prescribed. If you are taking Pancrease for cystic fibrosis, your doctor may also prescribe a special diet for you. Be sure to follow the diet closely, as well as taking Pancrease.

Do not change brands or dosage forms of this medication without first checking with your doctor.

If swallowing the Pancrease capsule is difficult, open the capsule and shake the contents (microspheres) onto a small amount of soft food, such as applesauce or gelatin, that does not require chewing, then swallow immediately. Avoid mixing it with alkaline foods, such as ice cream or milk. They can reduce the medication's effect.

Pancrease should be taken with meals and snacks. Drink plenty of fluids while you are taking Pancrease.

■ *If you miss a dose...*
  Resume taking the medication with your next meal or snack.

■ *Storage instructions...*
Store at room temperature in a tightly closed container away from moisture. Do not refrigerate.

What side effects may occur?
Side effects cannot be anticipated. If any develop or change in intensity, inform your doctor as soon as possible. Only your doctor can determine if it is safe for you to continue taking Pancrease.

■ *More common side effects may include:*
Stomach and intestinal upset

■ *Less common or rare side effects may include:*
Allergic-type reactions

Why should this drug not be prescribed?
Pancrease should not be used if you are sensitive to or have ever had an allergic reaction to pork protein.

Special warnings about this medication
If you develop an allergic reaction to Pancrease, stop taking the medication and inform your doctor immediately. If you have cystic fibrosis and develop any signs of an intestinal blockage, call your doctor.

Possible food and drug interactions
when taking this medication
If Pancrease is taken with certain other drugs, the effects of either can be increased, decreased, or altered. It is especially important that you check with your doctor before combining Pancrease with the following:

Certain antacids such as Tums and Milk of Magnesia
Ulcer medications classified as H_2 histamine antagonists, such as
Pepcid and Zantac

Special information
if you are pregnant or breastfeeding
The effects of Pancrease during pregnancy have not been adequately studied. If you are pregnant or plan to become pregnant, inform your doctor immediately.

Recommended dosage

ADULTS

The usual dose ranges from 4,000 units to 20,000 units (more if necessary) with each meal and with snacks. Any increase in dosage should be made slowly.

Overdosage

Although no specific information is available, any medication taken in excess can have serious consequences. If you suspect an overdose of Pancrease, seek medical treatment immediately.

Generic name:

PANCRELIPASE

See Pancrease, page 796.

Brand name:

PARAFON FORTE DSC

Pronounced: PAIR-a-fahn FOR-tay DEE-ESS-SEE
Generic name: Chlorzoxazone

Why is this drug prescribed?

Parafon Forte DSC is prescribed, along with rest and physical therapy, for the relief of discomfort associated with severe, painful muscle spasms.

Most important fact about this drug

Be careful using this drug if you have allergies or have ever had an allergic reaction to a drug. If you have a sensitivity reaction such as hives, redness, or itching of skin while you are taking Parafon Forte DSC, notify your doctor immediately.

How should you take this medication?

Take Parafon Forte DSC exactly as prescribed by your doctor. Do not increase the dose or take it more often than prescribed.

Parafon Forte DSC occasionally discolors urine orange or purple red.

■ *If you miss a dose...*
Take it as soon as you remember, if it is within an hour or so of the missed time. Otherwise, skip the dose and go back to your regular schedule. Do not take 2 doses a once.

■ *Storage instructions...*
Store a room temperature in a tightly closed container.

What side effects may occur?
Parafon Forte DSC is generally well tolerated and rarely produces undesirable side effects. However, if any develop or change in intensity, inform your doctor as soon as possible. Only your doctor can determine if it is safe for you to continue taking Parafon Forte DSC.

■ *Uncommon and rare side effects may include:*
Bruises, dizziness, drowsiness, feeling of illness, fluid retention, light-headedness, overstimulation, red or purple spots on the skin, severe allergic reaction, skin rashes, stomach or intestinal disturbances or bleeding, urine discoloration

Why should this drug not be prescribed?
If you have had any reaction to this drug, notify your doctor. Make sure he or she is aware of any drug reactions you have experienced.

Special warnings about this medication
If you have any sign of a liver problem, stop taking the drug and contact your doctor.

Possible food and drug interactions
when taking this medication
Parafon Forte DSC may intensify the effects of alcohol. Be cautious about drinking alcohol while taking this medication.

If Parafon Forte DSC is taken with certain other drugs, the effects of either could be increased, decreased, or altered. It is especially important to check with your doctor before combining Parafon Forte DSC with drugs that slow the action of the central nervous system, such as Percocet, Valium, and Xanax.

Special information
if you are pregnant or breastfeeding
The effects of Parafon Forte DSC during pregnancy have not been adequately studied. If you are pregnant or plan to become pregnant, inform your doctor immediately. This drug may appear in breast milk and could affect a nursing infant. If this medication is essential to your health, your doctor may advise you to discontinue breastfeeding until your treatment is finished.

Recommended dosage

ADULTS

The usual dosage of Parafon Forte DSC is 1 caplet taken 3 or 4 times per day. If you do not respond to this dosage, your doctor may increase it to one and a half caplets (750 milligrams) taken 3 or 4 times per day.

Overdosage

Any medication taken in excess can have serious consequences. If you suspect an overdose, seek medical treatment immediately.

- *Symptoms of Parafon Forte DSC overdose may include:*
  Diarrhea
  Dizziness
  Drowsiness
  Headache
  Light-headedness
  Nausea
  Vomiting

- *Symptoms that may develop after a period of time include:*
  Feeling of illness
  Loss of muscle strength
  Lowered blood pressure
  Sluggishness
  Troubled or rapid breathing

Brand name:

PARLODEL

Pronounced: PAR-luh-del
Generic name: Bromocriptine mesylate

Why is this drug prescribed?

Parlodel inhibits the secretion of the hormone prolactin from the pituitary gland, thereby preventing production of breast milk. It also mimics the action of dopamine, a chemical lacking in the brain of someone with Parkinson's disease. It is used to treat a variety of medical conditions, including:

- Infertility in some women
- Menstrual problems such as the abnormal stoppage or absence of flow

- Excessive or spontaneous flow of milk
- Growth hormone overproduction leading to acromegaly, a condition characterized by an abnormally large skull, jaw, hands, and feet
- Parkinson's disease
- Pituitary gland tumors

Some doctors also prescribe Parlodel to treat cocaine addiction, the eye condition known as glaucoma, erection problems in certain men, restless leg syndrome, and a dangerous reaction to major tranquilizers called neuroleptic malignant syndrome.

Parlodel is also used to interrupt milk production in women who should not breastfeed for medical reasons.

Most important fact about this drug
Notify your doctor immediately if you develop a severe headache that does not let up or continues to get worse. It could be a warning of the possibility of other dangerous reactions, including seizure, stroke, or heart attack.

How should you take this medication?
Parlodel should be taken with food (in your stomach.) Take the first dose while lying down. You may faint or become dizzy due to lower blood pressure, especially following the first dose.

You may not feel the full effect of this medication for a few weeks. Do not stop taking Parlodel without first checking with your doctor.

- *If you miss a dose...*
  Take it as soon as you remember if it is within 4 hours of the scheduled time. Otherwise, skip the dose you missed and go back to your regular schedule. Do not take 2 doses at once.

- *Storage information...*
  Store at room temperature in a tightly closed, light-resistant container. Protect from excessive heat.

What side effects may occur?
The number and severity of side effects depend on many factors, including the condition being treated, dosage, and duration of treatment. Side effects cannot be anticipated. If any develop or change in intensity, inform your doctor as soon as possible. Only your doctor can determine if it is safe for you to continue taking Parlodel.

■ *More common side effects may include:*
Abdominal cramps or discomfort, confusion, constipation, depression, diarrhea, dizziness, drop in blood pressure, drowsiness, dry mouth, fainting, fatigue, hallucinations (particularly in Parkinson's patients), headache, inability to sleep, indigestion, light-headedness, loss of appetite, loss of coordination, nasal congestion, nausea, shortness of breath, uncontrolled body movement, vertigo, visual disturbance, vomiting, weakness

■ *Less common side effects may include:*
Abdominal bleeding, anxiety, difficulty swallowing, frequent urination, heart attack, inability to hold urine, inability to urinate, nightmares, nervousness, rash, seizures, splotchy skin, stroke, swelling in feet and ankles, twitching of eyelids

Some of the above side effects are also symptoms of Parkinson's disease.

■ *Rare side effects may include:*
Abnormal heart rhythm, blurred vision or temporary blindness, cold feet, fast or slow heartbeat, hair loss, heavy headedness, increase in blood pressure, lower back pain, muscle cramps, muscle cramps in feet and legs, numbness, pale face, paranoia, prickling or tingling, reduced tolerance to cold, severe or continuous headache, shortness of breath, sluggishness, tingling of ears or fingers

Why should this drug not be prescribed?
You should not be using Parlodel if you have high blood pressure that is not being treated or blood poisoning called toxemia of pregnancy. You should also not take Parlodel if you are allergic to it or to any other drugs considered to be ergot alkaloids, such as Bellergal-S and Cafergot.

Special warnings about this medication
Your doctor will check your pituitary gland thoroughly before you are treated with Parlodel.

Since Parlodel can restore fertility and pregnancy can result, women who do not want to become pregnant should use a "barrier" method of contraception during treatment with this medication. Do not use "The Pill" or oral contraceptives, as they may prevent Parlodel from working properly.

Notify your doctor immediately if you become pregnant while you are being treated with Parlodel.

If you have kidney or liver disease, consult your doctor before taking Parlodel.

If you are being treated with Parlodel for endocrine problems related to a tumor and stop taking this medication, the tumor may grow back rapidly.

If you are being treated for Parkinson's disease, the use of Parlodel alone or Parlodel with levodopa may cause hallucinations, confusion, and low blood pressure. If this happens, notify your doctor immediately.

If you have an abnormal heartbeat rhythm caused by a previous heart attack, consult your doctor before taking Parlodel.

If you experience a persistent watery nasal discharge while taking Parlodel, notify your doctor.

This drug may impair your ability to drive a car or operate potentially dangerous machinery. Do not participate in any activities that require full alertness if you are unsure about your ability to do so.

Your first dose of Parlodel may cause dizziness. If so, check with your doctor.

Possible food and drug interactions
when taking this medication
Combining alcohol with Parlodel can cause blurred vision, chest pain, pounding heartbeat, throbbing headache, confusion, and other problems. Do not drink alcoholic beverages while taking this medication.

Certain drugs used for psychotic conditions, including Thorazine and Haldol, inhibit the action of Parlodel. It is important that you consult your doctor before taking these drugs while on Parlodel therapy.

■ *Other drugs that may interact with Parlodel include:*
  Blood pressure-lowering drugs such as Aldomet and Catapres
  Metoclopramide (Reglan)
  Oral contraceptives
  Other ergot derivatives such as Hydergine

Special information
if you are pregnant or breastfeeding
The use of Parlodel during pregnancy should be discussed thoroughly with your doctor. If Parlodel is essential to your treatment, your doctor will carefully monitor you throughout your pregnancy.

Because Parlodel prevents milk flow, it should not be used by mothers who wish to breastfeed their infants.

Recommended dosage

ADULTS

Parlodel is available as 2.5-milligram tablets and 5-milligram capsules. Dosage information given is for 2.5-milligram tablets.

Excess Prolactin Hormone

If you are being treated for conditions associated with excess prolactin, such as excessive milk production, menstrual problems, infertility, or pituitary gland tumors, the usual starting dose is one-half to 1 tablet daily. Your doctor may add a tablet every 3 to 7 days, until the treatment works. The usual longer term dose is 5 to 7.5 milligrams per day and ranges from 2.5 to 15 milligrams per day.

Growth Hormone Overproduction

Treatment for the overproduction of growth hormones is usually one-half to 1 tablet with food at bedtime for 3 days. Your doctor may add one-half to 1 tablet every 3 to 7 days. The usual treatment dose varies from 20 to 30 milligrams per day. The dose should not exceed 100 milligrams per day. Your doctor will do a monthly re-evaluation.

Parkinson's Disease

Parlodel taken in combination with levodopa may provide additional treatment benefits if you are currently taking high doses of levodopa, are beginning to develop a tolerance to levodopa, or are experiencing "end of dose failure" on levodopa therapy.

The usual starting dose of Parlodel is one-half tablet twice a day with meals. Your dose will be monitored by your doctor at 2-week intervals. If necessary, your doctor may increase the dose every 14 to 28 days by 1 tablet per day.

CHILDREN

The safety and effectiveness of Parlodel have not been established in children under 15 years of age.

Overdosage

Any medication taken in excess can have serious consequences. If you suspect an overdose of Parlodel, contact your doctor immediately or seek other medical attention.

Generic name:

PAROXETINE

See Paxil, page 807.

Brand name:

PATHOCIL

Pronounced: PATH-oh-sill
Generic name: Dicloxacillin sodium

Why is this drug prescribed?

Pathocil is a penicillin-like antibiotic that treats certain bacterial infections caused by staph (staphylococci).

Most important fact about this drug

If you are allergic to either penicillin or cephalosporin antibiotics in any form, consult your doctor *before taking Pathocil.* There is a possibility that you are allergic to both types of medication and if a reaction occurs, it could be extremely severe. If you take the drug and feel signs of a reaction, seek medical attention immediately.

How should you take this medication?

It is important to take the entire amount of Pathocil prescribed, even if fever or other symptoms have disappeared.

Unless your doctor has told you otherwise, Pathocil should be taken 1 to 2 hours before meals or 2 hours after eating.

If you have previously experienced an allergic reaction to penicillin, you should wear a medical identification tag or bracelet.

- *If you miss a dose...*
  Take it as soon as you remember. If it is almost time for your next dose, and you take 2 doses a day, take the one you missed and the next dose 5 to 6 hours later. If you take 3 or more doses a day, take the one you missed and the next dose 2 to 4 hours later. Then go back to your regular schedule.

- *Storage instructions...*
  Store Pathocil capsules at room temperature in a tightly closed container. Suspension should be stored in the refrigerator. Discard any unused medication after 14 days.

What side effects may occur?

Side effects cannot be anticipated. If any develop or change in intensity, inform your doctor as soon as possible. Only your doctor can determine if it is safe for you to continue taking Pathocil.

■ *Side effects may include:*

Allergic reactions—delayed or immediate, black or hairy tongue, diarrhea, feeling of being sick, fever, gas, hives, itching, loose stools, low blood pressure, nausea, rashes, serum sickness-like symptoms (joint and muscle pain with fever and hives), stomach pain, vomiting, wheezing

Why should this drug not be prescribed?

Do not take Pathocil if you have ever had an allergic reaction to any penicillin medication.

Special warnings about this medication

Your doctor will probably take a complete drug and allergy history before prescribing Pathocil. Serious and, in rare instances, fatal allergic reactions have occurred with penicillin use. If you develop any allergy symptoms, contact your doctor immediately.

If you experience shortness of breath, wheezing, skin rash, mouth irritation, black tongue, sore throat, nausea, vomiting, diarrhea, fever, swollen joints, or unusual bruising or bleeding, stop taking Pathocil and contact your doctor immediately.

If you take Pathocil over a long period of time, you may develop an infection—called a superinfection—due to an organism that cannot be killed by Pathocil. If you have any symptoms of infection, contact your doctor.

Possible food and drug interactions
when taking this medication

If Pathocil is taken with certain other drugs, the effects of either could be increased, decreased, or altered. It is especially important to check with your doctor before combining Pathocil with the following:

Chloramphenicol (Chloromycetin)
Erythromycin (PCE, E.E.S., others)
Oral contraceptives
Probenecid (Benemid)
Tetracycline drugs such as Achromycin V

Special information
if you are pregnant or breastfeeding
The effects of Pathocil during pregnancy have not been adequately studied. If you are pregnant or plan to become pregnant, inform your doctor immediately. Penicillin appears in breast milk and may affect a nursing infant. If this medication is essential to your health, your doctor may advise you to stop breastfeeding until your treatment with Pathocil is finished.

Recommended dosage

ADULTS

Mild to Moderate Infections
The usual dose is 125 milligrams every 6 hours.

Severe Infections
The usual dose is 250 milligrams every 6 hours.

CHILDREN

Children weighing 88 pounds or more should be given the adult dosage. The following doses are for children weighing less than 88 pounds:

Mild to Moderate Infections
The usual total daily dose is 12.5 milligrams per 2.2 pounds of body weight divided into equal doses and taken every 6 hours.

Severe Infections
The usual total daily dose is 25 milligrams per 2.2 pounds divided into equal doses and taken every 6 hours.

Overdosage
Any medication used in excess can have serious consequences. If you suspect a Pathocil overdose, seek medical attention immediately.

Brand name:

PAXIL

Pronounced: PACKS-ill
Generic name: Paroxetine hydrochloride

Why is this drug prescribed?
Paxil is prescribed for a serious, continuing depression that interferes with your ability to function. Symptoms of this type of depression often include

changes in appetite and sleep patterns, a persistent low mood, loss of interest in people and activities, decreased sex drive, feelings of guilt or worthlessness, suicidal thoughts, difficulty concentrating, and slowed thinking.

Most important fact about this drug

Your depression may seem to improve within 1 to 4 weeks after beginning treatment with Paxil. Even if you feel better, continue to take the medication as long as your doctor tells you to do so.

How should you take this medication?

Take this medication exactly as prescribed by your doctor. Inform your doctor if you are taking or plan to take any prescription or over-the-counter drugs, since they may interact unfavorably with Paxil.

■ *If you miss a dose...*
Skip the forgotten dose and go back to your regular schedule with the next dose. Do not take a double dose to make up for the one you missed.

■ *Storage instructions...*
Paxil can be stored at room temperature.

What side effects may occur?

Side effects cannot be anticipated. If any develop or change in intensity, inform your doctor as soon as possible. Only your doctor can determine whether it is safe for you to continue taking this medication.

Over a 4-to-6-week period, you may find some side effects less troublesome (nausea and dizziness, for example) than others (dry mouth, drowsiness, and weakness).

■ *More common side effects may include:*
Constipation, decreased appetite, diarrhea, dizziness, drowsiness, dry mouth, gas, male genital disorders, nausea, nervousness, sleeplessness, sweating, tremor, weakness

■ *Less common side effects may include:*
Agitation, altered taste sensation, anxiety, blurred vision, burning or tingling sensation, decreased sex drive, drugged feeling, increased appetite, muscle tenderness or weakness, pounding heartbeat, rash, tightness in throat, twitching, upset stomach, urinary disorders, vomiting, yawning

Why should this drug not be prescribed?

Do not take Paxil if you are also taking an MAO inhibitor antidepressant or within 14 days after you discontinue treatment with this type of medication.

Special warnings about this medication

Paxil should be used cautiously by people with a history of manic disorders.

If you have a history of seizures, make sure your doctor knows about it. Paxil should be used with caution in this situation. If you develop seizures once therapy has begun, the drug should be discontinued.

If you have a disease or condition that affects your metabolism or blood circulation, make sure your doctor is aware of it. Paxil should be used cautiously in this situation.

Paxil may impair your judgment, thinking, or motor skills. Do not drive, operate dangerous machinery, or participate in any hazardous activity that requires full mental alertness until you are sure the medication is not affecting you in this way.

Possible food and drug interactions
when taking this medication

Do not drink alcohol during your treatment with Paxil.

If Paxil is taken with certain other drugs, the effects of either could be increased, decreased, or altered. It is especially important to check with your doctor before combining Paxil with any of the following:

Antidepressants such as Elavil, Tofranil, Norpramin, Pamelor, Prozac,
    Nardil, Marplan, and Parnate
Cimetidine (Tagamet)
Diazepam (Valium)
Digoxin (Lanoxin)
Flecainide (Tambocor)
Lithium (Lithonate)
Phenobarbital
Phenytoin (Dilantin)
Procyclidine (Kemadrin)
Propafenone (Rythmol)
Propranolol (Inderal, Inderide)
Quinidine (Quinaglute)
Thioridazine (Mellaril)
Tryptophan
Warfarin (Coumadin)

Special information
if you are pregnant or breastfeeding

The effects of Paxil during pregnancy have not been adequately studied. If you are pregnant or plan to become pregnant, inform your doctor immediately. Paxil appears in breast milk and could affect a nursing infant. If this medication is essential to your health, your doctor may advise you to discontinue breastfeeding until your treatment with Paxil is finished.

Recommended dosage

ADULTS

The usual starting dose is 20 milligrams a day, taken as a single dose, usually in the morning. Your physician may increase your dosage by 10 milligrams a day, up to a maximum of 50 milligrams a day.

CHILDREN

The safety and effectiveness of this drug in children have not been established.

ELDERLY

The recommended initial dose for elderly or weak individuals or those with severe kidney or liver disease is 10 milligrams a day. Your doctor may increase the dosage if needed, but it should not exceed 40 milligrams a day.

Overdosage

Any medication taken in excess can have serious consequences. If you suspect an overdose, seek medical attention immediately.

■ *The symptoms of Paxil overdose may include:*
  Drowsiness
  Enlarged pupils
  Nausea
  Rapid heartbeat
  Vomiting

Brand name:

PBZ-SR

Pronounced: pee-bee-zee ess-ar
Generic name: Tripelennamine hydrochloride

Why is this drug prescribed?

PBZ-SR is an antihistamine that relieves nasal stuffiness and inflammation and red, inflamed eyes caused by hay fever and other allergies. It is also used to treat: itching, swelling, and redness from hives and other rashes that are caused by mild allergic reactions; allergic reactions to blood transfusions; and, with other medications, anaphylactic shock (severe allergic reaction).

Antihistamines work by decreasing the effects of histamine, a chemical the body releases in response to certain irritants. Histamine narrows air passages in the lungs and contributes to inflammation. Antihistamines reduce itching and swelling and dry up secretions from the nose, eyes, and throat.

Most important fact about this drug

PBZ-SR can make you drowsy and less alert. Be very careful driving, operating machinery, or engaging in other potentially dangerous activities until you know how this medication affects you.

How should you take this medication?

Take PBZ-SR exactly as prescribed. The tablets should be swallowed whole, not crushed or chewed.

- *If you miss a dose...*
  Take it as soon as you remember. If it is almost time for your next dose, skip the one you missed and go back to your regular schedule. Do not take 2 doses at once.

- *Storage instructions...*
  Store at room temperature in a tightly closed container, away from moisture.

What side effects may occur?

Side effects cannot be anticipated. If any develop or change in intensity, inform your doctor as soon as possible. Only your doctor can determine if it is safe for you to continue taking PBZ-SR.

- *More common side effects may include:*
  Disturbed coordination
  Dizziness
  Drowsiness
  Dry mouth, nose, and throat
  Extreme calm (sedation)
  Increased chest congestion
  Sleepiness
  Stomach upset

■ *Less common or rare side effects may include:*
Allergic reactions (including rash, hives, sensitivity to light, anaphylactic shock—severe allergic reaction), anemia, an exaggerated sense of well-being, blood disorders, blurred vision, chills, confusion, constipation, convulsions, diarrhea, difficulty sleeping, difficulty urinating, double vision, excitement, fatigue, frequent urination, headache, hysteria, inability to urinate, irritability, loss of appetite, low blood pressure, nausea, nervousness, pounding heartbeat, rapid heartbeat, restlessness, ringing in the ears, stuffy nose, tightness in chest, vertigo, vomiting, wheezing

Why should this drug not be prescribed?
PBZ-SR should not be used in newborn or premature infants or in mothers who are breastfeeding their infants.

Do not take this medication if you are taking MAO inhibitor drugs such as the antidepressants Nardil, Parnate, and Marplan; or if you have the eye condition called narrow-angle glaucoma, peptic ulcer, symptoms of an enlarged prostate, bladder or intestinal obstruction, asthma, or other breathing disorders. Also, do not take this drug if you are sensitive to or have ever had an allergic reaction to it or to other antihistamines.

Special warnings about this medication
Remember that PBZ-SR can cause drowsiness. In children the effect can be either drowsiness or excitation.

Antihistamines can cause dizziness and may cause low blood pressure in people over age 60.

PBZ-SR should be used cautiously if you have the eye condition called glaucoma, an overactive thyroid gland, heart disease, high blood pressure, circulatory problems, or a history of bronchial asthma.

Possible food and drug interactions
when taking this medication
PBZ-SR may increase the effects of alcohol. Do not drink alcohol, or at least limit your consumption, while taking this medication.

If PBZ-SR is taken with certain other drugs, the effects of either could be increased, decreased, or altered. It is especially important to check with your doctor before combining PBZ-SR with the following:

Antidepressant drugs classified as MAO inhibitors, including Marplan and Nardil
Sedatives such as Nembutal and Seconal
Tranquilizers such as Librium, Valium, and BuSpar

Special information
if you are pregnant or breastfeeding

The effects of PBZ-SR during pregnancy have not been adequately studied. If you are pregnant or plan to become pregnant, inform your doctor immediately. PBZ-SR should be used during pregnancy only if clearly needed. Antihistamines are not recommended for nursing mothers. If this medication is essential to your health, your doctor may advise you to discontinue breastfeeding until your treatment is finished.

Recommended dosage

ADULTS

The usual dose is one 100-milligram PBZ-SR tablet in the morning and 1 tablet in the evening. If necessary, your doctor may prescribe one 100-milligram tablet every 8 hours.

CHILDREN

PBZ-SR tablets should not be given to children.

Overdosage

Any medication taken in excess can have serious consequences. An antihistamine overdose can be fatal, especially in infants and children. If you suspect an overdose, seek medical treatment immediately.

- *Symptoms of a PBZ-SR overdose may include:*
  Cardiovascular collapse
  Coma
  Decreased alertness
  Drowsiness

- *Symptoms more common in children may include:*
  Convulsions
  Dry mouth
  Excitement
  Fever
  Fixed, dilated pupils
  Flushing
  Hallucinations
  Involuntary wringing of the hands
  Lack of coordination
  Stimulation

Brand name:

PCE

See Erythromycin, Oral, page 405.

Brand name:

PEDIAPRED

Pronounced: PEE-dee-uh-pred
Generic ingredients: Prednisolone sodium phosphate

Why is this drug prescribed?

Pediapred, a steroid drug, is used to reduce inflammation and improve symptoms in a variety of disorders, including rheumatic arthritis, acute gouty arthritis, and severe cases of asthma. It may be given to people to treat primary or secondary adrenal cortex insufficiency (lack of or insufficient adrenal cortical hormone in the body). It is also given to help treat the following disorders:

Blood disorders such as leukemia and various anemias
Certain cancers (along with other drugs)
Connective tissue diseases such as systemic lupus erythematosus
Digestive tract diseases such as ulcerative colitis
Eye diseases of various kinds
Fluid retention due to nephrotic syndrome (a condition in which damage to the kidney causes a loss of protein in the urine)
High serum levels of calcium associated with cancer
Lung diseases such as tuberculosis
Severe allergic conditions such as drug-induced allergic reactions
Skin diseases such as severe psoriasis

Studies have shown that high doses of Pediapred are effective in controlling severe symptoms of multiple sclerosis, although they do not affect the ultimate outcome or natural history of the disease.

Most important fact about this drug

Pediapred decreases your resistance to infection; thus it is possible for you to get a new infection while taking this medication. Pediapred may also mask some of the signs and symptoms of new infection, which makes it difficult for a doctor to diagnose the actual problem.

How should you take this medication?
Pediapred may cause stomach upset and should be taken with food. Take this medication exactly as prescribed.

■ *If you miss a dose...*
Take it as soon as you remember. If it is almost time for your next dose, skip the one you missed and go back to your regular schedule. Never take 2 doses at the same time.

■ *Storage instructions...*
Store Pediapred in a cool place, and keep the bottle tightly closed. This medication may be refrigerated.

What side effects may occur?
Side effects cannot be anticipated. If any develop or change in intensity, inform your doctor as soon as possible. Only your doctor can determine if it is safe for you to continue taking Pediapred.

■ *Side effects may include:*
Abnormal loss of bony tissue causing fragile bones, abnormal redness of the face, backbone break that collapses the spinal column, bruising, cataracts, convulsions, dizziness, fluid retention (edema), fracture of long bones, glaucoma (increased eye pressure), headache, high blood pressure, increased sweating, loss of muscle mass, menstrual irregularities, mental capacity changes, muscle disease, muscle weakness, peptic ulcer (stomach ulcer with possible bleeding), protrusion of eyeball, salt retention, slow growth in children, slow wound healing, sugar diabetes, swelling of the abdomen, thinning of the skin, vertigo

Why should this drug not be prescribed?
This drug should not be used for fungal infections of the body.

Special warnings about this medication
You should not be vaccinated against smallpox while being treated with Pediapred. Avoid other immunizations as well, especially if you are taking Pediapred in high doses, because of the possible hazards of nervous system complications and a lack of natural immune response.

People who have never had measles or chickenpox should avoid exposure to these diseases. They can cause a serious or, in children, even fatal reaction.

If you are taking Pediapred and are subjected to unusual stress, notify your doctor. The drug reduces the function of your adrenal glands, and they may be unable to cope. Your doctor may therefore increase your dosage of this rapidly acting steroid before, during, and after the stressful situation.

Prolonged use of steroids may produce posterior subcapsular cataracts (a disorder under the envelope-like structure at the back of the eye that causes the lens to become less transparent) or the eye disease glaucoma, and may intensify additional eye infections due to fungi or viruses.

Average and high doses of this medication may cause an increase in blood pressure, salt and water retention, and an increased loss of potassium. Your doctor may have you decrease your salt intake and increase your potassium intake.

The effects of Pediapred may be intensified if you have an underactive thyroid or long-term liver disease.

If you have ocular herpes simplex (painful blisters of the eye), you should be careful using this drug because of the possibility of corneal perforation (puncture of the outer, transparent part of the eye).

The use of Pediapred may cause mood swings, feelings of elation, insomnia, personality changes, severe depression, or even severe mental disorders.

If you are being treated for a blood clotting factor deficiency, use aspirin with caution when taking Pediapred. Do not use this drug for any disorder other than that for which it was prescribed.

Your doctor will prescribe this medication very cautiously if you have ulcerative colitis (inflammation of the colon and rectum) where there is a possibility of a puncture, abscess, or other infection; diverticulitis (inflammation of a sac formed at weak points of the colon); recent intestinal anastomoses (a surgical connection between two separate parts of the colon); active or inactive peptic (stomach) ulcers; unsatisfactory kidney function; high blood pressure; osteoporosis (brittle bones that may fracture); or myasthenia gravis (a long-term disease characterized by abnormal fatigue and weakness of certain muscles).

Do not discontinue the use of Pediapred abruptly or without medical supervision.

If you should develop a fever or other signs of infection while taking Pediapred, notify your doctor immediately.

Possible food and drug interactions
when taking this medication
If Pediapred is taken with certain other drugs, the effects of either could be increased, decreased, or altered. It is especially important to check with your doctor before combining Pediapred with the following:

Amphotericin B

Aspirin

Barbiturates such as phenobarbital and Seconal

Carbamazepine (Tegretol)

Cyclosporine (Sandimmune)

Diabetes drugs such as Glucotrol

Diuretics such as Lasix

Estrogens such as Premarin

Isoniazid (Nydrazid)

Ketoconazole (Nizoral)

Nonsteroidal anti-inflammatory drugs such as Motrin

Oral contraceptives

Phenytoin (Dilantin)

Rifampin (Rifadin)

Special information
if you are pregnant or breastfeeding

The effects of Pediapred during pregnancy have not been adequately studied. If you are pregnant or plan to become pregnant, inform your doctor immediately. This medication may appear in breast milk and could affect a nursing infant. If this drug is essential to your health, your doctor may advise you to discontinue breastfeeding until your treatment is finished.

Recommended dosage

The starting dosage of Pediapred may vary from 5 milliliters to 60 milliliters, depending on the specific disease being treated.

Your doctor will adjust the dose until he or she is satisfied with the results. If your condition does not improve after a reasonable period of time, your doctor may switch you to another medication.

Once you have a favorable response, your doctor will determine your maintenance dosage by gradually decreasing the doses until you are taking the smallest amount that will keep an adequate response.

If you stop taking Pediapred after long-term therapy, your doctor will have you withdraw slowly, rather than abruptly.

For acute flare-ups of multiple sclerosis (MS), the usual dose is 200 milligrams per day of Pediapred for 1 week followed by 80 milligrams every other day or 4–8 milligrams of dexamethasone every other day for 1 month.

Overdosage

Although no specific information is available, any medication taken in excess can have serious consequences. If you suspect an overdose of Pediapred seek medical treatment immediately.

Brand name:

PEDIAZOLE

Pronounced: PEE-dee-uh-zole
Generic ingredients: Erythromycin ethylsuccinate,
Sulfisoxazole acetyl

Why is this drug prescribed?
Pediazole is prescribed for the treatment of severe middle ear infections in children.

Most important fact about this drug
Sulfisoxazole is one of a group of drugs called sulfonamides, which prevent the growth of certain bacteria in the body. However, sulfonamides have been known to cause rare but sometimes fatal reactions such as Stevens-Johnson syndrome (a rare skin condition characterized by severe blisters and bleeding in the mucous membrane of the lips, mouth, nose, and eyes), sudden and severe liver damage, a severe blood disorder (agranulocytosis), and a lack of red and white blood cells because of a bone marrow disorder.

Notify your doctor at the first sign of a side effect such as skin rash, sore throat, fever, abnormal skin paleness, darkened urine, reddish or purplish skin spots, or yellowing of the skin or whites of the eyes.

How should you take this medication?
Be sure to keep giving Pediazole for the full time prescribed, even if your child begins to feel better after the first few days. Keep to a regular schedule; the medication works best when there is a constant amount in the blood.

Pediazole can be given with or without food. However, you should not give this medication with or immediately after carbonated beverages, fruit juice, or tea. If the child develops an upset stomach, give the medicine with crackers or a light snack.

To prevent sediment in the urine and the formation of stones, make sure that the child drinks plenty of fluids during treatment with Pediazole.

This medication increases the skin's sensitivity to sunlight. Overexposure can cause a rash, itching, redness, or sunburn. Keep the child out of direct sunlight, or provide protective clothing.

Shake well before using.

■ *If you miss a dose...*
Give the forgotten dose as soon as you remember, then give the rest of the day's doses at evenly spaced intervals.

■ *Storage instructions...*
Store Pediazole in the refrigerator. Keep tightly closed. Do not allow it to freeze. Use within 14 days; discard unused portion.

What side effects may occur?
Side effects cannot be anticipated. If any develop or change in intensity, inform your doctor as soon as possible. Only your doctor can determine if it is safe to continue giving Pediazole.

■ *More common side effects may include:*
Abdominal cramping and discomfort
Diarrhea
Lack or loss of appetite
Nausea
Vomiting

■ *Less common or rare side effects may include:*
Anxiety, blood disorders, blood or stone formation in the urine, bluish discoloration of skin, chills, colitis, convulsions, cough, dark, tarry stools, depression, difficulty in urinating or inability to urinate, disorientation, dizziness, drowsiness, exhaustion, fainting, fatigue, fluid retention, flushing, fever, gas, hallucinations, headache, hepatitis, hives, inability to fall or stay asleep (insomnia), increased urine, inflammation of the mouth, irregular heartbeat, itching, lack of muscle coordination, low blood sugar, palpitations, rapid heartbeat, redness and swelling of the tongue, ringing in the ears, scaling of dead skin due to inflammation, sensitivity to light, severe allergic reactions, severe skin welts or swelling, shortness of breath, skin eruptions, skin rash, Stevens-Johnson syndrome, stomach or intestinal bleeding, swelling around the eye, temporary hearing loss, tingling or pins and needles, vertigo, weakness, yellow eyes and skin

Why should this drug not be prescribed?
If your child is sensitive to or has ever had an allergic reaction to erythromycin, sulfonamides, or drugs of this type, do not use this medication. Make sure that your doctor is aware of any drug reactions that your child has experienced.

Pediazole should not be used if your child is taking Seldane or Hismanal.

This medication should not be prescribed for infants under 2 months of age.

Pediazole should not be taken by pregnant women at the end of their pregnancy or by mothers nursing infants under 2 months of age.

Special warnings about this medication
If your child has impaired kidney or liver function or a history of severe allergies or bronchial asthma, caution should be exercised when giving Pediazole. Consult with your doctor.

Prolonged or repeated use of Pediazole may cause new infections. If your child develops a new infection (called a superinfection), talk to your doctor. A different antibiotic may be needed.

Your doctor may recommend frequent urine tests while your child is taking Pediazole.

Possible food and drug interactions when taking this medication
If Pediazole is taken with certain other drugs, the effects of either could be increased, decreased, or altered. It is especially important to check with your doctor before combining Pediazole with the following:

Astemizole (Hismanal)
Blood thinners such as Warfarin (Coumadin)
Bromocriptine (Parlodel)
Carbamazepine (Tegretol)
Cyclosporine (Sandimmune)
Digoxin (Lanoxin)
Disopyramide (Norpace)
Ergotamine (Cafergot, Ergostat)
Lovastatin (Mevacor)
Methotrexate (Rheumatrex)
Oral antidiabetic drugs such as Micronase
Phenytoin (Dilantin)
Terfenadine (Seldane)
Theophylline (Theo-Dur)
Triazolam (Halcion)

Special information
if you are pregnant or breastfeeding
This drug is not prescribed for adults, and should never be taken at term of pregnancy or when breastfeeding.

Recommended dosage

CHILDREN

The recommended dose for children 2 months of age or older is determined by weight. The total daily dose should be given in equally divided doses 3 or 4 times a day for 10 days.

- *Four-times-a-day schedule*
  Less than 18 pounds: Determined by doctor
  18 pounds: ½ teaspoonful
  35 pounds: 1 teaspoonful
  53 pounds: 1½ teaspoonfuls
  Over 70 pounds: 2 teaspoonfuls

- *Three-times-a-day schedule*
  Less than 13 pounds: Determined by doctor
  13 pounds: ½ teaspoonful
  26 pounds: 1 teaspoonful
  40 pounds: 1½ teaspoonfuls
  53 pounds: 2 teaspoonfuls
  Over 66 pounds: 2½ teaspoonfuls

Overdosage

Any medication taken in excess can have serious consequences. If you suspect an overdose, seek medical treatment immediately.

Generic name:

PEMOLINE

See Cylert, page 257.

Brand name:

PENETREX

Pronounced: PEN-eh-trecks
Generic name: Enoxacin

Why is this drug prescribed?

Penetrex is used to treat urinary tract infections, including cystitis (inflammation of the inner lining of the bladder caused by bacterial infection), and certain sexually transmitted diseases such as gonorrhea. It is a quinolone antibiotic.

Most important fact about this drug
Penetrex, like other antibiotics, works best when there is a constant amount in the blood and urine. To help keep the level constant, try not to miss any doses, and take them at evenly spaced intervals around the clock.

How should you take this medication?
Penetrex should be taken with a full glass of water, either 1 hour before or 2 hours after a meal. Do not take more than the prescribed dosage. Use up all the medicine. If you stop taking Penetrex too soon, your symptoms may return.

Be sure to drink plenty of fluids while taking Penetrex.

- *If you miss a dose...*
  Take it as soon as you remember. If it is almost time for your next dose, skip the one you missed and go back to your regular schedule. Do not take 2 doses at the same time.

- *Storage instructions...*
  Store at room temperature.

What side effects may occur?
Side effects cannot be anticipated. If any develop or change in intensity, tell your doctor as soon as possible. Only your doctor can determine whether it is safe for you to continue taking this medication.

- *More common side effects may include:*
  Nausea
  Vomiting

- *Less common or rare side effects may include:*
  Abdominal pain, agitation, back pain, bloody stools, chest pain, chills, confusion, constipation, convulsions, cough, depression, diarrhea, difficult or labored breathing, dizziness, dry mouth and throat, emotional changeability, excessive sweating, fainting, fatigue, fever, fluid retention and swelling, fungal infection, gas, general feeling of illness, hallucinations, headache, hives, inability to hold urine, indigestion, inflammation of the large intestine, inflammation of the mouth, inflammation of the stomach, inflammation of the vagina, inflamed eyes, joint pain, kidney failure, lack of coordination, loss of appetite, loss of feeling of identity, loss of memory, mental disorders, muscle pain, nosebleed, overactivity, palpitations (throbbing or fluttering heartbeat), purple or red spots on the skin, rapid heartbeat, ringing in the ears, sensitivity to light, skin

eruptions, skin peeling, sleepiness, tingling or pins and needles, tremor, twitching, vaginal yeast infection, vision disturbances, weakness

Why should this drug not be prescribed?
You should not take Penetrex if you are sensitive to this medication or to other quinolone antibiotics such as Cipro and Floxin.

Special warnings about this medication
Use Penetrex cautiously if you have disorders such as epilepsy, severe hardening of the arteries in the brain, and other conditions that might lead to seizures. Penetrex may cause convulsions.

In rare cases, other drugs in this class have caused severe, even fatal reactions, sometimes after a single dose. These reactions may include confusion, convulsions, difficulty breathing, hallucinations, hives, itching, light-headedness, loss of consciousness, rash, restlessness, swelling in the face or throat, tingling, and tremors. If you develop any of these symptoms, you should immediately stop taking Penetrex and seek medical help.

If you have experienced diarrhea when taking other antibacterial medications or develop it after you start taking Penetrex, be sure to tell your doctor. Penetrex may cause an inflammation of the bowel, ranging from mild to life-threatening.

Penetrex may cause dizziness or light-headedness and could impair your ability to drive a car or operate potentially dangerous machinery. Do not participate in any activities that require full alertness if you are unsure about the drug's effect on you.

You should avoid excessive exposure to direct sunlight while taking Penetrex. Stop taking Penetrex immediately if you have a severe reaction to sunlight, such as a skin rash.

Possible food and drug interactions
when taking this medication
If Penetrex is taken with certain other drugs, the effects of either could be increased, decreased, or altered. It is especially important to check with your doctor before combining Penetrex with the following:

Antacids containing calcium, magnesium, or aluminum, such as Maalox and Tums
Bismuth subsalicylate (Pepto-Bismol)
Caffeine (including certain drugs, coffee, tea, chocolate, and some soft drinks)
Cyclosporine (Sandimmune)
Digoxin (Lanoxin)

Ranitidine (Zantac)
Sucralfate (Carafate)
Theophylline (Theo-Dur)
Vitamins or products containing iron or zinc
Warfarin (Coumadin)

Special information
if you are pregnant or breastfeeding

The effects of Penetrex during pregnancy have not been adequately studied. If you are pregnant or plan to become pregnant, notify your doctor. Penetrex may appear in breast milk and may affect a nursing infant. Your doctor may have you stop nursing while you are taking this medication.

Recommended dosage

ADULTS

Uncomplicated Urinary Tract Infections
The usual dose is 200 milligrams every 12 hours for 7 days.

Other Urinary Tract Infections
The usual dose is 400 milligrams every 12 hours for 14 days.

Sexually Transmitted Disease (Gonorrhea)
The usual dose is 400 milligrams take in a single dose.

CHILDREN

Safety and efficacy of Penetrex have not been established for children under 18 years of age.

Overdosage

There is no information on overdosage with Penetrex. However, any medication taken in excess can have serious consequences. If you suspect a Penetrex overdose, seek medical help immediately.

Generic name:

PENICILLIN V POTASSIUM

Brand names: Beepen VK, Pen-Vee K, V-cillin K, Veetids

Why is this drug prescribed?

Penicillin V Potassium is used to treat infections, including:

Dental infection

Infections in the heart

Middle ear infections

Rheumatic fever

Scarlet fever

Skin infections

Upper and lower respiratory tract infections

Penicillin V works against only certain types of bacteria—it is ineffective against fungi, viruses, and parasites.

Most important fact about this drug

If you are allergic to either penicillin or cephalosporin antibiotics in any form, consult your doctor before taking penicillin V. There is a possibility that you are allergic to both types of medication; and if a reaction occurs, it could be extremely severe. If you take the drug and feel signs of a reaction, seek medical attention immediately.

How should you take this medication?

Penicillin V may be taken on a full or empty stomach, though it is better absorbed when the stomach is empty. Be sure to take it for the full time of treatment.

Doses of the oral solution of penicillin V should be measured with a calibrated measuring spoon. Shake the solution well before using.

- *If you miss a dose...*
  Take it as soon as you remember. If it is almost time for the next dose, and you take 2 doses a day, take the one you missed and the next dose 5 to 6 hours later. If you take 3 or more doses a day, take the one you missed and the next dose 2 to 4 hours later, or double the next dose. Then go back to your regular schedule.

- *Storage instructions...*
  Store in a tightly closed container. The reconstituted oral solution must be refrigerated; discard any unused solution after 14 days.

  Tablets and powder for oral solution may be stored at room temperature.

What side effects may occur?

Side effects cannot be anticipated. If any develop or change in intensity, inform your doctor as soon as possible. Only your doctor can determine if it is safe for you to continue taking this medication.

■ *Side effects may include:*
Anemia
Black, hairy tongue
Diarrhea
Fever
Hives
Nausea
Skin eruptions
Stomach upset or pain
Swelling in throat
Vomiting

Why should this drug not be prescribed?

You should not be using penicillin V if you have had an allergic reaction to penicillin or cephalosporin antibiotics.

Special warnings about this medication

If any allergic reactions occur, stop taking penicillin V and contact your doctor immediately.

If new infections (called superinfections) occur, consult your doctor.

If you have ever had allergic reactions such as rashes, hives, or hay fever, consult with your doctor before taking penicillin V.

Before taking penicillin, tell your doctor if you have ever had asthma, colitis (inflammatory bowel disease), diabetes, or kidney or liver disease.

For infections such as strep throat, it is important to take penicillin V for the entire amount of time your doctor has prescribed. Even if you feel better, you need to continue taking this medication. If you stop taking this medication before your treatment time is complete, your infection may recur.

Possible food and drug interactions
when taking this medication

If penicillin V is taken with certain other drugs, the effects of either could be increased, decreased, or altered. It is especially important to check with your doctor before combining penicillin V with the following:

Chloramphenicol (Chloromycetin)
Oral contraceptives
Tetracyclines such as Achromycin V and Sumycin

Special information
if you are pregnant or breastfeeding

The effects of penicillin V in pregnancy have not been adequately studied. If you are pregnant or plan to become pregnant, inform your doctor immediately. Penicillin V should be used during pregnancy only if your doctor determines that the potential benefit justifies the potential risk to the fetus. Since penicillin V appears in breast milk, you should consult with your doctor if you plan to breastfeed your baby. If this medication is essential to your health, your doctor may advise you to discontinue breastfeeding until your treatment is finished.

Recommended dosage

ADULTS AND CHILDREN 12 YEARS OLD AND OVER

Continue taking penicillin V for the full time of treatment, even if you begin to feel better after a few days. Failure to take a full course of therapy may prevent complete elimination of the infection. It is best to take the doses at evenly spaced times, around the clock.

For mild to moderately severe strep infections of the upper respiratory tract and skin, and scarlet fever
The usual dosage is 125 to 250 milligrams every 6 to 8 hours for 10 days.

For mild to moderately severe pneumococcal infections of the respiratory tract, including middle ear infections
The usual dosage is 250 milligrams to 500 milligrams every 6 hours until you have been without a fever for at least 2 days.

For mild staph infections of skin
The usual dosage is 250 milligrams to 500 milligrams every 6 to 8 hours.

For mild to moderately severe gum infections known as Vincent's gingivitis
The usual dosage is 250 milligrams to 500 milligrams every 6 to 8 hours.

To prevent recurring rheumatic fever and/or chorea (infective disorder of the nervous system)
The usual dosage is 125 milligrams to 250 milligrams 2 times a day on a continuing basis.

Prevention of bacterial endocarditis (inflammation of the heart membrane) in people with heart disease who are undergoing dental or surgical procedures

For oral therapy, the usual dose is 2 grams of penicillin V one-half to 1 hour before the procedure, then 1 gram 6 hours later.

•Overdosage

Any medication taken in excess can have serious consequences. If you suspect an overdose, seek medical attention immediately.

■ *Symptoms of penicillin V overdose may include:*
Diarrhea
Nausea
Vomiting

Brand name:

PENTASA

See Rowasa, page 984.

Generic name:

PENTAZOCINE WITH ASPIRIN

See Talwin Compound, page 1066.

Generic name:

PENTOXIFYLLINE

See Trental, page 1144.

Brand name:

PEN-VEE K

See Penicillin V Potassium, page 824.

Brand name:

PEPCID

Pronounced: PEP-sid
Generic name: Famotidine

Why is this drug prescribed?

Pepcid is prescribed for the short-term treatment of active duodenal ulcer (in the upper intestine) for 4 to 8 weeks and for active, benign gastric ulcer (in the stomach) for 6 to 8 weeks. It is prescribed for maintenance therapy, at reduced dosage, after a duodenal ulcer has healed. It is also used for short-term treatment of GERD (gastroesophageal reflux disease), a condition in which the acid contents of the stomach flow back into the esophagus, and for resulting inflammation of the esophagus. And it is prescribed for certain diseases that cause the stomach to produce excessive quantities of acid, such as Zollinger-Ellison syndrome. Pepcid belongs to a class of drugs known as histamine H_2 blockers.

Most important fact about this drug

To cure your ulcer, you need to take Pepcid for the full time of treatment your doctor prescribes. Keep taking the drug even if you begin to feel better.

How should you take this medication?

It may take several days for Pepcid to begin relieving stomach pain. You can use antacids for the pain, but should avoid taking them within 1 hour of a dose of Pepcid.

If you are taking Pepcid suspension, shake it vigorously for 5 to 10 seconds before use.

- *If you miss a dose...*
  Take it as soon as you remember. If it is almost time for your next dose, skip the one you missed and go back to your regular schedule. Do not take 2 doses at once.

- *Storage instructions...*
  Store at room temperature. Protect the suspension from freezing. Discard any unused portion after 30 days.

What side effects may occur?

Side effects cannot be anticipated. If any develop or change in intensity, inform your doctor as soon as possible. Only your doctor can determine if it is safe for you to continue taking Pepcid.

The most common side effect is headache.

- *Less common or rare side effects may include:*
  Abdominal discomfort, acne, agitation, altered taste, anxiety, breast development in males, changes in behavior, confusion, constipation,

decreased sex drive, depression, diarrhea, difficulty sleeping, dizziness, dry mouth, dry skin, facial swelling due to fluid retention, fatigue, fever, flushing, grand mal seizures, hair loss, hallucinations, hives, impotence, irregular heartbeat, itching, loss of appetite, muscle, bone, or joint pain, nausea, pounding heartbeat, prickling, tingling, or pins and needles, rash, ringing in ears, severe allergic reaction, sleepiness, vomiting, weakness, wheezing, yellow eyes and skin

Why should this drug not be prescribed?

If you are sensitive to or have ever had an allergic reaction to Pepcid, you should not take this medication. Make sure your doctor is aware of any drug reactions you have experienced.

Special warnings about this medication

If you have stomach cancer, Pepcid may relieve the symptoms without curing the disease. Your doctor will be careful to rule out this possibility.

Use Pepcid with caution if you have severe kidney disease.

Possible food and drug interactions
when taking this medication

If Pepcid is taken with certain other drugs, the effects of either can be increased, decreased, or altered. It is especially important that you check with your doctor before combining Pepcid with the following:

Itraconazole (Sporanox)
Ketoconazole (Nizoral)

Special information
if you are pregnant or breastfeeding

The effects of Pepcid during pregnancy have not been adequately studied. If you are pregnant or plan to become pregnant, inform your doctor immediately. Pepcid may appear in breast milk and could affect a nursing infant. If this medication is essential to your health, your doctor may advise you to discontinue breastfeeding until your treatment with this medication is finished.

Recommended dosage

ADULTS

For Duodenal Ulcer

The usual starting dose is 40 milligrams or 5 milliliters (1 teaspoonful) once a day at bedtime. Results should be seen within 4 weeks, and this medication should not be used at full dosage longer than 6 to 8 weeks. Your doctor may have you take 20 milligrams or 2.5 milliliters (½ teaspoonful) twice a day. The normal maintenance dose after your ulcer has healed is 20 milligrams or 2.5 milliliters (½ teaspoonful) once a day at bedtime.

Benign Gastric Ulcer

The usual dose is 40 milligrams or 5 milliliters (1 teaspoonful) once a day at bedtime.

Gastroesophageal Reflux Disease (GERD)

The usual dose is 20 milligrams or 2.5 milliliters (½ teaspoonful) twice a day for up to 6 weeks. For inflammation of the esophagus due to GERD, the dose is 20 to 40 milligrams or 2.5 to 5 milliliters twice a day for up to 12 weeks.

Excess Acid Conditions (such as Zollinger-Ellison Syndrome)

The usual starting dose is 20 milligrams every 6 hours, although some people need a higher dose.

If your kidneys are not functioning properly, your doctor will adjust the dosage.

CHILDREN

The safety and effectiveness of Pepcid have not been established in children.

Overdosage

Any medication taken in excess can have serious consequences. If you suspect an overdose, seek medical attention immediately.

Brand name:

PERCOCET

Pronounced: PERK-o-set
Generic ingredients: Acetaminophen, Oxycodone hydrochloride
Other brand names: Roxicet, Tylox

Why is this drug prescribed?

Percocet, a narcotic analgesic, is used to treat moderate to moderately severe pain. It contains two drugs—acetaminophen and oxycodone. Acetaminophen is used to reduce both pain and fever. Oxycodone, a narcotic analgesic, is used for its calming effect and for pain.

Most important fact about this drug

Percocet contains a narcotic and, even if taken only in prescribed amounts, can cause physical and psychological dependence when taken for a long time.

How should you take this medication?

Percocet may be taken with meals or with milk.

■ *If you miss a dose...*
If you take Percocet on a regular schedule, take it as soon as you remember. If it is almost time for the next dose, skip the one you missed and go back to your regular schedule. Never take 2 doses at once.

■ *Storage instructions...*
Store at room temperature.

What side effects may occur?

Side effects cannot be anticipated. If any develop or change in intensity, inform your doctor as soon as possible. Only your doctor can determine if it is safe for you to continue taking Percocet.

■ *More common side effects may include:*
Dizziness
Light-headedness
Nausea
Sedation
Vomiting

You may be able to alleviate some of these side effects by lying down.

■ *Less common or rare side effects may include:*
Constipation, depressed feeling, exaggerated feeling of well-being, itchy skin, skin rash, slowed breathing (at higher doses)

Why should this drug not be prescribed?

You should not use Percocet if you are sensitive to either acetaminophen or oxycodone.

Special warnings about this medication

You should take Percocet cautiously and according to your doctor's instructions, as you would take any medication containing a narcotic. If you have ever had a problem with alcohol addiction, make sure your doctor is aware of it.

If you have experienced a head injury, consult your doctor before taking Percocet. The effects of Percocet may be stronger for people with head injuries, and using it may delay recovery.

If you have stomach problems, such as an ulcer, check with your doctor before taking Percocet. Percocet may hide the symptoms of stomach problems, making them difficult to diagnose and treat.

If you have ever had liver, kidney, thyroid gland, or Addison's disease (a disease of the adrenal glands), difficulty urinating, or an enlarged prostate, consult your doctor before taking Percocet.

Elderly people or those in a weakened condition should take Percocet cautiously.

This drug may impair your ability to drive a car or operate potentially dangerous machinery. Do not participate in any activities that require full alertness if you are unsure about the drug's effect on you.

Possible food and drug interactions
when taking this medication
Alcohol may increase the sedative effects of Percocet. You should not take Percocet with alcohol.

If Percocet is taken with certain other drugs, the effects of either could be increased, decreased, or altered. It is especially important to check with your doctor before combining Percocet with the following:

Antidepressants such as Elavil, Nardil, Pamelor, and Parnate
Antispasmodic drugs such as Cogentin, Bentyl, and Donnatal
Major tranquilizers such as Thorazine and Mellaril
Other narcotic painkillers such as Darvon and Demerol
Sedatives such as phenobarbital and Seconal
Tranquilizers such as Xanax and Valium

Special information
if you are pregnant or breastfeeding
It is not known whether Percocet can injure a developing baby or affect a woman's reproductive capacity. Using any medication that contains a narcotic during pregnancy may cause physical addiction for your newborn baby. If you are pregnant or plan to become pregnant, inform your doctor immediately. As with other narcotic painkillers, taking Percocet shortly before delivery (especially at higher dosages) may cause some degree of impaired breathing in the mother and newborn. It is not known whether

Percocet appears in breast milk, possibly harming a nursing infant. If you are breastfeeding use Percocet only under a doctor's directions.

Recommended dosage

ADULTS

The usual dose is 1 tablet every 6 hours as needed.

CHILDREN

The safety and effectiveness of Percocet have not been established in children.

Overdosage

A severe overdose of Percocet can be fatal. If you suspect an overdose, seek medical help immediately.

■ *Symptoms of Percocet overdose may include:*
Bluish skin, eyes or skin with yellow tone, cold and clammy skin, decreased or irregular breathing (ceasing in severe overdose), extreme sleepiness progressing to stupor or coma, heart attack, low blood pressure, muscle weakness, nausea, slow heartbeat, sweating, vague bodily discomfort, vomiting

Brand name:

PERIACTIN

Pronounced: pair-ee-AK-tin
Generic name: Cyproheptadine hydrochloride

Why is this drug prescribed?

Periactin is an antihistamine given to help relieve cold- and allergy-related symptoms such as hay fever, nasal inflammation, stuffy nose, red and inflamed eyes, hives, and swelling. Periactin may also be given after epinephrine to help treat anaphylaxis, a life-threatening allergic reaction.

Some doctors prescribe Periactin to treat cluster headache and to stimulate appetite in underweight people.

Most important fact about this drug

Like other antihistamines, Periactin may make you feel sleepy and sluggish. However, some people, particularly children, may have the opposite reaction and become excited.

How should you take this medication?
Take Periactin exactly as prescribed by your doctor.

- *If you miss a dose...*
  Take it as soon as you remember. If it is almost time for your next dose, skip the one you missed and go back to your regular schedule. Do not take 2 doses at once.

- *Storage instructions...*
  Store at room temperature in a tightly closed container.

What side effects may occur?
Side effects cannot be anticipated. If any develop or change in intensity, tell your doctor immediately. Only your doctor can determine whether it is safe for you to continue taking Periactin.

- *Side effects may include:*
  Anaphylaxis (life-threatening allergic reaction), anemia, appetite loss, chest congestion or tightness, chills, confusion, constipation, convulsions, diarrhea, difficulty urinating, dizziness, dry mouth, nose, or throat, earlier-than-expected menstrual period, exaggerated feeling of well-being, excessive perspiration, excitement, faintness, fatigue, fluttery or throbbing heartbeat, frequent urination, hallucinations, headache, hives, hysteria, inability to urinate, increased appetite and weight gain, insomnia, irritability, lack of coordination, light sensitivity, low blood pressure, nausea, nervousness, rapid heartbeat, rash and swelling, restlessness, ringing in the ears, sleepiness, stomach pain, stuffy nose, tingling or pins and needles, tremor, vertigo, vision problems (double vision, blurred vision), vomiting, weight gain, wheezing, yellow eyes and skin

Older people, in particular, are likely to become dizzy or drowsy, or develop low blood pressure in response to Periactin.

Why should this drug not be prescribed?
Do not take Periactin if you are sensitive to it, or have ever had an allergic reaction to it or to a similar antihistamine.

Do not take Periactin if you are taking an antidepressant drug known as an MAO inhibitor. Drugs in this category include Nardil, Parnate, and Marplan.

Do not take Periactin if you have the eye condition called angle-closure glaucoma, a peptic ulcer, an enlarged prostate, obstruction of the neck of the bladder, or obstruction of the outlet of the stomach.

Newborn or premature infants should not be given this drug, nor should it be used by women who are breastfeeding an infant.

The elderly and those in a weakened condition should not take this drug.

Special warnings about this medication

Like other antihistamines, Periactin may make you drowsy or impair your coordination. Be very careful about driving, climbing, or operating machinery, or doing hazardous tasks until you know how you react to this medication.

Be cautious about taking Periactin if you have bronchial asthma, the eye condition called glaucoma, an overactive thyroid gland, high blood pressure, heart disease, or circulatory problems.

Possible food and drug interactions
when taking this medication

Avoid alcoholic beverages while taking Periactin.

If Periactin is taken with certain other drugs, the effects of either could be increased, decreased, or altered. It is especially important to check with your doctor before combining Periactin with the following:

Antidepressant drugs classified as MAO inhibitors, including Marplan,
     Nardil, and Parnate
Sedatives such as Nembutal and Seconal
Tranquilizers such as Librium and Valium

Special information
if you are pregnant or breastfeeding

Because of possible harm to the unborn baby, Periactin should not be used during pregnancy unless it is clearly needed. Periactin should not be taken by a woman who is breastfeeding. If you have just given birth, you will need to choose between breastfeeding and taking Periactin.

Recommended dosage

ADULTS

The usual initial dose is 4 milligrams (1 tablet or 2 teaspoonfuls) 3 times daily. Dosage may range from 4 to 20 milligrams a day, but most people will take between 12 and 16 milligrams. Some may need as much as 32 milligrams a day.

CHILDREN

Ages 2 to 6 Years

The usual dose is 2 milligrams (½ tablet or 1 teaspoon) 2 or 3 times a day; your doctor may adjust the dose if necessary. A child this age should not take more than 12 milligrams a day.

Ages 7 to 14 Years

The usual dose is 4 milligrams (1 tablet or 2 teaspoons) 2 or 3 times a day; your doctor may adjust the dose if needed. A child this age should not take more than 16 milligrams a day.

Overdosage

Any drug taken in excess may have serious consequences. An overdose of Periactin can be fatal. If you suspect an overdose, seek medical attention immediately.

■ *Symptoms of Periactin overdose may include:*
Dilated pupils
Dry mouth
Extreme excitement and agitation
Fever
Flushing
Stomach or bowel distress
Stupor or coma

Overdosage in children may produce hallucinations and convulsions.

Brand name:

PERIDEX

Pronounced: PAIR-i-decks
Generic name: Chlorhexidine gluconate

Why is this drug prescribed?

Peridex is an oral rinse used to treat gingivitis, a condition in which the gums become red and swollen. Peridex is also used to control gum bleeding caused by gingivitis.

Most important fact about this drug
Peridex may stain front-tooth fillings, especially those with a rough surface. These stains have no adverse effect on the gums, and usually can be removed by a professional cleaning.

How should you take this medication?
You should get a thorough dental cleaning and examination before beginning treatment with Peridex.

After brushing, thoroughly rinsing, and flossing your teeth, rinse with Peridex by swishing ½ fluid ounce (marked in the cap) around in your mouth for 30 seconds, then spit it out. Do not dilute Peridex and do not eat or drink for several hours after using this medication.

- *If you miss a dose...*
  Resume your regular schedule the next time you brush.

- *Storage instructions...*
  Protect from freezing.

What side effects may occur?
Side effects cannot be anticipated. If any develop or change in intensity, inform your doctor as soon as possible. Only your doctor can determine if it is safe for you to continue using Peridex.

- *More common side effects may include:*
  Change in taste
  Increase in plaque
  Staining of teeth, mouth, tooth fillings, dentures, or other appliances in the mouth

- *Less common or rare side effects may include:*
  Irritation of the mouth
  Scaling of the lining of the mouth

Why should this drug not be prescribed?
Unless you are directed to do so by your doctor, do not use Peridex if you have shown a sensitivity to or are allergic to Peridex.

Special warnings about this medication
If you have both gingivitis and periodontitis (disease of the tissue that supports and attaches the teeth), remember that Peridex is used only for gingivitis. Periodontitis may require additional treatment by your doctor or dentist.

The use of Peridex may leave a bitter aftertaste. Rinsing your mouth with or drinking water after using Peridex may increase the bitterness.

In addition to staining, Peridex can also cause an excess of tartar build-up on your teeth. It is recommended that you have your teeth cleaned at least every 6 months.

Foods may taste different to you for several hours after rinsing with Peridex. In most cases, this effect becomes less noticeable after continued use. Taste should return to normal when treatment with Peridex is finished.

**Possible food and drug interactions
when taking this medication**
No interactions with other drugs have been reported.

**Special information
if you are pregnant or breastfeeding**
The effects of Peridex during pregnancy have not been adequately studied. If you are pregnant or plan to become pregnant, inform your doctor immediately. It is not known whether this medication appears in breast milk. If it is essential for you to use Peridex, your doctor may advise you to stop breastfeeding until your treatment is finished.

Recommended dosage

ADULTS

The usual dose of undiluted Peridex is ½ fluid ounce. Rinse for 30 seconds twice a day, morning and evening, after brushing. Peridex should be spit out after rinsing and never swallowed.

CHILDREN

The effectiveness and safety of Peridex have not been established in children under 18 years of age.

Overdosage
If you suspect that a child of 22 pounds or less has swallowed 4 or more ounces of Peridex, seek medical attention immediately.

Also seek immediate medical attention if any child shows signs of alcohol intoxication such as slurred speech, staggering, or sleepiness, and you suspect he or she has swallowed Peridex.

If a small child swallows 1 or 2 ounces of Peridex, he or she may have an upset stomach and nausea.

Brand name:

PERSANTINE

Pronounced: per-SAN-teen
Generic name: Dipyridamole

Why is this drug prescribed?
Persantine helps reduce the formation of blood clots in people who have had heart valve surgery. It is used in combination with blood thinners such as Coumadin.

Some doctors also prescribe Persantine in combination with other drugs, such as aspirin, to reduce the damage from a heart attack and prevent a recurrence, to treat angina, and to prevent complications during heart bypass surgery.

Most important fact about this drug
Persantine is sometimes used with aspirin to provide better protection against the formation of blood clots. However, the risk of bleeding may also be increased. To reduce this risk, take *only* the amount of aspirin prescribed by the *same* doctor who directed you to take Persantine. If you need a medication for pain or a fever, do not take extra aspirin without first consulting your doctor.

How should you take this medication?
Persantine must be taken exactly as your doctor prescribes, at regularly scheduled times.

It is best to take Persantine on an empty stomach, with a full glass of water. However, if this upsets your stomach, you can take the drug with food or milk.

Do not change from one brand of dipyridamole to another without consulting your doctor or pharmacist. Products manufactured by different companies may not be equally effective.

- *If you miss a dose...*
  Take it as soon as you remember. If it is within 4 hours of your next scheduled dose, skip the dose you missed and go back to your regular schedule. Never take 2 doses at the same time.

- *Storage instructions...*
  Store at room temperature. Protect from excessive heat.

What side effects may occur?

Side effects cannot be anticipated. If any develop or change in intensity, inform your doctor as soon as possible. Only your doctor can determine if it is safe for you to continue taking Persantine.

■ *More common side effects may include:*
Abdominal distress
Dizziness

■ *Less common or rare side effects may include:*
Angina pectoris (crushing chest pain), diarrhea, feeling flushed, headache, itching, liver problems, skin rash, vomiting

Why should this drug not be prescribed?

There is no known reason to avoid this drug.

Special warnings about this medication

Use this medication carefully if you have low blood pressure.

Tell the doctor that you are taking Persantine if you have a medical emergency, and before you have surgery or dental treatment.

Possible food and drug interactions
when taking this medication

If Persantine is taken with certain other drugs, the effects of either could be increased, decreased, or altered. It is especially important to check with your doctor before combining Persantine with the following:

Aspirin
Blood thinners such as Coumadin
Indomethacin (Indocin)
Ticlopidine (Ticlid)
Valproic acid (Depakene)

Special information
if you are pregnant or breastfeeding

The effects of Persantine during pregnancy have not been adequately studied. If you are pregnant or plan to become pregnant, inform your doctor immediately. This drug appears in breast milk and may affect a nursing infant. If this medication is essential to your health, your doctor may advise you to discontinue breastfeeding until your treatment with this medication is finished.

Recommended dosage

ADULTS

The usual recommended dose is 75 milligrams to 100 milligrams, 4 times a day.

CHILDREN

The safety and effectiveness of this medication have not been established in children under 12 years of age.

Overdosage

Low blood pressure is the most common symptom of overdose and usually lasts for a short period of time. If this occurs, contact your doctor or emergency room immediately.

Brand name:

PHENAPHEN WITH CODEINE

See Tylenol with Codeine, page 1171.

Generic name:

PHENAZOPYRIDINE

See Pyridium, page 926.

Generic name:

PHENELZINE

See Nardil, page 708.

Brand name:

PHENERGAN

Pronounced: FEN-er-gan
Generic name: Promethazine hydrochloride

Why is this drug prescribed?

Phenergan is an antihistamine that relieves nasal stuffiness and inflammation and red, inflamed eyes caused by hay fever and other allergies. It is also used to treat itching, swelling, and redness from hives and other rashes; allergic reactions to blood transfusions; and, with other medications, anaphylactic shock (severe allergic reaction).

Phenergan is also used as a sedative and sleep aid for both children and adults, and is prescribed to prevent and control nausea and vomiting before and after surgery and to prevent and treat motion sickness. It is also used, with other medications, for pain after surgery.

Antihistamines work by decreasing the effects of histamine, a chemical the body releases in response to certain irritants. Histamine narrows air passages in the lungs and contributes to inflammation. Antihistamines reduce itching and swelling and dry up secretions from the nose, eyes, and throat.

Most important fact about this drug

Phenergan may cause considerable drowsiness. You should not drive or operate dangerous machinery or participate in any hazardous activity that requires full mental alertness until you know how you react to Phenergan. Children should be carefully supervised while they are bike-riding, roller-skating, or playing until the drug's effect on them is established.

How should you take this medication?

Take Phenergan exactly as prescribed.

■ *If you miss a dose...*
If you are taking Phenergan on a regular schedule, take the forgotten dose as soon as you remember. If it is almost time for your next dose, skip the one you missed and go back to your regular schedule. Never take 2 doses at once.

■ *Storage instructions...*
Tablets should be stored at room temperature, away from light. Suppositories should be stored in the refrigerator, in a tightly closed container.

What side effects may occur?

Side effects cannot be anticipated. If any develop or change in intensity, inform your doctor as soon as possible. Only your doctor can determine if it is safe for you to continue taking Phenergan.

■ *More common side effects may include:*
Blurred vision
Dizziness
Dry mouth
Increased/decreased blood pressure

Nausea
Rash
Sedation (extreme calm)
Sleepiness
Vomiting

■ *Rare side effects may include:*
Abnormal eye movements, blood disorders, confusion, disorientation, protruding tongue, sensitivity to light, stiff neck

Why should this drug not be prescribed?
Phenergan should not be used to treat asthma or other breathing difficulties or if you are sensitive to or have ever had an allergic reaction to it or to related medications, such as Thorazine, Mellaril, Stelazine, or Prolixin.

Special warnings about this medication
If you are taking other medications that cause sedation, your doctor may reduce the dosage of these medications or eliminate them while you are using Phenergan.

If you have a seizure disorder, Phenergan may cause your seizures to occur more often.

Avoid this medication if you have sleep apnea (periods during sleep when breathing stops).

Use Phenergan cautiously if you have heart disease, high blood pressure or circulatory problems, liver problems, the eye condition called narrow-angle glaucoma, peptic ulcer or other abdominal obstructions, or urinary bladder obstruction due to an enlarged prostate.

Phenergan may affect the results of pregnancy tests and can raise your blood sugar.

Some people have developed jaundice (yellow eyes and skin) while on this medication.

Tell your doctor if you have any uncontrolled movements or seem to be unusually sensitive to sunlight.

Remember that Phenergan can cause drowsiness.

Possible food and drug interactions when taking this medication
Phenergan may increase the effects of alcohol. Do not drink alcohol, or at least substantially reduce the amount you drink, while taking this medication.

If Phenergan is taken with certain other drugs, the effects of either could be increased, decreased, or altered. It is especially important to check with your doctor before combining Phenergan with the following:

Certain antidepressant drugs, including Elavil and Tofranil
Narcotic pain relievers such as Demerol and Dilaudid
Sedatives such as Halcion, Dalmane, and Seconal
Tranquilizers such as Xanax and Valium

Special information
if you are pregnant or breastfeeding

The effects of Phenergan during pregnancy have not been adequately studied. If you are pregnant or plan to become pregnant, inform your doctor immediately. Phenergan may appear in breast milk and may affect a nursing infant. If this medication is essential to your health, your doctor may advise you to discontinue breastfeeding until your treatment is finished.

Recommended dosage

Phenergan is available in tablet, syrup, and suppository form. Phenergan tablets and suppositories are not recommended for children under 2 years of age.

ALLERGY

Adults

The average oral dose is 25 milligrams taken before bed; however, your doctor may have you take 12.5 milligrams before meals and before bed.

Children

The usual dose is a single 25-milligram dose at bedtime, or 6.25 to 12.5 milligrams 3 times daily.

MOTION SICKNESS

Adults

The average adult dose is 25 milligrams taken twice daily. The first dose should be taken one-half to 1 hour before you plan to travel, and the second dose 8 to 12 hours later, if necessary. On travel days after that, the recommended dose is 25 milligrams when you get up and again before the evening meal.

Children

The usual dose of Phenergan tablets, syrup, or rectal suppositories is 12.5 to 25 milligrams taken twice a day.

NAUSEA AND VOMITING

The average dose of Phenergan for nausea and vomiting in children or adults is 25 milligrams. When oral medication cannot be tolerated, use the rectal suppository. Your doctor may have you take 12.5 to 25 milligrams every 4 to 6 hours, if necessary.

For nausea and vomiting in children, the dose is usually calculated at 0.5 milligram per pound of body weight and will also be based on the age of the child and the severity of the condition being treated.

INSOMNIA

Adults

The usual dose is 25 to 50 milligrams for nighttime sedation.

Children

The usual dose is 12.5 to 25 milligrams by tablets or rectal suppository at bedtime.

Overdosage

Any medication taken in excess can have serious consequences. If you suspect an overdose, seek medical treatment immediately.

- *Symptoms of Phenergan overdose may include:*
  Difficulty breathing
  Dry mouth
  Fixed, dilated pupils
  Flushing
  Loss of consciousness
  Slowdown in brain activity
  Slowed heartbeat
  Stomach and intestinal problems
  Very low blood pressure

Children may become overstimulated and have nightmares; rarely, they may have convulsions. The elderly may also become overstimulated.

Brand name:

PHENERGAN WITH CODEINE

Pronounced: FEN-er-gan
Generic ingredients: Promethazine hydrochloride, Codeine
phosphate

Why is this drug prescribed?

Phenergan with Codeine is used to relieve coughs and other symptoms of allergies and the common cold. Promethazine, an antihistamine, helps reduce itching and swelling and dries up secretions from the nose, eyes, and throat. It also has sedative effects and helps control nausea and vomiting. Codeine, a narcotic analgesic, helps relieve pain and stops coughing.

Most important fact about this drug

Phenergan with Codeine may cause considerable drowsiness. You should not drive or operate dangerous machinery or participate in any hazardous activity that requires full mental alertness until you know how you react to this medication. Children should be carefully supervised while they are bike-riding, roller-skating, or playing until the drug's effect on them is established.

How should you take this medication?

Take this medication exactly as prescribed.

■ *If you miss a dose...*
If you take Phenergan with Codeine on a regular schedule, take the forgotten dose as soon as you remember. If it is almost time for your next dose, skip the one you missed and go back to your regular schedule. Never take 2 doses at once.

■ *Storage instructions...*
Store at room temperature, away from light.

What side effects may occur?

Side effects cannot be anticipated. If any develop or change in intensity, inform your doctor as soon as possible. Only your doctor can determine if it is safe for you to continue taking Phenergan with Codeine.

■ *Side effects may include:*
Blurred vision, constipation, convulsions, decreased amount of urine, depressed feeling, difficulty breathing, disorientation, dizziness, dizziness on standing, dry mouth, exaggerated sense of well-being, fainting,

faintness, fast, fluttery heartbeat, feeling of anxiety, restlessness, flushing, headache, hives, inability to urinate, increased/decreased blood pressure, itching, light-headedness, nausea, passing hallucinations, rapid heartbeat, rash, sedation (extreme calm), sleepiness, slow heartbeat, sweating, swelling due to fluid retention (including the throat), vision changes, vomiting, weakness, yellowed skin or whites of eyes

■ *Side effects seen rarely include:*
Abnormal eye movements, blood disorders, confusion, skin sensitivity to light, protruding tongue, stiff neck

Why should this drug not be prescribed?
Phenergan with Codeine should not be used if you have asthma or other breathing difficulties or if you are sensitive to or have ever had an allergic reaction to codeine, promethazine, or related medications, such as Thorazine, Mellaril, Stelazine, or Prolixin.

Special warnings about this medication
It is possible to develop psychological and physical dependence on codeine. Although the likelihood of this is quite low with oral codeine, be cautious if you have a history of drug abuse or dependence.

Never take more cough syrup than has been prescribed. If your cough does not seem better within 5 days, check back with your doctor.

Codeine can cause or worsen constipation.

Phenergan with Codeine should be used with extreme caution in young children.

Use this medication very carefully if you have a head injury, the eye condition called narrow-angle glaucoma, peptic ulcer or other abdominal obstruction, urinary bladder obstruction due to an enlarged prostate, heart disease, high blood pressure or circulatory problems, liver or kidney disease, fever, seizures, an underactive thyroid gland, intestinal inflammation, or Addison's disease (a disorder of the adrenal glands). Be cautious, too, if you have had recent stomach/intestinal or urinary tract surgery. The very young, the elderly, and people in a weakened condition may have problems taking Phenergan with Codeine.

This medication may make you dizzy when you first stand up. Getting up slowly can help prevent this problem.

If you are taking other medications with sedative effects, your doctor may reduce their dosage or eliminate them altogether while you are using Phenergan with Codeine.

If you have a seizure disorder, this medication may cause your seizures to occur more often.

Avoid using Phenergan with Codeine if you have sleep apnea (periods during sleep when breathing stops).

Phenergan with Codeine may affect the results of pregnancy tests; and it can raise your blood sugar.

Tell your doctor if you have any involuntary muscle movements or seem to be unusually sensitive to sunlight.

Possible food and drug interactions when taking this medication

Phenergan with Codeine may increase the effects of alcohol. Do not drink alcohol, or at least substantially reduce the amount you drink, while taking this medication.

If Phenergan with Codeine is taken with certain other drugs, the effects of either could be increased, decreased, or altered. It is especially important to check with your doctor before combining Phenergan with Codeine with the following:

All antidepressant drugs, including Marplan, Nardil, Elavil and Prozac
Narcotic pain relievers such as Demerol and Dilaudid
Sedatives such as Seconal, Halcion and Dalmane
Tranquilizers such as Xanax and Valium

Special information if you are pregnant or breastfeeding

The effects of Phenergan with Codeine during pregnancy have not been adequately studied. If you are pregnant or plan to become pregnant, inform your doctor immediately. Phenergan with Codeine may appear in breast milk and may affect a nursing infant. If this medication is essential to your health, your doctor may advise you to discontinue breastfeeding until your treatment is finished.

Recommended dosage

ADULTS

The usual dosage is 1 teaspoon (5 milliliters) every 4 to 6 hours, not to exceed 6 teaspoons, or 30 milliliters, in 24 hours.

CHILDREN 6 YEARS TO UNDER 12 YEARS

The usual dose is ½ to 1 teaspoon (2.5 to 5 milliliters) every 4 to 6 hours, not to exceed 6 teaspoons, or 30 milliliters, in 24 hours.

CHILDREN UNDER 6 YEARS

The usual dose is ¼ to ½ teaspoon (1.25 to 2.5 milliliters) every 4 to 6 hours. The total daily dose should not exceed 9 milliliters for children weighing 40 pounds, 8 milliliters for 35 pounds, 7 milliliters for 30 pounds, and 6 milliliters for 25 pounds.

Phenergan with Codeine is not recommended for children under 2 years of age.

Overdosage

Any medication taken in excess can have serious consequences. An overdose of codeine can be fatal. If you suspect an overdose, seek medical treatment immediately.

- *Symptoms of an overdose of Phenergan with Codeine may include:*
  Bluish skin, cold, clammy skin, coma, convulsions, difficulty breathing, dilated pupils, dry mouth, extreme sleepiness, flushing, low blood pressure, muscle softness, nightmares, overexcitability, slow heartbeat, small pupils, stomach and intestinal problems, stupor, unconsciousness

Generic name:

PHENINDAMINE, CHLORPHENIRAMINE, AND PHENYLPROPANOLAMINE

See Nolamine, page 742.

Generic name:

PHENOBARBITAL

Pronounced: fee-noe-BAR-bi-tal

Why is this drug prescribed?

Phenobarbital, a barbiturate, is used as a sleep aid and in the treatment of certain types of epilepsy, including generalized or grand mal seizures and partial seizures.

Most important fact about this drug

Phenobarbital can be habit-forming. You may become tolerant (needing more and more of the drug to achieve the same effect) and physically and psychologically dependent with continued use. Never increase the amount of phenobarbital you take without checking with your doctor.

How should you take this medication?
Take this medication exactly as prescribed.

If you are taking phenobarbital for seizures, do not discontinue it abruptly.

■ *If you miss a dose...*
Take it as soon as you remember. If it is almost time for your next dose, skip the one you missed and go back to your regular schedule. Never take 2 doses at once.

■ *Storage instructions...*
Store at room temperature in a tightly closed container.

What side effects may occur?
Side effects cannot be anticipated. If any develop or change in intensity, notify your doctor as soon as possible. Only your doctor can determine whether it is safe for you to continue taking phenobarbital.

■ *Side effects may include:*
Abnormal thinking, aggravation of existing emotional disturbances and phobias, agitation, anemia, angioedema (swelling of face around lips, tongue, and throat, swollen arms and legs, difficulty breathing), allergic reactions (localized swelling, especially of the eyelids, cheeks, or lips, skin redness and inflammation), anxiety, confusion, constipation, decreased breathing, delirium, difficulty sleeping, dizziness, drowsiness, excitement, fainting, fever, hallucinations, headache, increased physical activity and muscle movement, irritability and hyperactivity in children, lack of muscle coordination, low blood pressure, muscle, nerve, or joint pain, especially in people with insomnia, nausea, nervousness, nightmares, psychiatric disturbances, rash, residual drowsiness, restlessness, excitement, and delirium when taken for pain, shallow breathing, sleepiness, slow heartbeat, slowdown of the nervous system, sluggishness, softening of bones, temporary cessation of breathing, vertigo, vomiting

Why should this drug not be prescribed?
Phenobarbital should not be used if you suffer from porphyria (an inherited metabolic disorder), liver disease, or a lung disease that causes blockages or breathing difficulties, or if you have ever had an allergic reaction to or are sensitive to phenobarbital or other barbiturates.

Special warnings about this medication
Remember that phenobarbital may be habit-forming. Make sure you take the medication exactly as prescribed.

Phenobarbital should be used with extreme caution, or not at all, by people who are depressed, or have a history of drug abuse.

Be sure to tell your doctor if you are in pain, or if you have constant pain, before you take phenobarbital.

Phenobarbital may cause excitement, depression, or confusion in elderly or weakened individuals, and excitement in children.

If you have been diagnosed with liver disease or your adrenal glands are not functioning properly, make sure the doctor knows about it. Phenobarbital should be prescribed with caution.

Barbiturates such as phenobarbital may cause you to become tired or less alert. Be careful driving, operating machinery, or doing any activity that requires full mental alertness until you know how you react to this medication.

Possible food and drug interactions
when taking this medication
Phenobarbital may increase the effects of alcohol. Avoid alcoholic beverages while taking phenobarbital.

If phenobarbital is taken with certain other drugs, the effects of either could be increased, decreased, or altered. It is especially important to check with your doctor before combining phenobarbital with the following:

Antidepressant drugs known as MAO inhibitors, including Marplan and
    Nardil
Antihistamines such as Benadryl
Blood-thinning medications such as Coumadin and Panwarfin
Doxycycline (Doryx, Vibramycin)
Griseofulvin (Fulvicin-P/G, Grifulvin V)
Narcotic pain relievers such as Percocet
Oral contraceptives
Other epilepsy drugs such as Dilantin, Depakene, and Depakote
Other sedatives such as Nembutal and Seconal
Steroids such as Medrol and Deltasone
Tranquilizers such as Xanax and Valium

Special information
if you are pregnant or breastfeeding
Barbiturates such as phenobarbital may cause damage to the developing baby during pregnancy. Withdrawal symptoms may occur in an infant whose mother took barbiturates during the last 3 months of pregnancy. If you are pregnant or plan to become pregnant, inform your doctor immediately.

Phenobarbital appears in breast milk and could affect a nursing infant. If phenobarbital is essential to your health, your doctor may advise you to stop breastfeeding until your treatment is finished.

Recommended dosage

ADULTS

Sedation
The usual initial dose of phenobarbital is a single dose of 30 to 120 milligrams. Your doctor may repeat this dose at intervals, depending on how you respond to this medication.

You should not take more than 400 milligrams during a 24-hour period.

Daytime Sedation
The usual dose is 30 to 120 milligrams a day, divided into 2 to 3 doses.

To Induce Sleep
The usual dose is 100 to 200 milligrams.

Anticonvulsant Use
Phenobarbital dosage must be individualized on the basis of specific laboratory tests. Your doctor will determine the exact dose best for you. The usual dose is 60 to 200 milligrams daily.

CHILDREN

Anticonvulsant Use
The phenobarbital dosage must be individualized on the basis of specific laboratory tests. Your doctor will determine the exact dose best for your child.

The usual dose is 3 to 6 milligrams per 2.2 pounds of body weight per day.

ELDERLY

If you are elderly or debilitated, your dose may be lower than the regular adult dose. People who have liver or kidney disease may also require a lower dose of phenobarbital.

Overdosage
Barbiturate overdose can be fatal. If you suspect an overdose, seek medical treatment immediately.

■ *Symptoms of phenobarbital overdose may include:*
Congestive heart failure, diminished breathing, extremely low body temperature, fluid in lungs, involuntary eyeball movements, irregular heartbeat, kidney failure, lack of muscle coordination, low blood pressure, poor reflexes, skin reddening or bloody blisters, slowdown of the central nervous system

Generic name:

PHENOBARBITAL, HYOSCYAMINE, ATROPINE, AND SCOPOLAMINE

See Donnatal, page 360.

Generic name:

PHENTERMINE

See Fastin, page 422.

Generic name:

PHENYTOIN

See Dilantin, page 331.

Brand name:

PHOSPHOLINE IODIDE

Pronounced: FOS-foh-lin I-o-dide
Generic name: Echothiophate iodide

Why is this drug prescribed?

Phospholine Iodide is used to treat chronic open-angle glaucoma, a partial loss of vision or blindness resulting from a gradual increase in pressure of fluid in the eye. Because the vision loss occurs slowly, people often do not experience any symptoms and do not realize that their vision has declined. By the time the loss is noticed, it may be irreversible. Phospholine Iodide helps by reducing fluid pressure in the eye.

Phospholine Iodide is also used to treat secondary glaucoma (such as glaucoma following surgery to remove cataracts), for subacute or chronic angle-closure glaucoma after iridectomy (surgical removal of a portion of the iris) or when a patient cannot have surgery or refuses it. The drug is also prescribed for children with accommodative esotropia ("cross-eye").

Most important fact about this drug
Avoid exposure to certain pesticides or insecticides such as Sevin and Trolene. They can boost the side effects of Phospholine Iodide. If you work with these chemicals, wear a mask over your nose and mouth, wash and change your clothing frequently, and wash your hands often.

How should you use this medication?
To use Phospholine Iodide:

1. To minimize drainage of Phospholine Iodide into your nose, your doctor may instruct you to apply pressure with the middle finger to the inside corner of the eye for 1 to 2 minutes after placing the drops in your eyes.
2. Wipe off any excess Phospholine Iodide around the eye with a tissue.
3. Wash off any Phospholine Iodide that may get onto your hands.

■ *If you miss a dose...*
If you use 1 dose every other day: Apply the dose you missed as soon as you remember, if it is still the scheduled day. If you do not remember until the next day, apply it as soon as you remember, then skip a day and start your schedule again.

If you use 1 dose a day: Apply the dose you missed as soon as you remember. If you do not remember until the next day, skip the dose you missed and go back to your regular schedule.

If you use 2 doses a day: Apply the dose you missed as soon as you remember. If it is almost time for your next dose, skip the one you missed and go back to your regular schedule.

Never apply 2 doses at once.

■ *Storage instructions...*
The eyedrops can be kept in the refrigerator for up to 6 months or stored at room temperature if used within 1 month.

What side effects may occur?
Side effects cannot be anticipated. If any develop or change in intensity, tell your doctor immediately. Only your doctor can determine whether it is safe to continue taking Phospholine Iodide.

■ *Side effects may include:*
Ache above the eyes, blurred vision, burning, clouded eye lens, cyst formation, decreased pupil size, decreased visual sharpness, excess tears,

eye pain, heart irregularities, increased eye pressure, inflamed iris, lid muscle twitching, nearsightedness, red eyes, stinging

Why should this drug not be prescribed?

You should not use Phospholine Iodide if you have an inflammation in the eye.

Most people with angle-closure glaucoma (a condition in which there is a sudden increase in pressure of fluid in the eye) should not use Phospholine Iodide.

If you have ever had an allergic reaction to or are sensitive to Phospholine Iodide or any of its ingredients, you should not use this medication.

Special warnings about this medication

Drugs such as Phospholine Iodide should be used cautiously (if at all) if you have or have ever had:

    Bronchial asthma
    Detached retina
    Epilepsy
    Extreme low blood pressure
    Parkinson's disease
    Peptic ulcer
    Recent heart attack
    Slow heartbeat
    Stomach or intestinal problems

If you notice any problems with your heart, notify your doctor immediately.

Stop taking the drug and notify your doctor immediately if you experience any of the following: breathing difficulties, diarrhea, inability to hold urine, muscle weakness, profuse sweating, or salivation.

If you will be using Phospholine Iodine for a long time, your doctor should schedule regular examinations to make sure that Phospholine Iodide is not causing unwanted effects.

Phospholine Iodide may cause vision problems. Be careful when driving at night or performing tasks in dim or poor light.

Possible food and drug interactions
when taking this medication

If Phospholine Iodide is taken with certain other drugs, the effects of either could be increased, decreased, or altered. It is especially important to check with your doctor before combining Phospholine Iodide with drugs such as Enlon, Mestinon, or Tensilon, used to treat myasthenia gravis, a condition of muscle weakness that usually affects muscles in the eyes, face, limbs, and throat.

Special information
if you are pregnant or breastfeeding

If you are pregnant or plan to become pregnant, inform your doctor immediately. No information is available about the safety of Phospholine Iodide during pregnancy.

Phospholine Iodide should not be used by women who are breastfeeding.

Recommended dosage

ADULTS

For Glaucoma
A dose of 0.03 percent should be used 2 times a day, in the morning and at bedtime. Your doctor may increase the dose if necessary. Your doctor may have you take 1 dose a day or 1 dose every other day, instead.

CHILDREN

For Accommodative Esotropia
Place 1 drop of 0.125 percent solution in both eyes at bedtime for 2 or 3 weeks to diagnose the condition.

Your doctor may then change the schedule to 0.125 percent every other day or reduce the dose to 0.06 percent every day.

The maximum dose usually recommended is 0.125 percent solution once daily.

If the eye drops are slowly withdrawn after a year or two of treatment, and the eye problem returns, your doctor may want you to consider surgery.

Overdosage

Any medication used in excess can have serious consequences. If you suspect an overdose of Phospholine Iodide, seek medical help immediately.

Brand name:

PILOCAR

Pronounced: PYE-low-car
Generic name: Pilocarpine hydrochloride
Other brand names: Isopto Carpine, Pilopine HS Gel

Why is this drug prescribed?
Pilocar causes constriction of the pupils (miosis) and reduces pressure within the eye. It is used to treat the increased pressure of open-angle glaucoma and to lower eye pressure before surgery for acute angle-closure glaucoma. It can be used alone or in combination with other medications. Glaucoma, one of the leading causes of blindness in the United States, is characterized by increased pressure in the eye that can damage the optic nerve and cause loss of vision.

Most important fact about this drug
There is no cure for glaucoma. Pilocar and similar drugs can keep ocular pressure under control, but only as long as you take them. You will probably need to continue treatment for life; and you must be sure to take the medication regularly.

How should you use this medication?
Follow these steps to administer Pilocar:

1. Wash your hands thoroughly.
2. Gently pull your lower eyelid down to form a pocket next to your eye.
3. Brace the eye drop bottle on the bridge of your nose or your forehead.
4. Tilt your head back and squeeze the medication into your eye.
5. Close your eyes gently. Keep them closed for 1 to 2 minutes.
6. Do not rinse the dropper.
7. Wait for 5 to 10 minutes before using a second eye medication.

To avoid contaminating the dropper and solution, do not touch the eyelids or surrounding areas with the tip of the dropper.

Do not use if the solution is discolored.

- *If you miss a dose...*
  Apply it as soon as you remember. If it is almost time for your next dose, skip the one you missed and go back to your regular schedule. Do not take 2 doses at once.

- *Storage instructions...*
  Store away from heat and light. Do not freeze.

  Keep the bottle tightly closed when it is not being used.

What side effects may occur?
Side effects cannot be anticipated. If any develop or change in intensity, inform your doctor as soon as possible. Only your doctor can determine if it is safe for you to continue using Pilocar.

■ *More common side effects may include:*
   Cloudy vision
   Detached retina
   Headache over your eye
   Nearsightedness
   Reduced vision in poor light
   Spasms of the eyelids
   Tearing eyes

■ *Rare side effects may include:*
   Breathing difficulty, diarrhea, excessive salivation, fluid in lungs, high blood pressure, nausea, rapid heartbeat, sweating, vomiting

Why should this drug not be prescribed?
Pilocar should not be used if you are sensitive to or have ever had an allergic reaction to any of the components of this solution. Your doctor will not prescribe it for you if you have an eye condition in which your pupils should not be constricted.

Special warnings about this medication
Pilocar may make it difficult for you to see in the dark. Be careful driving at night, or taking part in any hazardous activity in dim light.

Possible food and drug interactions
when using this medication
No interactions have been reported.

Special information
if you are pregnant or breastfeeding
The effects of Pilocar during pregnancy have not been adequately studied. If you are pregnant or plan to become pregnant, inform your doctor immediately. Pilocar may appear in breast milk and could affect a nursing infant. If this medication is essential to your health, your doctor may advise you to stop breastfeeding until your treatment with Pilocar is finished.

Recommended dosage

ADULTS

The usual starting dose is 1 or 2 drops up to 6 times a day, depending on the severity of the glaucoma and your response. During a severe attack, your doctor will tell you to put drops into the unaffected eye as well.

Overdosage

Any medication taken in excess can have serious consequences. If you suspect an overdose, seek medical attention immediately.

Generic name:

PILOCARPINE

See Pilocar, page 857.

Brand name:

PILOPINE HS GEL

See Pilocar, page 857.

Generic name:

PINDOLOL

See Visken, page 1197.

Generic name:

PIROXICAM

See Feldene, page 428.

Brand name:

PLAQUENIL

Pronounced: PLAK-en-ill
Generic name: Hydroxychloroquine sulfate

Why is this drug prescribed?

Plaquenil is prescribed for the prevention and treatment of certain forms of malaria.

Plaquenil is also used to treat the symptoms of rheumatoid arthritis such as swelling, inflammation, stiffness, and joint pain. It is also prescribed for lupus erythematosus, a chronic inflammation of the connective tissue.

Most important fact about this drug

Children are especially sensitive to Plaquenil. Relatively small doses of this medication have caused fatalities. Keep this drug in a child-proof container and out of the reach of children.

How should you take this medication?

Take Plaquenil exactly as prescribed for the full course of therapy.

If you have been prescribed Plaquenil for rheumatoid arthritis, it will take several weeks for beneficial effects to appear. Take each dose with a meal or a glass of milk.

■ *If you miss a dose...*
  And you take 1 dose every 7 days, take it as soon as you remember, then go back to your regular schedule.

  If you take 1 dose a day and you miss your dose, take it as soon as you remember. If you do not remember until the next day, skip the one you missed and go back to your regular schedule.

  If you take more than 1 dose a day, take it as soon as you remember if it is within an hour or so of the missed time. If you do not remember until later on, skip the missed dose and go back to your regular schedule. Do not take 2 doses at once.

■ *Storage information...*
  Store away from heat, light, and moisture.

What side effects may occur?

Side effects cannot be anticipated. If any develop or change in intensity, inform your doctor as soon as possible. Only your doctor can determine if it is safe for you to continue taking Plaquenil.

■ *Side effects of treatment for an acute malarial attack may include:*
  Abdominal cramps
  Diarrhea
  Dizziness
  Lack or loss of appetite

Mild headache
Nausea
Vomiting

■ *Side effects of treatment for lupus erythematosus and rheumatoid arthritis may include:*
Abdominal cramps, abnormal eye pigmentation, anemia, bleaching of hair, blind spots, blood disorders, blurred vision, convulsions, decreased vision, diarrhea, difficulty focusing the eyes, dizziness, emotional changes, excessive coloring of the skin, eye muscle paralysis, "foggy vision," halos around lights, headache, hearing loss, hives, involuntary eyeball movement, irritability, itching, lack of muscle coordination, light flashes and streaks, light intolerance, loss of hair, loss or lack of appetite, muscle weakness, nausea, nervousness, nightmares, psoriasis (dry, scaly, red skin patches), reading difficulties, ringing in the ears, skin eruptions, skin inflammation and scaling, skin rash, vertigo, vomiting, weariness, weight loss

Why should this drug not be prescribed?
If you are sensitive to or have ever had an allergic reaction to Plaquenil or similar drugs such as Aralen and Chloroquine, you should not take this medication. Make sure your doctor is aware of any drug reactions you have experienced.

Plaquenil should not be prescribed if you have suffered partial or complete loss of vision in small areas while taking this medication or similar drugs. Notify your doctor of any past or present visual changes you have experienced.

This drug should not be used for long-term therapy in children.

Special warnings about this medication
Unless you are directed to do so by your doctor, do not take this medication if you have psoriasis (a recurrent skin disorder characterized by patches of red, dry, scaly skin) or porphyria (an inherited metabolic disorder affecting the liver or bone marrow). The use of Plaquenil may cause a severe attack of psoriasis and may increase the severity of porphyria.

Disorders of the retina causing impairment or loss of vision may be related to the length of time and the dose of Plaquenil given for lupus and rheumatoid arthritis. Problems have occurred several months to several years after beginning daily therapy. When you are on prolonged therapy your doctor will perform eye examinations at the beginning of treatment and every 3 months after that. Visual disturbances may progress, even after you have stopped taking this drug. If you have any problem with your vision or your eyes, notify your doctor immediately.

All people on long-term therapy with this drug should have a physical examination periodically, including testing of knee and ankle reflexes, to detect any evidence of muscular weakness.

Consult your doctor if you experience ringing in the ears, or other hearing problems.

If you are being treated for rheumatoid arthritis and have shown no improvement (such as reduced joint swelling or increased mobility) within 6 months, your doctor may decide to discontinue this drug.

Plaquenil should be used with caution by alcoholics and those who have liver disease or kidney problems.

Your doctor should conduct periodic blood cell counts if you are on prolonged therapy with this medication. If any severe blood disorder develops that is not attributed to the disease you are being treated for, your doctor may discontinue use of this drug.

Consult your doctor if you are taking a drug that has a tendency to produce dermatitis (inflammation of the skin), because you may have some skin reactions while taking Plaquenil.

Possible food and drug interactions
when taking this medication

If Plaquenil is taken with certain other drugs, the effects of either could be increased, decreased, or altered. It is especially important to check with your doctor before combining Plaquenil with the following:

   Any medication that may cause liver damage
   Aurothioglucose (Solganal)
   Cimetidine (Tagamet)
   Digoxin (Lanoxin)

Special information
if you are pregnant or breastfeeding

Use of this drug during pregnancy should be avoided except in the suppression or treatment of malaria when, in the judgment of your doctor, the benefit outweighs the possible hazard. This drug may appear in breast milk and could affect a nursing infant. If this medication is essential to your health, your doctor may advise you to discontinue breastfeeding until your treatment is finished.

Recommended dosage

ADULTS

Restraint or Prevention of Malaria

The usual dose is 400 milligrams taken once every 7 days on exactly the same day of each week. If circumstances permit, preventive therapy should begin 2 weeks prior to exposure. If this is not possible, your doctor will have you take a starting dose of 800 milligrams, which may be divided into 2 doses taken 6 hours apart. You should continue this suppressive therapy for 8 weeks after leaving the area where malaria occurs.

Acute Attack of Malaria

The usual starting dose is 800 milligrams, to be followed by 400 milligrams in 6 to 8 hours and 400 milligrams on each of 2 consecutive days.

Alternatively, your doctor may prescribe a single dose of 800 milligrams.

Lupus Erythematosus

The usual starting dose for adults is 400 milligrams once or twice daily. You will continue to take this dose for several weeks or months, depending on your response. For longer-term maintenance therapy, your doctor may reduce the dose to 200 to 400 milligrams per day.

Rheumatoid Arthritis

The usual starting dose for adults is 400 to 600 milligrams a day taken with a meal or a glass of milk. If your condition improves, usually within 4 to 12 weeks, your doctor will reduce the dose to a maintenance level of 200 to 400 milligrams daily.

CHILDREN

For the treatment of malaria, your doctor will calculate the dosage on the basis of your child's weight.

This drug has not been proved safe for treatment of juvenile arthritis.

Overdosage

Any medication taken in excess can have serious consequences. If you suspect an overdose, seek emergency medical treatment immediately.

- *Symptoms of an overdose of Plaquenil may occur within 30 minutes. They include:*
  Convulsions
  Drowsiness

Headache
Heart problems and failure
Inability to breathe
Visual problems

Brand name:

PLENDIL

Pronounced: PLEN-dill
Generic name: Felodipine

Why is this drug prescribed?
Plendil is prescribed for the treatment of high blood pressure. It is effective alone or in combination with other high blood pressure medications. A type of medication called a calcium channel blocker, Plendil eases the workload of the heart by slowing down its muscle contractions and the passage of nerve impulses through it. This improves blood flow through the heart and throughout the body, reduces blood pressure, and helps prevent angina pain (chest pain, often accompanied by a feeling of choking, usually caused by lack of oxygen in the heart due to clogged arteries).

Most important fact about this drug
If you have high blood pressure, you must take Plendil regularly for it to be effective. Since blood pressure declines gradually, it may be several weeks before you get the full benefit of Plendil; you must continue taking it even if you are feeling well. Plendil does not cure high blood pressure; it merely keeps it under control.

How should you take this medication?
Plendil can be taken with or without food. The tablets should be swallowed whole, not crushed or chewed.

Try not to miss any doses. If Plendil is not taken regularly, your blood pressure may increase.

- *If you miss a dose...*
  Take the forgotten dose as soon as you remember. If it is almost time for the next dose, skip the one you missed and go back to your regular schedule. Never try to "catch up" by doubling the dose.

- *Storage instructions...*
  Store at room temperature. Protect from light.

What side effects may occur?
Side effects cannot be anticipated. If any develop or change in intensity, inform your doctor as soon as possible. Only your doctor can determine if it is safe for you to continue taking Plendil.

■ *More common side effects may include:*
Flushing
Headache
Swelling of the legs and feet

■ *Less common or rare side effects may include:*
Anemia, angina pectoris (chest pain), ankle pain, anxiety disorders, arm pain, arthritis, back pain, blurred vision, bronchitis, bruising, constipation, cough, diarrhea, dizziness, decreased sex drive, depression, difficulty sleeping, dry mouth, enlarged gums, excessive nighttime urination, excessive perspiration, facial swelling, fainting, fatigue, flu, foot pain, frequent urination, gas, muscle pain, heart attack, hip pain, hives, impotence, inflammation of the nose, irregular heartbeat, irritability, itching, joint pain, knee pain, leg pain, low blood pressure, nausea, neck pain, nervousness, nosebleeds, painful or difficult urination, rapid heartbeat, rash, respiratory infections, ringing in the ears, shortness of breath, shoulder pain, sinus inflammation, sleepiness, sneezing, sore throat, stomach and intestinal pain, tingling sensation, tremor, urgent urination, vomiting, warm sensation, weakness

Why should this drug not be prescribed?
If you are sensitive to or have ever had an allergic reaction to Plendil or other calcium channel blockers, such as Calan and Procardia, you should not take this medication. Make sure your doctor is aware of any drug reactions you have experienced.

Special warnings about this medication
Plendil can cause your blood pressure to become too low. If you feel light-headed or faint, or if you feel your heart racing or you experience chest pain, contact your doctor immediately.

If you have congestive heart failure, Plendil should be used with caution, especially if you are also taking one of the "beta-blocker" family of drugs, such as Inderal or Tenormin.

Your legs and feet may swell when you start taking Plendil, usually within the first 2 to 3 weeks of treatment.

If you have liver disease or are over age 65, your doctor should monitor your blood pressure carefully while adjusting your dosage of Plendil.

Your gums may become swollen and sore while you are taking Plendil. Good dental hygiene will help control this problem.

Possible food and drug interactions when taking this medication

If Plendil is taken with certain other drugs, the effects of either could be increased, decreased, or altered. It is especially important to check with your doctor before combining Plendil with the following:

Beta-blocking blood pressure medicines such as Lopressor, Inderal, and Tenormin
Cimetidine (Tagamet)
Digoxin (Lanoxin)
Epilepsy medications such as Tegretol and Dilantin
Erythromycin (PCE, ERYC, others)
Phenobarbital
Theophylline (Theo-Dur)

Special information if you are pregnant or breastfeeding

Although the effects of Plendil during pregnancy have not been adequately studied in humans, birth defects have occurred in animal studies. If you are pregnant or plan to become pregnant, inform your doctor immediately. Plendil may appear in breast milk and may affect a nursing infant. If this medication is essential to your health, your doctor may advise you to discontinue breastfeeding until your treatment is finished.

Recommended dosage

ADULTS

Your doctor will adjust the dosage according to your response to the drug.

The usual starting dose is 5 milligrams once a day; your doctor will adjust the dose at intervals of not less than 2 weeks.

The usual dosage range is 5 to 10 milligrams once daily. The maximum recommended daily dose is 20 milligrams once a day.

CHILDREN

The safety and effectiveness of Plendil in children have not been established.

ELDERLY

If you are over 65 years of age, your doctor will monitor your blood pressure closely during dosage adjustment. In general, you should not take more than 10 milligrams a day.

Overdosage

Any medication taken in excess can have serious consequences. If you suspect an overdose, seek medical treatment immediately.

■ *Symptoms of Plendil overdose may include:*
Severely low blood pressure
Slow heartbeat

Brand name:

POLARAMINE

Pronounced: poll-AR-ah-meen
Generic name: Dexchlorpheniramine maleate

Why is this drug prescribed?

Polaramine is an antihistamine that relieves allergy symptoms, including: nasal stuffiness and inflammation and eye irritation caused by hay fever and other allergies; itching, swelling, and redness from hives and other rashes; allergic reactions to blood transfusions; and, with other medications, anaphylactic shock (severe allergic reaction).

Antihistamines work by decreasing the effects of histamine, a chemical the body releases in response to certain irritants. Histamine narrows air passages in the lungs and contributes to inflammation. Antihistamines reduce itching and swelling and dry up secretions from the nose, eyes, and throat.

Most important fact about this drug

Polaramine may cause drowsiness. You should not drive or operate dangerous machinery or participate in any hazardous activity that requires full mental alertness until you know how you react to this medication.

How should you take this medication?

If your mouth feels very dry while you are taking Polaramine, try using candy or gum or melt small chips of ice in your mouth.

Polaramine should be taken exactly as prescribed by your doctor.

■ *If you miss a dose...*
If you are taking Polaramine on a regular schedule, take the dose you missed as soon as you remember. If it is almost time for your next dose, skip the missed dose and go back to your regular schedule. Do not take 2 doses at once.

■ *Storage instructions...*
Store away from heat, light, and moisture. Protect the syrup from freezing.

What side effects may occur?
Side effects cannot be anticipated. If any develop or change in intensity, inform your doctor as soon as possible. Only your doctor can determine if it is safe for you to continue taking Polaramine.

■ *Most common side effects may include:*
Mild to moderate drowsiness
Thickening of mucus

■ *Less common or rare side effects may include:*
Anaphylactic shock (severe allergic reaction), blurred vision, chest congestion, chills, confusion, constipation, convulsions, diarrhea, difficulty sleeping, difficulty urinating, disturbed coordination, dizziness, dry mouth, nose and throat, early menstruation, excessive perspiration, excitement (especially in children), extreme fatigue, exaggerated sense of well-being, fever, frequent urination, headache, hives, hysteria, irritability, loss of appetite, low blood pressure, nausea, nervousness, nightmares, painful urination, pounding heartbeat, premature heart contractions, rapid heartbeat, rash, restlessness, ringing in ears, sedation (extreme calm), sensitivity to sun, sore throat, stomach upset or pain, stuffy nose, sweating, tightness in chest, tingling or "pins and needles", tiredness, tremor, unusual bleeding or bruising, urinary retention, vertigo, vomiting, weakness, wheezing

Why should this drug not be prescribed?
Polaramine should not be used in newborn or premature infants.

Do not take this medication if you are taking an antidepressant drug known as an MAO inhibitor (Parnate, Nardil, others), if you have asthma or other breathing difficulties, or if you are sensitive to or have ever had an allergic reaction to Polaramine or other medications with a similar chemical composition, such as Chlor-Trimeton.

Special warnings about this medication

Use Polaramine with care if you have the eye condition known as glaucoma, an obstructive peptic ulcer or other stomach problems, symptoms of an enlarged prostate, difficulty urinating, a history of bronchial asthma, an overactive thyroid, heart disease, circulatory problems, or high blood pressure.

Antihistamines may cause dizziness, and low blood pressure in the elderly (age 60 and over).

If you are taking large amounts of aspirin, for arthritis or rheumatism, for example, Polaramine may hide some effects of the aspirin, such as ringing in the ears.

Remember that Polaramine may make you feel drowsy.

Possible food and drug interactions
when taking this medication

Polaramine can cause extremely low blood pressure when taken with MAO inhibitor drugs such as the antidepressants Nardil and Parnate, and should never be taken with them.

Alcohol may increase the effects of Polaramine. Avoid alcohol while taking this medication.

If Polaramine is taken with certain other drugs, the effects of either could be increased, decreased, or altered. It is especially important to check with your doctor before combining Polaramine with the following:

Antidepressants such as Elavil and Tofranil
Blood-thinning medications such as Coumadin
Sedatives such as Nembutal, Seconal, Halcion
Tranquilizers such as Xanax, Valium

Special information
if you are pregnant or breastfeeding

The effects of Polaramine during pregnancy have not been adequately studied. The drug definitely should not be used in the third trimester. If you are pregnant or plan to become pregnant, inform your doctor immediately. Polaramine appears in breast milk and could affect a nursing infant. If this medication is essential to your health, your doctor may advise you to discontinue breastfeeding until your treatment is finished.

Recommended dosage

Your doctor will determine the dosage based on your needs and response.

POLARAMINE REPETABS TABLETS

Adults and Children 12 Years of Age and Older
The usual dose is one 4- or 6-milligram Polaramine Repetabs tablet at bedtime or every 8 to 10 hours during the day.

Children 6 Through 11 Years
The usual dose is one 4-milligram Repetabs tablet daily, usually at bedtime.

POLARAMINE TABLETS

Adults and Children 12 Years of Age and Older
The usual dose is 1 tablet every 4 to 6 hours.

Children 6 Through 11 Years
The usual dose is one-half tablet every 4 to 6 hours.

Children 2 Through 5 Years
The usual dose is one-quarter tablet every 4 to 6 hours.

POLARAMINE SYRUP

Adults and Children 12 Years of Age and Older
The usual dose is 1 teaspoonful (2 milligrams) every 4 to 6 hours.

Children 6 Through 11 Years
The usual dose is ½ teaspoonful (1 milligram) every 4 to 6 hours.

Children 2 Through 5 Years
The usual dose is ¼ teaspoonful (0.5 milligram) every 4 to 6 hours.

Overdosage
Any medication taken in excess can have serious consequences. Antihistamine overdose may cause hallucinations and convulsions and can be fatal, especially in infants and children. If you suspect an overdose, seek medical treatment immediately.

■ *Symptoms of Polaramine overdose may include:*
Blurred vision, cardiovascular collapse, convulsions, decreased alertness, difficulty sleeping, dizziness, hallucinations, lack of muscle coordination,

low blood pressure, ringing in ears, sedation, temporary failure to breathe, tremors

■ *Overdose symptoms more common in children include:*
Dry mouth
Extremely high body temperature
Fixed, dilated pupils
Flushing
Stimulation
Stomach and intestinal problems

Brand name:

POLYCILLIN

See Omnipen, page 772.

Generic name:

POLYMYXIN B, NEOMYCIN, AND HYDROCORTISONE

See Cortisporin Ophthalmic Suspension, page 241.

Brand name:

POLY-VI-FLOR

Pronounced: pol-ee-VIE-floor
Generic ingredients: Vitamins, Fluoride

Why is this drug prescribed?
Poly-Vi-Flor is a multivitamin and fluoride supplement with 10 essential vitamins plus the mineral fluoride. It is prescribed for children aged 2 and older to provide fluoride where the drinking water contains less than the amount recommended by the American Dental Association to build strong teeth and prevent cavities. Poly-Vi-Flor supplies significant amounts of other vitamins to avoid deficiencies. The American Academy of Pediatrics recommends that children up to age 16 take a fluoride supplement if they live in areas where the drinking water contains less than the recommended amount of fluoride.

Most important fact about this drug
Do not give your child more than the recommended dose. Too much fluoride can cause discoloration and pitting of teeth.

How should you take this medication?
Do not give your child more than your doctor prescribes.

Poly-Vi-Flor should be chewed or crushed before swallowing.

- *If you miss a dose...*
  Take it as soon as you remember. If it is almost time for the next dose, skip the one you missed and go back to your regular schedule. Do not take 2 doses at once.

- *Storage instructions...*
  Store away from heat, light, and moisture.

What side effects may occur?
Rarely, an allergic rash has occurred.

Why should this drug not be prescribed?
Children should not take Poly-Vi-Flor if they are getting significant amounts of fluoride from other medications or sources.

Special warnings about this medication
Do not give your child more than the recommended dosage. Your child's teeth should be checked periodically for discoloration or pitting. Notify your doctor if white, brown, or black spots appear on your child's teeth.

The fluoride level of your drinking water should be determined before Poly-Vi-Flor is prescribed.

Let your doctor know if you change drinking water or filtering systems.

Fluoride does not replace proper dental habits, such as brushing, flossing, and having dental checkups.

Recommended dosage
The usual dose is 1 tablet every day as prescribed by the doctor.

Overdosage
Although overdose is unlikely, any medication taken in excess can have serious consequences. If you suspect an overdose, seek medical treatment immediately.

Brand name:

PONSTEL

Pronounced: PON-stel
Generic name: Mefenamic acid

Why is this drug prescribed?

Ponstel, a nonsteroidal anti-inflammatory drug, is used for the relief of moderate pain (when treatment will not last for more than 7 days) and for the treatment of menstrual pain.

Most important fact about this drug

You should have frequent checkups with your doctor if you take Ponstel regularly. Ulcers or internal bleeding can occur without warning.

How should you take this medication?

Take Ponstel with food if possible. If it upsets your stomach, be sure to take it with food or an antacid or with a full glass of milk.

Take Ponstel exactly as prescribed by your doctor.

■ *If you miss a dose...*
   If you take Ponstel on a regular schedule, take the forgotten dose as soon as you remember. If it is almost time for your next dose, skip the one you missed and go back to your regular schedule. Do not take 2 doses at once.

■ *Storage instructions...*
   Store away from heat, light, and moisture.

What side effects may occur?

Side effects cannot be anticipated. If any develop or change in intensity, inform your doctor as soon as possible. Only your doctor can determine if it is safe for you to continue taking Ponstel.

■ *More common side effects may include:*
   Abdominal pain
   Diarrhea
   Nausea
   Stomach and intestinal upset
   Vomiting

- *Less common or rare side effects may include:*
Anemia, blurred vision, blood in the urine, changes in liver function, constipation, difficult or painful urination, dizziness, drowsiness, ear pain, eye irritation, facial swelling due to fluid retention, fluttery or throbbing heartbeat, gas, headache, heartburn, hives, inability to sleep, increased need for insulin in a diabetic, kidney failure, labored breathing, loss of appetite, loss of color vision, nervousness, rash, red or purple spots on the skin, sweating, ulcers and internal bleeding

Why should this drug not be prescribed?
Do not take Ponstel if you are sensitive to or have ever had an allergic reaction to it. You should not take it, either, if you have had asthma attacks, hay fever, or hives caused by aspirin or other nonsteroidal anti-inflammatory drugs, such as Motrin and Nuprin. Make sure your doctor is aware of any drug reactions you have experienced.

Do not take Ponstel if you have ulcerations or frequently recurring inflammation of your stomach or intestines.

Avoid this drug if you have serious kidney disease.

Special warnings about this medication
If you develop a rash, diarrhea, or other stomach problems, stop taking this medication and contact your doctor.

Ponstel should be used with caution if you have kidney disease, heart failure, or liver disease; it can cause liver inflammation in some people.

This drug may prolong bleeding time. If you are taking blood-thinning medication, take Ponstel with caution.

Possible food and drug interactions
when taking this medication
If Ponstel is taken with certain other drugs, the effects of either can be increased, decreased, or altered. It is especially important to check with your doctor before combining Ponstel with the following:

Aspirin
Blood-thinning medications such as Coumadin
Diuretics such as Lasix and HydroDIURIL
Lithium (Lithonate)
Methotrexate

Special information
if you are pregnant or breastfeeding

The effects of Ponstel during pregnancy have not been adequately studied. If you are pregnant or plan to become pregnant, inform your doctor immediately. You should not use Ponstel in late pregnancy because nonsteroidal anti-inflammatory drugs affect the heart and blood vessels of the developing baby. Ponstel may appear in breast milk and could affect a nursing infant. If this medication is essential to your health, your doctor may advise you to discontinue breastfeeding until your treatment is finished.

Recommended dosage

ADULTS AND CHILDREN OVER 14

Moderate Pain
The usual starting dose is 500 milligrams, followed by 250 milligrams every 6 hours, if needed, for 1 week.

Menstrual Pain
The usual starting dose, once symptoms appear, is 500 milligrams, followed by 250 milligrams every 6 hours for 2 to 3 days.

CHILDREN

The safety and effectiveness of Ponstel have not been established in children under 14.

Overdosage

Although there is no information available on overdosage with Ponstel, any medication taken in excess can have serious consequences. If you suspect an overdose of Ponstel, seek medical attention immediately.

Generic name:

POTASSIUM CHLORIDE

See Micro-K, page 658.

Brand name:

PRAVACHOL

Pronounced: PRAV-a-coll
Generic name: Pravastatin sodium

Why is this drug prescribed?

Pravachol is a cholesterol-lowering drug. Your doctor may prescribe it along with a cholesterol-lowering diet if your blood cholesterol level is dangerously high, and if you have not been able to lower it by diet alone.

The drug works by helping to clear harmful low-density lipoprotein (LDL) cholesterol out of the blood and by limiting the body's ability to form new LDL cholesterol.

Most important fact about this drug

Pravachol is usually prescribed only if diet, exercise, and weight loss fail to bring your cholesterol levels under control. It's important to remember that Pravachol is a supplement—not a substitute—for those other measures. To get the full benefit of the medication, you need to stick to the diet and exercise program prescribed by your doctor. All these efforts to keep your cholesterol levels normal are important because together they may lower your risk of heart disease.

How should you take this medication?

For an even greater cholesterol-lowering effect, your doctor may prescribe Pravachol along with a different kind of lipid-lowering drug such as Questran or Colestid. However, you must not take Pravachol at the same time of day as the other cholesterol-lowering drug. Take Pravachol at least 1 hour before or 4 hours after taking the other drug.

Pravachol should be taken once daily at bedtime. You may take it with or without food.

Your doctor will probably do blood tests for cholesterol levels every 4 weeks to determine the effectiveness of the dose.

■ *If you miss a dose...*
   Take the forgotten dose as soon as you remember. If it is almost time for your next dose, skip the one you missed and go back to your regular schedule. Do not take a double dose.

■ *Storage instructions...*
   Store at room temperature, in a tightly closed container away from moisture and light.

What side effects may occur?

Side effects from Pravachol cannot be anticipated. If any develop or change in intensity, inform your doctor as soon as possible. Only your doctor can determine if it is safe for you to continue taking Pravachol.

■ *Side effects may include:*
Abdominal pain, chest pain, cold, constipation, cough, diarrhea, dizziness, fatigue, flu, gas, headache, heartburn, inflammation of nasal passages, muscle aching or weakness, nausea, rash, urinary problems, vomiting

Why should this drug not be prescribed?
Do not take Pravachol if you are sensitive or have ever had an allergic reaction to it.

Do not take Pravachol if you have liver disease.

Special warnings about this medication
Pravachol should not be used to try to lower high cholesterol that stems from a medical condition such as alcoholism, poorly controlled diabetes, an underactive thyroid gland, or a kidney or liver problem.

Because Pravachol may cause damage to the liver, your doctor will do blood tests regularly. Your doctor should monitor you especially closely if you have ever had liver disease or if you are or have ever been a heavy drinker.

Since Pravachol may cause damage to muscle tissue, promptly report to your doctor any unexplained muscle pain, tenderness, or weakness, especially if you also have a fever or you just generally do not feel well.

Possible food and drug interactions
when taking this medication
If Pravachol is taken with certain other drugs, the effects of either could be increased, decreased, or altered. It is especially important to check with your doctor before combining Pravachol with the following:

Cholestyramine (Questran)
Cimetidine (Tagamet)
Colestipol (Colestid)
Erythromycin (E.E.S., Erythrocin, others)
Gemfibrozil (Lopid)
Immunosuppressive drugs such as Sandimmune
Niacin
Warfarin (Coumadin)

Special information
if you are pregnant or breastfeeding
You must not become pregnant while taking Pravachol. Because this drug lowers cholesterol, and cholesterol is necessary for the proper development of an unborn baby, there is some suspicion that Pravachol might cause birth

defects. Your doctor will prescribe Pravachol only if you are highly unlikely to become pregnant while taking the drug. If you do become pregnant while taking Pravachol, inform your doctor immediately.

Because Pravachol appears in breast milk, and because its cholesterol-lowering effects might prove harmful to a nursing baby, you should not take Pravachol while you are breastfeeding.

Recommended dosage

ADULTS

The usual starting dose is 10 to 20 milligrams once a day at bedtime.

For ongoing therapy, the recommended dose is 10 to 40 milligrams once a day at bedtime.

ELDERLY

The usual starting dose is 10 milligrams a day at bedtime; for ongoing therapy, the dose is 20 milligrams per day or less.

Overdosage
Although no specific information is available, any medication taken in excess can have serious consequences. If you suspect an overdose of Pravachol, seek medical attention immediately.

Generic name:

PRAVASTATIN

See Pravachol, page 876.

Generic name:

PRAZEPAM

See Centrax, page 189.

Generic name:

PRAZOSIN

See Minipress, page 671.

Brand name:

PRED FORTE

Pronounced: PRED FORT
Generic name: Prednisolone acetate

Why is this drug prescribed?
Pred Forte contains a steroid medication that eases redness, irritation, and swelling due to inflammation of the eye.

Most important fact about this drug
Do not use Pred Forte more often or for a longer period than you doctor orders. Overuse can increase the risk of side effects and can lead to eye damage. If your eye problems return, do not use any leftover Pred Forte without first consulting your doctor.

How should you use this medication?
Keep using Pred Forte for the full time prescribed.

To avoid spreading infection, do not let anyone else use your prescription.

Pred Forte may increase the chance of infection from contact lenses. Your doctor may advise you to stop wearing your contacts while using this medication.

Follow these steps to administer Pred Forte:

1. Wash your hands thoroughly.
2. Vigorously shake the dropper bottle.
3. Gently pull your lower eyelid down to form a pocket next to your eye.
4. Do not touch the applicator tip to any surface including your eye.
5. Brace the bottle against the bridge of your nose or your forehead.
6. Tilt your head back and squeeze the medication into your eye.
7. Close your eyes gently. Keep them closed for 1 to 2 minutes.
8. Do not rinse the dropper.
9. Wait for 5 to 10 minutes before using a second eye medication.

■ *If you miss a dose...*
 Apply it as soon as you remember. If it is almost time for your next dose, skip the one you missed and go back to your regular schedule.

■ *Storage instructions...*
 Store away from heat and direct light. Protect from freezing.

What side effects may occur?
Side effects cannot be anticipated. If any develop or change in intensity, inform your doctor as soon as possible. Only your doctor can determine if it is safe for you to continue taking Pred Forte.

■ *Side effects may include:*
Cataract formation
Increased pressure inside the eyeball
Perforation of the eyeball
Secondary infection with fungi or viruses

Since any one of these developments could affect your vision temporarily or permanently, it is important to keep in close contact with your doctor while using Pred Forte eyedrops, and to use the drops only as directed.

Occasionally, long-term use of Pred Forte eyedrops may cause bodywide side effects due to an overload of steroid hormone. Such side effects may include a "moon-faced" appearance, obese trunk, humped upper back, wasted limbs, and purple stretch marks on the skin. These effects are likely to disappear once the medication is withdrawn. If bodywide side effects occur, you will need to stop using the eye drops gradually rather than all at once.

Why should this drug not be prescribed?
Do not use Pred Forte if you have an untreated, pus-forming eye infection.

You should not take Pred Forte if you have herpes or other viral diseases of the eye, tuberculosis of the eye, or a fungal disease of the eye.

Do not use Pred Forte if you are allergic to prednisolone or any other ingredients.

Special warnings about this medication
You must stay in close touch with your doctor while using this medication, for the following reasons:

If you use Pred Forte eyedrops extensively and/or for an extended period of time, you may be at increased risk for cataracts.

If you use Pred Forte eyedrops for a condition that causes thinning of the cornea, you are at increased risk for perforation of the eyeball.

If you have a persistent ulceration of the cornea of your eye while using Pred Forte eyedrops, the problem may be a secondary fungus infection which Pred Forte cannot cure. An eye doctor should evaluate this possibility.

While you are using Pred Forte eyedrops, an eye doctor should check your intraocular pressure (pressure inside the eyeball) frequently, since steroids may increase this pressure. If increased pressure is allowed to continue, it may cause loss of vision.

Pred Forte contains sodium bisulfite, which can cause allergic-type reactions, including severe or even life-threatening asthmatic episodes. Sulfite sensitivity is seen more frequently in asthmatic than in non-asthmatic people.

Possible food and drug interactions
when using this medication
Prednisolone acetate, the active ingredient in Pred Forte eyedrops, is also available in tablet and injectable forms for the treatment of other disorders. If these other forms of prednisolone acetate are taken with certain other drugs, the effects of either could be increased, decreased, or altered. Therefore, it's wise to check with your doctor before combining Pred Forte eyedrops with other medications.

Special information
if you are pregnant or breastfeeding
If you are pregnant or plan to become pregnant, inform your doctor immediately. Pred Forte eyedrops should be used during pregnancy only if the potential benefit outweighs the potential risk to the developing baby.

It is not known whether the hormone in Pred Forte eyedrops appears in breast milk. If it does, the small quantity involved would be unlikely to harm a breastfeeding baby. Nevertheless, caution is advised when using Pred Forte eyedrops while breastfeeding.

Recommended dosage

ADULTS

Put 1 to 2 drops under the eyelid 2 to 4 times daily. During the first 24 to 48 hours, your doctor may want you to use more frequent doses.

Overdosage
A one-time accidental overdose of Pred Forte eyedrops ordinarily will not cause acute problems. Over time, however, overdosage may have serious consequences (see "What side effects may occur?"). If you suspect symptoms of a chronic overdose with Pred Forte eyedrops, seek medical attention immediately.

If you accidentally swallow Pred Forte eyedrops, drink fluids to dilute the medication. Call your local poison center or your doctor for assistance.

Generic name:

PREDNISOLONE ACETATE

See Pred Forte, page 880.

Generic name:

PREDNISOLONE SODIUM PHOSPHATE

See Pediapred, page 814.

Generic name:

PREDNISONE

See Deltasone, page 293.

Brand name:

PREMARIN

Pronounced: PREM-uh-rin
Generic name: Conjugated estrogens
Other brand names: Premphase, Prempro

Why is this drug prescribed?

Premarin is an estrogen replacement drug. The tablets are used to reduce symptoms of menopause, including feelings of warmth in face, neck, and chest, and the sudden intense episodes of heat and sweating known as "hot flashes." They also may be prescribed for teenagers who fail to mature at the usual rate, and to relieve the symptoms of certain types of cancer, including some forms of breast and prostate cancer.

In addition, either the tablets or Premarin vaginal cream can be used for other conditions caused by lack of estrogen, such as dry, itchy external genitals and vaginal irritation.

Along with diet, calcium supplements, and exercise, Premarin tablets are also prescribed to prevent osteoporosis, a condition in which the bones become brittle and easily broken.

Premphase and Prempro both combine a daily Premarin tablet with tablets of medroxyprogesterone acetate (Cycrin). The addition of progesterone to estrogen-replacement therapy has been shown to reduce the risk of uterine cancer.

Most important fact about this drug

Because estrogens have been linked with increased risk of endometrial cancer (cancer in lining of the uterus), it is essential to have regular checkups and to report any unusual vaginal bleeding to your doctor immediately.

How should you take this medication?

Take Premarin exactly as prescribed. Do not share it with anyone else.

If you are taking calcium supplements as a part of the treatment to help prevent brittle bones, check with your doctor about how much to take.

You should take a few moments to read the patient package insert provided with your prescription.

If you are using Premarin vaginal cream, apply it as follows:

1. Remove cap from tube.
2. Screw nozzle end of applicator onto tube.
3. Gently squeeze tube from the bottom to force sufficient cream into the barrel to provide the prescribed dose.
4. Unscrew applicator from tube.
5. Lie on back with knees drawn up. Gently insert applicator deeply into the vagina and press plunger downward to its original position.

To cleanse the applicator, pull the plunger out of the barrel, then wash with mild soap and warm water. Do not boil or use hot water.

■ *If you miss a dose...*
Take the forgotten dose as soon as you remember. If it is almost time for the next dose, skip the one you missed and go back to your regular schedule. Never try to "catch up" by doubling the dose.

■ *Storage instructions...*
Store at room temperature.

What side effects may occur?

Side effects cannot be anticipated. If any develop or change in intensity, inform your doctor immediately. Only your doctor can determine whether it is safe to continue taking Premarin.

■ *Side effects may include:*
Abdominal cramps, abnormal vaginal bleeding, bloating, breast swelling

and tenderness, depression, dizziness, enlargement of benign tumors in the uterus, fluid retention, gallbladder disease, hair loss from the scalp, increased body hair, intolerance to contact lenses, migraine headache, nausea, vomiting, sex-drive changes, skin darkening, especially on the face, skin rash or redness, swelling of wrists and ankles, vaginal yeast infection, vomiting, weight gain or loss, yellow eyes and skin

■ *Other possible side effects of Premphase and Prempro:*
Appetite changes, backache, blood clots, changes in blood pressure, excessive flow of breast milk, eye disorders, fatigue, fever, headache, nervousness, sleep disturbances, twitching

Why should this drug not be prescribed?
Do not take Premarin if you have ever had a bad reaction to it, or have undiagnosed abnormal vaginal bleeding.

Except in certain special circumstances, you should not be given Premarin if you have breast cancer or any other "estrogen-dependent" cancer.

Do not take Premarin if you have had any heart or circulation problem, including a tendency for abnormal blood clotting.

Special warnings about this medication
The risk of cancer of the uterus increases when estrogen is used for a long time or taken in large doses.

There may be an increased risk of breast cancer in women who take estrogen for a long time. If you have a family history of breast cancer or have ever had an abnormal mammogram, you need to have more frequent breast examinations.

Women who take Premarin after menopause are more likely to develop gallbladder disease.

Premarin also increases the risk of blood clots. These blood clots can cause stroke, heart attack, or other serious disorders.

While taking Premarin, get in touch with your doctor right away if you notice any of the following:

Abdominal pain, tenderness, or swelling
Abnormal bleeding from the vagina
Breast lumps
Coughing up blood
Pain in your chest or calves

Severe headache, dizziness, or faintness
Sudden shortness of breath
Vision changes
Yellowing of the skin

Possible food and drug interactions
when taking this medication

If Premarin is taken with certain other drugs, the effects of either could be increased, decreased, or altered. It is especially important to check with your doctor before combining Premarin with the following:

Barbiturates such as phenobarbital
Blood thinners such as Coumadin
Drugs used for epilepsy, such as Dilantin
Major tranquilizers such as Thorazine
Oral diabetics such as Micronase
Rifampin (Rifadin)
Thyroid preparations such as Synthroid
Tricyclic antidepressants such as Elavil and Tofranil
Vitamin C

Special information
if you are pregnant or breastfeeding

If you are pregnant or plan to become pregnant, notify your doctor immediately. Premarin should not be taken during pregnancy because of the possibility of harm to the unborn child. Premarin cannot prevent a miscarriage. Estrogens can decrease the quantity and quality of breast milk, and progestins appear in breast milk. Your doctor may advise you not to breastfeed while you are taking this drug.

Recommended dosage

Your doctor will start therapy with this medication at a low dose. He or she will want to check you periodically at 3- to 6-month intervals to determine the need for continued therapy.

PREMARIN TABLETS

Hot Flashes Associated with Menopause
The usual dosage is 0.3 to 1.25 milligrams daily. If you are still having periods, the doctor will start the Premarin on the fifth day of your cycle, have you take it for 3 weeks, then give you 1 week off.

Tissue Degeneration in the Vagina
The usual dosage is 0.3 to 1.25 milligrams or more daily. The drug is taken cyclically (3 weeks on and 1 week off).

Low Estrogen Levels Due to Reduced Ovary Function
The usual dosage is 2.5 to 7.5 milligrams daily, taken in several small doses, for 20 days, followed by a 10-day rest period. If you do not have your period by the end of this time, the same dosage schedule is repeated.

If you start to bleed before the end of the 10-day period, your doctor will start you on another 20-day cycle, with an oral progestin added during the last 5 days. If you start to bleed before the second cycle is over, stop taking the medication and tell your doctor.

Ovary Removal or Ovarian Failure
The usual dosage is 1.25 milligrams daily, cyclically (3 weeks on and 1 week off). Your doctor will adjust the dosage according to the severity of your symptoms and your response to treatment.

Osteoporosis (Loss of Bone Mass)
The usual dosage is 0.625 milligram daily, taken cyclically (3 weeks on and 1 week off).

Advanced Androgen-Dependent Cancer of the Prostate, for Relief of Symptoms Only
The usual dosage is 1.25 to 2.5 milligrams 3 times daily.

Breast Cancer (for Relief of Symptoms Only) in Appropriately Selected Women and Men with Metastatic Disease
The suggested dosage is 10 milligrams 3 times daily for a period of at least 3 months. Tell your doctor if you have any unusual bleeding.

PREMARIN VAGINAL CREAM

Given cyclically for short-term use only.

Degeneration of Genital Tissue or Severe Itching in the Genital Area
The recommended dosage is 2 to 4 grams (one-half to 1 applicator of cream) daily, inserted into the vagina, depending on the severity of the condition. You will use the cream for 3 weeks, then stop for 1 week. Tell your doctor if you notice any unusual bleeding.

PREMPHASE TABLETS

Take 1 maroon Premarin tablet every day for 28 days; on the 15th day, begin taking 1 light-purple Cycrin tablet along with the Premarin.

PREMPRO TABLETS

Take 1 maroon Premarin tablet and 1 white Cycrin tablet together each day.

Overdosage

Any medication taken in excess can have serious consequences. If you suspect an overdose of Premarin, seek medical attention immediately.

- *Symptoms of Premphase/Prempro overdose may include:*
  Nausea
  Vomiting
  Withdrawal bleeding

Generic name:

PREMPHASE

See Premarin, page 883.

Generic name:

PREMPRO

See Premarin, page 883.

Generic name:

PRENATAL VITAMINS AND MINERALS

See Stuartnatal Plus, page 1048.

Brand name:

PRILOSEC

Pronounced: PRILL-oh-sek
Generic name: Omeprazole

Why is this drug prescribed?

Prilosec is prescribed for the short-term treatment (4 to 8 weeks) of active duodenal ulcer, gastroesophageal reflux disease (backflow of acid stomach contents), and severe erosive esophagitis (inflammation of the esophagus).

It is also used for the long-term treatment of conditions in which too much stomach acid is secreted, such as Zollinger-Ellison syndrome, multiple endocrine adenomas (benign tumors), and systemic mastocytosis (cancerous cells).

Most important fact about this drug
Prilosec is not intended for long-term therapy after an ulcer has healed.

How should you take this medication?
Prilosec works best when taken before meals. It can be taken with an antacid.

The capsule should be swallowed whole. It should not be opened, chewed, or crushed.

Avoid excessive amounts of caffeine while taking this drug.

It may take several days for Prilosec to begin relieving stomach pain. Be sure to continue taking the drug exactly as prescribed even if it seems to have no affect.

■ *If you miss a dose...*
Take it as soon as you remember. If it is almost time for your next dose, skip the one you missed and go back to your regular schedule. Do not take 2 doses at once.

■ *Storage information...*
Store at room temperature in a tightly closed container, away from light and moisture.

What side effects may occur?
Side effects cannot be anticipated. If any develop or change in intensity, inform your doctor as soon as possible. Only your doctor can determine if it is safe for you to continue taking Prilosec.

■ *More common side effects may include:*
Abdominal pain
Diarrhea
Headache
Nausea
Vomiting

■ *Less common or rare side effects may include:*
Abdominal swelling, abnormal dreams, aggression, anemia, anxiety, apathy, back pain, breast development in males, blood in urine, changes in

liver function, chest pain, confusion, constipation, cough, depression, difficulty sleeping, discolored feces, dizziness, dry mouth, dry skin, fatigue, fever, fluid retention and swelling, fluttery heartbeat, frequent urination, gas, general feeling of illness, hair loss, hallucinations, hepatitis, high blood pressure, hives, irritable colon, itching, joint and leg pain, loss of appetite, low blood sugar, muscle cramps and pain, nervousness, nosebleeds, pain, pain in testicles, rapid heartbeat, rash, ringing in ears, skin inflammation, sleepiness, slow heartbeat, taste distortion, tingling or pins and needles, throat pain, tremors, upper respiratory infection, urinary tract infection, vertigo, weakness, weight gain, yellow eyes and skin

Why should this drug not be prescribed?

If you are sensitive to or have ever had an allergic reaction to Prilosec or any of its ingredients, you should not take this medication. Make sure your doctor is aware of any drug reactions you have experienced.

Special warnings about this medication

The safety of long-term use of this drug has not been established.

Possible food and drug interactions when taking this medication

If Prilosec is taken with certain other drugs, the effects of either could be increased, decreased, or altered. It is especially important to check with your doctor before combining Prilosec with the following:

Ampicillin-containing drugs such as Spectrobid
Cyclosporine (Sandimmune)
Diazepam (Valium)
Disulfiram (Antabuse)
Iron
Ketoconazole (Nizoral)
Phenytoin (Dilantin)
Warfarin (Coumadin)

Special information if you are pregnant or breastfeeding

The effects of Prilosec during pregnancy have not been adequately studied. If you are pregnant or plan to become pregnant, inform your doctor immediately. Prilosec may appear in breast milk and could affect a nursing infant. If this medication is essential to your health, your doctor may advise you to discontinue breastfeeding until your treatment with this medication is finished.

Recommended dosage

ADULTS

Short-term Treatment of Active Duodenal Ulcer
The usual dose is 20 milligrams once a day. Most people heal within 4 weeks.

Severe Erosive Esophagitis or Poorly Responsive Gastroesophageal Reflux Disease (GERD)
The usual dose is 20 milligrams daily for 4 to 8 weeks.

Pathological Hypersecretory Conditions
The usual starting dose is 60 milligrams once a day. If you take more than 80 milligrams a day, your doctor will divide the total into smaller doses. The dosing will be based on your needs.

CHILDREN

The safety and effectiveness of Prilosec in children have not been established.

Overdosage

No specific symptoms of Prilosec overdose are known, but any medication taken in excess can have serious consequences. If you suspect an overdose of Prilosec, seek medical attention immediately.

Generic name:

PRIMIDONE

See Mysoline, page 698.

Brand name:

PRINCIPEN

See Omnipen, page 772.

Brand name:

PRINIVIL

See Zestril, page 1230.

Brand name:

PRINZIDE

See Zestoretic, page 1226.

Generic name:

PROBUCOL

See Lorelco, page 606.

Generic name:

PROCAINAMIDE

See Procan SR, page 892.

Brand name:

PROCAN SR

Pronounced: PROH-can
Generic name: Procainamide hydrochloride
Other brand name: Pronestyl-SR

Why is this drug prescribed?

Procan SR is used to treat severe irregular heartbeats (arrhythmias). Arrhythmias are generally divided into two main types: heartbeats that are faster than normal (tachycardia), and heartbeats that are slower than normal (bradycardia). Irregular heartbeats are often caused by drugs or disease but can occur in otherwise healthy people with no history of heart disease or other illness.

Most important fact about this drug

Procan SR can cause serious blood disorders, especially during the first 3 months of treatment. Be sure to notify your doctor if you notice any of the following: joint or muscle pain, dark urine, yellowing of skin or eyes, muscular weakness, chest or abdominal pain, appetite loss, diarrhea, hallucinations, dizziness, depression, wheezing, cough, easy bruising or bleeding, tremors, palpitations, rash, soreness or ulcers in the mouth, sore throat, fever, and chills.

How should you take this medication?
Take only your prescribed doses of Procan SR; never take more.

Procan SR should be swallowed whole. Do not break or chew the tablet. You may see the tablet matrix of Procan SR in your stool, since it does not disintegrate following release of procainamide.

Try not to miss any doses. Skipping doses, changing the intervals between doses, or "making up" missed doses by doubling up later may cause your condition to worsen and could be dangerous.

■ *If you miss a dose...*
Take it as soon as you remember if it is within 4 hours of your scheduled time. If you do not remember until later, skip the dose you missed and go back to your regular schedule. Never take 2 doses at the same time.

■ *Storage instructions...*
Store away from heat, light, and moisture.

What side effects may occur?
Side effects cannot be anticipated. If any develop or change in intensity, inform your doctor as soon as possible. Only your doctor can determine if it is safe for you to continue taking Procan SR.

■ *More common side effects may include:*
Abdominal pain
Bitter taste
Diarrhea
Loss of appetite
Nausea
Symptoms similar to those of lupus erythematosus, an inflammatory disease of the connective tissue (joint pain or inflammation, abdominal or chest pain, fever, chills, muscle pain, skin lesions)
Vomiting

■ *Less common side effects may include:*
Depression, dizziness, fluid retention, flushing, giddiness, hallucinations, hives, itching, rash, weakness

■ *Rare side effects may include:*
Anemia, changes in blood counts, low blood pressure

Why should this drug not be prescribed?

Procan SR should not be taken if you have the heart irregularity known as complete heart block or incomplete heart block without a pacemaker, or if you have ever had an allergic reaction to procaine or similar local anesthetics.

Your doctor will not prescribe this drug if you have been diagnosed with the connective-tissue disease lupus erythematosus or the heartbeat irregularity known as torsades de pointes.

Special warnings about this medication

To check for the serious blood disorders that can develop during Procan SR therapy, your doctor will do a complete blood count weekly for the first 12 weeks and will continue to monitor your blood count carefully after that.

If you develop a fever, chills, sore throat or mouth, bruising or bleeding, infections, chest or abdominal pain, loss of appetite, weakness, muscle or joint pain, skin rash, nausea, fluttery heartbeat, vomiting, diarrhea, hallucinations, dizziness, depression, wheezing, yellow eyes and skin, or dark urine, contact your doctor immediately. It could indicate a serious illness.

Use Procan SR cautiously if you have ever had congestive heart failure or other types of heart disease.

Your doctor will prescribe Procan SR along with other antiarrhythmic drugs, such as quinidine or disopyramide, only if they have been tried and have not worked when used alone.

If you have ever had kidney disease, liver disease, or myasthenia gravis (a disease that causes muscle weakness, especially in the face and neck), your doctor will watch you carefully while you are taking Procan SR.

Make sure your doctor is aware of any drug reactions you have experienced, especially to procaine, other local anesthetics, or aspirin.

Possible food and drug interactions
when taking this medication

If Procan SR is taken with certain other drugs, the effects of either could be increased, decreased, or altered. It is especially important to check with your doctor before combining Procan SR with the following:

Antiarrhythmic drugs such as quinidine (Quinidex), propranolol (Inderal), and mexiletine (Mexitil)

Drugs that ease muscle spasms, such as Cogentin and Artane
Lidocaine
Neuromuscular blocking agents such as Anectine

Special information
if you are pregnant or breastfeeding

The effects of Procan SR during pregnancy have not been adequately studied. If you are pregnant or plan to become pregnant, inform your doctor immediately. Procan SR appears in breast milk and may affect a nursing infant. If this medication is essential to your health, your doctor may advise you to discontinue breastfeeding until your treatment is finished.

Recommended dosage

ADULTS

Dosages and intervals between doses will be adjusted for you, based on your doctor's assessment of the degree of underlying heart disease, your age, and the way your kidneys are functioning.

Younger people with normal kidney function will start with a total daily oral dose of up to 50 milligrams per 2.2 pounds of body weight, divided into smaller doses and taken every 6 hours.

Older people, especially those over 50 years of age, or those with reduced kidney, liver, or heart function will get lower doses or wait a longer time between doses; this may decrease the probability of side effects that are related to the size of the dose.

CHILDREN

The safety and effectiveness of this drug have not been established in children.

Overdosage

Any medication taken in excess can have serious consequences. If you suspect an overdose, seek medical treatment immediately.

- *Symptoms of Procan SR overdose may include:*
  Changes in heart function and heartbeat

Brand name:

PROCARDIA

Pronounced: pro-CAR-dee-uh
Generic name: Nifedipine
Other brand names: Procardia XL, Adalat

Why is this drug prescribed?

Procardia and Procardia XL are used to treat angina (chest pain caused by lack of oxygen to the heart due to clogged arteries or spasm of the arteries). Procardia XL is also used to treat high blood pressure. Procardia and Procardia XL are calcium channel blockers. They ease the workload of the heart by relaxing the muscles in the walls of the arteries, allowing them to dilate. This improves blood flow through the heart and throughout the body, reduces blood pressure, and helps prevent angina. Procardia XL is taken once a day and provides a steady rate of medication over a 24-hour period.

Most important fact about this drug

If you have high blood pressure, you must take Procardia XL regularly for it to be effective. Since blood pressure declines gradually, it may be several weeks before you get the full benefit of Procardia XL; and you must continue taking it even if you are feeling well. Procardia XL does not cure high blood pressure; it merely keeps it under control.

How should you take this medication?

Procardia and Procardia XL should be taken exactly as prescribed by your doctor, even if your symptoms have disappeared.

Procardia XL tablets are specially designed to release the medication into your bloodstream slowly. As a result, something that looks like a tablet may occasionally appear in your stool. This is normal and simply means that the medication has been released, and the shell that contained the medication has been eliminated from your body.

Procardia and Procardia XL tablets should be swallowed whole. Do not break, crush, or chew.

Procardia and Procardia XL can be taken with or without food.

Do not substitute another brand of nifedipine for Procardia or Procardia XL unless your doctor directs.

Procardia XL should be taken once a day. You can take it in the morning or evening, but should hold to the same time each day.

- *If you miss a dose...*
  Take the forgotten dose as soon as you remember. If it is almost time for your next dose, skip the one you missed. Never take 2 doses at the same time.

- *Storage instructions...*
  Procardia and Procardia XL can be stored at room temperature. Protect from moisture, light, humidity, and excessive heat.

What side effects may occur?
Side effects cannot be anticipated. If any develop or change in intensity, inform your doctor as soon as possible. Only your doctor can determine whether it is safe for you to continue taking Procardia or Procardia XL.

- *More common side effects may include:*
  Constipation, cough, dizziness, fatigue, flushing, giddiness, headache, heartburn, heat sensation, light-headedness, mood changes, muscle cramps, nasal congestion, nausea, sore throat, swelling of arms, legs, hands, and feet, tremors, wheezing

- *Less common side effects may include:*
  Abdominal pain, blurred vision, chest congestion, chills, cramps, diarrhea, difficult or labored breathing, difficulty in balance, difficulty sleeping, drowsiness, dry cough, dry mouth, excessive sweating, fever, fluttering heartbeat, gas, general chest pain, hives, impotence, indigestion, itching, jitteriness, joint pain, leg cramps, muscle and bone inflammation, nervousness, pain, production of large amounts of pale urine, rash, sexual difficulties, shakiness, shortness of breath, skin inflammation, sleep disturbances, sleepiness, stiff joints, tingling or pins and needles, weakness

- *Rare side effects may include:*
  Abnormal or terrifying dreams, anemia, anxiety, arthritis, back pain, belching, blood in the urine, breast pain, breathing disorders, dark stools containing blood, decreased sex drive, depression, distorted taste, dulled sense of touch, excessive urination at night, facial swelling, fainting, fever, gout, gum overgrowth, hair loss, hepatitis, hives, hot flashes, increased angina, increased sweating, inflammation of the sinuses, irregular heartbeat, migraine, muscle incoordination, muscle pain, muscle tension, nosebleeds, painful or difficult urination, paranoia, rapid heartbeat, reddish or purplish spots under the skin, ringing in the ears, swelling around the eyes, tearing eyes, temporary blindness, upper respiratory tract infection, vague feeling of illness, vertigo, vision changes, vomiting, weight gain

Why should this drug not be prescribed?

Procardia should not be used if you have ever had an allergic reaction to it or are sensitive to it or other calcium channel blockers (Adalat, Calan, others). Make sure your doctor is aware of any drug reactions you have experienced.

Special warnings about this medication

Procardia and Procardia XL may cause your blood pressure to become too low, which may make you feel light-headed or faint. This is more likely to happen when you start taking the medication and when the amount you take is increased. It is also more likely to occur if you are also taking a beta-blocker heart medication such as Tenormin or Inderal. Your doctor should check your blood pressure when you start taking Procardia or Procardia XL and continue monitoring it while your dosage is being adjusted.

There is a remote possibility of experiencing increased angina when you start taking Procardia or Procardia XL, or when your dosage is increased. If this happens, contact your doctor immediately.

You may have angina pain if you suddenly stop taking beta blockers when beginning Procardia therapy. Your doctor will taper you off the other drug.

If you have tight aortic stenosis (a narrowing of the aortic valve that obstructs blood flow from the heart to the body) and have been taking a beta blocker, your doctor will monitor you carefully while you are taking Procardia or Procardia XL.

If you develop swelling of the arms, hands, legs, and feet, your doctor can prescribe a diuretic (water pill) to relieve the problem.

Procardia XL should be used cautiously if you have any stomach or intestinal narrowing.

Notify your doctor or dentist that you are taking Procardia if you have a medical emergency, and before you have surgery or dental treatment.

Possible food and drug interactions
when taking this medication

If Procardia or Procardia XL is taken with certain other drugs, the effects of either could be increased, decreased, or altered. It is especially important to check with your doctor before combining Procardia or Procardia XL with the following:

Cimetidine (Tagamet)
Digoxin (Lanoxin)

Special information
if you are pregnant or breastfeeding

The effects of Procardia and Procardia XL during pregnancy have not been adequately studied, although new animal research points to possible birth defects in humans. If you are pregnant or plan to become pregnant, inform your doctor immediately. It is not known whether Procardia or Procardia XL appears in breast milk and can affect a nursing infant. If this medication is essential to your health, your doctor may advise you to discontinue breastfeeding until your treatment is finished.

Recommended dosage

ADULTS

The usual starting dose of Procardia is one 10-milligram capsule, 3 times a day. The usual range is 10 to 20 milligrams 3 times a day. Some people may need 20 to 30 milligrams, 3 or 4 times a day. Usually you will not take more than 120 milligrams in a day and should take no more than 180 milligrams.

The starting dose of Procardia XL is usually a 30- or 60-milligram tablet, taken once daily. Your doctor may increase the dose over 1 to 2 weeks if not satisfied with the way the drug is working. Doses above 120 milligrams per day are not recommended.

Although no serious side effects have been reported when Procardia XL is stopped, your doctor will probably have you lower the dose gradually under close supervision.

Overdosage

Any medication taken in excess can have serious consequences. If you suspect an overdose, seek medical treatment immediately.

■ *Symptoms of Procardia overdose may include:*
Dizziness
Drowsiness
Nausea
Slurred speech
Weakness

Generic name:

PROCHLORPERAZINE

See Compazine, page 233.

Generic name:

PROCTOCREAM-HC

See Anusol-HC, page 68.

Generic name:

PROMETHAZINE

See Phenergan, page 842.

Generic name:

PROMETHAZINE WITH CODEINE

See Phenergan with Codeine, page 847.

Brand name:

PRONESTYL-SR

See Procan SR, page 892.

Generic name:

PROPAFENONE

See Rythmol, page 995.

Brand name:

PROPINE

Pronounced: PROH-peen
Generic name: Dipivefrin hydrochloride

Why is this drug prescribed?

Propine is used to treat chronic open-angle glaucoma, the most common form of the disease. In glaucoma, the fluid inside the eyeball is under abnormally high pressure, a condition which can cause vision problems or even blindness.

Propine belongs to a class of medication called "prodrugs," drugs that generally are not active by themselves, but are converted in the body to an active form. This makes for better absorption, stability, and comfort and reduces side effects.

Most important fact about this drug
There is no cure for glaucoma. Propine and similar drugs can keep ocular pressure under control, but only as long as you take them. You will probably need to continue treatment for life; and you must be sure to take the medication regularly.

How should you use this medication?
Use this medication exactly as prescribed. If you use too much, or use it too often, Propine may cause side effects.

Wash your hands before and after you use the eyedrops. Once the drops are in your eye, keep your eye closed for 1 to 2 minutes, applying pressure to the inside corner of your eye, so the medicine can be properly absorbed.

To keep the medication free of contamination, do not touch the applicator tip to your eye or any other surface.

A number appears on the cap of the dropper bottle to tell you what dose you are taking. When you are ready to take the first dose, make sure the number 1 appears in the window. After each dose, replace the cap and rotate it to the next number. Turn until you hear a click.

- *If you miss a dose...*
  Apply it as soon as you remember. If it is almost time for your next dose, skip the one you missed and go back to your regular schedule. Never apply more than 1 dose at a time.

- *Storage instructions...*
  Keep Propine in the plastic dropper bottle it came in.

What side effects may occur?
Side effects cannot be anticipated. If any develop or change in intensity, inform your doctor as soon as possible. Only your doctor can determine if it is safe for you to continue taking Propine.

- *More common side effects may include:*
  Burning and stinging
  Red eye

- *Less common or rare side effects may include:*
  Allergic reactions, change in heart rhythm, conjunctivitis, extreme dilation of pupils, increased heart rate or blood pressure, increased sensitivity to light

Why should this drug not be prescribed?

If you are sensitive to or have ever had an allergic reaction to Propine or any of its ingredients, you should not use this medication. Make sure your doctor is aware of any drug reactions you have experienced.

Unless you are directed to do so by your doctor, do not use this medication if you have narrow-angle glaucoma.

Special warnings about this medication

Propine may cause vision problems, including blurry vision, for a short time after the eyedrops are applied. If this occurs, make sure you do not drive, use machinery, or participate in any hazardous activity that requires clear vision.

Possible food and drug interactions
when taking this medication

No significant interactions have been reported.

Special information
if you are pregnant or breastfeeding

The effects of Propine during pregnancy have not been adequately studied. If you are pregnant or plan to become pregnant, inform your doctor immediately. Propine may appear in breast milk and could affect a nursing infant. If this medication is essential to your health, your doctor may advise you to discontinue breastfeeding your baby until your treatment is finished.

Recommended dosage

ADULTS

The usual dose is 1 drop in the eye(s) every 12 hours. It usually takes about 30 minutes for Propine to start working. You should feel the maximum effects of the drug within 1 hour.

CHILDREN

The safety and effectiveness of Propine have not been established in children.

Overdosage

Any medication taken in excess can have serious consequences. If you suspect an overdose of Propine, seek medical attention immediately.

Generic name:

PROPOXYPHENE

See Darvocet-N, page 270.

Generic name:

PROPRANOLOL

See Inderal, page 514.

Generic name:

PROPRANOLOL WITH HYDROCHLOROTHIAZIDE

See Inderide, page 519.

Brand name:

PROPULSID

Pronounced: pro-PUHL-sid
Generic name: Cisapride

Why is this drug prescribed?
Propulsid is prescribed to treat nighttime heartburn caused by gastroesophageal reflux disease, a condition in which the valve between the esophagus and the stomach opens or leaks, allowing stomach acid to back up and cause burning or "heartburn."

Most important fact about this drug
Propulsid by itself rarely causes drowsiness. However, it may speed up the effects of alcoholic beverages and tranquilizers.

How should you take this medication?
Take your medication 15 minutes before meals and at bedtime. Take Propulsid exactly as prescribed, even if your symptoms disappear.

■ *If you miss a dose...*
  Take the forgotten dose as soon as you remember. If it is almost time for your next dose, skip the one you missed and go back to your regular schedule. Do not take 2 doses at once.

■ *Storage instructions...*
Store at room temperature. Protect from moisture.

What side effects may occur?
Side effects cannot be anticipated. If any develop or change in intensity, tell your doctor as soon as possible. Only your doctor can determine if it is safe for you to continue taking Propulsid.

■ *More common side effects may include:*
Abdominal pain
Bloating/gas
Constipation
Diarrhea
Headache
Inflamed nasal passages and sinuses
Nausea
Pain
Upper respiratory and viral infections

■ *Less common side effects may include:*
Abnormal vision, anxiety, back pain, chest pain, coughing, depression, dehydration, dizziness, fever, fatigue, frequent urination, indigestion, insomnia, itching, inflammation of the vagina, joint pain, muscle pain, nervousness, rash, sore throat, urinary tract infection, vomiting

Why should this drug not be prescribed?
You should not use Propulsid if you have bleeding, blockage, or leakage in the stomach or intestines. Do not take this drug at the same time as Nizoral, Sporanox, Monistat IV, or TAO. Also avoid Propulsid if you are sensitive to or have ever had an allergic reaction to it.

Special warnings about this medication
Propulsid is used only for nighttime heartburn. It has not been shown to be effective for daytime heartburn.

Rare, but serious, irregular heartbeats have occurred in some people taking Propulsid; tell your doctor if you have had any heart trouble.

Possible food and drug interactions
when taking this medication
If Propulsid is taken with certain other drugs, the effects of either could be increased, decreased, or altered. It is especially important to check with your doctor before combining Propulsid with the following:

Alcohol
Antispasmodic drugs such as Bentyl and Cogentin
Cimetidine (Tagamet)
Itraconazole (Sporanox)
Ketoconazole (Nizoral)
Miconazole (Monistat IV)
Ranitidine (Zantac)
Tranquilizers such as Librium, Valium, and Xanax
Troleandomycin (TAO)
Warfarin (Coumadin)

Remember that Propulsid may increase the effects of alcohol. If you are taking blood thinners (warfarin), your doctor will give you a blood test 1 week after you start on Propulsid and after your therapy is completed. Your blood-thinning medication may need to be adjusted.

Special information
if you are pregnant or breastfeeding
The effects of Propulsid during pregnancy have not been adequately studied. If you are pregnant or plan to become pregnant, tell your doctor immediately. The drug appears in breast milk and could affect a nursing infant. If this medication is essential to your health, your doctor may advise you to discontinue breastfeeding until your treatment is finished.

Recommended dosage

ADULTS

The usual starting dose is 10 milligrams of Propulsid 4 times daily, taken at least 15 minutes before meals and at bedtime.

Your doctor may need to adjust your dosage to 20 milligrams 4 times daily, depending on how well the drug works for you.

CHILDREN

The safety and effectiveness of Propulsid in children have not been established.

Overdosage
Any medication taken in excess can have serious consequences. If you suspect an overdose, seek medical attention immediately.

■ *Symptoms of Propulsid overdose may include:*
Frequent urination or bowel movements
Gas
Gurgling and rumbling in the stomach
Retching

Brand name:

PROSCAR

Pronounced: PRAHS-car
Generic name: Finasteride

Why is this drug prescribed?
Proscar is prescribed to help shrink an enlarged prostate.

The prostate, a chestnut-shaped gland present in males, produces secretions
that form part of the semen. This gland completely encloses the upper part
of the urethra, the tube through which urine flows out of the bladder. Many
men over age 50 suffer from a benign (noncancerous) enlargement of the
prostate. The enlarged gland squeezes the urethra, obstructing the normal
flow of urine. Resulting problems may include difficulty in starting urination,
weak flow of urine, and the need to urinate urgently or frequently.
Sometimes surgical removal of the prostate is necessary.

By shrinking the enlarged prostate, Proscar may alleviate the various
associated urinary problems, making surgery unnecessary.

Some doctors are also prescribing Proscar for baldness and as a preventive
measure against prostate cancer.

Most important fact about this drug
Different men have different responses to Proscar:

■ You may experience early relief from your urinary problems.
■ You may need to take the drug for 6 months or even a year before noticing
any improvement.
■ Or you may find that, even after a year of treatment, Proscar simply has
not helped you.

How should you take this medication?
You may take Proscar either with a meal or between meals.

- *If you miss a dose...*
Take it as soon as you remember. If it is almost time for your next dose, skip the one you missed and go back to your regular schedule. Never take 2 doses at the same time.

- *Storage instructions...*
Store at room temperature in a tightly closed container. Protect from light.

What side effects may occur?
Side effects cannot be anticipated. If any develop or change in intensity, inform your doctor as soon as possible. Only your doctor can determine if it is safe for you to continue taking Proscar.

- *Side effects may include:*
Decreased amount of semen per ejaculation
Decreased sex drive
Impotence

Why should this drug not be prescribed?
Proscar should never be taken by a woman or a child.

Do not take Proscar if you are sensitive to it or have ever had an allergic reaction to it.

Special warnings about this medication
Even if Proscar does relieve your urinary symptoms, periodic checkups are necessary to test for possible development of cancer of the prostate. Proscar is not an effective treatment for prostate cancer.

Benign enlargement of the prostate is not the only condition that can cause male urinary inefficiency and discomfort. Other possibilities include infection, obstruction, cancer of the prostate, and bladder disorders. Before prescribing Proscar, your doctor will want to do various tests to determine the cause of your urinary problems.

If accidentally absorbed by a pregnant woman who is carrying a male fetus, Proscar may cause abnormal development of the unborn baby's genital organs. Thus, a woman who is pregnant or who may become pregnant should never even touch a crushed Proscar tablet. If she is going to have intercourse with a man who is taking Proscar, she should insist that he wear a condom to protect her from his semen, which may contain small amounts of the medication.

It is important to read the patient information that comes in the Proscar package every time you renew your prescription so that you are aware of the latest information on the drug.

Possible food and drug interactions
when taking this medication
No significant drug interactions have been reported.

Special information
if you are pregnant or breastfeeding
As noted above, if a pregnant woman who is carrying a male fetus absorbs Proscar accidentally, the drug may cause defective development of the baby's genital organs. Any woman of childbearing age should be careful never to touch a crushed Proscar tablet. If her sexual partner is taking Proscar, he should always wear a condom when they have intercourse to avoid any possible transfer of the drug to her body via his semen.

Recommended dosage

ADULTS

The recommended dosage, for men only, is one 5-milligram tablet per day.

Overdosage
Although no specific information is available, any medication taken in excess can have serious consequences. If you suspect an overdose of Proscar, seek medical attention immediately.

Brand name:

PROSOM

Pronounced: PROE-som
Generic name: Estazolam

Why is this drug prescribed?
ProSom, a sleeping pill, is given for the short-term treatment of insomnia. Insomnia may involve difficulty falling asleep, frequent awakenings during the night, or too-early morning awakening.

Most important fact about this drug
As a chemical cousin of Valium and similar tranquilizers, ProSom is potentially addictive; thus, you should plan on taking this drug only as a temporary sleeping aid. Even after relatively short-term use of ProSom, you

may experience some withdrawal symptoms when you stop taking the medication.

How should you take this medication?

Take ProSom exactly as prescribed by your doctor. A typical schedule is 1 tablet every night at bedtime. For small, physically run-down, or older people, one-half a tablet may be a safer starting dose.

Avoid drinking alcoholic beverages while taking ProSom.

If you have ever had seizures, do not abruptly stop taking ProSom, even if you are taking antiseizure medication. Instead, taper off from ProSom under your doctor's supervision.

Even if you have never had seizures, it is better to taper off from ProSom than to stop taking the medication abruptly. Experience suggests that tapering off can help prevent drug withdrawal symptoms.

Typically, the only withdrawal symptoms caused by ProSom are mild and temporary insomnia or irritability. Occasionally, however, withdrawal can involve considerable discomfort or even danger, with symptoms such as abdominal and muscle cramps, convulsions, sweating, tremors, and vomiting.

■ *If you miss a dose...*
Take at bedtime only as needed. It is not necessary to make up a missed dose.

■ *Storage instructions...*
Store at room temperature.

What side effects may occur?

Side effects cannot be anticipated. If any develop or change in intensity, inform your doctor as soon as possible. Only your doctor can determine whether it is safe for you to continue taking ProSom.

■ *More common side effects may include:*
Abnormal coordination, cold symptoms, decreased movement or activity, dizziness, general feeling of illness, hangover, headache, leg and foot pain, nausea, nervousness, sleepiness, weakness

■ *Less common or rare side effects may include:*
Abdominal pain, abnormal dreaming, abnormal thinking, abnormal vision, acne, agitation, allergic reaction, altered taste, anxiety, apathy, arm and hand pain, arthritis, asthma, back pain, black stools, body pain, chest pain,

chills, confusion, constant, involuntary eye movement, constipation, cough, decreased appetite, decreased hearing, decreased reflexes, depression, difficult/labored breathing, double vision, dry mouth, dry skin, ear pain, emotional changeability, fainting, fever, flushing, frequent urination, gas, hallucinations, hostility, inability to hold urine, inability to urinate, increased appetite, indigestion, inflamed sinuses, itching, lack of coordination, little or no urine flow, loss of memory, menstrual cramps, muscle stiffness, nasal inflammation, neck pain, nighttime urination, nosebleed, numbness or tingling around the mouth, purple or reddish spots on the skin, rapid, heavy breathing, rash, ringing in the ears, seizure, sleep problems, sore throat, stupor, swollen breast, thirst, throbbing or fluttering heartbeat, tingling or "pins and needles", tremor, twitch, urgent need to urinate, vaginal discharge/itching, vomiting, weight gain or loss

Why should this drug not be prescribed?

Do not take ProSom if you are sensitive or allergic to it, or if you have ever had an adverse reaction to another Valium-type medication.

Do not take ProSom if you are pregnant or planning to become pregnant. Drugs in this class may cause damage to the unborn child.

Special warnings about this medication

Since ProSom may cloud your thinking, impair your judgment, or interfere with your normal physical coordination, do not drive, climb, or perform hazardous tasks until you know your reaction to this medication. It is important to remember that the tablet you took in the evening may continue to affect you well into the following day.

If you are older or physically run-down, or if you have liver or kidney damage or breathing problems, you will be particularly vulnerable to side effects from ProSom, and you should use this medication with special caution.

Possible food and drug interactions
when taking this medication

Do not drink alcohol while you are taking ProSom; this combination could make you comatose or dangerously slow your breathing.

For the same reason, do not combine ProSom with any other medication that might calm or slow the functioning of your central nervous system. Among such drugs are:

Anticonvulsants such as Dilantin, Tegretol, and Depakene
Antihistamines such as Benadryl and Chlor-Trimeton
Antipsychotics such as Haldol and Mellaril

Barbiturates such as phenobarbital
MAO inhibitor antidepressants such as Marplan, Nardil, and Parnate
Narcotics such as Percodan and Tylox
Tranquilizers such as Valium and Xanax

If you smoke, you will tend to process and eliminate ProSom fairly quickly compared with a nonsmoker.

Special information
if you are pregnant or breastfeeding

If you are pregnant, you must not take ProSom; it could cause birth defects in your child.

When a pregnant woman takes ProSom or a similar medication shortly before giving birth, her baby is likely to have poor muscle tone (flaccidity) and/or experience drug withdrawal symptoms.

Because ProSom is thought to pass into breast milk, you should not take this medication while breastfeeding.

Recommended dosage

ADULTS

The recommended initial dose is 1 milligram at bedtime; however, some patients may need a 2-milligram dose.

CHILDREN

There is no information on the safety and effectiveness of ProSom in patients under age 18.

ELDERLY

The recommended usual dosage for the elderly is 1 milligram. However, some patients may require only 0.5 milligram.

Overdosage

Any medication taken in excess can have serious consequences. If you suspect an overdose, seek medical attention immediately.

■ *Symptoms of a ProSom overdose may include:*
Confusion
Depressed breathing
Drowsiness and eventually coma
Lack of coordination
Slurred speech

Brand name:

PROSTEP

See Nicotine Patches, page 729.

Brand name:

PROTOSTAT

See Flagyl, page 444.

Brand name:

PROVENTIL

Pronounced: Proh-VEN-till
Generic name: Albuterol sulfate
Other brand names: Ventolin, Volmax Extended-Release
  Tablets

Why is this drug prescribed?
Drugs containing albuterol are prescribed for the prevention and relief of bronchial spasms. This especially applies to the treatment of asthma. This medication is also used for the prevention of bronchial spasm due to exercise.

Most important fact about this drug
Do not take albuterol more frequently than your doctor recommends. Increasing the number of doses can be dangerous and may actually make symptoms of asthma worse.

If the dose your doctor recommends does not provide relief of your symptoms, or if your symptoms become worse, consult with your doctor immediately.

How should you take this medication?
If you are using a metered-dose inhaler, follow the instructions carefully. If you are taking extended-release tablets, swallow them whole with some liquid—never chew or crush them.

- *If you miss a dose...*
  Take the forgotten dose as soon as you remember; then take any remaining doses for that day at equally spaced intervals. Never take a double dose.

- *Storage instructions...*
  This medication can be kept in the refrigerator or at room temperature.

What side effects may occur?
Side effects cannot be anticipated. If any develop or change in intensity, inform your doctor as soon as possible. Only your doctor can determine if it is safe for you to continue taking albuterol.

- *More common side effects may include:*
  Aggression, agitation, cough, diarrhea, dizziness, excitement, general bodily discomfort, headache, heartburn, increased appetite, increased blood pressure, indigestion, irritability, labored breathing, light-headedness, muscle cramps, nausea, nervousness, nightmares, nosebleed, overactivity, palpitations, rapid heartbeat, rash, ringing in the ears, shakiness, sleeplessness, stomachache, stuffy nose, throat irritation, tooth discoloration, tremors, vomiting, wheezing, worsening broncho-spasm

- *Less common side effects may include:*
  Chest pain (sometimes crushing) or discomfort, difficulty urinating, drowsiness, dry mouth and throat, flushing, high blood pressure, muscle spasm, restlessness, sweating, unusual taste, vertigo, weakness

- *Rare side effects following the use of inhaled albuterol include:*
  Hoarseness, increased breathing or wheezing, skin rash or hives, unusual and unexpected swelling of mouth and throat

Why should this drug not be prescribed?
If you are sensitive to or have ever had an allergic reaction to albuterol or other bronchodilators, you should not take this medication. Make sure that your doctor is aware of any drug reactions that you have experienced.

Special warnings about this medication
When taking albuterol inhalation aerosol, you should not use other inhaled medications before checking with your doctor.

Consult with your doctor before using this medication if you have a cardiovascular or convulsive disorder, high blood pressure, abnormal heartbeat, overactive thyroid gland, or diabetes.

Do not exceed your doctor's recommended dose of albuterol. Do not change brands without first consulting your doctor or pharmacist.

Possible food and drug interactions
when taking this medication

Albuterol inhalation aerosol should not be used with other aerosol bronchodilators.

If albuterol is taken with certain other drugs, the effects of either could be increased, decreased, or altered. It is especially important to check with your doctor before combining albuterol with the following:

Antidepressants such as Elavil and Nardil
Beta blockers (heart and blood pressure drugs such as Inderal, Tenormin, and Sectral)
Drugs similar to albuterol, such as Alupent, Brethaire, Isuprel, and epinephrine

Special information
if you are pregnant or breastfeeding

The effects of albuterol during pregnancy have not been adequately studied. If you are pregnant or plan to become pregnant, inform your doctor immediately. It is not known whether albuterol appears in breast milk. If this drug is essential to your health, your doctor may advise you to stop nursing your baby until your treatment is finished.

Recommended dosage

ADULTS

Inhalation Aerosol
Patient instructions are available with both products.

If you are being treated for a sudden or severe bronchial spasm or the prevention of asthma symptoms, the usual dosage of albuterol inhalation aerosol for adults and children aged 4 and over (Ventolin) or 12 and over (Proventil) is 2 inhalations repeated every 4 to 6 hours. More frequent use is not recommended. In some individuals, 1 inhalation every 4 hours may be sufficient.

The recommended dose of Proventil Inhalation Aerosol for prevention of recurring symptoms is 2 inhalations, 4 times a day.

For exercise-induced bronchial spasm, the usual dosage for adults and children 12 years and older is 2 inhalations, 15 minutes prior to exercise.

Tablets
The usual starting dose for adults and children 12 years of age and older is 2 or 4 milligrams 3 to 4 times a day.

Syrup
The usual starting dose for adults and children over 14 years of age is 1 or 2 teaspoonfuls 3 or 4 times a day.

Ventolin Rotacaps for Inhalation
The usual dosage for adults and children 4 years and older is the contents of one 200-microgram capsule inhaled every 4 to 6 hours using a Rotahaler inhalation device. Some people may require two 200-microgram capsules every 4 to 6 hours.

Inhalation Solution
.The usual dosage for adults and children 12 years of age and older is 2.5 milligrams administered 3 to 4 times daily by nebulization. To administer 2.5 milligrams, dilute 0.5 milliliter of the 0.5 percent solution for inhalation with 2.5 milliliters of sterile normal saline solution.

Ventolin Nebules Inhalation Solution
The usual dosage for adults and children 12 years and older is 2.5 milligrams of Ventolin taken 3 to 4 times a day by nebulization.

Proventil Repetabs and Volmax Extended-Release Tablets
The usual recommended dosage for adults and children 12 years of age and older is 8 milligrams every 12 hours. In some people, 4 milligrams every 12 hours may be sufficient. If the desired effect is not achieved with the standard dosage, your doctor may increase doses to a maximum of 32 milligrams per day, divided into two 16-milligram doses spaced 12 hours apart. Those taking Ventolin Tablets or Ventolin Syrup can switch to Volmax Extended-Release Tablets. One Volmax tablet every 12 hours is equivalent to one 2-milligram Ventolin Tablet every 6 hours.

CHILDREN

Inhalation Aerosol
Safety and effectiveness in children below the age of 12 (Proventil, Volmax) and below the age of 4 (Ventolin) have not been established. For dosage in children above these ages, see adult section.

Tablets
The usual starting dose for children 6 to 12 years of age is 2 milligrams 3 or 4 times a day. The dose can be increased with caution but should not exceed 24 milligrams per day.

Syrup
The usual starting dose for children 6 to 14 years of age is 1 teaspoonful 3 to 4 times a day. For children 2 to 6 years of age, the starting dose is 0.1 milligram per 2.2 pounds of body weight, to a maximum of 4 milligrams, 3 times a day.

ELDERLY

Oral Dosage
For elderly individuals, the usual starting dose of tablets or syrup is 2 milligrams 3 or 4 times a day.

Overdosage

■ *Symptoms of albuterol overdose may include:*
High blood pressure
Low potassium level
Radiating chest pain
Rapid heartbeat seizures

Exaggerated side effects may also be a sign of an overdose. If you suspect an overdose, seek medical attention immediately.

Brand name:

PROVERA

Pronounced: pro-VAIR-uh
Generic name: Medroxyprogesterone acetate
Other brand name: Cycrin

Why is this drug prescribed?
Provera is derived from the female hormone progesterone. You may be given Provera if your menstrual periods have stopped or a female hormone imbalance is causing your uterus to bleed abnormally.

Other forms of medroxyprogesterone, such as Depo-Provera, are used as a contraceptive injection and prescribed in the treatment of endometrial cancer.

Some doctors prescribe Provera to treat endometriosis, menopausal symptoms, premenstrual tension, sexual aggressive behavior in men, and sleep apnea (temporary failure to breathe while sleeping).

Most important fact about this drug
You should never take Provera during the first 4 months of pregnancy. During this formative period, even a few days of treatment with Provera might put your unborn baby at increased risk for birth defects. If you take Provera and later discover that you were pregnant when you took it, discuss this with your doctor right away.

How should you take this medication?
Provera may be taken with or between meals.

Do not change from one brand to another without consulting your doctor or pharmacist.

Your doctor will probably have you take Provera for 5 to 10 days and then stop; you should have your period within 3 to 7 days after the last dose.

If you are being treated for lack of regular menstrual periods, your doctor may have you start taking Provera at any time. If you are being treated for abnormal uterine bleeding due to a female-hormone imbalance, your doctor will probably have you start taking Provera on day 16 or 21 of your menstrual cycle (i.e., 16 or 21 days after the start of your last period). You should have your period within 3 to 7 days after the last dose.

- *If you miss a dose...*
  Take it as soon as you remember. If it is almost time for your next dose, skip the one you missed and go back to your regular schedule. Never take 2 doses at the same time.

- *Storage instructions...*
  Store at room temperature.

What side effects may occur?
Side effects cannot be anticipated. If any develop or change in intensity, inform your doctor as soon as possible. Only your doctor can determine if it is safe for you to continue taking Provera.

- *Side effects may include:*
  Acne, anaphylaxis (life-threatening allergic reaction), blood clot in a vein, lungs, or brain, breakthrough bleeding (between menstrual periods), breast tenderness or sudden or excessive flow of milk, cervical erosion or changes in secretions, depression, excessive growth of hair, fever, fluid retention, hair loss, headache, hives, insomnia, itching, lack of menstrua-

tion, menstrual flow changes, spotting, nausea, rash, skin discoloration, sleepiness, weight gain or loss, yellowed eyes and skin

Why should this drug not be prescribed?

Do not take Provera if you are sensitive to it or have ever had an allergic reaction to it.

If you suspect you may have become pregnant, do not take Provera as a test for pregnancy. Doctors once prescribed Provera for this purpose, but no longer do so for 2 reasons:

- Quicker, safer pregnancy tests are now available.
- If you are in fact pregnant, Provera might injure the baby.

Do not take Provera during your first 4 months of pregnancy. In the past, Provera was sometimes given to try to prevent miscarriage. However, doctors now believe that this treatment is not only ineffective but also potentially harmful to the baby.

Do not take Provera if you have:

- Cancer of the breast or genital organs
- Liver disease or a liver condition
- A dead fetus still in the uterus
- Undiagnosed bleeding from the vagina

Do not take Provera if you have, or have ever developed, blood clots.

Special warnings about this medication

Before you start to take Provera, your doctor will give you a complete physical exam, including examination of your breasts and pelvic organs. You should also have a cervical smear (Pap test).

Provera may cause some degree of fluid retention. If you have a medical condition that could be made worse by fluid retention—such as epilepsy, migraine, asthma, or a heart or kidney problem—make sure your doctor knows about it.

Provera may mask the onset of menopause. In other words, while taking Provera you may continue to experience regular menstrual bleeding even if your menopause has started.

Provera may make you depressed, especially if you have suffered from depression in the past. If you become seriously depressed, tell your doctor; you should probably stop taking Provera.

If you are diabetic, Provera could make your diabetes worse; your doctor will want to watch you closely while you are taking this drug.

There is some concern that Provera, like birth control pills, may increase your risk for a blood clot in a vein. If you experience any symptoms that might suggest the onset of such a condition—pain with swelling, warmth, and redness in a leg vein, coughing or shortness of breath, vision problems, migraine, or weakness or numbness in an arm or leg—see your doctor immediately.

Tell your doctor right away if you lose some or all of your vision or you start seeing double. You may have to stop taking the medication.

Possible food and drug interactions
when taking this medication

If Provera is taken with certain other drugs, the effects of either may be increased, decreased, or altered. It is especially important to check with your doctor before combining Provera with aminoglutethimide (Cytadren).

Special information
if you are pregnant or breastfeeding

You should not take Provera during pregnancy. If you are pregnant or plan to become pregnant, inform your doctor immediately.

Provera appears in breast milk. If you are a new mother, you may need to choose between taking Provera and breastfeeding your baby.

Recommended dosage

ADULTS

To Restore Menstrual Periods

Provera Tablets are taken in dosages of 5 to 10 milligrams daily for 5 to 10 days. Make sure you discuss what effect this will have on your menstrual cycle with your doctor. You should have bleeding 3 to 7 days after you stop taking Provera.

Abnormal Uterine Bleeding Due to Hormonal Imbalance

Beginning on the 16th or 21st day of your menstrual cycle, you will take 5 to 10 milligrams daily for 5 to 10 days. Make sure you discuss what effect this will have on your menstrual cycle with your doctor. You should have bleeding 3 to 7 days after you stop taking Provera.

Overdosage

Although no specific information is available, any medication taken in excess can have serious consequences. If you suspect an overdose of Provera, seek medical attention immediately.

Brand name:

PROZAC

Pronounced: PRO-zak
Generic name: Fluoxetine hydrochloride

Why is this drug prescribed?

Prozac is prescribed for the treatment of depression—that is, a continuing depression that interferes with daily functioning. The symptoms of major depression often include changes in appetite, sleep habits, and mind/body coordination; decreased sex drive; increased fatigue; feelings of guilt or worthlessness; difficulty concentrating; slowed thinking; and suicidal thoughts.

Prozac is also prescribed to treat obsessive-compulsive disorder. An obsession is a thought that won't go away; a compulsion is an action done over and over to relieve anxiety.

Prozac is thought to work by adjusting the balance of the brain's natural chemical messengers. It has also been used to treat obesity and eating disorders.

Most important fact about this drug

Serious, sometimes fatal, reactions have been known to occur when Prozac is used in combination with other antidepressant drugs known as MAO inhibitors, including Nardil, Parnate, and Marplan; and when Prozac is discontinued and an MAO inhibitor is started. Never take Prozac with one of these drugs or within 14 days of discontinuing therapy with one of them; and allow 5 weeks or more between stopping Prozac and starting an MAO inhibitor. Be especially cautious if you have been taking Prozac in high doses or for a long time.

If you are taking any prescription or nonprescription drugs, notify your doctor before taking Prozac.

How should you take this medication?

Prozac should be taken exactly as prescribed by your doctor.

Prozac usually is taken once or twice a day. To be effective, it should be taken regularly. Make a habit of taking it at the same time you do some other daily activity.

- *If you miss a dose...*
  Take the forgotten dose as soon as you remember. If several hours have passed, skip the dose. Never try to "catch up" by doubling the dose.

■ *Storage instructions...*
Store at room temperature.

What side effects may occur?
Side effects cannot be anticipated. If any develop or change in intensity, inform your doctor as soon as possible. Only your doctor can determine if it is safe for you to continue taking Prozac.

■ *More common side effects may include:*
Abnormal dreams, abnormal thinking, agitation, allergic reaction, anxiety, bronchitis, chest pain, chills, cough, diarrhea, dizziness, drowsiness and fatigue, dry mouth, flu symptoms, frequent urination, hay fever, headache, inability to fall or stay asleep, increased appetite, indigestion, itching, joint pain, lack or loss of appetite, light-headedness, limb pain, muscle pain, nausea, nervousness, sinus inflammation, sore throat, stomach/intestinal disorder, sweating, tremors, weakness, weight loss, yawning

■ *Less common side effects may include:*
Abnormal ejaculation, abnormal gait, abnormal stoppage of menstrual flow, acne, altered sense of taste, amnesia, apathy, arthritis, asthma, bone pain, breast cysts, breast pain, brief loss of consciousness, bursitis, chills and fever, confusion, conjunctivitis, convulsions, dark, tarry stool, decreased sex drive, difficulty in swallowing, dilation of pupils, dry skin, ear pain, eye pain, exaggerated feeling of well-being, excessive bleeding, facial swelling due to fluid retention, fever, fluid retention, fluttery heartbeat, gas, hair loss, hallucinations, hangover effect, hiccups, high or low blood pressure, hives, hostility, impotence, infection, inflammation of the esophagus, inflammation of the gums, inflammation of the stomach lining, inflammation of the tongue, inflammation of the vagina, intolerance of light, involuntary movement, irrational ideas, irregular heartbeat, jaw or neck pain, lack of muscle coordination, low blood pressure upon standing, low blood sugar, migraine headache, mouth inflammation, muscle spasm, neck pain and rigidity, nosebleed, ovarian disorders, paranoid reaction, pelvic pain, pneumonia, rapid breathing, rapid heartbeat, ringing in the ears, severe chest pain, skin inflammation, skin rash, thirst, tooth problems, twitching, uncoordinated movements, urinary disorders, vague feeling of bodily discomfort, vertigo, vision disturbances, vomiting, weight gain

■ *Rare side effects may include:*
Antisocial behavior, blood in urine, bloody diarrhea, bone disease, breast enlargement, cataracts, colitis, coma, deafness, decreased reflexes,

dehydration, double vision, drooping of eyelids, duodenal ulcer, enlarged abdomen, enlargement of liver, enlargement or increased activity of thyroid gland, excess growth of coarse hair on face, chest, etc., excess uterine or vaginal bleeding, extreme muscle tension, eye bleeding, female milk production, fluid accumulation and swelling in the head, fluid buildup in larynx and lungs, gallstones, glaucoma, gout, heart attack, hepatitis, high blood sugar, hysteria, inability to control bowel movements, increased salivation, inflammation of eyes and eyelids, inflammation of fallopian tubes, inflammation of testes, inflammation of the gallbladder, inflammation of the small intestine, inflammation of tissue below skin, kidney disorders, lung inflammation, menstrual disorders, miscarriage, mouth sores, muscle inflammation or bleeding, muscle spasms, painful sexual intercourse for women, psoriasis, rashes, reddish or purplish spots on the skin, reduction of body temperature, rheumatoid arthritis, seborrhea, shingles, skin discoloration, skin inflammation and disorders, slowing of heart rate, slurred speech, spitting blood, stomach ulcer, stupor, suicidal thoughts, taste loss, temporary cessation of breathing, tingling sensation around the mouth, tongue discoloration and swelling, urinary tract disorders, vomiting blood, yellow eyes and skin

Why should this drug not be prescribed?
If you are sensitive to or have ever had an allergic reaction to Prozac or similar drugs, you should not take this medication. Make sure that your doctor is aware of any drug reactions that you have experienced.

Do not take this drug while using an MAO inhibitor. (See "Most important fact about this drug.")

Special warnings about this medication
Unless you are directed to do so by your doctor, do not take this medication if you are recovering from a heart attack or if you have kidney or liver disease or diabetes.

Prozac may cause you to become drowsy or less alert and may affect your judgment. Therefore, driving or operating dangerous machinery or participating in any hazardous activity that requires full mental alertness is not recommended.

While taking this medication, you may feel dizzy or light-headed or actually faint when getting up from a lying or sitting position. If getting up slowly doesn't help or if this problem continues, notify your doctor.

If you develop a skin rash or hives while taking Prozac, discontinue use of the medication and notify your doctor immediately.

Prozac should be used with caution if you have a history of seizures. You should discuss all of your medical conditions with your doctor before taking this medication.

The safety and effectiveness of Prozac have not been established in children.

Possible food and drug interactions
when taking this medication
Combining Prozac with MAO inhibitors is dangerous.

Do not drink alcohol while taking this medication.

If Prozac is taken with certain other drugs, the effects of either could be increased, decreased, or altered. It is especially important to check with your doctor before combining Prozac with the following:

Carbamazepine (Tegretol)
Diazepam (Valium)
Digitoxin (Crystodigin)
Drugs that act on the central nervous system (brain and spinal cord) such as Xanax
Flecainide (Tambocor)
Lithium (Eskalith)
Other antidepressants (Elavil)
Phenytoin (Dilantin)
Tryptophan
Vinblastine (Velban)
Warfarin (Coumadin)

Special information
if you are pregnant or breastfeeding
The effects of Prozac during pregnancy have not been adequately studied. If you are pregnant or plan to become pregnant, inform your doctor immediately. This medication appears in breast milk, and breastfeeding is not recommended while you are taking Prozac.

Recommended dosage

ADULTS

The usual starting dose is 20 milligrams per day, taken in the morning. Your doctor may increase your dose after several weeks if no improvement is observed. Patients with kidney or liver disease, the elderly, and those taking other drugs may have their dosages adjusted by their doctor.

Dosages above 20 milligrams daily should be taken once a day in the morning or in 2 smaller doses taken in the morning and at noon.

The usual daily dose for depression ranges from 20 to 60 milligrams. For obsessive-compulsive disorder the customary range is 20 to 60 milligrams, though 80 milligrams is sometimes prescribed.

Overdosage

Any medication taken in excess or in combination with other drugs can cause symptoms of overdose. If you suspect an overdose, seek medical attention immediately.

- *Symptoms of Prozac overdose include:*
  Agitation
  Nausea
  Restlessness
  Vomiting

Brand name:

PSORCON

Pronounced: SORE-kon
Generic name: Diflorasone diacetate

Why is this drug prescribed?

Psorcon is prescribed for the relief of the inflammatory and itching symptoms of skin disorders that respond to the topical application (applied directly to the skin) of steroids (hormones produced by the body that have potent anti-inflammatory effects).

Most important fact about this drug

When you use Psorcon, you inevitably absorb some of the medication through your skin and into the bloodstream. Too much absorption can lead to unwanted side effects elsewhere in the body. To keep this problem to a minimum, avoid using large amounts of Psorcon over large areas, and do not cover it with airtight dressings such as plastic wrap or adhesive bandages unless specifically told to by your doctor.

How should you use this medication?

Use this medication exactly as prescribed.

Psorcon is for use only on the skin. Be careful to keep it out of your eyes.

- *If you miss a dose...*
  Apply it as soon as you remember. If it is almost time for the next dose, skip the one you missed and go back to your regular schedule.

■ *Storage instructions...*
Store at room temperature.

What side effects may occur?
Side effects cannot be anticipated. If any develop or change in intensity, inform your doctor as soon as possible. Only your doctor can determine if it is safe for you to continue taking Psorcon.

■ *Side effects may include:*
Burning, dryness, eruptions resembling acne, excessive discoloring of the skin, excessive growth of hair, inflammation of hair follicles, inflammation around the mouth, irritation, itching, prickly heat, secondary infection, severe inflammation of the skin, softening of the skin, stretch marks, stretching or thinning of the skin

Why should this drug not be prescribed?
If you are sensitive to or have ever had an allergic reaction to diflorasone diacetate or other drugs of this type (antifungals, steroids), you should not take this medication. Make sure your doctor is aware of any drug reactions you have experienced.

Special warnings about this medication
Remember that absorption of Psorcon through the skin can affect the whole body. Although it's unusual (most common if Psorcon is spread over large areas of the skin), you could develop symptoms of steroid excess such as weight gain, reddening and rounding of the face and neck, growth of excess body and facial hair, high blood pressure, emotional disturbances, loss of energy due to high blood sugar, and increase in frequency of urination.

Do not use this drug for any disorder other than the one for which it was prescribed.

The treated skin area should not be bandaged, covered, or wrapped unless otherwise directed by your doctor. Avoid covering a treated area with waterproof diapers or plastic pants. They can cause unwanted absorption of Psorcon.

If an irritation or allergic reaction develops while you are using Psorcon, notify your doctor.

Possible food and drug interactions
when taking this medication
No interactions with food or other drugs have been reported.

Special information
if you are pregnant or breastfeeding

If you are pregnant or plan to become pregnant, inform your doctor before using Psorcon. It is not known whether this medication appears in breast milk. If this drug is essential to your health, your doctor may advise you to discontinue breastfeeding until treatment with this medication is finished.

Recommended dosage

ADULTS

A thin film of Psorcon ointment should be applied to the affected area from 1 to 3 times a day, depending on the severity or resistant nature of the condition.

Your doctor may recommend airtight bandages for the management of psoriasis (chronic skin disorder) or stubborn skin conditions. If an infection develops, you should stop using airtight dressings.

CHILDREN

Your doctor will limit the use of Psorcon for your child to the least amount that is effective. Long-term treatment may interfere with the growth and development of children.

Overdosage

An acute overdosage is unlikely with the use of Psorcon; however, long-term or prolonged use can produce side effects throughout your body. If you suspect an overdose, seek medical attention immediately.

Brand name:

PYRIDIUM

Pronounced: pie-RI-di-um
Generic name: Phenazopyridine hydrochloride

Why is this drug prescribed?

Pyridium is a urinary tract analgesic that helps relieve the pain, burning, urgency, frequency, and irritation caused by infection, trauma, catheters, or various surgical procedures in the lower urinary tract. Pyridium is indicated for short-term use and can only relieve symptoms; it is not a treatment for the underlying cause of the symptoms.

Most important fact about this drug

Pyridium produces an orange to red color in urine, and may stain fabric. Staining of contact lenses has also been reported.

How should you take this medication?

Take Pyridium after meals, exactly as prescribed.

■ *If you miss a dose...*

Take it as soon as you remember. If it is almost time for your next dose, skip the one you missed and go back to your regular schedule. Never take 2 doses at the same time.

■ *Storage instructions...*

Store at room temperature.

What side effects may occur?

Side effects cannot be anticipated. If any occur or change in intensity, inform your doctor as soon as possible. Only your doctor can determine if it is safe for you to continue taking Pyridium.

■ *Side effects may include:*

Headache
Itching
Rash
Severe allergic reaction (rash, difficulty breathing, fever, rapid heartbeat, convulsions)
Upset stomach

Why should this drug not be prescribed?

Pyridium should be avoided if you have kidney disease, or if you are sensitive to or have ever had an allergic reaction to it.

Special warnings about this medication

If your skin or the whites of your eyes develop a yellowish tone, it may indicate that your kidneys are not eliminating the medication as they should. Notify your doctor immediately. If you are older, your doctor will watch you more closely, since the kidneys work less effectively as we age.

Possible food and drug interactions when taking this medication

No interactions have been reported.

Special information
if you are pregnant or breastfeeding

The effects of Pyridium during pregnancy have not been adequately studied. If you are pregnant or plan to become pregnant, inform your doctor immediately. To date, there is no information on whether Pyridium appears in breast milk. If this medication is essential to your health, your doctor may advise you to stop breastfeeding until your treatment with Pyridium is finished.

Recommended dosage

ADULTS

The usual dose is two 100-milligram tablets or one 200-milligram tablet 3 times a day after meals.

You should not take Pyridium for more than 2 days if you are also taking an antibiotic for the treatment of a urinary tract infection.

Overdosage

Any medication taken in excess can have serious consequences. If you suspect an overdose, seek emergency medical treatment immediately.

■ *Symptoms of Pyridium overdose may include:*
   Blood disorders
   Bluish skin color
   Impaired kidney and liver function

Generic name:

QUAZEPAM

See Doral, page 364.

Brand name:

QUESTRAN

Pronounced: KWEST-ran
Generic name: Cholestyramine
Other brand name: Questran Light

Why is this drug prescribed?

Questran is used to lower cholesterol levels in the blood of people with primary hypercholesterolemia (too much LDL cholesterol). Hypercholesterolemia is a genetic condition characterized by a lack of the LDL receptors that remove cholesterol from the bloodstream.

This drug is also prescribed for people with hypertriglyceridemia, a condition in which an excess of fat is stored in the body.

However, Questran is usually prescribed only when a low-fat, low-sugar, and low-cholesterol diet does not lower cholesterol levels enough.

This drug may also be prescribed to relieve itching associated with gallbladder obstruction.

It is available in two forms: Questran and Questran Light. The same instructions apply to both.

Most important fact about this drug
Questran is usually prescribed only if diet, exercise, and weight loss fail to bring your cholesterol levels under control. It's important to remember that Questran is a supplement—not a substitute—for these other measures. To get the full benefit of the medication, you need to stick to the diet and exercise program prescribed by your doctor. All these efforts to keep your cholesterol levels normal are important because together they may lower your risk of heart disease.

How should you take this medication?
Never take Questran in its dry form. Always mix it with water or other liquids *before* taking it. For Questran, use 2 to 6 ounces of liquid per packet or level scoopful; for Questran Light, use 2 to 3 ounces. Soups or fruits with a high moisture content, such as applesauce or crushed pineapple, can be used in place of beverages.

■ *If you miss a dose...*
Take the forgotten dose as soon as you remember. If it is almost time for the next dose, skip the one you missed and go back to your regular schedule. Never try to "catch up" by doubling the dose.

■ *Storage instructions...*
Store at room temperature. Protect from moisture and high humidity.

What side effects may occur?
Side effects cannot be anticipated. If any develop or change in intensity, inform your doctor as soon as possible. Only your doctor can determine if it is safe for you to continue taking Questran.

The most common side effect of Questran is constipation.

■ *Less common or rare side effects may include:*
Abdominal discomfort, anemia, anxiety, arthritis, asthma, backache, belching, black stools, bleeding around the teeth, blood in the urine, brittle bones, burnt odor to urine, dental cavities, diarrhea, difficulty swallowing, dizziness, drowsiness, fainting, fatigue, fluid retention, gas, headache, heartburn, hiccups, hives, increased sex drive, increased tendency to bleed due to vitamin K deficiency, indigestion, inflammation of the eye, inflammation of the pancreas, irritation around the anal area, irritation of the skin and tongue, joint pain, lack or loss of appetite, muscle pain, nausea, night blindness due to vitamin A deficiency, painful or difficult urination, rash, rectal bleeding and/or pain, ringing in the ears, shortness of breath, sour taste, swollen glands, tingling sensation, ulcer attack, vertigo, vitamin D deficiency, vomiting, weight gain or loss, wheezing

Why should this drug not be prescribed?
If you are sensitive to or have ever had an allergic reaction to Questran or similar drugs such as Colestid, you should not take this medication. Make sure that your doctor is aware of any drug reactions that you have experienced.

Unless you are directed to do so by your doctor, do not take this medication if you are being treated for gallbladder obstruction.

Special warnings about this medication
If you have phenylketonuria, a genetic disorder, check with your doctor before taking Questran because this product contains phenylalanine.

If you are being treated for any disease that contributes to increased blood cholesterol, such as hypothyroidism (reduced thyroid function), diabetes, nephrotic syndrome (kidney and blood vessel disorder), dysproteinemia, or obstructive liver disease, consult with your doctor before taking this medication.

Questran should begin to reduce cholesterol levels during the first month of therapy. If adequate reduction of cholesterol is not obtained, this medication should be discontinued. Therefore, it is important that your doctor check your progress regularly.

The use of this medication may produce or worsen constipation and aggravate hemorrhoids. If this happens, inform your doctor. Only your doctor can determine if your dose needs to be reduced or discontinued.

The prolonged use of Questran may change acidity in the bloodstream, especially in younger and smaller individuals in whom the doses are relatively higher. Again, it is important that you or your child be checked by your doctor on a regular basis.

Possible food and drug interactions when taking this medication

If Questran is taken with certain other drugs, the effects of either could be increased, decreased, or altered. It is especially important to check with your doctor before taking Questran with the following:

Chlorothiazide (Diuril)
Digitalis (Lanoxin, Crystodigin)
Oral diabetes drugs such as DiaBeta and Diabinese
Penicillin G (Pentids, others)
Phenobarbital
Phenylbutazone (Butazolidin)
Propranolol (Inderal)
Tetracycline (Achromycin V)
Thyroid medication such as Synthroid
Warfarin (Coumadin)

Your doctor may recommend that you take other medications at least 1 hour before or 4 to 6 hours after you take Questran.

If you are taking a drug such as digitalis (Lanoxin), stopping Questran could be hazardous, since you might experience exaggerated effects of the other drug. Consult your doctor before discontinuing Questran.

This drug may interfere with normal digestion and absorption of fats, including fat-soluble vitamins such as A, D, and K. If supplements of vitamins A, D, and K are essential to your health, your doctor may prescribe an alternative form of these vitamins.

There are no special considerations regarding alcohol use with this medication.

Special information if you are pregnant or breastfeeding

The effects of Questran during pregnancy have not been adequately studied. If you are pregnant or plan to become pregnant, inform your doctor immediately. Because this medication can interfere with vitamin absorption, it may have an effect on nursing infants. If this drug is essential to your health, your doctor may advise you to discontinue breastfeeding until your treatment is finished.

Recommended dosage

ADULTS

The recommended starting dose is 1 single-dose packet or 1 level scoopful, 1 to 2 times daily. The usual maintenance dosage is a total of 2 to 4 packets or scoopfuls daily divided into 2 doses preferably at mealtime (usually before meals). The maximum daily dose is 6 packets or scoopfuls. Although the recommended dosing schedule is 2 times daily, your doctor may ask you to take Questran in up to 6 smaller doses per day.

CHILDREN

Experience with the use of Questran in infants and children is limited. If this medication is essential to your child's health, follow your doctor's recommended dosing schedule.

Overdosage

No ill effects from an overdose have been reported. The main potential harm of an overdose would be obstruction of the stomach and intestines. If you suspect an overdose, seek medical attention immediately.

Brand name:

QUIBRON T/SR

See Theo-Dur, page 1102.

Generic name:

QUINAPRIL

See Accupril, page 1.

Brand name:

QUINIDEX EXTENTABS

Pronounced: KWIN-i-deks Eks-TEN-tabs
Generic name: Quinidine sulfate

Why is this drug prescribed?

Quinidex Extentabs are used to correct certain types of irregular heart rhythms and to slow an abnormally fast heartbeat.

Most important fact about this drug
It is important to take only the prescribed amount of this medication—no more and no less. Try to keep your doses at regularly spaced intervals, and be sure not to miss any.

How should you take this medication?
Quinidex Extentabs should be taken whole, not crushed or chewed, with a full glass of water, milk, or other liquid. Take them exactly as prescribed.

You should take this medication while you are sitting up or standing. This will make it easier to swallow the tablets.

■ *If you miss a dose...*
Take it as soon as you remember, if it is within 2 hours of your scheduled time. If you do not remember until later, skip the dose you missed and go back to your regular schedule. Do not take 2 doses at once.

■ *Storage instructions...*
Store at room temperature in a tightly closed container, away from light.

What side effects may occur?
Side effects cannot be anticipated. If any develop or change in intensity, inform your doctor as soon as possible. Only your doctor can determine if it is safe for you to continue taking Quinidex Extentabs.

■ *More common side effects include:*
Abdominal pain
Diarrhea
Hepatitis
Inflammation of the esophagus (gullet)
Loss of appetite
Nausea
Vomiting

■ *Less common or rare side effects may include:*
Allergic reaction (symptoms include: swelling of face, lips, tongue, throat, arms, and legs, sore throat, fever and chills, difficulty swallowing, chest pain), anemia, apprehension, asthma attack, blind spots, blood clots, blurred vision, changes in skin pigmentation, confusion, delirium, depression, dilated pupils, disturbed color perception, double vision, eczema, excitement, fainting, fever, fluid retention, flushing, headache, hearing changes, hepatitis, hives, inability to breathe, intense itching, intolerance

to light, irregular heartbeats, joint pain, lack of coordination, low blood pressure, lupus erythematosus (inflammation of connective tissue), mental decline, muscle pain, night blindness, psoriasis, rash, reddish or purplish spots below the skin, skin eruptions and scaling, skin sensitivity to light, vertigo, vision changes

Another possible side effect is a sensitivity reaction called cinchonism. Symptoms include ringing in the ears, loss of hearing, dizziness, light-headedness, headache, nausea, and disturbed vision.

Why should this drug not be prescribed?
Quinidex Extentabs should not be prescribed for certain heartbeat irregularities, including one known as heart block. This drug should also be avoided if you have myasthenia gravis (abnormal muscle weakness), or if you are sensitive to or have ever had an allergic reaction to quinidine or cinchona derivatives. (Quinidine comes from the bark of the cinchona tree.)

Special warnings about this medication
If you have poorly controlled heart disease or circulatory problems, Quinidex should be used cautiously. It can cause low blood pressure, slow heartbeat, or heart block.

Your doctor will carefully monitor your use of this medication if you have partial heart block. It can produce complete heart block.

If you have one or more fainting spells, notify your doctor at once.

Use Quinidex Extentabs cautiously if you have kidney or liver disease. Your doctor will check your blood count and liver and kidney function periodically during long-term therapy.

There have been cases of liver damage due to quinidine sensitivity. If you develop an unexplained fever, especially when you begin taking quinidine, your doctor will monitor your liver function for the first 4 to 8 weeks of therapy. Symptoms usually disappear when quinidine is stopped.

There have been rare cases of severe allergic reaction to quinidine, especially during the first few weeks of therapy. Discuss any allergic reactions you have experienced with your doctor.

Do not confuse Quinidex with quinine, which although related, is used to treat nighttime leg cramps and malaria.

Possible food and drug interactions
when taking this medication

Concentrations of digoxin (Lanoxin) in your blood may increase or even double when this drug is taken with Quinidex Extentabs. Your doctor may need to reduce the amount of digoxin you take.

If Quinidex Extentabs are taken with certain other drugs, the effects of either could be increased, decreased, or altered. It is especially important to check with your doctor before combining Quinidex Extentabs with the following:

Amiodarone (Cordarone)
Antacids containing magnesium, such as Maalox and Mylanta
Antispasmodic drugs such as Bentyl
Aspirin
Beta-blocking blood pressure medications such as Inderal and Tenormin
Blood thinners such as Coumadin
Certain antidepressants such as Elavil and Tofranil
Certain diuretic drugs such as Diamox and Daranide
Cimetidine (Tagamet)
Decamethonium
Disopyramide (Norpace)
Ketoconazole (Nizoral)
Major tranquilizers such as Stelazine and Thorazine
Nifedipine (Procardia)
Phenobarbital
Phenytoin (Dilantin)
Physostigmine (Antilirium)
Ranitidine (Zantac)
Reserpine (Diupres)
Rifampin (Rifadin)
Sodium bicarbonate
Sucralfate (Carafate)
Thiazide diuretics such as Dyazide and HydroDIURIL
Verapamil (Calan)

Special information
if you are pregnant or breastfeeding

The effects of Quinidex Extentabs during pregnancy have not been adequately studied. If you are pregnant or plan to become pregnant, inform your doctor immediately. Quinidex appears in breast milk and can affect a nursing infant. If this medication is essential to your health, your doctor may advise you to discontinue breastfeeding until your treatment is finished.

Recommended dosage

ADULTS

The usual dosage is 1 or 2 Quinidex Extentabs every 8 to 12 hours.

CHILDREN

The safety and effectiveness of this drug in children have not been established.

Overdosage

Any medication taken in excess can have serious consequences. If you suspect an overdose, seek medical treatment immediately.

- *The symptoms of Quinidex Extentabs overdose may include:*
  Abnormal heart rhythms
  Changes in heart function
  Coma
  Decreased breathing
  Decreased production of urine
  Fluid in the lungs
  Low blood pressure
  Seizures

Generic name:

QUINIDINE SULFATE

See Quinidex Extentabs, page 932.

Generic name:

RAMIPRIL

See Altace, page 35.

Generic name:

RANITIDINE HYDROCHLORIDE

See Zantac, page 1217.

Brand name:

REGLAN

Pronounced: REG-lan
Generic name: Metoclopramide hydrochloride

Why is this drug prescribed?
Reglan increases the contractions of the stomach and small intestine, helping the passage of food. It is given to treat the symptoms of diabetic gastroparesis, a condition in which the stomach does not contract. These symptoms include vomiting, nausea, heartburn, feeling of indigestion, persistent fullness after meals, and appetite loss. Reglan is also used, for short periods, to treat heartburn in people with gastroesophageal reflux disorder (backflow of stomach contents into the esophagus). In addition, it is given to prevent nausea and vomiting caused by cancer chemotherapy and surgery.

Most important fact about this drug
Reglan may cause mild to severe depression. If you have suffered from depression in the past, make sure your doctor is aware of it. Reglan may not be the best drug for you.

How should you take this medication?
Reglan is usually taken 30 minutes before a meal. If you suffer from heartburn that occurs only intermittently or only at certain times of day, your doctor may want you to schedule your Reglan therapy around those times.

You will probably take Reglan for only 4 to 12 weeks. Continuous treatment beyond 12 weeks is not recommended.

If you have diabetic "lazy stomach" (gastric stasis) that tends to recur, your doctor may want you to take Reglan at the first sign of a recurrence.

- *If you miss a dose...*
  Take it as soon as you remember. If it is almost time for your next dose, skip the one you missed and go back to your regular schedule. Do not take 2 doses at once.

- *Storage instructions...*
  Store at room temperature.

What side effects may occur?

Side effects cannot be anticipated. If any develop or change in intensity, inform your doctor as soon as possible. Only your doctor can determine if it is safe for you to continue taking Reglan.

■ *More common side effects may include:*
Drowsiness
Fatigue
Restlessness

■ *Less common or rare side effects may include:*
Breast development in males, confusion, continual discharge of milk from the breasts, depression, diarrhea, dizziness, fluid retention, frequent urination, hallucinations, headache, high or low blood pressure, high fever, hives, impotence, inability to hold urine, insomnia, menstrual irregularities, nausea, rapid or slow heartbeat, rash, rigid muscles, slow movement, swollen tongue or throat, tremor, vision problems, wheezing, yellowed eyes and skin

In addition, Reglan may cause symptoms similar to those of Parkinson's disease, such as slow movements, rigidity, tremor, or a mask-like facial appearance.

Reglan may produce tardive dyskinesia, a syndrome of jerky or writhing involuntary movements, particularly of the tongue, face, mouth, or jaw. Reglan may also cause involuntary movements of the arms and legs, and sometimes loud or labored breathing.

Reglan may cause intense restlessness with associated symptoms such as anxiety, agitation, foot-tapping, pacing, inability to sit still, jitteriness, and insomnia. These symptoms may disappear as your body gets used to Reglan, or if your dosage is reduced.

Why should this drug not be prescribed?

Do not take Reglan if you are sensitive to it or have ever had an allergic reaction to it.

You should not take Reglan if you have a condition such as obstruction, perforation, or hemorrhage of the stomach or small bowel that might be aggravated by increased stomach and small-bowel movement.

If you have pheochromocytoma (a nonmalignant tumor that causes hypertension), do not take Reglan; it could trigger a dangerous jump in blood pressure.

Do not take Reglan if you have epilepsy; it could increase the frequency and severity of seizures.

If you are taking a drug that is likely to cause side effects such as tremors, jerks, grimaces, or writhing movements, do not take Reglan; it could make such symptoms more severe.

Reglan is not recommended for patients under 18 years of age.

Special warnings about this medication

If you have Parkinson's disease, you should be given Reglan cautiously or not at all, since the drug may make your Parkinson's symptoms worse.

Because Reglan may make you drowsy and impair your coordination, you should not drive, climb, or perform hazardous tasks until you know how the medication affects you.

Use Reglan with caution if you have high blood pressure.

Possible food and drug interactions
when taking this medication

If Reglan is taken with certain other drugs, the effects of either could be increased, decreased, or altered. It is especially important to check with your doctor before combining Reglan with the following:

Acetaminophen (Tylenol)
Alcoholic beverages
Antispasmodic drugs such as Bentyl and Pro-Banthine
Cimetidine (Tagamet)
Cyclosporine (Sandimmune)
Digoxin (Lanoxin)
Insulin
MAO inhibitor antidepressants such as Marplan, Nardil, and Parnate
Levodopa (Dopar, Sinemet)
Narcotic painkillers such as Percocet and Demerol
Sleeping pills such as Dalmane, Halcion, and Restoril
Tetracycline (Achromycin, Sumycin, others)
Tranquilizers such as Valium and Xanax

If you take insulin for diabetes, your insulin dosage or dosing schedule may have to be adjusted while you are taking Reglan.

Special information
if you are pregnant or breastfeeding

The effects of Reglan during pregnancy have not been adequately studied. If you are pregnant or plan to become pregnant, inform your doctor immediately. Reglan should be used during pregnancy only if it is clearly needed. Reglan appears in breast milk. Your doctor may recommend that you discontinue Reglan while you are breastfeeding your baby.

Recommended dosage

ADULTS

Symptoms of Gastroesophageal Reflux

The usual dose is 10 milligrams to 15 milligrams of Reglan, up to 4 times a day, 30 minutes before each meal and at bedtime, depending upon the symptoms being treated and the effectiveness of the dose. Treatment usually lasts no longer than 12 weeks.

If symptoms occur only intermittently or at specific times of the day, your doctor may give you a single dose of up to 20 milligrams as a preventive measure.

Symptoms Associated with Diabetic Gastroparesis or Gastric Stasis

The usual dose is 10 milligrams 30 minutes before each meal and at bedtime for 2 to 8 weeks.

ELDERLY

Relief of Symptomatic Gastroesophageal Reflux
The elderly may need only 5 milligrams per dose.

Overdosage

Any medication taken in excess can have serious consequences. If you suspect an overdose, seek medical attention immediately.

■ *Symptoms of Reglan overdose may include:*
Disorientation
Drowsiness
Involuntary movements

Brand name:

RELAFEN

Pronounced: REL-ah-fen
Generic name: Nabumetone

Why is this drug prescribed?
Relafen, a nonsteroidal anti-inflammatory drug, is used to relieve the inflammation, swelling, stiffness, and joint pain associated with rheumatoid arthritis and osteoarthritis (the most common form of arthritis).

Most important fact about this drug
You should have frequent checkups with your doctor if you take Relafen regularly. Ulcers or internal bleeding can occur with or without warning.

How should you take this medication?
Relafen can be taken with or without food. Take it exactly as prescribed.

- *If you miss a dose...*
  Take the forgotten dose as soon as you remember. If it is almost time for your next dose, skip the one you missed and go back to your regular schedule. Never take a double dose.

- *Storage instructions...*
  Keep this medication in the container it came in, tightly closed, and away from moist places and direct light. It can be stored at room temperature.

What side effects may occur?
Side effects cannot be anticipated. If any develop or change in intensity, inform your doctor as soon as possible. Only your doctor can determine whether it is safe for you to continue taking Relafen.

- *More common side effects may include:*
  Abdominal pain, constipation, diarrhea, dizziness, fluid retention, gas, headache, indigestion, itching, nausea, rash, ringing in ears

- *Less common side effects may include:*
  Dry mouth, fatigue, inability to fall or stay asleep, increased sweating, inflammation of the mouth, inflammation of the stomach, nervousness, sleepiness, vomiting

■ *Rare side effects may include:*

Agitation, anxiety, confusion, dark, tarry, bloody stools, depression, difficult or labored breathing, difficulty swallowing, fluid retention, general feeling of illness, hives, increase or loss of appetite, large blisters, pins and needles, pneumonia or lung inflammation, sensitivity to light, severe allergic reactions, skin peeling, stomach and intestinal inflammation and/or bleeding, tremor, ulcers, vaginal bleeding, vertigo, vision changes, weakness, weight gain, yellow eyes and skin

Why should this drug not be prescribed?

Do not take this medication if you are sensitive to or have ever had an allergic reaction to Relafen, or if you have had asthma attacks, hives or other allergic reactions caused by Relafen, aspirin, or other nonsteroidal anti-inflammatory drugs.

Special warnings about this medication

Stomach and intestinal ulcers can occur without warning. Remember to get regular check-ups.

Make sure the doctor knows if you have kidney or liver disease. Relafen should be used with caution.

This drug can cause fluid retention and swelling. It should be used with caution if you have congestive heart failure or high blood pressure.

Relafen can cause increased sensitivity to sunlight.

Possible food and drug interactions
when taking this medication

If Relafen is taken with certain other drugs, the effects of either could be increased, decreased, or altered. It is especially important to check with your doctor before combining Relafen with blood-thinning drugs such as Coumadin and aspirin.

Other drugs with which Relafen could possibly interact include:

Diuretics (HydroDIURIL, Lasix)
Lithium (Lithonate)
Methotrexate

Special information
if you are pregnant or breastfeeding

The effects of Relafen during pregnancy have not been adequately studied. If you are pregnant or plan to become pregnant, inform your doctor immediately. Relafen may appear in breast milk and could affect a nursing infant. If this medication is essential to your health, your doctor may advise you to discontinue breastfeeding until your treatment with Paxil is finished.

Recommended dosage

ADULTS

The usual starting dose is 1,000 milligrams taken as a single dose. Dosage may be increased up to 2,000 milligrams per day, taken once or twice a day.

CHILDREN

The safety and effectiveness of this drug in children have not been established.

Overdosage

Any medication taken in excess can have serious consequences. If you suspect an overdose, seek medical attention immediately.

Generic name:

RESERPINE, HYDRALAZINE, AND HYDROCHLOROTHIAZIDE

See Ser-Ap-Es, page 1012.

Brand name:

RESTORIL

Pronounced: RES-tah-rill
Generic name: Temazepam

Why is this drug prescribed?

Restoril is used for the relief of insomnia (difficulty in falling asleep, waking up frequently at night, or waking up early in the morning). It belongs to a class of drugs known as benzodiazepines.

Most important fact about this drug

Sleep problems are usually temporary, requiring treatment for only a short time, usually 1 or 2 days and no more than 2 to 3 weeks. Insomnia that lasts longer than this may be a sign of another medical problem. If you find you need this medicine for more than 7 to 10 days, be sure to check with your doctor.

How should you take this medication?
Take this medication exactly as directed; never take more than the prescribed amount.

■ *If you miss a dose...*
Take only as needed.

■ *Storage instructions...*
Keep this medication in the container it came in, tightly closed, and out of the reach of children. Store it at room temperature.

What side effects may occur?
Side effects cannot be anticipated. If any develop or change in intensity, inform your doctor as soon as possible. Only your doctor can determine if it is safe for you to continue taking Restoril.

■ *More common side effects may include:*
Dizziness
Drowsiness
Fatigue
Headache
Nausea
Nervousness
Sluggishness

■ *Less common or rare side effects may include:*
Abdominal discomfort, abnormal sweating, agitation, anxiety, backache, blurred vision, burning eyes, confusion, constant, involuntary movement of the eyeball, depression, diarrhea, difficult or labored breathing, dry mouth, exaggerated feeling of well-being, fluttery or throbbing heartbeat, hallucinations, hangover, increased dreaming, lack of coordination, loss of appetite, loss of equilibrium, loss of memory, nightmares, overstimulation, restlessness, tremors, vertigo, vomiting, weakness

■ *Side effects due to rapid decrease in or abrupt withdrawal from Restoril:*
Abdominal and muscle cramps, convulsions, feeling of discomfort, inability to fall asleep or stay asleep, sweating, tremors, vomiting

Why should this drug not be prescribed?
If you are pregnant or plan to become pregnant, you should not take this medication. It poses a potential risk to the developing baby.

Special warnings about this medication

When you take Restoril every night for more than a few weeks, it loses its effectiveness to help you sleep. This is known as tolerance. You can also develop physical dependence on this drug, especially if you take it regularly for more than a few weeks, or take high doses.

When you first start taking Restoril, until you know whether the medication will have any "carry over" effect the next day, use extreme care while doing anything that requires complete alertness such as driving a car or operating machinery.

If you are severely depressed or have suffered from severe depression in the past, consult your doctor before taking this medication.

If you have kidney or liver problems or chronic lung disease, make sure your doctor is aware of it.

After you stop taking Restoril, you may have more trouble sleeping than you had before you started taking it. This is called "rebound insomnia" and should clear up after 1 or 2 nights.

Possible food and drug interactions
when taking this medication

Restoril may intensify the effects of alcohol. Do not drink alcohol while taking this medication.

If Restoril is taken with certain other drugs, the effects of either could be increased, decreased, or altered. It is especially important to check with your doctor before combining Restoril with the following:

Antidepressant drugs such as Elavil, Nardil, Parnate, and Tofranil
Antihistamines such as Benadryl
Barbiturates such as phenobarbital and Seconal
Major tranquilizers such as Mellaril and Thorazine
Narcotic pain relievers such as Percocet and Demerol
Oral contraceptives
Tranquilizers such as Valium and Xanax

Special information
if you are pregnant or breastfeeding

Do not take Restoril if you are pregnant or planning to become pregnant. There is an increased risk of birth defects. This drug may appear in breast milk and could affect a nursing infant. If this medication is essential to your health, your doctor may advise you to discontinue breastfeeding until your treatment with this medication is finished.

Recommended dosage

ADULTS

The usual recommended dose is 15 milligrams at bedtime; however, 7.5 milligrams may be all that is necessary, while some people may need 30 milligrams. Your doctor will tailor your dose to your needs.

CHILDREN

The safety and effectiveness of Restoril have not been established in children under 18 years of age.

ELDERLY

The doctor will prescribe the smallest effective amount in order to avoid side effects such as oversedation, dizziness, confusion, and lack of muscle coordination. The usual starting dose is 7.5 milligrams.

Overdosage

Any medication taken in excess can cause symptoms of overdose. If you suspect an overdose, seek medical attention immediately.

■ *The symptoms of Restoril overdose may include:*
Coma
Confusion
Diminished reflexes
Loss of coordination
Low blood pressure
Labored or difficult breathing
Seizures
Sleepiness
Slurred speech

Brand name:

RETIN-A

Pronounced: Ret-in-A
Generic name: Tretinoin

Why is this drug prescribed?

Retin-A is prescribed for the treatment of acne vulgaris (an inflammatory disease of the skin, usually affecting persons in puberty or early adult years).

Most important fact about this drug

While using Retin-A, exposure to sunlight, including sunlamps, should be kept to a minimum. If you have a sunburn, do not use this medication until you have fully recovered. Use of sunscreen products and protective clothing over treated areas is recommended when exposure to the sun cannot be avoided. Weather extremes, such as wind and cold, should also be avoided while using Retin-A.

How should you use this medication?

Retin-A gel, cream, or liquid should be applied once a day, at bedtime, to the skin where acne appears, using enough to cover lightly the affected area. The liquid may be applied using a fingertip, gauze pad, or cotton swab. If you use gauze or cotton, avoid oversaturation, which might cause the liquid to run into areas where treatment is not intended.

You may use cosmetics while being treated with Retin-A; however, you should thoroughly cleanse the areas to be treated before applying the medication.

■ *If you miss a dose...*
Resume your regular schedule the next day.

■ *Storage instructions...*
Store at ordinary room temperature. Protect from extreme heat. Keep the cream or gel tube tightly capped.

What side effects may occur?

If you have sensitive skin, the use of this medication may cause your skin to become excessively red, puffy, blistered, or crusted. If this happens, notify your doctor, who may recommend that you discontinue Retin-A until your skin returns to normal, or adjust the medication to a level that you can tolerate.

An unusual darkening of the skin or lack of color of the skin may occur temporarily with repeated application of Retin-A.

Why should this drug not be prescribed?

If you are sensitive to or have ever had an allergic reaction to any of the ingredients in Retin-A, you should not use this medication. Make sure that your doctor is aware of any drug reactions that you have experienced.

The safety and effectiveness of long-term use of this product in the treatment of disorders other than acne have not been established.

Special warnings about this medication

Retin-A should be kept away from the eyes, mouth, angles of the nose, and mucous membranes.

If use of this medication causes an abnormal redness or peeling of the skin where it has been applied, notify your doctor, who may suggest that you use Retin-A less frequently, discontinue use temporarily, or discontinue use altogether.

If you have eczema (skin inflammation consisting of itching and small blisters that ooze and crust over), use this medication with extreme caution, as it may cause severe irritation.

If a sensitivity reaction or chemical irritation occurs, notify your doctor. He may suggest that you discontinue using this medication.

Retin-A may cause a brief feeling of warmth or slight stinging when applied.

During the early weeks of therapy, a worsening of acne may occur due to the action of the medication on deep, previously unseen areas of inflammation. This is not a reason to discontinue therapy, but do notify your doctor if it occurs.

Retin-A gel is flammable and should be kept away from heat and flame.

Possible food and drug interactions
when taking this medication

If Retin-A is taken with certain other drugs, the effects of either could be increased, decreased, or altered. It is especially important to check with your doctor before combining Retin-A with the following:

  Preparations containing sulfur (ointments and other preparations used
    to treat skin disorders and infections)
  Resorcinol (a drug, used in ointments to treat acne, that causes skin to
    peel)
  Salicylic acid (a drug that kills bacteria and fungi and causes skin to
    peel)

"Resting" your skin is recommended between use of the above preparations and treatment with Retin-A.

Caution should be exercised when using Retin-A in combination with other topical medications, medicated or abrasive soaps and cleansers, soaps and cosmetics that have a strong drying effect, and products with high concentrations of alcohol, astringents, spices, or lime.

Special information
if you are pregnant or breastfeeding

There are no adequate and well-controlled studies in pregnant women. If you are pregnant or plan to become pregnant, inform your doctor immediately. It is not known if this drug appears in breast milk. If Retin-A is essential to your treatment, your doctor may advise you to discontinue breastfeeding until your treatment is finished.

Recommended dosage

ADULTS

Apply once a day at bedtime.

Results should be noticed after 2 to 3 weeks of treatment. More than 6 weeks of treatment may be needed before definite beneficial effects are seen.

Once acne has responded satisfactorily, it may be possible to maintain the improvement with less frequent applications or other dosage forms. However, any change in formulation, drug concentration, or dose frequency should be closely monitored by your doctor to determine your tolerance and response.

Overdosage

Applying this medication excessively will not produce faster or better results, and marked redness, peeling, or discomfort could occur.

Brand name:

RETROVIR

Pronounced: reh-troh-VEER
Generic name: Zidovudine

Why is this drug prescribed?

Retrovir is prescribed for adults infected with human immunodeficiency virus (HIV). HIV causes the immune system to break down so that it can no longer respond effectively to infection. This virus leads to the fatal disease known as acquired immune deficiency syndrome (AIDS). Retrovir slows down the progress of HIV.

This drug is also prescribed for HIV-infected children over 3 months of age who have symptoms of HIV or who have no symptoms but, through testing, have shown evidence of impaired immunity.

Signs and symptoms consistent with HIV disease are significant weight loss, fever, diarrhea, infections, and problems with the nervous system.

Most important fact about this drug

The long-term effects of treatment with zidovudine are unknown. However, treatment with this drug may lead to blood diseases, including granulocyto-penia (a severe blood disorder characterized by a sharp decrease of certain types of white blood cells called granulocytes) and severe anemia requiring blood transfusions. This is especially true in people with more advanced HIV and those who start treatment later in the course of their infection.

Also, because Retrovir is not a cure for HIV infections or AIDS, those who are infected may continue to develop complications, including opportunistic infections (infections not usually seen in humans that develop when the immune system falters). Therefore, frequent blood counts by your doctor are strongly advised. Notify your doctor immediately of any changes in your general health.

How should you take this medication?

Take this medication exactly as prescribed by your doctor. Do not share this medication with anyone and do not exceed your recommended dosage. Take it at even intervals every 4 hours around the clock (children every 6 hours).

- *If you miss a dose...*
  Take it as soon as you remember. If it is almost time for your next dose, skip the one you missed and go back to your regular schedule. Do not take 2 doses at once.

- *Storage instructions...*
  Capsules should be stored at room temperature, away from light and moisture. Syrup should be stored at room temperature, away from light.

What side effects may occur?

Side effects cannot be anticipated. If any develop or change in intensity, inform your doctor as soon as possible. Only your doctor can determine if it is safe for you to continue taking Retrovir.

The frequency and severity of side effects associated with the use of Retrovir are greater in people whose infection is more advanced when treatment is started. Sometimes it is difficult to distinguish side effects from the underlying signs of HIV disease or the infections caused by HIV.

- *More common side effects may include:*
  Change in sense of taste, constipation, diarrhea, difficult or labored breathing, dizziness, fever, general feeling of illness, inability to fall or stay

asleep, indigestion, loss of appetite, muscle pain, nausea, rash, severe headache, sleepiness, stomach and intestinal pain, sweating, tingling or pins and needles, vomiting, weakness

- *Less common side effects may include:*
  Acne, anxiety, back pain, belching, bleeding from the rectum, bleeding gums, body odor, changeable emotions, chest pain, chills, confusion, cough, decreased mental sharpness, depression, difficulty swallowing, dimness of vision, excess sensitivity to pain, fainting, fatigue, flu-like symptoms, frequent urination, gas, hearing loss, hives, hoarseness, increase in urine volume, inflammation of the sinuses or nose, itching, joint pain, light intolerance, mouth sores, muscle spasm, nervousness, nosebleed, painful or difficult urination, sore throat, swelling of the lip, swelling of the tongue, tremor, twitching, vertigo

Why should this drug not be prescribed?
If you have ever had a life-threatening allergic reaction to Retrovir or any of its ingredients, you should not take this drug.

Special warnings about this medication
This drug has been studied for only a limited period of time. Long-term safety and effectiveness are not known, especially for people who are in a less advanced stage of AIDS or AIDS-related complex (the condition that precedes AIDS), and for those using the drug over a prolonged period of time.

If you develop a blood disease, you may require a blood transfusion, and your doctor may reduce your dose or take you off the drug altogether. Make sure your doctor monitors your blood count on a regular basis.

The use of Retrovir has *not* been shown to reduce the risk of transmission of HIV to others through sexual contact or blood contamination.

Retrovir should be used with extreme caution by people who have a bone marrow disease.

Some people taking Retrovir develop a sensitization reaction, often signaled by a rash. If you notice a rash developing, notify your doctor.

Because little data are available concerning the use of this drug in people with impaired kidney or liver function, check with your doctor before using Retrovir if you have either problem.

Possible food and drug interactions
when taking this medication

If Retrovir is taken with certain other drugs, the effects of either could be increased, decreased, or altered. It is especially important to check with your doctor before combining Retrovir with the following:

Acetaminophen (Tylenol)
Amphotericin B (Fungizone, a drug used to treat fungal infections)
Doxorubicin (Adriamycin, a cancer drug)
Aspirin
Dapsone (a drug used to treat leprosy)
Flucytosine (Ancobon)
Indomethacin (Indocin)
Interferon (Intron A, Roferon)
Pentamidine (NebuPent, Pentam)
Phenytoin (Dilantin, an anticonvulsant)
Probenecid (Benemid, an antigout drug)
Vinblastine (Velban, a cancer drug)
Vincristine (Oncovin, a cancer drug)

The combined use of phenytoin and Retrovir will be monitored by your doctor because of the possibility of seizures.

Special information
if you are pregnant or breastfeeding

The effects of Retrovir during pregnancy are under study. Use during pregnancy has been shown to protect the developing baby from contracting HIV. If you are pregnant or plan to become pregnant, inform your doctor immediately. This drug may appear in breast milk and could affect a nursing infant. If this medication is essential to your health, your doctor may advise you to discontinue breastfeeding until your treatment is finished.

Recommended dosage

ADULTS

All dosages of Retrovir must be very closely monitored by your physician. The following dosages are general; your physician will tailor the dose to your specific condition.

Capsules and Syrup

For adults who have symptoms of HIV infection, including AIDS, the usual starting dose is 200 milligrams (two 100-milligram capsules or 4 teaspoonfuls of syrup) taken every 4 hours. After 1 month, your doctor may reduce your dose to 100 milligrams taken every 4 hours.

For adults who have HIV infection but no symptoms, the usual dose is 100 milligrams taken every 4 hours while awake.

CHILDREN

The usual starting dose for children 3 months to 12 years of age is determined by body size. While the dose should not exceed 200 milligrams every 6 hours, it must still be individually determined. Safety and efficacy have not been determined for infants under 3 months of age.

Overdosage
Any medication taken in excess can have serious consequences. If you suspect an overdose, seek emergency medical treatment immediately.

■ *Symptoms of Retrovir overdose may include:*
Nausea
Vomiting

Brand name:

REVIA

Pronounced: reh-VEE-uh
Generic name: Naltrexone hydrochloride

Why is this drug prescribed?
ReVia is prescribed to treat alcohol dependence and narcotic addiction. ReVia is not a cure and must be used as part of a comprehensive treatment program that includes professional counseling, support groups, and close medical supervision.

Most important fact about this drug
Before taking ReVia for narcotic addiction, you must be drug-free for at least 7 to 10 days. You must also be free of any drug withdrawal symptoms. If you think you are still in withdrawal, be sure to tell your doctor, since taking ReVia while narcotics are still in your system could cause serious physical problems. Your doctor will perform tests to confirm your drug-free condition.

How should you take this medication?
It is important to take ReVia on schedule as directed by your doctor, and to follow through with your counseling and support group therapy. If you take even small doses of heroin or other narcotic drugs while taking ReVia, the medication will not be effective. Large doses of heroin or other narcotic drugs combined with ReVia can be fatal.

- *If you miss a dose...*
  Take the missed dose as soon as possible. If you do not remember until the next day, skip the missed dose and go back to your regular dosing schedule. Do not take 2 doses at once.

- *Storage instructions...*
  Protect from light.

What side effects may occur?

Side effects cannot be anticipated. If any side effects develop or change in intensity, tell your doctor immediately. Only your doctor can determine whether it is safe for you to continue taking ReVia.

- *More common side effects of treatment for alcoholism may include:*
  Dizziness
  Fatigue
  Headache
  Nausea
  Nervousness
  Sleeplessness
  Vomiting

- *Less common side effects of treatment for alcoholism may include:*
  Anxiety, sleepiness

- *More common side effects of treatment for narcotic addiction may include:*
  Abdominal pain/cramps
  Anxiety
  Difficulty sleeping
  Headache
  Joint and muscle pain
  Low energy
  Nausea and/or vomiting
  Nervousness

- *Other side effects of treatment for narcotic addiction may include:*
  Acne, athlete's foot, blurred vision and aching, burning, or swollen eyes, chills, clogged and aching ears, cold sores, cold feet, confusion,

constipation, cough, decreased potency, delayed ejaculation, depression, diarrhea, disorientation, dizziness, dry mouth, fatigue, feeling down, fever, fluid retention, frequent urination, gas, hair loss, hallucinations, head "pounding", heavy breathing, hemorrhoids, hoarseness, "hot spells", increased appetite, increased blood pressure, increased energy, increased mucus, increased or decreased sexual interest, increased thirst, irregular or fast heartbeat, irritability, itching, light sensitivity, loss of appetite, nightmares, nosebleeds, oily skin, pain in shoulders, legs, or knees, pain in groin, painful urination, paranoia, restlessness, ringing in ears, runny nose, shortness of breath, side pains, sinus trouble, skin rash, sleepiness, sneezing, sore throat, stuffy nose, swollen glands, tremor, throbbing heartbeat, twitching, ulcer, weight loss or gain, yawning

Why should this drug not be prescribed?

If you are sensitive to or have ever had an allergic reaction to ReVia, you should not take it. If you have acute hepatitis (liver disease) or liver failure, do not start therapy with ReVia. Remember, too, that you must be narcotic-free before beginning ReVia therapy.

Special warnings about this medication

Since ReVia may cause liver damage when taken at high doses, if you develop symptoms that may signal possible liver problems, such as abdominal pain lasting more than a few days, white bowel movements, dark urine, or yellowing of your eyes, you should stop taking ReVia immediately and see your doctor as soon as possible. Your doctor may periodically test your liver function while you are on ReVia therapy. If you are narcotic-dependent and accidentally take ReVia, you may experience severe withdrawal symptoms lasting up to 48 hours, including confusion, sleepiness, hallucinations, vomiting, and diarrhea. If this occurs, seek help immediately. Ask your doctor to give you a Revia medication card to alert medical personnel that you are taking ReVia in case of an emergency. Carry this card with you at all times. If you do require medical treatment, be sure to tell the doctor that you are taking ReVia. You should also tell your dentist and pharmacist that you are taking ReVia. The safety of ReVia in children under 18 years of age has not been established.

Possible food and drug interactions
when taking this medication

Since studies to evaluate this interaction of ReVia with drugs other than narcotics have not been performed, do not take any medications, either over-the-counter or prescription, without first notifying your doctor. Do not use

Antabuse while you are taking ReVia; both drugs can damage your liver. Do not take Mellaril (a drug used to treat depression and anxiety) while on ReVia therapy, as the combination may cause you to feel very sleepy and sluggish. While taking ReVia, avoid medicines that contain narcotics, including cough and cold preparations, such as Actifed-C, Ryna-C, and Dimetane-DC; antidiarrheal medications such as Lomotil; and narcotic painkillers such as Percodan, Tylox, and Tylenol No. 3.

Special information
if you are pregnant or breastfeeding

The effects of ReVia during pregnancy have not been adequately studied. If you are pregnant or are planning to become pregnant, tell your doctor immediately. ReVia should be used during pregnancy only if clearly needed. ReVia may appear in breast milk. If this medication is essential to your health, your doctor may tell you to discontinue breastfeeding your baby until your treatment with ReVia is finished.

Recommended dosage

ALCOHOLISM

The usual starting dose is 50 milligrams once a day.

NARCOTIC DEPENDENCE

The usual starting dose is 25 milligrams once a day. If no withdrawal symptoms occur, the doctor may increase the dosage to 50 milligrams a day.

Overdosage

Any medication taken in excess can have serious consequences. If you suspect an overdose of ReVia, seek medical attention immediately.

Brand name:

RHEUMATREX

See Methotrexate, page 646.

Brand name:

RHINOCORT

Pronounced: RYE-no-kort
Generic name: Budesonide

Why is this drug prescribed?

Rhinocort is an anti-inflammatory steroid medication. It is prescribed for relief of the symptoms of hay fever and other nasal inflammations.

Most important fact about this drug

Because steroids can suppress the immune system, people taking Rhinocort may become more susceptible to infections, and their infections could be more severe. Anyone taking Rhinocort or other corticosteroids who has not had infections such as chickenpox and measles should avoid exposure to them. If you are taking Rhinocort and are exposed, tell your doctor immediately.

How should you take this medication?

Rhinocort is prescribed as a nasal inhaler. Instructions for use are provided with the product. Do not use doses that are larger than recommended.

Relief of symptoms usually occurs 24 hours to a few days after starting Rhinocort. If symptoms do not improve within 3 weeks, or if nasal irritation worsens, contact your physician.

Shake the Rhinocort container well before using it. Do not use near an open flame.

Rhinocort is to be used within 6 months after opening it.

■ *If you miss a dose...*
Take the forgotten dose as soon as you remember. If it is almost time for your next dose, skip the one you missed and go back to your regular schedule. Never take 2 doses at the same time.

■ *Storage instructions...*
Do not store near an open flame or heat above 120 degrees Fahrenheit. Do not store in areas of high humidity.

What side effects may occur?

Side effects cannot be anticipated. If any develop or change in intensity, inform your doctor as soon as possible. Only your doctor can determine if it is safe for you to continue taking Rhinocort.

■ *More common side effects may include:*
Increased coughing
Irritation of the nasal passages
Nosebleeds
Sore throat

■ *Less common side effects may include:*
Bad taste in mouth, dry mouth, facial swelling, hoarseness, indigestion, inflammation of the skin, itching, nasal sores or pain, nausea, rash, reduced sense of smell, yeast infection of the vagina or mouth, wheezing

Why should this drug not be prescribed?

If you develop an infection of your nose and throat, stop using Rhinocort and call your doctor. If you already have tuberculosis or any other kind of infection, be sure your doctor knows about it. If you are sensitive to or have ever had an allergic reaction to Rhinocort or any of its ingredients, you should not take this medication.

Special warnings about this medication

If you have been taking a steroid in tablet form, such as prednisone, and are switched to Rhinocort, you may have symptoms of withdrawal, such as joint or muscle pain, lethargy, and depression. If you have been taking another steroid for a long time for asthma, your asthma may get worse if your medication is cut back too quickly. Using Rhinocort with another steroid drug can decrease the body's normal ability to make its own steroid chemicals.

Possible food and drug interactions
when taking this medication

Talk to your doctor before using Rhinocort if you already take prednisone or any other steroid every other day.

Special information
if you are pregnant or breastfeeding

The effects of Rhinocort during pregnancy have not been adequately studied. If you are pregnant or plan to become pregnant, inform your doctor immediately. Rhinocort should be used during pregnancy only if clearly needed. The effects of Rhinocort on the infants of women who breastfeed also are unknown. Your doctor may have you stop breastfeeding while you are taking this drug.

Recommended dosage

The usual recommended starting dose for adults and children 6 years of age and older is 256 micrograms a day, either as two sprays in each nostril twice a day, morning and evening, or as four sprays in each nostril once a day in the morning. Your doctor may lower the dose once relief of symptoms occurs. Rhinocort is not recommended for use in children with nasal irritation not due to allergies.

Overdosage
Any medication taken in excess can have serious consequences. If you suspect an overdose, seek medical attention immediately.

Symptoms of Rhinocort overdose stem from a condition called hypercorticism, when the body produces an excess of its own steroid chemicals.

■ *Symptoms of overdose may include:*
Diabetes
Excess hair growth
Fatigue and weakness
Fluid retention
Impotence
Lack of menstrual periods
Skin discoloration

Brand name:

RIDAURA

Pronounced: ri-DOOR-ah
Generic name: Auranofin

Why is this drug prescribed?
Ridaura, a gold preparation, is given to help treat rheumatoid arthritis. Ridaura is taken by mouth, unlike other gold compounds, which are given by injection. It is recommended only for people who have not been helped sufficiently by nonsteroidal anti-inflammatory drugs (Anaprox, Dolobid, Indocin, Motrin, and others). Ridaura should be part of a comprehensive arthritis treatment program that includes non-drug forms of therapy.

You are most likely to benefit from Ridaura if you have active joint inflammation, especially in the early stages.

Most important fact about this drug
Unlike anti-inflammatory medications, Ridaura does not take effect immediately. In fact, you may have to wait for 3 to 6 months to get any benefit from Ridaura. Ridaura prevents or suppresses joint swelling, but does not cure rheumatoid arthritis.

How should you take this medication?
Read the patient information sheet provided with Ridaura, and take the medication exactly as prescribed.

You should observe good oral hygiene during therapy with Ridaura.

■ *If you miss a dose...*
If you take 1 dose a day, take the missed dose as soon as you remember. If you do not remember until the next day, skip the dose you missed and go back to your regular schedule.

If you take more than 1 dose a day, take the missed dose as soon as you remember. If it is almost time for your next dose, skip the one you missed and go back to your regular schedule.

Do not take 2 doses at once.

■ *Storage instructions...*
Store at room temperature in a tightly closed, light-resistant container.

What side effects may occur?
Side effects cannot be anticipated. If any side effects develop or change in intensity, tell your doctor immediately. Only your doctor can determine whether it is safe for you to continue taking Ridaura. Ridaura causes loose stools or diarrhea in about half of all people who take it; there may also be indigestion, abdominal pain and gas, loss of appetite, vomiting, or nausea.

■ *Other commonly reported side effects include:*
Blood-cell abnormalities that may result in bleeding, bronchitis, easy bruising, fever, gold dermatitis (inflammation of skin), itching, metallic taste, pinkeye, rash, sores in the mouth

■ *Less common or rare side effects may include:*
Altered sense of taste, anemia, black or bloody stools, blood in the urine, constipation, difficulty swallowing, fluid retention and swelling, hair loss, hives, inflammation of the tongue or gums, intestinal inflammation with ulcers, stomach or intestinal bleeding, yellowed eyes and skin

Why should this drug not be prescribed?
Do not take Ridaura if you have ever had any of the following reactions to a medication containing gold:

Anaphylaxis (life-threatening allergic reaction)
Blood or bone marrow abnormality
Fibrosis (scar tissue formation) in the lungs
Serious bowel inflammation
Skin peeling off in sheets

Special warnings about this medication

You should be monitored especially closely while taking Ridaura if you have any of the following:

History of a bone marrow abnormality
Inflammatory bowel disease
Kidney disease
Liver disease
Skin rash

Your doctor may order periodic blood and urine tests to check for unwanted effects.

Like other medications containing gold, Ridaura may cause serious blood abnormalities. If you start to bruise easily, or develop small red or purplish skin discolorations, see your doctor. He or she will have you stop taking Ridaura and will do some blood tests, including a platelet count.

Ridaura may cause protein or microscopic amounts of blood to spill into your urine. If a urine test shows that this is happening, your doctor will take you off of Ridaura immediately.

Gold compounds may cause your skin to become more sensitive to sunlight, so you may need to limit your exposure to the sun and wear a sunscreen.

Possible food and drug interactions
when taking this medication

If Ridaura is taken with certain other drugs, the effects of either could be increased, decreased, or altered. It is especially important to check with your doctor before combining Ridaura with the following:

Penicillamine (Cuprimine)
Phenytoin (Dilantin)

Special information
if you are pregnant or breastfeeding

If you are pregnant or plan to become pregnant, inform your doctor immediately. Because Ridaura may cause birth defects, it should not be taken during pregnancy.

Likewise, you should not take Ridaura while breastfeeding; although there are no data on Ridaura, injected gold appears in breast milk. If you are a new mother, you may have to choose between taking Ridaura and breastfeeding your baby.

Recommended dosage

The usual dosage of Ridaura is 6 milligrams daily in a single dose or divided into 2 smaller doses. After 6 months, your doctor may increase the dose to 9 milligrams, divided into 3 doses. Ridaura is prescribed only for adults.

Overdosage

Any medication taken in excess can have serious consequences. If you suspect an overdose of Ridaura, seek medical attention immediately.

Generic name:

RIFAMPIN, ISONIAZID, AND PYRAZINAMIDE

See Rifater, page 962.

Brand Name:

RIFATER

Pronounced: RIF-a-tur
Generic ingredients: Rifampin, Isoniazid, Pyrazinamide

Why is this drug prescribed?

Rifater is a combination antibiotic used to treat the initial phase of tuberculosis. After a 2-month period, your doctor may prescribe another combination of antituberculosis drugs (Rifamate), which can be continued for longer periods.

Most important fact about this drug

Isoniazid, one of the components of Rifater, sometimes causes liver damage. Contact your doctor immediately if you develop yellowing of the eyes or skin, fatigue, weakness, loss of appetite, nausea, or vomiting.

How should you take this medication?

Take Rifater exactly as prescribed. Do not stop without consulting your doctor. It is important to take all of the drug prescribed for you, even if you feel better, and not to miss any doses.

Take Rifater on an empty stomach, either 1 hour before or 2 hours after a meal, with a full glass of water. Wait at least 1 hour before taking an antacid, as antacids may interfere with the drug.

If needed, your doctor may suggest taking vitamin B$_6$ while you are on Rifater therapy.

■ *If you miss a dose...*
Take it as soon as you remember. If it is almost time for the next dose, skip the one you missed and go back to your regular schedule. Never take 2 doses at once.

■ *Storage instructions...*
Store at room temperature. Protect from moisture.

What side effects may occur?
Side effects cannot be anticipated. If any develop or change in intensity, tell your doctor as soon as possible. Only your doctor can determine if it is safe for you to continue taking Rifater.

■ *More common side effects may include:*
Angina (crushing chest pain), anxiety, bone pain, chest pain, chest tightness, cough, coughing up blood, diabetic coma, diarrhea, difficult breathing, digestive pain, fast, fluttery heartbeat, headache, hepatitis, hives, itching, joint pain, nausea, numbness or tingling of the legs, rash, reddened skin, skin peeling or flaking, sleeplessness, sweating, swelling of the legs, vomiting, yellowing of skin and eyes

■ *Less common side effects may include:*
High or persistent fever
Ringing in ears
Vertigo

Why should this drug not be prescribed?
Do not take this medication if you have ever had an allergic reaction to or are sensitive to rifampin, isoniazid, or pyrazinamide. If you have serious liver disease or have ever had a severe side effect from isoniazid (such as fever, chills, and arthritis), do not take Rifater. Also, if you have a history of liver disease or have had acute and painful joint swelling (gout), avoid this drug.

Special warnings about this medication
Rifater may cause your urine, sputum, sweat, and tears to turn a red-orange color. This is to be expected and is not harmful. The drug may also permanently discolor contact lenses.

Since Rifater may cause eye problems, you should have a complete eye examination before starting therapy and periodically during Rifater treatment.

Limit the amount of alcohol you drink while on this medicine. Daily users of alcohol may be more prone to liver problems.

Use this medicine with caution if you have diabetes or kidney disease.

When rifampin, one of the drugs in Rifater, is taken at high doses (more than 600 milligrams) once or twice a week, it is likely that side effects may increase, including "flu-like" symptoms such as fever, chills, fatigue, weakness, upset stomach, and shortness of breath.

Possible food and drug interactions
when taking this medication

If Rifater is taken with certain other drugs, the effects could be increased, decreased, or altered. Consider another form of birth control if you are taking oral contraceptives, since Rifater lowers their effectiveness. Also check with your doctor before combining Rifater with the following:

Antacids such as Maalox or Tums
Anticonvulsants such as Dilantin, Depakene, Mysoline, Tegretol
Barbiturates such as phenobarbital and Nembutal
Blood pressure medicines such as Inderal, Tenormin, and Vasotec
Blood thinners such as Coumadin
Chloramphenicol (Chloromycetin)
Ciprofloxacin (Cipro)
Clofibrate (Atromid-S)
Cotrimoxazole (Bactrim, Septra)
Cycloserine (Seromycin)
Cyclosporine (Sandimmune)
Dapsone
Diabetes medications such as Diabinese and Orinase
Disulfiram (Antabuse)
Fluconazole (Diflucan)
Haloperidol (Haldol)
Heart medications such Calan, Cardizem, Lanoxin, Norpace, Mexitil, Procardia, Quinidex, and Tonocard
Itraconazole (Sporanox)
Ketoconazole (Nizoral)
Levodopa (Sinemet)
Narcotic analgesics such as Darvon, Demerol, Percocet, Percodan
Nortriptyline (Pamelor)
Probenecid (Benemid)
Progestins such as Megace

Steroid drugs such as Deltasone and Prelone
Sulfasalazine (Azulfidine)
Theophylline (Theolair, Slo-Phyllin, Theo-Dur)
Tranquilizers such as Valium and Xanax

Foods such as cheese, fish, and red wine may cause reactions if you are taking a medicine containing isoniazid. Call your doctor immediately if fast or fluttery heartbeat, flushing, sweating, headache, or light-headedness occurs while you are taking this medication.

Special information
if you are pregnant or breastfeeding

If you are pregnant or plan to become pregnant, tell your doctor immediately. You may need to discontinue the drug. If needed for preventive treatment, Rifater should be started after delivery. An ingredient in Rifater may cause postnatal hemorrhaging in the mother and baby when given during the last few weeks of pregnancy.

Rifater can pass into breast milk and may affect the nursing infant. Your doctor may recommend that you stop breastfeeding until your treatment with Rifater is finished.

Recommended dosage

ADULTS

Take once a day, as follows:

If you weigh 97 pounds or less: 4 tablets
If you weigh 98 to 120 pounds: 5 tablets
If you weigh 121 pounds or more: 6 tablets

CHILDREN

Safety and effectiveness in children under the age of 15 have not been established.

Overdosage

Any medication taken in excess can have serious consequences. An untreated overdose of Rifater can be fatal. If you suspect an overdose, seek medical attention immediately.

■ *Symptoms of Rifater overdose may include:*
Blurring vision, coma, dizziness, hallucinations, increasing tiredness or sluggishness, liver enlargement or tenderness, nausea, seizures, slurring of speech, shallow or difficult breathing, stupor, vomiting, yellow eyes and skin

Brand name:

RISPERDAL

Pronounced: RIS-per-dal
Generic name: Risperidone

Why is this drug prescribed?
Risperdal is prescribed to treat severe mental illnesses such as schizophrenia.

Most important fact about this drug
Risperdal may cause tardive dyskinesia, a condition that causes involuntary muscle spasms and twitches in the face and body. This condition can become permanent and is most common among the elderly, especially women. Tell your doctor immediately if you begin to have any involuntary movement. You may need to discontinue Risperdal therapy.

How should you take this medication?
Do not take more or less of this medication than prescribed or use it for longer than the prescribed term of treatment as this may cause unwanted side effects.

Risperdal may be taken with or without food.

- *If you miss a dose...*
  Take it as soon as you remember. If it is almost time for your next dose, skip the one you missed and go back to your regular schedule. Do not take 2 doses at once.

- *Storage instructions...*
  Store at room temperature. Protect from light and moisture.

What side effects may occur?
Side effects cannot be anticipated. If any develop or change in intensity, tell your doctor as soon as possible. Only your doctor can determine if it is safe for you to continue taking Risperdal.

- *More common side effects may include:*
  Abdominal pain, abnormal walk, agitation, aggression, anxiety, chest pain, constipation, coughing, decreased activity, diarrhea, difficulty with orgasm, diminished sexual desire, dizziness, dry skin, erection and ejaculation problems, excessive menstrual bleeding, fever, headache, inability to sleep, increased dreaming, increased duration of sleep, indigestion, involuntary movements, joint pain, lack of coordination, nasal inflammation, nausea, overactivity, rapid heartbeat, rash, reduced salivation,

respiratory infection, sleepiness, sore throat, tremor, underactive reflexes, urination problems, vomiting, weight gain

■ *Less common side effects may include:*
Abnormal vision, back pain, dandruff, difficult or labored breathing, increased saliva, sinus inflammation, toothache

Why should this drug not be prescribed?

If you are sensitive to or have ever had an allergic reaction to Risperdal or other major tranquilizers, you should not take this medication.

Special warnings about this medication

You should use Risperdal cautiously if you have kidney, liver, or heart diseases, seizures, breast cancer, thyroid disorders, or any other diseases that affect the metabolism (conversion of food into energy), or if you are exposed to extreme heat.

Be aware that Risperdal may mask signs and symptoms of drug overdose and of conditions such as intestinal obstruction, brain tumor, and Reye's syndrome (a dangerous neurological condition that may follow viral infections, usually occurring in children).

Risperdal may cause neuroleptic malignant syndrome (NMS), a condition marked by muscle stiffness or rigidity, fast heartbeat or irregular pulse, increased sweating, high fever, and high or low blood pressure. Unchecked, this condition can prove fatal. Call your doctor immediately if you notice any of these symptoms. Risperdal therapy should be discontinued.

This drug may impair your ability to drive a car or operate potentially dangerous machinery. Do not participate in any activities that require full alertness if you are unsure of your ability.

Risperdal can cause orthostatic hypotension (low blood pressure when rising to a standing position), with dizziness, rapid heartbeat, and fainting, especially when you first start to take it.

Possible food and drug interactions
when taking this medication

If Risperdal is taken with certain other drugs, the effects of either can be increased, decreased, or altered. It is especially important to check with your doctor before combining Risperdal with the following:

Blood pressure medicines such as Aldomet, Procardia, and Vasotec
Bromocriptine mesylate (Parlodel)
Carbamazepine (Tegretol)
Clozapine (Clozaril)

Levodopa (Sinemet, Dopar)
Quinidine (Quinidex)

You may experience drowsiness and other potentially serious effects if Risperdal is combined with alcohol and other drugs that slow the central nervous system such as Valium, Percocet, Demerol, or Haldol.

Check with your doctor before taking any new medications.

Special information
if you are pregnant or breastfeeding

The safety and effectiveness of Risperdal during pregnancy have not been adequately studied. If you are pregnant or plan to become pregnant, tell your doctor immediately. It is not known whether Risperdal appears in breast milk. If this medication is essential to your health, your doctor may advise you to discontinue breastfeeding until your treatment with this medication is finished.

Recommended dosage

ADULTS

The usual starting dose is 1 milligram twice a day, with increases to 2 milligrams by the second day and 3 milligrams by the third day. Your doctor may further adjust the dosage at intervals of 1 week. For the longer term, dosage ranges from 4 to 6 milligrams daily, divided into 2 equal doses.

If you have a liver or kidney disease, your doctor will have you start with one-half of a 1-milligram tablet twice daily and may then increase your dosage by one-half tablet per dose.

CHILDREN

The safety and effectiveness of Risperdal in children have not been established.

ELDERLY

Elderly people generally take Risperdal at lower doses. The usual starting dose is one-half of a 1-milligram tablet twice daily. Your doctor may increase the dose gradually.

Overdosage

Any medication taken in excess can have serious consequences. If you suspect an overdose of Risperdal, seek medical attention immediately.

■ *Symptoms of Risperdal overdose may include:*
Drowsiness, low blood pressure, rapid heartbeat, sedation

Generic name:

RISPERIDONE

See Risperdal, page 966.

Brand name:

RITALIN

Pronounced: RIT-ah-lin
Generic name: Methylphenidate hydrochloride

Why is this drug prescribed?
Ritalin is a mild central nervous system stimulant used in the treatment of attention deficit disorders in children. (This is a general term for several behavior problems previously known as minimal brain dysfunction in children; other names being used are hyperkinetic child syndrome, minimal brain damage, minimal cerebral dysfunction, and minor cerebral dysfunction.) Ritalin is also occasionally used in adults to treat narcolepsy (an uncontrollable desire to sleep).

This drug should be given as an integral part of a total treatment program that includes psychological, educational, and social measures. Symptoms of attention deficit disorder include continual problems with moderate to severe distractibility, short attention span, hyperactivity, emotional changeability, and impulsiveness.

Most important fact about this drug
Excessive doses of Ritalin over a long period of time can produce addiction. It is also possible to develop tolerance to the drug, so that larger doses are needed to produce the original effect. Because of these dangers, be sure to check with your doctor before making any change in dosage; and withdraw the drug only under your doctor's supervision.

How should you take this medication?
Follow your doctor's directions carefully.

Ritalin is available in standard and sustained-release tablets (Ritalin-SR). It is recommended that Ritalin be taken 30 to 45 minutes before meals. If the drug interferes with sleep, give the child the last dose before 6 P.M. Ritalin-SR tablets should be swallowed whole, never crushed or chewed.

▪ *If you miss a dose...*
  Give it to the child as soon as you remember. Give the remaining doses for the day at regularly spaced intervals. Do not give 2 doses at once.

■ *Storage instructions...*
Keep out of reach of children. Store below 86°F in a tightly closed, light-resistant container. Protect Ritalin-SR from moisture.

What side effects may occur?
Side effects cannot be anticipated. If any develop or change in intensity, inform your doctor as soon as possible. Only your doctor can determine if it is safe for you to continue giving Ritalin.

■ *More common side effects may include:*
Inability to fall or stay asleep
Nervousness

These side effects can usually be controlled by reducing the dosage and omitting the drug in the afternoon or evening.

In children, loss of appetite, abdominal pain, weight loss during long-term therapy, inability to fall or stay asleep, and abnormally fast heartbeat are more common side effects.

■ *Less common or rare side effects may include:*
Abdominal pain, abnormal heartbeat, abnormal muscular movements, blood pressure changes, chest pain, dizziness, drowsiness, fever, head-ache, hives, jerking, joint pain, loss of appetite, nausea, palpitations (fluttery or throbbing heartbeat), pulse changes, rapid heartbeat, reddish or purplish skin spots, skin reddening, skin inflammation with peeling, skin rash, Tourette's syndrome (severe twitching), weight loss during long-term treatment

Why should this drug not be prescribed?
This drug should not be prescribed for anyone experiencing anxiety, tension, and agitation, since the drug may aggravate these symptoms.

Anyone sensitive or allergic to this drug should not take it.

This medication should not be taken by anyone with the eye condition known as glaucoma, anyone who suffers from tics (repeated, involuntary twitches), or someone with a family history of Tourette's syndrome (severe and multiple tics).

Ritalin is not intended for use in children whose symptoms may be caused by stress or a psychiatric disorder.

Ritalin should not be used for the prevention or treatment of normal fatigue, nor should it be used for the treatment of severe depression.

Special warnings about this medication

Your doctor will do a complete history and evaluation before prescribing Ritalin. He or she will take into account the severity of the symptoms, as well as your child's age.

Ritalin should not be given to children under 6 years of age; safety and effectiveness in this age group have not been established.

There is no information regarding the safety and effectiveness of long-term Ritalin treatment in children. However, suppression of growth has been seen with the long-term use of stimulants, so your doctor will watch your child carefully while he or she is taking this drug.

Blood pressure should be monitored in anyone taking Ritalin, especially those with high blood pressure.

Some people have had visual disturbances such as blurred vision while being treated with Ritalin.

The use of Ritalin by anyone with a seizure disorder is not recommended. Be sure your doctor is aware of any problem in this area.

Possible food and drug interactions when taking this medication

If Ritalin is taken with certain other drugs, the effects of either can be increased, decreased, or altered. It is especially important to check with your doctor before combining Ritalin with the following:

Anticonvulsants such as phenobarbital, Dilantin, and Mysoline
Antidepressant drugs such as Tofranil, Anafranil, and Norpramin
Blood thinners such as Coumadin
Drugs that restore blood pressure, such as EpiPen
Guanethidine (Ismelin)
MAO inhibitors (antidepressant drugs such as Nardil, Parnate, and Marplan)
Phenylbutazone (Butazolidin)

Special information if you are pregnant or breastfeeding

The effects of Ritalin during pregnancy have not been adequately studied. If you are pregnant or plan to become pregnant, inform your doctor immediately. It is not known if Ritalin appears in breast milk. If this medication is essential to your health, your doctor may advise you to discontinue nursing your baby until your treatment with this medication is finished.

Recommended dosage

ADULTS

Tablets

The average dosage is 20 to 30 milligrams a day, divided into 2 or 3 doses, preferably taken 30 to 45 minutes before meals. Some people may need 40 to 60 milligrams daily, others only 10 to 15 milligrams. Your doctor will determine the best dose.

SR Tablets

Ritalin-SR tablets keep working for 8 hours. They may be used in place of Ritalin tablets if they deliver a comparable dose over an 8-hour period.

CHILDREN

Ritalin should not be given to children under 6 years of age.

Your doctor will start your child on small doses, then increase the dose gradually at weekly intervals. Your child should not take more than 60 milligrams in a day. If you do not see any improvement over a period of 1 month, check with your doctor. He or she may wish to discontinue the drug.

Tablets

The usual starting dose is 5 milligrams taken twice a day, before breakfast and lunch; your doctor will increase the dose by 5 to 10 milligrams a week.

SR Tablets

Ritalin-SR tablets continue working for 8 hours. Your doctor will decide if SR tablets should be used in place of Ritalin tablets.

Your doctor will periodically discontinue this drug in order to reassess your child's condition. Drug treatment should not, and need not, be indefinite and usually can be discontinued after puberty.

Overdosage

If you suspect an overdose, seek medical attention immediately.

■ *Symptoms of Ritalin overdose may include:*
Agitation, confusion, convulsions (may be followed by coma), delirium, dryness of mucous membranes, enlarging of the pupil of the eye, exaggerated feeling of elation, extremely elevated body temperature, flushing, hallucinations, headache, high blood pressure, irregular or rapid heartbeat, muscle twitching, sweating, tremors, vomiting

Brand name:

ROBAXIN

Pronounced: Ro-BAKS-in
Generic name: Methocarbamol

Why is this drug prescribed?
Robaxin is prescribed, along with rest, physical therapy, and other measures, for the relief of pain due to severe muscular injuries, sprains, and strains.

Most important fact about this drug
Robaxin is not a substitute for the rest or physical therapy needed for proper healing.

Although the drug may temporarily make an injury feel better, do not let that tempt you into pushing your recovery. Lifting or exercising too soon may further damage the muscle.

How should you take this medication?
Take Robaxin exactly as prescribed. Do not take a larger dose or use more often than directed.

- *If you miss a dose...*
  If only an hour or so has passed, take it as soon as you remember. If you do not remember until later, skip the dose and go back to your regular schedule. Do not take 2 doses at once.

- *Storage instructions...*
  Store at room temperature in a tightly closed container.

What side effects may occur?
Side effects cannot be anticipated. If any develop or change in intensity, inform your doctor as soon as possible. Only your doctor can determine if it is safe for you to continue taking Robaxin.

- *Side effects may include:*
  Blurred vision, dizziness, drowsiness, fever, headache, hives, itching, light-headedness, nasal congestion, nausea, "pinkeye," rash

Why should this drug not be prescribed?
If you are sensitive to or have ever had an allergic reaction to Robaxin or other drugs of this type, you should not take this medication. Make sure your doctor is aware of any drug reactions you have experienced.

Special warnings about this medication
Robaxin causes drowsiness and blurred vision. Exercise extra caution while driving or performing tasks that require mental alertness.

Avoid or be careful using alcoholic beverages.

Robaxin may darken urine to brown, green, or black.

Possible food and drug interactions when taking this medication
If Robaxin is taken with certain other drugs, the effects of either can be increased, decreased, or altered. It is especially important to check with your doctor before combining Robaxin with drugs that slow the nervous system, including:

    Narcotic pain relievers such as Percocet and Tylenol with Codeine
    Sleep aids such as Halcion and Seconal
    Tranquilizers such as Xanax and Valium

Special information if you are pregnant or breastfeeding
The effects of Robaxin during pregnancy have not been adequately studied. If you are pregnant or plan to become pregnant, inform your doctor immediately. It is not known if this drug appears in breast milk. If this medication is essential to your health, your doctor may advise you to discontinue breastfeeding your baby until your treatment is finished.

Recommended dosage

ADULTS

Robaxin
The usual starting dose is 3 tablets taken 4 times a day. The usual long-term dose is 2 tablets taken 4 times a day.

Robaxin-750
The usual starting dose is 2 tablets taken 4 times a day. The usual long-term dose is 1 tablet taken every 4 hours or 2 tablets taken 3 times a day.

CHILDREN

The safety and effectiveness of Robaxin have not been established in children under 12 years of age.

Overdosage

Any drug taken in excess can have dangerous consequences. If you suspect an overdose of Robaxin, seek emergency medical treatment immediately.

Brand name:

ROCALTROL

Pronounced: Ro-CAL-trol
Generic name: Calcitriol

Why is this drug prescribed?

Rocaltrol is a synthetic form of vitamin D used to treat people on dialysis who have hypocalcemia (abnormally low blood calcium levels) and resulting bone damage. Rocaltrol is also prescribed to treat low blood calcium levels in people who have hypoparathyroidism (decreased functioning of the parathyroid glands). When functioning correctly, these glands help control the level of calcium in the blood.

Most important fact about this drug

While you are taking Rocaltrol, your doctor may want you to follow a special diet or take calcium supplements. This is an important part of your therapy. On the other hand, too high a calcium level can be harmful. If you are already taking any medications containing calcium or calcium supplements, make sure you doctor knows about it.

How should you take this medication?

Be sure to get enough fluids and avoid dehydration while taking Rocaltrol.

■ *If you miss a dose...*

If you take 1 dose every other day, and you remember before the next day, take the forgotten dose immediately, then go back to your regular schedule. If you do not remember until the next day, take the dose immediately, skip a day, then go back to your regular schedule.

If you take 1 dose every day, take it as soon as you remember. Then go back to your regular schedule. If you do not remember until the next day, skip the dose you missed and go back to your regular schedule.

If you take Rocaltrol more than once a day, take the forgotten dose as soon as you remember. If it is almost time for your next dose, skip the one you missed and go back to your regular schedule.

Do not take 2 doses at once.

■ *Storage instructions...*
Keep away from heat and light. Keep out of reach of children.

What side effects may occur?
Side effects cannot be anticipated. If any develop or change in intensity, inform your doctor as soon as possible. Only your doctor can determine if it is safe for you to continue taking Rocaltrol.

■ *More common side effects occurring early may include:*
Bone pain
Constipation
Dry mouth
Extreme sleepiness
Headache
Metallic taste
Muscle pain
Nausea
Vomiting
Weakness

■ *More common side effects occurring later may include:*
Abnormal thirst, decreased sex drive, elevated blood cholesterol levels, excessive urination, extremely high body temperature, high blood pressure, inflamed eyes, intolerance to light, irregular heartbeat, itchy skin, kidney problems, loss of appetite, nighttime urination, runny nose, weight loss, yellowish skin

■ *Rare side effects may include:*
Mental disturbances, red patches (irregular or circular shape) on arms and hands

Excessive amounts of Vitamin D may cause abnormally high calcium levels in the blood.

Why should this drug not be prescribed?
You should not use Rocaltrol if you have high blood levels of calcium, or if you have vitamin D poisoning.

Special warnings about this medication
You should not take additional doses of vitamin D while taking Rocaltrol. People who are on dialysis should not take antacids containing magnesium (such as Maalox) while taking Rocaltrol.

Your doctor will monitor your calcium levels while you are taking Rocaltrol.

While taking Rocaltrol, you should have an adequate daily intake of calcium, either from foods (such as milk and dairy products) or from a calcium supplement. Your doctor will estimate your daily calcium intake before you take this drug to see if you will require more calcium.

Possible food and drug interactions
when taking this medication
If Rocaltrol is taken with certain other drugs, the effects of either could be increased, decreased, or altered. It is especially important to check with your doctor before combining Rocaltrol with the following:

Antacids containing magnesium, such as Maalox
Calcium supplements
Cholestyramine (Questran)
Digitalis (Lanoxin)
Vitamin D pills

Special information
if you are pregnant or breastfeeding
The effects of Rocaltrol during pregnancy have not been adequately studied. If you are pregnant or plan to become pregnant, inform your doctor immediately. Pregnant women should use Rocaltrol only if the possible benefit outweighs any possible risk to the unborn baby.

Rocaltrol may appear in breast milk. Because it may affect a nursing infant, you should not use Rocaltrol while you are breastfeeding.

Recommended dosage

ADULTS

For People on Dialysis
The suggested beginning dose is 0.25 microgram daily. Your doctor may increase the dose.

People with normal or only slightly low blood calcium levels may find it helpful to take 0.25 microgram every other day.

For Low Calcium Levels Due to Hypoparathyroidism
The suggested beginning dose is 0.25 microgram daily, taken in the morning. Your doctor may increase the dose.

For most adults, regular doses ranging from 0.5 to 2 micrograms daily are effective.

CHILDREN

For Low Calcium Levels Due to Hypoparathyroidism
The starting dose is 0.25 microgram, taken in the morning.

For most children 6 years and older, doses ranging from 0.5 to 2 micrograms per day are effective.

Children from 1 to 5 years old are usually given 0.25 to 0.75 microgram a day.

Overdosage
Any medication taken in excess can have serious consequences. Severe overdosage of Rocaltrol may cause serious effects, such as extremely high blood levels of calcium. If you suspect an overdose, seek medical help immediately.

■ *Symptoms of Rocaltrol overdose may include:*
Coma
Confusion
Extreme drowsiness

Brand name:

ROGAINE

Pronounced: ROW-gain
Generic name: Minoxidil

Why is this drug prescribed?
Rogaine is a hair growth stimulant. It is applied directly to the scalp, and is used to treat baldness in men and thinning hair in women.

Most important fact about this drug
Rogaine must be used twice a day for at least 4 months before new hair growth can be expected. If you stop using Rogaine you will probably shed the new hair within a few months. Larger or more frequent doses do not speed up or increase hair growth, but do increase the possibility of side effects.

How should you use this medication?

Use this medication exactly as prescribed by your doctor. Do not use more than is recommended. Applying too much increases the chance of side effects.

You may wash your hair before applying Rogaine, but your hair and scalp should be dry before applying the medication. Be sure to apply Rogaine directly to the scalp; applying it to the hair will not help the hair grow.

After you apply Rogaine, it must remain on the scalp for at least 4 hours so it can be properly absorbed.

If you use your fingertips to apply Rogaine, be sure to wash your hands thoroughly when you are finished. You may see a slight residue on your hair after the Rogaine dries. This is harmless and does not affect Rogaine's action.

■ *If you miss a dose...*
Resume your regular schedule with the next application. Do not increase the amount you apply.

■ *Storage instructions...*
The spray attachment or applicator can be left on the bottle when not in use. It will not leak. The spray extender need be removed only when traveling. Store at room temperature out of reach of children.

What side effects may occur?

Side effects cannot be anticipated. If any develop or change in intensity, inform your doctor as soon as possible. Only your doctor can determine if it is safe for you to continue using Rogaine.

■ *Side effects may include:*
Aches and pains, arthritis symptoms, anxiety, back pain, blood disorders, bone fractures, bronchitis, changes in blood pressure, changes in pulse rate, chest pain, depression, diarrhea, dizziness, dry skin/scalp flaking, ear infections, eczema, exhaustion, facial swelling, faintness, fluid retention, genital infections and irritation, growth of excess body hair, headache, hives, increased hair loss, itching, light-headedness, menstrual and breast changes, nausea, pinkeye (conjunctivitis), pounding heartbeat, redness of skin, runny nose, sexual dysfunction, sinus inflammation, skin irritation and other allergic reactions, vision changes, vomiting, weight gain

Why should this drug not be prescribed?

Rogaine should not be used if you are sensitive to or have ever had an allergic reaction to any of its ingredients.

Special warnings about this medication

Rogaine is for external use only.

You should have a healthy, normal scalp before starting treatment with Rogaine.

Even though Rogaine is applied to your skin, it is absorbed into your bloodstream. If you use more medication than is recommended or suffer from irritations on your scalp, side effects can occur elsewhere in your body. In tablet form, minoxidil, a high blood pressure medication, can cause salt and water retention, generalized and local fluid retention, rapid heartbeat, angina (crushing pain, usually in the chest, accompanied by a choking feeling), and inflammation of the sac that surrounds the heart. Although the likelihood is very small, these symptoms could possibly occur with the use of Rogaine, and people with heart disease would be at particular risk. Rogaine could also have adverse effects when used by people taking medications to lower their blood pressure.

You should have a checkup after you have been using Rogaine for 1 month and every 6 months thereafter.

Rogaine contains alcohol. Be careful not to get it in your eyes. If it gets into your eyes or on sensitive parts of your skin, wash the area well with cool tap water. If the irritation does not subside, contact your doctor.

Rogaine should not be used with other topical medications, such as steroids, that increase skin absorption, or with petroleum jelly.

Possible food and drug interactions when using this medication

No interactions with Rogaine have been reported.

Special information if you are pregnant or breastfeeding

The effects of Rogaine during pregnancy have not been adequately studied. However, minoxidil may cause birth defects, and the use of Rogaine during pregnancy is not recommended. If you are pregnant or plan to become pregnant, inform your doctor immediately. Minoxidil appears in breast milk and could affect a nursing infant. Rogaine is not recommended for use by nursing mothers.

Recommended dosage

ADULTS

Apply 1 milliliter of Rogaine to the total affected areas of the scalp 2 times a day. The total daily dosage should not be more than 2 milliliters. Make sure the hair and scalp are dry before applying the medication. It could take up to 4 months of twice-daily use to see results. If hair regrowth occurs, continue to apply Rogaine 2 times a day for additional or continued hair regrowth.

CHILDREN

Safety and effectiveness in children under 18 have not been established.

Overdosage

Any medication taken in excess can have serious consequences. If you suspect an overdose, seek medical attention immediately.

Generic name:

ROLAIDS

See Antacids, page 62.

Brand name:

RONDEC

Pronounced: RON-dek
Generic ingredients: Carbinoxamine maleate,
  Pseudoephedrine hydrochloride

Why is this drug prescribed?

Rondec is an antihistamine/decongestant that relieves nasal inflammation and runny nose and the symptoms of hay fever and other allergies. Carbinoxamine, the antihistamine in this combination, fights the effects of histamine, a chemical released by the body in response to certain irritants. Histamine narrows air passages in the lungs and contributes to inflammation. Antihistamines reduce itching and swelling and dry up secretions from the nose, eyes, and throat. Pseudoephedrine, the decongestant, reduces nasal congestion and makes breathing easier.

Most important fact about this drug

Rondec may cause mild to moderate drowsiness. You should not drive or operate dangerous machinery or participate in any hazardous activity that requires full mental alertness until you know how you react to this medication.

How should you take this medication?

Rondec is available in four forms. You can take Rondec Drops, Syrup, and Tablets up to 4 times a day; Rondec-TR Tablets are taken twice a day.

- *If you miss a dose...*
  Take it as soon as you remember. If it is almost time for your next dose, skip the one you missed and go back to your regular schedule. Do not take 2 doses at once.

- *Storage instructions...*
  Store at room temperature in a tightly closed container.

What side effects may occur?
Side effects cannot be anticipated. If any develop or change in intensity, inform your doctor as soon as possible. Only your doctor can determine if it is safe for you to continue taking Rondec.

- *Side effects may include:*
  Convulsions, diarrhea, difficulty breathing, difficulty sleeping (insomnia), dizziness, double vision, dry mouth, excitability in children (rare), hallucinations, headache, heartburn, increased blood pressure, increased heart rate, increased production of urine, irregular heartbeat, loss of appetite, nausea, nervousness, painful or difficult urination, pallor, sedation (extreme calm), stimulation, tremors, vomiting, weakness

Why should this drug not be prescribed?
Do not take Rondec if you are taking an antidepressant drug known as an MAO inhibitor (Nardil, for example). Also avoid Rondec if you are undergoing an asthma attack, or if you have any of the following medical problems: the eye condition known as narrow-angle glaucoma, difficulty urinating, peptic ulcer, severe high blood pressure, or coronary artery disease.

Do not take this medication if you are sensitive to or have ever had an allergic reaction to any of its ingredients.

Special warnings about this medication
Use Rondec with care if you have high blood pressure, heart disease, asthma, an overactive thyroid gland, increased pressure within the eye, diabetes, or an enlarged prostate gland.

Use this medication cautiously if you are over age 60.

Remember that Rondec can cause moderate to severe drowsiness. Be careful driving, operating machinery, or using appliances until you know how the drug affects you.

Possible food and drug interactions
when taking this medication

Rondec may increase the effects of alcohol. Do not drink alcohol while taking this medication.

If Rondec is taken with certain other drugs, the effects of either may be increased, decreased, or altered. It is important that you consult your doctor before combining Rondec with the following:

Beta-blocking blood pressure drugs such as Tenormin and Inderal
Drugs for depression such as Elavil and Nardil
High blood pressure drugs such as Aldomet, Diupres, and Inversine
MAO inhibitor-type drugs (antidepressants such as Nardil and Parnate)
Sedatives such as Halcion and Restoril
Tranquilizers such as Xanax and Valium

Special information
if you are pregnant or breastfeeding

The effects of Rondec during pregnancy have not been adequately studied. If you are pregnant or plan to become pregnant, notify your doctor immediately.

Recommended dosage

RONDEC ORAL DROPS

Children

The usual dosage is:

1 to 3 months old, ¼ dropperful (¼ milliliter), 4 times a day.

3 to 6 months old, ½ dropperful (½ milliliter), 4 times a day.

6 to 9 months old, ¾ dropperful (¾ milliliter), 4 times a day.

9 to 18 months old, 1 dropperful (1 milliliter), 4 times a day.

RONDEC SYRUP AND TABLETS

Adults and Children 6 Years and Over

The usual dosage is 1 teaspoonful (5 milliliters) or 1 tablet, 4 times a day.

Children Under 6 years old

The usual dosage for children 18 months to 6 years old is ½ teaspoonful (2.5 milliliters), 4 times a day.

RONDEC-TR TABLETS

Adults and Children 12 Years and Over
The usual dose is 1 tablet, 2 times a day.

If you have a mild case or are particularly sensitive, your doctor may have you take Rondec less frequently or prescribe a reduced dose.

Overdosage
Any medication taken in excess can have serious consequences. If you suspect an overdose of Rondec, seek medical attention immediately.

Although no information is available for Rondec, the following symptoms have been reported with antihistamine and pseudoephedrine overdose:

Abdominal cramps, coma, convulsions, diarrhea, difficulty sleeping (insomnia), difficulty urinating, dizziness, drowsiness, dry mouth, excitement, fever, flushing, fluttery or throbbing heartbeat, headache, high blood pressure with subsequent low blood pressure, irregular heartbeat, irritability, loss of appetite, metallic taste, nausea, restlessness, talkativeness, tremor, vomiting

- *Symptoms more common in children are:*
  Coma
  Convulsions
  Death
  Excitement
  Fever
  Fixed and dilated pupils
  Flushed face
  Hallucination
  Lack of muscle coordination
  Tremors

Brand name:

ROWASA

Pronounced: ROH-ace-ah
Generic name: Mesalamine
Other brand name: Pentasa, Asacol

Why is this drug prescribed?
Rowasa Suspension Enema, Pentasa, and Asacol are used to treat mild to moderate ulcerative colitis (inflammation of the large intestine and rectum).

Rowasa Suspension Enema is also prescribed for inflammation of the lower colon, and inflammation of the rectum.

Rowasa Suppositories are used to treat inflammation of the rectum.

Most important fact about this drug

Mesalamine, the active ingredient in these products, has been known to cause side effects such as:

Bloody diarrhea
Cramping
Fever
Rash
Severe headache
Sudden, severe stomach pain

If you develop any of these symptoms, stop taking this medication and consult your doctor.

How should you use this medication?

To Use Rowasa Suspension Enema

1. Rowasa Suspension Enema comes in boxes of 7 bottles each. After the foil on the box has been unwrapped, all Rowasa Suspension Enemas should be used promptly, following your doctor's instructions. The Suspension Enema is normally off-white to tan in color, but may darken over time once its foil cover is unwrapped. You may still use the enema if it is slightly discolored, but do not use Rowasa Suspension Enema if it is dark brown. If you have any questions about using Rowasa Suspension Enema, contact your doctor.
2. Use Rowasa Suspension Enema at bedtime.
3. Shake the bottle thoroughly.
4. Uncover the applicator tip.
5. You may find it easier to use Rowasa Suspension Enema if you lie down on your left side, extending your left leg and bending your right leg forward for a comfortable balance. An alternative position is to squat with your knees to your chest.
6. Pointing the applicator tip up, gently insert the tip into the rectum.
7. Squeeze the bottle steadily to discharge the contents.
8. The enema should be retained all night (8 hours) for best results.

To Use Rowasa Suppositories

1. Rowasa Suppositories should be used twice a day.
2. You should handle the suppositories as little as possible, because they are designed to melt at body temperature.

3. Remove one suppository from the strip of suppositories.
4. While holding the suppository upright, carefully remove the foil wrapper.
5. Using gentle pressure, insert the suppository (with the pointed end first) completely into the rectum.
6. The suppository should be retained for 1 to 3 hours or longer for best results.

To take Pentasa or Asacol

Swallow the capsule or tablet whole. Do not break, crush, or chew it before swallowing.

You may notice what looks like small beads in your stool. These are just empty shells that are left after the medication has been absorbed into your body. However, if this continues, check with your doctor.

- ■ *If you miss a dose...*
  Take it as soon as you remember. If it is almost time for your next dose, skip the one you missed and go back to your regular schedule. Never take 2 doses at the same time.

- ■ *Storage instructions...*
  Store these products at room temperature.

What side effects may occur?

Side effects cannot be anticipated. If any side effects develop or change in intensity, tell your doctor immediately. Only your doctor can determine whether it is safe to continue using this medication.

- ■ *More common side effects of Rowasa Suspension Enema may include:*
  Flu-like symptoms
  Gas
  Headache
  Nausea
  Stomach pain/cramps

- ■ *Less common side effects of Rowasa Suspension Enema may include:*
  Back pain, bloating, diarrhea, dizziness, fever, hemorrhoids, itching, leg/joint pain, pain on insertion of enema tip, rash, rectal pain, sore throat, tiredness, weakness

- *Rare side effects of Rowasa Suspension Enema may include:*
  Constipation, hair loss, insomnia, swelling of the arms or legs, urinary burning

- *More common side effects of Rowasa Suppositories may include:*
  Diarrhea
  Dizziness
  Gas
  Headache
  Stomach pain

- *Less common side effects of Rowasa Suppositories may include:*
  Acne, cold symptoms, fever, inflammation of the colon, nausea, rash, rectal pain, swelling, weakness

- *More common side effects of Pentasa and Asacol may include:*
  Diarrhea
  Headache
  Nausea

- *Less common or rare side effects of Pentasa and Asacol may include:*
  Abdominal pain, abdominal swelling, acne, belching, blood in the urine, bloody diarrhea, breast pain, bruising, conjunctivitis, constipation, depression, difficulty sleeping, difficulty swallowing, dizziness, dry skin, duodenal ulcer, eczema, fever, fluid retention, general feeling of illness, hair loss, hives, inflammation of the pancreas, itching, joint pain, Kawasaki-like syndrome (rash, swollen glands, fever, mouth inflammation, strawberry tongue), lack or loss of appetite, leg cramps, menstrual irregularities, mouth sores and infections, muscle pain, nail problems, palpitations (rapid, fluttery heartbeat), rash, rectal bleeding, sensitivity to light, skin eruptions, sleepiness, stomach and intestinal bleeding, stool changes, sweating, thirst, tingling or pins and needles, ulcer of the esophagus, uncontrollable bowel movements, urinary frequency, weakness, worsening of ulcerative colitis, vomiting

Why should this drug not be prescribed?
These products should not be used by anyone who is allergic or sensitive to mesalamine or their other ingredients.

Pentasa and Asacol should not be used if you are allergic or sensitive to salicylates (aspirin).

Special warnings about this medication

Your doctor should check your kidney function while you are taking mesalamine, especially if you have a history of kidney disease or you are using other anti-inflammatory drugs such as Dipentum.

You should use mesalamine cautiously if you are allergic to sulfasalazine (Azulfidine). If you develop a rash or fever, you should stop using the medication and notify your doctor.

Some people using mesalamine have developed flare-ups of their colitis.

Rare cases of pericarditis, in which the membrane surrounding the heart becomes inflamed, have been reported with products containing mesalamine. Symptoms may include chest, neck, and shoulder pain, and shortness of breath.

Rowasa Suspension Enema contains a sulfite that may cause allergic reactions in some people. These reactions may include shock and severe, possibly fatal asthma attacks. Most people aren't sensitive to sulfites. However, some people with asthma might be sensitive and should take any medication containing sulfites cautiously.

Rowasa Suspension Enema may stain clothes and fabrics.

Possible food and drug interactions
when taking this medication

If these products are taken with certain other drugs, the effects of either could be increased, decreased, or altered. It is especially important to check with your doctor before combining Rowasa Suspension Enema or Rowasa Suppositories with Sulfasalazine (Azulfidine).

Special information
if you are pregnant or breastfeeding

Pregnant women should use mesalamine only if clearly needed. Mesalamine has been found in breast milk. If this medication is essential to your health, your doctor may advise you to discontinue breastfeeding until your treatment is finished.

Recommended dosage

ADULTS

Rowasa Suspension Enema
The usual dose is 1 rectal enema (60 milliliters) per day, preferably used at bedtime and retained for about 8 hours. Treatment time usually lasts from 3 to 6 weeks, although improvement may be seen within 3 to 21 days.

Rowasa Suppositories
The usual dose is one rectal suppository (500 milligrams) 2 times a day. To get the most benefit from a Rowasa Suppository, it should be retained for 1 to 3 hours or longer. Treatment time usually lasts from 3 to 6 weeks, although improvement may be seen within 3 to 21 days.

Pentasa Capsules
The usual dose is 4 capsules taken 4 times a day for a total of 16 capsules daily.

Asacol Tablets
The recommended dose is 2 tablets 3 times a day for 6 weeks.

CHILDREN

Safety and effectiveness in children have not been established.

Overdosage
There have been no proven reports of serious effects resulting from overdoses of Rowasa. An overdose of Pentasa or Asacol could cause any of the following symptoms:

Confusion
Diarrhea
Drowsiness
Headache
Hyperventilation
Ringing in the ears
Sweating
Vomiting

Any medication taken in excess can have serious consequences. If you suspect an overdose, seek medical attention immediately.

Brand name:

ROXICET

See Percocet, page 831.

Brand name:

RUFEN

See Advil, page 17.

Brand name:

RU-TUSS TABLETS

Pronounced: ROO-tus
Generic ingredients: Phenylephrine hydrochloride,
  Phenylpropanolamine hydrochloride, Chlorpheniramine
  maleate, Hyoscyamine sulfate, Atropine sulfate,
  Scopolamine hydrobromide

Why is this drug prescribed?
Ru-Tuss is an antihistamine/decongestant that relieves the runny, stuffy nose, nasal drip, itching, watery eyes, and scratchy, itchy throat caused by allergies, colds, and other irritations of the sinus, nose, and upper respiratory tract. Chlorpheniramine, the antihistamine, relieves watery eyes, dries up post-nasal drip, and reduces sneezing. Phenylephrine and phenylpropanolamine combine to reduce congestion and make breathing easier. Hyoscyamine, atropine, and scopolamine, commonly called belladonna alkaloids, enhance the drying effects of Ru-Tuss.

Most important fact about this drug
Ru-Tuss tablets may cause drowsiness. Do not drive, operate machinery or participate in any hazardous activity that requires full mental alertness until you know how you react to this medication.

How should you take this medication?
Take this medication exactly as prescribed. The tablets act continuously for 10 to 12 hours. Tablets should be swallowed whole, not crushed or chewed.

If this medicine dries out your mouth, sucking on hard candy or chewing gum may help.

■ *If you miss a dose...*
Take it as soon as you remember. If it is almost time for your next dose, skip the one you missed and go back to your regular schedule. Never take 2 doses at the same time.

■ *Storage instructions...*
Store it at room temperature.

What side effects may occur?
Side effects cannot be anticipated. If any develop or change in intensity, inform your doctor as soon as possible. Only your doctor can determine if it is safe for you to continue taking Ru-Tuss.

■ *Side effects may include:*
Allergic reactions (rash, hives), blood disorders, blurred vision, constipation, diarrhea, difficulty sleeping (insomnia), dilated pupils, dizziness, drowsiness, dry mouth, dry nose and other mucous membranes, exhaustion, faintness, frequent urination, giddiness, headache, hyperirritability, increased chest congestion, itching, lack of coordination, loss of appetite, low blood pressure/high blood pressure, nausea, nervousness, painful or difficult urination, pounding heartbeat, rapid heartbeat, ringing in the ears, stomach upset, tightness in the chest, vision changes, vomiting

Why should this drug not be prescribed?
Ru-Tuss should be avoided if you are pregnant, if you are sensitive to or have ever had an allergic reaction to antihistamines or any of the ingredients in this medication, if you have glaucoma or bronchial asthma, or if you are taking antidepressant drugs known as MAO inhibitors (Nardil, for example). Ru-Tuss should not be given to children under 12 years of age.

Special warnings about this medication
This medication can make you feel drowsy. Be careful driving, operating machinery, or using appliances.

Ru-Tuss should be used with care if you have a bladder obstruction, high blood pressure, cardiovascular disease, or an overactive thyroid.

Possible food and drug interactions when taking this medication
Ru-Tuss may increase the effects of alcohol. Do not drink alcohol while taking this medication.

Do not take Ru-Tuss while taking antidepressant drugs such as Nardil, Marplan, and Parnate.

If Ru-Tuss is taken with certain other drugs, the effects of either could be increased, decreased, or altered. It is especially important to check with your doctor before combining Ru-Tuss with the following:

Sleep medications such as Halcion and Dalmane
Tranquilizers such as Xanax and Valium

Special information
if you are pregnant or breastfeeding
Ru-Tuss is not recommended for use by pregnant women. If you are pregnant or plan to become pregnant, notify your doctor immediately.

Recommended dosage

ADULTS AND CHILDREN 12 YEARS OR OLDER

The usual dosage is 1 tablet in the morning and 1 tablet in the evening. This drug is not recommended for children under 12.

Overdosage
Any medication taken in excess can have serious consequences. Convulsions and death may occur from antihistamine overdose in children and infants. If you suspect an overdose, seek medical treatment immediately.

■ *Symptoms of Ru-Tuss overdose may include:*
Coma
Delirium
Fever
Rapid breathing
Respiratory failure
Stupor

Brand name:

RYNATAN

Pronounced: RYE-nuh-tan
Generic ingredients: Phenylephrine tannate,
    Chlorpheniramine tannate, Pyrilamine tannate

Why is this drug prescribed?
Rynatan is an antihistamine/decongestant that relieves runny nose and nasal congestion caused by the common cold, inflamed sinuses, hay fever, and other upper respiratory conditions. Chlorpheniramine and pyrilamine, the

antihistamines in the combination, reduce itching and swelling and dry up secretions from the eyes, nose, and throat. Phenylephrine, the decongestant, reduces congestion and makes breathing easier.

Most important fact about this drug
This medication can make you drowsy. You should not drive or operate dangerous machinery or participate in any hazardous activity that requires full mental alertness until you know how you react to Rynatan.

How should you take this medication?
Take this medication exactly as prescribed.

- *If you miss a dose...*
  Take it as soon as you remember. If it is almost time for the next dose, skip the one you missed and go back to your regular schedule. Do not take 2 doses at once.

- *Storage instructions...*
  Store at room temperature in a tightly closed container.

What side effects may occur?
Side effects cannot be anticipated. If any develop or change in intensity, inform your doctor as soon as possible. Only your doctor can determine if it is safe for you to continue taking Rynatan.

- *Side effects may include:*
  Drowsiness
  Dry nose, mouth, and throat
  Extreme calm (sedation)
  Stomach and intestinal problems

Why should this drug not be prescribed?
Rynatan should not be given to newborn babies, or used by nursing mothers or people who are sensitive to or have ever had an allergic reaction to any of its ingredients or to similar antihistamine and decongestant combinations.

Special warnings about this medication
Use Rynatan with care if you have high blood pressure, heart disease, circulatory problems, an overactive thyroid gland, diabetes, the eye condition known as narrow-angle glaucoma, or an enlarged prostate gland.

The antihistamines in Rynatan may cause dizziness, sedation, and low blood pressure in elderly people. In children they can cause excitement.

Possible food and drug interactions when taking this medication

Rynatan may increase the effects of alcohol. Do not drink alcohol while taking this medication.

If Rynatan is taken with certain other drugs, the effects of either could be increased, decreased, or altered. It is especially important to check with your doctor before combining Rynatan with the following:

Antidepressant drugs classified as MAO inhibitors, including Nardil and Marplan
Sedatives such as Halcion and Dalmane
Tranquilizers such as Xanax and Valium

Special information if you are pregnant or breastfeeding

The effects of Rynatan during pregnancy have not been adequately studied. If you are pregnant or plan to become pregnant, notify your doctor immediately. Rynatan should not be taken if you are breastfeeding.

Recommended dosage

RYNATAN TABLETS

Adults

The usual dosage is 1 or 2 tablets every 12 hours.

RYNATAN-S PEDIATRIC SUSPENSION

Children Over Age 6

The usual dosage is 1 to 2 teaspoonfuls (5 to 10 milliliters) every 12 hours.

Children Aged 2 Through 5

The usual dosage is ½ to 1 teaspoonful (2.5 to 5 milliliters) every 12 hours.

Children Under Age 2

Your doctor will determine the dose.

Overdosage

Any medication taken in excess can have serious consequences. Antihistamine overdose in young children can lead to convulsions and death. If you suspect an overdose, seek medical treatment immediately.

Symptoms of Rynatan overdose range from a slowdown of the central nervous system to overstimulation.

Brand name:

RYTHMOL

Pronounced: RITH-mol
Generic name: Propafenone

Why is this drug prescribed?
Rythmol is used to help correct certain life-threatening heartbeat irregularities (ventricular arrhythmias).

Most important fact about this drug
There is a possibility that Rythmol may cause new heartbeat irregularities or make the existing ones worse. Rythmol is therefore used only for serious problems, and should be accompanied by periodic electrocardiograms (EKGs) prior to and during treatment. Discuss this with your doctor.

How should you take this medication?
Rythmol may be taken with food or on an empty stomach.

Take Rythmol exactly as prescribed. It works best when there is a constant amount of the drug in the blood, so you should take it at evenly spaced intervals.

- *If you miss a dose...*
  Unless otherwise instructed by your doctor, take the forgotten dose as soon as possible. However, if it is almost time for your next dose or more than 4 hours have passed, skip the missed dose and go back to your regular schedule. Never take a double dose.

- *Storage instructions...*
  Keep this medication in the container it came in, tightly closed, away from direct light, at room temperature.

What side effects may occur?
Side effects cannot be anticipated. If any develop or change in intensity, inform your doctor as soon as possible. Only your doctor can determine if it is safe for you to continue taking Rythmol.

The most common side effects affect the digestive, cardiovascular, and nervous systems. The most serious are heartbeat abnormalities.

- *More common side effects may include:*
  Constipation
  Dizziness
  Heartbeat abnormalities
  Nausea
  Unusual taste in the mouth
  Vomiting

- *Other side effects may include:*
  Abdominal pain or cramps, anemia, angina (chest pain), anxiety, blood disorders, blurred vision, breathing difficulties, bruising, cardiac arrest, coma, confusion, congestive heart failure, depression, diarrhea, dreaming abnormalities, drowsiness, dry mouth, eye irritation, fainting or near fainting, fatigue, fever, flushing, gas, hair loss, headache, heart palpitations, heartbeat abnormalities (rapid, irregular, slow), hot flashes, impotence, increased blood sugar, indigestion, inflamed esophagus, stomach, or intestines, insomnia, itching, joint pain, kidney disease, kidney failure, lack of coordination, liver dysfunction, loss of appetite, loss of balance, low blood pressure, memory loss, muscle cramps, muscle weakness, numbness, pain, psychosis, rash, red or purple spots on the skin, ringing in the ears, seizures, speech abnormalities, sweating, swelling due to fluid retention, tingling or pins and needles, tremor, unusual smell sensations, vertigo, vision abnormalities, weakness

Why should this drug not be prescribed?
Do not take Rythmol if you have ever had an allergic reaction to or are sensitive to it. Your doctor will not prescribe Rythmol if you are suffering from any of the following conditions:

Abnormally slow heartbeat
Certain heartbeat irregularities, such as atrioventricular block or "sick sinus" syndrome, that have not been corrected by a pacemaker
Cardiogenic shock (shock due to a weak heart)
Chronic bronchitis or emphysema
Congestive heart failure that is not well controlled
Mineral (electrolyte) imbalance
Severe low blood pressure

Special warnings about this medication
If you have congestive heart failure, this condition must be brought under full medical control before you start taking Rythmol.

If you have a pacemaker, the pacemaker's settings must be monitored—and possibly reprogrammed—while you are taking Rythmol.

There is some risk that Rythmol may interfere with your body's normal ability to manufacture blood cells. Too few white blood cells may cause signs and symptoms that mimic infection. If you experience fever, chills, or sore throat while taking Rythmol—especially during the first 3 months of treatment—notify your doctor right away.

Rythmol may cause a lupus-like illness characterized by rashes and arthritic symptoms. If you have been taking Rythmol and testing shows that your blood contains ANA (antinuclear antibodies), your doctor may want to discontinue the medication.

Possible food and drug interactions
when taking this medication

If Rythmol is taken with certain other drugs, the effects of either could be increased, decreased, or altered. It is especially important to check with your doctor before combining Rythmol with the following:

Beta blockers such as Inderal and Lopressor
Cimetidine (Tagamet)
Digitalis (Lanoxin)
Local anesthetics (such as Novocain used during dental work)
Quinidine (Cardioquin)
Warfarin (blood thinners such as Coumadin)

Special information
if you are pregnant or breastfeeding

If you are pregnant or plan to become pregnant, inform your doctor immediately. Because of a possible risk of birth defects, Rythmol is not recommended during pregnancy unless the benefit to the mother outweighs the potential risk to the unborn baby.

It is not known whether Rythmol appears in breast milk. You are advised not to take Rythmol if you are nursing a baby. If treatment with Rythmol is essential to your health, your doctor may advise you to stop breastfeeding until your treatment is finished.

Recommended dosage

ADULTS

In most cases, treatment with Rythmol begins in the hospital.

Your doctor will tailor your dosage according to your individual condition and the presence of other disorders.

The usual initial dose of Rythmol is 150 milligrams every 8 hours. Your doctor may increase the dosage depending on how you respond to the initial dosage. The maximum recommended daily dosage of Rythmol is 900 milligrams.

CHILDREN

Safety and effectiveness have not been established in children.

ELDERLY

The doctor will increase the dosage more slowly at the beginning of treatment.

Overdosage

Any medication taken in excess can have serious consequences. If you suspect an overdose of Rythmol, seek medical attention immediately.

■ *Symptoms of Rythmol overdose, which are usually most severe within the first 3 hours of taking the medication, may include:*
Convulsions (rarely)
Heartbeat irregularities
Low blood pressure
Sleepiness

Generic name:

SALSALATE

See Disalcid, page 348.

Brand name:

SANDIMMUNE

Pronounced: SAN-dim-ewn
Generic name: Cyclosporine

Why is this drug prescribed?

Sandimmune is given after organ transplant surgery to help prevent rejection of organs (kidney, heart, or liver) by holding down the body's immune system. It is also used to treat long-term rejection in people previously treated with other immunosuppressant drugs, such as Imuran.

Some doctors also prescribe Sandimmune to treat alopecia areata (localized areas of hair loss), aplastic anemia (shortage of red and white blood cells and platelets), Crohn's disease (chronic inflammation of the digestive tract), and nephropathy (kidney disease). Sandimmune is sometimes used in the treatment of severe skin disorders, including psoriasis and dermatomyositis (inflammation of the skin and muscles causing weakness and rash). The drug is also used in procedures involving bone marrow, the pancreas, and the lungs.

Sandimmune is always given with prednisone or a similar steroid. It is available in capsules and liquid, or as an injection.

Most important fact about this drug
If you take Sandimmune orally over a period of time, your doctor will monitor your blood levels of cyclosporine to make sure your body is receiving the correct amount of Sandimmune. The reason for this repeated testing is that the absorption of this drug in the body is erratic. Constant monitoring is necessary to prevent toxicity due to overdosing or to prevent possible organ rejection due to underdosing. It is important to note that Sandimmune may need to be taken by mouth for an indefinite period following surgery.

How should you take this medication?
Take the Sandimmune capsule or oral liquid at the same time every day. You may take the medication either with a meal or between meals, but be consistent.

To make Sandimmune oral liquid more palatable, you may mix it with room-temperature milk, chocolate milk, or orange juice. Be sure to use the same type of beverage every day. Use a container made of glass, not plastic. Never let the mixture stand; drink it as soon as you prepare it. To make sure you get your full dose, rinse the glass with a little more liquid and drink that too.

You should maintain good dental hygiene and see your dentist frequently for cleaning to prevent tenderness, bleeding, and gum enlargement.

After you use the dosage syringe to transfer the oral solution to a glass, dry the outside of the syringe with a clean towel and put it away. Do not rinse or wash it. If you do have to clean it, make sure it is thoroughly dry before you use it again.

■ *If you miss a dose...*
If fewer than 12 hours have passed, take it as soon as you remember. If it is almost time for the next dose, skip the one you missed and go back to your regular schedule. Do not take 2 doses at once.

■ *Storage instructions...*
Store both the capsules and the oral solution below 86°F; do not store the liquid in the refrigerator. Sandimmune liquid, once opened, must be used within 2 months.

What side effects may occur?
Side effects cannot be anticipated. If any appear or change in intensity, inform your doctor immediately. Only your doctor can determine if it is safe for you to continue taking Sandimmune. The principal side effects of Sandimmune are high blood pressure, hirsutism (excessive hairiness), kidney damage, excessive growth of the gums, and tremor.

■ *Other common side effects may include:*
Abdominal discomfort, acne, convulsions, cramps, diarrhea, flushing, headache, liver damage, lymph system tumor, nausea, numbness or tingling, sinus inflammation, vomiting

■ *Less common side effects may include:*
Allergic reactions, anemia, appetite loss, brittle fingernails, confusion, conjunctivitis (pinkeye), fever, fluid retention, hearing loss, hiccups, high blood sugar, muscle pain, peptic ulcer, ringing in the ears, stomach inflammation

■ *Rare side effects may include:*
Anxiety, blood in the urine, breast development in males, chest pain, constipation, depression, hair breaking, heart attack, itching, joint pain, mouth sores, night sweats, sluggishness, stomach and upper intestinal bleeding, swallowing difficulty, tingling, visual disturbance, weakness, weight loss

Why should this drug not be prescribed?
You should not receive Sandimmune by injection if you have ever had an allergic reaction to an injection of the drug or you are especially sensitive to castor oil.

Special warnings about this medication
When your immune system is suppressed by Sandimmune, you are at increased risk of infection and of certain malignancies, including skin cancer and lymph system cancer.

High-dose Sandimmune is toxic to the liver and kidneys and may cause serious kidney damage. Because this toxicity has symptoms similar to those of transplant rejection, you must be monitored closely. If your body is trying

SANDIMMUNE / 1001

hard to reject a transplanted organ, your doctor will probably allow the rejection to occur rather than give you a very high dose of Sandimmune.

If you take large doses of a prednisone-like drug called methylprednisolone (Medrol) along with Sandimmune, you may be at increased risk of convulsions.

Use a barrier method of contraception, such as diaphragms or condoms, during Sandimmune therapy. Do not use oral contraceptive pills without your doctor's approval.

Possible food and drug interactions when taking this medication

Avoid getting vaccinations and immunizations while you are taking Sandimmune. The drug may make vaccinations less effective or increase your risk of contracting an illness from a live vaccine.

If Sandimmune is taken with certain other drugs, the effects of either could be increased, decreased, or altered. It is especially important to check with your doctor before combining Sandimmune with the following:

Bromocriptine (Parlodel)
Calcium-blocking heart and blood pressure medications such as Calan, Cardene, Procardia, and Cardizem
Carbamazepine (Tegretol)
Cimetidine (Tagamet)
Danazol (Danocrine)
Diclofenac (Voltaren)
Digoxin (Lanoxin, Lanoxicaps)
Erythromycin (E.E.S., Erythrocin, others)
Fluconazole (Diflucan)
Gentamicin (Garamycin)
Itraconazole (Sporanox)
Ketoconazole (Nizoral)
Lovastatin (Mevacor)
Melphalan (Alkeran)
Methylprednisolone (Depo-Medrol, Medrol, Solu-Medrol)
Metoclopramide (Reglan)
Phenobarbital
Phenytoin (Dilantin)
Potassium-sparing diuretics (Dyrenium, Midamor, Aldactone)
Prednisolone (Delta-Cortef)
Ranitidine (Zantac)
Rifampin (Rifadin, Rifamate, Rimactane)
Tobramycin (Nebcin)

Trimethoprim/sulfamethoxazole (Bactrim, Septra)
Vancomycin (Vancocin)

Special information
if you are pregnant or breastfeeding

The effects of Sandimmune in pregnancy have not been adequately studied. If you are pregnant or plan to become pregnant, inform your doctor immediately. Sandimmune should be used during pregnancy only if the benefit justifies the potential risk to the unborn child. Since Sandimmune appears in breast milk, it should not be used during breastfeeding. If you are a new mother, you may need to choose between taking Sandimmune and breastfeeding your baby.

Recommended dosage

Your doctor will tailor your dosage in accordance with your body's response. Expect a single dose of 15 milligrams per 2.2 pounds of body weight 4 to 12 hours before a transplant and 1 dose daily for 1 to 2 weeks after the operation. After that, the doctor may keep you on a daily dose of 5 to 10 milligrams per 2.2 pounds of body weight.

Overdosage

Although no specific information is available, an overdose of Sandimmune would be expected to cause liver and kidney problems. Any medication taken in excess can have serious consequences. If you suspect an overdose of Sandimmune, seek medical attention immediately.

Brand name:

SECTRAL

Pronounced: SEK-tral
Generic name: Acebutolol hydrochloride

Why is this drug prescribed?

Sectral, a type of medication known as a beta blocker, is used in the treatment of high blood pressure and abnormal heart rhythms. When used to treat high blood pressure, it is effective used alone or in combination with other high blood pressure medications, particularly with a thiazide-type diuretic. Beta blockers decrease the force and rate of heart contractions, thus reducing pressure within the circulatory system.

Most important fact about this drug

If you have high blood pressure, you must take Sectral regularly for it to be effective. Since blood pressure declines gradually, it may be several weeks before you get the full benefit of Sectral; and you must continue taking it even if you are feeling well. Sectral does not cure high blood pressure; it merely keeps it under control.

How should you take this medication?
Sectral can be taken with or without food. Take it exactly as prescribed, even if your symptoms have disappeared.

Try not to miss any doses. If this medication is not taken regularly, your condition may worsen.

■ *If you miss a dose...*
Take the forgotten dose as soon as you remember. If it's within 4 hours of your next scheduled dose, skip the one you missed and go back to your regular schedule. Never take 2 doses at the same time.

■ *Storage instructions...*
Store at room temperature. Keep the container tightly closed. Protect from light.

What side effects may occur?
Side effects cannot be anticipated. If any develop or change in intensity, inform your doctor as soon as possible. Only your doctor can determine if it is safe for you to continue taking Sectral.

■ *More common side effects may include:*
Abnormal vision, chest pain, constipation, cough, decreased sexual ability, depression, diarrhea, dizziness, fatigue, frequent urination, gas, headache, indigestion, joint pain, nasal inflammation, nausea, shortness of breath or difficulty breathing, strange dreams, swelling due to fluid retention, trouble sleeping, weakness

■ *Less common or rare side effects may include:*
Abdominal pain, anxiety, back pain, burning eyes, cold hands and feet, conjunctivitis, dark urine, excessive urination at night, eye pain, fever, heart failure, impotence, itching, loss of appetite, low blood pressure, muscle pain, nervousness, painful or difficult urination, rash, slow heartbeat, throat inflammation, vomiting, wheezing

Why should this drug not be prescribed?
If you have heart failure, inadequate blood supply to the circulatory system (cardiogenic shock), heart block (a type of irregular heartbeat), or a severely slow heartbeat, you should not take this medication.

Special warnings about this medication

If you have had severe congestive heart failure in the past, Sectral should be used with caution.

Sectral should not be stopped suddenly. This can cause increased chest pain and heart attack. Dosage should be gradually reduced.

If you suffer from asthma, seasonal allergies, other bronchial conditions, coronary artery disease, or kidney or liver disease, this medication should be used with caution.

Ask your doctor if you should check your pulse while taking Sectral. This medication can cause your heartbeat to become too slow.

This medication may mask the symptoms of low blood sugar or alter blood sugar levels. If you are diabetic, discuss this with your doctor.

Notify your doctor or dentist that you are taking Sectral if you have a medical emergency, or before you have any surgery.

Tell your doctor if you are taking over-the-counter cold medications and nasal drops. They may interact with Sectral.

If you experience difficulty breathing, or develop hives or large areas of swelling, seek medical attention immediately. You may be having a serious allergic reaction to the medicine.

Possible food and drug interactions
when taking this medication

If Sectral is taken with certain other drugs, the effects of either could be increased, decreased, or altered. It is especially important to check with your doctor before combining Sectral with the following:

Albuterol (the airway-opening drug Ventolin)
Certain blood pressure medicines such as reserpine (Diupres)
Certain over-the-counter cold remedies and nasal drops such as Afrin, Neo-Synephrine, and Sudafed
Nonsteroidal anti-inflammatory drugs such as Motrin and Voltaren
Oral diabetes drugs such as Micronase

Special information
if you are pregnant or breastfeeding

The effects of Sectral during pregnancy have not been adequately studied. If you are pregnant or plan to become pregnant, inform your doctor immediately. Sectral appears in breast milk and could affect a nursing infant. If this medication is essential to your health, your doctor may advise you to discontinue breastfeeding until your treatment with Sectral is finished.

Recommended dosage

ADULTS

Hypertension

The usual initial dose for mild to moderate high blood pressure is 400 milligrams per day. It may be taken in a single daily dose or in 2 doses of 200 milligrams each. The usual daily dosage ranges from 200 to 800 milligrams.

People with severe high blood pressure may take up to 1,200 milligrams per day divided into 2 doses. Sectral may be taken alone or in combination with another high blood pressure medication.

Irregular heartbeat

The usual starting dosage is 400 milligrams per day divided into 2 doses. Your doctor may gradually increase the dose to 600 to 1,200 milligrams per day. If your doctor wants you to stop taking this medication, he or she will have you taper off over a period of 2 weeks.

CHILDREN

The safety and effectiveness of Sectral have not been established in children.

ELDERLY

Your doctor will determine the dosage based on your particular needs. Do not take more than 800 milligrams per day.

Overdosage

Any medication taken in excess can have serious consequences. If you suspect an overdose, seek medical attention immediately.

■ *There is no specific information available on Sectral; however, overdose symptoms seen with other beta blockers include:*
   Difficulty breathing
   Extremely slow heartbeat
   Irregular heartbeat
   Low blood pressure
   Low blood sugar
   Seizures
   Severe congestive heart failure

Brand name:

SELDANE

Pronounced: SELL-dane
Generic name: Terfenadine

Why is this drug prescribed?

Seldane is an antihistamine that relieves the sneezing, runny nose, stuffiness, itching, and tearing eyes caused by hay fever. Another form of the drug, Seldane-D, also contains pseudoephedrine, which relieves nasal stuffiness.

Antihistamines work by decreasing the effects of histamine, a chemical the body releases in response to certain irritants. Histamine narrows air passages in the lungs and contributes to inflammation. Antihistamines reduce itching and swelling and dry up secretions from the nose, eyes, and throat.

Most important fact about this drug

Seldane is chemically different from other antihistamines and causes significantly less drowsiness.

How should you take this medication?

Take Seldane and Seldane-D only as needed. Do not take more than your doctor has prescribed.

- *If you miss a dose...*
  If you are taking Seldane regularly, take the missed dose as soon as you remember. If it is almost time for the next dose, skip the one you missed and go back to your regular schedule. Never take two doses at the same time.

- *Storage instructions...*
  Store at room temperature. Protect from moisture and extreme heat. Keep out of reach of children.

What side effects may occur?

Side effects cannot be anticipated. If any develop or change in intensity, inform your doctor as soon as possible. Only your doctor can determine if it is safe for you to continue taking Seldane or Seldane-D.

- *More common side effects of Seldane may include:*
Drowsiness
Fatigue
Headache
Stomach and intestinal problems (nausea, vomiting, change in bowel habits)

- *Less common or rare side effects of Seldane may include:*
Confusion, cough, depression, dizziness, dry mouth/nose/throat, excessive or spontaneous flow of milk, fainting, frequent urination, hair thinning or loss, hepatitis, hives, increased appetite, irregular heartbeat, insomnia, itching, low blood pressure, menstrual disorders and pain, nightmares, nosebleed, palpitations, rapid heartbeat, seizures, sensitivity to light, severe allergic reaction (anaphylactic shock), sore throat, sweating, tingling or pins and needles, tremor, vision changes, weakness, wheezing

- *More common side effects of Seldane-D may include:*
Drowsiness
Dry mouth, nose, and throat
Headache
Insomnia
Loss of appetite
Nausea
Nervousness

- *Less common or rare side effects of Seldane-D may include:*
Blurred vision, change in bowel habits, change in taste, confusion, cough, depression, disorientation, dizziness, excessive or spontaneous flow of milk, fatigue, flare-up of psoriasis, frequent urination, hair loss, hepatitis, hives, increased appetite, increased energy, increased physical activity, irregular heartbeat, irritability, itching, menstrual disorders, muscle twitches, nightmares, nosebleeds, palpitations, rapid heartbeat, rash, restlessness, seizures, sensitivity to light, severe allergic reaction, sore throat, stomach and intestinal upset, sweating, tingling or pins and needles, tremors, upper respiratory infection, vision problems, vomiting, weakness, wheezing

Why should this drug not be prescribed?
Rare, serious, heart-related side effects have been reported when Seldane or Seldane-D is used with erythromycin (PCE, E-Mycin), itraconazole (Sporanox), ketoconazole (Nizoral), clarithromycin (Biaxin), or troleandomycin (TAO). Do not combine Seldane or Seldane-D with any of these drugs.

Do not take Seldane or Seldane-D if you have liver disease, or if you are sensitive to or have ever had an allergic reaction to the drug.

In addition, Seldane-D should be avoided by nursing mothers, people with severe high blood pressure or heart disease, and people taking the antidepressant drugs known as MAO inhibitors (Nardil, Parnate, others).

Special warnings about this medication
Seldane and Seldane-D should be used cautiously if you have liver disease or heart disease. An irregular heartbeat can develop. Heartbeat irregularities also can occur when Seldane and Seldane-D are taken with a number of other medications such as Bepridil (Vascor), probucol (Lorelco), astemizole (Hismanal), diuretics (water pills), and certain drugs used to treat mental problems. If you develop an irregular heartbeat, stop taking Seldane and notify your doctor. If you have diabetes, glaucoma, or an enlarged prostate, you should take Seldane-D with caution.

Possible food and drug interactions when taking this medication
If Seldane or Seldane-D is taken with certain other drugs, the effects of either could be increased, decreased, or altered. It is especially important to check with your doctor before combining Seldane or Seldane-D with the following:

Amiodarone (Cordarone)
Astemizole (Hismanal)
Bepridil (Vascor)
Clarithromycin (Biaxin)
Disopyramide (Norpace)
Erythromycin (PCE, E-Mycin)
Itraconazole (Sporanox)
Ketoconazole (Nizoral)
Probucol (Lorelco)
Procainamide (Pronestyl, Procan)
Quinidine (Quinaglute, Quinidex)
Troleandomycin (TAO Capsules)

In addition, Seldane-D may interact with the following:

MAO inhibitors (antidepressant drugs such as Nardil and Parnate)
Mecamylamine (Inversine)
Methyldopa (an ingredient in some blood pressure medications)
Reserpine (Diupres)

Special information
if you are pregnant or breastfeeding
The effects of Seldane and Seldane-D during pregnancy have not been adequately studied. If you are pregnant or plan to become pregnant, inform your doctor immediately.

If you are breastfeeding, Seldane is not recommended and Seldane-D absolutely should not be taken. Animal studies have shown decreased weight gain in developing babies exposed to this drug.

Recommended dosage

ADULTS AND CHILDREN 12 AND OLDER

Seldane
The usual dose is 1 tablet (60 milligrams) 2 times a day.

Seldane-D
The usual dose is 1 tablet swallowed whole, morning and night.

CHILDREN

The safety and effectiveness of Seldane and Seldane-D in children below the age of 12 have not been established.

Overdosage
Any medication taken in excess can have serious consequences. If you suspect an overdose, seek medical attention immediately.

- *Symptoms of Seldane and Seldane-D overdose may include:*
Changes in heartbeat
Confusion
Fainting
Headache
Irregular heartbeat
Nausea
Seizures

Generic name:

SELEGILINE

See Eldepryl, page 391.

Brand Name:

SEMPREX-D

Pronounced: SEM-precks-dee
Generic ingredients: Acrivastine, Pseudoephedrine
  hydrochloride

Why is this drug prescribed?

Semprex-D is an antihistamine and decongestant drug that relieves sneezing, running nose, itching, watery eyes, and stuffy nose caused by seasonal allergies such as hay fever.

Most important fact about this drug

Semprex-D may cause drowsiness. Do not drive or operate dangerous machinery or participate in any hazardous activity that requires full mental alertness until you know how you react to this medication.

How should you take this medication?

Take Semprex-D exactly as prescribed by your doctor. Do not take more of this drug or use it more often than your doctor recommends.

- *If you miss a dose...*
  Take it as soon as you remember. If it is almost time for your next dose, skip the one you missed and go back to your regular schedule. Never take 2 doses at the same time.

- *Storage instructions...*
  Store at room temperature in a dry place; protect the drug from light.

What side effects may occur?

Side effects cannot be anticipated. If any develop or change in intensity, inform your doctor as soon as possible. Only your doctor can determine if it is safe for you to continue taking Semprex-D.

- *Side effects may include:*
  Cough, dizziness, drowsiness, dry mouth, headache, indigestion, menstrual problems, nausea, nervousness, skin eruptions, sleeplessness, sore throat, weakness, wheezing

Severe allergic reactions are rare. There have been isolated reports of swelling of the throat, lips, neck, face, hands, or feet. Pseudoephedrine, one of the ingredients of this drug, has also been known to cause rapid or fluttery heartbeat.

Why should this drug not be prescribed?

You should not take Semprex-D if you are sensitive to or have ever had an allergic reaction to acrivastine, pseudoephedrine, or similar drugs such as Actifed, Dimetane, Trinalin, or Seldane-D. Make sure your doctor is aware of any drug reactions you have experienced.

Avoid using Semprex-D if you have extremely high blood pressure or severe heart problems.

Do not take this drug within 14 days of taking any antidepressant drug known as an MAO inhibitor, including Nardil, Parnate, and Marplan.

Special warnings about this medication

Use this drug with caution if you have high blood pressure, diabetes, heart problems, peptic ulcer or other stomach problems, or an enlarged prostate gland. Use Semprex-D with care, too, if you have increased eye pressure, an overactive thyroid gland, or kidney disease. Make sure the doctor has taken these conditions into account.

Antihistamines are more likely to cause dizziness, extreme calm (sedation), bladder obstruction, and low blood pressure in the elderly (over age 60). The elderly are also more likely to have more side effects from the decongestant (pseudoephedrine) in Semprex-D.

Possible food and drug interactions
when taking this medication

If Semprex-D is taken with certain other drugs, the effects of either could be increased, decreased, or altered. It is especially important to check with your doctor before combining this drug with the following:

Alcoholic beverages
Antidepressants classified as MAO inhibitors, including Nardil, Marplan, and Parnate
Blood pressure medications such as Inderal and Lopressor
Other antihistamines such as Actifed, Seldane-D, and Entex
Other decongestants such as Quibron and Rynatan

Special information
if you are pregnant or breastfeeding

The effects of Semprex-D during pregnancy have not been adequately studied. If you are pregnant or plan to become pregnant, tell your doctor immediately.

It is not known whether acrivastine appears in breast milk, but pseudoephedrine does. If the drug is essential to your health, your doctor may tell you to stop nursing until your treatment is finished.

Recommended dosage

ADULTS

The usual dose for adults and children 12 years of age and older is 1 capsule, taken by mouth, every 4 to 6 hours, 4 times a day.

CHILDREN

The safety and effectiveness of Semprex-D in children less than 12 years old have not been established.

Overdosage

Although there have been few reports of overdosage with Semprex-D, overdosage with similar drugs has caused a variety of serious symptoms. If you suspect an overdose of Semprex-D, seek medical attention immediately.

- *Symptoms of overdose may include:*
  Anxiety, convulsions, difficult breathing, drowsiness, fear, hallucinations, heart failure with low blood pressure, irregular heartbeat, loss of consciousness, painful urination, paleness, restlessness, sleeplessness, tenseness, trembling, weakness

Brand name:

SEPTRA

See Bactrim, page 104.

Brand name:

SER-AP-ES

Pronounced: Sir-AP-ess
Ingredients: Serpasil (reserpine), Apresoline (hydralazine hydrochloride), Esidrix (hydrochlorothiazide)

Why is this drug prescribed?

Ser-Ap-Es is a combination drug used in the treatment of high blood pressure. It combines two high blood pressure medications—Serpasil and Apresoline—with a thiazide diuretic, Esidrix. Serpasil and Apresoline improve blood flow throughout your body. Esidrix helps your body produce and eliminate more urine, which also helps lower blood pressure.

Most important fact about this drug

You must take Ser-Ap-Es regularly for it to be effective. Since blood pressure declines gradually, it may be several weeks before you get the full benefit of Ser-Ap-Es; and you must continue taking it even if you are feeling well. Ser-Ap-Es does not cure high blood pressure; it merely keeps it under control.

How should you take this medication?

Take Ser-Ap-Es exactly as prescribed by your doctor, even if your symptoms have disappeared.

Try not to miss any doses. If this medication is not taken regularly, your condition may worsen.

■ *If you miss a dose...*
Take the forgotten dose as soon as you remember. If it is almost time for the next dose, skip the one you missed and go back to your regular schedule. Never try to "catch up" by doubling the dose.

■ *Storage instructions...*
Ser-Ap-Es can be stored at room temperature. Use the container it came in.

What side effects may occur?

Side effects cannot be anticipated. If any develop or change in intensity, inform your doctor as soon as possible. Only your doctor can determine if it is safe for you to continue taking Ser-Ap-Es.

■ *Side effects may include:*
Anemia, anxiety, blockage in the intestines, blood disorders, blurred vision, breast development in males, breast engorgement, change in potassium levels (dry mouth, excessive thirst, weak or irregular heartbeat, muscle pain or cramps), chills, conjunctivitis, constipation, cramping (stomach and intestinal), crushing chest pain (angina), deafness, decreased sex drive, depression, diarrhea, difficult or labored breathing, difficult or painful urination, disorientation, dizziness, dizziness when standing up, drowsiness, dry mouth, enlarged spleen, eye disorders, fainting, fever, fluid in the lungs, fluid retention, flushing, glaucoma, headache, hepatitis, high blood sugar, hives, impotence, inflammation of the lungs, inflammation of the pancreas, inflammation of the salivary glands, irregular heartbeat, irritation of the stomach, itching, joint pain, loss of appetite, low blood pressure, muscle aches, muscle cramps, muscle spasm, nasal congestion, nausea, nervousness, nightmares, nosebleeds, numbness, parkinsonian syndrome (tremors, muscle weakness, shuffling walk, stooped posture, drooling), pounding heartbeat, rapid heartbeat, rash, red or purple skin discoloration, respiratory distress, restlessness, skin peeling, skin sensitivity to light,

slow heartbeat, sugar in the urine, teary eyes, tingling or pins and needles, tremors, vertigo, vision changes, vomiting, weakness, weight gain, yellow eyes and skin

Why should this drug not be prescribed?

If you are being treated for depression, you should avoid this medication.

Ser-Ap-Es should not be prescribed if you have an active peptic ulcer, ulcerative colitis (chronic inflammation of the large intestine and rectum), coronary artery disease, or rheumatic heart disease, or if you are unable to urinate, or are receiving electroshock therapy. Make sure your doctor is aware of all your medical problems.

If you are sensitive to or have ever had an allergic reaction to Ser-Ap-Es, any of its ingredients, or sulfa drugs, do not take this medication. Inform your doctor of any drug reactions you have experienced.

Special warnings about this medication

Diuretics can cause your body to lose too much potassium. Signs of an excessively low potassium level include muscle weakness and rapid or irregular heartbeat. To boost your potassium level, your doctor may recommend eating potassium-rich foods such as bananas and orange juice, or may prescribe a potassium supplement.

Ser-Ap-Es can cause depression. It can last for several months after you have stopped taking the drug, and it can be severe. If you develop any signs of depression—despondency, waking early in the morning, loss of appetite, impotence, loss of self-esteem—contact your doctor immediately.

If you have a history of peptic ulcer, ulcerative colitis, or gallstones, you should use this medication cautiously.

Some people have developed symptoms similar to those of lupus erythematosus, a disease characterized by rash, fever, and sometimes the symptoms of arthritis. These symptoms usually disappear when the Ser-Ap-Es is discontinued.

If you already have lupus erythematosus, Ser-Ap-Es may activate or worsen its symptoms.

If you have coronary artery, kidney, or liver disease, you should be carefully monitored while taking Ser-Ap-Es.

This medication may mask the symptoms of low blood sugar or alter blood sugar levels. If you are diabetic, discuss this with your doctor.

Allergic reactions are more likely to occur if you have a history of allergies or bronchial asthma.

In rare cases, abnormal amounts of uric acid in the blood may develop while taking this medication, leading to an attack of gout.

Notify your doctor or dentist that you are taking Ser-Ap-Es if you have a medical emergency, or before you have surgery or dental treatment.

Possible food and drug interactions
when taking this medication

If Ser-Ap-Es is taken with certain other drugs, the effects of either could be increased, decreased, or altered. It is especially important to check with your doctor before combining Ser-Ap-Es with the following:

ACTH (adrenal hormone)
Amphetamines such as Dexedrine
Antidepressant and MAO inhibitors
Digitalis (Lanoxin)
Drugs for depression such as Elavil
Drugs that stimulate the central nervous system, such as Cylert and Desoxyn
Drugs that stimulate the sympathetic nervous system, such as epinephrine, ephedrine, isoproterenol, metaraminol, tyramine, and phenylephrine
Insulin
Lithium (Eskalith)
MAO inhibitors (antidepressant drugs such as Nardil, Parnate, and Marplan)
Nonsteroidal anti-inflammatory drugs (arthritis drugs and painkillers such as Motrin)
Norepinephrine (Levophed)
Other high blood pressure drugs such as Aldomet and Vasotec
Quinidine (Quinidex)
Steroids such as Deltasone

Special information
if you are pregnant or breastfeeding

The effects of Ser-Ap-Es during pregnancy have not been adequately studied. If you are pregnant or plan to become pregnant, notify your doctor immediately. Ser-Ap-Es appears in breast milk and could seriously affect a nursing infant. If this medication is essential to your health, your doctor may advise you to discontinue breastfeeding until your treatment is finished.

Recommended dosage

ADULTS

Your doctor will determine the dosage according to your specific needs. You should not take more than 0.25 milligrams of reserpine daily (the amount in 2½ tablets).

CHILDREN

The safety and effectiveness of this drug in children have not been established.

Overdosage

Any medication taken in excess can have serious consequences. If you suspect an overdose, seek medical attention immediately.

■ *Symptoms of Ser-Ap-Es overdose may include:*
Coma, confusion, constricted pupils, cramps of the calf muscles, decreased amounts of urine, diarrhea, dizziness, drowsiness, fatigue, flushing, headache, heart attack, inability to urinate, increased amounts of urine, increased salivation, irregular heartbeat, low blood pressure, low body temperature, nausea, rapid heartbeat, severe loss of fluid, shock, slow heartbeat, slowed breathing, thirst, tingling or pins and needles, vomiting, weakness

Brand name:

SERAX

Pronounced: SER-aks
Generic name: Oxazepam

Why is this drug prescribed?

Serax is used in the treatment of anxiety disorders, including anxiety associated with depression.

This drug seems to be particularly effective for anxiety, tension, agitation, and irritability in older people. It is also prescribed to relieve symptoms of acute alcohol withdrawal.

Serax belongs to a class of drugs known as benzodiazepines.

Most important fact about this drug

Serax can be habit-forming or addicting and can lose its effectiveness over time, as you develop a tolerance for it. You may experience withdrawal symptoms if you stop using the drug abruptly. When discontinuing the drug, your doctor will reduce the dose gradually.

How should you take this medication?
Take Serax exactly as prescribed.

■ *If you miss a dose...*
If you remember within an hour or so, take the dose immediately. If you do not remember until later, skip the dose you missed and go back to your regular schedule. Do not take 2 doses at once.

■ *Storage instructions...*
Store at room temperature in a tightly closed container.

What side effects may occur?
Side effects cannot be anticipated. If any develop or change in intensity, inform your doctor as soon as possible. Only your doctor can determine if it is safe for you to continue taking Serax. Your doctor should periodically reassess the need for this drug.

■ *More common side effects may include:*
Drowsiness

■ *Less common or rare side effects may include:*
Blood disorders, change in sex drive, dizziness, excitement, fainting, headache, hives, liver problems, loss or lack of muscle control, nausea, skin rashes, sluggishness or unresponsiveness, slurred speech, swelling due to fluid retention, tremors, vertigo, yellowed eyes and skin

■ *Side effects due to rapid decrease or abrupt withdrawal from Serax:*
Abdominal and muscle cramps, convulsions, depressed mood, inability to fall or stay asleep, sweating, tremors, vomiting

Why should this drug not be prescribed?
If you are sensitive to or have ever had an allergic reaction to Serax or other tranquilizers such as Valium, you should not take this medication. Make sure your doctor is aware of any drug reactions you have experienced.

Anxiety or tension related to everyday stress usually does not require treatment with Serax. Discuss your symptoms thoroughly with your doctor.

Serax should not be prescribed if you are being treated for mental disorders more serious than anxiety.

Special warnings about this medication

Serax may cause you to become drowsy or less alert; therefore, you should not drive or operate dangerous machinery or participate in any hazardous activity that requires full mental alertness until you know how this drug affects you.

This medication may cause your blood pressure to drop. If you have any heart problems, consult your doctor before taking this medication.

The 15-milligram tablet of this drug contains the coloring agent FD&C Yellow No. 5, which may cause an allergic reaction. If you are sensitive to aspirin or susceptible to allergies, consult your doctor before taking the tablet.

Possible food and drug interactions when taking this medication

Serax may intensify the effects of alcohol. It may be better not to drink alcohol while taking this medication.

If Serax is taken with certain other drugs, the effects of either could be increased, decreased, or altered. It is especially important to check with your doctor before combining Serax with the following:

Antihistamines such as Benadryl
Narcotic painkillers such as Percocet and Demerol
Sedatives such as Seconal and Halcion
Tranquilizers such as Valium and Xanax

Special information if you are pregnant or breastfeeding

Do not take Serax if you are pregnant or planning to become pregnant. There is an increased risk of birth defects. Serax may appear in breast milk and could affect a nursing infant. If this drug is essential to your health, your doctor may advise you to stop breastfeeding until your treatment with this medication is finished.

Recommended dosage

ADULTS

Mild to Moderate Anxiety with Tension, Irritability, Agitation
The usual dose is 10 to 15 milligrams 3 or 4 times per day.

Severe Anxiety, Depression with Anxiety, or Alcohol Withdrawal
The usual dose is 15 to 30 milligrams, 3 or 4 times per day.

CHILDREN

This medication is not intended for use in children under 6 years of age. Dosage guidelines for children 6 to 12 years of age have not been established. Your doctor will adjust the dosage to fit the child's needs.

ELDERLY

The usual starting dose is 10 milligrams, 3 times a day. Your doctor may increase the dose to 15 milligrams 3 or 4 times a day, if needed.

Overdosage

Although no specific information is available, any medication taken in excess can have serious consequences. If you suspect an overdose of Serax, seek medical attention immediately.

Brand name:

SEROPHENE

See Clomiphene Citrate, page 211.

Generic name:

SERTRALINE

See Zoloft, page 1241.

Brand name:

SERZONE

Pronounced: sur-ZONE
Generic name: Nefazodone hydrochloride

Why is this drug prescribed?

Serzone is prescribed for the treatment of depression severe enough to interfere with daily functioning. Possible symptoms include changes in appetite, sleep habits, and mind–body coordination, decreased sex drive, increased fatigue, feelings of guilt or worthlessness, difficulty concentrating, slowed thinking, and suicidal thoughts.

Most important fact about this drug

It may be several weeks before you feel the full antidepressant effect of Serzone. Once you do begin to feel better, it is important to keep taking the drug.

How should you take this medication?

Take Serzone exactly as prescribed by your doctor. It may take several weeks before you begin to feel better; once you do, it is important to keep taking the drug as prescribed. Your doctor should check your progress periodically.

■ *If you miss a dose...*
Take it as soon as you remember. If it is within 4 hours of your next dose, skip the one you missed and go back to your regular schedule. Do not take 2 doses at once.

■ *Storage instructions...*
Store at room temperature in a tightly closed container.

What side effects may occur?

Side effects cannot be anticipated. If any develop or change in intensity, tell your doctor as soon as possible. Only your doctor can determine if it is safe for you to continue taking Serzone.

■ *More common side effects may include:*
Blurred or abnormal vision, confusion, constipation, dizziness, dry mouth, light-headedness, nausea, sleepiness, weakness

■ *Less common side effects may include:*
Abnormal dreams, cough, decreased concentration, diarrhea, dizziness on getting up, flu-like symptoms, headache, increased appetite, water retention

■ *Rare side effects may include:*
Breast pain, chills, decreased sex drive, difficulty urinating, fever, frequent urination, lack of coordination, ringing in ears, stiff neck, taste change, thirst, urinary tract infection, vaginal inflammation

Why should this drug not be prescribed?

If you are sensitive to or have ever had an allergic reaction to Serzone or similar drugs, such as Desyrel, you should not take this medication.

Serious, sometimes fatal reactions have occurred when Serzone is used in combination with other antidepressant drugs known as MAO inhibitors, including Nardil, Parnate, and Marplan. Never take Serzone with one of these drugs; and do not begin therapy with Serzone within 14 days of discontinuing treatment with one of them. Also, allow at least 7 days between the last dose of Serzone and the first dose of an MAO inhibitor.

Special warnings about this medication

Your doctor will prescribe Serzone with caution if you have a history of seizures or mania (extreme agitation or excitability) or heart or liver disease. Serzone should also be used with caution if you have had a heart attack or stroke, or suffer from dehydration. Be sure to discuss all of your medical problems with your doctor before taking Serzone.

Serzone may cause you to become drowsy or less alert and may affect your judgment. Do not drive or operate dangerous machinery or participate in any hazardous activity that requires full mental alertness until you know how the drug affects you.

Before having surgery, dental treatment, or any diagnostic procedure requiring anesthesia, tell the doctor or dentist you are taking Serzone. If you develop an allergic reaction such as a skin rash or hives while taking Serzone, notify your doctor. If you are male and experience a prolonged or inappropriate erection while taking Serzone, discontinue this drug and call your doctor.

If you have ever been addicted to drugs, tell your doctor before you start Serzone.

Possible food and drug interactions
when taking this medication

If Serzone is taken with certain other drugs, the effects of either could be increased, decreased, or altered. It is especially important to check with your doctor before combining Serzone with the following:

    Alcohol
    Antidepressants classified as MAO inhibitors, including Nardil and
        Parnate
    Astemizole (Hismanal)
    Digoxin (Lanoxin)
    Sleep aids such as Halcion and Dalmane
    Terfenadine (Seldane)
    Tranquilizers such as Adapin and Xanax

Special information
if you are pregnant or breastfeeding

The effects of Serzone during pregnancy have not been adequately studied. If you are pregnant or are planning to become pregnant, tell your doctor immediately. Serzone should be used during pregnancy only if clearly needed. Serzone may appear in breast milk. If this medication is essential to your health, your doctor may tell you to discontinue breastfeeding until your treatment with Serzone is finished.

Recommended dosage

ADULTS

The usual starting dose for Serzone is 200 milligrams a day, divided into 2 doses. If needed, your doctor may increase your dose gradually to 300 to 600 milligrams a day.

CHILDREN

The safety and effectiveness of Serzone have not been established in children under 18 years of age.

ELDERLY

The usual starting dose for the elderly or debilitated is 100 milligrams a day, taken in 2 doses. Your doctor will adjust the dose according to your response.

Overdosage

Any medication taken in excess can have serious consequences. If you suspect an overdose, seek medical attention immediately.

- *Symptoms of Serzone overdose include:*
  Nausea
  Sleepiness
  Vomiting

Brand name:

SILVADENE CREAM 1%

Pronounced: SIL-vuh-deen
Generic name: Silver sulfadiazine

Why is this drug prescribed?

Silvadene Cream 1% is applied directly to the skin. The cream is used along with other medications to prevent and treat wound infections in people with second- and third-degree burns. It is effective against a variety of bacteria as well as yeast.

Most important fact about this drug

Silvadene is a sulfa derivative. If you have ever had an allergic reaction to sulfa drugs, such as Bactrim or Septra, you may have a similar reaction to this medication. Make sure your doctor is aware of any drug reactions you have experienced.

If burn wounds cover extensive areas of the body, Silvadene may be absorbed into the bloodstream. This could lead to side effects elsewhere in your body.

How should you use this medication?
Silvadene is for external use only.

Bathe the burned area daily.

You should continue using Silvadene Cream until the area has healed or is ready for skin grafting.

Clean your skin and apply Silvadene with a sterile, gloved hand. Apply a thin layer (about ⅟₁₆ inch) to the affected area.

- *If you miss a dose...*
  Keep the burn areas covered with Silvadene at all times. Reapply the medicine if it is rubbed or washed off.

- *Storage instructions...*
  Silvadene can be stored at room temperature.

What side effects may occur?
Side effects cannot be anticipated. If any side effects develop or change in intensity, tell your doctor immediately. Only your doctor can determine whether it is safe for you to continue using Silvadene.

- *Side effects may include:*
  Areas of dead skin
  Burning sensation
  Rash
  Red, raised rash on the body
  Skin discoloration

Why should this drug not be prescribed?
You should not use Silvadene if you are allergic to sulfa drugs such as Bactrim or Septra.

Do not use Silvadene at the end of pregnancy, on premature infants, or on newborn infants during the first 2 months of life.

Special warnings about this medication

Make sure your doctor knows about any kidney or liver problems you may have. If either organ becomes impaired, it may be necessary to stop using Silvadene.

There is a small chance of fungal infection when using Silvadene.

Possible food and drug interactions
when using this medication

If Silvadene is used with certain other drugs, the effects of either could be increased, decreased, or altered. It is especially important to check with your doctor before combining Silvadene with the following:

Topical enzyme preparations, such as Panafil and Santyl, that contain
   collagenase, papain, or sutilains
Cimetidine (Tagamet)

Special information
if you are pregnant or breastfeeding

If you are pregnant or plan to become pregnant, inform your doctor immediately.

The safety of Silvadene during pregnancy has not been fully studied, but you definitely should not take this drug at the end of your pregnancy, as it can lead to complications for the baby.

Although it is not known whether Silvadene appears in breast milk, other sulfa drugs are excreted in breast milk and can cause harm to a nursing infant. If this medication is essential to your health, your doctor may advise you to stop breastfeeding until your treatment is finished.

Recommended dosage

Apply Silvadene Cream 1% to the affected area once or twice daily to a thickness of 1/16 inch. Treatment with Silvadene should be continued until your doctor is satisfied that healing has occurred or determines that the burn site is ready for grafting.

Overdosage

Any medication taken in excess can have serious consequences. If you suspect an overdose, seek medical treatment immediately.

Generic name:

SILVER SULFADIAZINE

See Silvadene Cream 1%, page 1022.

Generic name:

SIMVASTATIN

See Zocor, page 1236.

Brand name:

SINEMET CR

Pronounced: SIN-uh-met see-are
Generic ingredients: Carbidopa, Levodopa

Why is this drug prescribed?
Sinemet CR is a controlled-release tablet that may be given to help relieve the muscle stiffness, tremor, and weakness caused by Parkinson's disease. It may also be given to relieve Parkinson-like symptoms caused by encephalitis (brain fever), carbon monoxide poisoning, or manganese poisoning.

Sinemet CR contains two drugs, carbidopa and levodopa. The drug that actually produces the anti-Parkinson's effect is levodopa. Carbidopa prevents vitamin B_6 from destroying levodopa, thus allowing levodopa to work more efficiently.

Parkinson's drugs such as Sinemet CR relieve the symptoms of the disease, but are not a permanent cure.

Most important fact about this drug
There is also a regular, non-controlled-release form of this medication, which is called Sinemet. Over a period of hours, Sinemet CR, the controlled-release form, gives a smoother release of the drug than regular Sinemet. If you have been taking regular Sinemet, be aware that you may need a somewhat higher dosage of Sinemet CR to get the same degree of relief. Your first morning dose of Sinemet CR may take as much as an hour longer to start working than your first morning dose of regular Sinemet.

How should you take this medication?
Take Sinemet CR after meals, rather than before or between meals. Swallow the tablets whole without chewing or crushing them.

Sinemet CR releases its ingredients slowly over a period of 4 to 6 hours. It is important to follow a careful schedule, taking your doses at the same time every day.

You should not change the prescribed dosage or add another product for Parkinson's disease without first consulting your doctor.

Sinemet CR works best when there is a constant amount in the blood. Try not to miss any doses, and take them at evenly spaced intervals day and night.

■ *If you miss a dose...*
if you forget to take a dose, take it as soon as you remember. If it is almost time for your next dose, skip the one you missed and go back to your regular schedule. Do not take 2 doses at once.

■ *Storage instructions...*
Store at room temperature in a tightly closed container.

What side effects may occur?
Side effects from Sinemet CR cannot be anticipated. If any develop or change in intensity, inform your doctor immediately.

Only your doctor can determine if it is safe for you to continue taking Sinemet CR.

■ *More common side effects may include:*
Confusion
Hallucinations
Nausea
Uncontrollable twitching or jerking

■ *Less common or rare side effects may include:*
Abdominal or stomach pain, abnormal dreams, agitation, anemia, anxiety, back pain, bitter taste, bizarre breathing patterns, bleeding from stomach, blurred vision, burning sensation of tongue, chest pain, clumsiness in walking, common cold, constipation, convulsions, cough, dark sweat, dark urine, delusions, depression, diarrhea, disorientation, dizziness, dizziness upon rising from a sitting or lying position, dream abnormalities, drooling, drowsiness, dry mouth, euphoria, eyelid twitching, faintness, falling, fatigue, fever, flatulence, fluid retention, flushing, hair loss, headache, heart attack, heart palpitations, heartburn, hiccups, high or low blood pressure, hoarseness, hot flashes, increased hand tremor, insomnia or other sleep problems, irregular heartbeat, leg pain, locked jaw, loss of appetite, malignant melanoma, memory problems, mental changes, muscle cramps, muscle twitching, nervousness, numbness, "on-off" phenomena, paralysis of certain muscles and unwanted movement of others, paranoia,

persistent erection, phlebitis (swelling of a vein), rash, shortness of breath, shoulder pain, slowed physical movements, sore throat, speech impairment, stomach ulcer, suicidal tendencies, swallowing difficulties, sweating, teeth-grinding, tingling or pins and needles, upper respiratory infection, upset stomach, urinary frequency, urinary incontinence, urinary retention, urinary tract infections, weakness, weight loss or gain, writhing or flailing movements, vomiting

Why should this drug not be prescribed?

Do not take Sinemet CR if you are sensitive to or have ever had an allergic reaction to its ingredients.

Sinemet CR should not be prescribed if you have a suspicious, undiagnosed mole or a history of melanoma.

Special warnings about this medication

Make sure your doctor knows if you have any of the following:

Bronchial asthma
Cardiovascular or lung disease (severe)
Endocrine (glandular) disorder
History of heart attack or heartbeat irregularity
History of active peptic ulcer
Kidney disorder
Liver disorder
Wide-angle glaucoma (pressure in the eye)

Your doctor will monitor your liver, blood, kidney and heart functions during extended therapy with Sinemet CR.

If you have been taking levodopa alone, you should stop taking levodopa for at least 8 hours before starting to take Sinemet CR.

The carbidopa contained in Sinemet CR cannot eliminate side effects caused by levodopa. Since carbidopa helps levodopa reach your brain, Sinemet CR may, in fact, produce some levodopa side effects—particularly twitching, jerking, or writhing—sooner and at a lower dosage than levodopa alone or even regular Sinemet. If such involuntary movements develop while you are taking Sinemet CR, you may need a dosage reduction.

Like levodopa, Sinemet CR may cause depression. Make sure your doctor knows if you have mental or emotional problems.

Muscle rigidity, high temperature, and mental changes may occur when Sinemet CR is reduced suddenly or discontinued. If you stop taking this medication abruptly, your doctor should monitor your condition carefully.

Possible food and drug interactions
when taking this medication

If Sinemet CR is taken with certain other drugs, the effects of either could be increased, decreased, or altered. It is especially important to check with your doctor before combining Sinemet CR with the following:

Antacids such as Di-Gel, Maalox, and Mylanta
Anticonvulsants such as Dilantin
Antispasmodic drugs such as Artane and Cogentin
Antihypertensives such as Aldomet and Clonidine
Iron products such as Feosol
Isoniazid (Nydrazid)
Major tranquilizers such as Haldol, Mellaril, and Thorazine
MAO inhibitor antidepressants such as Marplan, Nardil, and Parnate
Methionine drugs such as Odor-Scrip and Pedameth
Metoclopramide (Reglan)
Papaverine (Pavabid)
Pyridoxine (vitamin B$_6$)
Tranquilizers such as Dalmane, Valium, and Xanax
Tricyclic antidepressants such as Elavil and Tofranil

If you have been taking an MAO inhibitor antidepressant such as Marplan, Nardil, or Parnate, you must discontinue it at least 2 weeks before starting to take Sinemet CR.

Special information
if you are pregnant or breastfeeding

If you are pregnant or plan to become pregnant, inform your doctor immediately. Sinemet CR should be used during pregnancy only if the benefit outweighs the potential risk to the unborn child. It is not known whether Sinemet CR appears in breast milk. If this medication is essential to your health, your doctor may advise you to stop nursing your baby until your treatment with this drug is finished.

Recommended dosage

Your doctor will tailor your individual dosage carefully, depending on your response to previous therapy and symptoms.

ADULTS

For patients with mild to moderate symptoms, the initial recommended dose is 1 tablet of Sinemet CR taken 2 times a day.

Starting doses should be spaced out every 4 to 8 hours and then adjusted to each patient's individual response.

The usual long-term dose is 2 to 8 tablets per day, taken in divided doses every 4 to 8 hours during the waking day.

Higher doses (12 or more tablets per day) and shorter intervals (less than 4 hours) have been used, but are not usually recommended.

When doses of Sinemet CR are given at intervals of less than 4 hours, and/or if the divided doses are not equal, it is recommended that the smaller doses be given at the end of the day.

An interval of at least 3 days between dosage adjustments is recommended.

Dosage adjustment of Sinemet CR may be necessary if your doctor prescribes additional medications.

CHILDREN

Use of Sinemet CR in children under 18 is not recommended.

Overdosage
Too much Sinemet CR may cause muscle twitches, inability to open the eyes, or other symptoms of levodopa overdosage. Like other medications, Sinemet CR taken in excess can have serious consequences. If you suspect symptoms of a Sinemet CR overdose, seek medical attention immediately.

Brand name:

SINEQUAN

Pronounced: SIN-uh-kwan
Generic name: Doxepin hydrochloride
Other brand name: Adapin

Why is this drug prescribed?
Sinequan is used in the treatment of depression and anxiety. It helps relieve tension, improve sleep, elevate mood, increase energy, and generally ease the feelings of fear, guilt, apprehension, and worry most people experience. It is effective in treating people whose depression and/or anxiety is psychological, associated with alcoholism, or a result of another disease (cancer, for example) or psychotic depressive disorders (severe mental illness). It is in the family of drugs called tricyclic antidepressants.

Most important fact about this drug
Serious, sometimes fatal, reactions have occurred when Sinequan is used in combination with another type of antidepressant called MAO inhibitors. Any

drug of this type should be discontinued at least 2 weeks prior to starting treatment with Sinequan, and you should be carefully monitored by your doctor.

If you are taking any prescription or nonprescription drugs, consult your doctor before taking Sinequan.

How should you take this medication?
Take this medication exactly as prescribed. It may take several weeks for you to feel better.

■ *If you miss a dose...*
If you are taking several doses a day, take the missed dose as soon as you remember, then take any remaining doses for that day at evenly spaced intervals. If it is almost time for your next dose, skip the one you missed and go back to your regular schedule. Never take 2 doses at the same time.

If you are taking a single dose at bedtime and do not remember until the next morning, skip the dose. Do not take a double dose to make up for a missed one.

■ *Storage instructions...*
Store at room temperature.

What side effects may occur?
Side effects cannot be anticipated. If any develop or change in intensity, inform your doctor as soon as possible. Only your doctor can determine if it is safe for you to continue taking Sinequan.

The most common side effect is drowsiness.

■ *Less common or rare side effects may include:*
Blurred vision, breast development in males, bruises, buzzing or ringing in the ears, changes in sex drive, chills, confusion, constipation, diarrhea, difficulty urinating, disorientation, dizziness, dry mouth, enlarged breasts, fatigue, fluid retention, flushing, fragmented or incomplete movements, hair loss, hallucinations, headache, high fever, high or low blood sugar, inappropriate breast milk secretion, indigestion, inflammation of the mouth, itching and skin rash, lack of muscle control, loss of appetite, loss of coordination, low blood pressure, nausea, nervousness, numbness, poor bladder control, rapid heartbeat, red or brownish spots on the skin, seizures, sensitivity to light, severe muscle stiffness, sore throat, sweating, swelling of the testicles, taste disturbances, tingling sensation, tremors, vomiting, weakness, weight gain, yellow eyes and skin

Why should this drug not be prescribed?

If you are sensitive to or have ever had an allergic reaction to Sinequan or similar antidepressants, you should not take this medication. Make sure that your doctor is aware of any drug reactions that you have experienced.

Unless you are directed to do so by your doctor, do not take this medication if you have the eye condition known as glaucoma or difficulty urinating.

Special warnings about this medication

Sinequan may cause you to become drowsy or less alert; driving or operating dangerous machinery or participating in any hazardous activity that requires full mental alertness is not recommended.

Notify your doctor or dentist that you are taking Sinequan if you have a medical emergency, and before you have surgery or dental treatment.

Possible food and drug interactions
when taking this medication

Alcohol increases the danger in a Sinequan overdose. Do not drink alcohol while taking this medication.

Never combine Sinequan with the other antidepressants known as MAO inhibitors. Drugs in this category include Nardil, Parnate, and Marplan.

If Sinequan is taken with certain other drugs, the effects of either could be increased, decreased, or altered. It is especially important to check with your doctor before combining Sinequan with the following:

Carbamazepine (Tegretol)
Cimetidine (Tagamet)
Clonidine (Catapres)
Encainide (En Kaid)
Flecainide (Tambocor)
Guanethidine (Ismelin)
Major tranquilizers such as Compazine, Mellaril, and Thorazine
Other antidepressants such as Elavil, Paxil, and Prozac
Propafenone (Rythmol)
Quinidine (Quinidex)
Tolazamide (Tolinase)

Special information
if you are pregnant or breastfeeding

The effects of Sinequan during pregnancy have not been adequately studied. If you are pregnant or planning to become pregnant, inform your doctor immediately. Sinequan may appear in breast milk and could affect a nursing infant. If this medication is essential to your health, your doctor may advise you to discontinue breastfeeding your baby until your treatment is finished.

Recommended dosage

ADULTS

The starting dose for mild to moderate illness is usually 75 milligrams per day. This dose can be increased or decreased by your doctor according to individual need. The usual ideal dose ranges from 75 milligrams per day to 150 milligrams per day, although it can be as low as 25 to 50 milligrams per day. The total daily dose can be given once a day or divided into smaller doses. If you are taking this drug once a day, the recommended dose is 150 milligrams at bedtime.

The 150-milligram capsule strength is intended for long-term therapy only and is not recommended as a starting dose.

For more severe illness, gradually increased doses of up to 300 milligrams may be required as determined by your doctor.

CHILDREN

Safety and effectiveness have not been established for use in children under 12 years of age.

ELDERLY

A once-a-day dosage should be carefully adjusted by your doctor, depending upon the severity of your illness.

Overdosage

■ *Symptoms of Sinequan overdose may include:*
Blurred vision, coma, convulsions, decreased intestinal movement, dilated pupils, drowsiness, excessive dryness of mouth, high or low body temperature, irregular or rapid heartbeat, low or high blood pressure, overactive reflexes, severe breathing problems, stupor, urinary problems

If you experience any of these symptoms, seek medical attention immediately.

Brand name:

SLOW-K

See Micro-K, page 658.

Generic name:

SODIUM FLUORIDE

See Luride, page 619.

Brand name:

SODIUM SULAMYD

Pronounced: SOH-dee-um SOO-lah-mid
Generic name: Sulfacetamide sodium
Other brand name: Bleph-10

Why is this drug prescribed?

Sodium Sulamyd is used in the treatment of eye inflammations, corneal ulcer, and other eye infections. It may be used along with an oral sulfa drug to treat a serious eye infection called trachoma.

Most important fact about this drug

Sodium Sulamyd is similar to oral sulfa drugs such as Bactrim, Gantanol, and Gantrisin. If you are allergic to any of these medications, you may also be allergic to Sodium Sulamyd. In addition, if you have taken one of these medications in the past, you may have developed a "hidden" allergy to sulfa drugs that might show up when you take Sodium Sulamyd. Be alert for a rash, itching, or other signs of allergy. If any of these symptoms develop, stop taking Sodium Sulamyd immediately and consult your doctor.

How should you use this medication?

Sodium Sulamyd is available in eyedrop and ointment form. Use it exactly as prescribed. Your doctor may tell you to use both the eyedrops and the ointment.

To apply Sodium Sulamyd, pull down your lower eyelid to form a pouch, then squeeze in the medication. To avoid contaminating the eyedrops or the ointment, do not touch your eye with the dropper bottle or the tip of the tube. Keep the dropper bottle or tube poised slightly above your eye as you instill the drops or squeeze out the ointment.

■ *If you miss a dose...*
  Apply it as soon as you remember. If it is almost time for your next dose, skip the one you missed and go back to your regular schedule.

■ *Storage instructions...*
Store at room temperature. Protect the ointment from excessive heat.

What side effects may occur?
Side effects cannot be anticipated. If any develop or change in intensity, inform your doctor as soon as possible. Only your doctor can determine if it is safe for you to continue taking this medication.

Sodium Sulamyd may irritate your eye, causing stinging and burning. The irritation usually lasts only a short time. If it is very painful or lasts for a long time, you may have to stop using the medication.

In rare cases, people using Sodium Sulamyd have developed a severe blistering skin rash. Be alert for skin reactions. If a rash appears, stop using Sodium Sulamyd and call your doctor.

Why should this drug not be prescribed?
Do not use Sodium Sulamyd if you have ever had an allergic reaction to or are sensitive to this medication or any other sulfa drug.

Special warnings about this medication
Stay in close touch with your doctor while using Sodium Sulamyd. In some cases, an eye ointment may actually delay healing of the cornea. If you have a pus-producing eye infection, the pus may inactivate Sodium Sulamyd. Since sulfa drugs do not kill fungi, it is possible to develop a fungus infection in your eye while using Sodium Sulamyd.

Possible food and drug interactions
when taking this medication
Sodium Sulamyd should not be used with medications containing silver. Check with your doctor if you are unsure of any medications you are taking.

Special information
if you are pregnant or breastfeeding
If you are pregnant or plan to become pregnant, inform your doctor immediately. There is no information about the safety of Sodium Sulamyd during pregnancy.

It is not known whether Sodium Sulamyd appears in breast milk. If Sodium Sulamyd is essential to your health, it may be necessary to stop breastfeeding during treatment.

Recommended dosage

SODIUM SULAMYD OPHTHALMIC SOLUTION 30%

Inflamed Eyes or Corneal Ulcer
Place 1 drop inside the lower eyelid every 2 hours or less frequently; your doctor will determine the schedule according to the severity of the infection.

Trachoma (Contagious Inflammation)
Use 2 drops every 2 hours.

SODIUM SULAMYD OPHTHALMIC SOLUTION 10%

Place 1 or 2 drops inside the lower eyelid every 2 or 3 hours during the day, less often at night.

SODIUM SULAMYD OPHTHALMIC OINTMENT 10%

Apply a small amount of the ointment 4 times daily and at bedtime. The ointment may be used at the same time as either of the solutions.

Overdosage

Although no specific information is available on overdose with Sodium Sulamyd, any medication used in excess can have serious consequences. If you suspect you may have used too much Sodium Sulamyd, seek medical attention immediately.

Brand name:

SOMA

Pronounced: SOE-muh
Generic name: Carisoprodol

Why is this drug prescribed?

Soma is used, along with rest, physical therapy, and other measures, for the relief of acute, painful muscle strains and spasms.

Most important fact about this drug

Soma alone will not heal your muscles. You need to follow the program of physical therapy, rest, or exercise that your doctor prescribes. Do not attempt any more physical activity than your doctor recommends, even though Soma temporarily makes it seem feasible.

How should you take this medication?
Take Soma exactly as prescribed by your doctor.

- *If you miss a dose...*
  Take it as soon as you remember if only an hour or so has passed. If you do not remember until later, skip the dose you missed and go back to your regular schedule. Do not take 2 doses at once.

- *Storage instructions...*
  Store at room temperature in a tightly closed container.

What side effects may occur?
Side effects cannot be anticipated. If any develop or change in intensity, inform your doctor as soon as possible. Only your doctor can determine if it is safe for you to continue taking Soma.

- *Side effects may include:*
  Agitation, depression, dizziness, drowsiness, facial flushing, fainting, headache, hiccups, inability to fall or stay asleep, irritability, light-headedness upon standing up, loss of coordination, nausea, rapid heart rate, stomach upset, tremors, vertigo, vomiting

Allergic reactions usually seen between the first and fourth doses of Soma in patients who have never taken this drug before include: itching, red welts on the skin, and skin rash. A more severe allergic reaction may include symptoms such as asthmatic attacks, dizziness, fever, low blood pressure, shock, stinging of the eyes, swelling due to fluid retention, and weakness.

Why should this drug not be prescribed?
If you are sensitive to or have ever had an allergic reaction to Soma or drugs of this type, such as meprobamate (Miltown), you should not take this medication. Make sure your doctor is aware of any drug reactions you have experienced.

Unless you are directed to do so by your doctor, do not take this medication if you have porphyria (an inherited blood disorder).

Special warnings about this medication
In rare cases, the first dose of Soma may cause unusual symptoms that appear within minutes or hours of taking the medication. Symptoms reported include: agitation, confusion, disorientation, dizziness, double vision, enlargement of pupils, extreme weakness, exaggerated feeling of well-being, lack of

coordination, speech problems, temporary loss of vision, and temporary paralysis of arms and legs. These symptoms usually subside within a few hours. If you experience any of them, contact your doctor immediately.

Soma may impair the mental or physical abilities you need to drive a car or operate dangerous machinery. Do not participate in hazardous activities until you know how this drug affects you.

If you have a history of drug dependence, make sure your doctor is aware of it before you start taking this medication.

Withdrawal symptoms, including abdominal cramps, chilliness, headache, insomnia, and nausea, have occurred in people who suddenly stop taking Soma.

Take this drug cautiously if you have any kidney or liver problems.

Possible food and drug interactions
when taking this medication

Soma may intensify the effects of alcohol. Be careful drinking alcoholic beverages while you are taking this medication.

If Soma is taken with certain other drugs, the effects of either could be increased, decreased, or altered. It is especially important to check with your doctor before combining Soma with the following:

Antidepressant drugs such as Elavil, Tofranil, and Nardil
Major tranquilizers such as Haldol, Stelazine, and Thorazine
Sedatives such as Nembutal and Halcion
Tranquilizers such as Librium, Valium, and Xanax

Special information
if you are pregnant or breastfeeding

The effects of Soma during pregnancy have not been adequately studied. If you are pregnant or plan to become pregnant, inform your doctor immediately. This drug appears in breast milk and could affect a nursing infant. If this medication is essential to your health, your doctor may advise you to discontinue breastfeeding until your treatment is finished.

Recommended dosage

ADULTS

The usual dosage of Soma is one 350-milligram tablet, taken 3 times daily and at bedtime.

CHILDREN

The safety and effectiveness of this drug have not been established in children under 12 years of age.

Overdosage

A severe overdose of Soma can be fatal. If you suspect an overdose, seek medical help immediately.

■ *Symptoms of Soma overdose may include:*
Breathing difficulty
Coma
Shock
Stupor

Brand name:

SORBITRATE

See Isordil, page 538.

Brand name:

SPECTAZOLE CREAM

Pronounced: SPEK-tah-zole
Generic name: Econazole nitrate

Why is this drug prescribed?

Spectazole cream is prescribed for fungal skin diseases commonly called ringworm (tinea). It is used to treat athlete's foot (tinea pedis), "jock itch" (tinea cruris), a fungus infection of the entire body (tinea corporis), and a skin infection that causes yellow- or brown-colored skin eruptions (tinea versicolor). It is also prescribed for yeast infections of the skin caused by candida fungus (cutaneous candidiasis).

Most important fact about this drug

Do not use Spectazole in or near the eyes.

How should you use this medication?

Use Spectazole Cream exactly as prescribed by your doctor.

Continue using the medication for the full time prescribed even if your symptoms have been relieved.

When applied, the cream should completely cover the affected area.

■ *If you miss a dose...*
Apply it as soon as you remember. If it is almost time for your next dose, skip the one you missed and go back to your regular schedule.

■ *Storage instructions...*
Store at room temperature.

What side effects may occur?
Side effects cannot be anticipated. If any develop or change in intensity, inform your doctor as soon as possible. Only your doctor can determine whether it is safe for you to continue using Spectazole.

■ *More common side effects may include:*
Burning
Itching
Skin redness
Stinging

■ *Less common or rare side effects may include:*
Itching rash

Why should this drug not be prescribed?
Spectazole Cream should not be used if you are sensitive to it or have ever had an allergic reaction to any of its ingredients.

Special warnings about this medication
If you develop an irritation or an allergic reaction to Spectazole, stop using the cream and inform your doctor.

Spectazole is only for external use.

Possible food and drug interactions
when taking this medication
No interactions have been reported.

Special information
if you are pregnant or breastfeeding
Spectazole should be used during the first trimester (3 months) of pregnancy only if it is essential to your health, and during the remainder of your pregnancy only if your doctor feels it is clearly needed. If you are pregnant or plan to become pregnant, inform your doctor immediately. Spectazole may appear in breast milk and could affect a nursing infant. If this medication is essential to your health, your doctor may advise you to stop breastfeeding until your treatment with Spectazole is finished.

Recommended dosage

ATHLETE'S FOOT, JOCK ITCH, TINEA CORPORIS, TINEA VERSICOLOR

Apply sufficient Spectazole Cream to completely cover the affected area once a day. Athlete's foot is treated for 1 month; jock itch and tinea corporis are treated for 2 weeks. Tinea versicolor is usually treated for 2 weeks.

CUTANEOUS CANDIDIASIS

Apply sufficient Spectazole Cream to completely cover the affected area 2 times a day, once in the morning and once in the evening. Cutaneous candidiasis is treated for 2 weeks.

Overdosage

Although no specific information is available on Spectazole Cream overdosage, any medication used in excess can have serious consequences. If you suspect an overdose, seek medical attention immediately.

Generic name:

SPIRONOLACTONE

See Aldactone, page 27.

Generic name:

SPIRONOLACTONE WITH HYDROCHLOROTHIAZIDE

See Aldactazide, page 24.

Brand name:

SPIROZIDE

See Aldactazide, page 24.

Brand name:

SPORANOX

Pronounced: SPORE-ah-nocks
Generic name: Itraconazole

Why is this drug prescribed?

Sporanox is used to treat three types of serious fungal infection: blastomycosis, histoplasmosis, and aspergillosis. Blastomycosis can affect the lungs, bones, and skin. Histoplasmosis can affect the lungs, heart, and blood. Aspergillosis can affect the lungs, kidneys, and other organs. Sporanox is also used against fungal infections in people with weak immune systems, such as AIDS patients.

Most important fact about this drug

Be sure to take Sporanox for as long as your doctor prescribes. It will take 3 months or more to cure the infection completely. If you stop taking Sporanox too soon, the infection may return.

How should you take this medication?

Take Sporanox exactly as prescribed. To make sure the capsules are properly absorbed, you should take them with food. Continue taking Sporanox until all the medication is gone.

- *If you miss a dose...*

  Take the forgotten dose as soon as you remember. If it is almost time for the next dose, skip the one you missed and go back to your regular schedule. Never try to "catch up" by doubling the dose.

- *Storage instructions...*

  Store at room temperature. Protect from light and moisture.

What side effects may occur?

Side effects cannot be anticipated. If any develop or change in intensity, inform your doctor as soon as possible. Only your doctor can determine if it is safe for you to continue taking Sporanox.

- *More common side effects may include:*

  Diarrhea
  Fatigue
  Fever
  Headache
  High blood pressure
  Nausea
  Rash
  Swelling due to water retention
  Vomiting

- *Less common side effects may include:*
  Abdominal pain, decreased sexual drive, dizziness, extreme sleepiness, feeling of general discomfort, hives, itching, loss of appetite, reproductive disorders such as male impotence, spleepiness

- *Rare side effects may include:*
  Depression, gas, hepatitis, male breast development, male breast pain, ringing in the ears, severe allergic reaction, skin peeling, sleeplessness

Why should this drug not be prescribed?

If you are sensitive to or have ever had an allergic reaction to Sporanox or similar antifungal drugs such as Nizoral, you should not take this medication. Make sure that your doctor is aware of any drug reactions that you have experienced.

Serious heart problems, such as irregular heartbeats and even death, have occurred in people who have taken Sporanox at the same time as Seldane or Hismanal. Never take these drugs with Sporanox.

Special warnings about this medication

If you have liver disease, your doctor should monitor your liver function periodically while you are taking Sporanox. If you develop such symptoms of liver disease as unusual fatigue, loss of appetite, nausea, vomiting, jaundice, dark urine, or pale stool, report them to your doctor so that the appropriate laboratory testing can be performed.

Possible food and drug interactions
when taking this medication

If Sporanox is taken with certain other drugs, the effects of either could be increased, decreased, or altered. It is especially important to check with your doctor before combining Sporanox with any of the following:

Astemizole (Hismanal)
Blood-thinning drugs such as Coumadin
Cyclosporine (Sandimmune)
Digoxin (Lanoxin)
H_2 antagonists such as Tagamet and Zantac
Isoniazid
Oral diabetes medications such as DiaBeta, Diabinese, Glucotrol, Micronase, Orinase, and Tolinase
Phenytoin (Dilantin)
Rifampin (Rifadin, Rimactane)
Terfenadine (Seldane, Seldane-D)

Special information
if you are pregnant or breastfeeding
The effects of Sporanox during pregnancy have not been adequately studied. If you are pregnant or plan to become pregnant, inform your doctor immediately. Sporanox appears in breast milk and could affect a nursing infant. If this medication is essential to your health, your doctor may advise you to discontinue breastfeeding until your treatment with Sporanox is finished.

Recommended dosage

ADULTS

Blastomycosis and Histoplasmosis
The usual dose is two 100-milligram capsules, taken with food once a day. If you feel no improvement, or if there is evidence that the fungal disease has spread, your doctor will increase the dose 100 milligrams at a time to a maximum of 400 milligrams a day. Daily dosages above 200 milligrams a day should be divided into 2 smaller doses.

Aspergillosis
The usual dose is 200 to 400 milligrams a day.

Treatment usually continues for a minimum of 3 months, until tests indicate that the fungal infection has subsided.

Overdosage
Any drug taken in excess can have dangerous consequences. If you suspect an overdose, seek emergency medical treatment immediately.

Generic name:

STAVUDINE

See Zerit, page 1223.

Brand name:

STELAZINE

Pronounced: STEL-ah-zeen
Generic name: Trifluoperazine hydrochloride

Why is this drug prescribed?
Stelazine is used to treat severe mental disturbances as well as anxiety that does not respond to ordinary tranquilizers.

Most important fact about this drug

Stelazine may cause tardive dyskinesia—a condition marked by involuntary muscle spasms and twitches in the face and body. This condition may be permanent and appears to be most common among the elderly, especially women. Ask your doctor for information about this possible risk.

How should you take this medication?

If taking Stelazine in a liquid concentrate form, you will need to dilute it with a liquid such as a carbonated beverage, coffee, fruit juice, milk, tea, tomato juice, or water. You can also use puddings, soups, and other semisolid foods. Stelazine should be diluted just before you take it.

You should not take Stelazine with alcohol.

■ *If you miss a dose...*
If you take 1 dose a day, take the dose you missed as soon as you remember. Then go back to your regular schedule. If you do not remember until the next day, skip the missed dose and go back to your regular schedule.

If you take more than 1 dose a day, take the dose you missed if it is within an hour or so of the scheduled time. If you do not remember until later, skip the missed dose and go back to your regular schedule.

Do not take 2 doses at once.

■ *Storage instructions...*
Store away from heat, light, and moisture.

What side effects may occur?

Side effects cannot be anticipated. If any develop or change in intensity, inform your doctor as soon as possible. Only your doctor can determine if it is safe for you to continue taking Stelazine.

■ *Side effects may include:*
Abnormal secretion of milk, abnormal sugar in urine, abnormalities in movement and posture, agitation, allergic reactions (sometimes severe), anemia, asthma, blood disorders, blurred vision, body rigidly arched backward, breast development in males, chewing movements, constipation, constricted pupils, difficulty swallowing, dilated pupils, dizziness, drooling, drowsiness, dry mouth, ejaculation problems, exaggerated or excessive reflexes, excessive or spontaneous flow of milk, eye problems causing a state of fixed gaze, eye spasms, fatigue, fever or high fever, flu-like symptoms, fluid accumulation and swelling (including the brain), fragmented movements, headache, heart attack, high or low blood sugar, hives, impotence, inability to urinate, increase in appetite and weight,

infections, insomnia, intestinal blockage, involuntary movements of tongue, face, mouth, jaw, arms, and legs, irregular blood pressure, pulse, and heartbeat, irregular or no menstrual periods, jitteriness, light-headedness (especially when standing up), liver damage, lockjaw, loss of appetite, low blood pressure, mask-like face, muscle stiffness and rigidity, nasal congestion, nausea, persistent, painful erections, pill-rolling movement, protruding tongue, puckering of mouth, puffing of cheeks, purple or red spots on the skin, rapid heartbeat, restlessness, rigid arms, feet, head, and muscles, seizures, sensitivity to light, shuffling walk, skin inflammation and peeling, skin itching, pigmentation, reddening, or rash, spasms in jaw, face, tongue, neck, hands, feet, back, and mouth, sweating, swelling of the throat, totally unresponsive state, tremors, twisted neck, weakness, yellowing of skin and whites of eyes

Why should this drug not be prescribed?

You should not be using Stelazine if you have liver damage, or if you are taking central nervous system depressants such as alcohol, barbiturates, or narcotic pain relievers. Stelazine should not be used if you have an abnormal bone marrow or blood condition.

Special warnings about this medication

You should use Stelazine cautiously if you have ever had a brain tumor, breast cancer, intestinal blockage, the eye condition called glaucoma, heart or liver disease, or seizures. Be cautious, too, if you are exposed to certain pesticides or extreme heat. Be aware that Stelazine may hide the signs of overdose of other drugs and may make it more difficult for your doctor to diagnose intestinal obstruction, brain tumor, and the dangerous neurological condition called Reye's syndrome.

Tell your doctor if you have ever had an allergic reaction to any major tranquilizer similar to Stelazine.

Dizziness, nausea, vomiting, and tremors can result if you suddenly stop taking Stelazine. Follow your doctor's instructions when discontinuing this drug.

Tell your doctor immediately if you experience symptoms such as a fever or sore throat, mouth, or gums. These signs of infection may signal the need to stop Stelazine treatment. Notify your doctor, too, if you develop flu-like symptoms with fever.

This drug may impair your ability to drive a car or operate potentially dangerous machinery, especially during the first few days of treatment. Do not participate in any activities that require full alertness if you are unsure about your ability.

If you have any trouble with your vision, tell your doctor.

Stelazine concentrate contains a sulfite that may cause allergic reactions in some people, especially in those with asthma.

Stelazine can cause a group of symptoms called neuroleptic malignant syndrome. Signs are high body temperature, rigid muscles, irregular pulse or blood pressure, rapid or abnormal heartbeat, and excessive perspiration.

Possible food and drug interactions when taking this medication

Extreme drowsiness and other potentially serious effects can result if Stelazine is combined with alcohol, tranquilizers such as Valium, narcotic painkillers such as Percocet, antihistamines such as Benadryl, and barbiturates such as phenobarbital.

If Stelazine is taken with certain other drugs, the effects of either could be increased, decreased, or altered. It is especially important to check with your doctor before combining Stelazine with the following:

Anticonvulsants such as Dilantin
Atropine (Donnatal)
Blood thinners such as Coumadin
Guanethidine (Ismelin)
Lithium (Lithobid, Eskalith)
Propranolol (Inderal)
Thiazide diuretics such as Dyazide

Special information if you are pregnant or breastfeeding

Pregnant women should use Stelazine only if clearly needed. The effects of Stelazine during pregnancy have not been adequately studied. If you are pregnant or plan to become pregnant, inform your doctor immediately. Stelazine appears in breast milk and may affect a nursing infant. If this medication is essential to your health, your doctor may have you discontinue breastfeeding while you are taking it.

Recommended dosage

ADULTS

Nonpsychotic Anxiety

Doses usually range from 2 to 4 milligrams daily. This amount should be divided into 2 equal doses and taken twice a day. Do not take more than 6 milligrams a day or take the medication for more than 12 weeks.

Psychotic Disorders
The usual starting dose is 4 to 10 milligrams a day, divided into 2 equal doses; doses range from 15 to 40 milligrams daily.

CHILDREN
Doses are based on the child's weight and the severity of his or her symptoms.

Psychotic Children 6 to 12 Years Old Who Are Closely Monitored or Hospitalized
The starting dose is 1 milligram a day, taken all at once or divided into 2 doses. Your doctor will increase the dosage gradually, up to 15 milligrams a day.

ELDERLY
Elderly people usually take Stelazine at lower doses. Because you may develop low blood pressure while taking this drug, your doctor will watch you closely. Elderly people (especially elderly women) may be more susceptible to tardive dyskinesia—a possibly permanent condition characterized by involuntary muscle spasms and twitches in the face and body. Consult your doctor for information about these potential risks.

Overdosage
Any medication taken in excess can have serious consequences. If you suspect an overdose of Stelazine, seek medical help immediately.

■ *Symptoms of Stelazine overdose may include:*
Agitation, coma, convulsions, difficulty breathing, difficulty swallowing, dry mouth, extreme sleepiness, fever, intestinal blockage, irregular heart rate, low blood pressure, restlessness

Generic name:

STIMATE
See DDAVP, page 278.

Brand name:

STUARTNATAL PLUS

Pronounced: STU-art NAY-tal plus
Generic ingredients: Prenatal vitamins and minerals
Other brand names: Materna, Natalins Rx

Why is this drug prescribed?
Stuartnatal Plus contains vitamins and minerals including iron, calcium, zinc, and folic acid. The tablets are given during pregnancy and after childbirth to ensure an adequate supply of these critical nutrients. They may also be prescribed to improve a woman's nutritional status before she becomes pregnant.

Most important fact about this drug
Nutritional supplementation is especially important during pregnancy. Be sure to take Stuartnatal Plus regularly as prescribed.

How should you take this medication?
Take Stuartnatal Plus exactly as prescribed. The usual dosage is 1 tablet per day with or without food.

- *If you miss a dose...*
  Take it as soon as you remember, then return to your regular schedule.

- *Storage instructions...*
  Store at room temperature, away from excessive heat.

Why should this drug not be prescribed?
There are no known reasons to avoid this preparation.

Special information
if you are pregnant or breastfeeding
Pregnancy and breastfeeding impose special nutritional demands on the mother. A vitamin and mineral supplement can help ensure that there are enough nutrients for both you and your baby.

Recommended dosage

ADULTS

Before, during, and after pregnancy, take 1 tablet daily, or as directed by your doctor.

Overdosage

Although no specific overdose information is available, even a nutritional supplement in extremely large amounts can have serious consequences. If you suspect an overdose of Stuartnatal Plus, seek medical attention immediately.

Generic name:

SUCRALFATE

See Carafate, page 163.

Generic name:

SULFACETAMIDE

See Sodium Sulamyd, page 1033.

Generic name:

SULFASALAZINE

See Azulfidine, page 101.

Generic name:

SULFISOXAZOLE

See Gantrisin, page 460.

Generic name:

SULINDAC

See Clinoril, page 207.

Generic name:

SUMATRIPTAN

See Imitrex Injection, page 507.

Brand name:

SUMYCIN

See Achromycin V Capsules, page 8.

Brand name:

SUPRAX

Pronounced: SUE-praks
Generic name: Cefixime

Why is this drug prescribed?
Suprax, a cephalosporin antibiotic, is prescribed for bacterial infections of the chest, ears, urinary tract, and throat and for uncomplicated gonorrhea.

Most important fact about this drug
If you are allergic to either penicillin or cephalosporin antibiotics in any form, consult your doctor *before taking* Suprax. There is a possibility that you are allergic to both types of medication; and if a reaction occurs, it could be extremely severe. If you take the drug and feel signs of a reaction, seek medical attention immediately.

How should you take this medication?
Suprax can be taken with or without food. If the medication causes stomach upset, take it with meals. Food, however, will slow down the rate at which medication is absorbed into your bloodstream.

If you are taking a liquid form of Suprax, use the specially marked measuring spoon to measure each dose accurately. Shake well before using.

It is important that you finish taking all of this medication, even if you are feeling better, in order to obtain the medicine's maximum benefit.

■ *If you miss a dose...*
  If you are taking this medication once a day and you forget to take a dose, take it as soon as you remember. Wait at least 10 to 12 hours before taking your next dose. Then return to your regular schedule.

  If you are taking this medication 2 times a day and you forget to take a dose, take it as soon as you remember and take your next dose 5 to 6 hours later. Then go back to your regular schedule.

  If you are taking this medication 3 times a day and you forget to take a dose, take it as soon as you remember and take your next dose 2 to 4 hours later. Then return to your regular schedule.

■ *Storage instructions...*
  Suprax liquid may be kept for 14 days, either at room temperature or in the refrigerator. Keep the bottle tightly closed. Do not store in damp places.

Keep out of reach of children and away from direct light and heat. Discard any unused portion after 14 days.

What side effects may occur?

Side effects cannot be anticipated. If any develop or change in intensity, inform your doctor as soon as possible. Only your doctor can determine if it is safe for you to continue taking Suprax.

- *More common side effects may include:*
  Abdominal pain
  Gas
  Indigestion
  Loose stools
  Mild diarrhea
  Nausea
  Vomiting

- *Less common side effects may include:*
  Colitis, dizziness, fever, headaches, hives, itching, skin rashes, vaginitis

- *Rare side effects may include:*
  Bleeding, decrease in urine output, seizures, severe abdominal or stomach cramps, severe diarrhea (sometimes accompanied by blood), shock, skin redness

Why should this drug not be prescribed?

If you are sensitive to or have ever had an allergic reaction to Suprax, other cephalosporin antibiotics, or any form of penicillin, you should not take this medication. Make sure that your doctor is aware of any drug reactions that you have experienced.

Special warnings about this medication

Notify your doctor if you have had allergic reactions to penicillins or other cephalosporin antibiotics.

If you have a history of stomach or intestinal disease such as colitis, check with your doctor before taking Suprax.

If your symptoms of infection do not improve within a few days, or if they get worse, notify your doctor immediately.

If you suffer nausea, vomiting, or severe diarrhea while taking Suprax, check with your doctor before taking a diarrhea medication. Some of these medications, such as Lomotil and Paregoric, may make your diarrhea worse or cause it to last longer.

If you are a diabetic, it is important to note that Suprax may cause false urine-sugar test results. Notify your doctor that you are taking this medication before being tested for sugar in the urine. Do not change diet or dosage of diabetes medication without first consulting with your doctor.

When prescribing Suprax, your doctor may perform laboratory tests to make certain it is effective against the bacteria causing the infection. Some bacteria do not respond to Suprax, so do not give it to other people or use it for other infections.

If you have a kidney disorder, check with your doctor before taking Suprax. You may need a reduced dose of this medication because of your medical condition.

Repeated use of Suprax may result in an overgrowth of bacteria that do not respond to the medication and can cause a secondary infection. Therefore, do not save this medication for use at another time. Take this medication only when directed to do so by your doctor.

Possible food and drug interactions
when taking this medication
No interactions with food or other drugs have been reported.

Special information
if you are pregnant or breastfeeding
The effects of Suprax during pregnancy have not been adequately studied. If you are pregnant or plan to become pregnant, inform your doctor immediately. Suprax may appear in breast milk and could affect a nursing infant. If this medication is essential to your health, your doctor may advise you to discontinue breastfeeding your baby until your treatment with this medication is finished.

Recommended dosage

ADULTS

Infections Other Than Gonorrhea
The usual adult dose is 400 milligrams daily. This may be taken as a single 400-milligram tablet once a day or as a 200-milligram tablet every 12 hours. If you have kidney disease, the dose may be lower.

Uncomplicated Gonorrhea
A single 400-milligram oral dose is usually prescribed.

CHILDREN

The safety and effectiveness of Suprax in children less than 6 months old have not been established. The usual child's dose is 8 milligrams of liquid per 2.2 pounds of body weight per day. This may be given as a single dose or in 2 half-doses every 12 hours. Children weighing more than 110 pounds or older than 12 years of age should be treated with an adult dose.

If your child has a middle ear infection (otitis media), your doctor will probably prescribe Suprax suspension. The tablet form is less effective against this type of infection.

ELDERLY

Your doctor may start you on a low dosage because this drug is eliminated from your body by the kidneys and kidney function tends to decrease with age.

Overdosage

Any medication taken in excess can cause symptoms of overdose. If you suspect an overdose, seek medical attention immediately.

■ *Symptoms of Suprax overdose may include:*
Blood in the urine
Diarrhea
Nausea
Upper abdominal pain
Vomiting

Brand name:

SURMONTIL

Pronounced: SIR-mon-til
Generic name: Trimipramine maleate

Why is this drug prescribed?
Surmontil is used to treat depression. It is a member of the family of drugs known as tricyclic antidepressants.

Most important fact about this drug
Serious, sometimes fatal, reactions have been known to occur when drugs such as Surmontil are taken with another type of antidepressant called an MAO inhibitor. Drugs in this category include Nardil, Marplan, and Parnate. Do not take Surmontil within 2 weeks of taking one of these drugs. Make sure your doctor and pharmacist know of all the medications you are taking.

How should you take this medication?

Surmontil may be taken in 1 dose at bedtime. Alternatively, the total daily dosage may be divided into smaller amounts taken during the day. If you are on long-term therapy with Surmontil, the single bedtime dose is preferred.

It is important to take Surmontil exactly as prescribed, even if the drug seems to have no effect. It may take up to 4 weeks for its benefits to appear.

Surmontil can make your mouth dry. Sucking hard candy or chewing gum can help this problem.

■ *If you miss a dose...*
Take it as soon as you remember. If it is almost time for the next dose, skip the one you missed and go back to your regular schedule. Do not take 2 doses at once. If you take Surmontil once a day at bedtime and you miss a dose, do not take it in the morning. It could cause disturbing side effects during the day.

■ *Storage instructions...*
Store at room temperature in a tightly closed container. Capsules in blister strips should be protected from moisture.

What side effects may occur?

Side effects cannot be anticipated. If any develop or change in intensity, inform your doctor as soon as possible. Only your doctor can determine if it is safe for you to continue taking Surmontil.

■ *Side effects may include:*
Abdominal cramps, agitation, anxiety, black tongue, blocked intestine, blood disorders, blurred vision, breast development in the male, confusion (especially in elderly people), constipation, delusions, diarrhea, difficulty urinating, dilated pupils, disorientation, dizziness, drowsiness, dry mouth, excessive or spontaneous milk excretion, fatigue, fever, flushing, fluttery or throbbing heartbeat, frequent urination, hair loss, hallucinations, headache, heart attack, high blood pressure, high blood sugar, hives, impotence, increased or decreased sex drive, inflammation of the mouth, insomnia, irregular heart rate, lack of coordination, loss of appetite, low blood pressure, low blood sugar, nausea, nightmares, numbness, peculiar taste in mouth, purple or reddish-brown spots on skin, rapid heartbeat, restlessness, ringing in the ears, seizures, sensitivity to light, skin itching, skin rash, sore throat, stomach upset, stroke, sweating, swelling of breasts, swelling of face and tongue, swelling of testicles, swollen glands,

tingling or pins and needles, tremors, visual problems, vomiting, weakness, weight gain or loss, yellowing of the skin and whites of the eyes

Why should this drug not be prescribed?
Surmontil should not be used if you are recovering from a recent heart attack.

You should not take Surmontil if you are sensitive to it or have ever had an allergic reaction to it or to other similar drugs such as Tofranil.

Special warnings about this medication
Use Surmontil cautiously if you have a seizure disorder, the eye condition known as glaucoma, heart disease, or a liver disorder. Also use caution if you have thyroid disease or are taking thyroid medication. People who have had problems urinating should also be careful about taking Surmontil.

Nausea, headache, and a general feeling of illness may result if you suddenly stop taking Surmontil. This does not mean you are addicted, but you should follow your doctor's instructions closely when discontinuing the drug.

This drug may impair your ability to drive a car or operate potentially dangerous machinery. Do not participate in any activities that require full alertness if you are unsure of the drug's effect on you.

Possible food and drug interactions
when taking this medication
People who are taking antidepressants known as MAO inhibitors (Parnate, Nardil, or Marplan) should not take Surmontil. Wait 2 weeks after stopping an MAO inhibitor before you begin taking Surmontil.

If Surmontil is taken with certain other drugs, the effects of either could be increased, decreased, or altered. It is especially important to check with your doctor before combining Surmontil with the following:

Antispasmodic drugs such as Cogentin
Cimetidine (Tagamet)
Guanethidine (Ismelin)
Local anesthetics
Local decongestants such as Dristan Nasal Spray
Oral nasal decongestants such as Sudafed
Stimulants such as EpiPen
Thyroid medications such as Synthroid

Extreme drowsiness and other potentially serious effects may result if you drink alcoholic beverages while you are taking Surmontil.

Special information
if you are pregnant or breastfeeding
The effects of Surmontil in pregnancy have not been adequately studied. Pregnant women should use Surmontil only when the potential benefits clearly outweigh the potential risks.

Recommended dosage

ADULTS

The usual starting dose is 75 milligrams per day, divided into equal smaller doses. Your doctor may gradually increase your dose to 150 milligrams per day, divided into smaller doses. Doses over 200 milligrams a day are not recommended. Doses in long-term therapy may range from 50 to 150 milligrams daily. You can take this total daily dosage at bedtime or spread it throughout the day.

CHILDREN

Safety and effectiveness of Surmontil in children have not been established.

ELDERLY AND ADOLESCENTS

Dosages usually start at 50 milligrams per day. Your doctor may increase the dose to 100 milligrams a day, if needed.

Overdosage

Any medication taken in excess can have serious consequences. An overdose of Surmontil can be fatal. If you suspect an overdose, seek medical help immediately.

- *Symptoms of Surmontil overdose may include:*
  Agitation, coma, convulsions, difficulty breathing, dilated pupils, discolored bluish skin, drowsiness, heart failure, high fever, involuntary movement, irregular heart rate, lack of coordination, low blood pressure, muscle rigidity, rapid heartbeat, restlessness, shock, stupor, sweating, vomiting

Brand name:

SYNALGOS-DC

Pronounced: SIN-al-gose dee-cee
Generic ingredients: Dihydrocodeine bitartrate, Aspirin, Caffeine

Why is this drug prescribed?

Synalgos-DC is a narcotic analgesic prescribed for the relief of moderate to moderately severe pain.

Most important fact about this drug

Narcotics such as Synalgos-DC can be habit-forming or addicting if they are taken over long periods of time.

How should you take this medication?

Take Synalgos-DC exactly as prescribed. Do not increase the amount you take without your doctor's approval.

Avoid or reduce use of alcohol while taking Synalgos-DC.

■ *If you miss a dose...*
If you take this drug on a regular schedule, take the forgotten dose as soon as you remember. If it is almost time for your next dose, skip the one you missed and go back to your regular schedule. Do not take 2 doses at once.

■ *Storage instructions...*
Store at room temperature in a tightly closed container.

What side effects may occur?

Side effects cannot be anticipated. If any develop or change in intensity, inform your doctor as soon as possible. Only your doctor can determine if it is safe for you to continue taking Synalgos-DC.

■ *Side effects may include:*
Constipation
Dizziness
Drowsiness
Itching
Light-headedness
Nausea
Sedation
Skin reactions
Vomiting

Why should this drug not be prescribed?

If you are sensitive to or have ever had an allergic reaction to Synalgos-DC, other narcotic pain relievers, or aspirin, you should not take this medication.

Make sure your doctor is aware of any drug reactions you have experienced.

Special warnings about this medication

Synalgos-DC may cause you to become drowsy or less alert; therefore, you should not drive or operate dangerous machinery or participate in any hazardous activity that requires full mental alertness until you know how this drug affects you.

If you have ever been dependent on or addicted to drugs, consult your doctor before taking Synalgos-DC.

If you are being treated for a stomach ulcer or blood-clotting disorder, consult your doctor before taking this medication.

Possible food and drug interactions
when taking this medication

Synalgos-DC slows brain activity and intensifies the effects of alcohol. Therefore, you should reduce your intake of alcoholic beverages or avoid them altogether.

If Synalgos-DC is taken with certain other drugs, the effects of either could be increased, decreased, or altered. It is especially important to check with your doctor before combining Synalgos-DC with the following:

Narcotic pain relievers such as Percocet and Demerol
Sedatives such as Halcion and Seconal
Tranquilizers such as Valium and Xanax

Taking blood thinners such as Coumadin in combination with Synalgos-DC may cause internal bleeding.

The use of Synalgos-DC in combination with antigout medications such as Benemid may alter its effects.

Special information
if you are pregnant or breastfeeding

The effects of Synalgos-DC during pregnancy have not been adequately studied. If you are pregnant or plan to become pregnant, inform your doctor immediately. This drug may appear in breast milk and could affect a nursing infant. If this medication is essential to your health, your doctor may advise you to discontinue breastfeeding until your treatment is finished.

Recommended dosage

ADULTS

Your doctor will prescribe a dosage based on the severity of your pain and how you respond to this medication. The usual dose of Synalgos-DC is 2 capsules taken every 4 hours as needed.

CHILDREN

The safety and effectiveness of this medication have not been established in children 12 years of age and under.

ELDERLY

Synalgos-DC should be taken with caution by the elderly or anyone in a weakened or rundown condition. Therefore, your doctor will adjust the dosage accordingly.

Overdosage

Although no specific information is available, any medication taken in excess can have serious consequences. If you suspect an overdose of Synalgos-DC, seek medical attention immediately.

Brand name:

SYNTHROID

Pronounced: SIN-throid
Generic name: Levothyroxine
Other brand names: Levothroid, Levoxyl

Why is this drug prescribed?

Synthroid, a synthetic thyroid hormone available in tablet or injectable form, may be given in any of the following cases:

If your own thyroid gland is not making enough hormone;

If you have an enlarged thyroid (a goiter) or are at risk for developing a goiter;

If you need a "suppression test" to determine whether your thyroid gland is making too much hormone;

If your thyroid production is low due to surgery, radiation, cancer, or certain drugs.

Most important fact about this drug

If you are taking Synthroid to make up for a lack of natural hormone, it is important to take it regularly at the same time every day. You will probably need to take it for the rest of your life.

How should you take this medication?

Take Synthroid exactly as directed. Take no more or less than the prescribed amount. Take your dose at the same time every day for consistent effect.

If a child cannot swallow whole tablets, you may crush a Synthroid tablet and mix it into a spoonful of liquid or sprinkle it over a small amount of food such as cooked cereal or applesauce. Give this mixture while it is very fresh; never store it for future use.

While taking Synthroid, your doctor will perform periodic blood tests to determine whether you are getting the right amount.

■ *If you miss a dose...*
Take it as soon as you remember. If it is almost time for your next dose, skip the one you missed and go back to your regular schedule. Never take 2 doses at the same time. If you miss 2 or more doses in a row, consult your doctor.

■ *Storage instructions...*
Keep this medication in a tightly closed container. Store it at room temperature.

What side effects may occur?
Side effects from Synthroid, other than overdose symptoms, are rare. Children who are treated with Synthroid may initially lose some hair, but this effect is usually temporary. However, excessive dosage or a too-rapid increase in dosage may lead to overstimulation of the thyroid gland.

■ *Symptoms of overstimulation may include:*
Abdominal cramps, changes in appetite, chest pain, diarrhea, fever, headache, heat intolerance, increased heart rate, irregular heartbeat, irritability, nausea, nervousness, palpitations, sleeplessness, sweating, tremors, weight loss

Why should this drug not be prescribed?
You should not be treated with Synthroid if you have ever had an allergic reaction to it, your thyroid gland is making too much thyroid hormone, or your adrenal glands are not making enough corticosteroid hormone.

Although Synthroid will speed up your metabolism, it is not effective as a weight-loss drug and should not be used as such. An overdose may cause life-threatening side effects, especially if you take Synthroid with an appetite-suppressant medication.

Special warnings about this medication
You should receive low doses of Synthroid, under very close supervision, if you are an older person, or if you suffer from angina (chest pain caused by a heart condition) or other types of heart disease.

Notify your doctor immediately if you experience chest pain, increased pulse rate, heart palpitations (fast, fluttery heartbeat), heavy sweating, inability to tolerate heat, nervousness, or anything else unusual.

If you have diabetes mellitus or diabetes insipidus, or if your body makes insufficient adrenal corticosteroid hormone, Synthroid will tend to make your symptoms worse. If you take medication for any of these disorders, the dosage will probably have to be adjusted once you begin taking Synthroid.

Excessive doses of Synthroid in infants may cause the top of the skull to close too early.

Possible food and drug interactions when taking this medication

If Synthroid is taken with certain other drugs, the effects of either could be increased, decreased, or altered. It is especially important to check with your doctor before combining Synthroid with the following:

Antidepressants such as Elavil and Tofranil
Antidiabetic drugs such as Diabinese and Glucotrol
Blood thinners such as Coumadin
Cholestyramine (Questran)
Colestipol (Colestid)
Epinephrine (EpiPen)
Estrogen replacement drugs such as Premarin
Estrogen-containing oral contraceptives such as Ortho-Novum and Ovral
Insulin

If you are having a blood test to determine whether your dosage of Synthroid is correct, make sure your doctor knows about other medications you may be taking. Any of the following drugs may interfere with the results of the thyroid-level test:

Androgens such as Android-25 and testosterone
Corticosteroids such as Decadron and prednisone
Estrogens such as Premarin
Iodine-containing drugs such as SSKI
Oral contraceptive pills containing estrogen
Salicylate-containing drugs such as aspirin

Special information if you are pregnant or breastfeeding

If you need to take Synthroid because of a thyroid hormone deficiency, you can continue to take the medication during pregnancy. Once your baby is born, you may breastfeed while continuing to take carefully regulated doses of Synthroid.

Recommended dosage

Your doctor will tailor the dosage to meet your individual requirements, taking into consideration the status of your thyroid gland and other medical conditions you may have. He or she will monitor your thyroid hormone level with periodic blood tests.

Overdosage

If you suspect a Synthroid overdose, seek emergency medical attention immediately. Taken in excess, the drug may have serious consequences.

■ *Symptoms of Synthroid overdose may include:*
Abdominal cramps, chest pain, diarrhea, excessive sweating, fever, headache, heat intolerance, irregular heartbeat, nervousness, palpitations, rapid heartbeat, tremors, weight loss

Generic name:

TACRINE

See Cognex, page 222.

Brand name:

TAGAMET

Pronounced: TAG-ah-met
Generic name: Cimetidine

Why is this drug prescribed?

Tagamet is prescribed for the treatment of certain kinds of stomach and intestinal ulcers and related conditions. These include: active duodenal (upper intestinal) ulcers; active benign stomach ulcers; erosive gastroesophageal reflux disease (backflow of acid stomach contents); prevention of upper abdominal bleeding in those who are critically ill; and excess-acid conditions such as Zollinger-Ellison syndrome (a form of peptic ulcer with too much acid). It is also used for maintenance therapy of duodenal ulcer following the healing of active ulcers. Tagamet is known as a histamine blocker.

Some doctors also use Tagamet to treat acne and to prevent stress-induced ulcers. It may also be used to treat chronic hives, herpes virus infections (including shingles), abnormal hair growth in women, and overactivity of the parathyroid gland.

Most important fact about this drug

Short-term treatment with Tagamet can result in complete healing of a duodenal ulcer. However, there can be a recurrence of the ulcer after Tagamet has been discontinued. The rate of ulcer recurrence may be slightly higher in people healed with Tagamet rather than other forms of therapy. However, Tagamet is usually prescribed for more severe cases.

How should you take this medication?

You can take Tagamet with or between meals. Do not take antacids within 1 to 2 hours of a dose of Tagamet. Avoid excessive amounts of caffeine while taking this drug.

It may take several days for Tagamet to begin relieving stomach pain. Be sure to continue taking the drug exactly as prescribed even if it seems to have no affect.

- *If you miss a dose...*
  Take it as soon as you remember. If it is almost time for your next dose, skip the one you missed and go back to your regular schedule. Do not take 2 doses a once.

- *Storage instructions...*
  Store at room temperature in a tightly closed container, away from light.

What side effects may occur?

Side effects cannot be anticipated. If any develop or change in intensity, inform your doctor as soon as possible. Only your doctor can determine if it is safe for you to continue taking Tagamet.

- *More common side effects may include:*
  Breast development in men, headache

Less common side effects—agitation, anxiety, confusion, depression, disorientation, and hallucinations—may appear in severely ill individuals who have been treated for 1 month or longer. However, these reactions are not permanent and have cleared up within 3 to 4 days of discontinuation of the drug.

- *Rare side effects may include:*
  Allergic reactions, anemia, blood disorders, diarrhea, dizziness, fever, hair loss, impotence, inability to urinate, joint pain, kidney disorders, liver disorders, mild rash, muscle pain, pancreas inflammation, rapid heartbeat, skin inflammation or peeling, sleepiness, slow heartbeat

Why should this drug not be prescribed?
If you have ever had an allergic reaction to Tagamet, do not take this medication.

Special warnings about this medication
Ulcers may be more difficult to heal if you smoke cigarettes.

If you are being treated for a liver or kidney disorder, make sure the doctor is aware if it.

If you are over 50 years old, have liver or kidney disease, or are severely ill, you may experience temporary mental confusion while taking Tagamet. Notify your doctor.

Possible food and drug interactions
when taking this medication
If Tagamet is taken with certain other drugs, the effects of either can be increased, decreased, or altered. It is especially important that you check with your doctor before combining Tagamet with the following:

Antiarrhythmic heart medications such as Cordarone, Tonocard, Quinidex, and Procan
Antidiabetic drugs such as Micronase and Glucotrol
Antifungal drugs such as Diflucan and Nizoral
Aspirin
Augmentin
Benzodiazepine tranquilizers such as Valium and Librium
Beta-blocking blood pressure drugs such as Inderal and Lopressor
Calcium-blocking blood pressure drugs such as Cardizem, Calan, and Procardia
Chlorpromazine (Thorazine)
Cisapride (Propulsid)
Cyclosporine (Sandimmune)
Digoxin (Lanoxin)
Narcotic pain relievers such as Demerol and Morphine
Metoclopramide (Reglan)
Metronidazole (Flagyl)
Nicotine (Nicoderm)
Paroxetine (Paxil)
Pentoxifylline (Trental)
Phenytoin (Dilantin)
Quinine (Quinamm)
Sucralfate (Carafate)
Theophylline (Theo-Dur, others)
Warfarin (Coumadin)

Avoid alcoholic beverages while taking Tagamet. This medication increases the effects of alcohol.

Antacids can reduce the effect of Tagamet when taken at the same time. If you take an antacid to relieve the pain of an ulcer, the doses should be separated by 1 to 2 hours.

Special information
if you are pregnant or breastfeeding

The effects of Tagamet during pregnancy have not been adequately studied. If you are pregnant or plan to become pregnant, notify your doctor immediately. Tagamet appears in breast milk and could affect a nursing infant. If this medication is essential to your health, your doctor may advise you to discontinue breastfeeding until treatment with this drug is finished.

Recommended dosage

ADULTS

Active Duodenal Ulcer
The usual dose is 800 milligrams once daily at bedtime. However, other doses shown to be effective are:

300 milligrams 4 times a day with meals and at bedtime

400 milligrams twice a day, in the morning and at bedtime

Most people heal in 4 weeks.

If you require maintenance therapy, the usual dose is 400 milligrams at bedtime.

Active Benign Gastric Ulcer
The usual dose is 800 milligrams once a day at bedtime or 300 milligrams taken 4 times a day with meals and at bedtime.

Erosive Gastroesophageal Reflux Disease
The usual dosage is a total of 1,600 milligrams daily divided into doses of 800 milligrams twice a day or 400 milligrams 4 times a day for 12 weeks. The beneficial use of Tagamet beyond 12 weeks has not been firmly established.

Pathological Hypersecretory Condition
The usual dosage is 300 milligrams 4 times a day with meals and at bedtime. Your doctor may adjust your dosage based on your needs, but you should take no more than 2,400 milligrams per day.

CHILDREN

Safety and effectiveness have not been established in children under 16 years old. However, your doctor may decide that the potential benefits of Tagamet use outweigh the potential risks. Doses of 20 to 40 milligrams per 2.2 pounds of body weight have been used.

ELDERLY

Dosage in the elderly is generally the same as that for other adults. However, many elderly people require reduced doses of a variety of drugs. Your doctor will decide if any dosage adjustment of Tagamet is needed due to your age or other existing medical condition.

Overdosage

Information concerning overdosage is limited. However, respiratory failure, an increased heartbeat, exaggerated side effect symptoms or reactions such as unresponsiveness may be signs of Tagamet overdose. If you experience any of these symptoms, notify your doctor immediately.

Brand name:

TALWIN COMPOUND

Pronounced: TAL-win
Generic ingredients: Pentazocine hydrochloride, Aspirin

Why is this drug prescribed?

Talwin Compound combines the strong analgesic properties of pentazocine and the analgesic, anti-inflammatory, and fever-reducing properties of aspirin. It is used for the relief of moderate pain.

Most important fact about this drug

Talwin Compound can cause physical and psychological dependence. Do not share Talwin Compound with other people.

How should you take this medication?

Take Talwin Compound exactly as prescribed by your doctor. Do not increase the amount you take without your doctor's approval.

■ *If you miss a dose...*
   And you take this medication on a regular schedule, take the forgotten dose as soon as you remember. If it is almost time for your next dose, skip the one you missed and go back to your regular schedule. Do not take 2 doses at once.

- *Storage instructions...*
  Store away from heat, light, and moisture.

What side effects may occur?
Side effects cannot be anticipated. If any develop or change in intensity, inform your doctor as soon as possible. Only your doctor can determine if it is safe for you to continue taking Talwin.

- *More common side effects may include:*
  Confusion, disorientation, dizziness, feelings of elation, hallucinations, headache, light-headedness, nausea, sedation, sweating, vomiting

If any of these side effects occur, it may help if you lie down after taking the medication.

- *Less common side effects may include:*
  Blurred vision, constipation, depression, difficulty in focusing, disturbed dreams, fainting, flushing, inability to fall or stay asleep, lowered blood pressure, rapid heart rate, rash, weakness

- *Rare side effects may include:*
  Abdominal distress, chills, diarrhea, excitement, facial swelling, fluid retention, hives, inability to urinate, irritability, lack or loss of appetite, ringing in the ears, skin peeling, tingling sensation, tremors, troubled or slowed breathing

Why should this drug not be prescribed?
If you are sensitive to or have ever had an allergic reaction to pentazocine or salicylates (anti-inflammatory drugs such as aspirin), or other drugs of this type, you should not take this medication. Make sure your doctor is aware of any drug reactions you have experienced.

Because there is a possible association between aspirin and the dangerous neurological condition called Reye's syndrome, Talwin should not be given to children and teenagers who have chickenpox or flu, which predispose them to development of the condition.

Special warnings about this medication
Drug dependence and withdrawal symptoms—if you stop taking the drug abruptly—can occur with the use of pentazocine. If you have a history of drug dependence, Talwin should be used only under the close supervision of your doctor.

Talwin Compound may cause you to become drowsy, dizzy, or less alert; therefore, you should not drive or operate dangerous machinery or participate in any hazardous activity that requires full mental alertness until you know how this drug affects you.

Talwin Compound contains aspirin. If you have a stomach ulcer, consult your doctor before taking this medication. Aspirin may irritate the stomach lining and may cause bleeding.

If you have a kidney or liver disorder, or if you are prone to seizures, consult your doctor before taking Talwin.

Talwin Compound may cause breathing difficulties. If you have severe bronchial asthma or other respiratory problems, check with your doctor before taking this medication.

Talwin should be used with caution if you have had a heart attack or if you are nauseated or are vomiting.

Talwin Compound should be used with extreme caution in patients being treated by a doctor for a head injury. This medication may cause troubled breathing and pressure on the skull from increased brain and spinal fluid—which can be exaggerated by a head injury. This drug may also mask or hide the pain from head injury, making it difficult for your doctor to treat.

Use Talwin Compound only to relieve pain, not in anticipation of pain.

Possible food and drug interactions
when taking this medication
Talwin Compound slows brain activity and intensifies the effects of alcohol. Limit your intake of alcohol while taking this medication.

If Talwin Compound is taken with certain other drugs, the effects of either could be increased, decreased, or altered. It is especially important to check with your doctor before combining Talwin Compound with the following:

Benzodiazepines such as Valium and Xanax
MAO inhibitors (antidepressants such as Nardil)
Other analgesics (pain relievers such as Demerol)
Sleep aids such as Dalmane and Halcion

The use of these drugs with Talwin Compound increases their sedative or calming effects and may lead to overdose symptoms.

The use of blood thinners such as Coumadin in combination with Talwin Compound may cause bleeding. If you are taking a blood thinner, consult your doctor before taking this drug.

The use of narcotics, including methadone (prescribed for the daily treatment of drug dependence), with Talwin Compound may produce withdrawal symptoms.

Special information
if you are pregnant or breastfeeding

The effects of Talwin Compound during pregnancy have not been adequately studied. Consult your physician before taking Talwin Compound when pregnant. It is not known whether Talwin Compound appears in breast milk. If this medication is essential to your health, your doctor may advise you to discontinue breastfeeding until your treatment is finished.

Recommended dosage

ADULTS

The usual dose of Talwin Compound is 2 caplets, 3 or 4 times per day.

CHILDREN

The safety and effectiveness of Talwin Compound have not been established in children under 12 years of age.

Overdosage

Any medication taken in excess can have dangerous consequences. If you suspect an overdose, seek medical attention immediately.

■ *Symptoms of an overdose of Talwin Compound, because of its aspirin content, may include:*
Coma, confusion, convulsions, diarrhea, dizziness, gasping, headache, heavy perspiration, nausea, rapid breathing, rapid heart rate, ringing in the ears, thirst, vomiting

An inability to breathe may lead to death.

Brand name:

TAMBOCOR

Pronounced: TAM-ba-kore
Generic name: Flecainide acetate

Why is this drug prescribed?

Tambocor is prescribed to treat certain heart rhythm disturbances, including paroxysmal atrial fibrillation (a sudden attack or worsening of irregular heartbeat in which the upper chamber of the heart beats irregularly and very rapidly) and paroxysmal supraventricular tachycardia (a sudden attack or worsening of an abnormally fast but regular heart rate that occurs in intermittent episodes).

Most important fact about this drug
Tambocor may sometimes cause or worsen heartbeat irregularities and certain heart conditions, such as heart failure (the inability of the heart to sustain its workload of pumping blood). Before prescribing Tambocor, your doctor will explain the risks and benefits of Tambocor and how he or she will monitor your condition.

How should you take this medication?
In almost every case, your doctor will initiate Tambocor therapy in the hospital.

Take Tambocor exactly as prescribed by your doctor. Serious heartbeat disturbances may result if you do not follow your doctor's instructions, if you miss any regular doses, or if you increase or decrease the dosage without consulting your doctor.

Your doctor may order regular blood tests to monitor your therapy.

■ *If you miss a dose...*
Take it as soon as you remember if it is within 6 hours of your scheduled time. If you do not remember until later, skip the dose you missed and go back to your regular schedule. Do not take 2 doses at once.

■ *Storage instructions...*
Store at room temperature in a tightly closed container, away from light.

What side effects may occur?
Tambocor has a wide variety of possible effects on the heart, including new or worsened heartbeat abnormalities, heart attack, congestive heart failure, and heart block—an interference with the heart's contraction. If any develop, inform your doctor immediately. Only your doctor can determine whether it is safe for you to continue taking Tambocor.

■ *Other side effects may include:*
Abdominal pain, angina pectoris (crushing chest pain), anxiety, apathy, appetite loss, chest pain, confusion, constipation, convulsions, decreased sex drive, depression, diarrhea, difficult or labored breathing, dizziness (light-headedness, faintness, near fainting, unsteadiness), dry mouth, edema (accumulation of fluid in the tissues), exaggerated feeling of well-being, excessive urine, eye pain or irritation, fainting, fatigue, fever, flushing, gas, hair loss, headache, heart palpitations (fluttery heartbeat), high or low blood pressure, hives, impotence, inability to urinate,

indigestion, insomnia, intolerance of light, involuntary eye movements, itching, joint pain, lack of coordination, loss of sense of identity, lung inflammation or other conditions, malaise (feeling unwell or ill), memory loss, morbid dreams, muscle pain, nausea, numbness or tingling, paralysis, rash, reduced sensitivity to touch, ringing in the ears, skin inflammation and peeling, sleepiness, speech problems, stupor, sweating, swollen lips, tongue, and mouth, taste changes, tremor, twitching, vertigo, vision problems (blurred vision, difficulty in focusing, double vision, spots before the eyes), vomiting, weakness, wheezing

Why should this drug not be prescribed?
Your doctor should not prescribe Tambocor if you have ever had an allergic reaction to it or you are sensitive to it, if you have heart block (without a pacemaker), or if your heart cannot supply enough blood to the body.

Special warnings about this medication
If you have a pacemaker, you should be monitored very closely while taking Tambocor—your pacemaker may need to be adjusted.

If you have liver disease, Tambocor could build up in your system. Your doctor will prescribe the drug only if the benefits outweigh the risks. In addition, you should have frequent blood tests to make sure your dosage is not too high.

If you have a history of congestive heart failure or a weak heart, you may be at increased risk for dangerous cardiac side effects from Tambocor.

If you have very alkaline urine, perhaps caused by a kidney condition or by a strict vegetarian diet, your body will tend to process and eliminate Tambocor rather slowly and you may need a lower-than-average dosage.

If the potassium levels in your blood are too high or too low, your doctor will want to correct the condition before allowing you to take Tambocor.

If you have kidney failure, your doctor will want to watch you closely.

Possible food and drug interactions
when taking this medication
If Tambocor is taken with certain other drugs, the effects of either could be increased, decreased, or altered. It is especially important to check with your doctor before combining Tambocor with the following:

Amiodarone (Cordarone)
Beta blockers (blood pressure drugs such as Inderal, Tenormin, and Sectral)

Carbamazepine (Tegretol)
Cimetidine (Tagamet)
Diltiazem (Cardizem)
Disopyramide (Norpace)
Nifedipine (Procardia)
Phenobarbital
Phenytoin (Dilantin)
Verapamil (Calan, Isoptin)

Special information
if you are pregnant or breastfeeding

The effects of Tambocor during pregnancy have not been adequately studied. If you are pregnant or plan to become pregnant, inform your doctor immediately. Tambocor should be used during pregnancy only if the benefit justifies the potential risk to the unborn child. Tambocor appears in breast milk. Check with your doctor before breastfeeding your baby.

Recommended dosage

ADULTS

Treatment with Tambocor almost always begins in the hospital.

The usual starting dose is 50 to 100 milligrams every 12 hours, depending on the condition under treatment. Every 4 days, your doctor may increase your dose by 50 milligrams every 12 hours until your condition is under control.

Overdosage

An overdose of Tambocor is likely to cause slowed or rapid heartbeat, other cardiac problems, fainting, low blood pressure, nausea, vomiting, convulsions, and heart failure. Taken even in moderate excess, Tambocor may have serious consequences and can be fatal. If you suspect an overdose, seek medical attention immediately.

Generic name:

TAMOXIFEN

See Nolvadex, page 744.

Brand name:

TAVIST

Pronounced: TAV-ist
Generic name: Clemastine fumarate

Why is this drug prescribed?

Tavist is an antihistamine. Both Tavist and Tavist-1 are used in treatment of the sneezing, runny nose, itching, and watery eyes caused by hay fever. Tavist Tablets also relieve mild allergic skin reactions such as hives and swelling. Antihistamines reduce itching and swelling and dry up secretions from the eyes, nose, and throat.

Most important fact about this drug

Tavist may cause drowsiness. Be especially careful driving or operating dangerous machinery or participating in any hazardous activity that requires full mental alertness until you know how you react to this medication.

How should you take this medication?

Tavist should be taken exactly as prescribed.

Tavist may make your mouth dry. Sucking hard candy, chewing gum, or melting bits of ice in your mouth can provide relief.

- *If you miss a dose...*
  If you are taking this medication on a regular schedule, take the forgotten dose as soon as you remember. If it is almost time for your next dose, skip the one you missed and go back to your regular schedule. Do not take 2 doses at once.

- *Storage instructions...*
  Store at room temperature in a tightly closed container, away from light.

What side effects may occur?

Side effects cannot be anticipated. If any develop or change in intensity, inform your doctor as soon as possible. Only your doctor can determine if it is safe for you to continue taking Tavist.

- *More common side effects may include:*
  Disturbed coordination
  Dizziness
  Drowsiness

Extreme calm (sedation)
Sleepiness
Upset stomach

■ *Less common or rare side effects may include:*
Acute inflammation of the inner ear, anemia, blurred vision, chills, confusion, constipation, convulsions, diarrhea, difficulty sleeping, difficulty urinating, double vision, dry mouth, nose, and throat, early menstruation, exaggerated sense of well-being, excessive perspiration, excitement, fatigue, frequent urination, headache, hives, hysteria, inability to urinate, increased chest congestion, irregular heartbeat, irritability, loss of appetite, low blood pressure, nausea, nerve inflammation, nervousness, palpitations, rapid heartbeat, rash, restlessness, ringing in the ears, sensitivity to light, severe allergic reaction (anaphylactic shock), stuffy nose, tightness of chest, tingling or pins and needles, tremor, vertigo, vomiting, wheezing

Why should this drug not be prescribed?
Tavist should be avoided if you are breastfeeding, if you are taking antidepressant drugs known as MAO inhibitors (Nardil, Parnate, Marplan), or if you have asthma or other breathing problems. If you are sensitive to or have ever had an allergic reaction to clemastine fumarate or other antihistamines with a similar chemical composition, do not take this medication.

Special warnings about this medication
Use antihistamines very cautiously if you have the eye condition known as narrow-angle glaucoma, a peptic ulcer, intestinal blockage, a bladder obstruction, or an enlarged prostate. Antihistamines can make these problems worse.

Antihistamines are more likely to cause dizziness, sedation, and low blood pressure in the elderly (over age 60).

Use Tavist with care if you have a history of bronchial asthma, heart disease, circulatory problems, an overactive thyroid, or high blood pressure.

Possible food and drug interactions
when taking this medication
Tavist may increase the effects of alcohol. Do not drink alcohol—or at least limit your use—while taking this medication.

If Tavist is taken with certain other drugs, the effects of either could be increased, decreased, or altered. It is especially important to check with your doctor before combining Tavist with the following:

Antidepressant drugs known as MAO inhibitors such as Nardil, Marplan, and Parnate
Sedatives such as Nembutal and Seconal
Tranquilizers such as Xanax and Valium

Special information
if you are pregnant or breastfeeding

The effects of Tavist during pregnancy have not been adequately studied. If you are pregnant or plan to become pregnant, inform your doctor immediately. Tavist should not be used if you are breastfeeding.

Recommended dosage

TAVIST-1 TABLETS

The recommended starting dose is 1 tablet twice daily. Your doctor may increase the dose to a maximum of 6 tablets daily.

TAVIST TABLETS

The maximum recommended dosage is 1 tablet 3 times daily. Many people do well on a single dose. You should take no more than 3 tablets daily.

TAVIST SYRUP

Adults and Children 12 Years and Over

For Symptoms of Hay Fever
The starting dose of Tavist Syrup is 2 teaspoonfuls (1 milligram) 2 times a day. Your doctor may increase the dosage, but it should not be more than 12 teaspoonfuls (6 milligrams) daily.

For Hives and Swelling
The starting dose of Tavist Syrup is 4 teaspoonfuls (2 milligrams) twice a day; you should not take more than 12 teaspoonfuls (6 milligrams) daily.

Children 6 Through 11

For Symptoms of Hay Fever
The starting dose of Tavist Syrup is 1 teaspoonful (0.5 milligram) 2 times per day. Your doctor may increase the dosage to a maximum of 6 teaspoonfuls (3 milligrams) daily.

For Hives and Swelling
The starting dose of Tavist Syrup is 2 teaspoonfuls (1 milligram) twice a day, not to exceed 6 teaspoonfuls (3 milligrams) daily.

Overdosage
Any medication taken in excess can have serious consequences. If you suspect an overdose, seek medical treatment immediately.

- *Symptoms of Tavist overdose may include:*
  Coma
  Convulsions
  Drowsiness
  Dry mouth
  Fever
  Fixed, dilated pupils
  Flushing
  Stimulation, especially in children
  Stomach and intestinal problems

- *Symptoms of Tavist overdose in children may include:*
  Bluish color to the skin
  Convulsions
  Excitement
  Hallucinations
  High body temperature
  Slow, twisting movements of hand and arms
  Tremors
  Twitching
  Uncoordinated movements

Brand name:

TEGRETOL

Pronounced: TEG-re-tawl
Generic name: Carbamazepine
Other brand names: Epitol, Atretol

Why is this drug prescribed?
Tegretol is used in the treatment of seizure disorders, including certain types of epilepsy. It is also prescribed for trigeminal neuralgia (severe pain in the jaws) and pain in the tongue and throat.

In addition, some doctors use Tegretol to treat alcohol withdrawal, cocaine addiction, and emotional disorders such as depression and abnormally aggressive behavior. The drug is also used to treat migraine headache and "restless legs."

Most important fact about this drug
There are potentially dangerous side effects associated with the use of Tegretol. If you experience symptoms such as fever, sore throat, ulcers in the mouth, easy bruising, or reddish or purplish spots on the skin, you should notify your doctor immediately. These symptoms could be signs of a blood disorder brought on by the drug.

How should you take this medication?
This medication should only be taken with meals, never on an empty stomach.

Shake the suspension well before using.

■ *If you miss a dose...*
Take it as soon as you remember. If it is almost time for your next dose, skip the one you missed and go back to your regular schedule. Do not take 2 doses at once. If you miss more than 1 dose in a day, check with your doctor.

■ *Storage instructions...*
Store Tegretol at room temperature. Keep the container tightly closed. Protect the tablets from light and moisture. Keep the liquid suspension away from light.

What side effects may occur?
Side effects cannot be anticipated. If any develop or change in intensity, inform your doctor as soon as possible. Only your doctor can determine if it is safe for you to continue taking Tegretol.

■ *More common side effects, especially at the start of treatment, may include:*
Dizziness
Drowsiness
Nausea
Unsteadiness
Vomiting

■ *Other side effects may include:*
Abdominal pain, abnormal heartbeat and rhythm, abnormal involuntary movements, abnormal sensitivity to sound, aching joints and muscles,

agitation, anemia, blood clots, blurred vision, chills, confusion, congestive heart failure, constipation, depression, diarrhea, double vision, dry mouth and throat, fainting and collapse, fatigue, fever, fluid retention, frequent urination, hair loss, hallucinations, headache, hepatitis, hives, impotence, inability to urinate, inflammation of the mouth and tongue, inflamed eyes, involuntary movements of the eyeball, itching, kidney failure, labored breathing, leg cramps, liver disorders, loss of appetite, loss of coordination, low blood pressure, pneumonia, reddened skin, reddish or purplish spots on the skin, reduced urine volume, ringing in the ears, sensitivity to light, skin inflammation and scaling, skin peeling, skin rashes, skin pigmentation changes, speech difficulties, stomach problems, sweating, talkativeness, tingling sensation, worsening of high blood pressure, yellow eyes and skin

Why should this drug not be prescribed?

You should not use Tegretol if you have a history of bone marrow depression (reduced function), a sensitivity to Tegretol or a sensitivity to tricyclic antidepressant drugs such as amitriptyline (Elavil). You should also not be taking Tegretol if you are on an MAO inhibitor antidepressant such as Nardil or Parnate, or if you have taken such a drug within the past 14 days.

Tegretol is not a simple pain reliever and should not be used for the relief of minor aches and pains.

Special warnings about this medication

If you have a history of heart, liver, or kidney damage, an adverse blood reaction to any drug, glaucoma, or serious reactions to other drugs, you should discuss this history thoroughly with your doctor before taking this medication.

Anticonvulsant drugs such as Tegretol should not be stopped abruptly if you are taking the medication to prevent major seizures. There exists the strong possibility of continuous epileptic attacks without return to consciousness, leading to possible severe brain damage and death. Only your doctor should determine if and when you should stop taking this medication.

Since dizziness and drowsiness may occur while taking Tegretol, you should refrain from operating machinery or driving an automobile or participating in any high-risk activity that requires full mental alertness until you know how this drug affects you.

The elderly, especially, can become confused or agitated when taking Tegretol.

In very rare cases, some people have had severe, even fatal, skin reactions to Tegretol. Contact your doctor at the first sign of a skin problem.

Possible food and drug interactions
when taking this medication

The use of the antiseizure medications phenobarbital, phenytoin (Dilantin), or primidone (Mysoline) may reduce the effectiveness of Tegretol. Take other anticonvulsants along with Tegretol only if your doctor advises it. The use of Tegretol with other anticonvulsants may change thyroid gland function.

The effectiveness of haloperidol (Haldol) and valproic acid (Depakene) may be reduced when these drugs are taken with Tegretol.

The use of erythromycin, cimetidine (Tagamet), propoxyphene (Darvon), terfenadine (Seldane), isoniazid (Rifamate), fluoxetine (Prozac), or calcium channel blockers such as Calan may raise the amount of Tegretol in the blood to harmful levels.

Lithium (Lithonate) used with Tegretol may cause harmful nervous system side effects.

If you are taking an oral contraceptive and Tegretol, you may experience blood spotting and your contraceptive may not be completely reliable.

The activity of theophylline (Theo-Dur), doxycycline (Vibramycin), phenytoin (Dilantin), and the blood thinner warfarin (Coumadin) may be affected significantly by Tegretol.

Special information
if you are pregnant or breastfeeding

There are no adequate safety studies regarding the use of Tegretol in pregnant women. However, there have been reports of birth defects in infants. Therefore, this medication should be used during pregnancy only if the potential benefits justify the potential risk to the fetus. If you are pregnant or plan on becoming pregnant, you should discuss this with your doctor.

Tegretol appears in breast milk. If you are breastfeeding, your doctor may advise you to discontinue doing so if taking Tegretol is essential to your health.

Recommended dosage

ADULTS

Seizures

The usual dose for adults and children over 12 years of age is one 200-milligram tablet taken twice daily or 1 teaspoon 4 times a day. Your doctor may increase the dose at weekly intervals by adding 200-milligram or 2-teaspoon doses to a total of 3 or 4 times per day. Dosage should generally not exceed 1,000 milligrams daily in children 12 to 15 years old and 1,200 milligrams daily for adults and children over 15. The usual daily maintenance dosage range is 800 to 1,200 milligrams.

Trigeminal Neuralgia

The usual dose is one 100-milligram tablet twice or ½ teaspoon 4 times on the first day. Your doctor may increase this dose using increments of 100 milligrams every 12 hours or ½ teaspoonful 4 times daily only as needed to achieve freedom from pain. Doses should not exceed 1,200 milligrams daily and are usually in the range of 400 to 800 milligrams a day for maintenance.

CHILDREN

Seizures

The usual dose for children 6 to 12 years old is one 100-milligram tablet twice daily or ½ teaspoon 4 times a day. Your doctor may increase the dose at weekly intervals by adding 100 milligrams or 1 teaspoon 3 or 4 times a day. Total daily dosage should generally not exceed 1,000 milligrams and should be divided into 3 or 4 doses. The usual daily dosage range for maintenance is 400 to 800 milligrams. Safety and effectiveness in children under 6 years of age have not been established.

ELDERLY

To help determine the ideal dosage, your doctor may decide to periodically check the level of Tegretol in your blood.

Overdosage

Any medication taken in excess can have serious consequences. If you suspect an overdose, seek medical attention immediately. The first signs and symptoms of an overdose of Tegretol appear after 1 to 3 hours.

- *The most prominent signs of a Tegretol overdose include:*
  Coma, convulsions, dizziness, drowsiness, inability to urinate, involuntary rapid eye movements, irregular or reduced breathing, lack or absence of urine, lack of coordination, low or high blood pressure, muscular twitching, nausea, pupil dilation, rapid heartbeat, restlessness, severe muscle spasm, shock, tremors, unconsciousness, vomiting, writhing movements

Generic name:

TEMAZEPAM

See Restoril, page 943.

Brand name:

TEMOVATE

Pronounced: TIM-oh-vate
Generic name: Clobetasol propionate

Why is this drug prescribed?
Temovate relieves the itching and inflammation of moderate to severe skin conditions. Temovate Scalp Application is used for short-term treatment of scalp conditions; Temovate Cream and Ointment and the super-high potency Emollient Cream and Gel are used for short-term treatment of skin conditions on the body. Temovate is a steroid medication for external use only.

Most important fact about this drug
When you use Temovate, you inevitably absorb some of the medication through your skin and into the bloodstream. Too much absorption can lead to unwanted side effects elsewhere in the body. To keep this problem to a minimum, avoid using large amounts of Temovate over large areas, and do not cover it with airtight dressings such as plastic wrap or adhesive bandages unless specifically told to by your doctor.

How should you use this medication?
Use Temovate exactly as directed by your doctor. Remember to avoid covering or bandaging the affected area.

Temovate is for use only on the skin. Be careful to keep it out of your eyes.

A thin layer of cream or ointment should be gently rubbed into the affected area.

■ *If you miss a dose...*
   Apply it as soon as you remember. If it is almost time for the next dose, skip the one you missed and go back to your regular schedule.

■ *Storage instructions...*
Store at room temperature. Do not refrigerate the creams or the gel.

What side effects may occur?
Side effects cannot be anticipated. If any develop or change in intensity, inform your doctor as soon as possible. Only your doctor can determine if it is safe for you to continue using Temovate. This medication is generally well tolerated when used for 2 weeks. However, some side effects have been reported at the affected area.

CREAMS, OINTMENT, GEL

■ *Side effects are infrequent but may include:*
Burning
Cracking/fissuring
Irritation
Itching
Numbness of fingers
Patches
Reddened skin
Shrinking of the skin
Stinging

SCALP APPLICATION

■ *More frequent side effects may include:*
Burning
Stinging

■ *Less frequent side effects may include:*
Eye irritation, hair loss, headache, inflammation, itching, tenderness and/or tightness of the scalp

These additional side effects have been known to result from use of topical steroids and may be particularly apt to occur with the super-high potency Emollient Cream and Gel: acne, allergic skin inflammation, dryness, excessive hair growth, infection, inflammation around the mouth, loss of skin color, prickly heat, skin softening, streaking.

Why should this drug not be prescribed?
All forms of Temovate should be avoided if you are sensitive to or have ever had an allergic reaction to clobetasol propionate, other corticosteroids such as Valisone and Topicort, or any of their ingredients. Temovate Scalp Application should not be used if you have a scalp infection.

Special warnings about this medication

Temovate is a strong corticosteroid that can be absorbed into the bloodstream. It has caused Cushing's syndrome (a disorder characterized by a moon-shaped face, emotional disturbances, high blood pressure, weight gain, and, in women, abnormal growth of facial and body hair) and changes in blood sugar.

This medication should not be used for any condition other than the one for which it was prescribed.

Temovate should not be used by children under 12 years of age.

Treatment should not last for more than 2 weeks.

If you are being scheduled for surgery, let your doctor know you are using Temovate.

Possible food and drug interactions
when using this medication

No interactions have been reported.

Special information
if you are pregnant or breastfeeding

Although Temovate is applied to the skin, there is no way of knowing how much medication is absorbed into the bloodstream. Strong corticosteroids have caused birth defects in animals. Temovate, a strong corticosteroid, should be used only if the potential benefits outweigh the potential risks to the unborn baby; limit use to small amounts, on a limited area, for a short period of time. It is not known whether topical steroids are absorbed in sufficient amounts to appear in breast milk. If Temovate is essential to your health, your doctor may advise you to stop breastfeeding until your treatment with the medication is finished.

Recommended dosage

ADULTS AND CHILDREN 12 YEARS AND OLDER

Apply the medication to the affected area 2 times a day, once in the morning and once at night. Treatment should not last for more than 2 consecutive weeks, and the affected area should not be covered with a bandage. No more than 50 grams per week (approximately one large tube or bottle) should be used.

Overdosage

When absorbed into the bloodstream over a prolonged period, Temovate can cause disorders such as Cushing's syndrome. If you suspect an overdose of Temovate, seek medical attention immediately.

Brand name:

TENEX

Pronounced: TEN-ex
Generic name: Guanfacine hydrochloride

Why is this drug prescribed?
Tenex is given to help control high blood pressure. This medication reduces nerve impulses to the heart and arteries; this slows the heartbeat, relaxes the blood vessels, and thus reduces blood pressure. Tenex may be given alone or in combination with other high blood pressure medications, especially thiazide diuretics, such as Diuril, Esidrix, or Naturetin.

Most important fact about this drug
You must take Tenex regularly for it to be effective. Since blood pressure declines gradually, it may be several weeks before you get the full benefit of Tenex; and you must continue taking it even if you are feeling well. Tenex does not cure high blood pressure; it merely keeps it under control.

How should you take this medication?
Take Tenex exactly as prescribed by your doctor—usually 1 dose per day. Tenex should be taken at bedtime, since it will probably cause drowsiness.

After 3 or 4 weeks, if your blood pressure is still too high, your doctor may raise the dosage of Tenex. In some cases, you may take 2 evenly spaced doses per day rather than a single dose at bedtime.

- *If you miss a dose...*
  Take the forgotten does as soon as you remember. This will help to keep the proper amount of medicine in your body. However, if it is almost time for the next dose, skip the one you missed and go back to your regular schedule. Never try to "catch up" by doubling the dose. If you miss taking Tenex for 2 or more days in a row, check with your doctor.

- *Storage instructions...*
  Store Tenex at room temperature. Use the container it came in.

What side effects may occur?
Side effects cannot be anticipated. If any develop or change in intensity, inform your doctor as soon as possible. Only your doctor can determine whether it is safe for you to continue taking Tenex. This medication will probably make you drowsy, especially when you first begin to take it.

■ *More common side effects may include:*
Constipation
Dizziness
Dry mouth
Fatigue
Headache
Impotence
Sleepiness
Weakness

■ *Less common or rare side effects may include:*
Abdominal pain, amnesia, breathing difficulties, chest pain, confusion, conjunctivitis (red, puffy eyes), decreased sex drive, depression, diarrhea, difficulty swallowing, fainting, heart palpitations, indigestion, insomnia, itching, leg cramps, malaise (vague feeling of being sick), nausea, numbness or tingling of the skin, purplish spots on the skin, rash and peeling, ringing in the ears, "runny" nose, skin inflammation, slow heartbeat, stuffy nose, sweating, taste alterations, upset stomach, urinary incontinence, vision disturbance

Some of these side effects may lessen or disappear as your body gets used to Tenex.

Why should this drug not be prescribed?
Do not take Tenex if you are sensitive to it or have ever had an allergic reaction to it.

Tenex is not recommended for controlling the severe high blood pressure that accompanies toxemia of pregnancy (a disorder of pregnant women characterized by a rise in blood pressure, swelling, and leakage of protein into urine).

Special warnings about this medication
While taking Tenex, you should be monitored very closely by your doctor if you have any of the following medical conditions:

Chronic kidney or liver failure
Heart disease
History of stroke
Recent heart attack

Since Tenex causes drowsiness and may also make you dizzy, do not drive, climb, or perform hazardous tasks until you find out exactly how the medication affects you.

While taking Tenex, use alcoholic beverages with care; you may feel intoxicated after drinking only a small amount of alcohol.

If you have kidney damage and also take the antiseizure drug phenytoin (Dilantin), your body may process and eliminate Tenex rather quickly; in that case, you may need fairly frequent doses of Tenex to lower your blood pressure adequately.

If you have been taking Tenex for a while, do not stop taking it without consulting your doctor. Discontinuing abruptly may result in nervousness, rapid pulse, anxiety, heartbeat irregularities, and so-called rebound high blood pressure (higher than before you started taking Tenex). If you do have rebound high blood pressure, it will probably develop 2 to 4 days after your last dose of Tenex. Rebound high blood pressure, if it occurs, will usually diminish and then disappear over a period of 2 to 4 days.

Possible food and drug interactions
when taking this medication

If Tenex is taken with certain other drugs, the effects of either could be increased, decreased, or altered. It is especially important to check with your doctor before combining Tenex with the following:

Barbiturates such as Amytal, Seconal, Tuinal, and others
Benzodiazepines such as Tranxene, Valium, Xanax, and others
Phenothiazines such as Mellaril, Stelazine, Thorazine, and others
Phenytoin (Dilantin)

Special information
if you are pregnant or breastfeeding

If you are pregnant or plan to become pregnant, notify your doctor immediately. Tenex should be taken during pregnancy only if clearly needed. It is not known whether Tenex appears in breast milk. Check with your doctor if you plan to breastfeed.

Recommended dosage

ADULTS

The usual recommended dose of Tenex is 1 milligram daily, taken at bedtime. If necessary, after 3 to 4 weeks your doctor may increase the daily dosage to 2 milligrams.

CHILDREN

The safety and effectiveness of Tenex have not been established in children under 12 years of age.

Overdosage

Any medication taken in excess can have serious consequences. If you suspect an overdose of Tenex, seek medical attention immediately.

■ *Symptoms of Tenex overdose may include:*
Drowsiness
Lethargy
Slowed heartbeat
Very low blood pressure

Brand name:

TEN-K

See Micro-K, page 658.

Brand name:

TENORETIC

Pronounced: Ten-or-ET-ic
Generic ingredients: Atenolol, Chlorthalidone

Why is this drug prescribed?

Tenoretic is used in the treatment of high blood pressure. It combines a beta-blocker drug and a diuretic. Tenoretic can be used alone or in combination with other high blood pressure medications. Atenolol, the beta blocker, decreases the force and rate of heart contractions. Chlorthalidone, the diuretic, helps your body produce and eliminate more urine, which helps in lowering blood pressure.

Most important fact about this drug

You must take Tenoretic regularly for it to be effective. Since blood pressure declines gradually, it may be several weeks before you get the full benefit of Tenoretic; and you must continue taking it even if you are feeling well. Tenoretic does not cure high blood pressure; it merely keeps it under control.

How should you take this medication?

Tenoretic can be taken with or without food.

Take this medication exactly as prescribed by your doctor, even if your symptoms have disappeared.

Try not to miss any doses. If this medication is not taken regularly, your condition may worsen.

■ *If you miss a dose...*
Take the forgotten dose as soon as you remember. If it's within 8 hours of your next scheduled dose, skip the one you missed and go back to your regular schedule. Never take 2 doses at the same time.

■ *Storage instructions...*
Store Tenoretic at room temperature in the container it came in.

What side effects may occur?
Side effects cannot be anticipated. If any develop or change in intensity, inform your doctor as soon as possible. Only your doctor can determine if it is safe for you to continue taking Tenoretic.

■ *More common side effects may include:*
Dizziness, fatigue, nausea, slow heartbeat

■ *Less common or rare side effects may include:*
Blood disorders, constipation, cramping, decreased sexual ability, depression, diarrhea, difficult or labored breathing, dizziness when getting up, drowsiness, excessive thirst, hair loss, headache, high blood sugar, hives, impotence, light-headedness, loss of appetite, low potassium leading to symptoms like dry mouth, muscle pain or cramps, muscle spasm, Peyronie's disease (deformity of the penis), psoriasis-like rash, rash, reddish or purplish spots on skin, restlessness, skin sensitivity to light, sluggishness or unresponsiveness, stomach irritation, sugar in the urine, tingling or pins and needles, tiredness, vertigo, visual disturbances, vomiting, weak or irregular heartbeat, weakness, worsening of psoriasis, yellow eyes and skin

Why should this drug not be prescribed?
If you have a slow heartbeat; a history of serious heart block (conduction disorder); inadequate blood supply to the circulatory system (cardiogenic shock); heart failure; or inability to urinate; or if you are sensitive to or have ever had an allergic reaction to Tenoretic, its ingredients or similar drugs, or to other sulfonamide-derived drugs, you should not take this medication.

Special warnings about this medication
If you have a history of congestive heart failure, Tenoretic should be used with caution.

Tenoretic should not be stopped suddenly. It can cause increased chest pain and heart attack. When stopping the drug, your physician will gradually reduce your dosage.

When taking Tenoretic, if you suffer from asthma, seasonal allergies or other bronchial conditions, or liver or kidney disease, your doctor should monitor you more carefully.

Ask your doctor if you should check your pulse while taking Tenoretic. This medication can cause your heartbeat to become too slow.

This medication may mask the symptoms of low blood sugar or alter blood sugar levels. If you are diabetic, discuss this with your doctor.

Tenoretic can cause you to become drowsy or less alert; therefore, activity that requires full mental alertness is not recommended until you know how you respond to the drug.

Make sure the doctor knows that you are taking Tenoretic if you have a medical emergency, or plan to have surgery.

Possible food and drug interactions
when taking this medication
If Tenoretic is taken with certain other drugs, the effects of either could be increased, decreased, or altered. It is especially important to check with your doctor before combining Tenoretic with the following:

Blood pressure medicines containing reserpine
Clonidine (Catapres)
Epinephrine (EpiPen)
Insulin
Lithium(Eskalith)
Nasal decongestants
Other blood pressure drugs

Special information
if you are pregnant or breastfeeding
When taken during pregnancy, Tenoretic may cause harm to the developing baby. If you are pregnant, or plan to become pregnant, inform your doctor immediately. Tenoretic appears in breast milk and could affect a nursing infant. If this medication is essential to your health, your doctor may advise you to discontinue breastfeeding until your treatment with this medication is finished.

Recommended dosage

ADULTS

Dosage is always individualized.

The usual starting dosage is 1 Tenoretic 50 tablet taken once a day. Your doctor may increase the dosage to 1 Tenoretic 100 tablet taken once a day. Your doctor may gradually add other high blood pressure medications.

Your doctor will adjust your dosage if your kidney function is impaired.

CHILDREN

The safety and effectiveness of Tenoretic have not been established in children.

Overdosage

Any medication taken in excess can have serious consequences. If you suspect an overdose, seek medical attention immediately.

- *No specific information on Tenoretic is available, but common symptoms of overdose with the drug's atenolol component are:*
  Bronchospasm
  Congestive heart failure
  Low blood pressure
  Low blood sugar
  Slow heartbeat
  Sluggishness
  Wheezing

- *Symptoms of overdose with the chlorthalidone component include:*
  Dizziness
  Nausea
  Weakness

Brand name:

TENORMIN

Pronounced: Ten-OR-min
Generic name: Atenolol

Why is this drug prescribed?

Tenormin, a type of medication known as a beta blocker, is used in the treatment of high blood pressure, angina pectoris (chest pain, usually caused by lack of oxygen to the heart due to clogged arteries), and heart attack. When used for high blood pressure, it is effective alone or combined with other high blood pressure medications, particularly with a thiazide-type diuretic. Beta blockers decrease the force and rate of heart contractions.

Occasionally doctors prescribe Tenormin for treatment of alcohol withdrawal, prevention of migraine headache, and bouts of anxiety.

Most important fact about this drug
If you have high blood pressure, you must take Tenormin regularly for it to be effective. Since blood pressure declines gradually, it may be several weeks before you get the full benefit of Tenormin; and you must continue taking it even if you are feeling well. Tenormin does not cure high blood pressure; it merely keeps it under control.

How should you take this medication?
Tenormin can be taken with or without food. Take it exactly as prescribed, even if your symptoms have disappeared.

Try not to miss any doses, especially if you are taking Tenormin once a day. If this medication is not taken regularly, your condition may worsen.

- *If you miss a dose...*
  Take the forgotten dose as soon as you remember. If it's within 8 hours of your next scheduled dose, skip the one you missed and go back to your regular schedule. Never take 2 doses at the same time.

- *Storage instructions...*
  Store Tenormin at room temperature; protect from light.

What side effects may occur?
Side effects cannot be anticipated. If any develop or change in intensity, inform your doctor as soon as possible. Only your doctor can determine if it is safe for you to continue taking Tenormin.

- *More common side effects may include:*
  Dizziness
  Fatigue
  Nausea
  Slow heartbeat

- *Less common or rare side effects may include:*
  Depression, diarrhea, difficult or labored breathing, dizziness upon standing up, drowsiness, headache, heart failure, impotence, light-headedness, low

blood pressure, penile deformity, psoriasis-like rash, red or purple spots on the skin, rapid heartbeat, slow heartbeat, sluggishness, temporary hair loss, tiredness, vertigo, wheezing, worsening of psoriasis

Why should this drug not be prescribed?

If you have heart failure, inadequate blood supply to the circulatory system (cardiogenic shock), heart block (conduction disorder), or a severely slow heartbeat, you should not take this medication.

Special warnings about this medication

If you have a history of severe congestive heart failure, Tenormin should be used with caution.

Tenormin should not be stopped suddenly. It can cause increased chest pain and heart attack. Dosage should be gradually reduced.

If you suffer from asthma, seasonal allergies, or other bronchial conditions, coronary artery disease or kidney disease, this medication should be used with caution.

Ask your doctor if you should check your pulse while taking Tenormin. This medication can cause your heartbeat to become too slow.

This medication may mask the symptoms of low blood sugar or alter blood sugar levels. If you are diabetic, discuss this with your doctor.

Notify your doctor or dentist that you are taking Tenormin if you have a medical emergency, and before you have surgery or dental surgery.

Tenormin may cause harm to a developing baby when taken during pregnancy. If you are pregnant or become pregnant while taking this medication, inform your doctor immediately.

Possible food and drug interactions
when taking this medication

If Tenormin is taken with certain other drugs, the effects of either could be increased, decreased, or altered. It is especially important to check with your doctor before combining Tenormin with the following:

Ampicillin (Omnipen, others)
Calcium-containing antacids such as Tums
Calcium-blocking blood pressure drugs such as Calan and Cardizem
Certain blood pressure drugs such as reserpine (Diupress)
Clonidine (Catapres)
Epinephrine (EpiPen)
Insulin

Oral diabetes drugs such as Micronase
Quinidine (Quinidex)

Special information
if you are pregnant or breastfeeding

The use of Tenormin during pregnancy may cause harm to a developing baby. If you are pregnant, become pregnant, or plan to become pregnant, inform your doctor immediately. Tenormin appears in breast milk and could affect a nursing infant. If this medication is essential to your health, your doctor may advise you to discontinue breastfeeding until your treatment is finished.

Recommended dosage

ADULTS

Hypertension

The usual starting dose is 50 milligrams a day in 1 dose, alone or with a diuretic. Full effects should be seen in 1 to 2 weeks. Dosage may be increased to a maximum of 100 milligrams per day in one dose. Your doctor can and may use this medication with other high blood pressure medications.

Angina Pectoris

The usual starting dose is 50 milligrams in 1 dose a day. Full effects should be seen in 1 week. Dosage may be increased to a maximum of 100 milligrams per day. In some cases, a single dose of 200 milligrams per day may be given. Dosage will be individualized by your doctor.

Heart Attack

This medication may be used in the acute treatment of heart attack in both injectable and tablet form. Your doctor will determine the proper dosage.

CHILDREN

The safety and effectiveness of Tenormin have not been established in children.

ELDERLY

The doctor will determine the dosage for an elderly individual, according to his or her needs, especially in the case of reduced kidney function.

Overdosage

Any medication taken in excess can have serious consequences. If you suspect an overdose, seek medical attention immediately.

- *Symptoms of Tenormin overdose may include:*
  Bronchospasm
  Changes in breathing
  Congestive heart failure
  Low blood pressure
  Low blood sugar
  Slow heartbeat
  Sluggishness
  Wheezing

Brand name:

TENUATE

Pronounced: TEN-you-ate
Generic name: Diethylpropion hydrochloride

Why is this drug prescribed?
Tenuate, an appetite suppressant, is prescribed for short-term use (a few weeks) as part of an overall diet plan for weight reduction. It is available in two forms: immediate-release tablets (Tenuate) and controlled-release tablets (Tenuate Dospan). Tenuate should be used with a behavior modification program.

Most important fact about this drug
Tenuate will lose its effectiveness within a few weeks. When this begins to happen, you should discontinue the medicine rather than increase the dosage.

How should you take this medication?
Take this medication exactly as prescribed. Tenuate may be habit-forming and can be addicting.

If you are taking Tenuate Dospan (the controlled release formulation), do not crush or chew the tablets. Swallow the medication whole.

- *If you miss a dose...*
  If you are taking the immediate-release form of Tenuate, go back to your regular schedule at the next meal.

  If you are taking Tenuate Dospan, take the missed dose as soon as you remember. If you do not remember until the next day, skip the dose. Never take 2 doses at once.

■ *Storage instructions...*
Store at room temperature in a tightly closed container. Protect from excessive heat.

What side effects may occur?
Side effects cannot be anticipated. If any develop or change in intensity, inform your doctor as soon as possible. Only your doctor can determine if it is safe for you to continue using Tenuate.

■ *Side effects may include:*
Abdominal discomfort, abnormal redness of the skin, anxiety, blood pressure elevation, blurred vision, breast development in males, bruising, changes in sex drive, chest pain, constipation, depression, diarrhea, difficulty with voluntary movements, dizziness, drowsiness, dryness of the mouth, feelings of discomfort, feelings of elation, feeling of illness, hair loss, headache, hives, impotence, inability to fall or stay asleep, increased heart rate, increased seizures in epileptics, increased sweating, increased volume of diluted urine, irregular heartbeat, jitteriness, menstrual upset, muscle pain, nausea, nervousness, overstimulation, painful urination, palpitations, pupil dilation, rash, restlessness, shortness of breath or labored breathing, stomach and intestinal disturbances, tremors, unpleasant taste, vomiting

Why should this drug not be prescribed?
If you are sensitive to or have ever had an allergic reaction to Tenuate or other appetite suppressants, you should not take this medication. Make sure your doctor is aware of any drug reactions you have experienced.

Do not take this drug if you have severe hardening of the arteries, an overactive thyroid, glaucoma, or severe high blood pressure, or if you are agitated, have a history of drug abuse or are taking an MAO inhibitor (antidepressant drug such as Nardil) or have taken one within the last 14 days.

Special warnings about this medication
Tenuate or Tenuate Dospan may impair your ability to engage in potentially hazardous activities. Therefore, make sure you know how you react to this medication before you drive, operate dangerous machinery, or do anything else that requires alertness or concentration.

If you have heart disease or high blood pressure, use caution when taking this medication.

This drug may increase convulsions in some epileptics. Your doctor should monitor you carefully if you have epilepsy.

Psychological dependence has occurred while taking this drug. Talk with your doctor if you find you are relying on this drug to maintain a state of well-being.

The abrupt withdrawal of this medication following prolonged use at high doses may result in extreme fatigue, mental depression, and sleep disturbances.

Possible food and drug interactions
when taking this medication
Tenuate or Tenuate Dospan may interact with alcohol unfavorably. Do not drink alcohol while taking this medication.

If Tenuate or Tenuate Dospan is taken with certain other drugs, the effects of either could be increased, decreased, or altered. It is especially important that you consult your doctor before combining Tenuate with the following:

Blood pressure medications such as Ismelin
Insulin
Phenothiazine drugs such as the major tranquilizer Thorazine

Special information
if you are pregnant or breastfeeding
The effects of Tenuate or Tenuate Dospan during pregnancy have not been adequately studied. If you are pregnant or plan to become pregnant, inform your doctor immediately. This drug appears in breast milk. If the medication is essential to your health, your doctor may advise you to discontinue breastfeeding until your treatment is finished.

Recommended dosage

ADULTS

Tenuate Immediate-Release
The usual dosage is one 25-milligram tablet taken 3 times a day, 1 hour before meals; you may take 1 tablet in the middle of the evening, if you want, to overcome night hunger.

Tenuate Dospan Controlled-Release
The usual dosage is one 75-milligram tablet taken once daily, swallowed whole, in midmorning.

CHILDREN

Safety and effectiveness have not been established in children below 12 years of age.

Overdosage

Any medication taken in excess can have serious consequences. If you suspect an overdose, seek emergency medical treatment immediately.

■ *Symptoms of Tenuate overdose may include:*
Abdominal cramps, assaultiveness, confusion, depression, diarrhea, elevated blood pressure, fatigue, hallucinations, irregular heartbeat, lowered blood pressure, nausea, overreactive reflexes, panic state, rapid breathing, restlessness, tremors, vomiting

Brand name:

TERAZOL 3

Pronounced: TER-uh-zawl
Generic name: Terconazole

Why is this drug prescribed?

Terazol 3 Vaginal Cream and Suppositories are prescribed to treat candidiasis (a yeast-like fungal infection) of the vulva and vagina.

Most important fact about this drug

Keep using Terazol 3 for the full time of treatment, even if the infection seems to have disappeared. If you stop too soon, the infection could return. You should continue using this medicine during your menstrual period.

How should you use this medication?

Follow these steps to apply Terazol 3:

1. Load the applicator to the fill line with cream, or unwrap a suppository, wet it with warm water, and place it in the applicator as shown in the instructions you received with the product.
2. Lie on your back with knees drawn up.
3. Gently insert the applicator high into the vagina and push the plunger.
4. Withdraw the applicator and wash with soap and water.

To protect your clothing, wear a sanitary napkin. Do not use tampons, because they will absorb the medicine. Wear cotton underwear—avoid synthetic fabrics such as rayon or nylon. Do not douche unless your doctor tells you to do so.

Dry the genital area thoroughly after a shower, bath, or swim. Change out of a wet bathing suit or damp workout clothes as soon as possible. Moisture encourages the growth of yeast.

Try not to scratch. It can cause more irritation and can spread the infection.

■ *If you miss a dose...*
  Apply it as soon as you remember. If it is almost time for your next dose, skip the one you missed and go back to your regular schedule.

■ *Storage instructions...*
  Store at room temperature.

What side effects may occur?
Side effects cannot be anticipated. If any develop or change in intensity, inform your doctor as soon as possible. Only your doctor can determine if it is safe for you to continue using Terazol 3.

■ *More common side effects may include:*
  Body pain
  Burning
  Genital pain
  Headache
  Menstrual pain

■ *Less common side effects may include:*
  Abdominal pain, chills, fever, itching

Why should this drug not be prescribed?
If you have ever had an allergic reaction to or are sensitive to terconazole or any other ingredients of Terazol 3, you should not use this medication. Make sure your doctor is aware of any drug reactions you have experienced.

Special warnings about this medication
If irritation, an allergic reaction, fever, chills, or flu-like symptoms develop while using this medication, notify your doctor.

To avoid re-infection while using Terazol 3, either avoid sexual intercourse or make sure your partner uses a non-latex condom.

Terazol 3 suppositories can interact with latex products such as diaphragms and certain type of condoms. Use some other method of birth control while you are taking Terazol 3.

**Possible food and drug interactions
when taking this medication**
No interactions have been reported.

**Special information
if you are pregnant or breastfeeding**
Since Terazol 3 is absorbed from the vagina, it should not be used during the first trimester (first 3 months) of pregnancy unless your doctor considers it essential to your health. It is not known whether this drug appears in breast milk. Your doctor may advise you to discontinue breastfeeding your baby while using this medication.

Recommended dosage

ADULTS

Terazol 3 Vaginal Cream
The recommended dose is 1 full applicator (5 grams) of cream inserted into the vagina once daily at bedtime for 3 consecutive days.

Terazol 3 Vaginal Suppositories
The recommended dose is 1 suppository inserted into the vagina once daily at bedtime for 3 consecutive days.

CHILDREN

Safety and effectiveness have not been established in children.

Overdosage
There has been no reported overdose of this medication. Any medication used in excess, however, can have serious consequences. If you suspect an overdose of Terazol 3, seek medical attention immediately.

Generic name:

TERAZOSIN

See Hytrin, page 500.

Generic name:

TERBUTALINE

See Brethine, page 133.

Generic name:

TERCONAZOLE

See Terazol 3, page 1097.

Generic name:

TERFENADINE

See Seldane, page 1006.

Brand name:

TESSALON

Pronounced: TESS-ah-lon
Generic name: Benzonatate

Why is this drug prescribed?
Tessalon is taken for relief of a cough.

Most important fact about this drug
Tessalon should be swallowed whole, not chewed.

How should you take this medication?
Tessalon perles (soft capsule form) should be swallowed whole. If chewed, they can produce a temporary numbness of the mouth and throat that could cause choking or a severe allergic reaction.

■ *If you miss a dose...*
Take the forgotten dose as soon as you remember. If it is almost time for your next dose, skip the one you missed and go back to your regular schedule. Never double the dose.

■ *Storage instructions...*
Store Tessalon at room temperature.

What side effects may occur?
Side effects cannot be anticipated. If any occur or change in intensity, inform your doctor as soon as possible. Only your doctor can determine if it is safe to continue taking Tessalon.

■ *Side effects may include:*
Allergic reactions, burning sensation in the eyes, constipation, dizziness, extreme calm (sedation), headache, itching, mental confusion, nausea, numbness in chest, skin eruptions, stuffy nose, upset stomach, vague "chilly" feeling, visual hallucinations

Why should this drug not be prescribed?
Tessalon should not be used if you are sensitive to or have ever had an allergic reaction to benzonatate or similar drugs (such as local anesthetics).

Special warnings about this medication
Remember to swallow Tessalon perles whole.

Possible food and drug interactions
when taking this medication
There have been rare occurrences of bizarre behavior, including confusion and visual hallucinations, when Tessalon is taken with other prescribed drugs. Check with your doctor before taking Tessalon with other medications.

Special information
if you are pregnant or breastfeeding
The effects of Tessalon during pregnancy have not been studied adequately. Tessalon should be used during pregnancy only if clearly needed. If you are pregnant or plan to become pregnant, notify your doctor immediately. It is unknown if Tessalon appears in breast milk and could affect a nursing infant. If this medication is essential to your health, your doctor may advise you to stop breastfeeding until your treatment with Tessalon ends.

Recommended dosage

CHILDREN OVER AGE 10 AND ADULTS

The usual dose is a 100-milligram perle 3 times per day, as needed. The maximum dose is 600 milligrams, or 6 perles, a day.

Overdosage
If capsules are chewed or allowed to dissolve in the mouth, numbness of the

mouth and throat will develop rapidly. Symptoms of restlessness and tremors may be followed by convulsions.

If you suspect a Tessalon overdose, seek medical attention immediately.

Generic name:

TETRACYCLINE

See Achromycin V Capsules, page 8.

Brand name:

THALITONE

See Hygroton, page 496.

Brand name:

THEOCHRON

See Theo-Dur, page 1102.

Brand name:

THEO-DUR

Pronounced: THEE-a-door
Generic name: Theophylline
Other brand names: Quibron T/SR, T-Phyl, Theochron

Why is this drug prescribed?

Theo-Dur, an oral bronchodilator medication, is given to prevent or relieve symptoms of asthma, chronic bronchitis, and emphysema. The active ingredient of Theo-Dur, theophylline, is a chemical cousin of caffeine. It opens the airways by relaxing the smooth muscle that lines the tubes and blood vessels in the lungs.

Most important fact about this drug

Theo-Dur is a controlled-release medication. For an acute attack you should take an immediate-release medication instead of more Theo-Dur. If you develop *status asthmaticus* (a severe breathing difficulty that does not clear up with your usual medications), do not take extra Theo-Dur; instead, seek medical treatment immediately. Since even a little extra Theo-Dur may constitute an overdose, you should be treated in a place where close monitoring is possible.

Individual doses are determined by a patient's response (a decrease in symptoms of asthma). In order to avoid overdosing or underdosing, your doctor will perform regular tests to determine the amount of Theo-Dur in your bloodstream.

You should not change from Theo-Dur to another brand without first consulting your doctor or pharmacist. Products manufactured by different companies may not be equally effective.

How should you take this medication?
Take Theo-Dur exactly as prescribed by your doctor.

This drug is available in two forms. The extended-release tablets should be swallowed whole, not crushed or chewed. You may take the tablets with or without food. If you are taking them on a once-a-day basis, do not take the dose at night.

The other form, Theo-Dur Sprinkle sustained-action capsules, must be taken either 1 hour before or 2 hours after a meal. You may take the capsule whole or open it and empty the contents onto a spoonful of food that is soft but not hot. Without chewing, immediately swallow the spoonful of food and follow it with a glass of cool water or juice. Always take the complete contents of the capsule.

When taking Theo-Dur, you should avoid large amounts of caffeine-containing beverages, such as tea or coffee.

■ *If you miss a dose...*
Take it as soon as you remember. If it is almost time for your nest dose, skip the one you missed and go back to your regular schedule. Never take 2 doses at the same time.

■ *Storage instructions...*
Store at room temperature. Keep the container tightly closed. Make sure this medicine is kept out of reach of children.

What side effects may occur?
Side effects from Theo-Dur cannot be anticipated. Nausea and restlessness may occur when you first start to take Theo-Dur, but will probably disappear as your body becomes used to the drug. If side effects persist, see your doctor; the dosage may be too high.

■ *Other side effects may include:*
Convulsions, diarrhea, disturbances of heart rhythm, excitability, flushing, frequent urination, hair loss, headache, heart palpitations, high blood sugar, irritability, low blood pressure, muscle twitching, nausea, rapid breathing, rapid heartbeat, rash, restlessness, sleeplessness, stomach pain, vomiting, vomiting blood

Theo-Dur may cause or worsen heartbeat abnormalities. While you are taking this medication, any significant change in your heart rate or rhythm should be investigated promptly and thoroughly.

Why should this drug not be prescribed?
Do not take Theo-Dur if you are sensitive to it or have ever had an allergic reaction to it.

Do not take Theo-Dur if you have an active peptic ulcer. If you have epilepsy, you should be taking the correct dosage of antiseizure medication when you start treatment with Theo-Dur.

Special warnings about this medication
If you are a smoker, your body will tend to process and get rid of Theo-Dur rather quickly; thus, you may need to take more frequent doses than a nonsmoker. Even if you quit smoking, this quick-clearance effect may linger for 6 months to 2 years.

You should take Theo-Dur cautiously and under close medical supervision if you are over 55, especially if you are a male with chronic lung disease.

You should also take Theo-Dur cautiously and under close supervision if you have had a sustained high fever, or if you have heart disease or liver failure, high blood pressure, low blood oxygen, alcoholism, or a history of stomach ulcers.

Possible food and drug interactions
when taking this medication
If Theo-Dur is taken with certain other drugs, the effects of either could be increased, decreased, or altered. It is especially important to check with your doctor before combining Theo-Dur with the following:

Allopurinol (Lopurin, Zyloprim)
Cimetidine (Tagamet)
Ciprofloxacin (Cipro)
Ephedrine (in medications such as Primatene, Tedral, and Rynatuss)
Erythromycin (E.E.S., ERYC, Erythrocin, and others)
Lithium carbonate (Eskalith, Lithobid, and others)

Oral contraceptive pills
Phenytoin (Dilantin)
Propranolol (Inderal)
Rifampin (Rifadin, Rifamate, Rimactane)
Troleandomycin (Tao)

Special information
if you are pregnant or breastfeeding

If you are pregnant or plan to become pregnant, inform your doctor immediately. Theo-Dur should not be taken during pregnancy unless it is clearly needed, and unless the benefits to the mother outweigh the potential risk to the developing child.

Theo-Dur does find its way into breast milk; it may make a nursing baby irritable or harm the baby in other ways. If you are a new mother, you will probably need to choose between breastfeeding and taking Theo-Dur.

Recommended dosage

ADULTS

Theo-Dur Extended Release Tablets

The usual initial dose is 1 Theo-Dur 200-milligram table every 12 hours. If this is not effective, your doctor will gradually increase the dose until you respond, up a maximum of 900 milligrams per day. Once you have adjusted to the medication, your doctor may be able to put you on a once-a-day dose schedule.

Theo-Dur Sprinkle

The usual initial dose is no more than 200 milligrams every 12 hours. If this is not effective, your doctor will gradually increase the dose until you respond, up to a maximum of 900 milligrams per day. If a dose every 12 hours is inconvenient, your doctor may divide the daily total into 3 small doses taken every 8 hours.

CHILDREN UNDER 16 YEARS OLD

Theo-Dur Extended Release Tablets

For children under 55 pounds, a liquid preparation is recommended to establish proper dosage before switching to Theo-Dur tablets. Maximum regular daily dosages are calculated by body weight as follows.

55 through 76 pounds—500 milligrams
77 through 154 pounds—600 milligrams

Theo-Dur Sprinkle
For children under 55 pounds, a liquid preparation is recommended to establish proper dosage before switching to Theo-Dur Sprinkle. Maximum regular daily dosages are calculated by body weight as follows:

Children 6 through 8—24 milligrams per 2.2 pounds
Children 9 through 11—20 milligrams per 2.2 pounds
Children 12 through 15—18 milligrams per 2.2 pounds

Overdosage
Most of the symptoms listed in the "side effects" section are actually caused by slight overdosage.

Be aware that a flu shot, or influenza itself, may make your usual dose of Theo-Dur act like an overdose. Consult your doctor if you anticipate getting a flu shot, or if you think you have the flu; you may need a temporary dosage reduction.

A mild overdose of Theo-Dur may cause nausea and restlessness. A larger overdose may not give any warning before causing serious heartbeat irregularities, convulsions, or even death. If at any time you suspect symptoms of an overdose of Theo-Dur, seek medical attention immediately.

Generic name:

THEOPHYLLINE

See Theo-Dur, page 1102.

Generic name:

THERAGRAN

See Multivitamins, page 693.

Brand name:

THEROXIDE

See Desquam-E, page 308.

Generic name:

THIORIDAZINE

See Mellaril, page 640.

Generic name:

THIOTHIXENE

See Navane, page 713.

Brand name:

THORAZINE

Pronounced: THOR-ah-zeen
Generic name: Chlorpromazine

Why is this drug prescribed?

Thorazine is used for the reduction of symptoms of psychotic disorders such as schizophrenia; for the short-term treatment of severe behavioral disorders in children, including explosive hyperactivity and combativeness; and for the hyperenergetic phase of manic-depressive illness (severely exaggerated moods).

Thorazine is also used to control nausea and vomiting, and to relieve restlessness and apprehension before surgery. It is used as an aid in the treatment of tetanus, and is prescribed for uncontrollable hiccups and acute intermittent porphyria (attacks of severe abdominal pain sometimes accompanied by psychiatric disturbances, cramps in the arms and legs, and muscle weakness).

Most important fact about this drug

Thorazine may cause tardive dyskinesia—a condition marked by involuntary muscle spasms and twitches in the face and body. This condition may be permanent, and appears to be most common among the elderly, especially women. Ask your doctor for information about this possible risk.

How should you take this medication?

If taking Thorazine in a liquid concentrate form, you will need to dilute it with a liquid such as a carbonated beverage, coffee, fruit juice, milk, tea, tomato juice, or water. Puddings, soups, and other semisolid foods may also be used. Thorazine will taste best if it is diluted immediately prior to use. You should not take Thorazine with alcohol.

Do not take antacids such as Gelusil at the same time as Thorazine. Leave at least 1 to 2 hours between doses of the two drugs.

- *If you miss a dose...*
  If you take Thorazine once a day, take the dose you missed as soon as you remember. If you do not remember until the next day, skip the dose, then go back to your regular schedule.

  If you take more than 1 dose a day, take the one you missed as soon as you remember if it is within an hour or so of the scheduled time. If you do not remember until later, skip the dose, then go back to your regular schedule.

  Never take 2 doses at once.

- *Storage instructions...*
  Store away from heat, light, and moisture. Do not freeze the liquid. Since the liquid concentrate form of Thorazine is light-sensitive, it should be stored in a dark place, but it does not need to be refrigerated.

What side effects may occur?
Side effects cannot be anticipated. If any develop or change in intensity, inform your doctor as soon as possible. Only your doctor can determine if it is safe for you to continue taking Thorazine.

- *Side effects may include:*
  Abnormal secretion of milk, abnormalities in movement and posture, agitation, anemia, asthma, blood disorders, breast development in males, chewing movements, constipation, difficulty breathing, difficulty swallowing, dizziness, drooling drowsiness, dry mouth, ejaculation problems, eye problems causing fixed gaze, fainting, fever, flu-like symptoms, fluid accumulation and swelling, headache, heart attack, high or low blood sugar, hives, impotence, inability to urinate, inability to move or talk, increase of appetite, infections, insomnia, intestinal blockage, involuntary movements of arms and legs, tongue, face, mouth, or jaw, irregular blood pressure, pulse, and heartbeat, irregular or no menstrual periods, jitteriness, light-headedness (on standing up), lockjaw, mask-like face, muscle stiffness and rigidity, narrow or dilated pupils, nasal congestion, nausea, pain and stiffness in the neck, persistent, painful erections, pill-rolling motion, protruding tongue, puckering of the mouth, puffing of the cheeks, rapid heartbeat, red or purple spots on the skin, rigid arms, feet, head, and muscles (including the back), seizures, sensitivity to light, severe allergic reactions, shuffling walk, skin inflammation and peeling, sore throat, spasms in jaw, face, tongue, neck, mouth, and feet, sweating, swelling of breasts in women, swelling of the throat, tremors, twitching in the body, neck, shoulders and face, twisted neck, visual problems, weight gain, yellowed skin and whites of eyes

Why should this drug not be prescribed?

You should not be using Thorazine if you are taking substances that slow down mental function such as alcohol, barbiturates, or narcotics.

You should not take Thorazine if you have ever had an allergic reaction to any major tranquilizer containing phenothiazine.

Special warnings about this medication

You should use Thorazine cautiously if you have ever had: asthma; a brain tumor; breast cancer; intestinal blockage; emphysema; the eye condition known as glaucoma; heart, kidney, or liver disease; respiratory infections; seizures; or an abnormal bone marrow or blood condition; or if you are exposed to pesticides or extreme heat. Be aware that Thorazine can mask symptoms of brain tumor, intestinal blockage, and the neurological condition called Reye's syndrome.

Stomach inflammation, dizziness, nausea, vomiting, and tremors may result if you suddenly stop taking Thorazine. Follow your doctor's instructions closely when discontinuing Thorazine.

Thorazine can suppress the cough reflex; you may have trouble vomiting.

This drug may impair your ability to drive a car or operate potentially dangerous machinery. Do not participate in any activities that require full alertness if you are unsure about your ability.

This drug can increase your sensitivity to light. Avoid being out in the sun too long.

Thorazine can cause a group of symptoms called neuroleptic malignant syndrome, which can be fatal. Some symptoms are extremely high body temperature, rigid muscles, mental changes, irregular pulse or blood pressure, rapid heartbeat, sweating, and changes in heart rhythm.

If you are on Thorazine for prolonged therapy, you should see your doctor for regular evaluations, since side effects can get worse over time.

Possible food and drug interactions
when taking this medication

If Thorazine is taken with certain other drugs, the effects of either could be increased, decreased, or altered. It is especially important to check with your doctor before combining Thorazine with the following:

Anesthetics
Antacids such as Gelusil
Anticonvulsants such as Dilantin
Antispasmodic drugs such as Cogentin

Atropine (Donnatal)
Barbiturates such as phenobarbital
Blood-thinning drugs such as Coumadin
Captopril (Capoten)
Cimetidine (Tagamet)
Diuretics such as Dyazide
Epinephrine (EpiPen)
Guanethidine (Ismelin)
Lithium (Lithobid, Eskalith)
MAO inhibitors (antidepressants such as Nardil and Parnate)
Narcotics such as Percocet
Propranolol (Inderal)

Extreme drowsiness and other potentially serious effects can result if Thorazine is combined with alcohol and other mental depressants such as narcotic painkillers like Demerol.

Because Thorazine prevents vomiting, it can hide the signs and symptoms of overdose of other drugs.

Special information
if you are pregnant or breastfeeding
The effects of Thorazine during pregnancy have not been adequately studied. If you are pregnant or plan to become pregnant, notify your doctor.

Pregnant women should use Thorazine only if clearly needed. Thorazine appears in breast milk and may affect a nursing infant. If this medication is essential to your health, your doctor may advise you not to breastfeed until your treatment is finished.

Recommended dosage

ADULTS

Psychotic Disorders
Your doctor will gradually increase the dosage until symptoms are controlled. You may not see full improvement for weeks or even months.

Initial dosages may range from 30 to 75 milligrams daily. The amount is divided into equal doses and taken 3 or 4 times a day. If needed, your doctor may increase the dosage by 20 to 50 milligrams at semiweekly intervals.

Nausea and Vomiting
The usual tablet dosage is 10 to 25 milligrams, taken every 4 or 6 hours, as needed.

One 100-milligram suppository can be used every 6 to 8 hours.

Uncontrollable Hiccups
Dosages may range from 75 to 200 milligrams daily, divided into 3 or 4 equal doses.

Acute Intermittent Porphyria
Dosages may range from 75 to 200 milligrams daily, divided into 3 or 4 equal doses.

CHILDREN

Thorazine is generally not prescribed for children younger than 6 months.

Severe Behavior Problems, Nausea, and Vomiting
Dosages are based on the child's weight.

Oral: The daily dose is 0.25 milligram for each pound of the child's weight, taken every 4 to 6 hours, as needed.

Rectal: the usual dose is 0.5 milligram per pound of body weight, taken every 6 to 8 hours, as necessary.

ELDERLY

In general, elderly people take lower dosages of Thorazine, and any increase in dosage will be gradual. Because of a greater risk of low blood pressure, your doctor will watch you closely while you are taking Thorazine. Elderly people (especially elderly women) may be more susceptible to tardive dyskinesia—a possibly permanent condition characterized by involuntary muscle spasms and twitches in the face and body. Elderly people should consult their doctor for information about these potential risks.

Overdosage
Any medication taken in excess can have serious consequences. An overdose of Thorazine can be fatal. If you suspect an overdose, seek medical help immediately.

■ *Symptoms of Thorazine overdose may include:*
Agitation, coma, convulsions, difficulty breathing, difficulty swallowing, dry mouth, extreme sleepiness, fever, intestinal blockage, irregular heart rate, low blood pressure, restlessness

Generic name:

THYROID HORMONES

See Armour Thyroid, page 71.

Brand name:

TIGAN

Pronounced: TIE-gan
Generic name: Trimethobenzamide hydrochloride

Why is this drug prescribed?
Tigan is prescribed to control nausea and vomiting.

Most important fact about this drug
Antiemetics (drugs that prevent or lessen nausea and vomiting) are not recommended for the treatment of simple vomiting in children. Use of Tigan in children should be limited to prolonged vomiting caused by a known disease.

Caution should always be exercised when using this drug in children, since there may be a link between the use of antiemetic drugs to treat symptoms of viral illnesses such as chickenpox and the development of Reye's syndrome, which is a potentially fatal childhood disease of the brain.

How should you take this medication?
Take this medication exactly as prescribed.

If you are using the suppository form of Tigan and find it is too soft to insert, you can firm it up by chilling it in the refrigerator for about 30 minutes or running cold water over it before removing the wrapper.

To insert a suppository, first remove the wrapper and moisten the suppository with cold water. Then lie down on your side and use a finger to push the suppository well up into the rectum.

- *If you miss a dose...*
  Take it as soon as you remember. If it is almost time for your next dose, skip the one you missed and go back to your regular schedule. Do not take 2 doses at once.

- *Storage instructions...*
  Store away from heat, light, and moisture.

What side effects may occur?
Side effects cannot be anticipated. If any develop or change in intensity, inform your doctor as soon as possible. Only your doctor can determine if it is safe for you to continue taking Tigan.

- *Side effects may include:*
  Allergic-type skin reactions, blurred vision, coma, convulsions, depression, diarrhea, disorientation, dizziness, drowsiness, headache, muscle cramps, severe muscle spasm, tremors, yellowed eyes and skin

Why should this drug not be prescribed?
If you are sensitive to or have ever had an allergic reaction to Tigan, do not take this medication. Do not use the suppositories if you are allergic to benzocaine or other local anesthetics. Make sure your doctor is aware of any drug reactions you have experienced.

Unless you are directed to do so by your doctor, do not use suppositories in premature or newborn infants.

Special warnings about this medication
Tigan may cause you to become drowsy or less alert. Do not drive or operate dangerous machinery or participate in any hazardous activity that requires full mental alertness until you know how you respond to this drug.

Reye's syndrome has been associated with the use of Tigan during viral illnesses in children. Reye's syndrome is characterized by severe, persistent vomiting, sluggishness, irrational behavior, and a progressive brain disorder leading to coma, convulsions, and death.

Caution should be exercised when taking Tigan—especially in children, the elderly, or those in a weakened or run-down condition— if you have a severe illness accompanied by high fever, inflammation of the brain (encephalitis), inflammation of the stomach and intestines (gastroenteritis), or dehydration.

Severe vomiting should not be treated with Tigan alone. Your doctor should emphasize restoration of body fluids, the relief of fever, and the relief of the disease causing the vomiting. However, the overconsumption of fluids may result in cerebral edema (excessive accumulation of fluid in the brain).

The antinausea effects of Tigan may make it difficult to diagnose such conditions as appendicitis and may mask signs of drug poisoning due to overdosage of other drugs.

Possible food and drug interactions
when taking this medication
The use of alcohol in combination with this drug may produce an unfavorable reaction.

Caution should be exercised when taking Tigan in combination with central nervous system drugs such as phenothiazines (tranquilizers and antiemetics), barbiturates such as phenobarbital, and drugs derived from belladonna, such as Donnatal, if you are dehydrated or have a severe disease with fever or inflammation of the stomach, intestines, or brain.

Special information
if you are pregnant or breastfeeding
The effects of Tigan during pregnancy or breastfeeding have not been adequately studied. If you are pregnant or plan to become pregnant, inform your doctor immediately. If you are breastfeeding your baby, consult your doctor before taking this medication.

Recommended dosage
Dosage will be adjusted by your doctor according to your illness, the severity of your symptoms, and how well you do on the drug.

ADULTS

Capsules
The usual dosage is one 250-milligram capsule taken 3 or 4 times per day, as determined by your doctor.

Suppositories
The recommended dosage is 1 suppository (200 milligrams) inserted into the rectum 3 or 4 times per day, as determined by your doctor.

CHILDREN

Capsules
The usual dosage for children weighing 30 to 90 pounds is one or two 100-milligram capsules taken 3 or 4 times per day, as determined by the doctor.

Suppositories
The usual dosage for children weighing under 30 pounds is half a suppository (100 milligrams) inserted into the rectum 3 or 4 times a day, as determined by your doctor.

The usual dosage for children weighing 30 to 90 pounds is one-half to one 200-milligram suppository rectally 3 or 4 times a day, as determined by the doctor.

Pediatric Suppositories
The usual dosage for children weighing under 30 pounds is 1 suppository (100 milligrams) rectally 3 or 4 times a day, as determined by the doctor.

The usual dosage for children weighing 30 to 90 pounds is 1 to 2 suppositories (100 milligrams to 200 milligrams) rectally 3 or 4 times a day, as determined by the doctor.

Overdosage
Although no specific information is available, any medication taken in excess can have serious consequences. If you suspect a Tigan overdose, seek medical attention immediately.

Brand name:

TILADE

Pronounced: TILE-aid
Generic name: Nedocromil sodium

Why is this drug prescribed?
Tilade is an anti-inflammatory medication prescribed for use on a regular basis to control asthma symptoms in people with mild to moderate bronchial asthma.

Most important fact about this drug
Tilade must be used regularly to be effective, even if you have no symptoms. It improves your condition, but won't help during an acute attack.

How should you take this medication?
Proper inhalation of Tilade is essential for it to be effective. Make sure you understand how to use the medication correctly, and take it exactly as prescribed.

Tilade Inhaler should not be used with other mouthpieces.

- *If you miss a dose...*
  To work properly, Tilade must be inhaled every day at regular intervals. If you miss a dose, take it as soon as you remember. If it is almost time for your next dose, skip the one you missed and go back to your regular schedule. Do not take double doses.

- *Storage instructions...*
  Store Tilade Inhaler at room temperature. Because the contents are under pressure, do not puncture, incinerate, or place near heat.

What side effects may occur?

Side effects cannot be anticipated. If any develop or change in intensity, inform your doctor as soon as possible. Only your doctor can determine if it is safe for you to continue using Tilade.

■ *More common side effects may include:*
Chest pain
Coughing
Headache
Nausea
Inflamed nose
Sore throat
Unpleasant taste
Upper respiratory tract infection
Wheezing

■ *Less common side effects may include:*
Abdominal pain, bronchitis, diarrhea, difficult or labored breathing, difficulty speaking, dizziness, dry mouth, fatigue, increased sputum, indigestion, viral infection, vomiting

Why should this drug not be prescribed?

Tilade Inhaler should not be used if you are sensitive to or have ever had an allergic reaction to nedocromil sodium or any of Tilade's other ingredients. Make sure your doctor is aware of any drug reactions you have experienced.

Special warnings about this medication

This medication will not stop an asthma attack. However, you should continue to take it during an attack, along with a bronchodilator (a medication that increases air flow to your lungs) to relieve the acute symptoms.

Medications that are inhaled can cause coughing and wheezing in some people. If you experience these symptoms, stop taking Tilade and notify your doctor immediately.

Possible food and drug interactions
when taking this medication

No interactions have been reported.

Special information
if you are pregnant or breastfeeding

The effects of Tilade during pregnancy have not been adequately studied. If you are pregnant or plan to become pregnant, notify your doctor immediately.

Tilade may appear in breast milk and could affect a nursing infant. If this medication is essential to your health, your doctor may advise you to discontinue breastfeeding until your treatment is finished.

Recommended dosage

ADULTS AND CHILDREN 12 YEARS OF AGE AND OVER

The recommended dose is 2 inhalations 4 times a day at regular intervals. If you are doing well on that dosage, your doctor may try reducing the dose after a time.

CHILDREN

The safety and effectiveness of Tilade Inhaler have not been established in children under 12 years of age.

Overdosage

Any medication taken in excess can have serious consequences. If you suspect an overdose, seek medical attention immediately.

Generic name:

TIMOLOL MALEATE

See Timoptic, page 1117.

Brand name:

TIMOPTIC

Pronounced: Tim-OP-tic
Generic name: Timolol maleate

Why is this drug prescribed?

Timoptic is a topical medication (applied directly in the eye) that effectively reduces internal pressure in the eye. Timoptic is used in the treatment of glaucoma to lower elevated eye pressure that could damage vision and, with other glaucoma medications, to further reduce pressure in the eye.

Most important fact about this drug

Although Timoptic eyedrops are applied only to the eye, the medication is absorbed and may have effects in other parts of the body. If you have diabetes, asthma, or other respiratory disease, or decreased heart function, make sure your doctor is aware of the problem.

How should you use this medication?

Timoptic should be used exactly as prescribed by your doctor.

If you are using Timoptic in Ocudose, use the medication as soon as you open the individual unit and throw out any leftover solution.

If you are using Timoptic-XE, invert the closed container and shake it once—and only once—before each use.

If you need to use other eye medications along with Timoptic-XE, use them at least 10 minutes before you instill Timoptic-XE.

Handle the Timoptic solution carefully to avoid contamination. Do not let the tip of the dispenser actually touch the eye.

■ *To administer Timoptic, follow these steps:*

1. Wash your hands thoroughly.
2. Gently pull your lower eyelid down to form a pocket.
3. Brace the bottle against the bridge of your nose or your forehead.
4. Tilt your head back and squeeze the medication into your eye.
5. Close your eyes gently.
6. Keep your eyes closed for 1 to 2 minutes.

■ *If you miss a dose...*

If you use Timoptic once a day, apply it as soon as you remember. If you do not remember until the next day, skip the dose you missed and go back to your regular schedule. Do not take 2 doses at once. If you use it more than once a day, apply it as soon as you remember. If it is almost time for your next dose, skip the one you missed and go back to your regular schedule. Do not take 2 doses at once.

■ *Storage instructions...*

Store at room temperature, protected from light.

What side effects may occur?

Side effects cannot be anticipated. If any side effects develop or change in intensity, tell your doctor immediately. Only your doctor can determine whether it is safe to continue using this medication. If Timoptic is absorbed into the bloodstream, it can cause additional side effects.

■ *Side effects may include:*

Allergic reactions, anxiety, chest pain, confusion, conjunctivitis (pinkeye), cough, depression, diarrhea, difficult or labored breathing, disorientation, dizziness, double vision, drooping eyelid, dry mouth, eye discharge, eye irritation and inflammation, eye itching and tearing, fainting, fatigue, fluid in the lungs, hair loss, hallucinations, headache, heart failure, high blood pressure, hives, impotence, inability to breathe, increase in signs/symptoms of myasthenia gravis (severe muscle weakness), indigestion, inflammation of the eyelid, irregular heartbeat, loss of appetite, low blood pressure, nausea, nervousness, pain, rash, sensation of a foreign body in the eye, sleepiness, slow heartbeat, stroke, stuffy nose, throbbing or fluttering heartbeat, tingling or pins and needles, upper respiratory infection, visual disturbances, weakness, wheezing, worsened angina pectoris (crushing chest pain)

Why should this drug not be prescribed?

Do not use Timoptic if you have bronchial asthma, a history of bronchial asthma, or other serious breathing disorders such as emphysema, slow heartbeat, heart block (conduction disorder), active heart failure, or inadequate blood supply to the circulatory system (cardiogenic shock), or if you have ever had an allergic reaction or are sensitive to Timoptic or any of its ingredients.

Special warnings about this medication

Use Timoptic cautiously if you have a history of heart failure or poor cerebral circulation.

Tell your doctor if you have any type of allergy. The frequency and severity of allergic reactions may increase while you are using Timoptic.

Timoptic may mask the symptoms of low blood sugar. If you are diabetic, discuss this possibility with your doctor.

Tell your doctor or dentist that you are using Timoptic if you have a medical emergency or before you have surgery or dental treatment.

Timoptic should not be used with other topical beta blockers and should be used with caution if you are taking oral beta blockers such as Inderal and Tenormin.

Timoptic may mask symptoms of an overactive thyroid. If your doctor suspects you have excessive thyroid function, he or she will manage your case carefully to avoid such symptoms as rapid heartbeat, which can occur when the drug is withdrawn too abruptly.

Timoptic's antiglaucoma effects may decrease if you use the medication for a long time.

Some elderly individuals may be more sensitive to this product than younger people. If you develop an eye infection, check with your doctor. You may need to stop using Timoptic.

Possible food and drug interactions
when using this medication

If Timoptic is used with certain other drugs, the effects of either could be increased, decreased, or altered. It is especially important to check with your doctor before combining Timoptic with the following:

Epinephrine (EpiPen)
Catecholamine-depleting drugs, such as blood pressure drugs that
    contain reserpine (Serpasil)
Calcium antagonists such as Cardizem and Isoptin
Digitalis (Lanoxin)

Special information
if you are pregnant or breastfeeding

If you are pregnant or plan to become pregnant, inform your doctor immediately. No information is available about the safety of using Timoptic during pregnancy.

Timolol appears in breast milk and may harm a nursing infant. If using Timoptic is essential to your health, your doctor may advise you to stop breastfeeding until your treatment is finished.

Recommended dosage

ADULTS

Your doctor will tailor an individual Timoptic dosage depending on your medical condition and how you responded to any previous glaucoma treatment.

The usual recommended initial dose is to place 1 drop of 0.25 percent Timoptic in the affected eye(s) twice a day. If you do not respond satisfactorily to this dosage, your doctor may tell you to place 1 drop of 0. 5 percent Timoptic in the affected eye(s) twice a day.

The usual dose of Timoptic-XE is 1 drop of either 0.25 percent or 0.5 percent in the affected eye(s) once a day. Invert the closed container and shake it once before you use it.

Overdosage

Although there is no information available on Timoptic overdose, you should seek medical treatment immediately if you think you might have used too much Timoptic. Call your local poison control center or your doctor for assistance.

- *The following overdose symptoms have been reported with other beta blockers:*
  Extremely slow heart rate
  Low blood pressure
  Severe heart failure
  Wheezing

Generic name:

TOBRAMYCIN

See Tobrex, page 1121.

Brand name:

TOBREX

Pronounced: TOE-breks
Generic name: Tobramycin

Why is this drug prescribed?
Tobrex is an antibiotic applied to the eye to treat bacterial infections.

Most important fact about this drug
In order to clear up your infection completely, keep using Tobrex for the full time of treatment, even if your symptoms have disappeared.

How should you use this medication?

To apply Tobrex eyedrops:

1. Wash your hands thoroughly.
2. Gently pull your lower eyelid down to form a pocket between your eye and eyelid.
3. Brace the bottle on the bridge of your nose or your forehead.
4. Do not let the applicator tip touch your eye or any other surface.
5. Tilt your head back and squeeze the medication into the eye.
6. Close your eyes gently.
7. Keep your eyes closed for 1 to 2 minutes.
8. Do not rinse the dropper.
9. If you are using another eyedrop wait 5 to 10 minutes before applying it.

To apply the ointment form of this medication:

1. Tilt your head back.
2. Place a finger on your cheek just under your eye and gently pull down until a "V" pocket is formed between your eyeball and your lower lid.

3. Place about ½ inch of Tobrex in the "V" pocket. Do not let the tip of the tube touch the eye.
4. Look downward before closing your eye.

■ *If you miss a dose...*
   Apply it as soon as you remember. If it is almost time for your next dose, skip the one you missed and go back to your regular schedule.

■ *Storage instructions...*
   Store Tobrex at room temperature, away from heat, or in the refrigerator. Do not allow to freeze.

What side effects may occur?
Side effects cannot be anticipated. If any develop or change in intensity, inform your doctor as soon as possible. Only your doctor can determine if it is safe for you to continue to take Tobrex.

■ *Side effects may include:*
   Abnormal redness of eye tissue
   Allergic reactions
   Lid itching
   Lid swelling

Why should this drug not be prescribed?
If you are sensitive to or have ever had an allergic reaction to Tobrex or any of its ingredients, you should not use this medication. Make sure your doctor is aware of any drug reactions you have experienced.

Special warnings about this medication
If you experience an allergic reaction to this medication, discontinue use and inform your doctor.

Continued or prolonged use of Tobrex may result in a growth of bacteria that do not respond to this medication and can cause a secondary infection.

Ophthalmic ointments may slow healing of wounds of the cornea.

Possible food and drug interactions
when taking this medication
If you are taking any other prescription antibiotics for your eyes, check with your doctor before using Tobrex. Using this medication with certain other antibiotics in your system may cause an overdose.

Special information
if you are pregnant or breastfeeding
The effects of Tobrex during pregnancy have not been adequately studied. If you are pregnant or plan to become pregnant, inform your doctor immediately. Tobrex may appear in breast milk. Your doctor may advise you to discontinue breastfeeding until your treatment with this medication is finished.

Recommended dosage

ADULTS

Solution

If the infection is mild to moderate, place 1 or 2 drops into the affected eye(s) every 4 hours. In severe infections, place 2 drops into the eye(s) every hour until there is improvement. Then use less medication before you stop using it altogether.

Ointment

If the infection is mild to moderate, apply a half-inch ribbon into the affected eye(s) 2 or 3 times per day. In severe infections, apply a half-inch ribbon into the affected eye(s) every 3 or 4 hours until there is improvement. Then use less medication before stopping altogether.

CHILDREN
Your doctor will tailor a dose for the child.

Overdosage
Any medication used in excess can have serious consequences. If you suspect an overdose, seek medical assistance immediately.

- *Symptoms of Tobrex overdose may be similar to side effects. They include:*
  Corneal redness and inflammation
  Excessive eye tearing
  Lid itching and swelling

Generic name:

TOCAINIDE

See Tonocard, page 1131.

Brand name:

TOFRANIL

Pronounced: toe-FRAY-nil
Generic name: Imipramine hydrochloride

Why is this drug prescribed?
Tofranil is used to treat depression. It is a member of the family of drugs called tricyclic antidepressants.

Tofranil is also used on a short-term basis, along with behavioral therapies, to treat bedwetting in children aged 6 and older. Its effectiveness may decrease with longer use.

Some doctors also prescribe Tofranil to treat bulimia, attention deficit disorder in children, obsessive-compulsive disorder, and panic disorder.

Most important fact about this drug
Serious, sometimes fatal, reactions have been known to occur when drugs such as Tofranil are taken with another type of antidepressant called an MAO inhibitor. Drugs in this category include Nardil, Marplan, and Parnate. Do not take Tofranil within 2 weeks of taking one of these drugs. Make sure your doctor and pharmacist know of all the medications you are taking.

How should you take this medication?
Tofranil may be taken with or without food.

You should not take Tofranil with alcohol.

Do not stop taking Tofranil if you feel no immediate effect. It can take from 4 to 6 weeks for improvement to begin.

Tofranil can cause dry mouth. Sucking hard candy or chewing gum can help this problem.

- *If you miss a dose...*
  If you take 1 dose a day at bedtime, contact your doctor. Do not take the dose in the morning because of possible side effects.

  If you take 2 or more doses a day, take the forgotten dose as soon as you remember. If it is almost time for your next dose, skip the one you missed and go back to your regular schedule. Do not take 2 doses a once.

■ *Storage instructions...*
Store at room temperature in a tightly closed container.

What side effects may occur?
Side effects cannot be anticipated. If any develop or change in intensity, inform your doctor as soon as possible. Only your doctor can determine if it is safe for you to continue taking Tofranil.

■ *Side effects may include:*
Abdominal cramps, agitation, anxiety, black tongue, bleeding sores, blood disorders, blurred vision, breast development in males, confusion, congestive heart failure, constipation or diarrhea, cough, delusions, dilated pupils, disorientation, dizziness, drowsiness, dry mouth, episodes of elation or irritability, excessive or spontaneous flow of milk, fatigue, fever, flushing, frequent urination or difficulty or delay in urinating, hair loss, hallucinations, headache, heart attack, heart failure, high blood pressure, high or low blood sugar, high pressure of fluid in the eyes, hives, impotence, increased or decreased sex drive, inflammation of the mouth, insomnia, intestinal blockage, irregular heartbeat, lack of coordination, lightheadedness (especially when rising from lying down), loss of appetite, nausea, nightmares, odd taste in mouth, palpitations, purple or reddish-brown spots on skin, rapid heartbeat, restlessness, ringing in the ears, seizures, sensitivity to light, skin itching and rash, sore throat, stomach upset, stroke, sweating, swelling due to fluid retention (especially in face or tongue), swelling of breasts, swelling of testicles, swollen glands, tendency to fall, tingling or pins and needles, and numbness in hands and feet, tremors, visual problems, vomiting, weakness, weight gain or loss, yellowed skin and whites of eyes

■ *The most common side effects in children being treated for bedwetting are:*
Nervousness, sleep disorders, stomach and intestinal problems, tiredness

■ *Other side effects in children are:*
Anxiety, collapse, constipation, convulsions, emotional instability, fainting

Why should this drug not be prescribed?
Tofranil should not be used if you are recovering from a recent heart attack.

People who take antidepressant drugs known as MAO inhibitors, such as Nardil and Parnate, should not take Tofranil. You should not take Tofranil if you are sensitive or allergic to it.

Special warnings about this medication

You should use Tofranil cautiously if you have or have ever had: narrow-angle glaucoma (increased pressure in the eye); difficulty in urinating; heart, liver, kidney, or thyroid disease; or seizures. Also be cautious if you are taking thyroid medication.

General feelings of illness, headache, and nausea can result if you suddenly stop taking Tofranil. Follow your doctor's instructions closely when discontinuing Tofranil.

Tell your doctor if you develop a sore throat or fever while taking Tofranil.

This drug may impair your ability to drive a car or operate potentially dangerous machinery. Do not participate in any activities that require full alertness if you are unsure about your ability.

This drug can make you sensitive to light. Try to stay out of the sun as much as possible while you are taking it.

If you are going to have elective surgery, your doctor will take you off Tofranil.

Possible food and drug interactions
when taking this medication

If Tofranil is taken with certain other drugs, the effects of either could be increased, decreased, or altered. It is especially important to check with your doctor before combining Tofranil with the following:

Albuterol (Proventil, Ventolin)
Anticholinergics such as Cogentin
Antihypertensives such as Wytensin
Barbiturates such as Nembutal and Seconal
Carbamazepine (Tegretol)
Central nervous system depressants such as Xanax and Valium
Cimetidine (Tagamet)
Clonidine (Catapres)
Decongestants such as Sudafed
Epinephrine (EpiPen)
Fluoxetine (Prozac)
Guanethidine (Ismelin)
Methylphenidate (Ritalin)
Norepinephrine
Phenytoin (Dilantin)
Thyroid medications

Extreme drowsiness and other potentially serious effects can result if Tofranil is combined with alcohol or other mental depressants, such as narcotic painkillers (Percocet), sleeping medications (Halcion), or tranquilizers (Valium).

Special information
if you are pregnant or breastfeeding

The effects of Tofranil during pregnancy have not been adequately studied. Pregnant women should use Tofranil only when the potential benefits clearly outweigh the potential risks. If you are pregnant or plan to become pregnant, inform your doctor immediately. Tofranil may appear in breast milk and could affect a nursing infant. If this medication is essential to your health, your doctor may advise you to stop breastfeeding until your treatment is finished.

Recommended dosage

ADULTS

The usual starting dose in 75 milligrams a day. The doctor may increase this to 150 milligrams a day. The maximum daily dose is 200 milligrams.

Tofranil is not to be used in children to treat any condition but bedwetting, and its use will be limited to short-term therapy. Safety and effectiveness in children under the age of 6 have not been established.

Total daily dosages for children should not exceed 2.5 milligrams for each 2.2 pounds of the child's weight.

Doses usually begin at 25 milligrams per day. This amount should be taken an hour before bedtime. If needed, this dose may be increased after 1 week to 50 milligrams (ages 6 through 11) or 75 milligrams (ages 12 and up), taken in 1 dose at bedtime or divided into 2 doses, 1 taken at mid-afternoon and 1 at bedtime.

ELDERLY AND ADOLESCENTS

People in these two age groups should take lower doses. Dosage starts out at 30 to 40 milligrams per day and can go up to no more than 100 milligrams a day.

Overdosage

Any medication taken in excess can have serious consequences. An overdose of Tofranil can cause death. It has been reported that children are more sensitive than adults to overdoses of Tofranil. If you suspect an overdose, seek medical help immediately.

- *Symptoms of Tofranil overdose may include:*
  Agitation, bluish skin, coma, convulsions, difficulty breathing, dilated

pupils, drowsiness, heart failure, high fever, involuntary writhing or jerky movements, irregular or rapid heartbeat, lack of coordination, low blood pressure, overactive reflexes, restlessness, rigid muscles, shock, stupor, sweating, vomiting

Generic name:

TOLBUTAMIDE

See Orinase, page 780.

Brand name:

TOLECTIN

Pronounced: toe-LEK-tin
Generic name: Tolmetin sodium

Why is this drug prescribed?
Tolectin is a nonsteroidal anti-inflammatory drug used to relieve the inflammation, swelling, stiffness, and joint pain associated with rheumatoid arthritis and osteoarthritis (the most common form of arthritis). It is used for both acute episodes and long-term treatment. It is also used to treat juvenile rheumatoid arthritis.

Most important fact about this drug
You should have frequent checkups with your doctor if you take Tolectin regularly. Ulcers or internal bleeding can occur without warning.

How should you take this medication?
If Tolectin upsets your stomach, it may be taken with food or an antacid, and with a full glass of water. It may also help to prevent upset if you avoid lying down for 20 to 30 minutes after taking the drug.

Take this medication exactly as prescribed by your doctor.

- *If you miss a dose...*
  Take it as soon as you remember. If it is almost time for your next dose, skip the one you missed and go back to your regular schedule. Never take 2 doses at the same time.

- *Storage instructions...*
  Store at room temperature in a tightly closed container, away from light.

What side effects may occur?
Side effects cannot be anticipated. If any develop or change in intensity, inform your doctor as soon as possible. Only your doctor can determine if it is safe for you to continue taking Tolectin.

■ *More common side effects may include:*
Abdominal pain, change in weight, diarrhea, dizziness, gas, headache, heartburn, high blood pressure, indigestion, nausea, stomach and intestinal upset, swelling due to fluid retention, vomiting, weakness

■ *Less common or rare side effects may include:*
Anemia, blood in urine, chest pain, congestive heart failure, constipation, depression, drowsiness, fever, hepatitis, hives, inflammation of the mouth or tongue, kidney failure, painful urination, peptic ulcer, purple or reddish spots on skin, ringing in the ears, severe allergic reactions, skin irritation, stomach inflammation, stomach or intestinal bleeding, urinary tract infection, visual disturbances, yellow eyes or skin

Why should this drug not be prescribed?
If you are sensitive to or have ever had an allergic reaction to Tolectin, aspirin, or other nonsteroidal anti-inflammatory drugs, or if you have had asthma, hives, or nasal inflammation caused by aspirin or other nonsteroidal anti-inflammatory drugs, you should not take this medication. Make sure your doctor is aware of any drug reactions you have experienced.

Special warnings about this medication
Tolectin can cause kidney problems, especially if you are elderly, suffer from heart failure or liver disease, or take diuretics.

This drug can also affect the liver. If you develop symptoms such as yellow skin and eyes, notify your doctor. You should be taken off Tolectin.

Do not take aspirin or any other anti-inflammatory medications while taking Tolectin unless your doctor tells you to do so.

Tolectin can cause visual disturbances. If you experience a change in your vision, inform your doctor.

Tolectin prolongs bleeding time. If you are taking blood-thinning medication, this drug should be taken with caution.

This drug can increase water retention. Use with caution if you have heart disease or high blood pressure.

Tolectin causes some people to become drowsy or less alert. If it has this effect on you, driving or operating dangerous machinery or participating in any hazardous activity that requires full mental alertness is not recommended.

Possible food and drug interactions
when taking this medication

If Tolectin is taken with certain other drugs, the effects of either could be increased, decreased, or altered. It is especially important to check with your doctor before combining Tolectin with the following:

Aspirin
Blood thinners such as Coumadin
Carteolol (Cartrol)
Diuretics such as Lasix
Glyburide (Micronase)
Lithium (Lithonate)
Methotrexate

Special information
if you are pregnant or breastfeeding

The effects of Tolectin during pregnancy have not been adequately studied. If you are pregnant or plan to become pregnant, inform your doctor immediately. Tolectin appears in breast milk and could affect a nursing infant. If this medication is essential to your health, your doctor may advise you to discontinue breastfeeding until your treatment is finished.

Recommended dosage

ADULTS

Rheumatoid Arthritis or Osteoarthritis

The starting dosage is usually 1,200 milligrams a day divided into 3 doses of 400 milligrams each. Take 1 dose when you wake up and 1 at bedtime, and 1 sometime in between. Your doctor may adjust the dosage after 1 to 2 weeks. Most people will take a total daily dosage of 600 to 1,800 milligrams usually divided into 3 doses.

You should see the benefits of Tolectin in a few days to a week.

CHILDREN

The starting dose for children 2 years and older is usually a total of 20 milligrams per 2.2 pounds of body weight per day, divided into 3 or 4 smaller doses. Your doctor will advise you on use in children. The usual dose ranges from 15 to 30 milligrams per 2.2 pounds per day.

The safety and effectiveness of Tolectin have not been established in children under 2 years of age.

Overdosage

Although no specific information is available, any medication taken in excess can have serious consequences. If you suspect an overdose of Tolectin, seek medical attention immediately.

Generic name:

TOLMETIN

See Tolectin, page 1128.

Brand name:

TONOCARD

Pronounced: TAH-nuh-card
Generic name: Tocainide hydrochloride

Why is this drug prescribed?

Tonocard is used to treat severe irregular heartbeat (arrhythmias). Arrhythmias are generally divided into two main types: heartbeats that are faster than normal (tachycardia), or heartbeats that are slower than normal (bradycardia). Irregular heartbeats are often caused by drugs or disease but can occur in otherwise-healthy people with no history of heart disease or other illness. Tonocard works differently from other antiarrhythmic drugs, such as quinidine (Quinidex), procainamide (Procan SR), and disopyramide (Norpace). It is similar to lidocaine (Xylocaine) and is effective in treating ventricular arrhythmias (irregular heartbeats that occur in a particular part of the heart).

Most important fact about this drug

Tonocard can cause serious blood and lung disorders in some patients, especially in the first 3 months of treatment. Be sure to notify your doctor if any of the following occurs: painful or difficult breathing, wheezing, cough, easy bruising or bleeding, tremors, palpitations, rash, soreness or ulcers in the mouth, sore throat, fever, and chills.

How should you take this medication?

It is important to take Tonocard on a regular schedule, exactly as prescribed by your doctor. Try not to miss any doses. If this medication is not taken regularly, your condition can worsen.

■ *If you miss a dose...*
If less than 2 hours have passed, take the forgotten dose as soon as you remember. If you are more than 2 hours late, skip the dose. Never try to "catch up" by taking a double dose.

■ *Storage instructions...*
Keep the container tightly closed, and store it at room temperature. Protect from extreme heat.

What side effects may occur?
Side effects cannot be anticipated. If any develop or change in intensity, inform your doctor as soon as possible. Only your doctor can determine if it is safe for you to continue taking Tonocard.

■ *More common side effects may include:*
Confusion/disorientation, dizziness/vertigo, diarrhea/loose stools, excessive sweating, hallucinations, increased irregular heartbeat, lack of coordination, loss of appetite, nausea, nervousness, rash/skin eruptions, tingling or pins and needles, tremor, vision disturbances, vomiting

■ *Less common side effects may include:*
Arthritis, anxiety, chest pain, congestive heart failure, drowsiness, exhaustion, fatigue, headache, hearing loss, hot/cold feelings, involuntary eyeball movement, joint pain, low blood pressure, muscle pain, pounding heartbeat, rapid heartbeat, ringing in ears, sleepiness, slow heartbeat, sluggishness, unsteadiness, walking disturbances

■ *Rare side effects may include:*
Abdominal pain/discomfort, agitation, allergic reactions, anemia, angina, blood clots in lungs, blood disorders, changes in blood counts, changes in heart function, chills, cinchonism (a sensitivity reaction with symptoms including ringing in the ears, loss of hearing, dizziness, light-headedness, headache, nausea, and/or disturbed vision), cold hands and feet, coma, constipation, decreased mental ability, decreased urination, depression, difficulty breathing, difficulty speaking, difficulty sleeping, difficulty swallowing, disturbed behavior, disturbed dreams, dizziness on standing, double vision, dry mouth, earache, enlarged heart, fainting, fever, fluid in lungs, fluid retention, flushing, general bodily discomfort, hair loss, heart attack, hepatitis, hiccups, high blood pressure, hives, increased stuttering, increased urination, lung disorders, memory loss, muscle cramps, muscle twitching/spasm, myasthenia gravis, neck pain or pain extending from the neck, pallor, pneumonia, seizures, skin peeling, slurred speech, smell

disturbance, stomach upset, taste disturbance, thirst, weakness, yawning, yellow eyes and skin

Why should this drug not be prescribed?
If you have heart block (conduction disorder) and do not have a pacemaker, or if you are sensitive to or have ever had an allergic reaction to Tonocard or certain local anesthetics such as Xylocaine, do not take this medication.

Special warnings about this medication
Be alert for signs of the blood and lung disorders that can occur early in your treatment. (See "Most important fact about this drug.")

If you have congestive heart failure, make sure the doctor is aware of it. Tonocard could worsen this condition.

Also make certain that the doctor is aware of any kidney or liver problems that you have. You will need to be monitored more carefully.

Before any kind of surgery, including dental surgery and emergency treatment, make sure the surgeon knows that you are taking Tonocard.

Possible food and drug interactions
when taking this medication
If Tonocard is taken with certain other drugs, the effects of either could be increased, decreased, or altered. It is especially important to check with your doctor before combining Tonocard with any of the following:

The anesthetic Lidocaine (Xylocaine)
The blood pressure medicine Metoprolol (Lopressor)
Other anti-arrhythmics such as Quinidex, Procan, Mexitil

Special information
if you are pregnant or breastfeeding
The effects of Tonocard during pregnancy have not been adequately studied. However, animal studies have shown an increase in stillbirths and spontaneous abortions. If you are pregnant or plan to become pregnant, inform your doctor immediately. Tonocard may appear in breast milk and could affect a nursing infant. If this medication is essential to your health, your doctor may advise you to discontinue breastfeeding until your treatment is finished.

Recommended dosage

ADULTS

Dosages of Tonocard must be adjusted to its effects on each individual. Your doctor should monitor you carefully to determine if the dosage you are taking is working properly. He may divide your doses further or make other changes, such as shortening the time between doses, if side effects occur.

The usual starting dose is 400 milligrams every 8 hours.

The usual dose range is between 1,200 and 1,800 milligrams total per day divided into 3 doses. This medication can be taken in 2 doses a day with careful monitoring by your doctor.

Doses beyond 2,400 milligrams per day are rarely used.

Some people, particularly those with reduced kidney or liver function, may be treated successfully with less than 1,200 milligrams per day.

CHILDREN

The safety and effectiveness of this drug in children have not been established.

ELDERLY

Tonocard is prescribed cautiously for the elderly.

Overdosage

Any medication taken in excess can have serious consequences. If you suspect an overdose, seek medical attention immediately.

There are no specific reports of Tonocard overdose. However, the first and most important signs of overdose would be expected to appear in the central nervous system. Disorders of the stomach and intestines might follow. Convulsions and heart and lung slowing or stopping might occur.

Brand name:

TOPICORT

Pronounced: TOP-i-court
Generic name: Desoximetasone

Why is this drug prescribed?

Topicort is a synthetic steroid medication in cream, gel, or ointment form that relieves the inflammation and itching caused by a variety of skin conditions.

Most important fact about this drug

When you use Topicort, you may absorb some of the medication through your skin and into the bloodstream. Too much absorption can lead to unwanted side effects elsewhere in the body. To keep this problem to a minimum, avoid using large amounts of Topicort over large areas, do not use it for extended periods of time, and do not cover it with airtight dressings such as plastic wrap or adhesive bandages unless specifically told to by your doctor.

Children may absorb more medication than adults do.

How should you use this medication?
Topicort is for use only on the skin. Be careful to keep it out of your eyes.

Apply a thin coating of Topicort to the affected area. Rub in gently.

The treated area should not be covered unless your doctor has told you to do so.

If Topicort is being used for an infant or toddler with a genital rash, make sure the diapers or plastic pants are not too tight, so that air can circulate.

- *If you miss a dose...*
  Use Topicort only as needed, in the smallest amount required for relief.

- *Storage instructions...*
  Store Topicort at room temperature.

What side effects may occur?
Side effects cannot be anticipated. If any develop or change in intensity, inform your doctor as soon as possible. Only your doctor can determine if it is safe for you to continue using Topicort. The side effects listed below occur infrequently, but may occur more often if the treated area is covered with a bandage.

- *Side effects may include:*
  Acne-like pimples, blackheads, blistering, burning of the skin, dryness, excessive growth of hair, infection, inflammation of the hair follicles, irritation, itching, loss of skin pigmentation, prickly heat, skin inflammation around the mouth, rash, redness, stretch marks on the skin, thinning of the skin

Why should this drug not be prescribed?
Do not use Topicort if you are sensitive to it or have ever had an allergic reaction to any of its ingredients.

Special warnings about this medication
Remember to avoid getting Topicort in your eyes. Do not use Topicort to treat any condition other than the one for which it was prescribed.

Long-term use of steroids such as Topicort may interfere with the growth and development of children. They may also develop headaches, or bulging at the top of the head.

Avoid covering a treated area with tight waterproof diapers or plastic pants. They can increase unwanted absorption of Topicort.

If your skin becomes irritated or infected, stop using Topicort and call your doctor.

**Possible food and drug interactions
when using this medication**
No interactions have been reported.

**Special information
if you are pregnant or breastfeeding**
Topicort should not be used over large areas, in large amounts, or for long periods of time during pregnancy unless the benefit outweighs any potential risk to the unborn child. If you are pregnant or plan to become pregnant, inform your doctor immediately.

It is not known whether topical steroids are absorbed in sufficient amounts to appear in breast milk. If your doctor considers Topicort essential to your health, he or she may advise you to stop breastfeeding until your treatment with the medication is finished.

Recommended dosage

ADULTS

Apply a thin film of Topicort cream, gel, or ointment to the affected area 2 times a day. Rub in gently.

CHILDREN

Use the least amount of Topicort necessary to relieve symptoms. Ask your doctor for specific instructions.

Overdosage
Large doses of steroids such as Topicort applied over a large area or for a long time, especially when the treated area is covered, can cause increases in blood sugar and Cushing's syndrome, a condition characterized by a moon-shaped face, emotional disturbances, high blood pressure, weight gain, and, in women, baldness or growth of body and facial hair. Cushing's syndrome may also trigger the development of diabetes. If left uncorrected, Cushing's

syndrome may become serious. If you suspect your use of Topicort has led to this problem, seek medical attention immediately.

Brand name:

TORADOL

Pronounced: TOH-rah-dol
Generic name: Ketorolac tromethamine

Why is this drug prescribed?
Toradol, a nonsteroidal anti-inflammatory drug, is used to relieve pain. It is prescribed for a limited amount of time (about 8 days), not for long-term therapy.

Most important fact about this drug
You should have frequent checkups with your doctor if you take Toradol regularly. Ulcers or internal bleeding can occur without warning.

How should you take this medication?
Toradol works fastest when taken on an empty stomach, but an antacid can be taken if it causes upset. Take this medication exactly as prescribed.

Take Toradol with a full glass of water. Also, do not lie down for about 20 minutes after taking it. This will help to prevent irritation of your upper digestive tract.

■ *If you miss a dose...*
  If you take Toradol on a regular schedule, take it as soon as you remember. If it is almost time for your next dose, skip the one you missed and go back to your regular schedule. Never take 2 doses at the same time.

■ *Storage instructions...*
  Store at room temperature, away from excessive humidity and light.

What side effects may occur?
Side effects cannot be anticipated. If any develop or change in intensity, inform your doctor as soon as possible. Only your doctor can determine if it is safe for you to continue using Toradol.

■ *More common side effects may include:*
  Diarrhea
  Dizziness

Drowsiness
Headache
Indigestion
Itching
Nausea
Stomach and intestinal pain
Swelling due to fluid retention

■ *Less common side effects may include:*
Abdominal fullness, constipation, gas, high blood pressure, inflammation of the mouth, rash, red or purple spots on the skin, sweating, vomiting

■ *Rare side effects may include:*
Abnormal dreams, allergic reactions, anemia, asthma, belching, black stools, blood in the urine, convulsions, decreased amount of urine, difficult or labored breathing, exaggerated feeling of well-being, fainting, fever, fluid in the lungs, flushing, gastritis (inflammation of the lining of the stomach), hallucinations, hepatitis, hives, increased appetite, kidney failure, kidney inflammation, liver failure, loss of appetite, low blood pressure, nosebleeds, pallor, peptic ulcer, skin inflammation and flaking, Stevens-Johnson syndrome (skin peeling), stomach and intestinal bleeding, swelling of the throat or tongue, throbbing heartbeat, tremors, vertigo, weight gain, yellow skin and eyes

Why should this drug not be prescribed?
Do not take Toradol if it has ever given you an allergic reaction. Also avoid this medication if you have ever had an allergic reaction—such as nasal polyps (tumors), swelling of the face, limbs, and throat, hives, wheezing, light-headedness—to aspirin or other nonsteroidal anti-inflammatory drugs. Make sure your doctor is aware of any drug reactions you have experienced.

Special warnings about this medication
Remember that Toradol has been known to cause peptic ulcers and bleeding. Contact your doctor immediately if you suspect a problem.

This drug should be used with caution if you have kidney or liver disease. It may cause liver inflammation in some people.

Toradol is not recommended for long-term use, since side effects increase over time. This medication should be taken for as short a time as possible.

If you are elderly, use this drug cautiously.

Toradol can increase water retention. If you have heart disease or high blood pressure, use this drug with care.

This medication can prolong bleeding time. If you are taking blood-thinning medication, take Toradol with caution.

Possible food and drug interactions
when using this medication

If Toradol is taken with certain other drugs, the effects of either could be increased, decreased, or altered. It is especially important to check with your doctor before combining Toradol with the following:

Aspirin
Blood thinners such as Coumadin
Diuretics such as Lasix and Dyazide
Lithium (Lithonate)
Methotrexate
Probenecid (Benemid)

Special information
if you are pregnant or breastfeeding

The effects of Toradol during pregnancy have not been adequately studied. If you are pregnant or plan to become pregnant, inform your doctor immediately. Toradol appears in breast milk and could affect a nursing infant. If this medication is essential to your health, your doctor may advise you to discontinue breastfeeding until your treatment with this medication is finished.

Recommended dosage

ADULTS

The usual dose is 10 milligrams, taken as needed, every 4 to 6 hours for a limited time (5-14 days). You should not take more than 40 milligrams per day.

CHILDREN

The safety and effectiveness of Toradol in children have not been established.

ELDERLY

Doses are usually lower than younger people's. Your doctor will tailor the best dosage for you.

Overdosage

Although no specific information is available, any medication taken in excess can have serious consequences. If you suspect an overdose of Toradol, seek medical attention immediately.

Brand name:

TOTACILLIN

See Omnipen, page 772.

Brand name:

T-PHYL

See Theo-Dur, page 1102.

Brand name:

TRANDATE

See Normodyne, page 750.

Brand name:

TRANSDERM-NITRO

See Nitroglycerin, page 734.

Brand name:

TRANXENE

Pronounced: TRAN-zeen
Generic name: Clorazepate dipotassium
Other brand names: Tranxene-SD, Tranxene-SD Half
    Strength

Why is this drug prescribed?

Tranxene belongs to a class of drugs known as benzodiazepines. It is used in the treatment of anxiety disorders and for short-term relief of the symptoms of anxiety.

It is also used to relieve the symptoms of acute alcohol withdrawal and to help in treating certain convulsive disorders such as epilepsy.

Most important fact about this drug
Tranxene can be habit-forming if taken regularly over a long period. You may experience withdrawal symptoms if you stop using this drug abruptly. Consult your doctor before discontinuing Tranxene or making any change in your dose.

How should you take this medication?
Tranxene should be taken exactly as prescribed by your doctor.

■ *If you miss a dose...*
Take it as soon as you remember if it is within an hour or so of your scheduled time. If you do not remember until later, skip the dose you missed and go back to your regular schedule. Do not take 2 doses at once.

■ *Storage instructions...*
Store at room temperature. Protect from excessive heat.

What side effects may occur?
Side effects cannot be anticipated. If any develop or change in intensity, inform your doctor as soon as possible. Only your doctor can determine if it is safe for you to continue taking Tranxene.

■ *More common side effects may include:*
Drowsiness

■ *Less common or rare side effects may include:*
Blurred vision, depression, difficulty in sleeping or falling asleep, dizziness, dry mouth, double vision, fatigue, genital and urinary tract disorders, headache, irritability, lack of muscle coordination, mental confusion, nervousness, tremors, skin rashes, slurred speech, stomach and intestinal disorders, tremor

■ *Side effects due to rapid decrease of or abrupt withdrawal from Tranxene may include:*
Abdominal cramps, convulsions, diarrhea, difficulty in sleeping or falling asleep, hallucinations, impaired memory, irritability, muscle aches, nervousness, tremors, vomiting

Why should this drug not be prescribed?
If you are sensitive to or have ever had an allergic reaction to Tranxene, you should not take this medication. Make sure your doctor is aware of any drug reactions you have experienced.

Do not take this medication if you have the eye condition known as acute narrow-angle glaucoma.

Anxiety or tension related to everyday stress usually does not require treatment with such a strong drug. Discuss your symptoms thoroughly with your doctor.

Tranxene is not recommended for use in more serious conditions such as depression or severe psychological disorders.

Special warnings about this medication
Tranxene may cause you to become drowsy or less alert; therefore, you should not drive or operate dangerous machinery or participate in any hazardous activity that requires full mental alertness until you know how this drug affects you.

If you are being treated for anxiety associated with depression, your doctor will have you take a low dose of this medication. Do not increase your dose without consulting your doctor.

The elderly and people in a weakened condition are more apt to become unsteady or oversedated when taking Tranxene.

Possible food and drug interactions
when taking this medication
Tranxene slows down the central nervous system and may intensify the effects of alcohol. Do not drink alcohol while taking this medication.

If Tranxene is taken with certain other drugs, the effects of either could be increased, decreased, or altered. It is especially important to check with your doctor before combining Tranxene with the following:

Antidepressant drugs known as MAO inhibitors (Nardil, Parnate) and
    other antidepressants such as Elavil and Prozac
Barbiturates such as Nembutal and Seconal
Narcotic pain relievers such as Demerol and Percodan
Major tranquilizers such as Mellaril and Thorazine

Special information
if you are pregnant or breastfeeding
The effects of Tranxene during pregnancy have not been adequately studied. However, because there is an increased risk of birth defects associated with this class of drug, its use during pregnancy should be avoided. Tranxene may appear in breast milk and could affect a nursing infant. If this medication is

essential to your health, your doctor may advise you to discontinue breastfeeding until your treatment with this medication is finished.

Recommended dosage

ANXIETY

Adults
The usual daily dosage is 30 milligrams divided into several smaller doses. A normal daily dose can be as little as 15 milligrams. Your doctor may increase the dosage gradually to as much as 60 milligrams, according to your individual needs.

Tranxene can also be taken in a single bedtime dose. The initial dose is 15 milligrams, but your doctor will adjust the dosage to suit your individual needs.

Tranxene-SD, a 22.5-milligram tablet, and Tranxene-SD Half Strength, an 11.25-milligram tablet, can be taken once every 24 hours. Your doctor may switch you to this form of the drug after you have been taking Tranxene for several weeks.

Elderly
The usual starting dose for elderly people with anxiety is 7.5 to 15 milligrams per day.

ACUTE ALCOHOL WITHDRAWAL

Tranxene can be used in a multi-day program for relief of the symptoms of acute alcohol withdrawal.

Dosages are usually increased in the first 2 days from 30 to 90 milligrams and then reduced over the next 2 days to lower levels. After that, your doctor will gradually lower the dose still further, and will take you off the drug when you are ready.

WHEN USED WITH ANTIEPILEPTIC DRUGS

Tranxene can be used in conjunction with antiepileptic drugs. Follow the recommended dosages carefully to avoid drowsiness.

Adults and Children over 12 Years Old
The starting dose is 7.5 milligrams 3 times a day. Your doctor may increase the dosage by 7.5 milligrams per week to a maximum of 90 milligrams a day.

Children 9 to 12 Years Old
The starting dose is 7.5 milligrams twice a day. Your doctor may increase the dosage by 7.5 milligrams a week to a maximum of 60 milligrams a day.

Safety and effectiveness in children under 9 years of age have not been established.

Overdosage
Any medication taken in excess can have serious consequences. If you suspect an overdose, seek medical treatment immediately.

- *Symptoms of Tranxene overdose may include:*
  Coma
  Low blood pressure
  Sedation

Generic name:

TRAZODONE

See Desyrel, page 310.

Brand name:

TRENTAL

Pronounced: TREN-tall
Generic name: Pentoxifylline

Why is this drug prescribed?
Trental is a medication that reduces the viscosity or "stickiness" of your blood, allowing it to flow more freely. It helps relieve the painful leg cramps caused by "intermittent claudication," a condition resulting from poor blood supply to the leg muscles caused by hardening of the arteries.

Some doctors also prescribe Trental for dementia, strokes, circulatory and nerve problems caused by diabetes, and Raynaud's syndrome (a disorder of the blood vessels in which exposure to cold causes the fingers and toes to turn white). The drug is also used to treat impotence and to increase sperm motility in infertile men.

Most important fact about this drug
Trental can ease the pain in your legs and make walking easier but should not replace other treatments such as physical therapy or surgery.

How should you take this medication?

Trental comes in a controlled-release tablets. Do not break, crush, or chew the tablets; swallow them whole. Take Trental exactly as prescribed.

- *If you miss a dose...*

  Take it as soon as you remember. If it is almost time for your next dose, skip the one you missed and go back to your regular schedule. Never take 2 doses at the same time.

- *Storage instructions...*

  Keep this medication in the container it came in, tightly closed and away from light. Store it at room temperature.

What side effects may occur?

Side effects cannot be anticipated. If any develop or change in intensity, inform your doctor as soon as possible. Only your doctor can determine if it is safe for you to continue taking Trental.

Trental's side effects are fairly uncommon.

- *Side effects may include:*

  Allergic reaction (symptoms include: swelling of face, lips, tongue, throat, arms, or legs, sore throat, fever and chills, difficulty swallowing, chest pain), anxiety, bad taste in the mouth, blind spot in vision, blurred vision, brittle fingernails, chest pain (sometimes crushing), confusion, conjunctivitis (pink eye), constipation, depression, difficult or labored breathing, dizziness, dry mouth/thirst, earache, excessive salivation, flu-like symptoms, fluid retention, general body discomfort, headache, hives, indigestion, inflammation of the gallbladder, itching, laryngitis, loss of appetite, low blood pressure, nosebleeds, rash, seizures, sore throat/swollen neck glands, stuffy nose, tremor, vomiting, weight change

Why should this drug not be prescribed?

Do not take Trental if you have recently had a stroke or bleeding in the retina of your eye.

If you are sensitive to or have ever had an allergic reaction to Trental, caffeine, theophylline (medication for asthma or other breathing disorders), or theobromine, do not take this medication. Make sure that your doctor is aware of any drug reactions that you have experienced.

Special warnings about this medication

If you are taking a blood thinner, or have recently had surgery, peptic ulcers, or other disorders that involve bleeding, the doctor should test your blood periodically.

Most people tolerate Trental well, but there have been occasional cases of crushing chest pain, low blood pressure, and irregular heartbeat in patients with heart disease and brain disorders.

Possible food and drug interactions when taking this medication

If Trental is taken with certain other drugs, the effects of either could be increased, decreased, or altered. It is especially important to check with your doctor before combining Trental with the following:

Blood-thinning drugs such as Coumadin
Clot inhibitors such as Persantine
Ulcer medicines such as Tagamet

Special information if you are pregnant or breastfeeding

The effects of Trental during pregnancy have not been adequately studied. If you are pregnant or plan to become pregnant, inform your doctor immediately. Trental appears in breast milk and could affect a nursing infant. If this medication is essential to your health, your doctor may advise you to discontinue breastfeeding until your treatment with this medication is finished.

Recommended dosage

ADULTS

The usual dosage of Trental in controlled-release tablets is one 400-milligram tablet 3 times a day with meals.

While the effect of Trental may be seen within 2 to 4 weeks, it is recommended that treatment be continued for at least 8 weeks.

Any stomach or central nervous system (affecting the brain and spinal cord) side effects are related to the dose. If any of these side effects occur, the dosage should be lowered to 1 tablet, 2 times a day, for a total of 800 milligrams a day. If side effects persist at this lower dosage, your doctor may consider stopping this drug.

CHILDREN

The safety and effectiveness of this drug in children under age 18 have not been established.

Overdosage

Any medication taken in excess can have serious consequences. If you suspect symptoms of a Trental overdose, seek medical attention immediately. Symptoms appear within 4 to 5 hours and may last for 12 hours.

■ *Symptoms of Trental overdose may include:*
   Agitation
   Convulsions
   Fever
   Flushing
   Loss of consciousness
   Low blood pressure
   Sleepiness

Generic name:

TRETINOIN

See Retin-A, page 946.

Generic name:

TRIAMCINOLONE

See Azmacort, page 97.

Generic name:

TRIAMTERENE WITH HYDROCHLOROTHIAZIDE

See Maxzide, page 632.

Brand name:

TRIAVIL

Pronounced: TRY-uh-vill
Generic ingredients: Amitriptyline hydrochloride,
   Perphenazine

Why is this drug prescribed?

Triavil is used to treat anxiety, agitation, and depression. Triavil is a combination of a tricyclic antidepressant (amitriptyline) and a tranquilizer (perphenazine).

Triavil can also help people with schizophrenia (distorted sense of reality) who are depressed and people with insomnia, fatigue, loss of interest, loss of appetite, or a slowing of physical and mental reactions.

Most important fact about this drug

Triavil may cause tardive dyskinesia—a condition marked by involuntary muscle spasms and twitches in the face and body. This condition may be permanent and appears to be most common among the elderly, especially women. Ask your doctor for information about this possible risk.

How should you take this medication?

Triavil may be taken with or without food. You should not take it with alcohol.

■ *If you miss a dose...*
Take it as soon as you remember. If it is within 2 hours of your next dose, skip the one you missed and go back to your regular schedule. Do not take 2 doses at once.

■ *Storage instructions...*
Store at room temperature in a tightly closed container. Protect Triavil 2-10 tablets from light.

What side effects may occur?

Side effects cannot be anticipated. If any develop or change in intensity, inform your doctor as soon as possible. Only your doctor can determine if it is safe for you to continue taking Triavil.

■ *Side effects may include:*
Abnormal secretion of milk, abnormalities of movements and posture, anxiety, asthma, black tongue, blood disorders, blurred vision, body rigidly arched backward, breast development in males, change in pulse rate, chewing movements, coma, confusion, constipation, convulsions, delusions, diarrhea, difficulty breathing, difficulty concentrating, difficulty swallowing, dilated pupils, disorientation, dizziness, drowsiness, dry mouth, eating abnormal amounts of food, ejaculation failure, episodes of elation or irritability, excessive or spontaneous flow of milk, excitement,

exhaustion, eye problems, eye spasms, eyes in a fixed position, fatigue, fever, fluid accumulation and swelling (including throat and brain, face and tongue, arms and legs), frequent urination, hair loss, hallucinations, headache, heart attacks, hepatitis, high blood pressure, high fever, high or low blood sugar, hives, impotence, inability to stop moving, inability to urinate, increased or decreased sex drive, inflammation of the mouth, insomnia, intestinal blockage, intolerance to light, involuntary jerky movements of tongue, face, mouth, lips, jaw, body, or arms and legs, irregular blood pressure, pulse, and heartbeat, irregular menstrual periods, lack of coordination, light-headedness upon standing up, liver problems, lockjaw, loss or increase of appetite, low blood pressure, muscle stiffness, nasal congestion, nausea, nightmares, odd taste in the mouth, overactive reflexes, pain and stiffness around neck, palpitations, protruding tongue, puckering of the mouth, puffing of the cheeks, purple-reddish-brown spots on skin, rapid heartbeat, restlessness, rigid arms, feet, head, and muscles, ringing in the ears, salivation, sedation, seizures, sensitivity to light, severe allergic reactions, skin rash or inflammation, scaling, spasms in the hands and feet, speech problems, stomach upset, stroke, sweating, swelling of breasts, swelling of testicles, swollen glands, tingling, pins and needles, and numbness in hands and feet, tremors, twisted neck, twitching in the body, neck, shoulders, and face, uncontrollable and involuntary urination, urinary problems, visual problems, vomiting, weakness, weight gain or loss, writhing motions, yellowed skin and whites of eyes

Why should this drug not be prescribed?

You should not be using Triavil if you are taking drugs that slow down the central nervous system, including alcohol, barbiturates, analgesics, antihistamines, or narcotics.

Triavil should not be used if you are recovering from a recent heart attack, or if you have an abnormal bone marrow condition. Avoid Triavil if you have ever had an allergic reaction to phenothiazines or amitriptyline.

People who are taking antidepressant drugs known as MAO inhibitors (including Nardil and Parnate) should not take Triavil.

Special warnings about this medication

Before using Triavil, tell your doctor if you have ever had: the eye condition known as glaucoma; difficulty urinating; breast cancer; seizures; heart, liver, or thyroid disease; or if you are exposed to extreme heat or pesticides. Be aware that Triavil may mask signs of brain tumor, intestinal blockage, and overdose of other drugs.

Nausea, headache, and a general ill feeling can result if you suddenly stop taking Triavil. Follow your doctor's instructions closely when discontinuing Triavil. If your dose is gradually reduced, you may experience irritability, restlessness, and dream and sleep disturbances, but these effects will not last.

This drug may impair your ability to drive a car or operate potentially dangerous machinery. Do not participate in any activities that require full alertness if you are unsure about your ability.

If you develop a fever that has no other cause, stop taking Triavil and call your doctor.

Possible food and drug interactions when taking this medication

If Triavil is taken with certain other drugs, the effects of either could be increased, decreased, or altered. It is especially important to check with your doctor before combining Triavil with the following:

Airway-opening drugs such as Proventil
Anticonvulsants such as Dilantin
Antidepressant drugs classified as MAO inhibitors, including Nardil and Parnate
Antihistamines such as Benadryl
Antispasmodic drugs such as Bentyl
Atropine (Donnatal)
Barbiturates such as phenobarbital
Blood-thinning drugs such as Coumadin
Cimetidine (Tagamet)
Disulfiram (Antabuse)
Epinephrine (EpiPen)
Ethchlorvynol (Placidyl)
Fluoxetine (Prozac)
Furazolidone (Furoxone)
Guanethidine (Ismelin)
Major tranquilizers such as Haldol
Narcotic analgesics such as Percocet
Thyroid medications such as Synthroid

Extreme drowsiness and other potentially serious effects can result if Triavil is combined with alcohol or other central nervous system depressants such as narcotics, painkillers, and sleep medications.

Special information
if you are pregnant or breastfeeding
Triavil may cause false-positive results on pregnancy tests. Triavil should not be used by pregnant women or mothers who are breastfeeding.

Recommended dosage
Your doctor will individualize your dose.

You should not take more than 4 tablets of Triavil 4-50 or 8 tablets of any other strength in one day. It may be a few days to a few weeks before you notice any improvement.

ADULTS

For Non-Psychotic Anxiety and Depression
The usual dose is 1 tablet of Triavil 2-25 or 4-25 taken 3 or 4 times a day, or 1 tablet of Triavil 4-50 taken twice a day.

For Anxiety in People with Schizophrenia
The usual dose is 2 tablets of Triavil 4-25 taken 3 times a day. Your doctor may tell you to take another tablet of Triavil 4-25 at bedtime, if needed.

If you need to keep taking Triavil, your doctor will probably have you take 1 tablet of Triavil 2-25 or 4-25 from 2 to 4 times a day or 1 tablet of Triavil 4-50 twice a day.

CHILDREN

Children should not use Triavil.

ELDERLY AND ADOLESCENTS

For Anxiety
The usual dose is 1 tablet of Triavil 4-10, taken 3 or 4 times a day. People in these age groups usually take Triavil at lower doses.

Overdosage
Any medication taken in excess can have serious consequences. An overdose of Triavil can be fatal. If you suspect an overdose, seek medical help immediately.

■ *Symptoms of Triavil overdose may include:*
Abnormalities of posture and movements, agitation, coma, convulsions, dilated pupils, drowsiness, extreme low body temperature, eye movement

problems, high fever, heart failure, overactive reflexes, rapid or irregular heartbeat, rigid muscles, stupor, very low blood pressure, vomiting

Generic name:

TRIAZOLAM

See Halcion, page 480.

Brand name:

TRIDESILON

Pronounced: tri-DESS-ill-on
Generic name: Desonide
Other brand name: DesOwen

Why is this drug prescribed?
Tridesilon is a steroid preparation that relieves the itching and inflammation of a variety of skin problems. It is applied directly to the skin.

Most important fact about this drug
When you use Tridesilon, you inevitably absorb some of the medication through your skin and into the bloodstream. Too much absorption can lead to unwanted side effects elsewhere in the body. To keep this problem to a minimum, avoid using large amounts of Tridesilon over large areas, and do not cover it with airtight dressings such as plastic wrap or adhesive bandages unless specifically told to by your doctor.

How should you use this medication?
Use Tridesilon exactly as directed by your doctor.

Tridesilon is for use only on the skin. Be careful to keep it out of your eyes.

Remember to avoid wrapping the treated area with bandages or other coverings unless your doctor has told you to do so.

- *If you miss a dose...*
  Apply it as soon as you remember. If it is almost time for the next dose, skip the one you missed and go back to your regular schedule.

- *Storage instructions...*
  Store at room temperature.

What side effects may occur?
Side effects cannot be anticipated. If any develop or change in intensity, notify your doctor as soon as possible. Only your doctor can determine if it is safe for you to continue using Tridesilon. The side effects listed below are rare, but may occur more often if the affected area is covered with a bandage or treated for a long time.

■ *Side effects may include:*
Acne, additional infections, allergic reactions of the skin, burning, dryness, excessive hair growth, irritation, itching, loss of skin color, prickly heat, rash, skin inflammation around the mouth, skin loss, skin softening, stretch marks

■ *Side effects that may occur in children include:*
Delayed weight gain, headaches, slowed growth

Why should this drug not be prescribed?
You should not take this medication if you are sensitive or allergic to any of its ingredients.

Because steroid medications may interfere with their growth and development, children should be given the lowest strength that provides effective therapy.

Special warnings about this medication
If an irritation develops, inform your doctor.

Avoid covering a treated area with waterproof diapers or plastic pants. They can increase unwanted absorption of Tridesilon.

Large doses of steroids applied over a large area, and long-term use of these preparations, especially when the treated areas are covered, can cause increases in blood sugar or sugar in the urine, Cushing's syndrome (a condition characterized by a moon-shaped face, emotional disturbances, high blood pressure, weight gain, and, in women, growth of body hair), and effects on the adrenal gland, pituitary, and hypothalamus.

**Possible food and drug interactions
when using this medication**
No interactions have been reported.

Special information
if you are pregnant or breastfeeding

Although Tridesilon is applied to the skin, there is no way of knowing how much medication is absorbed into the bloodstream. The more powerful steroids have caused birth defects in animals. In general, these preparations should not be used extensively, in large amounts, or for prolonged periods of time by pregnant women. They should be used only if the potential benefits outweigh the potential risks to the unborn baby. If you are pregnant or plan to become pregnant, inform your doctor immediately. It is not known whether steroid creams and ointments are absorbed in sufficient amounts to appear in breast milk. If your doctor considers Tridesilon essential to your health, he or she may advise you to stop breastfeeding until your treatment with the medication is finished.

Recommended dosage

ADULTS AND CHILDREN

Tridesilon should be applied to the affected area as a thin film, from 2 to 4 times a day, depending on the severity of the condition.

A bandage or other covering may be prescribed by your doctor to apply over the affected area for psoriasis or conditions that are not responding as well as expected.

Overdosage

Any medication taken in excess can have serious consequences. With overuse or misuse of Tridesilon, too much medicine can enter the body, causing increases in blood sugar and Cushing's syndrome, with symptoms such as a moon-shaped face, emotional disturbances, high blood pressure, weight gain, and, in women, growth of body and facial hair.

Generic name:

TRIFLUOPERAZINE

See Stelazine, page 1043.

Generic name:

TRIHEXYPHENIDYL

See Artane, page 73.

Brand name:

TRILISATE

Pronounced: TRILL-ih-sate
Generic name: Choline magnesium trisalicylate

Why is this drug prescribed?
Trilisate, a nonsteroidal anti-inflammatory medication, is prescribed for the relief of the signs and symptoms of rheumatoid arthritis (chronic joint inflammation disease), osteoarthritis (degenerative joint disease), and other forms of arthritis. This drug is used in the long-term management of these diseases and especially for flare-ups of severe rheumatoid arthritis.

Trilisate may also be prescribed for the treatment of acute painful shoulder, for mild to moderate pain in general, and for fever.

In children, this medication is prescribed for severe conditions—such as juvenile rheumatoid arthritis—that require relief of pain and inflammation.

Most important fact about this drug
Because there is a possible association between the development of the rare but serious neurological disorder known as Reye's syndrome and the use of medicines containing salicylates or aspirin, Trilisate should not be used by children or teenagers who have chickenpox or flu symptoms unless otherwise advised by their doctor.

How should you take this medication?
Trilisate is available in tablet or liquid form. Take Trilisate exactly as prescribed by your doctor.

- *If you miss a dose...*
  If you take Trilisate on a regular schedule, take the forgotten dose as soon as you remember. If it is almost time for your next dose, skip the one you missed and go back to your regular schedule. Do not take 2 doses at once.

- *Storage instructions...*
  Store at room temperature.

What side effects may occur?
Side effects cannot be anticipated. If any develop or change in intensity, inform your doctor as soon as possible. Only your doctor can determine if it is safe for you to continue taking Trilisate.

- *More common side effects may include:*
  Constipation
  Diarrhea
  Heartburn
  Indigestion
  Nausea
  Ringing in the ears
  Stomach pain and upset
  Vomiting

- *Less common side effects may include:*
  Dizziness, drowsiness, headache, hearing impairment, light-headedness, sluggishness

- *Rare side effects may include:*
  Asthma, blood in the stool, bruising, confusion, distorted sense of taste, hallucinations, hearing loss, hepatitis, hives, inflammation of the upper gastric tract, itching, loss of appetite, nosebleed, rash, skin eruptions or discoloration, stomach or intestinal ulcers, swelling due to fluid accumulation, weight gain

Why should this drug not be prescribed?
If you are sensitive to or have ever had an allergic reaction to Trilisate or drugs of this type, such as aspirin, you should not take this medication. Make sure your doctor is aware of any drug reactions you have experienced.

Special warnings about this medication
Use Trilisate with caution if you have severe or recurring kidney or liver disorder, gastritis (inflammation of the stomach lining), or a stomach or intestinal ulcer. Consult your doctor regarding any medical problems you may have.

If you are an asthmatic allergic to aspirin, tell your doctor before taking Trilisate.

It may be 2 to 3 weeks before you feel the effect of this medication.

Possible food and drug interactions
when taking this medication
If Trilisate is taken with certain other drugs, the effects of either could be increased, decreased, or altered. It is especially important to check with your doctor before combining Trilisate with the following:

Antacids such as Gaviscon and Maalox
Antigout medications

Blood-thinners such as Coumadin

Carbonic anhydrase inhibitors such as acetazolamide (Diamox) used to treat heart failure, the eye condition called glaucoma, and certain convulsive disorders

Diabetes medications such as insulin, Micronase, and Tolinase

Methotrexate, an anticancer drug

Other salicylates used to reduce fever, inflammation, and pain such as aspirin

Phenytoin (the anticonvulsant Dilantin)

Steroids such as prednisone

Valproic acid (the anticonvulsant Depakene)

Special information
if you are pregnant or breastfeeding

The effects of Trilisate during pregnancy have not been adequately studied. If you are pregnant or plan to become pregnant, inform your doctor immediately. This drug does appear in breast milk and could affect a nursing infant. If this medication is essential to your health, your doctor may advise you not to breastfeed until your treatment is finished.

Recommended dosage

ADULTS

In rheumatoid arthritis, osteoarthritis, more severe arthritis, and acute painful shoulder, the recommended starting dose is 1,500 milligrams taken 2 times a day or 3,000 milligrams taken once a day. Your doctor will adjust the dosage based on your response to this medication.

If you have a kidney disorder, your doctor will monitor you and adjust your dose accordingly.

For mild to moderate pain or to reduce a high fever, the usual dosage is 2,000 to 3,000 milligrams per day divided into 2 equal doses as recommended by your doctor.

CHILDREN

For reduction of inflammation or pain, the recommended dose for children is determined by weight. The usual dose for children who weigh 81 pounds or less is 50 milligrams per 2.2 pounds of body weight, taken twice a day. For heavier children, the usual dose is 2,250 milligrams per day, divided into 2 doses.

Trilisate liquid can be taken by younger children and by adults who are unable to swallow a tablet.

ELDERLY

The usual dosage is 2,250 milligrams divided into 3 doses of 750 milligrams each.

Overdosage

Any medication taken in excess can have serious consequences. If you suspect an overdose, seek medical treatment immediately. An overdose of Trilisate can be fatal.

■ *Symptoms of Trilisate overdose may include:*
Confusion, diarrhea, dizziness, drowsiness, headache, hearing impairment, rapid breathing, ringing in the ears, sweating, vomiting

Generic name:

TRIMETHOBENZAMIDE

See Tigan, page 1112.

Generic name:

TRIMETHOPRIM WITH SULFAMETHOXAZOLE

See Bactrim, page 104.

Generic name:

TRIMIPRAMINE

See Surmontil, page 1053.

Brand name:

TRIMOX

See Amoxil, page 47.

Brand name:

TRINALIN REPETABS

Pronounced: TRIN-uh-lin
*Generic ingredients: Azatadine maleate, Pseudoephedrine
  sulfate*

Why is this drug prescribed?

Trinalin Repetabs is a long-acting antihistamine/decongestant that relieves nasal stuffiness and middle ear congestion caused by hay fever and ongoing nasal inflammation. It can be used alone or with antibiotics and analgesics such as aspirin or acetaminophen. Azatadine, the antihistamine in the combination, reduces itching and swelling and dries up secretions from the nose, eyes, and throat. Pseudoephedrine, the decongestant, reduces nasal congestion and makes breathing easier.

Most important fact about this drug

Trinalin Repetabs may cause drowsiness. You should not drive or operate dangerous machinery or participate in any hazardous activity that requires full mental alertness until you know how you react to this medication.

How should you take this medication?

Take this medication as indicated; do not take more than your doctor has prescribed.

- *If you miss a dose...*
  If you take Trinalin on a regular schedule, take the forgotten dose as soon as you remember. If it is almost time for your next dose, skip the one you missed and go back to your regular schedule. Do not take 2 doses at once.

- *Storage instructions...*
  Store at room temperature in a cool place.

What side effects may occur?

Side effects cannot be anticipated. If any develop or change in intensity, inform your doctor as soon as possible. Only your doctor can determine if it is safe for you to continue taking Trinalin.

- *Side effects may include:*
  Abdominal cramps, acute inflammation of the inner ear, anemia, anxiety, blood disorders, blurred vision, chest pain, chills, confusion, constipation, convulsions, diarrhea, difficulty breathing, dilated pupils, disturbed coordination, dizziness, dry mouth, nose, and throat, early menstruation, exaggerated feeling of well-being, excessive perspiration, excitement, extreme calm (sedation), fatigue, fear, fluttery heartbeat, frequent urination, hallucinations, headache, high blood pressure, hives, hysteria, increased chest congestion, increased sensitivity to light, insomnia, irregular heartbeat, irritability, loss of appetite, low blood pressure, nausea, nervousness, painful or difficult urination, pale skin, rapid

heartbeat, rash, restlessness, ringing in the ears, severe allergic reaction, sleepiness, stuffy nose, tension, tightness in chest, tingling or pins and needles, tremor, upset stomach, urinary retention, vertigo, vomiting, weakness, wheezing

Why should this drug not be prescribed?

Trinalin should be avoided if you have narrow-angle glaucoma or difficulty urinating, if you are taking antidepressant drugs known as MAO inhibitors or have stopped taking them within the past 10 days, if you have severe high blood pressure, severe heart disease, or an overactive thyroid, or if you are sensitive to or have ever had an allergic reaction to any of its ingredients.

This drug should not be used to treat asthma and other lower respiratory tract diseases.

Special warnings about this medication

Trinalin should be used with care if you have a peptic ulcer or other upper intestinal obstruction, bladder obstruction due to an enlarged prostate or other bladder problems, a history of bronchial asthma, heart disease, high blood pressure, increased eye pressure, or diabetes.

Pseudoephedrine can be habit-forming at high doses. Remember that this medication can make you feel drowsy. Be careful driving, operating machinery, or using appliances.

Trinalin may cause dizziness, extreme calm (sedation), and low blood pressure in people aged 60 and over. It is also more likely to cause such side effects as confusion, convulsions, hallucinations, and death in this age group.

Possible food and drug interactions
when taking this medication

Alcohol may increase the effects of Trinalin. Do not drink alcohol while taking this medication.

If Trinalin is taken with certain other drugs, the effects of either could be increased, decreased, or altered. It is especially important to check with your doctor before combining Trinalin with the following:

Antacids such as Maalox
Barbiturates such as phenobarbital
Beta-blocking blood pressure drugs such as Tenormin and Inderal
Blood thinners such as Coumadin
Digitalis (Lanoxin)
Drugs for depression such as Prozac and Elavil

High blood pressure drugs such as Aldomet and Inversine
Kaolin (Kaopectate)
MAO inhibitor drugs (antidepressants such as Nardil and Parnate)
Sedatives such as Nembutal and Seconal
Tranquilizers such as Xanax and Valium

Special information
if you are pregnant or breastfeeding

Although the effects of Trinalin during pregnancy have not been adequately studied, antihistamines have caused severe reactions in premature and newborn babies when used in the last 3 months of pregnancy. If you are pregnant or plan to become pregnant, notify your doctor immediately. Trinalin may appear in breast milk and could affect a nursing infant. If this medication is essential to your health, your doctor may advise you to discontinue breastfeeding until your treatment with Trinalin is finished.

Recommended dosage

ADULTS AND CHILDREN AGED 12 AND OVER

The usual dosage is 1 tablet twice a day.

Children under age 12 should not take Trinalin.

Overdosage

Any medication taken in excess can have serious consequences. An overdose of Trinalin can be fatal. If you suspect an overdose, seek medical attention immediately.

■ *Symptoms of Trinalin overdose may include:*
Anxiety, bluish color caused by lack of oxygen, blurred vision, chest pain, coma, convulsions, decreased mental alertness, delusions, difficulty sleeping, difficulty urinating, dizziness, excitement, extreme calm (sedation), exaggerated sense of well-being, fluttery heartbeat, giddiness, hallucinations, headache, high blood pressure/low blood pressure, irregular heartbeat, lack of muscle coordination, muscle tenseness, muscle weakness, nausea, perspiration, rapid heartbeat, restlessness, ringing in the ears, temporary interruption of breathing, thirst, tremors, vomiting

■ *Overdose symptoms more common in children may include:*
Dry mouth, fixed, dilated pupils, flushing, overstimulation, stomach and intestinal problems, very high body temperature

Generic name:

TRIPELENNAMINE

See PBZ-SR, page 810.

Brand name:

TRIPHASIL

See Oral Contraceptives, page 775.

Brand name:

T-STAT

See Erythromycin, Topical, page 409.

Brand name:

TUMS

See Antacids, page 62.

Brand name:

TUSSIONEX

Pronounced: TUSS-ee-uh-nex
Generic ingredients: Hydrocodone polistirex,
Chlorpheniramine polistirex

Why is this drug prescribed?

Tussionex Extended-Release Suspension is a cough-suppressant/antihista-
mine combination used to relieve coughs and the upper respiratory symptoms
of colds and allergies. Hydrocodone, a mild narcotic similar to codeine, is
believed to work directly on the cough center. Chlorpheniramine, an
antihistamine, reduces itching and swelling and dries up secretions from the
eyes, nose, and throat.

Most important fact about this drug

This medication can cause considerable drowsiness and make you less alert.
You should not drive or operate machinery or participate in any activity that
requires full mental alertness until you know how you react to Tussionex.

How should you take this medication?
Tussionex should be taken exactly as prescribed.

It should not be diluted with other liquids or mixed with other drugs. Shake well before using.

■ *If you miss a dose...*
If you take Tussionex on a regular schedule, take the forgotten dose as soon as you remember. If it is almost time for your next dose, skip the one you missed and go back to your regular schedule. Do not take 2 doses at once.

■ *Storage instructions...*
Store at room temperature in a tightly closed container.

What side effects may occur?
Side effects cannot be anticipated. If any develop or change in intensity, inform your doctor as soon as possible. Only your doctor can determine if it is safe for you to continue taking Tussionex.

■ *Side effects may include:*
Anxiety, constipation, decreased mental and physical performance, difficulty breathing, difficulty urinating, dizziness, drowsiness, dry throat, emotional dependence, exaggerated feeling of depression, extreme calm (sedation), exaggerated sense of well-being, fear, itching, mental clouding, mood changes, nausea, rash, restlessness, sluggishness, tightness in chest, vomiting

Why should this drug not be prescribed?
Do not take Tussionex if you are sensitive to or have ever had an allergic reaction to hydrocodone or chlorpheniramine. Make sure your doctor is aware of any drug reactions you have experienced.

Special warnings about this medication
Tussionex contains a mild narcotic that can cause dependence and tolerance when the drug is used for several weeks. However, it is unlikely that dependence will develop when Tussionex is used for the short-term treatment of a cough.

Like all narcotics, Tussionex may produce slowed or irregular breathing. If you have lung disease or a breathing disorder, use this medication cautiously.

Use Tussionex with care if you have the eye condition known as narrow-angle glaucoma, asthma, an enlarged prostate gland, urinary difficulties, an intestinal disorder, liver or kidney disease, an underactive thyroid gland, or Addison's disease (a disorder of the adrenal glands), or if you have recently suffered a head injury.

Extra caution should be used when giving Tussionex to the elderly and those in a weakened condition.

Remember that Tussionex can cause drowsiness.

Narcotics can cause intestinal blockage or mask a severe abdominal condition.

Possible food and drug interactions
when taking this medication

Tussionex may increase the effects of alcohol. Do not drink alcohol while taking this medication.

If Tussionex is taken with certain other drugs, the effects of either could be increased, decreased, or altered. It is especially important to check with your doctor before combining Tussionex with the following:

Antispasmodic medications such as Bentyl and Cogentin
Major tranquilizers such as Thorazine and Compazine
MAO inhibitor drugs (antidepressant drugs such as Nardil and Parnate)
Medications for anxiety such as Xanax and Valium
Medications for depression such as Elavil and Prozac
Other antihistamines such as Benadryl
Other narcotics such as Percocet and Demerol

Special information
if you are pregnant or breastfeeding

The safety of Tussionex during pregnancy has not been adequately studied. However, babies born to mothers who have been taking narcotics regularly before delivery will be born addicted. If you are pregnant or plan to become pregnant, inform your doctor immediately. Tussionex may appear in breast milk and could affect a nursing infant. If this medication is essential to your health, your doctor may recommend that you stop breastfeeding until your treatment with Tussionex is finished.

Recommended dosage

ADULTS

The usual dose is 1 teaspoonful (5 milliliters) every 12 hours. Do not take more than 2 teaspoonfuls in 24 hours.

CHILDREN AGED 6 TO 12

The usual dose is one-half teaspoonful every 12 hours. Do not take more than 1 teaspoonful in 24 hours.

Tussionex is not recommended for children under 6 years old.

Overdosage

Any medication taken in excess can have serious consequences. A narcotic overdose can be fatal. If you suspect an overdose, seek medical treatment immediately.

- *Symptoms of Tussionex overdose may include:*
  Blue skin color due to lack of oxygen
  Cardiac arrest
  Cold and clammy skin
  Decreased or difficult breathing
  Extreme sleepiness leading to stupor or coma
  Low blood pressure
  Muscle flabbiness
  Slow heartbeat
  Temporary cessation of breathing

Brand name:

TUSSI-ORGANIDIN NR

Pronounced: TUSS-ee or-GAN-i-din en are
Generic ingredients: Guaifenesin, Codeine phosphate
Other brand name: Brontex

Why is this drug prescribed?

Tussi-Organidin NR is used to relieve coughs and chest congestion in adults and children. It contains guaifenesin, which helps thin and loosen mucus in the lungs, making it easier to cough up. It also contains a cough suppressant, the narcotic codeine.

Most important fact about this drug

Tussi-Organidin NR may cause you to become drowsy or less alert. Alcohol will intensify this effect. Driving, operating dangerous machinery, or participating in any hazardous activity that requires your full mental alertness is not recommended until you know how you react to this medication.

How should you take this medication?
Take Tussi-Organidin NR exactly as described. When giving the liquid to a child, use a calibrated dropper to measure the dose.

- *If you miss a dose...*
  Take the missed dose as soon as you remember. If it is almost time for your next dose, skip the one you missed and go back to your regular schedule. Never take 2 doses at once.

- *Storage instructions...*
  Store at room temperature in a tightly closed container, away from light.

What side effects may occur?
Side effects cannot be anticipated. If any side effects develop or change in intensity, tell your doctor as soon as possible. Only your doctor can determine whether it is safe to continue taking Tussi-Organidin NR.

- *More common side effects may include:*
  Constipation
  Nausea
  "Pinpoint" pupils of the eye
  Vomiting

- *Less common side effects may include:*
  Dizziness, headache, rash

At higher doses, this medication may also cause light-headedness, drowsiness, slowed breathing, and an exaggerated sense of well-being.

Why should this drug not be prescribed?
Do not take Tussi-Organidin NR if you are allergic to codeine or guaifenisin.

Special warnings about this medication
Because it contains codeine, Tussi-Organidin NR may cause drug dependence and tolerance with continued use.

Do not use this product in children under 2 years of age. Be cautious if the child has an allergy.

Do not take Tussi-Organidin NR for the constant cough brought on by smoking, asthma, chronic bronchitis, or emphysema unless your doctor recommends it. If your cough lasts for more than 1 week, tends to come back, or is accompanied by fever, rash, or persistent headache, check with your doctor.

Be sure to tell the doctor if you have any breathing problems, a severe abdominal condition, kidney or liver problems, an underactive thyroid gland, or an enlarged prostate. Also alert the doctor if you suffer from seizures, have had a head injury, or have recently had stomach, intestinal, or urinary tract surgery.

Possible food and drug interactions
when taking this medication

If Tussi-Organidin NR is taken with certain other drugs, the effects of either could be increased, decreased, or altered. It is especially important to check with your doctor before combining Tussi-Organidin NR with the following:

Alcohol
Antihistamines such as Actifed or Benadryl
Drugs used to treat anxiety or depression, such as Librium and Prozac
Sedatives such as Dalmane

Special information
if you are pregnant or breastfeeding

If you are pregnant or plan to become pregnant, inform your doctor immediately. The safety of Tussi-Organidin NR during pregnancy has not been established. Tussi-Organidin NR should not be taken if you are breastfeeding.

Recommended dosage

ADULTS AND CHILDREN 12 YEARS AND OLDER

Tussi-Organidin NR
The usual dosage is 2 teaspoonfuls every 4 hours, not to exceed 12 teaspoonfuls in 24 hours.

Brontex
The usual dosage is 1 tablet or 4 teaspoonfuls every 4 hours.

CHILDREN 6 TO 12 YEARS OF AGE

Tussi-Organidin NR
The usual dosage is 1 teaspoonful every 4 hours, not to exceed 6 teaspoonfuls in 24 hours.

Brontex
The usual dosage is 2 teaspoonfuls every 4 hours. Do not give tablets.

CHILDREN 2 TO 6 YEARS OF AGE

Tussi-Organidin NR

Your doctor will determine the dosage according to weight. The recommended total daily dosage is 1 milligram per 2.2 pounds of body weight, divided into 4 small doses.

Overdosage

Any medication taken in excess can have serious consequences. If you suspect an overdose, seek medical treatment immediately.

- *Symptoms of Tussi-Organidin NR overdose may include:*
  Alternate periods of not breathing and rapid, deep breathing, bluish skin coloration, cold and clammy skin, constriction of the pupils of the eye, delirium, delusions, double vision, excitement, extreme sleepiness progressing to stupor or coma, flaccid muscles, hallucinations, low blood pressure, restlessness, slow, shallow, or labored breathing, slow heartbeat, speech disturbances, vertigo

Brand name:

TYLENOL

Pronounced: TIE-len-all
Generic name: Acetaminophen
Other brand names: Panadol, Aspirin Free Anacin

Why is this drug prescribed?

Tylenol is a fever- and pain-reducing medication that is widely used to relieve simple headaches and muscle aches; the minor aches and pains of bursitis, arthritis, rheumatism, neuralgia (nerve inflammation), sprains, overexertion, and menstrual cramps; and the discomfort of fever due to colds and the flu.

Children's Tylenol is used to relieve fever, pain and discomfort due to colds, flu, teething, immunizations, and tonsillectomy.

Most important fact about this drug

Do not use Tylenol to relieve pain for more than 10 days, or to reduce fever for more than 3 days unless your doctor has specifically told you to do so.

How should you take this medication?

Follow the dosing instructions on the label. Do not take more Tylenol than is recommended.

- *If you miss a dose...*
  Take this medication only as needed.

- *Storage instructions...*
  Store at room temperature. Keep the liquid form from freezing.

What side effects may occur?
Tylenol is relatively free of side effects. Rarely, an allergic reaction may occur. If you develop any allergic symptoms such as rash, hives, swelling, or difficulty breathing, stop taking Tylenol immediately and notify your doctor.

Special warnings about this medication
Remember that Tylenol should not be used for more than 10 days for pain, or 3 days for fever. Children's Tylenol should not be used for more than 5 days for pain, or 3 days for fever. If fever remains, or pain persists, contact your doctor. These symptoms could indicate a more serious illness.

If you generally drink 3 or more alcoholic beverages per day, check with your doctor about using Tylenol and other acetaminophen-containing products, and never take more than the recommended dosage. There is a possibility of damage to the liver when large amounts of alcohol and acetaminophen are combined.

**Possible food and drug interactions
when taking this medication**
If Tylenol is taken with certain other drugs, the effects of either could be increased, decreased, or altered. It is especially important to check with your doctor before combining Tylenol with the following:

    Alcohol
    Cholestyramine (Questran)
    Isoniazid (Nydrazid)
    Nonsteroidal anti-inflammatory drugs such as Dolobid and Motrin
    Oral contraceptives
    Phenytoin (Dilantin)
    Warfarin (Coumadin)
    Zidovudine (Retrovir)

**Special information
if you are pregnant or breastfeeding**
As with all medications, ask your doctor or health-care professional whether it is safe for you to use Tylenol while you are pregnant or breastfeeding.

Recommended dosage

ADULTS AND CHILDREN 12 YEARS AND OLDER

Tylenol Regular Strength
The usual dose is 1 to 2 tablets, 3 or 4 times daily.

Tylenol Extended Relief
The usual dose is 2 caplets every 8 hours, not to exceed 6 caplets in any 24-hour period. Swallow each caplet whole. Do not crush, chew, or dissolve the caplets.

CHILDREN 6 TO 12 YEARS OLD

Tylenol Regular Strength
One-half to 1 tablet 3 or 4 times a day.

Children's Tylenol
All doses of Children's Tylenol may be repeated every 4 hours, but not more than 5 times daily.

Chewable Tablets
The usual dose for children 6 to 8 years of age is 4 tablets; 9 to 10 years, 5 tablets; 11 to 12 years, 6 tablets

Elixir and Suspension Liquid
(A special cup for measuring dosage is provided.) The usual dose for children 6 to 8 years of age is 2 teaspoons; 9 to 10 years, 2½ teaspoons; 11 to 12 years, 3 teaspoons.

CHILDREN UNDER 6 YEARS OLD

Children under 2 years old should be given Children's Tylenol only on the advice of a physician.

Regular Strength Tylenol
Consult your physician or health care professional.

Children's Tylenol
All doses of Children's Tylenol may be repeated every 4 hours, but not more than 5 times daily.

Chewable Tablets
The usual dose for children 2 to 3 years of age is 2 tablets; 4 to 5 years, 3 tablets.

Elixir and Suspension Liquid

(A special cup for measuring dosage is provided.) The usual dose for children 4 to 11 months of age is ½ teaspoon; 12 to 23 months, ¾ teaspoon; 2 to 3 years, 1 teaspoon; 4 to 5 years, 1½ teaspoons.

Infants' Tylenol Drops and Suspension Drops

The usual dose for children 0 to 3 months of age is 0.4 milliliter; 4 to 11 months, 0.8 milliliter; 12 to 23 months, 1.2 milliliters; 2 to 3 years, 1.6 milliliters; 4 to 5 years, 2.4 milliliters.

Overdosage

Any medication taken in excess can have serious consequences. If you suspect an overdose, seek medical attention immediately. Massive doses of Tylenol may cause liver damage.

- **Symptoms of Tylenol overdose may include:**
  Excessive perspiration
  Exhaustion
  General discomfort
  Nausea
  Vomiting

Brand name:

TYLENOL WITH CODEINE

Pronounced: TIE-len-awl with CO-deen
Generic ingredients: Acetaminophen, Codeine phosphate
Other brand name: Phenaphen with Codeine

Why is this drug prescribed?

Tylenol with Codeine, a narcotic analgesic, is used to treat mild to moderately severe pain. It contains two drugs—acetaminophen and codeine. Acetaminophen, an antipyretic (fever-reducing) analgesic, is used to reduce pain and fever. Codeine, a narcotic analgesic, is used to treat pain that is moderate to severe.

People who are allergic to aspirin can take Tylenol with Codeine.

Most important fact about this drug

Tylenol with Codeine contains a narcotic (codeine) and, even if taken in prescribed amounts, can cause physical and psychological addiction if taken for a long enough time.

Addiction may be more of a risk for a person who has been addicted to alcohol or drugs. Be sure to follow your doctor's instructions carefully when taking Tylenol with Codeine (or any other drugs that contain a narcotic).

How should you take this medication?
Tylenol with Codeine may be taken with meals or with milk (but not with alcohol).

■ *If you miss a dose...*
If you take this medication on a regular schedule, take the forgotten dose as soon as you remember. If it is almost time for your next dose, skip the one you missed and go back to your regular schedule. Do not take 2 doses at once.

■ *Storage instructions...*
Store away from heat, light, and moisture. Keep the liquid from freezing.

What side effects may occur?
Side effects cannot be anticipated. If any develop or change in intensity, inform your doctor as soon as possible. Only your doctor can determine if it is safe for you to continue taking Tylenol with Codeine.

■ *More common side effects may include:*
Dizziness
Light-headedness
Nausea
Sedation
Shortness of breath
Vomiting

■ *Less common side effects may include:*
Abdominal pain, allergic reactions, constipation, depressed feeling, exaggerated feeling of well-being, itchy skin

■ *Rare side effects may include:*
Decreased breathing (when Tylenol with Codeine is taken at higher doses)

Why should this drug not be prescribed?
You should not use Tylenol with Codeine if you are sensitive to either acetaminophen (Tylenol) or codeine.

Special warnings about this medication

You should take Tylenol with Codeine cautiously and only according to your doctor's instructions, as you would take any medication containing a narcotic. Make sure your doctor is aware of any problems you have had with drug or alcohol addiction.

Tylenol with Codeine tablets contain a sulfite that may cause allergic reactions in some people. These reactions may include shock and severe, possibly life-threatening, asthma attacks. People with asthma are more likely to be sensitive to sulfites.

If you have experienced a head injury, consult your doctor before taking Tylenol with Codeine.

If you have stomach problems, such as an ulcer, check with your doctor before taking Tylenol with Codeine. Tylenol with Codeine may obscure the symptoms of stomach problems, making them difficult to diagnose and treat.

If you have ever had liver, kidney, thyroid, or adrenal disease, difficulty urinating, or an enlarged prostate, consult your doctor before taking Tylenol with Codeine.

If you generally drink 3 or more alcoholic beverages per day, check with your doctor before using Tylenol with Codeine and other acetaminophen-containing products, and never take more than the recommended dosage. There is a possibility of damage to the liver when large amounts of alcohol and acetaminophen are combined.

This drug may cause drowsiness and impair your ability to drive a car or operate potentially dangerous machinery. Do not participate in any activities that require full attention when using this drug until you are sure of its effect on you.

Possible food and drug interactions
when taking this medication

Alcohol may increase the sedative effects of Tylenol with Codeine. Therefore, do not drink alcohol while you are taking this medication.

If Tylenol with Codeine is taken with certain other drugs, the effects of either could be increased, decreased, or altered. It is especially important to check with your doctor before combining Tylenol with Codeine with the following:

Antidepressants such as Elavil, Nardil, Parnate, and Tofranil
Drugs that control spasms, such as Cogentin

Major tranquilizers such as Clozaril and Thorazine
Other narcotic painkillers such as Darvon
Tranquilizers such as Xanax and Valium

Special information
if you are pregnant or breastfeeding

It is not known if Tylenol with Codeine could injure a baby, or if it could affect a woman's reproductive capacity. Using any medication that contains a narcotic during pregnancy may cause babies to be born with a physical addiction to the narcotic. If you are pregnant or plan to become pregnant, you should not take Tylenol with Codeine unless the potential benefits clearly outweigh the possible dangers. As with other narcotic painkillers, taking Tylenol with Codeine shortly before delivery (especially at higher dosages) may cause some degree of breathing difficulty in the mother and newborn.

Some studies (but not all) have reported that codeine appears in breast milk and may affect a nursing infant. Therefore, nursing mothers should use Tylenol with Codeine only if the potential gains are greater than the potential hazards.

Recommended dosage

ADULTS

Dosage will depend on how severe your pain is and how you respond to the drug.

To Relieve Pain

A single dose may contain from 15 milligrams to 60 milligrams of codeine phosphate and from 300 to 1,000 milligrams of acetaminophen. The maximum dose in a 24-hour period should be 360 milligrams of codeine phosphate and 4,000 milligrams of acetaminophen. Your doctor will determine the amounts of codeine phosphate and acetaminophen taken in each dose. Doses may be repeated up to every 4 hours.

Single doses above 60 milligrams of codeine do not give enough pain relief to balance the increased number of side effects.

Adults may also take Tylenol with Codeine elixir (liquid). Tylenol with Codeine elixir contains 120 milligrams of acetaminophen and 12 milligrams of codeine phosphate per teaspoonful.

The usual adult dose is 1 tablespoonful every 4 hours as needed.

CHILDREN

The safety of Tylenol with Codeine elixir has not been established in children under 3 years old.

Children 3 to 6 years old may take 1 teaspoonful 3 or 4 times daily.

Children 7 to 12 years old may take 2 teaspoonsful 3 or 4 times daily.

ELDERLY

The elderly and anyone in a weakened or run-down condition should use Tylenol with Codeine cautiously.

Overdosage

Any medication taken in excess can cause symptoms of overdose. Severe overdosage of Tylenol with Codeine can cause death. If you suspect an overdose, seek medical attention immediately.

■ *Symptoms of Tylenol with Codeine overdose may include:*
Bluish skin, cold and clammy skin, coma due to low blood sugar, decreased, irregular, or stopped breathing, extreme sleepiness progressing to stupor or coma, general bodily discomfort, heart attack, kidney failure, liver failure, low blood pressure, muscle weakness, nausea, slow heartbeat, sweating, vomiting

Brand name:

TYLOX

See Percocet, page 831.

Brand name:

ULTRACEF

See Duricef, page 371.

Brand name:

ULTRASE

See Pancrease, page 796.

Brand name:

URISED

Pronounced: YOUR-i-said
Generic ingredients: Methenamine, Methylene blue, Phenyl
salicylate, Benzoic acid, Atropine sulfate, Hyoscyamine

Why is this drug prescribed?

Urised relieves lower urinary tract discomfort caused by inflammation or diagnostic procedures. It is used to treat urinary tract infections including cystitis (inflammation of the bladder and ureters), urethritis (inflammation of the urethra), and trigonitis (inflammation of the mucous membrane of the bladder). Methenamine, the major component of this drug, acts as a mild antiseptic by changing into formaldehyde in the urinary tract when it comes in contact with acidic urine.

Most important fact about this drug

Urised may give a blue to blue-green color to urine and discolor stools as well.

How should you take this medication?

If dry mouth occurs, hard candy or gum, saliva substitute, or crushed ice may provide temporary relief.

Take this medication exactly as prescribed; do not take more than the recommended dose.

Drinking plenty of fluids will help the medication work better and relieve discomfort.

▪ *If you miss a dose...*
  Take it as soon as you remember. If it is almost time for your next dose, skip the one you missed and go back to your regular schedule. Never take 2 doses at the same time.

▪ *Storage instructions...*
  Store Urised at room temperature, in a dry place.

What side effects may occur?

Side effects cannot be anticipated. If any develop or change in intensity, inform your doctor as soon as possible. Only your doctor can determine if it is safe for you to continue taking Urised.

- *Side effects with long-term use may include:*
  Acute urinary retention (in men with an enlarged prostate)
  Blurry vision
  Difficulty urinating
  Dizziness
  Dry mouth
  Flushing
  Rapid pulse
  Skin rash

Why should this drug not be prescribed?

Urised should be avoided if you have glaucoma, a bladder blockage, cardiospasm, or a disorder that obstructs the passage of food through the stomach. Also avoid Urised if you are sensitive to or have ever had an allergic reaction to any of its ingredients.

Special warnings about this medication

Urised should be used cautiously if you have heart disease or have ever had a reaction to medications that are chemically similar to atropine.

Your doctor may ask you to check your urine with phenaphthazine paper to see if it is acidic. Urine acidifiers, such as vitamin C, may be recommended if the urine is not acidic enough.

Possible food and drug interactions
when taking this medication

If Urised is taken with certain other drugs, the effects of either could be increased, decreased, or altered. It is especially important to check with your doctor before combining Urised with the following:

Acetazolamide (Diamox)
Potassium supplements such as Slow-K
Sodium bicarbonate antacids such as Alka-Seltzer
Sulfa drugs such as Gantrisin, Gantanol, Bactrim, and Septra

Drugs and foods that produce alkaline urine (such as sodium bicarbonate, antacids, and orange juice) should be limited.

Special information
if you are pregnant or breastfeeding

The effects of Urised during pregnancy have not been adequately studied. If you are pregnant or plan to become pregnant, inform your doctor immediately. Urised may appear in breast milk and could affect a nursing infant. If this medication is essential to your health, your doctor may advise you to stop breastfeeding until your treatment with Urised ends.

Recommended dosage

ADULTS

The usual dose is 2 tablets, 4 times a day.

CHILDREN 6 YEARS AND OLDER

The dosage must be determined by your doctor.

CHILDREN UNDER 6 YEARS

Use is not recommended in children under 6 years old.

Overdosage

Any medication taken in excess can have serious consequences. If you suspect an overdose, seek medical treatment immediately.

■ *Symptoms of Urised overdose may include:*
Abdominal pain, bladder and abdominal irritation, bloody diarrhea, bloody urine, burning pain in throat and mouth, circulatory collapse, coma, dilated pupils (large pupils), dizziness, dry nose, mouth, and throat, elevated blood pressure, extremely high body temperature, headache, hot, dry, flushed skin, painful and frequent urination, pallor (paleness), pounding heartbeat (pounding sensation against the chest), rapid heartbeat (increased pulse rate), respiratory failure, ringing in ears, sweating, vomiting, weakness, white sores in mouth

Brand name:

URISPAS

Pronounced: YOUR-eh-spaz
Generic name: Flavoxate hydrochloride

Why is this drug prescribed?

Urispas prevents spasms in the urinary tract and relieves the painful or difficult urination, urinary urgency, excessive nighttime urination, pubic area pain, frequency of urination, and inability to hold urine caused by urinary tract infections. Urispas is taken in combination with antibiotics to treat the infection.

Most important fact about this drug
Urispas can cause blurred vision and drowsiness. Be careful driving, operating machinery, or performing any activity that requires complete mental alertness until you know how you will react to this medication.

How should you take this medication?
Take this medication exactly as prescribed. Urispas may make your mouth dry. Sucking on a hard candy, chewing gum, or melting bits of ice in your mouth can provide relief.

■ *If you miss a dose...*
Take it as soon as you remember. If it is almost time for your next dose, skip the one you missed and go back to your regular schedule. Do not take 2 doses at once.

■ *Storage instructions...*
Store away from heat, light, and moisture.

What side effects may occur?
Side effects cannot be anticipated. If any develop or change in intensity, notify your doctor as soon as possible. Only your doctor can determine whether it is safe for you to continue taking Urispas.

■ *Side effects may include:*
Allergic skin reactions, including hives, blurred vision and vision changes, drowsiness, dry mouth, fluttery heartbeat, headache, high body temperature, mental confusion (especially in the elderly), nausea, nervousness, painful or difficult urination, rapid heartbeat, vertigo, vomiting

Why should this drug not be prescribed?
You should not take Urispas if you have stomach or intestinal blockage, muscle relaxation problems (especially the sphincter muscle), abdominal bleeding, or urinary tract blockage.

Special warnings about this medication
Use Urispas cautiously if you have the eye condition known as glaucoma.

**Possible food and drug interactions
when taking this medication**
No interactions involving Urispas have been noted.

**Special information
if you are pregnant or breastfeeding**

The effects of Urispas during pregnancy have not been adequately studied. If you are pregnant or plan to become pregnant, inform your doctor immediately. Urispas may appear in breast milk and could affect a nursing infant. If this medication is essential to your health, your doctor may advise you to stop breastfeeding until your treatment is finished.

Recommended dosage

ADULTS AND CHILDREN OVER AGE 12

The usual dose of Urispas is one or two 100-milligram tablets 3 or 4 times a day.

When your symptoms have improved, your doctor may reduce the dosage.

CHILDREN

The safety and effectiveness of Urispas in children under 12 years of age have not been established.

Overdosage

Any medication taken in excess can have serious consequences. If you suspect an overdose of Urispas, seek medical attention immediately.

■ *Symptoms of Urispas overdose may include:*
Convulsions
Decreased ability to sweat (warm, red skin, dry mouth, and increased body temperature)
Hallucinations
Increased heart rate and blood pressure
Mental confusion

Generic name:

URSODIOL

See Actigall, page 14.

Brand name:

VALIUM

*Pronounced: VAL-ee-um
Generic name: Diazepam*

Why is this drug prescribed?
Valium is used in the treatment of anxiety disorders and for short-term relief of the symptoms of anxiety. It belongs to a class of drugs known as benzodiazepines.

It is also used to relieve the symptoms of acute alcohol withdrawal, to relax muscles, to relieve the uncontrolled muscle movements caused by cerebral palsy and paralysis of the lower body and limbs, to control involuntary movement of the hands (athetosis), to relax tight, aching muscles, and, along with other medications, to treat convulsive disorders such as epilepsy.

Most important fact about this drug
Valium can be habit-forming or addictive. You may experience withdrawal symptoms if you stop using this drug abruptly. Discontinue or change your dose only on your doctor's advice.

How should you take this medication?
Take this medication exactly as prescribed. If you are taking Valium for epilepsy, make sure you take it every day at the same time.

- *If you miss a dose...*
  Take it as soon as you remember if it is within an hour or so of the scheduled time. If you do not remember until later, skip the dose you missed and go back to your regular schedule. Never take 2 doses at the same time.

- *Storage instructions...*
  Store away from heat, light, and moisture.

What side effects may occur?
Side effects cannot be anticipated. If any develop or change in intensity, inform your doctor as soon as possible. Only your doctor can determine if it is safe for you to continue taking Valium.

- *More common side effects may include:*
  Drowsiness
  Fatigue
  Light-headedness
  Loss of muscle coordination

- *Less common or rare side effects may include:*
  Anxiety, blurred vision, changes in salivation, changes in sex drive, confusion, constipation, depression, difficulty urinating, dizziness, double vision, hallucinations, headache, inability to hold urine, low blood pressure,

nausea, overstimulation, rage, seizures (mild changes in brain wave patterns), skin rash, sleep disturbances, slow heartbeat, slurred speech and other speech problems, stimulation, tremors, vertigo, yellowing of eyes and skin

■ *Side effects due to rapid decrease in dose or abrupt withdrawal from Valium:*
Abdominal and muscle cramps, convulsions, sweating, tremors, vomiting

Why should this drug not be prescribed?
If you are sensitive to or have ever had an allergic reaction to Valium, you should not take this medication.

Do not take this medication if you have the eye condition known as acute narrow-angle glaucoma.

Anxiety or tension related to everyday stress usually does not require treatment with such a powerful drug as Valium. Discuss your symptoms thoroughly with your doctor.

Valium should not be prescribed if you are being treated for mental disorders more serious than anxiety.

Special warnings about this medication
Valium may cause you to become drowsy or less alert; therefore, you should not drive or operate dangerous machinery or participate in any hazardous activity that requires full mental alertness until you know how this drug affects you.

If you have liver or kidney problems, use this medication cautiously.

Possible food and drug interactions
when taking this medication
Valium slows down the central nervous system and may intensify the effects of alcohol. Do not drink alcohol while taking this medication.

If Valium is taken with certain other drugs, the effects of either could be increased, decreased, or altered. It is especially important to check with your doctor before combining Valium with any of the following:

Anticonvulsants such as Dilantin
Antidepressant drugs such as Elavil and Prozac
Barbiturates such as phenobarbital
Cimetidine (Tagamet)
Digoxin (Lanoxin)
Disulfiram (Antabuse)

Fluoxetine (Prozac)
Isoniazid (Rifamate)
Levodopa (Larodopa, Sinemet)
Major tranquilizers such as Mellaril and Thorazine
MAO inhibitors (antidepressant drugs such as Nardil)
Narcotics such as Percocet
Omeprazole (Prilosec)
Oral contraceptives
Propoxyphene (Darvon)
Ranitidine (Zantac)
Rifampin (Rifadin)

Special information
if you are pregnant or breastfeeding

Do not take Valium if you are pregnant or planning to become pregnant. There is an increased risk of birth defects.

If this medication is essential to your health, your doctor may advise you to discontinue breastfeeding until your treatment is finished.

Recommended dosage

ADULTS

Treatment of Anxiety Disorders and Short-Term Relief of the Symptoms of Anxiety
The usual dose, depending upon severity of symptoms, is 2 milligrams to 10 milligrams 2 to 4 times daily.

Acute Alcohol Withdrawal
The usual dose is 10 milligrams 3 or 4 times during the first 24 hours, then 5 milligrams 3 or 4 times daily as needed.

Relief of Muscle Spasm
The usual dose is 2 milligrams to 10 milligrams 3 or 4 times daily.

Convulsive Disorders
The usual dose is 2 milligrams to 10 milligrams 2 to 4 times daily.

CHILDREN

Valium should not be given to children under 6 months of age.

The usual starting dose for children over 6 months is 1 to 2.5 milligrams 3 or 4 times a day. Your doctor may increase the dosage gradually if needed.

ELDERLY

The usual dosage is 2 milligrams to 2.5 milligrams once or twice a day, which your doctor will increase as needed. Your doctor will limit the dosage to the smallest effective amount because older people are more apt to become oversedated or uncoordinated.

Overdosage

Any medication taken in excess can have serious consequences. If you suspect an overdose, seek medical attention immediately.

■ *Symptoms of Valium overdose may include:*
    Coma
    Confusion
    Diminished reflexes
    Sleepiness

Generic name:

VALPROIC ACID

See Depakene, page 301.

Brand name:

VANCENASE

See Beclomethasone, page 110.

Brand name:

VANCERIL INHALER

See Beclomethasone, page 110.

Brand name:

VASERETIC

Pronounced: Vaz-err-ET-ik
Generic ingredients: Enalapril maleate,
    Hydrochlorothiazide

Why is this drug prescribed?

Vaseretic is used in the treatment of high blood pressure. It combines an ACE inhibitor with a thiazide diuretic. Enalapril, the ACE inhibitor, works by preventing a chemical in your blood called angiotensin I from converting into a more potent form that increases salt and water retention in your body. Enalapril also enhances blood flow throughout your blood vessels. Hydrochlorothiazide, a diuretic, prompts your body to produce and eliminate more urine, which helps in lowering blood pressure.

Most important fact about this drug
You must take Vaseretic regularly for it to be effective. Since blood pressure declines gradually, it may be several weeks before you get the full benefit of Vaseretic; and you must continue taking it even if you are feeling well. Vaseretic does not cure high blood pressure; it merely keeps it under control.

How should you take this medication?
Take this medication exactly as prescribed by your doctor.

■ *If you miss a dose...*
Take it as soon as you remember. If it is almost time for your next dose, skip the one you missed and go back to your regular schedule. Never take 2 doses at the same time.

■ *Storage instructions...*
Keep container tightly closed. Store at room temperature and protect from moisture. Keep out of reach of children.

What side effects may occur?
Side effects cannot be anticipated. If any develop or change in intensity, inform your doctor as soon as possible. Only your doctor can determine if it is safe for you to continue taking Vaseretic.

■ *More common side effects may include:*
Cough, diarrhea, dizziness, drop in blood pressure upon standing up, fatigue, headache, impotence, low potassium levels (leading to symptoms such as dry mouth, excessive thirst, weak or irregular heartbeat, muscle pain or cramps), muscle cramps, nausea, rash, tingling or pins and needles, weakness

■ *Less common or rare side effects may include:*
Abdominal pain, abnormal skin sensations such as numbness, prickling, or burning, allergic reactions, arthritis, back pain, black stools, blisters, blood clots in lungs, blurred vision, bronchitis, chest pain, confusion, conjunctivitis, constipation, decrease in sex drive, depression, disturbances in heart rhythm, dry eyes, dry mouth, excessive sweating, fainting, fluid in lungs, flushing, gas, gout, heart attack, hepatitis, hives, hoarseness, inability to

sleep, indigestion, inflammation of mouth and tongue, inflammation of the pancreas, itching, joint pain, kidney failure, liver failure, loss of appetite, loss of coordination, loss of hair, low blood pressure, muscle cramps, nervousness, rapid heartbeat, rash, restlessness, ringing in ears, runny nose, sensitivity to light, shortness of breath, sleepiness, sore throat, stroke, tearing, urinary tract infection, vomiting, yellow eyes and skin

Why should this drug not be prescribed?

If you are sensitive to or have ever had an allergic reaction to enalapril, hydrochlorothiazide, or similar drugs, or if you are sensitive to other sulfa drugs, you should not take this medication.

If you have a history of angioedema (swelling of face, extremities, and throat) or inability to urinate, you should not take this medication. Tell your doctor of all allergic reactions you have experienced.

Special warnings about this medication

If you develop swelling of your face, eyes, lips, tongue, or throat; swelling of your arms and legs; or difficulty swallowing, you should contact your doctor immediately. You may need emergency treatment.

If you are taking bee or wasp venom to prevent an allergic reaction to stings, you may have a severe allergic reaction to Vaseretic.

If you develop chest pain, a sore throat, or fever, you should contact your doctor immediately. It could indicate a more serious illness.

If you are taking Vaseretic, a complete assessment of your kidney function should be done. Kidney function should continue to be monitored. Some people on dialysis have had a severe allergic reaction to Vaseretic.

If you have liver disease or lupus erythematosus (a form of rheumatism), Vaseretic should be used with caution.

If your skin or the whites of your eyes turn yellow, stop taking Vaseretic and notify your doctor at once.

If you have severe congestive heart failure, you should be carefully watched for low blood pressure.

Excessive sweating, dehydration, severe diarrhea, or vomiting could cause you to lose too much water and cause your blood pressure to become too low. Be careful when exercising and in hot weather.

Vaseretic can cause some people to become drowsy or less alert. If it has this effect on you, driving or operating dangerous machinery or participating in any hazardous activity that requires full mental alertness is not recommended.

If you are diabetic, blood sugar levels should be monitored.

Vaseretic may increase your sensitivity to sunlight. Be careful to avoid overexposure.

Possible food and drug interactions
when taking this medication

Vaseretic may intensify the effects of alcohol. Do not drink alcohol while taking this medication.

If Vaseretic is taken with certain other drugs, the effects of either could be increased, decreased, or altered. It is especially important to check with your doctor before combining Vaseretic with the following:

Alcohol
Barbiturates such as phenobarbital
Certain other antihypertensives
Corticosteroids such as prednisone
Digitalis (Lanoxin)
Insulin
Lithium (Eskalith, Lithonate)
Narcotics (Percocet)
Nonsteroidal anti-inflammatory drugs such as Naprosyn, Advil, and
    Motrin
Norepinephrine
Oral antidiabetic drugs such as Micronase
Potassium supplements (K-Lyte, K-Tab, others)
Potassium-containing salt substitutes
Potassium-sparing diuretics such as Midamor

Special information
if you are pregnant or breastfeeding

Vaseretic can cause birth defects, prematurity, and death to the newborn baby. If you are pregnant or plan to become pregnant and are taking Vaseretic, contact your doctor immediately to discuss the potential hazard to your unborn child. Vaseretic appears in breast milk and could affect a nursing infant. If this medication is essential to your health, your doctor may advise you to discontinue breastfeeding until your treatment is finished.

Recommended dosage

ADULTS

Dosages of this drug are always individualized. Your doctor will determine what works best for you. This medication can and may be used in combination with other high blood pressure medications, and dosages will be adjusted accordingly. Dosages will also be modified and carefully monitored in people with reduced kidney function.

Once your doctor has determined that your blood pressure is stable, the usual starting dose is 1 or 2 tablets once a day. Maximum daily dosage is 2 tablets.

Diuretic use should, if possible, be stopped before using Vaseretic. If not, your doctor may give an initial dose under his or her supervision before any further medication is prescribed.

CHILDREN

The safety and effectiveness of Vaseretic in children have not been established.

Overdosage
Any medication taken in excess can cause symptoms of overdose. If you suspect an overdose, seek medical attention immediately.

No specific information on treatment of Vaseretic overdose is available.

■ *Symptoms of a Vaseretic overdose may include:*
Dehydration
Low blood pressure

Brand name:

VASOTEC

Pronounced: VAZ-oh-tek
Generic name: Enalapril maleate

Why is this drug prescribed?
Vasotec is a high blood pressure medication known as an ACE inhibitor. It works by preventing a chemical in your blood called angiotensin I from converting into a more potent form that increases salt and water retention in your body. It is effective when used alone or in combination with other medications, especially thiazide-type diuretics. It is also used in the treatment of congestive heart failure, usually in combination with diuretics and digitalis, and is prescribed as a preventive measure in certain conditions that could lead to heart failure.

Most important fact about this drug
If you have high blood pressure, you must take Vasotec regularly for it to be effective. Since blood pressure declines gradually, it may be several weeks

before you get the full benefit of Vasotec; and you must continue taking it even if you are feeling well. Vasotec does not cure high blood pressure; it merely keeps it under control.

How should you take this medication?

Vasotec can be taken with or without food.

Do not use salt substitutes containing potassium without first consulting your doctor.

Take this medication exactly as prescribed by your doctor.

■ *If you miss a dose...*
Take it as soon as you remember. If it is almost time for your next dose, skip the one you missed and go back to your regular schedule. Never take 2 doses at the same time.

■ *Storage instructions...*
Keep container tightly closed. Store at room temperature and protect from moisture.

What side effects may occur?

Side effects cannot be anticipated. If any develop or change in intensity, inform your doctor as soon as possible. Only your doctor can determine if it is safe for you to continue taking Vasotec.

■ *Side effects may include:*
Abdominal pain, abnormal skin sensations such as numbness or prickling, anaphylactoid reactions (severe allergic reactions), angina pectoris (chest pain, often accompanied by a feeling of choking or impending death), angioedema (swelling of face, lips, tongue, throat, arms and legs, difficulty swallowing), asthma, blisters, blood abnormalities, blood clots or foreign material in the lungs, blurred vision, breast enlargement in males, bronchitis, confusion, constipation, cough, dark, tarry stool containing blood, decreased urination, depression, diarrhea, difficulty breathing, difficulty sleeping, digestive difficulty and stomach discomfort, dizziness, dizziness upon standing, dry eyes, dry mouth, excessive perspiration, fainting, fatigue, flank pain, fluid in lungs, flushing, hair loss, headache, heart palpitations, heart rhythm disturbances, hepatitis, herpes zoster, hives, impotence, inflammation of the mouth, inflammation of the tongue, itching, lack of muscle coordination, liver failure, loss of appetite, loss of sense of smell, low blood pressure, low blood pressure upon standing, muscle cramps, nausea, nervousness, pinkeye (conjunctivitis), pneumonia, pounding heartbeat, rapid or slow heartbeat, rash, red skin (like sunburn),

ringing in ears, runny nose, sensitivity to light, sleepiness, sore throat and hoarseness, stroke, taste alteration, tearing, tingling or pins and needles or burning sensation, upper respiratory infection, upset stomach, urinary tract infection, vertigo, vomiting, weakness, wheezing

Why should this drug not be prescribed?

If you are sensitive or have ever had an allergic reaction to Vasotec or similar drugs, or if you have a history of angioedema (swollen throat and difficulty swallowing) related to previous treatment with ACE inhibitors, you should not take this medication. Make sure that your doctor is aware of any drug reactions that you have experienced.

Special warnings about this medication

Vasotec has been known to cause a serious allergic reaction called angioedema. The symptoms are swelling of the face, lips, tongue, or throat; swelling of arms and legs; and difficulty swallowing or breathing. If you notice any of these symptoms, call your doctor immediately.

If you are taking bee or wasp venom to prevent an allergic reaction to stings, you may have a severe allergic reaction to Vasotec.

If you are taking high doses of diuretics and Vasotec, you may develop excessively low blood pressure. You are at special risk if you have heart disease, kidney disease, or a potassium or salt imbalance. Some people on kidney dialysis have had a severe allergic reaction to Vasotec.

There have been cases of serious blood disorders reported with the use of Captopril, another ACE inhibitor drug. Your doctor should check your blood regularly while you are taking Vasotec.

ACE inhibitors can cause fetal abnormalities and fetal and newborn deaths when used in pregnancy during the second and third trimesters.

When pregnancy is detected, Vasotec should be discontinued as soon as possible.

If you develop a sore throat or fever, you should contact your doctor immediately. It could indicate a more serious illness. Also, if your skin and the whites of your eyes turn yellow, contact your doctor at once.

Excessive sweating, dehydration, severe diarrhea, or vomiting could cause you to lose too much water, causing your blood pressure to drop dangerously. Be careful when exercising or when exposed to excessive heat.

Possible food and drug interactions
when taking this medication

If Vasotec is taken with certain other drugs, the effects of either could be increased, decreased, or altered. It is especially important to check with your doctor before combining Vasotec with the following:

Diuretics such as Lasix and HydroDIURIL
Lithium (Eskalith, Lithotab)
Potassium-containing salt substitutes
Potassium-sparing diuretics such as Aldactazide and Moduretic
Potassium supplements such as K-Lyte and K-Tab

Special information
if you are pregnant or breastfeeding

Vasotec can cause birth defects, prematurity, and death to the developing or newborn baby. If you are pregnant or plan to become pregnant, inform your doctor immediately. Vasotec may appear in breast milk and could affect a nursing infant. If this medication is essential to your health, your doctor may advise you to stop breastfeeding until your treatment with Vasotec is finished.

Recommended dosage

ADULTS

Hypertension

The usual starting dose for people not using diuretics is 5 milligrams, taken once a day. The usual dose is 10 to 40 milligrams per day, taken as a single dose or divided into 2 smaller doses.

If you are taking a diuretic, your physician may ask you to stop for 2 to 3 days before using Vasotec. Otherwise, he or she may give an initial dose of 2.5 milligrams of Vasotec under medical supervision before any further medication is prescribed.

If you have a kidney disorder, your dosage will be adjusted according to its severity.

To Treat Heart Failure

This medication can be used in conjunction with digitalis and diuretics in people with heart disease. The usual starting dose is 2.5 milligrams twice a day.

The usual regular dose is 2.5 to 20 milligrams each day, taken in 2 separate doses. The maximum daily dose is 40 milligrams, in 2 separate doses.

To Prevent Heart Failure
The usual starting dose is 2.5 milligrams twice a day, to be gradually increased to 20 milligrams a day divided into smaller doses.

CHILDREN

The safety and effectiveness of Vasotec in children have not been established.

Overdosage

Any medication taken in excess can have serious consequences. If you suspect symptoms of a Vasotec overdose, seek medical attention immediately.

A sudden drop in blood pressure is the primary effect of a Vasotec overdose.

Brand name:

V-CILLIN K

See Penicillin V Potassium, page 824.

Brand name:

VEETIDS

See Penicillin V Potassium, page 824.

Brand name:

VELOSULIN

See Insulin, page 527.

Generic name:

VENLAFAXINE

See Effexor, page 380.

Brand name:

VENTOLIN

See Proventil, page 912.

Generic name:

VERAPAMIL

See Calan, page 146.

Brand name:

VERELAN

See Calan, page 146.

Brand name:

VIBRAMYCIN

See Doryx, page 367.

Brand name:

VIBRA-TABS

See Doryx, page 367.

Brand name:

VICODIN

Pronounced: VY-koe-din
Generic ingredients: Hydrocodone bitartrate,
   Acetaminophen
Other brand names: Anexsia, Lortab, Zydone

Why is this drug prescribed?
Vicodin combines a narcotic analgesic (painkiller) and cough reliever with a non-narcotic analgesic for the relief of moderate to moderately severe pain.

Most important fact about this drug
Vicodin can be habit-forming. If you take this drug over a long period of time, you can become mentally and physically dependent on it, and you may find the drug no longer works for you at the prescribed dosage.

How should you take this medication?
Take Vicodin exactly as prescribed. Do not increase the amount you take without your doctor's approval. Do not take this drug for any reason other than the one prescribed.

Do not give this drug to others who may have similar symptoms.

■ *If you miss a dose...*
If you take Vicodin regularly, take the forgotten dose as soon as you remember. If it is almost time for your next dose, skip the one you missed and go back to your regular schedule. Do not take 2 doses at once.

■ *Storage instructions...*
Store at room temperature in a tightly closed container, away from light.

What side effects may occur?
Side effects cannot be anticipated. If any develop or change in intensity, inform your doctor as soon as possible. Only your doctor can determine if it is safe for you to continue taking Vicodin.

■ *More common side effects may include:*
Dizziness
Light-headedness
Nausea
Sedation
Vomiting

If these side effects occur, it may help if you lie down after taking the medication.

■ *Less common or rare side effects may include:*
Allergic reactions, anxiety, blood disorders, constipation, decreased mental and physical capability, difficulty urinating, drowsiness, fear, mental clouding, mood changes, restlessness, skin rash, sluggishness, troubled, irregular, or slowed breathing

Why should this drug not be prescribed?
If you are sensitive to or have ever had an allergic reaction to hydrocodone or acetaminophen (Tylenol), you should not take this medication. Make sure your doctor is aware of any drug reactions you have experienced.

Special warnings about this medication
Vicodin may make you drowsy, less alert, or unable to function well physically. Do not drive a car, operate machinery, or perform any other potentially dangerous activities until you know how this drug affects you.

Use caution in taking Vicodin if you have a head injury. Narcotics tend to increase the pressure of the fluid within the skull, and this effect may be exaggerated by head injuries. Side effects of narcotics can interfere in the treatment of people with head injuries.

Use Vicodin with caution if you have a severe liver or kidney disorder, an underactive thyroid gland, Addison's disease (a disease of the adrenal glands), an enlarged prostate, or urethral stricture (narrowing of the tube carrying urine from the bladder).

The elderly or those in a weakened condition should be careful using this drug, since it contains a narcotic.

Narcotics such as Vicodin may interfere with the diagnosis and treatment of people with abdominal conditions.

Hydrocodone suppresses the cough reflex; therefore, be careful using Vicodin after an operation or if you have a lung disease.

High doses of hydrocodone may produce troubled, irregular, or slowed breathing; if you are sensitive to this drug, you are more likely to experience this effect.

Possible food and drug interactions
when taking this medication
Hydrocodone slows the nervous system. Alcohol can intensify this effect.

If hydrocodone is taken with certain other drugs, the effects of either may be increased, decreased, or altered. It is especially important to check with your doctor before combining Vicodin with the following:

Antianxiety drugs such as Valium and Librium
Antihistamines such as Tavist
Depression medications such as Elavil, Nardil, and Tofranil
Drugs that control muscle spasms, such as Cogentin
Major tranquilizers such as Thorazine and Haldol
Other narcotic analgesics such as Demerol and other nervous system
  depressants

Special information
if you are pregnant or breastfeeding
The effects of Vicodin in pregnancy have not been adequately studied. Do not take this drug if you are pregnant or plan to become pregnant unless you are directed to do so by your doctor. Drug dependence occurs in newborns when the mother has taken this drug regularly prior to delivery. If you take it shortly before delivery, the baby's breathing may be slowed. Acetaminophen does, and hydrocodone may, appear in breast milk and could affect a nursing

infant. If this medication is essential to your health, your doctor may advise you to discontinue breastfeeding your baby until your treatment is finished.

Recommended dosage

ADULTS

Your doctor will adjust the dosage according to the severity of the pain and the way the medication affects you.

The dosages given below are for Vicodin and Vicodin ES only. If your doctor prescribes other brands, your daily dose may vary.

The usual dose of Vicodin is 1 or 2 tablets taken every 4 to 6 hours for pain as needed. The total dose should not exceed 8 tablets a day.

The usual dose of Vicodin ES is 1 tablet every 4 to 6 hours for pain as needed. The total dose should not exceed 5 tablets a day.

CHILDREN

The safety and effectiveness of Vicodin have not been established in children.

Overdosage

Any medication taken in excess can have serious consequences. A severe overdose of Vicodin can be fatal. If you suspect an overdose, seek emergency medical treatment immediately.

■ *Symptoms of a Vicodin overdose include:*
Blood disorders, bluish tinge to skin, cold and clammy skin, extreme sleepiness progressing to a state of unresponsiveness or coma, general feeling of bodily discomfort, heart problems, heavy perspiration, kidney problems, limp muscles, liver failure, low blood pressure, nausea, slow heartbeat, troubled or slowed breathing, vomiting

Generic name:

VI-DAYLIN

See Multivitamins, page 693.

Brand name:

VIOKASE

See Pancrease, page 796.

Brand name:

VISKEN

Pronounced: VIS-kin
Generic name: Pindolol

Why is this drug prescribed?
Visken, a type of medication known as a beta blocker, is used in the treatment of high blood pressure. It is effective alone or combined with other high blood pressure medications, particularly with a thiazide-type diuretic. Beta blockers decrease the force and rate of heart contractions.

Most important fact about this drug
You must take Visken regularly for it to be effective. Since blood pressure declines gradually, it may be several weeks before you get the full benefit of Visken; and you must continue taking it even if you are feeling well. Visken does not cure high blood pressure; it merely keeps it under control.

How should you take this medication?
Visken can be taken with or without food.

Take this medication exactly as prescribed, even if your symptoms have disappeared. Try not to miss any doses. If this medication is not taken regularly, your condition may worsen.

- *If you miss a dose...*
  Take it as soon as you remember. If it's within 4 hours of your next scheduled dose, skip the one you missed and go back to your regular schedule. Never take 2 doses at the same time.

- *Storage instructions...*
  Store Visken at room temperature in a tightly closed, light-resistant container.

What side effects may occur?
Side effects cannot be anticipated. If any develop or change in intensity, inform your doctor as soon as possible. Only your doctor can determine if it is safe for you to continue taking Visken.

- *More common side effects may include:*
  Abdominal discomfort, chest pain, difficult or labored breathing, dizziness, fatigue, joint pain, muscle pain or cramps, nausea, nervousness, strange dreams, swelling due to fluid retention, tingling or pins and needles, trouble sleeping, weakness

■ *Less common or rare side effects may include:*
Hallucinations, heart failure, itching, palpitations, rapid heartbeat, rash

Why should this drug not be prescribed?

If you have bronchial asthma; severe congestive heart failure; inadequate blood supply to the circulatory system (cardiogenic shock); heart block (a heart irregularity); or a severely slow heartbeat, you should not take this medication.

Special warnings about this medication

If you have had severe congestive heart failure in the past, Visken should be used with caution.

Visken should not be stopped suddenly. It can cause increased chest pain and heart attack. Dosage should be gradually reduced.

If you suffer from asthma, chronic bronchitis, emphysema, seasonal allergies or other bronchial conditions, coronary artery disease, or kidney or liver disease, this medication should be used with caution.

Ask your doctor if you should check your pulse while taking Visken. This medication can cause your heartbeat to become too slow.

This medication may mask the symptoms of low blood sugar in diabetics or alter blood sugar levels. If you are diabetic, discuss this with your doctor.

Visken may cause you to become disoriented. If it has this effect on you, driving or operating dangerous machinery or participating in any hazardous activity that requires full mental alertness is not recommended.

If you have a history of severe allergic reactions, inform your doctor before taking Visken.

Notify your doctor or dentist that you are taking Visken if you have a medical emergency and before you have surgery or dental treatment.

Possible food and drug interactions
when taking this medication

If Visken is taken with certain other drugs, the effects of either could be increased, decreased, or altered. It is especially important to check with your doctor before combining Visken with the following:

Airway-opening drugs such as Proventil and Ventolin
Blood pressure drugs such as reserpine
Digoxin (Lanoxin)
Epinephrine (EpiPen)
Hydrochlorothiazide (HydroDIURIL)

Insulin or oral antidiabetic agents such as Micronase
Nonsteroidal anti-inflammatory drugs such as Motrin
Ritodrine (Yutopar)
Theophylline (Theo-Dur, others)
Thioridazine (Mellaril)
Verapamil (Calan, Verelan)

Special information
if you are pregnant or breastfeeding

The effects of Visken during pregnancy have not been adequately studied. If you are pregnant or plan to become pregnant, inform your doctor immediately. Visken appears in breast milk and could affect a nursing infant. If this medication is essential to your health, your doctor may advise you to discontinue breastfeeding until your treatment with this medication is finished.

Recommended dosage

ADULTS

Your doctor will determine the dosage according to your specific needs.

The usual starting dose is 5 milligrams, 2 times per day, alone or with other high blood pressure medication. Your blood pressure should be lower in 1 to 2 weeks. If blood pressure is not reduced sufficiently within 3 to 4 weeks, your doctor may increase your total daily dosage by 10 milligrams at a time, at 3- to 4-week intervals, up to a maximum of 60 milligrams a day.

CHILDREN

The safety and effectiveness of Visken have not been established in children.

ELDERLY

The doctor will determine dosage for an elderly individual based on his or her particular needs.

Overdosage

Any medication taken in excess can have serious consequences. If you suspect an overdose, seek medical attention immediately.

■ *Symptoms of Visken overdose may include:*
Bronchospasm (spasm of the air passages)
Excessively slow heartbeat
Heart failure
Low blood pressure

Brand name:

VISTARIL

See Atarax, page 80.

Generic name:

VITAMINS WITH FLUORIDE

See Poly-Vi-Flor, page 872.

Brand name:

VOLMAX EXTENDED RELEASE TABLETS

See Proventil, page 912.

Brand name:

VOLTAREN

Pronounced: vol-TAR-en
Generic name: Diclofenac sodium
Other brand name: Cataflam (Diclofenac potassium)

Why is this drug prescribed?

Voltaren and Cataflam, nonsteroidal anti-inflammatory drugs, are used to relieve the inflammation, swelling, stiffness, and joint pain associated with rheumatoid arthritis, osteoarthritis (the most common form of arthritis), and ankylosing spondylitis (arthritis and stiffness of the spine). Cataflam is also used in the treatment of menstrual pain.

Most important fact about this drug

You should have frequent checkups with your doctor if you take Voltaren regularly. Ulcers or internal bleeding can occur without warning.

How should you take this medication?

To minimize stomach upset and related side effects, your doctor may recommend taking this medicine with food, milk, or an antacid. However, this may delay onset of relief.

Take this drug with a full glass of water. Also, do not lie down for about 20 minutes after taking it. This will help to prevent irritation in your upper digestive tract.

Take this medication exactly as prescribed.

■ *If you miss a dose...*
If you take this medicine on a regular schedule, take it as soon as you remember. If it is almost time for your next dose, skip the one you missed and go back to your regular schedule. Do not take 2 doses at once.

■ *Storage instructions...*
Store at room temperature. Keep the container tightly closed and protect from moisture.

What side effects may occur?
Side effects cannot be anticipated. If any develop or change in intensity, inform your doctor as soon as possible. Only your doctor can determine if it is safe for you to continue taking Voltaren.

■ *More common side effects may include:*
Abdominal pain or cramps
Constipation
Diarrhea
Dizziness
Headache
Indigestion
Nausea

■ *Less common side effects may include:*
Abdominal bleeding, abdominal swelling, fluid retention, gas, itching, peptic ulcers, rash, ringing in the ears

■ *Rare side effects may include:*
Anaphylaxis (severe allergic reaction), anemia, anxiety, appetite change, asthma, black stools, blood disorders, bloody diarrhea, blurred vision, changes in taste, colitis, congestive heart failure, decrease in white blood cells, decreased urine production, depression, double vision, drowsiness, dry mouth, hair loss, hearing loss (temporary), hepatitis, high blood pressure, hives, inability to sleep, inflammation of mouth, irritability, kidney failure, low blood pressure, nosebleed, red or purple skin discoloration, rash, itching, sensitivity to light, skin eruptions, inflammation, scaling, or peeling, Stevens-Johnson syndrome (a severe form of skin

eruption), swelling of eyelids, lips, and tongue, swelling of the throat due to fluid retention, vague feeling of illness, vision changes, vomiting, yellow eyes and skin

Why should this drug not be prescribed?
If you are sensitive to or have ever had an allergic reaction to Voltaren or Cataflam, or if you have had asthma attacks, hives, or other allergic reactions caused by aspirin or other nonsteroidal anti-inflammatory drugs, you should not take this medication. Make sure your doctor is aware of any drug reactions you have experienced.

Special warnings about this medication
Remember, this medication has been known to cause peptic ulcers and bleeding. Contact your doctor immediately if you suspect a problem.

This drug should be used with caution if you have heart failure, kidney problems, or liver disease, and it can cause liver inflammation in some people.

If you are taking blood-thinning medication or diuretics, use this drug with caution.

Use with caution if you have heart disease or high blood pressure. This drug can increase water retention.

If you experience nausea, fatigue, lethargy, itching, yellowed eyes and skin, tenderness in the upper right area of your abdomen, or flu-like symptoms, notify your doctor at once.

Possible food and drug interactions
when taking this medication
If Voltaren or Cataflam are taken with certain other drugs, the effects of either could be increased, decreased, or altered. It is especially important to check with your doctor before combining Voltaren with the following:

Aspirin
Blood thinners such as Coumadin
Carteolol (Cartrol)
Cyclosporine (Sandimmune)
Digitalis drugs such as Lanoxin
Diuretics such as Dyazide, Midamor, and Lasix
Insulin or oral antidiabetes medications such as Micronase
Lithium (Lithonate)
Methotrexate

Special information
if you are pregnant or breastfeeding

The effects of Voltaren during pregnancy have not been adequately studied. If you are pregnant or plan to become pregnant, inform your doctor immediately. Voltaren appears in breast milk and could affect a nursing infant. If this medication is essential to your health, your doctor may advise you to discontinue breastfeeding until your treatment with Voltaren is finished.

Recommended dosage

ADULTS

Osteoarthritis

The usual dose is 100 to 150 milligrams a day, divided into smaller doses of 50 milligrams 2 or 3 times a day (for Voltaren or Cataflam) or 75 milligrams twice a day (for Voltaren).

Rheumatoid Arthritis

The usual dose is 150 to 200 milligrams a day, divided into smaller doses of 50 milligrams 3 or 4 times a day (for Voltaren or Cataflam) or 75 milligrams twice a day (for Voltaren).

People with rheumatoid arthritis should not take more than 225 milligrams a day.

Ankylosing Spondylitis

The usual dose is 100 to 125 milligrams a day, divided into smaller doses of 25 milligrams 4 times a day, with another 25 milligrams at bedtime if necessary.

Menstrual pain and discomfort

The usual starting dose of Cataflam is 50 milligrams 3 times a day, although some women will take 100 milligrams for the first dose, followed by 50-milligram doses. After the first day, you should not take more than 150 milligrams in a day.

CHILDREN

The safety and effectiveness of Voltaren have not been established in children.

Overdosage

Any medication taken in excess can have serious consequences. If you suspect an overdose, seek medical attention immediately.

■ *The symptoms of Voltaren overdose may include:*
Acute kidney failure
Drowsiness
Loss of consciousness
Lung inflammation
Vomiting

Generic name:

WARFARIN

See Coumadin, page 248.

Brand name:

WELLBUTRIN

Pronounced: Well-BEW-trin
Generic name: Bupropion hydrochloride

Why is this drug prescribed?
Wellbutrin, a relatively new antidepressant medication, is given to help relieve certain kinds of major depression.

Major depression involves a severely depressed mood (for 2 weeks or more) accompanied by sleep and appetite disturbances, agitation or lack of energy, feelings of guilt or worthlessness, decreased sex drive, inability to concentrate, and perhaps thoughts of suicide.

Unlike the more familiar tricyclic antidepressants, such as Elavil, Tofranil, and others, Wellbutrin tends to have a somewhat stimulating effect.

Most important fact about this drug
Although Wellbutrin occasionally causes weight gain, a more common effect is weight loss: Some 28 percent of people who take this medication lose 5 pounds or more. If depression has already caused you to lose weight, and if further weight loss would be detrimental to your health, Wellbutrin may not be the best antidepressant for you.

How should you take this medication?
Take Wellbutrin exactly as prescribed by your doctor. The usual dosing regimen is 3 equal doses spaced evenly throughout the day. Allow at least 6 hours between doses. Your doctor will probably start you at a low dosage and gradually increase it; this helps minimize side effects.

Since Wellbutrin may impair your coordination or judgment, do not drive or operate dangerous machinery until you find out how the medication affects you.

If Wellbutrin works for you, your doctor will probably have you continue taking it for at least several months.

Avoid alcoholic beverages.

■ *If you miss a dose...*
Take it as soon as you remember. If it is within 4 hours of your next dose, skip the one you missed and go back to your regular schedule. Never take 2 doses at the same time.

■ *Storage instructions...*
Store at room temperature. Protect from light and moisture.

What side effects may occur?
Side effects cannot be anticipated. If any develop or change in intensity, inform your doctor as soon as possible. Only your doctor can determine if it is safe for you to continue taking Wellbutrin.

Seizures are perhaps the most worrisome side effect.

■ *More common side effects may include:*
Agitation
Constipation
Dizziness
Dry mouth
Excessive sweating
Headache
Nausea, vomiting
Skin rash
Sleep disturbances
Tremor

■ *Other side effects may include:*
Acne, bedwetting, blisters in the mouth and eyes (Stevens-Johnson syndrome), blurred vision, breathing difficulty, chest pain, chills, complete or almost complete loss of movement, confusion, dry skin, episodes of overactivity, elation, or irritability, extreme calmness, fatigue, fever, fluid retention, flu-like symptoms, gum irritation and inflammation, hair color changes, hair loss, hives, impotence, incoordination and clumsiness, indigestion, itching, increased libido, menstrual complaints, mood instability, muscle rigidity, painful ejaculation, painful erection, retarded ejacula-

tion, ringing in the ears, sexual dysfunction, suicidal ideation, thirst disturbances, toothache, urinary disturbances, weight gain or loss

Why should this drug not be prescribed?
Do not take Wellbutrin if you are sensitive to or have ever had an allergic reaction to it.

Since Wellbutrin causes seizures in some people, do not take it if you have any type of seizure disorder.

You should not take Wellbutrin if you currently have, or formerly had, an eating disorder. For some reason, people with a history of anorexia nervosa or bulimia seem to be more likely to experience Wellbutrin-related seizures.

Do not take Wellbutrin if, within the past 14 days, you have taken a monoamine oxidase inhibitor (MAO inhibitor) type of antidepressant, such as Nardil, Marplan, or Parnate. This particular drug combination could cause you to experience a sudden, dangerous rise in blood pressure.

Special warnings about this medication
If you take Wellbutrin, you may be vulnerable to seizures if your dosage is too high or if you ever suffered brain damage or experienced seizures in the past.

Do not take other medications that might help trigger seizures (e.g., antipsychotics, other antidepressants).

If you have been taking Valium or a similar tranquilizer but are ready to stop, taper off gradually rather than quitting abruptly.

Possible food and drug interactions
when taking this medication
Do not drink alcohol while you are taking Wellbutrin; an interaction between alcohol and Wellbutrin could increase the possibility of a seizure.

If Wellbutrin is taken with certain other drugs, the effects of either could be increased, decreased, or altered. It is especially important to check with your doctor before combining Wellbutrin with the following:

Dilantin
Levodopa (Larodopa)
Major tranquilizers such as Thorazine and Mellaril
MAO inhibitors (antidepressants such as Parnate and Nardil)
Other antidepressants such as Elavil and Tofranil
Phenobarbital (Luminal)
Tagamet
Tegretol

Special information
if you are pregnant or breastfeeding

If you are pregnant or plan to become pregnant, notify your doctor immediately. Wellbutrin should be taken during pregnancy only if clearly needed.

Wellbutrin may pass into breast milk and cause serious reactions in a nursing baby; therefore, if you are a new mother, you may need to discontinue breastfeeding while you are taking this medication.

Recommended dosage

No single dose of Wellbutrin should exceed 150 milligrams.

ADULTS

At the beginning, your dose will probably be 200 milligrams per day, taken as 100 milligrams 2 times a day. After at least 3 days at this dose, your doctor may increase the dosage to 300 milligrams per day, taken as 100 milligrams 3 times a day, with at least 6 hours between doses. This is the usual adult dose. The maximum recommended dosage is 450 milligrams per day taken in doses of no more than 150 milligrams each.

CHILDREN

The safety and effectiveness in children under 18 years old have not been established.

ELDERLY

Because they are more sensitive to antidepressant drugs, older people may find smaller doses satisfactory.

Overdosage

Any medication taken in excess can have serious consequences. If you suspect an overdose of Wellbutrin, seek medical attention immediately.

- *Symptoms of Wellbutrin overdose may include:*
  Hallucinations
  Heart failure
  Loss of consciousness
  Rapid heartbeat
  Seizures

■ *An overdose that involves other drugs in combination with Wellbutrin may also cause these symptoms:*
Breathing difficulties
Coma
Fever
Rigid muscles
Stupor

Brand name:

WYMOX

See Amoxil, page 47.

Brand name:

WYTENSIN

Pronounced: why-TEN-sin
Generic name: Guanabenz acetate

Why is this drug prescribed?
Wytensin is used in the treatment of high blood pressure. It is effective used alone or in combination with a thiazide type of diuretic. Wytensin begins to lower blood pressure within 60 minutes after taking a single dose and may slow your pulse rate slightly.

Most important fact about this drug
You must take Wytensin regularly for it to be effective. Since blood pressure declines gradually, it may be several weeks before you get the full benefit of Wytensin; and you must continue taking it even if you are feeling well. Wytensin does not cure high blood pressure; it merely keeps it under control.

How should you take this medication?
Wytensin may be taken with or without food. Take it exactly as prescribed.

■ *If you miss a dose...*
Take it as soon as you remember. If it is almost time for the next dose, skip the one you missed and go back to your regular schedule. Do not take 2 doses at the same time. If you forget the medication 2 or more times in a row, contact your doctor.

■ *Storage instructions...*
Store at room temperature, in a tightly closed container, away from light.

What side effects may occur?
Side effects cannot be anticipated. If any develop or change in intensity, inform your doctor as soon as possible. Only your doctor can determine if it is safe for you to continue taking Wytensin.

■ *More common side effects may include:*
Dizziness
Drowsiness
Dry mouth
Headache
Weakness

■ *Less common side effects may include:*
Abdominal discomfort, aches in arms and legs, anxiety, blurred vision, breast development in males, changes in taste, chest pain, constipation, decreased sex drive, depression, diarrhea, fluid retention, frequent urination, impotence, irregular heartbeat, itching, lack of muscle coordination, muscle aches, nausea, pounding heartbeat, rash, shortness of breath, sleep disturbances, stomach pain, stuffy nose, vomiting

■ *Rare side effects may include:*
Heartbeat irregularities

Why should this drug not be prescribed?
Do not take Wytensin if you are sensitive to it or have ever had an allergic reaction to it.

Special warnings about this medication
Wytensin can make you drowsy or less alert. Driving or operating dangerous machinery or participating in any hazardous activity that requires full mental alertness is not recommended until you know how this drug affects you.

If you have severe heart disease, stroke or related disorders, or severe liver or kidney failure, or if you have recently had a heart attack, this drug should be used with caution.

Your doctor will monitor your blood pressure if you have disorders of the kidney or liver.

Possible food and drug interactions
when taking this medication

Wytensin may intensify the effects of alcohol. Use of alcohol should be avoided.

If Wytensin is taken with certain other drugs, the effects of either could be increased, decreased, or altered. It is especially important to check with your doctor before combining Wytensin with the following:

Antihistamines such as Benadryl, Clor-Trimeton, and Tavist

Drugs that depress the central nervous system such as Halcion, Valium, and phenobarbital

Special information
if you are pregnant or breastfeeding

The effects of Wytensin during pregnancy have not been adequately studied, but it may affect the fetus. If you are pregnant or plan to become pregnant, inform your doctor immediately. Wytensin may appear in breast milk and could affect a nursing infant. If this medication is essential to your health, your doctor may advise you to discontinue breastfeeding until your treatment is finished.

Recommended dosage

ADULTS

Your doctor will adjust the dosage of this medication to meet your individual needs.

The usual starting dose is 4 milligrams 2 times per day, whether Wytensin is used alone or with a thiazide type of diuretic.

Your doctor may increase the dosage in increments of 4 to 8 milligrams per day every 1 to 2 weeks, depending on your response.

The maximum reported dose has been 32 milligrams twice daily, but doses as high as this are rarely needed.

CHILDREN

The safety and effectiveness of this drug have not been established in children under 12 years of age.

ELDERLY

The elderly should use this drug with caution.

Overdosage

Any medication taken in excess can have serious consequences. If you suspect an overdose, seek medical attention immediately.

■ *Symptoms of Wytensin overdose may include:*
Excessive contraction of the pupils
Irritability
Low blood pressure
Sleepiness
Slow heartbeat
Sluggishness

Brand name:

XANAX

Pronounced: ZAN-ax
Generic name: Alprazolam

Why is this drug prescribed?

Xanax is a tranquilizer used in the short-term relief of symptoms of anxiety or the treatment of anxiety disorders. Anxiety disorder is marked by unrealistic worry or excessive fears and concerns.

Xanax is also used in the treatment of panic disorder, which appears as unexpected panic attacks and may be accompanied by a fear of open spaces called agoraphobia. Only your doctor can diagnose panic disorder and best advise you about treatment. Anxiety associated with depression is also responsive to Xanax.

Some doctors prescribe Xanax to treat alcohol withdrawal, fear of open spaces and strangers, depression, irritable bowel syndrome, and premenstrual syndrome.

Most important fact about this drug

Tolerance and dependence can occur with the use of Xanax. You may experience withdrawal symptoms if you stop using the drug abruptly. Only your doctor should advise you to discontinue or change your dose.

How should you take this medication?
Xanax may be taken with or without food. Take it exactly as prescribed.

■ *If you miss a dose...*
If you are less than 1 hour late, take it as soon as you remember. Otherwise skip the dose and go back to your regular schedule. Never take 2 doses at the same time.

■ *Storage instructions...*
Store Xanax at room temperature.

What side effects may occur?
Side effects cannot be anticipated. If any develop or change in intensity, inform your doctor as soon as possible. Only your doctor can determine if it is safe for you to continue taking Xanax. Your doctor should periodically reassess the need for this drug.

Side effects to Xanax are usually seen at the beginning of treatment and disappear with continued medication. However, if dosage is increased, side effects will be more likely.

■ *More common side effects may include:*
Abdominal discomfort, abnormal involuntary movement, agitation, allergies, anxiety, blurred vision, chest pain, confusion, constipation, decreased or increased sex drive, depression, diarrhea, difficult urination, dream abnormalities, drowsiness, dry mouth, fainting, fatigue, fluid retention, headache, hyperventilation (too frequent or too deep breathing), inability to fall asleep, increase or decrease in appetite, increased or decreased salivation, impaired memory, irritability, lack of coordination, lightheadedness, low blood pressure, menstrual problems, muscular twitching, nausea and vomiting, nervousness, palpitations, rapid heartbeat, rash, restlessness, ringing in the ears, sexual dysfunction, skin inflammation, speech difficulties, stiffness, stuffy nose, sweating, tiredness/sleepiness, tremors, upper respiratory infections, weakness, weight gain or loss

■ *Less common or rare side effects may include:*
Abnormal muscle tone, concentration difficulties, decreased coordination, dizziness, double vision, fear, hallucinations, inability to control urination or bowel movements, infection, itching, loss of appetite, muscle cramps, muscle spasticity, rage, sedation, seizures, sleep disturbances, slurred speech, stimulation, talkativeness, taste alterations, temporary memory loss, tingling or pins and needles, uninhibited behavior, urine retention, warm feeling, weakness in muscle and bone, weight gain or loss, yellow eyes and skin

- *Side effects due to decrease or withdrawal from Xanax:*
  Blurred vision, decreased concentration, decreased mental clarity, diarrhea, heightened awareness of noise or bright lights, impaired sense of smell, loss of appetite, loss of weight, muscle cramps, seizures, tingling sensation, twitching

Why should this drug not be prescribed?

If you are sensitive to or have ever had an allergic reaction to Xanax or other tranquilizers, you should not take this medication. Make sure that your doctor is aware of any drug reactions that you have experienced.

Do not take this medication if you have been diagnosed with the eye condition called narrow-angle glaucoma.

Anxiety or tension related to everyday stress usually does not require treatment with Xanax. Discuss your symptoms thoroughly with your doctor.

Special warnings about this medication

Xanax may cause you to become drowsy or less alert; therefore, driving or operating dangerous machinery or participating in any hazardous activity that requires full mental alertness is not recommended.

If you are being treated for panic disorder, you may need to take a higher dose of Xanax than for anxiety alone. High doses of this medication taken for long intervals may cause emotional and physical dependence. It is important that your doctor supervise you carefully when you are using this medication.

Remember that withdrawal symptoms can occur when Xanax is stopped suddenly.

Possible food and drug interactions
when taking this medication

Xanax may intensify the effect of alcohol. Do not drink alcohol while taking this medication.

If Xanax is taken with certain other drugs, the effects of either could be increased, decreased, or altered. It is important to check with your doctor before combining Xanax with the following:

Antihistamines such as Benadryl and Tavist
Carbamazepine (Tegretol)
Certain antidepressant drugs, including Elavil, Norpramin, and Tofranil
Cimetidine (Tagamet)
Digoxin (Lanoxin)
Disulfiram (Antabuse)
Major tranquilizers such as Mellaril and Thorazine

Oral contraceptives
Other central nervous system depressants such as Valium and Demerol

Special information
if you are pregnant or breastfeeding

Do not take this medication if you are pregnant or planning to become pregnant. There is an increased risk of respiratory problems and muscular weakness in your baby. Infants may also experience withdrawal symptoms. Xanax may appear in breast milk and could affect a nursing infant. If this medication is essential to your health, your doctor may advise you to stop breastfeeding until your treatment with this medication is finished.

Recommended dosage

ADULTS

Anxiety disorder

The usual starting dose of Xanax is 0.25 to 0.5 milligram taken 3 times a day. The dose may be increased every 3 to 4 days to a maximum daily dose of 4 milligrams, divided into smaller doses.

Panic disorder

You may be given a dose from 1 up to a total of 10 milligrams, according to your needs. The typical dose is 5 to 6 milligrams a day.

The usual starting dose is 0.5 milligram 3 times a day. This dose can be increased by 1 milligram a day every 3 or 4 days.

CHILDREN

Safety and effectiveness have not been established in children under 18 years of age.

ELDERLY

The usual starting dose for an anxiety disorder is 0.25 milligram, 2 or 3 times daily. This dose may be gradually increased if needed and tolerated.

Overdosage

Any medication taken in excess can have serious consequences. If you suspect an overdose, seek medical attention immediately.

■ *Symptoms of Xanax overdose may include:*
Confusion
Coma

Impaired coordination
Sleepiness
Slowed reaction time

An overdose of Xanax, alone or after combining it with alcohol, can be fatal.

Brand name:

YOCON

Pronounced: YOE-kon
Generic name: Yohimbine hydrochloride

Why is this drug prescribed?
Yocon is used in the treatment of male impotence. The drug is thought to work by stimulating the release of norepinephrine, one of the body's natural chemical regulators. This results in increased blood flow to the penis.

Most important fact about this drug
Yocon does not work for all men. Your doctor will determine if Yocon can be prescribed for you.

How should you take this medication?
Take this medication exactly as prescribed.

■ *If you miss a dose...*
Take it as soon as you remember. If it is almost time for your next dose, skip the one you missed and go back to your regular schedule. Never take 2 doses at the same time.

■ *Storage instructions...*
Keep this medication in the container it came in, tightly closed, and out of the reach of children. Store it at room temperature, away from moist places and direct light.

What side effects may occur?
Side effects cannot be anticipated. If any develop or change in intensity, inform your doctor as soon as possible. Only your doctor can determine if it is safe for you to continue taking Yocon.

■ *Side effects may include:*
Decreased urination, dizziness, flushing, headache, increase in blood pressure, increased heart rate, increased motor activity, irritability, nausea, nervousness, tremor

Why should this drug not be prescribed?
Yocon should not be used if you have kidney disease, or if you are sensitive to or have ever had an allergic reaction to yohimbine. Make sure your doctor is aware of any drug reactions you have experienced.

Special warnings about this medication
Yocon is generally not recommended for use by children, the elderly, or men with heart and kidney disease who also have a history of stomach or duodenal ulcer. The drug is also not recommended for men being treated for a psychiatric disorder.

Possible food and drug interactions
when taking this medication
It is important that you consult with your doctor before taking Yocon with drugs for depression such as Elavil or other drugs that change mood.

Special information
if you are pregnant or breastfeeding
Yocon is not recommended for use in women generally and certainly must not be used during pregnancy.

Recommended dosage

ADULTS

Dosages of this drug are based on experimental research in the treatment of male impotence.

This dosage is one 5.4-milligram tablet, 3 times a day.

If you experience nausea, dizziness, or nervousness, your doctor will reduce the dose to one-half tablet 3 times a day, and then increase it gradually back up to 1 tablet 3 times a day.

CHILDREN

This drug is not for use in children.

ELDERLY

This drug should not be used by the elderly.

Overdosage
Any medication taken in excess can cause symptoms of overdose. If you suspect an overdose, seek medical attention immediately. No specific symptoms of Yocon overdose have been reported.

Generic name:

YOHIMBINE

See Yocon, page 1215.

Brand name:

ZANTAC

Pronounced: ZAN-tac
Generic name: Ranitidine hydrochloride

Why is this drug prescribed?

Zantac is prescribed for the short-term treatment (4 to 8 weeks) of active duodenal ulcer and active benign gastric ulcer, and as maintenance therapy for duodenal ulcer, at a reduced dosage, after the ulcer has healed. It is also used for the treatment of conditions in which the stomach produces too much acid, such as Zollinger-Ellison syndrome and systemic mastocytosis, for gastroesophageal reflux disease (backflow of acid stomach contents) and for healing erosive esophagitis (severe inflammation of the esophagus).

Some doctors prescribe Zantac to prevent damage to the stomach and duodenum from long-term use of nonsteroidal anti-inflammatory drugs such as Indocin and Motrin, and to treat bleeding of the stomach and intestine. Zantac is also sometimes prescribed for stress-induced ulcers.

Most important fact about this drug

Zantac helps to prevent the recurrence of duodenal ulcers and aids the healing of ulcers that do occur.

How should you take this medication?

Take this medication exactly as prescribed by your doctor. Make sure you follow the diet your doctor recommends.

Dissolve "Efferdose" tablets and granules in 6 to 8 ounces of water before taking them.

You can take an antacid for pain while you are taking Zantac.

■ *If you miss a dose...*
Take it as soon as you remember. If it is almost time for your next dose, skip the one you missed and go back to your regular schedule. Never take 2 doses at the same time.

■ *Storage instructions...*
Store this medication at room temperature in the container it came in,
tightly closed and away from moist places and direct light. Keep Zantac
Syrup from freezing.

What side effects may occur?
Side effects cannot be anticipated. If any develop or change in intensity,
inform your doctor as soon as possible. Only your doctor can determine if it
is safe for you to continue taking Zantac.

■ *More common side effects may include:*
Headache, sometimes severe

■ *Less common or rare side effects may include:*
Abdominal discomfort and pain, agitation, changes in blood count
(anemia), changes in liver function, constipation, depression, diarrhea,
difficulty sleeping, dizziness, hair loss, hallucinations, heart block, hepatitis, hypersensitivity reactions, inflammation of the pancreas, involuntary
movements, irregular heartbeat, joint pain, muscle pain, nausea and
vomiting, rapid heartbeat, rash, reduced white blood cells, reversible
mental confusion, sleepiness, slow heartbeat, vague feeling of bodily
discomfort, vertigo, yellow eyes and skin

Why should this drug not be prescribed?
If you are sensitive to or have ever had an allergic reaction to Zantac or
similar drugs such as Tagamet, you should not take this medication. Make
sure that your doctor is aware of any drug reactions that you have
experienced.

Special warnings about this medication
A stomach malignancy could be present, even if your symptoms have been
relieved by Zantac.

If you have kidney or liver disease, this drug should be used with caution.

If you have phenylketonurea, you should be aware that the "Efferdose"
granules contain phenylalamine.

Possible food and drug interactions
when taking this medication
If Zantac is taken with certain other drugs, the effects of either could be
increased, decreased, or altered. It is especially important to check with your
doctor before combining Zantac with the following:

Alcohol
Blood-thinning drugs such as Coumadin
Glipizide (Glucotrol)
Glyburide (DiaBeta, Micronase)
Itraconazole (Sporanox)
Ketoconazole (Nizoral)
Metoprolol (Lopressor)
Midazolam (Versed)
Nifedipine (Procardia)
Phenytoin (Dilantin)
Procainamide (Procardia)
Sucralfate (Carafate)
Theophylline (Theo-Dur)

Special information
if you are pregnant or breastfeeding

The effects of Zantac in pregnancy have not been adequately studied. If you are pregnant or plan to become pregnant, inform your doctor immediately. Zantac appears in breast milk and could affect a nursing infant. If this medication is essential to your health, your doctor may advise you to discontinue breastfeeding until your treatment with this medication is finished.

Recommended dosage

ADULTS

Active Duodenal Ulcer

The usual starting dose is 150 milligrams 2 times a day or 10 milliliters (2 teaspoonfuls) 2 times a day. Your doctor might also prescribe 300 milligrams or 20 milliliters (4 teaspoonfuls) once a day, after the evening meal or at bedtime, if necessary for your convenience. The dose should be the lowest effective dose. Long-term use should be reduced to a daily total of 150 milligrams or 10 milliliters (2 teaspoonfuls), taken at bedtime.

Other Excess Acid Conditions (such as Zollinger-Ellison Syndrome)

The usual dose is 150 milligrams or 10 milliliters (2 teaspoonfuls) 2 times a day. This dose can be adjusted upwards by your doctor.

Benign Gastric Ulcer and Gastroesophageal Reflux Disease (GERD)

The usual dose is 150 milligrams or 10 milliliters (2 teaspoonfuls) 2 times a day.

CHILDREN

The safety and effectiveness of Zantac have not been established in children.

ELDERLY

Dosage should be tailored to your particular needs.

Overdosage

Any medication taken in excess can have serious consequences. If you suspect an overdose, seek medical attention immediately.

Information concerning Zantac overdosage is limited. However, an abnormal manner of walking, low blood pressure, and exaggerated side effect symptoms may be signs of an overdose.

If you experience any of these symptoms, notify your doctor immediately.

Brand name:

ZAROXOLYN

Pronounced: Zar-OX-uh-lin
Generic name: Metolazone
Other brand name: Mykrox

Why is this drug prescribed?

Zaroxolyn is a diuretic used in the treatment of high blood pressure and other conditions that require the elimination of excess fluid from the body. These conditions include congestive heart failure and kidney disease. When used for high blood pressure, Zaroxolyn can be used alone or with other high blood pressure medications. Diuretics prompt your body to produce and eliminate more urine, which helps lower blood pressure.

Zaroxolyn is also occasionally prescribed for kidney stones.

Most important fact about this drug

If you have high blood pressure, you must take Zaroxolyn regularly for it to be effective. Since blood pressure declines gradually, it may be several weeks before you get the full benefit of Zaroxolyn; and you must continue taking it even if you are feeling well. Zaroxolyn does not cure high blood pressure; it merely keeps it under control.

How should you take this medication?

Take Zaroxolyn exactly as prescribed. Stopping Zaroxolyn suddenly could cause your condition to worsen.

- *If you miss a dose...*
  Take it as soon as you remember. If it is almost time for the next dose, skip the one you missed and go back to your regular schedule. Do not take 2 doses at the same time.

- *Storage instructions...*
  Store a room temperature in a tightly closed, light-resistant container.

What side effects may occur?
Side effects cannot be anticipated. If any develop or change in intensity, inform your doctor as soon as possible. Only your doctor can determine if it is safe for you to continue taking Zaroxolyn.

- *Side effects may include:*
  Anemia, bloating of the abdomen, blood clots, blurred vision, chest pain, chills, constipation, depression, diarrhea, dizziness on standing up, dizziness or light-headedness, drowsiness, fainting, fatigue, gout, headache, hepatitis, high blood sugar, hives, impotence, inflammation of the skin, inflammation of the pancreas, joint pain, loss of appetite, low potassium levels (leading to dry mouth, excessive thirst, weak or irregular heartbeat, or muscle pain or cramps), muscle spasms or cramps, nausea, rapid, pounding heartbeat, rash, reddish or purplish spots on the skin, restlessness, sensitivity to light, sugar in the urine, tingling or pins and needles, upset stomach, vertigo, vomiting, weakness, yellow eyes and skin

Why should this drug not be prescribed?
If you are unable to urinate or have severe liver disease, you should not take this medication.

If you are sensitive to or have ever had an allergic reaction to Zaroxolyn or similar drugs, you should not take this medication.

Special warnings about this medication
Diuretics can cause your body to lose too much potassium. Signs of an excessively low potassium level include muscle weakness and rapid or irregular heartbeat. To boost your potassium level, your doctor may recommend eating potassium-rich foods or taking a potassium supplement.

If you are taking Zaroxolyn, your doctor will do a complete assessment of your kidney function and continue to monitor it.

Do not interchange Zaroxolyn and other formulations of metolazone such as Mykrox. The brands vary in potency of action.

If you have liver disease, diabetes, gout, or lupus erythematosus (a disease of the immune system), Zaroxolyn should be used with caution.

If you have had an allergic reaction to sulfa drugs, thiazides, or quinethazone, you may be at greater risk for an allergic reaction to this medication.

Dehydration, excessive sweating, severe diarrhea, or vomiting could deplete your fluids and cause your blood pressure to become too low. Be careful when exercising and in hot weather.

Notify your doctor or dentist that you are taking Zaroxolyn if you have a medical emergency and before you have surgery or dental treatment.

Possible food and drug interactions
when taking this medication
Zaroxolyn may intensify the effects of alcohol. Avoid drinking alcohol while taking this medication.

If Zaroxolyn is taken with certain other drugs, the effects of either could be increased, decreased, or altered. It is especially important to check with your doctor before combining Zaroxolyn with the following:

ACTH
Antidiabetic drugs such as Micronase
Barbiturates such as phenobarbital
Corticosteroids such as prednisone (Deltasone)
Digitalis glycosides such as Lanoxin
Insulin
Lithium (Lithonate)
Loop diuretics such as furosemide (Lasix)
Methenamine (Mandelamine)
Narcotics such as Percocet
Nonsteroidal anti-inflammatory agents such as Advil, Motrin, and
    Naprosyn
Norepinephrine (Levophed)
Other high blood pressure medications such as Aldomet
Tubocurarine

Special information
if you are pregnant or breastfeeding
The effects of Zaroxolyn during pregnancy have not been adequately studied. If you are pregnant or plan to become pregnant, inform your doctor immediately. Zaroxolyn appears in breast milk and could affect a nursing infant. If this medication is essential to your health, your doctor may advise you to discontinue breastfeeding until your treatment is finished.

Recommended dosage

ADULTS

Your doctor will adjust the dosage of this medication to your individual needs and will use the lowest possible dose with the maximum effect. The time it takes for this medication to become effective varies from person to person, depending on the diagnosis.

Most starting doses of this medication will be given once a day.

Edema Due to Heart or Kidney Disorders
The usual dosage is 5 milligrams to 20 milligrams once a day.

Mild to Moderate High Blood Pressure
The usual dosage is 2.5 milligrams to 5 milligrams once a day.

CHILDREN

The safety and effectiveness of Zaroxolyn in children have not been established.

Overdosage
Any medication taken in excess can have serious consequences. If you suspect an overdose, seek medical attention immediately.

- *Symptoms of Zaroxolyn overdose may include:*
  Difficulty breathing
  Dizziness
  Dizziness on standing up
  Drowsiness
  Fainting
  Irritation of the stomach and intestines
  Lethargy leading to coma

Brand name:

ZERIT

Pronounced: ZAIR-it
Generic name: Stavudine

Why is this drug prescribed?
Zerit is an antiviral drug in capsule form used to treat adults with human immunodeficiency virus (HIV) infection. HIV is the virus that causes the fatal

disease AIDS, a breakdown of the immune system. Zerit is prescribed for adults with advanced HIV infection who have already taken other antiviral drugs such as Retrovir (zidovudine, AZT) and who either have not improved on them or have experienced serious side effects or allergic reactions.

Most important fact about this drug

Zerit is not a cure for HIV infection or AIDS. At present, there is no evidence from studies that Zerit has increased the lifespan of people with HIV or lowered their risk of getting an opportunistic infection. (An opportunistic infection, such as a serious type of pneumonia called *Pneumocystis carinii* pneumonia, occurs only in people with a weak immune system.) People taking Zerit or any other antiviral drug may still develop infections or other complications of HIV infection. Consequently, if you are on Zerit, you should be closely monitored by your doctor and should see a doctor who is experienced in treating people with HIV infection.

How should you take this medication?

Take this medication at regular 12-hour intervals, exactly as prescribed. You may take it with meals or in between.

▪ *If you miss a dose...*
Take the forgotten dose as soon as you remember. If it is almost time for your next dose, skip the one you missed and go back to your regular schedule. Never take 2 doses at the same time.

▪ *Storage instructions...*
Store at room temperature in a tightly closed container.

What side effects may occur?

Side effects cannot be anticipated. If any develop or change in intensity, inform your doctor as soon as possible. Only your doctor can determine if it is safe for you to continue taking Zerit.

The major side effect associated with the use of Zerit is peripheral neuropathy, a usually temporary condition that causes numbness, tingling, burning, or pain in the feet or hands. If you develop peripheral neuropathy while taking Zerit, your doctor may take you off the drug, especially if your symptoms are severe. Sometimes, symptoms are temporarily worse when people stop taking Zerit.

▪ *More common side effects may include:*
Abdominal pain, allergic reaction, anxiety, back pain, chest pain, chills and fever, confusion, conjunctivitis (pinkeye), constipation, depression, diarrhea, difficult or labored breathing, dizziness, flu-like symptoms, general

feeling of illness, headache, hives, indigestion, inflammation and sores of the mouth, insomnia, itching, joint pain, loss of appetite, migraine, muscle pain, nausea, nervousness, pain, painful urination, pneumonia, rash, skin tumor, sweating, vision problems, vomiting, weakness, weight gain

■ *Less common or rare side effects may include:*
Asthma, blood in the urine, development of tumors, fainting, frequent urination, genital pain, high blood pressure, impotence, noncancerous skin tumors, painful menstruation, skin inflammation, sleepiness, tremors, vaginal inflammation

Why should this drug not be prescribed?
If you are sensitive to or have ever had an allergic reaction to Zerit, you should not take this drug.

Special warnings about this medication
Although Zerit attacks HIV in the bloodstream, people taking the drug can still transmit the virus to others. Zerit has not been shown to reduce the risk of transmitting HIV through sexual contact or exposure to blood.

Possible food and drug interactions when taking this medication
No interactions have been reported.

Special information if you are pregnant or breastfeeding
The effects of Zerit during pregnancy have not been adequately studied. Zerit should be used during pregnancy only if it is clearly needed. It is not known if Zerit appears in breast milk. Because it may affect a nursing infant, your doctor may instruct you not to breastfeed if you are taking Zerit.

Recommended dosage

ADULTS

The recommended starting dose is based on body weight. If you weigh 132 pounds or more, it is 40 milligrams twice a day. If you weigh less than 132 pounds, it is 30 milligrams twice a day.

If your doctor has taken you off Zerit because you have developed peripheral neuropathy, he may start giving you the drug again when your symptoms go away. The recommended dose when resuming Zerit therapy is 20 milligrams twice a day for people weighing 132 pounds or more, and 15 milligrams twice a day for those weighing less.

Your doctor may also give you a lower dose of Zerit if you develop liver or kidney problems.

Overdosage

Any medication taken in excess can have serious consequences. If you suspect an overdose, seek medical attention immediately.

■ *Symptoms of Zerit overdose may include:*
Peripheral neuropathy
Problems with liver functions

Brand name:

ZESTORETIC

Pronounced: zest-or-ET-ik
Generic ingredients: Lisinopril, Hydrochlorothiazide
Other brand name: Prinzide

Why is this drug prescribed?

Zestoretic is used in the treatment of high blood pressure. It combines an ACE inhibitor drug with a diuretic. Lisinopril, the ACE inhibitor, works by limiting production of a substance that promotes salt and water retention in your body. Hydrochlorothiazide, a diuretic, prompts your body to produce and eliminate more urine, which helps in lowering blood pressure.

Most important fact about this drug

You must take Zestoretic regularly for it to be effective. Since blood pressure declines gradually, it may be several weeks before you get the full benefit of Zestoretic; and you must continue taking it even if you are feeling well. Zestoretic does not cure high blood pressure; it merely keeps it under control.

How should you take this medication?

Zestoretic can be taken with or without food. Take it exactly as prescribed.

■ *If you miss a dose...*
Take the forgotten dose as soon as you remember. If it is almost time for your next dose, skip the one you missed and go back to your regular schedule. Never take a double dose.

■ *Storage instructions...*
Zestoretic should be stored at room temperature. Keep the container tightly closed.

What side effects may occur?

Side effects cannot be anticipated. If any develop or change in intensity, inform your doctor as soon as possible. Only your doctor can determine if it is safe for you to continue taking Zestoretic.

■ *More common side effects may include:*
Cough
Dizziness
Dizziness when standing up
Fatigue
Headache

■ *Less common side effects may include:*
Asthma, diarrhea, hair loss, impotence, indigestion, low blood pressure, muscle cramps, nausea, rash, tingling or pins and needles, upper respiratory infection, vomiting, weakness

■ *Rare side effects may include:*
Abdominal pain, anemia, arthritis, back pain, back strain, blurred vision, bronchitis, bruising, chest discomfort or pain, common cold, confusion, constipation, decreased sex drive, depression, difficulty breathing, difficulty falling or staying asleep, dry mouth, earache, excessive perspiration, fainting, fever, flu, flushing, foot pain, gas, general feeling of illness, gout, hay fever, heart attack, heartburn, heart rhythm disturbances, hepatitis, hives, itching, joint pain, knee pain, loss of appetite, lung congestion, muscle pain, muscle spasm, nervousness, palpitations, rapid heartbeat, red or purple areas on the skin, reduced urine output, restlessness, ringing in ears, sensitivity to light, shortness of breath, severe allergic reaction, shoulder pain, sinus inflammation, skin inflammation, sleepiness, sore throat, stomach and intestinal cramps, stroke, stuffy nose, swelling of the face, lips, tongue, throat, or arms and legs, trauma, urinary tract infection, vertigo, virus infection, vision abnormality in which objects have a yellowish hue, yellow eyes and skin

Why should this drug not be prescribed?

If you are sensitive to or have ever had an allergic reaction to lisinopril or hydrochlorothiazide or if you are sensitive to other ACE inhibitor drugs such as Capoten or sulfa drugs such as Gantrisin, you should not take this medication. If you suffered angioedema (swelling of face, lips, tongue, throat, arms, or legs) during previous treatment with an ACE inhibitor, you should not take this medication. You should also avoid Zestoretic if you are unable to urinate. Tell your doctor of all allergic reactions you have experienced.

Special warnings about this medication

If you develop swelling of your face, lips, tongue, or throat, or of your arms and legs, or have difficulty swallowing or breathing, you should contact your doctor immediately. You may need emergency treatment.

Zestoretic may cause your blood pressure to become too low. If you feel light-headed, especially during the first few days of treatment, inform your doctor. If you actually faint, stop taking Zestoretic until you have consulted your doctor.

Do not use salt substitutes containing potassium without first consulting your doctor.

Excessive sweating, dehydration, severe diarrhea, or vomiting could cause you to lose too much water and cause your blood pressure to drop dangerously.

If you develop chest pain, a sore throat, or fever and chills, contact your doctor immediately. It could indicate a more serious illness.

Make sure the doctor knows if you have congestive heart failure, diabetes, liver disease, a history of allergy or bronchial asthma, or lupus erythematosus (an arthritis-like disease sometimes accompanied by rashes). Zestoretic should be used cautiously. If you have kidney disease, your doctor should monitor your kidney function regularly.

This medication is not recommended for people on dialysis; severe allergic reactions have occurred.

If you are diabetic, your doctor will want to keep an eye on your blood sugar levels.

Make sure your doctor or dentist knows you are taking Zestoretic before you undergo surgery.

Possible food and drug interactions
when taking this medication

Zestoretic may intensify the effects of alcohol. Do not drink alcohol while taking this medication.

If Zestoretic is taken with certain other drugs, the effects of either could be increased, decreased, or altered. It is especially important to check with your doctor before combining Zestoretic with the following:

   Barbiturates such as Nembutal and Seconal
   Cholestyramine (Questran)
   Colestipol (Colestid)
   Corticosteroids such as prednisone

High blood pressure drugs such as Procardia XL and Aldomet
Indomethacin (Indocin)
Insulin
Lithium (Lithonate)
Narcotics such as Darvon and Dilaudid
Nonsteroidal anti-inflammatory drugs such as Naprosyn
Oral antidiabetic drugs such as Micronase
Potassium supplements such as K-Dur and Slow-K
Potassium-containing salt substitutes
Potassium-sparing diuretics such as Midamor

Special information
if you are pregnant or breastfeeding
During the second and third trimester, lisinopril can cause birth defects, prematurity, and death in the fetus and newborn. If you are pregnant or plan to become pregnant, contact your doctor immediately to discuss the potential hazard to your unborn child. Zestoretic may appear in breast milk and could affect a nursing infant. If this medication is essential to your health, your doctor may advise you to discontinue breastfeeding until your treatment with this medication is finished.

Recommended dosage

ADULTS

Dosages of this drug are always individualized. Your doctor will determine what works best for you. Dosages will also be modified and carefully monitored if you have reduced kidney function.

Once your doctor has determined that your blood pressure is stable, the usual dose is 1 or 2 tablets taken once a day. You should not take more than 4 tablets a day.

CHILDREN

Safety and effectiveness in children have not been established.

Overdosage
Any medication taken in excess can have serious consequences. If you suspect an overdose, seek medical treatment immediately.

■ *Symptoms of Zestoretic overdose may include:*
Dehydration
Low blood pressure

Brand name:

ZESTRIL

Pronounced: ZEST-rill
Generic name: Lisinopril
Other brand name: Prinivil

Why is this drug prescribed?

Lisinopril is used in the treatment of high blood pressure. It is effective when used alone or when combined with other high blood pressure medications. It may also be used with other medications in the treatment of heart failure.

Lisinopril is a type of drug called an ACE inhibitor. It works by reducing production of a substance that increases salt and water retention in your body.

Most important fact about this drug

If you have high blood pressure, you must take lisinopril regularly for it to be effective. Since blood pressure declines gradually, it may be several weeks before you get the full benefit of lisinopril; and you must continue taking it even if you are feeling well. Lisinopril does not cure high blood pressure; it merely keeps it under control.

How should you take this medication?

Lisinopril can be taken with or without food. Take it exactly as prescribed. Stopping lisinopril suddenly could cause your blood pressure to rise.

■ *If you miss a dose...*
Take the forgotten dose as soon as you remember. If it is almost time for your next dose, skip the one you missed and go back to your regular schedule. Never take 2 doses at the same time.

■ *Storage instructions...*
Store at room temperature, with the container sealed and dry. Avoid excessive heat or freezing cold.

What side effects may occur?

Side effects cannot be anticipated. If any develop or change in intensity, inform your doctor as soon as possible. Only your doctor can determine if it is safe for you to continue taking lisinopril.

- *More common side effects may include:*
  Abdominal pain, chest pain, common cold, cough, diarrhea, difficulty in breathing, dizziness, fatigue, headache, itching, low blood pressure, nausea, rash, respiratory infection, vomiting, weakness

- *Less common or rare side effects may include:*
  Arm pain, arthritis, asthma, back pain, blurred vision, breast pain, bronchitis, burning sensation, changes in heart rhythm, chills, confusion, constipation, coughing up blood, cramps in stomach/intestines, decreased sex drive, dehydration, depression, diabetes, difficult breathing at night, dizziness on standing, double vision, dry mouth, excessive sweating, fainting, feeling of illness, fever, flu, fluid retention, flushing, gas, gout, hair loss, heart attack, heartburn, hepatitis, hip pain, hives, impotence, inability to sleep or sleeping too much, incoordination, indigestion, inflamed stomach, intolerance of light, irregular heartbeat, irritability, joint pain, kidney failure, knee pain, leg pain, little or no urine, "little strokes," liver failure, loss of appetite, lung cancer, memory impairment, muscle pain or cramps, nasal congestion or inflammation, neck pain, nervousness, nosebleed, painful breathing, painful urination, pelvic pain, pneumonia, prickling or burning sensation, rapid or fluttery heartbeat, rash, reddening of skin, ringing in ears, runny nose, sensitivity to light, severe allergic reactions, skin eruptions, shoulder pain, sinus inflammation, sleepiness, sore throat, spasm, stroke, sweating, swelling of face or arms and legs, thigh pain, tremor, upset stomach, urinary tract infection, vertigo, virus infection, vision changes, weight loss or gain, wheezing, yellow eyes and skin

Why should this drug not be prescribed?
If you are sensitive to or have ever had an allergic reaction to lisinopril or other ACE inhibitors, you should not take this medication. Make sure your doctor is aware of any drug reactions you have experienced.

Special warnings about this medication
If you develop swelling of your face, lips, tongue, or throat, or of your arms and legs, or have difficulty swallowing or breathing, you should contact your doctor immediately. You may need emergency treatment.

If you are being given bee or wasp venom to guard against future reactions, you may have a severe reaction to lisinopril.

If you have kidney disorder or connective tissue disease such as lupus, your doctor may perform periodic blood tests while you are taking this medication.

If you are taking lisinopril, a complete assessment of your kidney function should be done and kidney function should continue to be monitored.

This drug should be used with caution if you are on dialysis. There have been reports of extreme allergic reactions during dialysis in people taking ACE inhibitor medications such as lisinopril.

If you are taking high doses of a diuretic (water pill) and lisinopril, you may develop excessively low blood pressure.

Lisinopril may cause some people to become dizzy, light-headed, or faint, especially if they are taking a water pill at the same time. Do not drive, operate dangerous machinery, or participate in any hazardous activity that requires full mental alertness until you are certain lisinopril does not have this effect on you.

If you develop chest pain, sore throat, fever, and chills, contact your doctor for medical attention.

If your skin and the whites of your eyes turn yellow, stop taking the medication and contact your doctor.

Avoid salt substitutes that contain potassium. Limit your consumption of potassium-rich foods such as bananas, prunes, raisins, orange juice, and whole and skim milk. Ask your doctor for advice on how much of these foods to consume.

Excessive sweating, dehydration, severe diarrhea, or vomiting could cause you to lose too much water and cause your blood pressure to drop dangerously.

Possible food and drug interactions
when taking this medication

If lisinopril is taken with certain other drugs, the effects of either could be increased, decreased, or altered. It is especially important to check with your doctor before combining lisinopril with any of the following:

 Diuretics such as HydroDIURIL and Lasix
 Indomethacin (Indocin)
 Lithium (Lithonate, Eskalith)
 Potassium preparations such as K-Phos and Micro-V
 Potassium-sparing diuretics such as Aldactone and Midamor

Special information
if you are pregnant or breastfeeding

If it is taken during the second and third trimesters, lisinopril can cause birth defects, prematurity, and death in the fetus and newborn. If you are pregnant or plan to become pregnant and are taking lisinopril, contact your doctor immediately to discuss the potential hazard to your unborn child. Lisinopril may appear in breast milk and could affect a nursing infant. If this medication is essential to your health, your doctor may advise you to discontinue breastfeeding until your treatment with this medication is finished.

Recommended dosage

ADULTS

Hypertension

For people not on diuretics, the initial starting dose is usually 10 milligrams, taken 1 time a day. After blood pressure is adjusted, dosage is usually 20 to 40 milligrams a day, taken in a single dose.

Diuretic use should, if possible, be stopped before using lisinopril. If not, your physician may give an initial dose of 5 milligrams under supervision before any further medication is prescribed.

People with kidney disorders must be carefully monitored, and dosages will be adjusted to the individual's needs, depending on kidney function.

Heart Failure

The recommended dose is 5 milligrams, once a day, along with diuretics and digitalis. This starting dose should be taken under your doctor's supervision. The usual dosage range is 5 to 20 milligrams taken once a day.

CHILDREN

The safety and effectiveness of lisinopril in children have not been established.

ELDERLY

The physician will adjust the dosage carefully, according to the elderly individual's needs.

Overdosage

Any medication taken in excess can cause symptoms of overdose. If you suspect an overdose, seek medical attention immediately.

A severe drop in blood pressure is the primary sign of a lisinopril overdose.

Generic name:

ZIDOVUDINE

See Retrovir, page 949.

Brand name:

ZITHROMAX

Pronounced: ZITH-roh-macks
Generic name: Azithromycin

Why is this drug prescribed?
Zithromax is an antibiotic related to erythromycin. It is prescribed to treat certain mild to moderate skin infections; upper and lower respiratory tract infections, including pharyngitis (strep throat), tonsillitis, and pneumonia; and sexually transmitted infections of the cervix or urinary tract.

Most important fact about this drug
There is a possibility of rare but very serious reactions to Zithromax, including angioedema (swelling of the face, lips, and neck that impedes speaking, swallowing, and breathing) and anaphylaxis (a violent, even fatal allergic reaction). If you develop these symptoms, stop taking Zithromax and call you doctor immediately.

How should you take this medication?
Take Zithromax at least 1 hour before or 2 hours after a meal. Do not take this medication with food, or with an antacid that contains aluminum or magnesium, such as Di-Gel, Gelusil, Maalox, and others.

Be sure to take all the Zithromax your doctor prescribes.

■ *If you miss a dose...*
Take the forgotten dose as soon as you remember. If you don't remember until the next day, skip the dose and go back to your regular schedule. Never try to "catch up" by doubling the dose.

■ *Storage instructions...*
Zithromax should be stored at room temperature.

What side effects may occur?
Side effects cannot be anticipated. If any develop or change in intensity, inform your doctor as soon as possible. Only your doctor can determine if it is safe for you to continue taking Zithromax.

■ *More common side effects may include:*
Abdominal pain
Diarrhea or loose stools
Nausea
Vomiting

■ *Less common side effects may include:*
Blood in the stools, chest pain, dizziness, drowsiness, fatigue, gas, headache, heart palpitations, indigestion, jaundice (yellowing of the skin and the whites of the eyes), kidney infection, light sensitivity, rash, severe allergic reaction including swelling (as in hives), sleepiness, vaginal inflammation, vertigo, yeast infection

The single large dose (4 capsules) of Zithromax that is prescribed to treat sexually transmitted infection of the cervix or urinary tract is more likely to cause stomach and bowel side effects than the smaller doses prescribed for a skin or respiratory tract infection.

Why should this drug not be prescribed?
Do not take Zithromax if you have ever had an allergic reaction to it or to similar antibiotics such as erythromycin (E.E.S., PCE, and others).

Special warnings about this medication
Like certain other antibiotics, Zithromax may cause a potentially life-threatening form of diarrhea called pseudomembranous colitis. Pseudomembranous colitis may clear up spontaneously when the drug is stopped; if it does not, hospital treatment may be required. If you develop diarrhea, check with your doctor immediately.

If you have a liver problem, your doctor should monitor you very carefully while you are taking Zithromax.

Possible food and drug interactions
when taking this medication
If Zithromax is taken with certain other drugs, the effects of either could be increased, decreased, or altered. It is especially important to check with your doctor before combining Zithromax with antacids containing aluminum or magnesium, such as Maalox and Mylanta.

Interactions with the following drugs can also occur with erythromycin, a similar drug.

Carbamazepine (Tegretol)
Certain antihistamines such as Hismanal and Seldane
Cyclosporine (Sandimmune)
Digoxin (Lanoxin, Lanoxicaps)
Ergot-containing drugs such as Cafergot and D.H.E.
Hexobarbital
Lovastatin (Mevacor)
Phenytoin (Dilantin)

Theophylline drugs such as Bronkodyl, Slo-Phyllin, Theo-Dur, and others
Triazolam (Halcion)
Warfarin (Coumadin)

Special information
if you are pregnant or breastfeeding

If you are pregnant or plan to become pregnant, inform your doctor immediately. You should take Zithromax during pregnancy only if it is clearly needed. It is not known whether Zithromax can make its way into breast milk. If the drug is essential to your health, your doctor may advise you to stop breastfeeding until your treatment is finished.

Recommended dosage

ADULTS

The usual dose of Zithromax for patients age 16 years and older is 500 milligrams in a single dose the first day. This is followed by 250 milligrams one time each day for the next 4 days. The total amount taken should be 1.5 grams.

For treatment of non-gonococcal urethritis and cervicitis (sexually transmitted disease) due to the organism *Chlamydia trachomatis*, the usual dose is a single gram (1,000 milligrams) one time only.

CHILDREN

This medication is not recommended for children under age 16.

Overdosage

Although no specific information on Zithromax overdose is available, any medication taken in excess can have serious consequences. If you suspect an overdose, seek medical attention immediately.

Brand name:

ZOCOR

Pronounced: ZOH-core
Generic name: Simvastatin

Why is this drug prescribed?

Zocor is a cholesterol-lowering drug. Your doctor may prescribe Zocor in addition to a cholesterol-lowering diet if your blood cholesterol level is too high, and if you have been unable to lower it by diet alone.

Most important fact about this drug
Zocor is usually prescribed only if diet, exercise, and weight loss fail to bring your cholesterol level under control. It's important to remember that Zocor is a supplement to—not a substitute for—those other measures. To get the full benefit of the medication, you need to stick to the diet and exercise program prescribed by your doctor. All these efforts to keep your cholesterol levels normal are important because together they may lower your risk of heart disease.

How should you take this medication?
Take Zocor exactly as prescribed.

- *If you miss a dose...*
  Take it as soon as you remember. If it is almost time for your next dose, skip the one you missed and go back to your regular schedule. Do not take 2 doses at once.

- *Storage instructions...*
  Store at room temperature.

What side effects may occur?
Side effects cannot be anticipated. If any develop or change in intensity, inform your doctor as soon as possible. Only your doctor can determine whether it is safe for you to continue taking Zocor.

- *More common side effects may include:*
  Abdominal pain
  Headache

- *Less common side effects may include:*
  Constipation, diarrhea, gas, nausea, upper respiratory infection, upset stomach, weakness

Why should this drug not be prescribed?
Do not take Zocor if you have ever had an allergic reaction to it or are sensitive to it.

Do not take Zocor if you have active liver disease.

Do not take Zocor if you are pregnant or plan to become pregnant.

Special warnings about this medication
Because Zocor may damage the liver, your doctor may order a blood test to check your liver enzyme levels before you start taking the drug. Blood tests

will probably be done every 6 weeks for the first 3 months of treatment, every 8 weeks for the rest of the first year, and about every 6 months after that. If your liver enzyme levels rise too high, your doctor may tell you to stop taking Zocor.

Since Zocor may cause damage to muscle tissue, be sure to tell your doctor of any unexplained muscle tenderness, weakness, or pain right away, especially if you also have a fever or feel sick. Your doctor may want to do a blood test to check for signs of muscle damage.

Possible food and drug interactions
when taking this medication

If you take Zocor with certain other drugs, the effects of either could be increased, decreased, or altered. It is especially important to check with your doctor before combining Zocor with any of the following:

Blood-thinning drugs such as Coumadin and Dicumarol
Cimetidine (Tagamet)
Clofibrate (Atromid-S)
Cyclosporine (Sandimmune)
Digoxin (Lanoxin, Lanoxicaps)
Erythromycin (PCE and others)
Gemfibrozil (Lopid)
Itraconazole (Sporanox)
Ketoconazole (Nizoral)
Nicotinic acid
Spironolactone (Aldactone, Aldactazide)

Special information
if you are pregnant or breastfeeding

You must not become pregnant while taking Zocor. This drug lowers cholesterol, and cholesterol is needed for a baby to develop properly. If you do become pregnant while taking Zocor, notify your doctor right away. Based on studies of other cholesterol-lowering drugs, it is assumed that Zocor could appear in breast milk and could cause severe adverse effects in a nursing baby. Do not take Zocor while breastfeeding your baby.

Recommended dosage

You will have to follow a standard cholesterol-lowering diet before starting treatment with Zocor and continue this diet while using Zocor.

All doses should be adjusted to your individual needs.

ADULTS

The usual starting dose is 5 to 10 milligrams per day, taken as a single dose in the evening. The maximum recommended dose is 40 milligrams per day. Dosage adjustments may be made every 4 weeks, and dose levels should be reduced as cholesterol levels come down.

Those who have severe kidney disease should use Zocor with caution. The recommended dose is 5 milligrams per day.

Zocor may be used with other drugs. Your doctor will determine the proper dose based on your individual needs.

ELDERLY

Reduction of cholesterol in the elderly may be achieved with doses of 20 milligrams per day or less.

Overdosage
Although no specific information about Zocor overdose is available, any medication taken in excess can have serious consequences. If you suspect an overdose of Zocor, seek medical attention immediately.

Brand name:

ZOFRAN

Pronounced: ZOH-fran
Generic name: Ondansetron hydrochloride

Why is this drug prescribed?
Zofran is used for the prevention of nausea and vomiting caused by radiation therapy and chemotherapy for cancer.

Most important fact about this drug
To ensure the maximum effect, it is important to take all doses of Zofran exactly as prescribed by your doctor.

How should you take this medication?
Try not to miss a dose. The first dose should be taken a half-hour prior to cancer chemotherapy, with two more doses 4 and 8 hours after the first one.

■ *If you miss a dose...*
Take the forgotten dose as soon as you remember.

■ *Storage instructions...*
Store Zofran at room temperature. Protect from light. Keep the drug in the carton it came in.

What side effects may occur?
Side effects cannot be anticipated. If any develop or change in intensity, inform your doctor as soon as possible. Only your doctor can determine if it is safe for you to continue taking Zofran.

■ *More common side effects may include:*
Abdominal pain
Constipation
Headache
Weakness

■ *Less common or rare side effects may include:*
Anaphylaxis (severe allergic reaction), dry mouth, rash, wheezing

Why should this drug not be prescribed?
If you are sensitive to or have ever had an allergic reaction to ondansetron hydrochloride, you should not take this medication. Make sure that your doctor is aware of any drug reactions that you have experienced.

Special warnings about this medication
There are no special warnings about Zofran.

Possible food and drug interactions
when taking this medication
No interactions with Zofran have been reported.

Special information
if you are pregnant or breastfeeding
The effects of Zofran during pregnancy have not been adequately studied. If you are pregnant or plan to become pregnant, inform your doctor immediately. Zofran may appear in breast milk and could affect a nursing infant. If this medication is essential to your health, your doctor may advise you to discontinue breastfeeding until your treatment with this medication is finished.

Recommended dosage

ADULTS AND CHILDREN 12 YEARS OF AGE AND OLDER

The recommended dose of Zofran is one 8-milligram tablet taken 3 times a day. For chemotherapy, the first dose should be taken 30 minutes before the start of treatment. The other 2 doses should be taken 4 and 8 hours after the first dose. One 8-milligram tablet should be taken 3 times a day (every 8 hours) for 1 to 2 days after completing chemotherapy.

For radiation therapy, the first dose should be taken 1 to 2 hours before each treatment. Your doctor will tell you how long to continue taking the drug.

CHILDREN 4 TO 12 YEARS OF AGE

The recommended dose of Zofran is one 4-milligram tablet taken 3 times a day. The first dose should be taken 30 minutes before the start of chemotherapy. The other 2 doses should be taken 4 and 8 hours after the first dose. One 4-milligram tablet should be taken 3 times a day (every 8 hours) for 1 to 2 days after completing chemotherapy.

Overdosage

There are no specific symptoms of Zofran overdose to report. However, any medication taken in excess can have serious consequences. If you suspect an overdose, seek medical attention immediately.

Brand name:

ZOLOFT

Pronounced: ZOE-loft
Generic name: Sertraline

Why is this drug prescribed?

Zoloft is prescribed for major depression—a persistently low mood that interferes with everyday living. Symptoms may include loss of interest in your usual activities, disturbed sleep, change in appetite, constant fidgeting or lethargic movement, fatigue, feelings of worthlessness or guilt, difficulty thinking or concentrating, and recurrent thoughts of suicide.

Some doctors also prescribe Zoloft for obsessive-compulsive disorders.

Zoloft is thought to work by adjusting the balance of the brain's natural chemical messengers.

Most important fact about this drug
Do not take Zoloft if, within the past 2 weeks, you have taken another type of antidepressant medication known as an MAO inhibitor. Drugs in this category include Nardil, Parnate, and Marplan. When medication like Zoloft are combined with MAO inhibitors, serious and sometimes fatal reactions can occur.

How should you take this medication?
Take Zoloft exactly as prescribed: once a day, in either the morning or the evening.

Improvement with Zoloft may not be seen for several days to a few weeks.

Zoloft may make your mouth dry. For temporary relief suck a hard candy, chew gum, or melt bits of ice in your mouth.

■ *If you miss a dose...*
Take the forgotten dose as soon as you remember. If several hours have passed, skip the dose. Never try to "catch up" by doubling the dose.

■ *Storage instructions...*
Store at room temperature.

What side effects may occur?
Side effects cannot be anticipated. If any develop or change in intensity, inform your doctor as soon as possible. Only your doctor can determine if it is safe for you to continue taking Zoloft.

■ *More common side effects may include:*
Agitation, confusion, constipation, diarrhea or loose stools, difficulty with ejaculation, dizziness, dry mouth, fatigue, fluttery or throbbing heartbeat, gas, headache, increased sweating, indigestion, insomnia, nausea, nervousness, sleepiness, tremor, vomiting

■ *Less common or rare side effects may include:*
Abdominal pain, abnormal hair growth, abnormal skin odor, acne, altered taste, anxiety, back pain, bad breath, breast development in males, breast pain or enlargement, bruise-like marks on the skin, changeable emotions, chest pain, cold, clammy skin, conjunctivitis (pinkeye), coughing, difficulty breathing, difficulty concentrating, difficulty swallowing, double vision, dry eyes, enlarged abdomen, excessive menstrual bleeding, eye pain, fainting, feeling faint upon arising from a sitting or lying position, female sexual problems, fever, fluid retention, flushing, frequent urination, hair loss,

heart attack, hemorrhoids, hiccups, high blood pressure, hot flushes, increased appetite, increased salivation, inflammation of nose or throat, inflammation of the penis, intolerance to light, itching, joint pains, lack of coordination, lack of menstruation, lack of sensation, loss of appetite, low blood pressure, menstrual problems, middle ear infection, migraine, movement problems, muscle cramps or weakness, muscle pain, need to urinate during the night, nosebleed, pain upon urination, painful menstruation, purple or red spots on the skin, racing heartbeat, rash, ringing in the ears, sensitivity to light, sinus inflammation, skin eruptions or inflammation, sleepwalking, sores on tongue, speech problems, stomach and intestinal inflammation, swelling of the face, swollen wrists and ankles, thirst, tingling or pins and needles, twitching, urinary trouble, vaginal inflammation or discharge, varicose veins, vision problems, weight loss or gain, yawning

- *Zoloft may also cause mental or emotional symptoms such as:*
  Abnormal dreams or thoughts, aggressiveness, exaggerated feeling of well-being, depersonalization ("unreal" feeling), hallucinations, memory loss, paranoia, rapid mood shifts, suicidal thoughts, tooth-grinding, worsened depression

Many people lose a pound or two of body weight while taking Zoloft. This usually poses no problem but may be a concern if your depression has already caused you to lose a great deal of weight.

In a few people, Zoloft may trigger the grandiose, inappropriate, out-of-control behavior called mania or the similar, but less dramatic, "hyper" state called hypomania.

Why should this drug not be prescribed?
There are no known reasons to limit the use of this medication.

Special warnings about this medication
If you have a kidney or liver disorder, take Zoloft cautiously and under close medical supervision.

Possible food and drug interactions
when taking this medication
You should not drink alcoholic beverages while taking Zoloft.

If Zoloft is taken with certain other drugs, the effects of either could be increased, decreased, or altered. It is especially important to check with your doctor before combining Zoloft with the following:

Cimetidine (Tagamet)
Diazepam (Valium, Valrelease)
Digitoxin (Crystodigin)
Lithium (Lithonate)
MAO inhibitors (antidepressant drugs such as Nardil, Parnate, and Marplan)
Other psychiatric drugs such as Elavil and Mellaril
Over-the-counter drugs such as cold remedies
Tolbutamide (Orinase)
Warfarin (Coumadin)

Special information
if you are pregnant or breastfeeding

The effects of Zoloft during pregnancy have not been adequately studied. If you are pregnant or plan to become pregnant, inform your doctor immediately. Zoloft should be taken during pregnancy only if it is clearly needed. It is not known whether Zoloft appears in breast milk. Caution is advised when using Zoloft during breastfeeding.

Recommended dosage

ADULTS

The usual starting dose is 50 milligrams once a day, taken either in the morning or in the evening.

Your doctor may increase your dose depending upon your response. You should not take more than 200 milligrams in a day.

Overdosage

Any medication taken in excess can have serious consequences. If you suspect an overdose, seek medical attention immediately.

■ *Symptoms of Zoloft overdose may include:*
Anxiety
Dilated pupils
Nausea
Rapid heartbeat
Sleepiness
Vomiting

Generic name:

ZOLPIDEM

See Ambien, page 42.
See Ambien, page 42.

Brand name:

ZOVIRAX

Pronounced: zoh-VIGH-racks
Generic name: Acyclovir

Why is this drug prescribed?

Zovirax liquid, capsules, and tablets are used in the treatment of certain infections with herpes viruses. These include genital herpes, shingles, and chickenpox. This drug may not be appropriate for everyone, and its use should be thoroughly discussed with your doctor. Zovirax ointment is used to treat initial episodes of genital herpes and certain herpes simplex infections of the skin and mucous membranes.

Some doctors use Zovirax, along with other drugs, in the treatment of AIDS, and for unusual herpes infections such as those following kidney and bone marrow transplants.

Most important fact about this drug

Zovirax does not cure herpes. However, it does reduce pain and may help the sores caused by herpes to heal faster. Genital herpes is a sexually transmitted disease. To avoid infecting your partner, forgo intercourse and other sexual contact when visible lesions are present.

How should you take this medication?

Your medication should not be shared with others, and the prescribed dose should not be exceeded. Zovirax ointment should not be used in or near the eyes.

To reduce the risk of spreading the infection, use a rubber glove to apply the ointment.

- *If you miss a dose...*
  Take it as soon as you remember. If it is almost time for your next dose, skip the one you missed and go back to your regular schedule. Never take 2 doses at the same time.

  If you are using the ointment, apply it as soon as you remember and continue your regular schedule.

- *Storage instructions...*
  Store Zovirax at room temperature in a dry place.

What side effects may occur?
Side effects cannot be anticipated. If any develop or change in intensity, inform your doctor as soon as possible. Only your doctor can determine if it is safe for you to continue taking Zovirax.

■ *More common side effects may include:*
  Confusion, constipation, diarrhea, dizziness, fever, fluid retention, general feeling of bodily discomfort, gland enlargement in the groin, hair loss, hallucinations, headache, hives, itching, muscle pain, nausea, pain, skin rash, sleepiness, stomach and intestinal problems, visual abnormalities, vomiting

■ *Less common or rare side effects may include:*
  Abdominal pain, anaphylaxis (severe allergic reaction), diarrhea, dizziness, fatigue, gas, headache, inability to sleep, leg pain, loss of appetite, medicinal taste, rash, retention of fluid, sore throat, tingling or pins and needles, vomiting, weakness

■ *Common side effects of Zovirax ointment may include:*
  Burning
  Itching
  Mild pain
  Skin rash
  Stinging
  Vaginal inflammation

Why should this drug not be prescribed?
If you are sensitive to or have ever had an allergic reaction to Zovirax or similar drugs, you should not take this medication. Make sure that your doctor is aware of any drug reactions that you have experienced.

Special warnings about this medication
If you are being treated for a kidney disorder, consult with your doctor before taking Zovirax.

Although decreased sperm count has been reported in animals given high doses of Zovirax, this effect has not been documented to occur in humans.

**Possible food and drug interactions
when taking this medication**
If Zovirax is taken with certain other drugs, the effects of either could be

increased, decreased, or altered. It is especially important to check with your doctor before combining Zovirax with the following:

Cyclosporine (Sandimmune)
Interferon (Roferon)
Probenecid (Benemid)
Zidovudine (Retrovir)

Special information
if you are pregnant or breastfeeding

The effects of Zovirax during pregnancy have not been adequately studied. If you are pregnant or plan to become pregnant, inform your doctor immediately. Zovirax appears in breast milk and could affect a nursing infant. If this medication is essential to your health, your doctor may advise you to discontinue breastfeeding your baby until your treatment with Zovirax is finished.

Recommended dosage

ADULTS

For Genital Herpes

The usual dose is one 200-milligram capsule or 1 teaspoonful of liquid every 4 hours, 5 times daily for 10 days. If the herpes is recurrent, the usual adult dose is 400 milligrams (two 200-milligram capsules, one 400-milligram tablet or 2 teaspoonfuls) 2 times daily for up to 12 months.

If genital herpes is intermittent, the usual adult dose is one 200-milligram capsule or 1 teaspoon of liquid every 4 hours, 5 times a day for 5 days. Therapy should be started at the earliest sign or symptom.

Ointment

Apply ointment to affected area every 3 hours, 6 times per day, for 7 days. Use enough ointment (approximately one-half inch ribbon of ointment per 4 square inches of surface area) to cover the affected area.

For Herpes Zoster (Shingles)

The usual adult dose is 800 milligrams (four 200-milligram capsules, two 400-milligram tablets, or 4 teaspoonfuls of liquid) every 4 hours, 5 times daily for 7 to 10 days.

If you have a kidney disorder, the dose will need to be adjusted by your doctor.

CHILDREN

The usual dose for chickenpox is 20 milligrams per 2.2 pounds of body weight, not to exceed 800 milligrams, taken orally 4 times daily for 5 days. Therapy should be initiated at the earliest sign or symptom.

The safety and effectiveness of Zovirax have not been established in children under 2 years of age. However, your doctor may decide that the benefits of this medication outweigh the potential risks.

ELDERLY

No special considerations apply.

Overdosage

Zovirax is generally safe; however, there have been cases of kidney disorder in patients taking Zovirax orally.

Any medication taken in excess can have serious consequences.

If you suspect an overdose, seek medical attention immediately.

Brand name:

ZYDONE

See Vicodin, page 1193.

Brand name:

ZYLOPRIM

Pronounced: ZYE-loe-prim
Generic name: Allopurinol
Other brand name: Lopurin

Why is this drug prescribed?

Zyloprim is used in the treatment of many symptoms of gout, including acute attacks, tophi (collection of uric acid crystals in the tissues, especially around joints), joint destruction, and uric acid stones. Gout is a form of arthritis characterized by increased blood levels of uric acid. Zyloprim works by reducing uric acid production in the body, thus preventing crystals from forming.

Zyloprim is also used to manage the increased uric acid levels in the blood of patients with certain cancers, such as leukemia. It is also prescribed to manage some types of kidney stones.

Most important fact about this drug
Zyloprim will not stop a gout attack that is already underway. However, when taken over a period of several months, this drug will begin to reduce your symptoms. It's important to keep taking it regularly, even if it seems to have no immediate effect.

How should you take this medication?
Take Zyloprim exactly as prescribed. Your doctor will probably start you on a low dosage, increasing it gradually each week until you reach the dosage that is best for you.

A typical starting dose is one 100-milligram tablet per day. You may want to take Zyloprim immediately after a meal to minimize the risk of stomach irritation.

You should avoid taking large doses of vitamin C because of the increased possibility of kidney stone formation.

While taking Zyloprim you should drink plenty of liquids—10 to 12 glasses (8 ounces each) per day unless otherwise prescribed by your doctor.

To help prevent attacks of gout, you should also avoid beer, wine, and purine-rich foods such as anchovies, sardines, liver, kidneys, lentils, and sweetbreads.

If you have been taking colchicine and/or an anti-inflammatory drug, such as Anaprox, Indocin, and others, to relieve your gout, your doctor will probably want you to continue taking this medication while your Zyloprim dosage is being adjusted. Later, when you have had no attacks of gout for several months, you may be able to stop taking these other medications.

If you have been taking a drug that promotes the excretion of uric acid in the urine, such as probenecid (Benemid) or sulfinpyrazone (Anturane), to try to prevent attacks of gout, your doctor will probably want to reduce or stop your dosage of this drug while increasing your dosage of Zyloprim.

■ *If you miss a dose...*
Take it as soon as you remember. If it is almost time for your next dose, skip the one you missed and go back to your regular schedule. Do not take 2 doses at once.

■ *Storage instructions...*
Store at room temperatures in a cool, dry place, away from light.

What side effects may occur?
Side effects cannot be anticipated. If any develop or change in intensity, inform your doctor as soon as possible. Only your doctor can determine if it is safe for you to continue taking Zyloprim.

Because a skin reaction, the most common side effect of Zyloprim, may occasionally become severe or even fatal, you should stop taking Zyloprim if you notice even the beginnings of a rash. Such a rash may be itchy or scaly or may make your skin peel off in sheets; it may be accompanied by chills and fever, aching joints, or jaundice.

■ *More common side effects may include:*
Acute attack of gout
Diarrhea
Nausea
Rash

■ *Less common or rare side effects may include:*
Abdominal pain, bruising, chills, fever, hair loss, headache, hepatitis, hives, indigestion, itching, joint pain, kidney failure, loosening of nails, muscle disease, nosebleed, rare skin condition characterized by severe blisters and bleeding on the lips, eyes, or nose, reddish-brown or purplish spots on skin, skin inflammation or peeling, sleepiness, stomach inflammation, taste loss or change, tingling or pins and needles, unusual bleeding, vomiting, yellowing of skin and eyes

Why should this drug not be prescribed?
Do not take Zyloprim if you have ever had a severe reaction to it in the past.

Special warnings about this medication
If you notice a rash or other signs of an allergic reaction, stop taking Zyloprim immediately and consult your doctor. In some people, a Zyloprim-induced rash may lead to a serious skin disease, generalized inflammation of a blood or lymph vessel, irreversible liver damage, or even death.

You may experience acute attacks of gout more often in the early stages of Zyloprim therapy, even when normal uric acid levels have been attained. These attacks will become shorter and less severe after several months of therapy.

A kidney problem may turn a normal dose of Zyloprim into an overdose. If you have a kidney disease, or a condition such as diabetes or high blood pressure that may affect your kidneys, your doctor should prescribe Zyloprim cautiously and order periodic blood and urine tests to assess your kidney function.

Because Zyloprim may make you drowsy, do not drive or perform hazardous tasks until you know how the medication affects you.

It may be 2 to 6 weeks before you see any results from this medication.

Possible food and drug interactions
when taking this medication

If Zyloprim is taken with certain other drugs, the effects of either could be increased, decreased, or altered. It is especially important to check with your doctor before combining Zyloprim with the following:

Amoxicillin (Amoxil, Larotid, Polymox)
Ampicillin (Amcill, Omnipen, Polycillin, Principen)
Azathioprine (Imuran)
Blood thinners such as Coumadin
Drugs for diabetes, such as Diabinese and Orinase
Mercaptopurine (Purinethol)
Probenecid (Benemid, ColBENEMID)
Sulfinpyrazone (Anturane)
Theophylline (Theo-Dur, Slo-Phyllin, and others)
Thiazide diuretics such as HydroDIURIL, Diuril, and others
Vitamin C

Special information
if you are pregnant or breastfeeding

The effects of Zyloprim during pregnancy have not been adequately studied. If you are pregnant or plan to become pregnant, notify your doctor immediately. Zyloprim should be taken during pregnancy only if it is clearly needed.

Zyloprim appears in breast milk; what effect it may have on a nursing baby is unknown. Caution is advised when Zyloprim is taken during breastfeeding.

Recommended dosage

ADULTS

Your doctor will tailor the dosage of Zyloprim individually to control the severity of symptoms and to bring the uric acid levels to normal or near normal.

Gout

The usual starting dose is 100 milligrams once daily. Your doctor may increase your dose by 100 milligrams per day at 1-week intervals until desired results are attained. The average dose is 200 to 300 milligrams per day for mild gout and 400 to 600 milligrams daily for moderate to severe gout. The most you should take in a day is 800 milligrams.

Recurrent Kidney Stones

The usual dose is 200 to 300 milligrams daily, divided into smaller doses or taken as one dose.

Management of Uric Acid Levels in Certain Cancers

The usual dose is 600 to 800 milligrams daily for 2 to 3 days, together with a high fluid intake.

CHILDREN

The usual recommended dose for children 6 to 10 years of age is 300 milligrams daily for the management of uric acid levels in certain types of cancer. Children under 6 years of age are generally given 150 milligrams daily.

Overdosage

Although no specific information is available regarding Zyloprim overdosage, any medication taken in excess can have serious consequences. If you suspect an overdose of Zyloprim, seek medical attention immediately.

APPENDIX 1

Safe Medication Use

Using medications safely is largely a matter of common sense and caution. The following are general guidelines to keep in mind:

You and your doctor

- Tell your doctor everything about your medical history, including reactions to medications you've used in the past.
- Tell the doctor about any medications you are using now, even if they are over-the-counter drugs.
- Keep track of your reactions to a medication and report them to your doctor.
- Ask your doctor what you can do when given a new drug. For example, are there any foods to avoid when taking the drug? Should you avoid alcohol?
- Never change your dose schedule unless your doctor tells you to do so.
- Ask about the addiction or dependence potential of any new drug.

You and your pharmacist

- See if there are any written instructions that you can take with you.
- Ask the pharmacist to explain clearly when and how to take the drug.
- Check the ingredients of over-the-counter drugs you may be taking to ensure that your prescription doesn't interact with them.
- If you are starting a new medication, ask your pharmacist to fill only half the prescription in case you have an adverse reaction and the drug is stopped.
- Ask how long the medication remains effective. Don't take it after its expiration date.
- If you are going on a vacation, make sure your drug can be used in different climates.

You and your medications

- Never take someone else's medication; and don't share your own medicines.

- Check the label each time you take a drug. Don't take a drug in the dark.
- Keep your medications in a dry, safe spot.
- Keep each medicine in the bottle from the drug store. Don't mix medicines together in a single bottle.
- If you think you are pregnant, consult with your doctor before using any medication.
- Destroy any unused portions of a drug and throw out the bottle.
- If you need a certain medicine (for instance, insulin) in case of emergency, carry the information with you.

Your medicines and your children

- Keep all medications in a locked cabinet or in a spot well out of the reach of children.
- Ask for child-proof safety bottles.
- Be alert and awake when giving a child medication.
- Make sure that children know medications can be dangerous if misused.
- Keep antidotes such as Syrup of Ipecac on hand.
- Keep the numbers of your EMS (emergency medical service) and poison control centers handy.

APPENDIX 2

Alcohol-Free Products

I f you must avoid alcohol, the following is a representative list of liquid preparations, both over the counter and prescription, that are alcohol-free. For easy identification, the drugs are listed by category.

Analgesics
Demerol Syrup
Halenol Children's Liquid
Liquiprin Infant's Drops
Motrin Children's
Panadol Children's Liquid
Panadol Infant's Drops
Tempra 1 Drops
Tempra 2 Syrup
Tylenol Children's Elixir
Tylenol Children's Suspension
Tylenol Infant's Drops
Tylenol Infant's Suspension Drops

Asthma Medications
Alupent Syrup
Aquaphyllin Syrup
Dilor G Liquid
Dyline-GG Liquid
Elixophyllin-GG Liquid
Metaprel Syrup
Slo-Phyllin GG Syrup
Slo-Phyllin 80 Syrup
Theoclear-80 Liquid
Theolair Liquid

Anticonvulsants
Mysoline Suspension
Tridione Solution
Zarontin Syrup

Antidiarrheals
Kaodene Non-Narcotic Liquid
Kaopectate Advanced Formula

Kaopectate Children's Liquid
Pepto-Bismol Suspension

Nausea Medications
Emetrol Solution

Cough/Cold/Allergy Preparations
Actifed Syrup
Anaplex HD Syrup
Anaplex Liquid
Chlorgest HD
Codegest Expectorant
Dallergy-D Syrup
Deconamine Syrup
Delsym Liquid
Diabetic Tussin DM Liquid
Diabetic Tussin EX Liquid
Donatussin DC Syrup
Donatussin Drops
Donatussin Pediatric Syrup
Dorcol Children's Cold Formula Liquid
Dorcol Children's Cough Syrup
Dorcol Children's Decongestant Liquid
Drixoral Syrup
Hayfebrol Liquid
Hycodan Syrup
Hycomine Pediatric Syrup
Hycomine Syrup
Ipsatol Cough Formula Liquid
Kolephrin GG/DM Liquid
Naldecon CX Adult Liquid
Naldecon DX Children's Syrup
Naldecon DX Pediatric Drops
Naldecon EX Children's Syrup

Naldecon EX Pediatric Drops
Naldecon Senior DX Liquid
Naldecon Senior EX Liquid
Organidin NR Liquid
PediaCare Cough-Cold Formula Liquid
PediaCare Infants' Decongestant Drops
PediaCare Night Rest Cough-Cold
    Formula
Pneumotussin HC Syrup
Poly-Histine CS Syrup
Poly-Histine DM Syrup
Robitussin Pediatric Cough & Cold
    Formula
Robitussin Pediatric Cough Suppressant
Rondec Oral Drops
Rondec Syrup
Ryna-C Liquid
Ryna-CX Liquid
Ryna Liquid
Rynatuss Pediatric Suspension
Safe Tussin 30 Liquid
Scot-Tussin DM Liquid
Scot-Tussin Original 5-Action Cold
    Formula
Scot-Tussin Original 5-Action Liquid
Sudafed Children's Liquid
Triaminic DM Syrup
Triaminic Expectorant Liquid
Triaminic Nite Lite Liquid
Triaminic Oral Infant Drops
Triaminic Syrup
Triaminicol Multi-Symptom Relief Syrup
Tussar DM Cough Syrup
Tussi Organidin DM NR Liquid
Tussi Organidin NR Liquid
Tussirex Sugar Free Liquid
Tussirex Syrup
Tylenol Children's Cold Multi-Symptom
    Liquid
Tylenol Children's Cold Plus Cough
    Multi-Symptom Liquid
Vicks Children's NyQuil Liquid
Vicks Pediatric Formula 44D Liquid
Vicks Pediatric Formula 44E Liquid
Vicks Pediatric Formula 44M Liquid
Vicodin Tuss Syrup

Mouth/Throat Products
Baby Orajel
Baby Orajel Nighttime
Chloraseptic Spray/Gargle
Fluorinse
Gly-Oxide Liquid

Electrolytes
Kolyum Liquid

Iron Preparations
Feostat Drops
Feostat Suspension
Troph-Iron Liquid

Laxatives
Agoral Emulsion
Colace Liquid
Haley's M-O Liquid
Kondremul Plain Liquid
Liqui-doss
Milkinol Emulsion
Neoloid Emulsion
Phillip's Milk of Magnesia Liquid

Major Tranquilizers
Haldol Concentrate
Stelazine Concentrate
Thorazine Syrup

Miscellaneous
Glandosane

Vitamins
Poly-Vi-Sol Drops
Poly-Vi-Sol Drops w/ Iron
Theragran Liquid
Tri-Vi-Sol ADC Drops
Tri-Vi-Sol ADC Drops w/ Iron
Vitalize SF Liquid

APPENDIX 3

Sugar-Free Products

The following is a selection of products that contain no sugar. Remember, however, that some may contain sorbitol, alcohol, or other sources of carbohydrates. Read the product label carefully for a listing of all the ingredients.

Analgesics
Children's Myapap Elixir
Children's Panadol Drops
Children's Panadol Liquid
Children's Panadol Tablets, Chewable
Children's Tylenol Tablets, Chewable
Children's Tylenol Suspension Liquid
Dolanex Elixir
Feverall Sprinkle Caps
Infant's Tylenol Drops
Infant's Tylenol Suspension Drops
Junior Strength Tylenol Chewable
  Tablets
Methadone HCl
Myapap Drops
St. Joseph Aspirin-Free Drops
St. Joseph Aspirin-Free Liquid
Tempra 1 Drops
Tempra 2 Syrup
Tempra 3 Tablets, Chewable
Tempra Tablets, Chewable

Antacids/Anti-gas Medications
Alka-Seltzer Lemon Lime Effervescent
  Tablets
Aluminum Hydroxide Concentrated
  Suspension
Calglycine Tablets
Citrocarbonate Granules
Di-Gel Liquid
Dimacid
Eno Powder
Extra Strength Maalox Suspension
Gaviscon Liquid

Gelusil Liquid
Gelusil II Suspension
Maalox HRF Suspension
Maalox Suspension
Magnesia and Alumina Oral Suspension
  USP
Mallamint Tablets, Chewable
Marblen Suspension
Milk of Magnesia USP
Nephrox Suspension
Pepto-Bismol Liquid
Pepto-Bismol Tablets
Phosphaljel Suspension
Riopan Plus Suspension
Riopan Suspension
Titralac Plus Liquid
Titralac Plus Tablets
Titralac Tablets

Asthma Medications
Elixophyllin-GG Liquid
Mudrane-GG Elixir
Organidin Solution
Potassium Iodide Solution
Slo-Phyllin Syrup
Theoclear-80 Syrup

Antidiarrheals
Diasorb Liquid
Kaolin with Pectin Suspension
Konsyl Powder
Pepto-Bismol Liquid
Pepto-Bismol Tablets
Pepto Diarrhea Control Liquid

Antihistamines/Decongestants
Dimetane D-C
Hay-Febrol Liquid
Novahistine Elixir
Ryna Liquid
Trind Liquid

Anti-mania Medications
Cibalith-S Syrup
Lithium Citrate Syrup

Corticosteroids
Dexamethasone Solution
Pediapred Oral Liquid

Cough/Cold/Allergy Preparations
Anatuss Syrup
Cerose-DM Liquid
Chlorgest HD
Codegest Expectorant
Codiclear DH Syrup
Codimal-DM Syrup
Dexafed Cough Syrup
Diabetic Tussin DM
Diabetic Tussin EX Liquid
Dimetane-DC Cough Syrup
Dimetane-DX Cough Syrup
Entuss-D Liquid
Hayfebrol Liquid
Hytuss 2X Capsules
Hytuss Tablets
Naldecon CX Adult Liquid
Naldecon DX Adult Liquid
Naldecon DX Children's Syrup
Naldecon DX Pediatric Drops
Naldecon EX Children's Syrup
Naldecon EX Pediatric Drops
Naldecon Senior DX Liquid
Naldecon Senior EX Liquid
Novahistine Elixir
Organidin NR Liquid/Tablets
Robitussin Pediatric Cough and Cold Liquid
Robitussin Pediatric Cough Suppressant Liquid
Rondec-DM Syrup
Ryna Liquid
Ryna-C Liquid

Ryna-CX Liquid
Safe Tussin 30 Liquid
S-T Forte 2 Liquid
S-T Forte SF Liquid
Scot-Tussin DM Cough Chasers
Scot-Tussin DM Liquid
Scot-Tussin Expectorant
Scot-Tussin Original Liquid
Tolu-Sed Cough Syrup
Tolu-Sed DM Liquid
Trind-DM Liquid
Trind Liquid
Tussar SF Syrup
Tuss-DM Tablets
Tuss-LA Tablets
Tussi-Organidin DM NR Liquid
Tussi-Organidin Liquid
Tussi-Organidin NR Liquid
Tussirex Sugar-Free Liquid
Vicodin-Tuss Syrup

Gastrointestinal Drugs
Reglan Syrup

Iron Preparations
Geritol Complete Tablets
Incremin with Iron Syrup
Kovitonic Liquid
Niferex Elixir
Nu-Iron Elixir

Laxatives
Agoral Marshmallow Emulsion
Agoral Plain Emulsion
Agoral Raspberry Emulsion
Citrucel Sugar Free Powder
Emulsoil
Fiberall Powder
Haley's M-O
Hydrocil Instant Powder
Kondremul Plain Emulsion
Konsyl D Powder
Konsyl Powder
Metamucil Sugar Free Powder

Miscellaneous
Bicitra Solution
Nicorette Chewing Gum

Nicorette DS Chewing Gum
Polycitra-K Solution/Crystals
Polycitra-LC Solution

Mouth/Throat Preparations
Anbesol Gel
Babee Teething Lotion
Baby Orajel
Chloraseptic Mouthwash/Gargle
Moi-Stir Solution
Mycinettes Lozenges
Mycinette Spray
N'ice Lozenges
Orajel Brace-Aid Gel
Orajel/d Gel
Orajel Mouth Aid Liquid
Rid-A-Pain Drops
Rid-A-Pain Gel
Salivart Solution
Sucrets Maximum Strength
    Mouthwash/Gargle
Sucrets Throat Spray
Tanac Liquid
Tanac Roll-On Liquid

Potassium Supplements
Cena-K Liquid
Kaochlor-S-F Liquid
Kaon-Cl 20% Liquid
Kaon Elixir
Kay Ciel Elixir
Kay Ciel Powder
Klor-Con Powder
Klor-Con/25 Powder
Klor-Con/EF Tablets
Klorvess Effervescent Granules
Kolyum Liquid

Psychotropics
Serentil Concentrate

Vitamins/Minerals
Bugs Bunny Complete Chewable
    Tablets
Bugs Bunny Plus Iron Chewable Tabs
Bugs Bunny with Extra C Chewable
    Tabs
Caltrate 600 Tablets
Decagen Tablets
Luride Drops
Luride Lozi-tabs
Luride-SF Lozi-tabs
One-A-Day Essential Tablet
One-A-Day Maximum Formula Tablets
One-A-Day Women's Formula Tablets
Oyst-Cal 500 Tablets
Pediaflor Drops
Phos-Flur Rinse/Supplement
Posture Tablets
Tri-Vi-Sol Drops
Vi-Daylin ADC Drops
Vi-Daylin Drops
Vi-Daylin/F ADC Drops
Vi-Daylin/F Drops
Vi-Daylin/F Plus Iron Drops
Vi-Daylin Plus Iron ADC Drops
Vi-Daylin Plus Iron Drops
Vitalize SF Liquid

APPENDIX 4

Drugs That Cause a Reaction to Sunlight

Some people may have what is known as a "photosensitivity reaction" when taking certain drugs. This means they may suffer an allergic reaction if exposed to bright sunlight. The following list of potential culprits is not all-inclusive, and shows only a representative brand name for each generic drug. When in doubt, always consult with your doctor or your pharmacist.

Generic Name (Brand)

Acetazolamide (Diamox)
Amantadine (Symmetrel)
Amiloride/hydrochlorothiazide (Moduretic)
Amiodarone (Cordarone)
Amitriptyline (Elavil, Endep)
Amoxapine (Asendin)
Astemizole (Hismanal)
Atenolol/chlorthalidone (Tenoretic)
Auranofin (Ridaura)
Azatadine (Optimine)
Azatadine/pseudoephedrine (Trinalin Repetabs)
Azithromycin (Zithromax)
Benazepril (Lotensin)
Benazepril/hydrochlorothiazide (Lotensin HCT)
Bendroflumethiazide (Naturetin)
Benzthiazide (Exna)
Bisoprolol/hydrochlorothiazide (Ziac)
Bromodiphenhydramine/codeine (Ambenyl)
Brompheniramine/phenylpropanolamine/codeine (Dimetane-DC)
Brompheniramine/pseudoephedrine/ dextromethorphan (Dimetane-DX)
Captopril (Capoten)
Captopril/hydrochlorothiazide (Capozide)

Carbamazepine (Tegretol)
Chlordiazepoxide/amitriptyline (Limbitrol)
Chlorhexidine gluconate (Hibistat)
Chlorothiazide (Diuril)
Chlorpheniramine (Chlorpheniramine)
Chlorpheniramine/D-pseudoephedrine (Deconamine)
Chlorpheniramine/phenylpranolamine (Ru-Tuss II, Ornade)
Chlorpromazine (Thorazine)
Chlorpropamide (Diabinese)
Chlorprothixene (Taractan)
Chlorthalidone (Hygroton, Thalitone)
Chlorthalidone/reserpine (Demi-Regroton, Regroton)
Cinoxacin (Cinobac)
Ciprofloxacin (Cipro)
Clemastine (Tavist)
Clemastine/phenylpropanolamine (Tavist-D)
Clofazamine (Lamprene)
Clomipramine (Anafranil)
Clonidine/chlorthalidone (Combipres)
Coal tar (Estar Gel, PsoriGel)
Contraceptive, oral (see Estrogen/Progestin)
Cyclobenzaprine (Flexeril)
Cromolyn sodium (Intal)

Cyproheptadine (Periactin)
Dacarbazine (DTIC-Dome)
Dantrolene sodium (Dantrium)
Dapsone (Dapsone)
Demeclocycline (Declomycin)
Desipramine (Norpramin, Pertofrane)
Dexchlorpheniramine (Polaramine)
Diclofenac (Voltaren, Cataflam)
Diflunisal (Dolobid)
Diltiazem (Cardizem)
Diphenhydramine (Benadryl)
Diphenylpyraline (Hispril)
Divalproex Sodium (Depakote)
Doxepin (Sinequan)
Doxycycline (Vibramycin, Doryx)
Enalapril (Vasotec)
Enalapril/hydrochlorothiazide (Vaseretic)
Enoxacin (Penetrex)
Erythromycin ethylsuccinate/
  sulfisoxazole (Pediazole)
Estazolam (ProSom)
Estrogen (Premarin)
Estrogen/progestin (Ortho-Novum,
  Ovral)
Ethionamide (Trecator-SC)
Etodolac (Lodine)
Etretinate (Tegison)
Felbamate (Felbatol)
Floxuridine (FUDR Injectable)
Flucytosine (Ancobon)
Fluorouracil (Adrucil, Efudex)
Fluphenazine (Prolixin, Permitil)
Flurbiprofen (Ansaid)
Flutamide (Eulexin)
Fluvastatin (Lescol)
Fosinopril (Monopril)
Furosemide (Lasix)
Glipizide (Glucotrol)
Glyburide (Diabeta, Micronase)
Gold Glynase compounds (Solganal)
Gold sodium thiomalate (Myochrysine)
Griseofulvin (Fulvicin, Gris-PEG)
Guanethidine/hydrochlorothiazide
  (Esimil)
Haloperidol (Haldol)
Hexachlorophene (pHisoHex)

Hydralazine/hydrochlorothiazide
  (Apresazide, Apresoline-Esidrix)
Hydrochlorothiazide (Esidrix,
  HydroDIURIL, Oretic)
Hydrochlorothiazide/deserpidine
  (Oreticyl)
Hydrochlorothiazide/triamterene
  (Dyazide, Maxzide)
Hydroflumethiazide (Diucardin, Saluron)
Hydroflumethiazide/reserpine
  (Salutensin)
Ibuprofen (Advil, Motrin, Nuprin)
Imipramine (Tofranil)
Indapamide (Lozol)
Interferon ALFA-2B (Intron A)
Interferon Alfa-N3 (Alferon N)
Interferon BETA-1B (Betaseron)
Isocarboxazid (Marplan)
Isotretinoin (Accutane)
Ketoprofen (Orudis, Oruvail)
Levamisole (Ergamisol)
Lisinopril (Prinivil, Zestril)
Lisinopril/hydrochlorothiazide (Prinzide,
  Zestoretic)
Lomefloxacin (Maxaquin)
Loratadine (Claritin)
Lovastatin (Mevacor)
Maprotiline (Ludiomil)
Meperidine/promethazine (Mepergan)
Mesalamine (Pentasa)
Mesoridazine (Serentil)
Methacycline (Rondomycin)
Methazolamide (Neptazane)
Methdilazine (Tacaryl)
Methotrexate (Folex, Mexate)
Methotrimeprazine (Levoprome)
Methyclothiazide (Aquatensen,
  Enduron)
Methyclothiazide/deserpidine
  (Enduronyl)
Methyclothiazide/reserpine
  (Diutensen-R)
Methyldopa/chlorothiazide (Aldoclor)
Methyldopa/hydrochlorothiazide
  (Aldoril)
Metolazone (Diulo, Mykrox)

Metoprolol/hydrochlorothiazide
  (Lopressor HCT)
Minocycline (Minocin)
Nabilone (Cesamet)
Nabumetone (Relafen)
Nadolol/bendroflumethiazide (Corzide)
Nalidixic acid (NegGram)
Naproxen (Aleve, Anaprox, Naprosyn)
Norfloxacin (Noroxin, Chibroxin)
Nortriptyline (Pamelor)
Ofloxacin (Floxin)
Olsalazine (Dipentum)
Oxaprozin (Daypro)
Oxytetracycline (Terramycin)
Oxytetracycline/sulfamethizole/
  phenazopyridine (Urobiotic-250)
Paroxetine (Paxil)
Pentostatin (Nipent)
Perphenazine (Trilafon)
Perphenazine/amitriptyline (Etrafon,
  Triavil)
Phenelzine (Nardil)
Phenylbutazone (Butazolidin)
Phenylpropanolamine/pheniramine/
  pyrilamine (Triaminic TR)
Piroxicam (Feldene)
Polythiazide (Renese)
Pravastatin (Pravachol)
Prazosin/polythiazide (Minizide)
Prochlorperazine (Compazine)
Promethazine (Phenergan)
Propranolol/hydrochlorothiazide
  (Inderide)
Protriptyline (Vivactil)
Pyrazinamide (Pyrazinamide)
Quinapril (Accupril)
Quinethazone (Hydromox)
Quinidine gluconate (Quinaglute Dura-
  Tabs)
Quinidine sulfate (Quinqdex, Quinora)
Ramipril (Altace)
Rauwolfia Serpentina/
  bendroflumethiazide (Rauzide)
Reserpine/chlorothiazide (Diupres)
Reserpine/hydralazine/hydrochloro-
  thiazide (Ser-Ap-Es)
Reserpine/hydrochlorothiazide
  (Hydropres, Serpasil-Esidrix)

Risperidone (Risperdal)
Selegiline (Eldepryl)
Sertraline (Zoloft)
Simvastatin (Zocor)
Sotalol (Betapace)
Spironolactone/hydrochlorothiazide
  (Aldactazide)
Sulfacetamide sodium/phenylephrine
  (Vasosulf)
Sulfadoxine/pyrimethamine (Fansidar)
Sulfamethizole (Thiosulfil Forte)
Sulfamethizole/phenazopyridine
  (Thiosulfil-A)
Sulfamethoxazole (Gantanol)
Sulfamethoxazole/phenazopyridine (Azo
  Gantanol)
Sulfamethoxazole/trimethoprim
  (Bactrim, Septra)
Sulfasalazine (Azulfidine)
Sulfisoxazole (Gantrisin)
Sulfisoxazole/phenazopyridine (Azo
  Gantrisin)
Sulfone (Dapsone)
Sulindac (Clinoril)
Terfenadine (Seldane)
Terfenadine/pseudoephedrine
  (Seldane-D)
Tetracycline (Achromycin, Sumycin)
Thioridazine (Mellaril)
Thiothixene (Navane)
Timolol/hydrochlorothiazide (Timolide)
Tolazamide (Tolinase)
Tolbutamide (Orinase)
Tranylcypromine (Parnate)
Tretinoin (Retin-A)
Triamterene (Dyrenium)
Trichlormethiazide (Metahydrin, Naqua)
Trifluoperazine (Stelazine)
Triflupromazine (Vesprin)
Trimeprazine (Temaril)
Trimethoprim (Trimpex)
Trimethoprim sulfate/polymyxin B
  sulfate (Polytrim)
Trimipramine (Surmontil)
Tripelennamine (PBZ)
Triprolidine (Actidil)
Triprolidine/pseudoephedrine (Actifed)

Triprolidine/pseudoephedrine/codeine
(Actifed with codeine)
Valproic acid (Depakene)

Venlafaxine (Effexor)
Vinblastine (Velban)
Zolpidem (Ambien)

Adapted from *Medications that Increase Sensitivity to Light: a 1990 Listing*, prepared by Jerome I. Levine, M.S., R.Ph., U.S. Department of Health and Human Services, Public Health Service/Food and Drug Administration Center for Devices and Radiological Health.

APPENDIX 5

Recommended Vaccinations

I t sometimes seems that modern medicine has all but eliminated many of the infections that plagued our forebears. But don't be deceived. These germs—from mumps and measles to polio and pertussis—are still very much with us, as occasional outbreaks clearly show.

With the host of vaccines readily available today, there's absolutely no reason to leave your child (or yourself) in danger of contracting these dangerous diseases. A few quick visits to a doctor or clinic are all that's needed to provide vital—possibly life-saving—protection. Use the following overview to brush up on the immunizations to request.

DIPHTHERIA, TETANUS, PERTUSSIS (DTP)

Protects against

This combined vaccine protects against diphtheria, tetanus, and pertussis (also known as whooping cough). All three are serious, contagious diseases.

- Diphtheria is contracted through the nose or mouth. It causes fever, weakness, and difficulty breathing. In severe cases, it can lead to paralysis and heart failure. About 1 in 10 people who get diphtheria may die from it. The disease is most dangerous in children and the elderly.
- Tetanus can occur when a cut or wound allows an organism into the body. Once inside, the organism produces a poison that can cause severe muscle spasms or lockjaw. Three in 10 people with tetanus die from it.
- Pertussis can be mild enough to be confused with the common cold. A more serious infection can make it difficult eat, drink, or breath. Pertussis is also called whooping cough because it can cause attacks of coughing and choking that end in a "whoop" sound as air is forced into the lungs. Pertussis is contracted through the air.

DTP vaccine can be combined with the vaccine against Haemophilus influenzae type B.

Recommended vaccination schedule

The first three doses of DTP should be given at 2, 4, and 6 months. A fourth dose should be given at 12 months but may be given up to 18 months. If the fourth dose is given at 15 months or older, your child may receive a modified form of the vaccine.

Delay vaccination if
An acute illness with fever may be reason to delay the vaccination. However, a child with a mild upper respiratory infection may still receive the vaccination.

Potential side effects
Side effects are generally mild and last only a short time. There may be slight pain, redness, hardness, swelling, or tenderness where the injection was given. Your child may also get a fever, be irritable and drowsy, vomit, or lose his appetite. Some reactions (fever, fretfulness, persistent inconsolable crying) are significantly more common when pertussis is included in the vaccination, but they are also self-limiting and can be treated with nothing more than acetaminophen to reduce fever. Nodules at the injection site occur occasionally. In rare cases, a sterile abscess may form.

The frequency of local reactions and fever following a DTP vaccination is significantly higher with later doses, while other reactions become significantly less frequent. Notify your doctor of any unusual reactions.

Rare side effects include anaphylactic reactions (hives, swelling at the mouth, difficulty breathing, or shock); high fever and persistent, inconsolable crying lasting more than three hours; and complications involving the nervous system.

Recommended boosters
A fifth dose is given as a booster between the ages of 4 and 6. Typically, this is given before your child starts kindergarten or elementary school. The Advisory Committee on Immunization Practices (ACIP), the American Academy of Pediatrics, and the American Academy of Family Physicians also recommend a tetanus/diphtheria booster at 11-12 years or 14-16 years.

FLU

Protects against
Flu or influenza is a viral respiratory disease that spreads very quickly. Many different strains of flu virus can cause the illness. Flu vaccines change each year depending on which strains are expected to become most prevalent in the coming flu season. The flu is not a cold or a 24-hour virus. It can cause high fever, headache, body pains, extreme fatigue and weakness, cough, and chest discomfort that last for three to four days. Flu may also be accompanied by runny, stuffy nose, sneezing, and a sore throat. Severe cases can lead to bronchitis and pneumonia and can be life threatening. You can be contagious before you begin to feel sick.

Recommended when

The best time to be immunized is between October and November, before flu season begins. Even if the vaccine doesn't prevent the flu, it may lessen its severity. Flu vaccine is recommended for infants 6 months and older and for the following:

- Those 65 and older
- Residents (of any age) of long-term care facilities
- Children and teenagers (6 months to 18 years) who receive long-term aspirin therapy
- Those with asthma, high blood pressure, heart or lung disease, anemia or a blood disorder, diabetes, kidney problems, immunosuppressive diseases, and those who have been diagnosed as HIV positive
- Healthy adults who want to avoid the flu.

Delay vaccination if

Do not get a flu shot if you have a history of hypersensitivity to chicken eggs or any component of the vaccine. You should delay getting a shot if you have a fever and an acute illness. You should also delay if you have a changing neurological disorder; but you may consider the vaccine once the disease has stabilized. Mild upper respiratory infections are usually not a reason for delay.

Potential side effects

The vaccine itself cannot cause the flu since it contains only killed viruses. The most common side effect is tenderness, redness, and hardness at the injection site. Other side effects are fever, headache, and body pains. Immediate reactions, such as hives and allergic asthma, are assumed to be allergic and are rare.

Recommended boosters

None.

HAEMOPHILUS INFLUENZAE TYPE B

Protects against

Haemophilus influenzae type b bacteria, which can cause serious infections in children, particularly those under age 5. This infection is not the "flu." In severe cases, it can take the form of pneumonia, meningitis (a dangerous infection of the covering of the brain and spinal cord), or epiglottitis (an inflammation of the mouth of the windpipe that can cause choking and death if not treated immediately).

Recommended vaccination schedule

At 2, 4, and 6 months. (A form of the vaccine can be given at 12 to 15 months if you miss this schedule.)

Delay vaccination if
You should speak to your pediatrician about delaying the vaccine if your child has an acute infection or fever, or is receiving immunosuppressive therapy. Also alert the doctor if the child has shown sensitivity to any previous shots of the vaccine.

Potential side effects
Side effects are generally mild and last only 24 to 48 hours. There may be slight pain, warmth, and redness at the vaccination site. Other side effects are fever, lethargy, irritability, and loss of appetite.

Recommended boosters
Between 12 and 15 months.

HEPATITIS B

Protects against
Hepatitis B, a serious and contagious viral disease that can strike at any age. Hepatitis is transmitted through infected blood or other body fluids, such as saliva or semen. Signs and symptoms of hepatitis B include loss of appetite, fatigue, vomiting, stomach pain, joint pain, and yellowish eyes and skin.

Recommended vaccination schedule
The hepatitis B vaccine is normally given in a series of 3 doses. The first is usually administered at birth, but may be given up to 2 months of age. The second dose should be given at 2 months but may be given between 2 and 4 months. The third dose should be given at 6 months but may be given between 6 and 18 months.

If you have a child who was not immunized against hepatitis B but comes in contact with someone with the disease or is at risk for the disease, that child should be vaccinated. Risk factors for older children and teenagers include sexual activity, use of intravenous drugs, or contact with infected blood or body fluids.

Adults should get a vaccination against hepatitis B if they live in areas with a high prevalence of the disease or are at increased risk of infection due to their work. Examples of those who should receive the vaccine are:

- Health-care personnel
- People at increased risk due to their sexual practices, including people with multiple partners and people who repeatedly contract sexually transmitted diseases
- Illicit drug users

If you think you may fall into any of these categories, consult your doctor.

Delay vaccination if

If your child has a fever or active infection, your pediatrician may recommend delaying vaccination. If the child is allergic to yeast, he should not receive this vaccine. Be sure to tell your pediatrician.

Potential side effects

The most common reaction is swelling or redness at the injection site. During clinical trials, 17 percent of the healthy infants and children who received the vaccine also experienced the following in decreasing order of frequency: irritability, tiredness, fever, crying, diarrhea, vomiting, diminished appetite, and insomnia. Reactions usually appear within 24 hours after the vaccine is given and disappear within 48 to 72 hours. If your child experiences hypersensitivity after a first injection, he should not receive further injections. Be sure to alert your doctor to any reactions.

Recommended boosters
None.

MEASLES, MUMPS, RUBELLA (MMR)

Protects against

This combined vaccine protects against measles, mumps, and rubella (also known as German measles), contagious viral diseases that can occur at any age, but are seen most frequently in infants and children. All three can be severe and may lead to other infections, such as pneumonia and meningitis. These three "childhood" diseases are especially dangerous if they occur in adults, where they can cause sterility or other problems with the sex organs.

- Measles appears as a rash that may cover the entire body. The rash is often accompanied by fever and inflammation of the linings of the nose and throat.
- Mumps appear as a swelling around the neck and throat.
- Rubella is also known as three-day measles. It is particularly dangerous because a pregnant women who contracts rubella could lose the baby or give birth to a baby with severe birth defects.

Individual vaccines against each of disease are also available in case revaccination becomes necessary.

Recommended vaccination schedule

The MMR vaccine is given between 12 and 15 months. Health-care and child-care workers, as well as those born after 1956 who lack documentation of measles immunity, should also be vaccinated.

Delay vaccination if

Alert the doctor if your child has a fever, active untreated tuberculosis, a lymphatic disease, or is receiving immunosuppresive therapy. A weakened immune system is cause for delay. If the child has had an anaphylactic or anaphylactic-like reaction to eggs or neomycin, or other immediate reactions (hives, swelling of the mouth and throat, and/or difficulty breathing), he should not receive this vaccination.

Potential side effects

The temporary side effects your child might experience from the MMR vaccine are the same as those that can be expected if the vaccines are given separately. These may include: burning, stinging, redness, hardness or irritation at the injection site, fever, rash, headache, general weakness, sore throat, cough, cold symptoms, nausea, diarrhea, vomiting, joint reactions, inflammation of the salivary gland or testes, skin eruptions, or inflammation of spinal nerves. Other side effects that have been reported include anaphylactic reactions, ear infections, conjunctivitis (pinkeye). High fevers and nervous system reactions have been reported but are rare.

Recommended boosters

Boosters are typically given either when a child is about to enter kindergarten (between ages 4 and 6) or between ages 11 and 12.

POLIO

Protects against

Polio vaccines protect against poliomyelitis, or polio, a very serious, infectious disease affecting the spinal cord. There is no cure for polio—once contracted, the disease must run its course. In its most severe form, it can cause paralysis and even death. It can also lead to severe muscle pain and difficulty breathing. The virus can also cause milder forms of the disease, marked by fever, sore throat, stomachache, and headache. There are two types of polio vaccine: a live oral polio vaccine, and an inactivated polio vaccine that is given by injection when the live vaccine cannot be used.

Recommended vaccination schedule

The first two doses of the oral polio vaccine are given at 2 and 4 months. The third dose is generally given at 6 months but may be given up until a baby is 18 months.

Delay vaccination if

You should speak to your pediatrician about delaying the vaccination if your child has a fever or active infection, persistent vomiting or diarrhea, or a suspected gastroenteritis infection. If the child, or anyone in the household, has a weakened immune system due to disease or treatment of disease, the doctor may administer the inactivated vaccine instead of the live oral vaccine.

Potential side effects

The most dangerous side effect of the live vaccine is that it can, in very rare cases, cause the disease. If the child receives an injection of the inactivated vaccine, there may be slight pain and redness where the vaccination was given. Since the recommended vaccine schedules for polio, Hib, and DTP are the same at 2 and 4 months and frequently the same at 6 months, other side effects you observe might be due to one of the other vaccines. See also Haemophilus Influenza b and DTP.

Recommended boosters

Your child should get a booster between ages 4 and 6. This booster is typically given on starting elementary school.

RABIES

Protects against

Rabies is a potentially fatal disease caused by a virus that affects the nervous system. You can get rabies if you are bitten or licked in an open cut by an animal with rabies. Dogs and cats that have not been vaccinated, as well as raccoons, bats, skunks, and foxes, are all possible carriers.

If you are bitten by an animal that may have rabies, wash the wound with soap and water, then seek medical attention immediately. If there is any possibility that the animal may be rabid, you will probably be treated for rabies. If possible, take the animal to a veterinarian for testing and observation—but be sure to wear gloves.

It can take from 9 days to 1 year for symptoms of the disease to appear, though most people will show symptoms within 60 days. Because of this incubation period, there is time to seek effective treatment. Early symptoms include pain or numbness at the site of the bite, fever, sore throat, nausea, vomiting, diarrhea, stomach pain, and fatigue. Left untreated, rabies can also cause paralysis, hallucinations, heart problems, coma, and death.

Recommended when

Pre-exposure immunizations and boosters are given to people whose jobs may bring them into contact with rabid animals or with the rabies vaccine, such as veterinarians, lab workers, animal handlers; people spending more than 1 month overseas where rabies is common; and people whose hobbies may bring them into contact with possibly rabid animals (for instance, hunters).

Postexposure shots are given to anyone who has been exposed to the rabies virus without pre-exposure immunization. A series of five vaccine injections is given on days 0, 3, 7, 14, and 28, with a dose of rabies immune globulin (RIG—the rabies antibody) given on day 0, if appropriate.)

Delay vaccination if
There is generally no reason to delay a postexposure rabies vaccine. However, if you are hypersensitive to any of the antibiotics in the vaccine; if you are taking corticosteriods or other immunosuppresive medications, or have an immunosuppressive illness; or if you are pregnant, be sure to inform the doctor, who will determine the best way to proceed. For pre-exposure immunization, if you have another illness with a fever, you should postpone the vaccination series.

Potential side effects
Side effects are generally mild and should not be used as a reason for interrupting or discontinuing treatment. Common local reactions, reported by 25 percent of those receiving the vaccine, are pain, redness, swelling, or itching at the injection site. Other mild reactions, reported by about 20 percent of those receiving the vaccine, are headache, nausea, abdominal pain, muscle aches, and dizziness.

Recommended boosters
Pre-exposure boosters should be given every 6 months for people at continuous risk (anyone who works with the live virus), and every 2 years for people at frequent risk—for example, veterinarians.

TETANUS (ADULT)

To provide added protection against diphtheria, the Immunization Practices Advisory Council of the U.S. Public Health Services recommends a combined diphtheria and tetanus vaccine, rather than tetanus vaccine alone, for both primary and booster injections, including shots following a wound.

Protects against
Tetanus can occur when a cut or wound allows an organism into the body. Once inside, the organism produces a poison that can cause severe muscle spasms or lockjaw. Three in 10 people with tetanus die from it.

Recommended when
If you have never been immunized against tetanus, either as a child as part of DTP immunization or as an adult, the course of immunization is as follows: two doses 4 to 8 weeks apart, followed by a third reinforcing dose 6 to 12 months after the second dose.

Delay vaccination if
If you have a fever or acute infection or are receiving immunosuppressive therapy, you should consider delaying this vaccine. If you have an allergic type of reaction to the vaccine or experience nervous-system complications after receiving it, you should not take it again.

Potential side effects

Local reactions such as redness, soreness and hardness around the injection site are common, but usually go away quickly. Nodules or a sterile abscess may also occur at the injection site. Other possible reactions are fever, chills, headaches, and muscle pain or tenderness. Hypersensitivity or high fever may occur in people who have overly frequent injections. Rare reactions reported are neurological complications, rash and other skin reactions, and severe anaphylactic reactions.

Recommended boosters

You should get a booster at 10-year intervals after completing the primary series. If a dose is given sooner because of a wound, the next booster is not needed until 10 years after that. Whether or not you should get a booster after a wound will depend on the severity of the injury and your immunization history.

APPENDIX 6

Poison Control Centers

If there is one phone number that no home should be without, it is the nearest poison control center. The following is a list of regional centers that are certified members of the American Association of Poison Control Centers. To be certified, they must be supervised by a medical director, have pharmacists and nurses available to answer questions, be open 24 hours a day, and be accessible by direct dialing or a toll-free number.

The centers are organized by region and are listed alphabetically by name.

Far West

Fresno Regional Poison Control Center
Valley Children's Hospital
3151 N. Millbrook
Fresno, CA 93703
(209) 445-1222

Los Angeles County Regional Poison Control Center
1200 N. State St., Rm. 1107 A&B
Los Angeles, CA 90033
(213) 222-3212
(800) 777-6476

Oregon Poison Center
Oregon Health Sciences University
3181 S.W. Sam Jackson Park Rd.
Portland, OR 97201
(503) 494-8968 (Local)
(800) 452-7165 (OR only)

San Diego Regional Poison Center
U.C.S.D. Medical Center
200 W. Arbor Dr.
San Diego, CA 92103-8925
(619) 543-6000
(800) 876-4766
(619 area code only)

San Francisco Bay Area Regional Poison Control Center
San Francisco General Hospital
1001 Potrero Ave.
Bldg. 80, Room 230
San Francisco, CA 94110
(415) 476-6600
(800) 523-2222 (N. CA)

U. C. Davis Medical Center Regional Poison Control Center
2315 Stockton Blvd.
Sacramento, CA 95817
(916) 734-3692
(800) 342-9293 (CA only)

Great Lakes

Blodgett Regional Poison Center
Blodgett Memorial Medical Center
1840 Wealthy St. S.E.
Grand Rapids, MI 49506
(800) 764-7661 (MI only)
(800) 356-3232 (TTY for deaf)

Central Ohio Poison Center
Columbus Children's Hospital
700 Childrens Dr.
Columbus, OH 43205-2696
(614) 228-1323
(800) 682-7625
(614) 228-2272 (TTY for deaf)

Indiana Poison Center
Methodist Hospital of Indiana
1701 N. Senate Blvd., P.O. Box 1367
Indianapolis, IN 46206-1367
(317) 929-2323
(800) 382-9097

Poison Control Center
Children's Hospital of Michigan
3901 Beaubien Blvd.,
Detroit, MI 48201
(313) 745-5711

**Regional Poison Control System
Cincinnati Drug and Poison
Information Center**
University of Cincinnati College of
    Medicine
P.O. Box 670144
Cincinnati, OH 45267-0144
(513) 558-5111
(800) 872-5111 (OH)

Great Plains

**Cardinal Glennon Children's
Hospital Regional Poison Center**
1465 S. Grand Blvd.
St. Louis, MO 63104
(314) 772-5200
(800) 366-8888

Hennepin Regional Poison Center
Hennepin County Medical Center
701 Park Ave. S.
Minneapolis, MN 55415
(612) 347-3141
(612) 337-7474 (TDD for deaf)

Minnesota Regional Poison Center
St. Paul-Ramsey Medical Center
640 Jackson St.
St. Paul, MN 55101
(612) 221-2113

The Poison Control Center
Children's Memorial Hospital
8301 Dodge St.
Omaha, NE 68114
(402) 390-5555 (Omaha)
(800) 955-9119 (NE,WY)

Middle Atlantic

Central Pennsylvania Poison Center
University Hospital
Milton Hershey Medical Center
P.O. Box 850
Hershey, PA 17033
(800) 521-6110

Delaware Valley Regional Poison Control Center
3600 Market St., Rm. 220
Philadelphia, PA 19104
(215) 386-2100

Hudson Valley Regional Poison Center
Nyack Hospital
160 North Midland Ave.
Nyack, NY 10960
(914) 353-1000
(800) 336-6997

Long Island Regional Poison Control Center
259 First St.
Mineola, NY 11501
(516) 542-2323

Maryland Poison Center
University of Maryland School of
    Pharmacy
20 N. Pine St.
Baltimore, MD 21201
(410) 528-7701
(800) 492-2414 (MD only)

National Capital Poison Center
3201 New Mexico Ave., N.W.
Suite 310
Washington, DC 20007
(202) 625-3333
(202) 362-8536 (TTY for deaf)

New Jersey Poison Information and Education System
Newark Beth Israel Medical Center
201 Lyons Ave.
Newark, NJ 07112
(800) 962-1253

New York City Poison Control Center
NYC Depatrment of Health
455 First Ave., Room 123
New York, NY 10016
(212) 340-4494
(212) POISONS

Pittsburgh Poison Center
Children's Hospital of Pittsburgh
3705 Fifth Ave.
Pittsburgh, PA 15213
(412) 681-6669

Mid South

Kentucky Regional Poison Center of Kosair Children's Hospital
Medical Towers So., Suite 572
P.O. Box 35070
Louisville, KY 40232-5070
(502) 629-7275
(800) 722-5725 (KY only)

West Virginia Poison Center
West Virginia University
3110 MacCorkle Ave., S.E.
Charleston, WV 25304
(304) 348-4211
(800) 642-3625 (WV only)

New England

Massachusetts Poison Control System
The Children's Hospital
300 Longwood Ave.
Boston, MA 02115
(617) 232-2120
(800) 682-9211

Rhode Island Poison Center
593 Eddy St.
Providence, RI 02902
(401) 444-5727

Rocky Mountains

Arizona Poison and Drug Information Center
University of Arizona Health Sciences
Center, Rm. 1156
1501 N. Campbell Ave.
Tucson, AZ 85724
(602) 626-6016
(800) 362-0101 (AZ only)

New Mexico Poison and Drug Information Center
University of New Mexico
Albuquerque, NM 87131-1076
(505) 843-2551
(800) 432-6866 (NM only)

Rocky Mountain Poison and Drug Center
645 Bannock St.
Denver, CO 80204
(303) 629-1123

Samaritan Regional Poison Center
Good Samaritan Medical Center
1111 E. McDowell Road
Phoenix, AZ 85006
(602) 253-3334

Utah Poison Control Center
University of Utah Hospital
410 Chipeta Way, Suite 230
Salt Lake City, UT 84108
(801) 581-2151
(800) 456-7707 (UT only)

South

Blue Ridge Poison Center
Blue Ridge Hospital
Box 67
Charlottesville, VA 22901
(804) 924-5543
(800) 451-1428

Florida Poison Information and Toxicology Resource Center
Tampa General Hospital
P.O. Box 1289
Tampa, FL 33601
(813) 253-4444
(800) 282-3171 (FL only)

Georgia Poison Center
Grady Memorial Hospital
80 Butler St. SE, Box 26066
Atlanta, GA 30335-3801
(404) 616-9000
(800) 282-5846 (GA only)

North Texas Poison Center
Parkland Memorial Hospital
5201 Harry Hines Blvd.
P.O. Box 35926
Dallas, TX 75235
(800) 764-7661

Regional Poison Control Center
Children's Hospital of Alabama
1600 Seventh Ave. S.
Birmingham, AL 35233-1711
(205) 939-9201
(800) 292-6678 (AL only)

Texas State Poison Control Center
University of Texas Trauma Center
Room 3-112
Galveston, TX 77555-1175
(409) 765-1420

Disease and Disorder Index

U se this index to find out which drugs are available for a specific medical problem. Both brand and generic names are listed; the generic names are shown in italics. Only brands covered in the drug profiles are included.

Miltown, 667
Oxazepam. See Serax
Prazepam. See Centrax
Prochlorperazine. See Compazine
Serax, 1016
Stelazine, 1043
Tranxene, 1140
Trifluoperazine. See Stelazine
Valium, 1180
Vistaril. *See* Atarax
Xanax, 1211
Arthritis
Advil, 17
Anaprox, 55
Ansaid, 59
Aspirin, 77
Auranofin. See Ridaura
Cataflam. *See* Voltaren
Choline Magnesium Trisalicylate.
    See Trilisate
Clinoril, 207
Daypro, 274
Decadron Tablets, 281
Deltasone, 293
Dexamethasone. See Decadron
    Tablets
Diclofenac. See Voltaren
Diflunisal. See Dolobid
Disalcid, 348
Dolobid, 357
Ecotrin. *See* Aspirin
Empirin. *See* Aspirin
Etodolac. See Lodine
Feldene, 428
Flurbiprofen. See Ansaid
Genuine Bayer. *See* Aspirin
Hydroxychloroquine. See Plaquenil
Ibuprofen. See Advil
Indocin, 522
Indomethacin. See Indocin
Ketoprofen. See Orudis
Lodine, 585
Medrol, 635
Methotrexate, 646
Methylprednisolone. See Medrol
Motrin. *See* Advil
Nabumetone. See Relafen
Naprosyn, 704

Naproxen. See Naprosyn
Naproxen Sodium. See Anaprox
Orasone. *See* Deltasone
Orudis, 786
Oruvail. *See* Orudis
Oxaprozin. See Daypro
Pediapred, 814
Piroxicam. See Feldene
Plaquenil, 860
Prednisolone Sodium Phosphate.
    See Pediapred
Prednisone. See Deltasone
Relafen, 941
Rheumatrex. See Methotrexate
Ridaura, 959
Rufen. *See* Advil
Salsalate. See Disalcid
Sulindac. See Clinoril
Tolectin, 1128
Tolmetin. See Tolectin
Trilisate, 1155
Voltaren, 1200
Asthma
AeroBid, 20
Albuterol. See Proventil
Alupent, 39
Atrovent, 86
Azmacort, 97
Beclomethasone, 110
Beclovent Inhalation Aerosol. *See*
    Beclomethasone
Brethaire. *See* Brethine
Brethine, 133
Bricanyl. *See* Brethine
Cromolyn. See Intal
Decadron Tablets, 281
Decadron Turbinaire and
    Respihaler, 285
Deltasone, 293
Dexacort. *See* Decadron Turbinaire
    and Respihaler
Dexamethasone. See Decadron
    Tablets
Dexamethasone Sodium Phosphate.
    See Decadron Turbinaire and
    Respihaler
Flunisolide. See AeroBid
Intal, 533

Infertility, female
Clomid. *See* Clomiphene Citrate
Clomiphene Citrate, 211
Serophene. *See* Clomiphene Citrate
Inflammatory diseases
Decadron Tablets, 281
Deltasone, 293
Dexamethasone. See Decadron
   Tablets
Medrol, 635
Methylprednisolone. See Medrol
Orasone. *See* Deltasone
Pediapred, 814
Prednisolone Sodium Phosphate.
   See Pediapred
Prednisone. See Deltasone
Inflammatory diseases of the eyes
Fluorometholone. See FML
FML, 457
Naphazoline with Pheniramine. See
   Naphcon A
Naphcon-A, 702
Pred Forte, 880
Prednisolone Acetate. See Pred
   Forte
Insomnia
Ambien, 42
Dalmane, 267
Doral, 364
Estazolam. See ProSom
Flurazepam. See Dalmane
Halcion, 480
ProSom, 908
Quazepam. See Doral
Restoril, 943
Temazepam. See Restoril
Triazolam. See Halcion
Zolpidem. See Ambien
Intestinal disorders, inflammatory
See Colitis
Irritable bowel syndrome
See Spastic colon
Jock itch
See Infections, fungal
Juvenile arthritis
See Arthritis
Kidney stones
Allopurinol. See Zyloprim

Lopurin. *See* Zyloprim
Zyloprim, 1248
Leg Cramps
See Circulation, impaired
Legionnaires' disease
E.E.S. *See* Erythromycin, Oral
E-Mycin. *See* Erythromycin, Oral
ERYC. *See* Erythromycin, Oral
Ery-Tab. *See* Erythromycin, Oral
Erythrocin. *See* Erythromycin, Oral
Erythromycin, Oral, 405
Ilosone. *See* Erythromycin, Oral
PCE. *See* Erythromycin, Oral
Lice
Kwell, 549
Lindane. See Kwell
Lupus
Decadron Tablets, 281
Deltasone, 293
Dexamethasone. See Decadron
   Tablets
Hydroxychloroquine. See Plaquenil
Medrol, 635
Methylprednisolone. See Medrol
Orasone. *See* Deltasone
Pediapred, 814
Plaquenil, 860
Prednisolone Sodium Phosphate.
   See Pediapred
Prednisone. See Deltasone
Lyme disease
See Infections, rickettsiae
Malaria
Hydroxychloroquine. See Plaquenil
Plaquenil, 860
Manic-depressive illness
Cibalith-S. *See* Lithonate
Eskalith. *See* Lithonate
Lithium. See Lithonate
Lithonate, 581
Lithotabs. *See* Lithonate
Meningitis
See Infections, central nervous
   system
Menopause
Conjugated Estrogens. See
   Premarin
Premarin, 883